LIFE ON AN OCEAN PLANET

Cover Photos (top to bottom)
Johnson Space Center, NASA
Harbor Branch Oceanographic
PADI

Back Cover Photos (top to bottom)
Ocean Explorer, NOAA
Harbor Branch Oceanographic
PADI
Brenda Konar, University of Alaska Fairbanks
Agalita Marine Research Foundation/
www.agalita.org

Life on an Ocean Planet®
Acknowledgements

Printed in Canada

2 3 4 5 6 7 8 09 11

Product Number 9781878663603
Version 2.01 (12/10)

National Marine Educators Association
making known the world of water

The NMEA Trademark is owned by National Marine Educators Association and its use herein is under license from National Marine Educators Association.

NMEA supports all rigorous, high-quality instructional materials that help teachers to bring the essential principles of Ocean Literacy to life for all students of all ages. *Life on an Ocean Planet* exemplifies the type of materials that NMEA would like to see in every classroom in America.

Staff Credits

Project Management
Lesley Alexander, Ph.D.
Heather Goodwin-Robinson
John Kinsella
Drew Richardson, Ed.D.
Celeste Tanguay
Bob Wohlers, M.A.

Project Editor
Karl Shreeves, M.A.

Instructional Design
Lesley Alexander, Ph.D.
Karl Shreeves, M.A.
Bob Wohlers, M.A.

Design Director
Janet Klendworth

Desktop Design Production
Jeanne Bryant
Alexandra Grevatt-Gillette
Matt Kilroy
Cynthia Knighton

Photo Research
Cheryl Regan

Photography
Al Hornsby
Cheryl Regan
Budd Riker
Bob Wohlers

Copyeditor
Susan E. Tate, B.P.R.

Proofreading
Sandi Beveridge
Bret Lorea
Cambria McConnell
Elaine Mihram
Bryan Till
LeRoy Wickham

Contributing Writers
Lesley Alexander, Ph.D.
Ania Budziak, M.P.A./M.S.E.S.
Dana Desonie, Ph.D.
Charlotte Kelchner, M.S., M.A.
Julie Lambert, Ph.D.
Todd Menzel, M.E.M.
Jenny Miller-Garmendia, M.A.
Karl Shreeves, M.A.
Susan Snyder, M.S.
Susan E. Tate, B.P.R.
Jamie Watts
Bob Wohlers, M.A.
Gary K. Wolfe, M.S.

Artwork
Victor Archer
Patrick Boaz
Jay Collins
Carla Kiwior
Marybeth Kucan
Kate Lee
Tony Walczak

Technical Advisor
Prof. Robert Stewart
Oceanography Department
Texas A & M University

Reviewers
Stephanie Dial
Marine Science Educator
Satsuma High School
Satsuma, Alabama

Jack Gilbert
Marine Science Educator
Roosevelt High School
Corona, California

Mary Henterly, M.S.Ed.
Marine Science Educator
Curtis Senior High School
University Place, Washington

Christine Kirch
Marine Science Educator
West Warwick High School
West Warwick, Rhode Island

A special thanks to the organizations, universities and individuals who have generously shared their time, knowledge, illustrations and images with Current Publishing Corp.

Argo Information Centre, Department of Agriculture, Harbor Branch Oceanographic Institute, Historical Diving Society, PADI, NASA, NBII, NOAA, NPS, Scripps Institute of Oceanography, Smithsonian Environmental Research Center, USAF, US Navy, USFWS, USGS, Woods Hole Oceanographic Institute.

Peter Cornillon-Uri, Ivo Girogorov, Gustaaf Hallegraeff-Unv. of Tasmaina, Al Hornsby, Brenda Konar-uaf, Dave McSchaffrey-Marrietta College, Phil Nuytten, Bruce Perry-UCLB, Cheryl Regan, Budd Riker, Dr. Jamie Seymour-JCU, Karl Shreeves, Ria Tan, Bob Wohlers.

Diane Lavarello
Marine Science Educator
Riverview High School
Sarasota, Florida

Melanie Lee, M.S. Chemisty
Marine Science/
Chemistry Educator
Winter Park High School
Winter Park, Florida

Cheryl Milliken, M.S.
Marine Science Educator
Falmouth High School
Falmouth, Massachusetts

Dawn Sherwood, M.S.
Marine Science Educator
Highland Springs High School
Highland Springs, Virginia

Mark Tohulka, M.S.
Marine Science Educator
MAST Academy
Miami, Florida

Shelly Thompson
Marine Science Educator
West High School
Torrance, California

Shari Whitlock
Marine Science Educator
Satsuma High School
Satsuma, Alabama

Erron Yoshioka
Marine Science Educator
Moanalua High School
Honolulu, Hawaii

Advisory Review

Rebecca Bell
Environmental Education
Specialist
Division of Instruction
Maryland State Department
of Education

Rita Bell
Director of Education
Monterey Bay Aquarium
Monterey, California

Paula G. Coble, Ph.D.
Associate Professor
Chemical Oceanography,
College of Marine Science
University of South Florida

Elizabeth A Day-Miller, Ph.D.
Education Program Leader
National Sea Grant and
College Program
Bridgewater Educational
Consulting LLC
Virginia

Milton Love, Ph.D.
Associate Research Biologist
Marine Institute
University of California at
Santa Barbara

Laura Murray, Ph.D.
Research Associate Professor
Horn Point Laboratory
University of Maryland Center
of Environmental Science

Dr. Daniel Pauly
Professor of Fisheries
Fisheries Centre
The University of
British Columbia
Vancouver, B.C.
Canada

Ashanti Pyrtle, Ph.D.
Assistant Professor
Education Division
College of Marine Science
University of South Florida

Marsha Winegarner
Florida Coordinator
"Building a Presence and K12
Science and Literacy" Education
Consultant
National Science Teacher
Association

Ocean Literacy Advisory Team

Alison Besch
Associate Museum Curator
Northern Carolina Maritime Museum
North Carolina

Beth Jewell
High School Biology &
Oceanography Teacher
West Springfield High School
Virginia

Mellie Lewis
Gifted & Talented Resource
Teacher, Retired
Howard County Public School System
Maryland

Meghan E Marrero
Director of Curriculum
U.S. Satellite Laboratory, Inc.
Rye, New York

Diana Payne, Ph.D.
Assistant Professor & Education
Coordinator
Connecticut Sea Grant
University of Connecticut at
Avery Point
Groton, Connecticut

Eric Simms
Science Education Specialist
Scripps Institution of Oceanography
La Jolla, California

Lynn Whitley
Director of Education
Wrigley Institute for
Environmental Studies and Sea
Grant Program
Co-Director, Centers for Ocean
Sciences Education- West
University of Southern California
Los Angeles, California

Mark Wiley
Extension Specialist
Marine Science Education
New Hampshire Sea Grant
University of New Hampshire
Cooperative Extension
Durham, New Hampshire

Preface

Whether it was the foggy coast of Maine or the sunny coast of Florida, my family always lived near the ocean and the ocean was part of our everyday lives. My father taught me how to sail and encouraged me to go out and explore the ocean by myself, sometimes not getting home until long after dark. I found new places, swam, explored tide pools, beach combed, and fished. Lazy discovering days of wonder and they always felt good. Everything about the ocean then seemed good and healthy. People talked about unlimited food and mineral resources from the ocean. Even the great environmentalist Rachel Carson once believed that "the ocean was too big and vast…to be much affected by human activity."

This is the ocean that fired my imagination but that ocean is in serious trouble and many people despair that we can never return to the idyllic seas of my youth. But I cannot agree. The stakes are too high to give up, not just for the food and resources we need, but for our very sense of ourselves and our role in the world of nature and the sheer fun of enjoying a healthy ocean again, to swim, to surf, to dive, and to play. These are things that we still can achieve though they will not be easy.

Now almost all of the news about the ocean is bad. Marine ecosystems are collapsing around the world and the ocean is in crisis. We are taking out far too much of what we want from the ocean and giving back in return all of our garbage and poisons that we want to discard. Most of the big fish are gone, large areas of the sea floor are flattened and barren of life because of trawling. The ocean is getting warmer with dire consequences for reef corals that lose their symbiotic algae and die, introduced species clog our shores and smother native inhabitants, and toxic chemicals like PCBs and mercury have built up to deadly levels in our most prized fish and shellfish. Most disturbing of all, large areas called "dead zones" are forming along our coasts where oxygen levels are so low that nothing survives but jellyfish and bacteria. Runoff of excess fertilizer and other nutrients from the land fuels massive growth of marine plankton. Decomposition of the dead plankton uses up all the oxygen and the only remaining fishery in these areas is jellyfish.

How could we all have been so caught by surprise? The myth of the ocean as wilderness blinded understanding. Until the 1980s, the ocean was described as natural or pristine with little attention to the obvious facts of collapsing fisheries and widespread pollution. "Natural" meant the way things used to be when we were children and "unnatural" meant all the bad things that had happened afterwards during our lives. Of course, what we first saw as natural was already unnatural and degraded by the standards of our parents. But children rarely listen to their parents, so that generation by generation, our standards for the health of the ocean declined until one day we woke up to disasters like global warming, no more fresh water, and no more fish.

This is the problem that Daniel Pauly called Shifting Baselines (www.shiftingbaselines.org). Changes seem sudden but the warning signs were always there. Change crept up unnoticed as each new generation shifted the baseline for what it accepted as natural or pristine. At first the effects were subtle and easy to miss but now they hit us in the face like a sledgehammer. Entire ocean ecosystems are breaking down in ways that all can see if they care to look. Moreover, the life support systems of the planet, including the natural cycles of carbon, oxygen, and nitrogen depend upon a healthy ocean. Conservationists rightly emphasize the species and habitats we are losing at an alarming pace, but we also need to ask what will replace what we are losing and what will be the consequences for our economic and social well being and even for our health.

How can we reverse this tragedy and achieve a healthy ocean again? The answer lies in being aware of shifting baselines, of holding the line to make sure they no longer shift, and working to reverse trajectories of degradation to restore some or most of what we have almost lost. This is the challenge for you the young readers of this wonderful new book about the ocean. Here you can learn the basics about how the ocean works, physically, chemically, geologically, and above all biologically, because in the final analysis it is the health of life in the ocean upon which so much of our well being depends. This book can give you the tools to not only enjoy the excitement of discovery of ocean science but to build your skills as citizens to develop your own opinions about human impacts on the ocean and what you believe should be done. This is where wise stewardship begins.

Just as the tides of the ocean eventually reverse themselves, I believe it is possible for us to reverse the long tide of ocean deterioration. There is hope, and success stories do exist. For example, consider the striped bass—*Morone saxitalis*. Striped bass have long been a commercially and recreationally valued species of the Chesapeake Bay. The partial moratorium imposed from 1984 to 1989 has allowed the striped bass to increase and once again become a species of major importance to the bay.

The task to heal our ocean may seem daunting, but as the great Jamaican poet Jimmy Cliff taught us a generation ago, "You can get it if you really want, but you must try, try and try. Try and try, you'll succeed at last."

Jeremy B. C. Jackson
William E. and Mary B. Ritter Professor of Oceanography
Scripps Institution of Oceanography
La Jolla, California

Contents

CHAPTER 6

A Survey of Life in the Sea: Introduction to
Marine Animals-Invertebrates

CHAPTER 7

A Survey of Life in the Sea:
Introduction to Marine Animals–Vertebrates

UNIT 3

A Water World

CHAPTER 8

The Nature of Water

CHAPTER 9

Water: A Physically Unique Molecule

Contents

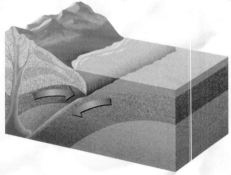

UNIT 6

The Present and Future of the Marine Environment

UNIT 1

Importance of

Institute of Nautical Archaeology

Courtesy of Richard Pyle

Ocean Exploration

Philip Nicholson

Ocean Explorer, NOAA

Photo courtesy of OAR/NURP

CHAPTER 1

Introduction to Marine Science

Courtesy of Richard Pyle

Russian Academy of Sciences/
Ocean Explorer, NOAA

Finding the Past in the Sea

I f someone asked you to draw an archaeologist, whom would you draw? The classic movie character Indiana Jones, complete with whip and machete in a cavern crawling with snakes? Maybe your archaeologist would look like adventure novelist Clive Cussler's main character, Dirk Pitt.

Although some archaeologists have adventures like Indiana Jones or Dirk Pitt, most have more in common with detective Sherlock Holmes. That's because what archaeologists really do is painstakingly dig through clues to solve mysteries. They spend days examining bits of information or spend hours in the laboratory, trying to fit together pieces of the puzzle.

The work of archaeological oceanographers differs little except that they carry out some of their work below the waves. Nearly all archaeological oceanographers spend many hours at a computer or digging through archives. Often, they spend more time there than in deep submersibles or using remotely operated vehicles. They need to do both to unlock questions about humanity's past that lie hidden in the ocean's depths.

Dr. Robert Ballard, the Director for the Institute for Archeological Oceanography at the University of Rhode Island, is recognized as one of the leading scientists studying the geology of continental margins. He has a particular interest in Earth formations of the North Atlantic Ocean in the New England region, but his interests range beyond natural history to human history.

"I am interested in numerous ocean subjects, with my favorite being marine geology, deep submergence technology, and my new area of interest—archaeological oceanography," explains Ballard. Ballard used remotely operated vehicle systems and telepresence technology to research volcanic, tectonic, and hydrothermal processes of the Mid-Ocean Ridge. In the mid 1980s, he began applying the same technologies to historic shipwrecks and archaeological research.

"My interest in science began very early in my childhood, about seven years of age, while living in San Diego near the largest oceanographic institute in the world – Scripps. Living next to Scripps turned my attention to oceanography. When I was a junior in high school I received a National Science Foundation scholarship to Scripps. During that summer I went on two separate oceanographic expeditions."

Dr. Robert Ballard has spent almost 30 years as a researcher at the Woods Hole Oceanographic Institution (WHOI), Woods Hole, Massachusetts – a private, non-profit research facility dedicated to the study of marine science and the education of marine scientists.

"When I went to undergraduate school at the University of California at Santa Barbara, I majored in chemistry and geology and minored in math and physics. This broad undergraduate training has served me well," says Ballard, who attended graduate school at the University of Southern California and the University of Hawaii's Graduate School of Oceanography. He received his PhD in marine geology and geophysics from the University of Rhode Island. Working on his doctorate when plate tectonics theory was still not widely accepted, he was one of the earliest proponents of using submersibles to do the field work that would confirm plate tectonics.

Robert Ballard, PhD
Director, Institute for Archeological Oceanography, University of Rhode Island

Figure 1-001

Argo.

Optical fiber technology has helped to redefine exploration of the ocean bottom. Scientists use *Argo* to map deep ocean archeological findings and transmit information, via real time video imagery, to the surface.

Figure 1-002

Alvin.

Alvin, operated by Woods Hole Oceanographic Institution and owed by the U.S. Navy, is one of the deepest diving manned submersible in use today. *Alvin* can carry two scientists and a pilot as deep as 4, 500 meters (14,760 feet), with each mission lasting six to ten hours.

In 1980, Dr. Ballard applied optical fiber technology to a new generation of towed sleds that transmit video pictures to the towing ship. This system, called *Argo*, was developed with funding from the US Navy. In 1985, *Argo* was tested by mapping the debris field and condition of the nuclear submarine *Thresher* that was lost in 1963, followed by a similar mission on the submarine *Scorpion*.

Dr. Ballard has led or participated in more than 100 deep-sea expeditions including the use of the deep diving submersibles *Alvin*, *Archimedes*, *Trieste II*, *Turtle*, *Ben Franklin*, *Cyana*, and *NR-1*. These expeditions included the first manned exploration of the Mid-Ocean Ridge, the discovery of warm water springs and their unusual animal communities in the Galapagos Rift, the first discovery of polymetallic sulfides, and the discovery of high-pressure "black smokers" (chimney-like structures made up of sulfur-bearing minerals or sulfides that come from beneath the Earth's crust).

"The undersea robots have greatly increased my ability to discover things beneath the sea," he says.

Dr. Ballard is perhaps best known for finding the R.M.S. *Titanic* in the cold, dark waters of the North Atlantic, as well as the discovery of the German battleship *Bismarck*, 11 warships from the lost fleet of Guadalcanal, and the U.S.S. *Yorktown*. Exploring the *Andrea Doria* and the luxury liner *Lusitania* are also among Dr. Ballard's scientific deep ocean archaeological accomplishments.

In 1989 Dr. Ballard founded the Jason Project after receiving thousands of letters from students like you wanting to know how he discovered the R.M.S. *Titanic*. The *Jason Project* is a non-profit educational organization working in partnership with teachers, students, corporations, educational institutions, and government to inspire in students a lifelong passion to pursue learning in science, math, and technology through exploration and discovery. The project's centerpiece is the Remote Operated Vehicle (ROV) *Jason.*

In the summer of 1997, Dr. Ballard and a team of scientists conducted the first deep ocean archaeological expedition using the Navy's deep-sea nuclear research submarine, *NR-1*. Dr. Ballard and his team went to the Mediterranean Sea in search of a fleet of ancient Roman shipwrecks dating to the fourth century A.D. They found more than they had anticipated – practically a fleet of ancient Roman ships, complete with cargo. The ships span five centuries of Roman history, beginning in the first century B.C.

"I think the most rewarding challenge is to take risks and gamble on the future and try to be five years ahead of others," says Ballard about his career. "I think young people need to understand that you need to take risks – to risk failing – before you can be successful."

Dr. Ballard has published more than 50 scientific articles, written books on his discoveries, and participated in the production of several undersea discovery and expedition television programs. He has earned numerous awards for his work. He offers this advice to science students like you when deciding on career avenues: "Most people who are interested in the ocean want to major in marine biology. This is a major mistake since your odds [of finding a job] are so low. Try the physical sciences and your chances are much better. Ocean engineering is a great major as well."

Figure 1-003

The R.M.S. *Titanic.*

In September 1985, the R.M.S. *Titanic* was found with its bow resting under approximately 3,800 meters (12,000 feet) of water.

Life on an Ocean Planet

The Scientist in You

What is a scientist?

Are you a scientist? Most people would answer "no." In modern culture, we view scientists as only those people with multiple college degrees who work in science. From that point of view, most people aren't scientists.

More accurately, though, a *scientist* is someone who uses the processes of science to find answers about how and why things work in the world and in the observable universe. Science isn't simply a body of facts, but the way you analyze those facts. This is what makes science an adventure full of discovery and wonder.

Think about your everyday actions. Have you ever gathered the facts of a problem and thought about how the facts relate to each other? Did this lead you to the probable cause of the problem? Perhaps you solved the problem based on eliminating the cause you uncovered. If your solution failed, did you then rethink the problem to find another solution? Then, in broad terms, this is the scientific process, and you *are* a scientist. Science involves testing *hypotheses* – educated guesses to answers to problems (more about hypotheses shortly). This is the heart of the scientific method. Using data to test hypotheses separates science from other methods of solving problems.

The purpose of this course and *Life on an Ocean Planet* is to expand your science knowledge and apply it to marine science – the study of the world's ocean. In this chapter, you'll learn why marine science is important to you. You'll start to see that the ocean affects your life every day. You'll also learn more about the process of science, and how to learn effectively from this book.

The Ocean Planet

What two influences and what three marine resources make the ocean important to life on Earth?

Have humans seen much of the ocean?

What effect can human interactions have on the ocean?

What is ocean literacy *and why is it important?*

There's a young lady named Karen. Under her parent's supervision, she is approached by dolphins while snorkeling, takes under-

STUDY QUESTIONS

Find the answers as you read.

1. What is a *scientist?*

2. What two influences and what three marine resources make the ocean important to life on Earth?

3. Have humans seen much of the ocean?

4. What effect can human interactions have on the ocean?

5. What is *ocean literacy* and why is it important?

Figure 1-1

Swimming with dolphins.

For Karen, biology and physics are experiences, not dreary school subjects.

water snapshots, and tugs her big sister's fin tips to tease her. For her, biology and physics are experiences, not dreary school subjects. She's seen sharks, frolicked with fish, raced rays, and watched whales. She's noted how light loses color at 10 meters (30 feet) compared to 5 meters (15 feet). On top of this, Karen is an aquanaut, having – more than once – spent 24 hours underwater and slept on the bottom of the sea in a habitat (at only 6 meters [20 feet]—but she's done it). She did all this before she turned 12.

Although still in high school, Karen is a marine scientist. She understands the basic principles of science and how they apply to this beautiful place full of fascinating life forms. Perhaps more importantly, Karen realizes that despite all we know about marine science, we barely understand the sea. She also realizes that her future and the Earth's future depend on the ocean.

If you look at Earth from space, you see a brilliant blue planet – an *ocean* planet. Look at a world map and you find the ocean borders most of the world's major cities. Study a diagram of ocean currents and you discover that they can affect global temperatures. If you could audit international economics, you would find that much of our material wealth comes from the sea.

The ocean produces two influences and many natural resources that make them vital to life on Earth. The weather and world climate patterns dictate how warm, cold, wet, or dry it will be. The ocean largely determines what organisms live on land, and where. The ocean provides important resources such as food and oxygen, and natural resources, such as oil. However, as you'll learn throughout this book, the ocean does far more than this for us.

Although humans have explored the seas for thousands of years, there's still more to learn than we know. We've seen all of the surface, but there's far, far more to discover *below* the surface than on it. To give you an idea of how little we've actually seen, if this page were the ocean, the part human eyes have seen would be the size of a period. For all we've learned, we haven't seen much.

However, human effects increasingly changes the ocean, too often in damaging ways. As we develop new technologies and the human population rises, these effects become more frequent, widespread and intense. Commercial fishing has severely depleted many types of fish. Pollution has deteriorated many marine environments. Crucial marine environments, such as coral reefs and mangroves, are dying off. The list could go on.

Fortunately, all isn't lost. There are ways to get the resources we need from the sea without destroying it. To make the necessary changes possible, people like you must understand the ocean, how it works, and why it's essential to all life. You and the rest of society benefit by understanding the marine environment because it gives you *ocean literacy*. Different groups have somewhat different specific definitions, but generally, *ocean literacy* means understanding the basic concepts related to how the ocean functions as an ecosystem, its importance to the Earth's ecosystem, and how and why it is vital to human existence.

Figure 1-2

Earth is really an ocean planet.

This NASA (National Aeronautic and Space Administration) photograph shows that the ocean covers more of the Earth's surface than does land.

Ocean literacy means you understand the consequences of human interactions with the sea. It makes you someone who can speak and act for marine preservation. It makes you part of the solution to the many problems.

Ocean literacy allows you to make responsible decisions related to the ocean. This includes voting, choosing what products and services to buy, and other decisions related to managing and preserving the ocean for our own sake and the future's sake. People who are unaware of what the ocean does and how it works are more likely to act in ways that jeopardize its future – and therefore, the planet's future. Those who *are* aware of these things understand why the ocean is vital and act accordingly, so it's important to make as many people ocean literate as possible.

Hopefully, you'll also find that understanding the marine environment benefits you because it's interesting and wonderful. The ocean holds opportunities for adventure, exploration, and discovery. One goal of *Life on an Ocean Planet* is to help show you these as you learn about the marine environment.

It doesn't matter whether you ultimately pursue a career as a marine archaeologist, engineer, physicist, mathematician, oceanographer, meteorologist, inventor, physician, businessperson, or a scientist in any specialty area. What you learn here can inspire daring ideas of investigation or discovery. It can help you design breakthroughs or world-changing technology. Regardless of your career choice, the science used to investigate and problem-solve in our ocean benefits you by making you a more capable person who contributes to society.

INTERNET PORTAL
SCiLINKS NSTA
Topic: Ocean Research
Go To: www.scilinks.org
Code: LOP2010

THINKING ABOUT THE PROCESS OF SCIENCE IN A CONCEPT MAP

Think about the process of science – not scientific facts you know, but how the process itself works. Write a list of ideas. After you read Chapter 1, you may want to change or add to the list. You may also find you know a lot more about the scientific process than you thought you did.

Investigation Question
You will construct a concept map that allows you to explore relationships between ideas and to discover new relationships about the process of science. (This activity fosters the development of critical thinking skills and the processes and skills of investigation. Drawing a concept map at the beginning of each chapter will help you to consider what you already know about the chapter topic. The concept map will also help you find what areas you need to learn more about. After reading the chapter, go back to your concept map and add the new things you have learned through reading.)

Hypothesis
The process of science is an ongoing, dynamic way of investigating the world.

Procedure
1. Write key words from the list of ideas you made on small pieces of paper. Decide which word will be the topic of your concept map. (A concept map is a representation of your understandings of a topic by arranging key ideas or concepts to show their relationships.) Place the topic at the top of the map. Underneath come concepts (thoughts or opinions, general notions or ideas) related to the topic, and under these are more concepts. The concepts become more specific, or more descriptive, as you move down the map away from the topic word.

2. Arrange your pieces of paper to show meaningful relationships to your topic and to each other. You will find that concept maps help you identify what you currently already know about a topic and what you need to know more about.

Results
1. After you complete an arrangement, copy it onto a large piece of paper. Connect concepts that you think relate with lines. To show a relationship more clearly, write one to three connecting words that make a logical statement about it.

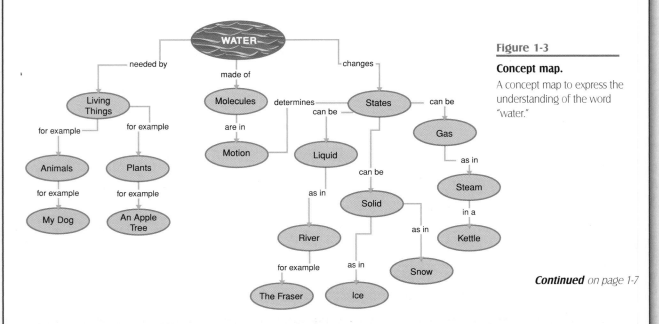

Figure 1-3

Concept map.

A concept map to express the understanding of the word "water."

Continued *on page 1-7*

Continued *from page 1-6*

2. Look for other connections between the concepts on your map. Draw lines and write connecting words. As you work on your map, you may wish to change the order of some of your words. That's fine. This is your concept map and it should represent what you currently think or know about the various concepts. You may think of other concepts that you could add to this map. Feel free to do this also until your concept map represents what you know about the process of science.

Conclude and Communicate

1. Compare your concept map with maps drawn by two or three classmates. Discussing your concept map with others may show you relationships you may not have thought of.

2. There is no "right" concept map. There are many ways of showing the relationships between ideas. Use the glossary list for each chapter to help you construct a concept map before reading the chapter. After reading the chapter, add to your concept map by reflecting on what you have learned through reading.

Reflecting on Your Learning: Concept Mapping as a Learning Tool

1. What is a concept map?

2. What is a concept?

3. What did you find easy about concept mapping? What did you find difficult?

4. How did you decide on the word for the top of your concept map?

5. Do you think concept mapping will help you to learn? Why or why not?

6. How did your concept map of the process of science differ from your classmates' maps?

7. After reading the chapter, how did your concept map change from your original?

ARE YOU LEARNING?

1. **A scientist is**
   A. someone with many college degrees.
   B. someone who knows a lot of science facts.
   C. someone who uses the processes of science to find answers.
   D. none of the above

2. **The ocean is important to life on Earth because it influences (choose all that apply)**
   A. weather.
   B. climate.
   C. Earth's orbit.
   D. solar flares.

3. **Three marine resources that are important include (choose all that apply)**
   A. food.
   B. trade.
   C. oxygen.
   D. natural resources including oil.

4. **Have humans seen much of the ocean?**
   A. Yes, humans have seen almost all of it.
   B. Yes and no. Humans have seen about half of it.
   C. No, humans have seen very, very little of it.
   D. There's not enough information to answer.

5. **Effects on the ocean from human interaction include (choose all that apply)**
   A. depleted fisheries.
   B. pollution.
   C. the loss of crucial marine environments.
   D. a general increase in marine life.

6. **Ocean literacy is important because**
   A. you'll be tested on it in college.
   B. you need it to be able to read books about the ocean.
   C. it allows you to make responsible decisions related to the ocean.

Defining Your Study

One of the most significant social changes in the last 150 years has been the increasing role of science in everyday life. As electronics and other technologies bring new capabilities and conveniences, the influence of science grows stronger. This is why science has become so important in your education. The National Science Education Standards state:

> In a world filled with the products of scientific inquiry, scientific literacy has become a necessity for everyone. Everyone needs to use scientific information to make choices that arise every day. Everyone needs to be able to engage intelligently in public discourse and debate about important issues that involve science and technology. And everyone deserves to share in the excitement and personal fulfillment that can come from understanding and learning about the natural world.

This is why studying marine science takes you beyond the ocean. It teaches you to draw on and integrate knowledge from other science areas. Through marine science, you learn about science as inquiry, science and technology, the history and nature of science, and science as personal and social perspectives. You also learn how science relates to other subjects.

Marine Science

What is marine science*?*

What is oceanography*?*

What are the four main branches of oceanography?

What has made the exploration of the ocean possible?

Because this is a book about *marine science*, maybe we should begin by formally defining marine science. Marine science is the process of discovering facts, processes, and unifying principles that explain the nature of the ocean, its associated life forms, and how the ocean interacts with other Earth systems. Marine science is an integral part of Earth science.

Marine science consists of four branches of *oceanography*. Oceanography is the science of recording and describing the ocean's contents and processes. That's very similar to marine science, and it's not unusual (or incorrect) to use the terms somewhat interchangeably.

STUDY QUESTIONS

Find the answers as you read.

1. What is *marine science*?

2. What is *oceanography*?

3. What are the four main branches of oceanography?

4. What has made the exploration of the ocean possible?

5. What traditional science disciplines does marine science draw on?

6. Why do most marine scientists have training in traditional science disciplines?

7. Beyond traditional science disciplines, what four study areas does marine science involve?

8. Why is the concept of *situatedness* important to marine scientists?

9. What disciplines apply basic marine science?

10. In what cross-discipline areas do marine scientists need education?

There are four main branches of oceanography: *biological oceanography, chemical oceanography, physical oceanography*, and *geological oceanography*. Each of these has subdivisions.

Biological oceanography (also called marine biology) studies the incredible diversity of life in the ocean, how life influences Earth systems, and ocean's role as their habitat.

Chemical oceanography studies the chemistry of seawater. Chemical oceanographers measure the rates and effects of chemical reactions in the ocean, and examine chemical changes brought about by nature and people.

Geological oceanography concerns itself with the geology of the ocean. It examines the composition of marine sediments and rocks. It also studies undersea volcanoes, seabed movement, undersea earthquakes, and other interactions between rock and sea.

Physical oceanography is the study of ocean influences on weather, climate and water movement, such as waves, currents, and tides. Physical oceanographers are also interested in how sound and light travel through water.

In *Life on an Ocean Planet*, you'll study all four types of oceanography. However, you'll quickly notice that these disciplines rarely stand alone. For example, if you study sound in the sea (physical oceanography), you quickly realize that it tells you something about how whales sense what's around them (biological oceanography). It's possible to use sound to study sediments (geological oceanography). Differences in water chemistry (chemical oceanography) affect how sound travels through the water. Because so much of oceanography revolves around marine life and how it survives, you'll find most references between biological oceanography and one of the other three.

Karen, the young marine scientist you read about earlier, may grow up to be a professional physical, biological, geological, or chemical oceanographer. The marine sciences have been around for hundreds of years. However, it is really only in the last five or so decades that true exploration of the ocean has become possible. What has made marine exploration and their associated careers possible is *technology*.

Imagine squeezing into a small submersible with Karen for a research dive to 2,000 meters (6,562 feet) or picture diving with Karen using special scuba gear and synthetic breathing gases to 100 meters (330 feet) to discover new fish species. Maybe you'd like to follow in the footsteps of Dr. Ballard and explore ancient shipwrecks with ROVs (remotely operated vehicles).

It is through these technologies that true marine exploration has become possible. But, it comes at a price. It can cost anywhere

Figure 1-4a

Biological oceanography – surveying fish.

Figure 1-4b

Chemical oceanography – water analysis.

Figure 1-4c

Geological oceanography – exploring deep-sea sediment.

Figure 1-4d

Physical oceanography – determining how the ocean affects weather.

Courtesy of Harbor Branch Oceanographic

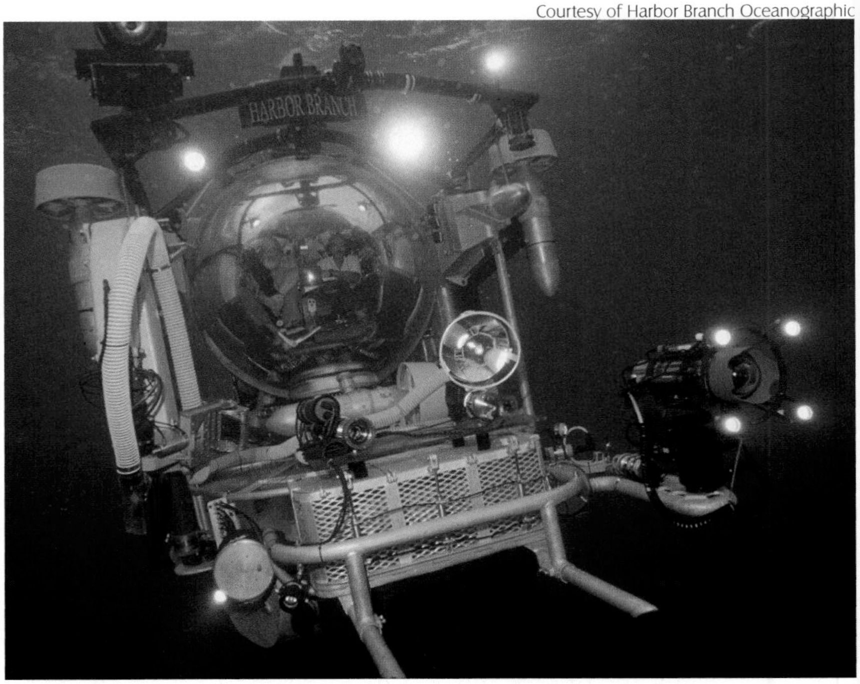

Figure 1-5

Johnson-Sea-Link (JSL) I. Submersibles take scientists to depths they cannot reach by any other means. Technology is used by all types of oceanographers.

from hundreds to hundreds of thousands of dollars to use state-of-the-art marine exploration technology. Therefore, those using these technologies must know exactly why, what, where, and how they're studying ahead of time.

Yet, this is one of the draws of marine science. Imagine a 10 hour dive in a submersible. The sunlight fades as you descend into the depths to a bottom never seen before. If you didn't understand oceanography, you could come upon a world-changing discovery and not even know it. But, as a marine scientist, that doesn't happen. Instead, you collect samples, take measurements, and listen through hydrophones, carefully entering the data into your computer. This is part of "doing" marine science – experiencing the unknown and carefully recording what you find and observe.

Later you will "do" marine science by examining your data and samples. You will spend hours trying to explain the facts and processes behind your observations. If that doesn't sound so exciting, picture this: One day, all your research adds up. Something new unfolds before you – a discovery. Perhaps it will be a new drug that cures disease. Perhaps it will be a compound used for high-tech aerospace engineering. Perhaps it will be a new species of bacteria. Whatever it is, it will be a contribution to knowledge and the well being of society. When you experience it, you'll realize it is far more rewarding and exciting than a submersible dive.

Integrating the Sciences

What traditional science disciplines does marine science draw on?

Why do most marine scientists have training in traditional science disciplines?

Just as each branch of oceanography interacts with the others, marine science also interacts with the more traditional science disciplines. Since all science is built on primarily on mathematics, oceanographers often spend more time in front of a computer than on the water. To understand ocean systems, marine scientists must be well versed in the traditional science disciplines of physical science, life science, and Earth and space science. Yet in a shared manner, marine scientists also help expand the knowledge of mathematics and the sciences – it's a two way street.

One advantage of studying marine science is that you can learn something about all scientific disciplines – especially the physical, life and Earth and space sciences. As a marine scientist, you integrate traditional science concepts and apply them to marine science. In many respects, this gives you a broader and more complete understanding of how the traditional sciences interrelate than if you studied each of them separately.

Physical science is the study of matter and energy. It involves examining and understanding the structure of atoms and molecules, and the properties of different energy forms such as light, heat, and sound. Chemistry and physics are two forms of physical science that you'll learn and apply from a marine perspective. For example, you'll study the chemical properties of water and how

Scott Bauer, US Department of Agriculture   Stephen Asumus, US Department of Agriculture

Figure 1-6a   **Figure 1-6b**

Physical science.

Physical science involves the study of matter and energy and their interactions. Chemistry and physics are two physical sciences.

Figure 1-7a

Figure 1-7b

Figure 1-7c

Life science.

Life science involves the study of any of the branches of natural science dealing with the structure and behavior of living organisms.

energy flows through the living and nonliving parts of the marine and Earth environment.

Life science is the study of living things and their interactions with their environments. Biology, physiology, and ecology are all forms of life science that apply to marine science. Among other topics, you'll study different types of marine organisms, how marine physiology differs from terrestrial physiology, evolution theory, and many other components of life science that apply to the ocean.

Earth and space science is the study of the physical Earth, the solar system, the universe, and their interrelationships. It studies the interactions among water, carbon, other cycles, and the relationships of the Earth, sun and moon. Geology, astronomy, and astrophysics are three types of Earth and space science. Among other phenomena, Earth and space science interests you as a marine scientist because it explains how the ocean formed. It also applies to how the moon causes the tides, how the Earth's orbit

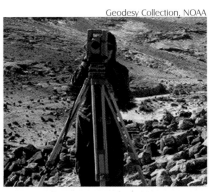

Figure 1-8a

Figure 1-8b

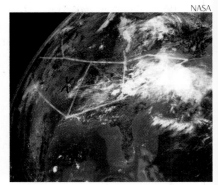

Figure 1-8c

Earth and space science.

Earth and space science involves the study of the energy in the Earth system, geochemical cycles, the origin and evolution of the Earth system, and the universe.

around the sun affects climate and weather, and the formation and the composition of ocean sediments.

Because marine science uses all three of the traditional science disciplines and mathematics, most marine scientists have training in them. Marine scientists draw on research from all three to understand what they observe in the ocean. In this way, marine science is truly an interdisciplinary course of study. You cannot really study marine science without studying physical science, life science, Earth and space science, mathematics and statistics.

Studying Science Itself

Beyond traditional science disciplines, what four study areas does marine science involve?

Why is the concept of situatedness *important to marine scientists?*

The study of marine science involves more than integrating the traditional science disciplines to examine the ocean. It is about studying science itself. Science is a way of thinking. It relates to technology, it has social influence, and it has a history. Therefore, marine science involves four study areas beyond the traditional science disciplines. They are *science as inquiry, science and technology, science in personal and social perspectives*, and the *historical nature of science*. You'll find these interwoven throughout each chapter as they relate to marine science.

Science as inquiry is learning to apply science as a way of solving problems and answering questions. It's not simply learning science as a process (though that is important), but combining the process with scientific knowledge and critical thinking. This book and the activities you will complete teach you how to choose the right method to solve a single problem. That's more important than doing page after page of the same type of problem.

The science-as-inquiry approach serves you five ways when you study marine science (or any science). First, it helps you to understand concepts. Second, it helps you to learn how to know that you know something. Third, it teaches you the nature of science – how science works. Fourth, it develops your ability to think critically and ask questions inde-

Courtesy of Harbor Branch Oceanographic

Figure 1-9

Integrating the traditional sciences.

Learning marine science involves integrating the traditional sciences and more. To understand the ocean and its surroundings you must study science as inquiry, the relationship of science to technology, how science affects personal and social perspectives, and the historical nature of science.

S. Bernhardt, FGBNMS/Ocean Explorer, NOAA

Figure 1-10

Science as inquiry.

Science as inquiry involves investigation as well as knowledge to explain.

Figure 1-11

The relationship between science and technology.

With a 1,361 kg (3,000 pound) payload grasped between them, the space station's new Canadian Arm 2 shakes hands with the space shuttle's Canadian-built robot arm. Technology can help us make sense of the natural world.

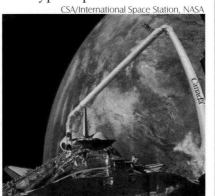

CSA/International Space Station, NASA

Figure 1-12

Science in personal and social perspective.

When studying marine science, we need to be aware of the social and economic effects of our decisions, specifically with issues that deal with the environment. Should this forest be cut for wood product to build homes for the homeless? Or, should groves of trees be cultivated to enhance physical and chemical processes essential to life on the planet?

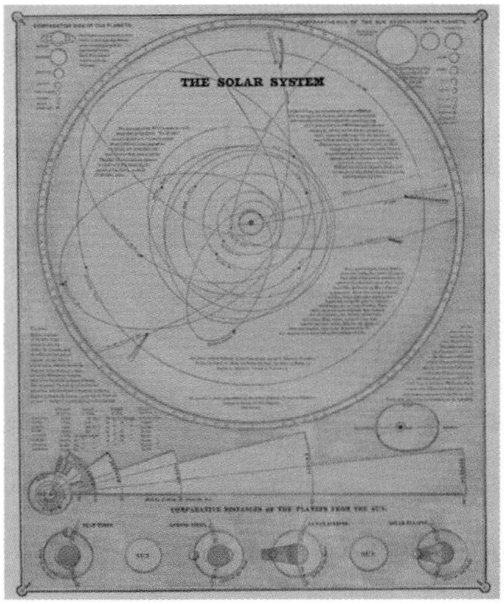

Figure 1-13

History and nature of science.

Foundations for what we know to be true come from historical examples such as this 1884 George Cram map of the solar system. We've built on this early understanding of the solar system to send probes to distant planets and beyond.

pendently. Fifth, it makes science something you'll use as you go through life.

Science and technology involves learning how science advances technology and vice-versa. Throughout *Life on an Ocean Planet*, you'll find examples of inventions created to solve problems for marine scientists. You'll also find examples of how new technologies lead to unexpected discoveries or new ways of researching. Aerospace technology, for example, now provides oceanographers the means to map the ocean's level and determine its surface temperature by satellite.

Each chapter starts with a marine scientist profile. You'll find that many of these reflect the relationship between science and technology. An excellent example is the one you just read about Dr. Robert Ballard. Without submersible and ROV technology, the science of deep water archaeology would be difficult.

Science in personal and social perspectives relates to how science affects you personally and society as a whole. It also relates to how society influences science. Science and technology affect personal health, the economy, natural resources, political thinking, warfare, and personal and social values, to name only a few. You'll see that marine science in particular relates to this issue. As described in Chapter 2, from the earliest times until now, much of ocean research grew out of humanity's desire for resources from the sea. Chapter 17 discusses how the need to keep resources sustainable drives much research today.

The personal nature of science also involves career choices you will make. More and more careers are built directly or indirectly on science and technology. The better you understand science and how it works, the better you can choose a career path that you find rewarding and productive. This is another reason for the marine scientist profiles at the start of each chapter. They give you an inside view from successful professionals who share their wisdom when it comes to choosing a career.

The historical nature of science involves understanding how science evolved as a discipline. This is important because, historically, discoveries in science accompany changes in technology and advances in understanding. You'll learn that advances in scientific understanding are *situated* – come about – within specific circumstances and contexts. *Situatedness* is the explanation of when, where, and why a concept came about. This helps us to understand the concept's past, its appropriateness today, and its usefulness in the future.

Situatedness is important to marine scientists because in oceanography, you may apply established scientific concepts that you will never personally demonstrate or observe. How do you know that these are valid? How do you know when to question these assumptions? A historical perspective of discoveries, the scientific method, and social influences on science – situatedness – gives you some basis for judging the validity of scientific concepts.

The Cross-Disciplinary Nature of Marine Science

What disciplines apply basic marine science?

In what cross-discipline areas do marine scientists need education?

Just as marine science draws on other sciences, other sciences, professions, and careers draw on basic marine science. These disciplines include atmospheric science, astronomy, ecology, biomedical research, environmental science, and marine engineering. Professionals such as marine lawyers, politicians, governmental policy makers, civil engineers, marine architects, and astronauts have backgrounds that include marine science. As discussed in Chapter 17, even United States presidents, including President Harry Truman in the 1940s and 1950s, have drawn on marine science to make national policy decisions.

Because marine science is a broad field, marine scientists need more than a formal education in the sciences. They also need education in *cross-discipline* subjects such as mathematics, history, technology, social sciences, literature, and the arts. *Life on an Ocean Planet* addresses this by bringing these cross-discipline subjects into your studies.

Mathematics is the universal "language" of science that helps you explain the physical nature of the ocean. Ocean chemistry, for instance, requires you to communicate your understandings in symbolic form (formal logic). You also solve many physical science problems using mathematics. You may be asked to explain what happens in a chemical reaction by using mathematical formulas or you may need to communicate your data with charts, graphs, or tables.

Mathematics is also relevant when studying life science. It applies to population surveys and estimating the quantities of energy and nutrients in living systems. You may use mathematics

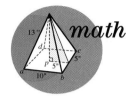

Figure 1-14

Math.
Learning science through the application of mathematical concepts.

Figure 1-15

History.
Learning science through historical review provides insight to the past, present, and future of our ocean.

Figure 1-16

Technology.
Some say technology causes our problems while others say technology increases our knowledge.

Figure 1-17

Social sciences.
Considering the decisions you make about the environment may affect the life of others on the planet.

Figure 1-18

Literature.
Science requires you to conclude and announce your conclusions to others. This is done using the literary form.

Figure 1-19

Arts.
Sometimes your method of experimentation will take the form of videography or ethnography rather than the typical experiment.

for determining whether patterns are significant or random. You even use mathematics when scuba diving or diving in a submersible to determine how long you can safely stay under water.

A *historical background*, as previously mentioned, provides a context of how and why the study of oceanography has changed over time. Through history, you learn that many people and events that seemed unrelated at the time came to influence marine science. By understanding how people and events shaped marine science in the past, you gain a perspective of how today's people and events shape marine science for tomorrow. It's hard to move forward in any discipline if you don't know what's behind you.

Technology will continue to link closely with studying the ocean. As you read previously, it is really the advances in technology that have made modern oceanography possible. More than likely, this trend will continue. In fact, a promising career opportunity is in developing marine exploration technologies.

Social sciences tremendously influence marine science and vice-versa. As we rely more and more on marine resources, the sea becomes increasingly socially significant. Issues such as pollution, global climate change, commercial fishing, and offshore oil drilling will have a direct effect on your life. The discovery of a huge new oil field by a marine geologist, for example, may change what you pay for gasoline. The policies of marine resource managers can affect what you pay for a can of tuna, or even whether it's a wise decision to buy tuna at all.

Over the years, the ocean has influenced *literature and the arts*. Homer's *Odyssey* is one example. More recent examples include Hemingway's The *Old Man and the Sea* and the wonderful graphics, clearly marked illustrations, and colorful photos in the book you are now reading. Literature and the arts also relate to your work in this course. Scientists must be able to write and communicate clearly. Your teacher may evaluate your learning and understanding based on what you present through writing.

Underwater imaging for television and magazines has become an art and craft practiced by amateurs and professionals. With today's well-educated readers, writers have to be accurate when writing novels or screen plays. When the story involves the ocean, they apply marine science to make their stories more realistic.

Given the cross-disciplinary nature of marine science, don't be surprised when your understanding of mathematics, history, technology, social science, literature, and the arts are put to the test. Undoubtedly, studying the wonders of the ocean will improve your knowledge and skill with each of these cross-disciplinary subjects.

1. **Marine science is (choose all that apply)**

    A. the study of fish and fish-like organisms.

    B. the process of discovering the facts, processes, and unifying principles that explain the nature of the ocean and its associated life forms.

    C. research carried on by the US Marines.

    D. none of the above

2. **Oceanography is the science of (choose all that apply)**

    A. recording and describing the ocean's processes and contents.

    B. studying the physical, but not biological, aspects of the sea.

    C. creating oceanic graphs.

    D. Latin and Greek applied to the sea.

3. **The four main branches of oceanography include (choose all that apply)**

    A. biological oceanography.

    B. spatial oceanography.

    C. physical oceanography.

    D. graphical oceanography.

4. **It is_____that has made true exploration of the ocean possible.**

    A. government funding

    B. changes in international law

    C. a declining interest in space exploration

    D. technology

5. **Marine science involves the traditional science disciplines of (choose all that apply)**

    A. physical science.

    B. life science.

    C. paranormal science.

    D. Earth and space science.

6. **Most marine scientists have training in the traditional science disciplines because marine science is interdisciplinary and draws extensively on traditional science research.**

    A. true

    B. false

7. **Beyond traditional science disciplines, marine science involves four study areas that include (choose all that apply)**

    A. science as inquiry.

    B. science and technology.

    C. science in personal and social perspectives.

    D. the historical nature of science.

8. **Situatedness is important because**

    A. it allows you to tell if you're in a situation.

    B. it gives you the right to dispute the experts.

    C. it is important to take your mind off science periodically.

    D. none of the above

9. **Other disciplines that draw on marine science may include (choose all that apply)**

    A. atmospheric science.

    B. ecology.

    C. astronomy.

    D. none of the above

10. **Marine scientists need cross-discipline training in (choose all that apply)**

    A. mathematics.

    B. history.

    C. technology.

    D. social sciences.

Find the answers as you read.

1. What is *science*?

2. What is a *technology*?

3. What effects have science and technology had on humans and other organisms?

4. What three broad actions can society take with respect to the effects of science and technology on the Earth's environment? Which of these appears to be the most logical?

5. When do you apply scientific process skills?

6. What are the five basic steps to the scientific method?

7. What is a *hypothesis*?

8. How do inductive and deductive reasoning apply to forming a hypothesis?

9. What is a *theory*?

10. Why is reporting results crucial to the scientific process?

11. How does science progress?

12. How does it benefit you to stay up to date with current trends, findings, and developments in science and technology?

Figure 1-20

Two marine scientists in a JSL submersible.
The *Johnson-Sea-Link (JSL) I* and *II* are owned and operated by Harbor Branch Oceanographic Institution. These highly maneuverable pieces of technology measure 12 meters (39 feet) long, 3.3 meters (10 feet) high, and 2.5 meters (8 feet) wide. These submersibles are capable of diving to 914 meters (3,000 feet) and travel at a maximum speed of 1.8 meters per second (1.2 mph). Scientist, aviator, inventor and oceanographer Edwin Link built the first JSL in 1971.

Science, Technology, Society, and You

Imagine that you and Karen, the young marine scientist, are going to venture to the bottom of the sea in a submersible. It took perhaps six months to put the expedition together, plus a week for the research ship to reach the dive site. The support crew needed 12 hours to prepare the submersible. From an immediate perspective, it took about six months, seven days, and 12 hours to set up the dive. The staff and crew consist of about 18 people.

From a broad perspective, it took centuries and thousands of people to make your dive possible. Submarine technology dates back to Alexander the Great (356-323 B.C.), with each generation of submarine inventors learning from the previous. Electronic advancements gave submarines instruments beyond imagination only 150 years ago. Chemical science makes it possible for your submarine to reuse the air you need on the dive. Your research submersible is the latest in perhaps a thousand years of marine engineering and submarine technology.

Next, consider the *reason* for your dive. If you're a biological oceanographer, the data you're gathering is the latest step in more than 2,000 years in the study of life. Now consider the technological advances in ships, seafaring instruments, wireless communications, computing, and even food storage for your expedition. The number of people and the work hours that led to these would be staggering.

The point is that science and technology build on each other. They affect our lives broadly and personally far beyond what we may see. For better and worse, the human condition revolves around them. You cannot escape them. Therefore, it's important for you to understand the foundational concepts of science and how they relate to technology.

Courtesy of Harbor Branch Oceanographic

Science—A Definition

What is science?

We've been using the term "science" quite a bit. Because you're reading *Life on an Ocean Planet*, it's reasonable to expect that you already basically understand what science is. But, since you're going to be studying marine science formally, it's important to know the precise definition.

Dictionaries say that science is a body of knowledge. That is, facts, explanations, and ideas that scientists use to describe the world and universe around us. That is correct, but not complete. *Science* (from the Latin *scire* meaning to *know*) is a body of knowledge and an *organized method* used to gain knowledge about the *observable* universe. Note the key words "organized method" and "observable." As you'll see shortly, these are pivotal to conducting true science.

Also, scientific knowledge is not "truth," but the best explanation available based on the existing objective and *observable* evidence. This means evidence that anyone can see, hear, taste, smell, feel, or detect with scientific instruments.

Technology—A Benefit and a Burden

What is a technology?

What effects have science and technology had on humans and other organisms?

What three broad actions can society take with respect to the effects of science and technology on the Earth's environment? Which of these appears to be the most logical?

Technology is a common word that we throw around meaning some kind of tool, especially an electronic one. Formally, however, a *technology* (from the Greek *technologia* meaning *systematic treatment*) is a material system that produces intended results. When we say "technology" in a general sense, we mean knowledge of those systems.

Today, science and technology go almost hand-in-hand, but technology predates science. Fire is a technology. People created water wheels, horse-drawn plows, and many other tools using simple science through trial and error.

It's obvious that technology has many effects on our lives and on the world around us. Two hundred years ago it took weeks to send a message from the Atlantic coast to the Pacific coast of North America. Today casual conversations go on between both places thousands of times a day. And, technology is accelerating. When your parents were young, to make a call you went to a telephone. Today you take a cell phone out of your pocket. If you're wearing a Bluetooth headset, you just press a button. Technology provides the tools that scientists use to make discoveries that lead to new technologies.

You can probably list hundreds of ways technologies have improved daily life just by looking around your house. Beyond that, consider health care, transportation, communication, exploration, and agriculture – you name it – and you will find there's almost no material area of human life that technology hasn't improved. Even our pets and livestock enjoy better medical care through technology. Clearly, one effect of science and technology has been to improve the lives of humans and other organisms.

Unfortunately, there's another side. Another effect of science and technology has been to threaten and degrade the lives of humans and other organisms. These may be minor effects, such as eye strain from watching too much television, or they may be major effects, such as pollution spills and overfishing wiping out huge populations of marine fish. Today we face problems such as global climate change that may be due to the burning fossil fuels, or air pollution that is definitely a result of burning such fuels. We are also facing other concerns about cancer-causing toxins, and destruction of our freshwater supplies from indiscriminant pollution. Technology raises social questions and problems. For example, questions about the ethics of human cloning and stem cell research didn't come up until technology made these possible.

Technology isn't going away. The most immediate negative effect concerning everyone is that on the environment. If we destroy the ability for Earth to support human life, we destroy ourselves. Basically, there are only three broad actions that society can take with respect to the effects of science and technology on the environment:

1. Consider the environment a lost cause and disregard the effects. The likely conclusion is that the global environment will become extensively degraded. There would be massive death among humans and organisms. Species could become extinct on a massive scale, and that could include *Homo sapiens* – us!

2. Dismiss the effects on the environment as overstated by scientists and therefore actually inconsequential. This is a different attitude but leads to the same result. A positive, long-term outcome relies on the wishful thinking that the environmental damage recorded by thousands of scientists for more than 40 years worldwide is wrong. That's not likely.

3. Prioritize the consequences to the environment in developing and applying technologies. This would mean phasing out or replacing damaging technologies (such as moving from an oil based energy society to something like hydrogen based energy) and finding ways to repair the environmental damage. The likely conclusion is that this has high short-term costs, but a high probability that the global environment will survive. No doubt there will always be damaging effects, but more than likely this damage would be limited and controlled.

Without a doubt, the last broad action appears the most logical.

TECHNOLOGY AROUND YOU

Examples of technology are all around – at school, at the gym, at the mall, in the business center, and in your home. Sometimes we take technology for granted.

Investigation Question
Look at the picture and list the products of technology.

Hypothesis
Technology has both positive and negative effects.

Procedure
1. In your notebook classify the technologies you listed. Use classifications such as:

    • involves energy or changes in energy

    • involves living or once-living components

    • synthetic—made from artificial materials rather than natural plants, animals, or minerals.

    Add classifications as appropriate. You may classify the same item under more than one classification.

2. Draw a picture of a kitchen scene 200 years ago. In your notebook, classify the technologies in your 200 year old kitchen into the same categories as above.

3. Identify and justify the product of technology that you think has affected your life the most.

Results
1. Use an example of each from both the modern and the 200 year old kitchen to illustrate the differences between science and technology.

2. Give an example of a technology in the modern kitchen that has both good and bad effects.

3. Suggest at least one environmental problem associated with technology in the modern kitchen.

Cheryl Regan

Figure 1-21

What technology is in this kitchen?
The digital home: cooking in the high-tech kitchen. Smart appliances may mean less time spent preparing meals.

Conclude and Communicate
Some people believe that all environmental problems arise from science and technology. Others think that problems can only be solved through science and technology. With one or more classmates debate your thoughts on the roles of science and technology in solving environmental problems.

Reflecting on Our Learning—Technology
1. Give two examples of science-related issues that you've seen in the news recently.

2. "Science and technology have changed the way we do things." Explain what this means with some examples from your two kitchens.

The Scientific Method

When do you apply scientific process skills?

What are the five basic steps to the scientific method?

What is a hypothesis?

How do inductive and deductive reasoning apply to forming a hypothesis?

What is a theory?

Why is reporting results crucial to the scientific process?

In the definition of science, you saw that science is an organized method and a body of knowledge. The formal, organized steps that scientists follow in proposing explanations for their observations and then testing their explanations are called the *scientific method.* Let's look at how the scientific method works.

CHANCE, SERENDIPITY, DISCOVERY, AND THE SCIENTIFIC METHOD

In science, chance is seldom acknowledged as a contributing factor in important discoveries. Yet, chance has played a key role in discoveries that reveal our natural world. For example, consider the discoveries of the antibiotic penicillin and of the hydrothermal vent communities on mid-ocean ridges.

In 1928, Alexander Fleming was researching the properties of the group of bacteria of the genus *Staphylococcus.* His problem during this research was the frequent contamination of culture plates with airborne molds. One day he observed a contaminated culture plate and noted that the *Staphylococci* bacteria were dead in the area immediately surrounding an invading mold growth. He realized that something in the mold was inhibiting growth of the surrounding bacteria. Subsequently, Fleming isolated an extract from the mold and he named it penicillin.

Ten years after Fleming's discovery, Ernst Chain, Howard Florey, and Edward Abraham of Oxford University were able to purify and stabilize a form of penicillin that enabled demonstration of its therapeutic potential. Again, chance favored their work. Unknown to them, the species of animal that they chose for laboratory studies turned out to be one of few species that do not find penicillin toxic. Had they chosen to work with a different species, they might have deemed penicillin too toxic for use, and humankind would have been deprived of the phenomenal life-saving ability of this drug.

In 1977, scientists studying plate tectonics (see Chapter 13) detected unusually hot water around rift valleys and mid-ocean ridges. Scientists on this first voyage to the Galapagos Rift found the hot water vents and much more. To their surprise, they also found a rich community of specialized organisms living at approximately 2,400 -2,700 meters (7,900 - 8,900 feet) – an area typically barren of most life. Organisms included clams, giant tubeworms, and crustaceans. They discovered a vast ecosystem based not on photosynthesis, but chemosynthesis. Until this chance discovery, all life was believed to be based on the photosynthetic process. This chance discovery shook the scientific world.

The scientific method is typically noted for its order and control. In fact, we are taught that without these characteristics, experimental research may yield invalid results. Therefore, chance should play little or no role in the process of the scientific method. But, what is chance? When is chance truly an accident and when is it foreseeable? Historically, some chance discoveries have led to startling new ideas that eventually directed important further scientific investigation of natural phenomena.

Although scientists pride themselves on the theories of science being based on methodical research and the scientific method, key discoveries often occur by chance or serendipity. The most interesting questions examine things that we neither know nor expect. In fact, revealing the unknown and unexpected is a good definition of discovery. With the current demands on scientific research to solve critical problems and provide modern amenities, the unexpected, chance event should not be discounted.

Basically, science is the process of asking a question about the observable world, making an educated guess at an answer to the question, and then testing whether the facts support your guess. This process isn't restricted to scientists, of course. You do this every day, informally, perhaps without even realizing it. Suppose you sit down at your desk and discover someone accidentally left a notebook behind. You ask other students if they know whose notebook it is. They tell you that Pat sits in the same desk during the previous period. You guess that the notebook is Pat's. You test your guess by asking Pat about the notebook. If it's not Pat's notebook, you ask more questions until you find out to whom it belongs.

Similarly, scientists interpret information from their observations to understand the natural world and how it works. They may come up with several plausible explanations for their observations, and then apply tests (experiments) to see which explanation best fits the facts. As they come across new evidence (observations or other experiments) that no longer fits their explanations, they revise their explanations or replace them entirely.

Prehistoric people studied nature primarily to develop early technologies and use resources. Many people credit the early Greeks, particularly the philosopher Aristotle (384-322 B.C.), with the birth of scientific thought. Aristotle was among the first naturalists to systematically record what he observed and draw conclusions from his observations.

Most historians date the birth of the scientific method to around 1500 A.D. This was the time of the European Renaissance, ending the Middle Ages. It was a time of new ways of thinking and an expansion of human knowledge and learning. At this time, naturalists began to formalize the steps used in science. The thinking was that, by making science formal and repeatable, it would

M. Grady/Ocean Explorer, NOAA

Figure 1-22

How do scientists solve problems?

Science is actually an ever-changing body of knowledge and an active process that thousands of people around the world engage in every day.

SCIENCE, PHILOSOPHY AND THE SEARCH FOR TRUTH

What is science? In a nutshell, it's a tool for finding out about how the universe and its components work and why. It's a search for truth, which leads to the question, what is truth? That's a harder question, but most people would agree that truth is the body of real things, events, and facts. In other words, when we look for truth, we're looking for the explanation that is always correct and accounts for all circumstances and all points of view.

Broadly, the search for truth is philosophy (from the Greek *philos* meaning *the love of* and *sophia* meaning *wisdom* or *knowledge*). Science is one of several philosophies seeking truth, but not the only one. In Western culture, science philosophy strongly influences how people think and how they perceive what is or is not true. However, science doesn't influence all cultures as strongly, nor all individuals to the same degree.

Science is a philosophy based on the principle that truth is discovered through evidence that you can observe directly or indirectly with instruments. The science philosophy says that only evidence that more than one person can observe is valid. In other words, science seeks to eliminate human subjectivity in determining what is truth.

Other philosophies approach the search for truth differently.

In the classic movie *Creator*, geneticist Dr. Harry Wolper (played by Peter O'Toole) says: "One day science will come galloping triumphantly over the hill only to find that religion has been there all along." Many philosophies accept faith, personal experiences, testimonies of personal experiences, and other evidence that one would not consider to be scientific.

But, despite our cultural biases, it's important to realize that lacking objectivity does not make such a philosophy necessarily wrong. In fact, if you apply science to itself, you must conclude that there's no objective evidence that science can provide all truths. Science is an ongoing process, so scientists don't even consider scientific findings "truths," but "theories" – the current best estimate of what the truth may be.

As a scientist, be scientific: be objective, get the best evidence possible, consider the evidence objectively, and reach an objective conclusion. Make the theory line up with the facts, not the other way around. That's what makes good science.

As a human being, however, remember that there are other ways to seek truth. Realize that while thinking like a scientist will help you with many of life's questions, it can't answer all of them. A balanced person uses science as a tool to answer the questions science can answer – but not necessarily the only tool to answer all questions.

---

be objective. This made science more reliable and credible. It also made it easier for scientists to build on each other's work.

When you apply the scientific method, you apply *scientific process skills.* These are skills such as identifying the problem (question), classifying data, communicating findings, comparing observations, constructing models, interpreting measurements, predicting outcomes, and recording data.

For science to work, you must apply scientific process skills in a logical sequence. You can't test your explanation until you create it. There are five basic steps to the scientific method, generally in this sequence:

1. identify the problem (or question)
2. make a hypothesis
3. test the hypothesis
4. interpret and analyze results
5. report results, procedures, and conclusions

Let's look at each step in more detail.

1. Identify the problem (or question). Generally, scientific research begins with a problem or question based on observations. The question can take either of two basic forms. The first form is to ask what process led to a set of facts. Facts are always actual observations – documentable evidence that you see, hear, taste, smell, touch, or detect with scientific instruments.

For instance, suppose you observe (fact) lots of fish around a human-made reef. You might ask: "Did the fish grow and breed on artificial reefs or did they relocate from natural reefs?"

The second form is to ask what facts you would observe if a process took place. For instance, a marine resources manager might ask: "What will happen to local fish populations if an industry dumps 20,000 metric tons of fertilizer in the bay?"

2. Make a hypothesis. Once you have a question, based on your observations and research, you make an educated scientific guess that you can test about the answer. This is called a *hypothesis* (plural *hypotheses*, from the Greek *hypo* meaning *under* or *less than*, and *thesis* meaning *set down* or *established*). It is a formulation of the best explanation you can think of based on what you know so far. It is based on previous observations and tests.

Creating your hypothesis can apply *inductive* or *deductive* reasoning. You use *inductive* reasoning to propose a process that explains the facts you observe. You use *deductive* reasoning to propose what you would observe should a known process take place.

For example, suppose you come into a room and smell smoke and sulfur, but no obvious source of fire. Through inductive reasoning and previous experience with match smells, you might explain your observations with "Someone probably lit a match." On the other hand, suppose you enter a room and find someone about to light a match. Through deductive reasoning and your past experience with matches, you might conclude: "If he lights the match, the room will probably smell of smoke and sulfur."

In forming your hypothesis, you may apply a law. In science, a law is an invariable relationship or process assumed to always exist. For example, the law of gravity says that all mass attracts other mass, and that it is an unwavering property of mass everywhere in the universe. There is no way to test that the principle is universal, so its universality is an assumption. A law is therefore considered valid until someone observes facts that contradict it (which is very rare). Laws are particularly common in the physical sciences. They provide the groundwork on which to build hypotheses and theories based on observed facts.

3. Test the hypothesis. A hypothesis may be an excellent guess, but until you have objective evidence (fact) that supports it, it's still only a guess, scientifically speaking. The most direct way of doing this is with an experiment or series of experiments. An experiment is an objective test of your hypothesis with observable results.

Suppose a hypothesis regarding dumping 20,000 metric tons of fertilizer in a bay were: "Dumping 20,000 metric tons of fertilizer in the bay will cause the zooplankton (animal plankton) to overpopulate and consume all the oxygen in the water, causing all the fish to die." To test this, you might take an aquarium and fill it with plankton, fish, and water from the bay. Next, you would put in enough fertilizer to have the same concentration as would exist with 20,000 metric tons dumped in the bay. You would determine this based on the physical laws that govern the solution and distribution of chemicals in water.

If the plankton blooms and the fish die, you have supported your hypothesis. To be more thorough and add credibility, you would fill two aquariums as described. You would add fertilizer to one (experimental) and not to the other (control). If the plankton bloom and fish die only in the experimental aquarium, you have strong evidence that the independent variable (adding the fertilizer) caused the fish deaths. It's even more convincing if you use instruments to measure the oxygen level in the water and find it significantly lower in the experimental aquarium after the plankton blooms.

Experiments aren't the only way to test a hypothesis. Sometimes you test a hypothesis by examining existing information. This is important because some experiments aren't always possible. For example, you cannot change an ocean current to see if it influences marine life near a particular coastal area. This particularly relates to studying the past. You cannot do an experiment to test whether Julius Caesar was a real person, for example. In such a case, scientists support a hypothesis based on the best evidence available (historical documentation). The conclusion will always rest with circumstantial evidence. We will never be able to observe directly that Julius Caesar ever lived. However, the surviving recorded testimonies of witnesses, along with other documentation and evidence provide such a strong case that he did that it would be difficult to dispute reasonably.

Practicality can be an issue. Researching large populations or large areas often relies on sampling because it's impossible to test every person or location. In this case, you base your experiment and gather your data (a set of facts derived from direct observation – singular *datum*) from randomly selected samples of the population or area. Then you would use statistical methods to estimate how reliably you can expect the information to apply to the entire population or area.

Sometimes you don't do an experiment because the data you need already exist. Suppose, based on some geological observations, that you develop a hypothesis about where volcanoes must form. You determine that if all volcanoes occur above approximately 36° north latitude in North America, you have support for your hypothesis. You could spend years searching the entire continent to record where you find volcanoes, but the information already exists. You need only to look at a map showing all US volcanoes to see if the facts support your hypothesis.

4. Interpret and analyze the results. The next step is to take the results of your experiment or other data search and organize them. You do this for two reasons. The first is to more easily and objectively analyze your findings. The second is so that other scientists can understand your work.

After organizing your data, you analyze them. Basically, you're trying to confirm whether your results support your hypothesis. Depending on the question you examine and your results, data may strongly support your hypothesis, data may partially support your hypothesis, data may refute your hypothesis, or data may neither support nor contradict your hypothesis. Good scientists analyze without emotion. The best scientists look for every possible flaw in their hypotheses using the data.

If the data support your hypothesis, you may have a *theory*. A theory is a scientific explanation with *observable* and *repeatable* evidence to support it. Further, keep in mind that the scientific meaning of the word "theory" differs from the way most of us use it in casual conversation. We casually use *theory* to mean a *guess* – "I have a theory about how he passed the test" – but actually, the correct term would be *hypothesis*.

If the data partially support your hypothesis, you can modify your hypothesis, based on the data, to arrive at a theory. In the fertilizer and aquarium example, suppose several species of bottom-dwelling fish in the experimental tank do not die or seem affected. Your final theory might be: "Dumping 20,000 metric tons of fertilizer in the bay will cause zooplankton (animal plankton) to overpopulate, killing or driving away all the fish that do not live on the bottom."

If the data refute your hypothesis, you discard the hypothesis. You may now have the basis for a new hypothesis requiring further testing. Suppose there is no plankton bloom or fish deaths in the experimental aquarium. Your new hypothesis might be: "Dumping up to 20,000 metric tons of fertilizer in the bay will have little effect on the plankton and fish populations." You might then follow this with a series of experiments that test the effects of various fertilizer levels.

If your data neither refute nor confirm your hypothesis, you still have only a hypothesis. This can happen because of unintended flaws in your experiment design or accidentally using an inappropriate data set. When this happens, and it happens to all scientists, you still analyze closely because you can still learn. You try to determine why your data aren't conclusive so that you can redesign your experiment or choose better data sources. You try to see what new information lies within your results.

HOW SCIENTISTS SOLVE PROBLEMS

Let's see how scientists go about solving problems.

Investigation Question
To become aware of the basic steps common to most scientific research.

Hypothesis
The approach to solving problems is always orderly, but not always exactly the same. Questions about living things in the ocean may require a different approach than questions about the universe.

Procedure
1. Take 14 slips of paper, about 10 cm (4 inches) by 4 cm (1 inch), and write each of the following phrases on a separate slip:

   Assembling equipment

   Carrying out the experiment

   Checking results against the original prediction

   Collecting equipment

   Designing new experiments to study the problem further

   Designing the experiment

   Researching the topic

   Identifying the problem

   Interpreting observations

   Looking for patterns or regularities in observations

   Making conclusions

   Making observations

   Predicting an answer to the problem

   Recording observations

2. Lay all your slips of paper face up on the desk in front of you. Sequence the slips into a list of steps that you think a scientist would follow in solving a problem.

Results
1. Compare your list with others.
2. Compare your list with library materials – perhaps a chemistry or physics textbook.
3. Once you complete your list, copy it onto a large piece of paper. Draw lines to connect the steps that you think relate. The lines show connections, or relationships, between the steps. To show relationships more clearly, write one to three connecting words that make a logical statement about the two steps.
4. Look for new connections between the steps. Draw lines and write connecting words. As you work, feel free to change the order of some of your steps. There is no one right sequence to the list. Feel free to add steps as well. Continue until your list represents what you know about the steps scientists follow in solving problems.

Conclude and Communicate
1. Compare your list of steps with two or three of your classmates' lists. Discuss your lists to explore relationships between ideas and to discover new ones you may not have thought of.
2. After finishing this chapter, add to your list of steps by reflecting on what you learned.

Reflecting on Our Learning—The Scientific Method
1. How was your list like and unlike other lists?
2. Which of these steps do you think are the five most important ones? Why?
3. What other steps could you add to this method of problem solving?
4. What other logical sequence of steps might be used to solve a problem?
5. Design an experiment of your own using these steps.

HYPOTHESIS, THEORY, AND THINKING CRITICALLY

In science you hear the terms *hypothesis* (plural *hypotheses*) and *theory*. It's important to recognize the difference.

The first step in explaining something scientifically is forming an idea to test by gathering evidence and experimentation. A hypothesis is a scientific guess. It is based on your observations and inductive or deductive reasoning, but has little objective data to support it. For example, suppose you notice that apples growing on a tree start out green and then turn red. Based on what you know about other types of fruit that ripen, you guess (hypothesize) that the color change from green to red indicates when apples become ripe.

A theory is a scientific explanation with objective data that support the explanation. A hypothesis becomes a theory through experimentation and research. Suppose you test your hypothesis by sampling apples while they're green and find lots of starch. When they turn red, you find that samples have less starch and more sugar. You now have a theory that the color change from green to red indicates when apples become ripe.

Scientists realize that a theory is not necessarily correct or complete. It is the best explanation for the evidence available, though new evidence may refute it or require revisions. Suppose in your research, you discover a variety of apples that does not turn red. You sample these at various times and confirm that they're green before and after they're ripe. So, you modify your theory to say that color change from green to red indicates when specific varieties of apples, but not all varieties of apples, become ripe.

So, what theories can you treat as "fact"? That's where critical thinking comes in. Some theories have so much support that we treat them as fact (even though we still call them theories). No reasonable person seriously doubts that the sun is the center of the solar system or that the Earth is a sphere. The evidence supporting these theories is overwhelming.

Other theories have some data supporting them, but the question is still so open that scientists realize we still know little. Physicists theorize about many subatomic particles for which they have some evidence. However, they know they're far from declaring the existence or attributes of these particles as practically proven "fact."

The difficult theories are those in between. You'll find some theories that are, in the opinions of some scientists, virtually fact. Yet other scientists (perhaps a minority) consider the theory still open to debate. Sometimes two or more groups of scientists have "competing" theories. In these cases, you have to apply critical thinking and/or look for more data in deciding what to accept as the most reasonable explanation. Try asking yourself these questions:

What's the source? Think about who supports a theory and who disputes it. What are their levels of expertise with the subject? What experience do they have? What do the majority of the experts think? Expertise and a majority view generally denote credibility, but don't disregard social pressures within a community. Sometimes a theory becomes so entrenched that those in that area of study have difficulty thinking any other way. In such circumstances it's often a newcomer or outsider who replaces the theory with a better one.

Is it really a theory? If there's no conceivable way that a claim could be proved wrong through objective observed data (experiments or evidence), then it's neither a scientific theory nor a hypothesis. For example, it is a theory that the Earth is round because it is *conceivable* that measurements and other observations *could* show that the Earth is flat (although it's not likely). A "theory" that 14 angels can dance on the head of a pin may or may not be true, but it is not a scientific theory because there's no way to objectively support or refute it with objective information.

How good are the data? Consider the quality and quantity of the evidence. Support from extensive, varied, and overlapping evidence carries more weight than only fragments of evidence, or evidence that is contradicted by other findings. Be careful of theories that rely on other theories. If a supporting theory lacks strong evidence to support it, so does any theory that relies on it.

Be cautious when the supporting data rely on statistics. Statistics are reliable and useful in many areas of science when used properly, but you have to understand *statistical significance*. Statistical significance is a calculation that determines how likely a result is by mere chance. The less likely a finding can happen by chance, the more you can trust the result as evidence for the theory.

For instance, suppose someone proposes a theory that a certain coin always lands heads up. Supporting evidence of two coin flips, both heads, is too small for a statistically significant result. That can happen pretty easily just by chance, so it doesn't support the theory in any meaningful way. One thousand flips that come up all heads, however, is highly unlikely by chance. In this case the evidence has high statistical significance and supports the theory strongly.

What is the simplest explanation? When comparing competing hypotheses, or theories with an equal balance of evidence, the rule of thumb is to assume the simplest explanation. This is called *Occam's razor*, after the scientist who devised

Continued *on page 1-30*

Continued *from page 1-29*
it to cut quickly to the best guess. Suppose two hypotheses for the salt in the ocean are that it flows there from dissolved minerals on land and that it was put into the ocean by an ancient civilization from outer space. The first hypothesis is the simpler and better explanation. Just remember that this is a useful guideline when you have no other information. Being simpler is not proof and Occam's razor may be wrong—but it's right more often than wrong.

Has the obvious been ruled out? In the story "The Sign of Four," Sir Arthur Conan Doyle's famous fictional detective, Sherlock Holmes, says: "How often have I said to you that when you have eliminated the impossible, whatever remains, however improbable, must be the truth?" Before dismissing a hypothesis or theory because it seems highly unlikely, consider whether the evidence has ruled out all other reasonably possible explanations. If so, then the hypothesis or theory may have merit. Einstein's theory that time stops at the speed of light seemed highly unlikely when he proposed it – but the evidence from math and physics ruled out any other possibility. Today, experimental evidence supports his theory.

Suppose both your control aquarium and your experimental aquarium have some plankton growth and fish deaths. The plankton growth is a bit higher and a few more fish die in the experimental aquarium, but the difference isn't significant. You cannot conclude with confidence that the fertilizer caused any of the bloom or fish fatalities, but neither can you conclude that it had no effect. Therefore, you're left with your hypothesis. But, have you learned anything worth investigating? Of course you have. You've learned that there may be factors other than the fertilizer causing plankton growth and fish deaths in the bay. You may have found that the fertilizer is only one possible factor in a complex problem.

It may sound odd, but data can prove a theory is wrong, but data *cannot* prove that a theory is right. That is, if the data contradict your hypothesis, then you know there's something wrong with your guess. If the data fail to contradict your hypothesis, then you may have a theory with factual support, but it still may not be a perfect. In the future, additional data may show your theory to be incorrect, incomplete, or inaccurate in some way even though your present data don't contradict it. The need to discard or revise theories that were once the best explanation for a phenomenon happens frequently – you'll learn about several examples in *Life on an Ocean Planet*. This is also why, even with strong data supporting your theory, you still have a theory – not a law.

5. Report results, procedures, and conclusions. The final reporting results step is one of the most critical in the scientific method. It's important because it allows other scientists to verify your work and conclusions. It's also important because it allows other scientists to build on what you've learned.

Typically, you share your work in journals dedicated to specific fields of science. Professional scientists review these journals so that they can benefit from each other's work. Sometimes a scientist will duplicate an experiment to confirm the results – and sometimes the second scientist gets different results! This often becomes the fuel for debate, formulating new hypotheses to explain the differences, and new research leading to new discoveries.

The Progress of Science

How does science progress?

Because science is a process, it changes. Science progresses through the revision of theories in the light of new evidence or better explanations of existing evidence. Throughout this book, you'll read several examples of how human concepts about the world and the universe changed over time through this process. However, just because someone proposes a new theory and new evidence does not mean things change overnight. They may, but scientific progress has social and scientific influences.

The arrangement of the solar system provides a classic example. Until the early 1500s, scientists held that the Earth was the center of the solar system. This concept dated back to at least the work of Greek Claudius Ptolemy, who popularized it in 150 A.D. The prevailing solar system model had the sun, planets, and all the stars orbiting the Earth. Based on this model, astronomers of the day accurately predicted eclipses, the location of planets, and constellations, and other astronomical events. The model worked, so mainstream science accepted it.

This started to change with Nicolaus Copernicus (1473-1543). Based on the same celestial observations, Copernicus proposed that the sun, not Earth, sits at the center. He further asserted that the Earth rotates on its axis (causing night and day) and orbits the sun annually.

Although we take these for granted today, at the time this was a radical assertion. It seemed to counter the view that man, God's special creation, was the center of the universe. The Copernicus model ran against established social and scientific thinking so much that it took more than 100 years before scientists accepted it widely. In 1633, Galileo Galilei (1564-1642) became the subject of public persecution and house arrest when he announced his support for the Copernicus model. He had to publicly recant to end the social pressure.

It may seem that scientists in Copernicus' day were being naive by disputing his evidence and theory. However, even today, scientists seldom accept radical changes in scientific thought until they're bolstered by ample evidence. Often, it takes acceptance by prominent scientists with noted credibility before the new theory replaces the old. While this may be counter-progressive at times, it acts as a filter that strains out frivolous and dubious theories.

Staying Current with Science

How does it benefit you to stay up to date with current trends, findings, and developments in science and technology?

Given the roles of science and technology in society, it's clear that you need to understand them. It's just as important to keep up with current trends, findings, and developments in science and technology.

If you're a scientist, researcher, or employed in technology, the need to do this seems clear. But, how does it benefit you to keep up with these findings and trends if you're a butcher, fireman, bus driver, or actor?

The answer is that science and technology affect all walks of life. A new medical discovery can reduce disease transmission in beef for the butcher. A new insulating textile can allow a fireman to walk safely through a blaze. Vehicle tracking programs keep the bus driver on time. New forms of media give actors new career opportunities.

As time progresses, whatever career you're in, you have two choices. You can anticipate changes caused by science and technology, prepare, and advance your career with them or you can disregard the current trends, findings, and developments and spend your time trying to catch up with those who don't.

Another benefit of staying current is that you can help society handle the effects of science and technology. You will be a society member who votes and expresses views based on accurate information. Unfortunately, many times government and the media have created outcries, implemented bans, and raised hysteria based on inaccurate, incomplete, or unscientific information. At other times, technologies become popularized and accepted without complete understanding of the drawbacks. This has happened many times with medicines, diets, nutritional supplements, electronics, and other technologies.

One example is the controversy over human cloning. Many decry this as something that should be outlawed. While human cloning does present potential ethical issues with strong significance, some of the protest comes from misinformation. Possibly because of science fiction movies, many people believe cloning creates a "photocopy" of a human being, complete with the same memories, personalities, and even scars of the cloned person. On this basis, some people have even said that a cloned human would have no soul (not that you could test this scientifically).

This view comes from not having sufficient understanding

SCIENCE AND SOCIAL PRESSURE

As illustrated here and elsewhere in *Life on an Ocean Planet*, social pressures influence science. These can be pressures within the science community or from outside.

What would *you* do if you made a discovery that ran contrary to scientific thinking? What if mainstream scientists ridiculed your theory? What if, despite your evidence and certainty that you are correct, pursuing your theory would probably end your career? What would you do?

It's easy to say we should fight for what we believe is true, but it's not always that simple. US Army General George S. Patton once said: "Never fight a battle where there's nothing to be gained by winning."

Suppose you're a medical research scientist using fruit flies to study HIV and AIDs. Purely by accident, you discover strong evidence that fruit flies are cross-eyed, which explains why they never fly in a straight line. You publish your findings and theory in an entomology (study of insects) journal.

The entomology community responds that you're crazy. They point out that fruit flies have compound eyes so they couldn't *possibly* be cross-eyed. They even attack your credibility by pointing out that you're in medicine, not insect research. The fuss grows so out of control that, under pressure from the natural sciences department, your sponsoring university tells you to withdraw your theory. Otherwise they'll have to cut your funds and let you go. Do you stick to your guns here?

Honestly, maybe not. You have seven years of graduate school under your belt, five years of experience, a spouse, two children, and a mortgage to pay. Furthermore, while your theory is interesting, it has no substantial significance. It won't change society or scientific direction. It's not even your field of expertise. You have everything to lose and little to gain. Without admitting you're wrong (you *know* your evidence), you might close the matter by responding: "The paper has my findings, but you folks are the experts on fruit-fly eyesight. Perhaps I missed something in my conclusions. I leave this question for your field to investigate further."

Suppose that, two years later, you discover a crucial element in the fight against HIV. Again you face outcry and protests. This time it's from medical scientists who protest that the fruit fly is the wrong subject for meaningful HIV research. You couldn't *possibly* have found anything that applies to human HIV, they say. Again a furor erupts. Again the university raises the possibility of cutting your funding.

But again, you have your facts. You have strong evidence from thousands of experiments that this one piece of the HIV problem can be solved with fruit flies and *was*. You've even quietly had a few key scientists confirm that your research is solid. Your discovery could change thousands of lives for the better. It could profoundly benefit society. In face of the pressure, do you stick to your guns?

Let's hope the answer would be "Yes."

---

about the science of genetics and technology of cloning. A clone is an organism with identical DNA to the original organism, but it is not a "photocopy." Duplicate DNA even happens naturally. Identical twins are natural clones, in a sense – two humans with the same DNA. But, they're not duplicate human beings. They share the same genetics, but go through life having different experiences, values, emotions, and other dimensions that make them distinct individuals.

The point here isn't to support or condemn human cloning. Rather, it is to point out that sometimes people, government, and the media take stances or act regarding science or technology issues based on inaccurate or incomplete information. By staying informed about science and technology, you can base your ethical evaluations, estimates, and other potential effects on accurate information. You can then vote and voice opinions based on reality rather than on misconceptions.

1. **Science is**

   A. a body of knowledge.

   B. static and unchanging.

   C. an organized method.

   D. both A and C

2. **Technology is a material system that produces intended results.**

   A. true

   B. false

3. **Science and technology have affected humans and other organisms (choose all that apply)**

   A. by improving many aspects of life.

   B. by threatening and degrading life in many ways.

   C. only slightly, with nothing documentable noted.

   D. by solving every imaginable problem.

4. **Of the three broad actions that society can take with respect to the effects of science and technology on the environment, the most logical appears to be to**

   A. consider the environment a lost cause and disregard the effects.

   B. dismiss the effects on the environment as overstated by scientists.

   C. abandon technology and return to a primitive lifestyle.

   D. prioritize the consequences to the environment in applying technologies.

5. **Scientific process skills include (choose all that apply)**

   A. identifying the problem.

   B. constructing models.

   C. comparing observations.

   D. predicting outcomes.

6. **Place the basic steps of the scientific method in their generally accepted order**

   A. Report results, procedures, and conclusions.

   B. Identify the problem (or question).

   C. Test the hypothesis.

   D. Make a hypothesis.

   E. Interpret and analyze results.

7. **A hypothesis is**

   A. the same thing as a theory.

   B. a wild guess.

   C. an educated scientific guess that you can test.

   D. all of the above

8. **You use _____ reasoning to propose a process that explains observed facts. You use _____ reasoning to propose what facts you would observe if a known process took place.**

   A. inductive, deductive

   B. deductive, abductive

   C. abductive, inductive

   D. deductive, inductive

9. **A theory is**

   A. the same thing as a hypothesis.

   B. an educated, scientific guess.

   C. a scientific explanation with observable supporting evidence.

   D. both A and B

10. **Reporting the results of your work is crucial in science because**

    A. it allows scientists to verify your work.

    B. it allows scientists to build on what you've learned.

    C. otherwise someone else will get the credit.

    D. both A and B

11. **Science progresses through revision of theories based on new evidence or better explanations of existing evidence**

    A. true

    B. false

12. **It benefits you to stay up to date with current trends, findings, and developments in science and technology because (choose all that apply)**

    A. the changes affect all walks of life.

    B. doing so can help you advance your career.

    C. failing to do so can put you behind in your career.

    D. you can help society adjust to the effects.

How to Learn Marine Science Most Efficiently

As you progress through this course, you should find learning marine science rewarding, challenging, and even fun. However, it's probably just one of several courses you're taking. You have to divide your time among other subjects, plus other dimensions of life that range from dating to sports.

There are two ways to go about learning and studying with *Life on an Ocean Planet*. The first is to read through it thoughtlessly and toss it aside. Although this is easy in the short run, it's really the long, slow way to study. You will either not do well or spend much more time trying to catch up with what you should have learned in the first place.

The second way to study is efficient and will help you easily remember most of what this course has to offer, allowing you to earn a higher grade *and* making you a better citizen of planet Earth. You'll have to spend a bit more time in your initial study, but you'll save time because you'll learn quickly. You'll do better and waste little time struggling with rereading or cramming for tests. If that sounds better than the first option, keep reading.

Study Elements and Visual References

How many basic study elements are in Life on an Ocean Planet?

What marine science fundamentals do these study elements cover?

How does Life on an Ocean Planet *help you prepare for a career in or related to marine science?*

What visual references help your learning in Life on an Ocean Planet?

Life on an Ocean Planet consists of six basic study elements (units) that divide marine science into meaningful segments.

These units are:

Unit 1– Importance of Ocean Exploration

Unit 2 – The Foundation of Life in the Ocean

Unit 3 – A Water World

Unit 4 – The Motion of the Ocean

Unit 5 – Voyage to the Bottom of the Sea

Unit 6 – The Present and Future of the Marine Environment

These six units cover the broad spectrum of marine science, which helps you prepare yourself as a steward of this planet or for a career related to marine science. It does this by showing you the various marine sciences and what related careers involve. Your ability to have a career in or related to marine sciences depends on many things. The most important, however, is your desire, passion, and interest in learning about Earth and marine science. One goal of *Life on an Ocean Planet* is to help you find what areas of marine science fit best with your interests and desires.

Life on an Ocean Planet contains visual references intended to focus your study and speed learning. By taking the time to use these, you save time by learning more efficiently. You've seen these references as you've read this chapter.

Look for headings and subheadings that divide each chapter. Main headings are **black**, followed by **blue** subheadings. Paying attention to these headings helps you to organize the material in your head. That's a key to effective learning.

Under each subheading, you'll find learning objectives in **green**. They're written as questions to guide your reading. **Important:** As you read, find the answers to each of the learning objective questions. More on how to "question" your reading in the next section.

In addition to the main text, you'll find relevant supplemental information in the sidebars with **purple** headings. These sidebars expand what you're learning by deepening your knowledge on specific aspects of the topic. Finally, look for photos and illustrations labeled in **red**. These provide important visual information to illustrate what you're reading. If you don't understand something when you read it, be sure to examine the photos and illustrations. Often, they bring everything together so what you're learning makes sense.

At the end of a main subject division, you'll find a quick quiz. These help you assess and reinforce your learning as you go. Be sure you can answer all the questions before moving on. If you can't answer the questions from memory, return to the related material to find the answer. This saves you time because subsequent study will be easier. If you continue without understanding a key concept, it becomes a stumbling block for learning subsequent material.

There's a chapter glossary at the end of each chapter. This glossary lists and defines all the new terms introduced in that chapter. Review the terms to confirm that you know what they mean. There's also a comprehensive glossary at the end of *Life on an Ocean Planet*. This is helpful if you come across a term introduced in a different chapter and need to quickly refresh your memory about what it means.

COMMUNICATION AND SEQUENCE IN SCIENCE AND *LIFE ON AN OCEAN PLANET*

In September 1985, Robert Ballard, PhD, located the remains of the famed ocean liner R.M.S. *Titanic*. The news of his find made international headlines, and even today remains perhaps the best known of more than 100 deep-sea expeditions that he's led. Discoveries made on the initial and subsequent expeditions to *Titanic* forever changed theories about what doomed the liner and how she sank. That she broke in half explains witness testimonies about the sinking that didn't seem to make sense. But, it's not just history that finding *Titanic* benefits. Because we know exactly when she sank, *Titanic* provides a marker against which scientists can examine sedimentation, organism growth and other environmental factors.

Imagine what would have happened if Ballard had found *Titanic* and told no one. History would still record that *Titanic* went down in one piece, instead of in two like we know today. Researchers wouldn't know where to find the remains for studying biology, geology, physics, marine construction and a dozen other sciences that *Titanic* has benefited.

What this tells you is that without communication, science doesn't progress. What we've learned from *Titanic* would not have been learned if Ballard hadn't reported what he'd found. Part of science necessarily includes writing about it so others can benefit from and build upon your work – just as you benefit from and build upon the work of those who've gone before you.

Ballard's discovery of *Titanic* reveals something else about communicating in science: sciences interact, overlap and benefit from each other. Different people can look at any discovery or topic in any science from different perspectives. A rainbow is a single phenomenon, yet the physicist, the digital camera engineer and the meteorologist all see it differently and will communicate about it differently. The physicist may report about light refraction, the engineer may record the sensor response and the meteorologist may analyze what it says about pending weather.

This tells you that in communicating about science, there are usually several ways to discuss or approach a subject, all of which have merit. But to communicate, you have to decide on an approach that works, and then use it. Skipping around a subject and changing points of view without any plan or logic will simply confuse those with whom you're trying to communicate.

The team of writers, educators and scientists who developed *Life on an Ocean Planet* had to do this. Together, we created a logical overview of oceanography that introduces you to the key concepts involved in marine science and how they interrelate with other sciences. The chapters were sequenced to establish principles progressively, so what you learn in one chapter builds upon what you learned before. The chapter and topic order before you is simply one that we found to work well for this purpose.

But, there's no "right" or "wrong" sequence. Therefore, you and your teacher may go through the book in some order other than the way the chapters are sequenced. Your teacher may do this based on your learning style, the teaching style, your environment and other topics you're studying. For example, if your teacher knows you've already studied the chemical properties of water and know them well from a physics class, there's no need to read that chapter again here. *Life on an Ocean Planet* was therefore also written with this flexibility in mind.

Titanic reveals another important aspect of communication: conveying thoughts in ways that your readers or viewers most easily understand them. If you want to tell the depth to a scientist who's planning a dive to the wreck, you would probably want to be very precise and say something like, "3800.9 meters (12,467 feet), depending upon tides." But, if you were speaking conversationally in more general terms, you might say the depth is "about 3800 meters (12,500 feet)," or even, "about 3800 meters (13,000 feet)." The latter examples are not only less precise, but the metric and imperial numbers are not equivalent. However, many people more easily grasp the depth, size, quantity or whatever else the number describes when given as a broad concept rather than as a precise figure. In these cases, the precision isn't important (or may not exist) and the number is clearly not intended to be exact.

In *Life on an Ocean Planet*, you'll find similar references. When discussing a number to give a concept of size, depth or range, the term will usually be conversational with qualifiers like "about" or "more than." They are typically (but not always) round numbers rather than exactly equal metric and imperial conversations. When discussing a number that has scientific precision (like the boiling point of water, for instance), however, the number will be exact (often within a decimal place) and metric and imperial conversions will be equal.

As you learn about oceanography while reading *Life on an Ocean Planet*, remember that learning to *communicate* about science as important as the science itself. Without communication, you cannot learn science because to learn you must ask questions about what you don't know. And, without communication, anything *you* discover will be lost forever.

At the end of each chapter, you'll find questions that review what you've been studying and how the topics interrelate. These questions help you assess and demonstrate your learning. Your teacher will probably have you answer these questions in your science journal. If you find you don't recall the material, look back through the chapter to relocate and review the information.

You'll also answer some critical thinking questions. Most of these don't have one "right" answer. Rather, your teacher will judge your responses based on several attributes. These include accurately applying information to problems, respect for differing views, original thinking, and your ability to defend your position. The critical thinking questions focus on what you do with information rather than whether you learned it.

Learning Effectively with *Life on an Ocean Planet*

How does surveying Life on an Ocean Planet *before reading it make learning more efficient and effective?*

What five study steps can you follow to learn from Life on an Ocean Planet *more quickly and effectively?*

What can you do to make what you learn in Life on an Ocean Planet *more relevant to other study areas and your day-to-day life?*

Now that you know the basic layout of the book, let's go through the steps to follow for study and learning. (Note: the study system outlined in this section will help you learn effectively from *any* textbook in *any* course you take. The study system outlined here is well researched and has been found to help both high school and college students learn more effectively).

If you have not done so already, the first thing to do is examine the entire book. First, read the table of contents. Note the chapter titles and subheadings. Look at the order of the topics and subjects that group together. Even if your teacher has you read the chapters in a different sequence, you'll have a grasp of where to find different topics for further reference and study.

Next, go through this book from cover to cover. You don't need to look at every page, but pay attention to the style and how it's laid out. Look for the pattern in the identifying elements, the marine scientist profiles, quizzes, reviews, and so on. Skim through the glossary, index, and references to see how they're laid out.

Why do this? Examining *Life on an Ocean Planet* before reading it makes learning more efficient and effective. It does this by establishing your mental framework about marine science. Research on how people learn shows that this is important because your brain builds on this framework as you study.

After surveying the entire book, there are five study steps to follow as you learn from *Life on an Ocean Planet* – topic by topic. The five steps are: Survey, Question, Read, Recite and Review (sometimes called the *SQ3R* study system). Let's look at the five steps.

FIVE STEPS TO LEARNING EFFECTIVELY

Learning steps		What to do?
Step One	Survey	Read marine scientist profile. Quickly scan the chapter.
Step Two	Question	Make questions out of the subheads and read the objective learning questions at the beginning of each topic.
Step Three	Read	While holding the questions clearly in mind, purposefully read the topic to answer your questions.
Step Four	Recite	Recite the answers to the questions.
Step Five	Review	Review by answering the questions at the end of the chapter.

Figure 1-23

Chart for the Five Steps to Learning Effectively.

Step One – Survey

Launch your study by preparing yourself mentally prior to reading. Do this by surveying the chapter. Surveying a chapter should not take you too long, but it's very valuable in helping you remember material. Here's how you survey a chapter:

1. Fix the name of the chapter in your mind. The name is the essence of the main idea you are trying to get from the chapter.

2. Read the chapter's marine scientist profile. The profile stimulates your learning by raising interest in the topic. You learn how the topic relates to a real career and applies in the real world. These are real people who have dedicated themselves to exploring the natural world and uncovering its mysteries. As you read about the struggles and triumphs of these professionals, you learn something about why the information matters.

3. Next, scan the entire chapter. Carefully read each of the subheads. Look at the photos and illustrations, sidebar titles, and generally explore the chapter's general flow. Pay attention to

bolded and Italicized words. New terms are *italicized* when they're introduced, along with their meanings. You'll find these terms listed in the glossary at the end of each chapter, and in the glossary at the end of the book. These are key ideas related to the content of the chapter.

Step Two – Question

After you've quickly surveyed the chapter, return to the first main topic subhead. Now begin to *question* what's in the chapter. To do this:

1. Turn the subhead into a question. Let's say the subhead is "Water's Unique Properties." In your mind or on your personal notes, ask, "What are water's unique properties?"

2. Next, carefully read all of the subhead's study questions printed in **green**. This will help you guide your reading because you will be looking for the answers.

Step Three – Read

Now read the content within the subhead. As you read the material under the subhead, look for each answer to the learning objective questions. You'll find the same questions at the end of the topic in the "Are You Learning" quiz. For every objective, there is a question. While holding the questions clearly in mind, read the topic to answer your questions. Doing this creates a clearly defined purpose for reading.

Next, reread all photo and illustration captions. Reduce your reading speed for difficult passages and stop and reread parts that are not clear.

Step Four – Recite

Steps three (reading) and four (recite) are accomplished together.

1. As you read, when you find the answer to a learning objective question *recite* it out loud or quietly to yourself. Restate the answer in your own words; don't look at the text.

2. Next, write down the "Are You Learning" questions *and* answers for the subhead (your teacher may require you to do this anyway in a personal notebook or marine science journal – don't write in your textbook). You can also recite the key information iby taking notes, writing down key material in your own words.

Reciting helps you learn much more effectively because it requires mental processes far beyond simply reading, or even rereading. Reciting promotes and speeds learning, whereas reading and re reading often slows, impedes, and in some cases, prevents learning.

Writing makes your learning even *more* effective because you engage even more mental processes. The act of writing helps to transfer the material from your short-term memory to long-term memory. Think of it as hitting "save" to send it to the hard drive. Experts on human learning put it this way:

Learning = Seeing or Hearing
Learning with Added Retention = Seeing *and* Hearing
Learning with Better Retention = Seeing, Hearing *and* Saying
Learning with Best Retention = Seeing, Hearing, Saying, *and* Writing

3. If you don't understand a question or know the answer, review the material until you understand and find the answer before moving on.

Step Five – Review

Very few students can remember the content of a whole chapter after reading it once. The "Question-Read-Recite" process divides a chapter into sections that you can learn separately, piece by piece. This allows you to move at a pace you find best for learning. Regular review puts a chapter back together again in your mind. In review, you study the answers you found from the questions. Using *Life on an Ocean Planet's* layout, here's how you can specifically conduct your review:

1. Answer the Chapter in Review and the Connecting Chapter Concepts – Science Scenarios questions at the end of each chapter, again writing the answers in your journal. Review previous material as necessary and answer completely. The Chapter in Review questions focus on what you learned by answering the Study Questions. The Connecting Chapter Concepts questions focus on the interrelationships of what you're studying.

2. Next, answer the Marine Science in the Real World questions. These questions apply critical thinking to the new concepts and materials you've studied. Use your observations, evidence, and explanations to support your conclusions and thinking. Note how your thinking may challenge accepted points of view and how others may challenge your thinking.

3. Review the SciLinks internet references on the topic you're studying. Also, if you find a topic of interest or something you don't understand, use the internet search engines to find more information on the topic.

4. Use the laboratory activities and field research excursions to further your review, to evaluate and to apply what you've learned. They may also raise questions not answered by *Life on an Ocean Planet*. Take the time to find the answers in your school library, on the internet, and through other resources your teacher suggests.

All of these steps involve reviewing each chapter's material. If you want to succeed at anything in life, persistence is most important – review, review, review. You learn by reading, but you are not reading a novel. *Life on an Ocean Planet* is a book you need to *learn* from, so follow the steps as listed – and get in the habit of doing the same thing with *all* your textbooks and study materials. The extra time it takes will be more than offset by the time you save in overall learning.

It's important that you make what you study in *Life on an Ocean Planet* more relevant to your other study areas and your day-to-day life. The more relevant something is, the more you benefit from knowing it. There are several things you can do to achieve this.

First, explore the provided references. You'll find internet SciLinks references throughout *Life on an Ocean Planet*, each placed with related material. Go to scilinks.org and follow the listed code to learn more about what you're reading with expanded detail, photos, graphs, video and other material. Similarly, look up the some of the references listed at the end of the chapter either online or in your school library. These will give you more detail about many of the topics.

Second, check out the internal references, too. When you see "as discussed in Chapter___," go to that chapter, find the material and review it. This will expand your comprehension and help you connect different aspects of marine science.

Third, when you come across something you learned in *Life on an Ocean Planet* that relates to another subject you're studying, or something you see in your everyday life, explore the connection to expand what you're learning. A great example of this has been used as an example in this chapter: *Titanic*. When studying the story of *Titanic* in your history class, for example, note how marine science has shaped what we know about what happened. Examine how knowing the history made it possible for science to find the wreck, and how what Ballard learned when looking for *Titanic* has made it easier to find other historic wrecks. Note how these two study areas overlap and help each other progress.

Fourth, apply what you learn in each chapter in the labs and activities your teacher has you complete. The topics relate. If you don't see how they connect, re-read *Life on an Ocean Planet* or ask your teacher for guidance.

Finally, follow your curiosity. If you find yourself particularly interested in something, find out more about it. This is the best way to discover what you're passionate about, and may help guide you to a satisfying career.

1. *Life on an Ocean Planet* has _____ basic study elements.

   A. two

   B. three

   C. four

   D. six

2. **Marine science fundamentals covered in the study elements include (choose all that apply)**

   A. theories on the foundation of life in the ocean.

   B. scientific submersibles and their origin.

   C. the present and the future of the marine environment.

   D. navigation considerations for oceanographic vessels.

3. *Life on an Ocean Planet* **helps prepare you for a career in or related to marine science by**

   A. teaching you everything you will need to know.

   B. showing you different marine sciences and what their careers involve.

   C. identifying the jobs that pay the best.

   D. all of the above

4. **In** *Life on an Ocean Planet*, **text written in green indicates**

   A. main headings.

   B. subheadings.

   C. learning objectives.

   D. photo and illustration captions.

5. **Surveying** *Life on an Ocean Planet* **before reading it makes learning more efficient and effective by**

   A. eliminating the need to read it word-for-word.

   B. allowing you to find all the answers to the questions.

   C. teaching you the material through the picture/illustration captions.

   D. none of the above

6. **During the _____ step in studying** *Life on an Ocean Planet*, **you should write the answers to the "Are You Learning" questions.**

   A. survey

   B. question

   C. recite

   D. review

7. **To make what you learn in** *Life on an Ocean Planet* **more relevant to other study areas and your day-to-day life, you should (choose all that apply)**

   A. explore the provided references.

   B. explore connections that relate to other subjects or everyday life.

   C. apply what you learn in the labs and activities.

   D. follow your curiosity.

New Terms You Learned

- **biological oceanography** (marine biology) the study of the life in the ocean and the ocean's role as a habitat for that life (p. 1-9)
- **chemical oceanography** the study of seawater chemistry (p. 1-9)
- **concept map** a representation of a topic made by arranging key ideas or concepts to show their relationships (p. 1-6)
- **deductive reasoning** concluding what facts will be observed as the result of a known process (p. 1-25)
- **Earth and space science** the study of the physical earth, the solar system, the universe and their interrelationships (p. 1-12)
- **geological oceanography** the study of the geology (see geology) of the ocean (p. 1-9)
- **geology** the study of the structure of the Earth or another planet, in particular its rocks, soil, and minerals, and its history and origins (p. 1-9)
- **hypothesis** a scientific guess based on observation, but with little data to support it; an untested scientific explanation for an observed phenomenon (p. 1-25)
- **inductive reasoning** concluding what process caused an observed fact or facts (p. 1-25)
- **life science** the study of living things and their interactions with their environments; a principal branch of science concerned with plants, animals, and other living organisms and including biology, botany, and zoology (p. 1-12)
- **marine science** the process of discovering the facts, processes and unifying principles that explain the nature of the ocean and its associated life forms (p. 1-8)
- **mathematics** the universal "language" of science; the study of the relationships among numbers, shapes and quantities (p. 1-15)
- **Occam's razor** the guideline that when you have two competing explanations for something and no evidence to support either, the simpler explanation is more likely to be correct (p. 1-29)
- **ocean literacy** understanding the basic concepts related to how the ocean functions as an ecosystem, its importance to the Earth's ecosystem, and how and why it is vital to human existence (p. 1-5)
- **oceanography** the science of recording and describing the ocean's contents and processes; four main branches – biological, chemical, geological, and physical (p. 1-8)
- **physical oceanography** the study of physics within the marine environment (p. 1-9)
- **physical science** the study of matter and energy; any of the sciences such as physics and chemistry that study nonliving things (p. 1-11)
- **science** a body of knowledge and an organized method used to gain knowledge about the observable universe (p .1-19)
- **scientific method** the formal, organized steps that scientists follow in proposing explanations for their observations and then testing their explanations (p. 1-22)
- **scientific process skills** skills used in conducting the scientific method, such as comparing, relating, inferring, applying, measuring, modeling, recording, etc. (p. 1-23)
- **scientist** someone who uses the processes of science to find answers about how things work and why in the observable universe (p. 1-3)
- **situatedness** the explanation of when, where, and why a concept came about (p. 1-15)
- **SQ3R** A well researched study method than can help anyone learn from a textbook; stands for Survey, Question, Read, Recite and Review (p. 1-39)
- **statistical significance** a calculation that determines how likely a result is by mere chance (p. 1-29)
- **technology** the study, development, and application of devices, machines, and techniques for manufacturing and productive processes (p. 1-19)
- **theory** a scientific explanation with observable evidence to support it (p. 1-27)

Chapter 1 in Review

1. What two influences and what three marine resources make the ocean important to life on Earth? Explain why each is important. Research and find out approximately how much of the oxygen we use is produced by marine plants.

2. How much of the ocean have humans seen? What area do we know the most about?

3. Explain how human interaction can affect the ocean. How does this relate to the benefits of understanding the marine environment?

4. Define *marine science* and *oceanography*. Include the four main branches of oceanography.

5. What has made modern exploration possible? Why? What traditional science disciplines does marine science draw on?

6. Beyond the traditional science disciplines, what four study areas does marine science involve? What is the concept of *situatedness*, and how does it relate to these four study areas?

7. What disciplines benefit from marine science? What disciplines does marine science benefit from? In what cross-discipline areas dop marine scientists need education? Why?

8. Explain what *science* and *technology* are, and give two examples that illustrate the difference. Explain how science and technology affect humans and other organisms. Of the three broad actions society can take with respect to these effects on the environment, which appears the most logical to you? Why?

9. What are scientific process skills? Based on what you've learned, give six examples of scientific process skills other than the examples given in the text.

10. List the basic steps to the *scientific method* and describe each. Explain what a *hypothesis* and a *theory* are. What is the difference between *inductive* and *deductive* reasoning? Include why the final step in the scientific method is critical.

11. Science isn't static, but changes over time. How does it progress? How does it benefit you to stay up to date with the progress of science and technology?

12. List the basic study elements covered by *Life on an Ocean Planet*. How does *Life on an Ocean Planet* help you prepare for a career in or related to marine science? How do these basic study elements relate to this preparation?

13. List and describe all the visual references that aid learning in *Life on an Ocean Planet*. By each item you list, explain how you use the reference to guide your study.

14. How does surveying *Life on an Ocean Planet* before reading it make learning more efficient and effective? What does this process do for you mentally?

15. List the five study steps to follow to learn from *Life on an Ocean Planet* effectively. Include what you should do at each step.

Connecting Chapter Concepts – Science Scenarios

1. The scientific method creates a hypothesis, tests the hypothesis, analyzes the results and reports the results and conclusions as a way of furthering scientific knowledge. The goal of this process is to eliminate subjectivity in understanding how the natural world works.

    A. With respect to a hypothesis, what is the difference between inductive and deductive reasoning?

    B. When does a hypothesis become a theory?

    C. People normally think of experiments as the way you test a hypothesis, but there are two situations in which you do *not* generally test your hypothesis with experiments. What are they, and what data do you use instead?

    D. Why is it sometimes necessary to experiment with samples of something and use statistical methods to see how your results would apply?

Marine Science and the Real World

1. Why call this book *Life on an Ocean Planet* instead of *Life on a Land Planet*? Support your answer by describing how the ocean influences the entire planet.

2. "*Life on an Ocean Planet* is a high-school marine science textbook that reflects the intellectual and cultural traditions that characterize contemporary science and technology." Explain what this statement means and support it with what you learned in this chapter. Look ahead into the book for further support.

3. Write two hypotheses – one using inductive reasoning and the other using deductive reasoning – about a question or problem you've observed regarding riding a bicycle.

4. Take either hypothesis from Question 3 and describe how you could use the scientific method to test your hypothesis.

5. You're in charge of an ocean awareness campaign. You've found that your target audience generally believes the ocean is important, but they don't know why. If you could only convey the one most significant reason why the ocean is important, what would it be? How would you get this message across? What examples would you use?

6. Pick a reason other than the one you gave in Question 5 to defend why it is actually the most significant reason for the ocean's importance.

7. Return to the photo of the kitchen in the *Technology Around You* sidebar. Which technologies in the picture may be usable to address an environmental problem? For each, explain why and how.

8. Imagine you're a scientist in a food-testing laboratory. An inventor visits your lab with a product he calls a Low Carb Chocolate Mix. He claims that it:

    A. sweetens foods and drinks with no carbohydrate intake.

    B. provides the human body with energy.

    C. is perfectly safe to consume.

    D. is inexpensive to produce and comes from a readily available source.

    Outline the steps you would take to test the validity of these claims.

9. Explain how you can use the scientific method to help you study *any* school subject. Give some examples based on studying English grammar.

References

Adams, Michelle, et al. 2001. Columbia Earthscape. Serendiptity! The Arctic Mid-Ocean Ridge Expedition. http://www.earthscape.org/rl/hea01/hea01g.html

Berliner, D. 1987. Ways Of Thinking About Students And Classrooms By More Or Less Experienced Teachers. In J. Calderhead (Ed.), *Exploring Teachers' Thinking*. London: Cassell.

Beyer, L. 1984. Field Experience, Ideology, And The Development Of Critical Reflectivity. *Journal of Teacher Education.* 35 (3).

Bloom, B.S. 1953. Thought Processes In Lectures And Discussions. *Journal of General Education.* 7 (3).

Brown, J.S., Q. Collins, and P. Duguid. 1989. Situated Cognition And The Culture Of Learning. *Educational Researcher.* 18 (1).

Carter, K. 1990. Teacher's Knowledge And Learning To Teach. In W.R. Houston (Ed.), *Handbook Of Research On Teacher Education.* New York: Macmillan.

Covey, S.R. 1990. *The Seven Habits Of Highly Effective People: Restoring The Character Ethic.* New York: Fireside, Simon and Schuster.

Dewey, J. 1933. *How We Think: A Restatement Of The Relation Of Reflective Thinking To The Educational Process.* Chicago: Henry Regnery Co.

Erickson, G., and A. MacKinnon. 1991. Seeing In New Ways: On Becoming A Science Teacher. In D. Schon (Ed.), *The Reflective Turn: Case Studies In Professional Practice.* New York: Teachers College Press.

Feiman-Nemser, S. 1983. Learning To Teach. In L. Shulman and G. Sykes (Ed.), *Handbook Of Teaching And Policy.* New York: Longman.

Gagne, E.D., C.W. Yekovich, and F.R. Yekovich. 1993. *The Cognitive Psychology Of School Learning.* Harper Collins College Publishers.

Garrison, T. 2004. *Essentials of Oceanography.* Pacific Grove, CA: Brooks/Cole, a division of Thomson Learning, Inc.

Grimmett, P.P. 1988. The Nature Of Reflection And Schon's Conception In Perspective. In P.P. Grimmett and G.L. Erickson (Eds.), *Reflection In Teacher Education.* New York: Teachers College Press.

Guba, E.G., and Y.S. Lincoln. 1994. Competing Paradigms In Qualitative Research. In Denzin, N.K. and Y.S. Lincoln (Eds.), *Handbook Of Qualitative Research.* Thousand Oaks, CA: Sage Publications.

Hazen, W.A. 1997. *Everyday Life Inventions.* Glenview, IL: Good Year Books.

Jennett, P.S. 1995. *Investigations In Science: Ecology Hands-On Experiments And Interdisciplinary Activities.* Cypress, CA: Creative Teaching Press, Inc.

Lave, J., and E. Wegner. 1991. *Situated Learning: Legitimate Peripheral Participation.* Cambridge, MA: Cambridge Press.

Llewellyn, D. 2002. *Inquiry Within: Implementing Inquiry-Based Science Standards.* Thousand Oaks, CA: Corwin Press, Inc.

National Research Council. 2000. *Inquiry And The National Science Standards: A Guide For Teaching And Learning.* Washington, DC: National Academy Press.

National Research Council. 1999. National Science Education Standards. Washington, DC: National Academy Press.

National Science Teachers Association. 1996. *Pathways To Science Standards: Guidelines For Moving The Vision Into Practice.* Virginia: NSTA.

Novak, J., and A. Gowin. 1984. *Learning How To Learn.* Cambridge University Press.

Ramig, J.E., J. Bailer, J., and J.M. Ramsey. 1995. *Teaching Science Process Skills.* Good Apple, CA: Frank Schaffer Publications, Inc.

Shulman, L.S., A.S. and Elstein. 1975. Studies Of Problem Solving, Judgment And Decision Making: Implications For Educational Research. In F.N. Kerlinger, (Ed.), *Review of Research in Education,* Volume 3. Itasca, Illinois: Peacock.

Sinclair, G.D., and D.A. Sinclair. 1994. Developing Reflective Performers By Integrating Mental Management Skills With The Learning Process. *The Sport Psychologist.* 8.

1994. *Usborn Science And Experiments: Our World.* New York, NY: Usborn Publishing Ltd.

1995. *Water, The Source Of Life.* New York, NY: Scholastic Inc.

Smith, L.M. 1982. Benefits Of Naturalistic Methods In Research In Science Education. *Journal Of Research In Science Teaching.* 19 (8).

Wikipedia. 2005. Scientific Method. http://en.wikipedia.org/wiki/Scientific_method

CHAPTER 2

History of Ocean Explor[ation] and Marine Sciences

Institute of Nautical Archaeolog[y]

Philip Nicholson

Preserving our Maritime Past for the Future

Much of human history lies in our maritime cultural heritage. Dating back to prehistory, seafaring has shaped events as instruments of exploration, expansion, commerce and war. The submerged remains of shipwrecks have stories to tell us about their important, and sometimes tragic, history. Because they are underwater, shipwrecks and the important information they yield about our past are often overlooked. But, like land-based history, our underwater cultural heritage is a valuable part of humanity's common heritage and, as such, deserving of study by archaeologists such as John Broadwater.

Broadwater has been working to protect the United States' underwater cultural heritage for 30 years. He has a PhD in Maritime Studies and is Chief Archaeologist of the National Marine Sanctuaries.

"I first became interested in science as a child. Many years later, I was working as an engineer and, already a certified diver, I made my first dive on a shipwreck and that dive changed everything. I knew immediately that I had found what I wanted to do with my life: To touch history and to learn the stories that only shipwrecks could tell."

Broadwater's specialty is maritime (of or relating to navigation or commerce on the sea) archaeology, the study of people and their interaction with the sea. "I think this field of study is important because we live on a water planet where most of Earth's inhabitants have a direct connection with the sea or at least are affected by the sea in important ways."

Shipwrecks and other archaeological sites attract peoples' interest. Preserving these sites and artifacts, either under water or in museums, allows people to experience them and to gain a better understanding of history. When archaeologists excavate sites they do so in such a way as to ensure that important cultural and historical information is not lost or destroyed. As a maritime archaeologist, Broadwater has participated in several challenging and rewarding *underwater* excavations.

"I directed the excavation of a Revolutionary War shipwreck that was challenging because of the difficulty in obtaining the necessary funding and support, but we were successful in spite of all obstacles. More recently, I headed up an effort by the National Oceanic and Atmospheric Administration to save parts of the famous Civil War ironclad ship, the U.S.S. *Monitor*. Working with US Navy divers we overcame many obstacles, including limited funding, deep water, and hazardous ocean conditions and we successfully raised many of the Monitor's most important components, including her steam engine and armored gun turret." These artifacts are now on exhibit at the U.S.S. *Monitor* Center at The Mariners' Museum, Newport News, Virginia.

To those who would follow in his footsteps, Broadwater says, "The marine sciences offer lots of exciting and challenging career opportunities. To get into the best schools and land the best jobs, you will need a solid science education. Try to learn about all branches of science and math because you will find that you will use bits and pieces of each discipline in college and beyond."

John D. Broadwater, PhD
Chief Archaeologist
Office of National Marine Sanctuaries
National Oceanic and Atmospheric Administration (NOAA)
http://maritimeheritage.noaa.gov

Figure 2-1a

Philip Nicholson

Figure 2-1b

US Naval Historical Center

Figure 2-1c

Courtesy of Harbor Branch Oceanographic

Figure 2-1d

Four stages of historical oceanography.

We can divide the history of oceanography into four stages: ancient uses and explorations, the Middle Ages, European voyages of discovery, and the birth and growth of modern sciences.

Today the United States is the longest standing democratic republic to ever exist. The successes and failures of this government offer tremendous lessons in political science and the nature of government. However, the establishment of this republic offers another important perspective.

Following the Constitutional Convention in Philadelphia in 1787, Alexander Hamilton, John Jay, and James Madison published 85 essays known today as the Federalist Papers. The purpose of these essays was to defend the proposed new Constitution for the United States of America and to encourage the states to ratify it. Throughout the 85 Federalist Papers, Hamilton, Jay, and Madison frequently cite prior failures of government and institutions as far back as ancient Greece. Their works show the many counterbalances written in to the US Constitution to cancel out these weaknesses.

The Federalist Papers show that in laying out the US Constitution, Hamilton, Jay, Madison, and the other members of the Constitutional Convention looked to history for lessons about what had succeeded and failed in government. For example, they examined the dismal track records of the early Greek democracies. Based on their failures, the convention determined that the US would not be a democracy. History showed them that a representative government elected by the people—a democratic republic—best preserves liberty.

The success of the United States' republic demonstrates that history is not irrelevant. It isn't simply names and dates that matter, but the lessons learned. In any field, whether politics or science, we avoid repeating errors by looking at history. Likewise, we repeat and build on success. The foundation of wisdom is history.

The History of Oceanography—Why Study It?

What are three reasons to learn the history of oceanography?

What are four main stages in the history of oceanography?

To learn to drive a car, you don't need to learn the history of cars. You can drive safely without knowing what a Model-T is or what the first sports car was. So, do you *need* to learn the history of oceanography to learn and apply modern marine sciences? To be honest, in many ways, no. Yet, unlike learning to drive a car, if you study oceanography without studying its past, you lose important dimensions that help you as a scientist.

Like oceanography, history is a branch of knowledge. History is the branch that records and explains past events. In the history of science, those events and explanations are more than curiosities. They form the basis for science as it exists today. You need to learn the history of oceanography for at least three reasons:

1. The history of oceanography isn't isolated from, but connected to, the world's overall history. In commerce, warfare, resources, and weather, the ocean has shaped humanity's past. Understanding the history of oceanography is part of understanding how the ocean has shaped human society and how they may shape the future.

2. Oceanography's past helps you understand why and how people apply marine sciences today. Based on the latest information, a scientist may challenge modern theories, procedures, or practices—this is how science progresses. But, it's difficult to objectively challenge the status quo without understanding its origin.

3. A good reason to study the history of oceanography is that it's interesting. It's not just a boring list of dates and famous fish nerds. Oceanography sometimes grew out of humanity's desire to explore and discover, sometimes out of naval combat and power struggles, and sometimes out of pure curiosity. As you're about to see, contributors to this science have ranged from the most powerful people on earth to those whose names history didn't record. Oceanography's history is about *people*, not just the ocean and test tubes.

We can divide the history of oceanography into four stages: ancient uses and explorations, the Middle Ages, European voyages of discovery, and the birth and growth of modern marine sciences. As you'll see, each of these periods marks distinct changes in how we interact with and study the ocean.

STUDY QUESTIONS

Find the answers as you read.

1. What are three reasons to learn the history of oceanography?

2. What are four main stages in the history of oceanography?

INTERNET PORTAL

SCiLINKS. NSTA

Topic: History of Oceanography
Go To: www.scilinks.org
Code: LOP2020

ARE YOU LEARNING?

1. **Reasons for studying the history of oceanography include (choose all that apply)**

   A. it is part of understanding how the ocean has affected society.

   B. it explains how and why marine sciences are conducted today.

   C. it's interesting.

2. **Four stages of the history of oceanography include (choose all that apply)**

   A. ancient uses and explorations.

   B. European voyages of discovery.

   C. the atomic era.

Find the answers as you read.

1. What were the three primary reasons for early civilization to interact with the ocean?

2. When was the first recorded sea voyage, and by what civilization?

3. What did the Phoenicians contribute to ocean exploration?

4. What was the significance of early Polynesian seafaring?

5. How did ancient explorers navigate near shore and in the open ocean?

6. What major ocean discovery is credited to the Greek Pytheas?

7. What two major contributions are credited to the Greek Eratosthenes?

8. What were the significances of the maps of Herodotus, Strabo, and Ptolemy?

9. What is the purpose of the latitude and longitude mapping system?

10. What is a *parallel*? What is another name for the 0° parallel?

11. What is a *meridian*? Through what city does the 0° meridian run?

Ancient Uses and Explorations (5000 B.C.–800 A.D.)

Prehistory and the Rise of Seafaring

What were the three primary reasons for early civilization to interact with the ocean?

When was the first recorded sea voyage, and by what civilization?

History doesn't record exactly who the first people were to explore the ocean, nor when. But, archaeologists date Native American primitive fishhooks and spears to approximately 5000 B.C. It's clear that the first reason early civilization interacted with the ocean was to obtain food. As societies grew, trade between cities and cultures grew, adding two new reasons: to discover new lands and as a means of trade. Although these were economic rather than scientific pursuits, these three motivations led to the invention of ships and seafaring (the use of the sea for travel or transportation).

When was the first sea voyage in a ship? No one is really sure. The earliest voyage in a ship may be that of Noah and his Ark. Some scholars say this event may have occurred approximately 4000 B.C. Along with the earliest Biblical reference; several ancient cultures have similar stories about a worldwide flood and a large boat full of animals. Regardless, the existence of the Ark is widely debated. In any case, escaping a flood is not really a sea voyage in the true sense of the term.

The earliest recorded sea voyage therefore appears to have taken place about 3200 B.C. under the auspices of the Egyptian Pharaoh Snefru. The Egyptian records say that he brought 40 ships to Egypt from Phoenicia, suggesting that seafaring had been commonplace for some time. Other Egyptian hieroglyphics (the symbols used in ancient Egyptian writing) record an expedition to the southern edge of the Arabian Peninsula and the Red Sea. This trip in about 2750 B.C. appears to be the first recorded sea voyage of exploration. The earliest seafaring craft known dates to about 2585-2560

www.stonehenge-info.org

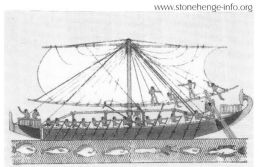

Figure 2-2

Egyptian seagoing vessel.

The earliest recorded sea voyage appears to have taken place about 3200 B.C. under the auspices of the Egyptian Pharaoh Snefru. Around 2750 B.C. the Egyptian Hannu led the first recorded sea voyage of exploration to the limits of their known world, the southern edge of the Arabian Peninsula and the Red Sea. These early vessels often used a single sail and oars for propulsion.

B.C., around the time the Egyptians built the Great Pyramids. The Egyptians entombed an entire ship in the Pyramid of Khufu (Cheops), surrounding it with hieroglyphics and paintings. This reed boat used a single sail and oars for propulsion.

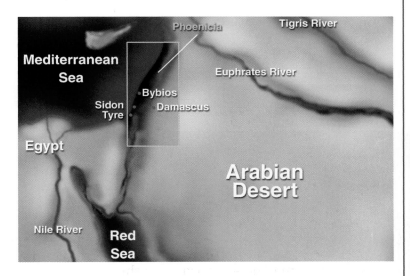

Figure 2-3

Location of Egypt and Phoenicia.

The ancient Phoenicians and Egyptians used sea voyages for trade and explorations.

THE NORTH STAR AND NAVIGATION

You may have heard that the North Star is significant in seafaring and navigation. The reason is that this star (called *Polaris* by astronomers) is almost directly over the Earth's axis at the North Pole. At night, all the other stars appear to move across the sky as the Earth turns. Due to the Earth's orbit around the sun, the timing and location of constellations also vary in their appearance with the seasons.

The North Star, however, doesn't appear to move much because it's nearly in line with the Earth's axis. This makes it a nearly steady point in the sky, which is why it became one of the first references for nighttime seafaring. It remained a primary navigation reference until the introduction of electronic navigation in the latter half of the 20th century.

Ancient Phoenician Explorations and Discoveries

What did the Phoenicians contribute to ocean exploration?

The ancient Phoenicians were among the most important early Western seafarers. Professor George Bass and archaeologists who studied what is probably the oldest underwater shipwreck known believe it was about 9 meters (30 feet) long and built in approximately 1200 B.C. Found off the coast of Turkey, evidence suggests the vessel was used by a Syrian merchant trader who specialized in buying and selling metals. Archaeologists think this Syrian culture was the forerunner of the Phoenician culture. In this sense, Phoenician seafaring probably predates the rise of Phoenicia itself.

Considering the broad area and strong influence of Phoenician seafaring and trade, today little is known about their explorations. Phoenicia was on the North African Mediterranean coast, where Libya is today. Motivated by trade, the Phoenicians traveled (for their day) incredible distances. They contributed to ocean exploration by establishing the first trade routes throughout the Mediterranean and as far north as Great Britain.

Archaeologists theorize that the Phoenicians sailed both along the shore and in open ocean. Coastal sailors traveled only by day

Figure 2-4

within sight of land, stopping at villages or other landfalls at night. Open ocean Phoenician sailors ventured farther from shore, but stayed within sight of land and sometimes traveled at night. They steered by observing the constellations and the North Star. In the ancient world, the North Star was called the Phoenician Star. This is one of the earliest historical references to using the North Star for navigation.

UNDERWATER ARCHAEOLOGY

Very few drawings of ancient ships have survived, and those that have lack construction details. Yet today we have a good idea of what Greek and Phoenician ships looked like, how builders put them together, the types of cargo they carried, and other details. Furthermore, every sunken ship is a time capsule for the era in which it sank. Much of what we know about ancient cultures comes from what we've found in old shipwrecks. This is possible thanks to the science of underwater archaeology.

Archaeology is the scientific study of fossils, antiquities, and artifacts relating to past human cultures and activities. By necessity it is a methodical science that records every detail of an ancient find before moving and preserving it. This is important because archaeologists learn as much (sometimes more) from the relationships of objects to each other as from the objects themselves.

Institute of Nautical Archaeology

Figure 2-5

Underwater archaeology.

Much of what we know about ancient cultures comes from what we've found in old shipwrecks. This is possible thanks to the science of underwater archaeology.

other archaeological sites under water. Marine archaeology is sometimes known as archaeological oceanography. Scientists commonly use both terms.

As you may imagine, underwater archaeology can be quite demanding. Scientists must meet archaeology's exacting requirements in an extreme environment. This means they must do so using scuba diving, submersibles, or ROVs (Remotely Operated Vehicles), or a combination of these. Archaeologists must not only do this underwater, but they must determine the best scientific methods to apply to each wreck—no two are exactly the same.

Early in the 20th century, hard-hat divers simply grabbed artifacts, which is salvage—not archaeology. This unscientific approach did not effectively study the finds and did more damage than good by causing the loss of significant potential information. In the late 1950s and early 1960s, Peter Throckmorton and George Bass conducted the first detailed, legitimate underwater archaeology on ancient wrecks in the

Underwater archaeology applies the same science to human fossils, antiquities, and artifacts found under water. This typically means ancient shipwrecks, sunken cities, and Mediterranean. By the end of the 1960s, underwater archaeology had become an established and accepted archaeological discipline.

Ancient Polynesian Explorations and Discoveries

What was the significance of early Polynesian seafaring?

Imagine you're on Hawaii. You cut down a tree, hollow it out, add a sail, load in some food and water, and then set out on the ocean headed for Tahiti, more than 3,200 kilometers (2,000 miles) away. It will take weeks, you have no navigation tools except your eyes, ears, and nose, and you're not sure what the weather will be. By modern standards, to even attempt this would seem absurd and foolhardy.

Yet, based on the findings of archaeologists and anthropologists, between 2000 and 500 B.C.—while European cultures were sailing within sight of shore—Polynesian seafarers in the South Pacific were doing exactly this. They routinely crossed thousands of kilometers of open ocean in canoes crafted with stone, bone, and coral tools.

It's theorized that Polynesians built these canoes from tree trunks or planks sewn together with fiber rope. They sealed cracks and seams with tree sap. For open ocean stability on shorter voyages, they attached an *outrigger*, which is an elongated float, such as a shaped log extending from the side of the boat to prevent capsizing. For longer trips, they lashed together two canoes with crossbeams and a deck. These crafts had sails. The Polynesians paddled them when there was no wind.

INTERNET PORTAL

SCILINKS. NSTA

Topic: Navigation
Go To: www.scilinks.org
Code: LOP2025

Figure 2-6

Polynesian vessels.

It's theorized that Polynesians built canoes from tree trunks or planks sewn together with fiber rope. They sealed cracks and seams with tree sap. For open ocean stability on shorter voyages, they attached an *outrigger*, which is an elongated float such as a shaped log extending from the side of the boat to prevent capsizing. For longer trips, they lashed together two canoes with crossbeams and a deck. These crafts had sails. The Polynesians paddled them when there was no wind.

Incredibly, these crafts were seaworthy enough to voyage the distance from Hawaii to Tahiti—more than 3,200 kilometers (2,000 miles). Although they didn't carry as much as the ships used by European explorers and traders, the Polynesian ships were faster.

The significance of Polynesian seafaring is that it is the earliest known regular, long-distance, open ocean seafaring beyond sight of land. Archaeologists think that the Polynesians spread eastward from Fiji, Tonga, and Samoa, settling islands in an area of about 26 million square kilometers (10 million square miles). It's estimated that it took more than 1,000 years for the area to be fully settled. By the time Europeans reached the Pacific Ocean in the 1500s, Polynesians had settled most of the habitable islands for hundreds of years.

Figure 2-7

The extent of Polynesian seafaring.

The significance of Polynesian seafaring is that it is the earliest known regular, long-distance, open ocean seafaring beyond sight of land. Archaeologists think that the Polynesians spread eastward from Fiji, Tonga, and Samoa, settling islands in an area of about 26 million square kilometers (10 million square miles). It's estimated that it took more than 1,000 years for the area to be fully settled.

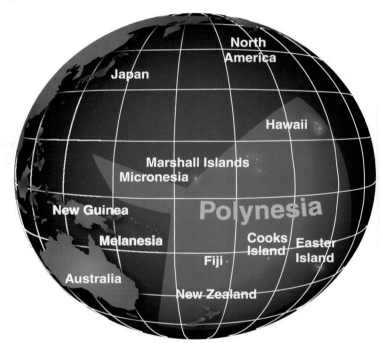

Ancient Greek Exploration and Discoveries

How did ancient explorers navigate near shore and in the open ocean?

What major ocean discovery is credited to the Greek Pytheas?

What two major contributions are credited to the Greek Eratosthenes?

What were the significances of the maps of Herodotus, Strabo, and Ptolemy?

If you've ever been out of sight of land on the ocean or a large lake, you know how difficult navigation can be. The sun and waves give you some directional clues, but these aren't steady or precise. Yet for seafaring to cross large expanses from one small point to another (from a port to an island), navigation is essential.

The Egyptians and other early ancient explorers probably stayed close to shore. They used references on shore to navigate. This kind of navigation is called *piloting*. As seafaring advanced, ancient explorers learned to use the sun, constellations, the North Star, and sea conditions to help them find their way on the open ocean. They learned to look for cloud patterns that form over islands and to watch for shore birds. It's even thought that they could smell land animals and plants some distance at sea.

It was primarily the ancient Greeks who first used mathematical principles and developed sophisticated maps for seafaring. By applying their advancements in early science and mathematics, this culture contributed to understanding the ocean in many ways. For example, although Western civilization would "lose" the knowledge during the Middle Ages, the Greeks knew that the Earth is a sphere, not flat.

While exploring the Mediterranean and the adjacent Atlantic up to modern-day Great Britain, the Greek Pytheas noted that he could predict tides in the Atlantic based on the phases of the moon. You'll learn more about how the moon creates tides in Chapter 10. Pytheas' major ocean discovery, however, was determining how far north or south you are from the North Star. He did this by measuring the angle between the horizon and the North Star. This significantly improved navigation.

About 150 years later, Eratosthenes (c. 264-194 B.C.) made two major contributions that furthered Pytheas' work. Eratosthenes calculated the Earth's circumference and invented the first latitude/longitude system. This is a system of imaginary grid lines on the Earth, used for navigation and mapping. Eratosthenes' system was irregular because he deliberately ran his gridlines through important landmarks. It wasn't until about 127 B.C. that another Greek, Hipparchus, invented the regular grid system that we use today. You'll learn more about this system shortly.

Early seafarers, including the Greeks, began gathering navigational information and writing it down as early maps. In about 450 B.C., Herodotus published a detailed history of Greece's struggles with the Persian Empire. This work included a map

www.nostos.com

Figure 2-8a

The Greek Pytheas.

While exploring the Mediterranean and the adjacent Atlantic up to modern-day Great Britain, the Greek Pytheas noted that he could predict tides in the Atlantic based on the phases of the moon. Pytheas' major ocean discovery, however, was determining how far north or south you are from the North Star. He did this by measuring the angle between the horizon and the North Star. This significantly improved navigation.

Figure 2-8b

Eratosthenes invents latitude and longitude.

Eratosthenes invented the first latitude/longitude system. This is a system of imaginary grid lines on the Earth, used for navigation and mapping. Eratosthenes' system was irregular because he deliberately ran his gridlines through important landmarks.

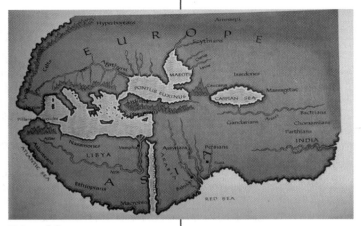

Figure 2-9

**The world according to
Herodotus, 450 B.C.**

Early seafarers, including the Greeks,
began gathering navigational information and writing it down as early
maps. In about 450 B.C., Herodotus
published a detailed history recording
Greece's struggles with the Persian
Empire. This work included a map
that is significant because it was one
of the earliest published maps of the
world the Greeks knew. Although no
known copies have survived, it has
been reconstructed based on surviving descriptions.

that is significant because it was one
of the earliest published maps of the
world the Greeks knew. Although no
known copies have survived, it has
been reconstructed based on surviving descriptions.

As sailors from Greece, Rome, and
other cultures continued their exploration, they returned from their voyages
with more information for mapping.
Strabo (63 B.C.–24 A.D.) was a Greek
historian, geographer, and philosopher. He published a 17-book work
called *Geographic*. It described the peo-
ples of the world the Greeks knew, and their histories. *Geographic*
contained a map that was significant because it demonstrated the
Greek's expanding knowledge, and its accuracy, about the world.

The next significant Greek map came from Ptolemy (c. 100-168
A.D.), an astronomer, mathematician, physicist, and geographer, in
about 150 A.D. Ptolemy's map was significant because it showed a
portion of the Earth as a sphere on flat paper. It was also significant
because it improved on Hipparchus' latitude/longitude system. It
did this by dividing the grid into degrees, minutes, and seconds.
This is the latitude/longitude system still in use today. Although
none of Ptolemy's maps have survived, it has been recreated from
descriptions.

Jim Siebold

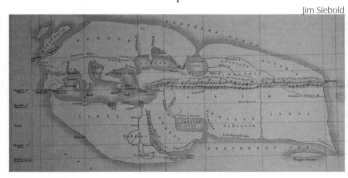

Figure 2-10

The world according to Strabo, c. 35 B.C.

As sailors from Greece, Rome, and other cultures continued their
exploration, they returned from their voyages with more information for mapping. Strabo gathered that information and developed
a map expanding knowledge and its accuracy, about the world.

Figure 2-11

Ptolemy's Earth as a sphere.

The Greek Ptolemy developed
the first known map to show a
portion of the Earth as a sphere
on flat paper.

MEASURING THE SIZE OF THE EARTH—ANCIENT GREEK STYLE

Imagine it's 200 B.C. and you want to make an accurate map. To do this, you need to know the circumference of the Earth. There are no satellites, surveying tools, or similar modern tools, so how do you do it? Can it even be done?

Eratosthenes did it by using basic geometry. Although his original work was lost long ago, his accomplishment survives through the works of other authors. It's thought his calculations went like this:

Eratosthenes knew that when a line crosses two parallel lines, the angles formed at the intersection of one line will always equal the angles formed at the intersection of the other line. Therefore, Eratosthenes determined he needed to measure the distance and angles between two parallel lines striking the Earth's surface. This would tell him the number of degrees of the Earth's circumference that the distance represents.

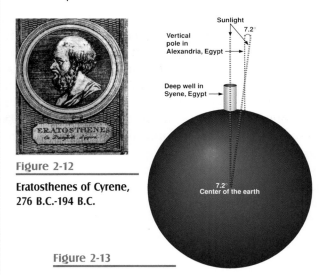

Figure 2-12

Eratosthenes of Cyrene, 276 B.C.-194 B.C.

Figure 2-13

First, Eratosthenes needed two parallel lines that intersected with the Earth's surface. For these, he decided to use the sun's rays. He probably knew that, technically, sun rays are not parallel. But, the sun is so far away that for his practical purposes, they were close enough to parallel to be accurate.

Next, Eratosthenes needed to know when sunlight was striking the Earth squarely so he would have one of his two lines perpendicular to the Earth. That would be when the sun was directly overhead. He had heard of a deep well in

Syene, Egypt, into which, at noon on the longest day of the year, sunlight shone directly down to the water at the bottom. That told him when the sun's rays gave him the parallel lines he needed. The well would be one line and the rays coming down anywhere else could be the other, provided he could measure and determine an angle from them.

In another Egyptian city, Alexandria, he had noticed a vertical pole that cast a very slight shadow on the same day at the same time. This meant that the sun was not directly overhead in Alexandria when it was directly overhead in Syene. The vertical pole's *shadow* therefore formed the intersecting angle he needed. Eratosthenes measured the angle and found it to be 7.2°. Now all he needed was the distance from the pole to the well, which was estimated as (in modern measurements) 800 kilometers (500 miles). From there it was determining a ratio with basic algebra:

$$\frac{7.2°}{800 \text{ km}} = \frac{360°}{\text{Earth circumference in km}}$$

The next step is to cross multiply:

7.2° x Earth circumference in km = 800 km x 360°

Then solve for the circumference:

Earth circumference in km = $\frac{800 \text{ km x } 360°}{7.2°}$

Earth circumference in km = $\frac{288,000° \text{ km}}{7.2°}$

Earth circumference in km = 40,000 km (24,840 miles)

The accepted measurement today using lasers, satellites, and other modern instruments is 40,032 km. Eratosthenes missed it by only 32 km (approximately 20 miles)! With the Earth's circumference in hand, Eratosthenes went on to invent the first latitude/longitude system.

Ironically, Ptolemy's later map, which used Hipparchus' improved latitude/longitude system, was based on an *inaccurate* Earth size. Ptolemy's map underestimated the Earth's circumference. His estimate became widely accepted and survived to Columbus' day. Columbus believed he had reached the west coast of Asia when he reached the Caribbean because he thought the Earth was smaller than it is.

The Latitude/Longitude System

What is the purpose of the latitude and longitude mapping system?

What is a parallel*? What is another name for the 0° parallel?*

What is a meridian*? Through what city does the 0° meridian run?*

One of the Greeks' primary contributions to oceanography and sea-faring is the latitude/longitude system. The purpose of this system is to identify specific locations on the Earth's surface. Since this system is important to seafaring and oceanography, and in many other applications, we'll detour from history for a moment to learn about it.

As you may be aware, the latitude/longitude system is simply an imaginary grid running over the face of the Earth. Latitude lines run east-west and longitude lines run north-south. To establish a given location, you determine the latitude line and the longitude line running through it. Because these lines run around the sphere of the Earth, they are numbered in degrees. For further accuracy, degrees are subdivided into 60 minutes, and minutes into 60 seconds (just like time). Scientists however, typically use decimal degrees (GPS coordinates) instead of degrees, minutes, and seconds. The use of decimal degrees instead of minutes and seconds allows the greatest precision.

Latitude lines never intersect, so they are also called *parallels* – circling the planet around the Earth's axis. The 0° degree parallel is called the *equator* and runs around the Earth at its widest point. Parallels above and below have increasing degree numbers until reaching the poles. The poles are 90°. Parallels above the equator are called *north* latitude and those below are called *south* latitude. As you go further north or south, each parallel becomes shorter because the distance around the Earth reduces.

Figure 2-14

Latitude lines.

Latitude lines run east-west and they never intersect, so they are also called *parallels*. The 0° degree parallel is called the *equator* and runs around the Earth at its widest point. Parallels above and below have increasing degree numbers until reaching the poles. The poles are 90°. Parallels above the equator are called north latitude and those below are called south latitude. As you go further north or south, each parallel becomes shorter because the distance around the Earth reduces.

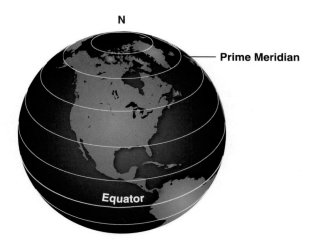

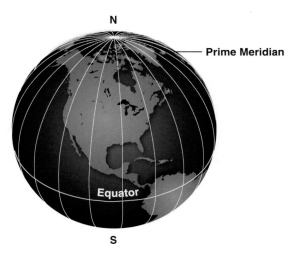

N

Prime Meridian

Equator

S

Longitude lines begin at one pole and end at the other. Sometimes called *meridians*, the 0° meridian runs through the Royal Naval Observatory in Greenwich, England. This is called the *prime meridian*. Directly on the other side of the world is the 180°

Figure 2-15

Longitude lines.

Longitude lines begin at one pole and end at the other. Longitude lines actually intersect with the Earth's axis at the poles.

Sometimes called meridians, the 0° meridian runs through the Royal Naval Observatory in Greenwich, England. This is called the prime meridian. Directly on the other side of the world is the 180° meridian. Meridians from the right of the prime meridian to the 180° meridian are called east longitude. Those to the left are called west longitude.

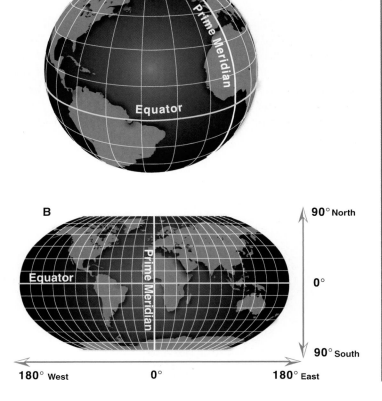

A

Prime Meridian

Equator

B

Prime Meridian

Equator

90° North

0°

90° South

180° West   0°   180° East

Figure 2-16

Prime meridian and equator.

An arctic (**A**) and flattened (**B**) map view of the Earth showing the prime meridian and equator.

meridian. If you are looking northward, the meridians on the right of the prime meridian are called east longitude, all the way to the 180° meridian.

By knowing the latitude and longitude of a place, you know where to find it. Suppose you're an oceanographer and you want to research organisms living on the wreck of the *Titanic*. You check with Woods Hole Oceanographic Institute and it sends you GPS coordinates (decimal degrees) like this: 49.9469° W, 41.7325° N. For a geographer, these coordinates look like this: 49° 56' 49" W, 41° 43' 57" N. This means 49 degrees, 56 minutes, and 49 seconds west longitude and 41 degrees, 43 minutes, and 57 seconds north latitude. Either of those coordinates will put you precisely on the *Titanic*, provided you have a *submersible* (a small underwater craft used especially for deep-sea research) that can dive the 3.2 kilometers (2 miles) of water to reach it.

Figure 2-17

Pinpointing the wreck of the Titanic.

The location of the wreck of the *Titanic* is 49.9469° W, 41.7325° N as expressed in decimal degrees. These are the GPS coordinates used by most scientists. Those coordinates will put you precisely on the *Titanic*, provided you have a submersible that can dive down the 3.2 kilometers (2 miles) of water to reach it.

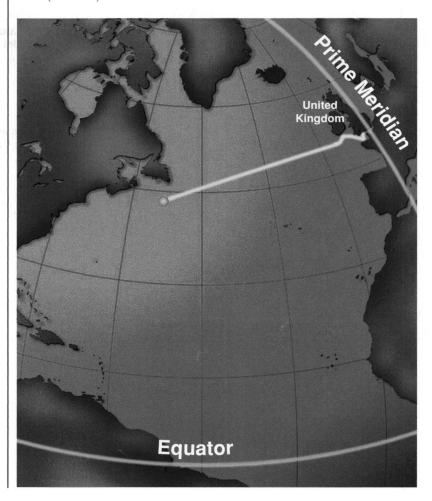

1. **The three primary reasons for early civilizations to interact with the ocean were food gathering, to discover new lands, and for trade.**

   A. true

   B. false

2. **The first recorded sea voyage of any kind was by the _____ and took place approximately _____.**

   A. Phoenicians, 1500 B.C.

   B. Egyptians, 2750 B.C.

   C. Phoenicians, 2750 B.C.

   D. Egyptians, 3200 B.C.

3. **The Phoenicians contributed to ocean exploration by**

   A. establishing the first trade routes through the Mediterranean.

   B. inventing the latitude/longitude system.

   C. calculating the circumference of the Earth.

4. **The significance of Polynesian seafaring is that**

   A. it brought Europeans to the Pacific Ocean.

   B. it is the earliest known regular open ocean seafaring beyond sight of land.

   C. it introduced the concept of the North Star.

5. **Historians think that, among other things, ancient explorers used their sense of smell to navigate.**

   A. true

   B. false

6. **The Greek Pytheas is credited with**

   A. using smell to navigate at sea.

   B. using the North Star to determine how far north or south you are.

   C. the Pythagorean Theorem.

7. **Eratosthenes' two major contributions were**

   A. using the North Star and the first latitude/longitude system.

   B. using the North Star and calculating the Earth's circumference.

   C. the first latitude/longitude system and calculating the Earth's circumference.

8. **Strabo's map was significant because it was one of the earliest published maps of the world.**

   A. true

   B. false

9. **The latitude and longitude mapping system is to**

   A. allow map makers to estimate the size of the Earth.

   B. identify specific locations on the Earth's surface.

10. **A parallel is another name for _____. The 0° parallel is called _____.**

    A. a latitude line, the equator

    B. the equator, the prime meridian

    C. a latitude line, the prime meridian

    D. a longitude line, the equator

11. **A meridian is another name for _____. The 0° meridian runs through _____.**

    A. a latitude line, the widest part of the Earth

    B. a latitude line, Greenwich England

    C. a longitude line, the widest part of the Earth

    D. a longitude line, Greenwich England

The Middle Ages (800 A.D.–1400)

STUDY QUESTIONS

Find the answers as you read.

1. What effect did the Middle Ages have on the knowledge of geography and science?

2. What climate change affected Scandinavia in the 9th century? What was the significance of this change to exploration?

3. By the year 1125, the Chinese were responsible for inventing what important navigational tool?

4. What two technological innovations did Chinese ships have by the mid 1400s?

The European Middle Ages

What effect did the Middle Ages have on the knowledge of geography and science?

The period of approximately 500 A.D. to 1500 in Europe is called the Middle Ages. This was the period that we think of when we think of knights, castles, and feudalism.

There's considerable speculation among historians as to what caused the Middle Ages. With the death of Romulus Augustus in 476, the Western Roman Empire ended. This may have contributed by beginning the breakup of a large European community into small, relatively isolated communities. The Catholic Church rose at about the same time. While there's much debate about its role and power, it was clearly a strong force that changed the interactions between government, church, and society. The end of the Middle Ages approximately coincides with the Catholic Church's decline in the mid 1500s. This supports the assertion that the Catholic Church of the period was a contributing factor to the social structure of the Middle Ages.

Whatever the causes, the Middle Ages suppressed further advancements in the knowledge of geography and science in the West. Europe entered an age of intellectual "darkness," which is why the period is sometimes called the Dark Ages. Communication between nations was poor, and invaders from the north swept across Europe.

Figure 2-18

Middle Ages map of the known world.
The Middle Ages suppressed further advancements in the knowledge of geography and science in the West. Europe entered an age of intellectual "darkness." Earlier, the Greeks correctly assumed that the Earth was round (compare this map to Figure 2-11 by Ptolemy). However, during the Middle Ages the prevailing belief was that the Earth was flat. To illustrate this point, here is a colorized recreation of a 6th century map by Cosmas Indicopleustes. Cosmas' map shows a somewhat warped perspective of the world based on his interpretation of descriptions given in the Bible.

Jim Siebold

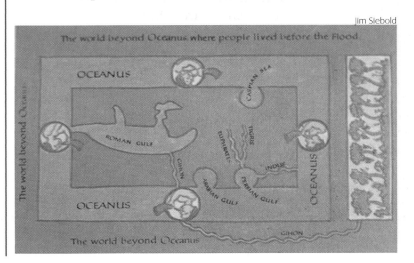

Education became less common, and many of the works of previous cultures were lost. Few people could read the works that survived, and myths replaced knowledge. For example, the Greeks knew the Earth is round, but the prevailing belief in the Middle Ages was that the Earth is flat.

Except for the Viking voyages, there was little ocean exploration by Europeans during this period. However, trade continued by ship. Seafaring for trade and passage may have been important in bringing the Middle Ages to a close by helping economic growth and restoring the spread of knowledge.

Viking Explorations and Discoveries

What climate change affected Scandinavia in the 9th century? What was the significance of this change to exploration?

The Viking period stretches from about 790 A.D. to 1100. During this period Vikings raided nearby lands, explored, and established trade routes throughout Britain, Ireland, Southern Europe, North Africa, and Central Asia. This was the only significant exploration taking place in Europe during this period.

In the 9th century, a warming global climate freed the North Atlantic of ice. This allowed the Vikings to explore westward. The Vikings discovered Iceland and Greenland. Eventually, a Viking expedition led by Leif Eriksson landed in North America at Newfoundland, Canada.

Many of the new Viking outposts didn't last. The Vikings abandoned them due to the harsh climates. The global climate became colder (the *Little Ice Age*) and the sea ice returned. This effectively cut off the northern sea routes from Scandinavia.

Archaeological findings show that Scandinavian vessel design progressed considerably from 11 A.D. to 1450. Because the Vikings often buried their dead in ships, more than 400 of their craft have been recovered by archaeologists from burial mounds. Findings indicate that the Vikings built some ships primarily for warfare and raiding and others as cargo carriers. Post-Viking Scandinavian ships show that seaworthy hull (the frame or body of a ship or boat exclusive of masts, yards, sails, and rigging) designs introduced by the Vikings continued into the mid 15th century. Evidence suggests that by the mid 1400s, Scandinavian merchants sailed frequently into the Mediterranean. At this point, shipbuilders began combining the best of both Scandinavian and Mediterranean ship design. This led to the ships that ushered in the European voyages of discovery.

Chinese Explorations and Discoveries

By the year 1125, the Chinese were responsible for inventing what important navigational tool?

What two technological innovations did Chinese ships have by the mid 1400s?

Although science and exploration lay idle in Europe during the Middle Ages, that wasn't the case in China. Among many important contributions in that era, the Chinese were responsible for inventing the magnetic compass.

Historians think that the Chinese were aware of magnetism as early as 240 B.C. However, the first definitive reference in Chinese literature to a true compass dates to approximately 1000 A.D. Chinese literature suggests that the compass was in use for seafaring around 1125. Compare this to European culture, where the first reference to a compass appears in a poem from 1190. It wasn't until the 1400s that European sailors fully understood compass navigation.

Artifacts and other archaeological evidence suggest that Chinese seafaring was well established by about 1000 A.D. Maps from the period show extensive trade routes along the eastern Chinese coast. Some routes extended as far as Korea, Japan, and Australia.

By the mid 1400s, shipbuilding was well established in China. More than 300 ships sailed under Chinese Admiral Zheng, known for traveling to 37 countries and around the tip of Africa. Chinese ships from that period had two technological innovations that are part of modern ships today: central rudders (underwater blades at a ship's stern that when turned cause the vessel to turn in the same direction) and watertight compartments.

Figure 2-19

Chinese ship circa 1450 A.D.
Although science and exploration lay idle in Europe during the Middle Ages, that wasn't the case in China. Among many important contributions in that era, the Chinese were responsible for inventing the magnetic compass. By the mid 1400s, shipbuilding was well established in China. More than 300 ships sailed under Chinese Admiral Zheng.

Philip Nicholson

1. **The Middle Ages are known for _____ the knowledge of geography and science in Europe.**

   A. improving

   B. suppressing advancements in

   C. motivating

2. **A global cooling trend in the 9th century affected Scandinavia. It was important because it built an ice bridge to Great Britain.**

   A. true

   B. false

3. **By the year 1125, the Chinese had invented**

   A. the astrolabe.

   B. the sextant.

   C. the compass.

4. **The two technological innovations found in Chinese ships by the mid 1400s were**

   A. the sail and the crow's nest.

   B. the central rudder and the steam turbine.

   C. the central rudder and watertight compartments.

   D. the steam turbine and the crow's nest.

European Voyages of Discovery (1400–1700)

The End of the Middle Ages and a Route Around Africa

What were the primary motivations that led to the ocean explorations of the 15th century?

What three explorers established the route around the Cape of Good Hope to India?

In Europe, the 1400s mark an important transition at the end of the Middle Ages. This period is called the Renaissance (from the Latin *renasci* meaning *to be born again*). It centered in Italy and spread throughout Europe through commerce and by those who had studied in Italy and traveled. It was a period marked by a "rediscovery" of principles and science put forth by the Greeks, Romans, and other cultures.

With the Renaissance came new interest in long ocean expeditions. The primary motives for these were economics, politics, and religion. In the early 1400s, Prince Henry the Navigator of Portugal set his sights on finding a route to the East around Africa. Using a compass—a new device among European sailors at the time—his expeditions brought back new information about the west African coast. Although he learned a great deal, he didn't find a route to the East.

Twenty years after Henry's death, Bartholomeu Dias completed the first voyage around the Cape of Good Hope in 1487. Ten years after Dias, Vasco da Gama (1469-1524) finally led the first expedition around the Cape of Good Hope to India.

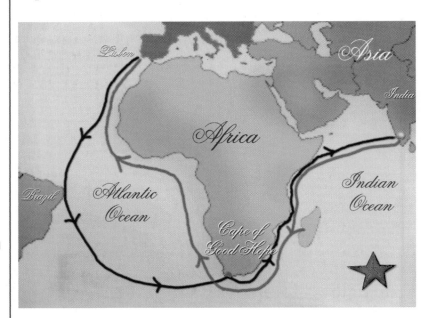

Figure 2-20

Vasco da Gama's journey to India.

A fleet of ships under da Gama's command left Lisbon harbor in July, 1497. After having passed the Cape of Good Hope and sailed up the east coast of Africa, da Gama first sighted the coast of India in May of 1498.

Exploration of the New World

What was the purpose of Christopher Columbus' four expeditions?

Who is credited as being the first European to recognize that South America was a new continent?

What was Vasco Nuñez de Balboa's accomplishment?

Who led the first expedition around the world? Over what years did the voyage take place?

Who led the second expedition around the world? Over what years did the voyage take place?

In 1492, Genovese (Italian) Christopher Columbus (1469-1524) set out on the first of his four famous voyages. His purpose was the same as Prince Henry's and Vasco da Gama's: to find a route to Asia and the East Indies. Because he was using Ptolemy's estimation of the Earth's size (which was too small), he believed he'd reached

Asia when he landed on a Caribbean island. Like all Europeans, the existence of the Americas was unknown to him.

Several expeditions followed Columbus. Sailing on behalf of Portugal and Spain, Italian Amerigo Vespucci (1454-1512) voyaged to South America several times. He explored much of its east coast and the mouth of the Amazon River. Vespucci is credited as the first European to recognize that South America was a new continent. A world map produced in 1507 honored Vespucci's discoveries by labeling the New World "America."

In the early 1500s, Vasco Nuñez de Balboa led an expedition that crossed the Isthmus of Panama in Central America. This expedition made him the first European to look out on the eastern shore of the Pacific Ocean.

News that the Pacific Ocean lay beyond the Americas restored the hope that you could reach the east by sailing west. That is, that you could sail around the world. The first expedition to do this set sail in 1519 under the command of Portuguese explorer Ferdinand Magellan. He, like Columbus, wanted to establish a trade route to the east. But, unlike Columbus, he had a better idea of how far he had to travel.

Magellan's trip was financed by Spain and began with five ships and about 260 men. Of these, a single ship and 18 men made it back in 1522. The rest died en route from disease and accidents. Magellan himself perished in the Philippines in a fight with islanders. Needless to say, the number of deaths and the stories of hard-

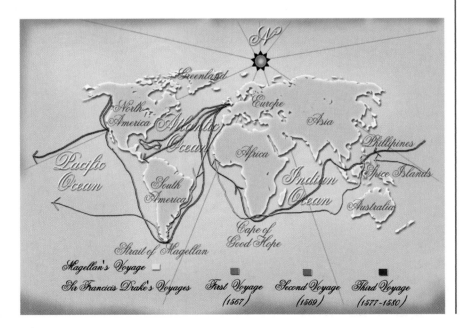

Figure 2-21

Magellan's and Drake's around-the-world voyages of discovery.

News that the Pacific Ocean lay beyond the Americas restored the hope that you could reach the east by sailing west. That is, that you could sail around the world. The first expedition to do this set sail in 1519 under the command of Portuguese explorer Ferdinand Magellan. He, like Columbus, wanted to establish a trade route to the east. But, unlike Columbus, he had a better idea of how far he had to travel. Many men, including Magellan, died on the trip and the crew returned to Spain in 1522. In 1577, Sir Francis Drake, a pirateer turned explorer, began the second circumnavigation of the globe.

ships discouraged anyone from trying to *circumnavigate*–completely sail around–the world again.

In 1577, Francis Drake left England on an expedition to the New World. His purpose was to raid Spanish ships and settlements for their treasure. His expedition rounded the southern tip of South America, then successfully raided Spanish territory along the west coast of South America. Loaded with treasure and knowing the Spanish would be waiting for him in the Atlantic, Drake decided to make for home by going westward. When he returned to London in 1580, Queen Elizabeth knighted him for his exploits. His cargo of treasure and spices was worth a fortune. This was the second successful circumnavigation of the world.

ARE YOU LEARNING?

1. **The primary motivations that led to the ocean explorations of the 15th century were**

   A. research, adventure, and sport.

   B. economics, politics, and religion.

2. **The three explorers who established the route around the Cape of Good Hope to India were**

   A. Prince Henry, Columbus, and Balboa.

   B. Columbus, Dias, and da Gama.

   C. Prince Henry, Dias, and da Gama.

   D. Prince Henry, da Gama, and Balboa.

3. **Columbus' purpose for his expedition was**

   A. to find a route to Asia and East India.

   B. to discover the New World.

4. **The first European to recognize that South America was a new continent was**

   A. Columbus.

   B. Ptolemy.

   C. Vespucci.

   D. da Gama.

5. **Balboa's accomplishment was**

   A. sailing around the world for the first time.

   B. sailing around the world for the second time.

   C. crossing the Isthmus of Panama and finding the Pacific Ocean.

6. **The first expedition around the world was led by _____ in the years _____.**

   A. Magellan, 1519-1522

   B. Columbus, 1492-1524

   C. Drake, 1577-1580

7. **The second expedition around the world was led by _____ in the years _____.**

   A. Magellan, 1519-1522

   B. Columbus, 1492-1524

   C. Drake, 1577-1580

The Birth of Marine Science (1700-1900)

The beginning of the 18th century marked a distinct change in sea exploration. While previous exploration had been motivated by specific military, trade, or conquest objectives, at this time exploration for its own sake began to take place.

Several factors contributed to the change. By 1700, global colonization saw a wide distribution of European outposts. This made repairs and resupply more available, and allowed seafarers to range farther without fear of being too far from food or the ability to make major repairs. Another important factor was the rise of Britain as a sea power.

As Britain began to compete with France and Spain for global conquest, it realized that the more it knew about the seas and the world, the more effective global power it would be. The Royal Navy launched voyages with the objectives of exploration, mapping, and projecting British presence around the world. The crews often included scientists and naturalists.

Cook's Expeditions

In what way did the voyages of James Cook differ from those of sea explorers before him?

What invention in 1735 was a major breakthrough for open ocean navigation?

What geographical discoveries did the Cook expeditions make?

The voyages of Captain James Cook largely receive credit as the first sea expeditions devoted to methodical, scientific oceanography. They differed from those of sea explorers that came before in that they were the first major expeditions launched with science and exploration as their only goals. They also documented their findings with more detail and attention to the scientific method than any previous major expeditions.

A major contribution to Cook's voyages was the invention of the *chronometer*. The chronometer was a very accurate clock or watch that wasn't affected by the waves and motion of the sea. Introduced in 1735, the chronometer was a major breakthrough for open-ocean navigation because knowing the time made it possible to determine longitude in the open sea. This meant that sailors could determine their exact position out of sight of land—even in uncharted waters—by determining both latitude (already possible with star sightings) and longitude. Chronometer accuracy was important in determining location because one hour of time equals

STUDY QUESTIONS

Find the answers as you read.

1. In what way did the voyages of James Cook differ from those of sea explorers before him?

2. What invention in 1735 was a major breakthrough for open-ocean navigation?

3. What geographical discoveries did the Cook expeditions make?

4. Which continent did the United States' Exploring Expedition prove exists?

5. Why do we remember Matthew Maury as the father of physical oceanography?

6. How did Charles Darwin explain the formation of coral reefs?

7. What theory did Darwin propose as a result of his observations during the H.M.S. *Beagle* expedition?

8. What expedition is commonly recognized as the first devoted entirely to marine science?

9. What accomplishments and discoveries did the H.M.S. *Challenger* make?

Figure 2-22

Captain James Cook.

The voyages of Captain James Cook largely receive credit as the first sea expeditions devoted to methodical, scientific oceanography. They differed from those of sea explorers that came before in that they were the first major expeditions launched with science and exploration as their only goals.

15° of longitude, so even relatively small time errors could cause large position errors.

Cook entered the Royal Navy in 1755 and soon proved himself an excellent navigator (one who navigates or is qualified to navigate). Shortly after he made officer rank in the mid 1760s, the Royal Society of London selected Cook to lead a scientific journey to Tahiti. The purpose was to document the path of the planet Venus as it passed between Earth and the sun. With these observations, Royal Society astronomers hoped they could calculate the distance from Earth to the sun.

The expedition departed August 25, 1768, with 94 crewmen and scientists. Besides the observation objectives, Cook carried secret orders to open after completing the science part of the mission.

Cook arrived in Tahiti on April 11, 1769. The expedition made its observations for several weeks, then Cook opened his secret orders. They instructed him to seek an undiscovered southern continent, find it if it existed, and claim it for England. *Cartographers* (map makers) since the 1570s had assumed that a continent exists at each pole. The Dutch sought the presumed southern continent in the early 1600s, but didn't find it.

Figure 2-23

The three voyages of Captain James Cook.

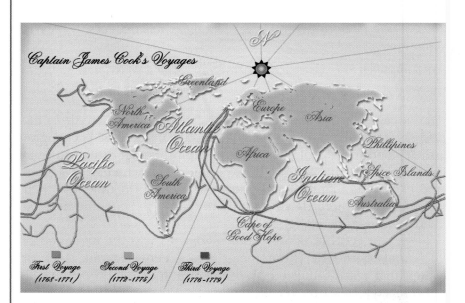

Cook headed from Tahiti to New Zealand, quickly concluding that it was not part of the southern continent. Next, he explored and documented the location of Australia. After exploring it for several months, Cook concluded it wasn't the fabled southern continent either and returned to England.

Cook's second voyage departed Plymouth, England, on July 13, 1772. Again with scientists included in his crew, his orders were to find the southern continent. To accomplish this, Cook planned to sail south and circumnavigate the globe as he searched.

After rounding the Cape of Good Hope, Cook crossed into the Antarctic circle in January, 1773. Ice fields blocked his path, so he headed for warm waters to the east, landing in New Zealand and Tahiti. Leaving there, the expedition continued through the south Pacific, discovering and documenting islands along the way. In

LONGITUDE AND CHRONOMETERS

James Cook led one of the first major sea voyages with the ability to determine longitude. The technology that made it possible was the chronometer—a special clock invented specifically for use at sea.

By using stars, sailors had long been able to determine their latitude, which told them how far north or south they were. This was helpful, but without the ability to determine longitude, they could only guess how far east or west they'd traveled.

Sailors knew they would be able to determine longitude accurately by comparing Greenwich Mean time to the local time based on the sun's posi-

©National Maritime Museum, London

Figure 2-24

John Harrison (1693-1776).

tion on the horizon. This is possible because the local time changes one hour for every 15° longitude you travel. Traveling eastward, the time moves forward one hour, and traveling west it moves back one hour.

©National Maritime Museum, London

Figure 2-25a

Harrison's first marine chronometer—designated H1.

Prior to 1735, however, clocks didn't run accurately on ships. Waves and rocking affected the clock mechanisms so much that they were unusable at sea. In 1714, the British government offered, by Act of Parliament, 20,000 British pounds sterling (about $12 million in today's US currency) to anyone who could solve the longitude problem to within half a degree of accuracy. The government established a Board of Longitude to administer and judge applications for the award.

Years went by. Along with legitimate attempts at a solution, the board received many weird and absurd ones. The phrase "finding the longitude" became an idiom for "the pursuit of a

fool." Many people believed the problem was beyond solution.

Eventually, a working class cabinet maker named John Harrison solved the problem in 1735 by inventing a clock that runs accurately at sea. Although lacking much formal education, Harrison trumped the scientific and academic establishment through extraordinary mechanical talent and determination.

His innovations included springs made of two metals to overcome accuracy problems with temperature changes, and jeweled bearing move-

©National Maritime Museum, London

Figure 2-25b

Harrison's H4 marine chronometer used by Captain James Cook.

ments to reduce friction. Many of these exist in mechanical clocks and watches today. Although his intent was to create a sea-going timepiece, Harrison's work also made possible two other timepieces that we've taken for granted for centuries: the pocket watch and the wrist watch.

November the expedition turned southward again, crossing back into the Antarctic Circle in January 1774. Although Cook went farther south than any explorer to that time, he never found the elusive southern continent. Returning to warmer water, the expedition furthered its exploration of the Pacific, then headed home, arriving in England on July 29, 1775.

Cook began his final voyage on July 12, 1776. Leading two ships with a crew that included scientists, his purpose was to find the fabled Northwest Passage. This was a hoped-for route through the Americas north of present-day Canada. Unlike previous attempts, Cook determined to explore from the Pacific side instead of the Atlantic. His expedition sailed south, rounded the Cape of Good Hope, and then headed north east.

On January 18, 1778, Cook sighted the Hawaiian Islands. He named them the Sandwich Islands after his friend, the Earl of Sandwich (remembered today for inventing the sandwich). According to Cook's reports, the Hawaiian people rowed out to greet him and were friendly. They thought that Cook was a god and that his men were supernatural beings.

Cook departed Hawaii about two weeks later, reaching the coast of present-day Oregon on March 7. He followed the coastline north and passed through the Bering Strait. After searching until August, Cook concluded that the Northwest Passage didn't exist and headed south for warmer waters.

By January 17, 1779, Cook's ships arrived again in Hawaii. This time they weren't welcomed so warmly, and with rising tensions, they departed by February 4. As fate would have it, however, they ran into a storm that broke a foremast. This forced them back to Hawaii for repairs, and the Hawaiians weren't very welcoming.

Cook died on February 14, 1779, during hostilities with the aboriginal Hawaiians. Accounts about what happened vary. One story was that the Hawaiians took one of Cook's smaller boats. To get it back, Cook took a Hawaiian chief hostage and died in the fighting that ensued. With morale low, his crew returned home rather than continuing the voyage, reaching England in August 1780.

Despite his untimely end and his failure to find Antarctica, Cook's contributions were extraordinary. Because of his thoroughness and accuracy in documenting his finds, many considered him more than a captain, but an oceanographer, anthropologist, and naturalist. His discoveries, maps, and reports changed the Western view of the world.

The United States Exploring Expedition

Which continent did the United States Exploring Expedition prove exists?

One of the first significant scientific expeditions launched by the US was the United States Exploring Expedition. This expedition, which is also referred to as the Wilkes Expedition, after its commander, Charles Wilkes, was authorized by an act of Congress in 1836. Its objective was to explore the southern Atlantic Ocean and the Pacific Ocean, which were areas becoming increasingly important to American traders and whalers.

The expedition of six small ships – *the Vincennes, Peacock, Porpoise, Relief, Flying Fish, and Sea Gull* – left Norfolk, Virginia, in August 1838. The crew included scientists and illustrators charged with studying and documenting the expedition's discoveries.

The Exploring Expedition sailed through the southern oceans for almost four years. By the time it returned to New York in June 1842, it had explored Madeira, both coasts of South America, Tierra del Fuego, many South Pacific islands, Australia, New Zealand, Hawaii, California, Oregon, the Philippines, Singapore, and St. Helena. The six ships had rounded the Cape of Good Hope and, perhaps most significant, visited and proved the existence of Antarctica—the elusive southern continent.

Besides mapping, the expedition gathered specimens of *flora* (plant life) and *fauna* (animal life) as it traveled. These were shipped back to the US when the expedition visited established ports. These specimens went into the trust of the Smithsonian Institution in 1858. After its conclusion, the United State's Exploring Expedition final report consisted of 19 volumes of maps, text, and illustrations states documenting its discoveries.

A Science Odyssey, NOAA History

Figure 2-26

Lt. Charles Wilkes—Commander of the US Exploring Expedition.

US Naval Historical Center

Figure 2-27

US Exploring Expedition.
One of the first significant scientific expeditions launched by the US was the United States Exploring Expedition. This expedition, which is also referred to as the Wilkes Expedition, after its commander, Charles Wilkes, was authorized by an act of Congress in 1836. Its objective was to explore the southern Atlantic Ocean and the Pacific Ocean, which were areas becoming increasingly important to American traders and whalers.

Matthew Maury—Father of Physical Oceanography

Why do we remember Matthew Maury as the father of physical oceanography?

Figure 2-28

Matthew Maury.

Often called the "father of physical oceanography," Matthew Maury became established as an authority on ocean exploration and science. His work began early in the century with three voyages that took him to Europe, around the world, and along the South American Pacific coast. From 1834 to 1841, Maury produced and published detailed works about sea navigation and his journeys.

US Naval Historical Center

During the same approximate period as the United States Exploring Expedition, a US naval officer named Matthew Fontaine Maury became established as an authority on ocean exploration and science. His work began early in the century with three voyages that took him to Europe, around the world, and along the South American Pacific coast. From 1834 to 1841, Maury produced and published detailed works about sea navigation and his journeys.

In 1842, the navy appointed Maury superintendent of the Depot of Charts and Instruments of the Navy Department in Washington D.C. In this position, he began collecting data from all navy ships, which he used to produce charts and sailing directions.

By 1853, Maury had earned global acclaim for organizing these data. Maury also gathered information from the logbooks of captains outside the US Navy. Their entries described weather and currents, which Maury knew could add to our knowledge of the ocean.

By using thousands of logbooks, Maury produced the first maps of winds, temperatures and currents around the world. In that year, he represented the US at an international congress on ocean exploration in Brussels. As a result, Maury's systems for recording oceanographic data from naval and merchant vessels were adopted worldwide.

By collecting data from ships from many countries, Maury was among the first to see a worldwide pattern for surface winds and currents. Based on his analysis of these patterns, he produced instructions for making long-distance sailing more efficient by using prevailing currents and winds. In 1855, he published *The Physical Geography of the Sea*, which is now considered the first textbook on modern oceanography. Thanks to his study of currents and other physical aspects of the sea, we remember Maury today as the father of physical oceanography.

Darwin and the H.M.S. *Beagle*

How did Charles Darwin explain the formation of coral reefs?

What theory did Darwin propose as a result of his observations during the H.M.S. Beagle *expedition?*

Of all the 19th century oceanographic expeditions, perhaps the best known is the five-year voyage of the H.M.S. *Beagle*. This voyage began on December 27, 1831. The *Beagle* sailed under the command of Robert Fitzroy, with the now-famous Charles Darwin aboard as the ship's naturalist. Departing from Plymouth, England, with a crew of 73, the *Beagle* ultimately circled the Earth studying the southern oceans. In its travels, it voyaged along both coasts of South America.

The route along South America proved especially interesting to Darwin. He spent much of his time studying the geology and biology of the coastline, with a particular interest in the unique animals in the Galapagos Islands off today's Ecuador. Darwin also noted the changes in organism characteristics and habitats that corresponded with latitude.

As the *Beagle* sailed through the warm South Pacific, Darwin turned his attention to coral and coral reefs. Among other observations, he noted that coral only grows in the relatively shallow, warm, upper depths. However, coral reefs themselves extended far deeper than coral grows. Darwin hypothesized that the massive coral reefs they saw could only result when the seafloor slowly sinks. As the seafloor descends, Darwin proposed, the coral grows upward from its base to remain in the shallow water it needs to survive. This hypothesis became the basis for Darwin's first major published work, *Structure and Distribution of Coral Reefs*. Darwin's

Figure 2-29

Charles Darwin.

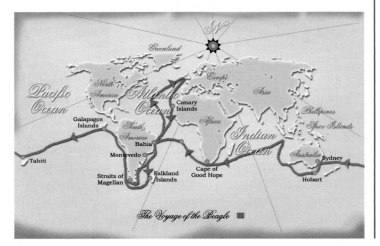

Figure 2-30

Map of voyage of the *Beagle*.

Departing from Plymouth, England, with a crew of 73, the Beagle ultimately circled the Earth studying the southern oceans. In its travels, it voyaged along both coasts of South America.

Figure 2-31

Sir Charles Wyville Thomson.

The H.M.S. *Challenger*, a warship converted and equipped for general oceanographic research sailed under the direction of Scottish professor Charles Wyville Thompson and British naturalist Sir John Murray.

Figure 2-32

Sir John Murray.

British naturalist who sailed on the four-year research mission of the H.M.S. *Challenger*.

explanation that coral reefs form by growing upward as the seafloor recedes is the explanation accepted by most scientists today.

Having returned to England in 1836, Darwin spent the next 20 years examining the data he had gathered. Based on this, Darwin ultimately proposed what we today call the theories of natural selection and the evolution of species. He proposed that new species result from natural selection favoring or disfavoring specific characteristics over long periods. He published his arguments, observations, and conclusions in 1859 in the now famous, *The Origin of Species.* The theory of evolution is discussed in more detail in Chapter 3.

From his study of finches (a small species of bird) on the Galapagos Islands, Darwin noticed that they were almost the same as finches that lived in South America. However, close observation by Darwin revealed that apparently the same birds from two locations had different beaks. The beak differences allowed them to eat different kinds of foods. Darwin noted that this meant the two birds were physically adapted to the different forms of foods found at their locations, and that the locations were separated by distance and water. Darwin later used this observation as evidence to support his work on natural selection.

The *Challenger* Expedition

What expedition is commonly recognized as the first devoted entirely to marine science?

What accomplishments and discoveries did the H.M.S. Challenger *make?*

While several expeditions devoted to exploration and science had sailed by 1872, the *Challenger* expedition, which launched that year, is recognized as the first devoted entirely to marine science. The H.M.S. *Challenger*, a warship converted and equipped for general oceanographic research, sailed under the direction of Scottish professor Sir Charles Wyville Thomson and British naturalist Sir John Murray. Its four-year mission was to gather detailed and consistent observations of various oceanographic phenomena across as much ocean as possible.

Using methodologies similar to those used by present-day oceanographers, the *Challenger* expedition gathered physical, geological, chemical, and biological oceanography data at regular intervals across the sea. From 1872 to 1876, the expedition sailed almost 130,000 kilometers (80,778 miles) in the Atlantic, Pacific, and Antarctic oceans. They documented temperature, currents, water chemistry, marine organisms, and marine bottom sediments at 362 stations scattered over 36 million square kilometers (14 million square miles) of ocean floor.

The *Challenger* expedition's accomplishments were so extensive that the expedition report took more than 23 years to complete. It was 29,500 pages long, in 50 volumes, and included the first systematic plot of currents and temperatures, a map of bottom deposits (still considered accurate), outlines of the main contours of the ocean basins, and the discovery of the Mid-Atlantic Ridge and the Marianas Trench. The expedition recorded a depth of 8,200 meters (26,900 feet) in the trench, the deepest known spot in the ocean at the time. Among its accomplishments and discoveries, the expedition:

• took the first soundings deeper than 4,000 meters (13,123 feet).

• captured biological samples in midwater and along the bottom with a towed device.

• discovered marine organisms in the deepest parts of the ocean. (Until that time, most oceanographers thought life would not be possible on the deep-sea bottom.)

• sampled and illustrated plankton in various habitats and depths not previously studied.

• cataloged and identified 715 new *genera* (the biological classification between family and species) and 4,717 new species. The next closest achievement in terms of species discovery is probably the late 1970s discovery of deep-sea hydrothermal vent (deep ocean hot

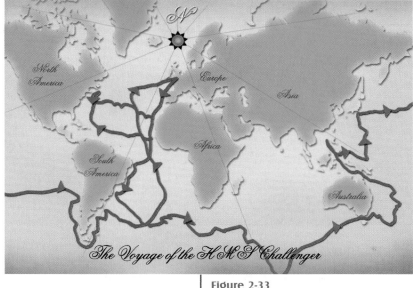

Figure 2-33

Voyage path of the Challenger expedition.

H.M.S. Challenger Volumes, NOAA

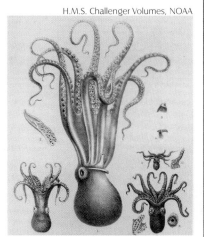

Figure 2-34a

Illustration plate of octopi from Challenger expedition report.

These plates are representative of the report's exquisite artistic detail.

H.M.S. Challenger Volumes, NOAA

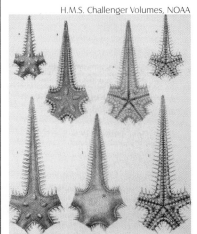

Figure 2-34b

Illustration plate of starfish from Challenger expedition report.

mineral springs) communities. These communities are covered in later chapters.

The *Challenger* expedition contributions were so vast that much of its work remains the foundation for several oceanographic disciplines. Even the illustrations it produced of plankton remain in use today. Recognizing the ship and expedition's role in furthering science, NASA named the second space shuttle *Challenger* in its honor.

ARE YOU LEARNING?

1. **The voyages of James Cook differ from those of sea explorers before him because**

   A. they were major military victories.

   B. he discovered Antarctica.

   C. they had science and exploration as their only goals.

   D. all of the above

2. **The invention of the _____ in 1735 was a major breakthrough for open ocean navigation.**

   A. chronometer

   B. sextant

   C. GPS

   D. compass

3. **The Cook expedition's geographical discoveries include (choose all that apply)**

   A. Antarctica.

   B. many south Pacific islands.

   C. Hawaii.

   D. that New Zealand isn't part of Antarctica.

4. **The United States Exploring Expedition proved the existence of**

   A. the United States.

   B. Australia.

   C. the Arctic.

   D. none of the above

5. **We remember Matthew Maury as the father of physical oceanography because of his studies of currents and other physical aspects of the sea.**

   A. true

   B. false

6. **Darwin's hypothesis explains that coral reefs form through a process of coral growth as**

   A. the seafloor subsides.

   B. it evolves.

   C. the seafloor rises.

   D. none of the above

7. **As a result of his observations during the H.M.S. *Beagle* expedition, Darwin proposed (choose all that apply)**

   A. the theory of natural selection.

   B. the theory of evolution of species.

   C. the theory of coral extinction.

   D. the theory of Galapagos current formation.

8. **The expedition commonly recognized as the first devoted entirely to marine science is**

   A. the first Cook expedition.

   B. the United States Exploring Expedition.

   C. the *Beagle* expedition.

   D. the *Challenger* expedition.

9. **Discoveries and accomplishments by the H.M.S. *Challenger* include (choose all that apply)**

   A. the first soundings deeper than 4,000 meters (13,123 feet).

   B. discovering marine organisms in the deep ocean.

   C. sampling and illustrating plankton.

   D. documenting physical, chemical, geological, and biological information in 362 stations in 36 million square kilometers (14 million square miles) of ocean.

Twentieth-Century Marine Science

The Oceanography Explosion

What change led to the growth and expansion of modern oceanography in the 20th century?

Oceanography in the modern sense really came into existence at the beginning of the 20th century. Ocean research accelerated from the early 1900s, so that by the 1950s, you could find marine science expeditions and projects in progress somewhere in the world at any given time. Especially in the latter half of the century, these became so numerous and frequent that it's impossible to list them all here. You'll touch on many of them as you go through *Life on an Ocean Planet*.

Although many factors contributed to the growth and expansion of marine sciences in the 20th century, most of these stem from a single, significant social change: the Industrial Revolution. The Industrial Revolution started around 1760 in England and it took time to spread to other countries. Although it was in progress, its most noticeable effects didn't appear until the last half of the 19th century, continuing into the 20th. During this period, science and technology began accelerating the pace of advancements that continues today.

One major change was the rise of steam engines and iron ships. As late as the 1870s, most vessels were wooden ships powered by sail. By 1900, these had largely given way to iron and steel steamships. This improved trade and oceanography because sea travel was no longer at the mercy of wind and current.

As the Industrial Revolution progressed, so did technologies that applied to ocean research. During the early 1900s, scientists and engineers began designing and building elaborate research equipment. Building on the work of the *Challenger* in the previous century, oceanographers became truly interdisciplinary in collecting data. Research increasingly included physical, geographic, chemical, and biological oceanography.

Although the dream of an underwater ship had been in the human mind for centuries, it was the invention of the diesel engine, electric motor, and the lead-acid battery that made the first useful submarines possible in the 20th century. This technology advanced rapidly. At the turn of the century there were few submarines and they were largely experimental. However, less than 15 years later, submarine warfare played an important strategic

Central Library, NOAA

Figure 2-35a

Rise of steam engines and iron ships.

T. Askew, OAR, NURP, NOAA/
Harbor Branch Oceanographic Institute

Figure 2-35b

Submersible.

OAR, National Undersea
Research Program, NOAA/U.S. Navy

Figure 2-35c

Nuclear submarine.
Although many factors contributed to the growth and expansion of marine sciences in the 20th century, most of these stem from a single, significant social change: the Industrial Revolution. The rise of steam engines, iron ships, submersibles, nuclear submarines, and modern sampling equipment helped further marine science in the 20th century.

role in World War I. The sinking of the *Lusitania* in May 1915 by a German submarine was a key motivator that propelled the US into the conflict.

As the pace of the Industrial Revolution picked up, the role and view of science took on new weight. More funding became available for research as Western societies became wealthier through industry. Applied research (science to create a specific product or solve a specific problem) grew. This research creates and meets demand for everything from new medicines to consumer goods. Pure research (no goal except science) also increased as government and industry recognized that pure research generates tangible economic benefits: it's worth the investment even when you don't know what the return will be.

Global conflict and the Cold War also drove science and technology in the 20th century. Countries invested in research to develop their military capabilities, but also to further their international stature. The 1960s and 1970s sea and space explorations by the United States and the Soviet Union were good examples. Both countries made great advances while competing for political prestige.

These trends continue today. The need for ocean resources has never been higher. The need for solutions to environmental problems concerning the sea has never been greater. Yet, as discussed in Chapter 1, most of the ocean remains unexplored. This suggests need and opportunity. It may well be that the oceanography explosion of the 20th century will pale in comparison to that of the 21st century.

Three Expeditions

For what accomplishment do we recognize the German Meteor *expedition?*

What was the significance of the Atlantis?

What noted discovery did the second H.M.S. Challenger *expedition make?*

Although there were hundreds of marine science expeditions and research vessels in the 20th century, three in particular stand out. These were the German *Meteor* expedition, the *Atlantis*, and the second H.M.S. *Challenger*.

The German *Meteor* expedition began in 1925 and is often cited as one of the first modern oceanographic research cruises. The *Meteor* crossed the Atlantic 14 times in just over two years, gathering physical, chemical, geological, and biological data. This included about 9,400 temperature, salinity, and chemical samples at varying depths. Analysis of these data established patterns for ocean water circulation, nutrient dispersal, and plankton growth.

The primary accomplishment for which we recognize this expedition, however, is mapping the Atlantic seafloor with echo-sounding technology to determine water depth by using sound waves. *Meteor* scientists used approximately 67,400 echo soundings to create the first detailed ocean floor map. They discovered a rugged, varied terrain instead of the long, flat bottom they expected. As discussed in Chapter 11, this was an important step in developing theories that explain the creation and destruction of the seafloor over time.

In 1931, the United States launched the *Atlantis*. The significance of the *Atlantis* is that it was the first ship specifically designed and built for ocean studies. Among many accomplishments, Atlantis built on the work of the *Meteor*. During its voyages, it confirmed the existence of the Mid-Atlantic Ridge and mapped it. As with *Challenger*, NASA named one of the space shuttles in honor of *Atlantis*.

In October 1951, a new H.M.S. *Challenger II* began a two-year voyage to measure the depths of the Atlantic, Pacific, and Indian Oceans. This effort used echo-sounding technology to further the mapping efforts started by Meteor and continued by Atlantis and other vessels. The most noted discovery made by the second *Challenger* was finding the deepest known part of the ocean. Located in the Marianas Trench (discovered by the first *Challenger*), they named it Challenger Deep in honor of the first *Challenger* expedition. At approximately 11,000 meters (36,000 feet), this is still the deepest known place in the world.

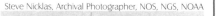
Steve Nicklas, Archival Photographer, NOS, NGS, NOAA

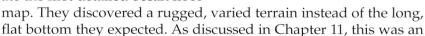

Figure 2-36

The *Meteor* research vessel.

The German *Meteor* expedition began in 1925 and is often cited as one of the first modern oceanographic research cruises. The *Meteor* crossed the Atlantic 14 times in just over two years, gathering physical, chemical, geological, and biological data. This included about 9,400 temperature, salinity, and chemical samples at varying depths. Analysis of these data established patterns for ocean water circulation, nutrient dispersal, and plankton growth.

Steve Nicklas, Archival Photographer, NOS, NGS, NOAA

Figure 2-37

***Meteor* research.**

Crew member handling plankton net for biological sampling.

Ship Collection, NOAA

Figure 2-38

Second *Challenger* expedition—1950s.

H.M.S. *Challenger II* seen here entering Suva, Fiji, in 1951, during her world voyage. The most noted discovery made by the second *Challenger* was finding the deepest known part of the ocean. Located in the Marianas Trench (discovered by the first *Challenger*), they named it the Challenger Deep in honor of the first *Challenger* expedition. At approximately 11,000 meters (36,000 feet), this is still the deepest known place in the world.

Figure 2-39a

US Navy submersible Asherah –1964.

Figure 2-39b

NOAA submersible Nekton.
This submersible is still in use by many research scientists.

Figure 2-39c

Access to the sea.
During the 1960s, modern submersibles and self-contained diving changed the study of the ocean. Instead of grabbing samples blindly, scientists could pick the specific samples they needed. They could take delicate samples without damaging them and living organisms without killing them. For many types of research, they no longer needed samples. Instead, they could directly observe the geology, organism behaviors, and other phenomena in their natural setting.

Submersibles and Self-Contained Diving

How have submersibles and self-contained diving changed the study of the ocean?

What are the three types of submersible that have been used for underwater research?

What are the advantages and disadvantages of submersibles and scuba?

Imagine trying to study terrestrial Earth from a balloon high in the atmosphere above the clouds. To learn what you can, you lower hooks and traps, grab things, and haul them up to study. Your views and impressions would come from whatever you happened to snag. Chances are, your ideas of what a forest or desert is like would be way off.

Until the 20th century, scientists studied the ocean floor essentially the same way. One of the biggest changes in the 1900s was opening the underwater world. Although diving and submersible technologies date back more than a thousand years, until the 20th century these were neither practical nor widespread. (See Underwater Exploration Historical Timeline at the end of this chapter for more about the history of undersea exploration.)

Modern submersibles and self-contained diving changed the study of the ocean. Instead of grabbing samples blindly, scientists could pick the specific samples they needed. They could take delicate samples without damaging them and living organisms without killing them. For many types of research, they no longer needed samples. Instead, they could directly observe the geology, organism behaviors, and other phenomena in their natural setting.

Submersibles. Over the years, scientists have used three basic types of submersible for research. The first was the *bathysphere* (from the Greek *bathys* meaning *deep*). Pioneered in the 1930s by William Beebe and Otis Barton, this submersible was essentially a steel ball with a window. It had an oxygen recirculating system so scientists could breathe and an umbilical that provided communications and power.

The bathysphere operated only vertically, raised and lowered by a cable from a ship. Since it dangled, it tossed up and down with the mother ship in rough seas, making it uncomfortable for the occupants. Although the bathysphere is no longer used because of its limitations, it allowed the first deep-water visits by scientists. In 1932, Beebe and Barton reached 661 meters (2,170 feet) in the bathysphere in the waters off of Bermuda.

The bathysphere gave way to the *bathyscaphe* (from the Greek *scaphe* meaning *boat*). In essence, a bathyscaphe is a more sophisticated bathysphere, with the sphere attached to a large float instead of a cable and ship. Bathyscaphes operate much like blimp airships. The float contains a liquid that's buoyant in water, such as gasoline, and heavy ballast. By releasing some of the ballast or the buoyant liquid, the bathyscaphe rises or descends. Small electric motors drive propellers to give it horizontal mobility. However, the horizontal motion is limited.

Bathyscaphes aren't widely used today because they're difficult to operate and limited in what they can accomplish. Their big advantage, however, is that they are the deepest diving submersibles ever made. Probably the best known bathyscaphe is the *Trieste*, which is the only submersible to have descended to the bottom of Challenger Deep.

The state of the art today is the deep-diving submersible. These are typically two- and three-person vessels that dive in moderate to deep depths, though not as deep as a bathyscaphe. However, they don't require the bulky float tanks of a bathyscaphe and they have excellent horizontal maneuverability. They're far less fragile than bathyscaphes, making them easier to launch and use in rough

Figure 2-40

A steel ball with a window.

Pioneered in the 1930s by William Beebe and Otis Barton, the bathysphere was essentially a steel ball with a window. It had an oxygen recirculating system so scientists could breathe and an umbilical that provided communications and power. The bathysphere operated only vertically, raised and lowered by a cable from a ship. Since it dangled, it tossed up and down with the mother ship in rough seas, making it uncomfortable for the occupants. Although the bathysphere is no longer used because of its limitations, it allowed the first deep-water visits by scientists.

Courtesy of Space and Naval Warfare Systems Center of San Diego

Figure 2-41a

Bathyscaphe *Trieste*.

A bathyscaphe is a more sophisticated bathysphere, with the sphere attached to a large float instead of a cable and ship. Bathyscaphes operate much like blimp air ships. The float contains a liquid that's buoyant in water, such as gasoline, and heavy ballast. By releasing some of the ballast or the buoyant liquid, the bathyscaphe rises or descends. Small electric motors drive propellers to give it horizontal mobility. However, the horizontal motion is limited.

OAR, NURP, NOAA

Figure 2-41b

Trieste II.

THE *TRIESTE*

In 1960, under the leadership of Dr. Andreas B. Rechnitzer, a graduate of the Scripps Institution of Oceanography, US Navy Lieutenant Don Walsh and Jacques Piccard carried out what is probably the most dangerous and daring deep dive to date. Piccard and Walsh descended in the bathyscaphe *Trieste* to the bottom of Challenger Deep in the Mariana Trench.

This is the one and only time man has visited very near the deepest known part of the ocean. The *Trieste* attained a record depth of 10,914 meters (35,807 feet).

While landing on the bottom, Piccard claims to have seen a fish, a shrimp, and a jellyfish through a tiny view port; proving that life exists even at this depth. Although this was more than four decades ago, Challenger Deep has not been visited since.

Figure 2-42

Trieste.

Project leader Dr. Andy Rechnitzer organized the journey of Jacques Piccard and Don Walsh aboard the bathyscaphe *Trieste* to Challenger Deep.

Figure 2-43

Augustus Siebe hard-hat diving equipment.

In the middle of the 19th century the first practical dive equipment emerged. This equipment was hard-hat (helmet) diving that supplied air from the surface through a hose. An Englishman named Augustus Siebe introduced the first commercially successful line of hard-hat equipment in 1840. Seibe's equipment looked very much like the basic helmet equipment still used today.

seas. These characteristics make them suitable for far more varied types of research. Some deep-diving submersibles have robotic arms that allow the pilot or scientist to grasp samples or perform experiments outside the sub.

Self-contained diving. For centuries, humans experimented with ways to stay underwater for longer than a single breath. Different types of bells to support divers and crude diving apparatus date back as far as 375 A.D.

Despite these efforts, however, it wasn't until the middle of the 19th century that the first practical dive equipment emerged. This equipment was *hard-hat* (helmet) *diving* that supplied air from the surface through a hose. An Englishman named Augustus Siebe introduced the first commercially successful line of hard-hat equipment in 1840. Seibe's equipment looked very much like the basic helmet equipment still used today.

Although Seibe's surface-supplied hard-hat diving became the basis for underwater labor (construction, salvage, ship maintenance), this type of dive equipment was limited for underwater research. It was heavy and required a support team and vessel. Although science was conducted in hard-hats to a limited degree, it was not ideal. What was needed for scientific diving was a lightweight, self-contained system—what we call scuba today.

Another Englishman, Henry Fleuss, introduced the first workable scuba in 1878. His unit recirculated pure oxygen. Caustic soda absorbed the carbon dioxide the diver exhaled, and the diver replaced consumed oxygen as needed from a pressurized cylinder. Although this system worked, it soon proved limited for scientific

IMPORTANT WORKING RESEARCH SUBMERSIBLES CURRENTLY USED BY SCIENTISTS

The *Alvin,* operated by Woods Hole Oceanographic Institution and owned by the US Navy, is considered the world's most productive submersible. Refurbished and upgraded numerous times over its career, *Alvin* is scheduled to be replaced by a new vehicle. In its present configuration, *Alvin* is capable of diving to 4,500 meters (14,764 feet). During its career, *Alvin* made over 150 dives per year. Dr. Robert Ballard used the *Alvin* for the first visits to the wreck of the *Titanic.*

©Woods Hole Oceanographic Institution (All)

Figure 2-44a

Alvin, 1956.

Figure 2-44b

Alvin, 1977.

Figure 2-44c

Alvin, 2001.

Courtesy of Harbor Branch Oceanographic

Figure 2-45

Johnson SeaLink.

Ifremer

Figure 2-46

Nautile.

Harbor Branch Oceanographic Institution in Fort Pierce, Florida, owns and operates two Johnson SeaLink submersibles. These manned submersibles are devoted primarily to marine research with an operating depth of 914 meters (3,000 feet). The forward 12.7 centimeter (5 inch) thick acrylic sphere accommodates the pilot and observer, allowing panoramic visibility. A second chamber in the rear can hold two additional scientists. Both SeaLinks have manipulator arms, suction devices, plankton samplers, active sonar, and broadcast quality video cameras for use by scientists in their research.

Nautile is a three-person French submersible operated by the Institute of Research and Exploitation of the Sea. This submersible also has a small, tethered ROV (remotely operated vehicle) named *Robin* that can inspect and image areas inaccessible to *Nautile* itself.

MIR-1 and *MIR-2* are three-person submersibles operated by the Shirshov Institute of Oceanology in Russia. Both submersibles have an operating depth of 6,000 meters (20,000 feet). The MIR submersibles have the second deepest rating of all deep submersibles. (The Japanese submersible *Shinkai* leads with a depth rating of 6,500 meters [21,325 feet]). The *MIR* submersibles were featured in the movie *Titanic.*

Operated by the Hawaii Undersea Research Laboratory at the University of Hawaii, *Pisces IV* and *V* both have a maximum operating depth of 2,000 meters (6,280 feet). International Hydrodynamics of Vancouver, Canada, built both *Pisces.* Scientists commonly use them for studies along the undersea volcano Lo'ihi, on submerged banks in the main Hawaiian Islands and on the banks and sea mounts in the Northwestern Hawaiian Islands.

Constructed by Nuytco Research in Canada, *DeepWorker* is a new breed of small, lightweight submersible. *DeepWorker* allows one or two explorers at a time to descend to 610 meters (2,000 feet). Due to its small size, *DeepWorker* easily travels by trailer and launches much like a regular submersible from a small support ship. With this capability, *DeepWorker* makes research by submersible more accessible by lowering logistical costs.

OAR, NURP, NOAA

Figure 2-47

MIR-1.

OAR, NURP, NOAA

Figure 2-48

Pisces V.

Courtesy of Phil Nuytten

Figure 2-49

DeepWorker **with its inventor Phil Nuytten.**

Figure 2-50

Fleuss rebreather, 1878.

Henry Fleuss introduced the first workable scuba in 1878. His unit recirculated pure oxygen. Caustic soda absorbed the carbon dioxide the diver exhaled, and the diver replaced consumed oxygen as needed from a pressurized cylinder. Although this system worked, it soon proved limited for scientific diving.

Courtesy of Historical Diving Society, USA

Courtesy of Historical Diving Society, USA

diving. The most substantial obstacle was that divers can't use pure oxygen deeper than approximately 10 meters (33 feet). This is because oxygen becomes toxic beyond a certain pressure. Despite this limitation, Fleuss' design went on to become the basis for early combat-diver equipment and submarine escape apparatus.

Frenchman Jacques Cousteau introduced the first practical scuba in 1943. Working with a compressed-gas engineer named Emile Gagnan, Cousteau developed a scuba system that delivered compressed air (not oxygen) to a diver. By automatically adjusting the breathing air pressure and providing air only when the diver inhaled, this new, self-contained equipment was easy to operate, reliable, and provided a reasonable underwater duration. It was relatively lightweight, simple, and required minimal support compared to hard-hat diving. This opened a new door to the underwater world. Divers swam freely like fish instead of walking awkwardly on the bottom. Within 20 years, scuba was in use by the military, science, and as a fast-growing recreation.

Today scientists use both submersibles and scuba for underwater research. Both tools have their place, with respective advantages and disadvantages. The primary advantages of submersibles compared to scuba are depth and duration. Submersibles can descend far deeper than scuba divers. Most of the ocean's volume is within reach of research submersibles, but out of reach of scuba. Submersibles can also continue for much longer than scuba dives. Four hours is a long scuba dive. Sometimes, a submersible needs longer than that just to reach the working depth!

The primary disadvantages of submersibles compared to scuba are cost, logistics, and accessibility. Submersible diving is

Figure 2-51a & b

Open-circuit scuba equipment.

Frenchman Jacques Cousteau introduced the first practical, open-circuit (meaning the diver's exhalation is breathed into the water as bubbles) scuba in 1943. This is basically the same equipment used today by recreational and scientific divers.

La Spirotechnique-Courtesy of Historical Diving Society, USA

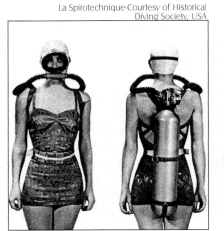

Figure 2-51a

Original Cousteau Aqualung.

Al Hornsby

Figure 2-51b

Modern Scuba Equipment.

substantially more expensive than scuba diving, so research from a submersible doesn't take place on a whim. Submersibles generally need support vessels (vessels used to tend a submersible from the surface) and a team for launching, retrieval, and maintenance. Finally, due to their size, there are places submersibles can't go, either because they're too big or too difficult to transport.

The primary advantages of scuba over submersibles are cost, simplicity, portability, size, and dexterity. Although the leading-edge scuba technologies can be very expensive, standard compressed air scuba is so inexpensive that it is a common recreation. Compressed-air scuba is simple, making training and maintenance relatively easy compared to a submersible.

Scuba is very portable. With scuba, scientists can dive from a wide range of vessels that would be unable to support a submersible. Similarly, they can go places with scuba that would be nearly impossible for submersible diving—like an underwater archaeological site in the middle of a dense rainforest. Because scuba equipment is compact, it gives specially trained divers access to small areas underwater where submersibles cannot go.

Although many research submersibles have robot claws and other devices scientists can use, none of these replace the human hand for many tasks and procedures. When a scientist needs to delicately lift a fragile archaeological find, it is much easier to do this by hand than with a robotic arm.

While scuba is very versatile, its drawbacks compared to submersibles are depth and duration. Working with conventional compressed-air equipment, scuba is limited to no more than about 40 or 50 meters (130 to 165 feet). Even with the leading-edge, highly sophisticated scuba using synthetic breathing gases, presently the practical working depth limit is no more than about 150 meters (492 feet). While there is a tremendous amount of research possible in this range, the vast majority of the ocean lies deeper.

Scientists cannot stay underwater on scuba as long as in a submersible. Because they're exposed to the water and pressure, divers have temperature, *decompression* (the release of gas absorbed by a diver while surfacing), and endurance considerations. Even with the most effective dive suits, in all but very warm water, a diver will eventually become cold. While breathing gas under pressure, a diver's body absorbs excess gas. The diver must surface in stages (*decompression stops*) that allow this gas to dissipate, or *decompression sickness* (the condition caused by inert nitrogen or other gas coming out of solution and forming bubbles within the body, sometimes called "the bends") may result. The longer a diver remains under water, the longer it takes to surface.

OAR, NURP, NOAA

Figure 2-52a

Preparing a submersible for work underwater.

OAR, NURP, NOAA

Figure 2-52b

Submersible and diver at depth.

Scientist at work outside of submersible.

INTERNET PORTAL

SCiLINKS. NSTA

Topic: Submarines and Undersea Technology
Go To: www.scilinks.org
Code: LOP2030

SUBMERSIBLES VERSUS SCUBA

	ADVANTAGES	DISADVANTAGES
Submersibles	Greater depth	High cost
	Duration	Large size
		Logistical complexity
Scuba	Simplicity	Limited depth
	Portability	Short duration
	Low cost	

Figure 2-53

Submersibles versus scuba.

Even without temperature or decompression considerations, fatigue is a factor. Water is denser than air, so every move underwater requires more effort than out of water. Breathing through scuba requires more energy than breathing at the surface. These may be small effort differences, but over time they add up, tiring the diver.

Therefore, even within scuba depths, if a scientist needs to stay down for hours to observe something, a submersible may be the best tool. Temperature, decompression, and fatigue may make diving impractical even in relatively shallow water.

Because of these relative advantages and disadvantages of submersibles and scuba, the hardsuit first emerged in the 1913. Essentially wearable submersibles, hardsuits try to strike a balance between the advantages and disadvantages of each. Hardsuits protect the diver from pressure and temperature and are far smaller and more mobile than conventional submersibles. They allow the diver to go deeper than with scuba, though not as deep as a conventional submersible. The drawbacks are cost and logistical complexity, which, while less than a conventional submersible, are greater than for scuba diving. The state of the art in hardsuits is the Nuytco Newt Suit.

OAR, NURP, NOAA

Figure 2-54a

1935 hardsuit.

Pictured is an early one-atmosphere, armored hardsuit.

Figure 2-54b

Modern one-atmosphere hardsuit.

Because of the relative advantages and disadvantages of submersibles and scuba, the hardsuit first emerged in 1913. Essentially wearable submersibles, hardsuits try to strike a balance between the advantages and disadvantages of each. Hardsuits protect the diver from pressure and temperature and are far smaller and more mobile than conventional submersibles. They allow the diver to go deeper than with scuba, though not as deep as a conventional submersible.

Courtesy of Phil Nuytten

ROVs, AUVs, Drifters, Satellites, and Electronic Navigation

What is the difference between an ROV and an AUV?

How do drifters send their information to marine scientists and what type of information do they collect?

What are three types of sea surface observations that satellites can make to benefit oceanographers?

How have Loran-C and GPS benefited seafaring and oceanography?

Among the many scientific and technological advances in the last half of the 20th century, electronics and space travel provided at least four other important contributions to oceanography. These were the inventions of electronic navigation, remotely operated vehicles (ROV), autonomous underwater vehicles (AUV), drifters, and ocean observation satellites.

The *ROV* is another technology that has expanded underwater research. An ROV is essentially a small, unmanned submarine with propellers, a video camera, and an umbilical to the surface. The operator at the surface controls the ROV (remotely) by watching the video image. ROVs range in size from a lawnmower to larger than a car, depending on their purpose. Some are basically underwater "eyes," while others have robotic arms, claws, and other tools.

ROVs became common beginning in the late 1970s and early 1980s as a bridge between the capabilities of submersibles and scuba. ROVs can match the depth and duration of submersibles, yet they're far more compact and inexpensive. This makes them usable from vessels and in locations that cannot support submersibles. They're not affected by pressure or temperature, so they're suitable for long observations without the expense of a submersible.

ROVs are also very useful for both submersible and scuba operations. For example, researchers may send an ROV down ahead of a submersible or diver to check the location. This confirms the location before committing to launching a manned submersible or exposing a diver. Sometimes ROVs work with submersibles and divers, providing light and other support. There are specialized ROVs operated from submersibles. In exploring the *Titanic* from *Alvin*, Dr. Robert Ballard used such an ROV to view inside the wreck. There was no way this could have been done by a submersible.

Another important tool used by oceanographers is the *AUV*. AUVs are untethered robotic devices controlled and piloted by

Figure 2-55

Cave diver being towed by ROV.

Figure 2-56

ROV *Phantom*.

Figure 2-57

ROV *Ventana*.

The ROV *Ventana*, built for the Monterey Bay Aquarium Research Institute (MBARI), is a highly sophisticated vehicle with data collection sensors, a high definition camera, and animal collection devices.

an onboard computer. AUVs are launched from the surface and maneuver in three dimensions. Some are propelled through the water by self-contained power systems, while others have a glider style that uses the temperature differential between the warm surface water and the cooler water below to create motion. Under most conditions, either system permits AUVs to follow precisely preprogrammed underwater paths. Sensors within an AUV sample the ocean along these paths.

Bluefin Robotics Corp.

Figure 2-58

Glider Style AUV.

The glider style AUV collects salinity, temperature, conductivity, depth, and other information. It uses the GPS system to provide location information and to navigate. About 1.5 meters (4.9 feet) long, it glides no faster than 30 meters (98.4 feet) per minute for durations of up to five years. The AUV can travel for this duration by using the temperature difference between the warm surface water and the cooler water below for propulsion. It does this by alternately floating up toward the warmer water and then descending toward the cooler water. Its wings cause the AUV to move forward like a glider as it ascends and descends.

Unlike ROVs, which get power and instructions through their tethers, AUVs must carry their "brains" and "brawn" with them. The first AUVs in the 1960s were either too large, inefficient, expensive, or a combination of all three because of this. In the 1980s, AUV technology matured, but computer and battery technologies still had not advanced to make AUVs widely useful.

This has changed over the last 20 years as the required computing and battery power have begun to arrive, though AUVs are still thought to be in their infancy. Today, AUVs are under development or are operational all over the world. The next generation of glider style AUVs may be important oceanographic tools capable of collecting all types of critical data.

More common than AUVs for collecting data are *drifters*. Drifters are instrument packages placed in the open ocean to measure primarily temperature, salinity, pressure, and currents. They drift, collecting information and transmitting it with their exact position to a satellite system. Today, there are thousands of surface and subsurface drifters. Many of these drifters are vertically mobile and can descend to an intermediate depth such as 1,000

Figure 2-59

Drifter buoy.

More common than AUVs for collecting data are drifters. Drifters are instrument packages placed in the open ocean to measure primarily temperature, salinity, pressure, and currents. They drift, collecting information and transmitting it with their exact position to a satellite system.

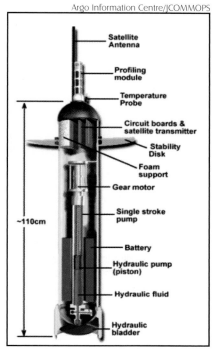

Figure 2-60

Electronics of a drifter buoy.

This is a diagram of a typical surface drifter buoy. Thousands of surface only drifters repeat their positions every few hours along with other critical oceanographic data. Both surface and subsurface drifters may operate autonomously for one to two years.

meters (3,280 feet). They drift at that depth for approximately 10 days collecting data, then descend further—as deep as 2,000 meters (6,560 feet). After collecting data for the programmed duration, the drifter slowly rises to the surface. It measures temperature and salinity as it rises. At the surface, the instrument transmits the data it collected to satellites. Thousands of surface only drifters repeat their positions every few hours along with other critical oceanographic data. Both surface and subsurface drifters may operate autonomously for one to two years.

In recent years, satellites have become an essential tool for oceanographers. Few oceanographers go to sea today without collecting satellite data. Today, satellites and drifters gather almost all data collected for areas far away from shore.

Satellites now give oceanographers global observations of the ocean, providing long-term, continuous measurements of many variables. These include sea-surface height, shape, and color, plus temperature, currents, winds, and tides over the entire planet. With this capability, they can detect algae blooms and river plumes, monitor pollution, and assist oceanographers in understanding the influence and effect of the ocean on the global climate system. They are an effective way for oceanographers to look at very large areas of the world in a very short period.

To obtain information about the ocean, scientists often go to sea and take measurements from ships or retrieve data from anchored or free-drifting buoys. However, satellite observations

INTERNET PORTAL

SCiLINKS. NSTA

Topic: Space Oceanography
Go To: www.scilinks.org
Code: LOP2035

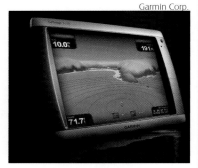

Figure 2-61

Modern GPS.

GPS navigation is very important for oceanography because with it, scientists know where they are when they take samples or conduct a search. They can reliably return to a specific study location, and can provide this information to other scientists who need to conduct research in the same location.

Figure 2-62

How GPS works.

A process called triangulation accurately determines a position on Earth using GPS (Global Positioning System). Satellite 1 transmits a signal that contains data on its location in space and the exact time the signal left the satellite. The GPS receiver collects and interprets this signal and is able to determine the distance from the satellite to the receiver. This creates an "area" of possible locations of the receiver. The process is repeated for satellites 2 and 3. Where the three signals meet at the GPS is its location expressed in specific coordinates. A fourth satellite signal is required to obtain the elevation of the GPS unit.

have mostly replaced measurements taken directly at sea. They provide oceanographers with data for studying global circulation and climate events such as El Niño. The information gathered from satellites is also used to build and validate computer models that numerically simulate the weather of the ocean and help to predict future events.

Another important breakthrough has been the invention of electronic navigation. After the invention of the chronometer, ships could determine their location accurately enough for navigational purposes. Plus or minus 2 kilometers (about a mile) is not much of an issue when you're in the open ocean. However, it is a huge difference if you're studying an archaeological shipwreck or a small, local, underwater community. Also, cloudy weather and haze sometimes meant that ships couldn't take a navigational fix for days at a time.

The first electronic navigation emerged in the late 1960s. Initially called LORAN (for LOng RAnge Navigation), it became known as *Loran-C*. Loran-C was based on radio signal transmitters along the coast. A ship that received signals from two or more transmitters could determine its position by plotting the signal directions and determining where they intersected. As electronics became more sophisticated, Loran-C receivers handled the plotting with software and simply displayed the latitude and longitude of the vessel.

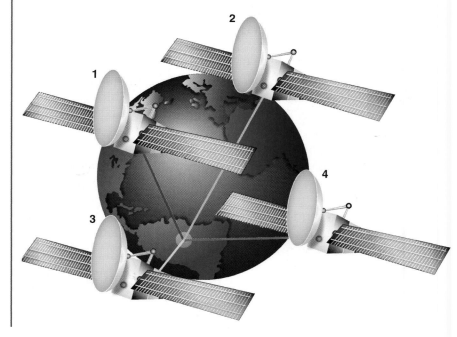

Loran-C changed navigation. Instead of accuracy within a kilometer (about half a mile), ships knew their location within a few meters. Loran-C also provided navigation information 24 hours a day in any weather. (This was the primary reason for its invention—to make shipping safer.)

Loran-C was a big step for navigation, but it had its limits. For these reasons, during the 1990s, *GPS* (*global positioning system*) largely replaced Loran-C. Developed and implemented by the US military, GPS is similar in concept to Loran-C, but provides signals from a series of orbiting satellites instead of transmitters on shore. GPS overcame the limits of Loran-C because it works everywhere (on land and at sea) and because it is much more accurate. With modern GPS receivers, accuracy to within 1 or 2 meters (3 to 6 feet) is possible, however accuracy to within 100 meters (328 feet) is more typical for commercial units. The most sophisticated GPS units display the ship's location, speed, and direction on top of a sea chart.

Electronic navigation has been very important for oceanography because with it, scientists know exactly where they are when they take samples or conduct a search. They can reliably return to a specific study location, and can provide this information to other scientists who need to conduct research in the same location.

The SeaWiFS Project and GeoEye, Scientific Visualization Studio/
Goddard Space Flight Center, NASA

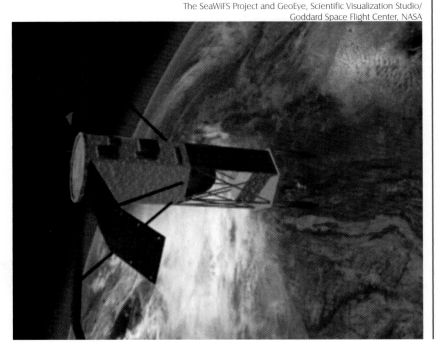

Figure 2-63

The *SeaStar* satellite with the SeaWiFS instrument.

The Sea-viewing Wide Field-of-view Sensor (or SeaWiFS) instrument is part of the *SeaStar* satellite. The *SeaStar* is an excellent example of a satellite used by oceanographers. It provides information on subtle changes in ocean color, which indicate the presence and concentration of microscopic marine plants called phytoplankton. The greener the water, the more phytoplankton is present.

1. **The change that led to the growth and expansion of marine sciences in the 20th century was primarily**

    A. the invention of scuba.

    B. World War II.

    C. the Industrial Revolution.

    D. the voyage of the *Challenger.*

2. **The accomplishment for which we recognize the German *Meteor* expedition was**

    A. the discovery of meteors in German waters.

    B. mapping the Atlantic seafloor.

    C. locating Challenger Deep.

    D. all of the above

3. **The *Atlantis* is significant because it was**

    A. the first ship constructed specifically for marine science.

    B. used to locate the Mariana Trench.

    C. the ship that discovered the lost continent of Atlantis.

    D. none of the above

4. **The noted discovery made by the second H.M.S. *Challenger* was**

    A. Challenger Deep.

    B. the deepest known point in the ocean.

    C. both A and B

    D. none of the above

5. **Submersibles and self-contained diving changed the study of the ocean by allowing scientists to (choose all that apply)**

    A. to pick specific samples.

    B. take living samples without killing them.

    C. directly observe organism behaviors.

    D. directly observe phenomena in their natural setting.

6. **Types of submersible that have been used for underwater research include (choose all that apply)**

    A. bathyspheres.

    B. bathyscaphes.

    C. deep-diving submersibles.

    D. none of these have been used for research

7. **One of the advantages of submersibles is _____, whereas one of the advantages of self-contained diving is _____.**

    A. cost, depth

    B. duration, depth

    C. depth, logistics

    D. cost, size

8. **A(n) _____ is remotely operated by a human being, whereas a(n) _____ has its own program and power.**

    A. Loran-C/GPS

    B. AUV/ROV

    C. ROV/AUV

    D. HIC/AUV

9. **Drifters are actually anchored to the seafloor. They gather information in place, which is downloaded periodically by scientists who tend them from a ship.**

    A. true

    B. false

10. **Surface observations that satellites can make to benefit oceanographers include (choose all that apply)**

    A. sea-surface height.

    B. color.

    C. temperature.

    D. shape.

11. **GPS has benefited seafaring and oceanography by**

    A. bridging the gap between submersibles and scuba.

    B. making it possible to see under water.

    C. increasing underwater duration.

    D. making navigation significantly more accurate.

Underwater Exploration Historical Timeline

360 B.C. Aristotle writes his *Problemata*. In it he refers to divers using equipment but does not clearly describe the equipment. He also describes a diving bell used by Alexander the Great.

Courtesy of Historical Diving Society, USA

Figure 2-64

This medieval French illustration shows Alexander the Great in an underwater vessel.

375 A.D. In ancient Rome, Flavius Vegetius Renatus was generally considered the leading authority on all military matters. Around 375 A.D. he produced a treatise on warfare titled *Epitome Institutionum Rei Militaris*. It was reprinted several times over the ensuing centuries, sometimes with added material, and is more commonly referred to as *Vegetius De Re Militari*. In 1511, an edition was printed in Germany, and it contained three images of diving apparatus, although the text does not mention diving. These images of men underwater are uncredited and untitled, and they undergo various alterations in later editions of the book. This is possibly the first printed design of a diver in equipment. It is doubtful that a diver could survive this apparatus for much longer than he could hold his breath. However, this early image does establish an interest in underwater activity.

Courtesy of Historical Diving Society, USA

Figure 2-65

1511, image from Vegetius De Re Militari.

1500s Leonardo da Vinci drafts first known scuba designs. His design combines air supply and buoyancy control in a single system and foreshadows later dive suits. There is no evidence that Da Vinci ever built his device.

Courtesy of Historical Diving Society

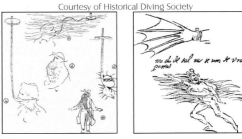

Figure 2-66

1500s, Leonardo da Vinci sketch of hand and foot fins and "snorkelers."

1551 Nicholas Tartaglia (actual name Niccolo Fontana) proposes a diving system that incorporated a large glass dome inside a wooden frame. The unit looked much like an hourglass with the bottom sphere removed. The diver stood inside the frame with his head inside the glass dome. A heavy weight attached to the frame base made the bell descend upright as the diver uncoiled a rope from a winch.

Underwater Exploration Historical Timeline

1660 In England, Robert Boyle studies the physical properties of compressed gas (air). His gas laws provide the foundations used in underwater exploration to determine changes in gas volume due to increases or decreases in pressure.

1665 Sturmius refers to a diving bell in his *Collegium Experimentale* of 1676. An illustration of it appears two years later in the French *Journal des Scavans* of 1678. The design of this bell has been credited to both Sturmius and Professor George Sinclair of Glasgow, Scotland.

1679-80 Italian physician Giovanni Borelli imagines a scuba design that recycles and replenishes air. His drawings show a giant bag using chemical components to regenerate exhaled air. Borelli also draws claw-like feet on his diver. Some recognize Borelli as the first to envision the free-swimming scuba diver as opposed to someone who walks on the bottom.

1690 Edmond Halley (noted as the astronomer who discovered the comet that now bears his name) is credited with staying submerged for 90 minutes in a diving bell he designed. Halley also produced the first contour chart showing the magnetic declination in the North Atlantic. This was necessary for accurate navigation.

Courtesy of Historical Diving Society, USA

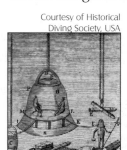

Figure 2-67

1690, Halley's Diving Bell.

1715 John Lethbridge develops his "Diving Engine" in Devon, England. A support crew lowered the diver to the seabed from a support vessel. Divers used the Lethbridge device with some success for salvage.

Courtesy of Historical Diving Society, USA

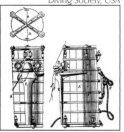

Courtesy of Historical Diving Society, USA

Figure 2-68a

Lethbridge "diving engine."

Figure 2-68b

1715, Salvage operations with Lethbridge "diving engine."

1797 Karl Heinrich Klingert develops a self-contained open diving helmet that features a double-hose system for inhaling and exhaling pressurized air. His dive suit attached to a large air tank equipped with an adjustable piston to control buoyancy.

Courtesy of Historical Diving Society, USA

Figure 2-69

1797, Klingert's diving apparatus.

1823-40 English brothers Charles Anthony Deane and John Deane develop the open diving helmet based on Charles' patented 1823 design for a smoke helmet for use by firefighters. They successfully use their open helmet to recover items from the seabed and wrecks around the British coast.

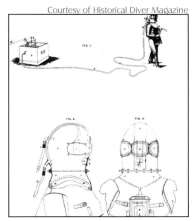

Figure 2-70

1823, The brothers' Deane equipment.

1825 William James makes the first practical proposal for a self-contained diving apparatus. His apparatus consists of a copper or leather helmet with a glass-plate window attached to a waterproof tunic sealed at the waist and wrists by elastic bandages. An iron reservoir in the form of a cylindrical belt around the diver's body supplies air to the helmet. Weights suspended below the reservoir maintain the diver's equilibrium. The device works by having the diver inhale through his nose and exhale through a mouthpiece connected by a short tube to an escape valve in the crown of the helmet. James suggested that with the reservoir charged to 30 bar (441 psi) the diver would have enough air for about one hour.

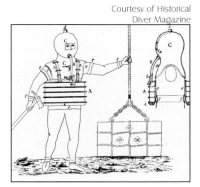

Figure 2-71

1825, James' self-contained apparatus.

1828 Frenchman Lemaire D'Augerville makes a device for cargo salvage from the wreck of the *Bellona*. The apparatus uses a large cylindrical reservoir of compressed air on the diver's back. A hand-operated valve allows the diver to control air flow from the reservoir to a flexible bag mounted on his chest from which he inhales through a tube. A copper facemask with eyepieces and an exhalation valve enclose the eyes and nose. The apparatus incorporates buoyancy control and ballast weights that can be released in an emergency.

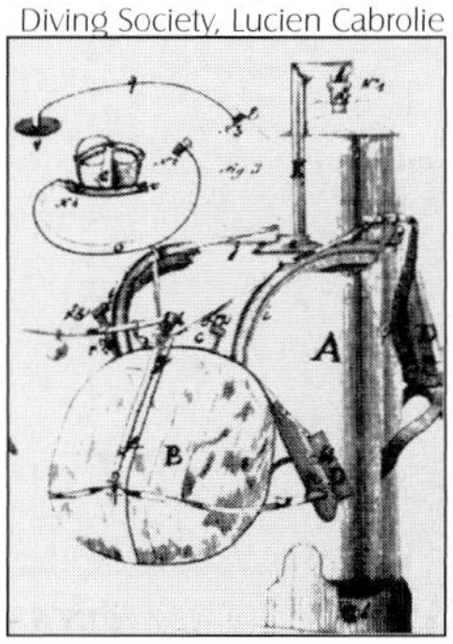

Figure 2-72

1828, D'Augerville device.

Underwater Exploration Historical Timeline

1831-32 American Charles Condert, a Brooklyn machinist, invents a self-contained diving dress similar to William James'. It consists of a two-piece suit of trousers and tunic that attaches to a helmet. The whole outfit is made of rubber-coated cloth. An air reservoir supplies the helmet, with surplus air escaping from a simple small hole in the crown of the helmet. Condert makes a number of well-recorded descents into the East River at Brooklyn. Unfortunately, he dies when the air tube to the helmet breaks.

1834 Leonard Norcross invents and patents the first US (and possibly the world's first) closed diving helmet apparatus. The Norcross equipment appears in the January 1835 edition of the *Journal of the Franklin Institute*. The report notes that the diver's helmet is attached to the suit by a "water tight juncture." It further notes that the "whole dress is inflated" when the diver closes the tube in the top of the helmet that is "for the escape of air ventilated by respiration." It is not certain if the Norcross apparatus ever went into mass production or if any of his equipment exists today.

Figure 2-73
1834 Norcross device.

1840s Augustus Siebe produces a closed (water-tight) diving apparatus that will become the world standard for more than 100 years. In 1840, his apparatus comes to the attention of Colonel Charles Pasley, who heads up efforts to remove the wreck of the *Royal George* at Spithead in England. Pasley praises the Siebe design. This important endorsement places Augustus Siebe at the forefront of equipment manufacturing. Using Siebe equipment, the trade of the diver started to flourish around the world. Augustus Siebe's company later becomes Siebe Gorman, a company that still exists today.

Figure 2-74
1865, Rouquayrol and Denayrouze diving equipment.

1860-65 Benoit Rouquayrol and Auguste Denayrouze introduce self-contained scuba equipment that is essentially the same as that introduced by Jacques Cousteau in the next century. It consists of a compressed-air reservoir and a single-stage demand valve with a rubber hose leading to a mouthpiece. This was the inspiration for Jules Verne's divers in his classic novel *Twenty Thousand Leagues Under the Sea.* The apparatus doesn't gain widespread application largely because compressed-gas cylinders of the period cannot withstand sufficient pressure to provide an adequate air supply.

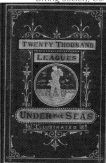

Figure 2-75

1870, *Twenty Thousand Leagues Under the Seas.*

1864   Confederate submarine *Hunley* sinks the Federal warship U.S.S. *Housatonic* during the US Civil War. This is the first successful sinking of an enemy ship by submarine during war. The *Hunley*, human-powered by volunteer sailors, never returns from the attack, however.

1878   Englishman Henry Fleuss invents the first practical self-contained diving apparatus, which recirculates and replaces oxygen consumed by the diver. It uses caustic soda to absorb carbon dioxide. Fleuss uses his device with considerable success, attracting a great deal of media interest. He develops it into a number of more practical forms for diving, and for mine-rescue purposes.

1880   French physiologist Paul Bert completes his pioneering work on breathing under hyperbaric (high-pressure) conditions. He recognizes that *caisson disease* (decompression sickness) is identical to problems experienced by divers and suggests that it is caused by the release of dissolved nitrogen from the bloodstream. He also shows that oxygen can become toxic when breathed under pressure.

Using the recently developed Fleuss scuba system, Alexander Lambert completes a legendary dive in the Severn Tunnel in Britain. He gains much fame and media attention for this accomplishment.

1893-98   Using a giant wet-plate camera, Louis Boutan takes the first underwater photographs.

1905   The US Navy publishes its first diving manual under the title *Handbook for Seaman Gunners.* It comprises only seven brief chapters and includes illustrations of some of the equipment of diverse origin being used at that time.

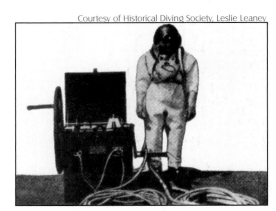

Figure 2-76

1905, US Navy Pump and diving dress.

Underwater Exploration Historical Timeline

1907 Professor John Scott Haldane develops the first decompression model and tables for the prevention of decompression sickness in divers. It revolutionizes diver safety and remains the foundational work behind decompression theory to the present, even in modern dive computers.

1911 The Draeger Company of Germany develops an oxygen rebreather that comes into wide use by the military. The company continues to develop rebreathers today.

Draeger-Courtesy of Historical Diving Society, USA

Figure 2-77
1911, Draeger oxygen scuba.

1912 Famed ocean liner R.M.S. *Titanic* sinks on her maiden voyage.

1913 Neufeldt and Kuhnke produce a one-atmosphere suit in Germany. The technology is essentially a submarine worn by a diver.

1915 Ocean liner R.M.S. *Lusitania* is sunk by German submarine. The event propels the US into World War I.

1917 Germany's Draeger produces a true scuba system that combines tanks containing a mixture of compressed air and oxygen (oxygen-enriched air) with rebreathing technology. It is sold for use at depths as deep as 40 meters (130 feet).

1918 Tokyo engineer Watanabe Riichi files an American patent for a respirator in 1918, which is granted in 1920. It is marketed under the name of Ohgushi's Peerless Respirator and uses air cylinders carried vertically on the diver's back. The diver inhales through the nose and exhales through the mouth. This unit went into service with the Japanese Navy.

1919 C. J. Cooke pioneers the use of helium and oxygen (*heliox*) as a breathing gas by divers. The mixture enables divers to avoid nitrogen narcosis while diluting oxygen to nontoxic concentrations. It allows commercial divers to extend their useful working depth well beyond previous limits.

1924 French Naval officer Yves Le Prieur develops the Fernez–Le Prieur self-contained diving apparatus that uses a high-pressure air cylinder carried on

Le Prieur—Courtesy of Historical Diving Society, USA

Figure 2-78
1924, Le Prieur device in use.

the diver's back. An adjustable regulator feeds air to the mouthpiece in a continuous stream.

1925 William Beebe, Director of the Department of Tropical Research of the New York Zoological Society, makes scientific dives in the Galapagos Islands. Over the following years he conducts several scientific expeditions that use basic open-helmet diving.

1925-27 The German *Meteor* expedition systematically surveys the South Atlantic with echo-sounding equipment and other oceanographic instruments, proving beyond a doubt the continuity of the Mid-Atlantic Ridge.

1930-34 William Beebe and Otis Barton begin deep-sea exploration with their bathysphere off Bermuda. They reach 925 meters (3,036 feet) in 1934

1930s Expatriate American writer Guy Gilpatric on the French Riviera waterproofs a pair of pilot's goggles by lining the edges with glazier's putty. Gilpatric pioneers the fledgling sport of goggle fishing.

1933 Frenchman Louis de Corlieu receives the first European patent for swimming "propellers," that is, swim fins. He files for an American patent the same year.

1935 Frenchman Rene Commeinhes invents a self-contained apparatus designed for use in fighting fires. The apparatus consists of two high-pressure air cylinders with a demand regulator mounted between them with a lever-operated valve attached to a rubber bag. Later, Rene's son Georges adapts the device for diving purposes and tests it to a depth of 53 meters (174 feet) off Marseilles on June 30, 1943 (about the same time Jacques Cousteau tests the first versions of his underwater breathing apparatus called the *Aqualung*). Georges dies in a military battle in 1944.

1937 Americans Jack Browne, Max Gene Nohl, and others form Diving Supply and Salvage Company (DESCO) in Milwaukee, Wisconsin. DESCO is still in business today. Using mixed gas and tables calculated by Edgar End, MD, Nohl completes a successful dive to a world record depth of 128 meters (420 feet).

Courtesy of Historical Diving Society, USA

Figure 2-79

1937, Max Gene Nohl prepares to descend on his record-breaking dive to 128 meters (420 feet).

1938 Austrian Hans Hass leads a group on a free-diving expedition from Vienna to the Yugoslavian coast. Hass, who will become renowned as an underwater photographer, takes his first underwater photographs.

Hans Hass—Courtesy of Historical Diver Magazine

Figure 2-80

1938, Hans Hass with his first underwater camera.

1939   Hans Hass publishes *Hunting Underwater with Harpoon and Camera* in Germany. The book is the first to cover underwater photography by free diving.

US Navy submarine *Squalus* sinks in 73 meters (240 feet) of water. Thirty-three of the crew escape with the use of the McCann submarine rescue bell. This is the first assisted escape from a sunken submarine. The salvage of the *Squalus* is the first substantial use of helium and oxygen by the US Navy in deep-diving operations.

Hans Hass leads a free-diving expedition to the Caribbean. He becomes the first to film under the sea at Bonaire and Curacao.

1940   Owen Churchill begins manufacturing fins in the United States. These become the first widely accepted fins used by divers. Later, in the 1950s, Churchill fins appear advertised in *Skin Diver Magazine* by Voit.

1941-42   Professor J. B. S. Haldane (son of John Scott Haldane) and Kenneth Donald conduct test dives to determine the limits of oxygen exposure. Their results remain the primary data set used in establishing oxygen exposure limits.

1941-43   Victor Berge develops a mask and breathing system used by the US Navy at Pearl Harbor and throughout World War II.

1942   Jacques-Yves Cousteau meets Emile Gagnan, an industrial gas-control systems engineer with L'Air Liquide et Cie. They combine their talents and begin work on the concept of the Aqualung, a compressed-air scuba device. Cousteau produces his first underwater film, *Par Dix-Huit Metres de Fond* (At a Depth of Eighteen Meters).

Courtesy of Historical Diving Society, La Spirotechnique

Figure 2-81

Early Cousteau regulator.

1943   Cousteau and two close friends, Philippe Tailliez and Frederic Dumas, test the new Cousteau/Gagnan scuba system in the Mediterranean Sea. The device proves to be safe, reliable, and remarkably easy to use. In July and August, they make hundreds of dives, thoroughly testing the system and seeking to determine its limits. In October, Dumas demonstrates the amazing reliability of the Aqualung with a dive to 64 meters (210 feet).

1945-46 La Spirotechnique of France begins commercial production of the Cousteau scuba regulator, the aqualung.

1950s Famed Swiss balloonist Augusta Piccard turns his attention to the deep sea. With son Jacques, he pioneers a new type of vessel called the bathyscaphe. On February 15, 1954, off the coast of French West Africa, a bathyscaphe exceeds Barton's 1948 diving record, reaching a depth of 4,050 meters (13,287 feet).

1950 Conrad Limbaugh forms a scientific diving team at Scripps Institution of Oceanography, California. This is one of the first organized programs to teach marine scientists how to use scuba for aquatic research.

Cousteau obtains his famed research vessel *Calypso*.

Courtesy of Scripps Institution of Oceanography

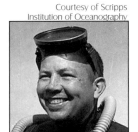

Figure 2-82

1950, Conrad Limbaugh.

1951 Rachel Carson publishes *The Sea Around Us*. Her scholarly yet poetic book about the ocean wins several prestigious awards and tops bestseller lists for almost seven months. The book brings a new awareness of the need to protect the world's ocean.

Cousteau takes *Calypso* on his first expedition to the Red Sea.

Courtesy of Historical Diving Society and Club Alpin Sous-Marin Magazine

Figure 2-83

Announcement of Cousteau's Red Sea Expedition.

1952 *National Geographic* magazine runs a 42-page article on Cousteau titled, "Fish Men Explore a New World Undersea."

1953 The *Silent World* by Cousteau and Frédéric Dumas is published in America. It is Cousteau's first English language book.

Dr. Eugenie Clark publishes *Lady with a Spear*. It becomes a Book-of-the-Month-Club selection and is translated into eight languages and braille.

Dr. Hugh Bradner from Scripps Institution of Oceanography develops and introduces the neoprene wetsuit. A full wetsuit cost $75.

Courtesy of Scripps Institution of Oceanography

Figure 2-84

1953, Bradner wetsuit design.

Underwater Exploration Historical Timeline

1954 The first nuclear-powered submarine, Nautilus, goes to sea. E. R. Cross publishes Underwater Safety, America's first modern-day dive manual. American diver Zale Parry sets a women's record dive to 64 meters (209 feet) at Catalina Island, California.

1957 Captain George Bond of the US Navy begins Project Genesis, which is the first series of experiments in saturation diving. Testing continues through 1963. Even before it concludes, Project Genesis becomes the basis for saturation diving worldwide.

1958 Ivan Tors produces the TV series *Sea Hunt* starring Lloyd Bridges. This series significantly raises public awareness about the underwater world and scuba diving. It becomes one of the longest-running programs in syndication.

Jacques Cousteau and Jean De Woutersk introduce the Calypso underwater 35mm camera (requires no special case to go under water). This is the first generation of the Nikon Nikonos camera series.

1960 *Trieste* descends to 10,914 meters (35,807 feet) in Challenger Deep. Both men aboard observe fish and invertebrates at the bottom, proving that life exists at all depths of the ocean.

US nuclear submarine *Triton* completes the submerged circumnavigation of the world in 84 days.

George Bass excavates a 3,500-year-old shipwreck in the waters of Turkey in the Mediterrean. Although other underwater archaeology efforts predate this, it is considered the first professional underwater archaeological effort. It proves that archaeologists can employ established methodologies underwater.

1962 Robert Stenuit completes a 24-hour experimental dive using heliox to 60 meters (200 feet). This is part of Edwin Link's Man-in-the-Sea program, which begin's Link's career as a leading marine scientist, visionary, and submersible engineer.

Cousteau conducts Conshelf I with a habitat housing two divers under water at 10 meters (35 feet) for seven days. In the next decade, several countries and institutions build and experiment with undersea habitats.

On December 3, Hannes Keller leads a world record dive using synthetic breathing gases to 304 meters (1,000 feet) off Catalina Island, California.

1963 Cousteau conducts Conshelf II in the Red Sea. This is the first multi-dwelling underwater habitat project. One of the most ambitious habitat projects to date, five divers lived at 10 meters (30 feet) for 30 days in a large habitat, and two aquanauts lived at 27.4 meters (90 feet) for a week in a smaller habitat close by. A third habitat was an underwater hanger for servicing a two-man submarine.

The first operational multibeam sounding system is installed on a USNS ship. This system observes a number of soundings to the left and right of a ship's head as well as vertically. This allows the development of a relatively accurate map of the sea floor as the ship proceeds on a survey line.

1964   Litton Systems builds the submersible *Alvin* and on May 26 delivers it to Woods Hole, where it was commissioned on June 5.

Supervised by Captain George Bond, the US Navy launches the SEALAB program, a series of projects involving divers living in habitats on the seafloor.

US Navy

Figure 2-85

1964, US Navy SEALAB I.

1965   The US Navy conducts SEALAB II. From 62 meters (205 feet) below the sea, former Mercury astronaut Scott Carpenter converses with astronaut Gordon Cooper in orbit above the Earth.

US Navy

Figure 2-86

1965, US Navy SEALAB II prior to launch.

1966   Underwater habitat *Hydrolab* begins operation off the coast of Florida. Periodically relocated and refitted, *Hydrolab* remains in use until 1984. It is one of the most-used research habitats of all time.

1968   JIM one-atmosphere dive suit introduced. This is the first widely produced and successful one-atmosphere suit.

1969   The US Navy launches SEALAB III at 186 meters (610 feet). An unfortunate fatality causes the navy to abandon the program.

The US Navy, NASA and the US Department of the Interior conduct the *Tektite I* program. Four aquanauts live underwater at 13.1 meters (43 feet) for 60 days.

Underwater Exploration Historical Timeline

1970 Dr. Sylvia Earle leads a team of women aquanauts for a two-week stay at 13 meters (42 feet) in the *Tektite* habitat. Earle goes on to become a major spokesperson for the care and protection of the marine environment.

OAR, NURP, NOAA

Figure 2-87

1970, Dr. Sylvia Earle and the women aquanauts of *Tektite*.

The National Oceanic and Atmospheric Administration is established. This U.S. Government agency is responsible for all U.S weather and climate forecasting, monitoring and archiving of ocean and atmospheric data, management of marine fisheries and mammals, mapping and charting all U.S. waters.

1972 The US Congress passes the Marine Protection, Research, and Sanctuaries Act.

1973 George Bass founds the Institute of Nautical Archeology at Texas A & M University. This is the oldest organization studying undersea sites.

1977 Jack Corliss leads a project using the Alvin submersible to look for the hydrothermal vents thought to be near the Galapagos Islands. Corliss, Jerry van Andel, and pilot Jack Donnelly were the crew of the *Alvin* that previously discovered the vents and the unexpected community of living around them (giant tubeworms, clams, crabs, shrimp and new species of bacteria). Corliss later proposes that the earliest life on Earth began in vents.

1981 Volunteer divers make a record 685 meter (2,250 foot) dive in a Duke Medical Center chamber. Three men live in the chamber complex for 43 days, breathing a mixture of nitrogen, oxygen, and helium. They beat their own previous record set in 1980.

1982 Major El Niño event leads to the installation of a Pacific equatorial oceanographic buoy array by NOAA's Pacific Marine Environmental Laboratory. Observations from this array have since predicted the onset of El Niño/La Niña events which has been a major step in understanding the coupling of the ocean/atmosphere system.

1983 The first commercially available dive computer, the Orca Edge, is introduced. In the next decade, dive computers will become common among recreational and scientific divers.

1984 Canadian diver and engineer Phil Nuytten introduces the Newtsuit one-atmosphere dive suit. This is the next generation one-atmosphere suit following in the footsteps of JIM and others, providing more mobility than previous designs.

Courtesy of Phil Nuytten

Figure 2-88

1984, Newtsuit.

1985-86 US-French team headed by Woods Hole researcher Robert Ballard finds the wreck of the *Titanic*. The wreck is explored with the submersible *Alvin*, ROVs, and other remote-operated instruments.

1986 The Marine Resource Development Foundation converts retired scientific underwater habitat *La Chalupa* into world's first underwater hotel, the *Jules Undersea Lodge*. Located in Key Largo, it remains operational.

1987 National Oceanic and Atmospheric Administration (NOAA) underwater habitat, *Aquarius,* begins scientific diving operations in the waters off St. Croix.

The United States Deep Cave Diving Team under the leadership of Dr. William Stone carries out the Wakulla Project. Exploring the cave in Wakulla Springs, Florida, the team executes dives as deep as 100 meters (330 feet) and 1,000 meters (3,300 feet) from the entrance. This is the first widespread use of helium-based diving gases with conventional scuba. It becomes the birth of technical diving, a discipline adopted in the 1990s by research divers to extend their performance, depths, and times.

1987-93 Ocean engineer Thomas Thompson and the Columbus-America Discovery Group locate, study, document, and salvage the gold-laden wreck of the *Central America*. Lying in 2,438 meters (8,000 feet) of water, this is the first major archaeological/salvage excavation carried out entirely by ROVs and other remote-operated technology. Thompson and his team invent, design, and build much of this technology for the task.

1990 Continuing the trend started by *Sea Hunt*, the number of people becoming recreational divers exceeds half a million annually in the US.

1991 Commercial diver and scientist Michael L. Gernhardt completes his PhD dissertation on a decompression model that accounts for the behavior of bubbles, not just dissolved gases. This is a major step in improving decompression models and becomes the basis for several bubble decompression models over the next two decades. Applying his research to the decompression stresses in human spaceflight, Dr. Gernhardt joins NASA and becomes a Mission Specialist astronaut who works on the International Space Station construction.

Underwater Exploration Historical Timeline

1992 Underwater habitat *Aquarius* relocates to Key Largo, Florida. It is currently the only operational scientific underwater habitat working in the open ocean in the world.

Nikon introduces the Nikonos RS, the first single-lens reflex underwater camera (no special case required). It remains in production less than five years.

Dr. Robert Ballard explores the World War II wrecks in the waters of Guadalcanal. He documents the remains of several US and Japanese warships lost during the heavy fighting in the south Pacific in 1942.

1992 Rutgers University installs the first undersea observatory off the New Jersey coast. It's now the "Mid-Atlantic Bight Center" of NOAA's Undersea Research Program.

1993 Dr. Robert Ballard explores the wreck of the *Lusitania* with submersibles and ROVs.

1995 Underwater search team funded by author Clive Cussler locates the wreck of the missing Confederate submarine, *Hunley*.

Declassification of Geosat satellite radar altimetry data leads to worldwide mapping of seafloor from space by Walter Smith and Dave Sandwell with observed data enhancing accuracy over images of the ocean basin drawn by Heezen and Tharpe in earlier years.

2000 Physiologists and others involved with the dynamics of human performance underwater meet to examine reverse profiles (making a shallow dive followed by a deeper dive). Data examination and comparison with theoretical decompression models lead to changes in how different types of diving should treat these profiles.

Wreck of the Confederate submarine *Hunley* raised and recovered for preservation, restoration, and archaeological study. The effort leads to the invention of new techniques for raising large submerged archaeological discoveries.

Friends of the Hunley/www.hunley.org

Figure 2-89

2000, *Hunley* in recovery sling.

2001 NASA begins using the *Aquarius* habitat to study human spaceflight dynamics. During NEEMO (NASA Extreme Environment Mission Operations) missions, astronauts live underwater for five to 14 days, replicating many of the conditions of living in space. Astronaut Michael Gernhardt, pioneer of the bubble decompression model, is among the astronaut crew of NEEMO I. Subsequent

NEEMO projects use live webcast technology, allowing students to see and talk to the astronauts while they dive.

NOAA/NURC

Figure 2-90

2001, NEEMO I astronauts in *Aquarius* habitat.

2002   NASA conducts NEEMO II, III and IV with NURC (National Underwater Research Center) in Aquarius.

2003   Research begins to suggest that the supply of large fish in the seas has dimished by 90% since 1950.

NASA conducts NEEMO V and NEEMO VI with NURC (National Underwater Research Center) in Aquarius.

2004   The Argo profiling float project deploys 1,000 floats (drifters). The project, an international effort to collect high quality temperature and salinity profiles down to 2,000 meters (6,562 feet) from around the world, provides an unprecedented look at the ocean interior.

NEEMO VII takes place.

2006   United States' President George W. Bush signs a proclamation creating the Northwestern Hawaiian Islands Marine National Monument. Called the Papahānaumokuākea Marine National Monument, the monument is the single largest United States conservation area and one of the largest in the world. Encompassing 362,073 square kilometers (139,797 square miles) the monument is larger than all the US national parks combined.

NEEMO IX, X and XI conducted by NASA/NURC

2007   Scientists from the J. Craig Venter Institute apply whole environment shotgun sequencing techniques originally developed for sequencing the human genome to the marine environment. As part of the Sorcerer II Global Ocean Sampling Expedition (a two year circumnavigation cruise), researchers discovered millions of new genes, nearly doubling the number of proteins known in the marine environment. These discoveries provide the bases for uncounted new avenues of marine research ranging from classifying organisms to developing new drugs.

NEEMO XII and XIII conducted by NASA/NURC.

New Terms You Learned

- **aqualung** brand name for the first practical scuba introduced by Jacques Cousteau (p. 2-55)

- **bathyscaphe** extremely deep diving vessels that operate much like a blimp airship, descending and rising without connection to the surface and with limited ability for horizontal movement; *Trieste* is an example (p. 2-37)

- **bathysphere** extremely deep diving underwater vessel, connected to a support ship by a cable, only capable of vertical movement (p. 2-36)

- **caisson disease** name for decompression sickness, name originated when the condition developed in workers emerging from pressurized caissons used for building bridge foundations (p. 2-53)

- **cartographer** person who practices cartography – map making (p. 2-24)

- **chronometer** sea going clock or watch used to determine longitude – time piece introduced in 1735 that would run accurately even in rough seas (p. 2-23)

- **circumnavigation** the act of going completely around something (p. 2-22)

- **decompression** the release of pressure; in diving, the term refers to the process of the body releasing gas absorbed during the dive when surfacing (p. 2-41)

- **decompression sickness** the conditions caused by inert nitrogen or other gas coming out of solution and forming bubbles with in the body (p. 2-41)

- **decompression stops** stops that divers make to release nitrogen or other gas accumulated at depth so they may safely surface (p. 2-41)

- **equator** 0° parallel latitude running around the Earth at its widest point (p. 2-12)

- **fauna** animal life (p. 2-27)

- **flora** plant life (p. 2-27)

- **genera** biological classification consisting of structurally similar or related species. This classification lies between family and species (p. 2-31)

- **Global Positioning System (GPS)** satellite-based navigation system made up of a network of 24 satellites placed into orbit by the US Department of Defense (p. 2-47)

- **hard-hat diving** diving that supplies air from the surface through a hose to a helmet the diver wears (p. 2-38)

- **heliox** a mix of helium and oxygen as a breathing gas for very deep diving (p. 2-54)

- **Loran-C** electronic navigation system that was based on radio signal transmitters along the coast (p. 2-46)

- **meridians** longitude lines (p. 2-13)

- **outrigger** an elongated float such as a shaped log extended from the side of the boat to prevent capsizing (p. 2-7)

- **parallels** latitude lines (p. 2-12)

- **piloting** navigating by using references on shore (p. 2-9)

- **Remotely Operated Vehicle (ROV)** an unmanned submersible that is remotely controlled (p. 2-43)

- **submersible** typically two and three-person, independently self-propelled vessels that dive in moderate to deep depths (p. 2-14)

Chapter 2 in Review

1. What are three reasons to learn the history of oceanography? Which of these do you think is the most important and why? What other reasons are there to learn the history of oceanography?

2. What are four main stages in the history of oceanography?

3. What were the three primary reasons for early civilization to interact with the ocean? Do you think these reasons exist today? Why or why not?

4. Explain the contributions and significance of Phoenician and Polynesian seafaring. Which, if either, do you feel did the most to advance seafaring? Why?

5. Explain how ancient explorers navigated near shore and in the open ocean. How did this influence the explorations of different cultures?

6. List and explain the discoveries and contributions of the Greeks Pytheas, Eratosthenes, Herodotus, Strabo, and Ptolemy. How would Ptolemy's work influence Christopher Columbus?

7. Explain and diagram the latitude and longitude mapping system. Show the location of the 0° parallel and the 0° meridian.

8. What were the Middle Ages? How did they affect the knowledge of geography and science?

9. What climate change affected Scandinavia in the 9th century? What was the significance of this change on exploration?

10. What navigational tool did the Chinese invent by 1125? What technological innovations did Chinese shipping have by the mid 1400s?

11. What were the primary motivations for ocean explorations in the 15th century? What three explorers established the route around the Cape of Good Hope to India in this period?

12. What was the purpose of Columbus' four expeditions? How did using Ptolemy's estimations of the Earth's size affect his expeditions? Who is credited as the first European recognizing that South America was a new continent?

13. What did Vasco Nuñez de Balboa accomplish? Why was this significant?

14. The first two expeditions all the way around the world were about 55 years apart. Who led the expeditions and for what purposes, respectively, and in what years? What explains the interval between the two expeditions?

15. How did the expeditions of James Cook differ from those of sea explorers before him? What geographical discoveries did he make? What invention was significant in Cook's travels? Why was this device important?

16. Which continent did the United States Exploring Expedition prove exists?

17. Why do we remember Matthew Maury as the father of physical oceanography?

18. What noted naturalist sailed with the H.M.S. *Beagle* expedition? How did this naturalist explain the formation of coral reefs? What theory did this person propose as a result of his observations during the expedition?

19. What distinguishes the H.M.S. *Challenger* Expedition of 1872 from previous oceanic research expeditions? What accomplishments and discoveries did this expedition make?

20. What change led to the growth and expansion of modern oceanography in the 20th century? Give examples of how this change contributed to modern oceanography.

21. Explain the accomplishments and significance of the German *Meteor* expedition, the *Atlantis*, and the second H.M.S. *Challenger* expeditions.

22. What are the three types of submersible that have been used for research? Which one is in use today? Compare the advantages and disadvantages of submersibles and scuba.

23. Explain why the ROV has become an important underwater research tool. What are the differences between an AUV and an ROV? Why are AUVs considered to still be in their infancy?

24. Explain why Loran-C and GPS are important to marine research.

Connecting Chapter Concepts – Science Scenarios

1. The latitude/longitude system, originally invented by the Greeks, allows you to identify specific locations on the Earth's surface. It is based on an imaginary grid over the Earth's face, with all locations identifiable based on where the imaginary lines intersect.

   A. What is the name and degree marking of the latitude line that runs around the Earth at its widest point?

   B. Why are latitude lines called "parallels"?

   C. Where do longitude lines begin and end? Where do you find 0° longitude, and what's it called?

   D. What are the two smaller units of latitude and longitude that subdivide degrees?

2. History generally records the birth of marine science as beginning in the 18th century. Several social and technological changes from 1700 to 1900 contributed to the emergence and evolution of marine science into the discipline we know of today.

   A. What distinct change in sea exploration began by the beginning of the 18th century?

   B. Which expeditions are credited as the first sea explorations largely devoted to methodical scientific oceanography?

   C. What technological introduction was important to the expeditions in B? Why was it so important?

   D. Why is the December 27, 1831 voyage of the H.M.S. *Beagle* significant?

Marine Science and the Real World

1. Is there any topic that does not benefit by studying its history? Explain your answer.

2. Why do you think Polynesian seafarers were sailing in open ocean hundreds of years before Western sailors? Propose a hypothesis as to why Polynesian sailors didn't end up traveling around the world like the Europeans did. How would you test this hypothesis?

3. Imagine you're a 17th century European sea captain. You can determine your latitude in the open sea, but not your longitude. Describe how you might navigate across the Atlantic without getting lost.

4. Do you agree that technology has been a major force in the growth and expansion of marine science? Support your answer. List at least five technological innovations that do not yet exist that would benefit marine science.

5. Imagine you're a biological oceanographer studying and documenting the breeding habits of a clam that lives in a depth range of 40 to 140 meters (130 to 459.3 feet). The clams are found only in the South Pacific about seven days sailing from the closest port. The breeding cycle takes place nightly and lasts four to six hours. Explain what underwater technologies you would use to accomplish this, and why.

References

Argo Profiling Float Project. http://www.argo.ucsd.edu/index.html

Captain Cook Society. 2004. http://www.captaincooksociety.com

Cornell University. Eratosthenes (276-195 B.C.). September 2004. http://astrosun2.astro.cornell.edu/academics/courses//astro201/eratosthenes.htm

David, Daniel. Fall 1999. Lemaire d' Augerville: A Great Forgotten Pioneer of Autonomous Diving. *Historical Diver Magazine (No. 21).*

Davis, Robert H. 1999. *Deep Diving and Submarine Operations: A Manual for Deep Sea Divers and Compressed Air Workers.* Great Britain: Siebe, Gorman and Company.

Duxbury, Alison B., Alyn C. Duxbury and Keith A. Sverdrup. 2002. *Fundamentals of Oceanography.* New York: McGraw-Hill.

Professional Association of Diving Instructors. 1999. *Encyclopedia of Recreational Diving* CD-ROM. Rancho Santa Margarita.

Garmin, Ltd. What is GPS?. 2005. http://www.garmin.com/aboutGPS/

Garrison, Tom. 2002. *Oceanography: An Invitation to Marine Science.* Pacific Grove, CA: Wadsworth/Thomson Learning.

Gross, M. Grant, and Elizabeth Gross. 1996. *Oceanography-A View of the Earth.* New Jersey: Prentice Hall.

Hanauer, Eric. 1994. *Diving Pioneers: An Oral History of Diving in America.* San Diego: Watersport Publishing.

Leaney, Leslie. Spring 1998. Cousteau and Hass: A Time line of their Early Careers. *Historical Diver Magazine (No. 15).*

Leaney, Leslie. Fall 1997. Jacques Yves Cousteau: The Pioneering Years. *Historical Diver Magazine (No. 13).*

Marx, Robert F. 1990. *The History of Underwater Exploration.* New York: Dover Publications.

Natural History Museum, London. The Voyage of H.M.S. Challenger (1872-1876). http://www.challengeroceanic.com/chal.htm

National Maritime Museum. Royal Observatory, Greenwich. John Harrison and the Longitude Problem. http://www.nmm.ac.uk/site/request/setTemplate:singlecontent/contentTypeA/conWebDoc/contentId/355

Papahanaumokuakea Marine National Monument. http://hawaiireef.noaa.gov/

Pinet, Paul R. 2003. *Invitation to Oceanography.* Massachusetts: Jones and Bartlett Publishers.

School of Mathematics and Statistics, University of St. Andrews, Scotland. Eratosthenes of Cyrene. January 1999. http://www-history.mcs.st-andrews.ac.uk/Mathematicians/Eratosthenes.html

South-Pole.com. 2004. Charles Wilkes 1798-1877. http://www.south-pole.com/p0000079.htm

Thurman, Harold V., and Elizabeth A. Burton. 2001. *Introductory Oceanography.* New Jersey: Prentice Hall.

J. Craig Venter Institute. 2007. More than Six Million New Genes, Thousands of New Protein Families and Incredible Degree of Microbial Diversity Discovered from First Phase of Sorcerer II Global Ocean Sampling Expedition. http://www.jvci.org

Viola, Herman, and Carolyn Margolis. 1985. *Magnificent Voyagers-The U.S. Exploring Expedition, 1938-1842.* Washington DC: Smithsonian Institution Press.

UNIT 2 | The Foundatio

Bob Wohlers

Marty Snyderman

Life in the Ocean

Bob Wohlers

Al Hornsby

Photo courtesy of NASA

Theories of the Origins of Life

European Space Agency/Peter Anders, Göttingen University
Galaxy Evolution Group, Germany, NASA

NURP

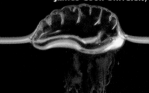

Dr. Jamie Seymour,
James Cook University

We Are Not Alone

A t least that's the hope of many legitimate scientists. Although alien hunting has traditionally been the domain of those obsessed with creatures coming to either save or destroy humanity, legitimate scientists are also looking for life beyond Earth.

The University of Washington's Professor James T. Staley, PhD, has been a leader in the field of astrobiology—the study of life in the universe. This life, as Staley puts it, isn't likely to be the long-limbed humanoid forms depicted in movies, magazines, and comic books. "We recognize that there is a good possibility that life exists in our solar system, but if life does exist it would be microbial, not the higher forms," he states. These potential sites of life are in relatively inhospitable environments, such as those found on Mars. Fortunately for scientists such as Staley, these conditions are somewhat duplicated in some of Earth's most extreme environments, such as undersea vents or within polar sea ice.

It might seem strange to have a microbiologist studying the ocean to find clues about the origin of life in our universe, but Staley isn't your average microbiologist. He's taken a love of science and a fascination with rockets, chemistry, and airplanes from 7th grade through to graduation from the University of Minnesota, Ohio State University, and the University of California, Davis and into some of the most extreme environments on the planet.

But, it wasn't until his graduate work that Staley became fascinated with aquatic microbial ecology. This fascination with microbial biodiversity focused his research on what bacteria reside in the ocean and what exactly they are doing there. Currently, he is looking at bacterial diversity in sea ice and in the Black Sea—both inhospitable environments.

These extreme environments have given him some of his most rewarding experiences. His work often takes him to interesting places and provides opportunity for discovery. It is this reward of discovery so fundamental to science that Staley relishes, "It is the finding of a new truth about the world that gives me a real thrill."

Not only a real thrill but also a chance to make a difference in the search for life. Although microbiology is only one of the many disciplines that make up astrobiology, it is also one of the most important. As the Director of a National Science Foundation graduate traineeship program on astrobiology at the University of Washington, Staley has helped the search for life achieve new levels.

James T. Staley, PhD
Professor, Microbiology Department,
University of Washington

INTERNET PORTAL

SCiLINKS. NSTA

Topic: Astrobiology
Go To: www.scilinks.org
Code: LOP2040

Where did Earth, the solar system, and the stars come from? Where did life come from? When we ask these questions, we're really asking where *we* came from. It's more than idle curiosity. This has been a question asked by humanity since recorded history. It is fundamental to all cultures and philosophies. It's a question that speaks to humanity's place in the universe. Many would suggest that it implies further questions about the purpose of life and whether good and evil are real universal concepts or arbitrary concepts created by humans. Without a doubt, these are important philosophical questions.

Since earliest recorded history, people have looked to the sky for answers about where we came from. The sky has appeared in prehistoric relics and paintings dating back thousands of years. Archaeologists think prehistoric cultures may have been charting the phases of the moon 30,000 years ago. Legends and mythologies based on constellations are a part of many cultures. The Greeks alone identified nearly 50 constellations.

Because of the regular appearance of the constellations, moon, and other celestial bodies at night, early cultures saw the sky as having a consistency and order with a direct bearing on Earth. This is evidenced by *astrology*, which is the study of the supposed influence of the stars and planets on human affairs. It is partly based on what particular constellation appears in the night sky when a person is born. Although its roots are quite ancient, astrology still has a following today. Most people treat it as entertainment, but some take it seriously.

Astrology is not considered a science in the modern sense, yet it's through early astrology that humankind recorded the basic observations on which *astronomy* would build. As astrologers sought meaning in the movements of the stars and planets in the night sky throughout the seasons, they recorded the appearances and cycles that would later help explain the structure of the solar system and Earth's place within it.

Early cultures viewed our existence as the intervention of a creator. A common belief was that Earth is the center of the universe—a notion that persisted in Western culture into the 1600s. Celestial observations were consistent with a belief that Earth was stationary and everything revolved around it.

Many credit the Greek philosopher Aristotle (384-322 B.C.) as the originator of scientific thought. The Greeks began studying nature and the sky objectively. They classified their observations more as natural phenomena than supernatural. Nonetheless, it would take about 2,000 years before the acceptance of the Copernicus model, which put the sun at the center of the solar system. As science evolved as a philosophy, though, scientists continued to look at the sky for answers about where everything began. As we move further into the 21st century, many astronomers and biologists increasingly wonder about the possibilities of life on other planets.

As you'll see, many of the theories behind the origins of the universe still come from the sky—from astronomy, not astrology. How our origin relates to the meaning and purpose of life now generally lies outside the scope of modern science. Scientists base their hypotheses about the origins of the universe on *empirical* findings. That is, modern science only considers objective facts based on what one can see, hear, touch, smell, taste, or detect with scientific instruments. Scientists develop models and hypotheses about the universe and life to help them predict relationships, behaviors, and future events. Understanding the past helps scientists understand what we observe in the present and expect to observe in the future.

The Universe, Solar System, and Earth

Origin of the Universe

What is the Big Bang?

What is a protostar?

How do scientists theorize that the first stars formed?

How do scientists theorize that heavy elements formed?

What is the theorized "life cycle" of a star?

Significant debate suggests several theories, but recent astronomical observations show clearly that the universe came into existence suddenly.

The common scientific theory is that the universe existed as a concentrated single point, containing all known matter and energy. Approximately 13.7 billion years ago, this single point began to expand—an event that has become known as the *Big Bang.* The universe has been expanding ever since.

According to the Big Bang theory, the young universe was very hot. It took about 1 million years for the matter in the universe to cool enough for the first elements to form. Most of the new matter was hydrogen and helium—two very simple elements.

STUDY QUESTIONS

Find the answers as you read.

1. What is the *Big Bang?*

2. What is a *protostar?*

3. How do scientists theorize that the first stars formed?

4. How do scientists theorize that heavy elements formed?

5. What is the theorized "life cycle" of a star?

6. According to theory, how did the solar system form?

7. How do scientists theorize the planets were formed?

8. What is the *nebular theory?*

9. According to theory, how did the Earth form?

10. What is *density stratification?*

11. How do scientists theorize the moon formed?

12. What is the common theory for how the early atmosphere formed?

13. According to theory, how did the ocean form?

14. According to theory, how is the formation of the ocean linked to atmospheric changes and the formation of life?

European Space Agency/Peter Anders, Göttingen University
Galaxy Evolution Group, Germany, NASA

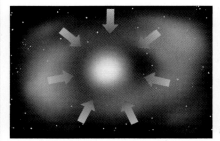

Figure 3-1

Galaxy NGC 1569.

A nearby dwarf galaxy that is producing stars.

Because matter isn't distributed uniformly throughout the universe, gravity, a natural property of matter, began attracting helium and hydrogen atoms. Theory says that matter accumulations became denser as gravity pulled them together. As the density increased, the matter collapsed and compacted under its own weight, causing a warm, dense core called a *protostar* (Greek *prot* meaning *before*). Given enough mass (accumulated matter), protostars continued to contract, becoming denser until the core pressure and density were so high that nuclear reactions began.

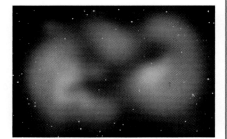

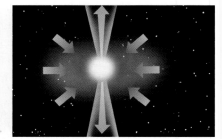

Figure 3-2

Star formation.

Unequal distribution of matter allows gravity to attract helium and hydrogen atoms. A protostar is created when the matter's density causes it to collapse and condense. A star is formed when the core pressure and density are high enough to allow nuclear fusion.

The *nuclear fusion* reaction from protostars creates the stars. Nuclear fusion is a reaction in which light atoms unite to form heavy atoms, releasing tremendous energy in the process. This is the reaction that gives a hydrogen bomb its destructive power.

Nuclear fusion and the theorized "life cycle" of stars provide an explanation of how heavy elements formed in a universe filled predominantly with helium and hydrogen. Once nuclear fusion begins, a star burns for millions to billions of years, consuming the hydrogen within it. Astronomers theorize that heavy elements form as hydrogen atoms fuse. As the hydrogen becomes exhausted, the star's core becomes denser. It eventually collapses under the extreme gravity forces generated by the density. This may cause a large nuclear explosion called a *supernova*. The explosion generates heavier atoms, such as iron, silicon, and aluminum, and blows them out into space. Eventually new stars and planets form.

The fusion core collapses and in the supernova, massive stars account for the origin and distribution of heavy elements throughout the universe.

Origin of the Solar System

According to theory, how did the solar system form?

How do scientists theorize the planets were formed?

What is the nebular theory?

Throughout the universe, stars are clustered in galaxies, each with hundreds of thousands of stars. The sun, Earth, and other planets in the solar system comprise only one of the millions of such systems thought to make up the Milky Way Galaxy.

The current theory among many scientists is that the solar system's current form, with planets orbiting the sun, began with a large cloud of hydrogen and helium, plus heavy elements such as iron, silicon, and aluminum from earlier supernovas. The shock wave of a supernova caused the cloud, called a *nebula,* to condense, which caused it to spin. As the cloud collapsed and became denser, it flattened into a disk due to the rotation, much as figure skaters spin faster when they pull in their arms. At the center a protostar developed, which when dense enough began nuclear fusion and became the sun. Some of the gas continued to revolve around the

Topic: Origin of the Solar System
Go To: www.scilinks.org
Code: LOP2045

Jet Propulsion Laboatory, NASA

Figure 3-3

Spiral galaxy.

This relatively close spiral shows a galaxy similar to the Milky Way that includes Earth.

sun, eventually condensing into masses too small to become stars. This is what formed the planets. This theory that the solar system originated as a nebula is called the *nebular theory*.

Figure 3-4

Nebular theory.

A nebula is given spin and begins to collapse due to a supernova shock wave. As the nebula continues to collapse and spin it flattens out into a disc around the central mass. A protostar forms at the center of the mass and matter continues to rotate into a flattened disc.

Origin of the Earth and Moon

According to theory, how did Earth form?

What is density stratification?

How do scientists theorize the moon formed?

According to the nebular theory, Earth and the other planets formed through *accretion*. Accretion is the process by which small particles clump together because of gravity. As a mass grows due to accretion, the more gravity it has, and the more additional mass it attracts.

Figure 3-5

The present solar system.

This is the end result of the nebular theory and shows the relative placement of the planets. This is not to scale.

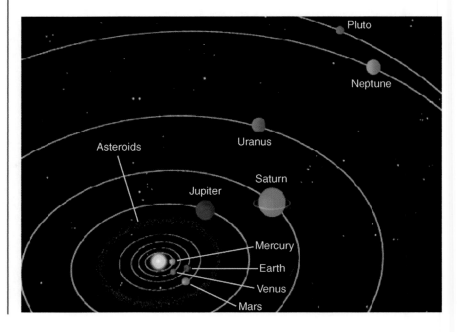

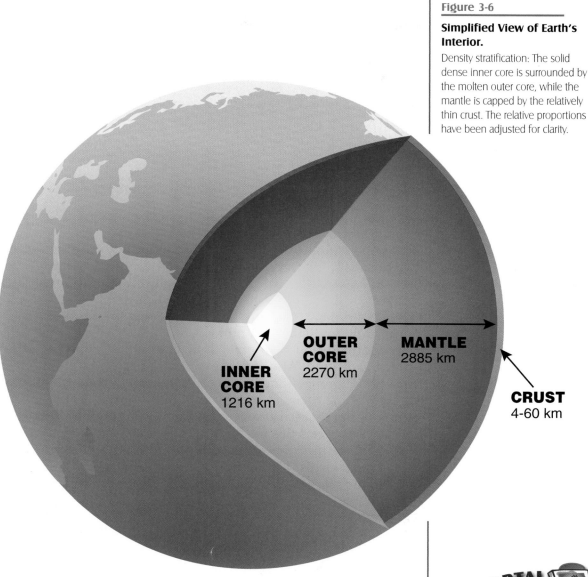

Figure 3-6

Simplified View of Earth's Interior.

Density stratification: The solid dense inner core is surrounded by the molten outer core, while the mantle is capped by the relatively thin crust. The relative proportions have been adjusted for clarity.

INNER CORE
1216 km

OUTER CORE
2270 km

MANTLE
2885 km

CRUST
4-60 km

INTERNET PORTAL

SCiLINKS. NSTA

Topic: Composition of the Earth
Go To: www.scilinks.org
Code: LOP2050

Although Earth didn't gain enough mass to form a protostar or star, its growing mass caused its core to compress. The core heated and became molten liquid (the outer core still is molten). Within this molten liquid, heavy matter, such as iron and nickel, sank toward the center, while light matter, such as oxygen and silicon, moved toward the surface. This process of *density stratification* formed the layers of the Earth.

How did Earth's moon form? The most widely accepted explanation for the moon's origin is the *Orpheus theory*. This theory says that a planet-sized body—possibly another planet about one-third the size of Earth—struck Earth during its early development and sent some of its material into orbit, forming the moon.

Origin of the Atmosphere and the Ocean

What is the common theory for how the early atmosphere formed?

According to theory, how did the ocean form?

According to theory, how is the formation of the ocean linked to atmospheric changes and the formation of life?

Scientists strongly believe that early Earth had no atmosphere. It was largely molten liquid and didn't allow any gases to escape. Scientists say that eventually it cooled enough for the surface to solidify into a crust. This allowed gases released by volcanic activity to escape, eventually accumulating as an early atmosphere of primarily water vapor, carbon dioxide, and nitrogen.

Conditions in the early atmosphere were still so hot that water vapor formed clouds and then rain, but the rain boiled off when it hit the ground. After further cooling, Earth's surface allowed rain to accumulate and the ocean formed as water vapor condensed. Some scientists hypothesize that comets or other water sources from space also contributed water vapor, although recent evidence suggests this may not be as likely as once thought.

Scientists also theorize that the development of the ocean began the process that allowed life to form. Carbon dioxide dissolved into the young ocean, leaving a nitrogen-rich atmosphere. Many scientists think that these were the conditions required for life. Interestingly, it is well accepted that there was *no oxygen* in the early atmosphere. Rocks dated to that time seem to indicate the atmosphere was a mixture of nitrogen, methane, water vapor, and possibly ammonia. *Ozone*, which is an oxygen molecule found high in the atmosphere, is also important because it protects life from ultraviolet radiation. (*Chapters 10 and 18 discuss the ozone layer in more detail.*)

Although oxygen is essential to almost all life today, according to data recorded in rocks, early life didn't use oxygen. Oxygen entered the atmosphere about 1.5 billion years ago, say scientists, when photosynthesizing organisms began using carbon dioxide and releasing oxygen. (*Chapter 4 discusses more about photosynthesis.*)

1. **The Big Bang is**

   A. the theorized beginning of the universe from a single point.

   B. the formation of Earth from a supernova.

   C. the formation of the moon from a volcanic explosion.

2. **A protostar is**

   A. a star that explodes into multiple protobodies.

   B. the theorized beginning of a star caused by gases accumulating and condensing into a dense core.

   C. an expanding cloud of water vapor.

3. **Scientists theorize that stars formed**

   A. because matter in the energy in the expanding universe is evenly distributed.

   B. when protostars became so dense that nuclear fusion began in their cores.

   C. as a result of comets striking protostars.

4. **Scientists theorize that heavy elements formed**

   A. when light atoms within stars fused, becoming heavier atoms.

   B. when the Big Bang hurled atoms into each other.

   C. when the universe collapsed.

5. **In a star's theorized life cycle, a supernova occurs when**

   A. the star consumes all the hydrogen fueling it.

   B. the star accretes from condensing gases.

   C. the star condenses and begins to spin.

6. **It's theorized that the solar system**

   A. was formed when stray planets spontaneously began to orbit the sun.

   B. resulted when a supernova shock wave caused a nebula to condense and spin.

   C. was formed from matter left by a passing comet.

7. **The planets were formed, according to theory,**

   A. when some condensing gas revolving around the sun collapsed into masses too small to become stars.

   B. when passing asteroids were captured by the sun's gravity and accreted into planets.

   C. when a passing comet left a trail of material.

8. **The nebular theory is the theory that**

   A. the solar system formed from a nebula.

   B. Earth is a nebula.

   C. the solar system will expand into a nebula.

9. **According to nebular theory, Earth and other planets formed due to a process called**

   A. transplantation.

   B. density stratification.

   C. accretion.

10. **The process by which matter became layered according to density during Earth's formation, with heavier matter near the core and lighter material closer to the crust, is called**

    A. transplantation.

    B. density stratification.

    C. accretion.

11. **The more accepted theory of the moon's origin is**

    A. that a planet-sized object struck young Earth, sending material into orbit that eventually became the moon.

    B. that the moon was a planet flung from another galaxy by a supernova that happened to fall into Earth's orbit.

    C. that the moon is a passing asteroid captured by Earth's gravity.

12. **It is theorized that the atmosphere formed**

    A. almost immediately when Earth formed.

    B. only after Earth cooled enough to have a crust.

    C. only in the last 40,000 years.

13. **It is theorized that the ocean formed**

    A. almost immediately on formation of the atmosphere.

    B. only after Earth cooled enough for water to accumulate on the surface.

    C. only in the last 40,000 years.

14. **Scientists theorize that the formation of the ocean**

    A. created the atmospheric changes required for terrestrial life to form.

    B. was helpful, but not important in the formation of life.

    C. was caused by the generation of oxygen.

The Origins of Life

Abiogenesis

What aspect of fossil evidence supports the theory that life began in the ocean?

According to theory, how did the first molecular building blocks of life originate?

By what processes do scientists theorize that nonliving chemicals became living organisms?

What are abiogenesis *and* spontaneous generation?

How life originated on Earth remains hotly debated. There are several theories, so rather than detail any one of them, we'll discuss the mainstream concepts accepted by the majority of biologists.

The fossil record indicates that life on Earth was first common in the shallows of the ocean. How is this known? Scientists have found that marine life fossils are significantly older than terrestrial fossils. Some of the oldest marine fossils are those of *cyanobacteria*, dated 3.5 billion years ago. Cyanobacteria are aquatic, photosynthetic bacteria (sometimes called blue-green algae—although they are not true algae). The oldest terrestrial fossils found are about one billion years old.

It's not clear exactly how the first molecules that comprise the building blocks of life originated. In 1929, scientist J.B.S. Haldane proposed that they could have originated from lightning or ultraviolet light in the atmosphere. In 1953, Stanley Miller and Harold Urey tested this hypothesis by discharging electricity within the gases Haldane proposed for the early atmosphere. These gases were water vapor, ammonia, methane, and hydrogen, but not oxygen.

The Urey-Miller experiment produced, among other substances, *amino acids*. Amino acids are the component molecules that living systems use to build protein. Similar experiments have also produced simple sugars, which are also used by living systems to construct more complex molecules.

STUDY QUESTIONS

Find the answers as you read.

1. What aspect of fossil evidence supports the theory that life began in the ocean?

2. According to theory, how did the first molecular building blocks of life originate?

3. By what processes do scientists theorize that nonliving chemicals became living organisms?

4. What are *abiogenesis* and *spontaneous generation?*

5. What are *heterotrophs* and *autotrophs?*

6. Why is oxygen important to life?

7. What is the theory of evolution?

INTERNET PORTAL

SCiLINKS. NSTA

**Topic: Cyanobacteria
Go To: www.scilinks.org
Code: LOP2540**

Figure 3-7

A Cambrian period trilobite.

A fossil from the Cambrian period found in Morocco. Scientists date this fossil at some 535 million years old. Trilobites are extinct arthropods. Living arthropods are discussed in Chapter 6.

The experiment did not produce life, of course. Scientists now theorize that methane and ammonia were not part of the early atmosphere. Astronomers also believe that these basic compounds exist in other parts of the solar system. Therefore, the precise origin of these compounds isn't entirely certain. The main point of the Urey-Miller experiment and subsequent discoveries, however, is that many basic molecules used by living systems readily form under certain conditions.

For many years, biologists proposed that early Earth's ocean acted as a "primordial soup" of simple compounds that are the building blocks of life. Proteins and other complex molecular chains formed when shallow pools evaporated, concentrating the "soup." Driven by sun energy, first life arose in this "soup" from increasingly complex chemical reactions.

More recently, however, scientists question this proposal. Many scientists theorize that volcanic activity, *meteorites*, and other influences were too destructive to allow life to develop in shallow surface pools. In addition, the early atmosphere would not have protected early life from the destructive influence of ultraviolet radiation. Therefore, these scientists propose that life arose deep in the ocean, protected by water. According to this theory, life origi-

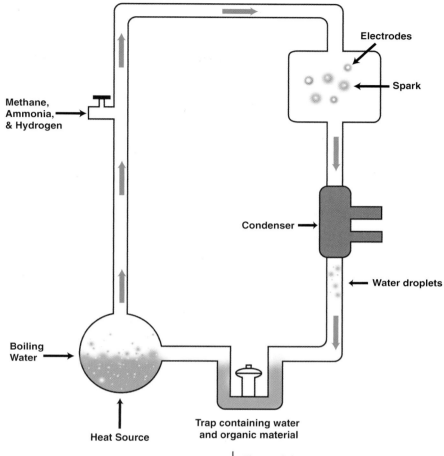

Figure 3-8

Stanley Miller and Harold Urey's 1953 experiment.

The experiment discharged electricity within water vapor, methane, ammonia, and hydrogen to create amino acids—the building blocks of life. The mixture was chosen to mimic Earth's early atmosphere and supported the idea that life arose from the "primordial soup."

ABIOGENESIS TODAY?

If you accept abiogenesis as the origin of life, it raises the question: Could it happen now under Earth's present conditions? The answer is "Not likely." Earth differs significantly from the conditions biologists think existed when life originated.

The most significant difference is that life already exists. Organisms compete for nutrients and energy. This means that some organism would almost certainly consume any useable energy source or compound long before new life could spontaneously generate independently from it.

nated using chemical energy and heat energy from hot mineral springs (*hydrothermal vents*) on the ocean bottom. Yet other hypotheses suggest that the first organic material or life itself arrived from space via a comet or meteor.

Regardless of the exact environment that allowed it to happen, biologists propose that simple molecules randomly combined and separated. Eventually, larger, more stable molecules formed by chance. When one of these combinations became capable of reproducing itself, say biologists, life was born. This origination of life from nonliving matter is called *abiogenesis*, sometimes referred to as *spontaneous generation*. You may also hear it called *biosynthesis*, although biosynthesis also means to use biological processes to manufacture products (such as alcohol through fermentation).

Oxygen and Evolution – Why do Scientists Believe Life Began in the Ocean?

What are heterotrophs *and* autotrophs?

Why is oxygen important to life?

What is the theory of evolution?

According to most biologists, the first organisms were very simple. They probably thrived by breaking down simple compounds in the "primordial soup" to supply their energy. Organisms that rely on consuming compounds to obtain chemical energy are called *heterotrophs*.

Most biologists theorize that as life became more advanced, about 3 to 3.5 billion years ago, the first *autotrophs* appeared. Unlike heterotrophs, autotrophs can create organic chemical energy compounds from inorganic compounds and an external energy source. (*Chapter 4 goes into more detail about heterotrophs and autotrophs*). The appearance of autotrophs was significant because they began breaking down carbon dioxide into oxygen. This

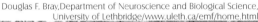
Douglas F. Bray, Department of Neuroscience and Biological Science, University of Lethbridge/www.uleth.ca/emf/home.html

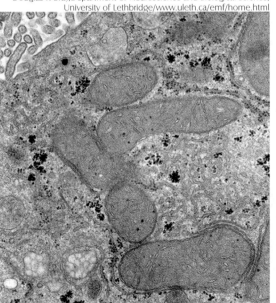

Figure 3-9

Cellular organelles.

This image of a liver cell shows mitochondria, glycogen, and rough endoplasmic reticulum.

raised the atmosphere's oxygen content from about 1% to the present 21%.

This was a significant change. Oxygen is important to life because oxygen reactions allow organisms to use chemical energy more effectively. Biologists theorize that the availability of oxygen allowed the development of *mitochondria*. Mitochondria are structures within cells that process oxygen as they use energy. Although some cells, such as bacteria, do not have mitochondria, they can still use oxygen. Mitochondria, however, make oxygen use more effective, and are found in more complex organisms.

How life transformed into the many types of organisms we see today is widely debated, with many specifics unresolved. Broadly, the most accepted explanations are based on the *theory of evolution*. Charles Darwin originally proposed this theory in his book *On the Origin of Species by Means of Natural Selection* in 1859, although he didn't use the term "evolution."

This theory is based on the principle that in nature, various characteristics affect survival. Organisms produce more offspring than can survive to adulthood, so those with favorable characteristics are more likely than those with less favorable characteristics to survive and reproduce. This is called *natural selection*. Sometimes new characteristics appear in an organism due to *mutation*. A mutation is an error in the genetic code (DNA). Most mutations are harmful, but some can create a survival advantage.

The theory of evolution says that over long periods (millions of years) natural selection and mutation caused the development of all the different life forms and their characteristics. In other words, organisms became more varied and complex over millions of years. The prevailing view in evolution is that changes come in spurts due to significant changes in the environment. These changes cause some species to become extinct. Existing organisms adapt and become new species as they fill niches left by extinct species. Through this process, life evolved from primitive organisms into single-cell organisms similar in many respects to those that exist today.

It is argued that some of these single-cell organisms then evolved from independent existence to life in colonies. Over millions of years, these colonies evolved into complex multicellular organisms. The first multicellular organisms lived in the ocean. Over time, evolutionary processes allowed organisms to adapt to life on land, and terrestrial and marine organisms have continued to evolve to this day. Biologists theorize that it is this process that specifically adapted organisms to the hundreds of environments in which they live.

TYPES OF EVOLUTION

Biologists distinguish between types of *macroevolution*.

Convergent evolution is the term for two or more different types of organisms evolving similar adaptations for a specific environment. A common example is the similarity between dolphins and fish. Although dolphins are mammals, they have fins and other adaptations similar to fish due to convergent evolution in the ocean environment.

Divergent evolution is when two or more related species develop adaptations that make them increasingly different due to differences in their environments.

Coevolution is when two organisms evolve together because they have a relationship. For example, an organism may evolve toward adaptations that allow it to better evade predators. However, the predators may simultaneously evolve new ways to capture their prey.

EARTH'S HISTORY IN TIME

Proterozoic Eon - Begins approximately 2.5 Billion Years ago and ends approximately 542 million years ago.

Hadean Eon	Archean Eon	Proterozoic Eon	Phanerozoic Eon
			Paleozoic Era Mesozoic Era Cenozoic Era

Hadean Eon -
Begins with the formation of the Earth 4.6 to 3.8 billion years ago.

The Eon's name comes from the underworld in Greek mythology and references the molten condition of the Earth at the time.

Archean Eon -
Begins approximately 3.8 to 4.6 billion years ago and ends approximately 2.5 billion years ago.

Scientists think the Earth cooled during this eon and a primitive anaerobic atmosphere enabled the first life - early bacteria - to develop about 3.5 billion years ago. Water was plentiful and the ocean likely formed along with the beginning of plate tectonics. Oxygen-producing organisms developed at the end of this eon.

Phanerozoic Eon - Begins approximately 542 million years ago and runs to the present.

Paleozoic Era

Paleozoic Era - approximately 540 million years ago to approximately 250 million years ago. Palentologists see the beginning of the Plaeozoic Era as marked by an explosion in multicellular diversity, and the development of the supercontinent Pangea. A major mass-extinction event - possibly the largest in history - signaled the end of the Paleozoic.

• **Cambrian Period** - 542 - 488 million years ago.
This is when many of the major groups of animals appeared. This is often called the "Cambrian Explosion".

• **Ordovician Period** - approximately 448 - 443 million years ago. During this time there was a proliferation of marine invertebrates and a suggestion that plans first appeared on land.

• **Silurian Period** - approximately 443 - 416 million years ago. Following the mass extinction event at the end of the Ordovician, distinct water-based ecosystems develop, including coral reefs and a proliferation of jawless fish.

• **Devonian Period** - 416 - 359 million years ago.
This, the Age of Fishes, saw two supercontinents on the Earth - Gondwana and Euramerica. The rest was covered by water. Primitive sharks were prevalent and the first bony fish appeared. On land, tetrapods and the first true trees appeared. The Devonian concluded with a large extinction event.

• **Carboniferous Period** - 359 - 299 million years ago. Named for the coal beds laid down during this time, the Carboniferous saw tetrapods that were truly land-based; dominated by amphibians and reptiles.

• **Permian Period** - 299 - 251 million years ago. In the Permian, amphibians and reptiles were dominant while insect diversity was intense. Gymnosperms dominated plants on land and Pangea formed. The Permian is most notable, however, for what is thought to be Earth's largest extinction event and brought the Paleozoic to a close.

When determining the history of the Earth, scientists find it impractical to use a linear time scale. Instead, they use Boundary Events – significant events that appear to have occurred in the Earth's history – to create manageable divisions.

Similar to the Linnaeus Classification System you'll learn about in Chapter 5, the geological time scale uses a hierarchical system to define events in the Earth's history.

Eons are the biggest intervals and are broken down into eras. Archean is an example of an eon, while Paleozoic is an example of an era. These eras are further broken down into periods and then Epochs. The Jurrasic is a Period you have probably heard of and the Holocene is the Epoch you're living in right now. Some also use an overarching category called an eon. This divides the Earth's history into two large groups - the Precambrian Eon (from about 543 million years ago to the present) and the Phanerozoic Era (more than about 543 million years ago).

Mesozoic Era

Mesozoic Era - approximately 250 - 65 million years ago. The Mesozoic is the age of the dinosaurs, which evolved to become the dominant animals of the time. The supercontinent Pangea split into Laurasia and Gondwana. The Mesozoic ended with the Cretaceous-Tertiary (K-T) mass extinction event that spelled the end - excluding birds - of the dinosaurs.

• **Triassic Period** - approximately 251 - 199 million years ago. Following the world's largest extinction event to date, the Triassic was notable as a recovery period as life grew and flourished to fill in the gaps. It also saw the introduction of the dinosaurs and large marine reptiles. It concluded with an extinction event setting the stage for the domination fo dinosaurs.

• **Jurassic Period** - approximately 199 - 145 million years ago. The Age of the Dinosaurs saw the supercontinent Pangea starting to separate and the Triassic's extinction event creating an opportunity for dinosaurs to flourish and diversify.

• **Cretaceous Period** - approximately 145 - 65 million years ago. Curing the Cretaceous, the split of Pangea led to the continents of Laurasia and Gondwana, and differing plant and animals among the two. Flowering plants made their first appearance but the Cretaceous is well known for the massive K-T extinction event that spelled the end of the dinosaurs.

Cenozoic Era

Cenozoic Era - 65 million years ago to the present. Marked by the end of the K-T extinction, the Cenozoic Era is frequently called Age of the Mammals.

Paleogene Period - 65 - 23 million years ago. This period is notable for the evolution and diversity of mammals following the K-T extinction event.

Neogene Period - approximately 23 - 2 million years ago. The Neogene currently consists of the Miocene and Pliocene Epochs but current debate may render this classification slightly different in the future. The Period saw mammal and bird evolution along with a cooling climate and the connection of North and South America.

Quaternary Period - approximately 2 million years ago to the present. Composed of the Pleistocene and Holocene Epochs, the Period saw the rise of recognizable humans and continues to the present.

ARE YOU LEARNING?

1. **The most compelling evidence that supports the theory that life began in the ocean is**

   A. based on how scientists interpret the fossil record.

   B. that the ocean is still a "primordial soup."

   C. completely without basis in the fossil record.

2. **According to theory, the first molecular building blocks of life**

   A. were caused by lightning striking the ocean.

   B. are readily formed under certain conditions by natural processes.

   C. formed with the Big Bang.

3. **Scientists theorize that nonliving chemicals became life when**

   A. a large, stable molecule formed by chance and became capable of reproducing itself.

   B. volcanic activity and electricity randomly shocked a protein structure.

   C. none of the above

4. **Abiogenesis is**

   A. the origin of life from nonliving matter.

   B. exactly the opposite of spontaneous generation.

   C. both a and b

5. **A(n) _____ is an organism that relies on consuming chemical compounds. A(n) _____ is an organism that can create organic chemical compounds from inorganic compounds and an external energy source.**

   A. heterotroph, mitochondria

   B. autotroph, mitochondria

   C. heterotroph, autotroph

   D. autotroph, heterotroph

6. **Oxygen is important to life because it allows organisms to use chemical energy more efficiently.**

   A. true

   B. false

7. **The theory of evolution says that modern organisms and their characteristics arose through the processes of _____ and _____ over millions of years.**

   A. natural selection, spontaneous generation

   B. abiogenesis, spontaneous generation

   C. spontaneous generation, mutation

   D. mutation, natural selection

Ocean Zones and Lifestyles

One of the amazing things about Earth is its diversity of environments and life. After the atmosphere, the ocean and life formed, organisms changed through processes still at work today. Uneven heating by the sun created regions with different relative temperatures and moisture. As discussed in Chapter 13, the current thinking is that this process even includes the movement of the continents. These processes explain the diversity of environments on Earth.

Characteristics that organisms need to survive vary with environment. As environments changed over millions of years, organisms developed and changed through the processes of natural selection and mutation.

Because the characteristics of an environment determine the adaptations of organisms that live there, we'll begin by looking at the basic marine environments and the types of organisms that live in them.

Environment Classification Methods

How do marine scientists classify marine environments?

Pretend you're visiting a local park. Your job is to define park areas for closer study. How would you go about it? You might observe that parts of the park consist of lawn, trees, and other plants. Other parts consist of small buildings, paved walkways, and swing sets for children. This may lead you to divide the park into the "natural zones" and the "developed zones." Or, you might notice that the park has outlying areas near the surrounding streets. The inner areas, on the other hand, lie a good distance from any motor traffic. This might call for a division into the "outer zone" and the "inner zone."

On the other hand, your interest may relate to how organisms live in the park. You notice birds, insects, dogs, trees, and people. Based on this, you may classify the life forms into "inhabitants" that live there and "visitors" that come from time to time but don't stay. Or, you may classify them as those that fly and those that don't.

None of these division methods are right or wrong; they are valid ways to define the park's areas. In studying the park, you may end up using more than one method, depending on what you're considering. Studying the effect of noise, you may consider the "inner" and "outer zones." Studying how people use the park, the "natural" and "developed" division may be more useful.

STUDY QUESTIONS

Find the answers as you read.

1. How do marine scientists classify marine environments?

2. What are the *pelagic* and *benthic zones?*

3. What are the *neritic* and *oceanic zones?*

4. What are the *epipelagic, mesopelagic, bathypelagic, abyssalpelagic,* and *hadalpelagic zones?*

5. Where are the *photic* and *aphotic zones?* Into which two smaller zones is the photic zone divided?

6. What are the *supralittoral, littoral, sublittoral, outer sublittoral, bathyal, abyssal,* and *hadal zones?*

7. What are *plankton, nekton,* and *benthos?*

8. What are *neuston?*

9. What are *epifauna, epiflora,* and *infauna?*

Scientists have the same concerns when they consider the ocean and its inhabitants. They divide the seas into many different regions based on physical characteristics. Scientists may classify parts of the ocean into different zones or regions based on the light, depth, temperature, nutrients, density, latitude, distance from shore, or a combination of these. For now, let's look at some of the basic classifications based on distance from shore and depth.

Location

What are the pelagic *and* benthic *zones?*

What are the neritic *and* oceanic *zones?*

What are the epipelagic, mesopelagic, bathypelagic, abyssalpelagic, *and* hadalpelagic *zones?*

Where are the photic *and* aphotic *zones? Into which two smaller zones is the photic zone divided?*

What are the supralittoral, littoral, sublittoral, outer sublittoral, bathyal, abyssal, *and* hadal *zones?*

The most basic division of the ocean based on location is between the water column and the bottom. The water portion is called the *pelagic zone* (Greek *pelagikos* meaning *sea*) and the bottom is called the *benthic zone* (Greek *benthos* meaning *depths of sea*). Each of these has subdivisions.

The pelagic zone is divided into two horizontal zones—*neritic* and *oceanic*. The *neritic zone* is the water area between the low tide mark to the edge of the continental shelf. Instead of neritic, many use the terms *continental shelf* or *coastal*.

The *oceanic zone* is the open water area beyond that. The oceanic zone is further divided into vertical regions called the *epipelagic zone, mesopelagic zone, bathypelagic zone, abyssalpelagic zone,* and *hadalpelagic zone*. These vertical regions can also be labeled as sunlit, twilight, midnight and abyssal (the very deep region).

The epipelagic zone is the top layer that sunlight penetrates (Greek *epi* meaning *over* or *before*). Think of it as the "sunlit" zone. Below that is a *"twilight"* zone, the mesopelagic zone (Greek *mesos* meaning *middle*). Sunlight reaches the mesopelagic zone, but not strongly enough to support much life.

The zones below are the bathypelagic, abyssalpelagic, and hadalpelagic. The bathypelagic zone (Greek *bathos* meaning *deep*) is the deep water in open ocean. The abyssalpelagic zone (Greek *abyssos* meaning *bottomless*) is even deeper water. Hadalpelagic

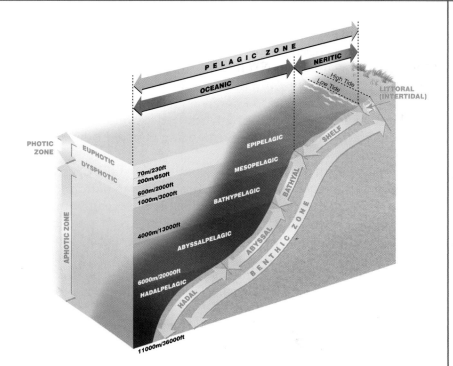

Figure 3-10

The pelagic, photic, and aphotic zones.

The pelagic zone is subdivided along both the horizontal and vertical axes. Horizontally there are the neritic and oceanic zones, which are delineated by the edge of the continental shelf or the coastal area. The neritic zone is shoreward of the shelf. Along the vertical axis the pelagic zone is divided by depth. The depth of light penetration defines the top layer, the epipelagic zone. The majority of the epipelagic zone receives sunlight and lies in the *photic zone*. The photic zone is divided between the *euphotic* (lighted) and *dysphotic* (dimly lit) *zones*. The aphotic zone and the remaining deeper zones are in constant darkness and comprise the seas below approximately 1,000 meters (3,280 feet).

(Greek Hades meaning *the underground abode of the dead*) is the deeper water in the ocean trenches. Collectively, these zones are simply called the "*midnight*" zone.

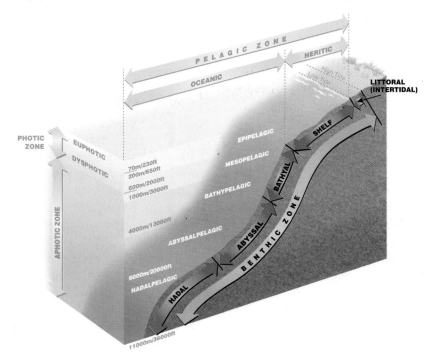

Figure 3-11

The benthic zone.

The benthic zone—the seafloor—is also subdivided. The littoral zone, also known as the intertidal zone, is submerged according to the tides. Past the low tide mark is the continental shelf. After the continental shelf break is the bathyal zone that extends down to the bottom of the continental slope. The abyssal zone runs from the base of the continental slope to the beginning of the deep ocean—after which is the hadal zone.

The benthic zone is divided based on depth. Moving from shore toward the open ocean, the first zone is the *supralittoral zone* (Latin *supra* meaning *upper* and *litus* meaning *shore*). This is the zone that water splashes, but does not remain submerged. Beyond that lies the *littoral zone* (also known as the intertidal zone), which is the bottom area between the high tide and low tide marks. In this zone, the bottom alternates between being covered by water and being exposed.

Beyond the littoral zone is the continental shelf. This area is divided into the *sublittoral zone*, which is the ocean bottom close to shore, and the *outer sublittoral zone*, which is the ocean bottom out to the edge of the continental shelf. The *bathyal zone* is the bottom along the continental slope down to the deep open ocean bottom. The deep open ocean bottom is called the *abyssal zone*. The deepest zone, areas below 6,000 meters (19,685 feet), is the *hadal zone*. Commonly you'll hear the bathyal, abyssal, and hadal zones called the *deep sea floor*.

The pelagic zone can also divided vertically by the depth of light penetration. The majority of the epipelagic zone receives sunlight and lies in the *photic zone* - also simply called the sunlit zone. The photic zone is further divided between the *euphotic* (lighted) and *dysphotic* (dimly lit) *zones*. The *aphotic zone* is in constant darkness and comprise the seas below approximately 1,000 meters (3,280 feet).

Figure 3-12

Vertebrate nekton.

Northern anchovies (*Engraulis mordax*).

Figure 3-13

Invertebrate nekton.

A northern shortfin squid (*Illex illecebrosus*).

Marine Lifestyles

What are plankton, nekton, *and* benthos?

What are neuston?

What are epifauna, epiflora, *and* infauna?

Chapters 5, 6 and 7 look at the thousands of different types of specific organisms living in the ocean. Marine life is incredibly diverse. With hundreds of thousands of species, it can be difficult to discuss them individually. Scientists therefore use groups and subgroups based on common physical characteristics.

This type of classification doesn't work for some discussions. Sometimes the organism itself is less important than how and where it lives. Very different organisms can exist in the same environment and have similar survival strategies. For those purposes, marine scientists classify marine life into three lifestyles called *plankton*, *nekton*, and *benthos*.

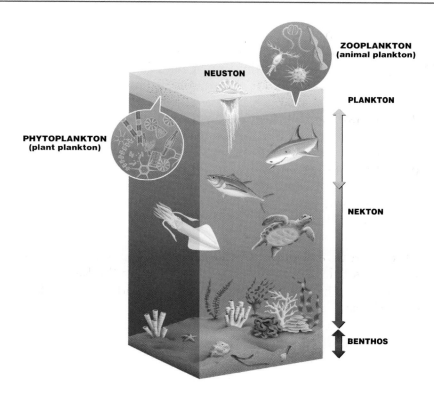

ZOOPLANKTON
(animal plankton)

NEUSTON

PLANKTON

PHYTOPLANKTON
(plant plankton)

NEKTON

BENTHOS

Figure 3-14

Marine lifestyles.

Organisms classified according to lifestyle are divided into three major groups. The plankton are the drifters (which also include the neuston while at the surface), nekton live in the water column, and benthic organisms live on or in the sea floor.

Al Hornsby

Figure 3-15

Benthic infauna.

A filter-feeding sea pen.

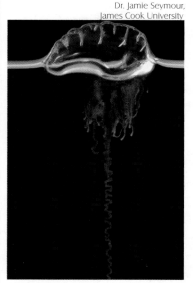

Dr. Jamie Seymour,
James Cook University

Figure 3-16

The neuston.

A Portuguese Man-of-War
(*Physalia physalis*).

Plankton (Greek *planktos* meaning *wanderer*) is a group of plants (phytoplankton) and animals (zooplankton) that exist adrift in ocean currents. Most plankton are very small or microscopic and can't swim against currents and waves. As discussed in more detail in Chapter 4, plankton are among the most important organisms on Earth, without which most life would die.

The nekton (Greek *nekton* meaning *swimming*) are what you probably visualize when you think of marine organisms. These are the organisms that swim, from small *invertebrates* to large whales. Most of the seas' predators are nekton. The majority of the nekton are *vertebrates* (animals with internal skeletons and backbones), such as fishes and whales. But, a few are invertebrates (animals without internal skeletons and backbones), such as squid.

The benthos are organisms that live on or in the bottom. Benthos can move about or be *sessile*. Sessile organisms are attached, like sea anemones, barnacles, and sea fans.

These classifications have subgroups. One important subgroup of plankton is called the *neuston* (Greek *neustos* meaning *swimming*). The neuston are those plankton that float at the surface. One example is the Portuguese Man-of-War, which has a special gas float that keeps it at the surface and allows the wind to push it to help it capture prey with its stinging tentacles.

The benthos are divided into the *epifauna* (*fauna* comes from *faun*, a class of Roman mythological deities that are part human and part animal), *epiflora* (Latin *flora*, Roman goddess of flowers), and *infauna*. The epifauna are those animals, such as crabs, that live on the sea floor. Epiflora are plants, such as seagrasses, that live on the sea floor. Infauna are organisms that are partially or completely buried in the sea floor. These include some species of clams, sand dollars, tubeworms, and sea pens. Most infauna are either *deposit feeders* or *suspension feeders*. Deposit feeders feed off *detritus* (loose organic and inorganic material) drifting down from above. Suspension feeders filter particles (mostly plankton) suspended in the water for food.

ARE YOU LEARNING?

1. Scientists may classify marine environments based on a wide range of physical characteristics, or a combination of physical characteristics.

    A. true

    B. false

2. The _____ zone refers to the water portion of the ocean. The _____ zone refers to the bottom.

    A. benthic, abyssal

    B. abyssal, benthic

    C. abyssal, pelagic

    D. pelagic, benthic

3. The zone between the low tide-mark and the edge of the continental shelf is the

    A. intertidal zone.

    B. neritic zone.

    C. oceanic zone.

4. A zone of deep water in the open ocean is the (choose all that apply)

    A. epipelagic zone.

    B. midnight zone.

    C. bathypelagic zone.

    D. abyssopelagic zone.

5. The photic zone is the _____ area of the open ocean, whereas the aphotic zone is the _____ area.

    A. dark, lighted

    B. lighted, nonlighted

    C. deep, shallow

6. Shore bottom that is splashed, but not submerged is the _____ zone of the benthic zone.

    A. supralittoral

    B. littoral

    C. inner sublittoral

    D. hadal

7. The marine lifestyle that consists of organisms that swim is called

    A. plankton.

    B. nekton.

    C. benthos.

8. The neuston are organisms that _____. They're a subgroup of the _____.

    A. live midwater, plankton

    B. live buried in the bottom, benthos

    C. float, plankton

    D. float, benthos

9. _____ refer(s) to organisms that live on the sea bottom. _____ are those organisms that live buried or partially buried in the sea bottom.

    A. Epifauna and epiflora, Neuston

    B. Neuston, Infauna

    C. Infauna, Epifauna and epiflora

    D. Epifauna and epiflora, Infauna

New Terms You Learned

- **abiogenesis** the formation of life from nonliving matter, also called spontaneous generation (p. 3-12)

- **abyssal zone** a division of the benthic zone, the ocean bottom in deep water (p. 3-20)

- **abyssalpelagic zone** a division of the oceanic zone consisting of the deepest water found in oceanic trenches; between 4,000 and 6,000 meters (13,123 and 19,685 feet) (p. 3-18)

- **accretion** the process in which small particles clump together due to gravity to form a solid body, such as a planet (p. 3-6)

- **amino acids** the component molecules used by living systems to build proteins (p. 3-10)

- **aphotic zone** the ocean zone of perpetual darkness below approximately 1,000 meters/3,280 feet (p. 3-20)

- **astrology** the study of the supposed influence of the stars and planets on human affairs (p. 3-2)

- **astronomy** the scientific study of the universe, especially of the motions, positions, sizes, composition, and behavior of celestial objects (p. 3-2)

- **autotrophs** organisms that can create organic chemical energy compounds from inorganic compounds and an external energy source (p. 3-12)

- **bathyal zone** a division of the benthic zone, the ocean bottom along the continental slope to the open ocean bottom (p. 3-20)

- **bathypelagic zone** a division of the oceanic zone consisting of deep water in open ocean; between 1,000 and 4,000 meters (3,280 and 13,123 feet) (p. 3-18)

- **benthic zone** the bottom portion of the ocean; pertaining to areas of water (and organisms) at the bottom of a water body, like the bottom of the ocean (p. 3-20)

- **benthos** marine organisms that live on or in the sea bottom (p. 3-22)

- **Big Bang** the theorized moment in which the universe began to expand from a single concentrated point (p. 3-3)

- **biosynthesis** a synonym for abiogenesis; also means the use of biological processes in the manufacture of products (p. 3-12)

- **coevolution** when two organisms evolve together because they have a relationship (p. 3-13)

- **continental shelf** the extended, underwater perimeter of a continent; an area that can stretch for many kilometers out to sea in some areas (p. 3-18)

- **convergent evolution** the process where two unrelated structures in unrelated organisms evolve to perform similar functions (p. 3-13)

- **cyanobacteria** a picoplankton bacteria belonging to a large group that have a photosynthetic pigment to carry out photosynthesis (p. 3-10)

- **deep sea floor** collective term that refers to the bathyal, abyssal and the hadal zones (p. 3-20)

- **density stratification** in the nebular theory, the process by which matter became layered according to density during the Earth's formation, with heavier matter near the core and lighter material closer to the crust (p. 3-7)

- **deposit feeders** organisms that feed off detritus drifting down from above (p. 3-22)

- **detritus** partially decomposed organic matter that makes up a portion of sediments in an aquatic environment; loose material from the breakup of organic and inorganic material (p. 3-22)

- **divergent evolution** when two or more related species develop adaptations that make them increasingly different due to differences in their environments (p. 3-13)

- **dysphotic zone** the dimly lit, deeper and less biologically productive portion of the photic zone (p. 3-20)

- **empirical** that which is based on something observed or experienced (p. 3-3)

- **epifauna** benthic animals that live on the sea floor; includes some species of crabs, sea stars, sea urchins (p. 3-22)

- **epiflora** benthic plants that live on the sea floor; includes seagrasses, some species of algae (p. 3-22)

- **epipelagic zone** the upper portion of the oceanic zone that sunlight reaches; between 0 and 70 meters (230 feet) (p. 3-18)
- **euphotic zone** the upper, most biologically productive portion of the photic zone (p. 3-20)
- **extremophiles** organisms that live in environments that have conditions fatal to most forms of life (p. 3-18)
- **hadal zone** The deepest zone, areas below 6,000 meters (19,685 feet) (p. 3-20)
- **hadalpelagic zone** a division of the oceanic zone, the deeper water in the ocean trenches, below 6,000 meters (19,685 feet) (p. 3-18)
- **heterotrophs** organisms that rely on external energy sources by digesting plant or animal matter (p. 3-12)
- **hydrothermal vent** a fissure in the Earth's surface from which geothermically heated water is forced out – found near volcanically active places, areas where tectonic plates are moving (p. 3-12)
- **infauna** benthic organisms that live buried or partially buried in the sea floor; includes some types of clams, tube worms, sea pens (p. 3-22)
- **invertebrate** animal lacking a backbone or spinal column; includes crabs, jellyfish, sea urchins, sea stars (p. 3-21)
- **littoral zone** ocean bottom zone between the high tide and low tide marks (p. 3-20)
- **mesopelagic zone** the division of the oceanic zone that sunlight reaches, but not strongly enough to support much life; between 200 and 1,000 meters (656 and 3,280 feet) (p. 3-18)
- **midnight zone** that zone of the deep ocean that is entirely dark—there is no light; also loosely associated with the aphotic, abyssalpelagic and hadalpelagic zones. (p. 3-19)
- **mitochondria** organelles (structures) within cells that process oxygen to produce energy (p. 3-13)
- **mutation** an abnormal characteristic in an individual organism caused by an error in the organism's DNA (p. 3-13)

- **natural selection** the process by which organisms with favorable characteristics tend to live longer and reproduce more (p. 3-13)
- **nebula** a large, hazy bright or dark cloud of hydrogen, helium, and interstellar dust in space (p. 3-5)
- **nebular theory** the theory that the solar system developed from a nebula (p. 3-6)
- **nekton** swimming organisms that are able to move independently of water currents; most fish, mammals, turtles, sea snakes (p. 3-21)
- **neritic zone** the water area between the low tide mark and the edge of the continental shelf v(p. 3-18)
- **neuston** plankton that lives on the water's surface; includes Portuguese Man-of-War (p. 3-21)
- **nuclear fusion** atomic reaction in which lighter atoms unite to form heavier atoms, releasing tremendous energy in the process (p. 3-4)
- **oceanic zone** the open water area beyond the continental shelf (p. 3-18)
- **organelle** microscopic structures ("organs") within an individual cell (p. 3-12)
- **Orpheus theory** the theory that a planetary object struck the Earth and hurled material into orbit, forming the moon (p. 3-8)
- **outer sublittoral zone** a division of the littoral zone, the ocean bottom away from shore out to the edge of the continental shelf (p. 3-20)
- **pelagic zone** the water portion of the ocean; pertaining to areas of water that are not near the surface or bottom of the water body (compare with benthic zone) (p. 3-18)
- **photic zone** upper sunlit zone of the ocean (p. 3-20)
- **plankton** organisms that exist adrift in the ocean, unable to swim against currents and waves, most, but not all, are very small or microscopic; includes dinoflagellates, diatoms, jellyfish, fish larva (p. 3-20)
- **protostar** theorized accumulation of gases that, due to gravitational attraction, forms a dense core that may, given enough mass, begin nuclear reactions and become a star (p. 3-4)

- **sessile** term for an organism that is permanently attached in place on the sea bottom; includes corals, barnacles, sea fans, mussels (p. 3-21)
- **spontaneous generation** the formation of life from non living matter, also called abiogenesis (p. 3-12)
- **sublittoral zone** a division of the littoral zone, the ocean bottom close to shore (p. 3-20)
- **sunlit zone** the top layer of the ocean, nearest the surface; also called the euphotic or epipelagic zone (p. 3-18)
- **supernova** a catastrophic explosion of a large star in the latter stages of stellar evolution, with a resulting short-lived luminosity from 10 to 100 million times that of the Sun (p. 3-5)
- **supralittoral zone** shore bottom that is splashed, but not submerged by water (p. 3-20)
- **suspension feeders** organisms that filter particles (mostly plankton) suspended in the water for food (p. 3-22)
- **twilight zone** the zone where only a small amount of light can penetrate the water; also loosely known as the dysphotic, mesopelagic and bathypelagic zones. (p. 3-18)
- **vertebrate** animal with a backbone or spinal column; includes fish, whales, sea lions (p. 3-21)

Chapter 3 in Review

1. Describe the theory generally accepted by scientists for the origin of the universe, stars, and heavy elements. Include a description of a protostar and a star's life cycle.
2. Describe nebular theory and how the solar system originated according to that theory. What is a nebula?
3. Continuing with nebular theory, describe the formation of Earth. Include and name the theory for how the moon originated.
4. Describe the common theory that explains the origin of the atmosphere and the ocean. Include how the formation of the ocean linked with the atmosphere to produce the theorized conditions under which life arose.
5. Describe the theory generally accepted by biologists for abiogenesis.
6. Why is oxygen important to life? According to theory, how did the atmosphere get its oxygen? What kinds of organisms existed before that?
7. In general terms, describe how the different organisms that exist today came to be according to the theory of evolution.
8. Explain how scientists classify different ocean zones. Why may they use more than one classification method?
9. Draw a diagram illustrating the pelagic zone and its subdivisions.
10. Draw a diagram illustrating the benthic zone and its subdivisions.
11. Define the terms plankton, nekton, benthos, neuston, epifauna, epiflora and infauna, and their grouped relationships.
12. Why is it important to group organisms based on lifestyle as well as on common physical characteristics?

Connecting Chapter Concepts— Science Scenarios

1. Based on astronomical observations, scientists theorize how the universe, stars, the solar system and the Earth and moon formed. According to prevailing theories:
   A. What is the name of the event at which the universe formed, and briefly, what happened?
   B. How did stars form? What natural property of matter made it happen?
   C. How does the nebular theory explain the origin of the solar system?
   D. What is the Orpheus theory?
2. Scientists divide the ocean into basic zones with similar environmental characteristics that determine the adaptations of the organisms that live there. The most basic division is the division between the water and the bottom, and each of these has subdivisions.
   A. Two broad divisions are the pelagic zone and the benthic zone. What is the difference between these zones?
   B. The Greek *epi* means *over* or *before*, and the Greek *bathos* means *deep*. At what level of the water column would one find the epipelagic zone? The bathypelagic zone?
   C. The Greek *supra* means *upper* and *litus* means *shore*. What is the supralittoral zone, and what adaptations would you expect to find in organisms that live there?
   D. Where is the bathyal division of the benthic zone?
   E. *Photos* means *light* and *a* means *not*. In which of the two zones that refer to light, would you find the majority of marine life and why?

Marine Science and the Real World

1. Support for theories of how the universe and solar system originated comes primarily from physics and astronomy rather than from biology and geology. Why do you suppose this is?
2. Thinking like a scientist means objectively analyzing a theory against the evidence. Choose a theory that you think is accurate and try to refute it based on the evidence. Use reasonable hypotheses to account for conflicting data. What does this exercise teach you about thinking critically?
3. In this chapter you learned two of several ways that marine scientists classify the ocean into divisions. Think of other divisions that you could use and how they could be useful. Be sure to consider cultural and political divisions (Hint: International and territorial seas).
4. Many biologists call oxygen "the first pollutant." Why would they say this? Do you agree? Why or why not?
5. Why are there no inflora?

References

Campbell, Neil. 1993. *Biology*. Redwood City: Benjamin/Cummings Publishing Company, Inc.

Castro, Peter and Michael E. Huber. 2003. *Marine Biology*. Boston: McGraw-Hill.

Garrison, Tom. 2002. *Oceanography: An Invitation to Marine Science*. Stamford, CT: Wadsworth/Thomson Learning.

Johnson, George B. and Peter H. Raven. 2001. *Biology: Principles and Explorations*. Austin: Holt, Rinehart and Winston.

Nybakken, James W. 2001. *Marine Biology: An Ecological Approach*. San Francisco: Benjamin Cummings.

Seeds, Michael A. 2000. *Horizons, Exploring the Universe*. Pacific Grove: Brooks/Cole Publishing Company.

Sumich, James. 1999. *An Introduction to the Biology of Marine Life*. Boston: WCB/McGraw-Hill.

Sverdrup, Keith A., Alyn C. Duxbury and Alison B. Duxbury. 2000. *An Introduction to the World's Oceans*. Boston: McGraw-Hill.

Tarbuck, Edward J. and Frederick K. Lutgens. 2000. *Earth Science*. Upper Saddle River: Prentice Hall.

Thurman, Harold V., and Elizabeth A. Burton. 2001. *Introductory Oceanography*. New Jersey: Prentice Hall.

Valiela, Ivan. 1995. *Marine Ecological Processes*. New York: Springer-Verlag.

CHAPTER 4

The Energy of Life

Al Hornsb

Bob Wohlers

How Human Activity Affects Plankton Communities

Plankton form the base of the food chain and, without them, few other life forms could survive in the ocean. This is why it is so important to understand how our activities, particularly the addition of nutrients to the marine environment in runoff from farms and from wastewater, have altered the dynamics of plankton communities.

Barbara K. Sullivan is currently researching whether jellyfish, in these nutrient-enriched waters, become abundant enough to consume sufficient numbers of larval fish to affect fish populations. Considering the decline of commercial fisheries, this is an important question with far-reaching environmental, cultural, and economic ramifications.

"When I was about seven, my mother read me a book called Puffin Island where there was a kid who captured smugglers, saved puffins, and carried around a fuzzy little mouse friend in his pockets. He had a female sidekick who did not do anything memorable in the story. In those days girls rarely led adventures, but that did not stop me from wanting to have the same kind of fun someday," says Sullivan. "My mother also shared her love of nature with me, so I grew to love the outdoors. And, when someone gave my Girl Scout troop a sailboat and lessons to go with it—how could I resist the attraction of oceanography?"

The most challenging part of Sullivan's career is writing the many research proposals necessary to obtain the funding to continue her work. According to Sullivan, "I need to obtain money for my own salary, for my assistants' salaries, for student tuition, for boats, and for laboratory materials."

However, Sullivan has had some fun travel opportunities, including a trip to Tasmania, Australia, where she worked with local fish farmers on the problems they were having with jellyfish. She has also ridden in manned submersibles, piloted unmanned submersibles with cameras, and met interesting people from all over the world.

Sullivan's research focuses mainly on zooplankton ecology, especially predator-prey interactions in estuaries and the coastal ocean. Recently, her research has included the increasing numbers of gelatinous predators, especially cteno-phores, in Narragansett Bay in relation to climate change and effects of invertebrate predators on fish eggs, fish larvae, and zooplankton in the Northeast Atlantic Georges Bank region.

To those considering careers in marine science, Sullivan has this to say, "It does take a willingness to work hard, and keep working at your goals, sometimes against discouraging odds. Getting a strong background in basic sciences and math is very important, as is honing your ability to write and to speak in public."

Barbara K. Sullivan, PhD
Senior Marine Research Scientist,
Adjunct Faculty,
Graduate School of Oceanography,
University of Rhode Island

In *A Brief History of Time* (Bantam Books, 1998), theoretical physicist Stephen Hawking writes, "The laws of science do not distinguish between the past and the future." Does this mean there's no difference between the past and the future? According to Hawking, there most certainly is a difference. Fires don't suck the heat out of a room, pull smoke out of the air, and assemble a piece of wood. People don't go from old to young. Spilled milk doesn't stream into a glass, which then pops upright and full.

The explanation for this is the *second law of thermodynamics* (though commonly referred to as a law, it is a actually a theory. See Chapter 1). It says that in a closed system (one that lets no new energy in or out), order decreases as time passes. Thermodynamics is one of three "arrows of time," according to Hawking. The other two are psychology and cosmology. The psychological arrow is our perception of time's direction from the past into the future. The cosmological arrow is based on the expansion of the universe, which is explained in Chapter 3.

Hawking argues that the thermodynamic arrow is essential for intelligent life, and that life itself is temporary order among growing disorder:

> In order to survive, human beings have to consume food, which is an ordered form of energy, and convert it into heat, which is a disordered form of energy… The progress of the human race in understanding the universe has established a small corner of order in an increasingly disordered universe.

As you'll see, this principle of physics, called *entropy*, or randomness, appears to be the driving force of all life in our universe.

The Nature of Life

Is fire alive? It moves, consumes, releases waste, and reproduces—all characteristics of life. Why do we say that fire isn't alive, but a tree is? Because the difference between life and nonlife seems obvious when we compare a fish and a rock, defining life would appear to be simple. However, from a scientific point of view, it's not quite so cut-and-dried. The same matter moves back and forth continuously between living and nonliving systems. On an atomic level, nothing distinguishes between matter that is involved in life processes and matter that is not. The carbon atoms in the breath you just exhaled do not differ from the carbon atoms in your tissue or a piece of coal, other than being part of a different molecular structure.

STUDY QUESTIONS

Find the answers as you read.

1. What makes something "alive"? What makes life differ from nonlife?

2. Why is energy required for life?

3. What is the *second law of thermodynamics*?

4. How does the second law of thermodynamics relate to the process of life?

Similarly, energy reactions found in a living system (an organism) also exist outside of life. For example, fire results when a reaction releases chemical energy within substances. Living systems use energy similarly—by releasing chemical energy for life processes.

As you're about to see, all life uses energy. Therefore, it's possible to define "life" based on the characteristics living systems have apart from nonliving systems with respect to matter and energy use.

PADI

Figure 4-1

Life and nonlife.

Energy reactions exist in living and nonliving systems.

ELEMENTS ESSENTIAL FOR LIFE

HYDROGEN:
Organic molecules

NITROGEN:
Proteins and
nucleic acids

OXYGEN:
Organic molecules

CARBON:
Organic molecules

IRON:
Electron transport

CALCIUM:
Bones, shells, coral

PHOSPHORUS:
Nucleic acids, etc.

1 H																	2 He
3 Li	4 Be											5 B	6 C	7 N	8 O	9 F	10 Ne
11 Na	12 Mg											13 Al	14 Si	15 P	16 S	17 Cl	18 Ar
19 K	20 Ca	21 Sc	22 Ti	23 V	24 Cr	25 Mn	26 Fe	27 Co	28 Ni	29 Cu	30 Zn	31 Ga	32 Ge	33 As	34 Se	35 Br	36 Kr
37 Rb	38 Sr	39 Y	40 Zr	41 Nb	42 Mo	43 Tc	44 Ru	45 Rh	46 Pd	47 Ag	48 Cd	49 In	50 Sn	51 Sb	52 Te	53 I	54 Xe
55 Cs	56 Ba	57 La	72 Hf	73 Ta	74 W	75 Re	76 Os	77 Ir	78 Pt	79 Au	80 Hg	81 Tl	82 Pb	83 Bi	84 Po	85 At	86 Rn
87 Fr	88 Ra	89 Ac	104 Unq	105 Unp	106 Unh	107 Uns	108 Uno	109 Une	110 Unn								

58 Ce	59 Pr	60 Nd	61 Pm	62 Sm	63 Eu	64 Gd	65 Tb	66 Dy	67 Ho	68 Er	69 Tm	70 Yb	71 Lu
90 Th	91 Pa	92 U	93 Np	94 Pu	95 Am	96 Cm	97 Bk	98 Cfr	99 Es	100 Fm	101 Md	102 No	103 Lr

■ = Elements accounting for 99% of the mass of all living things
▢ = Elements accounting for 1% of the mass of all living things

Figure 4-2

Elements essential for life.

All living organisms are composed of about 14 of 118 known elements from the periodic table. Carbon, hydrogen, oxygen, and nitrogen account for about 99% of the mass of all living things. Ten others account for almost all of the remaining 1%.

Matter and Energy

What makes something "alive"? What makes life differ from nonlife?

Why is energy required for life?

Life requires both matter and energy to exist. While this is also true of fire, the nature of matter and energy in living organisms differs in many ways from matter and energy in nonlife.

The matter making up living organisms consists of about 13 of 118 known elements. Carbon, hydrogen, oxygen, and nitrogen account for about 99% of the mass of all living things. Ten others account for almost all of the remaining 1%. Much of the hydrogen and oxygen in life exist in the compound water.

These elements, in various combinations, account for all biological chemicals. These range from very simple sugars to DNA, the most complex known molecule. Scientists recognize more than 1.6 million different species. Some biologists estimate that as many as 30 million may exist. Despite this huge number, all organisms organize matter into biological chemicals and into *cells*. A cell is the smallest whole structure that can be defined as a living system. Some organisms consist of single cells; others consist of billions of codependent cells. Either way, all life organizes matter into cells.

Here's the first way that fire differs from life: Fire consists of matter (gases), but it doesn't consist of cells. It also lacks any other structure that organizes matter in the way that living systems do.

Energy is defined as the capacity to do work. Energy is necessary for life because living systems use it to accomplish the processes of life: reproduction, growth, movement, eating, etc. Organisms need energy to break down complex molecules into simple molecules and to build distinct complex molecules from simple molecules.

The first law of thermodynamics states that energy cannot be created or destroyed. Therefore, although organisms require energy, they cannot create it. They can only transform it from one form to another and use it to perform useful work. All living systems acquire energy from outside sources, which you'll learn more about shortly.

Interestingly, a *machine* is a combination of matter capable of using energy to perform useful work. Does this mean that living

Figure 4-3

What's a "machine"?

A machine is a combination of matter capable of using energy to perform useful work. Therefore, both a submarine and a whale fit this definition. What separates living systems from other machines is that man-made machines are incapable of repairing and reproducing themselves. How would this definition change in the future if man-made machines gain these capabilities? And, what would this mean to the definition of "life"?

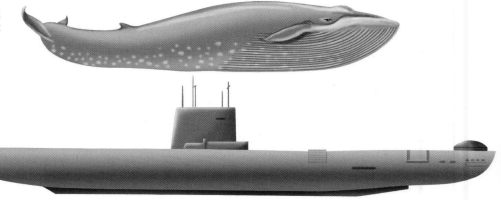

systems are machines? Arguably, yes. They're combinations of matter capable of using energy to perform useful work. What separates living systems from other machines is that they're the only machines known that were *not* created by human beings. And, at least so far, they're the only machines that are capable of reproducing themselves.

This is a second way fire differs from living systems. A fire results from the release of energy, but it is not performing useful work in the sense that it doesn't regulate energy use or matter acquisition to meet its needs. It simply burns the available fuel. A living system uses energy for the processes of life, including creating the organization that fire lacks.

Entropy

What is the second law of thermodynamics?

How does the second law of thermodynamics relate to the process of life?

An important law in physics is the second law of thermodynamics. This law states that disorder increases with the passage of time. It is the law that random processes lead to chaos and simplicity, not order and sophistication. In essence, the second law of thermodynamics says that the universe is "wearing out," or moving toward a state of disorganization.

The second law of thermodynamics is what allows energy to perform work. Energy is useful because it flows from areas of high concentration to areas of low concentration. It is this flow that living systems can harness to perform useful work. Similarly, it is this flow that we use in everyday items, such as an MP3 player. Whenever you use energy, taking it from one form to another to perform work, there's a price. The price is losing the energy as heat. Your MP3 player uses chemical energy from the battery transformed into electrical energy and sound energy. The electrical energy and sound energy ultimately transform into heat through friction.

Eventually all energy and matter will be distributed evenly throughout the universe. The distribution process isn't uniform as it progresses, of course. There are areas with high order and others with low order. *Entropy* (from the Greek *en* and *trepein*, meaning *to change*) is the measure of how much *un*available energy exists in a system due to even distribution. High entropy means low organization and low energy potential.

Because living systems create order, it might seem that life violates the second law of thermodynamics. This isn't the case.

Organisms use energy to organize matter and to gather and store potential (chemical) energy. Within the organism, matter exists in a low-entropy (organized) state. However, life gets energy externally—almost all of it directly or indirectly from the sun. The increased organization is local and temporary, and requires more energy to create than it retains.

A good example of this is protein synthesis within your muscles. It takes about 4,500 kilocalories (calories are an energy measure explained in Chapter 9) for your body to produce 0.45 kilograms (1 pound) of muscle tissue. However, 0.45 kilograms of muscle tissue itself only has about 650 kilocalories of stored chemical energy. About 85% of the energy required to organize protein into complex muscle tissue is ultimately lost as heat in creating the tissue.

This is a third way fire differs from life. Fire consumes energy, but it does not create temporary order within itself. In fact, fire is the opposite. It is the release of energy and the disorganization of matter. It is entropy in action.

ARE YOU LEARNING?

1. **What attributes make life differ from nonlife? (Choose all that apply)**

   A. organizes matter.

   B. uses energy to perform useful work.

   C. uses energy to create temporary order within itself.

   D. obeys the second law of thermodynamics.

2. **Life requires energy**

   A. to accomplish useful work—the processes of life.

   B. because life creates energy.

3. **The second law of thermodynamics says that with the passage of time, disorder increases.**

   A. true

   B. false

4. **Although matter exists in a low-entropy state within an organism, it is local and temporary, and requires more energy to create than it retains.**

   A. true

   B. false

How Matter and Energy Enter Living Systems

STUDY QUESTIONS

Find the answers as you read.

1. What are *autotrophy* and *heterotrophy*?

2. What is *cellular respiration*?

3. What is a *primary producer*?

4. What is *photosynthesis*?

5. How does photosynthesis relate to cellular respiration?

6. What is *chemosynthesis*? How is it similar to and different from photosynthesis?

Autotrophy and Heterotrophy

What are autotrophy *and* heterotrophy?

All living things obtain the matter and energy they need from external sources. Terrestrial organisms and most marine organisms get their energy directly or indirectly from the sun. Energy in the form of sunlight combines with inorganic compounds to become energy-rich organic compounds. These compounds provide energy when living systems break them down during cellular respiration, which you'll learn more about shortly.

Chapter 3 explains that there are organisms called autotrophs that obtain energy from the sun or chemical processes. *Autotrophy* is the process of self-feeding by creating energy-rich compounds called carbohydrates. Plants are autotrophs. They can feed themselves by converting the energy from sunlight and inorganic compounds (matter) into carbohydrates.

Organisms that rely on other organisms for sources of energy and matter are called heterotrophs. Many organisms, including virtually all animals, cannot produce their own carbohydrates. These heterotrophs get their energy and matter by consuming other organisms. This is called *heterotrophy* (from the Greek *heteros* meaning *other* and *trophikos* meaning *nourishment*). You are a heterotroph, of course. Therefore, you get the energy-rich compounds that supply your body with energy by consuming other organisms. You also get most of the matter that makes up your body the same way.

Cellular Respiration

What is cellular respiration?

Whether an organism is an autotroph or a heterotroph, it must convert carbohydrates into usable energy. To do this, most organisms use oxygen to engage in *cellular respiration*. Cellular respiration is the process of releasing energy from carbohydrates to perform the functions of life. (Note that *cellular respiration* differs from *respiration* commonly used to mean *breathing*.) The chemical process for this energy release may be written:

$$C_6H_{12}O_6 + 6O_2 \longrightarrow 6CO_2 + 6H_2O + \text{energy}$$

Figure 4-4

Photosynthesis and cellular respiration.

During photosynthesis, autotrophs use carbon dioxide, water (in a low-energy state), and sun energy to create high-energy carbohydrates. During cellular respiration, they consume oxygen, releasing and using the stored energy. This results in simpler (low-energy) molecules of carbon dioxide and water. Through photosynthesis and cellular respiration, carbon, oxygen, and water recycle continuously from inorganic to organic form.

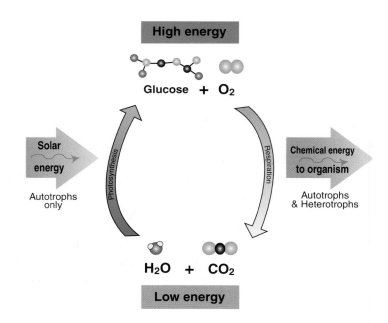

That is, sugar (glucose, a simple carbohydrate) plus oxygen convert to carbon dioxide, water, and energy. This chemical reaction is why you need oxygen to live and why you exhale carbon dioxide. It is part of the process of converting the food you eat into the energy your body uses.

Figure 4-5

The cycle of energy.

Radiant (electromagnetic) energy from the sun is converted into chemical energy through photosynthesis by autotrophs. These are eaten by heterotrophs (and some of the energy is used by the autotrophs themselves), releasing the chemical energy. But, much of that energy is released in the form of waste heat, which eventually dissipates back into space.

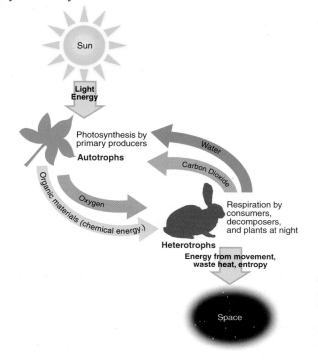

Photosynthesis

What is a primary producer?

What is photosynthesis?

How does photosynthesis relate to cellular respiration?

Because they create energy-rich compounds, autotrophs are also known as *primary producers*. They are the conduits through which the *biosphere* gets almost all its energy. The biosphere is the outer part of the Earth—land, water, and atmosphere—where all organisms live. Primary producers harness only about one two-thousandth of the light reaching Earth, yet this light powers life.

Organisms with *chlorophyll* account for the vast majority of primary producers. Chlorophyll is a compound found in specific plants, bacteria, and other microorganisms. It allows these organisms to capture sunlight energy to produce carbohydrates from inorganic material. These include simple carbohydrates called sugars (*saccharides*), such as glucose. Complex carbohydrates are long sugar chains called *polysaccharides*, commonly called starches.

The process of using light energy to create carbohydrates from inorganic compounds is called *photosynthesis* (from the Greek *photo* meaning *light*, and *syn + tithenai* meaning *to place together*). Carbohydrates consist of carbon, hydrogen, and oxygen. During photosynthesis, organisms use light energy to disassemble carbon dioxide and water molecules, rebuilding them into carbohydrates. Because carbon dioxide and water have more oxygen than is needed to make carbohydrates, the process also releases oxygen.

Note that even organisms with chlorophyll respire. They create carbohydrates through photosynthesis, then use the carbohydrates for the energy they need in the processes of life. If you look at photosynthesis, you can see that it is a complementary process to cellular respiration:

$$6CO_2 + 6H_2O + \text{light energy} \longrightarrow C_6H_{12}O_6 + 6O_2$$

Thus, during photosynthesis, autotrophs use carbon dioxide, water, and sun energy to create high-energy carbohydrates. During cellular respiration, they consume oxygen and release low-energy carbon dioxide. Through photosynthesis and cellular respiration, carbon, oxygen, and water recycle continuously from inorganic to organic form and back.

Cellular respiration as described above is *aerobic respiration*, meaning respiration that uses oxygen. Some organisms exist in environments without oxygen through anaerobic respiration.

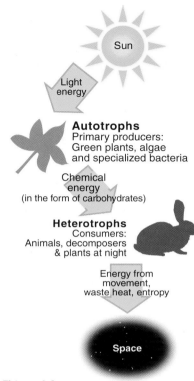

Figure 4-6

Energy transfer.

Most life on Earth is "solar powered." Energy from the sun is converted into chemical energy (food) by producers (autotrophs). Consumers (heterotrophs) capture the chemical energy through respiration. Eventually, most of the energy is converted to heat and dissipates into space.

Topic: Photosynthesis
Go To: www.scilinks.org
Code: LOP2075

Figure 4-7

The energy cycle.

(A) shows a generalization of how energy is required to assemble (synthesize) complex molecules. The complex molecules (food) are broken down through cellular respiration, releasing their energy for use by the cell. The result is, once again, simple molecules, and the cycle continues.

In **(B)**, note that the energy is supplied by the sun. The simple molecules are carbon dioxide and water. Through photosynthesis, the sun's radiant energy is transformed into chemical energy contained in the bonds holding together the complex glucose molecule.

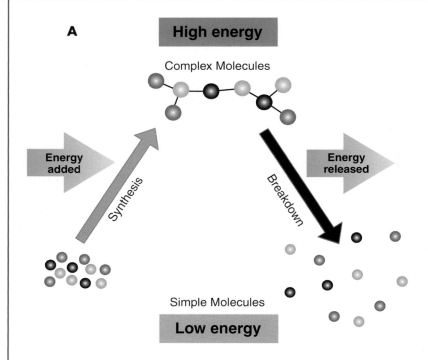

Anaerobic respiration releases energy for the processes of life through chemical reactions that do not require oxygen. Anaerobic respiration is not as efficient as aerobic respiration.

Without primary production—the photosynthesis in plants, bacteria, and other microorganisms all over the world—you would not have the oxygen you need for cellular respiration.

You would also not have the carbohydrates you need for energy. Humans, along with all other heterotrophs, rely on photosynthesizing plants, bacteria, and other microorganisms for life. This dependency is one reason why the health of the natural environment is a crucial issue. If pollution, deforestation, and other negative effects of humanity kill a substantial portion of the primary producers, it would compromise the ability for all other life to exist—including you.

Energy captured by photosynthesis powers life processes, including growth, repair, movement, and reproduction. The sun's energy moves from one organism to the next as heterotrophs consume autotrophs or other heterotrophs. Ultimately, the carbohydrates break down as they give up energy to life processes, turning into waste heat (entropy). The waste heat eventually emanates back into space.

Chemosynthesis

What is chemosynthesis? *How is it similar to and different from photosynthesis?*

Most primary producers use sunlight energy to produce carbohydrates. But, not all the energy used by living systems comes directly or indirectly from the sun. Some primary producers use *chemosynthesis*. Chemosynthesis is the process of using chemicals to create energy-rich organic compounds. Chemosynthesis is similar to photosynthesis because it produces carbohydrates. Both chemosynthesis and photosynthesis are forms of *fixation*. Fixation is the process of converting, or *fixing*, an inorganic compound into a usable organic compound. Chemosynthesis and photosynthesis fix carbon into carbohydrates.

Chemosynthesis differs from photosynthesis because it does not use sunlight as an energy source. Instead, it uses chemical energy within inorganic compounds. It's not as efficient as photosynthesis, and whereas the waste product of photosynthesis is oxygen, the waste products of chemosynthesis are different.

Although the existence of chemosynthesis has been known for some time, in 1977, scientists diving in the submersible *Alvin* discovered communities living around volcanic springs (hydrothermal vents) in the deep ocean. These communities live well below

Ocean Explorer, NOAA

Figure 4-8

A surprising discovery. Discovered only in the late 1970s, hydrothermal vent communities are not based on photosynthesis (light energy), but on chemosynthesis (chemical energy). The discovery of hydrothermal vent communities was one of the most important in the history of oceanography.

Topic: Chemosynthesis
Go To: www.scilinks.org
Code: LOP2080

the reach of sunlight and rely on chemical energy from minerals in the hot spring water. This was an important discovery of a major biological community relying on chemosynthesis. In addition, there are "cold seep" chemosynthetic communities, where primitive single-cell organisms use methane from seeps on the sea bottom. This process traps a lot of potential carbon dioxide, which is an issue with respect to climate change.

ARE YOU LEARNING?

1. **Heterotrophy refers to those organisms that must get their energy from other organisms.**

   A. true

   B. false

2. **Cellular respiration is**

   A. the act of breathing.

   B. the conversion of carbohydrate to usable energy.

   C. not carried out by primary producers.

   D. Both A and B

3. **Primary producers are**

   A. organisms that create energy-rich compounds.

   B. organisms that must get all their energy from other organisms.

4. **Photosynthesis is the process of converting light energy into carbon dioxide.**

   A. true

   B. false

5. **Photosynthesis is the production of high-energy compounds from light and low-energy compounds. Cellular respiration is the release of energy from high-energy compounds as they convert into low-energy compounds.**

   A. true

   B. false

6. **Chemosynthesis is similar to photosynthesis because it uses sunlight, but different because it doesn't produce carbohydrates.**

   A. true

   B. false

The Ocean's Primary Productivity

So far in this chapter, you've learned how energy enters living systems. In the marine environment, two variables affect the availability of energy. One is quantity of primary production and the other is the flow of energy. Let's start with quantity—the total energy primary producers bring into the ocean—because this dictates how much life can exist there. We'll look at the flow of energy in the next section.

Marine Biomass

What is the main "product" of primary production? How do scientists measure it?

What is biomass? *What is a* standing crop?

How do the primary productivities of land and ocean ecosystems compare?

Earlier you learned that photosynthesis and chemosynthesis are both forms of fixation. Both processes fix carbon into an energy-rich, usable form. Specifically, both processes take carbon from carbon dioxide and, using light or chemical energy, create carbohydrates.

Therefore, the main "products" of primary production are carbohydrates. Carbohydrates are the primary units of usable energy in living systems, plus a source of carbon used in an organism's tissues. Scientists measure primary productivity in terms of the carbon fixed (bound) into organic material. The unit of measurement of primary productivity is grams of carbon per square meter of surface area per year. This is abbreviated as $gC/m^2/yr$. Using this measure, the oceans' primary productivity averages from 75 to 150$gC/m^2/yr$.

Comparing the primary production of the seas to the primary production of the land, we find that the land's is slightly higher. The estimate for terrestrial productivity is about 50 to 70 billion metric tons of carbon annually. The estimated primary production from all marine ecosystems is 35 to 50 billion metric tons of carbon annually.

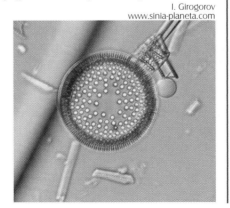

I. Girogorov
www.sinia-planeta.com

Find the answers as you read.

1. What is the main "product" of primary production? How do scientists measure it?

2. What is *biomass*? What is a *standing crop*?

3. How do the primary productivities of land and ocean ecosystems compare?

4. What is *plankton*? What is the difference between phytoplankton and zooplankton?

5. What organisms are responsible for most of the primary production in the sea?

6. What is a *diatom*?

7. What is a *dinoflagellate*?

8. What is a *coccolithophore*?

9. What is *picoplankton*? What is its role in primary productivity?

10. What are *cyanobacteria*?

11. What is a *limiting factor*?

12. How do nutrient availability and other variables in tropical, polar, and temperate ocean regions affect primary productivity? What ocean regions have the most primary productivity?

13. How does light availability affect primary production?

14. What is *compensation depth*? Why is it significant to primary production in the ocean?

Figure 4-9

Primary production in the sea.

Phytoplankton (shown here is a diatom) account for between 92% and 96% of the oceans' primary productivity.

Topic: Ocean Productivity
Go To: www.scilinks.org
Code: LOP2090

Primary production is an important issue in food production, both on land and in the sea. Because primary production brings energy and matter into the biosphere, it is one factor that determines how much food an environment produces. Based on the figures, then, you might think that land-based food production would be the most efficient. However, marine and terrestrial systems differ with respect to the *biomass* of the primary producers. Biomass is the mass of living tissue. The biomass at a given time is called the *standing crop*. Scientists express both terms as mass.

Typically, the standing crop in the ocean is one to two billion metric tons. On land, the standing crop is 600 to 1,000 billion metric

Figure 4-10

Primary productivity of some terrestrial and marine ecosystems.

Net primary productivity is a way of quantifying how much food autotrophs produce for consumption over the course of a year. This may be a difficult concept to grasp, so visualize one apple as containing about 50 grams of carbon. As you see, marine communities, particularly coral reefs and kelp forests, are among Earth's most productive ecosystems.

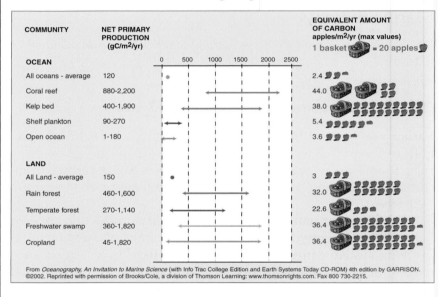

COMMUNITY	NET PRIMARY PRODUCTION (gC/m²/yr)	EQUIVALENT AMOUNT OF CARBON apples/m²/yr (max values) 1 basket = 20 apples
OCEAN		
All oceans - average	120	2.4
Coral reef	880-2,200	44.0
Kelp bed	400-1,900	38.0
Shelf plankton	90-270	5.4
Open ocean	1-180	3.6
LAND		
All Land - average	150	3
Rain forest	460-1,600	32.0
Temperate forest	270-1,140	22.6
Freshwater swamp	360-1,820	36.4
Cropland	45-1,820	36.4

From *Oceanography, An Invitation to Marine Science* (with Info Trac College Edition and Earth Systems Today CD-ROM) 4th edition by GARRISON. ©2002. Reprinted with permission of Brooks/Cole, a division of Thomson Learning: www.thomsonrights.com. Fax 800 730-2215.

tons. This is a huge difference in the average standing crops. So, how is it possible that the total primary production from marine ecosystems is only a bit less than that of terrestrial ecosystems?

The answer is that the marine ecosystem cycles its energy and nutrients much more rapidly. Hundreds of generations of *phytoplankton* (the sea's most important primary producers—more about these organisms shortly) will grow, be consumed, and pass their energy up through the trophic pyramid during the lifetime of a single land plant. The rate of this photosynthesis-respiration cycle is called *turnover*. Marine turnover is much shorter than terrestrial turnover. The shorter the turnover time, the faster the standing crop passes energy into the ecosystem.

In discussing primary productivity, scientists differentiate between *gross primary productivity* and *net primary productivity*. Gross primary productivity is the measure of all the organic material produced in an area by autotrophs. The primary producers use some of the energy for their own life processes and convert the rest into biomass (tissue and other organic material). Net primary productivity is the quantity of energy remaining after autotrophs have satisfied their respiratory needs.

COMPARISON OF NET PRIMARY PRODUCTIVITY IN MARINE AND LAND-BASED ECOSYSTEMS

Ecosystem	Net Primary Productivity (One billion metric tons/year)	Total Plant Biomass (One billion grams)	Turnover (years)
Marine	35-50	1-2	0.02-0.06
Terrestrial	50-70	600-1,000	9-20

From Oceanography, An Invitation to Marine Science (with Info Trac College Edition and Earth Systems Today CD-ROM) 4th edition by GARRISON ©2002. Reprinted with permission of Brooks/Cole, a division of Thomson Learning: www.thomsonrights.com. Fax 800 730-2215.

Figure 4-11

Net primary productivity.
Comparison of net primary productivity in marine and land-based ecosystems.

Plankton

What is plankton? *What is the difference between* phytoplankton *and* zooplankton?

What organisms are responsible for most of the primary production in the sea?

What is a diatom?

What is a dinoflagellate?

What is a coccolithophore?

What is picoplankton? *What is its role in primary productivity?*

What are cyanobacteria?

No discussion of primary productivity is complete without a look at plankton because many are vital marine autotrophs. You may already have an idea of what plankton is from Chapter 3. You've also learned the basic definitions of phytoplankton and zooplankton. Chapter 3 also discussed the neuston as the plankton subgroup that floats at the surface.

Plankton drift or swim weakly in the ocean and are at the mercy of currents, tides, and other water motion. It's important to know that plankton are not a species, but include many species from virtually every major group of organisms found in the sea. Most are very small, but some, such as the jellyfish, grow several meters long. Some organisms start life as planktonic larvae and then leave the plankton community as they grow large enough to

Florida Fish and Wildlife Conservation Commission's Fish and Wildlife Research Institute

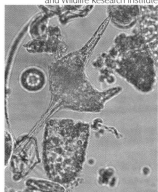

Figure 4-12

Plankton defined.

The term "plankton" doesn't describe a kind of organism, but a group of organisms with a common lifestyle and habitat. Plankton include autotrophs and heterotrophs, as well as predators and grazers.

swim as nektonic organisms or attach themselves to the bottom as benthic organisms.

The term "plankton," therefore, doesn't describe a kind of organism, but a group of organisms with a common lifestyle and habitat. Plankton include autotrophs and heterotrophs, as well as predators and grazers.

You already know that plankton consists of phytoplankton and zooplankton. Phytoplankton are primary producers because they photosynthesize. *Zooplankton* are primary and secondary consumers that feed on phytoplankton and other heterotrophic plankton.

The most important primary producers in the sea are phytoplankton. Phytoplankton account for between 92% and 96% of the oceans' primary productivity. Marine plants, kelp, and other multicellular photosynthesizing organisms account for only 2% to 5%, with the remainder from deep ocean chemosynthesis. Biologists are still trying to determine how much chemosynthesis contributes to primary production, which may be much higher than they currently think.

Because phytoplankton are responsible for more than 92% of marine primary production, let's focus on four of the most important kinds.

Diatoms are the most efficient photosynthesizers known. They convert more than half the light energy they absorb into carbohydrate chemical energy. There are thousands of known species, including bottom-dwelling (benthic) and planktonic species.

NOAA

Figure 4-13

Capturing plankton with nets.

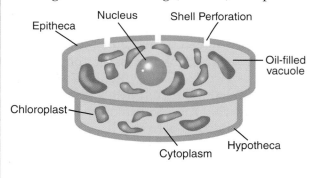

Epitheca · Nucleus · Shell Perforation · Oil-filled vacuole · Chloroplast · Cytoplasm · Hypotheca

Frustule

Figure 4-14

Marine autotrophs.

Diatoms are the most dominant and productive of the phytoplankton. They live inside a structure (frustule) made of silica. This helps make diatoms some of the most efficient photosynthesizers on Earth. Oil vacuoles help resist the tendency to sink.

Diatoms are the most dominant and productive of the phytoplankton. They are photosynthetic organisms characterized by a rigid cell wall made of silica. This cell wall, called a *frustule*, admits light much like glass. This is an ideal cell material for a photosynthesizer.

The second most abundant phytoplankton are the *dinoflagellates*. Dinoflagellates are (in most species) characterized by one or two whip-like *flagella*, which they move to change orientation or to swim vertically in the water. Most, but not all species of dinoflagellates are autotrophs. Besides planktonic species, other dinoflagellate species live within coral polyps and are the most significant primary producers in the coral reef community. Because they can reproduce rapidly, dinoflagellates are the principal organisms responsible for plankton blooms.

Coccolithophores are single-cell autotrophs characterized by shells of calcium carbonate. The shells are called *coccoliths*. Coccolithophores live in brightly lit, shallow water and in the tropics. It's hypothesized that their translucent coccoliths protect them by screening the light. Areas with high coccolithophore concentrations may appear milky or chalky.

Microbial Plankton Ecology – Microbial plankton ecology is now one of the most important topics in marine biology. Besides the larger phytoplankton, scientists are concentrating studies on extremely tiny marine bacteria, *archaea* and *viruses*. Oceanographers have found that each liter of seawater contains approximately 5 billion bacteria and archaea cells, and many more viruses. There are 100 million times more bacteria in the ocean than stars in the known universe, and there are a thousand times more viruses than bacteria. The total mass of bacteria in the ocean is thought to exceed the combined mass of zooplankton and fishes. Further, if marine viruses were stretched end to end they would span 10 million light years. In context, the total mass of carbon in viruses is equivalent to the mass of carbon in 75 million blue whales.

Traditionally, marine biologists considered tropical regions relatively unproductive. This view has now changed with an understanding of the role of *picoplankton* – extremely tiny (microbial) plankton with sizes between 0.2 and 2 micrometers. This community may account for as much as 79% of the photosynthesis in tropical waters and other marine habitats.

Many picoplankton are *cyanobacteria*, which are bacteria with chlorophyll. Recent research suggests that picoplankton play a significant role in producing oxygen and taking up carbon dioxide. The cyanobacteria are the most common type of bacteria in the ocean.

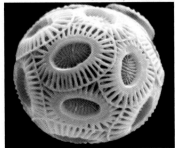

Gustaaf Hallegraeff, University of Tasmania

Figure 4-15

Coccolithophore.

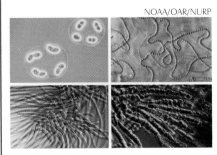

NOAA/OAR/NURP

Figure 4-16

The picoplankton.
Many picoplankton are cyanobacteria, which are bacteria with chlorophyll.

Stephen Giovannoni, Department of Microbiology, Oregon State University

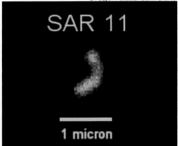

Figure 4-17

The SAR 11 marine bacteria.

The cyanobacteria are the most common type of bacteria in the ocean, and SAR 11 is the most common organism on earth. This organism accounts for roughly 25% of all the bacteria in the ocean.

PADI

Figure 4-18

Coral reef productivity.

Coral reefs are efficient ecosystems with very little nutrient loss to the open sea. Unlike most marine ecosystems, which rely on phytoplankton as their primary autotrophs, coral reefs rely on dinoflagellate autotrophs that live within the coral tissue. The relative lack of suspended nutrients and plankton is one of the reasons why there is typically clear water around coral reefs.

A bacterium called SAR 11 (*Pelagibacter clade*) is the most common organism on Earth, accounting for roughly 25% of all the bacteria in the ocean. *Prochlorococcus* and *Synechoccus* species dominate the microbial ecology of the ocean. Yet, they were mostly unknown until Sallie W. Chisholm, a professor at the Massachusetts Institute of Technology, first discovered *Prochloroccus* in 1988. Chapter 5 discusses more about marine bacteria, archea, cyanobacteria, and viruses.

In a sense, picoplankton productivity is unproductive. This is because they're too small for consumption by larger consumers in the food web. Instead, heterotrophic bacteria consume them and return the nutrients to their inorganic form. Picoplankton primary productivity contributes very little to the food webs larger organisms rely on. However, recent research suggests that picoplankton play a significant role in producing oxygen, taking up carbon dioxide, producing nitrogen compounds, and even producing vitamins necessary for marine organisms.

Limits on Marine Primary Productivity

What is a limiting factor?

How do nutrient availability and other variables in tropical, polar, and temperate ocean regions affect primary productivity? What ocean regions have the most primary productivity?

How does light availability affect primary production?

What is compensation depth? *Why is it significant to primary production in the ocean?*

Just from looking around on land, it's obvious that organisms are more common in some places than in others. The same is true in the ocean. Different areas have differing limiting factors. *Limiting factors* are physiological or biological necessities that restrict survival. Too much or too little of a limiting factor will reduce the population of an organism.

Most autotrophs require water, carbon dioxide, inorganic nutrients, and sunlight. In the ocean, water and carbon dioxide are almost never limiting factors. Inorganic nutrients such as nitrogen and phosphorus compounds, on the other hand, can be limiting factors. Sunlight can be a limiting factor due to season, depth, or water clarity.

Several factors can limit the availability of inorganic nutrients. A *plankton bloom* can deplete the nutrients available in a region. Plankton blooms are periods of very fast growth of numbers of a particular plankton species. The bloom deprives other species, the plankton, and themselves of nutrients by consuming them too rapidly.

In extreme cases, plankton blooms consume all the oxygen and release toxic by-products in such amounts that fish and other organisms cannot survive. Often the general public calls such events "*red tides.*" However, not all of these events are red, nor are they associated with tides. Marine scientists call them *Harmful Algal Blooms*, or HABs. Chapter 18 goes into more detail about these.

Plankton blooms occur naturally, but they may also be caused when pollution supplies a nutrient that is normally limited. Nutrient-rich pollution removes nutrients as a limiting factor, allowing the plankton to overpopulate.

Depth can limit nutrients. Dead organisms that would normally provide nutrients can sink below depths that sunlight can reach, making their nutrients unavailable to photosynthesizers. This creates a limiting factor until normal water motion brings the nutrients back to shallower water. However, water temperature can interfere with normal mixing. Waters of different temperatures resist mixing because they have different densities, which sets up a thermocline. This thermocline often traps nutrients in cold, deep water. Tropical waters tend to have low productivity because although there's ample sunlight and carbon dioxide, the warm upper water layer traps nutrients in the cold layers that are too deep for photosynthesizing autotrophs. To learn more about water layers in the ocean, see Chapter 9.

On the other hand, in the Arctic and Antarctic, there's little temperature difference between shallow and deep water, allowing nutrients to cycle to shallower water more easily. In temperate regions, coastal areas tend to have more primary productivity because there are more nutrients from rain run-off and because shallow water keeps them from sinking below the productive zone. Water movement also brings up nutrients from deep water. Chapter 8 provides more information about this process.

Besides depth, location can affect productivity. Coral reefs are an important exception to the low productivity of tropical waters. Coral reefs are the most efficient ecosystems on Earth. Unlike most marine ecosystems, which rely on phytoplankton as their primary autotrophs, coral reefs rely on dinoflagellates that live within coral tissue. This is a topic you can learn more about in Chapter 5.

Figure 4-19

Overview of yearly global phytoplankton production (primary productivity).

Note the concentration in near-shore regions, and moderate levels throughout extensive regions of the southern ocean. There is also high productivity off of Antarctica, but it is limited to the near continuous daylight conditions of late spring and early summer.

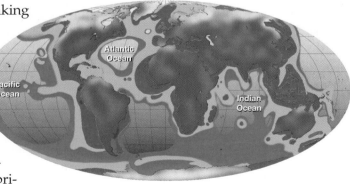

Phytoplankton Production (gC/m²/year)

■ 100 or Less ■ 101-150 ■ 151-250 ■ 251-500 ■ 501 or More

Source: Copyright © 2003 McGraw Hill Companies, Inc.

Although coral reefs are very efficient ecosystems, they make up less than 1% of the ocean's surface area. And, the coral reef recycles its nutrients efficiently, with very little loss to the open sea.

The regions extending westward from northern South America and northern Africa are also an exception to the relatively low productivity typical of tropical waters. These regions receive nutrients and cooler water from currents upwelling from deeper in the ocean. This is a topic you can learn more about in Chapter 11.

Some of the highest productivity takes place in the Antarctic Convergence Zone. Productivity can be well over $200gC/m^2/year$. Long summer days, water movement bringing nutrients to shallow water, and mineral runoff, cause explosive productivity. However, the short summer season makes this high productivity short-lived. Interestingly, the Arctic doesn't have comparable productivity intervals because the Arctic lacks a landmass comparable to the Antarctic. Without the landmass, there are fewer minerals in Arctic waters.

In temperate regions, productivity fluctuates with the seasons. During the summer, a warm-water upper layer traps nutrients in deeper water, but this layer disappears in the winter. Water motion from winter storms allows deep water nutrients to return to shallower water. During the spring, longer daylight hours combine with these nutrients for explosive phytoplankton growth.

Because of nutrient availability, the greatest total primary productivity occurs in near-shore temperate regions and southern subpolar waters. Typical productivity in the temperate zone is $120gC/m^2/yr$.

Besides nutrients, another factor that can affect primary productivity is light. The example of the Antarctic Convergence Zone demonstrates this factor. Although the zone has optimum nutrient availability, seasonal sunlight limits its productivity. The amount of daylight affects photosynthesis and primary productivity.

Depth also affects photosynthesis and primary productivity. Chapter 9 covers more about how water absorbs light, but the deeper the water, the less light is available. Suspended particles and the light's angle limit how much light penetrates water. Even in very clear water, little photosynthesis takes place below 100 meters (328 feet). Too much light can be an issue, too. *Photoinhibition* takes place when too much light overwhelms an autotroph. Therefore, some autotrophs cannot photosynthesize when the water is too shallow. Different phytoplankton species have different optimal depths. As light conditions change, the advantage shifts from species to species.

Autotrophs produce carbohydrates and oxygen during photosynthesis, but as you recall, they also respire. They use the carbohydrates they produce, as well as some oxygen, for cellular respiration. The less light there is, the less photosynthesis occurs, reducing carbo-

hydrate production. As you go deeper, therefore, autotrophs produce less carbohydrate.

At some point, the amount of carbohydrates produced exactly equals the amount required by the autotrophs for cellular respiration. This point of zero net primary production is called the *compensation depth*. The autotrophs lack sufficient energy to reproduce (in meaningful amounts), so there's no food source to pass energy up the food web. The compensation depth is typically the depth at which about 1% of the surface light penetrates.

The compensation depth varies with water clarity, surface disturbances, and sun angle. If phytoplankton remain below the compensation depth for more than a few days, they will die as they consume the available carbohydrate more quickly than they create it. This situation occurs during red tide and harmful algal blooms. Red tide and algal blooms can abruptly block light from penetrating more than a few meters. When conditions don't change within a couple of days, the loss of light begins killing deeper phytoplankton. This causes local primary productivity to fall, removing the food source for the ecosystem.

INTERNET PORTAL
SC*LINKS*. NSTA
Topic: Harmful Algae Blooms
Go To: www.scilinks.org
Code: LOP2100

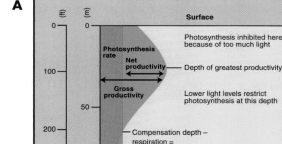

Source: Falkowski and Raren, 1997. *Oceanography—An Invitation to Marine Science*, by Garrison. Reprinted with permission, copyright © 2002 Thomson Learning, Inc.

Figure 4-20a

The compensation depth.

(A) The compensation depth is the point where the production of carbohydrates by autotrophs exactly equals the amount they require for cellular respiration. At this point there is no "surplus" to pass up the food web; it is defined as the point where 1% of the surface light remains.

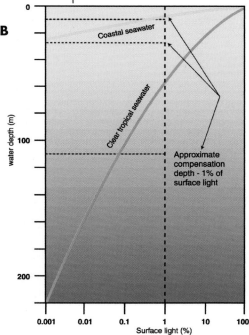

Figure 4-20b

The compensation depth.

(B) The compensation depth has no set point. Note that it can be very shallow in turbid coastal waters and very deep in the clear waters of the tropics.

1. **The primary product of primary production is_____. Scientists express measurements of it as _____.**

   A. carbohydrates, grams of carbon per square meter of surface area per year

   B. carbon, parts per thousand

   C. oxygen, grams per square meter of surface per year

   D. oxygen, parts per thousand

2. **Biomass means _____. Standing crop is the _____ in an ecosystem.**

   A. mass of living tissue, mass of primary consumers at a given time

   B. mass of primary consumers, mass of living tissue

   C. mass of living tissue at a given time, mass of living tissue

   D. mass of living tissue, mass of living tissue at a given time

3. **The primary production of land is higher than the primary production of the sea, but the sea's primary production is much more efficient.**

   A. true

   B. false

4. **Plankton describes**

   A. a particular species of organisms.

   B. a wide variety of organisms that share a habitat and lifestyle.

5. **Most primary production in the sea is from**

   A. algae.

   B. phytoplankton.

   C. zooplankton.

6. **A diatom is an organism characterized by**

   A. a rigid cell wall made of silica.

   B. a silica internal supporting structure.

   C. a calcium carbonate shell.

   D. two flagella.

7. **A dinoflagellate is an organism characterized by**

   A. a rigid cell wall made of silica.

   B. a silica internal supporting structure.

   C. a calcium carbonate shell.

   D. one or two flagella.

8. **A coccolithophore is an organism characterized by**

   A. a rigid cell wall made of silica.

   B. a silica internal supporting structure.

   C. a calcium carbonate shell.

   D. three flagella.

9. **Picoplankton are very small plankton, including bacteria and viruses.**

   A. true

   B. false

10. **Cyanobacteria are (choose all that apply)**

    A. picoplankton.

    B. the most common type of bacteria in the ocean.

    C. important in producing oxygen and taking up carbon dioxide.

11. **Limiting factors are**

    A. physiological or biological necessities that affect survival.

    B. the genetics that restrict an organism's maximum size.

12. **The ocean regions with the most primary productivity are**

    A. tropical regions.

    B. coastal temperate regions and subpolar regions.

13. **For the most part, the less light, the _____ primary productivity.**

    A. more

    B. less

14. **Compensation depth is the depth at which**

    A. the oxygen produced by autotrophs equals the oxygen they need for cellular respiration.

    B. the autotrophs compensate for too much oxygen through accelerated cellular respiration.

Energy Flow Through the Biosphere

Trophic Relationships

What is a trophic pyramid? *What is the relationship of organisms within a trophic pyramid?*

What is a primary consumer?

What is a secondary consumer?

Energy enters living systems and the biosphere through the primary production of autotrophs. Heterotrophs get their energy by consuming autotrophs or other heterotrophs. Energy flows through the biosphere when other heterotrophs consume these het-

STUDY QUESTIONS

Find the answers as you read.

1. What is a *trophic pyramid*? What is the relationship of organisms within a trophic pyramid?

2. What is a *primary consumer*?

3. What is a *secondary consumer*?

4. What happens to available energy at each level of a trophic pyramid?

5. What is a *food web*?

6. Why is it important that decomposition convert organic material back to an inorganic form?

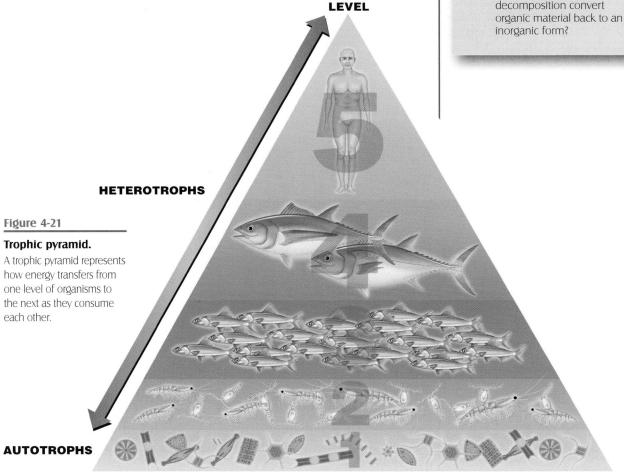

TROPHIC LEVEL

HETEROTROPHS

AUTOTROPHS

Figure 4-21

Trophic pyramid.

A trophic pyramid represents how energy transfers from one level of organisms to the next as they consume each other.

erotrophs. The hierarchy of what-eats-what can be illustrated with a *trophic pyramid*, which is simply a representation of how energy transfers from one level of organisms to the next as they consume each other.

Primary producers (mainly photosynthesizers) make up the pyramid base. As discussed previously, in the ocean, the phytoplankton are the most important primary producers.

The first level of heterotrophs eat the primary producers and photosynthesizing bacteria. These organisms are called *primary consumers*. *Herbivore* is a term given to those first level heterotrophs (animals) that exclusively eat plants.

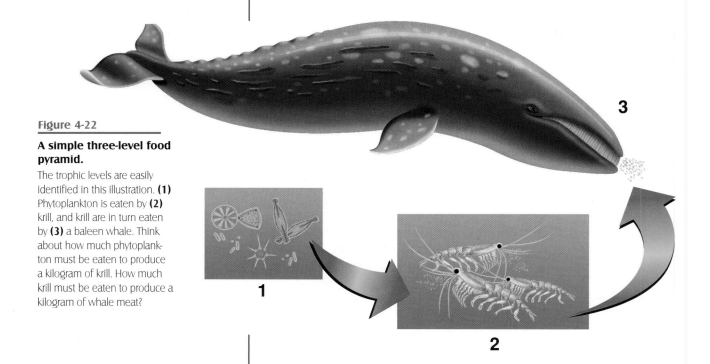

Figure 4-22

A simple three-level food pyramid.

The trophic levels are easily identified in this illustration. **(1)** Phytoplankton is eaten by **(2)** krill, and krill are in turn eaten by **(3)** a baleen whale. Think about how much phytoplankton must be eaten to produce a kilogram of krill. How much krill must be eaten to produce a kilogram of whale meat?

In the ocean, most phytoplankton are so small that the most important primary consumers are the zooplankton. Zooplankton are marine planktonic animals that eat phytoplankton or other heterotrophic plankton.

The next level includes the *secondary consumers*, which eat the primary consumers. In the ocean, secondary consumers feed primarily on zooplankton. There are additional levels of consumers above the secondary level. Each level in the pyramid eats the organisms of the level below it.

Energy Loss Through Trophic Levels

What happens to available energy at each level of a trophic pyramid?

Each level in the pyramid has significantly less biomass than the level below. This is important because energy is lost to entropy as each level uses energy in its life processes. The loss of energy from one level to the next is substantial. Only about 10% of the energy from one level transfers to the next. For this reason, each level is only about a tenth the size of the level below. At each level, 90% of the energy is lost to entropy.

As you can see, food fishes like tunas tend be quite high on the pyramid. Because they are high on the pyramid, there's a significant energy loss between tunas and primary producers.

It takes approximately 10,000 kilograms of primary producers to create every kilogram of tuna. This isn't just a biological curiosity. It is a significant economic and environmental issue influencing how human society feeds itself.

Consider a land-based example. If you eat a vegetable, you're eating a primary producer with only one level of energy loss. Cattle are primary consumers, so eating beef has two levels of energy loss. Tuna has *five* levels of energy loss. It takes a staggeringly high level of primary production to get a given amount of tuna versus vegetable or beef. As we face the issue of feeding the swelling human population, determining the most energy-efficient means of food production becomes increasingly more critical. This is an issue revisited in Chapter 17 concerning the topic of aquaculture – farming the sea. But, as you'll learn shortly, trophic levels aren't the only factors involved with this issue.

Food Webs

What is a food web?

The problem with a trophic pyramid is that it is only a simple model. It is a way to illustrate different levels of consumers and energy flow, but in real life different organisms consume across levels, not just the level below. You may be a good example. When you eat corn you're a primary consumer. When you eat beef or chicken you're a secondary consumer, and when you eat fish you may be a fifth-level consumer.

The concept of a *food web* better represents the flow of energy through consumption in nature. A food web shows that organisms often have different choices of prey and eat across the trophic pyramid's theoretical levels.

INTERNET PORTAL

SCiLINKS. NSTA

Topic: Food Chain/Web
Go To: www.scilinks.org
Code: LOP2085

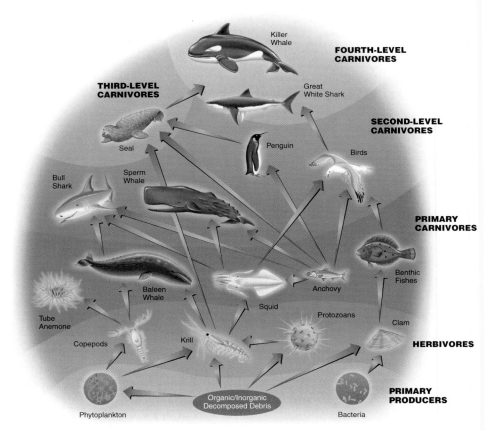

Figure 4-23

Food web.

Trophic (feeding) relationships are much more complex than a simple "chain" of one organism eating another; the concept of a food web better represents reality. It shows that organisms often have different choices of prey and eat across the trophic pyramid's theoretical levels.

Labels in figure: Killer Whale; FOURTH-LEVEL CARNIVORES; THIRD-LEVEL CARNIVORES; Great White Shark; SECOND-LEVEL CARNIVORES; Seal; Penguin; Birds; Bull Shark; Sperm Whale; PRIMARY CARNIVORES; Benthic Fishes; Anchovy; Baleen Whale; Squid; Protozoans; Clam; Tube Anemone; Copepods; Krill; HERBIVORES; Organic/Inorganic Decomposed Debris; PRIMARY PRODUCERS; Phytoplankton; Bacteria

Decomposition

Why is it important that decomposition convert organic material back to an inorganic form?

Decomposers break down organic material into inorganic form. These organisms take out the last remnants of usable energy from organic matter to sustain themselves. Primarily bacteria and fungi, they convert dead organisms and other organic waste into the compounds primary producers use. Decomposition is important because it completes the cycle of nutrients and matter. It renews the inorganic materials (matter) necessary for energy to enter life through primary production. Remember that within systems, energy *flows* and matter *cycles*.

Bacteria and *archaea*, both very simple organisms, are the most important decomposers. On average, there are 10^9 (1 billion) bacteria per liter of seawater. They are the most abundant organisms on Earth. Although you can't see these microbes, they are essential to life as decomposers (and as primary producers). Marine scientists have yet to fully understand how archaea take in nutrients, multiply, or what ecological role they play. Chapter 5 covers more about bacteria and archaea.

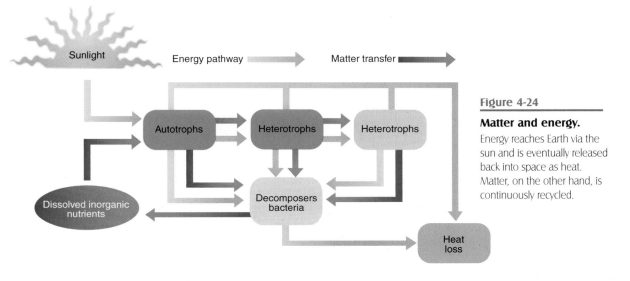

Figure 4-24

Matter and energy.
Energy reaches Earth via the sun and is eventually released back into space as heat. Matter, on the other hand, is continuously recycled.

ARE YOU LEARNING?

1. A trophic pyramid is

A. a representation of how energy transfers from one level of organisms to another.

B. a physical structure that directs food energy for cellular respiration.

2. A primary consumer is

A. an organism that photosynthesizes.

B. an organism that consumes primary producers.

C. an organism that consumes secondary consumers.

3. A secondary consumer is

A. an organism that photosynthesizes.

B. an organism that consumes primary producers.

C. an organism that consumes primary consumers.

4. About _____ of available energy transfers from each level of the trophic pyramid to the next.

A. 50%

B. 30%

C. 10%

D. 5%

5. A food web represents the flow of energy in nature better than a trophic pyramid because

A. organisms often eat across the theoretical levels of the trophic pyramid.

B. scientists don't really know what organisms consume.

6. Decomposition is essential to life because through it

A. organic compounds are recycled into organic energy that primary consumers use.

B. organic compounds are recycled into the inorganic compounds that primary producers use.

New Terms You Learned

- **aerobic respiration** respiration that uses oxygen in the release of energy (p. 4-9)
- **anaerobic respiration** respiration that does not use oxygen in the release of energy (p. 4-10)
- **Antarctic Convergence Zone** an area located at approximately 50° to 60° south latitude where the nutrient rich Antarctic water sinks under the warmer water of the more northern ocean (p. 4-20)
- **Archaea** domain of prokaryotes consisting of primitive organisms noted for being extremophiles (p. 4-17)
- **autotrophy** the process of self-feeding by producing energy-rich organic compounds (carbohydrates) (p. 4-7)
- **biomass** the mass of living tissue; tissue and other organic material created by living systems (p. 4-14)
- **biosphere** the outer part of the Earth—land, water and atmosphere—where all organisms live; the habitable space on Earth (p. 4-9)
- **carbohydrate** an organic compound derived from carbon, hydrogen, and oxygen that is an important source of food and energy for organisms; the primary units of usable energy in living systems and a source of carbon used in an organism's tissues (p. 4-9)
- **cell** the smallest whole structure that can be defined as a living system (p. 4-4)
- **cellular respiration** the process of releasing energy from carbohydrates to perform the functions of life (p. 4-7)
- **chemosynthesis** the process of using chemicals to create energy-rich organic compounds, such as carbohydrates (p. 4-11)
- **chlorophyll** compound that allows an organism to use sunlight energy to convert inorganic material into energy-rich organic compounds (carbohydrates) (p. 4-9)
- **coccolithophores** single-celled autotrophs characterized by shells of calcium carbonate (p. 4-17)
- **coccoliths** calcium carbonate scales that surround coccolithophores for protection (p. 4-17)

- **compensation depth** the depth at which the production of carbohydrates by photosynthesizing autotrophs equals the carbohydrates the autotrophs need for cellular respiration; at this depth, no energy is available to pass to higher trophic levels (p. 4-21)
- **cyanobacteria** a picoplankton bacteria with chlorophyll (p. 4-17)
- **decomposers** primarily bacteria and fungi that break down organic material into inorganic form (p. 4-26)
- **diatom** microscopic, one-celled photosynthetic plankton characterized by a rigid cell wall made of silica (p. 4-16)
- **dinoflagellates** phytoplankton characterized by flagella that allow them to orient themselves or swim (p. 4-17)
- **energy** the capacity to do work (p. 4-4)
- **entropy** a measure of the disorder that exists in a system; the measure of how much unavailable energy exists in a system due to even distribution; high entropy means low organization and low energy potential (p. 4-5)
- **fixation** the process of converting, or fixing, an inorganic compound into a usable organic compound (p. 4-11)
- **flagella** whip-like protrusion from a cell used for swimming, orientation or other motion (p. 4-17)
- **food web** an illustration that shows that organisms often have different choices of prey; represents the flow of energy through consumption in nature (p. 4-25)
- **frustule** silica cell wall of diatom (p. 4-17)
- **gross primary productivity** the measure of all the organic material produced in an area by autotrophs (p. 4-14)
- **Harmful Algal Blooms (HABs)** inappropriately called red tides; a rapid growth of certain marine algae due to the addition of nutrients in a local offshore area (p. 4-19)
- **herbivore** an animal that eats plants (p. 4-24)

- **heterotrophy** the process of obtaining energy-rich organic compounds by consuming other plants or animals (p. 4-7)
- **limiting factor** a physical or biological necessity that will limit an organism's normal function if present in inappropriate amounts (p. 4-18)
- **machine** a combination of matter capable of using energy to perform useful work; a device with moving parts, often powered to perform a task (p. 4-4)
- **net primary productivity** the quantity of energy remaining after autotrophs have satisfied their respiratory needs (p. 4-15)
- **photoinhibition** the condition in which excess light overwhelms an autotroph's ability to photosynthesize (p. 4-20)
- **photosynthesis** the organic synthesis of carbohydrates from light energy and inorganic compounds (p. 4-9)
- **phytoplankton** planktonic organisms that photosynthesize; autotrophic plankton (p. 4-14)
- **picoplankton** a community of extremely tiny plankton (p. 4-17)
- **plankton bloom** periods of explosive reproduction and growth of particular plankton species (p. 4-18)
- **polysaccharide** a complex carbohydrate (starch) (p. 4-9)
- **primary consumers** the first level of heterotrophs that eats the primary producers and photosynthesizing bacteria (p. 4-24)
- **primary producers** autotrophic organisms capable of synthesizing energy-rich organic compounds from inorganic material, effectively introducing new organic material into the environment that the primary consumers can feed upon and so forth (p. 4-9)
- **red tide** extreme plankton bloom that makes it difficult for organisms to survive due to oxygen consumption and toxin release (p. 4-19)
- **saccharide** a simple carbohydrate (includes sugars, such as glucose) (p. 4-9)

- **secondary consumers** organisms that eat primary consumers (p. 4-24)
- **standing crop** the biomass, total weight, or energy content of organisms at a given time (p. 4-14)
- **thermodynamics, second law of** in a closed system (one that lets no new energy in or out), order decreases as time passes (p. 4-2)
- **trophic pyramid** a representation of how energy transfers from one level of organisms to the next as they consume each other (p. 4-24)
- **turnover** the time required for the photosynthesis/respiration cycle in an ecosystem (p. 4-14)
- **zooplankton** planktonic animals that eat phytoplankton or other heterotrophic plankton (p. 4-16)

Chapter 4 in Review

1. How does the second law of thermodynamics relate to the processes of life? Life increases order rather than disorder – how is this possible without contradicting the second law of thermodynamics?

2. Define the terms *primary producer, autotrophy,* and *heterotrophy.*

3. Compare and contrast photosynthesis, chemosynthesis, and cellular respiration.

4. Define *primary consumer* and *secondary consumer.* How do they relate in a trophic pyramid and in a food web?

5. Explain what happens to energy as it passes from one level of the trophic pyramid to the next, and why this is significant. How does this tend to affect the number of organisms higher on the trophic pyramid?

6. Compare the productivity of the land's and the sea's ecosystems. Which is more productive? Which is more efficient?

7. List and explain the variables that affect primary productivity. Describe the concept of *compensation depth*, what happens to it as these variables change, and why compensation depth is important to an ecosystem.

8. What is *plankton*? What is *phytoplankton* and why is it important to primary productivity? Which phytoplankton organisms are the most important?

Connecting Chapter Concepts – Science Scenarios

1. According to the second law of thermodynamics, a closed system goes from a state of order to a state of disorder, and eventually will have all matter and energy evenly distributed within it. Increases in order are local and temporary, and require an external energy source to exist. Life is a temporary increase in order, so it must obtain energy from external sources.

   A. What is the primary source of energy for life, and what is the process that obtains this energy? What other energy source is used by a small fraction of organisms, and what is the process that obtains it?

   B. What is the difference between an autotroph and a heterotroph, and which of these is called a primary producer? Why do heterotrophs depend upon autotrophs for existence?

   C. How does oxygen relate to energy use by organisms? How do photosynthesis and the existence of oxygen relate?

   D. Is it possible for cellular respiration to take place without oxygen?

2. Trophic relationships describe how energy moves through the biosphere as primary consumers consume primary producers, and secondary consumers consume primary consumers. This relationship is sometimes illustrated as a trophic pyramid that represents the flow of energy as it transfers from one level of organisms to the next.

   A. About what percent of energy transfers from one level of the trophic pyramid to the one above it? How does this affect the size of the biomass of each level com-pared to the level below it?

   B. In theory, what would happen to the upper levels of a trophic pyramid if overfishing, pollution, or a natural factor eliminated all the organisms in a level between the primary producers and those levels?

   C. What is the flaw with the trophic pyramid concept? How does a food web explain trophic relationships?

   D. Primary producers use inorganic materials as well as sun or chemical energy to create carbohydrates. By what process does organic material return to inorganic form used by primary producers?

Marine Science and the Real World

1. Without primary producers, we don't have the oxygen we need to breathe, and toxic carbon dioxide may accumulate. How does the deforestation of large areas relate to this issue? Why might it be difficult for cultures with economic development not to deforest?

2. It takes significantly more primary production to make a kilogram of tuna than a kilogram of corn or beef. However, the marine environment is much more efficient in primary production. There are other factors that give both environments advantages and disadvantages for agriculture. Discuss the possible problems and considerations these issues raise for someone who is deciding whether to farm the land or the sea.

3. Discuss why it is as much of a concern to dump large concentrations of nutrients in the ocean as it is to dump large concentrations of toxins. (Hint: Red tides are only part of the issue.)

References

Boyd, P. W., et al. (2000). A mesoscale phytoplankton bloom in the polar Southern Ocean stimulated by iron fertilization. *Nature* 407 (6805), 695-702.

Des Marais, D. J. (2000). When Did Photosynthesis Emerge on Earth? *Science*, 289 (5485), 1703-1705.

Falkowski, P. G. and J. A. Raven. (1997). *Aquatic Photosynthesis*. Haldon, Massachusetts: Blackwell Science, Ltd.

Garrison, Tom. (2002). *Oceanography: An Invitation to Marine Science*. Stamford: Wadsworth/Thomson Learning.

Grahame, J. (1987). *Plankton and Fisheries*. London: Edward Arnold.

Hardy, A. (1956). *The Open Sea. Vol. 1: The World of Plankton*. London: Collins.

Hawking, Stephen (1988). *A Brief History of Time*, New York: Bantam Books

Liss, P. (1999). Take the shuttle - from marine algae to atmospheric chemistry. *Science* 285, (5431), 1217-8.

Malone, J. (1980). *Algal Size in the Physiological Ecology of Phytoplankton*, 433-63, edited by I. Morris. Berkeley: University of California Press.

McCartney, K. (1993). Silicoflagellates. pp. 143-154 in: Lipps, J.H., ed. *Fossil Prokaryotes and Protists*. Blackwell Scientific, Boston.

Milne, D. H. (1995). *Marine Life and the Sea*. Belmont, CA: Wadsworth.

Nixon, S. W. (1998). Enriching the Sea to Death. *Scientific American Presents: The Oceans*. Fall, 9, (3), 48-53.

Russell-Hunter, W. D. (1970). *Aquatic Productivity*. New York: Macmillan.

Smith, D. L. (1977). *A Guide to Marine Coastal Plankton and Marine Invertebrate Larvae*. Dubuque, IA: Kendall-Hunt.

Stewart, R. R. (2005). http://oceanworld.tamu.edu/resources/oceanography-book/microbialweb.htm

Wimpenny, R. S. (1966). *The Plankton of the Sea*. New York: Elsevier.

Xie, L, and W. W. Hsieh. (1995). The global distribution of wind-induced upwelling. *Fisheries Oceanography* 4, (1), 52-67.

Xie, L, and W. W. Hsieh. (1995). The global distribution of wind-induced upwelling. *Fisheries Oceanography* 4, (1), 52-67.

CHAPTER 5

A Survey of Life in the Sea

PAD

NURP

Searching for New Species in the
Twilight Zone

Richard Pyle, Ph.D.
Associate Zoologist, Database Coordinator
Hawaii Biological Survey Staff
Bishop Museum

R ichard Pyle, Ph.D. is an evolutionary biologist, taxonomist and adventurer. The Indiana Jones of fish hunters, in place of a whip and a fedora hat, Dr. Pyle uses a net and closed circuit scuba to catch fish under water.

Diving on coral reef habitats at depths between 60 –120 meters (200 – 500 feet), Dr. Pyle captures live fish he believes may be a new species. Because sunlight begins to dim at this extreme depth range, it is often known as the *twilight zone*. Over the years, Dr. Pyle and his team have discovered more than a hundred new species of fish previously unknown to humanity. Dr. Pyle, however, says that this is just the tip of the iceberg. "We estimate that between 1,000 and 2,000 organisms are still waiting to be found – for just fish. And for each new fish, there are probably hundreds of new invertebrates."

Dr. Pyle has been interested in fish as far back as he can remember. "Literally, my earliest memories have to do with fish," he says. "When I was a baby (I was born in Hawaii), our family had a small saltwater aquarium in the living room, and my mother says I used to stare at it for hours and it would calm me down. When I was about five and living outside of Washington D.C., I used to go down to a small pond near my house almost every day and catch bluegill sunfish. At age seven, we moved back to Hawaii and I was a complete fanatic about fish. I had multiple saltwater aquariums throughout my childhood – all populated with fish I caught myself."

In high school, Dr. Pyle's parents took him on several trips throughout the Pacific. He brought back fish for the several large saltwater aquariums he had built. These experiences solidified Dr. Pyle's interest in coral reefs and coral reef fish. When he entered high school, he learned how to scuba dive through the school's physical education program. He says that his marine biology teacher was one of the most important influences on his life. He taught Richard how to catch fish more effectively while scuba diving and helped him set his sights on his career.

Throughout all of this, Dr. Pyle's interest in studying fish increased. He was especially excited about rare fish, and for several years he wrote a monthly column in a major aquarium magazine focused on rare marine species. After his first semester at the University of Hawaii, he had an opportunity to catch fish in Palau. Taking a semester off from school, he searched for new species with the famous ichthyologist Jack Randall.

"I had an amazing time taking Dr. Randall diving," says Dr. Pyle, "But the trip ended with me paralyzed from a decompression accident. Dr. Randall felt so bad about the ordeal that he offered me a job working with the fish collection at Bishop Museum. He also mentored me throughout the rest of my undergraduate years, and was the chair of my PhD committee in graduate school. After more than 20 years, I'm still working at Bishop Museum."

Bishop Museum is a major museum in Hawaii, and has two primary focus areas – cultural history in Hawaii and the Pacific, and natural history. Dr. Pyle works in the Natural Sciences Department, which houses several

Dr. Richard Pyle underwater using his highly sophisticated rebreather diving equipment to explore deep and collect new fish species.

important specimen collections. Dr. Pyle started out processing fish specimens, but over the years he has become the Database Coordinator for Natural Sciences. He is in charge of all of the computer databases associated with the Natural Sciences Department.

Dr. Pyle has many responsibilities at Bishop Museum. In addition to database coordinator and taxonomist, he is also an associate zoologist, diving expert and closed circuit rebreather (CCR) engineer. He is actively involved in different efforts to bring together the world's biodiversity information using the internet (see the sidebar in this chapter on cybertaxonomy). Dr. Pyle even writes some of the software behind ZooBank.

"I see the living world around us as a tremendous library," says Dr. Pyle. "The information is contained in the collective genes of all living species. This information is the most valuable biological asset that ever has been, or ever will be on this planet. Evolutionary biology basically involves the processes by which the information in this vast biodiversity library came to be refined, edited, re-refined, and re-edited over the course of nearly 4 billion years. Each species is like a book containing its genetic information. Right now, we are like kindergarteners trying to read all the books in the Library of Congress. We are at a stage of reading an organism's genetic information that is roughly equivalent to reading *See Spot Run*. We know the letters, and the very basics of sentence structure, but we are a long way from being able to read.

"Someday scientists will be at that level, however I fear that only a fraction of the species on this planet will still be around to catalog. There is tremendous technical information and wisdom contained in the biodiversity of species, and it's terrifying to think that we will lose much of it before we have a chance to understand what it offers – cures to diseases, ways to feed the world, etc."

For high school students with an interest in the ocean science, Dr. Pyle has the following advice: "Follow your passion, and pay attention in math class. Learn to think critically. Seek multiple sources of evidence before jumping to any conclusion. And, don't just follow the money. There is big money science out there, and if it's the sort of science you find interesting and inspiring, that's wonderful. But, I strongly recommend you put your passion first. You may not earn as much money as a medical doctor, lawyer, or business executive, but you will enjoy almost every day of your life. You will wake up in the morning excited to go to your job. You will earn enough money to live comfortably, but more importantly, you will have a very rich and fulfilling life, filled with many exciting, happy, and fun moments. As you get older, you will come to realize that you can't buy such a life for all the money in the world."

I magine you have a jigsaw puzzle with 2 million pieces. Does that sound hard to put together? Now imagine you have no idea what the puzzle picture looks like. To make it more complicated, some pieces look like they go together, some look like they don't belong, and yet others go together even though they look like they shouldn't. If that's not enough, now imagine that every few days someone comes in and adds new pieces!

Now you can imagine what biologists deal with in trying to make sense of all the different organisms on Earth and how they relate to each other. Few people realize just how diverse life is. Scientists have been cataloging plants and animals for more than 250 years, but they still have no exact answer to how many species there are on Earth. Current estimates range from about 5 million to 100 million possible species, but scientists have only uncovered about 2 million.

Furthermore, scientists discover new species with surprising regularity. Undiscovered species primarily include fungi, fish, insects and microbes. New species are being classified at a rate of only about 15,000 a year. In some of the most diverse ecosystems, such as South Pacific coral reefs, you may find a thousand or more species in a region only a few meters or feet across. In the depths below conventional scuba ranges, researchers using special deep-diving equipment have discovered several new species on a single dive (see this chapter's profile of zoologist and deep diver, Dr. Richard Pyle).

This unimaginable diversity poses an important social question: What is the importance of any one species? The need to use land and resources to provide food and energy sometimes threatens the existence of species that depend on that land or those resources. The dilemma of west coast salmon species, particularly the Chinook, represents a good example of complex social issues.

All salmon are *anadromous,* meaning that they are born in fresh water, migrate to the sea, then migrate back to reproduce. When it is time to reproduce after a few years in the ocean, salmon swim up rivers and streams to return to the location of their birth. Shortly after reproducing, the adult salmon die. Their bodies provide essential nutrients for numerous creatures in the stream ecosystem, including the young salmon. The young salmon remain in slow-moving rivers and streams for about a year, grow and eventually migrate to the sea where they live most of their adult life.

The salmon provide an important fishery. Since the late 20th and early 21st centuries, however, fishing the salmon has become increasingly complex and controversial. One problem is that salmon numbers appear to be declining.

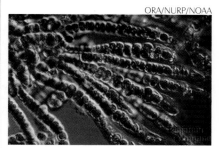
ORA/NURP/NOAA

Figure 5-1a

Cyanobacteria.

Bob Wohlers

Figure 5-1b

Squid.

Jürg Beeli/PADI

Figure 5-1c

Angel fish.
Imagine biologists classifying all the different organisms on Earth. What's the difference between the bacteria in Figure **5-1a**, the squid in Figure **5-1b**, and the angel fish in Figure **5-1c**? Few people realize just how diverse life is.

For Chinook salmon on the west coast, a combination of many factors appears to contribute to the decline. One of the primary factors is the construction of hydroelectric dams on rivers the salmon migrate. Dams impede adult salmon's efforts to swim up stream, cutting them off from their birth location. If they don't finish their journey, they don't reproduce and continue the species. It also denies the ecosystems the nutrients they supply after they die. On the other hand, the dams provide extremely valuable, clean (no fossil fuels used) hydroelectrical power. This power is exported throughout the west coast.

These facts create social and moral questions. Should the dams be removed, which would mean replacing the power they produce with methods that pollute more? What harm will that do? And, what about the species upstream that rely on the migrating salmon as food, such as bears? What will happen to the bear population once salmon migration halts altogether? Fishermen whose livelihoods depend on salmon will also be affected. What will happen to their income?

The fundamental question is, "How important are salmon?" We know that Earth can lose some species and survive, but we really don't know how important something like salmon are to the Earth's overall health. We know that the world's ecological balance relies on diversity, but we don't know how many species, or indeed which species can become extinct without disrupting it. These aren't easy questions, but they're important because, for now, once a species goes extinct, it is gone forever.

Naturalists and scientists have raised concerns regarding species extinction since the 1800s. However, it wasn't until the 1960s that the issue gained significant public attention in the United States. The 1960s marked many changes in social thinking, including a rising awareness about pollution, ecology, and the fragility of life. One possible contributor to this seems to have been space flight. In 1968, *Apollo 8* showed the Earth as seen from the moon on television. It was the first time most people realized how small Earth is for hundreds of millions of different organisms to share. It helped people realize that we exist in a global community of life that survives or perishes together.

Figure 5-2

Earth as seen from Apollo 8 in 1969.

From this single photo, we finally realized how small Earth actually is and how different it looks from other planets in our solar system. This photo helped launch the modern environmental movement, causing people to think about how we treat our planet and its resources.

Apollo 8 Crew, NASA

In this chapter, you'll learn how scientists organize and classify life on Earth. We'll look at the classification system, how it works, and why it changes. From there we'll apply the system to the marine environment. As you learn about the main groups that account for the majority of marine organisms, you may find some surprises. Sometimes you'll find seemingly dissimilar organisms classified closely together. At other times, you may find that organisms that seem related are not that close at all. Perhaps the most amazing thing about life in the sea is just how diverse it is.

The Linnaeus Classification System – Putting Life in Its Place

The Need for Classification

What are three reasons scientists have for classifying organisms?

It's not hard to imagine how difficult it would be for scientists to discuss important biological questions and interrelationships without a classification system for life. For example, without broad agreement on the name of a disease-bearing microbe, vital food species, or threatened animal, it's much harder to unite our knowledge to combat their potential harm, use them for possible human nutrition or conserve them, respectively.

There are at least three reasons why scientists classify organisms. First, classification helps identify the relationships between organisms. Through classification, it's easier to see how organisms are both similar and different. It creates a relationship theme that gives order to millions of life forms. This relationship also includes a description of the theorized evolutionary history of relationships among organisms. This evolutionary relationship between organisms is called *phylogeny* (from the Greek *phylon* meaning *tribe* or *race,* and *genesis* meaning *source*). Evolutionary relationships between organisms can be visualized with a *phylogenetic* or *taxa tree.* More on this later in the chapter.

Second, classification requires scientists to clearly identify key characteristics of each organism. This process avoids two individuals of the same species being mistaken for two different organisms because of minor individual differences. It also tells scientists which organisms are related but different. Through this classification process, for example, scientists know that a black house cat and a brown house cat are the same type of organism. The fur color does not make them different species. The same process shows that house cats are related to tigers, but are not a type of tiger.

A third reason for classification is to avoid confusion. The common names of many organisms differ with culture, language, and location. For example, among English-speaking cultures the long-finned pilot whale is also called a blackfish. Actually, it is neither a great whale nor a fish but a whale relative, the dolphin. The name "dolphin" highlights the opposite problem, which is that the same common name may apply to two different organisms. "Dolphin" can mean a marine mammal or it can be the food fish also called dolphin fish, mahi-mahi, or el dorado. The classification system used today avoids this issue by assigning every species its own Latin name. When a scientist hears that name, there's no question as to the species. Using our endangered salmon example discussed earlier, scientists communicating with each other can identify *which* salmon species they are talking about when working to solve specific environmental problems.

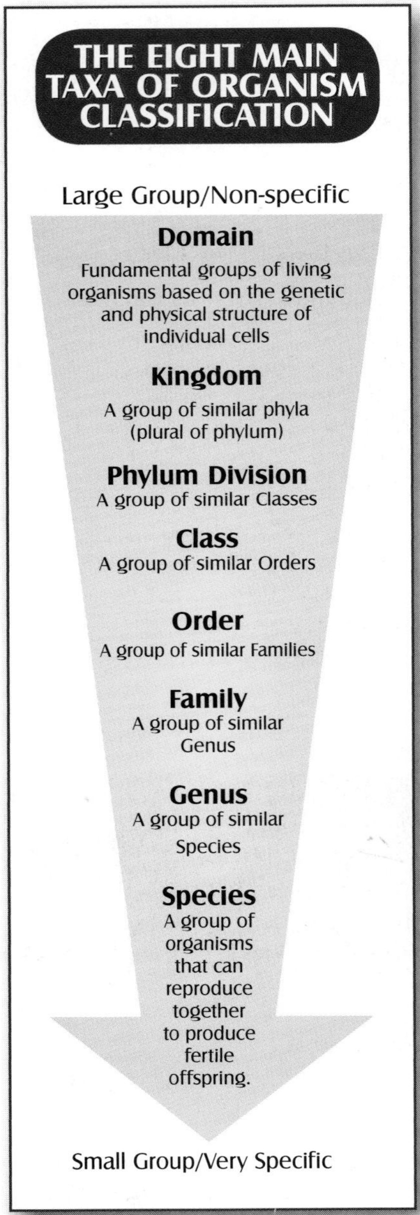

THE EIGHT MAIN TAXA OF ORGANISM CLASSIFICATION

Large Group/Non-specific

Domain
Fundamental groups of living organisms based on the genetic and physical structure of individual cells

Kingdom
A group of similar phyla (plural of phylum)

Phylum Division
A group of similar Classes

Class
A group of similar Orders

Order
A group of similar Families

Family
A group of similar Genus

Genus
A group of similar Species

Species
A group of organisms that can reproduce together to produce fertile offspring.

Small Group/Very Specific

Figure 5-4

PADI

Figure 5-3a

Neil Hammerschlag/www.neil4sharks.org

Figure 5-3b

Dolphin mammal or dolphin fish?

The same common name may apply to two different organisms. "Dolphin" can mean one of around 30 species of marine mammal **(5-3a)** or it can be the food fish called dolphin fish, mahi-mahi, or el dorado **(5-3b)**. The classification system used today avoids this issue by assigning every species its own Latin name. When a scientist hears that name, there's no question as to the species.

Classification Taxa

What two taxa does an organism's scientific name represent?

What are the eight main taxa into which scientists classify organisms?

When you consider the jigsaw puzzle with 2 million pieces you can imagine the problem facing scientists before they had a system for classifying organisms. It is hard to know what goes with what.

In 1758, Carolus Linnaeus (also known as Carl von Linne), a Swedish botanist, addressed this problem. In that year, he published *Systema Naturae*, which laid the framework for the classification system we use to this day. Linnaeus divided organisms into *taxa* (singular *taxon*, from the Latin *taxare* meaning *to appraise* or *handle*), which are divisions with subdivisions. From the most specific taxon (species) to the most general (domain) there are eight subdivision levels used by *taxonomists*. Taxonomists are scientists who study the relationships between organisms and classify them.

The most specific of the taxa is *species*, which is the Latin name for an individual organism. As you may know already, a species is considered to be a group of organisms that can reproduce together to produce fertile offspring. However, even this definition can be cause problems. For example, bacteria and other organisms reproduce asexually (individually). Some organisms that are considered different species and that do not normally reproduce in nature can produce fertile offspring under artificial circumstances.

Taxa above species level are often hard to define. These taxa tend to be based on similarities such as anatomical features, theorized

Figure 5-5

Carolus Linnaeus—the father of taxonomy.

In 1758, Carolus Linnaeus (also known as Carl von Linne), a Swedish botanist, addressed the problem of how to systematically classify organisms. On January 1 of that year, he published *Systema Naturae*, which laid the framework for the classification system we use to this day. The date January 1, 1758 is arbitrarily fixed by the International Code of Zoological Nomenclature as the starting point of all zoological nomenclature.

Al Hornsby

Figure 5-6a

Al Hornsby

Figure 5-6b

Genus and species.

The taxon above species is *genus*. A genus groups various species that are considered to be very closely related. For example, there are 34 species of reef shark, all belonging to the genus *Carcharhinus*. These include bull sharks (**5-6a**) (*Carcharhinus leucas*) and gray reef sharks (**5-6b**) (*Carcharhinus amblyrhynchos*).

evolutionary similarities, and genetic relationships. Taxonomists working within a specialized area usually classify a new organism, and the results are generally accepted. Like other areas in science, classifications change based on new information or new theories.

The taxon above species is *genus*. The species grouped in a genus are considered to be very closely related. For example, there are 34 species of reef shark all belonging to the genus *Carcharhinus*.

Newcomers to science sometimes wonder why scientific names are all from Latin. How did it start? Is it important?

Scientific names were originally Latin because in Linnaeus' time, scholars used Latin. It was the common language used by all scientists, much as English is today.

Latin has stayed on as the basis for scientific names for at least two apparent reasons. The first is tradition. The world has grown accustomed to it, so that when scientists see a binomial Latin name, they recognize it as the scientific name. A second reason is that since all organisms have only one scientific name, Latin provides a neutral language. No one from any culture need feel slighted because scientific names are in another scientist's native language. Today, Latin is no one's native language.

It's worth noting that while scientific names are in Latin *form,* not all scientific names originate from the Latin language. Sometimes a species takes the name of the discoverer of that species or in honor of someone. For instance, a new species of penguin discovered by Dr. Smith might be called *Spheniscus smithus.* It's also common for the name of a classification to borrow from Greek. For example phylum Arthropoda (includes crustaceans and insects) gets its name from the Greek *arthro* meaning *jointed* and *podos* meaning *foot.*

These include bull sharks (*Carcharhinus leucas*), Caribbean sharks (*Carcharhinus perezi*), and gray reef sharks (*Carcharhinus amblyrhynchos*).

Note that you identify each species by referring to *both* the genus *and* the species, with the genus capitalized and the species name in lower case. This is a species' scientific name, or *binomial Latin name* (from Latin *bis* meaning *twice* and *nomen* meaning *name*). The scientific name is unique to one organism. When an oceanographer in the United States talks to another in Russia about *Carcharhinus leucas,* both know exactly what organism they're discussing. Note also that you italicize the genus and species (or underline it when handwriting).

Genera (plural of genus) that share characteristics are grouped in a *family*. For example, *Carcharhinus* and several other genera of large sharks make up family Carcharhinidae. There are 51 species in this family.

Related families are grouped together into *orders*. Family Carcharhinidae is in order Carcharhiniformes, along with family Sphyrnidae (hammerhead sharks), family Scyliorhinidae (catsharks), and others. About 260 species make up this order.

Related orders make up a *class*. Class Chondrichthyes includes order Carcharhiniformes and several other orders of shark, rays, and their close relatives. This class includes more than 1,000 species.

Classes are grouped together by *phylum* (from the Greek *phylon* meaning *tribe, race*). In our example, class Chondrichthyes, along with the classes for mammals, birds, reptiles, amphibians, and bony fish, belong to phylum Chordata. Taxonomists define phylum Chordata as all the classes of animals that are chordates, meaning they possess a notochord and a dorsal nerve cord, either during development or for their entire lives. That's about 40,000 species. In botany and microbiology, *division* may be used in place of phylum.

Phyla (plural of phylum) are grouped together into *kingdoms,* which may also be called *supergroups*. For example, phylum Chordata and 32 other phyla make up kingdom Animalia. This includes an estimated 5 to 100 million species, from sponges and snails to elephants and whales, of which only about 2 million species have actually been identified.

Recent work, particularly in the field of genetics, has somewhat complicated the fundamentals of the higher level taxa. It has become widely accepted that there are more kingdoms than were previously thought. There are currently three clearly defined groups of kingdoms recognized. These groups of kingdoms have three fundamentally different genetic structures, and are grouped

CLASSIFICATION OF THREE DIFFERENT ORGANISMS

DOMAIN	Eukarya	Bacteria	Eukarya
KINGDOM	Animalia	Eubacteria	Animalia
PHYLUM/DIVISION	Chordata	Proteobacteria	Arthropoda
CLASS	Mammalia	Gramma Proteobacteria	Malacostraca
ORDER	Cetacea	Enterobacteriales	Euphausiacea
FAMILY	Delphinidae	Enterobacteriaceae	Euphausiidae
GENUS	*Globicephala*	*Escherichia*	*Euphausia*
SPECIES	*melas*	*coli*	*superba*
SCIENTIFIC NAME	*Globicephala melas*	*Escherichia coli*	*Euphausia superba*
COMMON NAME	long-finned pilot whale	lower intestinal bacteria	Antarctic krill

NOAA

NOAA

Jamie Hall, Gulf of Farallones Marine Sanctuary, NOAA

Figure 5-7a

Long-finned pilot whale.

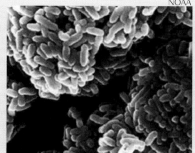

Figure 5-7b

Lower intestinal bacteria–*Escherichia coli*.

Figure 5-7c

Antarctic krill.

Figure 5-7

Classification of different organisms.

By looking at this table, you can see how taxonomists classify three very different organisms.

together as *domains.* Taxonomists use domains to define the largest groups of life.

Note there is no single, objective definition of domain, kingdom, family, order and so forth. These are determined based on groupings of common characteristics. By looking at the accompanying table, you can see how taxonomists classify three very different organisms.

David Fleetham

Figure 5-8

Classification problems.

A common problem taxonomists have is that some organisms don't fit neatly into defined classifications. Some organisms have the characteristics that define a classification along with other characteristics that separate them from it. For example, ratfish have characteristics that clearly fit with sharks and rays, yet have enough differences to require their own classification.

Determining Taxa

How do taxonomists determine into which taxon to classify an organism?

What common problem do taxonomists have in classifying organisms and how do they solve it?

The accepted taxa work very well as a framework for organizing life by defined characteristics. However, life has a way of defying simple definitions.

Linnaeus (and most taxonomists after him) classified macroorganisms based on anatomical features. This usually works well and it shows possible relationships between organisms. Classifying organisms based on anatomical features remains an important classification method. However, the study of genetics has become perhaps more important. Taxonomists find this especially useful when classifying single-cell organisms that all look the same. Studies of *DNA* and *RNA* also raise questions about existing taxonomy.

Taxonomists have found that some organisms don't fit neatly into defined classifications. Some organisms have the characteristics that define a classification, along with other characteristics that separate them from it. Yet, they don't belong in the classification above or below.

A good example of this is the relationship between sharks and rays. Both belong in class Chondrichthyes as taxonomists define it. The next level below, the order, would divide up all the sharks and rays, but here's the difficulty. You would have several orders with sharks and several orders with rays. However, rays and sharks are clearly different enough to be in two distinct groups. Adding to the problem, there are the chimaeras. Chimaeras have characteristics that clearly fit with sharks and rays, yet there are sufficient differences to require their own classification.

If taxonomists tried to subdivide class Chondrichthyes entirely with orders, there wouldn't be enough subsequent classifications. To make the classification system work for sharks and rays, taxonomists need more classification levels.

The solution is to insert intermediate classification levels. Taxonomists assign super- or sublevels to create new higher or lower divisions, respectively, within a classification. For example, class Chondrichthyes consists of two sublevels, subclass Holocephali and subclass Elasmobranchii. Subclass Holocephali consists of one order of chimaeras. Subclass Elasmobranchii consists of superorder Selachimorpha (orders of sharks) and superorder Batidoidimorpha (orders of rays).

It's important to realize that these intermediate classifications can sometimes have two names that mean essentially the same thing. For instance, the designations subphylum and superclass insert an intermediate level between phylum and class. Therefore, some taxonomists might call a particular classification a subphylum, while another taxonomist might call it a superclass. At other times, though, a superclass can be a division of a subphylum. Another example is that of supergroups and kingdoms. Both are large groups of organisms classified just below domain level. Some taxonomists use one term, and others use the other. At this time, there is not yet a single universally accepted scheme for the kingdom- or supergroup- level of classification. This may sound confusing, but in the context of actual organism classifications, you usually find the taxonomy readily understandable.

Consider the complexity taxonomists face trying to classify more than 25,000 bony fish, 100,000 mollusks, or the almost 1 million species of identified insects. It's an enormous task. Astoundingly, they accomplish it. By using intermediate classifications as appropriate, every known organism fits into the hierarchy from kingdom to species. New information may cause change or debate, but every species has an assigned taxonomy.

Figure 5-9

Super and sublevels of classification.

Taxonomists assign super or sublevels to create new higher or lower divisions, respectively, within a classification. Seen here is the complete classification of a California horn shark, demonstrating the use of intermediate classification levels. Compare its classification with that of a spotted eagle ray. Note that they have the same taxonomy until reaching super order.

COMPARISON OF SUPER AND SUBLEVELS OF CLASSIFICATION

California Horn Shark

Domain	Eukarya
Kingdom	Animalia
Phylum	Chordata
Subphylum	Vertebrata
Superclass	Gnathostomata (jawed vertebrates)
Class	Chondrichthyes (rays, sharks, and relatives)
Subclass	Elasmobranchii (sharks)
Superorder	Selachimorpha
Order	Heterodontiformes
Family	Heterodontidae
Genus	*Heterodontus*
Species	*francisci*

Bob Wohlers

Figure 5-9a

California Horn Shark.

Al Hornsby

Figure 5-9b

Spotted Eagle Ray.

Spotted Eagle Ray

Domain	Eukarya
Kingdom	Animalia
Phylum	Chordata
Subphylum	Vertebrata
Superclass	Gnathostomata (jawed vertebrates)
Class	Chondrichthyes (rays, sharks, and relatives)
Subclass	Elasmobranchii (sharks)
Superorder	Batidoidimorpha
Order	Rajiformes (rays, sawfishes, and skates)
Family	Myliobatoidea
Subfamily	Myliobatinae
Genus	*Aetobatus*
Species	*narinari*

CYBERTAXONOMY – WHAT'S ON YOUR PLANET?

Scientists estimate that millions of species remain unknown, unidentifiable, or inaccessible to science – particularly in the deep ocean. Categorizing the species of the world and their unique attributes are essential parts of understanding the history of life. Trustworthy taxonomic information is crucial to effective global communication about biodiversity, and hence its use and conservation. So, in scientific language, humans are *Homo sapiens* and honeybees are *Apis mellifera*. This is true all over the world – no matter what language you speak.

Traditional taxonomic tools and methods are not keeping pace with the growing need for knowledge. Taxonomists need to be able to communicate effectively with one another. Because taxonomy asks planetary scale questions about life on Earth, it requires direct comparisons of thousands of specimens housed in museums in dozens of countries. However, taxonomists cannot work efficiently without open access to instrumentation, other colleagues and especially, the museum specimens themselves. Further, it is estimated that taxonomists have only discovered and named about 10% of *all* species on Earth. A species that may be a key factor in the food chain might nearly be extinct, and we might not know. What can be done about this communication problem among taxonomists and the lack of information? How can researchers increase the pace at which species exploration progresses while maintaining the scientific rigor of traditional taxonomy? The answer is *cybertaxonomy*.

Cybertaxonomy is a mixture of taxonomy, internet technology, computer engineering and a new spirit of global partnership among taxonomists (a partnership that even includes *you* – read on). This new approach to taxonomy will create a modern and efficient science to confront the difficult challenge of discovering and describing millions of unknown species, while at the same time testing the almost 2 million already named species. Cybertaxonomy will enable international teams of scientists to create and test taxonomic knowledge to assure humanity's access to reliable information about Earth's species. This information will allow all scientists to guide public policy decisions regarding the health and welfare of our planet, food production, and diseases.

To further the initiative of cybertaxonomy, Arizona State University's International Institute for Species Exploration (www.planetbob.asu.edu) is partnering with international museums and botanical gardens to mount expeditions, describe species, build collections and engineer new tools for species explorers of the 21st century.

You can get involved with the discovery of new species. It's an incredibly exciting pastime. Begin with a group of plants or animals that interests you, and for which good field guides exist. With a little work learning appropriate terminology, and studying the group, you can learn the differences of the taxa and individual species. With familiarity, you will reach a point where you recognize organisms in the group that don't seem to fit any existing species definition – perhaps a new species.

If you think that identifying a new species is unlikely for you, consider that there are so many species and so few experts on each group. For this reason, amateur naturalists routinely make important scientific discoveries, including new species.

So, become part of discovering all the organisms that make up Earth. Make a plant or insect collection. Keep and enjoy a diversity of tropical fish. Get a pair of binoculars and bird watch. Learn to scuba dive and explore the depths for new species. The possibilities are endless and the excitement high. You never know what you'll find until you look.

Explore the following internet sites related to furthering cybertaxonomy:

International Commission on Zoological Nomenclature: www.iczn.org
ZooBank (in partnership with the ICZN): www.zoobank. org
Discover Life: www.discoverlife.org
Encyclopedia of Life: www.eol.org
Zootaxa: www. mapress.com/zootaxa/index.html
Biodiversity Information Standards: www.tdwg.org
ARKive: www.arkive.org
Catalogue of Life: www.catalgueoflife.org
Zoological Record: http://scientific.thomson.com/products/zr/

Dr. Gwen Goodman, CSULB

Figure 5-10

The Three Domain System of Classification

What are the names of the three domains?

As you just learned, living things are placed in groups on the basis of similarities and differences at the organism, cellular, and molecular levels. Taxonomic studies have led to the development of a system of classification in which all life-forms (with the exception of viruses) are divided into several kingdoms. However, one of the most contentious issues is the division of organisms into kingdoms.

Originally, there were just two kingdoms: animals (Animalia) and vegetables (Plantae). Gradually, as new discoveries revealed the diversity of life, taxonomists added more. The five-kingdom system (including Monera, Protista, Fungi, Plantae, and Animalia) proposed in 1959 by the American biologist Robert H. Whittaker won the support of most authorities and was the prevailing view for almost 50 years.

Today, the five-kingdom system has been superseded. Research concerning the organisms previously known as *archeabacteria* shows that these creatures form an entirely distinct group. In the 1970s, Carl Woese proposed that all terrestrial life is divided into three domains: Archaea, Bacteria, and Eukarya. Each of these domains contains two or more kingdoms. The three domains of life are now widely accepted.

Viruses—The Tiniest Fragments of Life

What are viruses?

Before we look at even the tiniest of cellular organisms, we need to consider the smallest forms of what could be considered marine life at all, the viruses. Unlike other organisms, viruses have no metabolism or cell structure of any kind. They are simply strands of DNA or RNA in a protective coat. In essence, a virus is a set of genetic instructions designed to break into an organism's cell and "hijack" its metabolism. The virus forces the cell to make hundreds to millions of copies of the virus.

We often think of viruses as airborne disease agents, but they are found everywhere there is organic material. Despite being far smaller than even the tiniest bacteria, viruses are so numerous that it has been calculated that the oceans contain hundreds of millions of tons of viruses. This makes these tiny bits of DNA and RNA a sizeable proportion of the mass of all marine life. Their total marine biomass may be greater than that of all marine mammals, and about the same biomass as fish. In fact, viruses are the most common biological agents in the sea.

HOW LIFE FITS TOGETHER – A PHYLOGENETIC TREE OF LIFE

As early biologists learned more about the world around them, they broadened their classification of living organisms. For many years, all living things were classified as either plant or animal. As new information was discovered, taxonomists developed a visual representation of how organisms fit with one another. The tree shows the theorized evolutionary relationships among various species that are thought to have a common ancestor. This visual representation is often called the *tree of life, phylogenetic tree,* or *taxa tree.* Although there are many versions of such trees, illustrated here is a simple view of how living organisms can be organized phylogenetically. It is important to realize that classification of organisms is ever changing and subject to opinion and debate among taxonomists.

The bottom or "root" of the tree begins with a common ancestor of all living things – life itself. Life is characterized by a nucleic-acid based genetic system (DNA or RNA), metabolism, and cellular structure. However, some parasitic life forms, such as viruses, have lost some of these features and rely on the host's cellular environment for these.

Phylogenetic Tree of Life

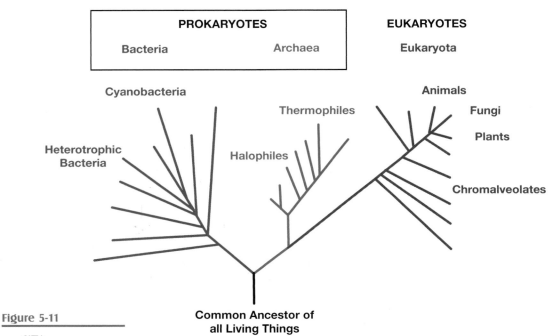

Figure 5-11

KEY:

Heterotrophic Bacteria – A group of bacteria that ingest food to obtain their energy and nutrition.

Cyanobacteria – A group of bacteria that obtain their energy through photosynthesis.

Halophiles – Organisms that can live in very high concentrations of salt.

Thermophiles – Organisms that can live at relatively high temperatures.

Animals – Multicellular organisms differing from plants in certain typical characteristics such as capacity for locomotion, nonphotosynthetic metabolism, pronounced response to stimuli, restricted growth, and fixed bodily structure.

Fungi – organisms lacking chlorophyll and vascular tissue and range in form from a single cell to a large body mass of branched filamentous hyphae that often produce specialized fruiting bodies. The group includes the yeasts, molds, smuts, and mushrooms.

Plants – Photosynthetic, multicellular organisms characteristically producing embryos, containing chloroplasts, having cellulose cell walls, and lacking the power of locomotion.

Chromalveolates – A group consisting of brown algae, diatoms and dinoflagellates.

Microbial oceanographic research in the 1970s and 1980s found that marine viruses measured approximately 10 billion per liter. This raised the question of whether viruses have a more fundamental role in marine ecologies than previously thought. Current research indicates that they appear to be part of the normal fauna of oceans, and play an essential role in the environment. Marine viruses interact with the primary producers in the food chain, plus they affect nutrient cycling, carbon recycling and other ecological processes.

ARE YOU LEARNING?

1. **Scientists classify organisms because (choose all that apply)**

   A. it helps identify relationships between organisms.

   B. it requires them to clearly identify key characteristics of each organism.

   C. it allows researchers to always use an organism's common name.

   D. it avoids confusion.

2. **An organism's scientific name represents**

   A. kingdom and order.

   B. family and genus.

   C. genus and class.

   D. genus and species.

3. **Which of the following are taxa used by scientists to classify organisms. (choose all that apply)**

   A. kingdom

   B. group

   C. species

   D. family

   E. type

   F. class

   G. phylum

   H. grade

4. **Taxonomists determine into which taxa to classify an organism based on (choose all that apply)**

   A. anatomical features.

   B. general color.

   C. genetics.

   D. environment.

5. **A common problem in taxonomy is that some organisms fit into different categories very easily. To solve this problem, taxonomists combine the taxa into one big division by eliminating intermediate levels.**

   A. true

   B. false

6. **Name the three domains.**

   _____ _____ _____

7. **Marine viruses (choose all that apply)**

   A. are deadly and can cause most waterborne diseases.

   B. are the smallest forms of what could be considered marine life.

   C. are very abundant in the world's ocean.

   D. have more biomass than that of marine mammals.

Prokaryotes—Small Yet Vital

STUDY QUESTIONS

Find the answers as you read.

1. What are the *prokaryotes*?

2. In what ways are *archaea* and *bacteria* similar?

3. What can some bacteria do that no other known organisms can do?

4. Why do scientists think the cyanobacteria are crucial to life?

Old and Simple

What are the prokaryotes?

Chapter 4 discusses that primary producers are responsible for all the life in the biosphere. Most life in the ocean exists as microbes and minute organisms are the most important primary producers in the ocean. Not only are they the most abundant life form in the ocean, they have extremely fast growth rates and life cycles.

The *prokaryotes* (from the Latin, *pro* meaning *before* and the Greek, *karyon* meaning *kernal, nucleus*) include among the most important of these in the ocean. Prokaryotes can be found all around us. You cannot see prokaryotes with the naked eye, yet they are the most numerous of all organisms on Earth. In the world's oceans they number more than 3×10^{28}. This is an almost unimaginable number – more than 100 million times as great as the number of stars in the visible universe.

Domain *Bacteria* and *Archaea* were classified as prokaryotes because they're structurally far simpler than the cells found in the organisms of the domain Eukarya. They don't have the same complex internal membrane structure. They lack chromosomes or a nucleus, and instead simply have a ring of DNA or RNA. Prokaryotes do not have mitochondria. Although many types of prokaryotes accomplish photosynthesis, they lack *chloroplasts*, which are structures used in photosynthesis by complex cells. Photosynthesis by prokaryotes is accomplished by having chlorophyll molecules in its membranes. These differences separate the prokaryotes from the complex-celled eukaryotes, which make up the single domain Eukarya.

Prokaryotes are also the smallest organisms (other than viruses), ranging from 1 to 10 microns in size (1 micron = 0.001 millimeters or 0.00004 inches). Although small in size, with respect to variety, prokaryotes win hands down. Besides being the simplest structurally, scientists think that the prokaryotes are by far the oldest types of organism, with the archaea originating 3.5 billion years ago. The eukaryotes evolved much later from prokaryotes that evolved to live within each other's cell membranes. This is thought to be the origin of the more complex and bigger cell structures of the eukaryotes. Chapter 4 discusses the theory that oxygen entered the atmosphere when organisms began photosynthesis. Scientists think that the responsible organisms were cyanobacteria of domain Bacteria. The theory is that the process of photosynthesis evolved with these early prokaryotes. It is also thought that these cyanobacteria evolved to become the chloroplasts now found within photosynthetic eukaryotes. *Endosymbiosis* is the state in which one organism lives inside another, and both organisms benefit. It is thought that prokaryote cells had a endosymbiotic relationship within other cells. These prokaryotes evolved into the chloroplasts and mitochondria found in complex cells.

Prokaryotes are found in nearly all environments, including the harshest. Some prokaryotes are *extremophiles* – which as explained in Chapter 3, are organisms that live in environments fatal to most forms of life. Some can be found living in hottest environments on Earth – even as hot as 121° C (249.8° F). These prokaryotes are called *hyperthermophiles* – heat-loving organisms. Other prokaryotes are found living in the coldest, most acidic, most alkaline and the saltiest (*halophiles* – salt-loving organisms) environments. Some need oxygen to survive, but others live where there is no oxygen at all. Many grow on plankton in the ocean, while others live in or on the bodies of other organisms, including humans.

Figure 5-12

Basic differences between prokaryotic and eukaryotic cells.

Bacteria and archaea were classified as prokaryotes because they're structurally far simpler than the cells found in the organisms of domain Eukaryote. They don't have the same complex internal membrane structure as eukaryotic cells. Prokaryotic cells lack chromosomes or a nucleus and instead simply have a ring of DNA or RNA. Prokaryotes do not have mitochondria. Although many types of prokaryotes accomplish photosynthesis, they lack chloroplasts, which are structures used in photosynthesis by complex cells. Many prokaryotes have simple locomotion flagella to assist them in movement. However, simply stated, prokaryotes are molecules surrounded by a membrane and cell wall. These characteristics separate the prokaryotes from the complex-celled eukaryotes. Prokaryotic cells are usually independent, while eukaryotic cells are often found in multicellular organisms.

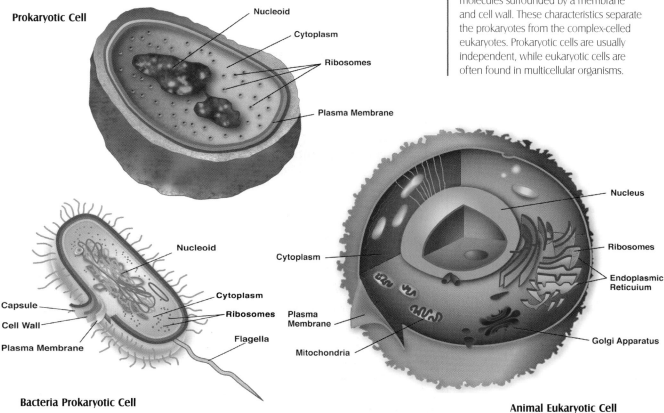

Prokaryotic Cell

Nucleoid
Cytoplasm
Ribosomes
Plasma Membrane

Bacteria Prokaryotic Cell

Nucleoid
Cytoplasm
Ribosomes
Flagella
Capsule
Cell Wall
Plasma Membrane

Animal Eukaryotic Cell

Nucleus
Ribosomes
Endoplasmic Reticuium
Golgi Apparatus
Cytoplasm
Plasma Membrane
Mitochondria

Archaea and Bacteria

In what ways are archaea *and* bacteria *similar?*

What can some bacteria do that no other known organisms can do?

Why do scientists think the cyanobacteria *are crucial to life?*

Recent genetic work has clearly separated bacteria and archaea into two different domains. These domains both share some characteristics of their cell structures. However, genetically they are clearly as different from each other as they are from eukaryotes. Because of their structural similarities, however, they are still commonly referred together as prokaryotes.

Archaea (from the Greek *archaio* meaning *old*) are extremely common in the ocean – they dominate the life of many deep-sea open ocean areas. As previously mentioned, domain Archaea includes many extremophiles. Archaea live near deep hydrothermal vents, in high salinity pools, in highly acidic environments, in sulfur pools, and even close to volcanoes. Other archaea species are chemosynthesizers, which many scientists think were the first autotrophs. This is one reason why scientists theorize that the archaea are the oldest forms of life in existence.

National Park Service

Ocean Explorer, NOAA

Figure 5-13

Archaea and Bacteria: masters of harsh environments.

The former kingdom Monera has become the separate domains Archaea and Bacteria. *Archaea* (from the Greek *archaio* meaning *old*) are best known for being *extremophiles*. Extremophiles live in environments that are inhospitable to most life. Hyperthermophiles (a specific type of extremophile – mostly archaea), have been found living in hot springs, such as the ones in the Morning Glory Pool in Yellowstone National Park, Wyoming. They are also found in deep-sea hydrothermal vents, including those near the Galapagos Islands off the coast of Ecuador.

The organisms in the domain Bacteria are also thought to be among the oldest life forms, but not as old as the Archaea. While you might think of bacteria as germs that cause disease, that's only a small fraction of this huge group. Scientists continue to find new and diverse bacteria. Bacteria are extremely adaptable and capable of processes that no other organisms can accomplish. One important example is a species of bacteria that creates organic nitrogen compounds by fixing inorganic nitrogen from the air. These organic nitrogen compounds are essential to most forms of life. Chapter 8 discusses more about nitrogen cycles.

Although there are hundreds of thousands of bacteria species, one important group is the *cyanobacteria* (from the Greek *kyan* meaning *dark blue*). Cyanobacteria used to be called blue-green

INTERNET PORTAL

SciLINKS. NSTA

Topic: Bacteria
Go To:www.scilinks.org
Code: LOP2105

OAR/NURP/NOAA

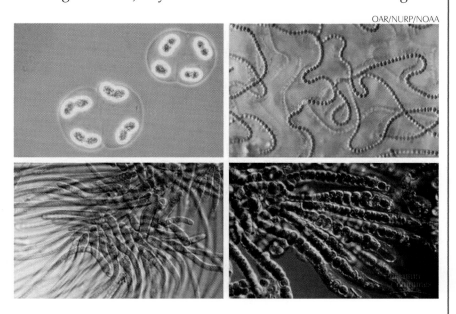

Figure 5-14

Microscopic marine cyanobacteria.

Cyanobacteria are enormously abundant and crucial to life. Cyanobacteria are a significant component of the marine nitrogen cycle and they are an important primary producer in many marine environments.

algae, which is amusing since they're not algae and not all varieties are blue-green. Despite the confusing common name, the cyanobacteria are perhaps the most ecologically important organisms on Earth, and crucial to life. Cyanobacteria are a significant component of the marine nitrogen cycle and they are an important primary producer in many marine environments. They also think that cyanobacteria created most of the oxygen in the atmosphere. Some scientists think that we presently underestimate the role cyanobacteria play in primary productivity.

Cyanobacteria are extremely abundant, and two cyanobacteria genera, *Prochlorococcus* and *Synechococcus* are possibly the most plentiful species on Earth as a single milliliter of seawater may con-

Figure 5-15

Pink flamingos and Cyanobacteria.

Although most cyanobacteria are blue-green, their colors include red. Interestingly, these pigments can contribute to the color of other organisms. African flamingos get their distinctive pink coloration from a red cyanophyte on which they feed.

Al Hornsby

tain over 100,000 cells. As mentioned in Chapter 4, cyanobacteria are picoplankton – very small plankton.

Although most cyanobacteria are blue-green, their colors include red. Interestingly, these pigments can contribute to the color of other organisms. African flamingos get their distinctive pink coloration from a red cyanobacteria on which they feed. On a more fundamental level, scientists think that different colored cyanobacteria evolved and became the various chloroplasts in the different groups of photosynthetic eukaryotes.

ARE YOU LEARNING?

1. **Prokaryotes are characterized by cells that are structurally _____ compared to the cells found in the organisms of other kingdoms.**

   A. more complex

   B. simpler

   C. symmetrical

   D. square

2. **Archaea and bacteria**

   A. have similar cell structures.

   B. have similar genetics and biochemical composition.

   C. have mitochondria and chloroplasts.

3. **Some bacteria can _____, which no other organisms can do.**

   A. photosynthesize

   B. fix inorganic carbon into organic carbon compounds

   C. fix inorganic nitrogen into organic nitrogen compounds

   D. live near the edge of volcanoes

4. **Cyanobacteria are crucial to life because scientists think that (choose all that apply)**

   A. photosynthesis evolved in cyanobacteria.

   B. cyanobacteria created most of the oxygen in the atmosphere.

   C. cyanobacteria convert carbon dioxide into nitrogen.

Eukaryotes — Diversity of Body Forms

Domain Eukarya – Major Groups

What types of organisms are included in the domain Eukarya?

How are eukaryote plant and animal cells different?

Domain Eukarya includes protists (mostly microbial eukaryotes, including those eukaryotes that aren't a plant, animal or fungus), fungi, plants and animals. These are all organisms with cells organized into complex structures enclosed within membranes. All organisms in this domain have cells that have a nucleus. It is the presence of a nucleus that defines the members of domain Eukarya. "Eukarya" comes from the Greek *eu*, meaning *good* or *true,* and *karyon* meaning *kernal, nucleus.*

Eukaryotes are a very diverse group and their cell structures are equally diverse. Eukaryotic cells are typically larger than prokaryote cells. Besides having a distinct nucleus, eukaryotic cells also have a variety of complex internal membranes and structures that prokaryotes do not (see figure 5-16). Further, eukaryotic animal and plant cells differ from each other. Plant eukaryotic cells have

STUDY QUESTIONS

Find the answers as you read.

1. What types of organisms are included in the domain Eukarya?

2. How are eukaryote plant and animal cells different?

Sharyn Hedrick, Phytoplankton Lab,
Smithsonian Environmental Research Center

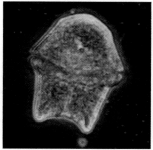

Dinoflagellates

PADI

Brown Algae

Heather Dine/NOAA

Sea Grass

Bob Wohlers

Angel Fish

Figure 5-16

Eukayotes.

The domain Eukarya includes organisms people are most familiar with – all protists, fungi, plants and animals. Although they show an extreme diversity in form, they share fundamental characteristics of cellular organization, biochemistry and molecular biology.

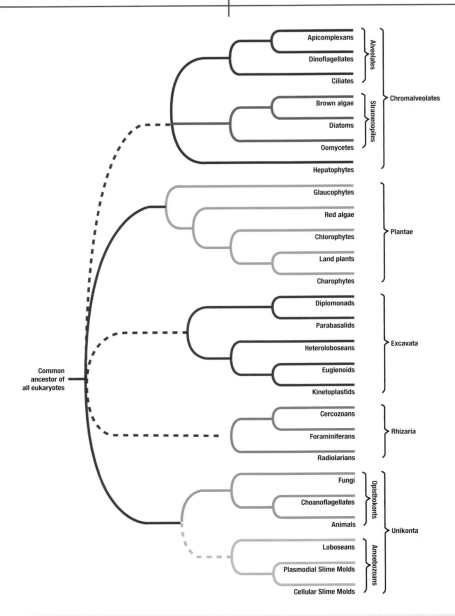

Figure 5-17

Major Eukaryote Groups.

The phylogeny of the domain Eukarya is currently in flux with continuing debate over how organisms are grouped. For the purposes of this text, domain Eukarya can be divided into five groups (also known by some taxonomists as "supergroups" or "Kingdoms") – Chromalveolates, Plantae, Excavates, Rhizaria, and Unikonts. Chromalveolates include the following marine eukaryotes: dinoflagellates, diatoms, and brown algae. Plantae include the following marine eukaryotes: red algae, chlorophytes or green algae and land plants that include the marine seagrasses and mangrove trees. Rhizaria include the following marine eukaryotes: foraminiferans and radiolarians. Unikonts include a diversity of marine animals such as dolphins, turtles, crabs and sea birds.

a cell wall – a fairly rigid layer outside the cell membrane. Cell walls provide plant cells with rigid structural support, protection and a filtering mechanism. Animal cells do not have a cell wall. Many types of plant cells also have chloroplasts, whereas animal cells do not. Chloroplasts contain *chlorophyll*, the pigment that give plants their green color and allows them to perform photosynthesis.

ARE YOU LEARNING?

1. **The following organisms are in the domain Eukaryota: (choose all that apply)**

    A. animals

    B. algae

    C. viruses

    D. bacteria

2. **Both eukaryote plant and animal cells have a cell wall and chloroplasts.**

    A. true

    B. false

Chromalveolates – Dinoflagellates, Coccolithophores, Diatoms and Brown Algae

Chromalveolata is a eukaryote supergroup (some taxonomists call it a kingdom) that includes several major marine organisms – dinoflagellates, diatoms, coccolithophores and brown algae. At one time, many chromalveolates were considered plants because most have cell walls and the ability to photosynthesize. Even now, this group's phylogeny is undergoing research and changes with new findings.

CLASSIFICATION OF CHROMALVEOLATES

Domain
Eukaryota

Kingdom/Supergroup
Chromalveolata

Phyla

Dinoflagellata – Dinoflagelates

Haptophyta – Coccolithophores

Heterokontophyta – Diatoms, Brown Algae

Figure 5-18

STUDY QUESTIONS

Find the answers as you read.

1. What are three primary characteristics of organisms in the phylum Dinoflagellata?

2. Why is the genus *Symbiodinium* important to coral reefs?

3. Where do coccolithophores live in the marine environment?

4. What is a *coccolith*?

5. What organisms make up the phylum Heterokontophyta?

6. About what percentage of the photosynthetic biomass do diatoms produce?

7. What is the largest of the brown algae? Why is it important?

8. How does brown algae differ from diatoms?

9. What commercial products are made from some species of brown algae?

Dinoflagellates

What are three primary characteristics of organisms in the phylum Dinoflagellata?

Why is the genus Symbiodinium *important to coral reefs?*

Chapter 4 explains that dinoflagellates are the second most productive group of primary producers, after diatoms. Dinoflagellates are mostly marine and they make up phylum Dinoflagellata. You may recall that dinoflagellates have flagella that they use to swim. At

Symbiodinium

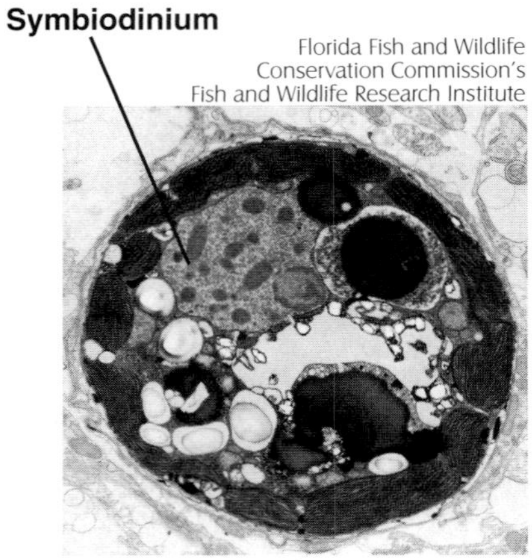

Figure 5-19

Coral polyp tissue.

Symbiodinium in the tissue of a zooxanthellate coral polyp. These autotrophic dinoflagellates provide food for the coral polyp tissue in return for nitrogenous wastes.

Figure 5-20

Coral reefs.

This coral reef wouldn't exist if it weren't for *Symbiodinium*. Without this key dinoflagellate, coral reefs could not have developed as we know them – along with the thousands of unique organisms that call reefs home.

30 to 150 microns across, most dinoflagellates are a bit larger than diatoms. That's still small enough to be classified as *microplankton*, though some species are larger than this. Microplankton are between 20 and 200 microns in size.

Most, but not all, dinoflagellates are autotrophs. An interesting genus of heterotrophic dinoflagellate is *Noctiluca*. The *Noctiluca* get their name from the Latin *nocturnus* meaning *night* and *lucent* meaning to *shine*. Members of this genus are capable of *bioluminescence*. Bioluminescence is the ability of an organism to emit light, like the flashes of a firefly. Bioluminescent organisms have specialized structures called *photophores*, which contain a compound called *luciferin* and an enzyme called *luciferase*. When luciferin and luciferase mix in the photophore, they produce light much like when you mix the chemicals in a light stick. Organisms use bioluminescence to attract prey, to fool predators, to attract mates, and sometimes as a light source for vision.

Noctiluca emit light when agitated, such as when a propeller stirs the water or when scuba divers kick their fins. At night, passing boats, ships, swimmers, and scuba divers can leave a glowing trail marked by hundreds of thousands of disturbed *Noctiluca*.

Members of the genus *Symbiodinium* (and other recently discovered dinoflagellate taxa) are particularly important autotrophic dinoflagellates. These symbiotic dinoflagellates are called *zooxanthellate*. Zooxanthellate are golden-brown, autotrophic dinoflagellates that live in the tissues of various marine animals – especially corals, anemones and jellyfish.

Symbiodinium multiply within coral polyps, providing their host with food via photosynthesis. In return, *Symbiodinium* receives nitrogenous wastes from the coral. This is an example of *mutualism*, which is when two species live together and benefit from the

Bob Wohlers

relationship. Besides coral, *Symbiodinium* species also live in giant clams and some species of sponges.

Without *Symbiodinium*, most species of hard coral could not exist as we know it. These species are the only corals that build massive coral reefs. Without coral and coral reefs, we wouldn't have the thousands of unique organisms that make up the world's most productive, diverse and beautiful ecosystems. This makes *Symbiodinium* a very important genus.

Even more so than diatoms, dinoflagellates can cause Harmful Algal Blooms (HABs – also know as "red tides"). Toxins produced by dinoflagellates are among the most toxic substances known. Some are far more toxic than cyanide. Because these toxins can accumulate over time in shellfish and fish, they can cause seafood poisoning. The presence or absence of these dinoflagellates can make a fish species safe to eat from one place and unsafe from elsewhere. Fish high in the food web, such as barracuda, have a higher toxin risk. This is because the toxins accumulate with each level and become more concentrated as you go up.

Coccolithophores

Where do coccolithophores live in the marine environment?

What is a coccolith?

Whether they realize it or not, the English know coccolithophores very well. The famous white cliffs of Dover are made primarily of the remains of these single-cell, microscopic, autotrophic organisms. Made of calcium carbonate, Dover's cliffs reach up to 106 meters (348 feet) and are thought to have originated approximately 136 million years ago with geological forces lifting fossil coccolith deposits.

Coccolithophores are in the phylum Haptophyta and all live in the upper layers of the ocean. Unlike other autotrophic plankton, they surround themselves with extremely tiny plates made of calcium carbonate. These scales, known as *coccoliths*, look like tiny hubcaps or buttons, and are thought to protect the organism.

Gary Turner/www.flickr.com/photos/perlworld

Figure 5-21

White cliffs of Dover.

The famous white cliffs of Dover are primarily made of the remains of these single-cell, microscopic, phytoplanktonic organisms. Made of calcium carbonate, Dover's cliffs reach up to 106 meters (348 feet) and are thought to have originated approximately 136 million years ago.

Gustaaf Hallegraeff, University of Tasmania

Figure 5-22

Individual coccolithophore cell.

A single coccolithophore can be surrounded by at least 30 scales. These scales, known as coccoliths, look like tiny hubcaps or buttons. The scales are dumped into the water when the coccolithophore multiply, die or simply make too many to surround the cell.

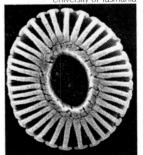

Figure 5-23

Individual coccolithophore scale or "coccolith."

This micrograph shows a detached coccolith. Scientists gather minute coccoliths by filtering the ocean with fine mesh during a coccolithophore bloom.

What coccoliths lack in size, they make up in numbers. A single coccolithophore can be surrounded by at least 30 scales. The scales are dumped into the water when the coccolithophores multiply, die or simply make too many to surround the cell. In waters where coccolithophores are abundant (such as the Mediterranean and Sargasso seas), release of coccoliths can turn the water milky. Scientists estimate that coccolithophores dump more than 1.4 million metric tons (1.5 million imperial tons) of calcium carbonate a year. This makes them the leading calcium carbonate producers in the ocean. Because of this abundance, coccoliths can build seabed deposits of calcium carbonate ooze.

Diatoms

What organisms make up the phylum Heterokontophyta?

About what percentage of the photosynthetic biomass do diatoms produce?

Chapter 4 explains that single-celled diatoms are very productive phytoplankton. Another organism in the eukaryote group Chromalveolates, diatoms often dominate the phytoplankton in particularly rich and productive seas. In some cool, productive waters, they may be even more important to primary production than the individually smaller, but more numerous, cyanobacteria. These primary producers make up phylum

Figure 5-24a

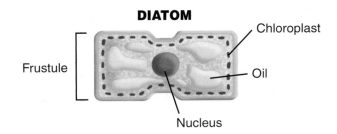

DIATOM

Frustule — Chloroplast — Oil — Nucleus

Figure 5-24b

Diatoms.

Diatoms are the most productive phytoplankton and, with brown algae, make up phylum Heterokontophyta. As viewed through a microscope, diatoms have silica exoskeletons.

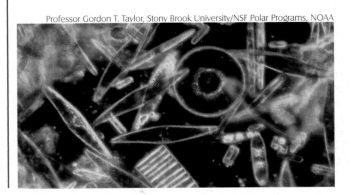

Heterokontophyta, a widely diverse group that also includes brown algae.

Scientists estimate that 5,000 to 50,000 species make up phylum Heterokontophyta. Diatoms are relatively large for single-celled algae, ranging from 20 to 80 microns across. As mentioned in Chapter 4, they have two-part silicon shells in an amazing array of shapes among the species. The trademark of diatoms is their cellular beauty. A diatom's architecture, on a cellular scale, is very eye-catching. Diatomaceous earth, used as an abrasive and filtration powder for pools, consists of fossilized remains of diatoms.

Because they're photosynthesizers, diatoms are relatively dormant during the winter months. When sunlight levels rise in the spring, they photosynthesize, grow, and reproduce rapidly. Diatoms reproduce asexually by budding, alternating with sexual reproduction. During peak growth, in two weeks more than a million diatoms can result from a single parent diatom. Because of this, diatoms are thought to account for about 25% of all the photosynthetic biomass on Earth. Fish, shellfish and other plankton feed on diatoms during these blooms.

Diatoms are one of the plankton species that can cause Harmful Algal Blooms (HABs). Some diatoms produce toxins. When HABs occur, these toxins can be concentrated in fish, shellfish and other species and may cause poisoning when people eat the contaminated animals. This is one reason why HABs harm the mussel (shellfish) and fishing industry. Even when the toxins don't kill many fish, it may be inappropriate to harvest seafood because of the toxin risk.

I. Girogorov/www.sinia-planeta.com

I. Girogorov/www.sinia-planeta.com

Figure 5-25

Diatom architecture.

Diatoms have two-part silicon shells in an amazing array of shapes among the species. The trademark of diatoms is their cellular beauty. A diatom's architecture, on a cellular scale, is very eye-catching.

OIL DEVELOPMENT AND PINHEAD SIZED ORGANISMS

In spite of what most people think, oil doesn't come from dead dinosaurs. Most oil found on Earth comes from ancient dead organisms no larger than a pinhead. This why it is called *fossil fuel.*

Minute diatoms, foraminifera and radiolaria (foraminifera and radiolaria are discussed later in this chapter) that die and settle to the bottom of the sea are what eventually turn into most available oil and natural gas. Under extreme pressure and over thousands of years, these marine organisms eventually form deposits of organic-rich sludge at the bottom of the ocean. In many places these oil deposits are many kilometers thick, locked in what is called reservoir rock – primarily porous sandstone and limestone.

Bob Wohlers

Figure 5-26

Offshore oil platform.

Drilling into reservoir rock to extract oil and natural gas left behind by ancient diatoms, foraminifera and radiolaria.

Brown Algae

What is the largest of the brown algae? Why is it important?

How does brown algae differ from diatoms?

What commercial products are made from some species of brown algae?

Brown algae are also members of the supergroup (or kingdom) Chromalveolates, phylum Heterokontophyta, but are more structurally complex than diatoms. Unlike diatoms, brown algae species are all multicellular. They range in size, with some individuals being gigantic.

Brown algae species have adapted to a variety of habitats. They can be found in tide pools and relatively deep, near-shore waters. Most prefer predominantly cold water with lots of nutrients, and water movement to help the algae absorb oxygen. Many species of brown algae have *holdfasts* (like the green algae), *blades*, leathery flexible *stipes*, and gas-filled *pneumatocysts* for floatation. The blades are the brown algae equivalent of leaves. Stipes are the equivalent of stems. Many species live in the littoral zone, so their stipes bend easily to resist breakage by waves. To keep the blades close to the surface and sun, many species have pneumatocysts. Pneumatocysts are natural gas-filled float structures that float the algae off the bottom. The cellular make up of some brown algae keeps them from drying out when stranded partially or wholly above surface during low tide.

Brown algae get their distinctive olive-green/brown color from the pigment *fucoxanthin*. Much of the cell biochemistry, particularly the photosynthetic pigments found in brown algae, is the same as the biochemistry found in diatoms and dinoflagellates.

Of the approximately 1,500 species of brown algae, the largest and most impressive are the various species of *kelp*. Kelp species have holdfasts, stipes, blades and

Figure 5-27

Giant kelp.

Brown algae, such as this kelp (*Macrocystis pyrifera*), are more structurally complex than other algae. They get their coloring from the pigment fucoxanthin. Anchored to the bottom by holdfasts, kelp stipes reach toward the surface and have blades buoyed by pneumatocysts. Giant kelp provides a foundation for many temperate coastal ecosystems, just as coral does in tropical marine ecosystems. Giant kelp grows quickly, up to 30 centimeters (11.8 inches) per day. Many growing in proximity form a kelp forest.

Budd Riker

pneumatocysts. Giant kelp (*Macrocystis pyrifera*) can grow more than 30 centimeters (11.8 inches) per day and reach the surface from 24 meters (79 feet) deep. Kelp is important because it is the foundation for many temperate coastal ecosystems, much as coral is the foundation for many tropical marine ecosystems. Among other locations, kelp forests dominate the coasts of California, much of the Mediterranean, and New Zealand.

Certain species of brown algae are commercially harvested for thickening agents in the textile, dental, cosmetic, and food industries. You can find these thickening agents in such products as toothpaste and ice cream. Some countries also harvest brown algae species for human food and cattle feed.

Not all species of brown algae live anchored by holdfasts. For example, members of the Sargassum genera are neuston. This brown alga forms huge drifting rafts that support entire communities of neuston. These drift rafts of Sargassum are ecosystems within themselves. The center of the North Atlantic Ocean is called the Sargasso Sea because of the large amounts of sargassum (the algae's common name and genus) found there.

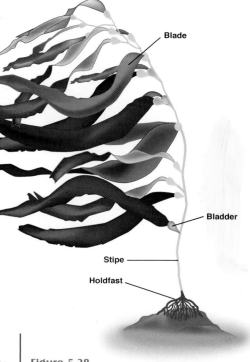

Bob Wohlers

Blade

Bladder

Stipe

Holdfast

Figure 5-28

Typical Brown Algae.

Many species of brown algae have *holdfasts* (like the green algae), *blades,* leathery flexible *stipes,* and gas-filled bladders or *pneumatocysts.*

Figure 5-29

Holdfasts.

Many species of algae have holdfasts. Algae holdfasts look like the roots of land plants, but they function differently. True roots allow land plants to anchor themselves firmly and absorb moisture from the ground. Algae do not need to absorb moisture from the holdfasts, so holdfasts only anchor the algae to solid substrates on the ocean bottom.

Brenda Konar, University of Alaska Fairbanks

Figure 5-30

Bull Kelp.

Bull kelp is recognized by its long, flexible stipe that ends at a single, bulbous pneumatocyst. Radiating from the gas float are long, flat, leaf-like blades that flow in currents. Some bull kelp can grow as large as 36 meters (118 feet).

Figure 5-31a

The Sargasso Sea.

Ocean Explorer, NOAA

Figure 5-31b

Sargasso brown algae.

The Sargasso Sea is at the center of the North Atlantic Ocean. It is named for the large floating rafts of the brown algae, Sargassum, that form there, shown at right.

Additionally, sargassum can be found drifting in North Atlantic currents. Early mariners feared that sargassum could ensnare their ships, though such dense concentrations are rare. However, because the Sargasso Sea exists in a relatively currentless portion of the Atlantic, when there was no wind, sailing ships seemed trapped there, which may account for the concerns early sailors had.

ARE YOU LEARNING?

1. **Characteristics of organisms in the phylum Dinoflagellata include (choose all that apply)**

   A. being unicellular.

   B. being multicellular.

   C. using a flagella to move.

   D. being planktonic.

   E. being autotrophs.

2. **Genus *Symbiodinium* is important to coral reefs because they live inside coral polyps and provide the coral with food via photosynthesis.**

   A. true

   B. false

3. **Coccolithophores live _____.**

   A. as plankton

   B. on the bottom

4. **Coccoliths are very minute calcium carbonate "scales" that cover a coccolithophore cell.**

   A. true

   B. false

5. **The phylum Heterokontophyta includes (choose all that apply)**

   A. all marine algae.   C. brown algae.

   B. diatoms.   D. corals.

6. **Diatoms produce about _____ of photosynthetic biomass.**

   A. 50%

   B. 25%

   C. 30%

7. **The largest of the brown algae is _____. It is important because _____.**

   A. Irish moss, it is eaten in Japan

   B. Sargassum, it is the foundation of tropical ecosystems

   C. kelp, it is the foundation of temperate coastal ecosystems

8. **Brown algae _____, diatoms _____. (choose all that apply)**

   A. is multicellular, are unicellular

   B. is unicellular, are multicellular

   C. are mostly anchored to the bottom, are planktonic

9. **Commercial products made from some species of brown algae include**

   A. food for humans and cattle.

   B. thickening agents in the textile, dental, cosmetic, and food industries.

Marine Plants – Red Algae, Green Algae, Seagrasses and Mangroves

The kingdom (or supergroup) Plantae includes several marine groups of organisms – red algae, green algae, seagrasses and mangrove trees. Kingdom Plantae also includes familiar terrestrial organisms such as trees, grasses, ferns, mosses, and pine trees.

Although plants dominate terrestrial environments, comparatively few members have a niche in the ocean. Algae are the ocean counterparts of plants, adding to Earth's primary productivity and oxygen production. The term *algae* is a loose term, however, and not very scientific (see sidebar).

CLASSIFICATION OF RED ALGAE, GREEN ALGAE, SEAGRASSES AND MANGROVE TREES

Domain:
Eukaryota

Kingdom/Supergroup:
Plantae

Phyla:
Rhodophyta (Red Algae)
Chlorophyta (Green Algae)
Magnoliphyta (flowering plants – sea grasses and mangroves)

Figure 5-32

STUDY QUESTIONS

Find the answers as you read.

1. What are chlorophyll *a* and *b*?

2. What allows red algae to live deeper than other algae?

3. Why are red algae important to coral reefs?

4. What evolutionary significance do scientists give the chlorophylls in green algae?

5. What is the greatest challenge for a plant to adapt to living in the sea?

6. What are *submergent* and *emergent* marine plants?

7. Other than food and oxygen, what do marine plants provide for other marine organisms?

8. What three reasons make mangrove swamps important to the environment?

ALGAE – A BROADLY APPLIED NON-SCIENTIFIC NAME

The term *algae* is loose and not scientific. Algae all produce carbohdrates by photosynthesis, but only the red algae and green algae are scientifically grouped with plants. As we've learned, brown algae are grouped differently – in the supergroup/kingdom Chromalveolates.

Over the years, the term algae has been used for bacteria, plants, and other organisms. Although the term "algae" is useful in some contexts, it does not correspond with the current theory of phylogeny, and some biologists try to avoid the term, except as part of a descriptive common name such as green algae, red algae or brown algae.

Taxonomists usually define eukaryote *algae* as those organisms that belong in one of several specific groups, notably Dinoflagellata, Heterokontophyta (diatoms, brown algae), Rhodophyta, and Chlorophyta. These groups are spread over several kingdoms or supergroups, some with very different cell chemistry. They vary from many single-celled forms to giant kelps that may be 50 meters (164 feet) long. Consequently, the algae phyla are quite diverse, and not necessarily closely related.

Department of Natural Resources and Parks, Water and Land Resources Division, Kings County, WA/CORIS, NOAA

Figure 5-33a

OAR, National Undersea Research Program, NOAA

Figure 5-33b

NURP

Figure 5-33c

Red algae.

Red algae from phylum Rhodophyta contain chlorophyll *a* but not *b* and have red pigments called phycoeryth- rins. This allows some red algae to live much deeper than other algae.

Figure 5-33d

Irish moss – a rhodophyte.

Phylum Rhodophyta—Red Algae

What are chlorophyll a *and* b*?*

What allows red algae to live deeper than other algae?

Why are red algae important to coral reefs?

Phylum Rhodophyta consists of freshwater and marine algae, known commonly as *red algae*. Most of the 4,000 or so red algae species are *macro algae*. Macro algae is a loose term that applies to several algae phyla, but refers to multicellular species includ- ing some of those that come to mind when you think of seaweed. Rhodophytes, like chlorophytes, have been classified as part of supergroup or kingdom Plantae by genetic analyses, along with true plants.

Members of this phylum have chlorophyll *a*, but not *b*. Chlorophyll *a* is a pigment directly involved with photosynthesis. Chlorophyll *b* assists chlorophyll *a* in capturing light for use in photosynthesis. Chlorophyll *a* and *b* absorb different colors of light. This means that organisms with both chlorophyll *a* and *b* use light more efficiently. The lack of chlorophyll *b* is one characteristic that distinguishes red algae from green algae and plants.

Although red algae don't have chlorophyll *b*, they have red pigments called *phycoerythrins*, which give them their color. This particular pigment has not been found in any other eukaryote, though it does exist in some cyanobacteria. (This is one reason that cyanobacteria are thought to be the ancestors of the chloroplasts found in the cells of Rhodophytes – another example of endosym- biosis.)

The significance of phycoerythrins is that they allow some red algae to live much deeper than any other algae. In clear water, some species live as deep as 200 meters (656 feet). This is because

Estuarine Research Reserve Collection, NOAA

phycoerythrins can absorb blue light, which penetrates deeper than any other color in the spectrum. (Chapter 9 tells you more about color absorption by water).

Red algae is also important for coral reefs. Think of the coral as the bricks in a coral reef wall. When it dies, a coral polyp leaves behind its calcium carbonate skeleton. The skeletons of each generation provide the basic building blocks for the next generation. Some species of red algae provides the cement that holds the reef together. These red algae species secrete a calcium carbonate shell. The secretions bond individual coral colonies and debris together, which in turn holds the coral reef structure together.

Not all red algae secrete calcium carbonate shells. Red algae of the genera *Chondrus* (commonly known as Irish moss because it was eaten during the Irish potato famine) and *Porphyra* (called nori) are leaf-like. They're harvested, dried, and eaten around the world, particularly in the North Sea and Japan. Both are rich in protein and minerals.

Bob Wohlers

Figure 5-34

Red algae cement.
Red algae species living on coral reefs secrete calcium carbonate shells that bond individual coral colonies and debris together. This helps hold the coral reef structure together.

Phylum Chlorophyta—Green Algae

What evolutionary significance do scientists give the chlorophylls in green algae?

Organisms of the phylum Chlorophyta, are also macro algae. Known as *green algae,* members of phylum Chlorophyta share the same green color as land plants. They also share the same pigments and have many similar biochemical characteristics. Among these, green algae and land plants both have chlorophyll *a* and chlorophyll *b.* As you just read, organisms with both chlorophyll *a* and *b* use light more efficiently.

Scientists think that the presence of chlorophyll *a* and *b* in green algae has evolutionary significance and indicates that land plants evolved from green algae. Other evidence of this is that both green algae and land plants have other pigments in common and have cell walls made of *cellulose.* Cellulose is a complex carbohydrate that gives plants their hardness and structure. Genetic analyses support a close relationship between plants and chlorophytes.

INTERNET PORTAL
SC*L*INKS. NSTA
Topic: Algae
Go To: www.scilinks.org
Code: LOP2095

Figure 5-35

Sea lettuce.

Sea lettuce (*Ulva* sp.) is among the approximately 7,000 species of green algae. Green algae contain chlorophyll *a* and *b* to photosynthesize.

There are approximately 7,000 species of green algae, making them the most diverse group of algae. Many, like sea lettuce (*Ulva* sp.) look like plants, though they're actually much simpler. They don't have the system of roots, veins, and stems that plants have, and some species are single-cell organisms. Some species have simple *holdfasts*. In green algae, these holdfasts are small and simple, and in general green algae are smaller than the large, rubbery brown algae like kelp.

Because of their similarities, yet their lack of the complex structures compared to land plants, many scientists view chlorophytes as intermediate forms. Green algae even vary in complexity within the classification, ranging from single-cell to multicell varieties. Many species of green algae live in shallow water and are eaten by a variety of marine snails such as periwinkles.

Marine Flowering Plants – Underwater Meadows and Shallow Nurseries

With the abundance and diversity of photosynthesizing prokaryotes and algae living in the ocean, you might expect similar abundance and diversity among marine flowering plants. This isn't the case. While there are perhaps a quarter of a million flowering plant species on land, so far scientists have only identified about 200 that live in the marine environment. Considering the small number of species, however, marine plants play a surprisingly important role in the health of the ocean and, ultimately, the Earth.

Plant Adaptation to the Marine Environment

What is the greatest challenge for a plant to adapt to living in the sea?

The salinity in the water is the greatest challenge to which plants must adapt to live in the sea. As terrestrial organisms, the vast majority of plants take in fresh water supplied directly or indirectly by rainfall. Exposure to salt water, however, dehydrates most plants. This is because the lower water concentration in seawater causes the fresh water in the plant to diffuse outward. (There's more about diffusion in Chapter 8.) Marine plants, on the other hand, resist dehydration through several adaptations, such as waxy coverings or other protection that reduces water loss and prevents dehydration.

Submergent and Emergent Plants

What are submergent *and* emergent *marine plants?*

Other than food and oxygen, what do marine plants provide for other marine organisms?

You can divide the approximately 200 species of marine plants into two basic types: *submergent* and *emergent*. Submergent plants live entirely underwater. Seagrasses are an example of these. Emergent plants live with their roots submerged, but with a significant portion of the plant growing above the surface. Mangrove trees are an example of emergent plants.

Like other marine primary producers, both submergent and emergent plants contribute food to the ocean's biosphere. Both produce oxygen, though emergent plants generally release oxygen into the air rather than into seawater. In addition, like macro algae such as kelp and sargassum, marine plants provide important habitats for other marine organisms.

Seagrasses

Seagrasses form extensive underwater meadows in shallow water. They are true flowering plants (*angiosperms*) from one of four plant families that grow exclusively in the marine environment – Posidoniaceae, Zosteraceae, Hydrocharitaceae, and Cymodoceaceae. Seagrasses undergo pollination while submerged and complete their entire life cycle underwater.

Seagrass (common names include *turtle grass, surf grass, eel grass*) meadows are highly diverse and productive ecosystems. They are home for juvenile fish, crustaceans, and other vertebrate and invertebrate animals. Conch, a mollusk known for its distinctive shell and as the primary ingredient in conch chowder, lives in seagrass meadows, as well as sand flats. There are even marine mammals –

Figure 5-37

Conch.
Conch, such as the queen conch shown here, live in seagrass meadows and sand flats.

Ria Tan/www.wildsingapore.com

PADI

Figure 5-36

Seagrasses.
A seagrass commonly called eelgrass, *Zostera marina* from the angiosperm family Zosteraceae.

Figure 5-38

Seagrass meadow.

Submergent plants are marine plants that live entirely under water. Seagrasses, such as those shown here, are an example of submergent marine plants.

dugongs and manatees – that specialize in grazing seagrass meadows. These are the only herbivorous marine mammals. Ecologically, seagrasses help stabilize bottom sediments and help to absorb excess nutrients from land run-off. When seagrass beds are damaged or disappear, bottom sediments and nutrients get stirred up into the water column, damaging water quality.

SEAGRASS CLASSIFICATION

Kingdom:
Plantae

Phylum/Division:
Magnoliphyta (angiosperms – flowing plants)

Class:
Lilopsida

Order:
Alismatales

Seagrass Families:
Posidoniaceae, Zosteraceae, Hydrocharitaceae, Cymodoceaceae

MANGROVE CLASSIFICATION

Kingdom:
Plantae

Phylum/Division:
Magnoliphyta (angiosperms – flowering plants)

Class:
Magnoliopsida

Order:
Rhizophorales

Family:
Rhizophoraceae

Figure 5-39

Mangroves

What three reasons make mangrove swamps important to the environment?

Mangrove trees form mangrove swamps, which are among the most important coastal marine ecosystems. Although mangrove swamps are often smelly, muddy, full of mosquitoes, and generally unappealing, their tangled root systems provide havens for many small organisms. Their murky waters provide nutrients for microorganisms that are in turn food for juvenile animals.

The combination of protection and food gives young animals a better chance for survival than they would have in the open sea. This is the first reason why mangrove swamps are important to the environment: they act as nurseries for adjacent marine ecosystems like coral reefs. Many of the species they nurture are commercially and economically important.

A second reason mangrove swamps are important to the environment is that they filter runoff water. By trapping runoff sediment, the mangroves protect sensitive offshore ecosystems (coral reefs in particular) that would be hurt or killed by settling sediment. Today, many ecologists consider mangroves transitional ecosystems, from marine to terrestrial.

A third benefit of mangrove swamps is that they hold sediments in place. They slow waves and reduce erosion while retaining the nutrients used by organisms living there. Mangrove swamps are particularly good for protecting shorelines from storm erosion by slowing down and dampening storm waves. Although a hurricane will still cause some erosion through a mangrove swamp, the sediment loss and erosion are negligible compared to the effects on unprotected shores.

The fate of mangrove swamps (commonly just called mangroves) has become an important issue related to urban expansion and bioproductivity. To those unfamiliar with their crucial role as a haven where juvenile organisms get a chance to survive to maturity, mangroves appear to be useless swampland. Consequently, at one time developers filled in mangroves and built housing and office buildings. An even bigger threat is the conversion of mangroves into shrimp mariculture farms.

The concern is that the loss of mangrove swamps is a loss to adjacent ocean ecosystems. Potential effects range from the damage or destruction of coral reefs to the decline of food fish populations. Chapter 16 discusses mangrove swamp environments in more detail.

Al Hornsby

Ms. Allison G. Delaplaine, America's Coastline Collection, NOAA

Figure 5-40

Mangroves.

Emergent plants, such as mangroves, are marine plants that live with their roots submerged but with a significant portion growing above the surface.

Ria Tan/www.wildsingapore.com

Figure 5-41

Mangrove swamp.

Mangrove trees form mangrove swamps, which are among the most important coastal marine ecosystems. Mangroves, such as those shown here in John Pennekamp Coral Reef State Park, act as nurseries for adjacent marine ecosystems, filter runoff water, and hold sediments in place.

1. **Chlorophyll *b* is a pigment**

   A. that assists chlorophyll *a* to capture light.

   B. that has no role in photosynthesis.

   C. found only in cyanobacteria.

   D. that is directly involved in photosynthesis.

2. **Red algae can live deeper than other algae because they produce cellulose, which resists water pressure better.**

   A. true

   B. false

3. **Red algae are important to coral reefs because**

   A. they help to cement the reef together.

   B. they are the coral polyp's primary food.

   C. they prevent sharks from feeding on coral.

   D.. they add desirable colors to underwater photographs.

4. **The presence of chlorophyll *a* and *b* in green algae leads some scientists to think that**

   A. green algae may have evolved from plants.

   B. land plants may have evolved from green algae.

   C. green algae are actually a type of bacteria.

   D. none of the above

5. **The greatest challenge for a plant to adapt to living in the sea is**

   A. water motion.

   B. predators.

   C. water salinity.

   D. nutrients.

6. **A(n) _____ plant lives partially in and out of the water. A(n) _____ plant lives entirely under water.**

   A. submergent, mangrove

   B. mangrove, emergent

   C. submergent, emergent

   D. emergent, submergent

7. **In addition to food and oxygen, marine plants provide important _____ for other marine organisms.**

   A. carbon dioxide

   B. light

   C. habitats

   D. all of the above

8. **Mangrove swamps are important to the environment because (choose all that apply)**

   A. they're nurseries for adjacent marine ecosystems.

   B. they're a good place to build houses.

   C. they filter runoff water.

   D. they hold sediments in place.

Rhizaria – Foraminiferans and Radiolarians

What two characteristics do foraminiferans and radiolarians share?

Rhizaria is a species-rich eukaryote supergroup (or kingdom) that includes two marine organism groups – Formaninifera and Radiolaria. Rhizaria vary considerably in form, but primarily they are microscopic and amoeboid in form.

Foraminifera (from the Latin *foramin* meaning *to bore a hole*) are found in all marine environments. While some foraminiferans live as plankton, most live on the sea bottom and have been found at the deepest known point in the world's ocean, Challenger Deep. They secrete external shells (*tests*) of calcium carbonate. The tests can either have one or multiple chambers, with some being quite elaborate.

US Geological Survey

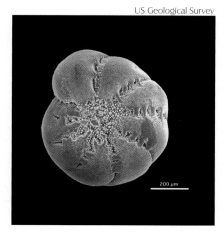

Figure 5-42a

Foraminiferans.

These electron micrographs of typical foraminiferans show the delicate intricacy of the organism's test or shell.

Randolph Femmer, National Biological Information Infrastructure

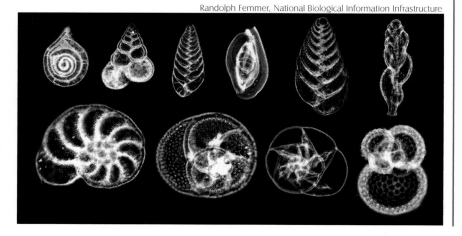

Figure 5-42b

STUDY QUESTIONS

Find the answers as you read.

1. What two characteristics do foraminiferans and radiolarians share?

RHIZARIA CLASSIFICATION

Domain:
Eukaryota

Kingdom/Supergroup:
Rhizaria

Phyla:
Formaninifera and Radiolaria

Figure 5-43

Figure 5-44

Live foraminifera.

This is an illustration of what a live foraminiferan looks like. Note the pseudopods used to catch smaller plankton for food and provide locomotion.

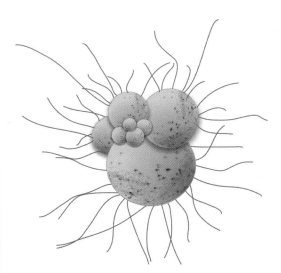

Long, slender branching threads of the cell body reach out through the pores in the foraminiferan's test. These threads or *pseudopods* are used to catch smaller plankton for food and to provide locomotion in some species.

Foraminiferans are important to the terrestrial environment as well. Scientists think that over millions of years, foraminiferans have created vast limestone deposits and sandy beaches around the world.

Radiolarians are found exclusively in marine environments as zooplankton (animal plankton), with most living in the photic zone. Practically all species secrete intricate mineral skeletons. These radiolarian skeletons lie within the cell's cytoplasm. Stiff, needlelike pseudopods radiating from around the cell increase the surface area. This speeds exchange of materials with the environment, and increases drag so the organism can drift effectively without sinking to the bottom.

I. Girogorov/www.sinia-planeta.com

Figure 5-45a

I. Girogorov/www.sinia-planeta.com

Figure 5-45b

Randolph Femmer, National Biological Information Infrastructure

Figure 5-45c

Radiolarians.

These electron micrographs of typical radiolarians show the delicate intricacy of the organism's skeleton.

ARE YOU LEARNING?

1. **Characteristics that foraminiferans and radiolarians share include (choose all that apply)**

    A. having planktonic species.

    B. being microscopic.

    C. having amoeboid form.

    D. building intricate mineral shells or skeletons.

New Terms You Learned

- **algae** a loose, non-scientific term for aquatic organisms that can produce carbohydrates by photosynthesis; taxonomists usually define eukaryote algae as those organisms that belong in one of several specific groups, notably Dinoflagellata, Heterokontophyta (diatoms, brown algae), Rhodophyta, and Chlorophyta (p. 5-31)

- **anadromous** describes fish such as salmon and shad that return from the sea to the rivers where they were born in order to breed (p. 5-3)

- **angiosperm** flowering plants; one of the major groups of seed plants including marine seagrasses (p. 5-35)

- **Archaea** domain of prokaryotes consisting of primitive organisms noted for being extremophiles (p. 5-18)

- **archaebacteria** One of the three domains of living organisms, recognized as the oldest living organisms on earth; are prokaryotes and unicellular (p. 5-13)

- **bacteria** unicellular microorganisms found in the Domain Bacteria (p. 5-19)

- **binomial Latin name** from Latin bis meaning twice and nomen meaning name; a species' scientific name consisting of genus and species, e.g., Carcharhinus leucas (common name: bull shark) (p. 5-8)

- **bioluminescence** the ability of an organism to emit light (p. 5-24)

- **blades** in brown algae, structures equivalent to leaves on plants (p. 5-28)

- **brown algae** members of the phylum Heterokontophyta, multicellular algae characterized by having holdfasts, blades, stipes and pneumatocysts (p. 5-28)

- **cellulose** a complex carbohydrate that gives plants their hardness and structure (p. 5-33)

- **chlorophyll** compound that allows an organism to use sunlight energy to convert inorganic material into energy-rich organic compounds (carbohydrates) (p. 5-22)

- **chlorophyll *a* and *b*** chlorophyll *a* is a pigment directly involved with photosynthesis; chlorophyll *b* assists chlorophyll *a* in capturing light for use in photosynthesis; each absorb different colors of light, meaning that organisms with both chlorophyll *a* and *b* use light more efficiently than organisms with either pigment alone (p. 5-32)

- **chloroplasts** organelles (structures) within cells used in photosynthesis (p. 5-16)

- **class** a major category in the taxonomic classification of related organisms, comprising a group of orders (p. 5-8)

- **coccoliths** calcium carbonate scales that surround coccolithophores for protection (p. 5-25)

- **cyanobacteria** a picoplankton bacteria belonging to a large group that have a photosythetic pigment to carry out photosynthesis (p. 5-19)

- **cybertaxonomy** a mixture of the science of taxonomy, internet technology, computer engineering an global partnership on the identification and cataloging of new and existing species (p. 5-12)

- **division** in botany and microbiology, may be used in place of phylum; a major category in the taxonomic classification of plants, comprising a group of classes (p. 5-8)

- **DNA** deoxyribonucleic acid contains the genetic instructions used in the development and functioning of all known living organisms and some viruses (p. 5-10)

- **emergent marine plant** a marine plant that lives partially submerged with its roots underwater and leaves and branches above water (p. 5-35)

- **endosymbiosis** symbiosis in which one organism lives inside another and both organisms benefit (p. 5-17)

- **eukaryote** domain taxon of those organisms with complex cell structures (p. 5-21)

- **extremophiles** organisms that live in environments fatal to most forms of life (p. 5-17)

- **family** a category in the taxonomic classification of related organisms comprising of one or more genera (p. 5-8)

- **fucoxanthin** pigment that gives brown algae their characteristic olive-green/brown coloration (p. 5-28)

- **genus** a category in the taxonomic classification of related organisms, comprising one or more species (p. 5-7)

- **green algae** members of the phylum Chlorophyta, multicellular algae characterized by sharing the same green color as land plants; typically found in shallow water (p. 5-33)

- **holdfast** an algae appendage that anchors the organism to rocks (p. 5-28)

- **kelp** a typically used common name for many larger species of brown algae in the phylum Phaeophyta; characterized by having holdfasts, stipes, blades and pneumatocysts (p. 5-28)

- **kingdom** in taxonomy, a group of similar phyla or divisions (p. 5-8)

- **luciferase** enzyme found in a photophore; used in the production of bioluminescent light by mixing with luciferin (p. 5-24)

- **luciferin** compound found in a photophore that produces light when mixed the enzyme luciferase (p. 5-24)

- **macro algae** multicellular species of algae (p. 5-32)

- **microplankton** plankton that is between 20 and 200 microns in size (p. 5-24)

- **order** a taxonomic classification made up of related families or organisms (p. 5-8)

- **photophore** specialized structure on an organism used to emit bioluminescent light (p. 5-24)

- **phycoerythrins** red pigments found in red algae and in some cyanobacteria that allow the organism to photosynthesize much deeper than they otherwise would (p. 5-32)

- **phylogeny** the evolutionary history of a particular group of organisms or their genes (p. 5-5)

- **phylum** a major taxonomic group into which animals are divided, made up of several classes (p. 5-8)

- **pneumatocysts** natural, gas-filled float structures that provide certain species of marine algae with buoyancy, lifting it off the bottom (p. 5-28)

- **prokaryote** structurally simple single celled organisms; thought to be the oldest forms of life (p. 5-16)

- **pseudopod** long, slender branching treads of a cell body used to catch food and provide locomotion in unicellular, amoeboid-type organisms (p. 5-40)

- **red algae** members of the phylum Rhodophyta, multicellular algae characterized by having the red pigment phycoerythrin, allowing this group to use blue light available in deeper water for photosynthesis; within this group is coralline algae – reef building species (p. 5-32)

- **Rhodophyta** a phyla characterized by multicellular red algae having only chlorophyll "a" and red pigments called phycoerythrins (p. 5-32)

- **RNA** ribonucleic acid made from a long chain of nucleotide units; similar to DNA, but usually exists in cells as a single strand; is central to the translation of some RNAs into proteins (p. 5-10)

- **species** a group of organisms that can reproduce together to produce fertile offspring (p. 5-7)

- **stipes** stem-like structure that supports algae but lacks the vascular system found in plants (p. 5-28)

- **submergent plant** a marine plant that lives entirely underwater (p. 5-35)

- **taxa** plural of taxon (p. 5-7)

- **taxon** any of the groups to which organisms are assigned according to the principles of taxonomy, including species, genus, family, order, class, and phylum; the divisions and subdivisions used to classify organisms (p. 5-7)

- **taxonomists** scientists who study the relationships between organisms and classify them (p. 5-7)

- **test** a shell or other hard covering on an invertebrate (p. 5-39)

- **zooxanthellae** golden-brown, autotrophic dinoflagellates that live intracellular (in the tissues) of various marine animals – especially corals and anemones (p. 5-24)

Chapter 5 in Review

1. Briefly describe the classification system used by taxonomists, including how they determine into which taxa to place an organism. Include the eight main taxa and explain why it is important to classify organisms.

2. What taxon is defined by "a group of organisms that can reproduce together to produce fertile offspring?"

3. Explain what the prokaryotes are, and the differences between archaea and bacteria.

4. What can some bacteria do that no other known organisms can do? Why is this important? Why do scientists think the Cyanobacteria are crucial to life?

5. Why is the term "algae" a non-scientific term or grouping?

6. List the algae that are important to coral reefs and explain their roles.

7. Explain why the presence of chlorophyll *a* and *b* in green algae may have significance related to the theory of evolution.

8. What is the largest brown algae? Why is it important?

9. Explain the difference between submergent and emergent marine plants. Describe the greatest challenge for a plant to adapt to living in the sea, and how some plant species manage that challenge.

10. Why are mangrove swamps important to the environment? What do mangroves and other plants provide beyond food and oxygen?

Connecting Chapter Concepts – Science Scenarios

1. Prokaryotes, algae and marine plants play pivotal roles in the ocean's ecosystems as primary producers, decomposers and through other roles.

   A. What is the significance of cyanobacteria – sometimes called blue-green algae? Why is "blue-green algae" a misnomer?

   B. Autotrophic dinoflagellates (some species are heterotrophs) are the second most productive primary producers among the algae. The genus *Symbiodinium* are important because they live in coral polyps. What does *Symbiodinium* provide, and what would happen to the world's coral reefs without it?

   C. Green algae, red algae and brown algae make up several phyla known as macro algae. What is the difference between macro algae and other algae, and macro algae and plants?

2. Scientists have evidence that mangrove swamps are important to the marine environments as protective environments for juvenile animal species, as filters that trap runoff sediments, and as barriers that absorb wave energy.

   A. What effect might you expect regarding species on adjacent marine ecosystems if local mangroves were to decline?

   B. How does the mangrove's ability to trap runoff sediments relate to the health of adjacent coral reefs?

   C. Why is the mangrove's ability to absorb wave energy important?

   D. What is the primary threat to mangroves?

Marine Science and the Real World

1. Imagine you've stumbled across what may be a new species. Explain how you would determine into what taxa it belongs. How would you use cybertaxonomy to assist you?

2. Do you agree that Latin is a neutral language for use in scientific names? Why or why not?

3. Assume you live near a coastline and recently read in the newspaper that there was a Harmful Algal Bloom (HAB – also known as a "red tide") offshore in your local area. You regularly visit a shellfish vendor down the street, where you know the owner obtains his mussels from the local waters. What questions might you ask him prior to buying and eating his mussels?

4. You own a house on a tropical island. Last year a hurricane completely destroyed the mangroves that existed on the shoreline, between the open ocean and your home. It's now June and it's heading into a new hurricane season. Are you worried about your home? Why? What would you do to protect your home?

References

ARKive. http://www.arkive.org

Beaugrand, G. 2004. Monitoring Marine Plankton Ecosystems I: Description Of An Ecosystem Approach Based On Plankton Indicators. *Mar Ecol Prog.* Ser 269.

Polistes Foundation. Discover Life. http://www.discoverlife.org

Encyclopedia of Life. http://www.eol.org

International Institute for Species Exploration. 2008. Arizona State University. http://species.asu.edu

The Internet Encyclopedia of Science. http://www.daviddarling.info/encyclopedia/V/virus.html

International Trust for Zoological Nomenclature. ZooBank. www.zoobank.org

Zootaxa. http://www.mapress.com/zootaxa/index.html

CHAPTER

6

A Survey of Life in the Sea

Bob Wohlers

Bob Wohlers

Cures from Beneath the Sea

Dr. Marc Slattery works in the field of *pharmacognosy*. Never heard of it? That's not surprising – few people have heard of this branch of science. Pharmacognosy (from the Greek *pharmakon* meaning *drug* and *gnosis* meaning *knowledge*) is the study of medicines derived from natural sources – including marine organisms.

Dr. Slattery's research focuses on the chemical make up of marine invertebrates (animals without backbones) in extreme or disturbed environments. He studies the adaptations that these organisms undergo to survive when the environment around them changes. These changes can be natural, or human made, such as pollution, climate change, disease or any other parameter.

As Dr. Slattery explains, "All animals live to reproduce, and reproduction takes a lot of energy. That means the production of defensive compounds may mean an organism produces fewer offspring. On the other hand, investing energy in defensive compounds may help an organism survive to reproduce, and in some cases those defensive compounds allow the offspring to survive as well."

Dr. Slattery explains that his research has many practical applications, with the development of new drugs one of the most prominent. "The toxic compounds produced by marine organisms to defend themselves against predators, have the potential to become the next important pharmaceutical to fight human diseases," he says.

Dr. Slattery is currently studying a number of species throughout the world that may yield chemicals from which important drugs can be made. Among these, he is studying sponges on deep reefs and in caves throughout the Caribbean, soft corals in the Pacific and Antarctic, and marine invertebrates that inhabit deep-sea vents and volcanoes. Often, Dr. Slattery has to scuba dive to deep depths and in uninviting undersea environments to find the important marine invertebrates he's researching.

Dr. Slattery decided he wanted to study marine life as a youngster. When he was five years old his parents moved his family to Jamaica, where he began snorkeling on Caribbean coral reefs. From the first time he snorkeled offshore he knew that he wanted to spend the rest of his life studying marine biology.

"When I was young, the Jamaican reefs were some of the most beautiful in the world, and I couldn't imagine a scenario where these magnificent ecosystems wouldn't be around forever." Years later while he was in college, however, a series of natural and human-related effects caused the same coral reefs to degrade and essentially collapse. "I was devastated, but I also wondered what allows some reefs to survive when others die, and what adaptations do marine organisms produce during times of stress. Since then my research has focused on a series of questions related to this general theme. Often I seek out stressed environments to study local adaptations by organisms. At other times, I collect marine organisms and stress them under laboratory conditions to see how they adapt. Either way, by better understanding how an organism copes with environmental stresses, we

Marc Slattery, Ph.D.
Professor & Director of National Institute
for Undersea Science and Technology
Ocean Biotechnology Center
Pharmacognosy
University of Mississippi

might learn how to regulate the responses in anticipation of changing environmental pressures."

Currently, Dr. Slattery is an academic researcher at the University of Mississippi (UM), within the School of Pharmacy. UM is also home to the National Institute for Undersea Science & Technology, and he directs the Ocean Biotechnology division within this research center. Dr. Slattery has two major duties: teaching and research.

"I teach future pharmacists about human disease and potential treatments, and I teach marine chemical ecology to UM graduate students. Teaching is an incredibly fulfilling career that allows me to mentor students eager to pursue their interests in marine sciences and drug discovery. Research is the backbone of that teaching experience because it provides hands-on opportunities for my students to learn techniques and gain knowledge. Research also allows me to continue to ask questions and seek answers about organism adaptation in the marine environment. Since Oxford is land-locked, I have to travel regularly to get to my field sites." Dr. Slattery and his students typically conduct research in coral habitats four times per year.

"I wake up everyday excited about my research and the questions I am addressing. I make a reasonable living, and I get to travel to exotic locations to dive and study the local sea-life. But, it can be difficult to find a job these days. As an individual you must stand out from the other job applicants. Since high school, I have taken advantage of any jobs, paid or unpaid, and other training opportunities to gain as much experience as possible. I worked hard in all my classes through college and graduate school, and I often put in long hours. But hard work pays off, and if you love what you do, the personal and financial rewards are fantastic."

To prepare for a marine science career, Dr. Slattery encourages high school students to take as many science classes as possible and pay particular attention in math, chemistry, and physics. "In high school you need to acquire the passion for marine science and develop good study habits," he says.

Invertebrates Introduction

Chapter 5 discusses prokaryotes, algae, and flowering marine plants. Chapters 5, 6, and 7 provide a survey of life in the sea, showing that ocean life ranges in size from the smallest virus to the largest animal (with respect to weight) that has ever lived on Earth, the blue whale.

Among multicellular organisms, animals dominate the sea in both quantity and variety. This contrasts with life on land, where plants (mainly trees) dominate the biomass of multi-celled organisms. When someone says "marine organism," chances are some type of animal comes to mind. The diversity of major groups of these organisms is much greater in the ocean than on land.

This chapter and Chapter 7 cover this diversity of marine animals. Marine animals range from very simple invertebrates that look and seem very plant-like, to some of the most complex and intelligent mammals on the planet. Considering that you could spend years studying the animals in any one of the hundreds of groups of marine animals, it's clearly impossible to cover marine animal diversity in detail in just two chapters.

However, this chapter and the next can cover *some* of the major animal groups and their overall characteristics. We'll begin by looking at creatures that are structurally simple, and progress toward those that are complex. In this chapter, we'll examine the major groups of marine invertebrates – animals without backbones. More than 95% of the Earth's animal species, and about 95% of their mass, are invertebrates, so this grouping is diverse, spectacular and abundant. Chapter 7 examines the major groups of marine vertebrates – animals with backbones. This group includes sharks and rays, fish, reptiles, sea birds and marine mammals.

Figure 6-1

Invertebrate Classification.

These invertebrate phyla are the most important. There are more invertebrate phyla than vertebrate. Most of the unlisted phyla are tiny, wormlike animals. Further, *unikonts* are a supergroup above kingdom Animalia. Unikonts are defined as eukaryotes, whose flagella, if present, are singular. The major groups of unikonts include amoebozoans, fungi and all animals groups. The simplest invertebrate phyla (like sponges) are at the top of this chart, the more complex phyla at the bottom.

INVERTEBRATE CLASSIFICATION OVERVIEW

Domain
Eukarya

Supergroup
Unikonts

Kingdom
Animalia

LESS COMPLEX

Phylum

1. Porifera – Sponges

2. Cnidaria – Corals, Sea Anemones, Hydroids, Sea Fans, Jellyfish

3. Platyhelminthes – Flat Worms

4. Nemertea – Ribbon Worms

5. Nematoda – Round Worms

6. Mollusca – Squid, Octopus, Sea Slugs, Snails, Oysters, Clams, Conches

7. Annelida – Complex Worms

8. Arthropoda – Barnacles, Copepods, Shrimp, Lobsters, Crabs

9. Echinodermata – Sea Lilies, Feather Stars, Sea Stars, Sea Urchins, Sea Cucumbers

MORE COMPLEX ANIMALS

Sponges—Filters of the Sea

STUDY QUESTIONS

Find the answers as you read.

1. What are the two major cell types in a sponge's tissue?

2. How do sponges feed?

3. How do sponges reproduce?

4. In what way are sponge larvae more animal-like than adult sponges?

SPONGE CLASSIFICATION

Domain
Eukarya

Supergroup
Unikonts

Kingdom
Animalia

Phylum
Porifera

Bob Wohlers

Figure 6-2

Caribbean azure vase sponge, *Cellispongia plicifera.*

Characteristics of Sponges

What are the two major cell types in a sponge's tissue?

How do sponges feed?

Sponges, members of phylum Porifera (from Latin *Porus* meaning *pore* and *ferre* meaning *to bear*), aren't very animal-like and they represent the simplest of animals. They don't have apparent eyes and they don't seem to move. Sponges don't have true tissues (like muscles and nerves) or any organs (like a heart or kidneys). In fact, they barely qualify as animals. It's no wonder that many people mistakenly think that sponges are plants.

Sponges do, however, have the minimum requirements for classification in the kingdom Animalia. Besides being multicellular heterotrophs, they have structural organization and different cell types. More than 5,000 species exist. Most are marine, but a few live in fresh water. They range from huge sponges more than 5 meters (16 feet) across, to fine, encrusting forms that resemble lumpy, spilled paint. They are found all over the world from tropical reefs to under the polar ice.

Sponges have two major cell types in their tissues. The first are *collar cells*. These cells have flagella that waft water through openings in the sponge's *epithelium*. The epithelium is the tissue that protects the sponge's outer surface. The epithelium has contractible pores through which water enters. Collar cells also absorb and digest food particles.

As the water passes through the sponge walls, *amoebocytes* (the second major cell type), pick up nutrient particles from the incoming flow. These mobile cells distribute the nutrients throughout the sponge, function as a crude immune system and assist in reproduction. Water passes into an internal cavity or cavities (depending on the species) and exits through one or more *oscula*. Oscula (singular *osculum*) are simply large openings to let the filtered water pass out of the mass of the animal.

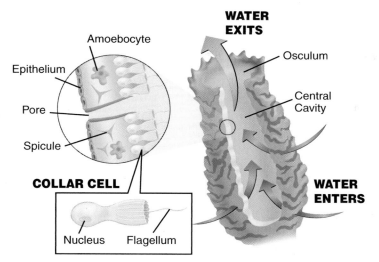

WATER EXITS

Amoebocyte

Epithelium

Osculum

Pore

Central Cavity

Spicule

COLLAR CELL

WATER ENTERS

Nucleus   Flagellum

Bob Wohlers

Figure 6-3

A typical sponge.

Sponges are very simple organisms without complex organs or nervous systems. *Collar cells* use flagella to draw water into the sponge's central cavity. As water passes through the sponge walls, *amoebocytes* pick up nutrients from the water. Water then exits the sponge through *oscula*.

Figure 6-4

Yellow tube sponge, *Aplysina fistularis*.

Note the small buds at the top of this sponge. A bud eventually breaks off and drifts to a new substrate beginning a new organism. Among many structurally simple animals, "budding" is one common form of asexual reproduction.

Oscula are primarily found at the upper and outer surfaces of the sponge.

Because of the way they feed, sponges are considered filter feeders. Some species filter up to 20 times their own volume of water per minute, capturing very minute food particles. Some species also benefit through mutualism with *Symbiodinium*, just as coral polyps do. You'll learn more about corals later in this chapter, and you can learn more about *Symbiodinium* in Chapter 5.

One problem sponges have is the same as with human-made filters: getting clogged with debris. Sponges avoid this problem two ways. First, they secrete a large quantity of mucus to cleanse their surface of debris and potential pathogens. Second, they provide a niche for mutualistic worms, sea cucumbers, and other organisms that live within and on the sponge and feed on the materials that can obstruct filtration.

Special Attributes of Sponges

How do sponges reproduce?

In what way are sponge larvae more animal-like than adult sponges?

Sponges reproduce both sexually and asexually. *Asexual* reproduction means there is no fusion of male and female sex cells (*gametes*). In sponges, this takes place by means of external buds. Buds grow from the surface of the sponge. Eventually, they break off and drift to a new substrate. Once the buds attach to the new substrate they begin to grow into new sponges.

Sexual reproduction takes place when sponges release sperm into the water. Currents disperse the sperm to neighboring sponges. Fertilization occurs internally in the tissues of the sponge, where

larval development occurs. While adult sponges look and act more like plants than animals as we typically think of them, that's not true with sponge larvae. Sponge larvae are more animal-like because they're free-swimming organisms with *cilia*. Cilia are short, hair-like structures similar to flagella that protrude from a cell for propulsion or to move liquid past the cell. The larvae swim and drift until colliding with a suitable spot on the reef, where they fix themselves in place and begin growing into adult sponges.

Because sponges can't swim, they may seem very vulnerable to predators. While some organisms do feed on sponges, they have their defenses. Most species are tough and fibrous with needlelike *spicules* throughout their tissue. These spicules provide structural support and can be made of a glass-like or calcium material. Some sponges use for support tough, elastic, protein fibers. The tough and fibrous nature of sponges makes them hard to feed on. Many species also produce toxic defense chemicals, some of which may have potential as drugs against diseases. Marine chemists, like this chapter's profiled marine scientist Dr. Marc Slattery, are studying the novel chemicals produced by sponges, looking for promising new cures. Chapters 15 and 17 talk more about finding drugs in the sea.

Finally, because they're very simple organisms without complex organs or nervous systems, many sponges can reassemble themselves. After being torn apart by a predator, remaining pieces in contact with each other may grow together, often in less than a day. Isolated pieces can regenerate into entirely new sponges.

ARE YOU LEARNING?

1. **The two major cell types in a sponge's tissues are**

   A. collar cells and epithelium.

   B. collar cells and amoebocytes.

   C. amoebocytes and ocscula.

   D. epithelium and oscula.

2. **Sponges feed by drawing water into the oscula and then filtering it out through the sponge walls.**

   A. true

   B. false

3. **Sponges reproduce (choose all that apply)**

   A. by breaking off buds – asexually.

   B. sexually by producing sperm that is released into the water.

   C. sexually by producing sperm that is transferred to the female through direct contact.

4. **Sponge larvae are more animal-like than adult sponges because**

   A. they're aggressive predators.

   B. they're free-swimming organisms.

   C. they make good pets.

   D. none of the above

Corals, Anemones, Sea Fans, and Jellyfish – Aquatic Stinging Nettles

Characteristics of Phylum Cnidaria

What marine organisms make up phylum Cnidaria?

What anatomical characteristics distinguish members of phylum Cnidaria?

The broad diversity of organisms in phylum Cnidaria (pronounced: nie'dare'ee'ah; from the Greek word *cnido* meaning *stinging nettle*) makes you wonder whether they have enough in common to constitute the same classification. Soft and hard corals, sea anemones, hydroids, sea fans, and jellyfish all make up phylum Cnidaria. Phylum Cnidaria also includes the colonial siphonophores, which are some of the longest animals in the world. Cnidarians are entirely aquatic, with most species living in the marine environment.

Despite their differences, all cnidaria share anatomical characteristics. They are *radially symmetrical*. Radial symmetry is symmetry around a point, like pie slices or a clock face. They have a cup or umbrella-shaped body made of two tissue layers of cells.

STUDY QUESTIONS

Find the answers as you read.

1. What marine organisms make up phylum Cnidaria?

2. What anatomical characteristics distinguish members of phylum Cnidaria?

3. What is the largest class in phylum Cnidaria? What marine organisms are in this class?

4. In what classes are jellyfish and box jellyfish?

5. What are two characteristics of the class Scyphozoa?

6. In what class are fire coral and siphonophores?

CNIDARIA CLASSIFICATION

Domain
Eukarya

Supergroup
Unikonts

Kingdom
Animalia

Phylum
Cnidaria

Classes
1. Anthozoa – Anemones, Corals
2. Scyphozoa – Jellyfish
3. Cubozoa – Box Jellies
4. Hydrozoa – Fire Corals, Portuguese Man-of-War, Siphonophores

Figure 6-6

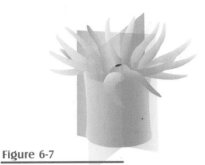

Figure 6-7

A typical cnidarian polyp.

Cnidarian polyps are one of two body forms found in this group of animals. Polyps are typically attached and can be found living as a solitary organism (like sea anemones) or in colonies (like many corals). Like the medusa body form, polyps have radial symmetry.

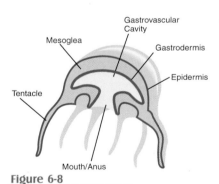

Figure 6-8

A typical cnidarian medusa.

The free-floating, medusa body forms have radial symmetry. Often called "jellyfish," medusae have mouths and tentacles that typically point downward. Anatomically, cnidarians are fairly simple organisms that have a mouth opening into a gastrovascular cavity, which is used for digestion and reproduction.

These two tissue layers are separated by a layer of jelly known as *mesoglea*. Around the rim of the umbrella-shaped body are tentacles. They have a mouth-like opening, which functions for feeding, reproduction and waste disposal. This opening also leads into the *gastrovascular cavity*, which is a space in the middle of their body. reproduction. They are structurally uncomplicated, with simple nerve net, muscle cells, and light receptors (simple "eyes").

Cnidarians take one of two body forms: polyp or medusa. Organisms that are attached, such as coral and sea anemones, are called *polyps*. Polyps are soft, though some species, including coral, secrete rigid protective calcium carbonate exterior "cups." Free-floating cnidarians, such as jellyfish, have essentially the same basic body design, but the mouth and tentacles typically point downward. These are called *medusae* (singular *medusa*).

All cnidarians share the ability to defend themselves with *nematocysts*, which are tiny structures on their tentacles that sting. These stinging structures are composed of special cells called *cnidocytes*. Nematocysts are essentially coiled darts that remain loaded, ready to strike and release toxins when triggered by contact with an animal. Although some of the toxins are quite potent, only a handful of the some 10,000 cnidarian species pose a threat to humans. In most cases, nematocysts aren't strong enough to penetrate skin and the toxin doses are minute. There are some noteworthy exceptions, however. More on this later.

Figure 6-9

Nematocysts.

Nematocysts are individual structures that are essentially coiled darts. They remain loaded, ready to strike and release toxins when triggered by contact with an animal.

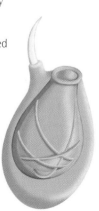
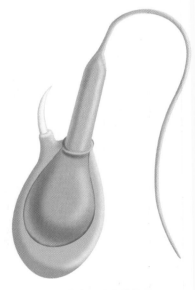

UNDISCHARGED CAPSULE **DISCHARGED CAPSULE**

Special Attributes of Corals and Anemones

What is the largest class in phylum Cnidaria? What marine organisms are in this class?

With more than 6,000 species, the largest class in phylum Cnidaria is class Anthozoa. In this class are the corals and anemones. All members of this class are polyps that attach to the reef or other substrate. Some of this class, including corals and soft corals, are colonial, while the anemones are individual organisms. A few corals are individual organisms, too.

The hard corals may be the most ecologically significant organisms of this class, thanks to the massive calcium carbonate reefs they build. Coral colonies can grow for centuries and become so large that they shape coastlines and build entire islands.

Hard corals look like colorful rock. As discussed in Chapter 5, dinoflagellates in genus *Symbiodinium* (zooxanthellae) live inside most species of hard coral, providing food and helping eliminate waste through photosynthesis. This is why corals with zooxanthellae grow best in tropical, well-lit, clear water. Most zooxanthellate coral polyps feed at night, opening up and spreading their tentacles to capture drifting plankton. The corals that look rock hard by day look soft and fuzzy at night when the polyps open and spread their tentacles to feed.

Because zooxanthellate corals live best in well-lit, clear water, they actually thrive in low-nutrient, less productive areas. This is because high nutrients cause plankton to proliferate, which obscures the water and reduces the sunlight making it through to

Bob Wohlers

Figure 6-10

Stalked anemone.

Bob Wohlers

Figure 6-11

Sea anemone.

Florida Fish and Wildlife Conservation Commission's Fish and Wildlife Research Institute

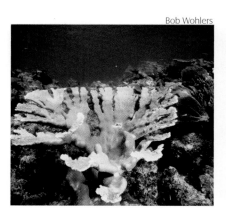

Bob Wohlers

Bob Wohlers

Figure 6-14

Coral bleaching.
When reef corals are stressed, they reject the zooxanthellae, which contain the pigments that give living coral its color. This rejection leaves the coral tissue colorless, allowing the white skeleton to show through – a phenomenon called *coral bleaching.*

Figure 6-12

Figure 6-13

Coral by day and night.
Most zooxanthellate coral polyps feed at night. Corals that look rock hard by day (**Figure 6-12**) look soft and fuzzy at night when the polyps feed (**Figure 6-13** - a close up photo).

Figure 6-15

Sea fan.

Sea fans are in class Anthozoa, order Gorgonacea, hence they are often called "gorgonians." Sea fans have thousands of individual tiny polyps living as one colony supported by an internal, central, wood-like, skeleton. Individual sea fan polyps are all interconnected by an internal tissue, making it a true colony.

Figure 6-16

Soft coral.

Like sea fans, soft corals are also colonial, but don't secrete solid calcium carbonate skeletons. Most grow into tree-like structures built on protein skeletons.

Figure 6-17

the coral. Hard corals are relatively sensitive to runoff of pollution, fertilizers, or any other nutrient source causing damage. When corals become stressed, they reject the zooxanthellae, which contain the pigments that give living coral its color. Without zooxanthellae, the coral polyp is translucent, so the rejection leaves them colorless. This is called *coral bleaching*, because the only color visible is the white of the polyp's skeleton. Coral bleaching is a stress response that can be a sign of a weakened and often dying colony.

Soft corals are also colonial, but don't secrete solid calcium carbonate skeletons. Most grow into tree-like structures built on protein skeletons. These proteins break down in the environment relatively quickly when the colony dies, so soft corals aren't reef builders. Sea fans are closely related to the soft corals. These colonial organisms attach to rocks and grow with the fans facing the prevailing current so the polyps can feed on drifting plankton.

Among other things, anemones are recognized for the mutualistic relationship they have in the tropical Indo-west Pacific or tropical Pacific, Indian Ocean, and Red Sea with various species of anemonefish (the most common species known as clownfish). The anemonefish receive protection by living among the stinging tentacles of an anemone. Although there is controversy as to a benefit to the anemone, some believe that the anemone receives food from the anemonefish. The anemonefish is *not* immune to anemone stings. Rather, by passing back and forth through the anemone, the anemonefish picks up anemone cells. From these cells, the anemone recognizes "its" anemonefish and doesn't sting it.

Special Attributes of Jellyfish

In what classes are jellyfish and box jellyfish?

What are two characteristics of the class Scyphozoa?

Cnidarians that have nematocysts that can hurt humans include some jellyfish species and box jellyfish. Because they all have this in common, you might expect them all to be closely related, but that's not the case.

Jellyfish are members of class Scyphozoa and range in size from smaller than a coin to more than 1 meter (3.28 feet) across with tentacles more than 3 meters (9.8 feet) long. Most are large planktonic organisms that swim, but also drift with the current. Jellyfish are weak swimmers that move by contracting and pulsating their rounded body, or bell. They feed on almost anything they catch with their tentacles. Some species have very short tentacles and very mild stings, making them more of an annoyance than a threat to swimmers. Others have long tentacles and can sting severely.

When small plankton bloom seasonally, the jellyfish that feed off them may reproduce, forming a secondary bloom. At these times, dense jellyfish clouds stretching for more than 160 kilometers (99 miles) may occupy the upper surface layers.

Although jellyfish are efficient predators, they are also prey. The leatherback turtle and several species of large fish, including the mola (also called "ocean sunfish"), feed on jellyfish and are relatively immune to the nematocysts. These predators appear to move seasonally with the jellyfish, staying near their food source. It turns out that human litter plays into this in a way that appears to threaten leatherbacks. Suspended in water, plastic bags, balloon fragments, and similar trash look much like jellyfish to the turtles. When eaten, they're indigestible and can clog their digestive system. This is one way that litter is not only ugly, but also an environmental hazard.

Among the most dangerous creatures in the ocean to humans are the box jellyfish. The name comes from tentacle clusters at the animal's four corners, giving a box-like appearance. Box jellyfish are members of class Cubozoa and a few species have stings that can kill an adult human within minutes. The box jellyfish's potent toxin causes paralysis and attacks blood cells. Like the jellyfish of class Scyphozoa, box jellyfish can swim and feed on plankton, but box jellyfish are much faster and more active hunters. Fortunately for swimmers and divers, they are rare in most parts of the world.

PADI

Figure 6-18

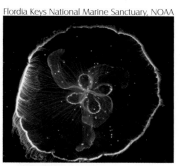

Flordia Keys National Marine Sanctuary, NOAA

Figure 6-19

PADI

Figure 6-20

Different types of jellyfish.
Jellyfish species come in a variety of shapes and sizes, but all are members of the class Scyphozoa. Some jellyfish can have tentacles up to 3 meters (9.8 feet) long. **Figures 6-18, 6-19** and **6-20** are all photos of typical jellyfish.

Dr. Jamie Seymour, James Cook University

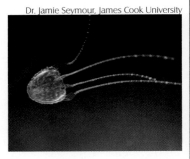

Figure 6-21

Box jellyfish.

One of the most dangerous creatures to humans is the box jellyfish. These members of the class Cubozoa have stings that can kill humans within minutes. They are rare in most parts of the world.

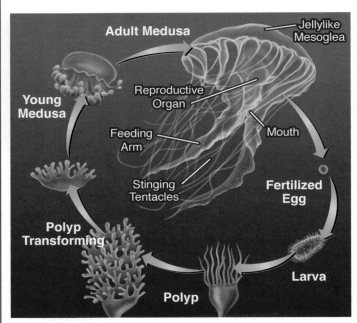

Figure 6-22

Typical jellyfish lifecycle.

The life cycle of a typical jellyfish involves alternating between two different body forms. The conspicuous medusa is the familiar, dominant form, while the smaller polyp form is restricted to the larval stage. The medusa males release sperm and females release eggs into the water. After an egg and sperm fuse and form a fertilized egg during sexual reproduction, a larva develops that attaches to a rock or other object. At this point, the larva develops into a polyp. Through asexual reproduction, the polyp transforms into a colony of polyps that resembles a stack of saucers. Each saucer in the stack detaches itself from the colony as a new medusa. From here the reproductive cycle repeats.

Marty Snyderman

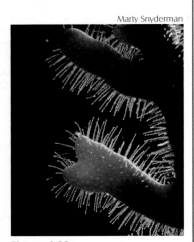

Figure 6-23

Fire coral.

Fire coral is a colonial organism that looks like a hard coral, but is actually a hydrozoan that can sting humans. This backlit photo shows the small tentacles protruding from the hard coral body. If you look carefully on each tentacle you can see the small bumps on each. These bumps are clumps of the stinging nematocysts.

Special Attributes of Fire Corals and Siphonophores

In what class are fire corals and siphonophores?

Fire coral is one of the cnidarians that can sting humans. It is a colonial organism that looks much like hard corals, but it belongs to a separate class, Hydrozoa. Organisms that form complex colonies or have more complex life cycles characterize this class. Most organisms in this class alternate between polyp and medusa forms during their life cycle.

Fire corals get their name from the mild burn you get from touching them. They have a waxy, yellow-tan appearance and grow in small tree-like colonies or as an encrusting, plate-like colony. Contact with fire coral is unpleasant but not considered serious unless the individual has an allergic reaction or the fire coral makes contact with a large portion of the body.

Siphonophores are another group within Class Hydrozoa. Siphonophores exist as colonies, yet within the colonies are specialized polyps adapted to feeding, reproduction, movement, and other functions. Thus, they're more than colonies, yet not as sophisticated as a complex animal, such as a fish or squid.

A good example of a siphonophore is the Portuguese Man-of-War, which has highly specialized polyps that perform different functions. Portuguese Man-of-War have distinct floats that allow the wind to push them through the water. This motion gives their long, hard-to-spot, trailing tentacles more opportunities to catch prey. As an interesting aside, the Portuguese Man-of-War fish lives among these tentacles, much as the anemonefish lives within anemone tentacles.

Ocean Explorer, NOAA

Figure 6-24

Portuguese Man-of-War.

The Portuguese Man-of-War (also called Man o' War) is a colonial organism with specialized colonial polyps for feeding buoyancy and reproduction.

AVOIDING JELLYFISH STINGS

Although jellyfish and Portuguese Man-of-War can have powerful stings, you don't need to be afraid of the water. Remember, many jellyfish stings are too small or weak to penetrate human skin. Apply some basic safety rules and common sense when you visit the ocean and you're much less likely to have an unpleasant experience.

1. Stay out of the water if you see jellyfish or if you see jellyfish warnings posted.
2. Cnidaria can't sting through wetsuits or fabric skin suits. Wearing these reduces your chances of getting stung.
3. Nematocysts on a dead jellyfish can still sting. Don't step on or handle jellyfish or other cnidarians that have washed up on the beach. When helping someone who has been stung, do not remove tentacles with your bare hands. Thoroughly rinse a protective suit before touching it with bare hands if it had contact with a jellyfish.
4. In the water, watch where you are swimming. If you're snorkeling or scuba diving, look up as you surface.

If you or someone you're with does get stung, remember these points:

1. For serious injuries or allergic reactions, call 911 and contact emergency medical help. Provide CPR if necessary.
2. Do not touch the injured area or tentacles with your bare hands. Lift them off gently with an instrument, or rinse them off gently with salt water, not fresh water.
3. Do not rub the injured area. Rubbing makes things worse by triggering unfired nematocysts.
4. Jellyfish stings should be liberally washed with vinegar (4% to 6% acetic acid solution) as soon as possible for at least 30 seconds to prevent further stinging and/or to inactivate nematocysts. If vinegar is not available, baking soda mixed with a small amount of seawater may be used instead. Topical application of meat tenderizer is not recommended for the relief of pain.
5. After the nematocysts are removed or deactivated, the pain caused by jellyfish stings should be treated with hot-water immersion when possible. The victim

should be instructed to take a hot shower or immerse the affected part in hot water (temperature as hot as tolerated) as soon as possible. The immersion should continue for at least 20 minutes, or for as long as pain persists. If hot water is not available, dry hot packs or, as a second choice, dry cold packs may also be helpful in decreasing pain.

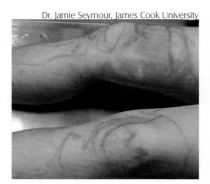
Dr. Jamie Seymour, James Cook University

Figure 6-25

Box jellyfish sting.

These extremely painful and potentially fatal stings can look dramatic. Shown here is the aftermath of a box jellyfish sting.

Figure 6-26

Planktonic Siphonophore.

Many siphonophores represent a bridge between colonial animals and complex organisms. The largest siphonophores can exceed 40 meters (131 feet) in length and many are major predators.

Budd Riker

The Portuguese Man-of-War has a very powerful sting that can be life-threatening. Although people call them jellyfish (class Scyphozoa), they're not. These animals are siphonophores in the class Hydrozoa.

Siphonophores are major predators, with some species consuming significant quantities of krill and copepods. Krill and copepods are planktonic crustaceans that also provide a major food source for most of the larger animals in the sea, such as fish and whales.

ARE YOU LEARNING?

1. Organisms in phylum Cnidaria include (choose all that apply)
   A. jellyfish.
   B. anemone.
   C. hard corals.
   D. sea fans.

2. Cnidarians have a radially symmetrical cup- or bag-like body made up of two layers of cells.
   A. true
   B. false

3. The largest class in phylum Cnidaria is class _____, which includes _____.
   A. Anthozoa, jellyfish
   B. Hydrozoa, siphonophores
   C. Anthozoa, corals and anemones
   D. Scyphozoa, jellyfish

4. Jellyfish are in class _____ and box jellyfish are in class _____.
   A. Scyphozoa, Cubozoa
   B. Cnidaria, Anthozoa
   C. Cubozoa, Scyphozoa
   D. Anthozoa, Scyphozoa

5. Like jellyfish, box jellyfish can swim and feed on plankton, but are weak swimmers.
   A. true
   B. false

6. Fire corals and siphonophores are in class
   A. Hydrozoa.
   B. Anthozoa.
   C. Scyphozoa.
   D. Protozoa.

Comb Jellies – Gelatinous Carnivores

Characteristics of Phylum Ctenophora

What are two differences between the jellyfish and Ctenophores?

What are the anatomical characteristics of Ctenophores?

What do Ctenophores eat?

STUDY QUESTIONS

Find the answers as you read.

1. What are two differences between the jellyfish and Ctenophores?

2. What are the anatomical characteristics of Ctenophores?

3. What do Ctenophores eat?

Organisms in phylum Ctenophora (pronounced teen-oh-FOUR-a; from the Greek *kteno* meaning *comb* and *phore*, meaning *bearer*) look like they should classified as cnidarians because they have gelatinous bodies similar to jellyfish. Common names for ctenophores include comb jellies, sea gooseberries, sea walnuts and Venus girdles. Of the approximately 100 to 150 oval and pear-shaped species, all live in the marine environment from polar to tropical, inshore to offshore waters.

Unlike true jellyfish, however, ctenophores lack the characteristic bag-like cnidarian body shape. Also, they do not have cnidocytes – stinging cells. Instead all ctenophres have eight "comb

Courtesy of Harbor Branch Oceanographic

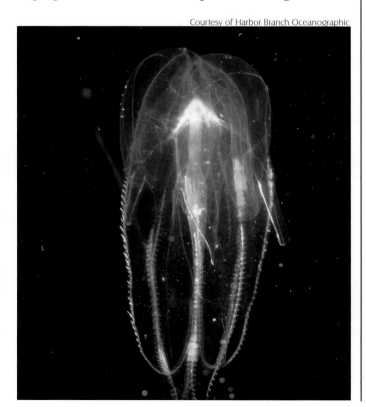

Figure 6-27

Comb jellyfish.

Although they appear to be jellyfish, comb jellyfish are actually members of phylum Ctenophora and lack stinging nematocysts.

rows" of cilia on their surfaces to help them move. Ctenophore's cilia beat synchronously and help propel them through the water. Some species also move with slow undulations of their body. Ctenophores are the largest organisms that use cilia for mobility.

Ctenophores are generally small. Most are only a few millimeters to several centimeters long. Generally, their bodies are nearly colorless, but most exhibit a rainbow colored light produced by the beating of their cilia. This appears as colors moving down the comb rows, beginning at one end of the body and ending at the other. Once thought to be chemical bioluminescence, the effect is actually diffraction or scattering of light by the moving cilia. Some ctenophores are also bioluminescent, but you can only see their light in the dark.

Like jellyfish, ctenophores have organized tissues but lack true organs. The body exterior is covered with a thin skin that also enters the mouth and lines the internal areas. Ctenophores have a well-developed nerve net and reproduce mostly through sexual reproduction. Some have a pair of sticky tentacles that can be retracted into the mouth area to aid in feeding.

Ctenophores are all carnivores, eating a variety of small planktonic animals – mainly copepods. Because plankton copepods are one of the greatest food sources on Earth, ctenophores populations can grow rapidly in productive seas. Like jellyfish, ctenophores may bloom abundantly in rich temperate and polar seas when plankton blooms.

ARE YOU LEARNING?

1. **Ctenophores differ from jellyfish by**

   A. being colorless.

   B. having stinging cells.

   C. using cilia for movement.

2. **Ctenophores are characterized by (choose all that apply)**

   A. having oval or pear-shaped, nearly colorless bodies.

   B. being generally small – only a few millimeters to several centimeters long.

   C. having stinging cells.

3. **Ctenophores eat**

   A. planktonic plants.

   B. planktonic animals.

   C. small fish.

Simple Marine Worms – Flat, Ribbon-Like and Round

Characteristics of Simple Worms

What characterizes members of phylum Platyhelminthes?

What characterizes members of phylum Nemertea?

What characterizes members of phylum Nematoda?

If the word "worm" makes you think of a simple, unexciting, and insignificant animal, think again. Of the 32 main animal phyla, 22 could be considered worms of various types. The worm body shape is highly adaptable, allowing these 22 phyla to dominate the habitats below the ground's surface. Scientists think the evolution of a wormlike body plan was the "blueprint" from which all complex body plans were derived. Worm anatomy makes up all the basics of a complex animal with organs. Most, but not all, have a complete one-way digestive system, a head, body cavities, and a brain-centered nervous system. There are three phyla of simple worms we want to look at with respect to marine biology.

Phylum Platyhelminthes is made up of flat worms. These are among the simplest animals, consisting of essentially a flattened

STUDY QUESTIONS

Find the answers as you read.

1. What characterizes members of phylum Platyhelminthes?

2. What characterizes members of phylum Nemertea?

3. What characterizes members of phylum Nematoda?

4. What is the longest animal in the world?

SIMPLE WORM CLASSIFICATION

Domain
Eukarya

Supergroup
Unikonts

Kingdom
Animalia

Phylum
Platyhelminthes – Flat Worms

Phylum
Nemertea – Ribbon Worms

Phylum
Nematoda – Round Worms

Figure 6-28

Figure 6-29

Turbellaria reef worm.

Although most flat worms are parasites, class Turbellaria is a notable exception. Many members are brightly colored tropical reef worms.

tube of muscle and a simple digestive system with a single opening that serves as both mouth and anus. It has no true body cavity, nor does it have the distinct body segments that characterize more complex worms. The vast majority of species in this phylum are parasites, but class Turbellaria is a noteworthy exception. This class includes species of brightly colored tropical reef worms.

The ribbon worms in phylum Nemertea are slightly more complex. While they also have a flattened shape, they have a one-way digestive system with separate mouth and anus and a simple blood vascular system. Nemerteans are carnivores that hunt in the sediments for prey. Phylum Nematoda consists of round worms that are structurally simple. A round body with a complete, one-way digestive system characterizes them (ie. having a mouth and an anus). They are more complex than phyla Platyhelminthes and Nemertea, but still lack true body segments. The vast majority of phylum Nematoda species are small parasitic worms. They're significant in marine biology because some of these parasites live in sea animals. However, this phylum also includes human parasite forms, including pinworms and hookworms.

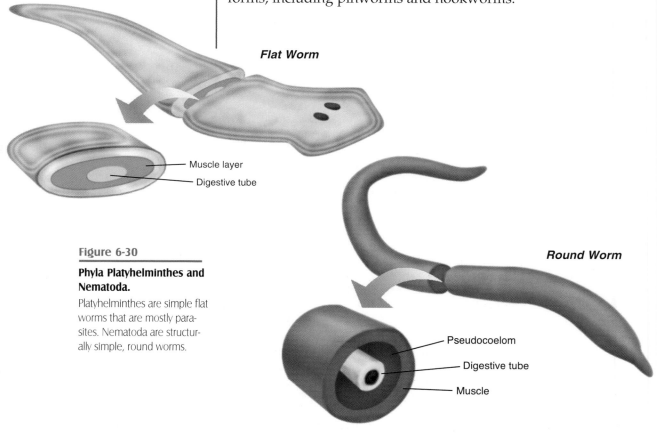

Flat Worm

Muscle layer
Digestive tube

Figure 6-30

Phyla Platyhelminthes and Nematoda.

Platyhelminthes are simple flat worms that are mostly parasites. Nematoda are structurally simple, round worms.

Round Worm

Pseudocoelom
Digestive tube
Muscle

Special Attributes of Simple Worms

What is the longest animal in the world?

Perhaps the most interesting distinction of any of the simple worms is that *Lineus longissimus* (the bootlace worm), a nemertean, is one of the longest known creatures in the world (note: the blue whale, by volume and weight, is the *largest* – not *longest* – known *animal* ever to have lived). Reaching up to 60 meters (197 feet) in length, this North Sea worm exceeds the length of the long, colonial siphonophores or blue whales.

Kare Telnes/www.seawater.no

Figure 6-31

Lineus longissimus.

Nemertean ribbon worms are carnivores that hunt in the sediment for prey. This North Sea species rivals siphonophores as possibly being the longest creature in the world. It has been estimated that when *Lineus longissimus* is stretched, it can reach 60 meters (197 feet). If this is the case, it is the longest known animal. The controversy goes on as to which creature is the longest on Earth.

ARE YOU LEARNING?

1. **Simple worms in phylum Platyhelminthes are characterized by**

   A. a round, structurally simple body, and a one-way digestive system.

   B. a flattened shape with a single opening that is both mouth and anus.

   C. a flattened shape with a one-way digestive system.

2. **Simple worms in phylum Nemertea are characterized by**

   A. a round, structurally simple body, and a one-way digestive system.

   B. a flattened shape with a single opening that is both mouth and anus.

   C. a flattened shape with a one-way digestive system.

3. **Simple worms in phylum Nematoda are characterized by**

   A. a round, structurally simple body, and a one-way digestive system.

   B. a flattened shape with a single opening that is both mouth and anus.

   C. a flattened shape with a one-way digestive system.

4. **_____ may possibly be the longest animal in the world.**

   A. The blue whale

   B. A siphonophore

   C. *Lineus longissimus*

   D. none of the above

Mollusks—A Bag, a Scraper, and a Foot

STUDY QUESTIONS

Find the answers as you read.

1. What organisms make up phylum Mollusca?

2. What three characteristics do members of phylum Mollusca share?

3. What mollusks belong to class Gastropoda?

4. What is *torsion* in gastropods? When does it happen?

5. What mollusks belong to class Bivalvia?

6. What mollusks belong to class Cephalopoda?

7. What are the major differences between the nautilus, cuttlefish, squid, and octopuses?

8. Which cephalopod is thought to be the most intelligent invertebrate?

Characteristics of Mollusks

What organisms make up phylum Mollusca?

What three characteristics do members of phylum Mollusca share?

Organisms from diverse environments and lifestyles make up phylum Mollusca – the mollusks. Ranging from squid and octopuses to snails, sea slugs (snails without shells), oysters, clams, and conches, the mollusks make up a successful animal group. Although there are around 50,000 mollusk species and 10 total classes, they all generally share the basic anatomical structures that categorize them in the phylum.

The first of these is a muscular bag called the *mantle*. The mantle surrounds the gills and most organs and is used to circulate water through the organism. Some mollusks use this circulation for feeding, while others use it to jet out water for propulsion. On many mollusks, the mantle secretes a calcium carbonate shell for protection.

A second feature common to most mollusks is a muscular foot beneath the head. Mollusks such as slugs and snails use this foot to crawl. In other mollusks, such as squid, the foot takes the form of tentacles.

The *radula* is a third distinguishing characteristic of some members within the phylum Mollusca. Think of it as a tongue bearing rough scraping teeth used for feeding. Different types of mollusks have different types of radula adapted to their feeding needs. In the case of predatory cone shells, the radula takes the form of a "harpoon" with a barb and venom that paralyzes. Some South Pacific

Figure 6-32

A typical mollusk.
The more than 50,000 mollusk species generally share the same basic anatomical structures. The mantle is a muscular bag surrounding the gills and most organs. The muscular foot is located beneath the head. The radula is a scraping mechanism used for feeding.

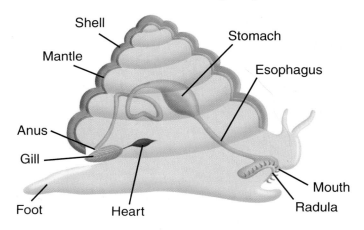

Shell

Stomach

Mantle

Esophagus

Anus

Gill

Mouth

Radula

Foot

Heart

cone shells can be very venomous to humans, even causing death. Divers are well advised to handle beautiful shells with caution.

Mollusks develop through distinct larval stages, starting with a *trochophore*, which resembles a spinning top. For most species, the next stage is as a planktonic *veliger*, which looks something like a translucent butterfly. The veliger settles on the bottom and matures into adult form.

Special Attributes of Class Gastropoda

What mollusks belong to class Gastropoda?

What is torsion *in gastropods? When does it happen?*

Snails, whelks, slugs, and most of the single-shelled mollusks belong in class Gastropoda. Members of this class undergo a unique developmental process called *torsion*. After the veliger settles and begins maturing, its body twists into a permanent loop that rearranges the organs and brings them all together. This allows the body to draw into the protective spiral shell common to this class. Many gastropods have single organs – gills and *nephridia* (simple kidneys) – that are separated pairs in other mollusks. Some scientists think the paired organs evolved into single organs because they're close together anyway.

Although they go through the same developmental process, not all gastropods have shells. Subclass Opisthobranchia consists of slugs, sea slugs, and nudibranchs. The protection these organisms lack from shells is offset by their ability to defend themselves with toxins. However, not all members of this subclass generate these protective toxins themselves. Nudibranchs feed on cnidarians, and have the ability to eat the nematocysts without firing or digesting them. The nematocysts are incorporated into *cerata* on the nudibranch's back. Cerata are unique organs that look like soft tufts and serve as both gills and a defensive weapon armed with stolen nematocysts.

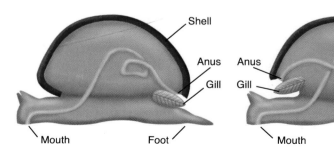

Shell
Anus
Gill
Mouth
Foot

Shell
Anus
Gill
Mouth
Foot

MOLLUSCA CLASSIFICATION

Domain
Eukarya
Supergroup
Unikonts
Kingdom
Animalia

Phylum
Mollusca

Major Classes
1. Gastropoda – Snails, Sea Slugs
2. Bivalvia – Clams, Oysters, Scallops, Mussels
3. Cephalopoda – Squid, Octopus, Cuttlefish, Nautilus

Figure 6-33

Bob Wohlers

Figure 6-34a

A classic gastropod.
California green abalone, *Haliotis fulgens* sp.

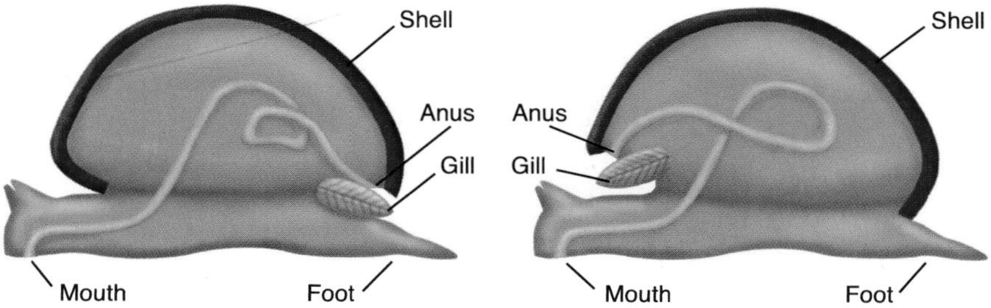

Figure 6-34b

Gastropod torsion.
Members of the class Gastropoda go through a developmental process called *torsion*. The body twists into a loop and rearranges organs to bring them together. This allows the body to draw into the protective shell common to this class.

Figure 6-35

Subclass Opisthobranchia.
Not all gastropods have
shells. Sea slugs and nudibranchs use toxins and cerata
to protect themselves. Some
species, such as this *Caloria
indica* incorporate ingested
nematocysts into the cerata
shown as soft tufts on the
organism.

Special Attributes of Class Bivalvia

What mollusks belong to class Bivalvia?

Mollusks that have two hinged shells belong to class Bivalvia (bi
meaning *two*). Mussels, clams, oysters, and scallops are all bivalves.
The approximately 10,000 species of bivalves are highly specialized,
with some interesting differences that set them apart from other
mollusks.

For one, bivalves lack any "head" in the sense that other mollusks
have them. Their nervous systems, eyespots, gills, and other sensory
organs spread out along the shell edges instead of being grouped
into a head-like location. The mantle bag acts as a pump, drawing
in water to supply oxygen to the gills and food to the mouth. Some
bivalves, like certain scallops, can "jump" short distances to escape
predators by jetting out water at high speed. Since they feed off particles filtered from the water flow, bivalves have no radula.

While shelled gastropods can withdraw into their single shell
for protection, bivalves can pull their two shells together with
powerful muscles. The insides of some bivalve shells are very
dense and smooth. This calcium carbonate shell lining is called
nacre, or mother-of-pearl. If sand or another irritant gets trapped
inside the shell, the organism will deposit nacre around it to protect itself. Over time, subsequent nacre layers enlarge it, forming
a pearl. Commercial pearl fishermen grow pearls by intentionally
inserting "seeds" inside pearl oysters. Given time, the oysters form
pearls around these seeds, which pearl fishermen later harvest
for jewelry.

Figure 6-36

A generic bivalve (oyster).
Bivalves, such as this oyster,
have two opposing shells
with their organs spread out
rather than in a central head-
like location. The mantle
pumps water to supply oxygen and food particles while
strong muscles let the bivalve
close. Some species can also
form pearls if an irritant gets
trapped inside the shell.

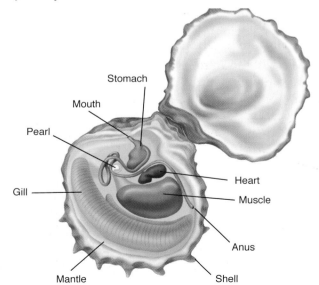

Stomach

Mouth

Pearl

Gill

Heart

Muscle

Anus

Mantle

Shell

Special Attributes of Class Cephalopoda

What mollusks belong to class Cephalopoda?

What are the major differences between the nautilus, cuttlefish, squid, and octopuses?

Which cephalopod is thought to be the most intelligent invertebrate?

The approximately 650 species of mollusks in class Cephalopoda (from Latin and Greek, *cephalopoda* means *head on foot*) differ significantly from the rest of the phylum. This class includes the nautilus, cuttlefish, squid, and octopuses, all of which share several attributes. For one, most cephalopods have little or no shell. Also, the muscular foot is divided and forms the arms and tentacles characteristic of cephalopods.

Nautiluses have a gastropod-like shell. Cuttlefish have an internal, leaf-shaped shell, while squid simply have a thin bar, and most octopuses have no shell at all. This class has a very specialized foot known as the *siphon*, which enables them to move through the water. Water is drawn into the mantle cavity and then forcibly expelled through the siphon. This creates a jet propulsion that shoots them forward, backward, upward, downward, or side-to-side, depending on the direction in which the siphon is pointed. Cephalopods have eyes and nervous systems developed to a degree not seen in any other invertebrates. Some cephalopods exhibit behavior typically found in higher-level animals.

Cephalopods are soft-bodied, but have several modes of defense. First, they can ward off attackers with their tentacles. Second, they have *chromatophores* – pigment sacs in their skin cells that allow them to change color – which make them excellent camouflage experts. Apparently, they also use these color changes to communicate mood or intention to rivals or mates. Last, most species have a sac that contains *sepia*, a black ink-like substance that can envelop and temporarily cloud the enemy's vision.

Cephalopods are fast moving, aggressive predators. They capture prey with tentacles that have muscular suckers for gripping. They bite prey with a parrot-like beak at the base of their tentacles and shred the meat with their radula.

The chambered nautilus (order Nautilida) is a native of the tropical Pacific and has the same general form of all cephalopods. It has a coiled, external shell that they use to control their buoyancy. They have up to 90 tentacles – the most of any cephalopod. The nautilus is thought to have changed little in the last 150 million years. Because of this, scientists think it's a living link to its cousin, the octopus.

Bob Wohlers

Figure 6-37

Chromatophores.

Chromatophores, such as those seen on this octopus, are specialized skin cells that allow the organism to change color or even form color patterns.

Bob Wohlers

Figure 6-38

Mating squid.

The California squid *Loligo opalescens* mating. The male squid (with the red tentacles) grabs the the female to provide her with sperm to fertilize her egg pouch.

The nautilus' tentacles are arranged into two circles, and unlike the tentacles of other cephalopods, they lack suckers. Nautilus tentacles have grooves and ridges that grip food and pass it into the mouth. Like squid and octopuses, nautiluses have a parrot-like beak that rips food apart, and a radula that further shreds the food. Also like squid and octopuses, they use their siphon to move forward, backward and sideways.

Found in the southwestern Pacific Ocean and Indian Ocean, the nautilus can live as deep as 1000 meters (3,280 feet). At night however, they often migrate up to a shallower 200 meter (650 feet) depth to feed. Their diet consists of crabs, shrimp and the remains of other animals.

Cuttlefish (order Sepioidea) differ from squid and octopuses by having an internal shell used primarily for buoyancy control. The shell, or cuttlebone, is very light and filled with tiny air chambers. Cuttlefish can vary their depth easily by changing the proportion of liquid to air in their internal shell. This is similar to what the nautilus does to control its buoyancy, but the nautilus has an external and proportionately larger shell.

Squid (order Teuthoidea) differ from cuttlefish and octopuses with their streamlined, torpedo-shaped bodies adapted to life in open water. Although some species live in reef communities, others, including giant squid, colossal squid and Humbolt squid, live their entire lives in open-ocean pelagic communities. Squid range in size from smaller than your hand to more than 13 meters (43 feet) long. Noted characteristics of squid are two opposing tentacles that are longer than the other eight the organism has. These special tentacles are especially suited to seizing prey in open water and drawing it within reach of the shorter tentacles.

Squid are important members of the world's food webs. In temperate and polar waters they consume krill and small fish and are prey for marine mammals and birds. The fishing industry catches about a million tons of squid annually. When you eat calamari in an Italian restaurant, you're consuming part of this catch. (*Calamari* is the Italian word for *squid*.)

Octopuses (order Octopoda) differ from squid and cuttlefish by having no shell and living in rocky reefs and coral. While they can jet away to escape a predator, they spend most of their time crawling through cracks and caves looking for prey and safety. They range from about fist size to the giant octopus. The giant octopus may be heavier than a large man and able to stretch its tentacles into a room-sized blanket.

Octopuses have venom glands in their beaks to paralyze struggling prey and avoid injury to their soft bodies. Most octopus venom is harmless to humans, though the blue-ringed octopus of the South Pacific is highly toxic to people and its bite can be fatal.

Many scientists think the octopus is the most intelligent invertebrate. Octopuses have demonstrated behaviors and thought patterns usually only associated with mammals. While most octopuses (even the giant octopus) are frightened of and flee from humans, divers have been able to tame reef octopuses. Octopuses are well

Bruce Avera Hunter

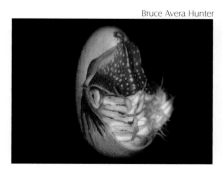

Figure 6-39a

Nautilus.

Al Hornsby

Figure 6-39b

Cuttlefish.

William Milhouser, National Ocean Service, NOAA

Figure 6-39c

Squid.

Al Hornsby

Figure 6-39d

Octopus.

Four cephalopods.

Although they are all members of the class Cephalopoda, nautilus, cuttlefish, squid, and octopuses differ in a number of respects. Nautiluses have a prominent head and tentacles, and an external, coiled shell. Cuttlefish have an internal shell and spend most of their time close to but off of reefs and bottom. Squid, on the other hand, have a streamlined body adapted to open water and possess two opposing tentacles longer than the others that are used to snare prey in open water. Octopuses have no shell and live in rocky reef and coral environments. They spend most of their time on the bottom crawling through cracks and caves looking for prey and safety.

known for their ability to escape from aquariums. In at least one incident, an octopus escaped from its tank, crawled across dry land, and climbed into another aquarium containing a potential mate. Octopuses have even learned how to unscrew a jar top to get to food visible inside.

ARE YOU LEARNING?

1. **Organisms in phylum Mollusca include (choose all that apply)**
   A. sea slugs.
   B. snails.
   C. squid.
   D. stingrays.

2. **Members of phylum Mollusca generally share _____, _____, and _____.**
   A. mantle, jet propulsion, tentacles
   B. mantle, foot, radula
   C. foot, tentacles, radula
   D. shells, radula, mantle

3. **The mollusks in class Gastropoda are**
   A. single-shelled mollusks, snails, and whelks.
   B. oysters, clams, and scallops.
   C. octopuses, squid, and clams.
   D. all of the above

4. **During torsion, gastropod bodies twist into a permanent line that separates the organs.**
   A. true
   B. false

5. **Mollusks in class Bivalvia**
   A. have two shells.
   B. lack a "head."
   C. do not have a radula.
   D. all of the above

6. **Mollusks in class Cephalopoda include**
   A. slugs and snails.
   B. oysters and scallops.
   C. nudibranchs.
   D. none of the above

7. **Squid differ from cuttlefish in that they're streamlined for open water living and have two tentacles that are longer than the others for seizing prey.**
   A. true
   B. false

8. **The _____ is thought to be the most intelligent invertebrate.**
   A. cuttlefish
   B. squid
   C. octopus
   D. whelk

Complex Worms – Segments and a Simple Heart

Characteristics of Annelids

What distinguishes worms in phylum Annelida from the simple worms of other phyla?

More worms! As you read earlier, worms are highly successful life forms thanks to their adaptable body shape and structure. Worms in phylum Annelida stand apart from the simple worms of other phyla because of their structural complexity. Annelids have *nephridia* (water-regulating tubules) as part of the excretory system, a heart, and, in some cases, jaws. Even more significant, annelids show *metamerism*. Metamerism is the division of the body into repeating blocks or segments. These repeating segments include muscle and nerve blocks that link to a central nervous system lying along the body axis. Some scientists think that the rise of metamerism was the evolutionary step that led to more complex body patterns, with some segments evolving into gills, jaws, and limb girdles from which appendages would evolve.

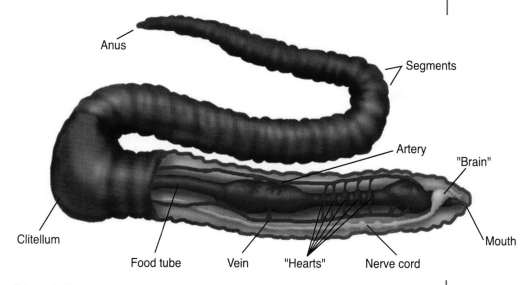

Figure 6-40

A typical annelid.

Annelids stand apart from the simple worms of other phyla because of their structural complexity. They have nephridia, a heart, and sometimes jaws. Most important, they exhibit metamerism the division of the body into repeating blocks or segments.

COMPLEX WORM CLASSIFICATION

Domain
Eukarya

Supergroup
Unikonts

Kingdom
Animalia

Phylum
Annelida – Segmented Worms

Class
Polychaeta
Tubeworms, Bristleworms

Figure 6-41

Special Attributes of Annelids

What class in phylum Annelida has many species in the marine environment?

Phylum Annelida has more than 15,000 species that range from the common earthworm to freshwater leeches. Class Polychaeta, however, has particular relevance to oceanography because many polychaete worms live in the marine environment. These include the tubeworms that live on coral reefs. Their distinct, flower-like "antennae" (actually filter-feeding organs) that withdraw in a blink at the slightest threat are familiar to recreational scuba divers. Bristleworms, which sting and burn when touched, live in the coral and beneath artificial underwater structures. Spongeworms live on sponges, as you might expect. Fireworms live on the surface of fire coral.

Bob Wohlers

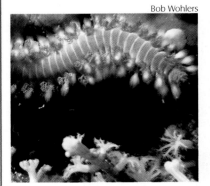

Figure 6-42a

Bristleworm.

Jürg Beeli/PADI

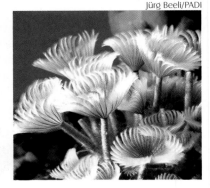

Figure 6-42b

Caribbean tubeworm.

These worms have distinct, flower-like "antennae" (actually filter-feeding organs) that withdraw in a blink at the slightest threat.

ARE YOU LEARNING?

1. **The characteristics that distinguish phylum Annelida worms from simple worms include(s) (choose all that apply)**
   - **A.** nephridia, a heart, and, in some cases, jaws.
   - **B.** the lack of a true digestive system.
   - **C.** metamerism.
   - **D.** the ability to swim.

2. **The class in phylum Annelida with many species in the marine environment is class**
   - **A.** Polychaeta.
   - **B.** Oakleaita.
   - **C.** Francsaeta.
   - **D.** Bolinaeta.

Crustaceans—Underwater Arthropods

Characteristics of Crustaceans

What characteristics do you find in organisms classified in phylum Arthropoda?

What characteristics do you find in organisms classified in superclass Crustacea?

Of all the complex and multicellular animal phyla, phylum Arthropoda is the most numerous. Scientists think at least 1 million arthropod species exist – far more than any other animal group. The majority of these are terrestrial insects, though this phylum also includes spiders, crustaceans, and all manner of organisms that we commonly think of as bugs. The number of arthropod species is likely to be well more than 1 million, because some *entomologists* (scientists who study insects) estimate there may be more than *20 million* insect species – though only a tiny fraction of these have been identified.

Taxonomists classify all these species into phylum Arthropoda because they generally share several characteristics. Arthropods have segmented bodies, jointed legs, and a chitinous *exoskeleton*. An exoskeleton is a hard external covering that provides support and protection for some invertebrates. *Chitin* (pronounced KI-tin) is the hard carbohydrate material that makes up arthropod exoskeletons.

Phylum Arthropoda has so many varied species that taxonomists must use several intermediate classifications. The one most important to marine sciences is superclass (sometimes called a

STUDY QUESTIONS

Find the answers as you read.

1. What characteristics do you find in organisms classified in phylum Arthropoda?

2. What characteristics do you find in organisms classified in superclass Crustacea?

3. What characteristic of barnacles sets them aside as class Cirripedia?

4. Why are organisms in class Copepoda important to ocean food webs?

5. What characteristics do crustaceans in order Decapoda have in common?

6. Why are the crustaceans in order Decapoda important to the fishing industry?

7. Why are krill important to ocean food webs?

Topic: Crustaceans
Go To: www.scilinks.org
Code: LOP2555

Bob Wohlers

Figure 6-43

Caribbean lobster—a classic marine arthropod.

Bob Wohlers

Figure 6-44

Crab.

subphylum) Crustacea. The approximately 40,000 crustaceans generally have the following characteristics: two pairs of antennae, mandibles for chewing, a pair of appendages on each body segment, and distinctive, teardrop-shaped larvae. All crustaceans molt (shed) their exoskeletons as they grow, leaving the old one behind as they grow into a new, larger one.

You're probably familiar with crustaceans such as crabs, lobsters, and shrimp, but barnacles and copepods fit in this category, too. Most, but not all, crustaceans are aquatic. A common terrestrial crustacean is the potato bug or "roly-poly."

Special Attributes of Class Cirripedia

What characteristic of barnacles sets them aside as class Cirripedia?

Barnacles have to be some of the least crustacean-like crustaceans, at least by appearance. Their unique lifestyle sets them apart into class Cirripedia. They begin life as free-swimming larvae like other crustaceans. When the larva finds a suitable surface on which to live – a rock, whale, boat bottom, or rope – it fuses itself in place "upside down." As an adult it uses its legs to gather and kick food floating by into its mouth. When danger threatens, it can withdraw into its *carapace* made of calcium carbonate plates. A *carapace* is a

Figure 6-46

A typical barnacle.
Barnacles begin their lives as free-swimming larvae, like other crustaceans, before settling on a hard surface and cementing themselves "upside down." The adult barnacle uses its legs (cirri) to gather food and withdraws into its carapace when threatened.

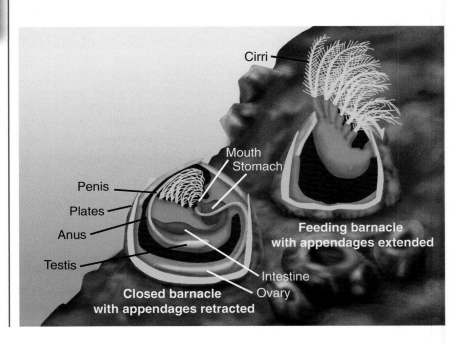

shell or hard surface an animal uses for protection. In this case, the barnacle's tough exoskeleton forms the carapace.

Some, but not all barnacles that live on other animals are parasitic. Barnacles known as Rhizocephlans have no carapace or organs and exist as an amorphous mass within the body of their host (usually crabs and shrimp). They are recognized as barnacles primarily due to their larval forms. These parasites not only feed of the tissues of the host, but render it sterile and cause the host's reproductive behaviors to aid the reproduction of the parasite.

Figure 6-47a

Gooseneck barnacles with "legs" extended for feeding.

Figure 6-47b

Barnacles.

Sometimes barnacles can attach in the most unlikely places. These barnacles have attached themselves to a gray whale.

Special Attributes of Copepods

Why are organisms in class Copepoda important to ocean food webs?

Copepods, which make up class Copepoda, are mostly very small crustaceans. Most are less than a millimeter long and teardrop shaped. To the naked eye, a copepod may look like a grain of sand swimming.

Despite their small size, copepods are important primary and secondary consumers of phytoplankton and smaller zooplankton. They're important for two reasons. First, they are by far the most numerous multicellular animals on Earth. They make up the majority of the mass of the zooplankton, and they grow and reproduce at incredible rates. The second reason for their importance is because relatively few larger animals can consume the tiniest plankton, but many can eat the larger copepods. Fish, krill, and giant plankton

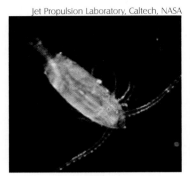

Figure 6-48

Copepods.

These crustaceans are shaped liked a teardrop, are less than a millimeter long, but are among the most important creatures in the ocean. Copepods form a crucial link mostly very small primary producers to the higher-level consumers.

feeders, including whale sharks, baleen whales, and manta rays, all eat copepods. Thus, copepods are important to ocean food webs because they link the tiny primary producers and consumers to the large animals higher up the web.

Another important function is that copepods concentrate the nutrients they consume as fecal pellets. These fecal pellets sink to the ocean bottom much more rapidly than the nutrients would in unconcentrated form. This makes copepod fecal pellets vital to shortening the nutrient cycles, and to removing carbon from the upper ocean layers and sequestering it to the seafloor. To learn more about how this process works, see Chapter 12.

Because of the importance of copepods to the ocean's productivity, scientists watch their physiology and ecology closely. This is likely to remain an active area of research as we cope with the effects of pollution and the need to feed the rising human population.

Special Attributes of Decapods and Krill

What characteristics do the crustaceans in order Decapoda have in common?

Why are the crustaceans in order Decapoda important to the fishing industry?

Why are krill important to ocean food webs?

Class Malacostraca includes two orders that particularly interest marine scientists because of their roles as food for humans and food for nature. The first is order Decapoda, which includes lobsters, shrimps, and crabs. All decapods have ten functional legs (from the Greek *deca* meaning *ten* and *poda* meaning *foot*). They have claws and an extended carapace that encloses the gills.

Figure 6-49

Shrimp net exclusion devices.

To reduce bycatch, fisheries and scientists have been working together to develop exclusion devices. Exclusion devices reduce the number of unwanted organisms caught and killed as bycatch, but it's still a problem. This illustration shows a shrimp net with a turtle exclusion device.

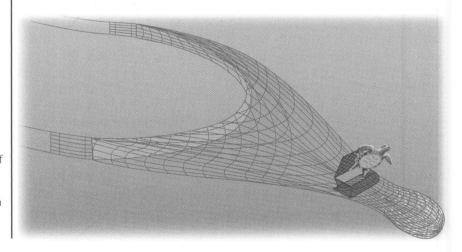

You might have immediately recognized that the crustaceans in order Decapoda are the organisms you may sometimes have for dinner. They're an important food source and resource on which the fishing industry relies. The capture of decapods for food isn't without concerns, however.

Most shrimp are free-swimming plankton feeders, making them readily catchable by net. Shrimp fisheries have come under increasing criticism for the amount of *bycatch* associated with netting shrimp. Bycatch is marine life captured but not wanted by fishermen – such as turtles, inedible fish and marine mammals. A lot of bycatch dies before being dumped back in the sea.

To reduce bycatch, fisheries and scientists have been working together to develop exclusion devices. Exclusion devices reduce the number of unwanted organisms caught and killed as bycatch, but it's still a problem. This is an important issue regarding the effects of fishing that's discussed more in Chapter 15.

Lobsters and crabs are benthic (bottom living) and are caught with traps, so the bycatch problem is not so serious. However, even these fisheries raise some concerns. American lobsters once exceeded a meter (3.28 feet) and 20 kilograms (44 pounds) regularly. Japanese spider crabs have been measured with leg spans exceeding 3 meters (9.8 feet). However, the fisheries for these organisms have become more and more efficient, and it's very rare for such large specimens to turn up. The popularity of lobsters and crabs for eating has put severe fishing pressure on some of these fisheries.

Order Euphausiacea consists of krill, which as you read earlier in this chapter, are small planktonic crustaceans consumed by larger predators. Although krill have been harvested as a food source for livestock, their primary importance is to ocean food webs. Like copepods, krill are important primary and secondary consumers that link the smaller plankton to the larger consumers higher in

Al Hornsby

Figure 6-50

Giant crab.

Bob Wohlers

Figure 6-51

California spiny lobster.

Jamie Hall, Gulf of the Farallones
National Marine Sanctuary, NOAA

Figure 6-52a

Antarctic krill.

Krill, like copepods, link primary producers to higher-level consumers. In the rich subpolar food webs, they are vital to the ecosystem.

Figure 6-52b

Humpbacks feeding.

Humpback whales (*Megaptera novaeangliae*) are among the many organisms that consume krill.

Commander John Bortniak, NOAA Corps

the web. In the rich subpolar food webs, they are vital. Most of the world's populations of great whales, seals, sea birds, and penguins only survive in the highly productive waters dominated by krill. These organisms rely directly or indirectly on krill.

As primary consumers, krill feed on diatoms and dinoflagellates during the annual summer plankton blooms. During the winter at poles, they graze on algae that grow on the underside of ice sheets. Krill can form *individual* swarms that exceed 10 million tons – an eighth of the entire global fisheries annual catch. Much of the food web above the krill depends on it for life. Just as scientists closely watch the health of copepods, they study the conditions that affect krill.

ARE YOU LEARNING?

1. **Animals in phylum Arthropoda generally have these characteristics in common: (choose all that apply)**

   A. chitinous exoskeleton.

   B. jointed legs.

   C. segmented bodies.

   D. no digestive system.

2. **The characteristics found in the members of super-class Crustacea include (choose all that apply)**

   A. two pairs of antennae.

   B. teardrop-shaped larvae.

   C. molting their exoskeletons as they grow.

   D. a pair of appendages on each body segment.

3. **The characteristic of barnacles that sets them apart in class Cirripedia is**

   A. their unique lifestyle of living "upside down" attached to something.

   B. their strong swimming ability as mature adults.

   C. their importance as secondary consumers.

   D. all of the above

4. **Copepods are important to the ocean food web because**

   A. dolphins won't eat anything else.

   B. few larger animals can eat them, making them a reservoir of nutrients.

   C. they form a link between the smaller plankton and the larger animals.

   D. none of the above

5. **Crustaceans in order Decapoda all have**

   A. eight legs.

   B. exposed gills.

   C. no claws of any kind.

   D. none of the above

6. **The crustaceans in order Decapoda are important to the fishing industry because they may replace shrimp, lobsters, and crabs as a food source.**

   A. true

   B. false

7. **Krill are important to the food web because**

   A. they are important primary and secondary consumers that link plankton to large animals high on the food web.

   B. copepods consume krill in large quantities.

   C. they are never found near the poles.

   D. none of the above

Echinoderms—Stars of the Sea

Characteristics of Echinoderms

What characteristics distinguish organisms classified in phylum Echinodermata?

How are members of phylum Echinodermata similar to chordates?

Like the sea anemones and jellyfish, many organisms in phylum Echinodermata don't look much like animals at first glance. To a casual observer, for instance, sea urchins and basket stars might look like prickly pears and small tumbleweeds. However, noticing that these organisms move and exhibit behaviors that are indeed animal-like will reward a patient observer. They move. They attack prey. They defend themselves. They just tend to do so very slowly.

Echinoderms take many forms, but they all share a radially symmetrical body. It is divided into five parts. Most echinoderms have hundreds of tiny tube feet for crawling, climbing, and holding on. In echinoderms such as sea stars and sea urchins, the water vascular system is used for motion by acting as a natural hydraulic system. They achieve motion by transmitting or withdrawing pressure through this vascular system. This causes the muscular tube feet or other appendages to extend or withdraw.

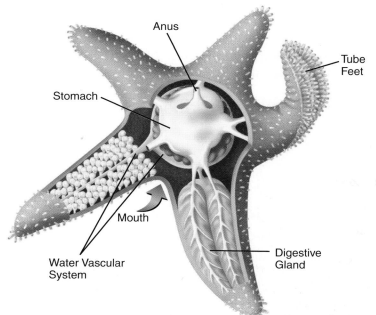

Anus

Tube Feet

Stomach

Mouth

Water Vascular System

Digestive Gland

INTERNET PORTAL

SCi LINKS. NSTA

Topic: Echinoderms
Go To: www.scilinks.org
Code: LOP2115

Figure 6-53

A typical echinoderm.

Echinoderms share a five-part, radially symmetrical body. Many, such as this star, have tube feet for motion and a water vascular system for circulating seawater to power the muscular tube feet.

STUDY QUESTIONS

Find the answers as you read.

1. What characteristics distinguish organisms classified in phylum Echinodermata?

2. How are members of phylum Echinodermata similar to chordates?

3. What class and characteristics do sea lilies and feather stars share?

4. What class and characteristics do the sea stars share?

5. What class and characteristics do the brittle stars share?

6. What class and characteristics do sand dollars and sea urchins share?

7. What class and characteristics do the sea cucumbers share?

ECHINODERM CLASSIFICATION

Domain
Eukarya

Supergroup
Unikonts

Kingdom
Animalia

Phylum
Echinodermata

Major Classes

1. Crinoidea– Feather Stars and Sea Lilies

2. Asteroidea – Sea Stars

3. Ophiuroidea – Brittle Stars

4. Echinoidea – Sand Dollars, Sea Urchins

5. Holothuroidea – Sea Cucumbers

Figure 6-54

Additionally, some echinoderms, including sea stars, have soft bumps on their body called *dermal branchiae*. These structures absorb oxygen from the water. Another type of skin adaptation is called *pedicellaria*. These pincher-like pairs of organs can be used to pluck objects off of the skin of the echinoderm – objects that might otherwise cause a problem for the organism.

Bob Wohlers

Figure 6-55

Sea star.

Perhaps the most common echinoderm is the sea star. Often called the starfish, sea stars are not actually fish. Marine scientists prefer to reserve the term "fish" for vertebrates with fins. Echinoderms have a five-part radially symmetrical body.

Although echinoderms look less animal-like than most invertebrates (Where is the head or eyes on a sea star?), they do, surprisingly, have traits that bring them close to the chordates. While the adult forms are radially symmetrical, the larvae are *bilaterally symmetrical*. This is symmetry along a vertical axis, which is what you see in mammals, fish, reptiles, and most of the more complex organisms. Echinoderms develop radial symmetry as they grow into adult form.

Special Attributes of Crinoids

What class and characteristics do sea lilies and feather stars share?

OAR, National Undersea Research Program, NOAA

Figure 6-56

Sea lily.

Many crinoids are nocturnal feeders. Deep water species, like this sea lily, feed 24 hours a day.

The 600 or so species in class Crinoidea include feather stars and sea lilies. The primary characteristics of this class are long, feather-like arms (hence the name feather star) and short, hook-like legs called *cirri*. They also have upward-facing mouths. Most are nocturnal feeders. By day, they hide in the reef, coiled up tightly. At night, they unfurl their arms, and climb out onto reef outcrops to capture plankton and other small particles carried into their paths by the current.

Most feather stars attach to the bottom by their cirri, but sea lilies are on stalks. Sea lilies stand off the bottom with their arms open as a net. Because sea lilies live at depths of about 185 meters (607 feet) and below, they feed 24 hours a day in perpetual darkness. Living at such depths, they weren't even seen alive in their natural habitat until viewed by scientists in submersibles in the mid 1970s.

Special Attributes of Sea Stars

What class and characteristics do the sea stars share?

There are about 1,500 species of sea stars in the class Asteroidea (from the Greek *asteroeid* meaning *star-like*, from which we also get the word *asteroid*). Sea stars usually have five arms (though a few species have more). They have downward-facing mouths and tube feet cover their undersides. A few species of sea stars (such as the crown-of-thorns) have toxic spines for protection.

Each arm carries an equal share of the animal's systems and organs. For this reason, sea stars are among the most complex animals that can regenerate a lost limb. Some species will grow into several new animals when cut into pieces.

Sea stars are predators. They feed on other invertebrates including gastropods (snails) and bivalves (mussels). With their organs

PADI

Figure 6-57

Feather star.

This feather star is filter feeding using its many feathery arms projecting from a central disk and mouth. The arms, called *pinnules*, are coated with a sticky substance that helps it catch food. Unlike sea lilies that are attached to the bottom, and cannot move, feather stars can move slowly.

Henry Ansley, Sanctuaries Collection, NOAA

Figure 6-58a

Fragile star.

Estuarine Research Reserve Collection, NOAA

Figure 6-58b

Sunflower star.

Bob Wohlers

Figure 6-58c

California sea star.

distributed throughout their bodies, sea stars can actually attack prey with their stomachs. A sea star can attack and digest prey by inverting its stomach. When feeding on a clam, for example, a sea star can insert its stomach through the small opening in the clam's shell to digest the meat inside.

Figure 6-59a

Figure 6-59b

Basket star.
Basket stars are brittle stars with highly developed arms that open as a tree-like net.

Special Attributes of Brittle Stars

What class and characteristics do the brittle stars share?

Although most brittle stars are, like sea stars, star-shaped with five legs, the 1,500 or so species in class Ophiuroidea differ significantly from sea stars. The characteristics this class shares include slender legs that are proportionately longer and thinner than those on sea stars. Brittle stars have a single set of organs in their central disks rather than the evenly distributed organs of sea stars. Brittle stars use their arms as well as their tube feet for locomotion, so they move relatively quickly. The skin of brittlestars is more like jointed plate armor than the mesh-like skin of seastars.

Brittle stars feed on detritus and small animals. One group, the basket stars, have highly developed arms that open as a tree-like net. Much like crinoids, basket stars feed at night by extending their arms to catch plankton.

Figure 6-60

Brittle star surrounding a small scallop.

Special Attributes of Sand Dollars and Sea Urchins

What class and characteristics do sand dollars and sea urchins share?

If you look at the underside of a sand dollar and a sea urchin, their similar shape is readily apparent. The 900 or so species in class Echinoidea have the characteristic five-section body, but no arms.

Figure 6-61a

Sea urchins.

Figure 6-61b

Keyhole sand dollar.

They have tube feet and you can think of them almost as sea stars with their arms pulled back and fused into a ball- or disk-shaped body (the exoskeleton or shell is called a *test*).

Because sea urchins graze on algae, they play an important role in the health of many ecosystems, particularly the coral reef. Algae can overrun and destroy coral. Urchins (along with herbivore fish) can help control algae growth to protect coral. They can also damage other ecosystems if their natural predators are removed. For example, in California's kelp forests, urchin populations have exploded. Years ago, sea otters ate the urchins, keeping them in check. Today there are few sea otters due to hunting (although they're now protected), which allows the urchins to over populate. One reason the kelp forests are dwindling is because of the large urchin population feeding on the kelp.

Swimmers and divers know to avoid sea urchins because of their spines. In a few species, the spines can inject venom for self-defense. Sea urchins can also move their spines to assist in locomotion.

Special Attributes of Sea Cucumbers

What class and characteristics do the sea cucumbers share?

Sea cucumbers make up class Holothuroidea. There are about 1,500 species that share the characteristics of an elongated five-segment body with tentacles around the mouth.

Most, but not all, sea cucumbers feed by moving along with their mouths open, allowing sand to flow through them. Because a lot of organic nutrients accumulate in marine sediments, this is a significant potential food source. A few species are filter feeders.

Sea cucumbers are visible and slow, and potentially easy prey for predators. Although they can't flee, sea cucumbers are not without defenses. Most have tough skins that aren't particularly

Art Howard, NAPRO Communications/ Ocean Explorer, NOAA

Figure 6-63a

A Portion of a Urchin shell.

A broken sea urchin "test" (shell) with an inside view of its mouth area. This mouth area is known as "Aristotle's Lantern," and is effective for scraping algae off rocks, a sea urchin's favorite food. Note the characteristic five sections to the test.

NOAA

Figure 6-63b

Sand dollar.

The underside of a sand dollar. In this photo you can see the five fused arms to form the shell.

Bob Wohlers

Figure 6-62

Sea cucumber.

Most, but not all sea cucumbers feed by moving along with their mouths open, allowing sand to flow through them.

palatable to predators. Another defense is to expel a substantial portion of their internal organs for the predator to consume, keeping enough to allow the sea cucumber to survive and recover. Some species spit out a sticky mass of white tubes covered with a toxin. These cling to predators' mouthparts, either killing them or at least sending them looking for easier prey.

ARE YOU LEARNING?

1. **Organisms in phylum Echinodermata are distinguished by characteristics including (choose all that apply):**
   A. radially symmetrical bodies.
   B. bilaterally symmetrical larvae.
   C. five-segment bodies.
   D. tube feet.

2. **Members of phylum Echinodermata are similar to chordates because**
   A. their larvae are bilaterally symmetrical.
   B. they have decentralized nervous systems.
   C. most species have no head.
   D. all of the above

3. **Sea lilies and feather stars are in class _____, which is characterized by _____ and _____.**
   A. Echinoidea, no arms, ball or disk shape
   B. Holothuroidea, elongated body, tentacles around the mouth
   C. Ophiuroidea, long thin legs, single organ set in central disk
   D. Crinoidea, upward-facing mouth, long feather-like arms

4. **Sea stars are in class _____, which is characterized by _____ and _____.**
   A. Echinoidea, no arms, ball or disk shape
   B. Holothuroidea, elongated body, tentacles around the mouth
   C. Ophiuroidea, long thin legs, single organ set in central disk
   D. Asteroidea, five arms with equal share of organs, downward-facing mouth

5. **Brittle stars are in class _____, which is characterized by _____ and _____.**
   A. Echinoidea, no arms, ball or disk shape
   B. Holothuroidea, elongated body, tentacles around the mouth
   C. Ophiuroidea, long thin legs, single organ set in central disk
   D. Asteroidea, five arms with equal share of organs, downward-facing mouth

6. **Sand dollars and sea urchins are in class _____, which is characterized by _____ and _____.**
   A. Echinoidea, no arms, ball or disk shape
   B. Holothuroidea, elongated body, tentacles around the mouth
   C. Ophiuroidea, long thin legs, single organ set in central disk
   D. Crinoidea, upward-facing mouth, long feather-like arms

7. **Sea cucumbers are in class _____, which is characterized by _____ and _____.**
   A. Echinoidea, no arms, ball or disk shape
   B. Holothuroidea, elongated body, tentacles around the mouth
   C. Ophiuroidea, long thin legs, single organ set in central disk
   D. Crinoidea, upward-facing mouth, long feather-like arms

Invertebrate Chordates

Characteristics of Chordates

What characteristics classify organisms as members of phylum Chordata?

Chordates (members of phylum Chordata) are characterized by having a *notochord* and a *dorsal nerve cord* at some point in their life cycle. The notochord is a support rod along the organism's dorsal (back) side. The dorsal nerve cord is a tube of nervous tissue just above the notochord. Chordates may have notochords and dorsal nerve cords their entire lives, or these may develop into more complex organs. Vertebrates, for example, have a dorsal nerve cord that develops into the spinal cord and brain before birth.

Special Attributes of Subphyla Urochordata and Cephalochordata

What organisms are found in subphylum Urochordata?

What organisms are found in subphylum Cephalochordata?

Although we tend to think of chordates as vertebrates, two subphyla of chordate invertebrates have an important place in marine biology. Subphylum Urochordata includes tunicates (sea squirts), colonial drifting salps, and larvaceans. Tunicates occupy a similar niche to sponges and have a similar lifestyle. Like sponges they pump water to filter feed, but tunicates are very complex organisms. Sponges are very simple multicellular animals.

STUDY QUESTIONS

Find the answers as you read.

1. What characteristics classify organisms as members of phylum Chordata?

2. What organisms are found in subphylum Urochordata?

3. What organisms are found in subphylum Cephalochordata?

INTERNET PORTAL

SCiLINKS. NSTA

Topic: Chordates
Go To: www.scilinks.org
Code: LOP2120

Budd Riker

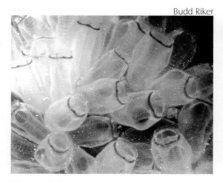

Figure 6-64

Tunicates.

Tunicates, such as these *Didemnid* species, are complex organisms that pump water to filter feed.

Gulf of the Farallones
National Marine Sanctuary, NOAA

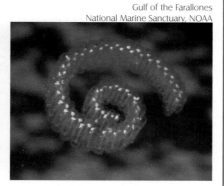

Figure 6-65

Salps.

Salps are gelatinous free-floating organisms that feed on microplankton.

Salps are gelatinous free-floating organisms. They're barrel-shaped and feed on micro plankton. Although their drifting lifestyle is similar to the jellyfish's, they are much more complex

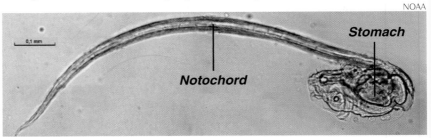

NOAA

Notochord

Stomach

0.1 mm

Figure 6-66

Larvacean.

These tadpole-like planktonic organisms drift in mucous structures they secrete to provide protection and trap food.

organisms. Salps are extremely abundant in more productive areas of the ocean. During spring and summer plankton blooms, salps, like other gelatinous organisms that feed on plankton, can quickly reproduce into their own blooms. Salps may be among the most abundant animals in the zooplankton, and can grow faster than any other multicellular animal.

Larvaceans are tadpole-like planktonic organisms thought to resemble the theorized ancestor of vertebrates. Larvaceans drift in mucous structures they secrete that provide protection and trap food. They must rebuild these structures every few hours because they become heavy and sink when they've trapped too much. The abandoned structures are a food source for other animals.

Subphylum Cephalochordata includes 25 species of lancelet. Common in sand and gravel, these small, fish-shaped filter feeders of genus *Amphioxus* are significant because they very much resemble vertebrates, except that they lack vertebrae.

NOAA

Figure 6-67

Lancelets.

These small, fish-shaped filter feeders resemble vertebrates but lack vertebrae.

ARE YOU LEARNING?

1. Organisms classified as members of phylum Chordata are characterized by having a _____ and a _____ at some point in their life cycle.

   A. notochord, vertebra

   B. dorsal nerve cord, vertebra

   C. notochord, dorsal nerve cord

   D. dorsal nerve cord, sinuses

2. Organisms in subphylum Urochordata include (choose all that apply)

   A. tunicates.   B. sponges.

   C. salps.   D. jellyfish.

3. Organisms in subphylum Cephalochordata include 25 species of _____, which are significant because they resemble _____.

   A. lancelets, cephalopods

   B. octopuses, vertebrates

   C. cephalopods, vertebrates

   D. lancelets, vertebrates

New Terms You Learned

- **amoebocytes** mobile cells in sponges that pick up and distribute nutrients from water drawn into a sponge (p. 6-4)

- **asexual** reproduction in which there is no fusion of male and female sex cells (gametes); as in sponge budding (p. 6-5)

- **bilateral symmetry** symmetry along a vertical axis, as seen in mammals, fish, reptiles and most of the more complex organisms (p. 6-36)

- **bycatch** marine life caught in a net or trap that is not the organism intended for capture (p. 6-33)

- **carapace** a shell or hard surface on all or part of an animal used for protection (p. 6-30)

- **cerata** organ on nudibranch back that functions as a gill and as a defensive weapon with nematocysts from consumed prey (p. 6-21)

- **chitin** the hard carbohydrate material that makes up arthropod exoskeleton (p. 6-29)

- **chromatophores** pigment sacs found in some organisms that allow them to change their skin color and pattern (p. 6-23)

- **cilia** short, hair-like structures similar to flagella that protrude from a cell for propulsion or to move liquid past the cell (p. 6-6)

- **cirri** short, hook-like legs on some echinoderm and arthropod species (p. 6-36)

- **cnidocytes** in Cnidarians, specialized stinging cells made up of nematocysts (p. 6-8)

- **collar cells** cells with flagella that direct water though a sponge's epithelium (p. 6-4)

- **coral bleaching** the white appearance of coral that has rejected its zooxanthellae dinoflagellates (symbiotic algae – Symbiodinium) due to stress (p. 6-10)

- **dermal branchiae** in some echinoderms, structures on the exoskeleton that absorb oxygen much like gills (p. 6-36)

- **dorsal nerve chord** a tube of nervous tissue just above the notochord (p. 6-41)

- **entomologist** scientist specializing in the study of insects (p. 6-29)

- **epithelium** a thin layer of tightly packed cells lining internal cavities, ducts and organs of animals and covering exposed bodily surfaces (p. 6-4)

- **exoskeleton** a hard protective covering the provides support and protection for some invertebrates (p. 6-29)

- **gametes** male and female reproductive cells that fuse to initiate the development of offspring (p. 6-5)

- **gastrovascular cavity** internal cavity of Cnidaria where digestion and reproduction takes place (p. 6-8)

- **mantle** in mollusks, a muscular bag that surrounds the gills and most organs, and is used to circulate water through the organism or as in squid and octopus, propulsion (p. 6-20)

- **medusa** in cnidarians, free-swimming, bell-shaped life cycle stage; such as a jellyfish (p. 6-8)

- **mesoglea** in Cnidaria, the jellylike material located between the two body tissues (p. 6-8)

- **metamerism** the division of the body into repeating segments, as found in phylum Annelida (worms) (p. 6-27)

- **nematocysts** stinging cells of Cnidarian organisms (p. 6-8)

- **nephridia** simple kidney organs found in less complex organisms (p. 6-21)

- **notochord** a firm tissue mass along the organism's dorsal (p. 6-41)

- **oscula** (singular osculum) openings in a sponge through which filtered water exits (p. 6-4)

- **pedicellaria** in echinoderms, pincher-like pairs of organs on the exoskeleton used to pluck foreign objects off the exterior of the organism (p. 6-36)

- **polyp** in Cnidarians, a sessile, vase-shaped life cycle stage (p. 6-8)

- **radial symmetry** symmetry around a point, like pie slices or a clock face (p. 6-7)

- **radula** specialized "tongue" in mollusks that is adapted for the particular species' feeding needs (p. 6-20)
- **sepia** the natural, black ink-like substance found in cuttlefish, squid and octopuses (p. 6-23)
- **siphon** in cephalopods (squids, octopus, nautilus), structure derived from the ancestral molluscan foot; used to manipulate the movement/ direction of the animal (p. 6-23)
- **spicules** in sponges, tiny structures providing support; made of glass or calcium material (p. 6-6)
- **test** in sea urchins, the globular external skeleton/shell on which the spines are attached (p. 6-39)
- **torsion** in gastropods, the developmental process that forms the body into a permanent loop so that the organism fits into a spiral shell (p. 6-21)
- **trochophore** initial larval stage of mollusks (p. 6-21)
- **unikont** a Supergroup above the Kingdom Animalia. Unikonts are defined as eukaryotes, whose flagella, if present, are singular. The major groups of unikonts include amoebozoans, fungi and all animals groups (p. 6-3)
- **veliger** planktonic larval stage of mollusks (p. 6-21)

Chapter 6 in Review

1. Describe the anatomy of sponges, including how they feed. Explain how sponge larvae are more "animal-like" than adult sponges.

2. Draw a diagram of a "typical" organism from phylum Cnidaria, labeling the common anatomical characteristics. What two body forms can cnidarians take?

3. Group the following organisms according to class, including the class names: hard coral, soft coral, fire coral, siphonophores, anemones, Portuguese Man-of-War, jellyfish, box jellyfish, and sea fans. Why don't comb jellies belong in this list?

4. Compare and contrast the characteristics of organisms in phyla Platyhelminthes, Nemertea, and Nematoda. In which of these does the longest animal in the world belong?

5. Compare and contrast the characteristics of organisms in classes Gastropoda, Bivalvia, and Cephalopoda. Give examples of organisms for each class and identify major differences between the cephalopods.

6. Compare and contrast the characteristics of complex worms in phylum Annelida with the simple worms. What class of annelids has many marine species?

7. List the characteristics of organisms in these classifications with examples: superclass Crustacea, class Cirripedia, class Copepoda, order Decapoda.

8. Explain why copepods, decapods and krill are important as primary consumers, and what why the role of primary consumer is crucial to the food web.

9. Compare and contrast the physical characteristics of sea lilies and feather stars, sea stars, brittle stars, sand dollars and sea urchins, and sea cucumbers. Identify their respective classes.

10. Describe the invertebrate chordates. What phyla do they comprise?

Connecting Chapter Concepts – Science Scenarios

1. Phylum Cnidaria consists of corals, anemones, sea fans and jellyfish.
   A. Although these organisms appear very different, what anatomical characteristics do they share?
   B. Why do corals with zooxanthellae grow best in tropical, well-lit, clear water?
   C. Why are comb jellies not jellyfish or cnidarians?
2. Crustaceans make up a superclass of phylum Arthropoda that consists almost (but not quite) entirely of aquatic animals. Some of the smallest crustaceans are vital to marine food webs.
   A. What are copepods, and what important role do they play in marine food webs?
   B. Why are crustaceans in order Decapoda important to the fishing industry? How does the issue of *bycatch* relate?
   C. What are krill? Why are they important to the health of oceanic food webs?

Marine Science and the Real World

1. Corals, sponges, and sea anemones don't seem much like animals. Having learned that they are, has it changed your perspective about their roles in the environment?
2. Devise an intelligence test for squid. Explain how you would conduct the test and what standard you would use to measure squid intelligence.
3. Due to increased sewage outflow in a particular area off the coast of California, a certain species of sea urchin had reproduced to the point were they covered the bottom and destroyed the kelp beds by eating the algae's holdfasts. In the 1970s there was a project initiated to have divers crush and break up sea urchins underwater. The hope was that this would restore the kelp. Once the project started, it was found that the urchins actually came back in larger numbers after being crushed underwater. Why do you think this project failed and the urchin population actually rose after the divers broke the urchins? HINT: Learn a bit more about the biology of sea urchins and how they reproduce.

References

Barnes, E. 1994. *Invertebrate Zoology.* Florida: Harcourt Brace.

Beaugrand, G. 2004. Monitoring Marine Plankton Ecosystems I: Description Of An Ecosystem Approach Based On Plankton Indicators. *Mar Ecol Prog. Ser 269.*

Crothers, J. 1997. A Key To The Major Groups Of British Marine Invertebrates. *Field Studies.* 9.

International Institute for Species Exploration. 2008. Arizona State University. http://species.asu.edu

Norman, M. 2001. *Cephalopods – A World Guide.* Conch Books

Roper, C.F.E., et al. 1984. *Cephalopods of the World.* FAO Species Catalogue.

UCMP. 1996. Berkeley Guides to Taxa. www.ucmp.berkeley.edu/help/taxa-form.html.

CHAPTER 7

A Survey of Life in the Sea

Al Hornsby

Bob Wohlers

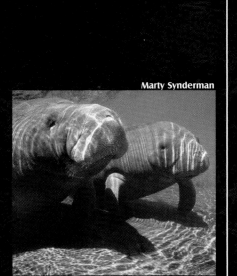

Marty Synderman

Love for the Fish

When you come to the "Love Lab" don't expect to get close to anyone but graduate students, researchers, and professors intent on unlocking the secrets of fish populations of the Southern California coastline. That's because the "Love Lab" is the home of Dr. Milton Love, Research Biologist at the Marine Science Institute at the University of California at Santa Barbara.

The charismatic leader of the "Love Lab's" interest in fish started at age six with a father-son fishing trip. After the trip, he announced he wanted to be an ichthyologist – a scientist who studies fish. He has spent practically his entire life since then studying fish.

Love completed a solid education – including an undergraduate degree in Environmental Biology and a Masters Degree and PhD from the University of California at Santa Barbara – to study the life history of economically important marine fish. Management of economically important species often flares passion among stakeholders such as fishermen and policy makers. To handle this, Dr. Love uses an unusual strategy to communicate his findings and research: humor. His presentations and articles for laypeople are known for making you laugh.

Although Dr. Love communicates with humor, his subject is serious. He works to obtain the best scientific information to help policy makers make fish management decisions. A case in point is his current research on the reefs that form on the subsurface structure of oil platforms off the California coast. A debate rages as to whether the platforms should be removed after they are no longer useful for pumping oil. Many feel the oil platforms are an eyesore and should be removed from the ocean, but some scientists are finding significant life around the undersea structures.

Since 1995, Dr. Love has conducted research on the fish that live around the platforms. He compares these artificial reefs to natural rock outcrops of central and southern California. His goal has been to determine the patterns of fish living around both platforms and outcrops, and to determine what processes may have generated these patterns. He is also attempting to understand the link between habitats and the various stages in fish life history. Love's want to determine whether or not oil platforms act as artificial reefs and help build fish populations, and how they compare to natural reefs. His data seem to suggest that certain key and overfished rockfish use the platforms as habitat to produce young.

As part of his research he has been fortunate to use the latest technology to go under the waves and take a look. Conventional scuba diving depths once limited scientists, but Dr. Love uses deep-sea submersibles, capable of diving to more than 305 meters (1,000 feet), to investigate the fish populations.

When you talk to Dr. Love, his passion for his research is obvious. He feels he is lucky to be able to do what he loves for a living. He offers prospective marine biologists with the following advice: "You're only on the planet once, so if you really want to go into marine science, go for it."

Milton Love, PhD
Associate Research Biologist, Marine Science Institute, University of California at Santa Barbara

STUDY QUESTIONS

Find the answers as you read.

1. What are the characteristics that classify an organism in subphylum Vertebrata?

2. What is the significance of organisms in classes *Petromyzontida* and *Myxini*?

3. What evolutionary development do scientists think occurred in the Cambrian period that gave rise to more complex fish?

Northeast Fisheries Science Center, NOAA

Figure 7-1

Hagfish.
Agnathans are jawless fish, including this hagfish in the class Myxini. They may also resemble the early ancestor of ray-finned fish and sharks.

Subphylum Vertebrata

Characteristics of Vertebrates

What are the characteristics that classify an organism in subphylum Vertebrata?

Organisms in subphylum Vertebrata of phylum Chordata have come to dominate the upper levels of almost all food webs. A dorsal nerve cord that has developed into a spinal cord, protected by vertebrae and a head with a brain characterize organisms in this subphylum. Vertebrates consist of the most complex, large, fast, and conspicuous organisms. They include the organism that has had the most effect on the global biosphere, namely us.

When most people think of animals, vertebrates usually come to mind. There's probably a degree of *anthropomorphism* involved. Anthropomorphism is subconsciously or consciously assigning human traits to inanimate objects or animals (like aquarium shows putting sunglasses on dolphins). Because we're vertebrates, there's a natural tendency to identify with other vertebrates. We have faces. They have faces. We have four limbs. Most vertebrates have four limbs (or fins). We have complex eyes. They have complex eyes. The list could go on.

Because of this, it's easy for emotion to become involved with what you observe. For example, watching a parrotfish eat coral has little emotional effect because we don't identify with the coral, only the fish. On the other hand, we may feel dismay watching a gray whale die as a pod of orcas attacks, kills, and eats it. This is because we can imagine ourselves in the gray whale's place. In truth, both feeding behaviors are a normal part of nature. Both coral and gray whales are, at times, food for other species. As a scientist, it's important to set anthropomorphism and feelings aside, especially when observing vertebrates.

Jawless Fish – The Living Ancestors of Sharks and Fish

What is the significance of organisms in classes Petromyzontida *and* Myxini?

What evolutionary development do scientists think occurred in the Cambrian period that gave rise to more complex fish?

There are more than 50,000 known vertebrate species. For the marine scientist, the majority of those of interest are in four classes of fish, though they also include organisms from every class of vertebrate. The simplest of these are the jawless fish, the *agnathans* –

from the Greek word *gnathos*, meaning "jaws;" *a-gnathos* = meaning "no jaws." The agnathans include two classes *Petromyzontida*, the lampreys, and *Myxini*, the hagfish.

The significance of agnathans is that they may represent the ancestor of ray-finned fish and sharks. Scientists think that a jawless fish similar to these species was probably the forerunner of the more complex fish during the Cambrian period. They theorize that during this period the first of three gill arches on a jawless fish evolved into the first jaws. Jaws allowed vertebrates to become very successful predators. Jaws put organisms in class Chondrichthyes (sharks and rays) and class Actinopterygii (ray-finned fish) near the top of marine food webs.

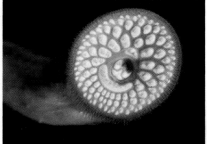

Figure 7-2a

Figure 7-2b

Sea Lampreys.

Sea Lampreys, another jawless agnathan, can live in the ocean or in fresh water. Lampreys migrate up rivers to spawn. Adult Sea Lamprey can reach 120 cm (47 in) and can weigh up to 1.4 kg (3 lbs). Sea Lamprey's have a mouth of sharp teeth with a sucking disk (**Figure 7-2a**). With this mouth they attach to their hosts by suction as in **Figure 7-2b**. Their sharp teeth then rasp at the skin of the host, allowing them to survive on the host's body fluids. The wound on the host fish stays open because the lamprey releases chemicals that prevent the host's blood from clotting. Often, the host fish dies from this attack.

VERTEBRATE CLASSIFICATION OVERVIEW

Domain
Eukarya

Supergroup
Unikonts

Kingdom
Animalia

Phylum
Chordata

Subphylum
Vertebrata

LESS COMPLEX ANIMALS

Classes

1. **Petromyzontida** - Lampreys
2. **Myxini** – Hagfish
3. **Class Chondrichthyes** – Rays and Sharks
4. **Class Actinopterygii** – Ray-Finned Fish
5. **Class Reptilia** – Sea Turtles, Sea Snakes, Marine Iguana
6. **Class Aves** – Sea Birds
7. **Class Mammalia** – Seals, Sea Lions, Dolphins, Whales, Porpoises, Dugongs, Manatees

MORE COMPLEX ANIMALS

Figure 7-3

1. Any organism with a notochord and a dorsal nerve cord is classified in subphylum Vertebrata.

   A. true

   B. false

2. Classes Petromyzontida and Myxin are significant because

   A. they dominate most food webs.

   B. scientists think they may resemble the early ancestor of ray-finned fish and sharks.

   C. all species of the class are extinct.

   D. all of the above

3. Scientists think that _____ evolved during the Cambrian period, allowing vertebrates to become very successful predators.

   A. cells

   B. photosynthesis ₹

   C. jaws

   D. none of the above

Find the answers as you read.

1. What organisms are in class Chondrichthyes? What characteristics do they have in common?

2. What traits make sharks and rays in subclass Elasmobranchii successful predators?

3. How do most sharks and rays reproduce?

4. What is the largest shark? What does it eat?

5. What organisms make up superorder Batidoidimorpha?

6. How does the anatomy of a ray compare to the anatomy of a "typical" fish?

Sharks and Rays—Teeth and Wings

Characteristics of Sharks and Rays

What organisms are in class Chondrichthyes? What characteristics do they have in common?

Sharks and rays are, without a doubt, supreme predators. Sharks in particular have this reputation because, on very rare occasions, they remind us that humans aren't always at the top of the food web. Many people think of sharks as large, aggressive, and dangerous animals that snap at anything and everything.

While that's a useful image for Hollywood, the truth is that of the 1,000 or so species of sharks, rays, and their close relatives in class Chondrichthyes, (pronounced: con'dric'these; from the Greek *chondros*, meaning *cartilage*, and *ichthys* meaning *fish*) very few are a potential threat to humans. Those that can be a threat very rarely are. The success of predatory sharks has more to do with efficiency and low energy use rather raw aggression.

Sharks and rays do not look very similar on the outside, but they share a basic anatomy that classifies them in class Chondrichthyes. They're all jawed fish that lack a swim bladder and have cartilaginous skeletons – they lack true bone. (Class Agnatha species also have skeletons made of cartilage, but lack jaws.) Subclass Elasmobranchii separates the sharks and rays from their close relatives, the chimaeras. Chimaeras (sometimes called "ghost sharks" or "ratfish") differ from elasmobranchs by having a relatively large head and no scales.

Image by Henry Firus at Melbourne Aquarium

Special Attributes of Sharks and Rays

What traits make sharks and rays in subclass Elasmobranchii successful predators?

How do most sharks and rays reproduce?

What is the largest shark? What does it eat?

Saving energy is one of several characteristics that have made the elasmobranchs successful predators. By being energy-efficient, sharks and rays do not have to eat as much as other organisms of the same size. They use less energy as they hunt, so they have ample energy to strike when they find their prey. Finally, being energy efficient makes these animals quick and inconspicuous. Many people who have survived a shark attack say that they weren't even aware of the shark until it hit.

Sharks and rays save energy several ways. Elasmobranchs have relatively simple cartilaginous skeletons. This characteristic saves energy because cartilage is much lighter than bone. Less weight means that even large sharks and pelagic rays sink slowly. Therefore, they use less energy trying to maintain neutral buoyancy. A few of the large sharks do have calcification similar to bone, but primarily in skeletal areas that need it because they're subject to high stress. Although scientists once considered having cartilage, as opposed to bone, a primitive characteristic, most no longer do.

Sharks and rays also store low-density organic compounds that minimize the energy they need to expend. They have buoyant oils in large livers. Sharks' fins sit at angles and

Figure 7-4

Chimaera.

Chimaeras are members of class Chondrichthyes but have their own subclass Holocephali. They differ from the sharks and rays of subclass Elasmobranchii in that they have a relatively large head and lack scales.

INTERNET PORTAL

SCiLINKS. NSTA

Topic: Sharks and Rays
Go To: www.scilinks.org
Code: LOP2125

Figure 7-5

External and internal basic shark anatomy.

Sharks are amazing creatures, well adapted to their environment. Most have long slender bodies, and use their pectoral fins for lift and steering. Sharks swim by undulating their muscular bodies and sweeping their caudal fin from side to side. Also shown here are the locations of the lateral line and the ampullae of Lorenzini.

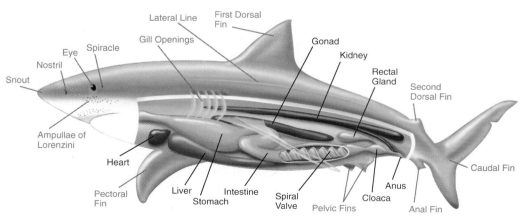

SHARK AND RAY CLASSIFICATION

Domain
Eukarya

Supergroup
Unikonts

Kingdom
Animalia

Phylum
Chordata

Subphylum
Vertebrata

Class
Chondrichthyes – Rays, Sharks and All Relatives

Subclass
Holocephali – Chimaeras

Subclass
Elasmobranchii – Sharks and Rays

Superorder
Selachimorpha – Sharks

Superorder
Batidoidimorpha – Rays and Skates

Figure 7-6

Marty Snyderman

Figure 7-7

Elasmobranch teeth.

Sharks have a "conveyor belt" of multiple rows of teeth that are constantly growing and swinging into place as the older teeth fall out.

act like wings to provide lift. Their asymmetrical tails produce lift, not simply forward propulsion. Rays have a wing-shaped body that does the same thing. In both cases, sharks and rays benefit from lift that holds them off the bottom as they glide through the water. Most ray-finned (bony) fish, by comparison, use considerably more energy remaining in the water column by controlling the gas in their swim bladders and sculling their fins.

The skin of elasmobranchs also contributes to saving energy. In sharks, the skin elasticity helps transfer energy to the tail for swimming. In both sharks and rays, scales called *denticles* point backwards. If you were to pet a shark, a stroke toward the tail feels smooth. A stroke toward the head feels very rough. The denticles (named that because they are very similar to shark teeth, though much smaller) trap a film of water close to the organism's body. This saves energy by reducing friction as the animals swim.

Compared to ray-finned fish, elasmobranchs save energy in the same way they maintain a balance with the surrounding saltwater environment. As discussed in Chapter 8, marine fish differ in how they keep fresh water from diffusing out of their bodies. Ray-finned fish literally pump the salt out. Sharks and rays, however, store urea and other chemicals in their tissues so the density matches the water density outside. The result is that they use very little energy to control buoyancy compared to ray-finned fish.

Yet another energy-saving characteristic is how elasmobranchs grow and replace teeth. Ray-finned fish have teeth fused to bones in their mouths. If they lose a tooth, it takes time for a new one to grow in to replace it. Sharks, in particular, have a "conveyor belt" of multiple rows of teeth. They're constantly growing and swinging into place as old teeth wear out and fall away. Some species produce more than 25 thousand teeth in a lifetime.

Beyond multiple energy-saving mechanisms, sharks and rays succeed as predators because of other characteristics, including their remarkable senses. Sharks in particular have a sense of smell that detects incredibly diluted substances, such as blood from a wounded fish. Tests have shown that sharks can smell fish extracts as dilute as one part extract per 10 billion parts water.

Both rays and sharks have *lateral lines*, as do ray-finned fish. Lateral lines are lines of sensory pores along the length of the body that detect water motion. The lateral line allows fish to detect vibrations of an approaching predator or, in the case of sharks and rays, struggling prey.

A unique elasmobranch characteristic is the sense of *electroreception*. Electroreception is the ability to sense the minute electricity created by muscles and nerves. Sharks and rays have organs called *ampullae of Lorenzini*, which you can see as visible pits near their snouts. The *ampullae of Lorenzini* detect the electrical current generated by living organisms. It's thought that rays, for example, use electro-reception to find prey concealed under sand. Many scientists think that electroreception explains why sharks occasionally bite power and telephone cables running through the ocean.

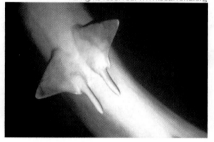
Marty Snyderman

Elasmobranchs also differ from other fish in their reproductive strategies. Ray-finned fish tend to produce large numbers of tiny offspring. A few manage to elude predation and reach maturity. Sharks and rays, however, produce fewer but more mature offspring. Most ray-finned fish fertilize their eggs externally, whereas most sharks and rays fertilize their eggs internally. The male deposits sperm in the female via a pair of copulatory organs called *claspers* found at the base of the pelvic fins.

After fertilization, most female sharks produce an egg case that is deposited in the sea, usually in coastal nurseries (see figure 7-10). The eggs mature and hatch outside the shark or ray's body, much like birds. The egg case protects and provides nutrients for the developing juvenile. This reproductive method is called *oviparous* or "egg" birth. Oviparous sharks include the horn, swell, and Port Jackson sharks.

A few shark species are *ovoviviparous* – producing live birth. With this reproductive method the mother retains within her body a thin-shelled egg and yolk. After a period of time, the embryo sheds the egg shell and the young continues to develop in the mother's uterus. Ovoviviparous sharks include the mako and tiger sharks.

Figure 7-8

Electroreception.

Sharks and rays have organs called ampullae of Lorenzini, which you can see as visible pits near their snout. The ampullae of Lorenzini detect the electrical current generated by living organisms.

Figure 7-9

Shark claspers.

Male elasmobranchs deposit sperm in the female via a pair of copulatory organs called claspers found at the base of the pelvic fin.

Bob Wohlers

Figure 7-10

Shark egg case.

This shark egg case is sometimes called a "mermaid's purse." Note the egg yolk inside the casing. The shark that laid this egg case is said to be oviparous – meaning it lays eggs that mature and hatch outside the body of the mother.

Bob Wohlers

Figure 7-11

Horned shark.

Most sharks are not "man-eaters." These small, slow moving sharks live on rocky reefs in kelp forests, often hiding in crevices or caves during the day, venturing out at night to feed. Diet includes sea urchins, crabs, worms and sea anemones.

Christopher L. Hale

Figure 7-12

Shark finning.

Sharks are sometimes fished for their fins. Because sharks reproduce in small numbers, scientists are worried that sharks are being caught more quickly than they can reproduce. Many shark populations are in serious decline today.

Figure 7-13

Whale shark.

The largest fish in the ocean is the whale shark. This shark can reach up to 14 meters (46 feet). Although these are huge fish, they are filter feeders that consume plankton.

One known species of shark, the hammerhead, is *viviparous* – producing a live birth much like mammals. The embryo's small yolk sac comes in contact with the mother's uterus, allowing the passage of nutrients from the mother to the embryo.

Whether a shark is ovoviviparous or not, scientists have concerns about their reproductive rates and overfishing. Because they reproduce later in life and in smaller numbers than ray-finned fish, some types of commercial fishing, such as for shark-fin soup, may be taking them from the ocean faster than they can breed. This could push many species to the brink of extinction in the near future.

Sharks range in size from small enough to fit in your hand to the largest fish in the ocean, the whale shark. The whale shark is one of three giant shark species. The other two are the basking shark and the megamouth shark. Whale sharks can reach 14 meters (46 feet), followed by basking sharks at 10 meters (33 feet), and megamouth sharks reaching 6 meters (20 feet). Although these are huge fish, they're filter feeders that consume zooplankton, such as copepods and krill.

THE PREDATORS' PREDATORS

While sharks and rays are successful predators, family Lamnidae, the mackerel sharks, stands out from the rest. This family consists of only five shark species: two species of mako shark, the salmon shark and porbeagle, and the notorious great white shark. However, these five sharks exhibit qualities that make them predators among predators.

Mackerel sharks are partially warm-blooded, maintaining body temperatures several degrees above the surrounding water. This gives them a faster metabolism, more powerful muscles, and an activity level higher than other sharks.

Their characteristic conical snouts and a nearly symmetrical tail create one of the most efficient swimming shapes known. This shape, coupled with powerful muscles, makes the mackerel sharks the fastest

Figure 7-14

Mako shark.

elasmobranchs. The makos are faster than dolphins and are the only sharks that chase the fastest ray-finned fish (tunas, swordfish, and billfish). Being a super predator has a price, however. Sitting at the apex of the trophic pyramid, the environment can support only a small population of such fish. Anything that disrupts the lower food web levels potentially threatens

Figure 7-15

Great white shark.

these fish. For this reason, apex predators are often good indicators of marine environment health.

One threat to the mackerel sharks has been human fear, which in the past has led to killing them indiscriminately. The great white shark, in particular, has been a target, partly motivated by its reputation for attacks on swimmers, surfers, and divers. So many great white sharks have been killed by man that this species is now on the CITES (Convention on International Trade in Endangered Species) list.

The truth is that sharks have more to fear from us than vice-versa. On average, fewer than 10 fatal shark attacks happen yearly. By contrast, humans kill tens of thousands of sharks every year. Statistically, sharks pose no greater threat than do mountain lions, tigers, or bees.

Special Attributes of Rays

What organisms make up superorder Batidoidimorpha?

How does the anatomy of a ray compare to the anatomy of a "typical" fish?

Superorder Batidoidimorpha of subclass Elasmobranchii consists of the rays, which includes skates and guitarfish – order Rajiformes. To the unfamiliar, a ray doesn't look much like a fish. When you compare a ray to a "typical" fish, however, you find the same basic anatomy modified to how rays live.

Ray anatomy is well suited to life on sandy bottoms. Their pectoral fins have become "wings" that stretch forward over the gills and are fused to the sides of the head. Their shoulder girdles are flattened, with many bones fused for rigidity not characteristic of other fish. With the pectoral fins prominent, rays no longer need their tails for swimming. Instead, the tail in some species has become a defensive whip. In the stingray, the whip has a venomous spine.

Rays literally fly through the water when they swim. They use their wings and body shape for lift and motion similar to how birds fly through the air. Some ray species have expanded "wings" and are especially well adapted to life in midwater. These species, which include the eagle ray and the manta ray, have broader, more pointed wings and body streamlining especially suited to underwater flying. These are the largest rays, with manta wingspans exceeding 8 meters (26 feet). Like the largest sharks, they feed on plankton.

Bob Wohlers

Figure 7-16

Southern stingray.
Dasyatis americana, lying in its preferred sandy habitat.

Bob Wohlers

Figure 7-17

Southern stingray and diver.
In the Cayman Islands there is a famous dive site called "Stingray City." On this shallow sandbar, divers can interact with stingrays with relatively little risk.

Marty Snyderman

Figure 7-18

Manta ray.
The manta is the largest of all rays. Like the whale shark, manta rays are plankton feeders. The ray shown here is scooping up minute plankton with its large mouth.

Al Hornsby

Figure 7-19

Spotted eagle ray.
Some rays, like this spotted eagle ray, have expanded, more pointed wings and streamlined shapes especially suited to underwater flying.

ARE YOU LEARNING?

1. Organisms in class Chondrichthyes include _____ and _____.

   A. sharks, ray-finned fish

   B. rays, ray-finned fish

   C. ray-finned fish, lampreys

   D. sharks, rays

2. Class Chondrichthyes characteristics include (choose all that apply)

   A. cartilaginous skeletons.

   B. no jaws.

   C. no swim bladder.

   D. none of the above

3. Traits that make sharks and rays successful predators include (choose all that apply)

   A. a light cartilage skeleton.

   B. backward-pointing denticles.

   C. ampullae of Lorenzini.

   D. lateral lines.

4. Most sharks and rays fertilize their eggs

   A. externally.

   B. internally.

   C. rarely.

   D. asexually.

5. The largest shark is the _____, which eats _____.

   A. great white shark, seals

   B. megamouth shark, squid

   C. basking shark, plankton

   D. none of the above

6. Organisms in superorder Batidoidimorpha include

   A. rays.

   B. skates.

   C. guitarfish.

   D. all of the above

7. When you compare a ray's anatomy to a "typical" fish anatomy you find

   A. no similarity at all.

   B. the same basic anatomy with adaptation to life on sandy bottoms.

   C. that rays are not actually fish.

   D. none of the above

Ray-Finned Fish—
Half the World's Vertebrates

Superclass Osteichthyes and Class Actinopterygii are the "bony" or "ray-fin" fish. These fish make up most of the vertebrate species in the ocean. The approximately 25,000 ray-finned fish species (a number that's rising with new discoveries) account for about half of all vertebrate species, terrestrial and aquatic. From tiny gobies to giant ocean sunfish to eels and bizarre deep water species, this group is so diverse that we can only touch on it superficially.

Characteristics of Ray-Finned Fish

What are the characteristics of ray-finned fish?

How do most ray-finned fish reproduce?

Why is there greater diversity among fish that live on reefs or the bottom than among those that school or live in the open ocean?

Although ray-finned fish make up a widely diverse group, they all generally share several characteristics. The first is that organisms in class Actinopterygii are jawed fish with skeletons made of bone. Most have a swim bladder and scales.

The majority of fish species control their buoyancy by adding or releasing gas to and from their swim bladder. This capability allows many species to hover nearly motionless in midwater, whereas most sharks seldom stop swimming, and if they do they rest on the bottom. In some species the fish gulps air or spits it out to control the swim bladder, but many fish don't normally come near the surface. These species control their swim bladders with gases exchanged to and from their blood. Many ray-finned fish have special organs called the *gas gland* and the *rete mirabile* that take up gases from the bloodstream for the swim bladder.

Most ray-finned fish reproduce *externally*. The female lays her eggs, usually in vast numbers that can reach millions in some cases. The male immediately fertilizes the eggs. Some species protect the eggs and juveniles, whereas other species leave larvae to fend for themselves as part of the plankton community. In contrast to the elasmobranch strategy of producing a few, relatively mature offspring, the strategy of many ray-finned fish is to produce a vast number of offspring. Of these, only a few survive to maturity.

Like sharks and rays, ray-finned fish have lateral lines that detect water motion and vibrations. You can see this in the movement of schooling fish. Fish in the school detect changes in the movement of

STUDY QUESTIONS

Find the answers as you read.

1. What are the characteristics of ray-finned fish?
2. How do most ray-finned fish reproduce?
3. Why is there greater diversity among fish that live on reefs or the bottom than among those that school or live in the open ocean?
4. What two orders of ray-finned fish are particularly important to worldwide fisheries? What types of fish are in these two orders?

RAY–FINNED FISH CLASSIFICATION

Kingdom
Animalia - see above

Phylum
Chordata

Subphylum
Vertebrata

Superclass
Osteichthyes

Class Actinopterygii

EXAMPLES:

Grouper
Halibut
Eels
Marlin
Gobies
Tuna
Angelfish

Figure 7-20

Figure 7-21

Basic external and internal ray-finned fish anatomy.

Classic external and internal anatomy of a ray-finned fish (class Actinopterygii). Compared to sharks and rays, ray-finned fish expend more energy because they are heavier per body size. Most species control their buoyancy by adding or releasing gas to and from a swim bladder. However, this capability allows many species to hover nearly motionless in midwater, whereas many sharks seldom stop swimming.

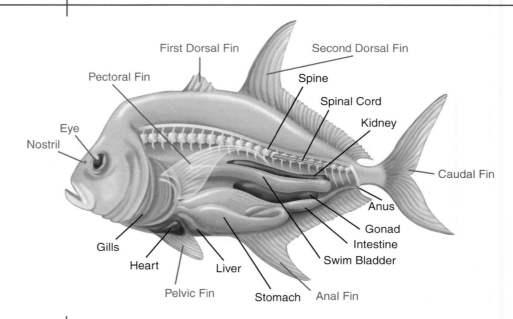

other fish and alter their motions accordingly. This coordinates the school to move almost as if it were a single organism.

Among ray-finned fish, most open ocean and schooling species are relatively similar in shape and coloration. This is because they all live in the same environment and have similar adaptations. They generally have a torpedo-like, streamlined shape that minimizes drag and turbulence. This *fusiform* shape has a characteristic spindle form, slightly broader at the head, and V-shaped tail. Tuna provide a good example of this. Most open ocean fish have a light underside to conceal them against the bright surface and a dark top to conceal them against the bottom or the dark color over a deep bottom. In fact, many pelagic marine animals are *countershaded* this way for concealment—penguins, killer whales, manta rays, and turtles.

Figure 7-22

Fast fish.

Fish adapted to the open ocean generally have a torpedo-like shape (called a fusiform shape) that reduces drag and turbulence. Most of these fish also have dark coloration on the top and light coloration on the bottom for camouflage. Can you name even one pelagic marine animal that is not countershaded like this?

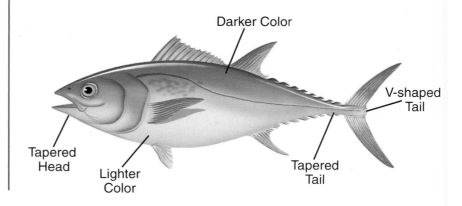

Figure 7-23

Caribbean French angelfish.

Ray-finned fish come in all shapes and sizes – the variety is amazing. Like other angelfish and butterflyfishes, French angelfish have tall narrow bodies. Having such narrow bodies, they can turn quickly and can maneuver down into narrow cracks between the corals to hunt their prey. Angelfish swim by rowing with their side, pectoral fins. Long dorsal (top), anal, and caudal (tail) fins enable angelfish to turn quickly.

Figure 7-24

California moray eel.

Eels are a ray-finned fish with an elongated, snake-like body and a dorsal fin that is continuous with the caudal and anal fin. Most species lack pectoral and pelvic fins. Eels typically live in crevices and small caves.

Figure 7-25

Flounder.

Flounders are bottom dwelling flat fish. As adults they have both eyes situated on one side of the head, but they are not born this way. As flounder larvae mature, a metamorphosis occurs during which one eye migrates to the other side of the body, so that as an adult, both eyes are situated on the upward-facing side of its body. Flounder are ambush predators that eat crabs, worms and small fish.

Ray-finned fish have adapted to many diverse bottom and reef habitats as well as midwater habitats. The survival strategies are likewise more diverse, and include concealment and armor instead of swimming. For this reason, you see far more variation in color and shape among reef and bottom fish than those that school or live in the open ocean.

Figure 7-26

Caribbean grouper.

Groupers have a robust body shape typical of medium-large reef predators.

Figure 7-27

Caribbean barracuda.

A barracuda's body shape is typical of an ambush predator.

Figure 7-28

Red Sea squirrel fish.

These species are brightly colored, medium-sized fish that are active mostly at night. A distinguishing characteristic is their large eyes – used for nocturnal hunting. Squirrel fish live in rocky or coral reefs in tropical and warm temperate seas.

Special Attributes of Orders Clupeiformes and Gadiformes

What two orders of ray-finned fish are particularly important to world-wide fisheries? What types of fish are in these two orders?

Today there are few ray-finned fish populations unaffected directly or indirectly by humans. Many fish populations have been reduced by 10% to 30% or more from their pre-fishing levels. Of particular interest and concern are the fisheries that provide a primary source of protein to the human population. Two orders in class Actinopterygii have a particularly important place in worldwide fisheries.

The first of these is order Clupeiformes, which includes herrings, pilchards, sardines, and anchovies. About one-quarter of all fish caught come from this group. These small, silvery fish are primary and secondary consumers living very low on the food web, and feeding off of diatoms, copepods, and other small plankton. Such a low place on the food web allows this order to take advantage of the enormous amount of food available in the plankton.

This order forms one of the most massive populations among all vertebrates. However, relatively few species of order Clupeiformes account for most of the catch. Scientists have concerns about this important food source because of natural and human influences.

One example came about in 1972 with the Peruvian anchovy (*Engraulis ringens*). Peak annual catches of this fish exceeded 10 million tons, accounting for a tenth of the entire world's fish haul. Besides being such an important commercial fish, this species supported local seabirds, penguins, fur seals, and sea lions. The export of seabird guano was itself an important related industry. An El Niño event (a climate pattern discussed in Chapter 11) brought warm, low-nutrient water to the Peruvian coast, reducing anchovy reproduction. The low egg production, plus overfishing, reduced catches to almost nothing over the next two years. To this day, the fishery has not fully recovered.

INTERNET PORTAL

SciLINKS. NSTA

Topic: Fish
Go To: www.scilinks.org
Code: LOP2130

Figure 7-29

Clupeiformes.

The species in order Clupeiformes account for about one-quarter of all fish caught. These small, silvery fish are primary and secondary consumers low on the food web.

Northeast Fisheries Science Center, NOAA

More important fisheries involve fish in the order Gadiformes, made up of cods, pollocks, haddock, whitings, and their relatives. The cod fishery in particular is an historical, worldwide fishery that has influenced politics and caused international disputes.

When Europeans arrived in the New World, they found a seemingly inexhaustible supply of cod. This proved not to be true, of course, but don't underestimate the economic significance of this fishery. Cod fishing rights were partly responsible for the internationally agreed 370.6 kilometers (200 nautical miles) Exclusive Economic Zone (EEZ). International disputes have arisen over cod, including the three Cod Wars between the United Kingdom and Iceland. These disputes arose in 1958, 1972-1973, and 1975-1976 as the two nations contested territories for cod fishing. Although neither nation involved their military and few shots were fired, fishing boats and other vessels received damage from intentional collisions in the heat of the dispute.

Kåre Telnes, www.seawater.no

Figure 7-30

Cod.

Kåre Telnes, www.seawater.no

Figure 7-31

Haddock.

Kåre Telnes, www.seawater.no

Figure 7-32

Pollock.

As extremely successful, high-level consumers, cod once dominated the North Atlantic food webs, with individuals reaching 95 kilograms (209 pounds). However, pressure from fishing has diminished stocks, with many researchers fearing that several cod stocks may have reached *commercial extinction*. Commercial extinction means that the species has become so scarce that it isn't a profitable fishery any more, and is unlikely to recover to fishable levels in the foreseeable future. For this reason, governments have closed cod fisheries in many areas to allow populations to recover.

Even with the cod fisheries closed, however, order Gadiformes continues to produce about a sixth of the world's fish catch. The Alaskan pollock, the haddock, and whitings have all become important fisheries. Chapter 17 discusses fisheries and concerns related to their future in greater detail.

STUDY QUESTIONS

Find the answers as you read.

1. What characteristics do organisms in class Reptilia share?

2. What three orders of reptiles have marine species? What types of animals do you find in each of these orders?

Marine Reptiles—Cold Blood and Warm Water

Characteristics of Reptiles

What characteristics do organisms in class Reptilia share?

While you might automatically think of fish when someone says "sea animal," you probably don't think of a reptile, except perhaps sea turtles. Many of the 6,000 or so species in class Reptilia live on land or in freshwater environments and relatively few live in the ocean.

Organisms in class Reptilia are generally cold-blooded. They breathe with lungs at all stages of their lives and have scales. Most species reproduce by laying internally fertilized eggs. Animals in this class include alligators, crocodiles, turtles, lizards, and snakes.

Special Attributes of Marine Crocodiles, Turtles, Snakes, and Lizards

What three orders of reptiles have marine species? What types of animals do you find in each of these orders?

Three of the four orders in class Reptilia have marine representatives. Because most are cold-blooded, you find all of these in relatively warm tropical and temperate waters.

The first of these is order Crocodilia, which includes alligators, crocodiles, and caimans. All members of this order are semiaquatic, with the vast majority living in freshwater swamps and in rivers. One species, the giant saltwater crocodile, ventures into the ocean and can live there for extended periods. However, the saltwater crocodile primarily lives in estuaries and other places where fresh water joins the sea. Some scientists suggest that the saltwater crocodile is a freshwater species that regularly visits the ocean more than a true marine species.

Order Chelonia includes turtles and tortoises. The seven species of marine turtles are probably what come to mind when you think of marine reptiles. All seven species live in relatively warm water, feeding on a variety of animals and plants and taking years to mature. At one time hunted as food, today all marine turtles are endangered or threatened.

Even with restrictions on capture, turtles continue to perish as bycatch. Marine turtles crawl up the beach and bury their eggs ashore. The eggs are vulnerable to predation, though more and more communities have taken steps to protect turtle nests from both poachers and animal predators. Hatchlings must dig their way out and scramble for the safety of the sea. If they hatch by day, seabirds and other predators snatch them up, so that very few make it to the water. Again, to help restore the endangered populations, a number of communities protects hatchlings so that a greater proportion at least make it to sea.

The largest of the turtles is the leatherback, *Dermochelys coriacea* (Figure 7-36). Reaching more than 450 kilograms (992 pounds), this reptilian giant ranges farther and swims faster than all the other marine turtle species. Unfortunately, the number of turtle-nesting beaches has declined rapidly, especially in

Bob Wohlers

MARINE REPTILE CLASSIFICATION

Domain
Eukarya

Supergroup
Unikonts

Kingdom
Animalia

Phylum
Chordata

Subphylum
Vertebrata

Class
Reptilia

Orders
1. Crocodilia – Alligators, Crocodiles
2. Chelonia – Turtles, Tortoises
3. Squamata – Snakes, Lizards

Figure 7-33

Marine Reptile Classification.

Figure 7-34

Green sea turtle.
Order Chelonia includes turtles and tortoises.

Figure 7-35

Marine turtles—order Chelonia.

The seven species of marine turtles are probably what come to mind when you think of marine reptiles. All live in warm water, feeding on a variety of animals and plants, plus taking years to mature. At one time hunted as food, today all marine turtles are endangered. Shown here are hawksbill (**Figure 7-35**) and leatherback turtles (**Figure 7-36**). The leatherback turtle shown in the middle is being fitted with a transmitter, allowing scientists to follow its migration.

Figure 7-36

Figure 7-37

Sea turtle nesting.

Sea turtles crawl up the beach and bury their eggs ashore. The hatchlings later dig their way out of the sand and head for the ocean. With both eggs and hatchlings vulnerable to predation, there are ongoing efforts to protect them so these endangered species may survive. Here a loggerhead turtle returns to the ocean after laying eggs.

the Pacific. Without strong conservation measures, the species faces imminent extinction.

Snakes and lizards make up order Squamata. The 61 species of sea snake are true marine organisms. They're related to cobras, but have a flattened tail adapted to swimming. They breathe air (as do all reptiles), but some species can absorb oxygen from the water through their skin. Sea snakes can remain under water for hours at a time.

Sea snakes are known for having the most toxic venom of any snake. This seems to be an adaptation to hunting small fish, which can escape into crevices when not immediately paralyzed. Although fatal sea snake bites occur, they're not as big a hazard to humans as venomous terrestrial snakebites. The reason is that sea snake fangs are small and at the back of the mouth, making it difficult (but not impossible) to deliver a toxic bite to a human. Sea snakes are also far less defensive than their terrestrial counterparts and therefore less likely to attempt to strike. However, because a bite is likely to be fatal unless antivenin is

Figure 7-38a&b

Sea snake.

Sea snakes are members of order Squamata and are true marine organisms. They are also known for having the most toxic venom of any snake. Although they have been known to bite humans, the size and position of sea snake fangs makes a toxic bite difficult compared to the bite of a terrestrial snake.

immediately available, swimmers and divers need prudence around sea snakes. Calmly leave the area if you spot a sea snake, and do not swim or dive where they've been seen.

There's only one lizard that's considered a true marine reptile, the marine iguana. Found in the Galapagos Islands, *Amblyrhynchus cristatus* is an unusual lizard not only because it swims and dives, but also because it is herbivorous. Most lizards are carnivorous.

Although marine iguanas are cold blooded, they feed on algae in the relatively cold waters of the Galapagos. To maintain an adequate body temperature, the iguanas sun themselves before and after every dive.

Al Hornsby

Figure 7-39a

Marine iguanas.
Order Squamata also includes a single species of marine iguana, which is found on the Galapagos Islands. These iguanas differ from their terrestrial counterparts in that they eat algae.

M. Elsbeth McPhee

Figure 7-39a

STUDY QUESTIONS

Find the answers as you read.

1. What characteristics are shared by organisms in class *Aves*?
2. What roles do birds play in marine ecosystems?
3. What adaptations to the marine environment do the various bird species exhibit?
4. In what parts of the world can penguins be found?

Seabirds—At Flight Over and In the Ocean

Characteristics of Birds

What characteristics are shared by organisms in class Aves*?*

What roles do birds play in marine ecosystems?

What adaptations to the marine environment do the various bird species exhibit?

Birds and the ocean go hand-in-hand. Every coastal marine environment has bird species that have found a niche there. Many scientists consider birds indicators of a marine ecosystem's richness and health. The more types and quantities of birds, the greater the richness and health.

Birds are vertebrates in class *Aves,* a huge group consisting of about 10,000 species. Members of this class share several characteristics, including feathers, which are unique to this class. Birds are also classified based on having forelimbs that are wings, a four-chambered heart, and laying internally fertilized eggs.

Birds play a myriad roles in marine ecosystems. They're predators that consume fish, crustaceans, and mollusks. At times, they're also prey to marine mammals and even sharks. Seabirds supply guano (droppings), which is a significant source of nutrients to the marine ecosystem. This is especially true of organic nitrogen, which scientists think is produced primarily on land (you can read more about organic nitrogen cycles in Chapter 8). Thus, birds that drop guano near the ocean help provide the marine ecosystem with organic nitrogen compounds.

Figure 7-40

Sea Birds.

Alaska Fisheries Science Center, Marine Observation Program/Fisheries Collection, NOAA

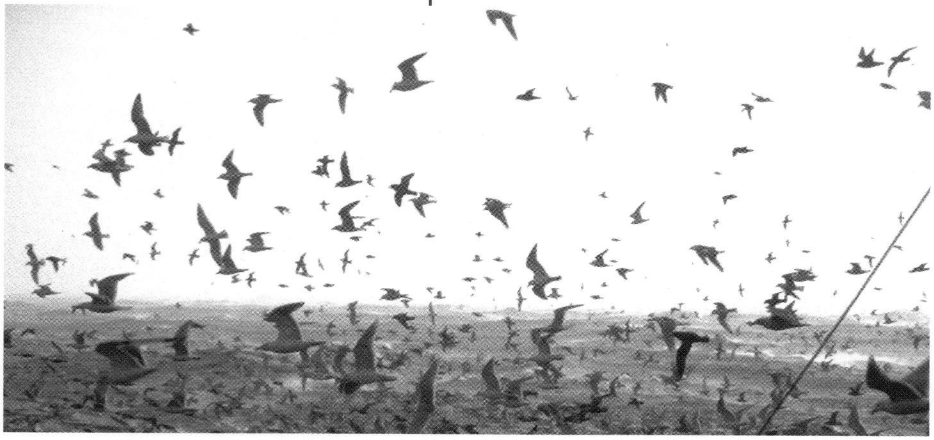

Because of their role in the marine and other aquatic environments, many species of birds exhibit related adaptations. Seabirds have webbed feet for swimming efficiently while floating on the surface. Most species have bill adaptations suited to their marine prey. For instance, the pelican is well known for its pouched lower jaw that aids it in capturing fish.

The cormorant not only flies over the water, but in it, descending many meters in pursuit of its prey. Some birds, like the albatross, have wings and flight characteristics adapted to low energy, long-duration flying over wide expanses of water.

Special Attributes of Penguins

In what parts of the world can penguins be found?

Incredibly, the most successful group of birds on Earth (in terms of biomass) is one of the few bird species that doesn't fly. Penguins, order Sphenisciformes, all live in the Southern Hemisphere. Penguins make up about 80% of the biomass of all Antarctic birds. However, not all species live in cold places. Penguins are found on the coasts of South America, Africa, Australia, New Zealand, and the nutrient-rich waters surrounding the Galapagos Islands near the equator.

Penguins spend as much as 75% of their time under water, searching for food in the ocean. When they are in the water, they swim, using their wings for propulsion. It looks just like they are flying! These birds thrive in massive nesting colonies. Most species breed in the less frigid subantarctic islands. Only the Emperor penguin remains on the Antarctic continent year round.

As consumers of krill, squid, and small fish, and as prey, penguins are an important link in the Antarctic and southern food webs. Penguins can't fly, but they're as at home under water as other birds are in the air. They dive hundreds of times daily hunting for food, reaching depths of 100 meters (328 feet) and deeper.

MARINE BIRD CLASSIFICATION

Domain
Eukarya

Supergroup
Unikonts

Kingdom
Animalia

Phylum
Chordata

Subphylum
Vertebrata

Class
Aves

Figure 7-41

Marine Bird Classification.

Glenn Grant, National Science Foundation

Figure 7-42

Penguins.

Penguins, members of order Sphenisciformes, are adapted to a totally marine existence. They thrive in massive nesting colonies and consume krill, squid, and small fish. Although they can't fly, they are at home under water and regularly make deep dives for food.

Marine Mammals—Warm Blood in Cold Water

Marine mammals are, in the opinion of many, the world's most spectacular animals. They include the largest animals that have ever lived and predators more powerful than the largest sharks. Their social behaviors, intelligence, and sensory capabilities fascinate us. Marine mammals sit near the top of their respective food webs.

Characteristics of Marine Mammals

What characteristics do organisms in class Mammalia have in common?

What challenges and adaptations to life in the sea do we find among marine mammals?

Marine mammals share the characteristics common to all organisms in class *Mammalia*. They all have hair on some part of the body (minimal on some marine mammals) and nourish their young with milk provided by mammary glands. Mammals are warm-blooded (also called *homeothermic*—how marine organisms deal with temperature is discussed in Chapter 9), meaning that they maintain constant internal temperature. By far the majority of mammals, including all marine mammals, give birth to live young.

Scientists think that mammals evolved on land, and that marine mammals evolved from land mammals that returned to the sea. The marine environment poses several challenges to mammalian physiology.

The first challenge is that, compared to living in air, life in water demands high oxygen consumption. Water cools a mammal's body, so marine mammals must generate enough heat to maintain their internal temperature. Water is much denser than air, requiring more energy to move. On top of this, mammalian physiology is already more metabolically active than fish or reptilian physiology, demanding more energy. All of these energy demands translate into high oxygen demand.

It is difficult to extract enough oxygen from water to maintain a stable body temperature, move rapidly though water, and support high metabolism. Marine mammals meet this challenge the way you do: they breathe air. Air has ample oxygen to allow marine mammals to meet their energy requirements. This is also why, so far, no one has created a practical artificial gill for divers. It's very difficult to extract sufficient oxygen for an air-breathing metabolism from the comparatively low levels dissolved in seawater.

Breathing air solves one challenge but creates another. Marine mammals cannot exist chained to the surface by their need to breathe. They need to breathe air, but they also need to dive holding their breath for reasonable periods. Several adaptations make this possible.

The first is *myoglobin*. Myoglobin is a protein similar to hemoglobin found in the tissues of marine mammals. Like hemoglobin, myoglobin binds reversibly with oxygen to make it available for use in metabolism. However, myoglobin binds with oxygen far more readily than does hemoglobin. All mammals have myoglobin, but not to the extent that marine mammals do. Their high myoglobin allows them to store much more oxygen in their bodies than can terrestrial mammals.

A second adaptation to breath-hold diving is the *mammalian diving reflex*. At the surface, marine mammals have high pulse rates with their metabolisms running at full speed. They consume oxygen at a very high rate. When they dive, however, their pulse rate slows and blood flow diverts from

Marty Snyderman

MARINE MAMMAL CLASSIFICATION

Domain
Eukarya

Supergroup
Unikonts

Kingdom
Animalia

Phylum
Chordata

Subphylum
Vertebrata

Class
Mammalia

Orders

1. Pinnipedia – Seals, Sea Lions, Walrus

2. Cetacea – Dolphins, Whales, Porpoises

3. Sirenia – Dugongs, Manatees

Figure 7-43

Marine Mammal Classification.

Figure 7-44

Mammalian diving reflex. At the surface, marine mammals have high pulse rates with their metabolisms running at full speed. They consume oxygen at a very high rate. When they dive, however, their pulse rate slows and blood flow diverts from the muscles to the sensitive heart and brain.

the muscles to sensitive organs, including the heart and brain. They may allow themselves to sink or glide more than they swim. Both responses cause their oxygen use to plummet, greatly extending their time under water. The mammalian diving reflex is pronounced in marine mammals, but it has also been documented in humans under some conditions.

A third challenge comes from water pressure. Have you ever experienced discomfort in your ears when you swim to the bottom of a swimming pool? This sensation is caused by water pressure compressing the air in your middle ears. This forces your ear drums to bend inward, causing pain. Scuba divers learn to equalize the pressure in their middle ears so this doesn't happen, but this process would be cumbersome for creatures that live their entire lives ascending and descending far faster and deeper than do scuba divers.

Marine mammal adaptations offset the problem. In marine mammals, the lungs and sinuses are very flexible, allowing these airspaces to compress significantly without pain or injury. They can exhale more than 95% of their total lung volume – humans can only exhale about 75%. In addition, the deep diving mammals, such as dolphins and whales, have lungs that engorge with blood, offsetting the compressed space. Through these adaptations, marine mammals can dive deeper and faster than human divers without injury.

A fourth challenge is movement through the dense medium of water. Marine mammal adaptations include streamlining and hydrodynamics. For a long time engineers couldn't figure out how dolphins could swim faster than their calculations said was possible. The answer, when finally discovered, was that their skin isn't rigid like the hull of a boat, but elastic and responsive. Dolphin skin has tiny grooves and actually changes to prevent turbulence against the surface. Furthermore, their skin constantly loses cells, which acts like a lubricant that minimizes water drag.

A fifth challenge for marine mammals is the senses. In terrestrial mammals, sight, hearing, and smell are the primary senses used for finding food and eluding predators. Water reduces the ability to see and smell, limiting the usefulness of these senses for marine mammals while under water.

Marine mammals have various adaptations to address this. Dolphins and some whales are well known for using *echolocation*, which is essentially natural sonar. By transmitting clicks and listening to their echoes, dolphins and some whales can determine an object's distance, size, density, and shape. (You can read more about echolocation in Chapter 9.) Seals and sea lions don't echolocate, but they have very sensitive hearing under water, and make

INTERNET PORTAL

SCiLINKS. NSTA

Topic: Marine Mammals
Go To: www.scilinks.org
Code: LOP2135

use of acoustics in other ways. They can hear potential prey or threats, and they have excellent under water eyesight. It appears that seals and sea lions do not have good eyesight above water; however, they have a keen sense of smell in air.

Special Attributes of Seals and Sea Lions

In what order do the seals and sea lions belong? How do seals and sea lions differ?

Seals and sea lions have many similar characteristics, but there's some disagreement over how to classify them. The prevailing view is that they belong in order Pinnipedia. Some taxonomists classify them in order Carnivora, which includes bears, otters, and cats. For our purposes, however, we'll treat seals and sea lions as members of order Pinnipedia.

Seals and sea lions belong to two different families because, despite their similarities, they have important differences. Seals are often called the "true" seals. They don't have ear flaps and their rear flippers point backward. Because of this, they cannot rotate their hind flippers forward. When a seal comes out of the water, it more or less crawls on its stomach. True seals swim with side to side movements of their powerful hind legs. True seals tend to be deeper divers than eared seals.

Sea lions, which include the misnamed fur "seals," have ear flaps. Their hind flippers can rotate underneath them, giving them more mobility out of the water. Sea lions can sit more fully upright. They can also run awkwardly by pivoting alternately on their fore and hind flippers. Under water, sea lions and fur seals swim with "flying" movements of their powerful forelimbs. Eared seals tend to live in shallower waters than true seals, and are more agile and active.

The walrus belongs in a third family between the seals and sea lions. Like a seal, the walrus has no ear flaps, yet can rotate its hind flippers forward like a sea lion.

Figure 7-45a

Sea lions.

PADI

Figure 7-45b

Sea lions.

Marty Snyderman

Figure 7-47

Sea lion.
Sea lions have ear flaps and can rotate their hind flippers underneath their body, which gives them additional mobility.

Figure 7-46

Harbor seal.
True seals don't have ear flaps and cannot rotate their hind flippers underneath them.

Special Attributes of Dolphins, Whales, and Porpoises

In what order do whales, porpoises, and dolphins belong?

Dolphins, whales, and porpoises come from different families organized under the order Cetacea. Mammals in this order show the most adaptation to living in the sea, leading scientists to think their ancestors returned to the ocean earlier than other marine mammal ancestors.

The 90 or so cetaceans have fish-like bodies and breathe air through a blowhole on the top of their head. They have no hind limbs, but have a huge, muscular tail that moves vertically to propel them through the water. These organisms have almost no hair, but have thick layers of fat called *blubber*, which provides insulation and reserve energy.

Cetaceans are divided into suborder Mysticeti, the baleen whales, and the suborder Odontoceti, the toothed whales. The baleen whales are filter feeders that include the humpback whale, the gray whale, the blue whale, and most of the other largest whales.

Baleen is a brush-like fringe that hangs from the roof of the whale's mouth. The whale takes in a mouthful of water, then filters it out through the baleen, trapping krill, other zooplankton, and small fish for food. Baleen whales have no teeth, but attain great size because filtering through baleen allows them to consume directly from the lowest levels of the food web.

Figure 7-48

Relative sizes of the baleen whales grouped in the suborder Mysticeti of the order Cetacea.

This suborder includes humpback, gray and blue whales. They are large filter feeders that use baleen to strain food from the water.

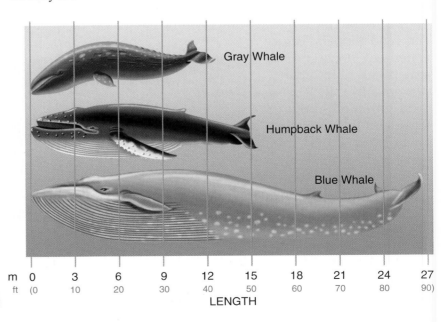

| m | 0 | 3 | 6 | 9 | 12 | 15 | 18 | 21 | 24 | 27 |
| ft | (0 | 10 | 20 | 30 | 40 | 50 | 60 | 70 | 80 | 90) |

LENGTH

The toothed whales include the sperm whale, the orca and other dolphins, and the porpoise. These whales are predators, with the sperm whale noted for feeding on deep ocean squid, including the giant squid. Most cetacea use echolocation and communicate by sound, with the toothed whales benefiting by using this ability for hunting.

Figure 7-49

Bottlenose dolphin.

Figure 7-50

Orca – killer whale.

Family Delphinidae, the dolphins, is one of the most varied and successful groups among the toothed whales. Although "dolphin" brings to mind the bottlenose dolphin made famous on television and in movies, this group includes the orca, also known as the killer whale. Orcas are considered very intelligent predators that hunt in packs and protect their young. Because of their distinct black-and-white coloration and their ability to learn, seaquariums commonly feature orcas, such as the famed Shamu.

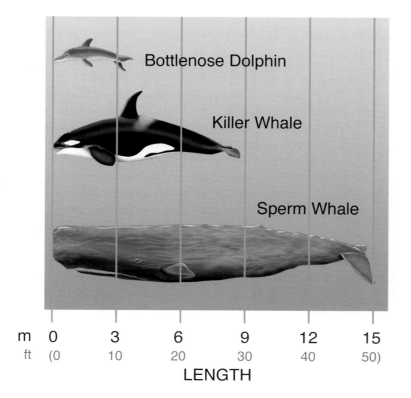

Bottlenose Dolphin

Killer Whale

Sperm Whale

| m | 0 | 3 | 6 | 9 | 12 | 15 |
| ft | (0 | 10 | 20 | 30 | 40 | 50) |

LENGTH

Figure 7-51

Relative size of toothed whales that are grouped in the suborder Odontoceti of the order Cetacea.

This suborder includes sperm whales, dolphins, and orcas. Toothed whales are predators that use echolocation and communication to help find their prey.

Marty Snyderman

Figure 7-52

Manatees.

Special Attributes of Dugongs and Manatees

In what order do dugongs and manatees belong?

Dugongs and manatees (sometimes called sea cows) belong to order Sirenia, which has four species. All four animals are the only herbivorous marine mammals. Manatees are noted for migrating between freshwater and saltwater environments. These relatives of the elephant are rare and endangered, having once been hunted for food. Today their primary threats are being accidentally run over by boat propellers as they lie just beneath the surface and the destruction of their habitats. In West Africa and Brazil, they're threatened by being hunted for meat.

This order gets its name from the Greek *Seiren*, the name of mythological Greek sirens, which were half woman and half bird. Legend has it that sirens lured sailors to their death with their beauty and singing. Taxonomists gave manatees and dugongs this name because of the similarity with mermaid myths. It's thought that early sightings of manatees and dugongs by sailors gave rise to stories about mermaids. If that's the case, the sailors who mistook manatees for mermaids must have been at sea for a long time!

Marine Mammals and Human Interaction

What human activities have endangered or may endanger marine mammals?

Under the slogan "Save the Whales," cetaceans and other marine mammals have been a conspicuous cause of environmentalists since the 1960s. Without a doubt, human activities have endangered marine mammals and continue to do so. Populations of many marine mammals have plummeted in recent years.

As explained earlier, mammalian physiology requires a lot of energy, especially in the marine environment. Marine mammals have been calculated to consume about a fifth of the entire food production of the world's ocean each year. Over the years, commercial fishing has demanded more and more from the ocean, and now probably takes nearly this much. This means that in effect, humans and marine mammals compete for much of the same productivity. Commercial fishing reduces the food available to marine mammals.

Beyond competing for their food, humans have a long history of whaling. North Atlantic populations of bowhead, grey and right whales declined from the 16th century onwards, primarily the result of English and Dutch

Figure 7-53

Manatee interaction.
Manatee encounters are popular in Florida when manatees come inshore to warmer rivers during the winter. Snorkelers often get a glance of the endangered marine mammal.

Al Hornsby

whaling. By the end of the 19th century, the use of explosive harpoons, special winches, and the ability to process the whales at sea increased the number of whales killed. The increase was so dramatic that several species went from common to the verge of extinction in fewer than 50 years. Today whaling is banned or greatly limited by international convention, but a few nations still actively engage in it. Although concerns remain for many whale species, the numbers for some species seem on the rise. Other species, unfortunately, do not seem to be recovering. Later chapters discuss whaling in more detail.

In addition to whales, people have historically hunted seals for fur and manatees for meat. Both practices have declined and are in fact illegal in most countries. A more recent concern has been the dolphins killed as bycatch in tuna fishing. Thanks to public pressure and media attention, the tuna-fishing industry responded with exclusion devices that reduce the dolphin bycatch, although the issue remains to some extent.

In the future, human interaction with marine mammals will probably remain a concern. While most countries, including the United States, now protect marine mammals, pollution and overfishing raise new threats. Because of their high metabolisms and energy demands, marine mammals require highly productive environments to survive. The loss of food due to overfishing or pollution is a potential threat that both scientists and environmentalists watch closely.

Archival Photography by Sean Linehan, NOS, NGS, NOAA

Figure 7-54

Old-school whaling operation.

Technological improvements in the whale hunt increased the number of whales killed so dramatically that several species were brought to the verge of extinction. Today whaling is banned or greatly limited by international convention.

Fisheries Collection, NOAA

Figure 7-55

Man and marine mammals.

In the future, human effects on marine mammals will likely remain a concern. While most countries, including the United States, now protect marine mammals from hunting, pollution, overfishing, and habitat destruction still threaten them.

1. **Organisms in class Mammalia have characteristics that include (choose all that apply)**

   A. hair.

   B. nourishing their young with milk provided by mammary glands.

   C. being homeothermic.

   D. that almost all give birth to live young.

2. **Marine mammal adaptations to the challenges of living in the sea include**

   A. the mammalian diving reflex.

   B. myoglobin for storing oxygen.

   C. breathing air to meet oxygen demands.

   D. all of the above

3. **Seals and sea lions belong to order _____, but have differences including that seals _____ and sea lions _____.**

   A. Cetacea, have ear flaps, lack ear flaps

   B. Pinnipedia, have ear flaps, lack ear flaps

   C. Cetacea, lack ear flaps, have ear flaps

   D. Pinnipedia, lack ear flaps, have ear flaps

4. **Whales, porpoises, and dolphins belong to order _____.**

   A. Carnivora

   B. Cetacea

   C. Pinnipedia

   D. any of the above, depending on the taxonomist

5. **The marine mammals in order Sirenia include (choose all that apply)**

   A. manatees.

   B. mermaids.

   C. sirens.

   D. dugongs.

6. **Human activities that have endangered or may endanger marine mammals include (choose all that apply)**

   A. whaling.

   B. overfishing.

   C. tuna fishing.

   D. fur hunting.

New Terms You Learned

- **Actinopterygii** the class of all ray-finned fish; jawed fish with skeletons made of bone; most have a swim bladder and scales (p. 7-3)

- **agnathan** a group of Vertebrata, characterized by marine animals similar to fish, but lacking both jaws and paired fins; includes two classes Petromyzontida, the lampreys, and Myxini, the hagfish. (p. 7-2)

- **ampullae of Lorenzini** organ in sharks and rays that detects weak electrical currents; see electro-reception (p. 7-7)

- **anthropomorphism** subconsciously or consciously assigning human traits to inanimate objects or animals (p. 7-2)

- **Aves** a class in the phylum Chordata, animals characterized by having feathers, forelimbs that are wings, a four-chambered heart and laying internally fertilized eggs (p. 7-20)

- **blubber** thick fat layer found in members of order Cetacea that provides insulation and reserve energy (p. 7-26)

- **Chondrichthyes** a class in the subphylum Vertebrata, fish characterized by lacking true bone and having a skeleton made of cartilage and having five to seven gill slits on each side of the body; includes sharks, skates and rays (p. 7-4)

- **claspers** male copulatory organs found on sharks and rays (p. 7-7)

- **commercial extinction** the reduction of a species to a population too low to exploit commercially (p. 7-15)

- **countershading** natural coloration of organism that conceals them against the bottom when viewed from above and against the surface when viewed from below (p. 7-12)

- **denticles** shark and ray scales, named for their characteristics that are much like shark teeth (p. 7-6)

- **echolocation** natural click transmissions from some marine mammals who listen to the echos to determine an object's distance, size, density, and shape (p. 7-24)

- **electroreception** the ability to sense the tiny, minute electricity created by muscles and nerves of other organisms (p. 7-6)

- **fusiform shape** open ocean fish shape characterized by spindle shape, slightly larger head and V-shaped tail; as in tuna (p. 7-12)

- **gas gland** organ in ray-finned fish that, along with another organ called the rete mirabile, takes oxygen from the bloodstream to inflate the swim bladder (p. 7-11)

- **homeothermic** designation for organisms that maintain a constant internal temperature; also called warm-blooded (p. 7-22)

- **lateral line** lines of sensory pores along the length of the body of fish that detect differences in water pressure; allows fish to detect vibrations of an approaching predator or struggling prey (p. 7-6)

- **Mammalia** class in the phylum Vertebrata, animals characterized by hair on the body, nourishing young with milk provided by mammary glands, being warm-blooded and with the majority giving live birth; includes whales, dolphin, sea lions, seals, walrus (p. 7-22)

- **mammalian diving reflex** especially pronounced in marine mammals, an adaptation to immersion in water that slows the pulse and diverts blood flow to extend breath-hold time (p. 7-23)

- **myoglobin** protein similar to hemoglobin that binds reversibly with oxygen, allowing marine mammals to extend their breath-hold time underwater (p. 7-23)

- **Myxini** class that include lampreys (p. 7-3)

- **Osteichthyes** a superclass in the phylum Vertebrata, animals characterized by having jaws and true bone; ray-finned fish, includes bass, eels, snappers, sea horses, tuna, flounder (p. 7-11)

- **oviparous** reproduction in which the mother lays eggs that mature and hatch outside the mother's body (p. 7-7)

- **ovoviviparous** reproduction in which eggs hatch and develop inside the mother with the young born live; as in some sharks and rays (p. 7-7)
- **Petromyzontida** class that includes sea lampreys (p. 7-3)
- **Reptilia** class in the phylum Vertebrata, animals characterized by air breathing, cold-blooded species that reproduce by laying internally fertilized eggs; includes alligators, crocodiles, turtles, lizards, snakes (p. 7-16)
- **rete mirabile** organ in ray-finned fish that, along with another organ called the gas gland, takes gas from the bloodstream to inflate the swim bladder (p. 7-11)
- **viviparous** reproduction in which the young develop inside the mother and are born live; mammalian live birth (p. 7-9)

Chapter 7 in Review

1. Explain what makes an animal a vertebrate. What is the significance of class Agnatha?
2. Describe what distinguishes sharks and rays from other organisms in class Chondrichthyes. Include classifications. How does the anatomy of a ray compare to the anatomy of a "typical" fish? In fish, what is dorso-ventrally flattened verses laterally flattened?
3. Compare and contrast how sharks and rays reproduce with how ray-finned fish reproduce. How do their reproduction strategies differ?
4. List and explain the traits that make sharks and rays successful predators. Include what the largest shark is and what it eats.
5. What characteristics make a fish a member of class Actinopterygii? What two types of fish, and their orders, are particularly important to worldwide fisheries?
6. Compare and contrast the diversity of fish that live on reefs and bottom with those that school or live in the open ocean. What is the explanation for this difference?
7. What characteristics distinguish an organism as a reptile? What reptiles are marine organisms?
8. Explain the role birds play in marine ecosystems. What adaptations to marine environments do you find in birds? In what parts of the world can penguins be found?
9. Explain the characteristics that classify an organism as a mammal. What are the challenges and adaptations to life in the sea found among marine mammals?
10. List the orders and physical differences for the following marine mammals: seals, sea lions, whales, porpoises, dolphins, dugongs, and manatees.
11. How have human activities endangered marine mammals in the past? What activities present concerns for the future?

Connecting Chapter Concepts – Science Scenarios

1. Sharks and rays make up class Chondrichthyes and ray-finned fish make up class Actinopterygii.
   A. What characteristics differentiate sharks and rays from ray-finned fish?
   B. What unique ability do sharks and rays in subclass Elasmobranchii have thanks to organs called ampullae of Lorenzini?
   C. What characteristics of shark reproduction make scientists concerned about commercial fishing for sharks? Why do these cause concerns?
   D. What do lateral lines do for fish? Which fish have lateral lines?
2. The marine environment creates several challenges to mammalian physiology. As a result, seals, sea lions, dolphins, whales and other marine mammals have specific adaptations to the marine environment.
   A. How do marine mammals obtain enough oxygen to support a mammalian physiology? Why does this provide more oxygen compared to how fish breathe?
   B. Marine mammals breathe air, but they have to be able to go under water for extended periods holding their breath. Explain two adaptations that allow them to do this.
   C. In air, sight is a primary way animals locate prey and elude predators. Sight is restricted by comparison under water. What adaptations in marine mammals offset this? Why is sight restricted under water?

Marine Science and the Real World

1. Tuna and shrimp fisheries have bycatch problems that they're attempting to solve with exclusionary devices. These devices work to varying degrees, but they increase the cost of catching tuna and shrimp, which makes the price of these foods high. Argue the cases for and against the need to bear this cost.
2. Some people point out that lightning and bees kill more people every year than do sharks. Do you agree that it is a realistic argument that sharks are not a substantial threat to people? Why or why not?
3. Assume that whale populations have returned to the levels that existed before 1900. Would you allow the resumption of whaling? Why or why not?
4. The military has trained dolphins for warfare roles that include detecting and killing enemy frogmen or placing explosives on enemy ships. Argue the cases for and against such a practice.

References

Bonner, N. 1994. *Seals and Sealions of the World.* Portland, OR: Book News.

Butler, P. J. 2004. Metabolic Regulation In Diving Birds And Mammals. *Respiratory Physiology & Neurobiology.* 141.

Cawardine, M. 1995. *Whales, Dolphins and Porpoises.* London: Dorling Kindersley.

Collette, B. B., et al. 1983. *Scombrids of the World.* FAO Species Catalogue.

Compagno, L.J.V. 2001. *Sharks of the World.* FAO Species Catalogue.

Hayward, P.J and J.S. Rylan. 2000. *Handbook of the Marine Fauna of North Western Europe.* Oxford: Oxford University Press

Jefferson, T.A., et al. 1993. *Marine Mammals of the World.* FAO Species Catalogue.

Kurlansky, M. 1997. *Cod: A Biography of the Fish That Changed the World.* New York: Penguin Books.

Marquez, M. R. 1990. *Sea Turtles of the World.* FAO Species Catalogue.

Nakamura, I. 1985. *Billfish of the World.* FAO Species Catalogue.

Nelson, J. 2006. *Fishes of the World.* New Jersey: John Wiley & Sons, Inc.

Science Encyclopedia. 2008. Squirrel Fish. http://science.jrank.org/pages/6422/Squirrel-Fish.html

The Marine Fauna Gallery of Norway. 2008. http://www.seawater.no

UCMP. 1996. Berkeley Guides to Taxa. www.ucmp.berkeley.edu/help/taxaform.html

Whitehead, H. 2002. Estimates Of The Current Global Population Size And Historical Trajectory For Sperm Whales. *Mar Ecol Prog.* Ser 242.

Whitehead, P.J.P., et al. 1985. *Clupeoid Fish of the World.* FAO species Catalogue.

Williams, T.D. 1995. *The Penguins.* Oxford: Oxford University Press

UNIT 3

A Water World

Bob Wohlers

Bob Wohlers

Rear Admiral Harley D. Nygren, NOAA Corps

Photo courtsey of Al Hornbsy

CHAPTER 8

The Nature of Water

NASA

Exploring the Deep Sea

H ydrothermal vents allow us to study a part of our planet that we can barely imagine. We still do not completely understand them. In 2008, seismologists discovered that the water in the world's ocean recycles through hydrothermal vents at a rate of perhaps 378 billion liters (1 billion gallons) per year in a process called hydrothermal circulation. Scientists, including Richard Lutz, think that hydrothermal vents offer clues to the origin of life on Earth and the possibility of life on other planets.

Although it is one of his scientific pursuits, Richard Lutz did not start out looking for the answer to the question of the origin of life on Earth.

Richard A. Lutz, PhD
Director, Center for Deep-Sea Ecology and Biotechnology
Professor, Institute of Marine and Coastal Sciences, Rutgers University

"When I was a child in elementary school, I would go to a creek and collect frogs, tadpoles, and the like. I think that's when I first became interested in science, though at the time, I didn't realize my collecting creatures would lead me to the study of hydrothermal vents. But, while I was attending the University of Virginia, I had an opportunity to go to the Chesapeake Biological Laboratory, a marine lab in Maryland (part of the University of Maryland) and spend the summer working on a research project. That's when I knew a career in science and exploration was what I would do with my life."

These days, Lutz does not collect many frogs or tadpoles. His main area of research is the ecology of deep-sea hydrothermal vents.

"The study of hydrothermal-vent environments is important because these are environments where life may have originated. They may also be similar to those of other extraterrestrial bodies, which means they may also provide clues regarding the possibility of life on other planets."

Lutz says his career is rewarding and has allowed him to see things no one else has ever seen before. He admits that there are certain challenges.

"The challenges and, yes, dangers associated with being in this field involve designing and conducting experiments on the bottom of the ocean. The submarine I go down in most is called Alvin. Alvin has made more than 4,000 dives and has only been stuck on the bottom once – while I was on board. It was a frightening experience because at first we couldn't figure out why we weren't able to move. We soon realized that the front of the sub had come loose and had scooped up about 800 pounds of mud. After some time, several maneuvers, and many gray hairs, we managed to get free and back to the surface."

For those students looking for a career in marine science, Lutz recommends waiting to concentrate on marine science until graduate school. First obtain a solid background in science and math at the undergraduate level.

"Marine science is an exciting field, and the most exciting discoveries in it are yet to be made. To any students considering careers in marine science: You will be part of the generation that gets to make these discoveries. The excitement of science is in figuring out the unknown as opposed to knowing the known. I wish you luck."

The Water Planet

You may have heard that water covers about 71% of the Earth's surface. Based on that, you might think that there's plenty of water to go around, but it's not that simple. Politically, water has always been an issue.

The vast majority of water on Earth can't be used directly for drinking, irrigation, or industry for the simple reason that it's salt water. But, the sea provides many other resources such as food, transport by shipping, oil and gas, and recreation. However, as revealed by the Cod Wars discussed in the previous chapter, as big as the ocean is, it's not always big enough.

Humans primarily need fresh water. There's just not as much as we'd like, and not all the sources are accessible.

Plenty of water exists at the poles, for instance, but it's frozen and located far from population centers. We can condense water vapor from the atmosphere by artificial means, but only at an astounding cost. Most of the fresh water we rely on comes from underground aquifers and rivers.

Historically, the lack of accessible, usable, fresh water has been a source of political tension. Rivers do not always go where people want them to, or people downstream dispute the use of water by people upstream. It's easy to recognize that if a group upstream pollutes a river or diverts its flow, those downstream may suffer.

Consider the situation in Africa between Ethiopia and Egypt. One of the world's longest rivers, the Nile, supplies Egypt with fresh water. Egypt is in one of the world's driest places. Without the Nile, Egypt would have little water for agriculture, industry, and its people. However, the Blue Nile (one of two rivers that merge to form the Nile in Egypt) originates in Ethiopia, which struggles economically. To promote agriculture and industry, the Ethiopian government wants to divert some of the Nile's water. The potential damage to Egypt isn't hard to imagine; hence, the two countries have been in conflict over this issue for some time.

Similar issues arise within the United States. Farmers in California's Tulelake agricultural region rely on water from Klamath Lake in Oregon. Questions regarding native-American rights and the protection of endangered species have led to Oregon periodically cutting off water to the farmers, damaging their crops and livelihood.

Figure 8-1a

Figure 8-1b

The ocean planet as seen from space.

From this perspective it is easy to see how much of our planet is covered by water—71% of the Earth's surface.

INTERNET PORTAL

SCiLINKS. NSTA

Topic: Properties of Water
Go To: www.scilinks.org
Code: LOP2140

In the southeast, faced with drought, Georgia planned to contain more water from the rivers that flow from it into northern Florida. This created huge concerns in Florida. Many feared such a drop in freshwater flow would affect commercial fishing and the economy of the Florida panhandle. The governors of Georgia, Alabama and Florida ultimately met and created a unified plan for managing their water needs.

In both cases, the dispute arose from two states that value the same water in two important, but different ways. And, in both cases, the states have found immediate, short term solutions but face long term issues that still need solving.

As the human population increases, so does the need for water. Part of the solution to meeting this demand lies in understanding what water is, where it goes, and how it cycles through nature.

Set aside the human perspective and look at water as if you lived in the sea like a dolphin or a fish. From this point of view, the ocean is vast. The ocean covers about 71% of the Earth's surface area. When you consider depth and volume, however, the world's ocean provides more than 99% of the *biosphere* – the habitable space on Earth.

On land, the habitable space comprises the ground, a few feet or meters below ground, and rarely more than 30 meters

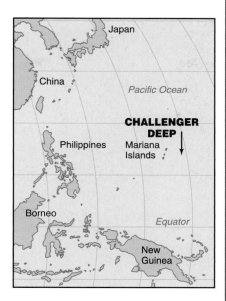

Figure 8-2

Challenger Deep.

The deepest known point in any ocean is the Challenger Deep in the Mariana Trench– almost 11,000 meters (36,000 feet). Challenger Deep got its name from the British Royal Navy ship *Challenger II*, which located the area east of the Mariana Islands in 1951. In 1997 and 2001, the Hawaii Institute of Geophysics and Planetology found a new super-deep spot near the island of Guam using an underwater sonar mapping system towed behind a research vessel. The new map reveals previously undiscovered faults, landslides, and undersea volcanoes in Mariana Trench at depths close to Challenger Deep. The new low point is called HMRG Deep— Hawaii Mapping Research Group Deep.

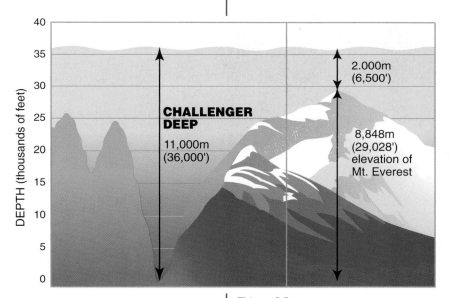

Figure 8-3

Challenger Deep and Mt. Everest comparison.

Challenger Deep is so deep that Mt. Everest could be placed within it and still have approximately 2,000 meters (6,500 feet) of water above it. The only visit to Challenger Deep was made in 1960 (you can review the story of the *Trieste* in Chapter 2). There is no submersible in use today that can reach the bottom of Challenger Deep.

STUDY QUESTIONS

Find the answers as you read.

1. What is a *polar molecule*?

2. What properties does water have because it is a polar molecule?

3. Why does ice float? How is this important to the thermal conditions on Earth?

(98 feet) above ground in trees. Some birds and insects fly high in the air, but they do not live there. This is why much of the atmosphere isn't considered part of the biosphere. But, many whales, fish, and other organisms live midwater – neither at the surface nor on the bottom – and seldom, if ever, near the seafloor or shore. Hydrothermal vents shoot hot, mineral-rich water into the ocean, providing flourishing habitats in the deepest parts of the sea. This makes the entire ocean, which averages 3,730 meters (12,238 feet) deep, part of the biosphere. While humans need fresh water for drinking, bathing, agriculture, and industry, the ocean provides resources for most life, including human life.

The deepest known point in any ocean is the Challenger Deep in the Mariana Trench. At approximately 11,000 meters (36,000 feet), it's so deep that if you put Mt. Everest into it, the top would still be more than 2,000 meters (6,500 feet) under water. As discussed in Chapter 9, this depth creates water pressure of an amazing 8 tons per square inch. That's about the weight of four automobiles

THE CYCLE OF WATER

Compared to Earth's total volume and mass, the outer layer in which we find life is as thin as paper wrapped around an egg. Yet except for sunlight, all the organisms on Earth get what they need from the resources in this layer.

Life would rapidly exhaust Earth's oxygen and vital elements if they were used only once. These resources exist to support life because they cycle between the air, land, water, and organisms.

The water around us has been here for a long time. Scientists think that the same water you drink or swim in today is billions of years old. Water travels in a hydrologic cycle, changing form as organisms take it in, as it evaporates, as it condenses, and as it flows from one location to another.

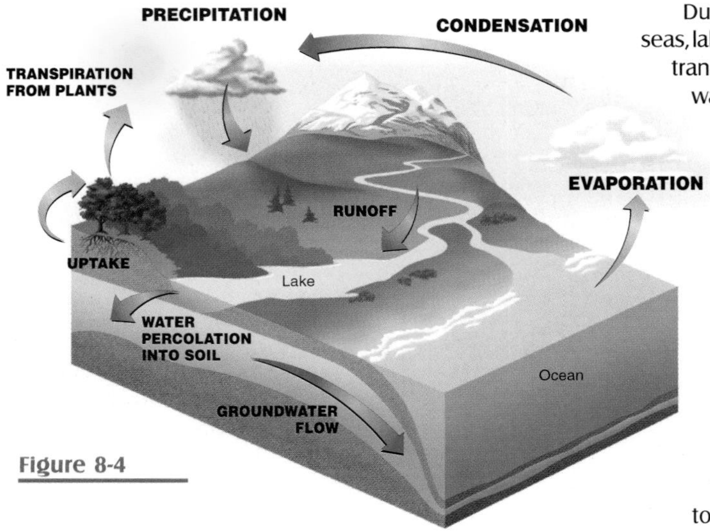

Figure 8-4

During the cycle, heat from the sun turns water from the seas, lakes, and streams into water vapor – evaporation. Through transpiration, even plants give off water vapor into the air. The water vapor rises into the atmosphere, eventually releasing its heat, and condenses. It then returns to Earth as rain, snow or other precipitation. It flows into streams and rivers, picking up minerals and compounds that it carries to the ocean. Organisms consume some of the water, later releasing it as water vapor, with waste products, or as a consequence of death and decomposition. From there it returns to the sea, river, and eventually, the air.

The same water molecule, over time, may have flowed through dozens of rivers and been part of every ocean. It may have been in the tears of an Egyptian pharaoh and, centuries later, joined a glistening dewdrop on corn in Thomas Jefferson's plantation fields. It's something to think about the next time you have a glass of water.

pressing down on an area the size of a typical postage stamp. The world's ocean holds more than 1.18 trillion cubic kilometers (285 million cubic miles).

Chapters 5, 6 and 7 discuss the many organisms in the sea, ranging from phytoplankton to whales. The ocean holds more life and diversity than any other place on Earth. To understand this life, you need to understand water itself. In this chapter, you'll learn about water's fundamental physical and chemical properties. You'll see why it's an unusual molecule with characteristics that shape the nature of life on Earth. You'll also learn how water cycles vital inorganic and organic compounds to and from the biosphere. Perhaps most important, you'll learn that we shouldn't take water for granted.

Water's Unique Properties

The Polar Molecule

What is a polar molecule?

Compared to many other important molecules, the water molecule is simple. You probably recognize its chemical symbol—H_2O. This means water consists of three atoms: two hydrogen and one oxygen. In contrast, the DNA molecule (deoxyribonucleic acid), which contains all of an organism's genetic information, consists of thousands of atoms.

Although water is a relatively simple molecule, the way it's held together gives it unique properties. The hydrogen atoms bond to the oxygen atom with a covalent bond. A *covalent bond* is formed

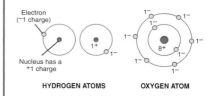

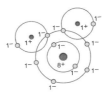

HYDROGEN ATOMS   OXYGEN ATOM

WATER MOLECULE

Figure 8-5

Covalent bonding.

Two atoms of hydrogen and one atom of oxygen share electrons in covalent bonds to become stable. Covalent bonds result in the formation of molecules. Molecules are the simplest part of a substance. They retain all the properties of the substance and can exist in a free state.

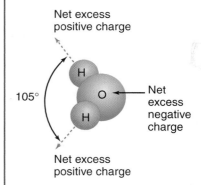

Figure 8-6

Water molecule has polarity.

Water molecules have positively and negatively charged ends, giving them *polarity*. The two hydrogen atoms have a net excess positive charge, while the oxygen atom has a net excess negative charge. Because water has two positively charged and slightly separated hydrogen atoms, it technically has two positive poles, one for each hydrogen atom. A molecule with positively and negatively charged ends is said to have polarity and is called a polar molecule.

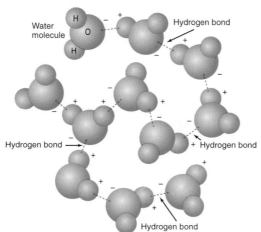

Figure 8-7

Hydrogen bonding.

The water molecule's polarity allows it to bond with adjacent water molecules. This happens because the positively charged hydrogen end of one water molecule attracts the negatively charged end of another water molecule. This is called a hydrogen bond.

HOW MICROWAVES COOK

One of the advantages of cooking with a microwave oven is that the microwaves heat the food but not the container (though the container may get hot from heat conducted away from the food). Why doesn't the plate heat up, too? Good question.

The reason is that microwave ovens produce heat by taking advantage of water's polar nature. Because a microwave creates a wave with an alternating positive and negative charge, it alternately attracts opposite ends of water molecules, which causes the water molecules to shift back and forth as the wave passes through the food. This happens more than 2.5 billion times per second, causing molecules to collide and generate heat through friction. That's how the microwave oven cooks your food.

Because there's very little water in glass or plastic, the microwaves have little effect on them. This is why the plate or cup doesn't heat up directly from the microwaves.

Topic: Properties of Ocean Water
Go To: www.scilinks.org
Code: LOP2145

by atoms sharing electrons. In water, the oxygen atom shares the electrons of two single-electron hydrogen atoms. This makes water a very stable molecule.

In water, the oxygen atom attracts the shared electrons close to its large nucleus, creating a lopsided molecule with two hydrogen atoms on one side and an oxygen atom on the other. This puts the hydrogen nuclei, with their positively charged protons, toward the outside of the molecule on one end. The oxygen atom's negatively charged electrons end up on the opposite side. This unequal electron sharing gives each water molecule a positive charge on the hydrogen end and a negative charge on the oxygen end, like a magnet. A molecule with positively and negatively charged ends is said to have *polarity* and is called a *polar molecule*. (Because of the presence of this charge on each of these atoms, water is sometimes called a *dipolar* molecule – *di* meaning *two*.)

The water molecule's polarity allows it to bond with adjacent water molecules. This happens because the positively charged (hydrogen) end of one water molecule attracts the negatively charged (oxygen) end of another water molecule. This bond between water molecules is called a *hydrogen bond*.

Individual hydrogen bonds are weak compared to covalent bonds. In fact, hydrogen bonds are only 6% as strong as covalent bonds, so they easily break and reform. However, the bonds have a cumulative strength in numbers. They are strong enough to give water some of its unique properties, all of which have profound effects on organisms on Earth, including you.

The Effects of Hydrogen Bonds

What properties does water have because it is a polar molecule?

Why does ice float? How is this important to the thermal conditions on Earth?

Liquid Water. The most important characteristic of hydrogen bonds is their ability to make water a liquid at room temperature. Without them, water would be a gas (water vapor or steam) at room temperature. This is because the hydrogen bonds hold the molecules together, requiring more energy (heat) to form steam. Without hydrogen bonds, Earth would be the *steam* planet instead of the liquid water planet.

Cohesion/Adhesion. Because hydrogen bonds attract water molecules to each other, water molecules tend to stick together. This is called *cohesion*. Cohesion gives water a more organized structure than most liquids. Water also sticks to other materials due to its polar nature. This is called *adhesion*. An example of this is the tendency for a raindrop to cling to the surface of a leaf. Only when there's a lot of water and the weight exceeds the force of adhesion does the droplet flow off the leaf.

Viscosity. *Viscosity* is the tendency for a fluid (gas or liquid) to resist flow. Most fluids change viscosity as they change temperature. Maybe you've put cooking oil in a cool pan and noticed that at first it flows very slowly when you tilt the pan. But, as the pan gets hot from the stove, the oil flows quickly because it becomes less viscous.

Because hydrogen bonds tend to hold water molecules together, they make water more viscous than it might otherwise be. As water cools, the viscosity rises proportionately more than it does in most other liquids. This is because the molecular motion caused by the heat helps offset the hydrogen bonds. Cooler water has less molecular motion to counteract the hydrogen bonds, so the water molecules "stick together" more than when the water is warmer. For example, a 20°C (68°F) drop in temperature increases water's viscosity by more than 60%. This is important because it affects the energy aquatic organisms expend. In cool water, the high viscosity means drifting organisms (plankton) use less energy to keep from sinking. However, swimming animals use more energy moving through it.

Surface Tension. The polar nature of water allows it to form a skin-like surface. This is called *surface tension*. Surface tension is water's resistance to objects attempting to penetrate its surface. The cohesive nature of water at its surface (caused by hydrogen bonds holding the water molecules together) makes surface tension possible.

To you, a large organism, surface tension is so weak you don't notice it when you step into a puddle or dive into a swimming pool. To small creatures, such as the water strider (*Halobates sericeous*), however, surface tension is a strong force. It allows the water strider to literally stand on water. As explained in Chapter 3, neuston are plankton that live on the water's surface. Many small organisms of this community rest on surface tension rather than float.

Scientists have a particular interest in the air/water boundary created by surface tension because they're trying to understand how it affects gas exchange between the ocean and the atmosphere. Surface tension affects how quickly the ocean takes up atmospheric carbon dioxide and release oxygen into the atmosphere. This issue has become particularly important as carbon dioxide increases in the atmosphere from air pollution. Surface tension affects how much

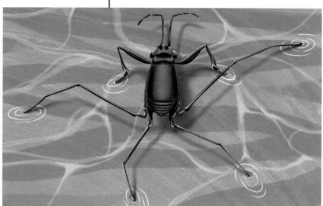

Figure 8-8

Surface tension.
Liquid molecules stick together (cohesive forces) causing the phenomenon known as *surface tension*. Water molecules at the surface do not have other water molecules above them. Consequently, they hydrogen bond more strongly with the water molecules beside and below them. This forms a surface "film," which makes it more difficult to penetrate through the surface than to move the same object when it is completely submerged. The small marine insect species, *Halobates sericeous*, use surface tension to literally stand on the water.

Figure 8-9

Ice floats.

As water cools enough to turn from a liquid into solid ice, the hydrogen bonds pull the molecules into a crystal structure that takes up more space than does liquid water. Ice is therefore less dense than liquid water, so it floats.

carbon dioxide the ocean absorbs to offset pollution.

Another concern is how pollutants affect the neustonic community. Many chemicals, including soaps and detergents, tend to reduce hydrogen bonding and negate surface tension. Many insects supported by surface tension cannot stand on water with soap in it because the water can no longer support their weight. The insects sink just like large animals would.

Ice Floats. When you fill a glass with water and put ice in it, the ice floats. You probably don't even think about it. But, it is actually very unusual for the solid form of a substance to float in the liquid form. Most substances become denser and sink when they cool and turn from liquid to solid. They lose density as they heat and turn from liquid to gas. Water also becomes less dense as it heats and denser as it cools, but only to a point. As water cools enough to turn from a liquid into solid ice, the hydrogen bonds spread the molecules into a crystal structure that takes up more space than liquid water. With more volume, ice is less dense than liquid water, so it floats. Chapter 9 discusses more about how water freezes.

This property has a huge effect on this planet. By floating, ice forms a layer that insulates the water below, allowing it to retain heat and remain a liquid. Surface ice insulates the water below from further cooling. With a cover of ice, the ocean retains more heat than it would otherwise. If ice sank, the ocean would be entirely frozen – or at least be substantially cooler – because water would not be able to retain as much heat. The Earth's climate would therefore be substantially colder – perhaps too cold for life at all.

ARE YOU LEARNING?

1. **What is a polar molecule?**

   A. a molecular combination only possible in freezing conditions such as those found at the North and South Poles

   B. a molecule with a configuration that causes it to have a positively charged end and a negatively charged end

2. **Properties of water that are possible only because it is a polar molecule include**

   A. being a liquid at room temperature, surface tension, and that ice floats.

   B. the ability to evaporate and reduce resistance to flow.

3. **If ice did not float, the Earth's entire climate would be markedly different because the ocean would be frozen solid or substantially cooler.**

   A. true   B. false

The Inorganic Chemistry of Water

Solutions and Mixtures in Water

What are the two kinds of mixtures? *What is a* solution?

Stir a spoonful of sugar in water and watch it dissolve. You have just created a *solution,* which occurs when the molecules of one substance are evenly dispersed among the molecules of another substance. In this example, water acts as the *solvent.* A solvent is the more abundant substance in a solution, and usually a liquid. The *solute* (in this case, sugar) is the substance being dissolved. It is in less abundance and is usually a solid or gas.

A solution is one of two forms of *mixture.* A mixture is the combination of two or more substances that are not chemically bonded, and not in fixed proportions to each other. There are two kinds of mixtures – *homogeneous* mixtures and *heterogeneous* mixtures. A homogeneous mixture is one that has a uniform appearance throughout and either entirely liquid or entirely gas.

A heterogeneous mixture is one that is not uniform and consists of visibly different substances. The mixture may include different phases of matter (liquid, solid or gas).

An example of a heterogeneous mixture would be India ink stirred into water. The water darkens, but if left to stand for a while, the ink settles to the bottom of the glass, leaving clear water above. When stirred, the ink and water molecules spread out evenly, creating a mixture heterogeneous mixture. A heterogeneous mixture with solid particles that tend to settle like this is called a *suspension.*

The difference between a homogeneous and a heterogeneous mixture is the size of the particles of substances in the mixture. In

STUDY QUESTIONS

Find the answers as you read.

1. What are the two kinds of *mixtures*? What is a *solution*?

2. What is *salinity*? What are the major sea salts?

3. What are the *colligative properties* of seawater? Does fresh water have these properties?

4. What is *the principle of constant proportions*?

5. Besides hydrogen and oxygen, what are the most abundant chemicals in seawater?

6. How is the principle of constant proportions used to determine salinity? How do marine scientists determine salinity?

7. Where do sea salts come from? Is the ocean getting saltier? Why or why not?

8. How do temperature and salinity affect seawater density?

9. What factors affect seawater's pH? Why does pH change with depth?

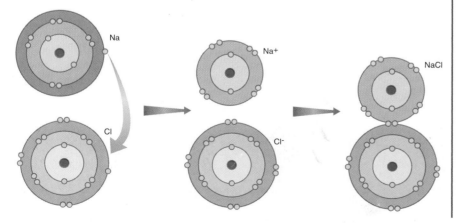

Figure 8-10

Ionic bonding.

Salt molecules are made up of one sodium and one chlorine atom—sodium chloride (NaCl). By losing its outermost electron, a sodium atom becomes a positively charged sodium ion. By gaining one electron, a chlorine atom becomes a negatively charged sodium ion. Because opposite charges attract, the Na+ and Cl- ions form a NaCl molecule with an ionic bond.

a solution, the particles are atoms or molecules and so small that they will remain in solution indefinitely. The solute particles don't separate from the solvent unless a change (temperature, pressure, evaporation of solvent, etc.) occurs. A *colloid* is a homogeneous mixture between a solution and a heterogeneous mixture. A colloid consists of very, very small particles that are larger than atoms or molecules. They may settle, but will take a very long time to do so. Milk, fog, smoke and stirred up dust in the air are examples.

Water can be part of both homogeneous and heterogeneous mixtures. Water is a good solvent, which is another characteristic derived in part from its polar nature. The way salt dissolves illustrates this. The water molecule's polar characteristics pull apart (*dissociate*) the salt (sodium chloride—NaCl) crystal. In the process, the dissociated sodium and chloride become charged particles (*ions*) and attract the positive and negative ends of the water molecules. The negative oxygen end of the water molecule attracts the positive sodium ions, and the positive hydrogen end attracts the negative chloride ions. These bonds tend to keep the salt in solution.

Substances that do not separate into ions can still dissolve in water through other mechanisms. Sugar crystals, for example, break into individual molecules when dissolved. These molecules have no charge and are therefore neutral. Because of this, the molecule remains intact in solution, and the solution is said to be *non-ionic*. As carbohydrates, sugar molecules do have carbon, hydrogen, and oxygen. Because of the individual charges of the atoms in the molecule, sugar molecules and water molecules will form hydrogen bonds.

Because many substances can dissolve into water in various ways, water is sometimes called the "universal solvent."

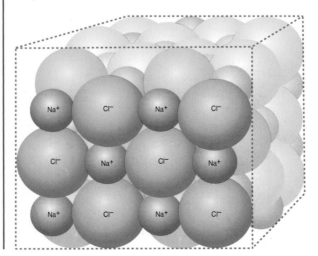

Figure 8-11

Salt.

Salt (sodium chloride—NaCl) in its crystal or solid state.

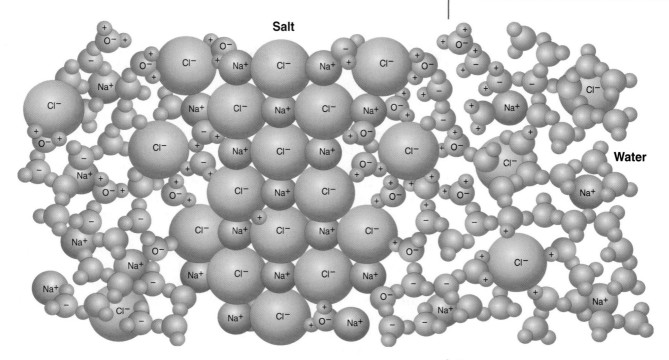

Salt

Water

Salts and Salinity

What is salinity? What are the major sea salts?

Although you may think salinity refers only to the sodium chloride (NaCl) dissolved in seawater, there are many other salts, including potassium chloride (KCl). *Salinity*, therefore, includes the total quantity or concentration of all dissolved inorganic solids, or more precisely, ions. This is the sodium chloride and everything else, commonly called the *dissolved salts*.

Scientists measure salinity in various ways. The most current methods use equipment that determine salinity based on how well water conducts electricity. The equipment uses the ratio of the conductivity of the sample to the conductivity of a standard solution of potassium chloride (KCl). Salinity values determined by this method are dimensionless – without units – because ratios have no units. This method for determination and expression of salinity is the Practical Salinity Scale (PSS). The ocean's average salinity is 35, which is equivalent to 35‰ salinity as determined by an older method. The abbreviation ‰ stands for "parts per thousand," so 35‰ means 35 parts per thousand, meaning 35g/kg. (Note: To convert parts per thousand into percent, you divide by 10, so that 35‰ = 3.5%.) Variations in salinity as small as 0.01 are of great significance to oceanographers.

Figure 8-12

Water as a solvent.

The water molecule's polar characteristics pull apart (dissociate) the salt molecules. In the process, dissociated sodium and chloride atoms become charged particles (ions) and attract the positive and negative ends of the water molecules. The negatively charged oxygen end of the water molecule attracts the positive sodium ions, and the positively charged hydrogen end attracts the negative chloride ions. The bonds tend to keep the salt in solution. As more water molecules come in contact with salt crystals, the water attacks the salt and breaks it down.

Generally the ocean's salinity varies very little, although there is a great deal of variation in specific areas: from near zero at the mouths of rivers to more than 40‰ in confined, arid regions such as the Red Sea. As discussed below, the *proportion* of the various dissolved salts in seawater does not change, only the relative amount of water. The salinity changes when fresh water enters the ocean—such as from a river or from rain—or as water evaporates. For instance, *brackish water* results when fresh water mixes with seawater in estuaries. Brackish water has a salinity of 0.6‰ to 30‰. *Brine,* which is water saturated or nearly saturated with dissolved salt, develops in areas with high evaporation and little inflow of fresh water. Brine also develops where salt domes dissolve at the seafloor, as is common in the Gulf of Mexico.

Most dissolved salts in seawater exist as dissociated ions. Sodium chloride (rock salt, also called *halite*) is the most abundant of these. You can see the dissolution of sodium chloride in Figure 8-12. In the middle, the salt is depicted as a set of stacked molecules; on the left and right, it dissolves into water, becoming dissociated ions. The dissociated ions separate in solution and recombine when the water evaporates. Because the different salts exist as dissociated ions, they interact with water molecules and each other. This changes some of water's physical properties primarily by disrupting the hydrogen bonds.

The properties of a liquid that may be altered by the presence of a solute are called *colligative properties*. Since pure water doesn't have anything dissolved in it, it does not have colligative properties. We associate colligative properties primarily with seawater. However, natural fresh water usually has some quantity of solutes and can have colligative properties to some degree. The strength of the colligative properties depends on the quantity of solute.

Figure 8-13

Colligative property—creating osmotic pressure.

A law of chemistry is that fluids flow or diffuse from areas of high concentration to areas of low concentration until the concentration equalizes. Because it contains dissolved salts, water in seawater exists in lower concentration than in fresh water. Therefore, if there's seawater on one side of a semipermeable membrane and fresh water on the other **(A)**, a pressure exists from the fresh water's tendency to diffuse through it. In **(A)**, water moves from left to right, trying to equalize the solute concentration on both sides of the membrane. Over time, the concentration on both sides of the membrane becomes equal **(B)**.

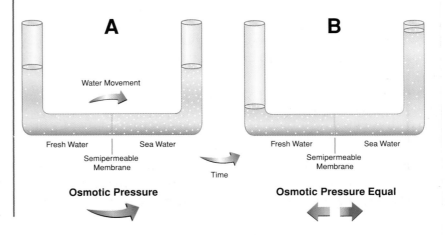

Colligative Properties of Seawater

What are the colligative properties of seawater? Does fresh water have these properties?

The properties of a liquid that may be altered by the presence of a solute are called *colligative properties*. Since pure water doesn't have anything dissolved in it, it does not have colligative properties. We associate colligative properties primarily with seawater. However, natural fresh water usually has some quantity of solutes, and can have colligative properties to some degree. The strength of the colligative properties depends on the quantity of solute.

Raised boiling point. Seawater boils at a slightly higher temperature than pure fresh water.

Decreased freezing temperature. As salinity increases, water resists freezing. This is why salt is sometimes used on the road during ice and snowstorms. Seawater freezes at a slightly lower temperature than fresh water.

Ability to create osmotic pressure. A law of chemistry is that fluids diffuse from areas of high concentration to areas of low concentration until the concentration equalizes. You can think of this as flowing downhill from a high area to a low area. *Osmosis* (from the Greek *osmos* meaning to *thrust*) occurs when this happens through a semipermeable membrane, such as a cell wall. (A *semipermeable membrane* allows some substances to pass through, but not others.) Because it contains dissolved salts, water in seawater exists in lower concentration than in fresh water. Therefore, if there's seawater on one side of a semipermeable membrane and fresh water on the other, a pressure exists from the fresh water's tendency to diffuse through the membrane. This is called *osmotic pressure*. Remember that water flows from the lower solute concentration to the higher solute concentration. Equilibrium is reached once enough water has moved to equalize the solute concentration on both sides of the membrane. Osmosis and osmotic pressure are crucial to many biological processes; we'll look at some of them more closely later on in this chapter.

Electrically conductive. The salts in seawater act as *electrolytes*, substances that can conduct electricity when dissolved in water.

Decreased heat capacity. It takes less heat to raise the temperature of seawater than to raise fresh water to the same degree.

Slowed evaporation. The attraction between ions and water molecules keeps water from evaporating easily. Seawater will evaporate more slowly than fresh water, all else being equal.

Photo of the 556 instrument courtesy of YSI, Inc.

Figure 8-14a

Salinometer.

Today's oceanographers often use an advanced type of *salinometer* to measure salinity. This device determines conductivity and calculates the salinity based on the water's electrical conductivity. When calibrated against known conductivity samples, it is very accurate.

Jim Abernethy/www.scuba-adventures.com

Figure 8-14b

The Principle of Constant Proportions

What is the principle of constant proportions?

Almost all known, naturally occurring elements – and since the development of nuclear explosives, even some non-naturally occurring ones – exist in seawater. They don't exist in the same amounts, of course. However, no matter how much the salinity varies, the proportions of several key inorganic elements and compounds do not change. This is useful because it means that if you know how much of one element there is, you can determine how much there is of all the others. Only the amount of water, and therefore the salinity, changes.

This constant relationship of proportions in seawater is called the *principle of constant proportions*. The dissolved salts are called *conservative constituents* because they do not change proportions.

Dissolved Solids in Seawater

Besides hydrogen and oxygen, what are the most abundant chemicals in seawater?

Let's suppose you have one kilogram of seawater with average salinity (35‰). This means that 3.5%, or 35 grams, would be dissolved solids. Based on constant proportions, this would break down to these approximate numbers:

(Cl^-) Chloride	18.98 g	(HCO_3) Bicarbonate	0.14 g
(Na^+) Sodium	10.56 g	(Ca^{2+}) Calcium	0.40 g
(SO_4^{2-}) Sulfate	2.65 g	(K^+) Potassium	0.38 g
(Mg^{2+}) Magnesium	1.28 g	Other	0.61 g

Determining Salinity, Temperature, and Depth

How is the principle of constant proportions used to determine salinity? How do marine scientists determine salinity?

You can't measure salinity by evaporating seawater and measuring what's left. Nor can you apply heat without causing chemical reactions that would change the results. Some of the salts don't release all the water molecules adhering to them, and if you try to dry it out with heat, chemicals decompose and react, forming gases and new compounds not found in seawater. So much for that approach.

Fortunately, the principle of constant proportions comes to our aid. If you know how much you have of any one seawater chemical, you can figure out the salinity. It turns out that chloride accounts for 55.04% of dissolved solids. Determining a sample's chlorinity (the total weight of the chloride, bromine, and iodine ions) is relatively easy. The following formula for determining salinity is based on *all* the chloride compounds (not just rock salt – sodium chloride).

salinity ‰ = 1.80655 x chlorinity ‰

Using some very basic arithmetic, you can figure out the salinity when you know how much chloride there is in parts per thousand. For example, suppose you have a seawater sample that tests 19.2‰ chlorinity.

salinity ‰ = 1.80655 x 19.2‰

salinity ‰ = 34.68‰

Likewise, when you know the salinity you can determine the chlorinity.

34.68‰ = 1.80655 x chlorinity ‰

$$\frac{34.68‰}{1.8065} = \frac{1.80655 \times chlorinity ‰}{1.80655}$$

19.2‰ = chlorinity ‰

Most commonly, salinity is determined with a *salinometer*, which determines the electrical conductivity of the water. When calibrated against samples with known conductivity, salinometers are accurate to 0.01‰.

One tool for measuring the properties of seawater is the conductivity, temperature, and depth (*CTD*) sensor. The CTD is a torpedo-shaped instrument that may be deployed by itself, but often is attached to a water-sampling rosette or a submersible. The CTD's primary function is to profile temperature and salinity (the two variables that determine density) with depth. Temperature is usually measured by a *thermistor*, which is a semiconductor having resistance that varies rapidly and predictably with temperature. Conductivity is determined by measuring the current flowing between two platinum electrodes sealed in a tube of nonconducting glass. Pressure measurements are made by measuring the natural frequency of a quartz crystal. As the CTD is lowered into the water on an electrical cable, conductivity, temperature, and depth data are transmitted to the ship and fed into computers for analysis by researchers. As further discussed in Chapter 11 and the sidebar later in this chapter, the *Argo* floats are now an important tool for oceanographers. *Argo* is a global array of 3,000 free-drifting profiling floats that measures the temperature and salinity of the

Frank Ruopoli, Coastal Services Center, NOAA

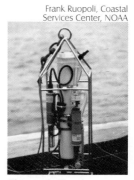

Figure 8-15

Jeff Pollack, Ocean Exlporer, NOAA

Figure 8-16

CTD sensor.

The CTD sensor (shown in 8-15) is a torpedo-shaped instrument for measuring the conductivity (salinity), temperature, and depth of seawater. A CTD is deployed to a predetermined depth with an array of water sampling bottles (8-16). Devices such as these give oceanographers a profile of conditions at depth.

Figure 8-17

Simple refractometer.

Dupree, Inc.

South Carolina Department of Natural Resources

Figure 8-18

Science as inquiry.
Student using refractometer.

MEASURING SALINITY WITH LIGHT

Refractometers measure salinity based on the principle of light refraction. Notice how a straw placed into a glass of water appears bent due to a shift in the light rays passing through the water. The refractive index (amount of refraction) that occurs in a substance relates to its density.

Because water with dissolved salts is denser than pure water, a straw appears more bent in salt water than in pure water. The more dissolved salt, the greater the density, and the more refraction and apparent bending. Refractometers put this phenomenon to practical use. By measuring the refractive index, the instrument determines the water density and therefore the salinity. Ernst Karl Abbe, a German scientist, invented refractometers in the early 1900s.

Pure Water   Salt Water

Figure 8-19

Refraction.
Because water with dissolved salts is denser than pure water, refraction makes a straw appear more bent in salt water than in pure water. The more dissolved salt, the greater the density, and the more refraction and apparent bending. You can try this simple experiment at home.

upper 2000 m of the ocean. *Argo* communicates its data directly to scientists through satellite transmissions.

Why the Seas are Salty

Where do sea salts come from? Is the ocean getting saltier? Why or why not?

With constant rain, runoff, erosion, and other natural forces, you may think that oceanic salinity is rising or falling. However, that doesn't appear to be the case. Most oceanographers think that salinity is not changing. It is in a steady state, and there's no sign of the ocean becoming more or less salty. The thinking is that the sources of salt removal and addition cancel each other out.

But, where do the salts come from in the first place? One source appears to be minerals and chemicals eroding and dissolving into fresh water flowing into the ocean. This means that rivers, runoff, and rain percolating through the ground into the sea bring in salts. However, the salts in seawater differ from the salts delivered by rivers, so there must be other sources. Waves and surf contribute by eroding coastal rock. Hydrothermal vents change seawater by adding some materials while removing others. (Chapter 13 discusses

DATA FROM THE DEPTHS

To understand the ocean better, oceanographers must measure salinity, temperature, dissolved gases, nutrients, suspended matter, pH, and other characteristics of seawater. They do this *in situ* (in the natural location at depth) but they can't simply lower a bottle on a piece of string.

Seawater is obtained from a predetermined depth with specialized water-sampling bottles, such as Nansen bottles and Niskin bottles. Nansen bottles are lowered singly on a cable. A signal weight dropped down the cable trips the bottle's release mechanism. The bottle turns upside down, sealing sample water in the bottle. Niskin bottles are mounted twelve to thirty-six on a rosette sampler. They are lowered into the water on a wire that supports an electrical conductor. An electrical command from the ship closes the spring-loaded end caps of each of the bottles when

Oceangraphic Museum of Monaco/NOAA

Figure 8-20

Nansen bottle.

characteristics of the water column in that location. Scientists can also tow winged CTD sensors behind a vessel to gather continuous data over a wide area. Oceanographers also leave instruments (buoys) on the surface or at depth. Some buoys are anchored to the bottom, others drift with currents. These buoys transmit sensor data and GPS location information via satellite or radio link to researchers. They can collect and transmit data actively for a number of years, making them extremely useful for studies of long-term variability in the ocean. Project Argo is an international deployment of a global array of 3,000 free-drifting temperature/salinity profiling floats that began in 2000. One major focus is to monitor global climate continuously in an effort to understand climate change.

Small manned submersibles allow oceanographers to collect seawater samples along with biological and geological specimens, video, and still photos. This is perhaps the most expensive way to collect seawater samples, but no doubt the most fun.

Monterey Bay Aquarium Research Institute

Figure 8-22

SeaSoar.

Captain Robert A. Pawlowski, NOAA Corps

Figure 8-21a

CTD rossette sampler.

Figure 8-21b

Niskin bottle array.

CTD sensors are in the center of the device, surrounded by a rossette of 12-36 water-sampling bottles.

desired. Rosette samplers are usually used with CTD sensors, which measure conductivity, temperature, and depth. They may also include sensors to measure pH, chlorophyll, water transparency, and oxygen. Combining data from Niskin bottles and CTDs will yield a profile of the important

© JAMSTEC

Figure 8-23

Argos float.

OAR, NURP, NOAA/Harbor Branch Oceanographic Institution

Figure 8-24

Johnson Sea-Link manned submersible.

Figure 8-25

Sources of salt in the ocean.

Salt and other important ions enter the ocean in various ways. Positive ions – sodium, magnesium, and potassium – can enter the ocean by the weathering of rocks. Carried by rivers, these ions are dispersed into the ocean. Negative ions – chlorine and sulfide – can enter the ocean through hydrothermal vent discharge and volcanic precipitation. Salts and other ions are removed from the ocean by sea spray, and biological processes. Scientists believe that the sources of salt removal and addition cancel each other out.

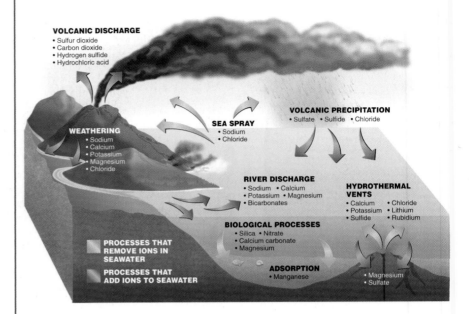

hydrothermal vents in more detail.) Other biological and chemical processes and reactions within the seawater and on the seafloor tend to remove salts. Scientists think these processes all counterbalance so that the average salinity of seawater remains constant. In this way, the ocean is said to be in *chemical equilibrium*.

Salinity, Temperature, and Water Density

How do temperature and salinity affect seawater density?

Most of the ocean surface has average salinity, about 35‰ (34.7‰ to be precise). Waves, tides, and currents mix waters of varying salinity to make them more uniform. Even so, surface ocean salinity varies slightly with the season and with the weather, particularly with rainfall and evaporation. Locations with salinity different from the average include primarily bays, semi-enclosed seas, and the mouths of large rivers.

Precipitation and evaporation have opposite effects on salinity. Rainfall decreases salinity by adding fresh water. Evaporation increases salinity by removing fresh water. Freshwater input from rivers lowers salinity. The average salinity is 40‰ at the surface of the Red Sea and 38‰ at the surface of the Mediterranean, because of low freshwater input and high evaporation. Conversely, abundant river input and low evaporation have resulted in salinities well below the average in the Black and the Baltic Seas, with 18‰ and 8‰, respectively.

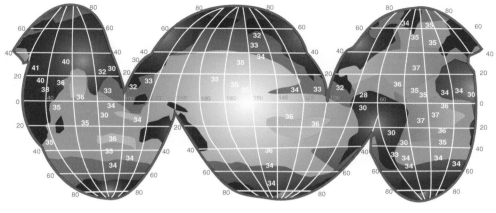

Figure 8-26

Global salinity.

Global salinity of the ocean can vary markedly from one area to the next. Tropical regions tend to be saltier than temperate regions.

Salinity greater than 36 parts per thousand   Salinity 34-36 parts per thousand   Salinity less than 34 parts per thousand

Surface ocean temperatures vary as well. The most important factor is latitude; water in the equatorial region is warmer than water near the poles. Surface temperatures also vary with the seasons. The greatest seasonal variation is in the temperate ocean, in the middle latitudes, where seasonal differences in sea surface temperatures are about 10°C (18°F).

Salinity and temperature also vary with depth. Density differences cause water to separate into layers. High-density water lies beneath low-density water. Water's density is the result of its temperature and salinity characteristics: low temperature and high salinity are features of high-density water. Relatively warm, low-density surface waters are separated from cool, high-density deep waters by the thermocline (from the Greek *therm* meaning *heat*, and *clinare* meaning *slope*), the zone in which temperature changes rapidly with depth.

Salinity differences overlap temperature differences and the transition from low-salinity surface waters to high-salinity deep waters is known as the *halocline* (*halo* meaning *salt*). The thermocline and halocline together make the *pycnocline*, the zone in which density increases with increasing depth. Below the pycnocline, temperature and salinity tend to be uniform. Temperature differences tend to dominate changes in water density, except at temperatures near 0°C, or in places where fresh water mixes with seawater. Chapters 9 and 11 discuss more about how water stratifies into layers.

Karl Shreeves

Figure 8-27

Halocline.

Water can form layers characterized by an abrupt change in salinity. The interface between these two layers is called a *halocline*. This is common in water-filled caves near the ocean. Less dense fresh water from the land forms a layer over salt water from the ocean. Underwater cave explorers passing through the halocline may stir up the layers. The blurred effect comes from the mixing of the different layers.

Acidity and Alkalinity

What factors affect seawater's pH? Why does pH change with depth?

Earlier you learned that, in the process of dissolving into water, sodium chloride dissociates and forms ions in solution. When something dissolves in water, some of the water molecules also dissociate and form ions, depending on the solutes. The water molecules can dissociate into positively charged hydrogen ions and negatively charged hydroxide ions. You can write this as:

$$H_2O \longrightarrow H^+ + OH^-$$

The relative concentration of positively charged hydrogen ions or negatively charged hydroxide ions determines the water's acidity or alkalinity. Acidity and alkalinity are measured as *pH*, a scale that represents the balance between the positive hydrogen ions (H+) and the negative hydroxide ions (OH-) in a liquid.

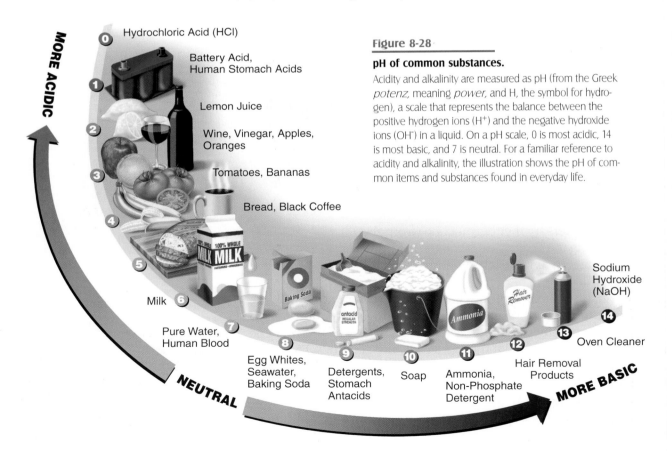

MORE ACIDIC

0 Hydrochloric Acid (HCl)

1 Battery Acid, Human Stomach Acids

2 Lemon Juice

2 Wine, Vinegar, Apples, Oranges

3 Tomatoes, Bananas

Bread, Black Coffee

4

5

Milk 6

Pure Water, Human Blood 7

8 Egg Whites, Seawater, Baking Soda

9 Detergents, Stomach Antacids

10 Soap

11 Ammonia, Non-Phosphate Detergent

12 Hair Removal Products

13 Oven Cleaner

14 Sodium Hydroxide (NaOH)

NEUTRAL

MORE BASIC

Figure 8-28

pH of common substances.

Acidity and alkalinity are measured as pH (from the Greek *potenz,* meaning *power,* and H, the symbol for hydrogen), a scale that represents the balance between the positive hydrogen ions (H$^+$) and the negative hydroxide ions (OH$^-$) in a liquid. On a pH scale, 0 is most acidic, 14 is most basic, and 7 is neutral. For a familiar reference to acidity and alkalinity, the illustration shows the pH of common items and substances found in everyday life.

When a solution has a lot of hydrogen ions, it is considered an acid. An acid has a pH value of 0 to less than 7. A pH of 0 indicates a very concentrated acid that would burn your skin, whereas a dilute acid has a pH of 4.0 or 5.5. For example, citric acid, which gives lemons their sour taste, is a dilute acid. The pH scale is logarithmic, meaning that every number in the scale is multiplied by a fixed number. In the case of pH, the fixed number is 10, so that each step in the scale represents a tenfold change. Therefore, going from a pH of 6 to a pH of 7, for example, represents a tenfold decrease in acidity.

Solutions with lots of hydroxyl ions are considered alkaline, also called basic solutions. The pH is higher than 7, with anything over 9 considered a concentrated alkaline solution. Sodium hydroxide, for example, has a pH of 14 and is dangerous to touch. Baking soda, by comparison, has a pH of about 8.

You can measure pH chemically or electronically. By exposing certain chemicals or chemically treated paper (litmus strips) to a sample, you can estimate pH by color change. For more precision, scientists use electronic instruments. These measure the hydrogen ions as potential voltage, which is proportional to the pH.

Pure water has a pH of 7, which is neutral. Seawater pH

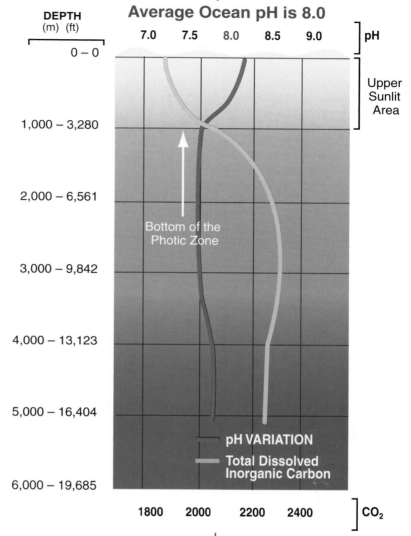

Figure 8-29

The variation in pH and total dissolved inorganic carbon with depth.
Although seawater pH is relatively stable, it changes with depth. It does this because the amount of total dissolved inorganic carbon dioxide tends to vary with depth.

Topic: Acids, Bases, Buffers
Go To: www.scilinks.org
Code: LOP2155

How the ocean maintains its pH balance is very complex. Many factors determine actual oceanic pH. However, when carbon dioxide dissolves in seawater, it forms carbonic acid and other compounds that decrease seawater's pH by making it more acidic. By absorbing carbon dioxide from the atmosphere and from the human-induced carbon dioxide emissions, the world's seas function as a giant buffer for the Earth's life support system.

The chemical balance of the sea has long been regarded as immovable. However, since the beginning of the industrial revolution, ocean pH has dropped globally by 0.12 pH – approximately 25%. While this change is not alarming, the recent *rate* of change is cause for concern. Scientists have never observed such a rapid ocean acidification.

If carbon dioxide concentrations continue to rise and the rate continues to accelerate, we may expect to see changes in pH that are three times greater and 100 times faster than those thought to occur during the transitions from glacial to interglacial periods. Such large changes in ocean pH have probably not been experienced on the planet for the past 21 million years.

How marine ecosystems, coral reefs, and fisheries would respond to such rapid acidification is unknown. Marine scientists are currently studying the effects of increased ocean acidification. Human-induced carbon dioxide emissions are also connected to global climate change – a topic discussed at length in Chapter 18.

typically ranges from 7.8 to 8.3, which is very mildly alkaline. Freshwater bodies can have a very broad pH range, from highly acidic to highly alkaline. However, the ocean's pH remains relatively stable due to buffering. A *buffer* is a substance that reduces the tendency of a solution to become too acidic or too alkaline. Seawater is buffered primarily through carbon dioxide content. Carbon dioxide combines with water in several chemical reactions that either free up or release hydrogen ions. One of these is to combine with the water itself to create carbonic acid:

$$H_2O + CO_2 \longrightarrow H_2CO_3$$

Carbonic acid is relatively unstable and tends to react further with water to create bicarbonate and other compounds. These reactions are reversible. When the water is too basic, the reactions release hydrogen ions, making it more acidic. Alternatively, when the water is acidic, other reactions bind with hydrogen ions, making it more basic. The carbon cycle is a vital but complex process that tends to keep pH relatively stable.

Although seawater pH is relatively stable, it changes with depth. It does this because the amount of carbon dioxide tends to vary with depth. The upper, sunlit depths (photic zone) have the greatest density of photosynthetic organisms. These organisms use carbon dioxide, which means less reaction into carbonic acids and subsequent compounds. This makes the water slightly less acidic. Also, surface water is relatively warm, which tends to reduce carbon dioxide in solution. Generally, warm productive water has a pH around 8.5.

In the ocean's middle depths, pH can change slightly. There may be more carbon dioxide present from the respiration of marine animals and other organisms. This makes the water somewhat more acidic with a lower pH.

At about 1,000 meters (3,281 feet) depth, there's less organic activity. This results in a decrease in respiration and, consequently, carbon dioxide, so that mid-level seawater tends to be more alkaline. At about 3,000 meters (9,843 feet) and deeper, the water becomes more acidic again. This is because the decay of sinking organic material produces carbon dioxide, but there are no photosynthetic organisms to remove it. The transition between less acidic and more acidic water is known as the *carbonate compensation depth* (CCD). Water below the CCD is acidic enough to dissolve the sinking calcium carbonate shells of dead organisms.

The Organic Chemistry of Water

Biogeochemical Cycles

How do the proportions of organic elements in seawater differ from the proportions of sea salts?

What is the biogeochemical cycle?

Although the sea salts—the dissolved inorganic solids in seawater—account for the majority of dissolved solids, there are others that are organic or that interact with organisms on a significant scale. These elements are crucial to life and differ from the sea salts in several ways.

STUDY QUESTIONS

Find the answers as you read.

1. How do the proportions of organic elements in seawater differ from the proportions of sea salts?

2. What is the *biogeochemical cycle?*

3. What element is fundamental to all life?

4. What are the roles of carbon in organisms?

5. What are the roles of nitrogen in organisms?

6. Why is phosphorus important to life?

7. What is the role of silicon in marine organisms?

8. What are the roles of iron and other trace metals in marine organisms?

Topic: Carbon Cycle
Go To: www.scilinks.org
Code: LOP2160

One difference is that the principle of constant proportions does not apply to these substances. These *nonconservative constituents* have concentrations and proportions that vary independently of salinity. They vary due to biological and geological activity. For example, some organic material may be in short supply in marine environments with a high biological activity and populations. In other areas, substances may be overabundant from pollution or discharge from mineral springs.

All life depends on material from the nonliving part of the Earth. The continuous flow of elements and compounds between organisms (biological form) and the Earth (geological form) is called the *biogeochemical cycle.*

Organisms require specific elements and compounds to stay alive. Aside from gases used in respiration or photosynthesis, those substances required for life are what we call *nutrients.* The primary nutrient elements related to seawater chemistry are carbon, nitrogen, phosphorus, silicon, iron, and a few other trace metals.

When organisms die, what scavengers do not consume sinks, eventually reaching the bottom at depths below the photic zone. Bacteria and other microorganisms decompose some of the organic material as it sinks and on the seafloor. Decomposition leaves inorganic nutrients. Upwelling, which is an upward water flow is one force that returns inorganic nutrients to shallow water. Once in the photic zone, photosynthesis returns the nutrients to the food chain. Chapter 11 discussed more about upwelling.

Not all elements and compounds cycle at the same rate. Some cycle rapidly, whereas others may be isolated or trapped on the seafloor for long periods. The biogeochemical cycle of the various nutrients affects the nature of organisms and where they live in the sea.

Carbon

What element is fundamental to all life?

What are the roles of carbon in organisms?

Carbon is the fundamental element of life. Organisms can form long carbon chains to which other atoms can attach during biosynthesis, so that every organic compound consists of carbon chains. It is a versatile foundation for a wide range of diverse chemicals. Carbon compounds form the basis for chemical energy and for building tissues.

The seas have plenty of carbon in several forms. Carbon dioxide from the air dissolves into the ocean. Natural mineral sources, such as carbonate rock, also contribute to the ocean's carbon as sediments dissolve into the water. Dissolved organic carbon is formed from organisms' excretion and from the decomposition of organic material. It is transported in global current patterns. Most of the organic carbon that finds its way into the deep sea is broken down into inorganic forms by bacteria. This action creates a "biological pump" that tends to concentrate carbon and other nutrients with depth; this plays a central role in the global carbon cycle. This "pump" transfers carbon from the atmosphere to the deep sea, where it concentrates and remains for centuries. Scientists think this accounts for about 75% of the difference between dissolved inorganic carbon concentrations at the surface and in the deep sea.

Carbon compounds are found in air and water and within rocks and minerals. They exist in the air as carbon dioxide, which is a by-product of respiration. Carbon dioxide also enters the atmosphere from volcanic activity and fires, particularly forest fires. Humans increase the amount of carbon dioxide in the atmosphere by burning fossil fuels. Carbon dioxide is created by burning fossil fuels because carbon is part of all plants and animals. When the organisms die, much of their carbon combines with water to form hydrocarbons that get buried in ocean sediments. These hydrocarbons

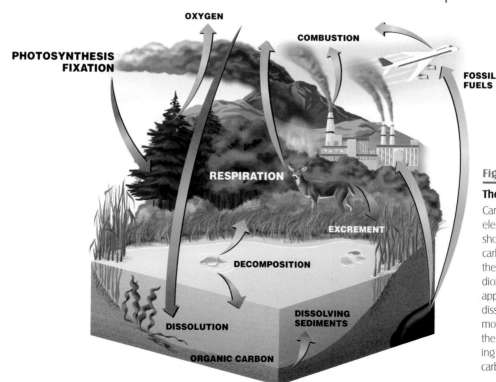

OXYGEN

PHOTOSYNTHESIS FIXATION

COMBUSTION

FOSSIL FUELS

RESPIRATION

EXCREMENT

DECOMPOSITION

DISSOLUTION

DISSOLVING SEDIMENTS

ORGANIC CARBON

Figure 8-30

The carbon cycle.

Carbon is the fundamental element of life and this figure shows the major steps of the carbon cycle. In addition to the 700 billion tons of carbon dioxide in the atmosphere, approximately 1 trillion tons are dissolved in the ocean. The movement of carbon between the biosphere and the nonliving world is described by the carbon cycle.

MARINE BIRDS AND THE NITROGEN AND PHOSPHORUS CYCLES

Chapter 7 discusses the roles marine birds play in the ecological balance. One of these is helping the sea obtain organic nitrogen and phosphorus. They do this through their guano, or bird droppings.

Guano is abundant on coasts and islands frequented by sea birds. It is rich in phosphates and ammonia, making it a powerful source of nutrients for the natural world and for agriculture. Guano can be used as a fertilizer for indoor and outdoor agriculture and has even been found to be effective in hydroponics.

The value of guano has long been recognized. The Incas in Chile and Peru guarded the deposits and delivered a death penalty to those who removed them unlawfully. In the mid 1800s, the US government passed a law that protected the people who discovered guano. The act authorized people to take possession of guano found on any unclaimed land and granted them exclusive rights to the guano for private use.

Because it supplies fast- and slow-release nutrients, guano plays an important role in the biological system. Marine birds consume approximately 80 million metric tons of fish annually. Most of their droppings fall onto the sea where they are broken down by nitrogen-fixing bacteria and the nutrients are recycled. Terrestrial nitrogen-fixing bacteria break down guano on land, providing a mechanism by which this organic nitrogen can make its way back to the sea.

take the form of petroleum, coal, natural gas and other fossil fuels. When burned, the hydrocarbons react with oxygen to produce carbon dioxide and water, which get released into the atmosphere.

Prior to the Industrial Revolution, the carbon dioxide concentration in the air was an estimated 280 ppm (parts per million). Today it averages about 365 ppm and is increasing rapidly. Carbon dioxide is a greenhouse gas and is thought to be a major contributor to the increase in temperatures known as global warming.

Carbon dioxide must be transformed into other carbon compounds for use by heterotrophs. The movement of carbon between the biosphere and the nonliving world is described by the carbon cycle.

As discussed in previous chapters, in terrestrial and aquatic environments, plants, phytoplankton, algae, and other primary producers with chlorophyll, convert carbon dioxide into carbohydrates through photosynthesis. Photosynthesis is a form of fixation, which as discussed in Chapter 4, is the process by which an element, such as one found in a gas, is converted, or fixed, into a new compound. This is an important process because many organisms can only use key elements essential to life when fixed into an organic molecule. Photosynthesis brings carbon from carbon dioxide into the food chain by converting it into more complex carbon compounds.

The role of organic carbon converting to hydrocarbons that get buried in ocean sediments has another profound effect. Many scientists think that this process is essential for the existence of oxygen in the atmosphere. The thinking is that if *all* organic carbon decomposed to carbon dioxide and water, then all the oxygen produced by photosynthesis would be used up. There would be little in the atmosphere. This makes the burial of organic carbon into ocean sediments crucial. By removing carbon from the carbon cycle, there is free oxygen from photosynthesis for use by heterotrophs.

Nitrogen

What are the roles of nitrogen in organisms?

Nitrogen is another element crucial to life. Organisms require nitrogen for organic compounds such as protein, chlorophyll, and nucleic acids. Nitrogen makes up about 78% of air and 48% of gases dissolved in seawater. However, gaseous nitrogen must be converted to a chemically usable form before it can be used by living organisms. Chapter 5 discusses bacteria, and notes that only bacteria can fix nitrogen from the air into other compounds. This happens in the nitrogen cycle, during which gaseous nitrogen is fixed into nitrate (NO_3^-), nitrite (NO_2^-), and ammonium (NH_4^+).

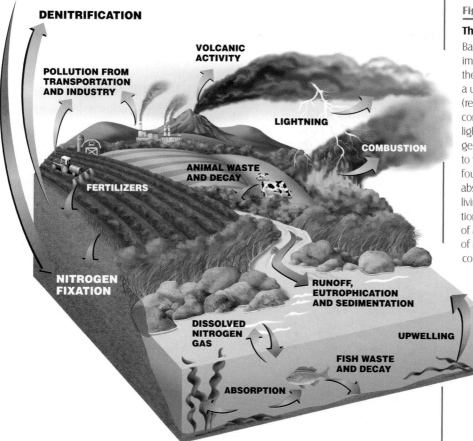

DENITRIFICATION

POLLUTION FROM TRANSPORTATION AND INDUSTRY

VOLCANIC ACTIVITY

LIGHTNING

COMBUSTION

FERTILIZERS

ANIMAL WASTE AND DECAY

NITROGEN FIXATION

RUNOFF, EUTROPHICATION AND SEDIMENTATION

DISSOLVED NITROGEN GAS

UPWELLING

FISH WASTE AND DECAY

ABSORPTION

Figure 8-31

The nitrogen cycle.

Bacteria and people carry out many of the important steps of the nitrogen cycle, including the conversion of atmospheric nitrogen into a usable form (ammonia), and denitrification (returning nitrogen to the air and water). Even combustion (from fossil fuels and forest fires), lightning, and volcanic activity can form nitrogen oxides and nitric acid that return nitrogen to the soil and water. The nitrogen cycle has four important stages: 1) Assimilation: the absorption and incorporation of nitrogen into living systems, 2) Decomposition: the production of ammonia by bacteria during the decay of animal urine, 3) Nitrification: the production of nitrate from ammonia, 4) Denitrification: the conversion of nitrate to nitrogen gas.

In these forms, autotrophs take up the nitrogen and incorporate it into their systems as protein. The nitrogen passes up the food web through trophic feeding and returns through the cycle after death. At this point, the nitrogenous compounds break down during decomposition, becoming ammonia. Plants take up some of the ammonia, and the rest either dissolves into water or remains in the soil. Microorganisms convert the ammonia into nitrates and nitrites (*nitrification*). Nitrates from decomposed material can be buried into sediments on the ocean floor or they can go through *dentrification* during which the nitrogen returns to the water column as a gas.

Since the industrial revolution, human nitrogen production has become the dominating source of nitrogen entering the nitrogen cycle. Rain runoff picks up ammonia, fertilizers and other human-produced nitrogen compounds, which then flow into the ocean. This can cause Harmful Algae Blooms, which Chapter 18 discusses in more detail.

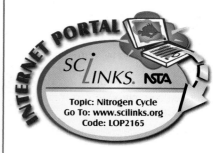

INTERNET PORTAL

SCiLINKS. NSTA

Topic: Nitrogen Cycle
Go To: www.scilinks.org
Code: LOP2165

Phosphorus and Silicon

Why is phosphorus important to life?

What is the role of silicon in marine organisms?

Phosphorus is another element important to life because it is used in the ADP/ATP cycle, by which cells convert chemical energy into the energy required for life. Phosphorus is also part of DNA and other nucleic acids, the molecules that pass genetic information from parent to offspring. Phosphorus also combines with calcium carbonate as the primary component of bones and teeth.

In the marine environment, some organisms, including diatoms and radiolarians, similarly use silicon for their shells and skeletons. Within these organisms, silicon exists as silicon dioxide, commonly called *silica*. In addition, most sand is made of silica because it is a common component of rocks and minerals and does not break down easily.

Phosphorus and silicon convert relatively rapidly into phosphate and silica, respectively, for consumption by phytoplankton and bacteria. When they become part of shells and skeletons, however, the cycle can be considerably longer because they sink into marine sediments. Once in sediment, it takes a long time for these elements to return to the biosphere for further availability to organisms. However, in the sediments they are used by benthic organisms that rely on them for survival.

Figure 8-32

The phosphorus cycle.

Phosphorus is another element important to life because it is used in the ADP/ATP cycle, by which cells convert chemical energy into the energy required for life. Dissolved phosphorus is carried to the sea by runoff and leaching from land. The phosphorus is used by plants, then recycled through animals until it is released from waste and decay. Bird guano is also a primary source of phosphorus in seawater.

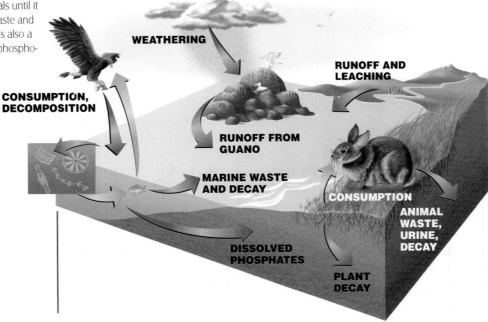

WEATHERING

RUNOFF AND LEACHING

CONSUMPTION, DECOMPOSITION

RUNOFF FROM GUANO

MARINE WASTE AND DECAY

CONSUMPTION

ANIMAL WASTE, URINE, DECAY

DISSOLVED PHOSPHATES

PLANT DECAY

Iron and Trace Metals

What are the roles of iron and other trace metals in marine organisms?

Iron, along with several other trace metals, fits into the definition of a *micronutrient*. Micronutrients are substances essential to organisms in very small amounts. Organisms use iron for constructing specialized proteins, including hemoglobin and enzymes. In addition, plants need iron to produce chlorophyll, although iron is not part of the chlorophyll molecule. Other trace metals used in enzymes include manganese, copper, and zinc.

Iron is essential to marine life, especially phytoplankton, and is one of the most abundant metals on Earth. However, it's not readily available in the sea because it does not dissolve well in seawater. The small amount that does dissolve readily reacts with other chemicals and tends to bond with particles that sink to the bottom.

Scientists have found that a lack of iron limits phytoplankton productivity in some parts of the ocean. Thus, adding iron to seawater on a large scale would trigger a phytoplankton bloom that would draw carbon dioxide from the atmosphere. This could help reduce global warming, which is thought to be caused by rising carbon dioxide levels resulting from burning fossil fuels.

If this controversial proposal were enacted, it would probably be in parts of the southern hemisphere that have the longest distances from the nearest major land mass. Land is the source of iron in the ocean, so these areas have less iron because there is less land for it to run off of or blow off of as dust. Levels of other nutrients are high there, and it is sometimes iron that limits phytoplankton populations.

Small-scale experiments have shown that this technique is valid. In one 2002 experiment, just over 1 metric ton (2,200 pounds) of iron was added to an area of 15 square kilometers (about 5 square miles). The scientists studied the amount of particulate organic carbon that sank from the surface and estimated that over an area of 400 square miles (1,036 square kilometers), 1,800 tons (about 4 million pounds) of carbon would have been lost from the ocean surface. Although this seems like a large number, this carbon flux is small compared to the variation that occurs naturally in this region.

Despite these successes, there's no widespread support for fertilizing the ocean with iron. First, there are no data to show that the carbon dioxide decline would be permanent. Second, there would be consequences on benthic, local and global ecosystems, but these have not been studied and are hard to estimate.

1. **The proportions of organic elements in seawater are constant, just like the proportions of sea salts.**

   A. true

   B. false

2. **A biogeochemical cycle is**

   A. the process of inorganic salts entering and leaving seawater.

   B. the process of elements and compounds moving continuously to and from organisms and the Earth.

3. **_____ is fundamental to all life.**

   A. Silicon

   B. Carbon

4. **Carbon is fundamental to all life because**

   A. it reacts with hydrogen to form energy.

   B. it provides a versatile foundation for diverse chemicals.

5. **Organisms use nitrogen**

   A. as an inhaled energy source.

   B. for the formation of organic compounds such as proteins, chlorophyll, and nucleic acids.

6. **Phosphorus is essential to life because**

   A. it combines with nitrogen to form shells.

   B. it is an important component of DNA and other nucleic acids.

7. **Silicon is important to some marine organisms**

   A. because it aids digestion.

   B. because it is used for shells and skeletons in some organisms.

8. **Iron and trace metals in marine organisms are essential for**

   A. constructing specialized proteins, such as hemoglobin and enzymes.

   B. sinking to the seafloor.

Chemical Factors That Affect Marine Life

Diffusion and Osmosis

How can diffusion and osmosis affect marine organisms?

STUDY QUESTIONS

Find the answers as you read.

1. How can diffusion and osmosis affect marine organisms?

2. What are *passive* and *active transport*?

3. What are *osmoregulators* and *osmoconformers*?

Earlier in this chapter you learned that seawater can create osmotic pressure and that osmosis is diffusion through a semipermeable cell membrane. Diffusion is the tendency for a liquid, a gas, or a solute to flow from an area of high concentration to an area of low concentration. Heat facilitates diffusion by causing molecules to move. High temperatures speed up diffusion by speeding up the molecules.

Semipermeable membranes surround all living cells. They allow nutrients in and wastes out. When photosynthesis in a plant cell produces oxygen, the amount of oxygen in the cell rises. Because there's more oxygen inside the cell than outside, the oxygen diffuses out through the cell membrane. Likewise, when an animal cell consumes oxygen, there is less oxygen inside the cell than outside. The oxygen diffuses through the cell membrane into the cell.

Most cell membranes allow water to move through them, which means that when there's water with different concentrations of solutes on opposite sides of a membrane, water will diffuse to the higher concentration. This has important implications with respect to marine animals.

The concentration of water inside an aquatic organism's cells must be the same as the surrounding water, or water will tend to diffuse in or out of the organism's cells. When the same concentration exists inside a cell as outside, the cells are said to be *isotonic*, and there is no osmotic pressure in either direction.

Marine fish cells have the same water concentration as the surrounding seawater and are therefore isotonic. When you put a marine fish in fresh water, however, the fish's cells, having a higher concentration of salt than the surrounding fresh water, are then said to be *hypertonic*. This means they have a higher salt concentration, and water will diffuse into the cells. The cells would eventually burst from excess water pressure.

INTERNET PORTAL

SCiLINKS. NSTA

Topic: Osmosis
Go To: www.sclinks.org
Code: LOP2170

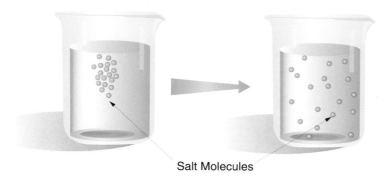

Salt Molecules

Figure 8-33

Diffusion.

Diffusion is the tendency for a liquid, a gas, or a solute to flow from an area of high concentration to an area of low concentration. Heat facilitates diffusion by causing molecules to move. High temperatures speed up diffusion by speeding up the molecules.

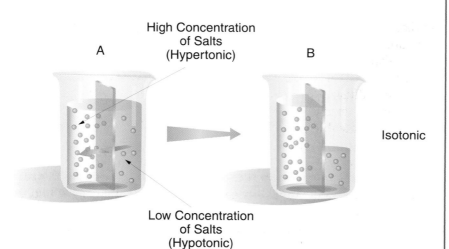

A

High Concentration
of Salts
(Hypertonic)

B

Isotonic

Low Concentration
of Salts
(Hypotonic)

Figure 8-34

Osmosis.

Osmosis is diffusion through a semipermeable cell membrane. In **(A)**, a semipermeable membrane divides a solution with a high concentration of salts (hypertonic) from a solution with a low concentration of salts (hypotonic). In **(B)**, water moves from the hypotonic side of the membrane to the hypertonic side. This occurs because water diffuses much faster than salt. If it did not, salt would cross the membrane and the water volume would not change. Eventually the concentration of salt water on both sides of the membrane will become equal, creating isotonic solutions.

OSMOSIS

Water is absorbed

A

Lower salt concentration outside
(fresh water)

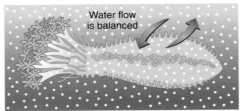

Water flow is balanced

B

Equal salt concentration
(standard seawater)

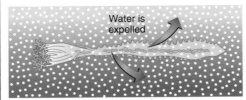

Water is expelled

C

Higher salt concentration outside
(extreme salt water)

Figure 8-35

Hypertonic, isotonic, and hypotonic states.

The concentration of water inside an aquatic organism's cells must be the same as the surrounding water, otherwise water will tend to diffuse in or out of the organism's cells. When the same concentration exists inside a cell as outside, the cells are said to be *isotonic,* and there is no osmotic pressure in either direction **(B)**. If you place a marine animal in fresh water **(A)**, the animal is *hypertonic* to its surroundings; water will move into the animal through its cell membranes. If the animal has no way to eliminate the water, it would swell and burst. If the same marine organism were placed in Utah's Great Salt Lake, where the salinity is greater than the ocean, the animal would be *hypotonic* to its surroundings; water would move out of the animal and into the lake. Eventually the animal would dehydrate and die **(C)**.

Suppose you put a freshwater fish in seawater. This reverses the situation. The fish cells would be *hypotonic,* meaning they have a lower salt concentration than the surrounding water. Water would diffuse out of the cells, and the fish would die of dehydration.

Active Transport, Osmoregulators, and Osmoconformers

What are passive and active transport?

What are osmoregulators *and* osmoconformers?

So far, we've been discussing osmosis through a semipermeable cell membrane, which is called *passive transport.* Passive transport moves materials in and out of a cell by normal diffusion. The materials move through the cell naturally from areas of high concentration to areas of low concentration.

Active transport is the process of a cell moving materials from low concentration to high concentration. Because active transport goes against the flow of diffusion, it requires energy.

Active transport is important because it is one way marine organisms control the water concentration within their cells.

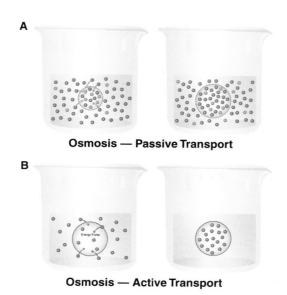

A

Osmosis — Passive Transport

B

Osmosis — Active Transport

Figure 8-36

Passive and active transport.
Basic diffusion and water movement through a semipermeable cell membrane, osmosis, are forms of *passive transport* **(A)**. Purple dots represent dissolved particles, and blue dots represent water molecules. The materials move through the cell naturally from areas of high concentration to areas of low concentration. In this illustration the cell actually swells because water has entered it through osmosis.

(B) shows *active transport*. Active transport is the process of a cell moving materials from low concentration to high concentration. Because active transport runs opposite the diffusion flow, it requires energy. Active transport allows a cell to accumulate molecules even when there are more inside the cell than outside. Cells may also expel molecules by active transport.

Marine fish in particular have a regulation process that allows them to use active transport to adjust the water concentration within their cells. This allows them to adapt to changes in the salinity of the surrounding seawater. Organisms with this ability are called *osmoregulators*.

Although all fish are osmoregulators, they don't regulate the same way. Ray-finned fish have an efficient system for maintaining a constant internal salinity, even though their internal salinity is only about one-third that of the surrounding water. To replace water lost by osmosis, they consume a great deal of seawater and excrete only a small amount of urine. They have specialized glands in their gills to eliminate the excess salts taken in with the water.

Sharks, on the other hand, adapt by using waste urea and other chemicals to maintain their internal tissue balance with the external salinity. When the external salinity changes, so does their internal salinity to remain isotonic. The urea required to maintain salinity explains why some shark species aren't suitable food fish—their flesh smells like urine!

Many marine organisms, especially invertebrates, cannot control their internal water concentration. Their internal salinity rises and falls along with the surrounding seawater's salinity. These organisms are called *osmoconformers*. Some osmoconformers can tolerate significant variations in salinity, but others can't and suffer a great deal of stress.

Figure 8-37

Osmoregulation.

Marine fish have a regulation process that allows them to use active transport to adjust the water concentration within their cells. This allows them to adapt to changes in the salinity of the surrounding seawater. Organisms with this ability are called *osmoregulators*. Although all fish are osmoregulators, they don't regulate the same way. Ray-finned fish consume water to replace what is lost through osmosis, and they have specialized glands in their gills to excrete excess salts taken in with the water. Sharks, on the other hand, adapt by using waste urea and other chemicals to maintain their internal tissue balance with the external salinity. When the external salinity changes, their internal salinity changes to remain isotonic.

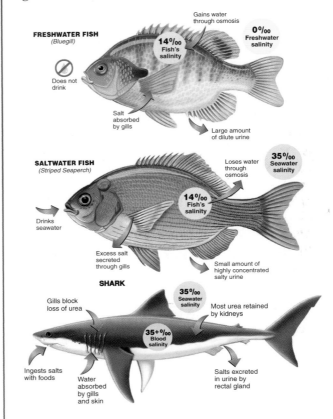

FRESHWATER FISH (Bluegill)
Gains water through osmosis
0°/oo Freshwater salinity
14°/oo Fish's salinity
Does not drink
Salt absorbed by gills
Large amount of dilute urine

SALTWATER FISH (Striped Seaperch)
Loses water through osmosis
35°/oo Seawater salinity
14°/oo Fish's salinity
Drinks seawater
Excess salt secreted through gills
Small amount of highly concentrated salty urine

SHARK
Gills block loss of urea
35°/oo Seawater salinity
Most urea retained by kidneys
35+°/oo Blood salinity
Ingests salts with foods
Water absorbed by gills and skin
Salts excreted in urine by rectal gland

ARE YOU LEARNING?

1. **Diffusion can affect marine organisms because changes in salinity can cause osmotic pressure between their cells and the outside environment.**

   A. true

   B. false

2. _____ **transport is the movement of materials through diffusion.** _____ **transport requires energy to move materials from areas of low concentration to areas of high concentration.**

   A. Active, Passive

   B. Passive, Active

3. _____ **can control the water concentration in their cells. The water concentration in the cells of** _____ **changes with the salinity of the surrounding seawater.**

   A. Osmoconformers, osmoregulators

   B. Osmoregulators, osmoconformers

New Terms You Learned

- **active transport** the process of a cell moving materials from low concentration to high concentration (p. 8-33)
- **adhesion** the tendency of water molecules to stick to other substances due to water's polar nature (p. 8-6)
- **Argo float** a global array of 3,000 free-drifting profiling floats that measures the temperature and salinity of the upper 2000 m of the ocean (p. 8-15)
- **biogeochemical cycle** the process of elements and compounds moving continuously to and from organisms and the earth (p. 8-24)
- **brackish water** water with a salinity of 0.6 to 30‰ (p. 8-12)
- **brine** water saturated or nearly saturated with dissolved salts (p. 8-12)
- **buffer** a substance that lessens the tendency for a solution to become too acid or too alkaline (p. 8-22)
- **chemical equilibrium** the state in which processes add and remove solutes from a solution at the same rate (p. 8-18)
- **cohesion** the tendency of water molecules to stick together due to hydrogen bonding (p. 8-6)
- **colligative properties** the properties of a liquid that may be altered by the presence of a solute (p. 8-12)
- **colloid** a homogeneous mixture such as fog or smoke consisting of very small particles that are larger than atoms and molecules (p. 8-10)
- **conservative constituents** dissolved inorganic salts in seawater that do not change proportion over time (p. 8-14)
- **covalent bond** a bond formed by atoms sharing electrons (p. 8-5)
- **CTD** conductivity, temperature, and depth sensor; a device often attached to a water-sampling device (p. 8-15)
- **denitrification** the release of free nitrogen into the atmosphere from the breakdown of nitrogen compounds (p. 8-27)
- **dissociation** the separation of a molecule into atoms and/or smaller molecules while in solution (p. 8-10)
- **dissolved salts** the sodium chloride and other dissolved inorganic solids in seawater (p. 8-11)
- **electrolyte** a solution that can conduct an electrical current (p. 8-13)
- **halite** table or rock salt, which is sodium chloride (NaCl) (p. 8-12)
- **halocline** an abrupt change in salinity that marks two different water layers (p. 8-19)
- **heterogeneous mixture** a mixture that is not uniform, consisting of visibly different substances (p. 8-9)
- **homogeneous mixture** a mixture that has a uniform appearance throughout, such as a solution (p. 8-9)
- **hydrogen bond** bond between water molecules caused by attraction of positive hydrogen end of one molecule to the negative oxygen of another (p. 8-6)

- **hypertonic** the condition of having a higher concentration of water or other substance that exerts osmotic pressure; a solution that contains a higher concentration of electrolytes than that found in living cells (p. 8-31)

- **hypotonic** the condition of having a lower concentration of water or other substance that exerts osmotic pressure; a solution in which the concentration of an electrolyte is below that in cells (p. 8-32)

- **in situ** on location or at the actual site of something rather than in the laboratory or an artificial condition (p. 8-17)

- **ion** a charged particle (atom or molecule) (p. 8-10)

- **ionic bond** an electrical attraction between two oppositely charged atoms or groups of atoms; as in sodium chloride (p. 8-9)

- **isotonic** the condition of having an equal concentration of water or other substance that exerts osmotic pressure (p. 8-31)

- **micronutrients** essential substances that organisms use in very small amounts (p. 8-29)

- **mixture** the combination of two or more substances that are not chemically bonded, and not in fixed proportions to each other (p. 8-9)

- **nitrification** when microorganisms convert ammonia into nitrates and nitrites (p. 8-27)

- **nonconservative constituents** dissolved substances in seawater that change over time and vary in proportion due to biological and geological activity (p. 8-24)

- **non-ionic** a solution in which solute particles remain intact and do not separate into ions (p. 8-10)

- **nutrients** elements and compounds required for life, other than oxygen or carbon dioxide used for respiration or photosynthesis (p. 8-24)

- **osmoconformers** marine organisms that cannot regulate the water concentration inside their cells (p. 8-34)

- **osmoregulators** marine organisms that can regulate the water concentration inside their cells (p. 8-33)

- **osmosis** diffusion through a semipermeable membrane, such as a cell wall (p. 8-13)

- **osmotic pressure** the pressure differential caused when a substance exists in differing concentrations on two sides of a semipermeable membrane (p. 8-13)

- **passive transport** the process of moving substances into or out of a cell by normal diffusion (p. 8-32)

- **pH** a scale that represents the balance between the positive hydrogen ions (H^+) and the negative hydroxide ions (OH^-) in a liquid, thereby measuring the acidity or alkalinity, with 7 being neutral, lower numbers acidic and higher numbers alkaline (p. 8-20)

- **polar molecule** a molecule with positively and negatively charged ends (p. 8-6)

- **polarity** the characteristic of having positive and negative poles (p. 8-6)

- **principle of constant proportions** principle that the proportions of dissolved elements in sea water are constant (p. 8-14)

- **pycnocline** a thermocline and halocline together creating a boundary between layers of differing water density (p. 8-19)

- **refractometer** optimal instrument that determines salinity based on light refraction through a seawater sample (p. 8-16)
- **salinity** the total quantity or concentration of all dissolved inorganic solids (p. 8-11)
- **salinometer** electronic instrument that determines salinity based on the conductivity of seawater (p. 8-15)
- **semipermeable membrane** a membrane that will allow some substances to pass through, but not others (p. 8-13)
- **silica** common name for silicon dioxide (p. 8-28)
- **solute** the part of a solution that is less abundant (p. 8-9)
- **solution** the state in which the molecules of a solute are evenly dispersed amid the molecules of a solvent (p. 8-9)
- **solvent** the part of a solution that is more abundant, usually a liquid (p. 8-9)
- **surface tension** water's resistance to being penetrated by something trying to break through the surface (p. 8-7)
- **suspension** a hetergeneous mixture with solid particles that tend to settle (p. 8-9)
- **thermistor** a semiconductor that has current flow resistance that varies predictably with temperature (p. 8-15)
- **viscosity** the tendency for a fluid to resist flow (p. 8-7)

Chapter 8 in Review

1. Explain what makes water a polar molecule, and how this allows water molecules to bond to each other.
2. What special properties does water have because of its polar nature? Explain how and why Earth's climate would differ without each of these.
3. Explain the principle of constant proportions and why it is significant.
4. If you had seawater that tested 18.3‰ chlorinity, what would the salinity be?
5. Suppose you test seawater and determine it has a pH of 9.2. Would you suspect the water is polluted? Why or why not?
6. How do the proportions of dissolved organic substances differ from the proportions of dissolved sea salts? Why?
7. When you dissolve salt in distilled water, what happens to the density? Is the water concentration now higher or lower? What properties will the water have that it did not have before? What are these properties called?
8. Explain the difference between an osmoregulator and an osmoconformer. How do passive transport and active transport affect the movement of materials to and from a cell, and how does this relate to an organism's response to changes in salinity?

Connecting Chapter Concepts – Science Scenarios

1. Water probably has the most commonly recognized chemical name – H_2O – because it consists of two hydrogen and one oxygen molecules. Water is very unusual, however, because the molecular shape puts the two positively charged hydrogen atoms on one end of the molecule and the negatively charged oxygen atom at the other.

   A. What do we call the water molecule due to its unusual structure, and why?

   B. What properties does this unusual structure give water that are significant to life on Earth?

2. Chapter 4 discusses entropy and the second law of thermodynamics, which says that a closed system moves from a state of order to a state of uniform disorder. In this chapter, you learned about diffusion, osmosis and active transport.

   A. How do entropy and diffusion relate?

   B. What is osmosis? How does it relate to diffusion?

   C. Active transport is the process of a cell moving materials from an area of low concentration to an area of high concentration. What do the second law of thermodynamics and diffusion tell us is therefore necessary for active transport?

   D. With respect to marine fish in particular, why is active transport important?

Marine Science and the Real World

1. Given what you've just learned about water's chemical properties, what concerns can you envision regarding

   A. pollutants that break down surface tension?

   B. industrial processes that heat water in a local area?

   C. evaporation processes that remove water but leave behind the salts in a local area?

2. Some marine animals, such as the striped sea bass, can adjust to and survive in fresh water. What potential concerns can you envision when introducing such a marine organism to a freshwater environment?

3. Scientists are very curious about the carbon cycle and how much carbon dioxide the ocean can hold. Why?

4. In coastal areas such as south Florida and the Mexican Yucatan Peninsula, in the underground water table, fresh water lies on top of seawater, creating unique habitats above and below the halocline. Due to development, however, fresh water is being pumped from underground at an increasing rate. What effects would you expect this to have?

5. Their weight canceled out by buoyancy, many marine organisms spend their lives in a three-dimensional existence. What advantages does this have compared to the two-dimensional existence common to land-based organisms? What disadvantages?

References

Broecker, W. S. 1983. The Ocean. *Scientific American.* September.

Elmhurst College. 2008. Virtual Chembook, Elmhurst, IL www.elmhurst.edu /~chm/vchembook/106Amixture.html

Garrison, T. 2004. *Essentials of Oceanography.* Brooks/Cole, a division of Thomson Learning, Inc. Pacific Grove, CA.

Garrison, T. 2004. *Oceanography: An Invitation to Marine Science.* Brooks/ Cole, a division of Thomson Learning, Inc. Pacific Grove, CA.

Kerr, R. A. 1999. A Cooler Way to Balance the Sea's Salt Budget. *Science.* 285 (no. 5427). July.

Kerr, R. A. 1988. Ocean Crust's Role in Making Seawater. *Science.* 239 (no. 4837).

MacIntyre, F. 1970. Why the Sea Is Salty. *Scientific American.* November.

Open University Course Team. 1998. *Seawater: Its Composition, Properties and Behavior.* New York: Pergamon Press.

The Ocean Acidification Network. 2008. http://www.ocean-acidification.net

The Physics
of Water

How Water
Physics Affect
Marine Life

Rear Admiral Harley D. Nygren, NOAA Corps

Bob Wohlers

Light in the Deep

Edith A. Widder, PhD
President and Senior Scientist,
Ocean Research & Conservation
Association (ORCA)

Contrary to popular belief, the deepest ocean depths aren't completely dark. Bioluminescent animals and organisms emit blue flashes and glows that help them communicate, hunt, find mates, and avoid predators.

The study of bioluminescence by scientists such as Dr. Edith Widder allows us to learn about marine life in the deepest ocean. She studies where we find certain organisms, how they interact, and how pollution, water temperature, light, and salinity affect them.

Widder's love affair with marine biology began at the age of 11, when she went to Fiji and explored the reefs there. It wasn't until years later (during her undergraduate training) that Widder realized the career path she'd chosen might be difficult, due to lack of funding for ocean-related research. But, marine biology was in her blood, so she looked to other sciences, hoping to combine disciplines in new ways to further the study of marine organisms.

"I got my master's degree in biochemistry and my PhD in neurobiology. My interest in bioluminescence grew out of my PhD research on a bioluminescent dinoflagellate – a type of phytoplankton that creates a flash of light. I was studying the action potential that triggers the flash. But, I was also intrigued by the phenomenon of bioluminescence, and the more I learned about it, the more I wanted to know what it really looked like in the ocean. A colleague who was putting together an expedition to test a submersible agreed to let me be part of that study, and what I saw changed the course of my career. I was astonished by how much light I saw, and felt that bioluminescence must be one of the most important processes in the ocean. I couldn't understand why more people weren't studying it."

As she was studying bioluminescence, Dr. Widder saw a challenge impeding research: a lack of instruments sensitive enough to measure the light.

"Much of my career has been spent developing and adapting instrumentation for measuring bioluminescence in the ocean. Most recently, I've been developing a coastal monitoring system called Kilroy, which uses those measurements to protect marine ecosystems. Although I didn't have a degree in engineering, I studied whatever I needed to and called on engineers for help. The biggest asset to this change in career direction was that I had a solid background in mathematics. It has been more valuable than I imagined when I first started out to be a marine biologist."

Dr. Widder has spent many years exploring the ocean and learning its secrets. "I have seen such incredible things, like siphonophore chains (jellyfish-like colonies) that are so long that both ends disappear into the distance. When you brush against one of these chains, the luminescence lights up the surrounding ocean like a Times Square marquee. I've seen deep-sea octopuses that produce light from their suckers and breathtaking displays of planktonic luminescence on almost every dive that still thrill me as much as the first time I saw them. If I had it to do all over again I wouldn't change a thing. This is the best job in the world."

Figure 9-1

Diving's early history.

In the mid 1600s the extremely inventive Italian scientist Giovanni Borelli was the first to visualize a diver as a free-swimming frogman, complete with swim fins.

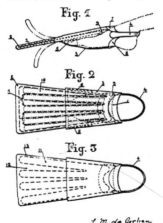

Figure 9-2

Frenchman de Corlieu's patented swim fin.

Figure 9-3

Early Churchill swim fins.

I n 1938 an American named Owen Churchill visited the South Pacific. There he saw local spearfishermen taking advantage of water's density. They wore crude homemade fin-like devices on their feet that allowed them to push against the water. This put their strong leg muscles to work for swimming and diving without using their hands.

After returning to the United States, Churchill made some improvements in design and patented his invention. He thought he was on to something, and he was right. By 1954 he had sold more than 2 million pairs of swim fins. Buyers included the military (Allied frogmen wore fins during World War II), as well as enthusiasts in a young sport called "scuba diving." Today scuba divers no longer use Churchill fins, but they remain popular with surfers.

Churchill's fins were the first commercial success for swim fins, but they were hardly a new idea. Churchill himself knew this, in fact. An honest man, he'd searched patents before releasing his fins and found a French patent for very similar fins by Louis de Corlieu. Churchill obtained a license from de Corlieu and patented his own improvements. Over the years, he paid de Corlieu hundreds of thousands of dollars in royalties.

But, even de Corlieu didn't invent the first swim fins. Sketches left by Leonardo da Vinci include illustrations of "hand fins" for swimmers. In the mid 1600s the extremely inventive Italian scientist Giovanni Borelli was the first to visualize a diver as a free-swimming frogman, complete with swim fins. Even Benjamin Franklin described how he had experimented with hand paddles. Natives in the Marquesas Islands were said to have tied palm fronds to their feet to help them swim long before de Corlieu and Churchill.

Today fins are standard equipment in recreational, technical, and military diving. Surfers, lifeguards, and water rescue specialists use them. Swimmers use hand fins to strengthen their upper body for competition or fitness.

As simple as this invention is, it took some imagination to turn water density into an advantage instead of a disadvantage for humans moving through water. On land, humans walk, but that's an ineffective way to move under water. The invention of the fin highlights one of the main differences between life in the sea and in the air.

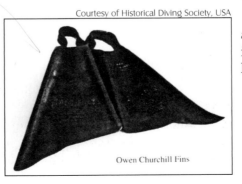

Courtesy of Historical Diving Society, USA

Owen Churchill Fins

The Physics of Water

As explained in Chapter 8, to understand marine life, you have to understand the chemical processes that affect it. Seawater's chemical properties affect how life functions in the ocean. In this chapter, you'll learn about the physical characteristics of water and how they affect life in water. Water's physical properties not only affect the life processes of marine organisms, but of human beings in the water. These effects are not only important for understanding marine life, but for marine scientists and others who enter the underwater world as scuba divers.

Bob Wolhers

Figure 9-4

Diving as a scientific tool.

The physical characteristics of water are not only important for understanding marine life, but for marine scientists and others who enter the underwater world as scuba divers.

Heat and Heat Capacity

What is heat? What is temperature? How do they differ?

What are the two common systems used to measure temperature? Which one is most used by scientists?

What is heat capacity? How do you measure it?

What implications does heat capacity have on Earth's climate?

Temperature is crucial in determining where organisms can live in the ocean. Many aquatic organisms can only live in the narrow temperature range to which they are adapted. Therefore, a temperature increase of only a few degrees can kill fish and other organisms in the environment.

STUDY QUESTIONS

Find the answers as you read.

1. What is *heat*? What is *temperature*? How do they differ?

2. What are the two common systems used to measure temperature? Which one is most used by scientists?

3. What is *heat capacity*? How do you measure it?

4. What implications does heat capacity have on Earth's climate?

5. What unique characteristics does water exhibit as it turns from vapor to liquid to ice?

6. What is *latent heat of fusion*? What is the difference between *sensible* and *non-sensible heat*?

7. What is *latent heat of vaporization*?

8. What are *thermal inertia* and *thermal equilibrium*? Why are these concepts important to life and Earth's climate?

9. What are the relationships between the salinity, temperature, and density of seawater?

10. How and why is the ocean stratified by density?

11. What are the three density layers of the ocean? Approximately what proportion of the ocean does each layer account for?

12. What is a *thermocline*?

CELSIUS TO FAHRENHEIT AND BACK

With online communication and international cooperation in science and reporting, it's not unusual to have water or weather information in one temperature system but need to apply it in another. For that, it's helpful to be able to convert from Celsius to Fahrenheit and vice-versa.

One degree Celsius equals 1.8 degrees Fahrenheit. To convert a Celsius temperature to Fahrenheit, multiply Celsius times 1.8 and add 32. For example, what is 15°C in Fahrenheit?

$$15° \times 1.8 = 27°$$

$$27° + 32° = 59°$$

To convert Fahrenheit to Celsius, subtract 32 and divide by 1.8. For example, what is 89°F in Celsius?

$$89° - 32° = 57°$$

$$57° \div 1.8 = 31.67°$$

Figure 9-5

Heat and temperature.

Simply put, heat is energy and temperature is a measurement. Heat is the energy in the random movement, or vibration, of individual atoms and molecules in a substance. Temperature measures only how fast the molecules vibrate. In **(A)** the atoms and molecules of the liquid are moving very quickly due to high heat. A thermometer reads the quick movement as a high temperature. In **(B)** the atoms and molecules of the liquid are vibrating slowly due cooling as the heat transfers from the liquid to the surrounding air. The thermometer reads this as a lower temperature.

The concept of temperature comes from the need to measure the relative heat of two bodies, or the same body after removing or adding heat. In the case of two bodies at different temperatures, heat flows from the hot body to the cold body until their temperatures become equal. This is entropy – the flow of energy from an area of high concentration to an area of low concentration. However, it's important to realize that heat and temperature, while interrelated, are two different concepts.

Suppose you've filled a bathtub with warm water and scooped out a glassful. If you take the temperatures of the water in the glass and the water in the tub, you'll find they are the same. But, which has more heat? Drop an ice cube in the glass and another one in the tub, let them melt, and take the temperatures again. You would find the ice made the temperature in the glass substantially lower, whereas it didn't cool the tub water enough to make a measurable difference.

This highlights the difference between *heat* and *temperature*. Heat is the kinetic energy in the random movement, or vibration, of individual atoms and molecules in a substance. The faster the molecules move, the more heat the substance has. The total heat energy is measured based on *both* the quantity and speed of vibrating molecules. *Temperature* measures the degree of molecular vibration only.

The glass and tub of water both had the same temperature, but the tub had far more heat because it contained many times more moving molecules. The ice cube made little difference to the tub's temperature because the heat change was insignificant among the large number of molecules. But, the glass of water had many fewer molecules, so the ice made it much colder.

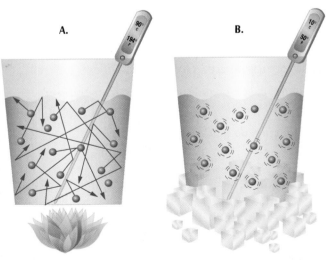

Suppose you wanted to raise the temperature of the water in the tub and the glass to the same degree. Using a given heat source, which would you have to heat longer, the glass or the tub? You would have to heat the tub longer, of course. It has many more molecules that must vibrate faster.

Although temperature measures only the degree of molecular motion, it's one of the most basic measurements in studying marine science. Temperature differences influence how quickly heat travels from one substance to another, and therefore affect weather, climate, and marine life. As you're probably aware, the two most common temperature systems are Fahrenheit and Celsius. Fahrenheit is used in the United States and a few other countries, whereas Celsius is used in countries that use the metric system. Celsius is the scale most used in science because it is based on water's physical properties: 0°C is the freezing point of water, and 100°C is its boiling point.

To measure the actual amount of energy – not just how quickly the molecules vibrate – you commonly use *calories*. A calorie is the amount of energy needed to raise 1 gram of water 1 degree Celsius. It takes more energy – more calories – to raise a tub of water a given number of degrees than to raise a glass of water the same number of degrees. (Note: The term *calorie* as listed for the energy content in food items differs from calories as discussed here. The nutritional calorie is actually a "giant" calorie or kilocalorie—1,000 calories. Also note that scientists also measure energy in *joules*. 4.2 joules = 1 calorie.)

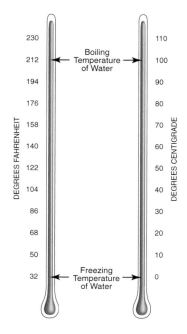

Figure 9-6

Fahrenheit and Celsius.

The two most common temperature systems are Fahrenheit and Celsius. Fahrenheit is the common temperature system used in the United States and a few other countries, whereas Celsius is used in metric system countries. Celsius (also called Centigrade) is also the scale most used in science because it is based on water's physical properties: 0°C is the freezing point of water, and 100°C is the boiling point.

HEAT CAPACITY OF COMMON SUBSTANCES

Substance	Heat Capacity (cal/g/°C)
Ammonia	1.13
Pure Water	1.00
Acetone	0.51
Gasoline	0.50
Grain Alcohol	0.23
Aluminum	0.22
Granite	0.20
Copper	0.09
Silver	0.06
Lead	0.03
Mercury	0.03

Figure 9-7

Heat capacity of common substances.

Heat capacity is measured as the amount of heat energy needed to change the temperature of 1 gram of a substance by 1°C. As shown in the table, substances have varying heat capacities. The heat capacity of water is 1 calorie per gram.

With climate change a rising concern, scientists are studying how much heat the ocean can absorb and release. At NASA, scientists use a computer model of the global climate to simulate how Earth's climate may change as the ocean changes in heat absorption. Current evidence suggests that the ocean has been acting as a "global heat sponge" since about 1951. Some scientists think that the ocean has reduced the rise in global surface temperature and will continue to do so for some time. However, they theorize that regional climates will change due to the increased amount of heat stored in the ocean.

Figure 9-8

This leads us to heat capacity. *Heat capacity* is the amount of heat energy required to raise a given amount of a substance by a given temperature. Heat capacity is measured in calories per gram. As you just learned, the value for water is 1.00 calorie per gram. This is because calories are defined based on the heat capacity of pure water. Substances have varying heat capacities, mostly lower than 1 calorie per gram.

Compared to most substances, water has a very high heat capacity. Chapter 8 explains that water's hydrogen bonds hold water molecules together, which is why water is liquid rather than vapor at room temperature. Because hydrogen bonds hold water molecules together, water resists molecular motion. This means it takes more heat energy to raise water's temperature than it does for most other substances. Therefore, water can absorb or release a lot of heat with little temperature change.

This is more than an interesting fact. Water's heat capacity affects you and everyone on Earth every day. It influenced what you wore to school today, because it influences the world's climate and weather. Among other things, it does this by carrying heat to areas that would otherwise be cooler, and by absorbing heat in areas that would otherwise be hotter.

A great example is the island of Bermuda. Bermuda has a moderately tropical climate year round, even though it lies above 30° north latitude. That's about the same latitude as Birmingham, Alabama, or Fort Worth, Texas, both of which experience some snow and freezing rain in the winter. The difference is that the warm Gulf Stream current flows around Bermuda. The tremendous heat capacity of water offsets the normally moderate temperature of this latitude. By carrying so much heat north, the Gulf Stream gives Bermuda a tropical climate. Chapter 11 goes into more about how ocean currents affect the world's climates.

Figure 9-9

Water's heat capacity influences the world's climate.

The warm flow of the Gulf Stream around Bermuda gives it a moderately tropical climate even in winter. This is an interesting fact considering that Bermuda lies at about the same latitude as Birmingham, Alabama, or Fort Worth, Texas, both of which experience some snow and freezing rain in the winter.

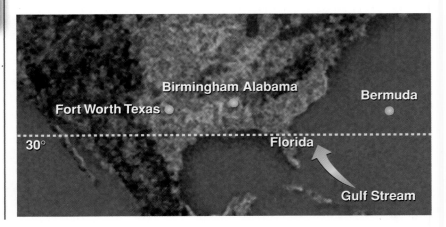

Water Temperature and Density

What unique characteristics does water exhibit as it turns from vapor to liquid to ice?

What is latent heat of fusion? What is the difference between sensible and non-sensible heat?

Chapter 8 explains that water is unusual because it becomes less dense as it freezes. Most substances become denser as they cool and less dense as they warm.

The maximum density of pure water is approximately 1 gram per cubic centimeter (1g/cm^3 or 62.4 pounds per cubic foot). Water becomes denser as it cools, but only to a point. At 3.98°C (39.16°F), it reaches maximum density. As water cools below the point of maximum density, it begins to crystallize into ice. As it moves into a solid state (*state* is an expression of a substance's form, which changes from solid, to liquid, to gas with the addition of heat), it becomes less dense. At 0°C, pure water freezes into ice and the density drops abruptly. This is because the crystal structure of the water molecules changes the bond angle between the oxygen and hydrogen atoms from 105° to 109°. The crystal structure forms a hexagon (structure with six sides) that acts like a raft because it increases the space the molecules take up by 9%. This space increase is why the density decreases. Note that salt water freezes at slightly below 0°C.

Ice becomes denser as the temperature drops below 0°C, but the density never rises above that of liquid water. The density of ice is approximately 0.917 grams per cubic centimeter (0.917g/cm^3 or 57.2 pounds per cubic foot). This is less than the density of liquid water, which is why ice floats. It's also why ice forms on top of the water – freezing over – whereas most liquids turn solid from the bottom up. Also, ice doesn't form all at once at its freezing point (0°C) but crystallizes continuously until all the liquid turns solid. The temperature does not drop any further until all the liquid water freezes, even though heat continues to leave.

This produces the phenomenon of *non-sensible heat*. As water cools, you can read the temperature drop with a thermometer—this is *sensible heat* (i.e., heat that you can sense with a thermometer). If 1 gram of liquid water loses 1 calorie of heat, the temperature will drop 1°C. Once water cools to 0°C, however, 1 gram must lose 80 calories to form ice, and the temperature does not change while that heat diminishes. This is called non-sensible heat because there's a change in heat energy, but you can't sense it with a thermometer. The non-sensible heat lost when water goes from

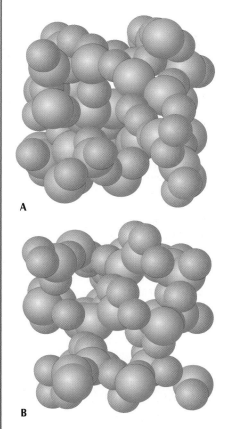

A

B

Figure 9-10

Why ice floats.

Liquid water molecules bonded together are shown in **(A)**. In **(B)** notice the empty spaces within the ice structure. The crystal structure of the water molecules changes the bond angle between the oxygen and hydrogen atoms from 105° to 109°. The crystal structure is a hexagon (structure with six sides) that acts like a raft because it increases the space the molecules take up by 9%. This space increase is why the density decreases and ice floats on top of liquid water.

Figure 9-11

Relationship of density to temperature in pure water.

This graph shows the relationship of density to temperature in pure water. Note that at 25°C (77°F) – point **(A)** – the density of pure water is approximately 0.997g/cm³. As the temperature of pure water decreases to 3.98°C (39°F) – point **(B)** – the density of water reaches its highest level at 1.0g/cm³. At point **(C)**, where the temperature reaches 0°C (32°F), liquid water begins to turn to solid ice. Just before the change from liquid to ice, water has a density of 0.999g/cm³. As the liquid water quickly becomes solid ice, you can see in the graph that the density of the ice drops off dramatically, going from 0.999g/cm³ to 0.917g/cm³ (note the break in the density scale on the graph). Even at lower temperatures the water basically stays at this density. Ice floats because the density of ice is less than the density of liquid water.

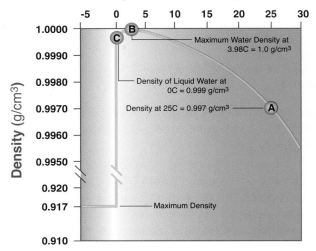

liquid to solid state is called the *latent heat of fusion*. (*Latent* means present, not noticeable, but capable of being active; from Latin meaning to *lie hidden*). On the graph of water's temperature and density, the abrupt density drop at 0°C represents the latent heat of fusion.

Latent heat of fusion also comes into play when ice melts back into water. The 80 calories per gram required to freeze all the water into ice must go back into the ice to turn all of it back into liquid water. Just as the ice doesn't change temperature until all the water freezes, when melting, ice doesn't change temperature until all of it turns into liquid. This is why ice cubes cool beverages so effectively.

Figure 9-12

Relationship of density to temperature in most substances.

Compare this temperature/density graph to the graph above for pure water. This graph could be for most substances, such as steel. At 0° C (32° F) and lower, steel continues to become more dense and contract. As steel heats up, it becomes less dense and expands.

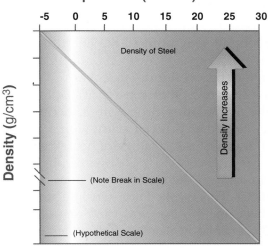

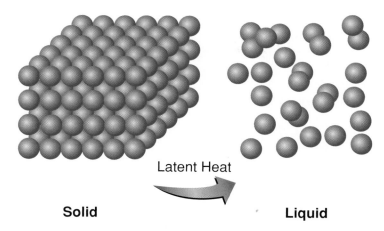

Latent Heat

Solid   **Liquid**

Latent Heat of Vaporization

What is latent heat of vaporization?

Hydrogen bonds give water its high heat capacity and make it resist evaporation. When you apply enough heat energy, however, individual water molecules begin to vibrate with enough force that hydrogen bonds cannot hold together. The molecules evaporate by diffusing into the air. This process begins at 100°C (212°F) at sea level. (Note that pressure affects the temperature at which water evaporates – an important point covered in greater detail in Chapter 13.)

Just as ice doesn't become any cooler until it all freezes, water does not get any warmer until it all vaporizes (changes its state from a liquid to a vapor). A good example is when you cook something in boiling water. Although you continue to heat the boiling water, the temperature doesn't increase, which is why boiling provides an even cooking temperature.

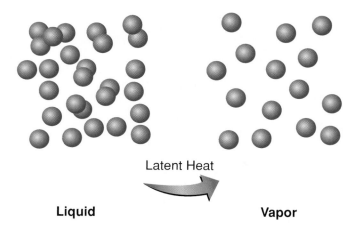

Latent Heat

Liquid   **Vapor**

Figure 9-13

Changing from a solid to a liquid.

When a solid substance changes to a liquid state, energy must be supplied to overcome the molecular attractions between the particles. This energy must be supplied externally, normally as heat, and does not bring about a change in temperature. We call this energy *latent heat* (latent comes from the Latin for to *lie hidden*). The latent heat is the energy released or absorbed during a change of state. Latent heat of fusion is the amount of heat required to convert a unit mass of the solid into the liquid. The temperature does not rise during this change, even though the substance is taking up heat.

Figure 9-14

Changing from a liquid to a vapor.

The heat required to change a liquid to a vapor (gas) is called the *latent heat of vaporization.* This implies that while a liquid undergoes a change to the vapor state at the normal boiling point, the temperature of the liquid will not rise beyond the temperature of the boiling point. The latent heat of evaporation is the energy required to overcome the molecular forces of attraction between the particles of a liquid and bring them to the vapor state, where such attractions are minimal.

Figure 9-15

Latent heat of vaporization and fusion in pure water.

This figure graphs temperature versus heat as pure water changes from ice to liquid to vapor. Area **(A)** is where water is solid ice. Area **(B)** is water's latent heat of fusion, showing that while the temperature remains at 0°C, heat energy must be lost to turn water into ice. Area **(C)** is where water remains a liquid. Area **(D)** is the latent heat of vaporization, showing that while the temperature holds at about 100°C, heat energy must increase from approximately 200 to 780 calories/gram to change water into steam. Area **(E)** is where water is in a gaseous, vapor form.

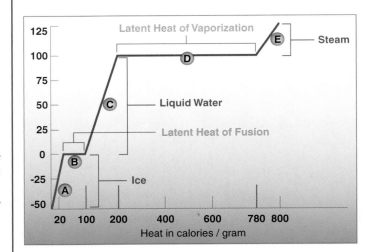

Topic: Phases of Matter
Go To: www.scilinks.org
Code: LOP2185

Figure 9-16

Hydrological cycle.

The hydrological cycle shows the movement of water around the Earth. Water is constantly changing from liquid to solid to gas and back again. Solar heat evaporates water into the air from the ocean, rivers, lakes, and land. Some water vapor also enters the atmosphere from plants in a process called *transpiration* – the passage of water vapor from living organisms. The atmospheric moisture spreads over the surface of the planet and condenses into clouds before falling again as precipitation – rain or snow. Precipitation is the main source of fresh water in rivers, lakes, and on the ground. Runoff and ground water flow ultimately return the water to the ocean.

The heat required to vaporize a substance is called *latent heat of vaporization*. At 540 calories per gram, water has the highest latent heat of vaporization of any known substance. It takes much more latent heat to vaporize water than to freeze it (540 calories per gram versus 80) because when water freezes only some of the hydrogen bonds break. When it vaporizes, all the hydrogen bonds must break, which requires more energy. Evaporation is another way that water affects you every day. Annually, enough water evaporates from the ocean to reduce their depth by a meter – 334,000 cubic kilometers (about 80,000

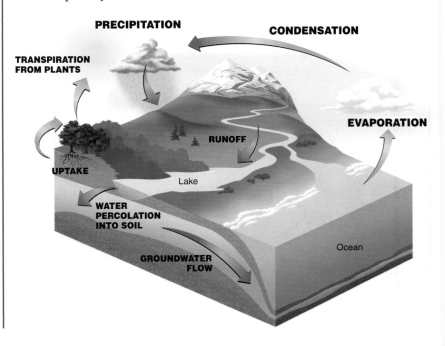

cubic miles) of water. The energy for evaporation comes from the sun's heat, which causes water to change from liquid to vapor. Eventually water vapor in the atmosphere condenses into liquid water (rain) and releases the heat energy into the atmosphere, heating it. Condensation is a major source of energy for the atmosphere; it powers storms, winds, wind waves, and ocean currents. As explained in Chapter 8, the rain and runoff replace the evaporated water in the hydrological cycle, so the sea level doesn't drop.

Thermal Inertia

What are thermal inertia *and* thermal equilibrium*? Why are these concepts important to life and Earth's climate?*

Water's high heat capacity provides the Earth with *thermal inertia,* which is the tendency to resist temperature changes. Because of its high heat capacity, seawater temperature doesn't rise or fall much, even when gaining or losing large quantities of heat. Therefore, temperature changes in the sea tend to be much less severe and more gradual over time. By comparison, temperatures on land may vary widely – 20°C/68°F or more in a single day in some climates at some times of the year.

However, *thermal inertia* is important to organisms on land as well as in the sea because the Earth receives a tremendous amount of energy from the sun – 10,000 times the amount of energy consumed by humans. About half of this energy makes it through the atmosphere, much of it being absorbed by the ocean. Through evaporation, radiation, and convection, the heat returns to the atmosphere before radiating back into space. Over time, the incoming solar radiation and Earth's internal heat sources balance with the outward radiating heat. This keeps the Earth in *thermal equilibrium,* meaning that it cools at about the same rate that it heats. Over time, it grows neither significantly warmer nor colder.

Daily and seasonally, seawater acts as a global thermostat, preventing broad temperature swings caused by uneven solar heating across the globe. Seawater absorbs heat during the day and during the summer and then releases it back into the atmosphere at night and during the winter. Also, sea ice found in the polar regions absorbs heat as it melts during the day and releases heat as it refreezes in the night. The temperature differences between day and night or winter and summer would be much greater without the ocean providing thermal equilibrium. Without the thermal inertia provided by water, many – perhaps most – of the organisms on Earth could not survive the drastic temperature changes that would occur every night.

INTERNET PORTAL

SciLINKS. NSTA

Topic: Water Cycle
Go To: www.scilinks.org
Code: LOP2180

UNEVEN SOLAR HEATING RESULTS IN THE SEASONS

This figure shows the seasons specific to the northern hemisphere. The 23.5° tilt of the Earth's rotational axis relative to the plane of its orbit around the sun causes the seasons. Close to the summer solstice, days are long, and the northern hemisphere receives more sunlight than at any other time during the year. For months, above the Arctic Circle, the sun doesn't set and the region receives 24 hours of daylight every day. Close to the winter solstice, days are short, and the northern hemisphere receives the least amount of sunlight of any time of year. Above the Arctic Circle, the sun doesn't rise for months.

On a day-to-day basis, seawater acts as a global thermostat, preventing broad temperature swings caused by uneven solar heating across the face of the Earth. Polar ice absorbs heat during the day and releases it back into the atmosphere as it refreezes during the night. The temperature differences between day and night, or even winter and summer, would be much broader without the oceans providing thermal equilibrium. Without the thermal inertia provided by water, many—perhaps most—of the organisms on Earth could not survive the drastic temperature changes that occur every night.

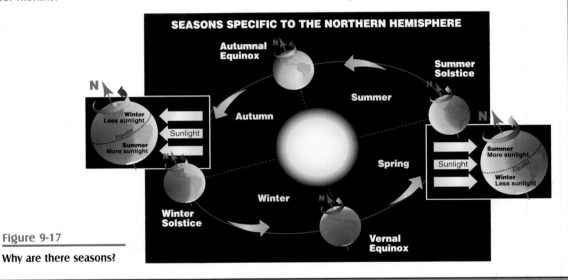

SEASONS SPECIFIC TO THE NORTHERN HEMISPHERE

Figure 9-17

Why are there seasons?

Every species has a range of conditions in which it can live and beyond which it can't. These conditions include temperature, salinity, and light intensity, among many others. Some species can tolerate a wide variety of environmental conditions and so can live in a large number of places. Others can tolerate only a narrow range of conditions and are more restricted in where they can live. An organism may have a wide range of tolerance for one condition (e.g., temperature) and a narrow range for another (e.g., salinity).

Tolerance ranges tend to affect each other. For example, sea stars can tolerate a wide range of temperatures. But, if they are living near their temperature limit, they are under stress and are less tolerant of changes in other environmental factors, such as salinity. An organism's tolerance range partly defines the ecological community in which it can live.

Ocean Water Density

What are the relationships between the salinity, temperature, and density of seawater?

How and why is the ocean stratified by density?

What are the three density layers of the ocean? Approximately what proportion of the ocean does each layer account for?

What is a thermocline?

As discussed in Chapter 8, seawater density varies with salinity and temperature. Seawater density typically varies between 1.02g/cm³ and 1.03g/cm³. This means seawater weighs about 2%–3% more than pure water, which has a density of 1g/cm³.

Seawater density increases with increasing salinity and decreasing temperature. Cold, salty water is denser than warm, fresh water. Water pressure also plays a role, although a smaller one than temperature and salinity. Deep water is somewhat denser than shallow water because of the weight of the water above it. You can see the relationship between temperature, salinity, and density in the accompanying graph. Notice that seawaters with different salinity can have the same density due to temperature differences, and vice-versa.

Because temperature and salinity affect water density, seawater *stratifies*, or forms layers. Dense water is heavy and sinks below less dense layers. Generally, there are three distinct layers (or zones) found in the ocean. Oceanographers usually define the zones based on temperature variations (although they could also use salinity or density). They are the *mixed layer*, the *thermocline*, and the deep zone. Defining the layers can be complex because they vary regionally, depending on the winds and conditions that affect temperature and salinity. (You can read more about density stratification layers in Chapter 11.)

Temperature and salinity are relatively constant because waves and breaking waves continually mix the water, although, as covered in Chapter 8, variations do exist. The surface zone is the most biologically productive because it's exposed to sunlight, yet it

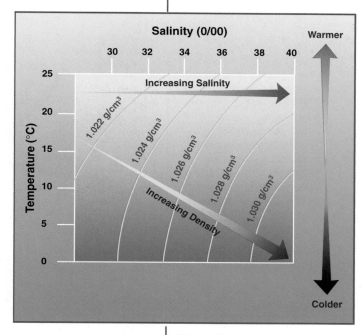

Figure 9-18

Relationship between temperature, salinity, and density.

The density of a substance or object is the ratio of its mass to its volume. This graph shows the variation of seawater density as a function of temperature and salinity. From the graph you can see that cold, salty water is denser than warm, less salty water. In other words, as temperature decreases and salinity increases, density increases, and vice-versa. Notice also that seawaters with different salinity can have the same density due to temperature differences and vice-versa. Small seawater density differences can produce very strong currents by causing water to rise or sink. The determination of seawater density, and its variation, is therefore one of the most important tasks in oceanography.

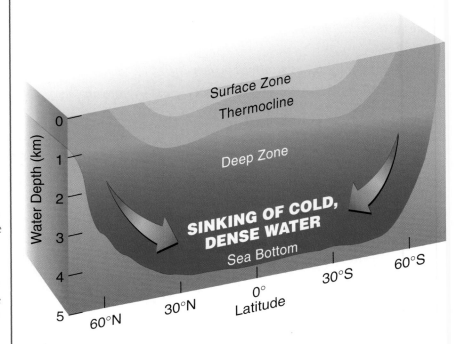

Figure 9-19

Density layers.

Because temperature and salinity affect water density, seawater *stratifies,* or forms layers. Dense water is heavy and sinks below less dense layers. Ocean layers vary regionally, depending on conditions that affect temperature and salinity. Defining the layers can be complex, but generally, there are three distinct density layers commonly found in the ocean. These are the surface zone, the thermocline, and the deep zone.

accounts for only about 2% of the ocean's volume. The surface zone extends from the surface to about 100 meters (328 feet) in most places, although it may be as deep as 500 meters (1,640 feet).

These relatively warm, low-density surface waters are separated from cold, high-density deep waters by the *thermocline,* the zone in which temperature changes rapidly with depth. The top of the thermocline varies with season, storms, currents, and other conditions. It depends in part on the amount of heat the surface zone receives from the sun and is therefore more pronounced in tropical and temperate waters. Thermoclines are weaker in polar regions because the surface water there is cold. The thermocline separates warm low-density surface waters from cold high-density deep waters. Thermocline zones account for about 18% of ocean water.

Below the thermocline is the deep layer. This layer is cold, dense, and fairly uniform because it originates in the polar regions. It begins deeper than about 1,000 meters (3,280 feet) in the middle latitudes but becomes shallower until it reaches the surface in the polar regions. The deep zone makes up about 80% of the ocean's volume.

1. **Heat is _____, and temperature is _____.**

   A. a measurement of average molecular motion speed, the total energy in the random motion of molecules and atoms

   B. the total energy in the random motion of molecules and atoms, a measurement of average molecular motion speed

2. **The _____ system is most often used in science to measure temperature.**

   A. Celsius

   B. Fahrenheit

3. **Heat capacity is**

   A. the amount of heat required to raise the temperature of a substance by a given amount.

   B. the temperature of something.

4. **The heat capacity of water**

   A. has little real effect.

   B. allows the ocean to heat areas that would otherwise be cooler, and cool areas that would otherwise be hotter.

5. **Water becomes _____ as it freezes. This is _____ most substances.**

   A. less dense, different from

   B. more dense, different from

   C. less dense, the same as

   D. more dense, the same as

6. **The heat that is lost without a change in temperature when water freezes is called**

   A. latent heat of vaporization.

   B. heat capacity.

   C. latent heat of fusion.

7. **The heat required to vaporize a substance is called**

   A. latent heat of vaporization.

   B. heat capacity.

   C. latent heat of fusion.

8. **The tendency for water to resist temperature change is called _____. It is one of the factors in establishing _____.**

   A. thermal equilibrium, global warming

   B. thermal inertia, global warming

   C. thermal equilibrium, thermal inertia

   D. thermal inertia, thermal equilibrium

9. **Low temperature and high salinity make seawater _____ dense.**

   A. less

   B. more

10. **The ocean is stratified with _____ layers below _____ layers.**

    A. less dense, denser

    B. denser, less dense

11. **The surface zone accounts for approximately _____ percent of the ocean's volume.**

    A. 1

    B. 2

    C. 18

    D. 80

12. **The thermocline is the boundary between layers of water with differing _____.**

    A. colors

    B. temperatures

    C. organisms

    D. none of the above

How Water Physics Affect Marine Life

STUDY QUESTIONS

Find the answers as you read.

1. How does water scatter and absorb light?

2. What are the *photic, euphotic, dysphotic,* and *aphotic zones*?

3. What advantage does ocean-based existence have over land-based existence with respect to temperature?

4. What are an *ectotherm,* an *endotherm,* a *homeotherm* and a *poikilotherm*?

5. How does temperature affect metabolism? What's the advantage of being an endotherm?

6. How does water affect sound? How do some marine mammals use sound in water to their advantage?

7. What is *hydrostatic pressure*? What effects does it have on marine life?

8. How do surface-to-volume ratios change as cell size increases?

9. Why is a high surface-to-volume ratio important to cell function?

10. How does buoyancy affect both swimming and drifting marine organisms?

11. What characteristics allow marine organisms to avoid sinking? What characteristics do marine organisms have to handle water resistance?

12. How does water movement affect the distribution and survival of marine life?

Living in the sea differs significantly from living on land. Although marine and terrestrial organisms must deal with most of the same physical factors, such as light, temperature, pressure, and movement, their environments are very different. As you probably guessed, the majority of differences relate to how these factors function in water compared to in air.

Light

How does water scatter and absorb light?

What are the photic, euphotic, dysphotic, and aphotic zones?

As you've already learned, light only penetrates the upper regions of the sea – an area called the *photic zone.* In the clearest conditions, light cannot penetrate in significant amounts much deeper than 600 meters (1,968 feet); penetration to 100 meters (328 feet) is typical. Significant light reaches no more than about 2% of the ocean because water scatters and absorbs light.

Scattering occurs initially when light reaches the water's surface. Most light penetrates the surface, but, depending on the sun's angle, some may reflect back out of the water. Within the water, some light reflects off light-colored suspended particles, sending some of the light back to the surface and out of the water. Dark, suspended particles and algae absorb some of the light.

Water – even pure water with no suspended particles – also absorbs light directly. As light travels through water, it strikes water molecules. The water molecules absorb the energy, converting the light into heat. However, water doesn't absorb light uniformly.

White light from the sun is actually the combination of all visible colors, each with a different wavelength and radiant energy. Colors at the red end of the spectrum have low energy and a long wavelength; colors at the blue end have high energy and a short wavelength. Water absorbs fractions of various colors as light travels through it, more easily removing the long wavelength/low energy colors. In other words, water absorbs colors at the red end of the spectrum more easily than at the blue end. The first meter of water absorbs nearly all infrared light. Infrared light is invisible to the human eye. The color red is almost totally absorbed at 4 meters (13 feet). As light passes through more water, orange is almost completely absorbed next, followed by yellow, green, blue, indigo, and violet. At 300 meters (984 feet) in clear water, almost all visible light has been absorbed.

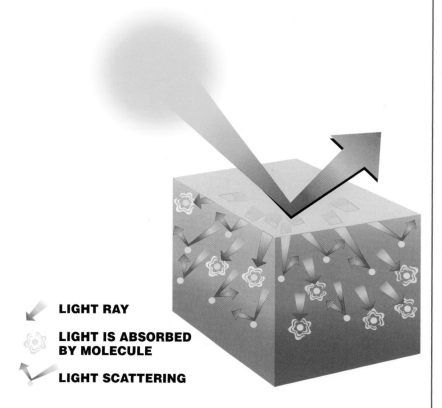

LIGHT RAY

LIGHT IS ABSORBED BY MOLECULE

LIGHT SCATTERING

Figure 9-20

Reflection, scattering, and absorption of light.

Depending on the sun's angle, as light hits the ocean's surface, much may simply reflect off the water. Within the water, light reflects off light-colored suspended particles, sending some of the light back to the surface and out of the water. Dark suspended particles and algae absorb some of the light. Water – even pure water with no suspended particles – also absorbs light directly. As light travels through water, it strikes water molecules. The water molecules absorb the energy, converting the light into heat.

While water absorbs colors in the order listed, it's a gradual process. That is, the color red doesn't suddenly disappear at 4 meters (13 feet). The water absorbs it gradually so very little is left at 4 meters (13 feet). Even then, some of each color may continue deeper, although not necessarily in significant amounts.

Blue is the strongest color and must travel through the most water before it's completely absorbed. This is why very clear water (without a high plankton concentration or suspended particles) looks blue. Light enters the water, scattering and reflecting in different directions. As the light travels, almost all the other colors get absorbed. Blue light remains when it reflects and emerges back from the water.

How deeply light penetrates depends on how clear or turbid the water is. In coastal areas with lots of runoff, penetration may be limited to less than 3 meters (10 feet). In the clearest water, a spectrophotometer may detect light as deep as 590 meters (1,936 feet). However, as mentioned, significant light penetration is limited to about 100 meters (328 feet). Nonetheless, in ideal conditions there can be enough visible light from the surface at 150 meters (492 feet) for the human eye to see by.

Figure 9-21

The electromagnetic spectrum and its transmission in water.

White light from the sun is actually the combination of all the visible colors, each with a different wavelength and potential energy. Colors at the red end of the spectrum have low energy and a long wavelength compared to the blue end, which has high energy and a short wavelength. Water absorbs fractions of various colors as light travels through it, more easily removing the long wavelength/low energy colors. In other words, water absorbs colors at the red end of the spectrum more easily than at the blue end.

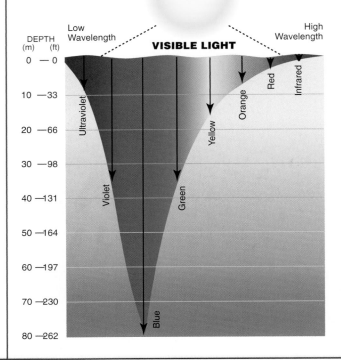

UNDERWATER PHOTOGRAPHERS FIGHT FOR LIGHT

Ask underwater photographers why it's so hard to take photos under water and they'll blurt out two words: visibility and light. Visibility is the distance one can see under water. Typically, it's reduced by the amount of particulate matter suspended in the water. One professional photographer compared underwater photography to taking photos of the goal posts on a football field in a dense fog while standing on the 50-yard line. Visibility isn't the only problem underwater photographers have to contend with. Color absorption is another. As you've learned, many colors are absorbed in very shallow water. If a diver tries to photograph a scene at 20 meters (66 feet) without a strobe, the result is a blue-green tinted picture. However, using an underwater strobe replaces the colors lost to water absorption. Also, modern digital cameras can adjust their color sensitivity to compensate for lost colors. By using both capabilities, underwater photographers can render images that show the true colors of the reef.

Bob Wohlers

Figure 9-22a

No strobe.

Bob Wohlers

Figure 9-22b

Absorbed colors replaced by camera strobe.

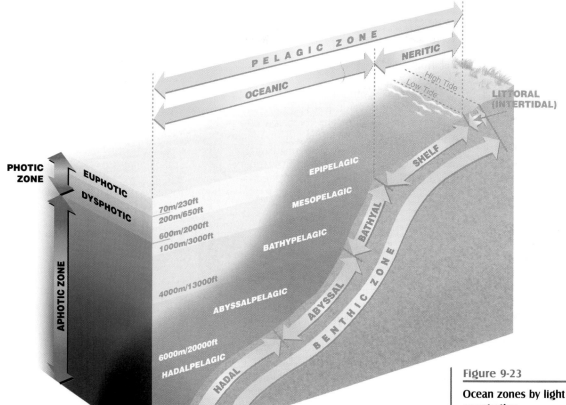

PELAGIC ZONE

OCEANIC

NERITIC

High Tide

Low Tide

LITTORAL (INTERTIDAL)

PHOTIC ZONE

EUPHOTIC

DYSPHOTIC

EPIPELAGIC

SHELF

MESOPELAGIC

BATHYAL

70m/230ft
200m/650ft

600m/2000ft
1000m/3000ft

BATHYPELAGIC

BENTHIC ZONE

APHOTIC ZONE

4000m/13000ft

ABYSSALPELAGIC

ABYSSAL

6000m/20000ft

HADALPELAGIC

HADAL

11000m/36000ft

Figure 9-23

Ocean zones by light penetration.

How deep light penetrates depends on how clear or turbid the water is. Significant light penetration is limited to about 200 meters (656 feet). Two basic zones exist with respect to light penetration: the *photic* and *aphotic* zones. The photic zone is the area where light penetrates, whereas the aphotic zone is one of total darkness. The photic zone can further be divided into the *euphotic* and *dysphotic* zones. The euphotic zone comprises only about 1% of the ocean, yet the vast majority of marine life exists there and depends on the light for survival. This is the zone where photosynthetic organisms bring light energy into the biological cycle. Light reaches the dysphotic zone, but there's not enough for photosynthetic life.

Two zones exist with respect to light penetration: the photic (sunlit) zone and the aphotic zone. Although the photic zone may reach as deep as 200 meters (656 feet), the most biologically productive region is the upper, shallow portion. This subzone of the photic zone is called the *euphotic zone* (from the Greek *eu* meaning *good*.) The euphotic zone comprises only about 1% of the oceans, yet the vast majority of marine life exists there and depends on the light for survival. This is the zone where photosynthetic organisms bring light energy into the biological cycle. The lower region of the photic zone is the *dysphotic zone* (from the Greek *dys* meaning *difficult*). Light reaches this region, but there's not enough for photosynthetic life.

The *aphotic zone* is where light doesn't reach. It begins at approximately 1,000 meters (3,280 feet). It actually makes up the vast majority of the ocean, though only a small portion of all marine organisms live there.

COLOR AND CONCEALMEANT

Figure 9-24

The North American, west coast sculpin fish (*Scorpaena sp.*) uses its reddish and brown color along with skin patterns, appendages, and shape to hide from predators.

Figure 9-25

Squirrel fish (*Holocentreidae sp.*) are nocturnal hunters. The red color of these fish helps them blend in with dark backgrounds.

Figure 9-26

This comb jelly uses its transparent body to hide while floating mid-water, which is its normal habitat.

In both terrestrial and aquatic ecosystems, many animals enhance their survival by being less visible to predators or prey. Their natural camouflage uses color and often shape to blend in with the background. You can find several types of camouflage in the marine environment.

The most common are coloration and patterns on the animal that match its environment. If the animal remains motionless, it's difficult for a predator to spot. Likewise, prey may wander within striking range of a concealed predator and never know what hit it. Fish that live in the open tend to be darker on top, concealing them against the dark bottom when seen from above by a predatory. They are silvery underneath, concealing them against the bright surface when seen from below. This is called *countershading*.

Other organisms combine color and shape. For example, trumpetfish have a color and long slender shape that resemble soft corals. They orient themselves vertically among these soft corals, disguised as a branch, waiting for unwary prey.

Some organisms have vivid colors that, to the human eye, seem to make them conspicuous. However, nature is smarter than that. Several species of nocturnal (active at night) fish have red or orangish coloration. Water absorbs these colors very rapidly, however, so at night or in dark crevices, where they usually hide during the day, these species blend in with dark backgrounds.

Some of the most complex concealment occurs in animals that can change their color and patterns to match the sea floor. Some species of flounder have this ability, as do several mollusks, such as the octopus and cuttlefish. As described in Chapter 6, cephalopods with this ability have chromatophores in their skin. Each *chromataphore* (from the Greek *chroma* meaning *color*) contains a colored pigment that the animal can reveal by constricting a muscle around it. The different chromatophores have different colors. So, by revealing the colors in some chromatophores and not others, the animal can change both its skin color and pattern. Some species not only change color to hide themselves, but as part of mating, to appear threatening, or when frightened.

Another concealment strategy is to have no color at all, like jellyfish and comb jellies. These organisms have translucent tissue, allowing light and color to pass through them. This makes them harder to spot because from any angle they tend to blend in with what is behind them.

Figure 9-27

Found on Australia's Great Barrier Reef, the stone fish (*Synanceja sp.*) is a master of concealment. A benthic dweller, it sits quietly waiting for its next meal to swim close to its large mouth.

Figure 9-28

The octopus is a master of rapid color change, capable of mimicking almost any pattern or color.

Temperature

What advantage does ocean-based existence have over land-based existence with respect to temperature?

What are an ectotherm, an endotherm, a homeotherm and a poikilotherm?

How does temperature affect metabolism? What's the advantage of being an endotherm?

As you learned earlier, seawater doesn't fluctuate in temperature nearly as much as air does. Marine organisms rarely encounter temperatures below 1.9°C or above 30°C. Compared to land-based climates, this narrow range provides an advantage. Marine organisms live in a much less challenging environment with respect to temperature range.

Generally, temperature dictates the rate of chemical reaction. The higher the temperature, the more quickly reactions take place. This is true in biological reactions and in reactions not related to life.

The higher the temperature within an organism, the more quickly energy-releasing chemical processes happen. Generally, these processes *(metabolism)* double in rate for each 10°C increase. Metabolic rate is proportional to how quickly an organism moves or reacts. For example, refrigeration is effective in preserving food because the low temperature greatly slows organisms that reproduce in and decompose the food, keeping it fresh.

Most marine organisms have an internal temperature close to that of surrounding seawater. Their internal temperature changes with seawater temperature. An organism with this characteristic is called an *ectotherm* (from the Greek *ektos* and *therme* meaning *outside* and *heat*, respectively). Ectotherms are commonly called "cold-blooded" organisms, and include terrestrial as well as marine organisms.

Opposite of ectotherm organisms are "warm-blooded" organisms. Warm-blooded animals are capable of generating sufficient amounts of heat energy to maintain a core temperature higher than the surroundings by metabolic means (burning energy). These animals are called *endotherms* (from the Greek *endon* meaning *inside*).

Endothermic animals with insulation such as birds and mammals that regulate their core body temperature at a relatively constant level are referred to as *homeotherms* (from the Greek *homeo* meaning *same*). However, some endotherms that lack this type of insulation, such as some large reptiles and many large fish. These organisms are called *poikilotherms* (from the Greek *poikolos* meaning *changeable*). Poikilotherms have a body temperature above the temperature of their surroundings, but it is not constant. Their internal temperature varies with the surrounding temperature, though remains above it. They generate internal heat through muscle activity.

All organisms (marine and terrestrial) live within an ideal temperature range. However, they can tolerate some variations above and below their ideal range. Ectotherms generally cannot tolerate temperatures much above their ideal range. Below their ideal range is usually more tolerable to them.

An advantage of being an endotherm is the ability to tolerate a wider range of external temperatures. This is because these organisms maintain their own internal temperature. Internal heat regulation allows endotherms, in general, to live in habitats with wider temperature ranges than can ectotherms. Homeotherm metabolic rates remain the same regardless of external temperature.

Being an endotherm (especially a homeotherm) can also have some disadvantages. For one, endotherms like whales and polar bears tolerate very little change in their internal temperature. Maintaining the internal temperature requires a high metabolic rate to generate heat or to eliminate heat. Therefore, compared to ectotherms, endotherms need more energy and a more efficient gas exchange. This means that these organisms must take in more food and oxygen to maintain their *internal* temperatures. The greater the difference between the external temperature and the required internal temperature, the more energy endotherms require, all else being equal. However, many endotherms have adaptations that help maintain their internal temperature. One example is the insulating layer of blubber that whales have so that they can retain body heat even in polar waters.

Sound

How does water affect sound? How do some marine mammals use sound in water to their advantage?

Sound is energy that travels in pressure waves. It can only travel through matter, which is why there's no sound in outer space. Sound travels well in air, but even better in water.

In distilled water at 20°C/68°F, sound travels at 1,482.4 meters (4863.4 feet) per second, which is about five times faster than in air. Density and temperature affect the speed of sound. It travels through warm water faster than cool water, and it travels faster in deep water due to the pressure. Much like light, sound bounces off suspended particles, water layers, the bottom, and other obstacles, and is eventually absorbed by water as heat. However, sound travels many times farther through water than light does.

Topic: Sound in the Sea
Go To: www.scilinks.org
Code: LOP2195

You can experience this by scuba diving or snorkeling in Hawaii or other areas frequented by humpback whales. Male humpbacks "sing" during mating season. Often you can hear their songs under water, even though there are no humpbacks in sight or within many kilometers.

Because sound travels effectively in water, marine mammals including dolphins and whales use *echolocation*, which is using sound to sense objects under water. These organisms echolocate by sending out a sound wave, then sensing the reflected sound wave that bounces back off an object. Dolphins and whales can determine an object's size, distance, density, and position with echolocation. Because the human body is mostly water, sound can travel through it. Some studies indicate that a dolphin can tell when a woman is pregnant by sensing echoes off an unborn child within her.

Marty Snyderman

Figure 9-29

Singing humpback whales.

Male humpback whales "sing" during mating season. In Hawaii and other places frequented by humpbacks, scuba divers and snorkelers often hear their songs under water, even though there are no humpbacks in sight or within many kilometers.

SONAR AND ECHOLOCATION

Human sonar replicates what whales, dolphins, and bats do naturally – use sound to obtain information. Human sonar has progressed considerably in the century since its introduction. Today, sonar can draw pictures of the sea bottom and objects found on it, sometimes so accurately that it's possible to pick out features on a shipwreck.

This, however, pales in comparison to echolocation – natural sonar. Experimental evidence shows that bat echolocation can detect size differences the width of a human hair. Similarly, a dolphin can determine the difference between a kernel of corn and a ball bearing at distance of 15 meters (49 feet).

Recent research suggests that dolphin and whale sonar carries spatial information from an object. This means that a single echo tells the animal the shape, size, density, and location of an object. It is likely that whales, dolphins, and bats, travel in darkness with an awareness of their surroundings comparable to a human's in broad daylight.

Dolphins emit a click – comparable to a human sonar ping – from behind a special organ in their heads called the melon. The melon acts like a sound "lens," allowing the dolphin to control the shape and intensity of the click for precise information in different situations. The dolphin receives the click echo in its jawbone, which transmits the sound to the middle ear. The ear hears the echo and sends it to the brain for processing. A dolphin often sends out another click after receiving an echo, so that the clicking/listening process is almost continuous.

Human sonar has two forms, active and passive. Active sonar is generating sound and listening for its echoes. Passive sonar (used extensively in the military) is simply listening to sound already in the environment. Evidence suggests that dolphins and whales also use passive sonar. They can obtain information from natural sounds, and may be able to "read" the echoes from clicks sent out by other dolphins or whales.

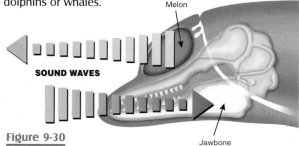
Melon

SOUND WAVES

Jawbone

Figure 9-30

Echolocation in dolphins.

Figure 9-31

Marine mammal echolocation.

Because sound travels effectively in water, marine mammals including dolphins and whales use echolocation to sense objects under water. These organisms echolocate by sending out a sound wave, then sensing the reflected sound wave that bounces back off an object. Dolphins and whales can determine an object's size, distance, density, and position with echolocation.

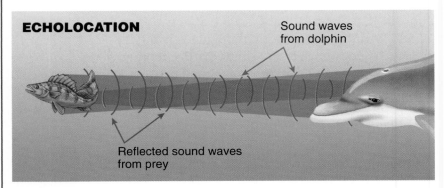

ECHOLOCATION

Sound waves from dolphin

Reflected sound waves from prey

As you've learned, deep water in the ocean is colder than the upper layers. However, pressure is greater with depth, too. The result is that sound travels more slowly in deep water due to the cold, but only to a point.

At about 1,000 meters (3,280 feet), the increasing pressure begins offsetting the effect of lower temperature. Beyond about 1,000 meters (3,280 feet), the speed of sound increases so that in very deep water it travels faster than at the surface. There's some evidence that whales use deep water to transmit sound across thousands of kilometers of ocean.

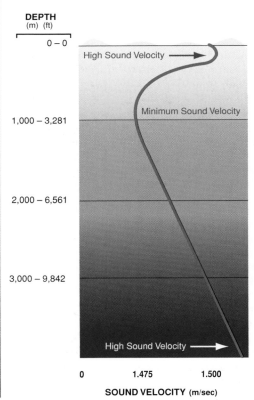

DEPTH (m) (ft)

0 – 0

High Sound Velocity ⟶

Minimum Sound Velocity

1,000 – 3,281

2,000 – 6,561

3,000 – 9,842

High Sound Velocity ⟶

0   1.475   1.500

SOUND VELOCITY (m/sec)

Figure 9-32

Speed of sound relative to depth.

Pressure

What is hydrostatic pressure? What effects does it have on marine life?

Right now, you're under pressure. If you're at sea level, you're under the pressure of the atmosphere, which is literally the weight of the air. Atmospheric pressure exerts a force of 1 kg/cm². For simplicity, scientists sometimes measure pressure in terms of the atmosphere. At sea level the pressure is one *bar* (metric system, from the Greek *baros* meaning *heavy*) also called one *atmosphere* (imperial system, abbreviated "ata"). "Bar" is always singular (i.e., 1 bar, 2 bar, 100 bar). Technically an atmosphere is about 1% greater than a bar, but for most practical purposes when discussing water pressure, you can treat them as equal.

Water weighs far more than air, so marine organisms exist in an environment with greater surrounding pressure than land-based organisms do. Pressure exerted by water is called *hydrostatic pressure* (from the Greek *hydro* meaning *water*). Hydrostatic pressure is the weight of the water column above a given depth.

Because water weighs more than air, it doesn't take much depth to produce a hydrostatic pressure equal to atmospheric pressure. It only takes approximately 10 meters (33 feet) of seawater to pro-

DEPTH (m) (ft)	PRESSURE
0 – 0	1 BAR/ATA
10 – 33	2 BAR/ATA
20 – 66	3 BAR/ATA
30 – 99	4 BAR/ATA

Figure 9-33

Air and water.

Ten meters (33 feet) of seawater exerts the same pressure as 1 bar/ata. Therefore, you add one bar/ata pressure for every 10 meters (33 feet) of depth.

EXPRESSIONS OF PRESSURE

Besides expressing pressure in atmospheres or bar, you can express pressure as a force over a given area, such as pounds per square inch (psi) or kilograms per square centimeter (kg/cm²). For example, you might use such measurements to determine how strong an aquarium window has to be. Other pressure measurements reflect the prevailing practice in a particular field. For example, meteorologists express atmospheric pressure in millimeters or inches of mercury because they originally measured the pressure with mercury barometers. Pressure can also be measured as the meters or feet of seawater (msw/fsw) that would exert a given amount of pressure. In other words, 1 atmosphere (ata) of pressure would also be:

> = 1.013 bar
> = 1.033 kg/cm²
> = 14.7 psi (pounds per square inch)
> = 760 mmHg (millimeters of mercury)
> = 29.92 in. Hg (inches of mercury)
> = 10.06 msw (meters of seawater)
> = 33 fsw (feet of seawater)

Oceanographers commonly use the unit decibar or one-tenth of a bar to express pressure. A bar of pressure is defined as the pressure exerted by 10 meters of pure water. This converts to a tenth of a bar or a decibar (dbar) to a close approximation of a meter in depth.

duce a hydrostatic pressure of 1 bar or 1 ata. At that depth, the total (absolute) pressure is 2 bar—one bar from atmospheric pressure, plus one bar from hydrostatic pressure. Therefore, a marine organism living at 10 meters experiences twice the pressure present at sea level. The pressure increases 1 bar for each additional 10 meters.

At 30 meters (98 feet), the pressure is 4 bar, or four times the surface pressure. Thirty meters isn't that deep considering that some marine organisms live thousands of meters deep. Thirty meters is within the depth range of experienced scuba divers, so even humans can go that deep. Why doesn't hydrostatic pressure affect these organisms or divers?

The reason is that while the pressure can be great, it is the same inside marine organisms as it is outside. Living tissue is made primarily of water, which is (within limits) incompressible and transmits pressure evenly. Since everything's in balance, the pressure doesn't crush or harm marine organisms. Very high pressure can affect chemical reactions and metabolism, but only at extreme depths well beyond where the vast majority of marine life exists. Organisms that do live at such depths are adapted to the specific effects of pressure.

Hydrostatic pressure is primarily an issue only for organisms that have gas spaces in their bodies. This is because gases compress, so hydrostatic pressure can distort or even collapse these spaces. This can affect the tissues surrounding the gas space. If you've dived down into the deep end of a pool, you may have experienced this as discomfort in your ears. Your ears have an air space behind the eardrum, and the discomfort comes from the hydrostatic pressure pushing your eardrum in against the compressible air space.

Many fish have a gas bladder that they use to control their buoyancy. They must add or release gas from the bladders when they change depth to keep the pressure in balance. Similarly, scuba divers learn to add air to the space in their ears so they can descend without discomfort. There are several techniques for *equalizing* (so-called because it equalizes the pressure inside the air space

PADI

Figure 9-34

Scuba diver equalizing an air space.

Scuba divers learn to add air to the air space in their ears (a technique called equalizing because it equalizes the pressure inside the air space with the pressure outside). Equalizing allows them to dive without discomfort. Failure to equalize can cause the increased water pressure to rupture the diver's ear drums.

PRESSURE AND GAS VOLUME RELATIONSHIPS

When it comes to gases, there's a predictable relationship between the pressure and the volume. Boyle's Law says that the volume of a gas is inversely proportional to the pressure. In other words, if you double the pressure, the volume (space the gas occupies) will reduce by half. If you halve the pressure, the volume will double. Knowing this allows scuba-diving scientists and other underwater explorers to determine how their depth will affect gases. This is important for calculating how long a tank of air will last, or how much air you need to put in a lifting device to recover an archaeological artifact.

Let's see how this works. At the surface, the pressure is 1 bar. If you descend to 10 meters, the pressure is now 2 bar – 1 from the pressure of the atmosphere and 1 from the pressure of the water. The pressure has doubled. This means that if you took an inverted glass full of air with you, assuming it was full at the surface, it would be only half full at 10 meters. The pressure has doubled, so the volume reduces by half.

DEPTH (m) (ft)	PRESSURE	AIR VOLUME	
0 – 0	1 BAR/ATA	1	
10 – 33	2 BAR/ATA	1/2	
20 – 66	3 BAR/ATA	1/3	
30 – 99	4 BAR/ATA	1/4	Inverted Container

Figure 9-35

Same air, less space.

When you take an air volume under water in an inverted jar, the volume changes proportionately with pressure.

DEPTH (m) (ft)	PRESSURE
0 – 0	1 BAR/ATA
10 – 33	2 BAR/ATA
20 – 66	3 BAR/ATA
30 – 99	4 BAR/ATA

Open Container   Closed Container

Figure 9-36

Expanding air during ascent.

To maintain a volume of air at depth, air is added to an air space. With an open container, the excess expanding air simply bubbles out into the surrounding water. In a closed, flexible container, the air volume grows proportionately with the decreasing pressure. If you inflated a sealed bag at 30 meters (98 feet), it would expand to four times the volume on the way to the surface, or burst during ascent.

If you were to go to 20 meters, the pressure is 3 bar – 1 from the pressure of the atmosphere, and 1 for each 10 meters of water. The pressure has tripled, so a gas is compressed to one-third what it was. Your glass would only be one-third full.

The same principle applies when you reduce the pressure by ascending to a shallower depth or to the surface. If your glass is half full of air at 10 meters and 2 bar of pressure, it will be when you return to the surface, at 0 meters and 1 bar of pressure. The pressure has reduced by half, so the volume doubles.

Suppose, then, that while scuba diving at 20 meters you fill a toy balloon with air and let it go. As it rises to the surface, the air in it expands as the pressure decreases. At the surface, the pressure is only one-third (1 bar) what it was at 20 meters (3 bar), so the balloon will be 3 times larger. This assumes the balloon has that much room to stretch. More than likely, the expanding air would burst the balloon before reaching the surface.

This can happen with a scuba diver's lungs! When scuba divers breathe under water, their scuba gear provides air equal to the surrounding pressure. Taking a breath, then, is like filling a toy balloon at depth. For this reason, scuba divers must be certain to breathe normally when ascending to allow expanding air to escape. Otherwise, it can rupture their lungs much as it would burst a toy balloon. This is one of the most serious injuries that can happen to a diver. To avoid this, scuba training emphasizes the most important rule in scuba diving: Breathe normally and never hold your breath.

with the pressure outside) that include swallowing, wiggling the jaw and blowing gently and momentarily against pinched nostrils. Failure to equalize can cause the pressure to rupture the diver's ear drums, so learning to do this is an important part of learning to dive.

Size and Volume

How do surface-to-volume ratios change as cell size increases?

Why is a high surface-to-volume ratio important to cell function?

Marine organisms thrive by getting all the resources they need from the water around them. Each cell gets the nutrients and gas it needs from the surrounding environment and excretes waste products into that environment. Single-cell organisms, such as protozoa or bacteria, make these exchanges directly to and from seawater. A multicellular organism, such as a sea cucumber or a fish, uses systems to gather nutrients and gas from the environment and excrete waste. The cells within a multicellular organism make the exchanges via the organism's systems rather than directly with the surrounding water.

This brings up some questions: Why are all large organisms multicellular? Why are single-cell organisms always small? Why couldn't a single-cell marine organism be the size of a multicellular organism and thrive by exchanging nutrients, gas, and wastes directly to and from seawater?

The reason is that for each cell to live, all gases, nutrients, and wastes must pass back and forth through the cell membrane. Although cells have many shapes, for the purposes of this discussion assume they're roughly spherical.

The volume of a sphere increases with the cube of its radius, and the surface area increases with the *square* of its radius. If a cell were to grow so its diameter were 24 times its original size, its volume would increase 64 times, but its surface area would increase only 16 times. Therefore, as a cell gets larger, the ratio between the surface area (i.e., the cell membrane) and the volume declines. The bigger the cell, the lower the surface-to-volume ratio. This means that there's less relative area through which to exchange gases, nutrients, and waste. That's why a high surface-to-volume ratio is important for cell function, and why large organisms are multicellular rather than giant single cells.

Diameter (cm)	0.5	1.0	1.5
Surface area (cm²)	0.79	3.14	7.07
Volume (cm³)	0.06	0.52	1.77
Surface - to - Volume Ratio	13.17:1	6.04:1	3.99:1

Figure 9-37

Surface-to-volume ratio.

The volume of a sphere increases with the cube of its radius, and the surface area increases with the square of its radius. In other words, as the diameter increases, the volume increases more quickly than the surface area. This is why a high surface-to-volume ratio is important for cell function, and why large organisms are multicellular rather than giant single cells.

Buoyancy

How does buoyancy affect both swimming and drifting marine organisms?

Although pressure doesn't affect marine organisms substantially, *buoyancy* profoundly affects life in water compared to life on land. The principle of buoyancy states that an object immersed in a gas or liquid is buoyed up by a force equal to the weight of the gas or liquid displaced. This is known as *Archimedes' Principle.*

The fact that you're immersed in air means that buoyancy is affecting you right now—an upward force equal to the weight of the air volume you displace. Air isn't very dense, though. If you were to figure out the weight of the air you displace, you'd discover that the upward force is so tiny that it has no meaningful effect. That's why we don't float in air.

Water is far denser than air (about 800 times), so buoyancy in water is a more significant force. The density of seawater is almost exactly the same as that of most living tissue. This means that most organisms in water are buoyed up by a force nearly the same as their own weight. Some organisms – from microscopic plankton to the great whales – live in the open ocean and never have contact with the bottom. It would be impossible for a bird to live without

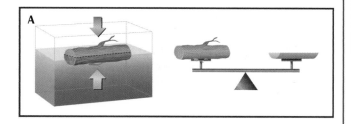

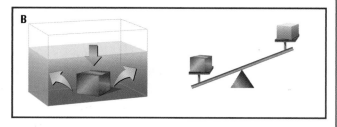

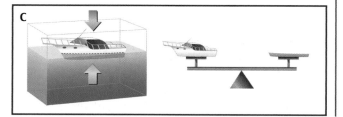

SPHERE CALCULATIONS

To determine a sphere's surface area:

$$\text{surface area} = 4\pi r^2$$

To determine a sphere's volume:

$$\text{volume} = \frac{4\pi r^3}{3}$$

The surface area to volume ratio:

$$\frac{\text{surface area}}{\text{volume}} = \frac{4\pi r^2(3)}{4\pi r^3} = \frac{3}{R}$$

Suppose a sphere has a radius of 10 centimeters. The volume would be

$$\text{volume} = \frac{4\pi 10 \text{ cm}^3}{3}$$

$$\text{volume} = \frac{12,560 \text{cm}^3}{3}$$

$$\text{volume} = 4186.7 \text{ cm}^3$$

To determine a sphere's surface area:

$$\text{surface area} = 4\pi r^2$$

The same sphere's surface area would be

$$\text{surface area} = 4\pi 10 \text{ cm}^2$$

$$\text{surface area} = 1256 \text{ cm}^2$$

Figure 9-38

Archimedes' principle.

The principle of buoyancy states that an object immersed in a gas or liquid is buoyed up by a force equal to the weight of the gas or liquid displaced. In **(A)** a wood log floats on the water. In **(B)** a solid steel block sinks in the water. In **(C)** the steel hull of a boat floats. The log floats because its density is less than that of water. The rock sinks because its density is greater than that of water. The ship floats because the average density is less than that of water. Even though the ship may weigh many tons, its hull shape displaces a substantial amount of water. The water it displaces weighs more than the ship itself. This allows it to float.

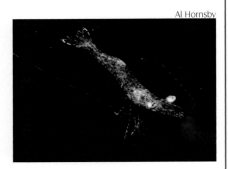

Figure 9-39

Midwater wanderer.

Most organisms in water are buoyed up by a force nearly the same as their own weight. Some organisms – from microscopic plankton to the great whales – live in the open ocean and never have contact with the bottom.

ever landing, yet in the marine environment this type of existence is not only possible, but common.

Some living tissue and organic structures like bone, teeth, and shells, have a greater density than water and therefore sink. Organisms have various adaptations to handle this. Chapter 9 explains that some fish have gas bladders to control their buoyancy. These bladders give them the buoyancy to offset the weight of bones or teeth. Other fish don't have bladders because they hinder rapid depth changes. These species may have light skeletons or produce tissue high in oil (oil is less dense than water and is therefore buoyant). Some organisms produce ammonium chloride, which is less dense than seawater.

Still other organisms have different adaptations for dealing with buoyancy. Large shell-bearing invertebrates don't rely on a midwater existence and instead live on the bottom. Planktonic organisms store food in lightweight waxes and oils, which provide buoyancy.

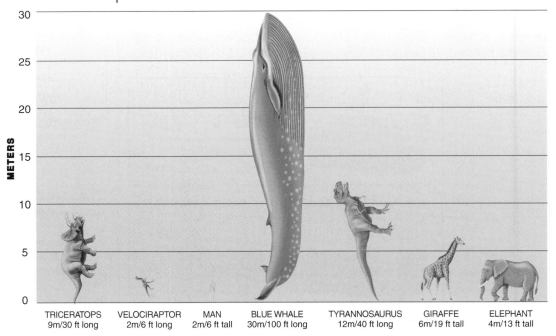

TRICERATOPS 9m/30 ft long	VELOCIRAPTOR 2m/6 ft long	MAN 2m/6 ft tall	BLUE WHALE 30m/100 ft long	TYRANNOSAURUS 12m/40 ft long	GIRAFFE 6m/19 ft tall	ELEPHANT 4m/13 ft tall

ANIMAL

Figure 9-40

Buoyancy makes size possible.

Because of buoyancy, marine organisms don't have to expend much energy to offset their own weight compared to land-based existence. This allows marine organisms to grow larger than those on land. This is particularly evident in whales, which grow significantly larger than any terrestrial animal ever has, living or extinct. Due entirely to weight, it would be physiologically impossible for a terrestrial animal the size of a blue whale to exist.

Because of buoyancy, marine organisms don't have to expend much energy to offset their own weight compared to land-based existence. This is what allows entire communities to exist simply by drifting in the ocean. It allows many swimming creatures to live most of their lives without ever actually coming into contact with the bottom. It allows organisms to grow larger than those on land. This is particularly evident in whales, which grow significantly larger than any terrestrial animal ever has, living or extinct. Due entirely to weight, which would crush its bones and internal organs, it would be physiologically impossible for a terrestrial animal the size of a blue whale to exist.

Movement and Drag

What characteristics allow marine organisms to avoid sinking? What characteristics do marine organisms have to handle water resistance?

While marine organisms have an advantage over land-based organisms with respect to buoyancy, the situation is reversed when it comes to drag. Because water has a far higher viscosity than air, water resists movement far more than air does. Consider what happens when you're in a swimming pool – it takes very little effort to push yourself off the bottom thanks to buoyancy. However, it takes far more effort to swim a long distance than to run the same distance. This is due to *drag*.

Viscosity affects small organisms, plankton in particular, much, much more than it does large organisms like fish. Their small size means that viscosity dominates their movement. These organisms may have plumes, hairs, ribbons, spines, and other protrusions that increase their drag and help them resist sinking. Many have buoyancy adaptations that help them remain suspended in the water column.

Even large organisms that swim must contend with water drag, but do so differently from small organisms. Drag is the resistance to movement caused by friction with water (or any other gas or fluid). Drag increases with viscosity, but also with the speed, shape, and size of the moving organism. Reducing drag is important because it affects an organism's ability to capture food or elude a predator.

Several adaptations help organisms overcome drag. Some organisms move or swim very slowly so that drag isn't a substantial factor. Some excrete mucus or oil that actually lubricates the organism to help it "slip" through the water. However, the most

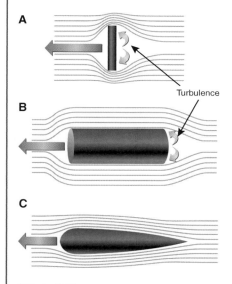

A

B

Turbulence

C

Figure 9-41

Drag, streamlining, and turbulence.

While marine organisms have an advantage over land-based organisms with respect to buoyancy, the situation is reversed when it comes to drag. Because water has a far higher viscosity than air, it resists movement through it far more than air does. **(A)**, **(B)** and **(C)** show the drag on a flat disk, cylinder, and teardrop-shaped object, respectively. Note how the top view of a tuna in **figure 9-42** closely resembles the teardrop-shaped object, the best shape for a fast-moving fish with reduced turbulence and drag.

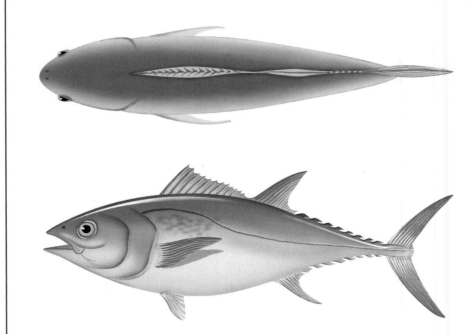

Figure 9-42

A streamlining champion.

common adaptation is *streamlining*, which is having a shape that reduces drag.

As you can see in the diagram, different shapes move through water with more or less drag. Some shapes create significant *turbulence*, which is chaotic water movement. Turbulence increases drag. A teardrop or torpedo shape produces the least turbulence and allows an organism to swim with the greatest efficiency and lowest drag. This is why fast-moving fish and other marine organisms have their characteristic torpedo shape. It is also why engineers design rockets, jets, submarines, sports cars, and other fast-moving craft with this shape.

Currents

How does water movement affect the distribution and survival of marine life?

The buoyancy characteristics that allow marine organisms to exist midwater have an interesting advantage with respect to survival. As you've learned, entire marine communities exist entirely in the open ocean, drifting in ocean currents without contact with shore or bottom.

Some marine organisms take advantage of this type of existence at some point during their life cycle. For organisms to drift as larvae provides advantages over remaining in the same location as the original community. First, drifting disperses the organisms to new habitats, maximizing the chances of species survival should something happen to the original community. Second, drifting may take organisms to nutrient-rich areas, preventing too many offspring from competing for the same resources in the original community.

ARE YOU LEARNING?

1. Particles in water _____ light, and water _____ light, turning it into heat.

   A. absorb and scatter, absorbs

   B. generate, magnifies

2. The _____ zone is the area of the ocean that sunlight never reaches.

   A. photic

   B. euphotic

   C. dysphotic

   D. aphotic

3. The advantage of ocean-based existence over land-based existence, with respect to temperature, is that the coolness of the water makes organisms live longer.

   A. true

   B. false

4. An _____ is an organism with an internal temperature the same as or close to the surrounding seawater's temperature.

   A. ectotherm

   B. endotherm

5. The advantage of being an endotherm is

   A. it requires a smaller food source.

   B. it allows the organism to live in habitats with wider temperature ranges.

6. Sound travels through water _____ in air.

   A. about a fourth as fast as

   B. about half as fast as

   C. about twice as fast as

   D. about five times faster than

7. Hydrostatic pressure has a/an _____ effect on marine organisms. This is because the pressure inside their tissues is _____ the surrounding pressure.

   A. significant, greater than

   B. significant, less than

   C. insignificant, equal to

   D. insignificant, greater than

8. The ratio between a cell's surface and its volume _____ as the diameter increases.

   A. decreases

   B. increases

   C. remains the same

9. A high surface-to-volume ratio is important to cell function because

   A. it affects cell buoyancy and drag as the organism moves.

   B. it affects the efficiency of nutrients, gas, and wastes passing through the cell membrane.

10. Buoyancy affects marine organisms by

    A. minimizing the effect of their weight.

    B. maximizing the effect of their weight.

11. The most common adaptation for overcoming water resistance is

    A. a gas bladder.

    B. streamlining.

    C. swimming slowly.

12. Drifting with water movement may

    A. carry organisms to new habitats.

    B. cause many organisms to compete for the same nutrients.

New Terms You Learned

- **absolute pressure** the total pressure, so that the zero point is a vacuum (p. 9-26)
- **aphotic zone** the ocean zone of perpetual darkness below the photic zone beginning at approximately 1,000 meters/3,280 feet (p. 9-19)
- **Archimedes' principle** an object immersed in a gas or liquid is buoyed up by a force equal to the weight of the gas or liquid displaced (p. 9-29)
- **atmospheric pressure** measurement equal to the air pressure at sea level, roughly equal to one bar (p. 9-25)
- **bar** pressure measurement equal to the air pressure at sea level, roughly equal to one atmosphere (p. 9-25)
- **buoyancy** the upward force on an object immersed in a gas or liquid that is equal to weight of the displace gas or liquid (p. 9-29)
- **calorie** the amount of heat needed to raise one gram of water one degree Celsius (p. 9-5)
- **chromatophores** pigment sacs found in some organisms that allow them to change their skin color and pattern (p. 9-20)
- **countershading** natural coloration of organism that conceals them against the bottom when viewed from above and against the surface when viewed from below (p. 9-20)
- **drag** resistance to movement caused by friction from contact with a fluid (or any gas or fluid) (p. 9-31)
- **dysphotic zone** the dimly lit, deeper and less biologically productive portion of the photic zone (p. 9-19)
- **echolocation** the use of sound by organisms to sense and locate objects underwater (p. 9-23)
- **ectotherm** an organism with an internal temperature that is close to and varies with the external temperature (p. 9-21)
- **endotherm** an organism with an internal temperature that varies with, but is constantly higher than, the surrounding temperature (p. 9-21)

- **equalizing** the technique divers use to add air to a body air space to balance it with the increased pressure outside the air space (p. 9-26)
- **euphotic zone** the upper, most biologically productive portion of the photic zone (p. 9-19)
- **gauge pressure** useable pressure, as when using gas from a cylinder, so that the zero point is one atmosphere (p. 9-26)
- **heat** the kinetic energy in the random movement or vibration of individual atoms and molecules in a substance (p. 9-4)
- **heat capacity** how much heat energy it takes to raise one gram of a substance 1° Celsius (p. 9-6)
- **homeotherm** an organism with a stable internal temperature ("warm-blooded" organisms) (p. 9-21)
- **hydrostatic pressure** pressure exerted by water (p. 9-25)
- **joule** a unit of energy measure; 4.2 joules = 1 calorie (p. 9-5)
- **latent** present, not noticeable, but capable of being active (p. 9-8)
- **latent heat of fusion** the non-sensible heat lost when water goes from liquid to ice (p. 9-8)
- **latent heat of vaporization** the heat required to vaporize a substance (p. 9-10)
- **metabolism** the energy-releasing chemical processes within an organism (p. 9-21)
- **non-sensible heat** heat change at a substance's state change that does not cause a temperature change and cannot be measured with a thermometer (p. 9-7)
- **photic zone** upper sunlit zone of the ocean (p. 9-16)
- **poikilotherm** endotherms (warm-blooded animals) such as large fish and reptiles that lack a layer of insulation and whose body temperature varies with the temperature of its surroundings (p. 9-21)

- **sensible heat** heat that is measurable as a change in temperature and readable with a thermometer (p. 9-7)
- **state** an expression of a substance's form as solid, liquid, or gas (p. 9-7)
- **streamlining** having the characteristic of a shape that reduces drag (p. 9-32)
- **temperature** the measurement of how fast molecules/atoms in a substance move (vibrate) (p. 9-4)
- **thermal equilibrium** the state in which heating and cooling balance so that temperature neither increases nor decreases substantially (p. 9-11)
- **thermal inertia** the tendency for water to resist temperature changes (p. 9-11)
- **thermocline** transition between a colder, deeper water layer and a warmer, upper layer of water) (p. 9-14)
- **transpiration** the passage of water vapor from living organisms (p. 9-10)
- **turbulence** chaotic water movement caused by an object passing through the water (p. 9-32)

Chapter 9 in Review

1. Heat and temperature are related yet different concepts. Explain the difference and why, given two bodies of water, one with a lower temperature may have more heat.
2. Define heat capacity and explain how the heat capacity of water affects the Earth's climate.
3. Describe the characteristics of water as it freezes and as it vaporizes. Include the definitions of latent heat of fusion, latent heat of vaporization, sensible heat, and non-sensible heat.
4. Explain why thermal inertia and thermal equilibrium are important to life and to the Earth's climate.
5. Explain the variables that cause water to stratify and why.
6. Make a diagram of the three density layers of the ocean, labeling each. Indicate where a thermocline would be expected in these three layers.
7. Explain how water scatters and absorbs light. How does this affect the photic zone?
8. Make a diagram showing the photic, euphotic, dysphotic, and aphotic zones of the ocean.
9. Define ectotherm, endotherm, homeotherm and poikilotherm. What are their similarities and differences?
10. Explain how sound behaves in water, and contrast it to the behavior of sound in air and to the behavior of light in water. What are some adaptations that marine organisms have to take advantage of sound in water?
11. Describe how buoyancy, water resistance, and water movement affect life in the sea. What adaptations do different organisms have to cope with these factors?

Connecting Chapter Concepts— Science Scenarios

1. Water's hydrogen bonds give it a high heat capacity, so that it takes a high amount of heat energy to raise it a given temperature, and it must lose a high amount of heat to lower a given temperature.

   A. How does water's high heat capacity affect the Earth's climate?

   B. What is non-sensible heat? What are latent heat of fusion and latent heat of vaporization?

   C. How does latent heat of fusion give ice the ability to cool beverages or climates so effectively?

2. Light does not travel through water the same way it travels through air. Water scatters and absorbs light to a far greater degree than air does.

   A. What two zones are defined by how much light penetrates the ocean? What are the sub zones of the upper of these two zones? What region does each zone represent?

   B. The euphotic zone comprises only about 1% of the ocean, yet the vast majority of life is found there. Why?

   C. What three factors reduce the amount of light that penetrates the water?

   D. Water doesn't absorb light uniformly. In what order does water absorb the colors visible to the human eye (from first to last).

Marine Science and the Real World

1. Large masses of seawater can produce severe weather patterns. El Niño is a hot mass of water in the Pacific Ocean that periodically develops, bringing substantial rain to the otherwise arid southwestern United States and other areas. Why is this a concern? How do concerns about El Niño relate to global climate change?

2. Suppose someone proposed to study the ocean by using very powerful sound waves over an extended period. What concerns, if any, would you have with respect to the marine organisms?

3. The blue whale is the largest animal ever known to exist. What specific reason related to its physiology, as well as any other factors, would make it difficult or impossible for a land-based animal of the same size to exist?

References

Amato, I. 1993. A Sub Surveillance Network Becomes a Window on Whales. *Science*. 261 (no. 5121).

Bowditch, N. 1966. *American Practical Navigator*. Publication 9. Washington, DC: U.S. Navy Hydrographic Office.

Buckingham, M.J., J.R. Porter, and C.L. Epifanio. 1996. Seeing Underwater with Background Noise. *Scientific American*. 274 (2).

Cromie, A. H. 1974. *Physics for the Life Sciences*. New York: McGraw-Hill.

Garrison, T. 2004. *Essentials of Oceanography*. Pacific Grove, CA: Brooks/Cole, a division of Thomson Learning, Inc.

Garrison, T. 2004. *Oceanography: An Invitation to Marine Science*. Pacific Grove, CA: Brooks/Cole, a division of Thomson Learning, Inc.

Hellemans, A. 1999. Getting to the Bottom of Water. *Science*. 283 (no. 5402). 29 January.

Lynch, D. K. 1995. *Color and Light in Nature*. Cambridge, England: Cambridge University Press.

Watson, L. 1988. *The Water Planet*. New York: Crown.

UNIT 4 The Motion of

Al Hornsby

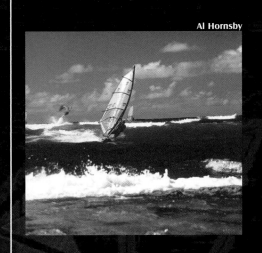

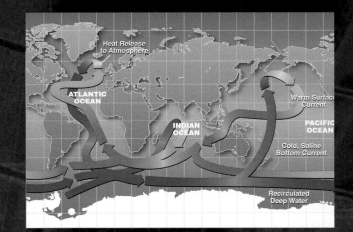

Heat Release
to Atmosphere

ATLANTIC
OCEAN

INDIAN
OCEAN

Warm Surface
Current

PACIFIC
OCEAN

Cold, Saline
Bottom Current

Recirculated
Deep Water

the Ocean

Photo Courtesy of NOAA's Ark Collection/NOAA

CHAPTER 10

Air–Sea Interaction

Visible Earth/http://visibleearth.nasa.gov, NASA

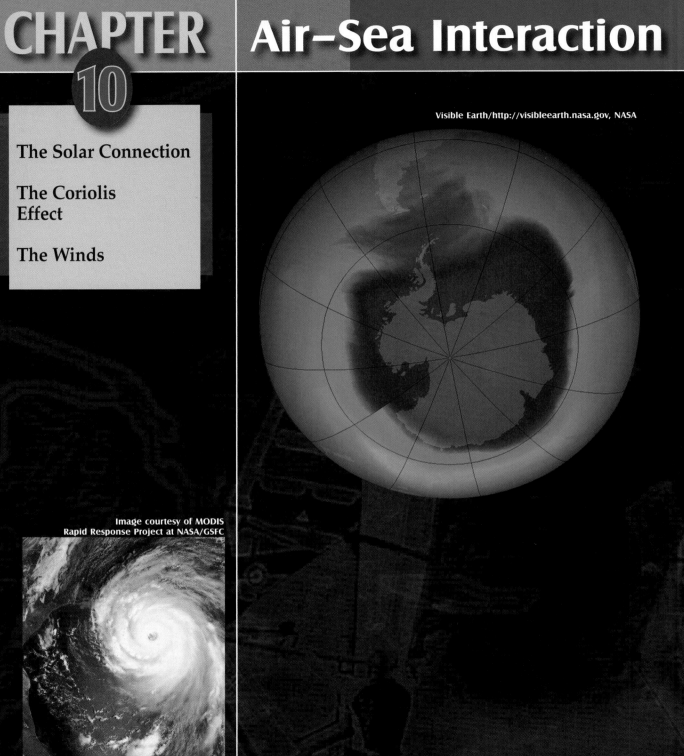

Image courtesy of MODIS
Rapid Response Project at NASA/GSFC

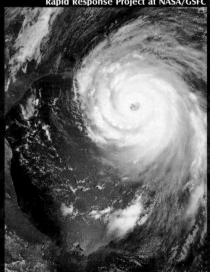

The Role of the Ocean in Earth's Climate

O ver the past 50 years, the use of fossil fuels (e.g., for cars, in industry) has increased dramatically. One concern regarding their use is that they release carbon dioxide (CO_2) into the atmosphere. The problem is that carbon dioxide is one of several greenhouse gases that cause the Earth to retain heat. Thus, increasing atmospheric carbon dioxide may be contributing to global climate change, drastically altering the Earth's climate. This could have wide-ranging effects on life. Fortunately, the ocean is helping by absorbing some of the excess carbon dioxide. The question is, just how much is the ocean helping and how? Will the ocean have problems too?

Dr. Claudia Benitez-Nelson, a chemical oceanographer at the University of South Carolina, is on the leading edge of answering these crucial questions.

"What I love about being an oceanographer is that I'm working on real applied problems and issues," says Dr. Benitez-Nelson. "I can explain what I do to everyday people and it makes sense to them. People understand air pollution and global warming."

As a little girl, Dr. Benitez-Nelson didn't imagine growing up to be a chemist at the forefront of science. Even as a youngster, however, she showed a curiosity about how things work. She frequently dismayed her mother by disassembling and reassembling things. When she was attending the University of Washington, she discovered her aptitude for chemistry.

"It never occurred to me that I could have a career as an oceanographer," explains Dr. Benitez-Nelson, "but then I took an introductory oceanography course in college and really loved it. My professor introduced me to the oceanography department, and that's how I became a chemical oceanographer."

Dr. Benitez-Nelson's research focuses in part on the role phytoplankton play in converting atmospheric carbon dioxide during photosynthesis into compounds, such as carbohydrates, that may eventually settle to the ocean floor. This process essentially traps the carbon produced from fossil fuels in the ocean for hundreds to thousands of years. Known as the "biological pump," this phenomenon has attracted a great deal of attention because some scientists estimate that as much as 50% of the carbon dioxide produced by fossil fuel emissions ultimately resides in the ocean and not the atmosphere. Dr. Benitez-Nelson will tell you that working on problems like these is what makes her career exciting. "I love having a question and figuring out the answer, or finding out something that I never planned or imagined. The latter is also the most challenging because then you have to figure out why!" Dr. Benitez-Nelson says. "It takes patience to conduct real science, but finding evidence that supports or refutes your theory is a lot of fun."

To those interested in pursuing a career in marine sciences, Dr. Benitez-Nelson offers this advice: "Take as many math and science courses as you can. Then, go with what your instincts tell you. Oceanography is a very diverse field. Try different research avenues. Don't let anyone tell you that you can't do what you want to do. It may be hard, but if you want it enough, you will succeed."

Claudia Benitez-Nelson, PhD
Associate Professor, Department of Geological Sciences & Marine Science Program,
University of South Carolina

Most of *Life on an Ocean Planet* pertains to the ocean of *water* that covers most of Earth's surface. In this chapter, we turn our attention to a different ocean – the atmosphere, which is an ocean of *air* that blankets all parts of Earth. If studying the atmosphere seems a surprising topic in marine science, you should understand that the air and the sea are fluid media that interact. As you'll see, you really can't study one without the other. What you learn in this chapter forms the basis for learning about currents, wind, and waves, which Chapters 11 and 12 cover.

To live, people must breathe air. You might think that people generally took air for granted prior to the Industrial Revolution. They did to the extent that they weren't worried about air quality like we are today. Air quality was only a concern at times in large cities or with respect to large fires or volcanic action.

In another way, however, people in the past were *more* concerned about air. With the majority of people subsisting on agriculture, the amount of moisture and heat in the air and the direction of its flow were crucial. Before modern irrigation, early farmers relied on qualities of the air for their crops to grow. These were adequate sunshine, heat, and rain. People involved in seafaring and trade also depended on another air quality – motion – that is, wind to propel their vessels.

Today, we depend more and more on accurate short and long-term weather predictions in planning our activities. In addition, we're concerned with air quality in new ways. You may be aware of smog, acid rain, and increasing levels of greenhouse gases, all of which reflect changes caused by industrialization and human activities. We are also concerned with changes that have altered how the atmosphere shields us against radiation from space.

Air quality issues have become important in international politics because air flows from one place to another. Much as people up river can affect water quality for those down river, people in one place can affect air quality for everyone. Smog may be an issue that affects a local area, but regardless of where they originate, greenhouse gases affect the whole world by altering the planet's heat balance.

Today scientists realize that the air, land, and water constantly exchange material and energy. As discussed relating to sediments in Chapter 14, the wind can pick up dry Sahara desert soil and drop it in the Caribbean Sea, changing the underwater environment. As explained more in Chapter 11, heated water rising from the central and western equatorial Pacific may raise the temperature of the air above it, causing a wind pattern change that ultimately causes flooding, destroys fisheries, and wipes out crops in North and

South America. You cannot study the health of the Earth's land and water environments and how they affect human needs without also studying the ocean of air around us.

The Solar Connection

Chapter 4 explains that life gets almost all its energy from the sun. Except for chemosynthesizers, primary producer organisms combine light energy from the sun with water and carbon to make carbohydrates. Primary consumers eat the primary producers, which are eaten by secondary consumers, and so on up the food web. The energy that's making your heart beat right now came indirectly from the sun.

It turns out that solar energy does more than provide energy for life on Earth. It drives the wind, and as discussed in later chapters, it drives currents in the ocean. The currents and water temperature, in turn, influence winds and weather. The Earth's surface is heated by solar energy (sunlight). Therefore, the sun not only powers life, but also provides the temperature conditions necessary for life.

Air and Sun

What components make up the air?

What are the four layers of the atmosphere?

What is the relationship between water vapor, air temperature, and air density?

What causes rain or snow?

What is air? It's the mixture of gases that surrounds us, but let's look at this mixture more closely. Chapter 8 explains that air consists of approximately 78% nitrogen. The components, on average, of clean dry air are:

Nitrogen	78.08%
Oxygen	20.95%
Argon	0.93%
Carbon dioxide	0.03%
All other gases	0.01%

STUDY QUESTIONS

Find the answers as you read.

1. What components make up the air?

2. What are the four layers of the atmosphere?

3. What is the relationship between water vapor, air temperature, and air density?

4. What causes rain or snow?

5. Approximately what percent of solar energy directed toward Earth reaches Earth's surface?

6. What would happen if the solar radiation coming to Earth and energy being reradiated into space were imbalanced?

7. What factors cause Earth to heat unevenly?

8. What causes *convection*?

INTERNET PORTAL

SCiLINKS. NSTA

Topic: Solar Energy
Go To: www.scilinks.org
Code: LOP2205

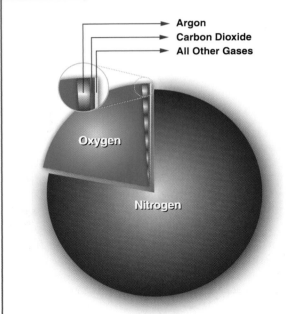

Argon
Carbon Dioxide
All Other Gases

Oxygen

Nitrogen

Figure 10-1

The composition of air.

This pie chart shows the proportion of each gas in one unit of air in the troposphere.

Actually, this is the composition of the *troposphere*, which is the lowest layer of the atmosphere and the one that concerns us most. The troposphere extends from the surface of the Earth to about 15,000 meters (49,200 feet) above sea level. The next layer is the *stratosphere*, which continues to about 50,000 meters (164,000 feet). Above the stratosphere lies the *mesosphere*, which extends to about 90,000 meters (295,200 feet). The top layer is the *thermosphere*, which goes beyond 110,000 meters (360,800 feet) into space.

Figure 10-2

Atmospheric layers.

The troposphere is the lowest layer of the atmosphere and extends from the surface of the Earth to about 15,000 meters (49,200 feet) above sea level. The stratosphere continues to about 50,000 meters (164,000 feet) followed by the mesosphere, which extends to about 90,000 meters (295,200 feet), and finally the thermosphere, which goes beyond 110,000 meters (360,800 feet – about 70 miles) into space.

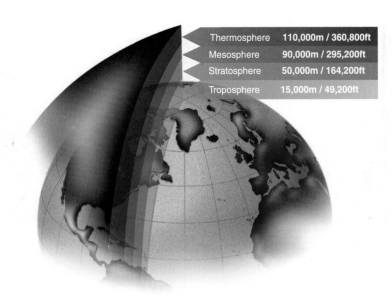

Thermosphere	110,000m / 360,800ft
Mesosphere	90,000m / 295,200ft
Stratosphere	50,000m / 164,200ft
Troposphere	15,000m / 49,200ft

A HOLE IN THE SKY

One marked difference between the troposphere and the stratosphere is that the stratosphere has a significant amount of ozone. *Ozone* is a gas composed of molecules of three oxygen atoms. The oxygen gas molecules we breathe consist of two atoms. The three-atom structure makes ozone unstable and highly reactive with other substances.

At sea level, ozone is rare, which is fortunate because it is a toxic health hazard. However, it is more abundant in the stratosphere, where it absorbs most of the ultraviolet radiation from the sun. Without this ozone layer in the stratosphere, ultraviolet radiation would kill off life on Earth's surface. A substantial decrease in this protection would kill essential microorganisms, slow the growth of primary producers, and lead to widespread effects on the body ranging from skin cancer to cataracts.

In 1974, scientists F. Sherwood Roland, Paul Crutzen, and Mario Molina showed that *chlorofluorocarbons* (CFCs) released into the atmosphere react with ozone. This led to the hypothesis that the industrial use of CFCs might deplete the ozone layer. This was alarming news because CFCs were used as common aerosol propellants in spray cans, as a refrigerant in air conditioners, and for other purposes.

Subsequent finds show that there is an ozone "hole" over Antarctica with an approximately 80% reduction in ozone that develops each spring in the Southern Hemisphere. The connection between CFCs and the ozone "hole" has been confirmed. The international community has reacted quickly to the problem. Today most countries have banned or greatly restricted the use of CFCs. However, CFCs continue to be smuggled and used illegally. Scientists continue to watch the yearly ozone hole to track whether it's growing, contracting, or stabilizing.

Visible Earth/http://visibleearth.nasa.gov, NASA

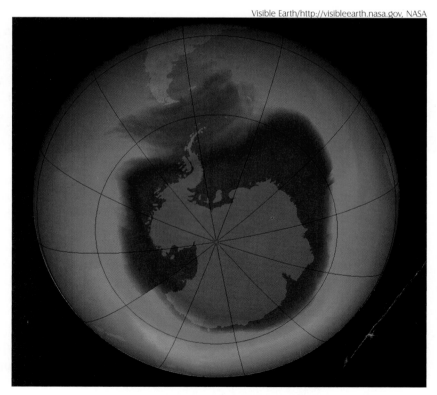

Figure 10-3

Antarctic ozone hole.

This image from NASA's Total Ozone Mapping Spectrometer on the Earth Probe satellite shows the ozone layer over Antarctica in September 2008. Ozone concentration is represented in this image with bright colors indicating a higher concentration and dark colors indicating less ozone. The hole is the dark blue region centered over the continent. The concentration of ozone plummets in spring, which begins in the Southern Hemisphere at the end of September.

Air compresses under its own weight. So, while the atmosphere extends more than 100 kilometers (approximately 70 miles) above sea level, most of the mass of the atmosphere exists close to Earth in the troposphere. The effects that concern our study – air quality, weather, and air-sea interactions – take place in this layer.

Besides the gases listed earlier as components of air, the atmosphere has two other components that account for up to 4% of its total volume. These are water vapor and *aerosols*. Aerosols are liquid and solid particles suspended in the air, such as dust, pollen, or ash.

Water vapor is invisible. You can see clouds because water vapor has condensed. The amount of water vapor in the air relates

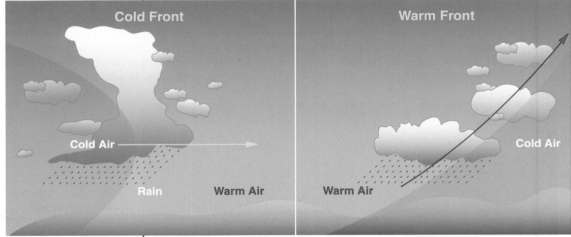

A.

Figure 10-4

Weather fronts.

When two air masses of different temperatures collide, cooling and precipitation usually result. In a cold front **(A)**, the cold air pushes into the warm air. In a warm front **(B)**, the warm air slides up and over the cool air.

to the air temperature, density, and pressure. As the temperature rises, air pressure decreases and density decreases. When you add water vapor, the density decreases even more. This is because the density of water vapor is less than the average density of air, so as water vapor molecules displace oxygen and nitrogen molecules, the air density decreases. This means that warm, moist air is less dense than cool, dry air. Two air masses of the same temperature can have different densities depending on the amount of water vapor. These differences cause precipitation.

Evaporation adds water vapor to the air, and condensation removes it. In *saturated air*, the rate of evaporation balances the rate of condensation, and the total amount of water vapor doesn't change. The amount of water vapor in saturated air varies with temperature. As saturated air cools, condensation temporarily increases, removing water vapor until a new balance is reached. As saturated air warms, it becomes unsaturated. Evaporation can add water vapor until the air is again saturated.

When saturated or nearly saturated air cools, its molecules vibrate more slowly. When water vapor molecules slow down enough, they condense into liquid water droplets or into ice crystals when the temperature is sufficiently cold. This releases the latent heat of vaporization, warming the air. (As discussed in Chapter 9, latent heat of vaporization is the heat required to overcome the polar bonds when water changes from a liquid to water vapor.) Initially these droplets or crystals are very small and tend to remain suspended. However, they can collide and form bigger drops or clusters of crystals that fall as rain or snow, and you get out your umbrella or boots.

When a warm, moisture-laden air mass collides with a cooler air mass, precipitation often occurs. This happens where the two air masses meet, because the warmer air cools and cannot hold as much water vapor, and becomes saturated. When you hear meteorologists talk about a weather front, they're referring to the place where two air masses meet. Rain and snow can also occur when warm moist ocean air travels over comparatively cool land.

From a marine science perspective, this is an important process for several reasons. One is that these movements redistribute heat around the Earth. A second is that precipitation is our primary source of fresh water. Ultimately, all aquifers (underground water),

AEROSOLS AND HEALTH

While water vapor isn't a health hazard, aerosols can be. Smoke, air pollution, dust, and pollen can all be detrimental to your respiratory system, and the respiratory systems of other organisms. The effects can range from irritation and allergies to lung disease.

If you live in an urban area, chances are that you're familiar with smog, which gets its name from smoke and fog combined. Most forms of smog and atmospheric haze result from auto exhaust, second-hand smoke, industrial processes, and other air pollution sources. Although some sources are natural, humans put millions of metric tons of aerosols into the air annually.

Fortunately, because dust, smoke, pollen, and similar aerosols exist in nature, our bodies have mechanisms for reducing their effects. Your sinuses protect your lungs by trapping many particles with each breath. Additionally, your trachea and other breathing passages have cilia (microscopic hairs) and coatings that capture particles before they can enter your lungs. One of the dangers of smoking is that it overwhelms or destroys these natural cleaning mecha-

nisms. Cigarette smoke particles and other aerosol particles accumulate far faster than your systems can remove them, impairing lung function and commonly resulting in lung disease.

Natural defenses don't protect us effectively from particles smaller than about 2.5 microns. Particles that small don't make up a significant volume of most natural aerosols, but they are common in human-produced aerosols. You may have heard that some rescue workers at the 2001 World Trade Center disaster have ongoing respiratory problems that resemble asthma. Their symptoms are caused by aerosols that lodged in the tiny, branching airways in their lungs that would normally trap pockets of air.

Modern efforts to reduce and control air pollution are helping. In addition, you may have heard of HEPA (High Efficiency Particulate Air) filters for portable air cleaners, vacuum cleaners, and central air conditioning systems. These filters remove particles as small as 0.1 microns, effectively eliminating many of the harmful aerosols.

rivers, and lakes get their fresh water from rain or snow. This is the part of the hydrologic cycle (see Chapter 9) that returns water from the sea back to land, giving it the potential to carry essential nutrients (including nitrogen compounds that originated in living material) into the ocean.

The Earth's Heat Balance

Approximately what percent of solar energy directed toward Earth reaches Earth's surface?

What would happen if the solar radiation coming to Earth and energy being reradiated into space were imbalanced?

As you've learned, the sun is the major source of energy for the Earth's surface. However, not all of the solar energy (sunlight) directed toward Earth makes it to Earth's surface. The atmosphere

INTERNET PORTAL

SCILINKS. NSTA

Topic: Heat Budget
Go To: www.scilinks.org
Code: LOP2215

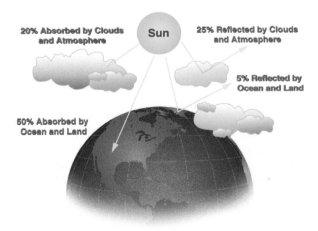

Incoming Solar Energy

20% Absorbed by Clouds and Atmosphere

Sun

25% Reflected by Clouds and Atmosphere

5% Reflected by Ocean and Land

50% Absorbed by Ocean and Land

Figure 10-5

Energy balance.

About 70% of the sun's energy reaching Earth is absorbed by the atmosphere and the Earth's surface. The remaining 30% is reflected back into space. To maintain a balance with the energy coming from the sun, the atmosphere, land, and ocean reradiates infrared radiation through various paths back into space.

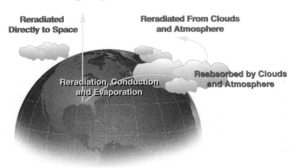

Outgoing Radiation

Reradiated Directly to Space

Reradiated From Clouds and Atmosphere

Reradiation, Conduction and Evaporation

Reabsorbed by Clouds and Atmosphere

either absorbs or reflects about 45% of it. This is a good thing – the atmosphere protects us from ultraviolet radiation, and life as we know it couldn't exist if the atmosphere transmitted all of the sun's energy. Of the 55% of the sun's energy that does reach the surface, 5% is reflected and 50% is absorbed. Half of the Earth's surface receives solar energy at any time. Of that, each square centimeter (0.15 square inches) receives about 2 calories per minute of solar energy.

That's a lot of energy, and it raises a question. Where does all the energy go? As discussed in Chapter 4, due to entropy, ultimately all energy ends up as heat. The Earth must be losing heat or it would be quite hot by now—too hot for life. The explanation is that the Earth sends exactly the same amount of energy coming in through radiation back into space. This is easiest to understand by looking at the path energy follows once it enters the atmosphere.

Solar energy consists primarily of visible, ultraviolet, and infrared light. Visible light makes it through the atmosphere to the Earth's surface with little absorption. The ozone layer in the stratosphere absorbs most of the ultraviolet light.

One third of the solar energy that reaches Earth reflects back into space off clouds and atmospheric particles, and off snow and reflective objects on the Earth's surface. The measure of the amount of energy something reflects is called *albedo* and the higher the albedo, the higher the reflectivity. Snow has a high albedo, whereas black sand has a low albedo.

The ocean, other water bodies and the land absorb much of the infrared radiation that reaches the Earth's surface. When water evaporates from these surfaces, it rises and releases latent heat into the atmosphere. Since most evaporation is from tropical ocean latitudes, this is the major source of heat for Earth's atmosphere. Tropical air, rich in water vapor, absorbs the heat. This drives the circulation of the atmosphere.

To maintain a balance with the energy coming from the sun, eventually much of the energy Earth absorbs reradiates through various paths back into space as infrared radiation. If this process were unbalanced over the long term with more energy coming in than leaving, the Earth would grow hotter and hotter until life perished.

Because the atmosphere absorbs infrared radiation, it tends to reradiate a lot of the heat back to the Earth's surface in the troposphere and stratosphere. This is called the *greenhouse effect*, and it effectively keeps the Earth habitable. Without the greenhouse effect, the Earth's temperature would be on average about 35°C (95°F) colder.

INTERNET PORTAL

SCiLINKS. NSTA

Topic: Light Absorption
Go To: www.scilinks.org
Code: LOP2220

Figure 10-6

Angle of incidence.
Light from a single source doesn't strike all parts of a sphere evenly. **(A)** Where light strikes the sphere at an angle of incidence of 90° degrees, energy is concentrated in a smaller area on the sphere than **(B)** where the sphere curves away from the light source and the angle of incidence is greater.

Uneven Heating

What factors cause Earth to heat unevenly?

What causes convection?

Unless you live close to the equator, you only have to watch the seasons to realize that the sun doesn't heat the Earth evenly. If it did, there would be little change in temperature over the course of a year. There are two primary factors that cause the Earth to heat unevenly. The first is that the Earth is spherical. The second is that the Earth's axis of rotation is tilted.

As you can see in figure 10-6, light from a single source doesn't strike a sphere evenly. A small part of the sphere receives perpendicular light rays, but most of the sphere receives slanted rays.

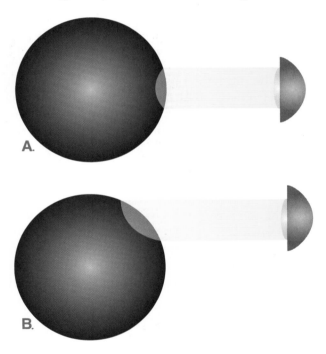

This means, for instance, that one square meter of sunlight traveling toward Earth will fall on roughly a square meter of ground when the sun is directly overhead. Because the angle of incidence differs near the poles, however, a square meter of sunlight will shine on a much larger area. The result is that the same amount of solar energy spreads over a wider area. This is why the Arctic and Antarctic are colder than the low latitudes around the equator. The farther north or south you go, the more slanted the solar energy is that reaches the surface.

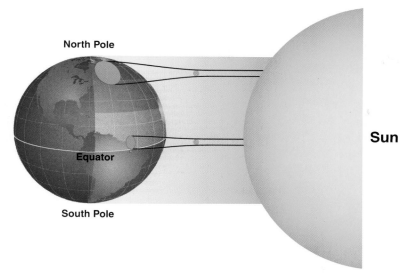

North Pole

Equator

South Pole

Sun

Figure 10-7

Angle of incidence on the Earth.

One square meter of sunlight traveling toward Earth will fall on roughly a square meter of ground if it shines onto the equator. Because the angle of incidence differs near the poles, however, a square meter of sunlight will shine on a much larger area. This spreads the same amount of solar energy over a larger area.

Another influence is the tilt of the Earth. The Earth rotates with its axis approximately 23.5° from perpendicular to the plane of its orbit around the sun. This is called the Earth's *axial inclination*. Due to this tilt, the latitude of the Earth receiving perpendicular rays from the sun isn't always the equator. Rather, the latitude changes throughout the year. It "migrates" between the Tropic of Cancer (23.5° north latitude) and the Tropic of Capricorn (23.5° south latitude). On the longest day of the year for each hemisphere, the sun is directly overhead at the Tropic line.

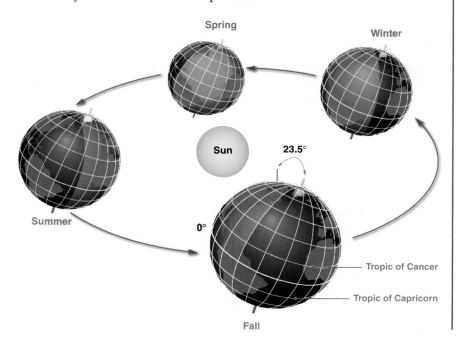

Spring

Winter

Sun

23.5°

0°

Summer

Tropic of Cancer

Tropic of Capricorn

Fall

Figure 10-8

Seasonal Changes.

Because the Earth's axis is offset from that of Earth's orbit around the sun by 23.5°, the part of the Earth where the sun is directly overhead "migrates" between the Tropic of Cancer (23.5° north latitude) and the Tropic of Capricorn (23.5° south latitude). During summer in the Northern Hemisphere, the Earth is tilted with the North Pole toward the sun. During the winter in the Northern Hemisphere, the Earth is tilted with the North Pole away from the sun.

Topic: Seasons
Go To: www.scilinks.org
Code: LOP2225

Figure 10-9

Elliptical orbit.

Because the Earth's orbit around the sun is slightly elliptical, the Earth receives more solar energy when its orbit comes closer to the sun, during the Northern Hemisphere's winter. The Earth is approximately 146 million kilometers (91 million millions) from the sun at the closest point, and 152 million kilometers (94.5 million miles) at its most distant point. The ellipse in the illustration is exaggerated to show the concept. If the orbit were drawn to scale, the elliptical shape would be so slight that to the eye, it would simply look like a circle. The land and water mass distributions of the hemispheres moderate the slight differences in solar energy. Therefore, the difference in the orbital distance is not considered a significant factor in seasonal temperatures.

Animals Collection, NOAA's Ark

Figure 10-10

Gray whale.

Aerial view of a gray whale (*Eschrichtius robustus*).

Because the angle of incidence changes as the Earth orbits the sun, the amount of solar energy falling on a particular location changes, causing the seasons. During summer in the Northern Hemisphere, the Earth is tilted with the North Pole toward the sun. During the winter in the Northern Hemisphere, the Earth is tilted with the North Pole away from the sun. This is why the Southern Hemisphere is always in the "opposite" season from the Northern Hemisphere. The amount of solar energy doesn't change much close to the equator, no matter what the time of year, so there's little noticeable seasonal change in most equatorial climates.

Another cause of uneven heating is that the Earth's orbit around the sun isn't circular, but very slightly elliptical. The Earth

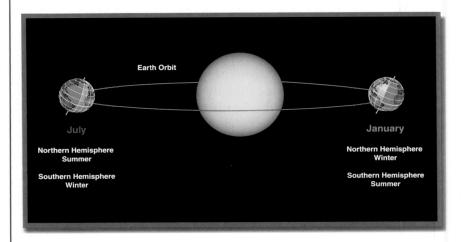

receives slightly more solar energy when its orbit brings it closer to the sun. However, the effect on Earth's temperature is minor, and it is the opposite of what you might at first think. The Earth is actually closer to the sun during the winter in the Northern Hemisphere and farther away during the summer. This has a negligible effect on seasonal temperatures, however, because the differences in land and water mass in the two hemispheres tend to balance and moderate seasonal differences.

The biological importance of the seasons is easy to notice in most areas of the United States. For example, in most of the east, the color change and falling of leaves marks autumn. In addition, many species of terrestrial birds and other animals migrate with the seasons. This is also true in the marine environment. Along the west coast, gray whales annually migrate to Arctic waters to feed off blooming krill and other plankton in the summer. As winter approaches, the gray whales swim south to breed in the warm waters around the Mexican Baja Peninsula. This predictable pattern, at one time economically important for whaling, has become economically important for whale watching and ecotourism.

The uneven heating of the Earth does more than cause the seasons. It also causes weather, due in part to *convection*. Convection is the vertical movement of currents caused by temperature differences in a fluid such as air. As explained in Chapter 13, convection currents occur in the Earth's interior as well as in the atmosphere.

Convection results when the sun warms the Earth's surface, which in turn warms the air above it. The warm air becomes less dense and rises. As the warm air rises, cool, dense air comes in to replace it. If there's a local heat source, airflow from a convection current can result. Imagine a hot fireplace. The fireplace heats the air in the room, which rises toward the ceiling. Cool air comes in to replace the heated air, which in turn warms and rises. As the warm air rises away from the fireplace, it moves to a cooler part of the room. The air then cools and sinks. This process continues, creating a circular airflow pattern.

Figure 10-11

Convection.

Convection results when air is warmed, becomes less dense, and rises. Then, cool, dense air replaces it. The fireplace heats the air, which rises to the ceiling. Cool air comes in to replace the heated air, which in turn warms and rises. This creates a circular airflow pattern.

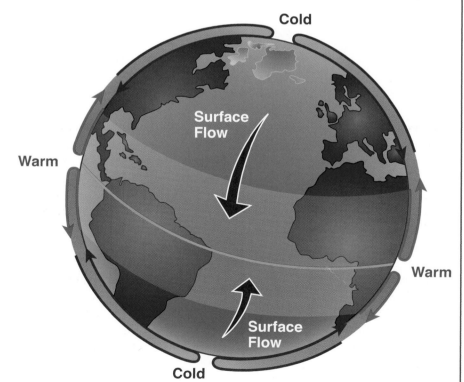

Figure 10-12

Idealized convection flow.

In a simplistic convection current, air in the tropics heats and rises. Cool air from the poles replaces the rising air. The warm air circulates toward the poles, where it cools and sinks. This movement creates a general global pattern of winds moving air between the poles and the equator.

Topic: Convection within the Atmosphere
Go To: www.scilinks.org
Code: LOP2230

On the Earth, you can think of the tropics as the fireplace and the poles as the cold parts of the room away from the fireplace. Air at the tropics is heated by rain, which releases latent heat. It is also heated by absorbing infrared radiation from the ocean. This heated, warm air rises. Cool air from the higher latitudes replaces the rising air. The warm air circulates toward the poles, where it cools and sinks. This is how solar energy absorbed by Earth's surface, mostly by the ocean, causes a general global pattern of winds moving air between the poles and the equator. As you'll see shortly, however, there's a bit more to it than this, or there would be no east or west winds.

ARE YOU LEARNING?

1. Air is about _____ % nitrogen.

   A. 78
   B. 75
   C. 21
   D. 0.03

2. The layer of the atmosphere next to the ground is the _____. The layer that extends into space is the _____.

   A. stratosphere, thermosphere
   B. thermosphere, troposphere
   C. troposphere, mesosphere
   D. troposphere, thermosphere

3. As the amount of water vapor in air increases, the air's density

   A. increases.
   B. decreases.

4. _____ can result when an air mass rapidly cools, causing water vapor to condense.

   A. Rain or snow
   B. Thunder
   C. A wave front
   D. Drought

5. About _____% of the sunlight that reaches the top of the atmosphere is absorbed by the Earth's surface.

   A. 75
   B. 66
   C. 50
   D. 25

6. If the Earth consistently absorbed more energy from the sun than it radiated to space,

   A. the Earth would grow hotter and hotter.
   B. there would be no noticeable effect.
   C. the energy would be absorbed and the Earth would be colder.
   D. there would be less energy radiated from the sun.

7. The sun heats the Earth unevenly because (choose all that apply)

   A. the Earth is a sphere.
   B. the Earth is tilted on its axis.
   C. the Earth has a solid core.
   D. the Earth is in an elliptical orbit.

8. Convection is caused by

   A. warm air rising and cool air flowing in to replace it.
   B. changes in the wind.
   C. large flocks of migrating birds.
   D. all of the above

The Coriolis Effect

Deflection to the Right or Left

What is the Coriolis effect?

If global convection currents cause air to move between the equator and the poles, how is it we have winds that blow east and west as well as north and south? The answer lies in a phenomenon called the *Coriolis effect*, named for Gaspard-Gustave Coriolis (1792-1843), a French civil engineer and mathematician who explained it. The Coriolis effect is the tendency for the path of a moving object to deflect to the right in the Northern Hemisphere and to the left in the Southern Hemisphere.

The Coriolis effect is a significant concept. As you'll read below, it explains why we have winds in all directions, not just to and from the north. Chapter 11 explains that the Coriolis effect also influences ocean currents. The Coriolis effect is a major factor affecting the distribution of the Earth's heat, nutrients, and many types of life by shaping the flow of wind and currents. Without the Coriolis effect, Christopher Columbus would not have had the winds he needed to reach the New World.

STUDY QUESTIONS

Find the answers as you read.

1. What is the *Coriolis effect*?

2. What causes the Coriolis effect?

INTERNET PORTAL

SCiLINKS. NSTA

Topic: The Coriolis effect
Go To: www.scilinks.org
Code: LOP2235

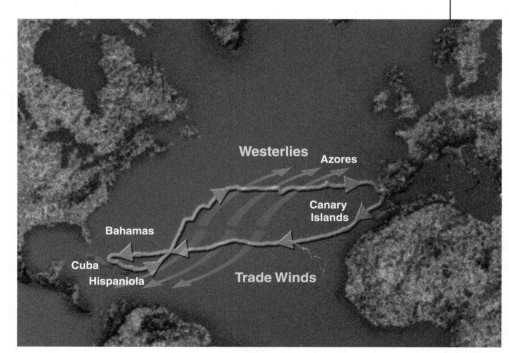

Westerlies   Azores

Canary
Islands

Bahamas

Cuba

Hispaniola

Trade Winds

Figure 10-13

Columbus and the Coriolis effect.

Christopher Columbus reached the New World thanks to the Coriolis effect, which provided the necessary trade winds for his journey.

The Earth's Rotation

What causes the Coriolis effect?

The Coriolis effect is caused by the Earth's rotation, which adds an apparent sideways motion to objects moving over the Earth's surface. To understand this, first assume you're standing on the equator and that a friend is standing near the North Pole. The ground doesn't seem to be moving to either of you. However, suppose someone watches from a fixed point in space far away from the Earth. Because the Earth rotates, this person sees that you and your friend are traveling in circles around the Earth's axis. Because of your location, you move through a larger circle for each rotation than your friend does. However, you and your friend both complete your circle in the same time – one day. Therefore, you are moving much more quickly than your friend.

Now suppose your friend stands on top of the North Pole while another friend stands at 45° north latitude, between you and your friend at the pole. If you could see your friends, they would appear motionless to you. But, someone watching from a fixed point in space would see otherwise. To that person, your friend on the North Pole turns around but otherwise doesn't move. Your friend at 45° north is moving in a circle around the Earth's axis, but not as quickly as you.

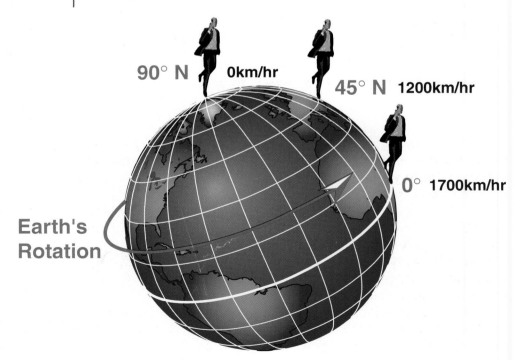

Figure 10-14

Relative motion.

In this perspective from space there are three people—one at the North Pole, one at 45° north latitude, and one on the equator. Relative to each other, the three people on Earth are motionless. To the observer in space, the three move at different rates.

90° N   0km/hr

45° N   1200km/hr

Earth's Rotation

0°   1700km/hr

A. View From Space

B. View From A Fixed Point Above The Earth

Let's suppose you and your two friends have really strong throwing arms. Your friend at the North Pole throws a baseball in a straight line to you at the equator. The throw misses, and to you it looked like it curved to your friend's right. What happened?

Let's look at it from a point in space. The throw was straight, but as the ball flew, the Earth continued to rotate eastward, *and you with it*. To anyone standing on the Earth, facing in the same direction the ball moved, it looked like the ball deflected to the right, but what's actually happening is that you rotate away with the Earth's spin as the ball travels.

Now let's consider your other friend at 45° north latitude. If this friend throws a ball to you, the same apparent deflection to the right happens. Your friend *is* moving with the Earth's rotation, but

Figure 10-15

Apparent deflection.

(A) From space it appears that the throw was straight, but as the ball flew through the air, the Earth (and the catcher) continued to rotate eastward, so the ball missed its target. **(B)** From the perspective of a person standing at the North Pole, a ball thrown straight to the equator misses its target and appears to curve to the right. Although it appears to the pitcher that the ball curved, what actually happened was the target rotated away during the ball's flight.

Figure 10-16

Major ocean gyres.

The Coriolis effect also affects air and water currents. The Earth's rotation tends to cause them to deflect to the right in the Northern Hemisphere and to the left in the Southern Hemisphere. In this way, the Coriolis effect creates circular airflow and current patterns such as the major ocean gyres, which you can read more about in Chapter 11.

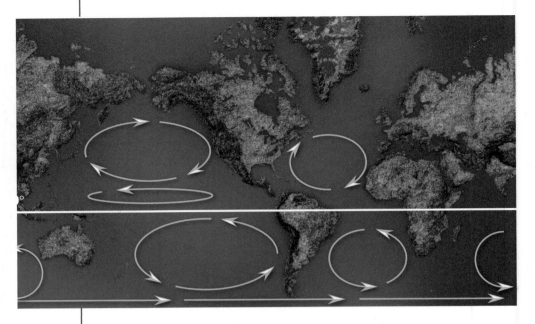

IT DOESN'T AFFECT YOUR TOILET

It's a common myth that because of the Coriolis effect, toilet water swirls clockwise when you flush in the Northern Hemisphere and counterclockwise in the Southern Hemisphere. A toilet is far too small for the Coriolis effect to have any influence. The swirl direction results from the toilet's design and can go either way in either hemisphere.

Similarly, when you're playing ball, the Coriolis effect isn't a concern. Ball-playing distances are too short for it to have any meaningful influence on a throw. Likewise, it doesn't affect the car when someone drives north or south. The friction of the tires against the road is far more powerful than the Coriolis effect. So don't try to blame a bad softball pitch or bad driving on the Coriolis effect.

more slowly than you are. Therefore, the Earth rotates you farther than your friend as the ball travels.

Finally, what happens when you throw the ball north to either of your friends? Again, the ball appears to deflect to your right. Before you throw the ball, it is *already* moving with you and the Earth's rotation. As the ball flies northward, it keeps the rotational velocity it had at the equator. But, as distance increases from the equator, the Earth's surface rotates eastward more slowly. Therefore, the ball appears to curve to the right because it moves eastward more quickly than the Earth's surface underneath it.

If you travel north or south on the Earth's surface near the poles, your rotational velocity changes more quickly than if you traveled a similar distance near the equator. Therefore, the Coriolis effect is greater at higher latitudes. If you travel along the equator, the Coriolis effect is zero, because your rotational velocity does not change.

You can think of the billions of molecules that make up air and water currents as tiny balls thrown by nature. As they travel, the Earth's rotation tends to deflect them to the right in the Northern Hemisphere and to the left in the Southern Hemisphere. You can see this tendency in Figure 10-16, which shows large ocean circulation patterns.

Remember, though, that many factors influence moving fluids. These factors include friction and the tendency of fluids to flow from high pressure to low pressure. Sometimes, such factors overcome the Coriolis effect.

ARE YOU LEARNING?

1. **The Coriolis effect is the tendency for the path of a moving object to shift to the right in the Northern Hemisphere and to the left in the Southern Hemisphere.**

   A. true

   B. false

2. **The Coriolis effect is caused by**

   A. the influence of a point in space.

   B. the rotation of the Earth.

   C. the Earth's currents.

   D. none of the above

The Winds

The Coriolis Effect and the Wind

How does the Coriolis effect influence the wind?

What is an atmospheric circulation cell?

Where are the trade winds found and what causes them?

Where are the westerlies found and what causes them?

Now let's see how convection and the Coriolis effect influence the wind. You recall that convection creates a general circulation pattern that moves air between the equator and the poles. The Coriolis effect deflects the air to the right in the Northern Hemisphere and to the left in the Southern Hemisphere. This gives the air a circular flow pattern rather than a straight north-south pattern. However, it's not as simple as a circular flow between the poles and the equator. The wind patterns exist in smaller regions called *atmospheric circulation cells*. Atmospheric circulation cells are six distinct air masses (three in each hemisphere) with individual airflow patterns.

The most important atmospheric circulation cells are the *Hadley cells*. These lie between the equator and approximately 30° north or south latitude. Using the Northern Hemisphere Hadley cell as an example, here's what happens.

Warm air rises at the equator and moves northward due to convection, as you learned. However, the air doesn't make it all the way to the North Pole. By the time it reaches approximately 30°N, it has become dense enough from cooling and moisture loss to sink. Most of the air descends and flows back toward the equator, deflecting to the right (westward) as it flows. This is what causes the trade winds, which flow westward between approximately 30°

STUDY QUESTIONS

Find the answers as you read.

1. How does the Coriolis effect influence the wind?

2. What is an *atmospheric circulation cell*?

3. Where are the trade winds found and what causes them?

4. Where are the westerlies found and what causes them?

5. What are the differences between the *geographic equator* and the *meteorological/intertropical convergence zone (ITCZ) equator*?

6. What causes Earth's major deserts to exist in their current locations?

7. What effects do you expect on the ocean's salinity near a desert?

8. What are *monsoons*?

9. What are *extratropical cyclones* and *tropical cyclones*?

10. How do cyclones form?

11. Why does air circulate counterclockwise in a Northern Hemisphere cyclone?

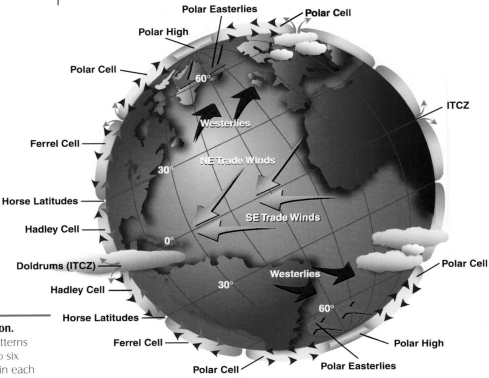

Figure 10-17

Global circulation.
Global wind patterns are divided into six regions (three in each hemisphere) called atmospheric circulation cells. The polar cells extend from about 60° to 90° latitude in each hemisphere. Ferrel cells extend from about 30° to 60°, and Hadley cells occupy the regions between about 30° and the equator. These atmospheric circulation cells produce the trade winds, the westerlies, and the polar easterlies in both hemispheres.

latitude and the equator. The trade winds were vital during the age of sail because they brought ships from Europe to the Americas.

Between approximately 30° and 60° latitude you find the *Ferrel cells*. Ferrel cells exist because *some* of the wind that descends from the Hadley cells doesn't turn toward the equator. Instead, it continues on toward the poles, again shifting to the right (to the left in the Southern Hemisphere) as it moves. This airflow forms the westerlies, which blow toward the east (they're called "westerlies" because they come *from* the west).

This gives you some idea of how sailing vessels traveled between Europe and America. To reach America from Europe, they sailed west in the low latitudes with the trade winds. To reach Europe from America, they sailed north and caught the westerlies to sail east. Chapter 11 goes into more detail about this.

The last are the *Polar cells*, which lie between approximately 50° to 60° and the poles. The airflow in a Polar cell is similar to a Hadley cell. Warm air at 60° rises and flows toward the pole, where it cools, descends, and flows back toward the equator. The Coriolis effect deflects it, so that the prevailing polar winds go to the west.

The south-flowing cold air from the Polar cells affects the air flowing north and eastward in the Ferrel cells. The two air masses don't easily mix due to differing densities and temperatures. It is convection and released latent heat at the poles that drives the Ferrel and Polar cells, especially in winter storms.

Intertropical Convergence Zones and Atmospheric Heat Engine

What are the differences between the geographic equator *and the* meteorological/intertropical convergence zone (ITCZ) equator?

What causes the Earth's major deserts to exist in their current locations?

What effects do you expect on the ocean's salinity near a desert?

If you locate the Earth's major deserts on a map, you'll see that the 30° north or south latitude line runs through most of them. At about 30° latitude, dry air sinks along the edge of each hemisphere's Hadley cell. Much of this air forms the trade winds, which gain moisture and heat from warm ocean water as they blow toward the equator. The trade winds meet and rise in a region called the ITCZ, or *intertropical convergence zone.* Vertical movement of air in the ITCZ releases large amounts of heat and moisture. Water vapor condenses in the rising air, warming the air relative to the air that surrounds it. Convection and rainstorms result. Some of the world's wettest climates are in the ITCZ. Surface winds are weak. Sailors called this area the *doldrums* because they could be stranded there for long periods without wind.

The ITCZ strongly influences climate and weather, and the seasons and landmasses affect the ITCZ. For this reason, there's a difference between the geographic equator and the *meteorological, or ITCZ, equator.* The *geographic equator* is at 0° latitude. The ITCZ equator is an imaginary line marking the temperature equilibrium between the hemispheres that shifts north and south of the geographic equator with seasonal changes. It shifts because land has lower heat capacity than water, and there is more landmass in the Northern Hemisphere. It's also not a straight line because landmasses affect its location. The ITCZ equator is important because atmospheric circulation is approximately symmetrical on either side of it—not the geographic equator.

Now let's return to 30° latitude, where dry air sinks along the boundary of the Hadley and Ferrel cells in each hemisphere. Here,

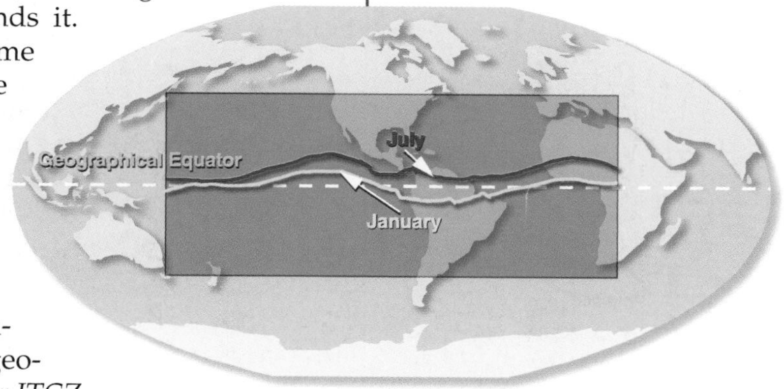

Figure 10-18a

The geographic and meteorological equators and world precipitation.

The geographic equator (dotted line) lies at 0°. The meteorological (ITCZ) equator - red and blue lines - shifts north and south of the geographic equator.

Figure 10-18b

Annual total precipitation map.

As you can see, most precipitation occurs in the tropics, where the rain releases latent heat, warming the atmosphere, and driving winds. Almost all the heating of the atmosphere occurs in this region, mostly in the west Pacific and eastern Indian Ocean. On this chart, yellow is low precipitation and red is high. Precipitation numbers are in centimeters.

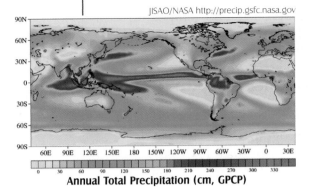

JISAO/NASA http://precip.gsfc.nasa.gov

Annual Total Precipitation (cm, GPCP)

too, winds can cease for extended periods. Sailors called these regions the *horse latitudes*. The name came from the carcasses of horses thrown overboard after stranded ships ran out of enough fresh water for both the sailors and the livestock.

The downward flow of dry air at about 30° latitude leads to widespread areas at the surface of the Earth that experience significant evaporation and little rainfall. This is why you find most of the Earth's major deserts at this latitude. In the ocean, more water evaporates than is returned to the ocean by rainfall or by the flow of rivers from land. Therefore, the ocean's surface salinity around 30° latitude is higher than at most other latitudes.

Figure 10-19

The world's major deserts.

Most of the Earth's major deserts lie along 30° latitude because dry air is brought to the surface, leading to significant evaporation and little rainfall.

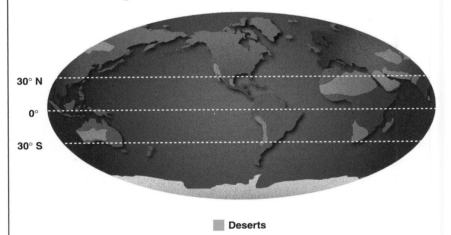

■ **Deserts**

Monsoons and Cyclones

What are monsoons?

What are extratropical cyclones *and* tropical cyclones?

How do cyclones form?

Why does air circulate counterclockwise in a Northern Hemisphere cyclone?

Convection, the Coriolis effect, and atmospheric circulation cells explain the general wind and climate patterns, but what about monsoons and cyclones?

Monsoons (from the Arabic *mausim* meaning *season*) are seasonal wind pattern changes caused by heating or cooling on the continents. Monsoons cause summers with significant rainfall and winters with very little. Monsoons result when air warmed by a hot landmass rises. Warm, moist air from the ocean flows in to replace it; this air in turn also rises. As the moisture-filled air ascends, it cools, causing rain. When winter comes, the cycle reverses. The wind reverses and the land has very little rain.

Monsoons are common on the west coast of India and in other parts of southeast Asia. The weather pattern is so strong and predictable that early traders used to plan their voyages based on the monsoon season. They would sail with the wind toward land during the summer and then sail away with the wind during the winter.

Cyclones are large rotating storm systems of low-pressure air with converging winds at the center. Cyclones can become the particularly intense storms that you know as typhoons (in the Northwest Pacific Ocean) or hurricanes (in the Northeast Pacific and North Atlantic Ocean). There are two main types: *extratropical* and *tropical*. You might think that extratropical cyclones form outside the tropics and tropical cyclones form within the tropics, but there's more to it than that.

Tropical cyclones form within a single atmospheric cell. They form in the low latitudes; hence, they're called "tropical." Extratropical cyclones form at higher latitudes.

In both cases, cyclones form where moist winds get drawn into a low-pressure area. The Coriolis effect causes the winds to spiral inward. Convection cells form in the rising air and produce rain as water vapor condenses. The formation of rain high in the storm releases latent heat, warms the atmosphere, causes air pressure to decrease further, and pulls more air into the system at the surface. The cyclone winds intensify as long as these processes continue. A tropical cyclone can experience explosive growth because of extremely rapid transport of heat and moisture into the atmosphere from the surface of the warm, tropical ocean. The storm can intensify until it reaches typhoon or hurricane strength. (*Typhoon* comes from the Chinese *tai fung*, meaning *great wind*; *hurricane* comes from the name of the Caribbean Taino tribe's god *Huracan*.) As the storm passes over land or cool water, however, there's no more water vapor supplying heat to continue the pattern, and it loses its source of energy and dissipates. This is why hurricanes and typhoons quickly lose strength when they move inland, even though they can still bring torrential rains and floods.

An extratropical cyclone also forms as an area of low air pressure intensifies. This frequently occurs along the boundary between the westbound polar winds and the eastbound westerlies. Because

Image courtesy of MODIS Rapid Response Project at NASA/GSFC

Figure 10-20

A tropical cyclone.

This satellite image shows Hurricane Katrina as it approached the Gulf Coast on August 29, 2005.

the air masses that meet along this boundary have different densities, they don't mix easily. If the westerlies become stronger, they push more northward and bulge into the polar cell. This creates a low-pressure area on the western side of the bulge, so the polar air turns in that direction, still carrying the wind energy it already has. As the warm air of the westerlies rises, cool polar air replaces it. At the surface, winds spiral in towards the center of the low-pressure area. Higher in the atmosphere, the system receives energy as rain forms, releasing heat. The extratropical cyclone travels along the boundary between the Hadley cell and the polar Ferrel cell.

Extratropical cyclones don't become hurricanes or typhoons, but they cause weather patterns like the "nor'easters" that cause hurricane-strength winds, huge ocean waves, and rain-or snowstorms in latitudes outside of the tropics. These are the storms that each year cost human lives and millions of dollars in weather damage, energy for heating, and a cessation in fishing and shipping.

Note that a cyclone rotates to the left (counterclockwise) in the Northern Hemisphere and to the right (clockwise) in the Southern Hemisphere. A strong difference in air pressure at the Earth's surface acts to pull winds directly into an area of low air pressure. The Coriolis effect deflects the winds to the right in the Northern Hemisphere. The combined influence of the pressure gradient, the Coriolis effect, and friction at the surface causes winds to blow in a counterclockwise, spiral pattern into the low-pressure area.

You might think that we'd be better off without cyclones, because they are capable of causing widespread devastation and intense human suffering. Actually, though, these cyclones serve an important purpose in nature. They move tremendous amounts of heat from the tropics to higher latitudes very quickly – far more quickly than simple convection would. A typical tropical cyclone can, in a single day, release about as much energy as the US uses in an entire year! Extratropical cyclones mix warmth from the tropics with polar air, helping to redistribute the heat that is important to life on the Earth.

Figure 10-21

Extratropical cyclone formation.

Extratropical cyclones are commonly much larger than tropical cyclones. They can be immensely powerful, causing weather patterns like the "nor'easters" that cause strong winds, huge ocean waves, and rain or snowstorms at high latitudes.

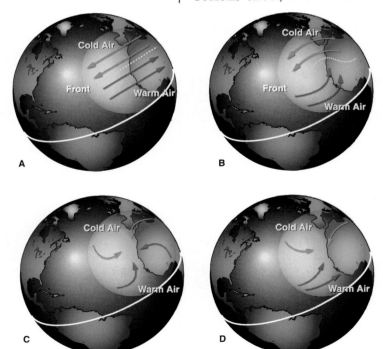

A   B   C   D

1. **The Coriolis effect tends to influence the wind by giving it a(n)**

    A. circular flow pattern.

    B. unpredictable flow pattern.

    C. north-south flow pattern.

    D. none of the above

2. **An atmospheric circulation cell is a distinct air mass that has the same airflow pattern as all other cells, but different weather.**

    A. true

    B. false

3. **The trade winds are found between approximately _____, and blow _____.**

    A. 30° and 60° latitude, toward the poles

    B. 0° and 30° latitude, toward the poles

    C. 30° and 60° latitude, toward the equator

    D. 0° and 30° latitude, toward the equator

4. **The westerlies are found between approximately _____, and blow _____.**

    A. 30° and 60° latitude, toward the poles

    B. 0° and 30° latitude, toward the poles

    C. 30° and 60° latitude, toward the equator

    D. 0° and 30° latitude, toward the equator

5. **The _____equator is at 0° latitude. The _____ equator is an imaginary line marking the temperature equilibrium between the hemispheres.**

    A. geographic, ITCZ/meteorological

    B. ITCZ/meteorological, geographic

6. **Most of the Earth's major deserts occur (choose all that apply)**

    A. at about 30° latitude.

    B. where the vertical airflow is downward.

    C. where the Hadley and Ferrel cells meet.

    D. only on the geographic equator.

7. **You would expect the ocean's surface near a desert to have _____ salinity compared to the average ocean salinity.**

    A. the same

    B. lower

    C. higher

    D. the answer cannot be determined from the question

8. **A monsoon is**

    A. a local seasonal weather pattern that causes summers to be very dry.

    B. a local seasonal weather pattern that causes winters to be very dry.

    C. a large rotating storm.

    D. none of the above

9. **A(n) _____ forms within a single atmospheric cell, whereas a _____ forms where Polar and Ferrel cells meet.**

    A. extratropical cyclone, monsoon

    B. monsoon, tropical cyclone

    C. tropical cyclone, monsoon

    D. none of the above

10. **Cyclones form where**

    A. high-pressure air pushes wind away, causing a drain effect.

    B. wind is drawn into a low-pressure area at the Earth's surface, forming a spiral pattern.

    C. two air masses meet head on and roll backwards, causing a typhoon and a hurricane.

    D. all of the above

11. **Air circulates counterclockwise in a Northern Hemisphere cyclone because the low pressure that draws in the winds is stronger than the Coriolis effect.**

    A. true

    B. false

New Terms You Learned

- **aerosols** suspensions of fine liquid and/or solid droplets in the air (p. 10-6)

- **albedo** a measure of reflectivity; the higher the albedo, the higher the reflectivity (p. 10-9)

- **atmospheric circulation cells** six distinct air masses (three in each hemisphere) with individual air flow patterns (p. 10-19)

- **axial inclination** the angle of tilt measured with 0° at perpendicular between a planet's rotation axis and the plane of its orbit around the sun (p. 10-11)

- **chlorofluorocarbon (CFC)** a hydrocarbon gas that includes fluorine and chlorine in the hydrocarbon molecule; used in the manufacture of aerosol sprays, packing materials, solvents and refrigerants; known to destroy ozone in the atmosphere (p. 10-5)

- **convection** a vertical circulation pattern in a gas or liquid caused by hot material rising and cold material sinking (p. 10-13)

- **Coriolis effect** the tendency for the path of an object moving in the North Hemisphere to deflect to the right, or to deflect left when moving in the Southern Hemisphere (p. 10-15)

- **cyclone** large rotating storm system of low pressure air with converging winds at the center (p. 10-23)

- **doldrums** a region near the equator where the Trade Winds cease for extended periods (p. 10-21)

- **extratropical cyclone** large rotating storm system of low pressure air that forms where the Ferrel and Polar cells meet (p. 10-23)

- **Ferrel cells** atmospheric circulation cells between approximately 30° and 60° latitude (p. 10-20)

- **geographic equator** an imaginary line around the Earth that separates the Northern and Southern hemispheres and is at 0° latitude (p. 10-21)

- **greenhouse effect** the ability of the Earth's atmosphere to hold and reuse energy close to the Earth's surface (p. 10-9)

- **Hadley cells** atmospheric circulation cells between the equator and approximately 30° latitude (p. 10-19)

- **horse latitudes** region at 30° latitude in both hemispheres where dry air sinks along the boundary of the Hadley and Ferrel cells; winds can cease for extended periods; name came from carcasses of horses thrown overboard by stranded ships (p. 10-22)

- **intertropical convergence zone (ITCZ)** an area where weather and climate are affected by the meeting of the Northern and Southern Hadley cells (p. 10-21)

- **intertropical convergence zone equator (ITCZ equator)** an imaginary line marking temperature equilibrium between the hemispheres that shifts slightly north and south of the geographic equator with seasonal changes; roughly the same as the meteorological equator (p. 10-21)

- **mesosphere** layer of atmosphere from 50,000 to 90,000 meters (31 to 56 miles) above sea level (p. 10-4)

- **meteorological equator** an imaginary line marking temperature equilibrium between the hemispheres that shifts slightly north and south of the geographic equator with seasonal changes; roughly the same as the ITCZ equator (p. 10-21)

- **monsoon** local seasonal wind pattern caused by heat from the continents that results in summers with significant rainfall and winters with very little rainfall (p. 10-22)

- **ozone** highly reactive oxygen gas molecule made up of three oxygen atoms (p. 10-5)

- **Polar cells** atmospheric circulation cell between approximately 50° to 60° latitude and the North or South pole (p. 10-20)

- **saturated air** air in which the rate of evaporation balances the rate of condensation (p. 10-6)

- **stratosphere** layer of atmosphere from 15,000 to 50,000 meters (9 to 31 miles) above sea level (p. 10-4)

- **thermosphere** outermost layer of atmosphere; from 90,000 meters (56 miles) above sea level into space (p. 10-4)
- **tropical cyclone** inward circulation of air around a low-pressure system; it forms within a single atmospheric cell, usually in low latitudes (p. 10-23)
- **troposphere** layer of atmosphere in contact with the surface Earth up to 15,000 meters (9 miles) above sea level (p. 10-4)

Chapter 10 in Review

1. List the components that make up air and diagram the atmosphere layers, labeling each one and its approximate location. Explain why most of the atmosphere is in the lower two layers.

2. Describe what causes rain and snow. How does the relationship between water vapor, air temperature, and air density relate?

3. Approximately what percent of solar energy directed toward Earth reaches Earth's surface? Explain why the Earth doesn't get significantly hotter despite all the solar energy that falls on it. What would happen if this process became imbalanced? What might cause an imbalance?

4. Identify the factors that make the Earth heat unevenly and explain why they do so. Why is it summer in the Northern Hemisphere even though the Earth is farther from the sun than it is in winter?

5. Describe the process of convection and how it relates to airflow on Earth. How does the relationship between water vapor, air temperature, and density relate to convection?

6. Explain what causes the Coriolis effect, and the influence it has on the wind.

7. Explain where the trade winds and the westerlies are located and explain what causes these winds. Describe the airflow patterns that characterize the six global atmospheric circulation cells and describe the role of these cells play in distributing heat on our planet.

8. What is the meteorological/ITCZ equator and why does it move?

9. Explain why the Earth's major deserts exist at approximately 30° latitude. How and why does this affect salinity in the nearby ocean?

10. Prepare a chart to show how monsoons, extratropical cyclones, and tropical cyclones are different and how they are similar.

11. Explain how cyclones form, where they get their energy, and what their role is in redistributing heat on Earth. Draw diagrams to show how their rotation develops.

Connecting Chapter Concepts – Science Scenarios

1. As evidenced by the seasons, sunlight doesn't fall evenly on the Earth. If it did, all parts of the world would have one continuous season.

   A. What is the *primary* cause of the four seasons, and how does this explain why seasons in the northern and southern hemisphere are opposite?

   B. Why do lower latitudes near the equator tend to be warmer than cooler latitudes near toward the poles?

   C. In what ways do seasonal changes affect the marine environment?

2. In the northern hemisphere, winds tend to flow in clockwise circular patterns with the bottom roughly at the equator and the top at about 30° north latitude.

   A. What is convection and how does it contribute to this wind pattern?

   B. What accounts for the clockwise flow of the winds?

   C. In the northern Atlantic, what do we call the winds that result from this flow?

Marine Science and the Real World

1. In urban environments, sometimes indoor air has more particulate matter than outdoor air. What would cause this? What can you do to reduce aerosols indoors?

2. Assume you're a scientist giving the federal government recommendations on how to restore the ozone layer. What recommendations would you present and why?

3. Pretend scientists are not sure whether the Earth rotates. However, you have empirical evidence through an experiment that the Coriolis effect is present. Use this as evidence to support an argument that the Earth must be rotating.

4. Although carbon dioxide and other greenhouse gases have increased since the Industrial Revolution, it's not conclusive that this alone will lead to significant global warming. Propose some reasons why.

5. Scientists think that global warming would, among other effects, increase the number of tropical cyclones. Why would this happen?

6. Some scientists believe it may be possible one day to stop tropical storms like typhoons and hurricanes. What would be reasons not to do so if it were possible?

References

Adler, R.F., G.J. Huffman, A. Chang, R. Ferraro, P. Xie, J. Janowiak, B. Rudolf, U. Schneider, S. Curtis, D. Bolvin, A. Gruber, J. Susskind, and P. Arkin. 2003. The Version 2 Global Precipitation Climatology Project (GPCP). Monthly Precipitation Analysis. (1979-Present). J. Hydrometeor. 4, 1147-1167

Cunningham, William P., Mary Ann Cunningham and Barbara Woodworth Saigo. 1999. *Environmental Science: A Global Concern.* Boston: McGraw-Hill.

Garrison, T. 2004. *Essentials of Oceanography.* Pacific Grove, CA: Brooks/ Cole, a division of Thomson Learning, Inc.

Gosline, Anna. 2004. CT Scans Explain Mysterious 9/11 Cough. *New Scientist.* 16:20. November. http://www.newscientist.com/article. ns?id=dn6741 http://www.newscientist.com/article.ns?id=dn6741

Klemm, Barbara, Francis M. Pottenger III, Thomas W. Speitel, S. Arthur Reed and Ann E. Coopersmith. 1991. *Hawaii Marine Science Studies: The Fluid Earth. Physical Science and Technology of the Marine Environment.* Honolulu, HI: Curriculum Research and Development Group.

Physical Oceanography. 1992. *Oceanus.* Special Issue 35 (no. 2).

Pickard, George, L., and William Emery. 1990. *Descriptive Physical Oceanography.* Oxford: Butterworth-Heinemann, Ltd.

Pond, Steven, and George L. Pickard. 1983. *Introductory Dynamical Oceanography.* Oxford: Butterworth-Heinemann Ltd.

Sverdrup, Keith A., Alyn C. Duxbury and Alison B. Duxbury. 2000. *An Introduction to the World's Oceans.* Boston: McGraw-Hill.

Tarbuck, Edward J. and Frederick K. Lutgens. 2000. *Earth Science.* Upper Saddle River: Prentice Hall.

The Delta Group. 2002. Trade Center Air Held Unprecedented Amounts of Very Fine Particles, Silicon, Sulfates, Metals, Say UC Davis Scientists. University of California, Davis. http://delta.ucdavis.edu/wtc_air.htm]

Thurman, Harold V., and Elizabeth A. Burton. 2001. *Introductory Oceanography.* New Jersey: Prentice Hall.

CHAPTER 11

Highways in the Sea

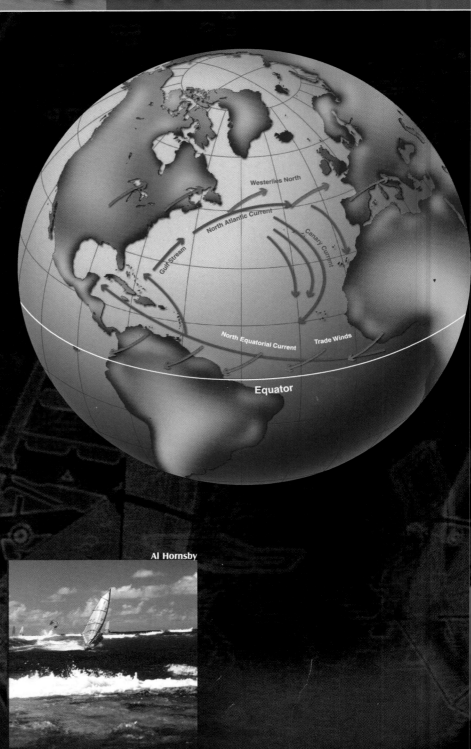

Photo Courtesy of Niagara Tourism & Convention Corp.

Al Hornsby

Going With the Flow

Ocean circulation plays a key role in controlling global climatic change. Its study helps scientists, including Steven Jayne, determine connections between circulation in the ocean and its effect on the Earth's climate.

"Large-scale ocean circulation is important to understand because it lets us know how the ocean interacts with the atmosphere and provides insight into the causes behind large-scale ocean circulation – crucial information when we consider the effects of global warming on the Earth's ocean and weather systems," says Jayne.

He first became interested in marine science in junior high school. "I was always interested in marine biology in general, but after watching one too many Jacques Cousteau specials, I knew my career path would include marine science and ocean research."

Jayne's principal research area is global ocean dynamics. He is currently hard at work developing statistical estimation techniques, for the Global Ocean Observing System (GOOS), for mapping ocean velocity and heat content. These techniques include using profiling floats, satellite gravimetry (information gathered from twin satellites launched in 2002 that accurately map variations in the Earth's gravity field), and satellite altimetry (which measures changes in sea level related to ocean circulation). He is also working on the development and application of new remote sensing techniques.

"Going on ships to do fieldwork is probably the most exciting part of my job. I've also worked in Greenland, drilling an ice core there for studies related to climate and temperature changes over the years. But, I would have to say that the most challenging part of this career has just been getting to where I am today; making my way through graduate school and all the work involved with that, like completing my thesis and developing my own research. These required a great deal of self-discipline and self-motivation – things that took time to develop."

To those planning on following in his footsteps, Jayne offers this advice: "To do well in this field, you'll need a good background in math and various science disciplines, such as biology, physics, geology, etc., to find that aspect of marine science that you enjoy and in which you can remain interested on a daily basis. That's what I did and things have worked out quite well for me. I truly enjoy what I do and can't imagine myself doing anything else."

Steven Jayne, ScD
Assistant Scientist, Department of Physical Oceanography, Woods Hole Oceanographic Institution

The English word *ocean* comes from the Greek word *okeanos* and the Latin *oceanus*. What's interesting is that *okeanos* and *oceanus* mean river, not ocean. The English word apparently dates back to Greek mariners who encountered a strong southerly current when they sailed out of the Mediterranean Sea. The Canary Current, as it's called today, is so strong that the Greeks thought they had sailed into an enormous river. Hence the word *okeanos* for what today we call the Atlantic Ocean.

In a sense, the Greeks were right. Ocean currents behave in many ways like rivers within the seas. It's amazing how much currents have shaped culture by influencing the early days of sea exploration. Islands such as Bermuda were settled and gained influence because they sat along the routes that the winds and currents forced merchants to travel. As you'll see in this chapter, currents have shaped battles at sea, ultimately leading to the decline of empires.

Although currents have had less influence on the transport of materials since the rise of powered shipping, modern concerns still relate to currents. Because ocean currents interconnect the various parts of the world, currents distribute pollution. As you'll see when you read about deep-sea currents, the source of pollution is not always obvious.

For example, scientists have been concerned about the declining health of many of the coral reefs around the Florida Keys. The problem was once thought to be the result of nutrients in runoff. (Chapter 6 explains that hard corals generally live in warm, *low-nutrient* water.) The question is "Where does the pollution come from?"

Many have looked to Miami and other major urban centers north of the Keys as the likely sources. However, recent evidence has called this into question, or at least provided an alternative explanation. The Gulf Stream, a great "river of the sea," tends to move urban water from south Florida north, away from the Keys. Preliminary studies by the National Underwater Research Center (NURC) in Key Largo, Florida provide some surprising results. The center is studying seawater samples from deep-water currents that come to the surface near the Keys. It turns out that these currents sometimes bring high levels of nutrients from well off shore, possibly from thousands of kilometers away. So which is the origin of the pollution – high levels of land-based nutrients from urban areas or seaborne nutrients from the depths? Perhaps, as is often the case in science, it may turn out to be both. For now it shows how little we know about the other 71% of our planet.

Surface Currents

Understanding what causes water and air currents and where they flow is fundamental to almost all marine sciences. It helps explain how heat, sediments, nutrients, and organisms move within and above the seas. This makes currents important whether you're studying climate, weather, minerals, sediments, or a regional ecosystem.

Causes of Currents

What forces are responsible for currents? What influences the direction and nature of these currents?

Deep and shallow areas of the sea have currents. Surface currents are generally from 0 to about 400 meters (1,300 feet) deep, although some go much deeper. Deep currents are those whose upper portions remain below the ocean surface. Different processes drive surface and deep currents. In this chapter, we will consider surface currents first and deep currents later.

There are two major factors that set ocean currents in motion: wind and variations in water density. Wind transfers momentum to the water it blows across by creating friction on the water's surface. Wind causes both surface currents and waves. (You can read more about waves in Chapter 12.) If the wind blows long enough in the same direction, it will cause a water current to develop. What happens if the wind then stops blowing? The current continues to flow until internal friction, or friction with the sea floor, dissipates its energy.

Wind-driven currents cause changes in sea level across horizontal distances. *Sea level* is defined as the average level of the sea's surface. You might think that if all waves were to disappear, the ocean's surface would be completely flat. This is not so. Wind driven currents at the sea surface cause slopes to develop. Also, when a landmass interrupts a current's flow, water mounds up against the land. The slope in the water surface causes a horizontal difference in water pressure. The water will tend to flow and even out this difference, which is called a pressure gradient. The steeper the "mound" of water, the larger and faster the current will be that carries the water away. The force that drives this current is called the *pressure gradient force.*

Differences in water density also cause horizontal differences in water pressure. The horizontal pressure gradient between two

STUDY QUESTIONS

Find the answers as you read.

1. What forces are responsible for currents? What influences the direction and nature of these currents?

2. What is a *gyre?*

3. How many gyres are there? Where are they?

4. What is *Ekman transport?* What is its role in wind-driven circulation?

5. Why do currents tend to flow around the periphery of an ocean basin?

6. What are *geostrophic currents?* How do they relate to ocean basin circulation patterns?

7. Why are western ocean boundary currents faster than eastern ocean boundary currents? How do western ocean boundary currents differ from eastern ocean boundary currents?

8. What is a *countercurrent?* What is an *undercurrent?*

9. What makes *upwelling* and *downwelling* occur? What biological effects do they have?

10. What role do currents play in transporting heat? How do currents affect climate?

11. What happens when an *El Niño Southern Oscillation (ENSO)* occurs? What effect does it have on weather, marine habitats, and human activity?

areas of different densities initiates a current. More dense water sinks below less dense water. For example, the atmosphere cools surface water near Greenland. As this happens, the water becomes denser and it sinks below water layers of less density. Later in this chapter, you will learn more about how density differences create deep currents.

As you have just learned, persistent winds set surface currents in motion. And, as discussed in the last chapter, the trade winds

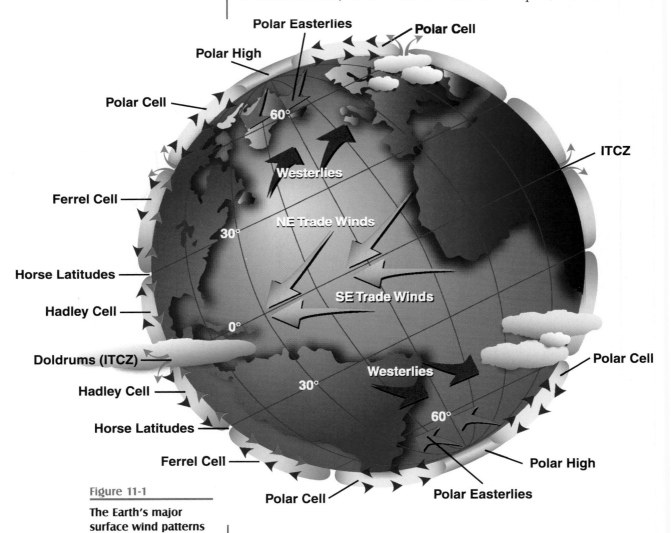

Figure 11-1

The Earth's major surface wind patterns in the Atlantic Ocean.

and the westerlies account for most the Earth's wind energy. If you compare a map of wind direction at the Earth's surface and a map of surface ocean currents, you'll notice similarities. You'll also notice differences. For example, continents force currents to turn.

Gyres

What is a gyre?

How many gyres are there? Where are they?

Large persistent currents in the ocean eventually run into land. (The Antarctic Circumpolar Current, which runs around Antarctica, is a notable exception.) Chapter 10 explains the Coriolis effect, which tends to deflect winds to the right in the Northern Hemisphere and to the left in the Southern Hemisphere. It tends to do the same thing with currents.

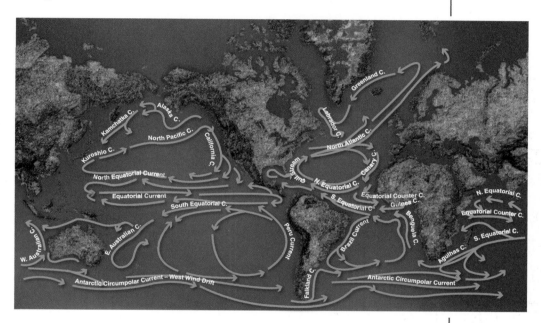

Figure 11-2

The major currents of the world ocean.

There are five major gyres: North and South Atlantic, North and South Pacific, and Indian.

The combination of the westerlies pushing water eastward along the upper latitudes of the Atlantic, the trade winds pushing it westward near the equator, and the Coriolis effect results in a circular flow in each ocean basin. This flow is called a *gyre* (pronounced "gi'er," from the Greek *gyros* meaning *circle*). There are five major gyres, one in each major ocean basin. The North Atlantic Gyre is perhaps the most studied, and since ocean gyres are generally similar, we'll use the North Atlantic Gyre as an example of how they work.

The North Atlantic Gyre is a single water flow, though oceanographers divide it into four interconnected currents. Each of these has distinct flow characteristics and temperatures, even though they're all part of the same gyre. Currents in other gyres are similarly interconnected.

In Figure 11-3, you can see that some, but not all, of the currents that make up the North Atlantic Gyre flow in the same general direction as the average winds. Obviously, winds alone do not determine the paths of surface currents. We have already mentioned the importance of ocean boundaries in deflecting currents. But, the flow of currents in all parts of the ocean is a balance of various factors, including the wind pressure gradient force, friction, and the Coriolis effect.

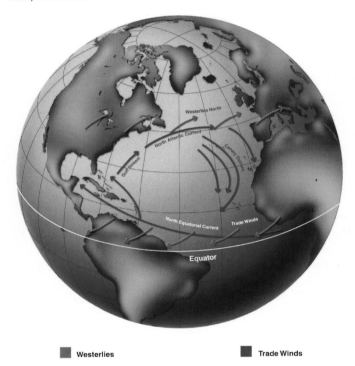

Figure 11-3

The North Atlantic Gyre.
Although the North Atlantic Gyre is a single phenomenon, like all gyres it's divided into separate currents. For the North Atlantic they are: the Gulf Stream (western ocean boundary), North Atlantic Current (transverse), Canary Current (eastern ocean boundary), and North Equatorial Current (transverse). The direction of flow of all of these currents results from a balance of factors that include wind, friction, and the Coriolis effect.

■ Westerlies   ■ Trade Winds

Ekman Transport

What is Ekman transport? What is its role in wind-driven circulation?

You've already learned that currents have a tendency to flow to the right in the Northern Hemisphere and to the left in the Southern Hemisphere because of the Coriolis effect. This results in an interesting phenomenon called *Ekman transport.*

One way to understand Ekman transport is to look at how it was discovered. During the 1890s, oceanographer Fridtjof Nansen led a polar research expedition in which his ship was deliberately allowed to freeze into Arctic ice for two years. He noticed that his ship tended to drift to the right of the wind. Nansen realized that he was observing an important phenomenon, which he eventually

concluded was related to the Coriolis effect. His ship was drifting with a current generated by friction with the wind. The current shifted to the right of the wind due to the Coriolis effect in the Northern Hemisphere.

When Nansen returned, he asked his graduate student, B. Walfrid Ekman, to determine how wind causes surface currents. Ekman understood that the friction of the wind on the surface of water, or on floating ships and icebergs, sets them in motion. Movement at the surface drags deeper water along, too, and the Coriolis effect acts on water moving at most depths. He hypothesized, therefore, that progressively deeper water must flow to the right of the water immediately above it. Moving water transfers energy through friction to deeper water, and the deeper water shifts to the right of the water pushing it. As a result, the current as a whole moves to the right of the wind.

This spiraling effect of water continually moving slightly to the right of the water above it (to the left in the Southern Hemisphere) is called an *Ekman spiral*. Ekman described the effect mathematically in 1908.

In picturing an Ekman spiral, *don't* think of it as a whirlpool. Instead, think of extremely thin layers of water, each flowing independently but affected by and provided energy by the layer above. Each water layer uses some of the energy transferred from the wind, but some energy is lost as heat due to turbulence in the water. The velocity of the current decreases with depth as more and more energy dissipates. As velocity decreases, the ability of shallower water to drag deeper water along also decreases. Eventually, a depth is reached where the wind-driven current dies out. Until this depth is reached, however, the Ekman spiral keeps shifting the flow of water to the right. It is important to realize that, although it is convenient to think of water moving in distinct layers, it really forms a continual spiral.

Although the Ekman spiral keeps shifting water to the right throughout the depth of the current, there's a net motion imparted to the water column down to *friction depth*. This motion is called Ekman transport. The net effect

Figure 11-4

The Ekman spiral.

The Coriolis effect influences water below the surface because water tends to flow in what can be imagined as layers. As depicted, the angular deflection of the Coriolis effect is initially quite small, but each water layer affects the one below it. The phenomenon is like the way a dealer can twist a deck of cards. Each individual water layer, like a card, acts independently but influences the one below it.

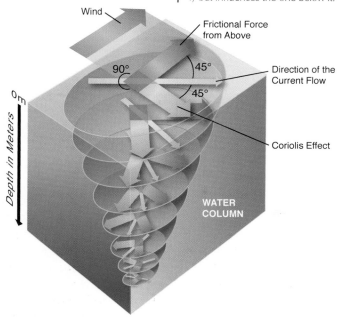

of Ekman transport in wind-driven circulation, averaging all the speeds and directions of the Ekman spiral, is to move water 90° to the right of the wind in the Northern Hemisphere, and to the left in the Southern Hemisphere.

Western Ocean Boundary Currents and Eastern Ocean Boundary Currents

Why do currents tend to flow around the periphery of an ocean basin?

What are geostrophic currents? How do they relate to ocean basin circulation patterns?

Why are western ocean boundary currents faster than eastern ocean boundary currents? How do western ocean boundary currents differ from eastern ocean boundary currents?

Anyone who's been on or near the ocean frequently can tell you it is rarely flat or calm. Although small areas can be completely calm and flat at times, if you looked at it overall, you'd find it has a "hilly" topography. The surface of the sea, as you learned earlier, would not really be flat even if you removed all the waves. Satellite pictures show that, in some areas, ocean circulation causes water to pile up, creating a dome or "hill." In other areas, water diverges, and "valleys" form. These differences rarely amount to more than a meter or so, yet they dramatically influence how currents flow.

Now let's see how a dome might form in the North Atlantic Gyre and how its presence will influence circulation in the gyre. As the westerlies and the trade winds push water along, Ekman transport tends to make the water go to the right, toward the center

Figure 11-5

A water dome in the North Atlantic.

In this satellite image, color represents height, with red the highest elevation and purple the lowest. Note how a conspicuous dome of water lies in the western Atlantic. The contour lines also show that the dome has a much steeper western boundary than eastern.

Adapted from Jet Propulsion Laboratory, NASA

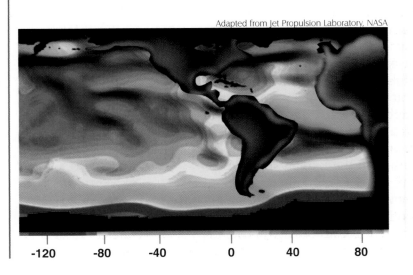

-120   -80   -40   0   40   80

of the gyre. This action piles up water to form a hill. The high point of this hill is about 1 meter (3 feet) higher than at the outside of the gyre. The flow away from the high surface level in the center pushes the currents against the periphery of the ocean basin. The slope between a high area and a low area on the ocean surface sets up a pressure gradient force that causes water to flow. The greater the slope, the more quickly the water moves.

All five oceanic gyres behave like the North Atlantic Gyre. These gyres are called *geostrophic currents. Geostrophic* means related to the Earth's rotation. After a geostrophic current is set in motion, its flow is a balance between the pressure gradient force

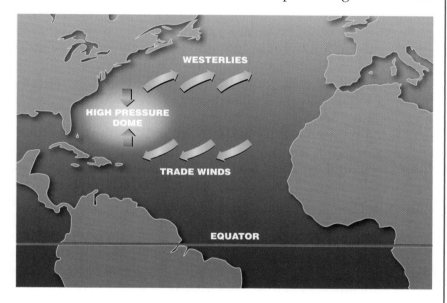

Figure 11-6

How domes form.

Ekman transport, shown by the red arrows in this figure, pushes warm surface water toward the center of the gyre, piling up warm water to form a dome. Note that the dome is offset to the west. A balance is achieved between Ekman transport, and the pressure gradient force, which tries to move water down the slope of the dome in response to gravity. Thus, a dynamic balance keeps the currents flowing around the outside edge of the ocean basin.

and the Coriolis effect. A geostrophic current results from the balance between the pressure gradient force and the Coriolis effect. The two large gyres in the Northern Hemisphere rotate clockwise. These are the North Pacific Gyre and the North Atlantic Gyre. The three large gyres in the Southern Hemisphere are the South Atlantic Gyre, the South Pacific Gyre, and the Indian Ocean Gyre. These rotate counterclockwise. The sixth rotating current is the Antarctic Circumpolar Current. Although this current moves continuously to the east, it is technically not a gyre because an ocean basin does not contain it. Powerful and nearly unceasing winds drive the Antarctic Circumpolar Current. No continent deflects or slows it, so it is very powerful with very large seas of 9-meter (30-foot) waves and bigger.

The five geostrophic gyres mentioned above are comprised of many of the world's major currents. Each of these gyres is made up of four currents. Western ocean boundary currents are those along eastern continental coasts and eastern ocean boundary currents are those along western continental coasts. In the North Atlantic, the Gulf Stream is a western ocean boundary current and the Canary Current is an eastern ocean boundary current. In the North Atlantic Gyre, the North Equatorial Current and the North Atlantic Current are the major east-west currents. Gyres are powered primarily by the trade winds and the westerlies, which provide most of the energy for the world's surface currents.

Western ocean boundary currents and eastern ocean boundary currents have very different characteristics. The narrowest, fastest, and deepest surface currents are the western ocean boundary currents. Western ocean boundary currents move warm water from the equator toward the poles. Besides the Gulf Stream, other major western ocean boundary currents include the Kuroshio Current in the North Pacific, the Brazil Current in the South Atlantic, the Agulhas Current in the Indian Ocean, and the East Australian Current in the South Pacific.

Of the western ocean boundary currents, the Gulf Stream is the most studied. As mentioned in Chapter 2, this current has been studied a long time. Benjamin Franklin was responsible for the creation of the first detailed map of the Gulf Stream in the 18th century. (You probably know of Franklin from his role in the Revolutionary War and the birth of the United States, and from the famous story of proving that lightning is an electric current by flying a kite in a thunderstorm.) As Deputy Postmaster General for the colonial American government, Franklin received complaints that it took much longer for a letter to come from England than to send one there. His cousin, a whaling captain, informed Franklin that the cause was the Gulf Stream. The current delayed ships sailing westward. Franklin commissioned the Gulf Stream map based on what he had learned.

The Gulf Stream is one of the deepest surface currents, reaching depths greater than 1 kilometer (0.6 miles). In places, its surface velocity exceeds a rate of 7 kilometers (4 miles) per hour. The Gulf Stream transports more than 55 sverdrup (sv). The *sverdrup* is a unit of measure invented to express volume transported in ocean currents. Named for oceanographer Harald Sverdrup, one sverdrup equals 1 million cubic meters of water per second.

The Gulf Stream's average flow is just over 55 sv, which means it's moving more than 55 million cubic meters of water per second. To picture this, think of the water flowing from a total of 10,000 Niagara Falls.

INTERNET PORTAL

SCiLINKS. NSTA

Topic: Gulf Stream
Go To: www.scilinks.org
Code: LOP2260

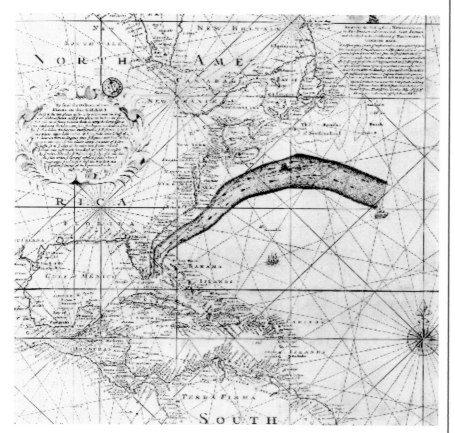

Figure 11-7

Franklin's chart of the Gulf Stream published in 1769.

Not only a founding father in US history, Benjamin Franklin was a scientist. Although most famous for his work in electricity, he was also the first person to commission a chart of the Gulf Stream, shown in this illustration from 1769.

Gyre currents flow in a general area along the periphery of ocean basins, but they don't flow within perfectly defined pathways. Their paths vary somewhat depending on wind strength. In addition, friction with adjacent water can create swirling currents, called *eddies*. Imagine a meandering river; eddies form when the river meanders too much, causing a bend to pinch off on its own and form a circular looping current that migrates.

In the ocean, these small, temporary currents can be either *cold-core* or *warm-core eddies*. The temperature of an eddy determines the direction it will rotate. Like gyres, warm- and cold-core eddies flow in opposite directions in the Northern and Southern Hemispheres. In response to the direction of the pressure gradient, warm-core eddies flow clockwise and cold-core eddies flow counterclockwise in the Northern Hemisphere, with the reverse in the Southern Hemisphere. Warm- and cold-core eddies travel slowly for periods ranging from days to months and sometimes years.

Eddies are important because they can profoundly affect local temperatures and water conditions. Commercial fishing vessels

Figure 11-8

How strong is the Gulf Stream?

The water flowing in the Gulf Stream is 10,000 times the volume of Niagara Falls.

use eddies to locate fish. These currents can also affect shipping by influencing ship speed. Eddies can affect local climates by redistributing heat.

The term "small" is relative when we're talking about oceanic currents and eddies. In the North Atlantic, for example, these eddies are commonly 200 kilometers (320 miles) across. They not only move water with them, but also the water's inhabitants. During the summer, warm-core eddies have been known to carry tropical fish from Florida and the Caribbean as far north as Long Island, New York, and southern New England.

Just as there are western ocean boundary currents, there are eastern ocean boundary currents, such as the Canary Current in the North Atlantic, the Benguela Current in the South Atlantic, the California Current in the North Pacific, the West Australian Current in the Indian Ocean, and the Peru Current in the South Pacific.

Eastern ocean boundary currents and western ocean boundary currents differ in almost every aspect. Eastern ocean boundary currents carry cool water toward the equator. Also, they tend to be wide – sometimes more than 1,000 kilometers (620 miles) across – and relatively shallow. Their borders are less distinct, and eddies do not commonly spin off from them. Flow rate and total volume of water transported are significantly less in eastern ocean boundary currents. For example, the rate of flow in the Canary Current, and the amount of water it transports, are both less than one-third of the Gulf Stream's.

THE NORTH ATLANTIC CURRENT AND THE DEFEAT OF THE SPANISH ARMADA

Because of their influence on shipping, both weather and currents have changed human events. One example occurred in 1588 with the defeat of Spain's Armada, at the time considered the most powerful navy in the world.

Spain and England were at war. Planning to invade England, Spain sent its Armada to rendezvous with, and protect, its invasion fleet. The Armada ships were considered invincible. Built in the days when sea battles were decided by boarding enemy ships, the Spanish ships were the largest and could hold more soldiers to swarm aboard an enemy vessel. The Armada also used the tactic of keeping its fleet close together to unite its strength.

Smaller and outnumbered, the English fleet sailed to intercept and prevent the Spanish invasion. They knew that they could not take on the Armada at close range because the Spanish could easily board and overwhelm them. Therefore, the English began the fight at a distance, with two advantages: they had superior cannons that could be more rapidly reloaded, and their ships were far more agile.

As the Armada moved into the English Channel, the English attacked but could not stop the fleet. At that point, the weather changed history. Erratic winds complicated sailing for the more cumbersome Armada, so it missed joining up with the invasion fleet. Although the Armada anchored to wait and regroup, the nimble English vessels had less trouble with the wind and ran the Armada off their anchorage.

This caused the Armada to lose its unity. With the Spanish ships relatively divided, the English moved in and pounded them with their superior gunfire. The Armada withdrew, but the English blocked a southerly retreat directly to Spain. Forced to head north, the Armada planned to sail into the North Sea around Great Britain and then turn south to Spain in the open Atlantic.

Almost half the Armada didn't make it home. At least 14 ships ended up wrecked on the north shores of Scotland and Ireland. To this day, it's not clear why. Although some historians attribute the wrecks to weather, many argue that, based on the reports, it wasn't a likely issue. As the most powerful navy in the world at the time, the Spanish had some of the best navigators in service, so poor navigation wasn't a likely cause either.

One theory is the effect of the North Atlantic Current – a strong current above the Gulf Stream flowing north. While sailors knew about the North Atlantic Current, at the time it wasn't known that it flows into the North Sea. In calculating their speed, the fleet navigators may not have realized that they were sailing into a current. This meant that they were moving more slowly than they thought. Consequently, they turned south too soon to clear Great Britain, and wrecked ashore before realizing their errors.

With the Armada defeated and nearly half the remaining fleet and men lost, Spain's military power diminished substantially. Spain was unable to invade England, much less defeat it. This marked the rise of England's era as the dominant sea power.

Western ocean boundary currents are much stronger than eastern ocean boundary currents because of a phenomenon called *western intensification*, to which the Coriolis effect is a major contributor. Remember that the Coriolis effect is stronger at high latitudes than at low latitudes. Water in the eastward-flowing currents of major ocean gyres turns more strongly toward the equator than water flowing in the westward-flowing currents near the equator turns toward a pole. Therefore, over much of the surface of the ocean, there is a weak flow of water toward the equator. The strong flow of the western ocean boundary currents occurs in part to balance this slow drift of water toward the equator. These factors, plus some additional ones beyond the scope of this discussion, combine to make western ocean boundary currents narrower and stronger than eastern ocean boundary currents.

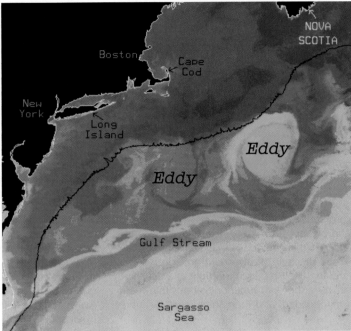

Professor Peter C. Cornillon, Graduate School of Oceanography, University of Rhode Island

Figure 11-9

Formation of eddies.

In this satellite photograph of the North Atlantic, the Gulf Stream is orange. As the Gulf Stream moves along, meandering loops develop and sometimes become so coiled that they break off into distinct circulating masses called eddies. The swirling cold-core eddy shown here was pinched off from the Gulf Stream and moved south-east. A similar phenomenon occurs in the atmosphere to create high- and low-pressure centers.

East-west (transverse) currents link the eastern and western ocean boundary currents. Most of them travel to the west at low latitudes and to the east in the high latitudes. The trade winds tend to drive the west-flowing currents at low latitudes, providing much of the energy for the ocean's gyres. The westerlies drive east-flowing currents in the high latitudes. The Antarctic Circumpolar Current is one of the best examples of an east-flowing current. The Antarctic Circumpolar Current carries more water than any other surface current, with an estimated 100 sv flow rate in some places.

Figure 11-10

Characteristics of western and eastern ocean boundary currents.

OCEAN BOUNDARY CURRENTS		
CHARACTERISTIC	WESTERN	EASTERN
Temperature	warm	cold
Width	narrow	wide
Depth	deep	shallow
Volume	high	low
Speed	fast	slow
Direction of flow	toward poles	toward equator
Eddies present	common	rare

YOU CAN'T GET THERE FROM HERE

The course to follow on a modern ship with engines and propellers is relatively straightforward. You have to account for bottom topography and the effects of currents and winds, but basically you head directly from point A to point B.

This was not always true. In the age of sail, you couldn't go straight from one place to another when that meant sailing against the winds and currents.

A good example is the routes between Europe and the New World. Coming to North America, you couldn't just sail straight west. That would require sailing directly into the westerlies. Instead, you sailed south until you reached the low latitudes with the trade winds. The trade winds then took you west.

To return to Europe, you had to sail in the northern waters carried by the westerlies. If you were south of the westerlies, in the Caribbean for example, you sailed north aided by the Gulf Stream. You turned east when you entered the westerlies. This is why the island of Bermuda became important in early trade. One of only a few islands in the flow of the westerlies, it was an important navigational reference and an opportunity to make landfall on the voyage. However, dozens of reefs that can be navigation hazards surround Bermuda. Over the years, before modern navigation, these reefs caused many ships to run aground. As a result, Bermuda has one of the world's highest concentrations of shipwrecks.

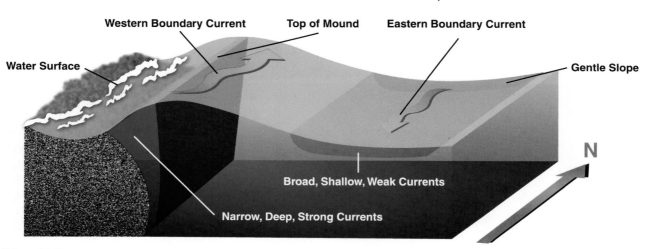

Figure 11-11

Asymmetrical flow around gyres.

Because of the higher elevation of the western portion of the dome, the water in the western ocean boundary current shown must squeeze past its steeper western side. However, the volume of water in the western and eastern ocean boundary currents is the same. So, the "squeezed" western ocean boundary current must flow much more deeply and swiftly than the eastern ocean boundary current. Vertical dimensions in this diagram have been exaggerated for explanation purposes. The actual height of the dome is only about 1 meter (3 feet), but the slope can be hundreds or even thousands of miles long. Western intensification tends to be obscured in the Southern Hemisphere due to the influence of the Antarctic Circumpolar Current (also known as the West Wind Drift) and the flow of surface water from the Pacific into the Indian Ocean adjacent to Indonesia.

Countercurrents

What is a countercurrent? *What is an* undercurrent?

Ekman spirals are not the only way water flows in directions that differ from the major ocean currents. *Countercurrents* and *undercurrents* are two other examples.

As the name implies, a countercurrent flows in a direction opposite an adjacent current. The North Equatorial Current (NEC) and the South Equatorial Current (SEC) flow west until they encounter continents. There the water piles up and some of it turns toward higher latitudes as a result of the Coriolis effect and Ekman transport and becomes a western ocean boundary current.

A hypothesis to explain the formation of the Equatorial Countercurrent is based on what is thought to happen to the water that does not turn toward higher latitudes. Since the NEC and the SEC turn in opposite directions, there is divergence of Ekman transport in the region between the doldrums and the trade winds. This creates a region of lower sea level. Some of the water from the NEC and SEC curls back on itself into this region of lower sea level and flows east to form the Equatorial Countercurrent.

Countercurrents that flow beneath adjacent currents are called *undercurrents*. Like other countercurrents, they probably form

Figure 11-12

Geostrophic flow in the tropics.

In the Pacific, the prevailing trade winds carry large quantities of surface water westward via the Northern Equatorial Current (NEC) and Southern Equatorial Current (SEC). In the NEC, some of this water flows northward in the Kuroshio Current **(A)** and back across the north Pacific. Water "piles up" in the western regions from the SEC **(B)**. As a result of divergence of Ekman transport in the NEC and SEC, an area of lower sea level forms. The "piled-up" water flows east into the area of lower sea level as the Equatorial Countercurrent. A similar phenomenon occurs in the tropical Atlantic. However, note that Brazil deflects the South Equatorial Current across the equator. This weakens and restricts the Atlantic Countercurrent to only the eastern portion of the basin **(C)**.

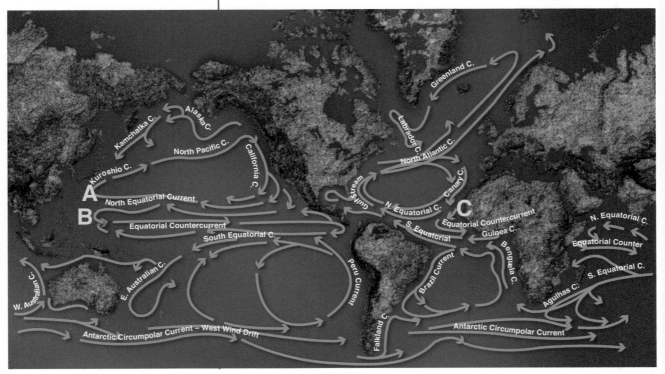

where divergence of Ekman transport occurs, but their origin isn't really clear. One significant undercurrent is the Pacific's Cromwell Current, named for Townsend Cromwell, who discovered it in 1956. The Cromwell Current flows more than 14,000 kilometers (8,700 miles) from New Guinea to Ecuador at a depth of approximately 100 to 200 meters (300 to 600 feet). It flows at an average speed of 5 kilometers (3 miles) per hour and carries a volume about half that of the Gulf Stream. Since the discovery of the Cromwell Current, undercurrents have been found beneath most major currents.

Upwelling and Downwelling

What makes upwelling *and* downwelling *occur? What biological effects do they have?*

Up to this point, we've looked at horizontal water flow. However, wind-driven currents sometimes cause a vertical flow called *upwelling* or *downwelling*. An upwelling is an upward vertical current that brings deep water to the surface. A downwelling is a downward vertical current that pushes surface water deeper into the ocean.

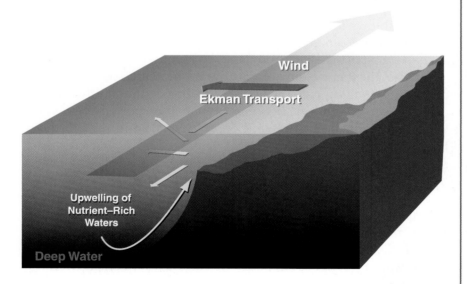

Figure 11-13

Coastal upwelling.

This illustration depicts coastal upwelling in the Southern Hemisphere. Wind blowing from the south causes Ekman transport to move offshore. As the surface layer of water moves away, the nutrient-rich water replaces it from below. Once this cold nutrient water reaches the sunlit surface waters, life explodes. What would happen if in this situation the wind were blowing the opposite direction?

A coastal upwelling occurs when the wind blows offshore or parallel to shore. Whether wind blowing parallel to shore causes an upwelling depends on the hemisphere, the coast, and the wind direction.

Upwelling occurs when a wind blowing parallel to shore pushes surface water out to sea due to Ekman transport, which moves

Prime Hook National Wildlife Refuge
U.S. Fish and Wildlife Service

Figure 11-14a

Brush fire.

Along with coastal upwelling, dry Santa Ana winds often bring wildfires to Southern California.

Al Hornsby

Figure 11-14b

Wind surfing.

Winds that drive coastal upwelling can also have positive consequences. They're a delight to windsurfers.

PADI

Figure 11-14c

Scuba diving.

Upwelling water brings deeper cold and very clear water near shore that scuba divers enjoy.

the water column 90° to the right or left of the wind (depending on the hemisphere). An upwelling can develop in a matter of hours. If the wind blows for more than a few hours, Ekman transport starts to develop and offshore winds produce currents along the shore. Ekman transport is away from land, so an upwelling results.

In the Northern Hemisphere, a wind blowing southward will cause an upwelling only on a west coast of a continent (the eastern ocean basin boundary). Because Ekman transport drives water 90° to the right, the same wind on an east coast in the Northern Hemisphere sends surface water *toward* shore. This creates a downwelling, in which the surface water is forced downward at the shoreline. It flows back seaward along the bottom.

Upwelling and downwelling have strong biological effects. An upwelling tends to bring nutrients up into shallow water. This can significantly increase biological productivity, often on a large scale. For example, the productive fishing grounds off the South American west coast exist because of frequent upwelling. Upwelling can also influence weather patterns that have multiple social and environmental effects. An excellent example is the southern California Santa Ana winds. These hot winds flow with significant force seaward from the inland coastal mountain area. Santa Ana winds are dry and help feed the famous brush fires that periodically threaten local communities and forests. These winds also have positive effects. They can clean the air and provide good

INTERNET PORTAL
SCiLINKS. NSTA
Topic: Science of Surfing
Go To: www.scilinks.org
Code: LOP2265

scuba-diving conditions. Over time, the winds tend to flatten incoming waves. Santa Ana winds also cause water at and near the ocean's surface to mix. If the Santa Ana Winds blow strongly for more than a few hours, Ekman transport starts to develop, and upwelling is created.

The biological effect of downwelling is to carry nutrients and other essential materials to the deep ocean. Normally throughout the ocean, some nutrients are returned to deeper water when they sink. However, surface organisms recycle most of the organic matter before it can sink. Downwelling removes organic nutrients from the surface. The effect may be a reduction in the productivity of some surface species and an increase in the productivity of some bottom species.

In addition to coastal upwelling regions, there are important open ocean upwelling regions. Chapter 4 explains that tropical waters generally tend to have low nutrient levels and low productivity. An exception to this exists in some equatorial regions, especially in the Pacific. In these locations, significant upwelling brings nutrients into the sunlit zone, thus supporting biological productivity.

Equatorial upwelling results from the trade winds blowing along the equator. Recall that the Coriolis effect and Ekman transport cause water to travel to the right of the wind in the Northern Hemisphere and to the left in the Southern Hemisphere. This

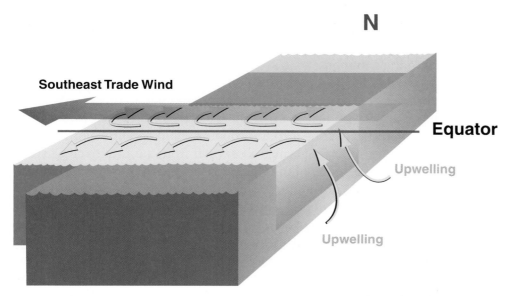

N

Southeast Trade Wind

Equator

Upwelling

Upwelling

Figure 11-15

Equatorial upwelling.
The Coriolis effect and Ekman transport deflect water movement to the right in the Northern Hemisphere and to the left in the Southern. This affects what happens when winds blow along the equator. While the wind is still in the Southern Hemisphere, the water column is deflected to the left (counterclockwise). But, when it crosses the equator, the deflection is toward the right (clockwise). The result is that surface water near the equator flows in opposite directions away from the equator. Cold, nutrient-rich water moves up from below to take the place of the surface water moving north and south.

means that along the equator water tends to move in *two* directions: to the right on the north side and to the left on the south side. With water flowing away in opposite directions, deep water rises to fill the void. This is upwelling.

Heat Transport and Climate

What role do currents play in transporting heat? How do currents affect climate?

Previous chapters explain that water's high heat capacity is the reason that the ocean affects weather and climate. Currents play a critical role by transporting heat from warm areas to cool areas, and vice versa.

Currents redistribute about a third of the heat in the tropics. According to estimates, the ocean transfers 8 X 1013 calories out of the tropics each second. To put it in perspective, that's more than 230 times the energy all the people in the world consume in a second.

Transporting this heat affects climate by moderating temperatures. Without currents and winds moving heat, the world's climates would be more extreme. The Earth's cold regions would be colder and the warm regions would be warmer. Winters in northern Europe would be significantly colder without the Gulf Stream bringing heat from the tropics. Southern California owes its mild climate to the moderating effects of the Pacific Ocean. The southerly current along the California coast brings cool water from the north, keeping southern California cooler than it would otherwise be in the summer.

As it is, the heat redistribution isn't perfectly even, so heat transported by currents affects some places more than others. Earlier in this chapter you learned that the Galapagos are much cooler than you would expect near to the equator, thanks to upwelling due to Ekman transport that brings cool water from the Cromwell Current to the surface. Many of the Galapagos species require a cool climate and would not normally thrive at low latitudes.

As was mentioned earlier, another example is the United Kingdom and much of Europe. Although the United Kingdom and northern Europe lie at the same latitudes as Canada, they enjoy a warmer climate. The reason is that the Gulf Stream warms the atmosphere, which carries the heat to Europe. The North Atlantic Current also keeps the seas around Europe ice-free year round, further moderating Europe's climate.

INTERNET PORTAL

SCiLINKS. NSTA

Topic: El Niño
Go To: www.scilinks.org
Code: LOP2270

El Niño Southern Oscillation (ENSO)

What happens when an El Niño Southern Oscillation (ENSO) *occurs? What effect does it have on weather, marine habitats, and human activity?*

Chapter 10 discusses that weather and climate result from the interactions of the ocean and the atmosphere. Some examples of these interactions occur all of the time, such as the moderation of the climate of the United Kingdom due to the Gulf Stream. But, some significant weather and climate phenomena are not regular or constant. One significant example is the *El Niño Southern Oscillation (ENSO)*, which is a buildup of warm water in the Central and Eastern Equatorial Pacific. (*Niño* is Spanish for *boy child*. Pronounce it NEE-nyo.) When it occurs, this event tremendously affects world weather patterns.

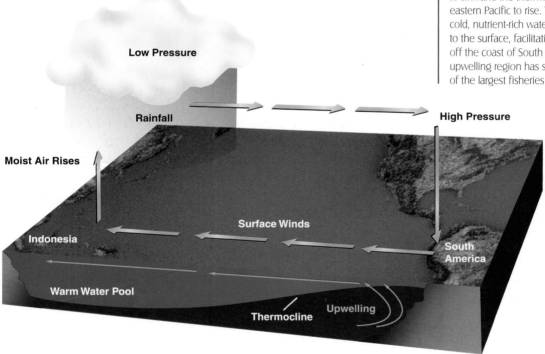

Figure 11-16

Pacific circulation (normal).

In a normal (non-El Niño) year, there is a stable low-pressure center in the western Pacific, which gives the region its typical high rainfall. An equally stable dry high-pressure center forms in the eastern Pacific. This pressure differential contributes to the consistent trade winds, which blow along the equator from east to west. In turn, the winds push and maintain a mass of water that pools in the western Pacific. The increased pressure of the additional surface water causes the thermocline in the western Pacific to sink and the thermocline in the eastern Pacific to rise. This brings cold, nutrient-rich water very close to the surface, facilitating upwelling off the coast of South America. This upwelling region has sustained one of the largest fisheries on Earth.

To understand ENSO, let's begin with the pattern of surface winds in the Pacific during the cold phase of ENSO. The trade winds blow strongly westward along the equator. Other winds blowing toward the equator parallel to the coast of South America create an upwelling and make the surface water relatively cool.

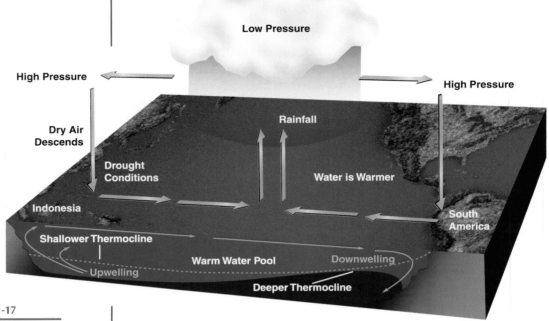

High Pressure

Low Pressure

High Pressure

Dry Air
Descends

Rainfall

Drought
Conditions

Water is Warmer

Indonesia

South
America

Shallower Thermocline

Upwelling

Warm Water Pool

Downwelling

Deeper Thermocline

Figure 11-17

Pacific circulation (El Niño).

During an El Niño year, for reasons that are still not clear to scientists, a rearrangement of the high and low-pressure systems occurs. Low pressure moves westward (the Southern Oscillation), and along with it comes the mass of warm surface water normally held in the western Pacific (the El Niño). This happens on a cycle of every three to eight years. This El Niño Southern Oscillation (ENSO) phenomenon has occurred at least ten times since the middle of the 20th century.

The warm surface water, pushed by the trade winds, tends to accumulate in the Western Pacific. This results in a typical weather pattern of low pressure and high rainfall in the Western Pacific, with high pressure and less rainfall in the Eastern Pacific.

For reasons still being studied, every three to eight years the pattern changes. The warm phase of ENSO occurs. The trade winds in the western Pacific weaken or reverse and blow toward the east for several weeks. These occurrences are called westerly wind bursts. Without winds holding it west, the warm water of the western Pacific migrates east, crossing the ocean and arriving off the coast of South America. The warm water from the west deepens the thermocline in the east. This shuts off the upwelling of cold water, and the eastern tropical Pacific becomes warmer. Because there is less temperature difference between the eastern and western Pacific, the circulation becomes weaker. This further weakens the trade winds. Rain moves eastward to the central equatorial Pacific. The warm water typically arrives along South America's coast around Christmas, which is why Peruvian fishermen named it *el corriento del Niño,* or *the current of the little boy* (Christ child). The loss of upwelling along the Peruvian coast deprives the water

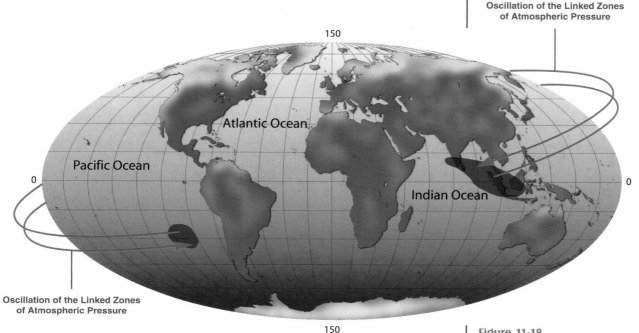

Oscillation of the Linked Zones
of Atmospheric Pressure

150

Atlantic Ocean

Pacific Ocean

0

Indian Ocean

0

Oscillation of the Linked Zones
of Atmospheric Pressure

150

Figure 11-18

The Pacific "see-saw."
The Southern Oscillation gets
its name from the back-and-
forth movement, or oscillation, of atmospheric pressure
systems in the eastern and
western Pacific. The dark-
ened regions represent the
linked zones of atmospheric
pressure.

of nutrients. This normally productive region declines, collapsing local fisheries and natural marine ecosystems.

El Niño is linked to the *Southern Oscillation*, a "seesaw" in air pressure. When air pressure is high in the eastern Pacific, it is low in the western Pacific near Indonesia and northern Australia, and vice-versa. Because El Niño and the Southern Oscillation are connected, scientists refer to them as a single phenomenon, ENSO. Although ENSO occurs in the Pacific, it affects the entire world because it changes where the troposphere's heat is the greatest. Because the hottest region of the troposphere moves eastward during an El Niño by about 120° or a third of the way around the Earth, the circulation in the troposphere changes.

So far, the two most severe ENSO events on record occurred in 1982-83 and 1997-98. These events caused flooding, tornados, drought, and other weather events that cost lives and caused damage. The 1997-98 ENSO caused an estimated 23,000 deaths and more than $33 billion in damages. Both of these ENSO events decimated the southern California kelp beds by warming the water. Kelp only thrives in moderate to cold water. This affected local fish populations and ecosystems, with damage to the kelp-harvesting industry, sport fishing, and other activities.

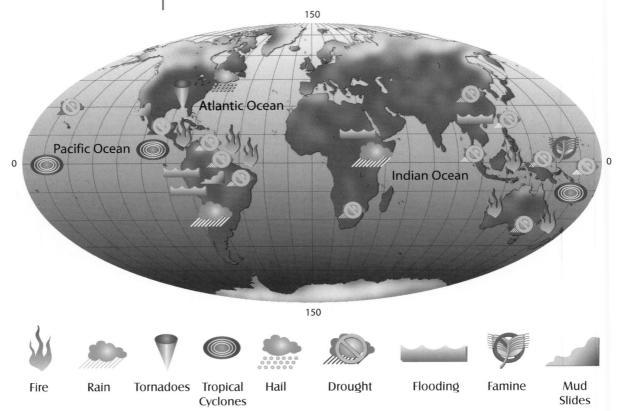

150

Atlantic Ocean

Pacific Ocean

0

Indian Ocean

0

150

| | | | | | | | | |
| Fire | Rain | Tornadoes | Tropical Cyclones | Hail | Drought | Flooding | Famine | Mud Slides |

Figure 11-19

Effects of ENSO.

While ENSO is a phenomenon of the Pacific, its effects are global. This illustration shows worldwide events related to the 1997-98 event.

After a strong ENSO, sometimes the "normal" conditions return with more intensity than usual. The eastern Pacific may experience unusually powerful upwelling of cold water and stormy conditions. This colder-than-normal condition is sometimes called *La Niña*, which is Spanish for *the girl child*. Apparently this name simply resulted from *girl* being the opposite of boy, just as the La Niña event is the opposite of the El Niño event.

Although scientists have yet to determine exactly what causes the warm phase of ENSO events, they're becoming adept at predicting changes in weather patterns once an El Niño begins. Some scientists believe that the eruption of El Chichon, a volcano in Mexico, triggered the 1982-83 warm-phase ENSO event. The eruption pumped huge amounts of volcanic ash and dust into the atmosphere, where it reflected enough incoming solar energy to affect the climate before it settled back to the Earth's surface. But, most warm-phase ENSO events, including the strong event in 1997-98, lack any such readily identifiable trigger.

1. **The primary force(s) that provide energy for surface currents include (choose all that apply)**

   A. wind.

   B. Coriolis effect.

   C. Ekman spiral.

   D. ocean gyres.

2. **The circular flow in each ocean basin is called a gyre.**

   A. true

   B. false

3. **There are _____ gyres and one is found in _____.**

   A. two, equatorial regions

   B. five, each major ocean basin

   C. two, polar regions

   D. three, the North Atlantic

4. **Currents tend to flow around the periphery of an ocean basin because**

   A. of the elevated surface level in the center and the Coriolis effect.

   B. the edge of the basin is deeper.

5. **Gyres are called _____ currents. They tend to flow _____.**

   A. equatorial, quickly

   B. geostrophic, only clockwise

   C. equatorial, clockwise in the Northern Hemisphere and counterclockwise in the Southern Hemisphere

   D. geostrophic, clockwise in the Northern Hemisphere and counterclockwise in the Southern Hemisphere

6. **Western boundary currents flow more quickly than eastern boundary currents partly because the trade winds pile water on the western ocean boundary.**

   A. true

   B. false

7. **Although different water layers move in different directions in an Ekman spiral, the overall effect of Ekman transport is to move a current directly in line with the wind.**

   A. true

   B. false

8. **A countercurrent is a _____. An undercurrent is a _____.**

   A. current that runs in the opposite direction and beneath a surface current, current that runs in the opposite direction of an adjacent current

   B. current that runs in the opposite direction of an adjacent current, current that runs in the opposite direction and beneath a surface current

9. **An undercurrent runs _____ an adjacent current. The reason why it forms is _____.**

   A. perpendicular to, the same as for a countercurrent

   B. beneath, unclear

   C. perpendicular to, unclear

   D. beneath, the same as for a countercurrent

10. **Both upwellings and downwellings can result from a wind parallel to shore.**

    A. true

    B. false

11. **Without currents, the world's climates would be**

    A. more extreme.

    B. more moderate.

    C. no different.

12. **During a warm-phase ENSO event, warm water _____. This event causes _____.**

    A. accumulates in the Western Pacific, dramatic weather changes

    B. accumulates in the Eastern Pacific, stable weather

    C. accumulates in the Western Pacific, stable weather

    D. accumulates in the Eastern Pacific, dramatic weather changes

Deep Currents

So far in this chapter, we've looked at surface currents. Surface currents have historically been the most obvious because of their effect on shipping and trade. The wind is the primary energy source for surface currents. But, about 90% of the ocean volume lies too deep for the wind and surface currents to affect it directly. These deep ocean layers do have currents, driven by much different processes. As you will learn later in this chapter, these currents influence changes in climate.

Deep Circulation and Water Masses

How does deep circulation differ from surface wind-driven circulation?

What five distinct water masses result from density stratification?

Earlier, you learned that differences in water density are one of several causes of currents. In the deep ocean layers, mixing, not wind, is the primary cause of currents. *Deep circulation* is water motion caused by mixing water of different densities. Mixing drives most of the vertical motion of seawater and the ocean's overall circulation. Deep circulation begins when water density increases due to cooling and increased salinity. When water becomes denser than the water below it, the denser water sinks. The cold dense water will stay at the bottom until mixing brings it back to the surface. If

STUDY QUESTIONS

Find the answers as you read.

1. How does *deep circulation* differ from surface wind-driven circulation?

2. What five distinct water masses result from density stratification?

3. Where and how do the distinct deep water masses of the ocean form?

4. What is the general pattern of deep water circulation?

5. What is the *ocean conveyor belt phenomenon*? Why is it important?

Figure 11-20

Layers in the sea.

This illustration represents a stylized view of ocean stratification. An actual depth profile would appear much more complex because of the many factors affecting circulation patterns in the sea.

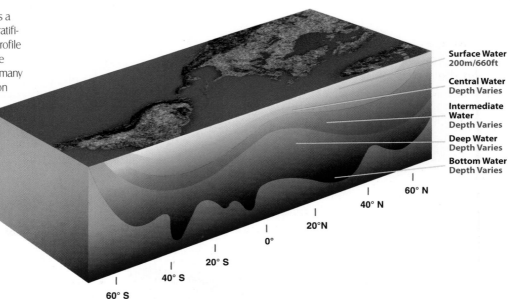

Surface Water
200m/660ft

Central Water
Depth Varies

Intermediate
Water
Depth Varies

Deep Water
Depth Varies

Bottom Water
Depth Varies

60° N

40° N

20°N

0°

20° S

40° S

60° S

there were no mixing, the ocean basins would fill with cold water and then become stagnant because no more water would sink. It is the tides and internal waves that keep deep water mixed.

The ocean stratifies into density layers (you can read more about this in Chapter 9). Each water layer has specific temperature and density characteristics. Stratification is generally more pronounced in temperate and tropical regions because there's a significant temperature difference between surface and deep water. Stratification is less pronounced or entirely absent at very high latitudes.

You may recall that water layer masses don't easily mix with water layers of differing density characteristics. Instead, the lower density layers ride over the higher density layers. Unlike air masses, which are relatively temporary, water masses tend to last for long periods. Based on density stratification, there are five generally recognized primary water masses:

- Surface water extends to a depth of about 200 meters (600 feet)
- Central water extends to the thermocline; its depth varies with latitude
- Intermediate water extends to about 1,500 meters (5,000 feet)
- Deep water is below intermediate water, but not in contact with the bottom; its maximum depth is about 4,000 meters (13,000 feet)
- Bottom water is in contact with the seafloor

Wind-driven currents move the surface and central water layers. Surface waters show the greatest variation in temperature and salinity, whereas the intermediate, deep, and bottom layers show the least. The most abrupt boundary with the biggest change is between the central and intermediate water layers.

The reason for these differences is that water mass characteristics develop at the surface. Evaporation of seawater or dilution with fresh water can only happen at the surface. Density also depends on heating or cooling. Temperature, salinity, and depth all affect density, so that two water masses with different salinities and temperatures can have the same density. In Figure 11-21, note the S-shaped curve on the temperature-salinity diagram. The curve shows that as depth increases, temperature and salinity

INTERNET PORTAL

SCiLINKS. NSTA

Topic: Deep Ocean Currents
Go To: www.scilinks.org
Code: LOP2560

Figure 11-21

A temperature-salinity (T-S) diagram.

Note the S-shaped curve, the top of which shows the sea surface and bottom the seafloor. The curve shows that, as depth increases, temperature and salinity vary. However, through the differing combinations of salinity and temperature, the density (orange lines - grams per cubic centimeter) continues to increase with depth. Note that in this example the salinity varies only slightly – ranging only about 2‰ – while the temperature ranges about 27°C.

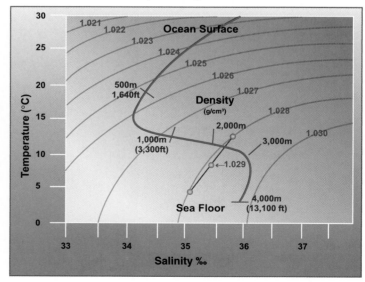

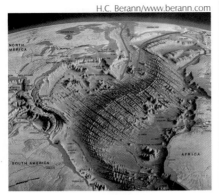

Figure 11-22

The flow of Atlantic Deep Water.

After its formation off Greenland and other polar regions, very dense Atlantic Deep Water follows the contours of the seafloor and enters the Atlantic primarily by the pathways depicted here.

rise and fall in successive layers, although density continues to increase. Because water stratifies into distinct water masses, these layers may form and flow into an ocean basin from entirely different areas.

How Deep Water Masses Form

Where and how do the distinct deep water masses of the ocean form?

Since water mass characteristics form at the surface, you may wonder how the deeper layers get to the bottom. The answer is that the intermediate, deep, and bottom water masses form *primarily*, but not entirely, at high latitudes (around 70° North and South). Two deep masses, Antarctic Bottom Water and North Atlantic Deep Water, make up most of the world's deep water. Pacific Intermediate Water and Mediterranean Deep Water are also important. Let's look at each of these masses.

The bottom layer comes primarily from the Antarctic and North Atlantic. The densest ocean water forms near the Antarctic during the winter. This Antarctic Bottom Water has a salinity of about 34.65‰ and temperature of -0.5°C (31°F). At the surface, its density is 1.0279 grams per cubic centimeter, or almost 3% higher than pure fresh water.

This high density is due to low temperature and high salinity. As explained in Chapter 8, as seawater freezes, it leaves salt behind. The water that remains therefore becomes saltier. This is why Antarctic Bottom Water has high salinity.

Figure 11-23

Formation of deep, bottom, and intermediate waters.

The illustration depicts regions of the world ocean where deep and bottom waters form, along with the location of the slightly less dense intermediate waters. It also shows the locations where major upwelling occurs.

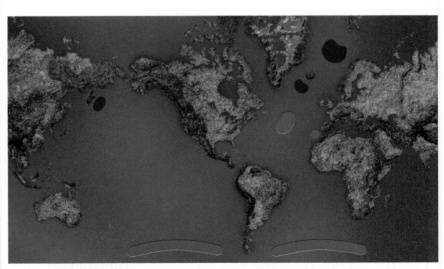

■ Zones where deep and bottom waters form and sink

■ Zones where intermediate and bottom waters form and sink

According to estimates, about 8 million cubic meters of Antarctic Bottom Water form every second. This very dense water descends to the bottom, spreads along the Antarctic deep-sea continental shelf and creeps northward. Antarctic Bottom Water is thought to reach as far as about 40° north latitude, taking somewhat less than 1,000 years to get there. Antarctic Bottom Water is a primary source for both the deep and bottom water layers.

In the North Atlantic, deep water forms as high-salinity surface water cools and sinks. Much of the North Atlantic Deep Water forms off Norway, Greenland, and in the Labrador Sea. It moves south through deep channels around Scotland, Ireland, and Greenland. Deep water currents must flow around, not over, bottom obstacles that rise above the top of the currents. Bottom currents that are significantly influenced by bottom topography are called *contour currents*.

Pacific water that forms in the Northern Hemisphere along the east coast of the Siberian Kamchatka Peninsula is not as dense as deep bottom water, so it forms Pacific Intermediate Water. Intermediate water also develops in the North Atlantic, South

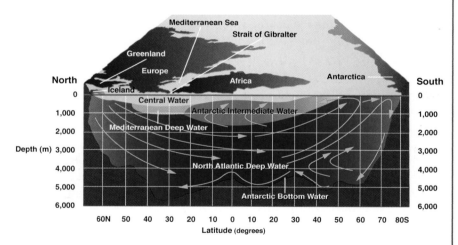

Figure 11-24

Water masses.

This illustration shows a cross-section of the entire Atlantic Ocean looking eastward. Note how the different water masses float or sink, depending on their relative density. Circulation patterns are also indicated.

Atlantic, and South Pacific at latitudes that are not quite as cold as that of the Arctic or Antarctic.

Mediterranean Deep Water forms due to evaporation rather than cooling. The high evaporation rate in the Mediterranean raises salinity, so that during the winter, Mediterranean Deep Water with a salinity of 38‰ flows through the Strait of Gibraltar into the Atlantic. This water is saltier than Antarctic Bottom Water, but warmer and not as dense. Mediterranean Deep Water tends to rest above the North Atlantic Deep Water layer. Mediterranean Deep Water has been traced as far as the Antarctic Ocean basins.

Deep Water Flow Patterns

What is the general pattern of deep water circulation?

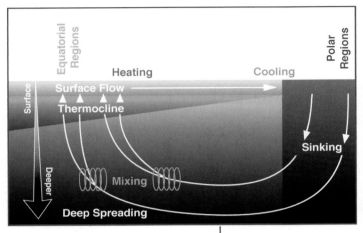

Figure 11-25

Deep circulation.

An idealized model of deep circulation in the world ocean. Note how deep water forms in polar regions and then disperses, eventually mixing with water of other densities. As it rises to the surface, it warms. The rising water keeps the thermocline stable. Otherwise, the thermocline in low latitudes would progress deeper and deeper.

The enormous water quantities sinking at the poles and in the Mediterranean are the source of the deep water masses and circulation. The dense water tends to descend relatively quickly into deep areas, displacing and mixing with the water already there. As deep or bottom water is mixed upward, it warms. When it rises close enough to the surface to enter wind-driven currents, it is carried to higher latitudes. The currents carry warm water as far north as Norway, keeping the far Northeast Atlantic ice-free in the winter and helping warm Europe. In the high latitudes, the water cools, becomes denser, and sinks again, repeating the process.

This general pattern of deep circulation is a slow process. Some estimates suggest that it can take about 1,000 years for a water mass to complete the cycle from the North Atlantic to the North Pacific via the Antarctic Circumpolar Current. Deep water only flows at an estimated average of one to two meters (three to six feet) daily, though it may flow much faster at times.

The Ocean Conveyor Belt

What is the ocean conveyor belt *phenomenon? Why is it important?*

When we look at both deep water and surface currents, we can see how they influence the Earth's climate. The interconnected flow of currents that redistribute heat is called the *ocean conveyor belt*. Some oceanographers call the system the Earth's "air conditioner."

If you look at Figure 11-26, you can see the general pattern. Deep water forms primarily at high latitudes, as you read earlier. North Atlantic Deep Water flows south along the Atlantic bottom, merging with Antarctic Bottom Water. From there it flows eastward, with some flowing into the Indian Ocean, but most flowing to the South Pacific and on to the North Pacific. As the water mixes with water of lower density, it rises, warms, and eventually reaches the surface. From there it is pushed by the trade winds around the ocean . It carries heat from the equatorial regions north and south toward the poles. There it cools and descends, and starts the cycle all over.

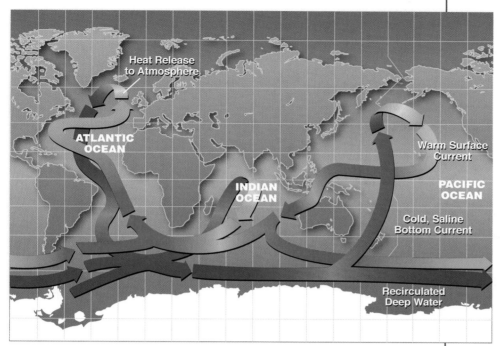

Figure 11-26

The ocean conveyor belt.
The global ocean conveyor belt serves essentially as the Earth's air conditioning system. This marriage of surface and deep water circulation carries heat away from the tropics and, in turn, keeps the tropics from getting too hot. Many scientists think that past events, such as the flooding of the North Atlantic with fresh water, may have, at times, halted the conveyor belt. In such cases, the inability to disperse heat may be one contributor to past ice age conditions.

This description is very generalized. If you were to follow a single water molecule, in theory it would take 1,000 to 2,000 years to complete a cycle on the ocean conveyor belt.

As you may guess from previous discussions about how currents move heat, the ocean conveyor belt is important because of its great effect on the world's climate. When cold water sinks off Norway, it must be replaced by surface water from warmer latitudes. As you learned earlier, as this water moves north, it warms the atmosphere. Some scientists hypothesize that some of the coldest intervals within ice ages have resulted from disruption of the ocean conveyor belt. They hypothesize that dilution of the North Atlantic Ocean with excess fresh water decreases the sinking of North Atlantic Deep Water. If this thinking is correct, then global warming may, ironically, lead to an ice age. The hypothesized cause is that global warming increases the melting of glaciers and ice caps. This dilutes the seawater, preventing the high-density, salty water from forming. Without this high-density water, there's no downwelling to pull warm tropical water into the North Atlantic to feed the deep water currents. This would disrupt the ocean conveyor belt by shutting down the transport of relatively warm water to the far North Atlantic. Such events would cause large parts of the Northern Hemisphere, especially Europe, to become much colder.

Scientists think these events did occur during the last ice age, but the possibility of their happening now is speculative. Some researchers have found a decrease in the production of North Atlantic Deep Water and Antarctic Bottom Water. If the trends continue, pronounced changes in the Earth's climate may occur by 2050.

Another way that the ocean conveyor belt affects climate is by removing some carbon dioxide from the atmosphere. Burning fossil fuels releases carbon dioxide into the air. Nearly half of this carbon dioxide dissolves into the surface water of the ocean. After being absorbed, the conveyer belt carries it deep into the ocean, where it may potentially remain for hundreds to thousands of years. Carbon dioxide is a greenhouse gas associated with concerns about climate change and global warming. The ocean conveyor belt phenomenon may be extremely important in helping moderate climate change by removing carbon dioxide from the atmosphere.

ARE YOU LEARNING?

1. **Deep circulation is water movement caused by**

   A. changes in the wind.

   B. an increase in the productivity of pelagic organisms.

   C. the mixing of water masses of different water densities.

2. **Based on density stratification, the primary water mass classifications include**

   A. surface water, deep water, and photic water.

   B. central water, intermediate water, and deep water.

   C. intermediate water, deep water, and photic water.

   D. photic water, surface water, and bottom water.

3. **The primary source of deep and bottom water is from**

   A. the equator, where evaporation causes an increase in salinity and density.

   B. high latitudes, where freezing and cooling cause an increase in salinity and density.

4. **The general pattern of deep water circulation begins with dense water sinking. It flows along the bottom, mixes with other water, rises and warms, and eventually becomes part of a surface current.**

   A. true

   B. false

5. **The ocean conveyor belt is important because**

   A. it is the primary method fishermen have to process what they catch.

   B. it enables benthic organisms to travel quickly.

   C. it enables transport ships to travel quickly.

   D. it redistributes heat and moderates the Earth's climate.

Studying Ocean Currents

So far in this chapter, you've learned a great deal about the ocean's currents. But, how do scientists study currents? How did they determine what you just read about? Let's turn our attention to how scientists investigate currents.

Three Distinct Approaches

What are three distinct approaches to studying currents?

There are quite a few instruments and methods used for studying currents. No matter what aspect of a current you're interested in or what instrument you use, however, there are three main approaches.

The first is the *Lagrangian method,* also called the *float method.* With this approach, you study the current by tracking a drifting object. The Lagrangian method involves floating something in the current that records information as it drifts. Although this is normally an instrument, it can also be a vessel. The *Ben Franklin,* a specialized submersible, studied the Gulf Stream by floating in it for weeks with a team of scientists aboard.

The second is the *Eulerian method,* also called the *flow method.* With this approach, you study the current by staying in one place and measuring the velocity of the water as it flows past. The Eulerian method uses fixed instruments that meter the current as it passes.

These first two methods were named for mathematicians Joseph-Louis Lagrange (1736-1813) and Leonhard Euler (1707-1783). Both are known for multiple contributions to mathematics and physics. Lagrange established many of the principles in fluid dynamics. Euler published many papers on mathematics and is responsible for standardizing most of the modern mathematical symbols.

The third method uses altimeter satellites to measure the highs and lows of the sea surface. Because geostrophic currents flow around highs and lows in the surface, satellite altimeters can produce maps of ocean currents everywhere on the ocean surface. This technology has revolutionized our knowledge of currents and tides.

STUDY QUESTIONS

Find the answers as you read.

1. What are three distinct approaches to studying currents?

2. What are five examples of instruments or methods that scientists use for studying currents?

SeaWIFS, Goddard Space Flight Center, NASA

Figure 11-27

The *Ben Franklin.*

This specialized submersible studied the currents of the Gulf Stream. It was named after Benjamin Franklin, who commissioned the first chart of the Gulf Stream.

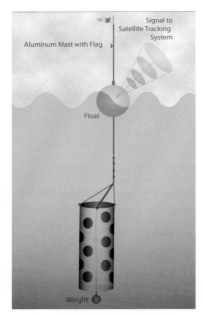

Figure 11-28

Collecting information on surface currents.

A drogue is a simple apparatus enabling scientists to study surface currents. The "holey sock" is attached so the drogue will be dragged by the current instead of blown by surface winds.

Figure 11-29

Collecting information on subsurface currents.

The Argo, named after a ship in Greek mythology, is a subsurface float that periodically adjusts its buoyancy to rise to the surface. On the surface, it transmits its position to a communication satellite. Once the uplink is complete, Argo returns to deep water to track current flow for ten days.

Instrumentation and Methods

What are five examples of instruments or methods that scientists use for studying currents?

People can carry out Lagrangian studies with something as simple as a bottle tossed into the water, but oceanographers have improved on this. A more useful float is called is a drogue. The advantage of a drogue over a simple surface float is that the "holey sock" shown in Figure 11-28 ensures that the current and not the wind determine where it drifts.

A second type of float, the *Argo* float, drifts at depths typically ranging from 1,500 to 2,000 meters (5,000 to 6,500 feet) before periodically rising to the surface to transmit to a satellite a temperature and salinity profile of the water it rose through. It then sinks back to its drifting depth.

For Eulerian study methods, researchers use various types of flow meters. These devices measure and record the speed and direction of passing currents. The information is either transmitted electronically or stored for retrieval later.

A more sophisticated device is the Doppler Acoustic Current Meter. This instrument also determines current direction and speed. The instrument is named for the *Doppler shift*, which is a change in frequency due to speed or direction change. By measur-

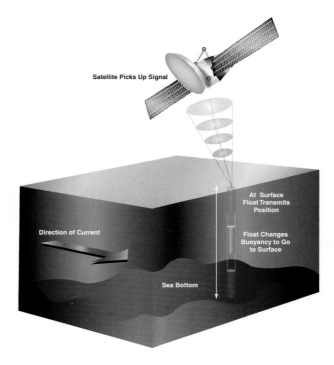

ing sound bouncing off particles suspended in the water and analyzing the echo frequencies, the Doppler Acoustic Current Meter can determine changes in flow speed and direction. The Doppler shift is also used in weather radar and police radar, among other instruments. Doppler Acoustic Current Meters are very accurate.

As you have learned, oceanographers use altimeter satellites to measure surface geostrophic currents. As shown in Figure 11-32, by using a ground tracking station, GPS satellite information, and radar, the Jason II satellite, launched in 2008, measures sea level height around the world. This information is used to make maps

Figure 11-30

Researchers use a flow meter.

These researchers are using a type of flow meter. This device uses an internal propeller and a vane to measure and record current speed and direction.

Narrow Beam Sound Pulses

Sea Bottom

Figure 11-31a

Using Doppler in the sea.

The Doppler Acoustic Current Meter represents some of the most sophisticated technology used to study ocean currents. Like the Doppler radar now commonly described by television weather forecasters, these devices can determine the direction and speed of currents by the change in sound frequency caused by water flow. (The frequency increases as the current approaches the instrument, and decreases as it moves away.)

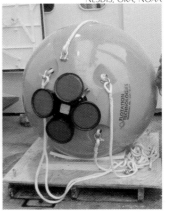

Figure 11-31b

The Doppler Acoustic Meter.

These are very expensive, but extremely accurate, systems.

of the currents and to evaluate and forecast weather and climate changes. The latest image from the satellite is updated every two weeks. Satellite altimeters have revolutionized our knowledge of currents and tides.

In addition to the methods described already, there are additional ways to learn about currents. Researchers use chemical tracers such as certain radioactive elements and fluorocarbons to track deep currents. If scientists know where and when the tracer entered the water, they can measure its presence to determine flow patterns and velocities. This method is the basis for studying North Atlantic Deep Water and its connection to the ocean conveyor belt.

Scientists also take advantage of accidental opportunities to

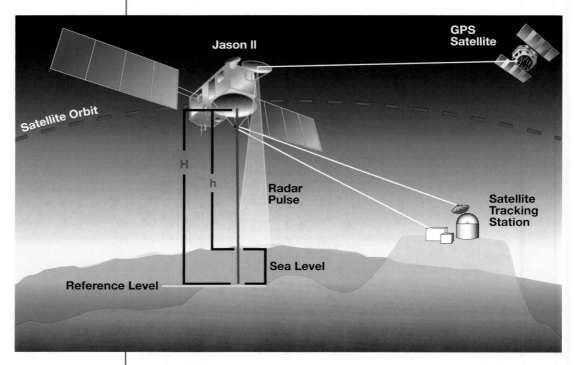

Figure 11-32

Ocean surface topography from space.

The Jason II satellite measures geostrophic currents using altimetry. A ground tracking station along with a GPS satellite measures the satellite's height **(H)** above a reference level of Earth's interior. Jason II sends out a radar pulse that reflects off the sea. The time it takes to go down and back is used to calculate the height **(h)** of the satellite from the seas surface. **H-h** = the height of sea level.

study currents. This is called the *flotsam method*. An example of this method occurred in May 1990, and another in January 1992. In both cases, ships in storms lost readily identifiable cargo overboard. In the first incident, a cargo carrier en route to Seattle, Washington, from Korea lost 30,000 pairs of athletic shoes. Six months later, they started washing up on the beaches of British Columbia and Oregon. Oceanographer Curtis Ebbesmeyer asked the public to help by reporting the date, place, and time they found the shoes. Based on these data, he was able to improve computer models of currents in the North Pacific.

In the second case, a ship lost 29,000 rubber ducks, frogs, and turtles while sailing from China to Seattle. Some of the toys washed up along the North Pacific coast at various locations from Oregon to Alaska, moving at a rate predicted by the improved current model. Eventually other toys drifted through the Bering Strait. By 2000, some rubber ducks had reached the North Atlantic. Although the thought of these rubber ducks helping scientists sounds amusing, more than 10,000 containers fall off ships annually, contributing to marine pollution and litter.

Similar to studying the incidents with shoes and ducks, scientists study seeds and pods found adrift for clues about currents. Seeds that redistribute themselves by drifting in the current are called *sea beans*, and include coconuts and the seeds of mangroves. When gathering support for his expedition to reach east by sailing west, Columbus used seeds washed up in Portugal as evidence of another landmass.

Cheryl Regan

Figure 11-33

Oceanography by accident.

Almost anything that falls into the water and floats – including toys and athletic shoes – can give scientists insight into the behavior of surface ocean currents.

ARE YOU LEARNING?

1. The _____ method studies currents by traveling with their flow. The _____ method studies currents by measuring the water that flows by a fixed point.

    A. Eulerian, Lagrangian
    B. Eulerian, Doppler
    C. drogue, Lagrangian
    D. Lagrangian, Eulerian

2. Examples of instruments or methods used to study currents include (choose all that apply)

    A. drogues.
    B. Argo float.
    C. flow meters.
    D. Doppler Acoustic Current Meters.
    E. satellites.
    F. radioactive chemicals.
    G. rubber ducks.

New Terms You Learned

- **cold-core eddies** circular loops of water that break away from currents, flow counterclockwise in the Northern Hemisphere, and have cool water centers (p. 11-11)
- **contour currents** bottom currents that flow around obstacles and that are influenced by bottom topography (p. 11-29)
- **countercurrent** current that runs in the opposite direction of an adjacent current (p. 11-16)
- **deep circulation** movement of water created by the mixing of water masses of different densities (p. 11-26)
- **Doppler shift** the change in a wave frequency caused by a change in speed or direction (p. 11-34)
- **downwelling** a downward vertical current that pushes surface water toward the bottom (p. 11-17)
- **eddies** large circular loops that break away from currents; caused by friction from the flow of a current (p. 11-11)
- **Ekman spiral** the spiral of water layers flowing to the right of the layer above in the Northern Hemisphere and to the left of the layer above in the Southern Hemisphere due to Ekman transport (p. 11-17)
- **Ekman transport** the net motion of the water column down to friction depth, which is 90° to the right in the Northern Hemisphere or 90° to the left in the Southern Hemisphere (p. 11-7)
- **ENSO** abbreviation for El Niño-South Oscillation and commonly referred to as El Niño; during ENSO, characterized by the build up of high pressure in the Western Pacific and low pressure to the east; trade winds weaken, and upwelling along the South American coast stops (p. 11-21)
- **Eulerian method** the study of currents through the use of fixed instruments that measure water characteristics as it flows by (p. 11-33)
- **flotsam method** the studying of currents by tracking the highly identifiable items accidentally or naturally adrift in the water (p. 11-37)
- **friction depth** the depth in an Ekman Spiral at which there is insufficient wind energy to overcome friction and move the water below (p. 11-7)
- **geostrophic** related to the Earth's rotation (Coriolis effect) (p. 11-9)
- **geostrophic currents** currents created by the rotation of the Earth (Coriolis effect) (p. 11-9)
- **gyre** the circular flow of currents in an ocean basin due to the Coriolis effect (p. 11-5)
- **Lagrangian method** also known as the float method; a study of currents performed by tracking a drifting object (p. 11-33)
- **ocean** from the Greek word okeanos and the Latin oceanus; a large expanse of salt water; includes any of the Earth's five largest oceans – Atlantic, Pacific, Indian, Arctic and Antarctic; covering about 71% of the Earth's surface (p. 11-2)
- **ocean conveyor belt** the interconnected surface and deep water currents that redistribute heat throughout the world (p. 11-30)
- **pressure gradient force** the force of water flowing away from a mound water where a current interrupts its flow (p. 11-3)
- **sea beans** seeds that redistribute themselves by drifting in current (p. 11-37)
- **sea level** the average level of the sea's surface at its mean level between high and low tide (p. 11-3)
- **Southern Oscillation** part of the ENSO event; a "seesaw" in air pressure. When air pressure is high in the eastern Pacific, it is low in the Western Pacific and vice-versa (p. 11-23)
- **sverdrup** unit of measurement for current flow that equals one million cubic meters per second (p. 11-10)
- **undercurrent** current that runs in the opposite direction and beneath a surface current (p. 11-16)
- **upwelling** upward vertical current that brings deep water to the surface (p. 11-17)

- **warm-core eddies** circular loops of water that break away from currents, flow clockwise in the Northern Hemisphere, and have warm water centers (p. 11-11)
- **western intensification** the flow of major ocean currents against western ocean basin boundaries caused by the Coriolis effect (p. 11-13)

Chapter 11 in Review

1. Describe the primary and secondary forces responsible for creating ocean currents.

2. Explain what a gyre is and how it is made up of geostrophic currents.

3. How many major ocean currents are there, where are they located, and what causes them to form? How do western ocean boundary currents differ from eastern ocean boundary currents and why? How do the differences affect the relative speed of these currents?

4. Describe the phenomenon of Ekman transport and the interaction of the forces that are responsible for its occurrence. What is an Ekman spiral?

5. What makes coastal upwelling and downwelling occur? How do they affect the biological productivity where they occur?

6. What role do currents play in transporting heat? Why is this important? What happens when a warm-phase ENSO (El Niño) occurs?

7. How does deep circulation differ from wind-driven surface circulation? What is its general pattern?

8. Diagram and label the five distinct water masses that result from density stratification.

9. Explain where and how the distinct deep water masses form. Explain how the mixing of water masses helps create deep circulation. Explain what the ocean conveyor belt is and how it affects Earth's climate. What do some scientists think will happen if something disrupts the ocean conveyor belt? Why would this happen?

10. What are three approaches to studying currents? List an example of how scientists have used each approach.

Connecting Chapter Concepts – Science Scenarios

1. Currents are "rivers" within the ocean that move vast amounts of water across Earth's surface. This water carries with it heat and nutrients, making currents important influences on climates and ecosystems.
   A. What is the primary force that causes surface ocean currents?
   B. What phenomena results from the combination of current flow and the Coriolis effect in the large ocean basins? What are their key characteristics?
   C. What major ocean current is not part of an ocean basin gyre? Why?
   D. What is the current-related hypothesis of some historians regarding 14 ships of the 1588 Spanish Armada that wrecked on the north shores of Scotland and Ireland?

2. Currents redistribute about a third of the heat the tropics receive, which cools their climates and warms other areas that would be cooler. As a result, some areas have climates that differ substantially from what they would have without the currents.
   A. What role does current play in the climate of Southern California?
   B. The Galapagos Islands lie in the Pacific Ocean just off the coast of South America very near the equator. Most areas at this latitude have a very hot, tropical climate, but the Galapagos have a cool climate. Explain why.
   C. How does a weakening of the Trade Winds in the Eastern Pacific every three to eight years affect weather patterns? What is the name of this back-and-forth pattern?

Marine Science and the Real World

1. Look at the maps showing the world's surface currents and the ocean conveyor belt. How could these currents relate to international politics? Consider fishing resources, pollution, trash dumping, and the cost of shipping.

2. Imagine you're a scientist who has just discovered not only what causes a warm-phase ENSO event, but also a way to stop it from happening. Considering the damage and death such events have caused, would you prevent the next one? Why or why not?

3. Speculate on how a decrease in the movement of the ocean conveyor belt would affect diverse aspects of society. Include the effects on habitable areas, agriculture, tourism, politics, and recreation.

4. Suppose a ship must abandon its cargo, like those ships that lost athletic shoes and rubber ducks. Which do you think would make a better "instrument" for studying currents – 50,000 empty, bright colored, capped plastic bottles or 50,000 neutral-colored biodegradable sponges? Would one type of cargo be better in some situations but not in others? Why or why not?

5. Find information on the Sargasso Sea in Chapter 5. What relationship, if any, do you find with the North Atlantic Gyre?

References

Bird, J. 1991. Supercomputer Voyages to the Southern Seas. *Science.* 254 (no. 5032).

Blankenberg, F. 1999. Tracing Past Ocean Circulation. *Science.* 286 (no. 5446). December.

Cramer, D. 2001. *Great Waters: An Atlantic Passage.* New York: W.W. Norton and Company.

DeVries, T. J., et al. 1997. Determining the Early History of El Niño. *Science.* 276 (no. 5314). May.

Garrison, T. 2004. *Essentials of Oceanography.* Pacific Grove, CA: Brooks/Cole, a division of Thomson Learning, Inc.

Garrison, T. 2004. *Oceanography: An Invitation to Marine Science.* Pacific Grove, CA: Brooks/Cole, a division of Thomson Learning, Inc.

Hollister, C. D., and A. Nowell. 1984. The Dynamic Abyss. *Scientific American.* March.

Kerr, R. 1997. A New Driver for the Atlantic's Moods and Europe's Weather? *Science.* 275. February.

MacLeish, W. H. 1989. Painting a Portrait of the Stream from Miles 41 Above and Below. *Smithsonian.* March.

MacLeish, W. H. 1989. *The Gulf Stream: Encounters with the Blue God.* New York: Houghton Mifflin.

Physical Oceanography. 1992. *Oceanus.* Special issue 35 (no. 2).

Philander, S. G. 1990. *El Niño, La Niña, and the Southern Oscillation.* San Diego: Academic Press.

Rasmussen, E. M. 1999. El Niño and Variations in Climate. *American Scientist.* 73 (no. 2).

Richardson, P. L. 1991. SOFAR Floats Give a New View to Ocean Eddies. *Oceanus.* 34 (no. 1).

Rothstein, L. M. and D. Chen. 1996. The El Niño/Southern Oscillation Phenomenon — Seeking Its "Trigger" and Working Toward Prediction. *Oceanus.* 39 (no. 2). Fall/Winter.

Stommel, H. 1987. *A View of the Sea.* Princeton: Princeton University Press.

Wiebe, P. 1982. Rings of the Gulf Stream. *Scientific American.* March.

Windows to the Universe team. 2000. *Deep Waters of the Ocean.* Boulder, CO: The Regents of the University of Michigan. http://www.windows.ucar.edu

http://www.pmel.noaa.gov/tao/elnimo/faq.html

http://seawifs.gsfc.nasa.gov/OCEAN_PLANET/HTML/oceanography_currents_1.html

CHAPTER 12

Waves and Tides

Tristan Bawn/http: uk-active.co.uk

Storm Hunter

Hurricanes have threatened human life and property since the first settlers made camp along the United States' Gulf and Atlantic coastlines. As our coastal population continues to swell, the potential for catastrophe increases dramatically. Oceanographers, including Evan Forde, however, are applying their expertise in various related disciplines to the problem. They are learning to better detect forming hurricanes and forecast the intensity levels with better hurricane prediction models.

Forde's interest in oceanography surfaced while he was in his teens. "My high school teacher was an avid scuba diver and always had interesting ways to help us understand the undersea world. One day, my teacher released a live crab into our octopus-inhabited classroom aquarium (often used for demonstrations of actual undersea scenarios). The octopus eventually ate the crab, but we were stunned that the crab, while defending itself, cut off two of the octopus' tentacles before he was subdued and consumed. I was fascinated, entertained, and hooked. I went on to receive my bachelor's degree in geology and my master's degree in marine geology and geophysics, both from Columbia University."

Forde, who has worked for the United States National Oceanic and Atmospheric Administration (NOAA) since 1973, now uses satellites to identify not only oceanic weather systems favorable to hurricane development, but also the effects of long-term climate change on hurricane development.

Forde isn't behind a computer crunching numbers all day every day. He also spends time aboard research submersibles. This has helped him to understand the development, morphology, and present-day evolution of submarine canyons, and to discover previously uncatalogued anemones and several small deep-sea creatures.

To aspiring oceanographers, Forde offers the following advice: "Get a diverse undergraduate science background and take as many writing and computer programming classes as you can. Good writing skills are often under-emphasized, but are essential for any scientific researcher. Students need to have a good understanding of basic computer programming, logic, and mathematics to manipulate, plot, and analyze data. These diverse skills will prepare you for the ever-changing world of scientific research. Above all, be persistent if you are sure this is the career for you. It can be hard to break into, but the effort is worthwhile. One of my strongest assets is that I am very determined and refuse to give up – ever. I love my job and would do scientific research even if I were a billionaire."

Evan B. Forde, MA
Research Oceanographer,
Atlantic Oceanographic and
Meteorological Laboratory (AOML)
Satellite Remote Sensing Group,
National Oceanic and Atmospheric
Administration (NOAA)

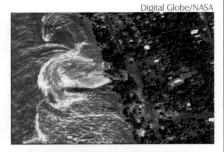

Figure 12-1

2004 Indian Ocean tsunami.

This aerial image shows the tsunami actually moving beyond the beach and heading inland causing great destruction.

T*sunamis* have historically been a problem for Hawaiians. Triggered by geological events up to thousands of kilometers away, tsunamis can come ashore at more than 33 meters (108 feet) above sea level. These unpredictable giant waves crash ashore with devastating force. In 1946, a tsunami hit Hilo, Hawaii, killing more than 150 people. However, in a tragedy almost beyond comprehension, a tsunami struck the edges of the Indian Ocean in 2004, killing more than 225,000 people.

The 1946 Hawaiian tsunami disaster prompted the development of the International Tsunami Warning System for the Pacific Ocean. In 1957, a larger tsunami hit Hawaii, but no one died. This time, Hawaiians knew that the wave was on its way and cleared the beaches. Unfortunately, no such system was available in the Indian Ocean in 2004.

Today, the Pacific Ocean Tsunami Warning System (TWS) is one of the most successful measures we can use against a natural disaster. When seismologists record a major earthquake or other event that can initiate a tsunami, they trigger the TWS. Islanders throughout the Pacific evacuate the low-lying, at-risk areas. Monitoring stations measure the wave size as it passes and transmit the information to other areas.

Thanks to this system, people in Hawaii usually know about a tsunami's arrival, hours ahead of time. They have plenty of time to clear the beaches and move away from other threatened areas. They know exactly when it will hit because of measurements that are made as it travels, but they do not know how far it will come ashore.

Figure 12-2

Tsunami aftermath.

This image shows the incredible devastation caused by the 2004 Indian Ocean tsunami.

Other natural disasters are not as easy to predict as tsunamis. Tornados are short-lived yet tremendously destructive and deadly. So far, there is no way to give warnings greater than a few minutes for a tornado. Hurricanes give plenty of warning; however, scientists cannot predict precisely where they will strike. Consequently, evacuations can be inefficient because they have to be broad.

Hawaii's tsunami warning system provides an important lesson. It shows that with adequate warning, we can save lives and reduce damage caused by natural events. In 2006, the Indian Ocean Tsunami Warning System became active. The investment made in such a system more than pays for itself. It gives people time to evacuate before a tsunami hits and it gives people greater peace of mind as they rebuild their homes or decide to vacation in a coastal area.

The Nature of Waves

Anatomy of a Wave

What is a wave?

What are three types of progressive waves?

What are the crest, trough, height, wavelength, period, *and* frequency *of a wave?*

How do wavelength and period relate to a wave's speed?

Before we can look at what waves do in the sea and how they affect life there, it is useful to know something about waves themselves. They are more complex than they appear. By understanding the basic principles of waves, you will understand how different types of waves produce different effects in the marine environment.

A *wave* is the transmission of energy through matter. When energy moves through matter as a wave, the matter moves back and forth or rotates, but then it returns to its original position. It transmits the energy to adjacent matter, allowing the energy to continue. For instance, imagine dropping a stone in a pond. Waves ripple away from the splash. The water particles do not move away, only the energy.

As you watch the rippling, you can see the energy move as a series of waves away from the disturbance as a *progressive wave*. It is called a progressive wave because you can see the energy progress from one point to another. There are three types of progressive waves – *longitudinal*, *transverse*, and *orbital*.

A longitudinal wave occurs when the matter moves back and forth in the same direction that the energy travels. This type of wave can move through all states of matter, transmitted

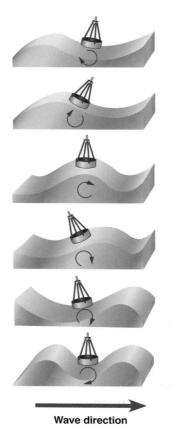

Wave direction

STUDY QUESTIONS

Find the answers as you read.

1. What is a *wave*?

2. What are three types of *progressive waves*?

3. What are the *crest, trough, height, wavelength, period,* and *frequency* of a wave?

4. How do wavelength and period relate to a wave's speed?

5. What *disturbing forces* cause waves?

6. What *restoring forces* resist waves?

7. What are the differences between *deepwater waves* and *shallow-water* waves?

8. What three factors affect the maximum wave size?

9. How can a *fully developed sea* have waves that are bigger or smaller than the maximum theoretical size?

10. What causes *internal ocean waves*?

Figure 12-3

Orbital wave motion.

As a wave approaches a buoy, the buoy moves forward on the wave face. It rises, goes over the crest, and slides backward down the rear of the wave. Individual particles of water move in circular patterns (shown by curved arrow) as the wave's energy moves through the water.

through the compression and decompression of particles, much like a spring or Slinky toy. Sound is a longitudinal wave.

When transverse waves occur in matter, the motion of the matter is perpendicular to the direction in which the wave as a whole is moving. For example, when you shake one end of a taut, horizontal

Figure 12-4

Major wave components and orbital pattern.

The wavelength is the horizontal distance between the identical points on two waves – in this illustration the horizontal distance from **A** to **B**. The crest is the highest wave point above the average water level. The trough is the lowest point, and the height is the vertical measurement from the trough to the crest. Period is the time it takes for the same spot on two waves to pass a single point, while frequency is the number of waves that pass a fixed point in one second. Note the orbital wave pattern tapering in intensity down to a depth equal to one half the wave's wavelength.

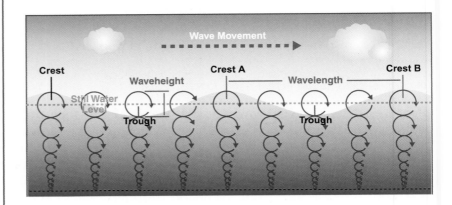

rope up and down, the rope moves vertically, but the wave travels horizontally along the length of the rope.

Orbital waves only transmit through fluids. With respect to the ocean, these are primarily the waves that concern us. They occur when the energy moves the fluid in a circular motion as it passes. Imagine a floating buoy as shown in Figure 12-1. As the wave approaches, the buoy moves forward on the wave face. It rises, goes over the crest, and slides backward down the rear of the wave.

Although the water (fluid) travels through an orbital motion, it returns to its original place. Only the energy moves along. Looking at the buoy, it looks like the orbital motion occurs only in a single plane. Actually, the orbital motion continues in progressively smaller orbits down to a depth of about half the wave's *wavelength*. Wavelength is one of several terms that we use to discuss waves. Others include the *crest, trough, height, period,* and *frequency*. The crest is the highest point above the average water level, the trough is the lowest point, and the height is the vertical distance from the trough to the crest. Wavelength is the horizontal distance between the identical points on two waves, such as crest to crest (Figure 12-4). Period is the time it takes for the same spot on two waves to pass a single point, while frequency is the number of waves that pass a fixed point in one second.

Wave characteristics can be expressed mathematically. This is useful because it allows you to calculate wave behaviors based on the information you have. *H:L* is the ratio of the wave height to wavelength. Later, you will see how we use this to determine when a wave will break.

If you know the wavelength (L: distance in meters) and the period (T: time in seconds), you can determine the *speed* of waves (S: speed in meters per second):

speed = wavelength ÷ period

This is sometimes abbreviated:

S = L ÷ T

The chart below compares the period, wavelength, and speed of wind-generated waves and tsunami waves.

Wind-Generated Wave:

Example 1	T = 4 s	L = 60 m	S = 60 m ÷ 4 s = 15 m/s
Example 2	T = 5 s	L = 100 m	S = 100 m ÷ 5 s = 20 m/s
Example 3	T = 10 s	L = 150 m	S = 150 m ÷ 10 s = 15 m/s

Tsunami: (converted to seconds and meters)

Example 1	T = 15 min	L = 192 km	
	T = 900 s	L = 192,000 m	S = 192,000 m ÷ 900 s = 213 m/s
Example 2	T = 16 min	L = 200 km	
	T = 960 s	L = 200,000 m	S = 200,000 m ÷ 960 s = 208 m/s

Wave Causes and Characteristics

What disturbing forces *cause waves?*

What restoring forces *resist waves?*

What are the differences between deepwater waves *and* shallow-water waves?

What three factors affect the maximum wave size?

How can a fully developed sea *have waves that are bigger or smaller than the maximum theoretical size?*

You now know the definition of a wave, the three types of progressive waves, and the anatomy of a wave. Let's look at what causes waves and how they behave in the ocean. *Disturbing forces* create waves and *restoring forces* resist their creation. The intensity and duration of a disturbing force and the interaction of restorative forces give waves their characteristics.

Fluids tend to remain at rest on the Earth. They move only when something imparts energy to them and disturbs them. Disturbing forces that cause ocean waves include wind, changes in gravity, and seismic activity. Wind is the most common disturbing force. As wind blows over water, friction creates waves. Changes in gravity cause waves you probably don't think of as waves; these are the tides. These have characteristics that distinguish them significantly from what we normally think of as waves, so we will look at them separately toward the end of this chapter. Seismic activity includes earthquakes and volcanic eruptions, which can cause tsunamis.

Each kind of disturbing force tends to produce waves with distinct wavelengths. Wind commonly creates wavelengths of about 60 to 150 meters (200 to 500 feet). The wavelength of the tides is about the size of the ocean basins, and tsunamis have wavelengths of about 200 kilometers (120 miles).

Restoring forces that resist ocean wave formation include gravity, the Coriolis effect, and surface tension. Gravity is the main restoring force for large waves and seismic waves. It tends to flatten waves by pulling water back to level. Gravity and the Coriolis effect are the primary restoring forces for the tides, because their wavelengths are so long. Surface tension is an important restoring force for the tiniest waves, called *capillary waves*, which have wavelengths of about 1.7 centimeters (0.7 inches) or less. Surface tension is caused by the strongly polar nature of bonds in water, which resist surface disturbances.

You can classify waves based on which restoring force has the most effect. *Capillary waves* are classified as such because the primary force countering them is surface tension. Capillary waves are the first to form as wind blows across still water. As waves grow larger, however, surface tension becomes relatively insignificant as a primary restoring force. Gravity – the weight of the wave – takes over, so we call large waves *gravity waves*. For practical purposes, most of the waves that concern us in oceanography are gravity waves.

Figure 12-5

Wavelengths, disturbing, and restoring forces of ocean waves.

WAVELENGTHS, DISTURBING FORCES, AND RESTORING FORCES OF OCEAN WAVES

Wave type	Standard wavelength	Primary disturbing force	Primary restoring force
Wind wave (capillary)	Less than 1.73 centimeters	Wind	Surface tension
Wind wave (gravity)	Up to 150 meters	Wind	Gravity
Seismic wave	200 kilometers	Seismic activity	Gravity
Tide	Up to 17,000 kilometers	Sun's and moon's gravity	Gravity and Coriolis effect

Although disturbing forces can be somewhat random in their intensity, duration, and place of origin, waves tend to organize themselves into patterns. Waves that are not so organized travel at different speeds. The longest waves outrun the smaller ones. Eventually only waves of similar wavelengths are left traveling together. They are called a *swell,* which is simply the rise and fall of waves with nearly the same frequency and wavelength.

Groups of swells with similar characteristics tend to travel together in *wave trains.* The first wave in the train gradually loses energy, which is picked up by new waves forming in the trailing portion of the train. As the leading waves dissipate, the trailing waves form and join the train. The entire train moves at half the speed of individual waves through this process of dissipation and reformation. When the wave train reaches shallow water, the individual and group speeds become the same. This is because as depth changes, so do wave characteristics. Waves are classified as *deepwater waves, transitional waves,* or *shallow-water waves.*

Deepwater waves occur in water that is deeper than half their wavelength. Water motion in orbital waves decreases very quickly with depth. A fish swimming at 20 meters (66 feet) would not notice any effects from a wave passing overhead if the wavelength is 40 meters (131 feet) or less. If the water is deeper than half the wavelength, then no interaction with the bottom can affect the wave characteristics. Because the bottom does not affect deepwater waves, their orbital motion progresses unaffected.

When the water is shallower than one-fourth the wavelength, the bottom affects the orbital motion. This tends to flatten the circular motion into an ellipse. When the depth is about one-twentieth of the wavelength, the wave becomes a shallow-water wave. In depths between one-half and one-twentieth the wavelength, waves are transitional, progressing from deepwater to shallow-water characteristics.

Deepwater and shallow-water waves can exist at the same time. A good example is the giant wave created by the tides. By defini-

Figure 12-6

Deepwater and shallow-water waves.

(A) When water depth is greater than half the wavelength, waves are called deepwater waves. Water motion in these orbital waves decreases rapidly as depth increases. At a depth equal to one-half the wavelength, there is less than 5% of the motion that exists at the water's surface. When the depth is less than one-fourth the wavelength, there is no room for the waves to move in circles and wave motion becomes elliptical. **(B)** When water is shallower than one-twentieth the wavelength, waves are classified as shallow-water waves.

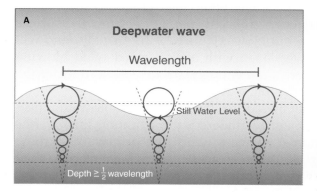

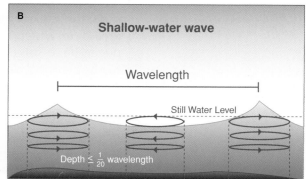

tion, this is always a shallow-water wave because the wavelength is about the size of its ocean basin. For a tide to be a deepwater wave, the ocean would have to be deeper than the diameter of the Earth! The wind creates waves, which can be deepwater waves on top of the tides. Capillary waves are almost always deepwater waves because the water only needs to be 0.9 centimeters (0.35 inches) deep.

As previously mentioned, wind waves grow due to friction with the air transferring energy to the water. As a wave grows, it presents a larger surface area to the wind, allowing more energy to transfer. The three factors that affect the growth of a wind wave are wind speed, wind duration, and *fetch*.

Figure 12-7

Fetch.

In this illustration, the winds are originating along the Sefton coast of England and heading toward Scotland and Ireland. If the wind speed and duration were the same in all areas shown on this map, the waves would be highest along the Ireland coast. The waves would be highest because the fetch is the longest, 200 km (124 miles). The longer the fetch length and the faster the wind speed, the larger and stronger the waves will be.

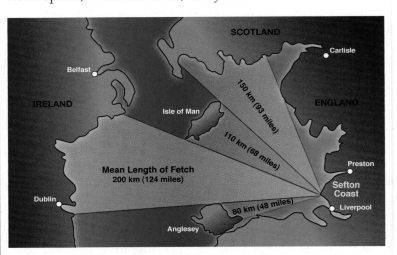

Distances of fetch affecting the Sefton Coast.
Reproduced from the Sefton Coast Database.

Wind speed is important because the wind must be blowing faster than the wave to give it energy. Wind duration is the length of time the wind blows in a single direction. Even a high-speed wind will not cause large waves when the duration is short or the direction makes frequent significant changes. Fetch is the surface area over which the wind blows (Figure 12-7). A small pond will never have huge waves, even with a high-speed wind blowing for hours, because there's not enough surface area to transfer the required energy to form a big wave.

The combination of these three factors yields a maximum theoretical wave size. Above this theoretical maximum, gravity (the primary restoring force) balances wind (the primary disturbing force) and waves break. When an area's waves have reached their maximum size, the region is called a *fully developed sea*.

With wind speed, duration, and fetch all acting as independent variables, a fully developed sea is not necessarily a sea with huge waves. As you can see in Figure 12-8, average wave heights for fully developed seas range from about a third of a meter (about one foot) to about 14 meters (46 feet).

As in the example of the small pond, these three factors also influence the largest waves that an ocean can have. Remember that an ocean often has large, unobstructed stretches of water over which wind waves can develop.

At times a wave can be larger than the maximum theoretical size for a fully developed sea. Scientists believe such a *rogue wave* results from the interaction of two closely related wave trains.

When wave trains come together from different areas, they affect each other in the form of constructive or destructive interference. If the waves are *in phase*, the crests and troughs coincide so the heights of the waves are constructive and combine to make larger waves. Also, anomalously large waves can result when waves go against the direction of a current, which makes the waves steeper. This second mechanism is probably a more important cause of rogue waves.

If wave trains are *out of phase*, so that the crests of one train coincide with the troughs of the other, the waves cancel each other out. Neither constructive nor destructive interference can act over distances greater than a few wavelengths. Therefore, for example, destructive interference cannot result in a relatively calm sea during strong winds.

It is relatively rare for trains coming together to have exactly the same wavelength and to be synchronized. They are usually timed slightly differently, and interacting trains tend to alternate between

CONDITIONS FOR A FULLY DEVELOPED SEA WITH A GIVEN WIND SPEED

wind speed (kilometers per hour)	average wave height (meters)
30	.88
40	1.8
50	3.2
60	5.1
70	7.4
80	10.3
90	13.9

Figure 12-8

Conditions for a fully developed sea with a given wind speed.

British Antarctic Survey/Global Carbon Project

Figure 12-9a

Figure 12-9b

Antarctic sea waves.
Some of the largest wind waves in the world occur near Antarctica. They can circle the continent without encountering obstructing landmasses.

N. Metzl, August 2000, Global Carbon Project

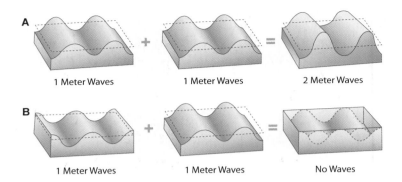

A

1 Meter Waves + 1 Meter Waves = 2 Meter Waves

B

1 Meter Waves + 1 Meter Waves = No Waves

Figure 12-10

Constructive and destructive interference.

When wave trains come together from different areas, they affect each other in the form of constructive or destructive interference. If the waves are in phase **(A)**, the crests and troughs coincide so the wave energies are constructive and combine into larger waves. If they are out of phase **(B),** so that the crests of one train coincide with the troughs of the other, the waves cancel each other out. Note that real waves at sea never exactly conform to these ideal models of wave interference.

Courtesy of www.sf-raum.de

Figure 12-11

Internal wave demonstration.

This desk top wave machine shows an internal wave involving two liquids of differing densities.

Figure 12-12

Internal ocean waves.

Internal ocean waves can occur within different density layers. The wave motion in a deep layer can cause a thermocline, halocline, or pycnocline (a region of a water column where density increases rapidly with depth) to slowly rise and fall as the wave passes. Here two water layers of differing density create an internal wave.

being constructive and destructive. This results in a mixed sea with periods of large and small waves. You have probably seen surf patterns that cycle from periods of calm, build to large waves, then, regress to calm again, and so on. This is the effect of two slightly different wave trains coming together.

Internal Waves

What causes internal ocean waves?

We think of waves as phenomena that occur on the sea surface. However, a wave is energy that travels through matter, not just on top of it. Wind waves are progressive and occur where two fluids—water and air—meet. However, waves can move inside the ocean.

Internal ocean waves can occur within different density layers. These waves can be more than 30 meters (100 feet) tall, but they move slowly compared to surface waves. The wave motion in a deep layer can cause a thermocline or halocline to slowly rise and fall as the wave passes. A great example of internal waves is found in the wave machines available in science stores. These consist of two liquids with differing densities (and colors for visual effect) that you rock back and forth. The waves you generate in the lower, denser liquid are internal waves.

Scientists do not exactly know what causes internal waves. It is likely that they get their energy mostly from tides and storms. Breaking internal waves mix the ocean and drive deep circulation.

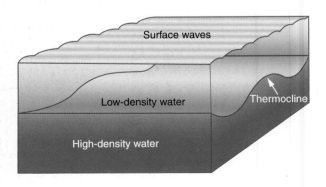

Surface waves

Low-density water

Thermocline

High-density water

1. **An ocean wave is an energy transmission that moves matter along with the energy.**

    A. true

    B. false

2. **_____ are progressive waves. (choose all that apply)**

    A. Orbital

    B. Radial

    C. Longitudinal

    D. Tidal

3. **_____ is the distance between the identical spot on two waves.**

    A. Period

    B. Height

    C. Frequency

    D. Wavelength

4. **Wave speed equals**

    A. wavelength divided by height.

    B. period divided by wavelength.

    C. wavelength divided by period.

    D. height divided by wavelength.

5. **Disturbing forces include (choose all that apply)**

    A. wind.

    B. gravity.

    C. Coriolis effect.

    D. seismic activity.

6. **Restoring forces include (choose all that apply)**

    A. wind.

    B. gravity.

    C. Coriolis effect.

    D. seismic activity.

7. **Deepwater waves occur when the depth is _____. Shallow-water waves occur when the depth is _____.**

    A. greater than half the wavelength, less than half the wavelength

    B. greater than half the wavelength, less than one-twentieth of the wavelength

    C. less than half the wavelength, less than one-twentieth of the wavelength

    D. none of the above

8. **Factors that affect maximum wave size include (choose all that apply)**

    A. wind speed.

    B. wind duration.

    C. fetch.

    D. thermocline.

9. **Fully developed seas can have waves that are bigger or smaller than maximum theoretical size due to**

    A. tides.

    B. greenhouse gases.

    C. constructive and destructive interference.

    D. all of the above

10. **Scientists are not sure what causes internal ocean waves.**

    A. true

    B. false

When Waves Hit the Shore

Surf and Breaking Waves

What makes a wave break?

What happens when a wind wave breaks on shore?

How do wave refraction, diffraction, *and* reflection *affect the behavior of waves?*

What is a standing wave?

If you have ever been to the beach, you've seen waves break and spill their energy as surf. Have you ever thought about *how* a wave breaks?

In deep water, a wave breaks when its H:L ratio exceeds 1:7. That means, when the height exceeds one-seventh of the wavelength, the wave breaks as whitecaps. The same ratio applies in shallow water, though through a different process.

Wind waves (deepwater waves) become transitional when they enter water that is shallower than half their wavelength. At this point, the bottom begins to affect the wave. As it moves shoreward, the orbital motion flattens, becoming elliptical. Interaction with the bottom slows the wave, decreasing the wavelength and packing the wave's energy into a tighter area. This causes the wave height to rise.

As the wave continues moving shoreward (Figure 12-13a), the wavelength continues to decrease and the height continues to

STUDY QUESTIONS

Find the answers as you read.

1. What makes a wave break?

2. What happens when a wind wave breaks on shore?

3. How do *wave refraction, diffraction,* and *reflection* affect the behavior of waves?

4. What is a *standing wave?*

5. What causes storm surges?

6. What causes *seiches?*

7. What causes tsunamis?

8. Why are tsunamis always shallow-water waves?

9. Why don't tsunamis destroy ships in the open sea?

Figure 12-13a

Breaking waves.

Deepwater waves become transitional when they enter water that is shallower than half their wavelength. At this point, the bottom begins to affect the wave. The trough starts to travel more slowly than the crest, decreasing the wavelength and causing the wave height to rise. As the wavelength continues to decrease and the height continues to increase, the wave's H:L ratio moves closer to 1:7. When the wave passes the 1:7 ratio, the bottom of the wave travels more slowly than the top. This topples the upper part of the wave forward, causing it to break.

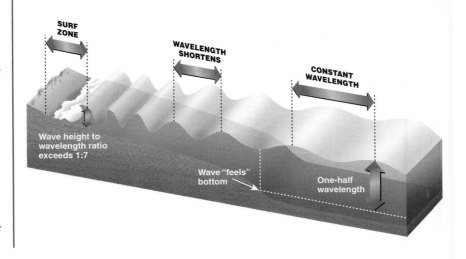

SURF ZONE

WAVELENGTH SHORTENS

CONSTANT WAVELENGTH

Wave height to wavelength ratio exceeds 1:7

Wave "feels" bottom

One-half wavelength

Depth	Wavelength	Height of Wave	H:L Ratio
Decreasing	Decreasing	Increasing	Decreasing
12 m	150 m	1 m	1:150
6 m	90 m	2 m	1:45
4 m	21 m	3 m	1:7

Figure 12-13b

Characteristics of a wave approaching a shore.

This chart depicts what happens to a wave as it approaches a beach. The height of the wave increases and the depth, wavelength, and ratio of height to wavelength decreases. At 1:7 the wave topples.

increase, moving the wave closer and closer toward an H:L ratio of 1:7. The wave passes the 1:7 ratio when the depth is 1.3 times the height (Figure 12-13b). Because the crest of the wave is now traveling faster than its trough, and because its height is more than 1.7 times its length, the wave becomes unstable. The instability causes the wave to break, and its crest topples forward.

There are three basic types of breaking waves. *Plunging breakers* (Figure 12-14a) are characterized by a curl, created as the top of the wave pitches through the air before splashing into the bottom. These occur on moderately steep beaches that decelerate the wave quickly, so the top of the wave literally flies ahead of the bottom. *Spilling breakers* occur on gentle slope beaches (Figure 12-14b). The top of the wave tumbles and slides down the front of the wave as it decelerates slowly. *Surging breakers* occur on very steep beaches that are almost like walls rising out of deep water. Since there is little or no bottom contact, the waves do not slow down, but surge virtually unbroken. Surging waves can be very destructive because they do not lose much energy until they reach the shore.

This description of surf is somewhat idealized because it assumes that when wave crests strike the shore, they are parallel to the shore. In reality, that rarely happens. *Refraction, diffraction,* and *reflection* affect wave behavior.

You may already be familiar with refraction as the bending of light rays. It also means the bending of ocean waves. This happens when waves approach the shore at an angle. The crest closest to shore reaches shallow water first and slows sooner than the crest away from shore. Because of this uneven slowing, the waves refract, or bend, until the wave crests become more parallel to the shore. (Figure 12-15a). When the shoreline is irregular, refraction tends to concentrate wave energy toward headlands because the wave crest nearest to the headland slows first, turning the wave toward it (Figure 12-15b).

Figure 12-14a

Plunging breaker.

Figure 12-14b

Spilling breaker.

Bruce Perry

Figure 12-15a

Wave refraction.

Refraction occurs when waves approach a shore at an angle. As they approach, wave crests become parallel to shore.

Figure 12-15b

Wave refraction at a headland.

When the shoreline is irregular, refraction tends to concentrate wave energy toward headlands because the wave crest nearest to the headland slows first, turning the wave toward it.

Wave diffraction (Figure 12-16) occurs when waves pass an obstacle, such as a jetty or a point of land. Energy shifts within the wave, allowing a new wave pattern to form past the obstacle or through an opening. Diffraction is what allows very heavy seas to rock an otherwise well-protected harbor. Waves diffracted after passing through island channels can alter swell patterns well offshore. Evidence suggests that the early Polynesian seafarers discussed in Chapter 2 used diffracted waves to aid their navigation.

Reflection occurs when waves hit an abrupt obstacle that is nearly perpendicular in the water, such as a sea wall. The wave retains most of its energy and bounces back toward the open water.

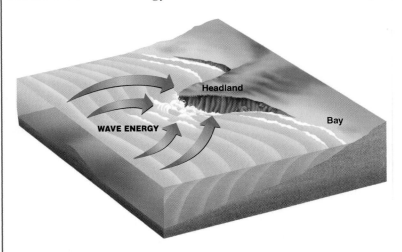

Reflected wave energy can bounce around the inside of an enclosed area, creating complex wave patterns. A good example is the pattern that you get with a single splash in a still swimming pool. At first a single wave set travels from the splash, but when it reaches a wall, it reflects in a new direction as a new set of waves. Meanwhile, the other side of the wave reaches another wall, doing the same thing. Soon, there is no discernible pattern as the reflected waves interact and continue to reflect.

Reflection can also cause a *standing wave*. A standing wave (Figure 12-17) is a vertical oscil-

Michael Rymer

Figure 12-16

Wave diffraction.

Wave diffraction occurs when waves pass an obstacle. Energy shifts within the wave, allowing a new wave pattern to form past the obstacle or through an opening.

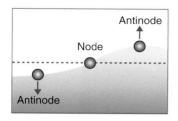 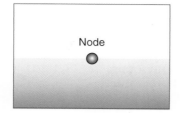 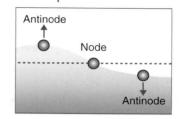

lation in which water rocks back and forth, rising and falling at the ends but relatively motionless near the center, like coffee sloshing back and forth after you bump the cup. A standing wave is not orbital, but has a trough and crest that alternate in a single position. The point in the wave that is stationary is called its *node*; the *antinodes* occur where there is maximum vertical change.

Destructive Waves

What causes storm surges?

What causes seiches?

What causes tsunamis?

Why are tsunamis always shallow-water waves?

Why don't tsunamis destroy ships in the open sea?

On the open sea, even very large waves can seem harmless. A ship rides up and over them. When they reach shallow water and unleash their energy, however, their power becomes visible. Waves driven by storm winds can be dangerous to coastal areas. There are three distinct types of waves noted for their destructive power: storm surge, seiche, and tsunami.

Storm surge (Figure 12-18) is a destructive wave that forms when high winds push water against the shore, where it piles up. The shallower the water offshore, and the further it extends offshore, the greater the surge. This is why the US Gulf Coast has the biggest storm surges, which can exceed 9 meters (30 feet) for a Category 5 hurricane. Much of the damage caused by Hurricane Ike, which struck the Houston, Texas area in September 2008, resulted when storm surge flooded coastal communities.

National Weather Service Collection, NOAA

Figure 12-17

Standing wave.

A standing wave is a vertical oscillation in which water rocks back and forth, rising and falling at the ends but remaining relatively motionless near the center. The point in the wave that is stationary is called its node; the antinodes occur where there is maximum vertical change.

Figure 12-18

Storm surge.

In September 1975, 4.9 meter (16 foot) storm surge struck the Florida Panhandle during Hurricane Eloise.

Seiche

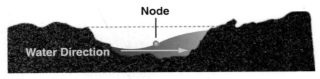

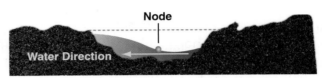

Figure 12-19

Seiche.

A seiche is the sloshing of a closed body of water, as in an ocean harbor or bay. The back-and-forth water movement can be caused by a local earthquake or when a strong wind blowing in one direction suddenly stops.

When the storm moves ashore, the storm surge builds on top of the tide. The damage to low-lying coastal areas can be tremendous when storm surge and an extremely high tide coincide. Although hurricane winds cause the most structural damage, about 90% of deaths in a hurricane result from the storm surge. Storm surge is not a progressive wave, it is a pile of water and exists only in cyclonic storms.

Seiche (pronounced "SAYsh") is a form of standing wave that can be destructive. Seiches (Figure 12-19), which form in large bays and lakes as a wave that rocks back and forth, can result from a local earthquake and a strong wind that pushes the water level up on one side of a lake or basin. When the wind abates, the water rocks back and forth in the basin at a frequency determined by the size and depth of the basin.

Lake Geneva, Switzerland, is known for seiches and is, in fact, where scientists first described the phenomenon. All the Great Lakes have seiches regularly. When combined with storm waves, seiches sometimes cause damage to waterfront property.

A *tsunami* results from sudden water displacement caused by a landslide, an iceberg falling into the sea from a glacier, a volcanic eruption, or, most commonly, an earthquake. Tsunamis get their name from the Japanese word for *harbor wave* because of their particular destructiveness in harbors and bays. You may have also heard them called tidal waves, though this is a misnomer because they are not caused by the tides or directly related to the tides in any way.

Initially it may seem strange, but all tsunamis are shallow-water waves in the same way that the tides are shallow-water waves.

Topic: Tsunamis
Go To: www.scilinks.org
Code: LOP2290

The typical tsunami has a wavelength of about 200 kilometers (120 miles), yet the deepest point in the ocean (Marianas Trench) is about 11 kilometers (6.8 miles) deep. There is no ocean deep enough to make a tsunami behave as a deepwater wave.

Figure 12-20a

Tsunami.
This tsunami inundated Hilo, Hawaii.

Figure 12-20b

Tsunami damage.
This 1963 tsunami swept fishing boats into the town of Kodiak, Alaska.

Tsunamis are fast-moving waves that can travel thousands of kilometers. They are not much of an issue in the open sea. They have very long wavelengths and are nearly imperceptible as they travel. Vessels may rise and fall about 1 meter when a tsunami passes, but they do so very gradually. Japanese folklore relates an incident in which fishermen at sea all day sailed home to find their village wiped out by a tsunami. The fishermen were unaware that it had passed under them.

When a tsunami reaches shore, it becomes much higher. The wave surges ashore, breaks and hurls a tremendous water mass and energy onto land as shown in Figure 12-20a&b. If the trough precedes the crest to shore, the wave water recedes as if a massive low tide were in progress. The building period can take several minutes and has accounted for many fatalities. Curious beachgoers,

CLOCKING A TSUNAMI

Care to outswim a tsunami? Just how fast are tsunamis, anyway? If you know the depth, you can figure it out for yourself. The velocity of a shallow-water wave is determined by this equation:

$$V = \sqrt{gd}$$

where:

V = velocity

g = the acceleration of gravity (9.8 meters per second squared)

and

d = the water depth.

That is, velocity = square root of gravity times depth.

Suppose a tsunami originates in water that is 4,000 meters deep.

$$V = \sqrt{(9.8 \text{ m/s}^2) \times (4,000 \text{ m})}$$

$$V = \sqrt{39,200 \text{ m}^2/\text{sec}^2}$$

$$V = 198 \text{ m/sec}$$

Therefore, the velocity of the tsunami would be 198 meters per second. That works out to 712.8 kilometers (442.9 miles) per hour.

unaware of the danger, have wandered out onto the drained sea-bed, only to be drowned by the wave a few minutes later. History records a tsunami surging up a hillside 530 meters (1,740 feet) high in Lituya Bay, Alaska, in 1958 when a landslide smashed into the other side of the bay.

Figure 12-21

Tsunami formation.

A tsunami results from sudden water displacement caused by a landslide, iceberg, volcanic eruption, or most commonly, an earthquake. The long period and wavelength make them nearly unnoticeable at sea. When the wave reaches shore, it can unleash a tremendous water mass and energy onto land.

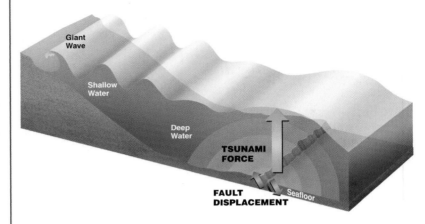

LEARNING MARINE SCIENCE CAN SAVE LIVES

The undersea Indian Ocean earthquake that occurred on December 26, 2004 produced tsunamis that rank among the deadliest natural disasters in modern history. Tsunami waves reaching 15 meters (50 feet) high devastated the shores of Indonesia, Sri Lanka, India, Thailand, and other countries. The tsunami even reached as far as Somalia on the east coast of Africa, 4,500 kilometers (2,800 miles) west of the epicenter.

The tsunamis resulted from a rare megathrust earthquake, which is a large earthquake produced by one tectonic plate suddenly slipping beneath another. The earthquake took place at 7:58:53 local time in the Indian Ocean off the western coast of northern Sumatra, Indonesia. At a magnitude of 9.0, it was the largest since the 9.2-magnitude Good Friday Earthquake off Alaska in 1964. The 2004 Indian Ocean earthquake was the third largest since 1900, when accurate global seismographic record keeping began.

As reported by Reuters news service, on the morning of the earthquake, a 10-year-old British girl saved 100 other tourists from the Asian tsunami. She warned them that a giant mass of water was on its way after learning about the phenomenon weeks earlier at school. "I was on the beach and the water started to go funny," Tilly Smith told the news service in Phuket, Thailand. "There were bubbles and the tide went out all of a sudden. I recognized what was hap-

pening and had a feeling there was going to be a tsunami. I told Mummy."

While other holidaymakers stood and stared as the disappearing waters left boats and fish stranded on the sands, Tilly recognized the danger signs because she had recently completed a school project on tsunamis. Quick action by Tilly's mother and Thai hotel staff cleared Maikhao beach, just minutes before a huge wave crashed ashore. The beach was one of the few on the island of Phuket where no one was killed.

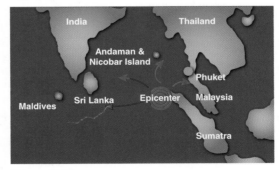

Figure 12-22

The 2004 undersea earthquake created tsunami waves that killed nearly 250,000 people.

1. **Waves break**

   A.   when their H:L ratio exceeds 1:7.

   B.   when they reach a depth 1.3 times the wave height.

   C.   when water is deep and the circumstances are right.

   D.   all of the above

2. **When a wind wave breaks on shore, (choose all that apply)**

   A.   the H:L ratio exceeds 1:7.

   B.   the water depth is 1.3 times the wave height.

   C.   the top of the wave is traveling more quickly than the bottom.

   D.   contact with the bottom decreases the wavelength and increases the height.

3. **Wave _____ tends to bend waves parallel to shore or toward a protrusion. Wave _____ causes wave energy to bounce back toward open water.**

   A.   diffraction, refraction

   B.   refraction, diffraction

   C.   reflection, refraction

   D.   refraction, reflection

4. **A standing wave is**

   A.   a horizontal energy flow that knocks down anything standing.

   B.   a null wave (i.e., water that is standing still).

   C.   a misnomer for tidal wave.

   D.   a vertical wave that doesn't travel, but has a trough and crest that alternate.

5. **Storm surges are caused by (choose all that apply)**

   A.   earthquakes.

   B.   landslides.

   C.   heavy winds.

   D.   cyclonic storms.

6. **Seiches are caused by (choose all that apply)**

   A.   earthquakes.

   B.   refraction.

   C.   heavy winds.

   D.   cyclonic storms.

7. **Tsunamis are caused by (choose all that apply)**

   A.   earthquakes.

   B.   landslides.

   C.   heavy winds.

   D.   cyclonic storms.

8. **Tsunamis are always shallow-water waves because**

   A.   earthquakes only occur in shallow water.

   B.   they cannot travel toward deep water.

   C.   their energy dissipates into the deep water.

   D.   they have such long wavelengths that no water is deep enough for them to be deepwater waves.

9. **Tsunamis do not destroy ships in the open sea because**

   A.   tsunamis do not move through the sea.

   B.   the tsunami warning system gives ships time to get out of the way.

   C.   tsunami periods are so long that ships rise and fall very slowly when a tsunami passes under them.

   D.   none of the above is correct; ships are frequently destroyed on the open sea by tsunamis.

Tides

STUDY QUESTIONS

Find the answers as you read.

1. What causes the tides?

2. How does Newton's *equilibrium theory of the tides* differ from Laplace's *dynamic theory*?

3. What influences besides lunar and solar gravity affect the tides?

4. What are *amphidromic points*?

5. What are *diurnal, semidiurnal,* and *mixed tides*?

6. What are *tidal currents* and a *tidal bore*?

7. What are the relative positions of the sun and moon during *spring tides* and *neap tides*?

INTERNET PORTAL
SCiLINKS. NSTA

Topic: Tides
Go To: www.scilinks.org
Code: LOP2295

Figure 12-23

A simple view of tides.

Tides result from the gravitational pull of the moon and, to a lesser degree, the sun. In principle, the sun and moon's gravities each create two bulges on opposite sides of the Earth. As Earth rotates on its axis throughout the day, the bulges rotate around the Earth. As the bulge reaches a coastline, the tide rises. As it rotates past the coastline, the tide falls.

The Cause of Tides

What causes the tides?

How does Newton's equilibrium theory of the tides *differ from Laplace's* dynamic theory?

What influences besides lunar and solar gravity affect the tides?

What are amphidromic points?

If you have ever spent a day at the seashore, you have probably seen the tides. You may find water high on the beach at one time of the day and low at another. Rocky areas may lie under water part of the day and above water the rest of the day.

Tides are daily variations in the ocean's sea level. They affect the whole ocean, but they are most noticeable at the shore. Tides result from the gravitational pull of the moon and, to a lesser degree, the sun. They pull ocean water into a huge wave with a wavelength the size of an ocean basin. In principle, the sun and moon each create two bulges on opposite sides of the Earth. The relative positions of the sun and moon change slowly, so the bulge rotates around the Earth. As a coastline rotates into the bulge, the tide rises. As it rotates out, the tide falls.

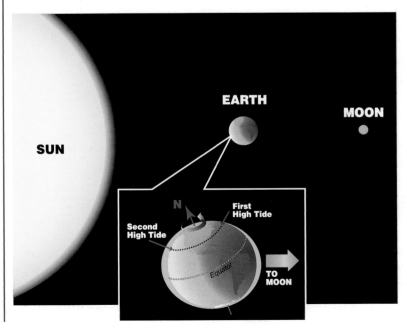

Arlo Thomas, Ph.D.   Arlo Thomas, Ph.D.

Figure 12-24a   **Figure 12-24b**

High tide at the Bay of Fundy.   **Low tide at the Bay of Fundy.**

Extreme tides such as those in Canada's Bay of Fundy demonstrate that tides are much more complex than Newton's simple model. Each day the tides move a volume of more than 100 km³ in and out of the Bay of Fundy. That is four times the combined volume of the world' rivers.

Isaac Newton proposed this simplistic explanation of the tides. It is called the *equilibrium theory*, which assumes that the Earth is perfectly uniform, that water is very, very deep, and that there are no landmasses.

The problem with the equilibrium theory is that it is too simple to explain the actual tides on the Earth. Some places have two tides in a day, others have one. In some places, the tides are very extreme, in others they are not. How could this happen if the Earth was perfectly uniform and nothing influences the tides except the gravitational pull of the moon and sun? It couldn't. The Earth is not perfectly spherical and it is not covered uniformly with water. The tides do not move like an unobstructed wave in the open sea. They are waves that are forced through and around obstacles. Understanding this requires a more complex model.

Pierre-Simon Laplace modified Newton's model to account for tidal variations. His model, called the *dynamic theory of tides*, shows that there are not only two tidal bulges; rather, there are many additional tidal bulges. This is because, in addition to lunar and solar gravity, the imperfect sphere of the Earth, the season, the time of the month, the shape of the ocean basin, and the Coriolis effect all influence the tides. Tides rotate around more than a dozen *amphidromic points* (from the Greek *amphidromos* meaning *to run around*). These are points where the water does not rise and fall with the tides. The tides occur in a pinwheel-shaped, standing-wave pattern. There is no vertical tidal movement at an amphidromic point, but away from that point there may be magnified tidal motion as the tides change throughout the day.

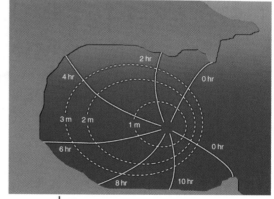

Figure 12-25

Tidal flow around an amphidromic point.

Tides rotate around amphidromic points – points where the water does not rise and fall with the tides. The tides occur in a pinwheel-shaped, standing wave pattern. In this case, the tidal magnitude is shown on the dotted lines and the pinwheel represents the progression of the tide around the basin.

Tidal Patterns and Currents

What are diurnal, semidiurnal, *and* mixed tides?

What are tidal currents *and a* tidal bore?

Because there are multiple tidal bulges and other influences, tidal patterns vary with location (Figure 12-26). Some places have a single high and low tide daily. This pattern is called a *diurnal tide* (from the Latin *diurnalis* meaning *daily*). Some places in the Gulf of Mexico have diurnal tides. The east coast of the United States has

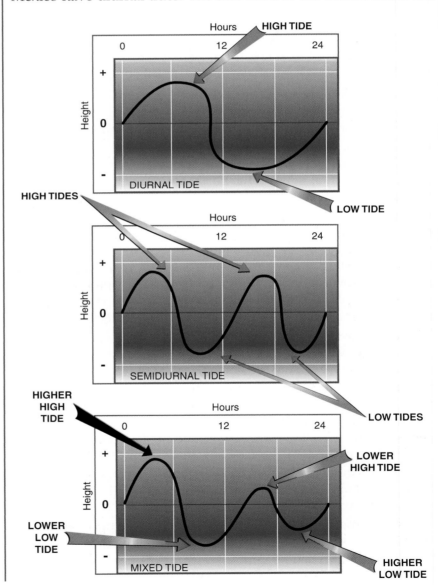

Figure 12-26

Three tidal patterns.

Tidal patterns vary with location. Some places have a single high and low tide daily. This pattern is called a diurnal tide and is shown in the top diagram. Other areas have semidiurnal tides – two roughly equal high and low tides daily. This is shown in the middle diagram. The bottom diagram shows a mixed tide where there are two unequal high and low tides daily.

Figure 12-27

Tidal patterns of the United States.

The continental United States has examples of all three tidal patterns. On the west coast and in parts of the Gulf of Mexico mixed tides predominate. Other parts along the Gulf of Mexico have diurnal tides. The east coast of the United States is dominated by semi-diurnal tides.

semidiurnal tides. This means having two roughly equal high and lw tides daily, as predicted by Newton's model. The Pacific coast of the US, however, has *mixed tides*. This pattern consists of two unequal high and low tides daily. Figure 12-27 shows tidal patterns around the United States.

The shape and depth of the ocean basins affect tidal patterns. The range – the difference between high and low tides – depends mostly on the basin shape and size. Large, wide basins tend to have a smaller tidal range than narrow, shallow basins.

The daily tides create a current that flows into and out of bays, rivers, harbors, and other restricted spaces. The inflow is called a *flood current* and the outflow is called an ebb tide or *slack current*. The midpoint between high and low tides is *slack tide*. At slack tide, little water moves. These tidal variations are important to people who work on and around the sea. Large ships may only be able to enter or exit a harbor during high tide to ensure sufficient water depth for travel. Sailing ships often use the slack current to take advantage of the flow carrying them seaward.

At a few places in the world, as shown in Figure 12-28, a *tidal bore* can form. This is when the incoming tide produces a wave that flows into a river, bay, or other relatively narrow area. This is a true tidal wave and can be several meters high. On the Amazon River in South America and the Severn River in England, surfers can take long rides on the tidal bore.

Figure 12-28

Tidal bore.

Tidal bores form when the incoming tide produces a wave that flows into a river, bay, or other relatively narrow area.

Tristan Bawn/http: uk-active.co.uk

The Sun, Moon, and Types of Tide

What are the relative positions of the sun and moon during spring tides *and* neap tides?

The influence of the moon on the tides is about twice the influence of the sun. The sun has a stronger gravitational pull, but affects the tides less than the moon because it is so much farther away. Solar and lunar gravity affect the tides differently, depending on the positions of the sun and moon relative to the Earth.

When the sun, the moon, and the Earth are aligned, their gravitational strength works together. Constructive interference creates two bulges of tidal water as shown in Figure 12-29. You can tell when this happens by observing and comparing the tides during the different phases of the moon. When there is a new moon (no moon visible), both the sun and the moon are aligned on the same side of Earth, and during a full moon, the sun and moon are aligned on opposite sides of Earth. Both positions create the highest and lowest tides of each month, called *spring tides.*

When the moon is in a quarter phase, the arrangement in space of the moon, the sun, and the Earth forms a right angle. The gravitational force of the sun pulls in a perpendicular direction to the

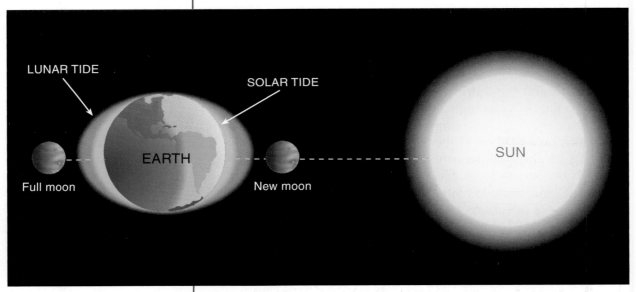

Figure 12-29

Spring tides.

When the sun and moon align during the new moon and full moon, their gravity works together to increase the height of the tidal bulges. Both the new moon and full moon create the highest and lowest monthly tides, called spring tides.

moon's tidal bulge. This tends to raise the low tide and lower the high tide. These weaker tides, created by destructive interference, are called *neap tides* (Figure 12-30).

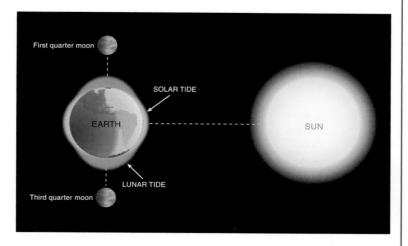

Figure 12-30

Neap tides.

When the moon is in its first and third quarter phases, the configuration in space of the moon, sun, and Earth is a right angle. The sun's gravitational pull is perpendicular to the gravitational pull of the moon. The result is weaker tides, called neap tides.

WHY IS THE MOON STRONGER THAN THE SUN?

Physicists tell us that all mass creates gravity, but compared to other natural forces, such as magnetism, it is weak. However, the larger the mass, the more gravity, so the large masses of planets and stars produce powerful gravitational forces.

Since the sun is about 27 million times the mass of the moon, you might expect it to be far more powerful than the moon with respect to generating tides. Actually, it has roughly half the tide-pulling power of the moon.

The reason is that gravity's effect decreases substantially with distance. The sun is about 149,800,000 kilometers (93 million miles) away, but the moon is only about 384,800 kilometers (239,110 miles) away. This huge difference in distance makes the sun's ability to generate a tide weaker than the moon's.

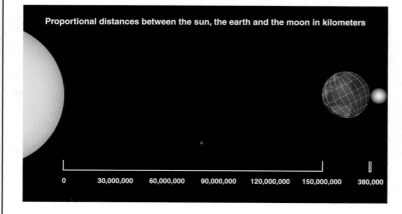

Figure 12-31

The Earth, sun, and moon.

The sun has roughly half the tide-pulling power of the moon because of its distance from Earth. The moon has a much greater effect because of its proximity to the Earth. Here the sun, Earth, and moon are shown with their distances to scale.

LUNAR EFFECTS ON LIFE

There may not be life *on* the moon, but there are organisms *affected by* the moon. As discussed in Chapter 3, the littoral zone is the sea bottom area that is sometimes, but not always, under water. This is the seafloor that the tides cover and uncover daily.

Tide pools harbor organisms that are adapted to the rise and fall of the ocean water. These can include hardy algae and crustaceans that can survive several hours out of water during low tide. Other littoral organisms survive in tide pools, which are places that trap water when the tides recede (Figure 12-32).

Cheryl Regan

Figure 12-32

Tide pool.

Marty Snyderman

Figure 12-33

Grunion spawn off the California coast.

Non-littoral organisms also have adaptations related to the tides. Grunion, a 12-15 centimeter (4.7-5.9 inch) fish, congregates at night to spawn just after the highest spring tide on southern California beaches. Taking advantage of the unusually high water, they deposit their eggs in the sand and return to sea. Although the annual grunion run is a predictable event enjoyed by beachgoers, scientists still are not sure how the fish know when to come ashore (Figure 12-33).

Marty Snyderman

Interestingly, it was discovered in 1981 that corals time their spawning with the tides. The corals release their sperm and eggs into the water column together during the neap tide when there is minimal tidal variation. The calm water appears to benefit reproduction by letting the sperm mix with and fertilize the eggs more effectively (Figure 12-34).

Figure 12-34

Coral spawning.

This photo shows a Caribbean coral spawning at night. Corals time their release of sperm and eggs into the water during neap tides when there is minimal tidal variation. The calm water appears to benefit reproduction.

1. **Tides are caused by**

   A. the Coriolis effect.

   B. the sun's gravity only.

   C. primarily the sun's gravity, with some effect from the moon.

   D. primarily the moon's gravity, with some effect from the sun.

2. **Newton's equilibrium theory is more complex and explains more of the variables in tides than does Laplace's dynamic theory.**

   A. true

   B. false

3. **Besides lunar and solar gravity, influences on the tides include (choose all that apply)**

   A. the season.

   B. the Coriolis effect.

   C. ocean basin shape.

   D. that the Earth is not perfectly spherical.

4. **Amphidromic points are**

   A. points with maximum tidal variation.

   B. the locations ancient sailors dropped amphorae at high tide.

   C. points with no net water motion around which tides occur.

   D. none of the above

5. **A single high and low tide daily is called a _____ tide. Two unequal high and low tides daily is called a _____ tide.**

   A. diurnal, mixed

   B. mixed, semidiurnal

   C. diurnal, semidiurnal

   D. mixed, diurnal

6. **Tidal currents are incoming tide flow. Tidal bore is outgoing tide flow.**

   A. true

   B. false

7. **During _____ tides the sun and moon align relative to Earth. During _____ tides, the configuration in space of the moon, sun, and Earth form a right angle.**

   A. neap, spring

   B. summer, neap

   C. spring, summer

   D. spring, neap

New Terms You Learned

- **amphidromic points** location with no net water motion, about which the tides move away in a pinwheel type pattern (p. 12-21)
- **antinodes** in a standing wave, the points where there is maximum vertical change in the water level (p. 12-15)
- **capillary waves** waves with wavelengths of 1.73 centimeters (.68 inches) or smaller, with surface tension being the primary restoring force that acts on them (p. 12-6)
- **crest** the highest wave point above the average water level (p. 12-4)
- **deepwater waves** waves in water that is deeper than half their wavelength (p. 12-7)
- **diffraction, wave** the tendency of energy to shift within a wave upon reaching an obstacle, allowing a new wave pattern to form (p. 12-13)
- **disturbing forces** energy sources that cause waves to form (p. 12-5)
- **diurnal tide** the tidal pattern of a single high and low tide daily (p. 12-22)
- **dynamic theory (of tides)** tide theory that accounts for various influences in explaining why there are multiple tidal bulges (p. 12-21)
- **equilibrium theory (of tides)** simplistic tide theory that assumes earth is perfectly uniform and that solar and lunar gravity are the only tidal influences (p. 12-21)
- **fetch** the area over which the wind blows (p. 12-8)
- **flood current** the incoming tidal flow (p. 12-23)
- **frequency** the number of waves that pass a fixed point in one second (p. 12-4)
- **fully developed sea** an area where the waves have reached the maximum possible size for the wind speed, duration and fetch (p. 12-8)
- **gravity waves** waves with wavelengths longer than 1.73 centimeters (.68 inches); gravity is their primary restoring force (p. 12-6)
- **H:L** symbol for the ratio of the wave height to wavelength (p. 12-4)

- **height, wave** the vertical measurement from the trough to the crest of a wave (p. 12-4)
- **internal ocean waves** energy that occurs within different density layers (p. 12-10)
- **longitudinal wave** wave in which the energy moves in the same direction that the energy travels through the compression and decompression of particles. (p. 12-3)
- **mixed tides** the tidal pattern of two unequal high and low tides daily (p. 12-23)
- **neap tides** the weaker monthly tidal extremes of high and low tide, created when the arrangement in space of the moon, sun, and Earth form a right angle; they result when the gravitational force of the sun pulls in a perpendicular direction to the gravitational force of the moon (p. 12-25)
- **node** in a standing wave, the point where there is no vertical change in the water level (p. 12-15)
- **orbital wave** a wave that only transmits through fluids; a wave that occurs when energy moves the fluid in a circular motion as it passes (p. 12-4)
- **period** the time it takes for the same spot on two waves to pass a single point (p. 12-4)
- **plunging breakers** surf waves characterized by a curl that forms as the top of the wave pitches through the air and then splashes into the bottom of the wave (p. 12-13)
- **progressive wave** a wave that allows you to observe its energy moving from one point to another; progressive waves are classified as longitudinal, transverse, and orbital (p. 12-3)
- **reflection, wave** wave energy bouncing off a nearly perpendicular object in the water; may cause a standing wave (p. 12-14)
- **refraction, wave** bending of waves (p. 12-13)
- **restoring forces** energy sources that resists wave formation (p. 12-5)
- **rogue wave** wave that exceeds the maximum theoretical size in a fully developed sea (p. 12-9)
- **seiche** a form of standing wave that can be destructive; formed in large bays, harbors, and lakes as a wave that rocks back and forth as a result of a strong wind or local earthquake (p. 12-16)

- **semidiurnal tides** the tidal pattern of two roughly equal high and low tides daily (p. 12-23)

- **shallow-water waves** waves in water that is shallower than one-twentieth their wavelength (p. 12-7)

- **slack current** an outgoing tidal flow (p. 12-23)

- **slack tide** the relative lack of water motion between tides (p. 12-23)

- **speed, wave** wavelength divided by period (p. 12-5)

- **spilling breakers** surf waves characterized by the top of the wave tumbling and sliding down the front of the wave as it decelerates slowly on gentle slope beaches (p. 12-13)

- **spring tides** the highest and lowest monthly tides, caused by the alignment of the sun and moon with respect to Earth (p. 12-24)

- **standing wave** a vertical oscillation in which water rises and falls with alternating trough and crests in a single position (p. 12-14)

- **storm surge** bulge or wave caused by low pressure at the center of a cyclonic storm (p. 12-15)

- **surging breaker** surf waves that rise onto an abrupt, near vertical beach rising out of deep water; so named because they surge ashore before breaking (p. 12-13)

- **swell** a long line of waves that have the same frequency and wavelength (p. 12-7)

- **tidal bore** a wave created where an incoming tide flows into a narrow area (p. 12-23)

- **transverse wave** wave in which the energy motion is perpendicular to the travel direction (p. 12-4)

- **trough** the lowest wave point above the average water level (p. 12-4)

- **tsunami** a destructive wave caused by a sudden water displacement that results from an underwater landslide, volcanic eruption, earthquake or an iceberg falling into the sea from a glacier (p. 12-16)

- **wave** the transmission of energy through matter (p. 12-3)

- **wavelength** the horizontal distance between the identical point on two waves (p. 12-4)

- **wave diffraction** the tendency of energy to shift within a wave upon reaching an obstacle, allowing a new wave pattern to form

- **wave height** the vertical measurement from the trough to the crest of a wave

- **wave reflection** wave energy bouncing off a nearly perpendicular object in the water; may cause a standing wave

- **wave refraction** bending of waves

- **wave speed** wavelength divided by period

- **wave trains** a series of swells traveling together with the leading wave dissipating and the following waves forming (p. 12-7)

- **weathering** involves mechanical and chemical processes that break rocks into smaller particles

Chapter 12 in Review

1. Diagram a wave and identify its components.
2. Explain what a wave is and compare and contrast the three types of progressive waves.
3. Calculate the speed of a wave that has a wavelength of 100 meters (330 feet) and a period of 8 seconds.
4. List and describe disturbing forces and restoring forces that relate to waves.
5. Contrast the differences between deepwater waves and shallow-water waves. What three factors normally affect the maximum size of a wave? Explain how waves larger or smaller than the maximum theoretical size can exist in a fully developed sea.
6. Where do internal waves occur? What causes them?
7. Explain what makes a wave break and what happens when a wave breaks on shore. What distinguishes a plunging breaker from a spilling breaker?
8. Describe and diagram how wave refraction, diffraction, and reflection affect wave behavior.
9. Describe and diagram a standing wave. What type of destructive wave does this relate to and what causes it?
10. Explain what causes storm surge and how it causes damage.
11. What causes a tsunami? Explain why tsunamis are always shallow-water waves and why they don't destroy ships in the open sea.
12. Explain the causes of daily tides, spring tides, and neap tides. Include a diagram that illustrates these tides. Explain why tides are classified as shallow-water waves.
13. Describe the differences between Newton's equilibrium theory for tides and Laplace's dynamic theory. In your description, discuss what influences tides in addition to gravity, and explain amphidromic points.
14. Define diurnal, semidiurnal and mixed tides. Describe the locations where these tides occur.
15. What is a tidal current? How is a tidal bore related to tidal current?

Connecting Chapter Concepts – Science Scenarios

1. Waves are the transmission of energy through matter, and this is true for both sound waves in the air, or waves you see on the surface of the ocean.
   A. What are the three types of waves, and which one of these is the type of wave you find in water?
   B. What is the largest ocean wave, and what are its disturbing forces and its restoring forces?
   C. What is the disturbing force that causes most of the waves you see on the ocean, and what is the restoring force that causes these waves to subside?
   D. What is a deepwater wave, and what two kinds of waves are never deepwater waves? Why?
   E. What interaction causes the difference between deepwater waves and shallow-water waves?

2. Tidal patterns vary with location, which means there can be pronounced differences in how tides affect different places. The three kinds of tidal patterns are diurnal, semidiurnal and mixed.
   A. Define the tidal patterns for each of the three kinds of tides.
   B. According to Newton's equilibrium theory, there should be two high and two low tides daily everywhere, with the greatest variation at the equator. However, this is far from what actually happens. Why?
   C. What does Laplace's dynamic theory say about where tidal bulges occur, and why?

Marine Science and the Real World

1. Only wind waves can be deepwater waves. Why is this?

2. Besides ocean waves, what other phenomena have in-phase and out-of-phase effects?

3. Newton's equilibrium theory does not adequately explain how tides actually occur around the world. Is it still a useful theory? Why or why not?

4. Tides affect us more than you may realize. What human activities do the tides affect and how? Compare your list with a classmate's list.

5. Imagine that Mars has an ocean and that its two moons, Phobos and Deimos, affect the tides. Mars rotates in about 24 hours (same as Earth). Phobos orbits Mars three times daily and Deimos orbits Mars every 1.26 days. For simplicity, assume both moons would have an approximately equal tidal pull. Assuming a simple equilibrium model, what would the tidal patterns on Mars be like? Use diagrams to illustrate and do not forget the effects of the sun.

6. Detecting and predicting tsunamis is only half the purpose of a tsunami warning system. Warning the populations who live in the areas that will be affected is critical. Why do you think multiple forms of communication must be used? Why don't tsunami warning systems work well when earthquakes occur close to land?

References

Cunningham, William P., Mary Ann Cunningham and Barbara Woodworth Saigo. 1999. *Environmental Science: A Global Concern.* Boston: McGraw-Hill.

Klemm, Barbara, Francis M. Pottenger III, Thomas W. Speitel, S. Arthur Reed and Ann E. Coopersmith. 1991. *Hawaii Marine Science Studies: The Fluid Earth. Physical Science and Technology of the Marine Environment.* Honolulu, HI: Curriculum Research and Development Group.

Pond, Steven and George L. Pickard. 1983. *Introductory Dynamical Oceanography.* Oxford: Butterworth-Heinemann, Ltd.

Pickard, George L. and William Emery. 1990. *Descriptive Physical Oceanography.* Oxford: Butterworth-Heinemann, Ltd.

Seeds, Michael A. 2000. *Horizons, Exploring the Universe.* Pacific Grove: Brooks/Cole Publishing Company.

Sverdrup, Keith A., Alyn C. Duxbury and Alison B. Duxbury. 2000. *An Introduction to the World's Oceans.* Boston: McGraw-Hill.

Tarbuck, Edward J. and Frederick K. Lutgens. 2000. *Earth Science.* Upper Saddle River: Prentice Hall.

Thomas, Abbie. 2002. Hard Core Spawn. http://www.abc.net.au/science/scribblygum/october2002/default.htm

Thurman, Harold V. and Alan Trujillo. 1996. *Essentials of Oceanography.* Upper Saddle River: Prentice Hall.

Thurman, Harold V. and Elizabeth A. Burton. 2001. *Introductory Oceanography.* New Jersey: Prentice Hall.

UNIT 5

Voyage to the

Bob Wohlers

Image Courtesy of Monika Bright,
University of Vienna, Austria/Ocean
Explorer, NOAA

Bottom of the Sea

Photo courtesy of PDPhoto.org

CHAPTER 13

A Revolution in Science:
The Theory of Plate Tectonics

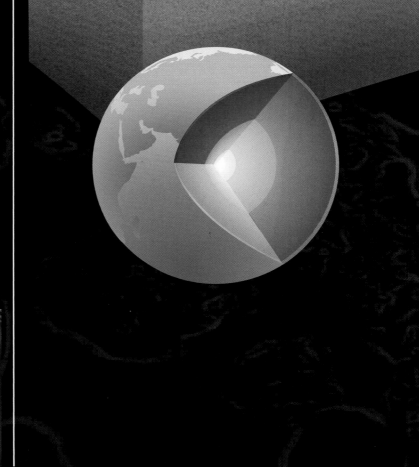

Ring of Fire

Challenger Deep

Mapping the Ocean Floor

Geological oceanographers study seafloor sediments, including their color, size, shape, weight, age, origins, and distribution and composition, to discover how the Earth and ocean formed and how ongoing geologic processes may alter them in the future.

The study of geological oceanography and its related disciplines help scientists, including Dr. Dawn Wright (also called "Deepsea Dawn"), understand plate tectonics (the theory that the Earth's outermost layer, the lithosphere, is divided into plates that move at different speeds in different directions) and how plate movement results in earthquakes and volcanoes.

"I grew up in the Hawaiian Islands, which had a lot to do with my interest in oceanography. I remember having very, very good teachers who always encouraged us to read a lot. I really got interested in reading books about the sea. I started out reading *Twenty Thousand Leagues Under the Sea, Mutiny on the Bounty, Treasure Island* — anything that had to do with sea adventures. I imagined myself as a pirate or adventurer. Then I thought, 'Why not consider doing something like this for real?' By the time I was eight, I had pretty much decided to become an oceanographer. By high school, I had read up on what oceanographers do and I was really interested in geology, so I decided to put myself on the path to geological oceanography."

Dr. Wright is actually involved in two separate oceanographic disciplines. She is a marine geologist who studies coral reef platforms and underwater volcanic chains, and in the past has also studied hydrothermal vents and the unique ecosystems the vents support along mid-ocean ridges. Dr. Wright is also a geographer and a leading authority on the use of *geographic information systems* (GIS). This is the software oceanographers use to map the seafloor. When working in geology, Dr. Wright's research focuses on seafloor cracks – *fissures* – that act as passageways for seawater and magma (molten rock) rising from the Earth's mantle. When seawater seeps down through cracks in the ocean's crust, it heats through contact with magma. The hot seawater rises back up through the cracks, creating geyser-like *hydrothermal vents*. Research into these seafloor cracks provides important information about the nature of volcanic eruptions, as well as about the birth and death of hydrothermal vents.

As a geographer, Wright uses her expertise in GIS to map volcanic features and coral reef zones on the ocean floor, looking at its roughness and complexity as places where different kinds of creatures may be living. This is especially important if these areas are candidates for future marine protected areas. She also uses GIS to manage and link together many different kinds of large databases that can be exchanged on the web with people all over the world.

To those considering careers in oceanography, Dr. Wright advises, "Do well in school, but also have a balance of other interests. There is no escaping mathematics – even if it isn't your strongest subject, it's a good idea to stick with it. You should also try and get as much experience as possible with computers. That's a big part of oceanography today. Even if you are not a computer geek, you need basic computer knowledge and expertise to be successful in this field."

Dawn Wright, PhD
Professor, Department of Geosciences, Oregon State University

Chapter 1 explains how and why theories change in science. Science slowly modifies and discards theories and hypotheses based on new information and findings. By constantly proposing, questioning, and testing theories and hypotheses, science progresses.

However, human nature often affects this fundamental concept of science. There is a tendency to fear change, sometimes leading people to resist changing or questioning concepts. Sometimes these influences come from what a culture accepts. For example, there was outrage when in 1633 Galileo Galilei (1564-1642) publicly supported the Copernicus model of the solar system in which the sun, not the Earth, is at the center. This went against the prevailing belief that, because God had given mankind a unique place in creation, Earth must be at the center of the universe (as well as the solar system). Under heavy social pressure – which included being placed under house arrest and excommunication from the church – Galileo recanted publicly, though he lived to see the Copernicus model widely accepted by science.

Similar resistance to change also comes from *within* the scientific community. At times, scientists become so comfortable with a theory that they resist contradictory evidence or refuse to question the assumptions on which it rests. They may arbitrarily ignore or refuse to consider the alternative explanations for the same evidence. In 1643, a prevailing view was that "nature abhors a vacuum," and that a vacuum could not exist. Mathematician Evangelista Torricelli (1608-1647) proposed an experiment, later performed by his colleague Vincenzo Viviani (1622-1703), that showed this principle to be invalid. The experiment called for inverting a tube of mercury sealed on one end with its opening submerged in mercury. This was the first mercury barometer. Because atmospheric pressure cannot hold the weight of the mercury the full height of the tube, a space forms at the top. This space, Torricelli pointed out, would be a vacuum. The mercury's height in the tube resulted from atmospheric pressure, not nature abhorring a vacuum.

Despite this evidence, debate continued. To show that atmospheric pressure explained the height of the mercury column in the tube, Blaise Pascal (1623-1662) climbed a mountain with Torricelli's device. As Pascal climbed, the mercury in the tube dropped. This change, he asserted, was because there was less atmospheric pressure to push the mercury toward the vacuum. Pascal argued that this further demonstrated that atmospheric pressure, not nature abhorring a vacuum, was the accurate explanation. Incredibly, legend has it that one scientist responded that the experiment merely proved that nature abhors a vacuum less at the top of a mountain than at the bottom.

The *theory of plate tectonics* is another example of resistance to change. As you will learn, this theory says that the continents float on the Earth's molten interior, gradually moving over millions of years. However, the rise of this theory required several fundamental changes in how scientists think about natural processes and the Earth's structure. The development of the theory began more than 200 years ago.

Until the late 18th century, virtually all scientists thought Earth was much younger than the prevailing scientific views today. In the 18th century, however, an important social change began to shape Europe and the Americas. It was a time of growing acceptance of new ideas and new ways of thinking. This was the period that gave rise to the democratic republics in the United States and France. Adam Smith published *An Inquiry into the Nature and Causes of the Wealth of Nations* (Edinburgh, 1776), which was the first comprehensive economic theory. The so-called Scottish Enlightenment took place in this era, around 1750. This name came from a group of scientists, inventors, politicians, and other intellectuals in Edinburgh, Scotland, who began contributing new thinking to science, politics, and other areas.

This period was also the beginning of the Industrial Revolution. As the revolution moved toward the 19th century, the rise of the steam engine created a demand for coal. The search for coal sparked an interest in geology. At this time, a physician, natural philosopher, and geologist named James Hutton of Edinburgh (1726-1797) proposed a dynamic Earth, with changes that are largely gradual and continuous. His concept was modified by Sir Charles Lyell (1797-1875), eventually becoming the *principle of uniformitarianism*. This principle is that processes such as weathering, erosion, and sediment layering that are taking place today were happening in the past, and will continue to do so in the future. This is the cornerstone of many theories and hypotheses.

The principle of uniformitarianism changed the thinking about the age of the Earth. If these slow, gradual processes were responsible for the Earth's present form, scientists reasoned, then Earth must be much older than originally thought. Hutton's idea became a basis for considering the past in many scientific areas, ranging from theorizing the life cycles of stars to estimating the ages of rocks and fossils. It was also a necessary principle for the acceptance of plate tectonic theory, itself one of the most significant revolutions in geological theory.

This chapter takes you through the principles behind the theory of plate tectonics and describes the thinking and discoveries that led to them. You'll learn about the layers that scientists theorize

STUDY QUESTIONS

Find the answers as you read.

1. What are the internal layers of the Earth? How do scientists study them?

2. How does the Earth's crust differ from the *lithosphere*?

3. What are the three types of rock? How does the *rock cycle* account for their formation?

4. How does Archimedes' Principle relate to the structure of the Earth?

5. What is *isostatic equilibrium*?

6. What links some earthquakes with isostatic equilibrium? Where do such earthquakes occur?

INTERNET PORTAL

SCiLINKS. NSTA

Topic: The Inner and Outer Core
Go To: www.scilinks.org
Code: LOP2300

make up the Earth's interior, the differences between oceanic and continental crusts, and the theories about how ocean basins form. You'll also learn the basic principles behind the theory of plate tectonics, and how it unified other theories about how the Earth's crust changes over time. You'll also see how this theory, combined with the theory of evolution, explains some of the similarities and differences found among organisms on different continents.

The Earth Inside and Out

In 1864, Jules Verne published his classic novel, *Journey to the Center of the Earth*. Although a fantastic tale of imagination, it reveals the fundamental changes in what scientists believed about the Earth's interior compared with what they think today. Verne was unaware of the tremendous heat and pressure that would make such a journey impossible, at least with the technology available then, now, or in the foreseeable future. Actually, the deepest hole drilled into the Earth is about 12.1 kilometers (7.5 miles) in the Russian Kola Peninsula. It is not drilling or fantastic journeys that scientists use to theorize about the Earth's interior. Instead, they measure volcanic gases, gravity variations, and *seismic* (earthquake) *waves*.

Earth's Internal Layers

What are the internal layers of the Earth? How do scientists study them?

How does the Earth's crust differ from the lithosphere?

The Earth's interior consists of multiple layers: the inner core, the outer core, the mantle, and the crust. This structure has been proposed from numerous seismic wave studies detailing the different properties that are found within the Earth. In 2008, using new and historic seismic data, geologists at the University of Illinois determined that the inner core is solid and composed mainly of iron crystals. They also determined that the inner core has a core. The diameter of the innermost core is 1,180 kilometers (733 miles), slightly less than half the diameter of the 2,400 kilometers (1,491 miles) inner core. Although thought to have a temperature of about 5,000°C (9,032° F), which is nearly the same temperature as the surface of the sun, scientists theorize that the reason the inner core is solid is because of its intense pressure. The enormous pressure holds the atoms and molecules close together so that the materials remain solid.

Scientists conclude that the outer core consists of the same elements at the same temperature as in the inner core. However, they theorize that with less pressure, it is liquid. The thickness of the outer core is 2,270 kilometers (1,411 miles). In some places, the outer core has *thermal plumes*, which are localized areas of high heat release that might possibly be related to volcanic activity. This is currently being debated.

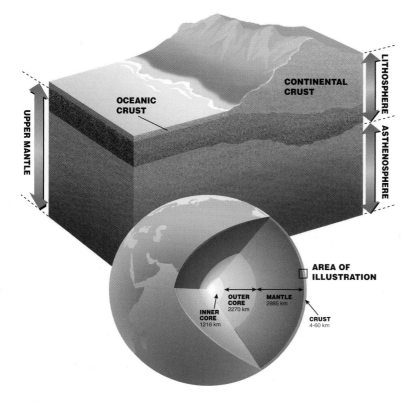

Figure 13-1

Cross-section of the Earth.
Earth has a solid inner core, surrounded by a liquid outer core. The mantle surrounds that core and is thick and fluid-like. The crust is the outermost layer, varying in thickness from 5 kilometers (3 miles) for oceanic crust to 30-40 kilometers (20-25 miles) for continental crust. The outermost, rigid layer consists of the crust and the uppermost mantle and is known as the lithosphere. Beneath the lithosphere lies the soft, relatively weak layer known as the asthenosphere.

Above the core lies the mantle. The mantle is thought to contain mostly silicon and oxygen, with some iron and magnesium. The estimated thickness of the mantle is about 2,900 kilometers (1,802 miles). Seismic wave studies have given scientists a picture of the mantle's structure. It consists of the lower mantle and the upper mantle.

The lower mantle is made of very hot, dense *magma* (molten rock). Until recently, not much was known about the lower mantle. In 2005, Dr. Christine Thomas, a University of Liverpool scientist, discovered a layer within the lower mantle near the boundary between the mantle and the core. Her discovery will allow geophysicists to measure temperature variations at the mantle-core boundary.

Figure 13-2

The rock cycle.

The rock cycle is a graphic representation of how the three major types of rock change from one kind to another over long periods of time. The three classes of rock—igneous, sedimentary, and metamorphic—may melt to form magma, be weathered into sediments, or undergo heat and pressure.

Igneous rocks form when molten material cools and hardens. Over time, igneous, sedimentary, and metamorphic rocks may be broken apart. This process is called weathering and the broken pieces of rock are called sediments. Water, wind, glaciers, and gravity carry the sediments away. This process is called erosion. The sediments are then deposited in a new location. Over time sediments may be pressed or cemented together to form sedimentary rocks. As layers of sedimentary rock are buried under more layers of sediment, they are heated and pressed even closer together. Metamorphic rock forms when the heat and pressure are great enough to change the rock. Sedimentary and metamorphic rocks may melt and become igneous rocks again.

The upper mantle is composed of the *asthenosphere* (from the Greek *astheneia* meaning *weakness)* and a portion of the *lithosphere.* The asthenosphere is solidified magma that flows slowly over time. The *lithosphere* (from the Greek *lithos* meaning *rock*) is the uppermost, rigid part of the upper mantle and the crust. This is the cool solid rock portion of the outer Earth that rests on the warmer asthenosphere.

The outermost layer of the Earth is the crust. It is composed mainly of oxygen, silicon, magnesium, and iron. It varies in thickness and is the outer layer of the lithosphere. Low density magma from the asthenosphere rises and can eventually flow from a volcano or other opening in the crust. When the molten rock exits the opening, it is called *lava.*

Scientists separate the uppermost mantle from the crust because they think the mantle's elemental composition changes little. The crust, however, consists of different rock types thought to undergo change over long periods. Besides chemical properties, conditions such as temperature and pressure differentiate the crust from the mantle.

The Rock Cycle

What are the three types of rock? How does the rock cycle *account for their formation?*

The three types of rock found in the crust are *igneous, sedimentary,* and *metamorphic.* Rocks form or change over long periods due to the processes of the *rock cycle.* You can think of this as the Earth's recycling machine, endlessly converting rock from one type to another.

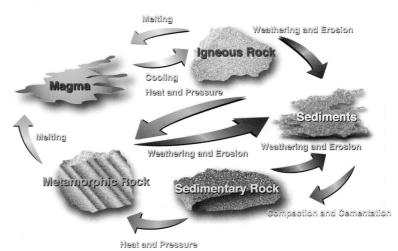

Igneous (from the Latin *igneus* meaning *fire*) *rocks* form when magma or lava cools and hardens. Granite is a common example of igneous rock. Igneous rocks and all other types of rocks are affected by *weathering.*

Weathering involves mechanical and chemical processes that break rocks into smaller particles. For example, water may contain dissolved acids that react with rock, chemically changing it so that its particles separate from one another. Once the particle size is small enough, erosion transports the particles. *Erosion* is the process that carries weathered rock and other loose material like soil and organic matter from one place to another. Water, wind, glaciers, and gravity are erosion agents.

When the erosion agent slows or stops, particles may be deposited as *sediment.* Sediment consists of organic and inorganic particles accumulated in an unconsolidated form. Based on geological evidence, scientists have concluded that, over time, sediments are compressed and cemented together to form *sedimentary rocks.* Because sediments contain organic matter, sedimentary rocks are a rich source of fossils. Coal, petroleum, and other fossil fuels in sedimentary rock provide us with energy resources. Sedimentary rocks are important when studying extinct organisms such as dinosaurs. Chapter 14 discusses more about sediments and their role in the ocean.

INTERNET PORTAL

SCi**LINKS.** NSTA

Topic: Sedimentary Rock
Go To: www.scilinks.org
Code: LOP2310

As layers build up on top of each other, the upper layers subject lower layers to increasing pressure and heat. *Metamorphic* (from the Greek *meta* meaning *change*, and *morphe* meaning *form*) *rock* forms when pressure and heat become great enough to change the rock chemically.

Rock may return to the mantle as part of the plate tectonic processes you will learn about shortly. Subjected to the heat of the Earth's interior, rocks re-melt and become magma, returning to the crust as igneous rock. By understanding the rock cycle, you can better understand the ocean's past.

Isostatic Equilibrium

How does Archimedes' Principle relate to the structure of the Earth?

What is isostatic equilibrium?

What links some earthquakes with isostatic equilibrium? Where do such earthquakes occur?

Even before the plate tectonics theory emerged, scientists thought that the crust floated on the denser mantle below. The prevailing theory still is that the crust doesn't sit on anything rigid, but liter-

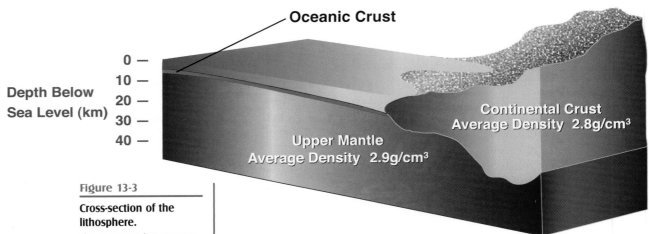

Oceanic Crust

Depth Below
Sea Level (km)

0 —
10 —
20 —
30 —
40 —

Upper Mantle
Average Density 2.9g/cm³

Continental Crust
Average Density 2.8g/cm³

Figure 13-3

Cross-section of the lithosphere.

The continental crust varies in thickness from approximately 30 to 60 kilometers (20 to 40 miles) and the oceanic crust is approximately 4 kilometers (2.5 miles) thick. Because the continental crust is composed of granite, it is less dense (2.8 g/cm³) and floats higher than the oceanic crust, which is composed of denser (2.9 g/cm³) basalt rock. The continental and oceanic crust and the uppermost mantle make up the lithosphere. The lithosphere floats on the asthenosphere.

ally floats on the mantle. The *continental crust* (the crust under the continents) consists primarily of granite, whereas the *ocean crust* (the crust under the ocean basins) consists primarily of basaltic rock.

With the crust floating on the mantle, there must be a balance between the weight of the crust and the upward force of buoyancy. This is an application of Archimedes' Principle of buoyancy, which says an object immersed in a fluid (gas or liquid) is buoyed up by a force equal to the weight of the fluid displaced. An object that weighs less than the fluid it displaces will float. (You can review Archimedes' Principle in Chapter 9.)

If the weight of the crust changes, according to Archimedes' Principle the landmass must rise or subside (sink) to compensate. Think of a raft in a swimming pool. The raft sinks lower in the water when you climb on to it, and rises higher in the water when you get off.

The balance between the weight of the crust and the buoyancy provided by the mantle is called *isostatic equilibrium*. As material adds to the oceanic crust (from deposition by sedimentation, glaciers, and volcanic activity) or leaves the continental crust (from erosion), this balance becomes disrupted. The additional weight will cause the crust to deflect downwards, while the removal of material causes the crust to deflect upwards. This is called *isostatic rebound*. Isostatic rebound is one theorized cause of earthquakes. To restore equilibrium, landmasses will sink or rise slightly along a weak area called a *fault*. During an earthquake, the landmasses (continental or ocean basin) on either side of the involved fault do not move together.

Until the last half of the 20th century, the prevailing view in science was that earthquakes and continental movement only involved vertical rises and falls. The theory of plate tectonics shows that the continents move in horizontal directions and that earthquakes result from both horizontal and vertical movement.

ARE YOU LEARNING?

1. Going from the center of the Earth outward, the four major layers in order are

    A. the mantle, the inner core, the outer core, and the crust.

    B. the crust, the mantle, the inner core, and the outer core.

    C. the inner core, the outer core, the crust, and the mantle.

    D. the inner core, the outer core, the mantle, and the crust.

2. The lithosphere is

    A. another name for the crust.

    B. the uppermost solid portion of the mantle.

    C. the uppermost solid portion of the mantle and the crust.

    D. the liquid layer that the crust floats on.

3. According to the rock cycle, _____ rocks form when accumulated organic and inorganic particles are compressed and cemented together.

    A. igneous

    B. sedimentary

    C. metamorphic

    D. all of the above

4. Archimedes' Principle relates to the structure of the Earth because scientists theorize that the lithosphere floats on the asthenosphere.

    A. true

    B. false

5. Isostatic equilibrium is the balance between the weight of land and the weight of water that keeps the continents from sinking into the ocean.

    A. true

    B. false

6. When isostatic equilibrium becomes disrupted, landmasses will restore the balance by

    A. rising or falling along a fault.

    B. shifting the level of the ocean.

    C. creating a volcano.

The Theory of Continental Drift

STUDY QUESTIONS

Find the answers as you read.

1. What are *Pangaea* and *Panthalassa*?

2. What is the *theory of continental drift*?

3. What evidence did Alfred Wegener use to support the theory of continental drift?

4. Why did scientists not widely accept the theory of continental drift when Wegener originally proposed it? What further evidence might have strengthened his theory?

INTERNET PORTAL

SCiLINKS. NSTA

Topic: Continental Drift
Go To: www.scilinks.org
Code: LOP2320

Alfred Wegener and Pangaea

What are Pangaea *and* Panthalassa?

What is the theory of continental drift?

In 1912, a German meteorologist and polar explorer named Alfred Wegener proposed what was at the time a startling idea. He proposed that in the distant past all the continents had been a single, giant continent. Wegener called this continent *Pangaea* (pronounced pan-GEE-ah, from the Greek *pan* meaning *all*, and *Gaea*, the Greek goddess of the Earth – *all the Earth.*) Surrounding Pangaea, he said, was a single large ocean he called *Panthalassa* (pan-tha-LA-sa, from the Greek *thalassa* meaning the *sea*).

Over the years, since the first accurate maps, others (including Leonardo da Vinci and Sir Francis Bacon) had observed how well the continents could be pieced together like a puzzle. However, Wegener was the first to formally propose a process that explained the fit and present placement of the continents.

Wegener theorized that because the less dense continents floated on the molten rock of the mantle, Pangaea broke by floating apart into separate pieces. The separate continents reached their present locations by drifting apart for more than 200 million years. The theory that the continents were once a single landmass that drifted apart and continue to drift is called the *theory of continental drift.*

Figure 13-4

Pangaea and Panthalassa.

Pangaea as it was thought to have appeared 200 million years ago. (Adapted from R. S, Dietz and J. C, Holden. Journal of Geophysical Research 75:49443.)

Evidence for Continental Drift

What evidence did Alfred Wegener use to support the theory of continental drift?

Why did scientists not widely accept the theory of continental drift when Wegener originally proposed it? What further evidence might have strengthened his theory?

In the 1600s, the first accurate world maps became available. People noticed that the continents apparently fit together like jigsaw-puzzle pieces. This was the first evidence of continental drift. It was hundreds of years later that Wegener began to see further evidence from other sources.

In 1855, the German scientist Edward Suess found fossils of the *Glossopteris* fern in South America, Africa, Australia, India, and

Antarctica. The seeds of this fern are too heavy to travel by wind and too fragile to survive significant sea crossings. To Wegener and other early advocates of continental drift, this suggested that these landmasses must have once been much closer together for the fern to have spread so widely.

Continental drift proponents also studied the distribution of animals and fossils. Two examples were the extinct aquatic reptile *Mesosaurus* and an extinct bear-like animal called *Lytrosaurus*. Based on the distribution of fossils for these animals, Wegener and others who supported the theory of continental drift hypothesized that Pangaea had split into two continents about 200 million years ago. They called the hypothetical northern continent Laurasia. It included today's North America, Greenland, and Eurasia. They named the southern continent Gondwanaland, which included the remaining continents.

Wegener also saw the distribution of coal as evidence. In 1908, the famed polar explorer Ernest Shackleton discovered coal in the

Figure 13-5

Laurasia and Gondwanaland.
About 200 million years ago, Pangaea broke into two large landmasses. The northern continent was known as Laurasia, and included the current landmasses of North America, Greenland, and Eurasia. The southern continent was known as Gondwanaland and included South America, Africa, Antarctica, Australia, and India.

Evidence and Explanations

Today, most scientists accept the theory of continental drift. Evidence supporting the concept includes direct measurement of plate motion. Evidence of past plate movement includes glacial rock deposits on landmasses too far from the cold latitudes where glaciers form – even during an ice age. The conclusion is that these areas must have once been closer to the poles. Similarly, salt deposits dated hundreds of millions of years old have been found at latitudes where salt deposits do not form. Limestone deposits, which scientists attribute to the remains of coral reefs, have been found in the north-central United States and other places far from the latitudes where corals grow. Again, the conclusion is that these areas must have once been at latitudes with different climates.

Scientists also point to similarities in mountain ranges. The Caledonian mountain range in Scotland is thought to have been as high as the Himalayas 400 to 500 million years ago. According to the current theories of continental drift, mountains in Norway, northern Africa, Greenland, Canada (Newfoundland), and the US (the Appalachians) were at one time part of the same Caledonian range. Similarly, the Cape Mountains in South Africa were part of the Sierra Mountains of Argentina, South America.

Although the continents fit together like a puzzle, it is not a perfect fit when you line up the shorelines. A partial explanation is that over time, weathering and erosion change shorelines. However, if you compare the edges of the continental shelves, which are the true edges of the continents, the pieces fit together much more closely. This is also evidence for continental drift.

Because the theory of continental drift has been widely accepted, it has become an important explanation for some of the puzzles facing biologists. One example is the unique animals found in Australia, such as the kangaroo. Why do such distinct animals exist there with no closely related animals on the other continents? One explanation is that Australia broke away from the other continents and became isolated long before distinct species evolved there. Scientists use the same principle to explain the diverse species in Southeast Asia.

More broadly, when applied to the theory of evolution, the theory of continental drift helps explain differences in apparently related species. Scientists theorize that in the past, continental drift has separated a single species into two groups. According to the theory of evolution, separation drives speciation. When two populations of the same species become isolated, they no longer interbreed with one another. Thus they may continue along different paths according to differing natural selection pressures, eventually evolving into similar but different species.

An example of this is the difference between Old World and New world monkeys. Scientists theorize that South America and Africa split apart about 45 million years ago, allowing monkeys to evolve into two groups. South American monkeys live primarily in trees and have tails adapted for hanging onto branches and for balance. African monkeys include some that live in trees, but none have the tail adaptations found in South American monkeys.

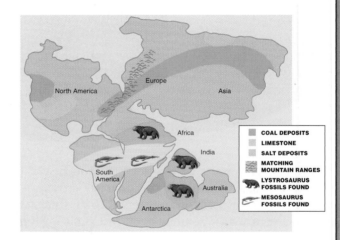

Figure 13-6

Evidence to reconstruct Pangaea.

Many forms of evidence were used to reconstruct the supercontinent Pangaea. This map of Pangaea shows evidence from fossils of the same organisms found on widely separated continents, mountain ranges that match on both sides of the Atlantic Ocean, rock deposits in areas far from a climate that would have created them, and glacial striations in rocks far from polar latitudes.

Antarctic. Scientists theorize that coal originates when geological processes bury vegetation in warm, swampy climates faster than it can decompose. Pressure and heat alter the vegetation, eventually turning it into coal. Since Antarctica does not presently have the appropriate climate for this kind of vegetation, Wegener reasoned, it must have in the past been in a different place with a different climate.

Despite these examples and other evidence, the theory of continental drift was not widely accepted until many years after Wegener's death. A major scientific weakness in Wegener's theory was that he could not adequately explain how continents drift. He suggested that the Earth's rotation and tides moved the continents. However, an English physicist of the period, Harold Jeffries, calculated mathematically that continents cannot drift. Because Jeffries was much more famous than Wegener, his view was accepted. Another criticism was that the jigsaw puzzle of the continents had gaps. Finally, many in the geological community did not take Wegener seriously because he was a meteorologist, not a geologist.

Wegener disappeared in 1930 during an expedition in Greenland. Many years later, the plate tectonics theory would provide an explanation for how continents move, making his theory widely accepted and proving Jeffries' calculations wrong. Additionally, it was found that by including the submerged parts of the continental shelves, most of the gaps in the jigsaw puzzle were filled.

ARE YOU LEARNING?

1. The theory of continental drift says that

A. all of the continents were once one continent that broke up and drifted apart over hundreds of millions of years.

B. the continents have always been separate but may one day drift together to form a single continent.

2. Pangaea is the theorized _____. Panthalassa is the theorized _____.

A. single continent hundreds of millions of years ago, single sea that surrounded it

B. single sea hundreds of millions of years ago, single continent that it surrounded

C. original northern continent, original southern continent

D. original southern continent, original northern continent

3. Evidence Wegener used to support the theory of continental drift included (choose all that apply)

A. that the shapes of the continents fit together.

B. the discovery of coal in Antarctica.

C. the distribution of fossils.

D. that nature abhors a vacuum.

4. If Wegener could have explained _____, his theory of continental drift might have been more widely accepted in his day.

A. why Australia has organisms like kangaroos

B. what causes the tides

C. how coal forms

D. what forces could move continents

The Theory of Seafloor Spreading

STUDY QUESTIONS

Find the answers as you read.

1. How did the invention of sonar contribute to information about the ocean bottom?

2. What are *mid-ocean ridges*, *rift valleys*, and *trenches*?

3. According to the theory of seafloor spreading, where and how does new crust form?

4. What evidence supports the theory of seafloor spreading?

New Technology and Seafloor Knowledge

How did the invention of sonar contribute to information about the ocean bottom?

What are mid-ocean ridges, rift valleys, *and* trenches?

At about the same time Wegener proposed his theory of continental drift and partly in response to the *Titanic* disaster, a new technology was born that would change what we know about the seafloor. This technology was sonar (an acronym for SOund Navigating And Ranging). With sonar, it became possible to "see" through long distances under water.

As explained in Chapter 9, sonar detects objects under water by transmitting a sound and receiving an echo. Based on the echo's angle, how long it takes to return, and changes in frequency, sonar operators can determine where an object is, its distance, and whether it's moving. Sonar made it possible, for example, to detect otherwise invisible icebergs up to 5 kilometers (3.1 miles) away. Sonar underwent improvements and played a pivotal role in World War II by providing the Allies with a way to counter the German U-boat threat.

Scientists almost immediately recognized that they could map the ocean bottom with sonar. Using an echo sounder – essentially a sonar modified specifically for mapping bottom terrain – the German *Meteor* expedition mapped the contours and depths of the South Atlantic in 1925. This became the basis for the first worldwide seafloor map of deep ocean ridges.

The seismograph, used to locate and measure earthquakes, had been invented in the late 1800s. In 1940, geologist Hugo Benioff began using seismographic information to pinpoint and map deep earthquakes in the Pacific. This was the beginning of the discovery of a pattern of earthquakes and volcanoes today called the *Ring of Fire*. As you will see shortly, further discoveries and the theory of plate tectonics would later explain this pattern. Scientists say it marks the boundary of what we now call the Pacific Plate.

Following World War II, sonar and echo sounder technology improved. The ability to map the seafloor in greater detail revealed important new features to scientists. One of the most important discoveries was a 70,000-kilometer (43,497-mile) mountain range that extends through the Atlantic, Indian, and Pacific Oceans. The portion running through the middle of the Atlantic Ocean is called the

Archival photography by Sean Linehan, NOS, NGS, Ship Collection NOAA

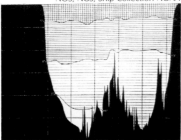

Profil VII. 22°S. Temperatur

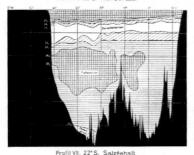

Profil VII. 22°S. Salzéehalt

Figure 13-7

Early map of the seafloor.

Using an echo sounder, this early seafloor map was made during the *Meteor* expedition.

Figure 13-8

Ring of fire.

This is the major earthquake and volcano zone that extends around the edge of the Pacific Ocean.

Mid-Atlantic Ridge. This was one of the first *mid-ocean ridges* discovered. Scientists also discovered *trenches*, which are deep ravines in the seafloor, and *rift valleys*, which are deep valleys running through the center of the Mid-Atlantic Ridge and other mid-ocean ridges. They began to notice patterns in the mid-ocean ridges, trenches, and rift valleys that proved pivotal in developing new theories.

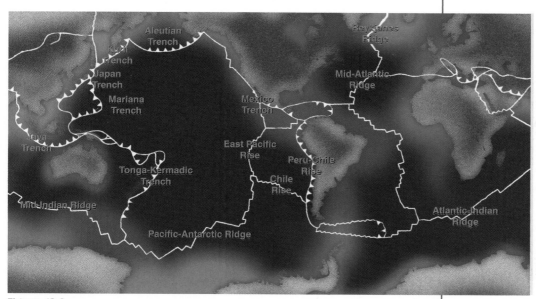

Figure 13-9

Patterns of ridges and trenches.

A mid-ocean ridge extends from the Atlantic Ocean (Mid-Atlantic Ridge) through the Indian Ocean (Atlantic-Indian Ridge) and Pacific Ocean (East Pacific Rise). Trenches are found around most of the Pacific Ocean basin.

The Creation and Destruction of Seafloor

According to the theory of seafloor spreading, where and how does new crust form?

In 1960, geologists Harry Hess and Robert S. Dietz proposed an explanation of seafloor features. They hypothesized that the seafloor is in a constant state of creation and destruction through a process called *seafloor spreading.*

In the theory of seafloor spreading, new crust emerges from the rift valley in a mid-ocean ridge. Magma from the asthenosphere pushes up through the rift and solidifies into new crust. As more magma comes up from below, it pushes new crust away on each side of the ridge. Through this process, new seafloor near the ridge continuously pushes old seafloor away from the ridge.

As the theory became accepted, other scientists proposed that old seafloor subsides (sinks) at the trenches. The old seafloor is drawn downward by gravity and inertia, eventually reaching the asthenosphere and melting into magma again. Therefore, the theory of seafloor spreading says that new seafloor forms at the rift valleys and mid-ocean ridges, spreading away from the ridges until it returns as part of the rock cycle at subduction zones (trenches). Scientists estimate that the interval from creation at the rift valley to subsiding at the trenches takes 185 to 200 million years. They estimate the rate of seafloor spreading to be about the same rate at which your fingernails grow.

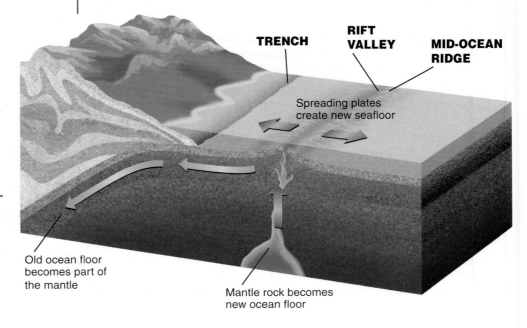

TRENCH

RIFT VALLEY

MID-OCEAN RIDGE

Spreading plates create new seafloor

Old ocean floor becomes part of the mantle

Mantle rock becomes new ocean floor

Figure 13-10

Creation and destruction of the seafloor.

New seafloor is created at a rift valley in the middle of a mid-ocean ridge. Old seafloor subsides at a trench and becomes molten rock.

Evidence of Seafloor Spreading

What evidence supports the theory of seafloor spreading?

Five forms of evidence support the theory of seafloor spreading. The first evidence came from *radiometric dating*. Radiometric dating is used to determine the age of rocks. Natural radioactive elements within a rock are unstable and decay into new, stable elements. Based on this decay rate being stable over time (this rate is called the *half-life*), scientists can estimate a rock's age. They calculate the age by examining the ratio of radioactive and stable atoms of a particular element in the rock sample. For example, scientists sometimes determine age based on the decay of potassium into argon.

By using radiometric dating, scientists have found seafloor rock to be significantly younger than rock in the center of the continents. Radiometric dating estimates the oldest seafloor rock to be 200 million years old. Rock in continental centers has been dated as old as 3.9 billion years. This difference in rock age supports the theory of seafloor spreading, because according to the theory, continental rock does not subside, whereas seafloor rock does. In addition to this, dating finds younger ocean crust close to the mid-ocean ridge and older crust further away. This age difference also supports the theory.

The second evidence comes from ocean-bottom sediment samples. In 1968, scientists aboard the research ship *Glomar Challenger* began drilling holes in the seafloor to gather sediment samples. This process is called coring. They found the sediment layers were thin or absent at the ridges and thicker away from the ridges. They found the thickest layers near the continents. These findings are consistent with the theory. The youngest seafloor, at the ridges, would have accumulated sediment for the least amount of time and would therefore have the thinnest layers. The seafloor furthest from the mid-ocean ridge would have accumulated sediment for the most amount of time and would therefore have the thickest layers.

Scientists have visited rift valleys in deep-diving submersibles, such as the *Alvin* of the Woods Hole Oceanographic Institute. Beginning in the mid-1970s, dives to the Mid-Atlantic Ridge and other ridges and rift valleys found recent lava formations with little sediment—all consistent with the coring data.

A third supporting piece of evidence is supplied by *rheology*. Rheology is the study of how matter flows. The model proposed for sea floor spreading predicts that the temperature should be high at the mid-ocean ridge and get relatively cooler as you move away from the ridge. Temperature data show that this predicted pattern exists.

Ocean Drilling Program, Texas A&M University/US Geological Survey

Figure 13-11

The *Glomar Challenger*. Aboard the *Glomar Challenger*, researchers collected core samples of ocean sediments.

Ocean Explorer, NOAA

Figure 13-12

***Alvin* on descent.** Researchers making dives to mid-ocean ridges and rift valleys in *Alvin* found recent lava formations had little sediment.

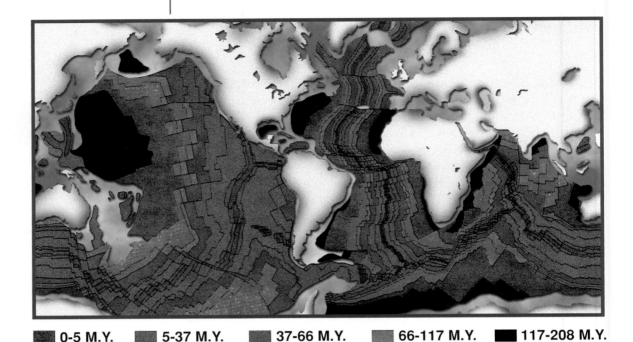

0-5 M.Y.   **5-37 M.Y.**   **37-66 M.Y.**   **66-117 M.Y.**   **117-208 M.Y.**

Figure 13-13

Radiometric dating of the seafloor.

Radiometric dating indicates that the youngest oceanic rocks are located near the mid-ocean ridges and the oldest rocks are located at the greatest distance from the ridges. (M.Y. = millions of years.)

A fourth form of evidence for seafloor spreading comes from *magnetometer* data. A magnetometer is an instrument that measures the polar orientation and intensity of magnetism of minerals. In the late 1950s, researchers began towing magnetometers over the seafloor. In 1961, Ronald Mason and Arthur Raff, researchers at the Scripps Institution of Oceanography, mapped a symmetrical pattern in the polar orientation of the magnetism of seafloor basalt rock. The seafloor on either side of the mid-ocean ridges roughly mirrors each other's polar orientation. This evidence actually came to light several years after Hess and Dietz proposed their seafloor spreading theory.

In 1963, British geologists Fred Vine and Drummond Matthews developed a model that explained the seafloor magnetic pattern. Their model was based on the principle that the Earth itself is a magnet. When magma cools and hardens into rock, magnetic minerals in the rock tend to align their polar orientation with the Earth's magnetic polar orientation. Assuming no force reorients the rock, the rock records the Earth's polar orientation at the time it solidified.

Geological evidence suggests that the Earth's magnetic field reverses at times. Scientists theorize that the last reversal was about 1 million years ago and that it has reversed about ten times in the last 4 million years. Vine and Matthews proposed that the alternating magnetic pattern reveals how seafloor spreading reflects these reversals.

Upward moving magma creates new seafloor at the mid-ocean ridge. The magma solidifies with its magnetic minerals aligned with the Earth's magnetic polar orientation. The seafloor spreads

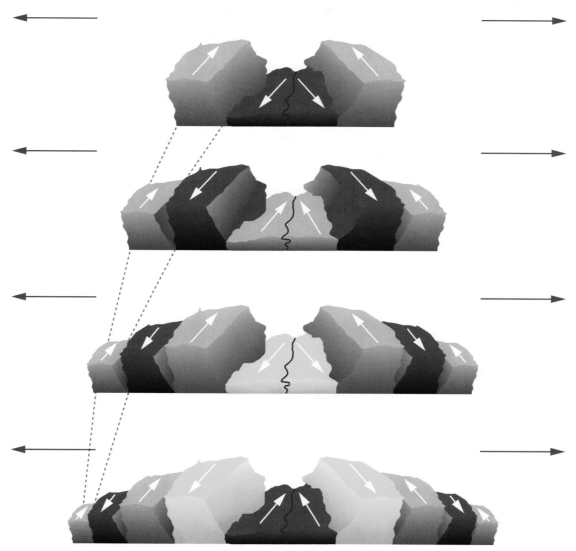

Figure 13-14

The Vine and Mathews model.

Vine and Mathews observed the same pattern of alternating polarity on each side of the mid-ocean ridge. They proposed that as the magma rises through a rift valley and cools to form new rock, magnetic particles align in the direction of the current polarity of Earth.

away at roughly an even rate on both sides of the mid-ocean ridge. Even when the Earth's poles reverse, the seafloor spreading process continues. The emerging magma solidifies with its magnetic minerals aligned with the Earth's new polar orientation. The symmetrical magnetic pattern found on the seafloor reflects the pole reversals during the creation and spreading of the seafloor.

The fifth supporting evidence for the theory of seafloor spreading is that since about 1990, geodesists have been directly measuring plate movements. They have been doing this on either side of the Juan de Fuca Ridge off Washington State. (A *geodesist* is a person who engages in the field of geodesy. *Geodesy* is the branch of science that deals with measurement of Earth's gravitational field, crustal motion, tides, and polar motion.) Geodesists can measure crustal motion of less than 1 mm/year.

ARE YOU LEARNING?

1. **Sonar contributed to information about the ocean bottom by**

   A. allowing scientists to detect submarines.

   B. giving scientists a way to map the bottom terrain.

2. **A _____ is an underwater mountain range with a _____ running through the center of it.**

   A. trench, rift valley

   B. trench, mid-ocean ridge

   C. rift valley, trench

   D. mid-ocean ridge, rift valley

3. **According to the theory of seafloor spreading, new seafloor _____ due to _____.**

   A. emerges from the rift valley, magma pushing up from the asthenosphere

   B. subsides at the trenches, polar reversal

   C. emerges from the mid-ocean ridge, basaltic orientation in the trenches

   D. all of the above may be correct at different times

4. **Evidence of seafloor spreading includes (choose all that apply)**

   A. the pattern of sediment layers.

   B. mineral patterns consistent with moon rocks.

   C. radiometric dating of seafloor and midcontinent rocks.

   D. the magnetic patterns found on the seafloor.

LIFE IN THE EXTREME: HYDROTHERMAL VENT COMMUNITIES

Beginning in the early 1970s, scientists predicted that hot springs, called hydrothermal vents, should form by mid-oceanic ridges. Peter Lonsdale was the first person to actually detect a hot plume of water. Using a deep-tow vehicle developed at the Scripps Institution of Oceanography, he made his discovery in 1976 along the Galapagos Rift. Over the years, scientists have suspected that hydrothermal vents form when cold seawater seeps into large faults along the rift valleys. Hot magma below the crust superheats the water and the heated water then rises back through the crust much like a hot spring or geyser found in terrestrial environments.

P. Rona/OAR/National Undersea
Research Program, NOAA

Figure 13-15

Hydrothermal vent.

Fluid rising from hydrothermal vents provides nutrients for organisms.

There have been many bizarre discoveries made at hydrothermal vents. In 1977, Tjeerd "Jerry" van Andel, Jack Corliss, and Jack Donnelly returned to the Galapagos Rift to follow up on Lonsdale's discovery. They explored the vents from inside the submersible Alvin. It is uncertain who was the first to discover the very strange animals living near the vents, but in 1977, Lonsdale published the first scientific paper describing them. Instead of the relatively barren sea bottom typical of the deep ocean at approximately 2,400 – 2,700 meters (7,874 – 8,858 feet), an entire community of specialized organisms lives near hydrothermal vents. Despite living well below the photic zone, this hydrothermal vent community includes diverse organisms such as clams, giant tubeworms, and crustaceans. The question was, how can life exist in such abundance without sunlight?

Topic: Hydrothermal Vents
Go To: www.scilinks.org
Code: LOP2325

After studying the communities for more than 20 years now, marine biologists think they have some of the answers. The heated vent water provides the local area with adequate temperature to support a productive ecosystem. Temperatures range from 17°C to 400°C (63°F to 752°F) compared to a typical deep-sea temperature of 2°C (36°F).

Along with the heat, however, the water carries high levels of dissolved hydrogen sulfide picked up during its trip through the crust. For hydrothermal vent organisms, hydrogen sulfide is the equivalent of sunlight.

As explained in Chapter 4, the primary producers for these communities are chemosynthesizers. Much as photosynthesizing plankton bring sunlight energy into the biosphere in the photic zone, primitive organisms metabolize the dissolved sulfides and bring chemical energy into the biosphere. Other microorganisms eat the bacteria, which are in turn eaten by other organisms. This passes the chemical energy up through the local food web.

Today scientists have multiple hypotheses about the origin of the hydrothermal vent communities. Some hypothesize that life spread to the vents from the photic zone. Other scientists hypothesize that life originated at the vents and spread to the rest of the Earth.

Many questions remain regarding the theory of plate tectonics, hydrothermal vents, and vent communities. Hydrothermal vents will continue to be important research areas for both biologists and geologists for the foreseeable future.

Image Courtesy of Monika Bright,
University of Vienna, Austria/Ocean Explorer, NOAA

Figure 13-16

Hydrocarbon-vent tubeworms.

Giant tubeworms rely on chemosynthesis for energy.

Find the answers as you read.

1. What two theories does the theory of plate tectonics unite?

2. According to the theory of plate tectonics, of what does the lithosphere consist?

3. How do mid-ocean ridges, rift valleys, and trenches relate to plate tectonic concepts?

4. According to the theory of plate tectonics, what happens at a *transform boundary*?

5. According to the theory of plate tectonics, what happens at a *divergent boundary*?

6. According to the theory of plate tectonics, what happens at a *convergent boundary*?

7. What is the *hot spot theory*?

8. What forces do scientists think cause tectonic plates to move?

9. According to the theory of plate tectonics, what changes will occur to the ocean and the continents over the next millions of years?

Topic: Plate Tectonics
Go To: www.scilinks.org
Code: LOP2330

The Unifying Theory: Plate Tectonics

Seafloor Spreading and Continental Drift Combine

What two theories does the theory of plate tectonics unite?

According to the theory of plate tectonics, of what does the lithosphere consist?

How do mid-ocean ridges, rift valleys, and trenches relate to plate tectonic concepts?

According to the theory of plate tectonics, what happens at a transform boundary*?*

According to the theory of plate tectonics, what happens at a divergent boundary*?*

According to the theory of plate tectonics, what happens at a convergent boundary*?*

In 1965, geophysicists John Tuzo Wilson and Fred Vine, along with geologist Henry Hess, introduced a new theory. It united the theories of continental drift and seafloor spreading, along with some of the original isostatic equilibrium concepts. This was the birth of today's theory of plate tectonics. As you will recall, Alfred Wegener's 1912 continental drift theory was criticized because he could not explain how continents move. More than 50 years later, the theory of plate tectonics built upon concepts developed in the theory of seafloor spreading to help explain how they move.

According to plate tectonics, the Earth's lithosphere consists of many separate plates. Coring and studies of types of rock formation showed that some plates have entirely oceanic crust, some have continental crust, and some have both types. The plates are rigid and float on the asthenosphere.

Scientists can now measure the rate of plate movement. Studies of Earth's structure show that the mantle is molten. This allows the plates to move a few centimeters a year, propelled by convection under the plate, pull from the subduction zones, and the force of magma pushing up between plates. Where plates meet at plate boundaries, there are three possible motions relative to each other: passing side-by-side, spreading apart, or pushing together.

At a *transform boundary* or *fault*, two plates slide past each other. In the United States, perhaps the most well-known of these is the San Andreas Fault in California. The San Andreas Fault marks

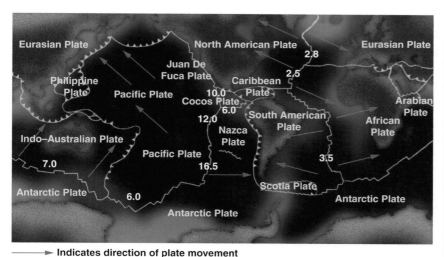

→ **Indicates direction of plate movement**
▲▲▲▲▲ **Indicates convergent boundaries**

Figure 13-17

Earth's crustal plates.
Crustal plates are defined by different types of boundaries. Plates move beside each other at transform boundaries, diverge at spreading boundaries, and converge at colliding boundaries. Crustal plates move an average of a few centimeters a year while individual plates move at different rates (indicated in centimeters per year on map).

the boundary between the Pacific Plate on the west and the North American Plate on the east. The plate to the west of the fault is moving north, while the plate to the east is moving south. Earthquakes result as rocks move when the plates slide next to each other.

At a spreading or *divergent boundary*, two plates are moving apart. As this happens, the crust pulls apart and forms valleys. Mid-ocean ridges and rift valleys mark divergent boundaries. Magma from the asthenosphere flows up through the rift valley where the plates separate, creating new crust and widening the seafloor.

Besides forming new seafloor, volcanic activity at a divergent boundary may build mountains higher than sea level. This process builds islands such as Iceland, which is thought to have formed from oceanic crust built up between the North American and Eurasian plates. Because new crust forms there, divergent boundaries are also called constructive boundaries.

Figure 13-18

The San Andreas Fault.
The San Andreas Fault is a break in the Earth's crust and is an example of a transform boundary. It is located between the Pacific and North American plates. The land to the west of the San Andreas Fault is moving north and the land to the east is moving south.

Figure 13-19

Divergent boundary.

Where two ocean plates diverge, magma rises up through a rift valley, new ocean crust forms, and the seafloor widens.

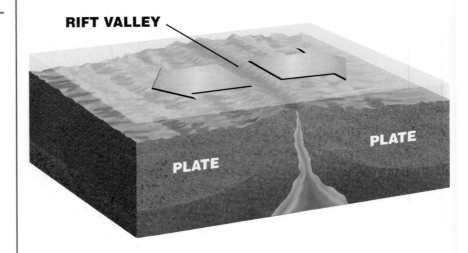

At a colliding or *convergent boundary*, two plates are pushed together. Convergent boundaries are also called destructive boundaries because movements along these boundaries destroy crust. There are three types of plate collision: ocean – ocean, ocean – continent and continent – continent.

The first occurs between two oceanic plates. In this collision, one plate is *subducted* under (is pushed beneath) the other. A chain of volcanic islands, called an *island arc,* characterizes this type of collision. According to the theory of plate tectonics, the islands of Japan were formed by the *subduction* of the Philippine Plate under the Eurasian Plate. Similarly, the Aleutian Islands resulted from the subduction of the Pacific Plate under the North American Plate. Earthquakes and volcanoes, common in island arcs, are further evidence of plate movement or plate boundaries.

Figure 13-20

Island arcs.

When two oceanic plates collide, the denser plate will be subducted. Some of the material from the melting oceanic plate rises upward to form a volcanic island arc.

The second type of plate collision occurs between oceanic and continental plates. The more dense oceanic plate is subducted under the less dense continental plate. This subduction zone is characterized by ocean trenches. A range of volcanic mountains may form at the edge of the continental plate as molten rock from the melting oceanic plate rises. Benioff's Ring of Fire and trenches around the Pacific Plate demonstrate this type of plate collision.

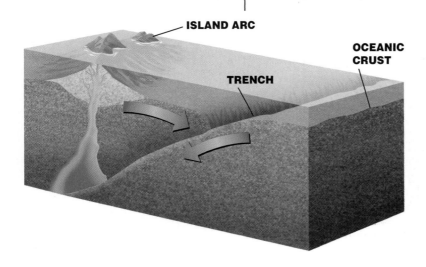

A similar pattern exists in the Andes Mountains, which sit adjacent to the Chile-Peru Trench, where the Nazca Plate subducts under the South American Plate. Still another example is the Cascade Mountain range. Here the Juan de Fuca Plate subducts under the North American Plate. Deep earthquakes, like those that identified the Ring of Fire, correlate with these subduction zones. The Mount St. Helens eruption was yet another example of volcanic activity related to subduction.

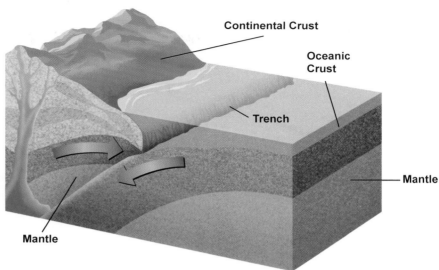

Continental Crust

Oceanic Crust

Trench

Mantle

Mantle

The third type of collision occurs between two continental plates. According to the theory, when two continental plates collide, mountains form as the crust folds. Because both continental plates have similar densities, the plates buckle rather than one sinking below or floating above the other. The Himalayas are thought to still be forming as the Indo-Australian Plate pushes into the Eurasian Plate.

Figure 13-21

Subduction zones.
A trench forms as a more dense oceanic plate moves under a less dense continental plate. As subduction occurs, some of the material from the melting oceanic plate rises upward to form volcanoes on the continent.

Mountain Range

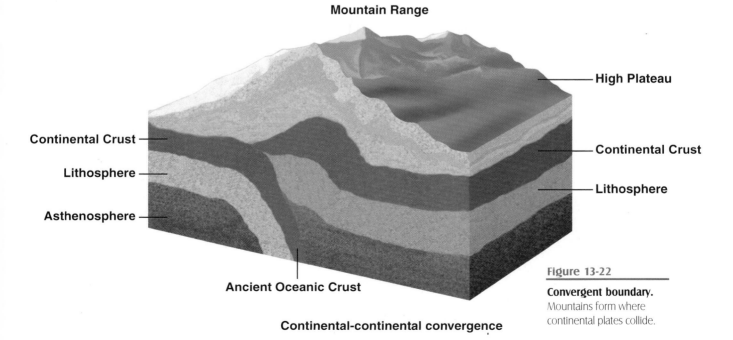

Continental Crust

Lithosphere

Asthenosphere

High Plateau

Continental Crust

Lithosphere

Ancient Oceanic Crust

Continental-continental convergence

Figure 13-22

Convergent boundary.
Mountains form where continental plates collide.

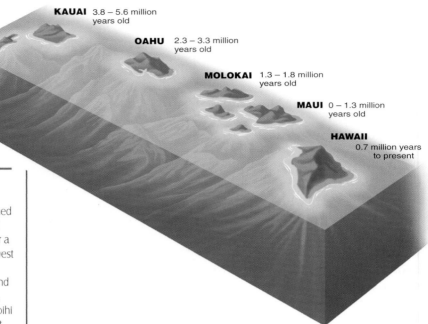

KAUAI 3.8 – 5.6 million years old

OAHU 2.3 – 3.3 million years old

MOLOKAI 1.3 – 1.8 million years old

MAUI 0 – 1.3 million years old

HAWAII 0.7 million years to present

Figure 13-23

Hot spots and the Hawaiian Islands.

The Hawaiian Islands formed as the Pacific Plate moved toward the northwest over a hot spot. The most northwest island, Kauai, is the oldest of the Hawaiian Islands, and the most southeast island, Hawaii, is the youngest. Loihi is a seamount forming just southeast of Hawaii.

Hot Spots

What is the hot spot theory?

Besides contributing to the plate tectonic theory, J. Tuzo Wilson also proposed the *hot spot theory* in 1963. Wilson observed that some volcanoes exist far from plate boundaries. His theory is that hot spots are small melting areas within the mantle where thermal plumes cause magma columns to push up intensely, breaking through the crust. Hot spots can occur at plate boundaries, though most are far from the plate edge. Scientists cite the geysers and other geological activity found at Yellowstone National Park as an example of hot spot effects.

What makes the hot spot theory significant is the concept that hot spots do not move with tectonic plates. Hot spots originate in the mantle, so the volcanic areas change on the plate as it moves over the hot spot. This results in a line or row of volcanic formations. Volcanic island chains, for example, result from the plate moving over a hot spot.

Hot spot theory is important to oceanographers because it explains the nature of features forming away from plate boundaries. Perhaps the most prominent of these is a hot spot under the Pacific Plate that scientists think created the Emperor Seamounts and the Hawaiian Islands. They formed from a hot spot as the plate moved northwest over the last 35 million years.

Plate Movement

What forces do scientists think cause tectonic plates to move?

According to the theory of plate tectonics, what changes will occur to the oceans and the continents over the next millions of years?

As you read earlier, the theory of continental drift wasn't accepted early in its conception because no one could explain how continents could move. The theory of plate tectonics provided the explanation.

Convection is a primary force driving seafloor spreading and continental drift. Chapter 10 explains that convection is a vertical circulation pattern in a gas or liquid caused by hot material rising and cold material sinking. This occurs in the mantle when warm molten rock rises and cool magma sinks. This circulation creates a current that moves the plates away from each other at the divergent boundaries, toward each other at the convergent boundaries, and past each other at the transform boundaries.

Scientists theorize that a secondary driving force comes from seafloor spreading. As new seafloor forms, the plates tend to slide away from the elevated mid-ocean ridges. The leading (older) edge of oceanic plates tends to be dense and will sink downward at the subduction zone.

The theory of plate tectonics says that the relative positions of the continental plates change as the oceanic plates subduct in places and new seafloor emerges in others. Continental plates also change their relative positions as they slide past other plates along transform boundaries. This explains how continental drift could occur.

As you read earlier, according to the theory of continental drift, Pangaea split into Laurasia and Gondwanaland about 200 million years ago. Gondwanaland then split into two landmasses, one that corresponds with today's South America, Africa, and India, and the other with today's Antarctic and Australia. South America and Africa separated about 135 million years ago, with the Atlantic Ocean forming between them.

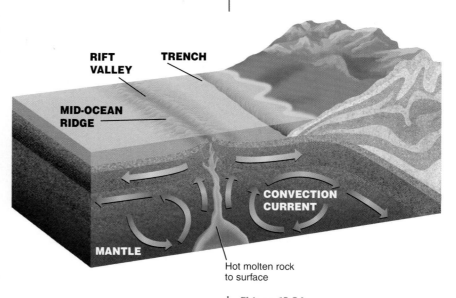

RIFT VALLEY · TRENCH · MID-OCEAN RIDGE · CONVECTION CURRENT · MANTLE · Hot molten rock to surface

Figure 13-24

Plate motion.

Scientists believe that the circular motion of convection currents in the mantle cause Earth's crustal plates to move. Convection currents form as warm material rises and cool material sinks. The spreading of plates occurs where the rising magma reaches the surface. Plates are carried along as though on a conveyor belt.

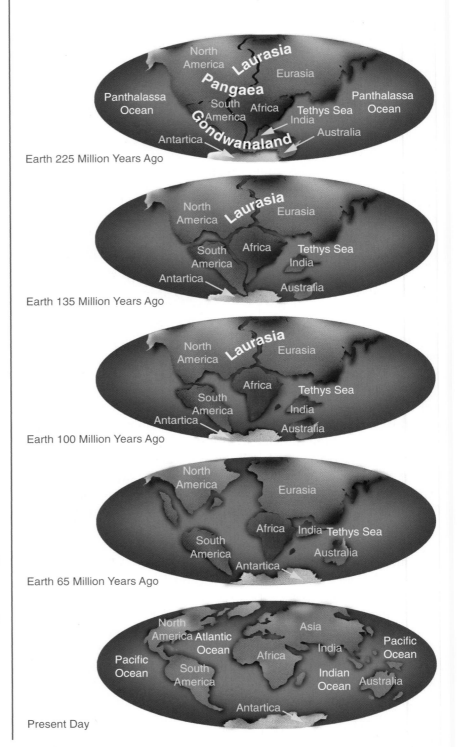

Figure 13-25

Continental drift.

Pangaea began to break apart about 200 million years ago. Laurasia (North America and Eurasia) separated from Gondwanaland. India moved away from Antarctica northward toward Asia. About 135 million years ago, South America and Africa began to separate. By 65 million years ago, South America and Africa had separated, Africa had moved northward, and the Mediterranean Sea had formed. Australia and Antarctica began to separate. During the last 16 million years, North America and Eurasia separated, creating the North Atlantic Ocean. North and South America united. India collided with Asia to form the Himalayas. Robert Dietz and John Holden predict that in 50 million years, the Baja Peninsula will have moved past and apart from the North American Plate. They predict that a new sea will form in eastern Africa and that Australia will move toward the equator while Africa pushes toward Europe. The Atlantic and Indian Ocean will continue to grow while the Pacific will become smaller.

Earth 225 Million Years Ago

Earth 135 Million Years Ago

Earth 100 Million Years Ago

Earth 65 Million Years Ago

Present Day

Scientists hypothesize that Laurasia broke apart to form North America and Eurasia about 16 million years ago. Then Greenland separated from Europe, and the Mediterranean Sea opened between Europe and Africa. Australia drifted away from Antarctica to the northeast, and India collided with Eurasia. This collision produced the Himalayas.

Based on present theorized plate movements, what will happen over the next several million years? Will the plates ever rejoin as a super continent? According to current theory, the Atlantic Ocean and Indian Ocean will expand while the Pacific Ocean will shrink. Australia will continue to drift toward Eurasia. Southern California will pass San Francisco as it moves to the northwest, and a new ocean will form in the East African rift valley. The Mediterranean Sea will close as Africa moves northward.

ARE YOU LEARNING?

1. **The theory of plate tectonics unites the theory of seafloor spreading and the theory of evolution.**

   A. true

   B. false

2. **According to the theory of plate tectonics, the lithosphere consists of**

   A. an unbroken solid mass that surrounds the molten interior.

   B. several rigid plates that float on the asthenosphere.

   C. hot spots that float up from the mantle.

3. **Mid-ocean ridges, rift valleys, and trenches are thought to**

   A. mark the boundaries between tectonic plates.

   B. occur in the middle of tectonic plates.

   C. have no relationship to plate tectonics.

   D. reverse roles in the Southern Hemisphere.

4. **According to the theory of plate tectonics, at a divergent boundary**

   A. plates spread apart from each other.

   B. plates collide with each other.

   C. plates slide past each other.

5. **According to the theory of plate tectonics, at a convergent boundary**

   A. plates spread apart from each other.

   B. plates collide with each other.

   C. plates slide past each other.

6. **According to the theory of plate tectonics, at a transform boundary**

   A. plates spread apart from each other.

   B. plates collide with each other.

   C. plates slide past each other.

7. **According to the hot spot theory, a hot spot**

   A. is a local rising column of magma that does not move with the plate above it.

   B. is a local rising column of magma that moves with the plate above it.

   C. never forms away from a plate boundary.

   D. always forms away from a plate boundary.

8. **One primary force that scientists think causes plates to move is**

   A. subduction.

   B. rotation.

   C. convection.

   D. vaporization.

9. **According to the theory of plate tectonics, over the next millions of years**

   A. the Atlantic Ocean will shrink.

   B. the Mediterranean Sea will widen.

   C. a new ocean will form in the East Africa rift valley.

   D. southern California will drift below Mexico.

New Terms You Learned

- **asthenosphere** theorized upper layer of the mantle characterized by hot solid material that flows slowly over time, much like old glass (p. 13-6)
- **continental crust** the crust under the continents (p. 13-8)
- **continental drift, theory of** the theory that the continents were once a single land mass that drifted apart and are still moving (p. 13-10)
- **convergent boundary** in the theory of plate tectonics, the boundary between two tectonic plates that are coming together; also called a colliding boundary (p. 13-24)
- **divergent boundary** in the theory of plate tectonics, the boundary between two tectonic plates that are spreading apart; also called a spreading boundary (p. 13-23)
- **erosion** the process of water, wind, glaciers, and gravity carrying away rock, soil and organic particles (p. 13-7)
- **fault** a weak area in the crust where landmasses will sink, rise, or slide by one another (p. 13-8)
- **fissures** seafloor cracks that act as passageways for seawater and molten rock to rise from Earth's mantle (p. 13-1)
- **geodesist** a person who engages in geodesy (p. 13-20)
- **geodesy** a branch of earth science that deals with measurement of Earth's gravitational field, crustal motion, tides, and polar motionv (p. 13-20)
- **geographic information systems (GIS)** software oceanographers use to map the seafloor (p. 13-1)
- **half-life** the rate of radioactive decay of an unstable element expressed as the time required for half the element present to decay into a stable element (p. 13-17)
- **hot spot theory** the theory that small melting spots in the mantle send magma up through the crust; these spots do not move in relation to the tectonic plate above it (p. 13-26)
- **hydrothermal vents** hot mineral springs on the deep ocean floor; formed by water sinking through cracks in the ocean crust near a rift valley, becoming heated by magma, and rising again through the ocean crust, somewhat like a geyser (p. 13-1)
- **igneous rock** rock created by cooling magma or lava (p. 13-7)
- **island arc** a chain of volcanic islands created at a subduction zone (p. 13-24)
- **isostatic equilibrium** the balance between the weight of the crust and the force of buoyancy provided by the mantle (p. 13-8)
- **isostatic rebound** a deflection in the Earth's crust thought to be a cause of earthquakes that results from a change in weight distribution between the oceanic crust and continental crust (p. 13-8)
- **lava** molten rock that emerges through the crust via a volcano or other opening (p. 13-6)
- **lithosphere** the uppermost, rigid part of the upper mantle and the crust; cool solid rock portion of the outer Earth (p. 13-6)
- **magma** molten rock inside the Earth (p. 13-5)
- **magnetometer** instrument that measures the polar orientation and intensity of magnetism of minerals (p. 13-18)
- **metamorphic rock** rock that forms when pressure and heat become great enough to change the rock chemically (p. 13-7)
- **mid-ocean ridge** a mountain range on the bottom of the ocean, created where plates diverge; each mid-ocean ridge has a rift valley running through its center (p. 13-15)
- **ocean crust** the crust under the ocean basins (p. 13-8)
- **Pangaea** the theorized single continent in the distant past before the continents broke apart and drifted away from each other (p. 13-10)
- **Panthalassa** the theorized single large ocean that existed when the Earth's landmasses consisted of the single continent Pangaea (p. 13-10)
- **plate tectonics, theory of** theory states that the continents float on the Earth's molten interior, gradually moving over millions of years (p. 13-3)
- **principle of uniformitarianism** the principle that processes acting on the Earth's surface today were the same in the past (p. 13-3)

- **radiometric dating** method of estimating a rock's age based on the decay rate of radioactive elements in the rock (p. 13-17)
- **rheology** the study of how matter flows (p. 13-17)
- **rift valley** valley running through the center of mid-ocean ridges thought to be the origin of new seafloor in the process of seafloor spreading (p. 13-15)
- **Ring of Fire** an area bordering the Pacific Ocean where many earthquakes and volcanoes occur (p. 13-14)
- **rock cycle** the processes that account for the changes in the types of rock (p. 13-6)
- **seafloor spreading** the theory that the seafloor forms in and spreads from rift valleys in mid-ocean ridges, eventually pushing underground in trenches (p. 13-16)
- **sediment** organic and inorganic particles accumulated together in a loose, unconsolidated form (p. 13-7)
- **sedimentary rock** rock formed by the compression and cementing together of sediments (p. 13-7)
- **seismic waves** waves that travel through the Earth that result from movement of the plates; also known as earthquake waves (p. 13-4)
- **subducted** sinks beneath (p. 13-24)
- **subduction** in the theory of plate tectonics, where one plate sinks beneath another during plate collision (p. 13-24)
- **thermal plumes** localized areas of high heat release in the outer core thought to be associated with volcanic activity (p. 13-5)
- **transform boundary** in the theory of plate tectonics, the boundary between two tectonic plates that are sliding past each other (p. 13-22)
- **trench** deep ravine in the ocean floor thought to mark where two tectonic plates meet, one being pushed under the other (p. 13-15)
- **weathering** involves mechanical and chemical processes that break rocks into smaller particles (p. 13-7)

Chapter 13 in Review

1. Draw and label a diagram of the theorized internal structure of the Earth. Include the lithosphere and indicate how it overlaps other defined layers.

2. Describe how scientists think the three different types of rock form. Include an explanation of the rock cycle.

3. What does Archimedes' Principle tell us? Explain how it relates to the Earth's theorized structure.

4. Define the concept of isostatic equilibrium and explain how it appears to be linked to some earthquakes. Where do such earthquakes occur?

5. Explain the theory of continental drift and list the early evidence used to support it. Include a description of Pangaea and Panthalassa.

6. Why did scientists not widely accept the theory of continental drift when Wegener originally proposed it? What further evidence might have strengthened his theory?

7. Explain how sonar contributed to information about the ocean bottom.

8. Explain the theory of seafloor spreading and some of the evidence that supports it. Include a sketch of the process with labels indicating mid-ocean ridge, rift valley, and trench.

9. What two theories does the theory of plate tectonics unite? How does it unite them? Explain the structure of the lithosphere according to this theory, and how mid-ocean ridges, rift valleys and trenches relate to plate tectonic concepts.

10. According to the theory of plate tectonics, what happens at transform, divergent, and convergent boundaries? Include a sketch for each boundary.

11. Describe and explain the hot spot theory. What type of geographic feature does the hot spot theory explain and why? Give an example of such a geographic feature.

12. Explain the forces and processes scientists think cause tectonic plates to move. Include a diagram.

13. According to the theory of plate tectonics, what changes will occur to the ocean basins and the continents over the next millions of years? Include a rough diagram.

Connecting Chapter Concepts – Science Scenarios

1. Current theory suggests that the Earth's crust floats on the denser mantle layer below. The continental crust consists primarily of granite, and the ocean crust consists primarily of basaltic rock.
   A. What principle explains how the crust floats on the mantle?
   B. According to this principle, what must happen if the weight of the crust changes? What phenomena does this process partially explain?
   C. What causes landmasses to gain or lose weight?
2. The theory of plate tectonics, introduced by John Tuzo Wilson in 1965, unified two theories that, when introduced, were disputed by many scientists.
   A. What two theories does the theory of plate tectonics unify?
   B. The theory of plate tectonics proposes three kinds of boundaries where plates that make up the Earth's crust meet. What are the names of each of these boundaries and what characterizes each?
   C. What are two forces that scientists think move the crust plates?
   D. What are Pangaea, Laurasia and Gondwanaland?

Marine Science and the Real World

1. Do you agree that the theory of plate tectonics was a revolution in scientific thinking about the development of the Earth? Why or why not? What other changes in thinking mark a similar revolution? Are all such changes positive? Why or why not?
2. Use the theories of hot spots and plate tectonics to estimate the age of the listed Pacific islands. Assume the hot spot that formed the islands is under Loihi now and that the Pacific Plate moves 108 millimeters per year.
3. Plate tectonic theory and other theories relating to the Earth's age and prehistory rely on the principle of uniformitarianism. What discoveries might significantly alter or make obsolete the theory of plate tectonics? What theories might be obsolete or in doubt if the principle of uniformitarianism were to prove wholly or partially inaccurate?
4. How does the theory of plate tectonics relate to present concerns about air pollution and global warming?
5. Pretend that humans can live millions of years and you're a real estate investor who specializes in tropical waterfront properties. Knowing the theories of plate tectonics and continental drift, where might you want to invest expecting a return in several million years? What areas where you might have properties today should you sell before too many million years go by? Account for possible changes in sea level.

Island	Distance from Loihi (km)	Age in Millions of Years
Loihi	0	
Oahu	390	
Kauai	550	
Midway	2,400	
Kammu	3,450	
Ojin	4,160	
Meiji	6,400	

References

Duxbury, A. 1994. *An Introduction to the World's Oceans.* Dubuque, IA: William C. Brown Publishers.

Garrison, T. 2004. *Oceanography: An Invitation to Marine Science.* Pacific Grove, CA: Brooks/Cole, a division of Thomson Learning, Inc.

Klemm, Barbara, Francis M. Pottenger III, Thomas W. Speitel, S. Arthur Reed and Ann E. Coopersmith. 1991. *Hawaii Marine Science Studies: The Fluid Earth. Physical Science and Technology of the Marine Environment.* Honolulu, HI: Curriculum Research and Development Group.

Segar, D. A. 1998. *Introduction to Ocean Sciences.* Belmont, CA: Wadsworth Publishing Company.

Tarbuck, E. J. and Lutgens, F. K. 2000. *Earth Science.* New Jersey: Prentice-Hall.

Thurman, Harold V. and Elizabeth A. Burton. 2001. *Introductory Oceanography.* New Jersey: Prentice Hall.

CHAPTER 14

Sediments in the Sea

Bob Wohlers

NASA

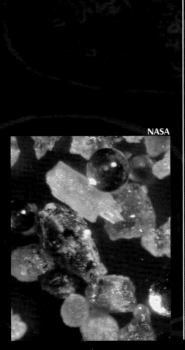

Bob Wohlers

Keeping an Eye on the Future

D r. Ashanti Pyrtle is a detective disguised as an Assistant Professor in the College of Marine Science at the University of South Florida in St. Petersburg. Specifically, she's an expert at tracking radionuclides in the aquatic environment.

What's a radionuclide? A radionuclide is an isotope (an element in which only the number of neutrons differs) of a radioactive element. Although some radionuclides occur naturally, others are the by-product of humans splitting the atom to supply energy or create atomic weapons. One radionuclide she tracks is Cesium-137, which results from the fission of uranium or plutonium – two of the most common elements used in nuclear operations. Unfortunately, this by-product of nuclear energy production or weapons manufacturing is harmful to aquatic environments as well as to humans.

Dr. Pyrtle is helping track what happens to these radionuclides following their production. Currently she is studying radionuclides in Puerto Rico and Georgia to see how this man-made material has been transported to coastal areas via rivers, streams, and groundwater movement. Dr. Pyrtle faces challenges tracking the Cesium-137 because different mechanisms affect its distribution. This not only includes the water transport, but also the radionuclides' affinity for chemically binding to positively charged particles, such as the clay sediment that lines the bottom of the environment.

Her work isn't just about uncovering the past, but also about predicting the future. By helping predict the movement and transport of radionuclides through aquatic environments, her work could be vital in the event of a nuclear accident or attack.

But, Dr. Pyrtle isn't just focused on her research. She's looking behind her to help those following in her footsteps. Part of her success is due to those supporting her. "You really do need a network and a support system because things do get hard sometimes. When they do, you need people who will help and encourage you."

She is intent on giving back and providing a support network for those following in her footsteps by directing the Minority Striving and Pursuing Higher Degrees of Success (MS PHD'S) in Earth System Science initiative. Through the MS PHD'S experience, undergraduate and graduate students from underrepresented minorities are assigned mentors who work with them during professional society conferences, field trips, discussions, and workshops. Mentors also interact with their students via web-based video conferencing, email, bulletin boards, and through live chat discussions. All of these activities help MS PHD'S participants join the Earth System Science professional community (one that includes the ocean sciences), while assisting them in identifying and achieving their academic and career goals. Through her work outside of the lab, Dr. Pyrtle shows how being a scientist is much more than doing scientific research. Part of being a scientist is helping others follow your lead.

Ashanti Pyrtle, PhD
Assistant Professor, College of Marine Science, University of South Florida

J ust as seawater constantly changes with the flow of currents and wind, so does the sea bottom. Most of the bottom receives a constant rain of sediment. As discussed in Chapter 13, sediment consists of organic and inorganic particles accumulated in a loose, unconsolidated form. As you'll see, sediment has many origins. Weather, erosion, hard-shelled organisms, chemical processes, volcanic activity, and outer space all contribute to the formation of sediments.

Sedimentary processes are an important part of Earth systems. Chapter 8 outlines why they are essential to the carbon, nitrogen, oxygen, and phosphorous biogeochemical cycles. Sediments also provide a window into the planet's past. They played a principal role in the development of plate tectonics theory, as discussed in Chapter 13. Scientists use sediments to understand Earth's past climate, ocean circulation patterns, and biological developments, among other things.

Figure 14-1

Why study sediments?

Understanding the methods and consequences of marine sedimentation can lead to unlocking some of the mysteries of the ocean and will give us insight into Earth's past.

Ocean Explorer, NOAA

Studying sediments yields practical information as well. Deep within some ocean sediments we find oil and natural gas, vital resources for continued economic growth in a current oil-based energy delivery system. These resources have tremendous political influence. Natural resources found in sediments have sparked dispute and led to international agreements about which nations can drill for or recover particular resources. They have sparked local debates about oil platforms being pollution sources and eyesores that clutter the beauty of the horizon. Even after the oil is gone, controversy continues. For example, in California there is a growing consensus that oil platforms shouldn't be removed completely when they're no longer needed for drilling. Over the years the underwater portions have become massive artificial reefs that support significant ecosystems and should therefore be left in place.

Sediments have given us clues to solving some big mysteries. For example, scientists have used information from sediments to develop hypotheses about what killed off the dinosaurs and about how dust from Africa may be damaging corals in the Caribbean. As you will read, the study of sediments even played a pivotal role in one of the most intriguing Cold-War interplays between the United States and the former Soviet Union.

The Study of Sediments

The study of marine sediments has been ongoing for more than a century. As you'll see in this chapter, scientists learn a great deal about biological productivity and ecological concerns by studying them. Before looking specifically at types of sediment and where they're found, let's start with how scientists study them to learn where to find resources and to learn about the past.

Sediment Study Tools and Techniques

What techniques do scientists use to study ocean sediments?

As you would expect, modern oceanographers use tools far more sophisticated than those used a hundred years ago to study the ocean bottom. However, some study methods have not changed much in decades because they are simple and effective.

When a scientist needs a large sample of the top sediment, the instrument of choice is the *clamshell sampler* (also known as a *grab sampler*). The clamshell sampler has a set of jaws much like those you may have seen on earth-moving cranes. The sampler descends to the bottom with the jaws locked open. When it hits the sediment, the jaws unlock automatically or via a trip line. This allows them to close, scooping up a sample when the researcher hauls the sampler back up.

The clamshell sampler brings up a lot of material, but it does not reveal much about the different sediment layers. To study that, the oceanographer chooses a box or piston corer. Both corers penetrate the sediment and bring up samples with the layers intact. They work similarly, but the piston corer retrieves samples from deeper in the sediment.

Ship Collection, NOAA

Figure 14-2a

Clamshell sampler.

This instrument is limited to capturing only the top layers of sediment.

STUDY QUESTIONS

Find the answers as you read.

1. What techniques do scientists use to study ocean sediments?

2. How do scientists use ocean sediments to study the past?

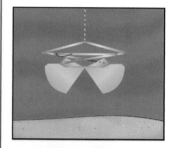

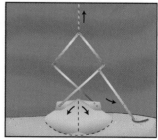

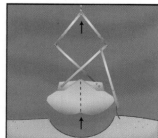

Figure 14-2b

How a Clamshell sampler operates.

The sampler is lowered to the bottom with its jaws open. Upon contact with the bottom, the jaws close, and the sampler is hauled to the surface.

Figure 14-3a

Piston Corer.

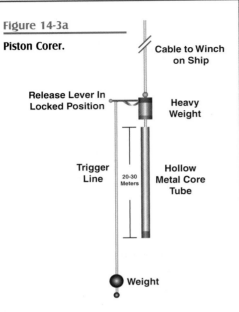

Cable to Winch on Ship

Release Lever In Locked Position

Heavy Weight

Trigger Line

20-30 Meters

Hollow Metal Core Tube

Weight

Exploring the Seas Collection, NOAA

Figure 14-4a

Piston corers aboard ship.

US Geological Survey

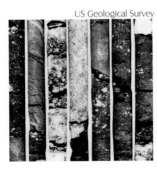

Figure 14-4b

Core samples from Chesapeake Bay taken by the *Glomar Explorer*.

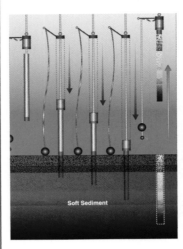

Soft Sediment

Figure 14-3b

Piston corer operation.

The piston corer is lowered from a ship and sinks into the sediment, driven by its own weight. An integrated piston creates a partial vacuum in the tube. This drives the tube deeper into the bottom. Then the corer, containing a layered sediment sample, is hauled to the surface.

A *piston corer* is an open tube on a cable that is dropped from a ship. It sinks and is driven into the sediment by its weight. An integrated piston creates a partial vacuum in the tube. This drives the tube deeper into the bottom. Then the scientists haul up the corer containing a layered sediment sample. Large piston corers can take samples as deep as 25 meters (82 feet) into the bottom.

To sample even deeper, scientists use drilling equipment on specialized research vessels. The JOIDES *Resolution*, a drilling ship in the Integrated Ocean Drilling Program, has drilled holes more than 2,000 meters (6,500 feet) deep.

Scientists also study sediments using *seismic refraction*. This is a technique that involves using an air gun and a hydrophone. An air gun is lowered over the side of a ship and suspended below the water's surface. Compressed air in the gun generates sound waves

John Beck, Integrated Ocean Drilling Program/IODP-USIO

Figure 14-5

Deep-sea drilling.

Piston corers are limited to sampling down to about 25 meters (82 feet) of sediment. For deeper samples, scientist must employ drilling techniques similar to those used in the oil industry. Special ships have been designed for this purpose.

that travel through the water and penetrate into the seafloor. As the sound passes through rock layers of different densities, it is refracted back to the surface. A *hydrophone* (underwater microphone), towed behind the ship records the refracted sound. The speed of the returning waves depends on the density of the material they travel through. Therefore, the signal can yield detailed information about the geologic structure and composition of the ocean floor sediments and underlying rocks. Marine geologists commonly use this method when looking for oil and gas.

Figure 14-6a

Air gun.

For bottom profiling using seismic refraction, this air gun is used to emit a loud sound underwater.

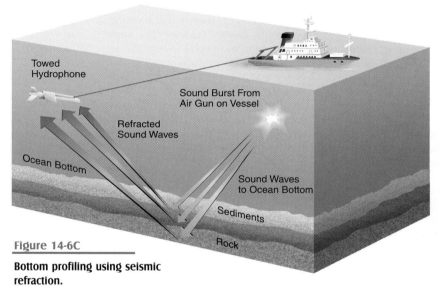

Figure 14-6C

Bottom profiling using seismic refraction.

One way of getting detailed information about what lies beneath the sea bottom is through seismic refraction. The research vessel uses an air gun that sends sound waves to the seafloor. The waves refract off the sediment and rock layers and return to the ship where they are recorded by a towed hydrophone. The air gun under the vessel is detonated every 30-60 seconds; in this way a profile of the seafloor is made.

Figure 14-6b

Air gun "bubble."

Once the air gun is discharged underwater, a bubble can can be seen at the surface.

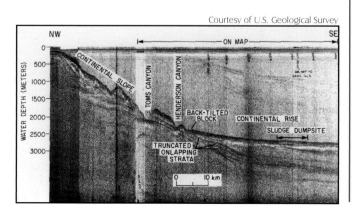

Figure 14-7

A seismic profile.

When bottom sampling is not practical, sound waves can be quite effective in determining the layering beneath the seafloor.

COLD WAR "SEDIMENT STUDY"

Built in 1973, one of the deepest drilling research ships is the Hughes *Glomar Explorer*. Although capable of drilling in water as deep as about 3,500 meters (11,483 feet) and unveiled as a deep-sea mining vessel, the *Glomar Explorer* was actually intended for another, secret purpose. The vessel was designed for deep-sea studies – but not of sediments. The *Glomar Explorer's* secret was that she was built to recover a lost Soviet submarine!

The story begins April 11, 1968, when a Soviet Golf-II class ballistic missile submarine sank in about 5,200 meters (17,060 feet) of water, some 1,200 kilometers (746 miles) northwest of Hawaii. US Naval intelligence had tracked the sub, heard the disaster with underwater listening equipment, and knew where it sank. The Soviet Navy came looking, but couldn't locate it. The US Navy realized that they alone knew where it lay. Unfortunately, the technology to reach it did not yet exist.

Recognizing an intelligence bonanza, the US Central Intelligence Agency (CIA) hired the Hughes Corporation to design and build a ship that could recover the Soviet sub. Under the cover of being a deep-sea mining ship that would recover nodules, the *Glomar Explorer's* actual purpose was such a closely guarded secret that even most of the people building her did not know it.

In June 1974, the *Glomar Explorer* brought up the Soviet submarine using a specialized, massive, deep-grappling system designed to bring it up in one piece. Unfortunately the device partially failed, and only a portion of the sub made it to the surface. Reportedly, the material recovered included nuclear missiles and torpedoes and Soviet codebooks and coding equipment. There were also the remains of Soviet sailors, who were buried at sea according to Soviet naval protocols.

The secret was too good to last. Less than a year later, the *Los Angeles Times* ran a story linking the *Glomar Explorer* to secret US government operations. The CIA did not admit the *Glomar Explorer's* true mission until much later, but it became quickly known that the ship was not what people had claimed she was.

In the end, though, the *Glomar Explorer* became what she was supposed to be all along. After years in storage by the US Navy, Global Marine Drilling leased the *Glomar Explorer*, refit her, and put her to work as one of the deepest sediment drillers ever built.

Federation of American Scientists

Figure 14-8

Glomar Explorer.

Stratigraphy and Paleoceanography

How do scientists use ocean sediments to study the past?

As you will learn in more detail shortly, sedimentation is an ongoing process. Sediments from different sources constantly enter the ocean and settle to the bottom. Because of this, at one time scientists expected that the sea bottom would tell them about the earliest days of the Earth. In the 19th century, most scientists thought that ocean sediments would be very thick throughout the ocean basins. Some hypothesized that perhaps a billion years lay buried in the sediments.

This is not what scientists have found. For example, there is little or no sediment on the Mid-Atlantic Ridge, or any other sea floor spreading ridge. The previous chapter discusses how plate tectonics theory explains this. The theory says that new ocean crust forms at mid-ocean ridges as part of the seafloor spreading process. Because the crust is new, little sediment has had a chance to fall onto it. As new ocean floor moves away from the ridge, it ages and accumulates sediment. So, sediment thickness increases with distance from the ridge. When it finally reaches a trench, the seafloor subducts. Subduction destroys old ocean crust, so there are no sediments on the ocean crust that are dated older than 200 million years. Despite this, scientists learn a great deal from ocean sediments.

The study of sediment layers is called *stratigraphy* (from the Greek *stratum* meaning *layer*, and *graph* meaning *drawing*). Scientists use deep-sea stratigraphy to look for clues, such as rock composition, microfossils, deposition patterns, and other physical properties. Based on these clues, scientists estimate the age of the

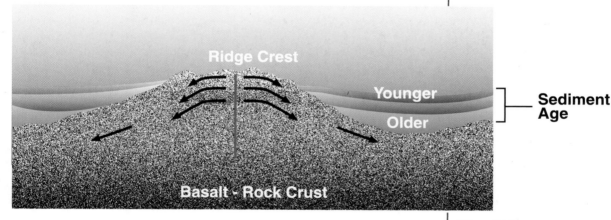

sediment layers and draw conclusions about the past. Stratigraphy provides evidence used by scientists to understand changes in the ocean and atmosphere. These include previous circulation patterns, former sea levels, and trends in biological productivity.

The use of stratigraphy and deep-sea drilling has led to a relatively new science called *paleoceanography* (from the Greek *palaios* meaning *ancient*). Paleoceanography is the study of prehistoric ocean. Paleoceanographers study chemical ratios and radioactive isotopes found in microfossils to obtain evidence about prehistoric ocean conditions. By examining deep ocean sediments called oozes, they have been able to make estimates about prehistoric ocean temperatures and climatic conditions that are thought to be highly accurate.

Stratigraphy, paleoceanography, and marine geology interrelate with broader studies about the Earth. These studies are not confined to the ocean. For example, scientists use stratigraphy to

Figure 14-9

Plate motion at a mid-ocean ridge.

At the crest of the mid-ocean ridge, there is little or no sediment. This crust is too new for sediments to have time to accumulate. As the crust is pushed away from the crest, sediments begin accumulating. A cross section shows that younger deposits form layers on top of older deposits. The oldest sediments on the ocean floor are at the greatest distance from the ridges, directly above the basalt-rock crust. These sediments were the first to be deposited.

study core samples from glaciers much as they do ocean sediments. As another example, because scientists think that at one time an ancient sea covered the Grand Canyon region, paleoceanographers and marine geologists often go to this region and similar sites to conduct research. Oceanographers have even played a key role in developing current hypotheses regarding the past existence of an ocean on Mars. In 2008, using instruments aboard NASA's Mars Reconnaissance Orbiter (MRO), clay-like minerals, which form only in the presence of large quantities of water, were found covering about half the planet. This confirms the hypothesis that Mars once had a lot of water.

Malin Space Science Systems/JPL, NASA

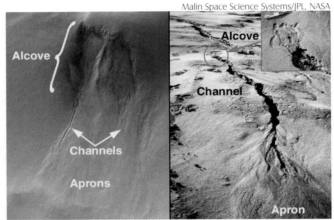

Figure 14-10

Water on Mars?

In the Earth picture on the right, rainwater flowing under and seeping along the base of a recently deposited volcanic ash layer has created a gully. The similarity to the Martian gully on the left is striking.

ARE YOU LEARNING?

1. Methods scientists use to study sediments include (choose all that apply)

   A. radar.

   B. clamshell sampler.

   C. piston corer.

   D. drilling ships.

2. To examine the past using stratigraphy, scientists study the sediment layers to look for clues in the rock composition, microfossils, and other physical properties.

   A. true

   B. false

DEATH FROM ON HIGH?
A K–T EXTINCTION HYPOTHESIS

Figure 14-11

Scientists have long wondered what killed off the dinosaurs and many other organisms (about two-thirds of all Earth's plants and animals) about 65 million years ago. The existence of the K-T extinction, as scientists call it, has been known for decades, but evidence for its possible cause did not come to light until 1980. K-T is a designation from the geologic time scale. K stands for Cretaceous, the last period in the Mesozoic era, and T for Tertiary, the first period in the Cenozoic era. Geologists use the mass extinction event to define the boundary between these two periods.

The most widely accepted explanation for the mass extinction was proposed in 1980 by the father-and-son team of Luis and Walter Alvarez. Walter is a geologist who thought that the secret to the end of the dinosaur's reign might lie in a clay layer found right at the K-T boundary. He asked his chemist and Nobel laureate father, Luis, how to determine how long it took for the clay to be deposited. Since iridium is a component of cosmic dust that comes in from outer space at a low, but known rate, they used the amount of iridium in the clay layer to determine the time it took for the clay to be deposited. What they found surprised them: there was nearly 100 times as much iridium as they expected. They knew that so much iridium could only have come from

an extraterrestrial source, such as an asteroid. This led to their hypothesis, which was published the following year. Over the past three decades, many other researchers have found other data to fill in additional details that support what is now considered a theory.

The theory as it stands is this: The K-T extinction was triggered when a giant asteroid, 10 kilometers (6 miles) in diameter, struck the Earth. Heat from the impact raised the atmospheric temperature to that of a kitchen oven on broil. Animals roasted and forests burned. Dust and smoke enshrouded the planet, blocking out the sun so the temperature went from burning hot to freezing cold. The dust and smoke temporarily shut down photosynthesis. The only life to survive this holocaust were small animals that burrowed into the ground or lived in fresh water and plants with seeds that could survive for long periods in the soil. Marine species were decimated, although deep-sea animals survived fairly well.

One decade after the Alvarez's proposed their hypothesis, researchers found an impact crater that supported the hypothesis. It is a 180 kilometer (110 mile) diameter hole buried beneath nearly 2 kilometers (1.2 miles) of sediment near the northern coast of the Yucatan Peninsula, Mexico.

While scientists have strong evidence that the dinosaurs and other life went extinct 65 million years ago and that a giant asteroid struck at that time, not all scientists accept the link between the two events. One camp of scientists blames the extinction on a massive volcanic eruption. They hypothesize that the volcano discharged high volumes of poisonous gases into the atmosphere and brought about tremendous acid rains for years. These scientists point to an eruption at the Deccan Traps in India, where approximately 500,000 km$_2$ (200,000 mi$_2$) of lava came out of a huge set of volcanoes at about the same time as the K-T extinctions.

Either or both catastrophes could have caused the mass extinctions. Alternatively, they could have been the last straw in a decline in animal and plant populations that was already taking place for some other reason, like changing climate. Since 65 million years is a such long time, there is little evidence remaining and what is there is difficult to find and not conclusive. It is possible that we will never know for sure what killed the dinosaurs.

Types of Sediment

Scientists, engineers, and others classify sediments in many ways, depending on what they are studying. Two of the most common classification systems use origin and size.

Sediment Origins

How are sediments classified by origin?

What are the characteristics and relative abundance of sediments based on their classification by origin?

Scientists learn a great deal by classifying sediments based on where they originate. As you may imagine, this is important for understanding the processes that created them, the environmental conditions at the time they were formed and deposited, and what sorts of deposits they become. This is why determining sediment origins is one of the cornerstones of paleoceanography. Sediments may be classified into four origin categories: *lithogenous*, *biogenous*, *hydrogenous*, and *cosmogenous*.

Lithogenous sediments come from the land (from Greek *lithos* meaning *stone*, and Latin *generare* meaning to *produce*). Also known as *terrigenous sediments*, they result primarily from erosion by water, wind, and ice carrying rock and mineral particles into the sea. Other lithogenous sediments enter the sea from landslides and volcanic eruptions.

Lithogenous sediments make up the majority of sediments found near continents and islands. This is because they come from weathering and erosion of the land. Quartz, which is a major mineral in the rock granite, is the most common mineral in lithogenous sediments because it is hard and does not easily break down physically or chemically. Feldspar is also abundant in granite. Although it is found in sands, feldspar often breaks down to form clay. Clay is common in lithogenous sediments. It consists of small particles that travel far in the water before settling to the bottom. For this reason, clay is often found far from shore.

It is estimated that rivers carry up to 15 billion metric tons of lithogenous sediments into the ocean annually. Human activities, such as agriculture, disturb the land and enhance stream erosion. Another approximately 100 million metric tons of sediment transfer from land to sea as fine dust and volcanic ash. Lithogenous sediments usually surround volcanic islands due to the breakdown of basalts and other volcanic rocks that make up the islands.

STUDY QUESTIONS

Find the answers as you read.

1. How are sediments classified by origin?

2. What are the characteristics and relative abundance of sediments based on their classification by origin?

3. How are sediments classified by size?

4. How do sediment grain size and current velocity affect the erosion and deposition of sediments?

True Color Earth, MODIS, NASA

Figure 14-12

Lithogenous sediment.

Sediments that originate on land, such as material eroded from mountains, are carried by rivers to the sea. Shown in this satellite photograph, a delta made from lithogenous sediments forms where the Mississippi River water spills into the Gulf of Mexico.

Biogenous sediments originate from organisms (from the Greek *bios* meaning *life*, and *generare* meaning to *produce*). The particles in these sediments come from shell and hard skeletons. Although lithogenous sediments are the most abundant with respect to their total volume, biogenous sediments cover a larger area of sea floor.

The vast majority of biogenous sediments come from planktonic organisms that obtain *siliceous* (contains silica) and *calcareous* (contains calcium carbonate) compounds from seawater. These organisms use the compounds to form shells or skeletons, which later settle as sediment when the organisms die. Some sediment comes from large organisms' shells and hard corals. Important deep water sediments, called oozes, are biogenous. You'll learn more about these later in this chapter.

Biogenous sediments are most plentiful where there is a lot of productivity and where there are not a lot of other sediments. Although organisms are abundant along continental margins where there are ample nutrients, biogenous sediments do not make up a large proportion of the total sediments in that area. This is because they are overwhelmed by the loads of lithogenous sediments coming off the continent, especially near the mouths of rivers. In the deep ocean, where productivity is much lower, biogenous sediments are the most common because there are few other types of sediments in the region.

Over time, biogenous sediments accumulate into layers. Under the right conditions, organic carbon molecules in these sediments form crude oil (petroleum) and natural gas.

Hydrogenous sediments result from chemical reactions within seawater (from the Greek word *hydro* meaning *water*). The reactions cause minerals to come out of solution and form particles that settle on the bottom. The sources of the dissolved minerals vary, including the dissolution of submerged rock and sediments, materials coming from new crust forming at mid-ocean ridges, chemicals dissolved in hydrothermal vent water, and material dissolved in river runoff.

Although this accounts for less than 1% of the seafloor sediments, it is the process that produces important mineral deposits, such as ferromanganese and phosphorite nodules, which you will learn more about later in this chapter. Hydrogenous sediments usually form slowly (but can form quickly under certain conditions) and are found among biogenous and lithogenous sediments.

Cosmogenous sediments come from outer space (from the Greek *kosmos* meaning *space*). They are primarily made up of small particles the size of sand or smaller called cosmic dust. Some of

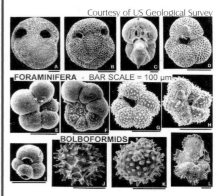
Courtesy of US Geological Survey

FORAMINIFERA - BAR SCALE = 100 µm

BOLBOFORMIDS

Figure 14-13

Biogenous sediment.
Sediments that originate from biological organisms, such as the limestone or silica remnants of plankton, are termed *biogenous*.

INTERNET PORTAL
SCiLINKS. NSTA

Topic: Seafloor Sediments
Go To: www.scilinks.org
Code: LOP2305

these are thought to result from collisions between objects in space, such as asteroids and comets.

Cosmic dust particles continually settle through the atmosphere, much as particles settle through water. Large and fast-moving objects that enter the atmosphere are called *meteors*. A meteor heats up in the atmosphere from friction with the air, usually getting hot enough to melt and vaporize. This is why the space shuttle requires special tiles to protect it from burning up when it reenters the atmosphere. The meteor streaks you see at night come from space rocks burning up as they hurtle through the air. A meteor that strikes the ground is called a *meteorite*.

Most meteors vaporize before they reach the ground. However, cosmic dust and meteorites account for an estimated 15,000 to 30,000 metric tons of material from space that reaches the Earth's surface each year. Although large meteor strikes are rare, they can produce tremendous effects locally or even globally, depending on their size. Sometimes cosmogenous sediments contain micro-tektites. *Microtektites* are glass particles that form when a large meteorite impacts the Earth. The tremendous impact energy results in enough heat to melt the Earth's crust and hurl some of it into space. The crust bits melt again as they reenter the atmosphere, forming raindrop shapes as they plummet through the air. The ancient Egyptians valued tektites as jewelry for royalty, and sent people specifically to find dark tektites on the desert sand.

Cosmogeneous sediments are the least abundant of the sediments. Typically they make up no more than a few parts per million of a marine sediment layer.

NASA

Figure 14-14

Microtektites.

Although these extraterrestrial materials account for only a tiny fraction of Earth's sediments, cosmogenous sediments have yielded important clues about our planet's past.

Much of the ocean bottom consists of lithogenous sediments carried out to sea as dust by the wind. That may not sound like a major material source, but wind-carried dust, especially from Africa, has become a growing concern for scientists.

For years, scientists have been trying to determine what is causing the decline of Caribbean coral reefs. While local human effects are obviously the cause in some places, remote reefs show decline too rapidly to be accounted for by local pollution. The answer now appears to relate to dust carried all the way across the Atlantic from the Sahara Desert.

Scientists estimate that more than a billion metric tons of dust travels through the atmosphere each year. African dust alone accounts for several hundred million tons of it. This is not new – scientists think it is a natural process going back eons – but what is new is the increase in African dust since the 1970s. Since then, drought, poor agricultural processes, and other environmental effects have broadened the Sahara and increased the amount of dust blowing from the continent. The problem with African dust appears to be twofold: iron and organisms. Iron is an important nutrient for algae. Because African dust is high in iron, scientists hypothesize that it increases algae growth on coral reefs. The algal growth blocks the sunlight that would normally reach the tiny coral animals. As discussed in Chapter 6, *Symbiodinium*, a dinoflagellate algae, lives inside the tissue of corals. These algae photosynthesize and provide food for the coral animals. When something blocks light to the corals, *Symbiodinium* cannot photosynthesize and the coral animals starve to death.

African dust also carries living microorganisms. Many researchers are beginning to think that these organisms are responsible for diseases found in coral community organisms. For example, sea fans in Florida waters began dying due to something growing on them. Scientists found the culprit – a soil fungus that can grow under water but not reproduce there. This means that there has to be a continuous external source of spores for the fungus to spread – and a likely candidate is the African dust. This also relates to human infections. A growing concern is that germs causing respiratory and other ailments may be traveling with the dust.

At the moment, a lot of this is hypothesis. Scientists don't really know for sure how much African dust affects the coral communities and other ecosystems, and they are still gathering data. This will probably be a key research area for the next few decades.

Sediment Sizes

How are sediments classified by size?

How do sediment grain size and current velocity affect the erosion and deposition of sediments?

When scientists and engineers need to study how water motion affects sediments, origin is less important than size. Sediments are therefore also classified based on *grain size*, which is the diameter of an individual particle. This classification system identifies sediment ranging in size from a *boulder* (largest grain size) to *clay* (smallest grain size). This is shown in the *Wentworth Scale* (Figure 14-15).

Figure 14-15

Wentworth Scale.
This classifies sediment according to grain size.

WENTWORTH SCALE		
Classification	**Grain diameter**	**Example**
clay	smaller than 0.004 mm	talc or fine powder
silt	0.004 mm to 0.0625 mm	powder
sand	0.0625 mm to 2 mm	sugar crystals
granule	2 mm to 4 mm	aquarium gravel
pebble	4 mm to 64 mm	grape
cobble	64 mm to 256 mm	cobblestone
boulder	256 mm and larger	a brick or larger

In addition, scientists sometimes use terms to describe mixes of different grain sizes. For example, *mud* is a mixture of silt and clay.

As you may imagine, the smaller a particle, the slower it falls. Settling times become longer as particles get smaller. For instance, in water 2 kilometers (1.24 miles) deep, medium sand takes about a day to settle, whereas a clay-sized particle takes much longer. Heavy particles require more energy to move and therefore do not travel as far as fine particles.

Because of this, current and waves tend to distribute sediment according to particle size. You commonly find coarse grain sizes together in one area with increasingly finer sizes as you move away. However, this is not always the case. This is because other processes affect settling time. For example, clay particles tend to be spherical like other particles, but they are more cohesive (meaning that they cling together) than other particles. For this reason, clay particles may clump together into larger particles and settle quickly.

Grain size and current velocity affect the erosion and deposition of sediments. The relationship is interesting because the smallest and the largest particles behave similarly with respect to transportation and erosion. *Hjulström's diagram* (Figure 14-16) illustrates the relationship.

Notice that sand, in about the middle of the graph, takes the least amount of energy to erode. Large particles require more energy to erode because they are heavy and it takes a strong current to lift them off the bottom. Interestingly, particles smaller than sand also require more energy to erode. This is because small particles (especially clays) tend to be cohesive. Sand is the smallest of the non-cohesive particles, so it is the easiest to erode.

Figure 14-16

Hjulström's diagram.

This shows the relationship that particle size and energy (rate of flow of water or current) have on erosion, transportation, and deposition of sediments. For particles larger than sand, the energy required for erosion increases because the particles weigh more. For particles smaller than sand, the energy required for erosion also increases because very small particles are cohesive – they stick together. Sand is easily eroded because it is small and not cohesive. As energy decreases, particles are deposited according to size (weight), with largest first and smallest last. More energy is required to erode than to transport a particle.

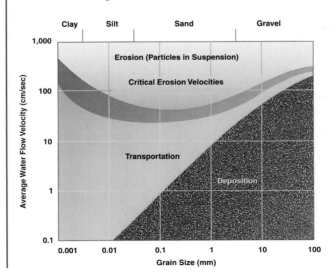

If you look at the deposition field in the diagram, you see that particles return to the bottom in a roughly linear relationship with the current strength. The stronger the current, the larger the particles it will keep in suspension. Or, put another way, the smaller the particle, the less water motion it takes to keep the particle from settling to the bottom. When a current is strong enough, even pebbles will not settle. On the other hand, silt remains suspended with very little current, and clay can stay suspended almost indefinitely.

Sorting results from the nature of water movement in the region. When the water movement does not fluctuate much, sediment tends to be *well sorted*. This means that you find sediments of primarily one grain size. As explained in Chapter 11, deepwater currents tend to be slow, progressive, and constant. This results in well sorted sediments.

When water movement changes frequently, sediment will be *poorly sorted*. This means that you have sediments with a mix of grain sizes. A common example of this is wave erosion against an unprotected (no barrier reef or islands) shoreline. Because wave energy changes substantially with the weather, the waves sometimes erode the coast with high energy and sometimes with low energy. Some types of current carry sediments that tend to be poorly sorted.

Mary Hollinger, NODC biologist, NOAA

Figure Figure 14-17a

Well sorted sediment.

Mary Hollinger, NODC biologist, NOAA

Figure 14-17b

Poorly sorted sediment.

ARE YOU LEARNING?

1. **Sediments that originate from organisms are called**

   A. lithogenous.

   B. biogenous.

   C. hydrogenous.

   D. cosmogenous.

2. **_____ include sand and clay. These sediments _____.**

   A. Lithogenous sediments, cover the most sea bottom

   B. Biogenous sediments, cover most of the sea bottom

   C. Lithogenous sediments, are the most abundant by volume

   D. Biogenous sediments, are the most abundant by volume

3. **Sediments are classified by size based on the**

   A. weight of an individual particle.

   B. the diameter of an individual particle.

4. **Because it is a small but non-cohesive particle, sand is the most easily eroded sediment.**

   A. true

   B. false

Continental Shelf Sediments

As you have already learned, you can divide the ocean bottom into two distinct areas: the continental shelf and the deep ocean basin. The continental shelf is relatively shallow and near land, whereas the deep ocean basin is farther from shore and far away from any sources of lithogenous sediments. The differences in depth and proximity to land account for sedimentation processes on the continental shelf that differ from those in the deep ocean basin.

Sedimentation Processes on the Continental Shelf

What processes affect sedimentation on the continental shelf?

Tides, waves, and currents strongly control continental shelf sedimentation. Shoreline turbulence from waves is one of the most notable influences because it keeps small particles from settling. Surf and waves carry the smallest particles out to sea, which is why most beaches and immediate shorelines are sandy rather than muddy.

STUDY QUESTIONS

Find the answers as you read.

1. What processes affect sedimentation on the continental shelf?

2. What are *recent* and *relict* sediments?

3. How does the rate of continental shelf sedimentation compare to the rate of deep ocean sedimentation?

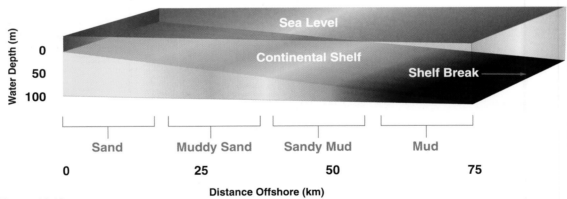

Figure 14-18

Shelf sediments.
Idealized model of how sediments are sorted on the continental shelf.

Because waves and tides have less effect in deep water, mud can be present further offshore. As you move toward deep water, sediments tend to have smaller particles. For this reason, the "ideal" continental shelf sediment would be sand from shore to about 20 kilometers (12.4 miles) out. There, the sediment would be muddy sand to about 30 kilometers (18.6 miles) out. Going further out on the shelf, the sediment would be more muddy and less sandy from sorting. From about 60 kilometers (37.3 miles) from shore out to the edge of the shelf, you would expect to find mud with almost no sand in it.

Recent and Relict Sediments

What are recent *and* relict *sediments?*

In reality, you do not find the "ideal" continental shelf you would expect. Although the expected pattern is evident, you actually find coarse sediment near shore and finer sediment as you follow the bottom deeper and seaward. Suddenly, you find coarse sediment again. Moving still further out on the shelf it gets finer and then coarse again.

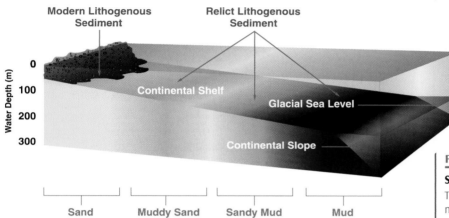

This is the result of fluctuations in the sea level over time. *Recent sediments* have accumulated since the sea level stabilized. *Relict sediments* accumulated and were left stranded when the sea level was lower.

Figure 14-19

Shelf sediments.
This model shows how sediments actually occur on the continental shelf. The reason for the intermixing is the effect of past sea level fluctuations.

Continental Shelf Sedimentation Rates

How does the rate of continental shelf sedimentation compare to the rate of deep ocean sedimentation?

The sedimentation rate on the continental shelf varies with region. However, in virtually all regions, sedimentation on the shelf is more rapid than in the deep ocean. At the mouths of large rivers, for example, sedimentation can occur at a rate of one meter per thousand years, but there is a lot of variation. For example, sedimentation is relatively slow along most of the US east coast, despite its many rivers. This is because many of the rivers enter estuaries rather than flow directly into the ocean. The estuaries trap most of the river sediment. This suggests that the continental shelf sediments off the US east coast are primarily relict sediments left from a lower sea level during the last ice age.

Interestingly, continental shelf sedimentation processes also affect the adjoining deep ocean. Just as only so much snow can accumulate

Figure 14-20

Evidence from the past.

The spectacular sediments seen in the Grand Canyon were laid down long ago when the region was at the bottom of an ancient sea.

on a land mountain before it avalanches, accumulating sediment on the continental shelf avalanches down the continental slopes. These are called *turbidity currents* and consist of thick, muddy fluid that rushes down with such force that it carries sediment deposits all the way to the abyssal plain. These deposits are called *turbidites*. Turbidites consist of layers of lithogenous sand embedded with the more typical, fine deep-sea sediments. Turbidity currents travel with so much force that they cut the large submarine canyons found on continental slopes.

The continental shelves undergo processes that produce biogenous sediments, which also affect the sedimentation rate. Biogenous sedimentation depends on local productivity, which tends to be high in coastal waters. Continental shelf sediments tend to have a mix of both biogenous and lithogenous materials. In tropical climates, calcareous biogenous sediments dominate, especially where there are no rivers to carry in lithogenous sediments.

Chapter 13 explains the rock cycle, which includes the formation of sedimentary rocks that result from compression and chemical processes occurring over millions of years. Continental shelf sediments are part of this cycle. *Lithification* (the formation of rock) sometimes transforms sediments into rocks that eventually become part of the terrestrial environment. Scientists attribute this to the movement of tectonic plates pushing the seafloor up, as well as processes associated with sea level changes. In many states like Florida, Texas, and Ohio, limestone deposits are so extensive that the rock is mined. It is an important building material and a necessary ingredient in cement. Limestone is sedimentary rock made of biogenous marine sediment. The presence of limestone in these states helps explain their geologic history.

Figure 14-21

Ice rafting.

Glacial sediments are deposited on the sea bottom when rafting ice breaks away from a glacier and floats offshore. As the ice melts, the sediment is released and falls to the bottom and accumulates over time.

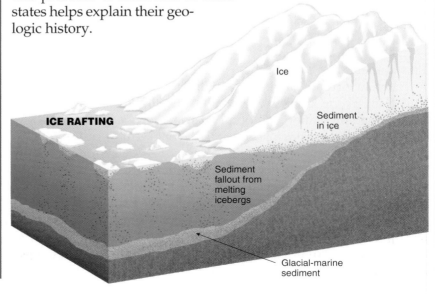

Deep Ocean Sediments

Sedimentation Processes on the Deep Ocean Bottom

What processes affect sedimentation in the deep ocean?

Like the processes that affect the continental shelf, sedimentation processes in the deep ocean vary regionally. Since most biological productivity takes place near land, you might expect that seafloor samples taken far from land would have a lower proportion of biogenous material. Actually, the opposite is true. Deep ocean sediments tend to be high in biogenous material.

The explanation for this is that there is significantly less lithogenous sediment far from land. Therefore, proportionately there is a high concentration of biogenous material from planktonic organisms. Deep ocean sediments that consist of 30% or more biogenous sediment are called *ooze.* Oozes have various names, depending on the dominant plankton remains that make them up. As you have learned, some planktonic organisms have skeletons or *tests* (shell-like outer coverings of the organisms) made primarily of calcium carbonate. Oozes composed primarily of these plankton are called *calcareous ooze.* Other plankton have silica skeletons. They form *siliceous ooze.*

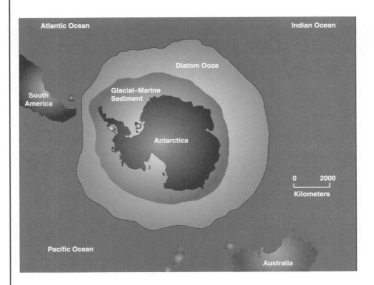

Figure 14-22

Deep-sea deposits around Antarctica.

Sediment deposition has created a 1,000 km (620 mile) zone of glacial sediments around Antarctica. Beyond this zone, deposits from diatoms in this highly productive area cover the sea bottom.

Oozes accumulate slowly. The rate is about 1 to 6 centimeters (0.39 to 2.36 inches) per thousand years. You will note, however, this is still 10 times or more faster than deep ocean lithogenous sediment accumulation.

Ooze accumulation rates vary due to several influences. One is the abundance of organisms at the surface above the deep ocean. Another is the rate at which lithogenous sediments accumulate in the area. A third is the rate at which the calcium carbonate dissolves into seawater on the bottom.

Clays and other lithogenous materials cover about 38% of the deep-sea floor. The small grain size of clay makes it easy for cur-

Monterey Bay National Marine Sanctuary/NOAA

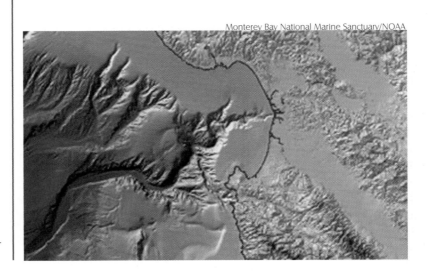

Figure 14-23

Lithogenous sediments in a submarine canyon.

This figure shows a sonar map of Monterey Bay Canyon as it plunges to over 1829 meters (6000 feet) just offshore. Research geologists determined that during winter storms, currents carry thousands of tons of sand parallel to the shoreline. Offshore the water carries these sediments down into the deep Montery Canyon.

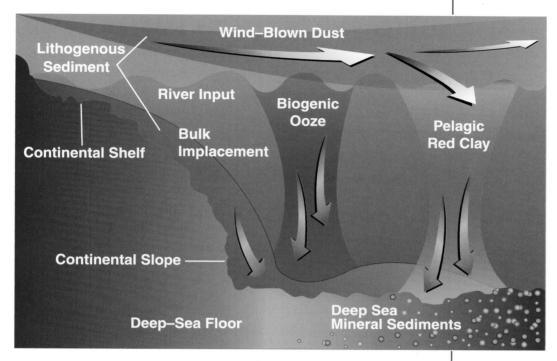

Wind–Blown Dust

Lithogenous Sediment

River Input

Biogenic Ooze

Pelagic Red Clay

Continental Shelf

Bulk Implacement

Continental Slope

Deep–Sea Floor

Deep Sea Mineral Sediments

rents to carry it a long distance before it settles. Wind-borne dust and volcanic ash also settle to the deep ocean floor. These result in fine brown, olive, and reddish clays. Clays typically accumulate very slowly – at a rate of about 2 millimeters (0.079 inches) per thousand years.

The variation in the quantity of sediments that sink to deep water causes tremendous variations in sediment accumulation. One of the most conspicuous examples is the difference between sediment thickness in the Pacific and Atlantic Oceans. The average sediment thickness in the deep Pacific Ocean is a bit under 0.5 kilometers (0.3 miles) – half the average thickness in the Atlantic Ocean. The explanation for this is that the Atlantic has more sediment flowing into it than does the Pacific. This is because the rivers flowing into the Atlantic drain from wide areas on the continents. Rivers flowing in the Pacific drain less continental area and accumulate less sediment. Portions of the Pacific have deep trenches that trap sediment, reducing accumulation over the rest of the sea floor, whereas the Atlantic do not have the same deep trenches.

The thickness of sediments in the deep ocean also varies with topography. As previously discussed, sediments are thickest on the abyssal plans and thinnest or absent on the mid-ocean ridges and seamounts.

Figure 14-24

Near-shore and offshore deposition.

Lithogenous sediments, except for clays, are generally confined near shore. Biogenic sediments – primarily the remnants of plankton – dominate the sediments offshore waters. Because of its very small grain size, clay can remain suspended in the water for great distances and be carried by wind, allowing it to deposit in the deep-sea.

The Carbonate Compensation Depth and Ooze Distribution

Why are calcium carbonate sediments found in some places on the ocean floor, while silaceous sediments are found in other locations?

Why do siliceous deposits dominate sediments below the carbonate compensation depth?

Chapter 8 discussed the dissolution of calcium carbonate in seawater and introduced you to the *carbonate compensation depth* (CCD). It is an important phenomenon because it explains why, below a certain depth, the characteristics of deep ocean sediments change significantly. The planktonic organisms that leave behind calcareous tests when they die live everywhere at the ocean surface, yet you will not find calcareous oozes everywhere on the ocean floor.

Figure 14-25

Carbonate compensation depth.

Calcium carbonate becomes more soluble in cold water and under pressure. Additionally, deep ocean water holds more carbon dioxide, making it more acidic and able to dissolve calcium carbonate more easily. The depth range at which this dissolution occurs is the *carbonate compensation depth*, or CCD. Below the CCD, the tiny tests and skeletons of calcium carbonate dissolve, preventing formation of calcareous ooze. Although the CCD varies between the Atlantic and Pacific, it is generally considered to occur around 4,500 meters (14,760 feet). Above this depth calcareous sediments dominate the deep-sea floor.

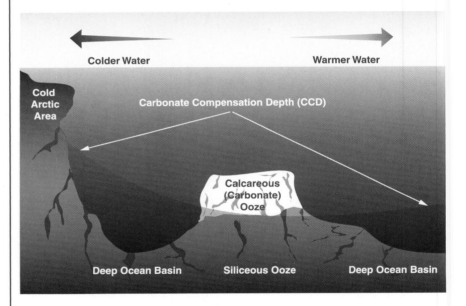

The greater the amount of carbon dioxide in water, the greater the acidity of the water. Acidic water dissolves calcium carbonate, the molecule found in calcareous shells and tests. Seawater below about 3,000 meters (9,840 feet) contains more carbon dioxide than surface water because carbon dioxide becomes more soluble in colder water and under greater pressure. When calcareous shells and tests fall to 3,000 meters, they encounter higher acidity and begin to dissolve. When this happens, no calcareous sediment is left to accumulate on the ocean floor. The effects of acidity, temperature, and water pressure combine so that there is a point at which calcium carbonate dissolves just as fast as it accumulates. This is the CCD. Above the CCD, calcareous oozes are the most abundant biogenous sediments. Below the CCD, this is not the case.

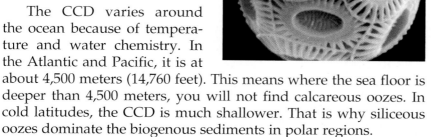

Gustaaf Hallegraeff, University of Tasmania

The CCD varies around the ocean because of temperature and water chemistry. In the Atlantic and Pacific, it is at about 4,500 meters (14,760 feet). This means where the sea floor is deeper than 4,500 meters, you will not find calcareous oozes. In cold latitudes, the CCD is much shallower. That is why siliceous oozes dominate the biogenous sediments in polar regions.

Siliceous oozes consist primarily of the silaceous tests of diatoms and amoeba-like animals called *radiolarians* – two organisms discussed in Chapters 4 and 5. Their tests dissolve many times more slowly than calcareous tests at all depths. The slow dissolution of siliceous material and high diatom productivity allows siliceous oozes to accumulate throughout the sea floor. Although you find siliceous ooze at shallow depths, they are the dominant biogenous sediments below the CCD. Siliceous ooze is most common in the Antarctic due to strong ocean currents and seasonal upwelling. Siliceous ooze is also found in equatorial regions west of South America, where diatoms are quite abundant.

Fecal Pellets

Why does deep ocean sediment tend to have the same particle composition as the surface water above it?

Based on what you learned earlier, you know that the smaller the particle size, the more slowly it settles. Clay particles on the deep ocean floor should take 20 to 50 years to sink. When you consider ocean gyres and other water motion, you would expect material to drift a long way from where it originates before it reaches the bottom.

Surprisingly, scientists find that bottom composition is usually similar to the particle composition of the water above it. How can this be? It seems to be due to fecal pellets. Large planktonic organisms, such as copepods, consume the calcareous or siliceous organisms that also dominate the bottom ooze. These large organisms eliminate their waste as dense fecal pellets of multiple skeletal and shell remains compressed together. Although still very small by human standards, these pellets are much larger and sink more

Figure 14-26

Photomicrograph of coccolithophore.

Coccolithophores are tiny planktonic organisms that leave behind calcareous tests (shells) when they die. Their tests are a major component of calcareous ooze. More on coccolithophores in Chapter 5.

Courtesy of Smithsonian Environmental Research Center

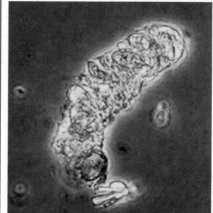

Figure 14-27

Photomicrograph of fecal pellet.

quickly than individual skeletal remains. They reach the bottom in about two weeks instead of 20 to 50 years. On the bottom, the pellets break up from decomposition and chemical processes.

Mineral Nodules

How do scientists think ferromanganese and phosphorite nodules form?

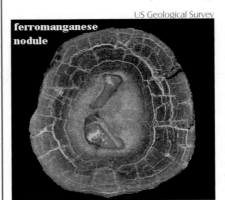

US Geological Survey

ferromanganese nodule

An unusual sediment with possible commercial value is the *ferromanganese nodule*, which is found mostly in water 4,000 to 6,000 meters (13,000 to 19,700 feet) deep. Originally discovered in 1803, and studied by the HMS *Challenger* in the mid-1800s, these nodules are irregular lumps about the size of potatoes, though some more than a meter (three feet) across have been found. Ferromanganese nodules consist of iron and manganese (from the Latin *ferrum* meaning *iron*) and small amounts of cobalt, nickel, chromium, copper, molybdenum, and zinc. Phosphorite nodules have also been found. They consist of phosphorite, as well as other trace minerals.

Nodules are hydrogenous sediments thought to be produced by some of the slowest chemical reactions in nature. Nodules grow at a rate of 1 to 200 millimeters (0.039 to 7.9 inches) per million years. This makes many nodules 10 or more million years old.

Scientists are not entirely sure what causes the chemical precipitation that forms nodules. Thoughts on their formation involve the initial presence of organic material since nodules often form around a nucleus, such as a shark's tooth or rock fragment.

In addition to understanding how they form, other questions remain. One question is why accumulating sediment does not bury the nodules. Hypotheses range from currents to the actions of benthic organisms, which is the prevailing theory.

Whatever the answer, scientists find nodules in significant amounts. They are found in all of the world's oceans and may be distributed over as much as 50% of the deep Pacific floor alone. Phosphorite nodules are found on the shallow banks and the continental shelves off California, Argentina, and Japan. Both types of nodules have the potential to be important resources because of the minerals they contain. So far, however, it costs more to recover them from the ocean floor than the minerals are worth.

Figure 14-28

Cross-section of Ferromanganese nodule.

These nodules are rich in valuable and important metals. Because they form by precipitation, they are considered to be hydrogenous sediments. Note this nodule's shark tooth nucleus. Ferromanganese nodules cover vast expanses of the sea floor, especially in the Pacific.

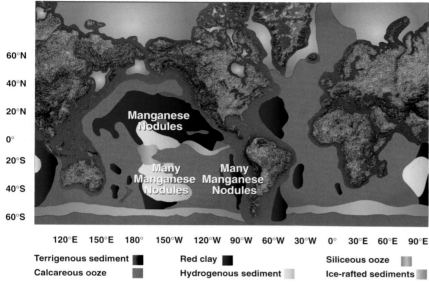

Figure 14-29

Global sediment distribution.

This is a simplified view of the worldwide distribution of marine sediments. Note how siliceous oozes are found in very high latitudes, especially off Antarctica, and as a band extending west from equatorial South America. The siliceous oozes in high latitudes are diatomaceous; the ones near the equatorial Pacific are radiolarian. As is shown, there is a broad expanse of calcareous ooze covering major portions of the Atlantic, South Pacific, and Indian Ocean sea floor. The broad, deep, and relatively old Pacific contains extensive clay deposits, most deposited from airborne dust. Poorly sorted ice-rafted glacial deposits are found near the poles.

ARE YOU LEARNING?

1. Deep ocean sediments tend to have proportionately _____ biogenous sediment than continental shelf sediment.

   A. less

   B. more

2. Siliceous deposits tend to dominate below the carbonate compensation depth because

   A. calcareous organisms cannot live that deep.

   B. siliceous organisms are more productive below the carbonate compensation depth.

   C. at or below the carbonate compensation depth, calcareous material dissolves as quickly as it accumulates.

3. Deep ocean sediment tends to have the same particle composition as the surface water above it because

   A. small particles actually sink more quickly than large particles.

   B. surface water is made primarily of deep water.

   C. the dense fecal pellets of larger planktonic organisms carry material to the bottom relatively quickly.

   D. all of the above

4. Scientists are not exactly sure how ferromanganese and phosphorite nodules form, but they think a biological process may be involved.

   A. true

   B. false

Find the answers as you read.

1. What are four ocean sediments that have economic importance? Why are they important?

2. Why are sand and gravel economically important sediments?

3. What is an *evaportie*?

Sediments as Economic Resources

What are four ocean sediments that have economic importance? Why are they important?

Chapter 17 discusses important or potentially important economic resources that come from ocean sediments. The ferromanganese and phosphorite nodules you just read about are examples. Although Chapter 17 goes into more detail, no discussion on sediments would be complete without touching on their crucial roles in the world economy.

Petroleum and Natural Gas

By far, oil and natural gas are the minerals with the greatest economic value of all minerals mined from the ocean. Many geological oceanographers work in the gas and petroleum industry. This is an important component of the world economy. More than a third of the world's crude petroleum and a quarter of its natural gas come from sedimentary deposits on the continental shelf. This is on the rise, with hundreds of billions of dollars in annual revenues worldwide coming from this source. Sedimentary deposits may account for a third or more of the world's oil and gas reserves.

In August and September 2005, Hurricanes Katrina and Rita hit the Gulf Coast of the United States, destroying 109 oil platforms and damaging five drilling platforms. Destruction by these hurricanes, combined with supply worries related to importing oil from other

Bob Wohlers

Figure 14-30

Black gold.

Accounting for hundreds of billions of dollars in annual revenues world wide, more than a third of the world's crude petroleum and a quarter of its natural gas come from sedimentary deposits on the continental shelf.

countries, sent oil prices to a record high. It took several months for petroleum production in the storm damaged areas to return to its prestorm levels. Today, there is a lot of debate over opening up more regions of the continental shelves of the US for drilling. The belief is, this would relieve dependence on oil imports and reduce political and diplomatic problems caused by increasing demand by developing countries. Some people have environmental concerns.

OIL PLATFOMS—A CHANGING PERSPECTIVE

In the ongoing debate between environmental and economic interests, offshore oil platforms have historically been a target. Many people consider them an eyesore, and raise concerns about damage to the local environment. The original thinking was that when an oil platform outlives its purpose, the oil company must remove it completely, all the way to the seabed.

Today, many people think differently. While one may still argue they are an eyesore above water, under water they are not. Under water, oil platforms create new habitats and become artificial reefs, supporting a myriad organisms. Many biologists think these organisms are new productivity that only exists because the rig provides a habitat.

In addition, the artificial reefs created by oil platforms provide a place for sports fishermen and scuba divers to enjoy. This allows oil platforms to continue to generate revenue for the economy even after they are inactive.

A growing number of people believe that at least in some environments, a better approach is to remove only the top levels of an inactive oil rig so it's no longer an eyesore or a hazard to shipping and to leave the lower levels as an artificial reef. This keeps the artificial reef in place to continue supporting the organisms that have made it a home. It also provides a spot for recreation and continued research.

Bob Wohlers

Figure 14-31a

Underwater views of an oil platform.
Figure 14-31a shows the amount of life attached to and living around the support structures of a California oil platform. **Figure 14-31b** is a photo of a marine biologist conducting a fish survey.

Bob Wohlers

Figure 14-31b

Other Sediments With Economic Importance

Why are sand and gravel economically important sediments?

What is an evaporite?

Although petroleum and natural gas are probably the most obvious examples of sediments with economic significance, there are others that are important or potentially important. Metal sulfides, found at deep sea hydrothermal vents are important. Dissolved minerals in the hot vent water precipitate out when the water mixes with the cold surrounding water. These deposits are rich enough, especially in the Red Sea, that mining them could be economically feasible. Currently these deposits are not being mined, but as the value of these deposits keeps rising, several mining companies are exploring possible ways of extracting the metals. As you have learned, hydrothermal vents provide a unique environment for some organisms. There are environmental impact concerns involved with mining these areas.

Yet another example of an economically important deposit is an evaporite. *Evaporites* form at the surface and comprise the salts left behind when seawater evaporates. During the process of evaporation, water molecules change from a liquid to a gas, but atoms such as calcium, sodium, and chlorine are left behind. As a result, the remaining water becomes enriched in these atoms which begin to precipitate from the water. The salts precipitate in landlocked and isolated seas. This provides a source of calcium carbonate, calcium sulfate, gypsum, and sodium chloride — that is, table salt. Both sulfide deposits and evaporites are examples of hydrogenous sediments that have economic importance.

Calcium carbonate forms hydrogenous sediments that are deposited when seawater acidity drops or temperature increases. This can happen in shallow, tropical seas where phytoplankton rapidly consume carbon dioxide and the acidity drops. Alternatively, the tropical sun may elevate water temperature and cause calcium carbonate to come out of solution. Calcium carbonate is ordinarily deposited around shell fragments or other particles, forming round, white grains called *ooliths* or *ooids* (from the Greek *oon* meaning *egg*). When this happens on a large scale, oolithic sand results. Oolithic sands are very common on the Bahamas Banks. The limestone forming the lower Florida Keys is the remnant of lithified oolithic sands.

You may not think of sand and gravel as important resources, but they are crucial for the construction industry. Although it amounts to less than 1% of the world's needs, the seas account for about $500 million in sand and gravel each year.

Still another sediment-based resource is *diatomaceous earth*. Chances are you put diatomaceous earth in your mouth every day! This is because it is mined for use in water filters, paints, and mild abrasives, including car polish and toothpaste. Scientists attribute the formation of diatomaceous earth to lithification and uplifting of deep ocean siliceous sediments. The White Cliffs of Dover, England, are one example. The cliffs are formed primarily of foraminifera and coccolithophore remains.

ARE YOU LEARNING?

1. **Ocean sediments are economically important if _____.**

   A. they can be easily mined

   B. the sediments are found as nodules

   C. they are found in very deep water

   D. the cost of mining the sediment is less than the economic value of the sediment

2. **Sand and gravel are economically important sediments because they are used**

   A. for fuel.

   B. to make mild abrasives.

   C. as a source of iron and manganese.

   D. as a source of metal sulfides.

3. **An evaporite _____.**

   A. settles to the sea floor, ready for mining

   B. falls from the atmosphere into the ocean

   C. such as calcium carbonate, calcium sulfate, gypsum, and sodium chloride (table salt) forms when the process of water evaporation occurs in landlocked and isolated seas

   D. forms when deep ocean siliceous sediments are uplifted

New Terms You Learned

- **biogenous sediment** sediment that originates from life, consisting of primarily shells and hard skeleton (p. 14-11)

- **boulder** the largest grain size on the Wentworth Scale (p. 14-13)

- **calcareous** calcium carbonate containing (p. 14-11)

- **calcareous ooze** ooze composed primarily of planktonic organisms that have calcium carbonate skeletons or shells (p. 14-19)

- **Carbonate Compensation Depth (CCD)** the depth at which calcium carbonate dissolves as fast as it accumulates, generally considered to be about 4,500 meters (14,760 feet) (p. 14-22)

- **clamshell sampler** ocean sediment sampler with a set of jaws, designed to scoop up bottom sediment for research purposes; also called a grab sampler (p. 14-3)

- **clay** the smallest grain size on the Wentworth Scale (p. 14-13)

- **cosmogenous sediments** sediment that originates from outer space (p. 14-11)

- **diatomaceous earth** soil composed of diatom remains; thought to have been created by the uplifting of siliceous sediments (p. 14-29)

- **evaporites** the salts/compounds left behind when seawater evaporates (p. 14-28)

- **ferromanganese nodules** irregular lumps of iron and manganese with small amounts of cobalt, nickel, chromium, copper, molybdenum, and zinc found on some deep ocean bottoms (p. 14-24)

- **grab sampler** ocean sediment sampler with a set of jaws, designed to scoop up bottom sediment for research purposes; also called a clamshell sampler (p. 14-3)

- **grain size** the diameter of an individual sediment particle (p. 14-13)

- **Hjulström's diagram** a graph that illustrates the relationship of transportation, erosion, and deposition of particles of different sizes (p. 14-14)

- **hydrogenous sediment** sediment that originates from chemical reactions in seawater (p. 14-11)

- **hydrophone** an underwater microphone (p. 14-5)

- **ice rafting** the process by which polar ice floats to sea carrying sediments that sink when the ice melts (p. 14-18)

- **lithification** the formation of rock (p. 14-18)

- **lithogenous sediments** (also known as terrigenous sediments) sediment that originates on land, primarily through erosion carrying particles into the sea (p. 14-10)

- **meteor** material entering the Earth's atmosphere from space (p. 14-12)

- **meteorite** a meteor that strikes the ground (p. 14-12)

- **microtektites** glass particles that form when a large meteorite impacts the Earth (p. 14-12)

- **mud** a mixture of clay and silt (p. 14-14)

- **nodules** irregular lumps of rock about the size of potatoes that are found in deep water; classified as hydrogenous sediments and thought to be produced by some of the slowest chemical reactions in nature; types of nodules include ferromanganese and and phosphorite (p. 14-24)

- **ooliths (ooids)** round, white grains that form when calcium carbonate is deposited around shell fragments or other particles (p. 14-28)

- **ooze** deep ocean sediments that contain 30% or more biogenous sediments; includes calcareous and siliceous oozes (p. 14-19)

- **paleoceanography** the study of prehistoric ocean (p. 14-7)

- **piston corer** research device used to study bottom sediment; an open tube on a cable that is dropped from a ship, retrieves layers of bottom sediment (p. 14-4)

- **poorly sorted sediment** sediment of mixed grain sizes created when water movement changes frequently (p. 14-15)

- **radiolarians** tiny amoeba-like marine animals whose complex skeletons are made of silica and contribute to siliceous ooze (p. 14-23)

- **recent sediments** sediments that have accumulated since sea level stabilized (about 5,000 years ago) where it is today (p. 14-17)

- **relict sediments** sediments that accumulated and were left stranded when the sea level was lower than present day (about 5,000 years ago); much of the continental shelf is blanketed with sand deposits that are mainly relict sands (p. 14-17)

- **seismic refraction** a technique used to study marine sediments; equipment includes an air gun aboard a vessel to produce the reflected sound and a towed hydrophone to detect the reflected sound waves (p. 14-4)

- **siliceous** silicon containing (p. 14-11)

- **siliceous ooze** ooze composed primarily of planktonic organisms that have silica skeletons (p. 14-19)

- **stratigraphy** the study of sediment layers (p. 14-7)

- **terrigenous sediment** (also known as lithogenous sediments) sediment that originates on land, primarily through erosion carrying particles into the sea (p. 14-10)

- **tests** shell-like coverings of organisms (p. 14-19)

- **turbidites** sediment deposits created by turbidity currents; they consist of layers of litho-genous sand embedded with fine deep-sea sediments (p. 14-18)

- **turbidity currents** underwater avalanches of thick, muddy sediments accumulated on the continental shelf that speed down the continental slope into deep water (p. 14-18)

- **well sorted sediment** sediment of primarily one-grain size, resulting when water move-ment in a region does not fluctuate very much (p. 14-15)

- **Wentworth Scale** the classification of sediments by size; a boulder is the largest grain size and clay is the smallest grain size in this classification system (p. 14-13)

Chapter 14 in Review

1. List four sediment study methods and explain how scientists use tools for these studies. Which sediment study method do scientists commonly use in looking for oil and natural gas?

2. Explain how scientists use different studies of sedimentation to explain the Earth's past. Why do scientists think that no more than about 200 to 180 million years worth of sediment exists anywhere on the ocean floor? See Chapter 13 if you need to refresh what you learned. Discuss how different sciences integrate into the study of the ocean.

3. List the four sediment classifications by origin, their characteristics, and their relative abundance.

4. Describe how scientists classify sediments by size. Compare a cobble to a boulder.

5. Explain how grain size and current velocity affect the erosion and deposition of sediment. Why is sand the most easily eroded particle?

6. Explain how waves and currents sort grain sizes on the continental shelf, include the roles of recent and relic sediments. Explain whether continental shelf sedimentation is faster or slower than deep ocean sedimentation and why.

7. List four economically important or potentially economically important sediment resources. Why are some ocean sediments with potential economic importance not being mined?

8. Explain why deep ocean sediments above and below the calcium carbonate compensation depth are significantly different. What causes this depth to vary?

Connecting Chapter Concepts— Science Scenarios

1. Scientists classify ocean sediments different ways. Two ways of classifying them are by origin, and by size.
   A. What are the four categories used when classifying sediments by origin, and what are the characteristics of each category?
   B. What do scientists study at times that makes sediment size more important than origin? How does size relate to this?
   C. Why does sand take the least energy to erode, even though there are particles both larger and smaller than sand?
   D. Under what circumstances would you expect to find poorly sorted particles and under what circumstances would you expect to find well-sorted particles? Why?
2. Deep ocean sediments differ in many respects from continental shelf sediments because sedimentation processes differ.
   A. Do deep ocean sediments tend to have proportionately more or less biogenous material than do continental shelf sediments? Why?
   B. What is an ooze? What are two different kinds of oozes?
   C. Rivers flowing into the Atlantic Ocean drain larger continental areas than do the rivers flowing into the Pacific Ocean. How would you expect this to affect deep water sedimentation in the ocean? Do the facts support this?
   D. Why might you expect the bottom composition of deep water sediments to differ from the water above it? Why is the composition actually roughly similar to the water above it?

Marine Science and the Real World

1. Imagine you want to start a deep-sea mining operation to recover ferromanganese nodules. What challenges do you need to overcome to launch such an operation? Include the technical challenges as well as the political, environmental, and economic problems that could arise.
2. Research the concept of *nuclear winter*. Explain how this relates to the hypothesis that the K-T extinction resulted from a meteor impact.
3. Suppose you're interested in studying the origin and distribution of dust around the world. How might you go about doing so? Use your imagination. Don't neglect opportunities in the air, on land, or underwater.
4. Why would an oceanographer studying deep ocean sediments be interested in a shipwreck such as the *Titanic?* What could the *Titanic* or similar wrecks tell the oceanographer about the processes of sedimentation?

References

Arrhenius, G. 1963. Pelagic Sediments. *In The Sea.* 3: 655-727. Edited by M. N. Hill. New York: Interscience.

Cronan, David S. (editor). 2000. *Handbook of Marine Mineral Deposits.* Boca Raton, FL: CRC Press.

Dietz, R. S. 1978. IFO's (Identified Flying Objects). *Sea Frontiers.* 24 (no. 6).

Erickson, J. 1996. *Marine Geology: Undersea Landforms and Lifeforms.* New York: Facts On File.

Garrison, T. 2004. *Oceanography: An Invitation to Marine Science.* Pacific Grove, CA: Brooks/Cole, a division of Thomson Learning, Inc.

Garrison, T. 2004. *Essentials of Oceanography.* Pacific Grove, CA: Brooks/Cole, a division of Thomson Learning, Inc.

Gehrels, T. T. 1996. Collisions with Asteroids and Comets. *Scientific American.* 274 (no. 3).

Cronan, David S. (editor). 2000. *Handbook of Marine Mineral Deposits.* Boca Raton, FL:.CRC Press.

Heezen, B., and C. Hollister. 1971. *The Face of the Deep.* New York: Oxford University Press.

Karst Research Group. 2004. University of South Florida. http://uweb.cas.usf.edu/~vacher/karsthome.htm

Kennett, J. P. 1982. *Marine Geology.* Englewood Cliffs, NJ: Prentice-Hall.

Libes, S. M. 1992. *Iron-Manganese Nodules And Other Hydrogenous Minerals. In: Introduction To Marine Biogeochemistry.* New York: John Wiley and Sons.

Prospero, J. 1985. Records of Past Continental Climates in Deep-Sea Sediments. *Nature.* 315 (23 May).

Schlee, S. 1973. *The Edge of an Unfamiliar World: A History of Oceanography.* New York: Dutton.

Siebold, E., and W. H. Berger. 1993. *The Sea Floor: An Introduction to Marine Geology* Second Edition. New York: Springer-Verlag.

Spencer, D. W., and S. Honjo. 1978. Particles And Particle Fluxes In The Ocean. *Oceanus.* 21 (no. 1).

CHAPTER 15

The Dynamic Coast

Coastal Classification

Coastal Dynamics

Biological Processes
and Human Activity

John J. Mosesso, National Biological Information Infrastructure

U.S. Department of Interior,
U.S. Geological Survey

Rear Admiral Harley D. Nygren, NOAA Corps

Playing with Mud for a Living

Humans dump tons of pollutants into the ocean every day. These include toxins, nutrients and other compounds that are either directly dangerous or cause environmental havoc. Not all of these toxins remain in the water, but become part of the ocean bottom. Then what happens to toxins? As a coastal chemical oceanographer, Dr. Linda Kalenjais looks for the answer to that question.

Linda Kalnejais PhD
**Assistant Professor of Oceanography
University of New Hampshire**

"I play with mud for a living," says Dr. Kalenjais. "I do this because I love to be outside and on the water collecting samples, but also because the chemical processes that occur at the bottom of the sea can have a big impact on the water quality and environmental health of the coastal zone." She explains that many pollutants stick to the fine-grained particles that settle from the water and make up muddy sediments. Consequently, many muddy ocean sediments are contaminated with dangerous levels of heavy metals, toxic organic compounds and excessive nutrients.

Dr. Kalenjais studies what happens to contaminants in muddy sediments. She's trying to determine whether they can return to the water or whether they remain buried – and if so, for how long. These are crucial questions for effective coastal area management.

Much of Dr. Kalenjais' work begins with sample collection. "The chemical reactions that occur within the mud hold the key to understanding the fate of contaminants. To study these reactions we use a research vessel to very carefully collect a core of mud. We then slice the mud up into little slabs and extract samples that can be measured back in the laboratory."

Dr. Kalenjais says she's always been fascinated by water. Growing up near the beach in Australia, she found herself fascinated by the beach: what caused the special sea smell, how did the sand ripples form, why did the temperature change so much from day to day.

"I knew I wanted to learn more about how the natural world worked and how we could protect it, so after high school I enrolled in Environmental Engineering at the University of Western Australia. At the same time I knew I loved chemistry, so I also obtained a chemistry degree."

After graduating from university, she began working for the government agency that manages the water quality of rivers and estuaries in Western Australia. Interested in learning more about what was happening in sediments, she went to the Woods Hole Oceanographic Institution and started working on her PhD in chemical oceanography. Today she continues to study sediments as an Assistant Professor of Oceanography at the University of New Hampshire.

"Any high school student interested in marine sciences should take classes in math and basic sciences such as chemistry, physics and biology as well as Earth science," Dr. Kalenjais advises. "Spend time outside, thinking about how the processes they see happening around them are driven by the ocean, sun and atmosphere. I suggest that interested students spend time at science museums and investigate volunteering if possible. The best advice I have is to be curious about how the world works, and pursue what interests and motivates you the most."

Figure 15-1

Egyptian pyramids.

Without coastal dynamics – the processes that create and shape the oceans' coastlines – world history would be significantly different. While the effects of nature have had varying influences on civilizations, there is one civilization that owes its existence to coastal dynamics. It is ancient Egypt, home of the pyramids. Egypt introduced one of the earliest 365-day calendars in 2772 B.C. It was perhaps the first culture to use scientific principles. The word chemistry comes from the ancient name of Egypt – Alchemy.

Situated on the arid Mediterranean coast of North Africa, Egypt lies adjacent to the Sahara Desert. It would be the last place for an advanced civilization to develop were it not for the Nile River. The

Jacques Descloitres, MODIS Rapid Response Team, NASA/GSFC

Figure 15-2

Nile Delta and flood plain.

The Nile Delta is important because it provides fertile ground for agriculture. Rain in central Africa leads the Nile to overflow its banks. The nutrient-rich sediments that settle out and accumulate in the floodplain provide far better soil than the local red earth. Shown here is the delta and flood plain with the city of Cairo at the base of the delta.

Nile was literally life for ancient Egypt, not just because it supplies water to the region, but because of the Nile Delta.

The importance of the Nile Delta is the fertile ground it provides for agriculture. Prior to the building of the Aswan Dam, described later in this chapter, each year, rain in central Africa caused the Nile to rise and overflow its banks. This covered the floodplain at the Nile's mouth with river water laden with nutrient-rich black sediment from Ethiopia and inner Africa. The sediments settled out, accumulating in the delta floodplain, providing far better soil than the local red earth. Each year when the water receded, Egypt had naturally fertilized land in which to plant crops. This cycle was so predictable that the Egyptians called the season *Akhet,* meaning *inundation.*

Few civilizations have had their histories shaped so significantly by a recurring natural event. Although somewhat predictable, the flooding of the Nile varied. Several seasons of excessive flooding or insufficient flooding have directly affected Egypt's politics and government by causing famine and hardship. One hundred years of low flooding beginning about 2250 B.C. brought about the decline of the earliest Egyptian dynasties. About seven decades of high inundation starting around 1840 B.C. unseated the second generation of dynasties.

Even in modern times, the Nile continues to affect Egyptian culture. It also teaches us lessons about trying to tame nature. In 1960, the Aswan Dam was built to tame the Nile's flooding and to produce hydroelectric power. This resulted in the creation of Lake Nasser, which now regulates the annual flooding of the delta. It also traps most of the sediments that would flow into the Mediterranean.

That's the problem. Many scientists fear that taming the Nile, while certainly improving Egyptian agriculture, has had far-reaching environmental and economic consequences. The Mediterranean is a relatively low-nutrient sea, so the loss of the Nile's sediment seems to be reducing bioproductivity. The reduction in sediments reaching the sea causes extensive erosion on the Egyptian coast. Solving one type of environmental problem, flooding, has caused another, the sinking and loss of the Nile Delta.

In this chapter, you will read about the processes that create different types of coasts, how scientists classify coasts based on the processes that create them, and why they are important to understanding the marine environment. You will also see how human activities influence the processes that shape the world's shorelines.

Coastal Classification

Two Classification Systems

What are the differences between an active coast *and a* passive coast?

What are the differences between primary coasts *and* secondary coasts?

As in other aspects of marine science, scientists classify the coasts in various ways. The classification systems they use depend on what they are studying. This is similar to classifying sediments by size or by origin, as discussed in Chapter 14. Scientists classify coasts many ways, but we'll consider two.

The first system is based on geology. When examining long-term coastal dynamics, geologists classify coasts as *active coasts* and *passive coasts* based on plate dynamics. Active coasts are close to plate collisions that result in volcanic activity and earthquakes. The Ring of Fire, as discussed in Chapter 13, correlates with the effects of plate collisions around much of the Pacific basin. Passive coasts lie far away from active plate boundaries. These coasts have little volcanic activity and few earthquakes.

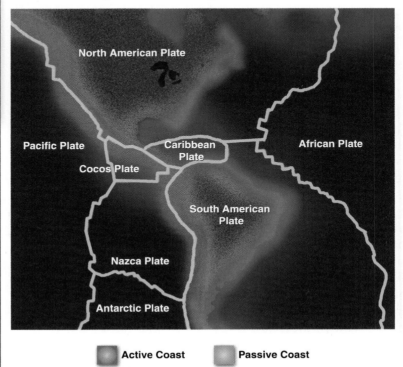

Active Coast   **Passive Coast**

Figure 15-3

Active and passive coasts.
Active coasts, shown in orange, are close to plate collisions that result in volcanic activity and earthquakes. Passive coasts, shown in turquoise, lie far away from active plate boundaries. These coasts have little volcanic activity and few earthquakes.

The problem with the geologists' classification is that it is based on processes that take place over very long periods. Oceanographers think that many other coastal processes occur much more quickly. The second coastal classification addresses short-term coastal dynamics.

In this system, scientists classify coasts into *primary coasts* and *secondary coasts*. Geologic processes not directly related to the ocean form primary coasts. Secondary coasts are formed by marine action. Primary coasts form over more extended periods than secondary coasts. A coast can therefore be both primary and secondary. This is sometimes called a *combination coast.*

Based on this primary division in coastal types, Francis Shepard, who was at the Scripps Institution of Oceanography, La Jolla, California, detailed further classifications in 1937. His basic system appears in the accompanying table.

INTERNET PORTAL
SCILINKS. NSTA

Topic: Coastal Geology
Go To: www.scilinks.org
Code: LOP2350

SHEPARD COASTAL CLASSIFICATION SYSTEM

Primary Coasts

Sinking coasts
Drowned river valleys
Dendritic
Trellis
- Drowned glacial erosion coasts
- Fjord coasts
- Glacial troughs
Drowned Karst topography

Land-deposition coasts
River deposition coasts
Deltaic coasts
Compound delta coasts
Compound alluvial fan coasts straightened by wave erosion
Glacial deposition coasts
- Partially submerged moraines
- Partially submerged drumlins
- Partially submerged drift features
Wind-deposition coasts
- Dune prograded coasts
- Dune coasts
- Fossil dune coasts
Landslide coasts

Volcanic coasts
Lava-flow coasts
Tephra coasts
Volcanic collapse or explosion coasts

Tectonic coasts
Fault coasts
- Fault scarp coasts
- Fault trough or rift coasts
- Overthrust
- Fold coasts
- Sedimentary extrusions
  – Salt domes
  – Mud lumps

Ice coasts

Secondary Coasts

Wave-erosion coasts
Wave-straightened coasts
- Cut in homogenous materials
- Hogback strike coasts
- Fault-line coasts
- Elevated wave-cut bench coasts
- Depressed wave-cut bench coasts
Irregular through wave erosion
- Heterogeneous formation coasts

Marine-deposition coasts
Barrier coasts
- Barrier beaches
- Barrier islands
- Barrier spits
- Bay barriers
- Overwash fans
Cuspate forelands
Beach plains
Mud flats or salt marshes

Coasts built by marine organisms
Coral reef coasts
- Fringing reef
- Barrier reef
- Atolls
- Elevated reef coast
Serpulid reef coasts
Oyster reef coasts
Mangrove coasts
Marsh grass coasts

Primary Coasts

What forces do scientists think cause primary coasts?

What kind of coasts do scientists attribute to sinking?

What kind of coasts do scientists attribute to land deposition?

What kind of coast do scientists attribute to volcanic activity?

What kind of coasts do scientists attribute to tectonic activity?

Scientists attribute primary coast development to nonmarine processes. These include sinking, land deposition (from running water, wind, or land ice), volcanism, and tectonic (plate) movement. Scientists think that primary coasts have remained relatively unchanged since sea level rose after the last ice age.

Sinking coasts. Coasts formed by sinking are among the most dramatic. These include *fjord coasts* and *drowned river valleys*. These occur from erosion cutting into the land during periods of low sea level. Then the sea level rises, flooding the eroded area.

Scientists explain that fjord coasts form when glaciers moved toward the coastline during the last ice age. The glaciers cut large, deep grooves in the land, which then flooded when the sea level rose. Southern Alaska has many fjord coasts.

Drowned river valleys are thought to form similarly, but the erosion comes from a river. The river forms a valley, which floods

Glow Images/Getty Images

Figure 15-4

Fjord coasts.

Norway is famous for its many fjords.

Courtesy of Chesapeake Bay Program

Figure 15-5

The Chesapeake Bay drowned river valley.

Drowned river valleys are created when an ancient river forms a valley, which floods when the sea level rises. Chesapeake Bay is an example of a drowned river valley. In this figure, the ancient Susquehanna River is seen as the deep water forming a channel down the center of the bay.

when the sea level rises. Chesapeake Bay is an example of a sinking coast. Both fjord coasts and drowned river valleys can form *estuaries.*

Estuaries are partially enclosed water bodies where fresh water from rivers and salt water from the sea mix. They are important ecosystems with a constant flushing and exchange of nutrients carried into the estuary by a river or rivers. The daily tide flushes seawater to and from estuaries. This allows a steady flow of nutrients to adjacent marine environments. Chapter 16 presents the significant roles that estuaries play in the biosphere.

Scientists classify estuaries based on circulation patterns and flow. A *salt wedge estuary* occurs when high-salinity seawater from the ocean slips into the estuary under the less dense fresh water coming in from the river. This results in a saltwater layer under a freshwater layer.

INTERNET PORTAL

SCiLINKS. NSTA

Topic: Sea Level Change
Go To: www.scilinks.org
Code: LOP2355

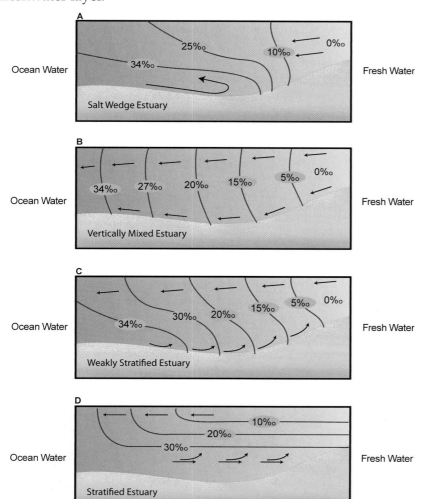

Figure 15-6

Four types of estuary.

A salt wedge estuary **(A)** occurs when dense, high-salinity seawater from the ocean slips into the estuary under the less dense fresh water coming in from the river. This results in a saltwater layer under a freshwater layer.

A vertically mixed estuary **(B)** is brackish throughout, with the salinity lower near the head of the estuary and higher near the mouth.

Weakly stratified estuaries **(C)** have significant vertical mixing, but there are still clearly defined saltwater and freshwater layers.

Stratified estuaries **(D)** have distinct upper freshwater layers and lower saltwater layers. However, the freshwater layer becomes more saline toward the mouth and the saltwater layer becomes less saline toward the head.

Figure 15-7

Land-deposition coasts.

Land-deposition coasts form when materials carried by rivers flow into the ocean, are deposited, and accumulate. This happens most readily where there is a wide continental shelf and no drowned rivers to form estuaries. Two of the most famous are the Nile Delta in Egypt and the Mississippi River Delta in the United States, shown here.

A *vertically mixed estuary* does not have distinct water layers. In these estuaries, the flow and topography cause seawater and fresh water to mix. This creates brackish water throughout the estuary. The salinity varies with location, however. Near the estuary head, where the freshwater river flows in, salinity is low. At the mouth, by the ocean, the salinity is high.

Between these two extremes are *weakly stratified estuaries* and *stratified estuaries.* With both of these, the salt water and fresh water partially mix, but still form layers. Weakly stratified estuaries have significant degrees of vertical mixing. However, there are defined saltwater and freshwater layers. Stratified estuaries have distinct upper freshwater layers and lower saltwater layers. However, the freshwater layer becomes more saline toward the mouth of the river. Similarly, the saltwater layer becomes less saline toward the head of the river.

Land-deposition coasts. Sedimentation forms coasts when materials carried by rivers flow into the ocean, deposit, and accumulate. This happens most readily where there is a wide continental shelf for accumulation and no drowned rivers to form estuaries. The area of accumulated sediment often forms a wide triangular shape, so this type of coast is called a *delta.* It gets its name from the triangle-shaped Greek letter delta (Δ).

Deltas form flat expanses with very fertile ground. Two of the most famous are the Nile Delta in Egypt, and the Mississippi River Delta in the United States.

Volcanic coasts. The coasts most recognizable as having been formed by volcanic activity occur in the Hawaiian Islands. As discussed in Chapter 13, according to hot-spot theory, this type of island chain forms as the oceanic plate migrates over a plume where magma rises from the mantle, breaking through the crust. This results in volcanoes that build up on the seafloor, eventually breaking the ocean surface. Continued lava flow adds to and enlarges the island coasts. This process continues in Hawaii.

Figure 15-8

Volcanic coasts.

Volcanic islands are some of the most recognizable coasts formed by volcanic activity. Here steam rises as lava flows into the ocean in Hawaii.

Tectonic coasts. Coasts formed by tectonic activity primarily include *fault coasts*. These coasts form as plates collide; the collisions force the earth to move upward, downward, or side-by-side. A fault coast results when the collision uplifts a section of seafloor above the water surface or when a fault opens and spreads, allowing the sea to flood a new area. Tomales Bay in California is a good example of the latter.

Secondary Coasts

What forces do scientists think cause secondary coasts?

How do scientists think wave erosion coasts form?

How do scientists think marine deposition coasts form?

How do scientists think marine organisms build coasts?

Secondary coasts result from marine processes. These include wave erosion, material deposited by seawater motion, and marine life. Most of these processes happen in relatively short periods. However, some secondary coast formation processes, such as coral reef building, take a long time.

Wave-erosion coasts. Constant pounding by waves erodes and changes a coastline over time. Geological processes are thought to give coastlines an irregular shape, with wave action straightening them over time. Generally, this happens as wave energy focuses on areas that protrude, as discussed in Chapter 12. This wears away at the coastline and can result in spectacular formations where the coast rises well above the sea. Sea caves, arches, and sea stacks are good examples of wave-erosion coastal formations (Figure 15-11 a, b).

Marine-deposition coasts. Deposition coasts form when sea action causes ocean sediments to accumulate in one place. Barrier islands, beaches, salt marshes, and mud flats are all examples of deposition coasts. Note that although both secondary marine-deposition coasts and primary land-deposition coasts involve sediment accumulation, they differ. Secondary marine-deposition coasts involve ocean sediments

Mr. David Sinson, Office of Coast Survey, NOAA

Figure 15-9

Fault coasts.

This photograph shows large-scale folding and faulting in metamorphic and sedimentary rocks.

Landsat Satellite Image by M. Rymer, USGS

Figure 15-10

Tomales Bay.

Tomales Bay in northern California is an example of a fault coast. There, the San Andreas Fault opened and spread, allowing the sea to flood a new area.

Rear Admiral Harley D. Nygren, NOAA Corps

Figure 15-11a

Wave-erosion Coast.
Arch rock at Depoe Bay, Oregon

Becky Stamski, SIMoN, NOAA

Figure 15-11b

Sea Stack.
This is a photo of a sea stack, typical from a wave-erosion coast.

Figure 15-12

Barrier islands.

Barrier islands form on deposition coasts when material accumulates parallel to shore, forming a barrier between the sea and the existing coast. These islands are important because they protect the main coast from the energy of storm waves. Shown here is a barrier beach in New Jersey.

Landsat satillite image source: U.S. Geological/Survey, Courtesy of Grant F. Walton Center for Remote Sensing and Spatial Analysis, Rutgers Universty

0 2.5 5 Miles

SIMoN, NOAA

Figure 15-13

Iron Shore.

This coast line built by marine organisms in the Cayman Islands is typical of Caribbean islands. It is a coast built by ancient coral reefs. Often it is called "iron shore."

moved by water motion in the sea. Primary land-deposition coasts involve sediments carried from land into the sea by rivers.

Barrier islands form when material accumulates parallel to shore, forming a barrier between the sea and the existing coast. These islands are important because they protect the main coast from the energy of storm waves. Barrier islands tend to move over time, but the migration is slow from a human standpoint. Many barrier islands are well developed and inhabited.

Globally, barrier islands form in relatively few places, but you commonly find the typical sand. This is also a type of deposition coast. There are many types of beaches, but generally a *beach* is defined as an accumulation of loose sediment near the edge of a large water body.

Salt marshes and mud flats form along coastlines where the bottom topography prevents large waves from breaking. This allows sea sediments to accumulate on shore. Salt marshes and mud flats flood with the tides and tend to be rich environments full of life.

Coasts built by marine organisms. Many coasts emerge as a result of biological activity. Marine organisms build coasts by providing a structure that reduces the effects of waves and current. Perhaps the best-known are the barrier reefs built by coral. Successive generations of coral polyps in colonies grow and build on the calcium skeletons of previous generations. Over time, this can create massive reefs, including the largest barrier reef in the world, the Great Barrier Reef of Australia.

Other organisms can build coasts, too. Oysters leave behind shells that can accumulate along shores. Marine plants help hold sediments and reduce wave and current erosion, which results in bigger beaches. Examples of these plants are seagrasses and marsh grass. Mangrove trees form mangrove swamps, as discussed in Chapter 5. These are environmentally important coasts discussed in Chapter 16.

We will look more closely at the dynamics that build and change secondary coasts in the next sections.

1. A(n) _____ coast occurs near where tectonic plates collide. A(n) _____ coast occurs away from tectonic plate boundaries.

   A. active, passive

   B. passive, active

   C. primary, secondary

   D. secondary, primary

2. _____ coasts are formed by geologic processes not directly related to the ocean. _____ coasts are those formed by marine action.

   A. Active, Passive

   B. Passive, Active

   C. Primary, Secondary

   D. Secondary, Primary

3. Forces that scientists think form primary coasts include (choose all that apply)

   A. land-based erosion.

   B. marine life.

   C. volcanic activity.

   D. tectonic activity.

4. Coasts formed by erosion include (choose all that apply)

   A. barrier islands.

   B. fjord coasts.

   C. fault coasts.

   D. drowned river valleys.

5. Coasts formed by land-deposition (sedimentation) include (choose all that apply)

   A. volcanic islands.

   B. estuaries.

   C. deltas.

   D. fault coasts.

6. Coasts formed by volcanic activity include (choose all that apply)

   A. volcanic islands.

   B. estuaries.

   C. deltas.

   D. fault coasts.

7. Coasts formed by tectonic activity include (choose all that apply)

   A. volcanic islands.

   B. estuaries.

   C. deltas.

   D. fault coasts.

8. Forces that scientists think form secondary coasts include (choose all that apply)

   A. land-based erosion.

   B. marine life.

   C. volcanic activity.

   D. tectonic activity.

9. Scientists think wave-erosion coasts form

   A. as wave energy focuses on areas that protrude.

   B. as waves form coral reefs.

   C. a lack of waves in certain areas.

   D. all of the above

10. Scientists think marine-deposition coasts form

    A. as a result of the ocean carrying sediments into deep water.

    B. as a result of the accumulation of ocean sediments in one place.

    C. as a result of marine organism deposits.

    D. none of the above

11. Scientists think that marine organisms build coasts by

    A. moving sediment.

    B. creating waves.

    C. triggering volcanic activity.

    D. none of the above

Coastal Dynamics

Coasts constantly change. In most areas the beach constantly moves inland. Wind, waves, currents, tides, sea level change, and erosion are the dynamic marine forces that create and change primary and secondary coasts. Let's look at these processes in more detail.

Longshore Drift

How does longshore drift *move material along the coastline?*

One of the most significant forces shaping the coast is *longshore drift,* which is the net transport of sediments along the coast by a *longshore current.* Longshore currents result from waves approaching the beach at an angle and wind pushing water on shore.

Usually, waves approach a beach at an angle because of the direction of the prevailing wind (see Figure 15-14). The waves break on the shore and stir up sediment. Sediments become suspended in the longshore current that develops parallel to the shore. The sediments move down the beach as shown by the black arrows in Figure 15-14, which represent backwash of sediment and longshore drift. The water molecules are also moved in the process so there is a net movement of water as well. This establishes a longshore current.

Because the longshore current flows with the approaching waves, longshore drift tends to move sand and sediment primarily with the prevailing winds. On both coasts of North America, for example, the prevailing winds (particularly storms, which generate the most powerful waves) tend to be angled from the north. Therefore, longshore currents tend to move material south along both US coastlines.

Figure 15-14

Longshore current and longshore drift.

Usually, waves approach a beach at an angle because of the direction of the prevailing wind. The waves break when their crests are traveling faster than their troughs. Sediments become suspended in the longshore current that develops parallel to the shore. The sediments move down the beach as shown by the black arrows, which represent longshore drift.

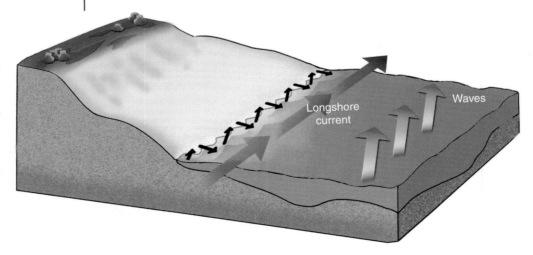

Beach Dynamics

Where does sand come from?

A beach is composed of what three sections?

What factors affect the shape and appearance of a beach?

What is a coastal cell?

Longshore drift explains one of the major ways that sand moves along the coast. But, where does sand come from in the first place? How does it form beaches?

Most sand comes from erosion. Erosion may be the effect of waves pounding the shoreline or it may be inland erosion. In the latter case, streams and rivers carry the sand to the ocean. Sand can accumulate on a beach that is a long distance from where it originates. As an example, the primary sand source for the US east coast and the Gulf of Mexico is erosion of the Appalachian Mountains.

Not all sand comes from a long distance away. The only sand source for some islands is erosion of the local rock. Hawaii's distinctive black sand beaches, for example, come from eroded volcanic rock.

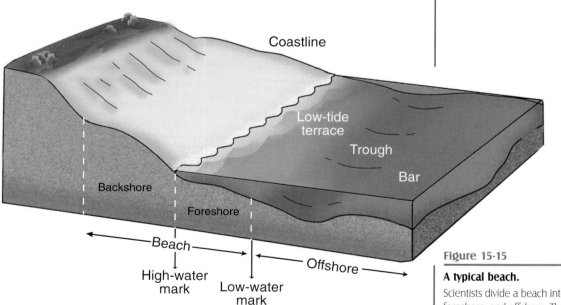

Figure 15-15

A typical beach.

Scientists divide a beach into the backshore, foreshore, and offshore. The backshore is the region rarely touched by water. The foreshore is the part of the beach between the high-tide mark and the low-tide mark. The offshore is the region beyond the low-tide mark.

In tropical regions, much sand comes from biological sources, such as corals. Erosion wears away at the nonliving portions of coral reef, creating coral sand. A few species, such as parrotfish, eat coral polyps and the polyps' limestone skeletons. The parrotfish therefore excrete sand as digestive waste. This is called *bioerosion*. There are several bioeroding invertebrates also, including sea urchins.

Beaches are very dynamic. Water motion constantly shapes and changes them. Scientists divide a beach into three basic sections, each with differing characteristics related to these changes.

The *foreshore* and *backshore* are the two sections we normally think of when we think "beach." The foreshore is the part of the beach that water sometimes covers. It is the region from the high-tide mark to the low-tide mark. The *low-tide terrace* is the flat portion of the foreshore where waves break. The backshore is the region rarely touched by seawater. It includes dunes or grasses that help stabilize this section, and extends all the way to "non-beach" ground.

Offshore is the area beyond the low-tide terrace. It typically includes a slightly deeper *longshore trough* and, further out, a shallow sandbar. Both are parallel to shore. Longshore currents flow along the trough between the sandbar and the beach. Beyond the sandbar is not considered beach because sediment movement ceases, at least with respect to beach dynamics.

The shape and appearance of a beach depend on many interacting factors. These include the grain size of beach sediments, wave energy, and the degree of beach slope. As discussed in Chapter 14, grain size ranges from very small (clay and silt) to large boulders. As the grain size increases, so does the beach's slope and wave size.

The reason is that it takes more wave energy to move large sediments up onto a beach than it does to move small ones. It also takes more energy to move sediments up a steep beach than up a gradual one. High-energy waves tend to sort the sediments by carrying large sediments high onto the beach. There is less energy in the backwash, so the heavier sediments tend to stay behind while the smaller ones rush back to sea with the water. In very heavy waves, the smallest particles may not be able to settle at all due to constant wave action and backwash.

A flat, low-energy beach has the opposite effect. This type of beach provides a large area over which wave energy dissipates. This allows small particles to settle, forming a sandy beach.

Because wave energy varies with season in many areas, the beach tends to change seasonally. Winter storms have more powerful waves and tend to carry sand offshore. During the summer, gentler waves prevail, moving sand onshore.

In nature, the dynamics of deposition and erosion of sand on a beach are usually in balance. However, people have interfered with this balance through development, such as dam and harbor construction. This topic will be discussed later in this chapter. The accumulation and dispersion of sand is generally controlled through a *coastal cell*. A coastal cell is a local region of material transport mechanisms that, when combined, form an area with no net sand gain or loss.

As an example, sand may continuously enter a coastal cell through river runoff and wave erosion. The sand accumulates offshore, moving down the coast with longshore drift. Eventually it meets a submarine canyon or the edge of the continental shelf. From there it falls off into deep water, leaving the system as shown in Figure 15-16.

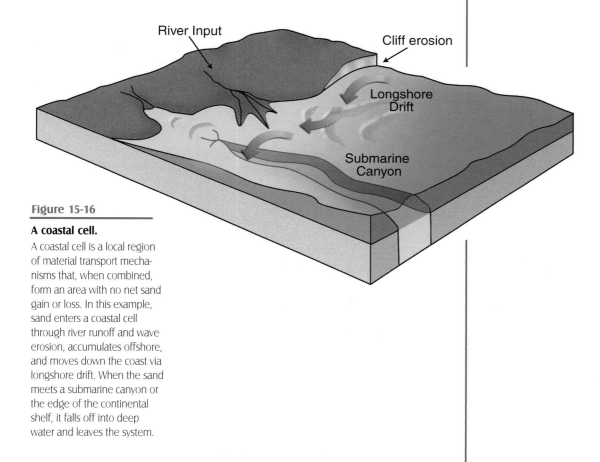

Figure 15-16

A coastal cell.

A coastal cell is a local region of material transport mechanisms that, when combined, form an area with no net sand gain or loss. In this example, sand enters a coastal cell through river runoff and wave erosion, accumulates offshore, and moves down the coast via longshore drift. When the sand meets a submarine canyon or the edge of the continental shelf, it falls off into deep water and leaves the system.

Large-Scale Sand Features

What causes a spit to form?

What causes tombolos to form?

Why are barrier islands temporary coastal features?

What five features make up a "typical" barrier island?

What are differences between river-dominated, tide-dominated, and wave-dominated deltas?

Sand movement and accumulation form significant coastal features. These features affect water flow and shape the environment.

Figure 15-17

A spit.

A spit is a length of accumulated sand attached to land at one end, pointing in the direction of the longshore drift.

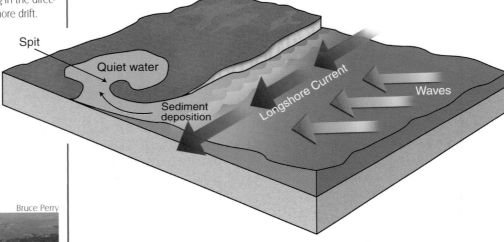

Figure 15-18

Bay mouth barrier.

Because spits form as a longshore current turns a beach corner into the calm water of a bay, they often form a hook shape. If the spit is large enough, it may form a bay mouth barrier, closing the bay to boat traffic. Natural and human-made inlets often cut through the barrier, providing boat access to the bay as shown here at Mission Bay, California.

Bruce Perry

Spits and tombolos. A *spit* is a length of accumulated sand attached to land at one end, pointing in the direction of the longshore drift. It forms when a longshore current turns a beach corner into the relatively calm water of a bay. The current slows and cannot carry as much sediment. Sand settles out of the water, forming the spit.

Spits often have a hook shape due to wave refraction as the waves bend around it. When a spit grows large enough, it may form a *bay mouth barrier*. Natural and human-made inlets often cut through the barrier, providing boat access to the bay.

Tombolos (from the Latin *tumulus* meaning *mound*) are spits that extend between two islands or from an island to the mainland. The islands or island create a wave "shadow" where there is less water turbulence. This causes the longshore current to slow around two

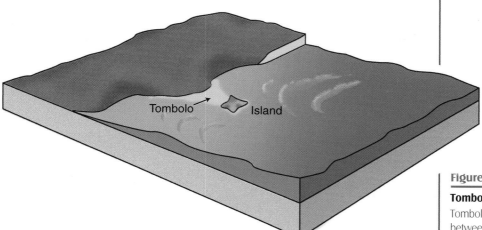

Tombolo → Island

sides of land. The current cannot carry as much sand with slower water flow, so it doesn't carry as much sand away. Some sand in the current may also settle out. Sand therefore accumulates and forms two spits that eventually grow together into a tombolo, as shown in Figure 15-19a.

Barrier islands. As you read in the last section, barrier islands are large sediment deposits that form between the ocean and the shoreline. You also read that many barrier islands are inhabited and developed. Although barrier islands can last thousands of years, and they appear to be stationary, they are actually temporary features. Barrier islands are never the same from day to day. They are gradually moving inland as the sea erodes the coast and the inlets migrate along the coastline. The effects of high wind and storm surge can alter barrier islands dramatically in a short period. This is why people and buildings on barrier islands are especially vulnerable during hurricanes.

Barrier islands can be quite large. They can be several kilometers wide and more than 60 kilometers (37.3 miles) long. They can occur 30 kilometers (18.6 miles) or more offshore. Although barrier islands comprise a small proportion of the global coastline, they are important to coastal communities. Barrier islands surround much of the US eastern and Gulf coasts. The Outer Banks of North Carolina is an example of a broad chain of barrier islands.

A "typical" barrier island has five features: an ocean beach, sand dunes, a barrier flat, a salt marsh, and a lagoon. The ocean beach differs little from other beaches. Behind the ocean beach, dunes accumulate sand as the wind blows it inland. Grasses and other vegetation grow in the dunes, stabilizing them. These dunes protect the

Figure 15-19a

Tombolo formation.

Tombolos are spits that extend between two islands or from an island to the mainland. Because waves cannot carry sediments in the shadow of the island, sand accumulates on both sides of the island. Over time, the two spits grow together forming the tombolo.

Captain Albert E. Theberge, NOAA Corps

Figure 15-19b

Tombolo off Pt. Sur Lightstation in California.

INTERNET PORTAL

SC*i*LINKS. NSTA

Topic: Barrier Islands
Go To: www.scilinks.org
Code: LOP2365

islands from storms and tides by dissipating storm energy. The dunes also help reduce the energy reaching the main coastline behind the barrier island. However, large storms can penetrate the dunes and the wind and storm surge will move the island inland.

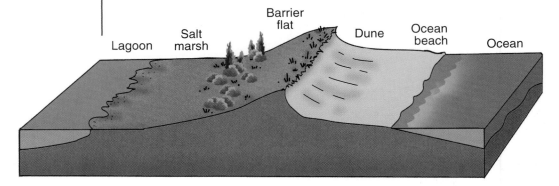

Figure 15-20

Barrier islands.

Barrier islands are large sediment deposits that form between the ocean and the shoreline and have five features: an ocean beach, ocean dunes, a barrier flat, a salt marsh, and a lagoon.

Beyond the dunes is the *barrier flat*, which is a broad, relatively level area with vegetation ranging from grasses to woodlands. Winds create the flats as they sweep over the dunes. Beyond the flats is a *salt marsh*, which is an intertidal grassland that is usually biologically diverse and productive. The salt marsh leads into the *lagoon*, which is relatively shallow water enclosed between the island and the mainland. Lagoons are the nursery for many types of fish and shrimp.

Storms constantly change barrier islands. A storm surge can wash over barrier islands, flooding the barrier-flat vegetation with salt water. This can kill many plants and force the biological succession of plants to have to start over. Overwash can cut a new inlet through a barrier island and damage or destroy structures built on the island.

Storms and rising sea level gradually move barrier islands shoreward. They do this by eroding the leading edge while depositing sand on the lagoon side. This is a slow process, but it has already been an issue for communities built on barrier islands.

Figure 15-21

Hurricane damage.

Storm energy can dramatically change barrier islands. In 2003, when Hurricane Isabel hit Hatteras Island in North Carolina, the overwash destroyed many structures and created a new inlet.

U.S. Geological Survey

Deltas. In the last section, you read that deltas form when sediments carried by a river accumulate at the river's mouth. Deltas cannot form at the mouths of all rivers. There has to be enough sediment deposited by the river that it can accumulate and not be carried away by the oceanic water energy. The ideal areas for deltas are those with broad continental shelves, low tidal range, and relatively mild waves and currents. You do not find deltas on the US west coast because the continental shelf is too narrow. They are not common on the east coast because estuaries tend to trap river sediments. The Gulf of Mexico coast, however, has good delta conditions, and the Mississippi River Delta is a prime example.

Scientists classify deltas several ways based on distinguishing characteristics. William Galloway classified deltas into three basic types in 1975: *river-dominated deltas*, *tide-dominated deltas*, and *wave-dominated deltas*.

River-dominated deltas have strong rivers and mild wave and tidal action. The river's flow therefore acts as the primary force shaping the delta. River-dominated deltas have the characteristic delta (triangle) shape that give deltas their name. The Mississippi River delta is an example.

Tide-dominated deltas occur in areas with strong tidal changes. The tides redistribute the sediments, commonly creating tidal sand ridges perpendicular to shore. Over time, the ridges accumulate sediment and form a tidal channel. The Essex River in Massachusetts has a tide-dominated delta.

Wave-dominated deltas have significant wave energy that redistributes river sediments. As the sediment reaches the ocean, wave action tends to straighten and redistribute the sediment along the beaches as dunes and spits. The Senegal delta in west Africa is one example of a wave-dominated delta.

Jacques Descloitres, MODIS Rapid Response Team, NASA/GSFC

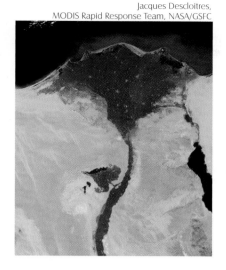

Figure 15-22

River-dominated delta.

River-dominated deltas, like the Nile Delta shown here, have strong rivers, mild tidal action, and mild wave action.

NASA

Figure 15-23

Tide-dominated delta.

Tide-dominated deltas are characterized by strong tidal changes that commonly create sand ridges perpendicular to shore, as shown here in Teignmouth, UK on the English Channel.

NASA

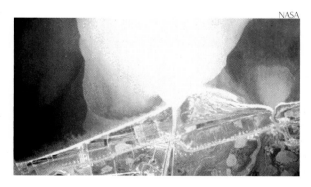

Figure 15-24

Wave-dominated delta.

Wave-dominated deltas have significant wave energy that redistributes river sediments.

1. Longshore drift moves material along the coastline (choose all that apply)

   A. because of the effect of a longshore current.

   B. only if the particle size is larger than a cobble.

   C. primarily with the prevailing winds.

   D. to the north along both US coastlines.

2. Sand comes from (choose all that apply)

   A. meteor showers.

   B. the digestive wastes of organisms, such as parrotfish.

   C. wave erosion of the shoreline.

   D. sources that are inland and carried to the ocean by streams and rivers.

3. Of the three sections that comprise a beach, the _____ is that part between the high-tide mark and the low-tide mark.

   A. barrier flat

   B. backshore

   C. foreshore

   D. offshore

4. Factors that affect the shape and appearance of a beach include (choose all that apply)

   A. sediment grain size.

   B. wave energy.

   C. beach slope.

   D. inland vegetation.

5. A coastal cell is

   A. a weather pattern that affects the shoreline.

   B. a submarine canyon.

   C. another name for longshore drift.

   D. a local region with no net sand gain or loss.

6. A spit forms when a longshore current turns a beach corner into the relatively calm water of a bay, allowing sand to settle out.

   A. true

   B. false

7. A tombolo forms when a large wave piles sediment between two islands or an island and the mainland.

   A. true

   B. false

8. A barrier island is a temporary coastal feature because (choose all that apply)

   A. the sea erodes the coast of a barrier island.

   B. subduction of the barrier island forces it to sink.

   C. rising sea level gradually moves a barrier island shoreward.

   D. storms move a barrier island shoreward.

9. A "typical" barrier island has five features that include (choose all that apply)

   A. an ocean beach.

   B. a tombolo.

   C. a barrier flat.

   D. a lagoon.

10. Of the three delta types identified by William Galloway, a _____ delta has the characteristic delta shape that gives deltas their name.

   A. river-dominated

   B. tide-dominated

   C. wave-dominated

   D. all deltas have the characteristic delta shape

Biological Processes and Human Activity

Coral Reefs

What part of a coral polyp creates the structure of a coral reef?

What are the differences between fringing reefs, barrier reefs, *and* atolls?

As you read earlier, not all coasts result from physical processes. Biological processes also shape the coastline. The role of coral in building reefs is discussed in several chapters of *Life on an Ocean Planet.* Coral is perhaps the most significant of all the biological processes that affect the coast.

A coral reef can be massive, but only the outside layer, where the coral polyps exist, is alive. Individual polyps create a calcium carbonate external skeleton as they grow. It is this part of its structure that creates coral reefs. As successive generations of polyps live and die, each generation grows on the skeleton of the previous. Although each generation adds only a fraction to the reef, given enough time (hundreds of years), enormous reefs emerge.

Like other forms of coast, scientists divide coral reefs into different types with respect to how they affect the coastline. Charles Darwin created one of the first coral reef classification systems. He divided coral reefs into *fringing reefs, barrier reefs,* and *atolls.*

Fringing reefs lie along an island or mainland coast. They form the fringe of the coast, hence the name. Fringing reefs have a *fore reef,* which is the outer, ocean side with most of the biological activity. The *reef crest* is the top of the reef that takes most of the wave energy. The *back reef* is on the land side and has less biological activity.

Jack Hollingsworth, Digital Vision/Getty Images

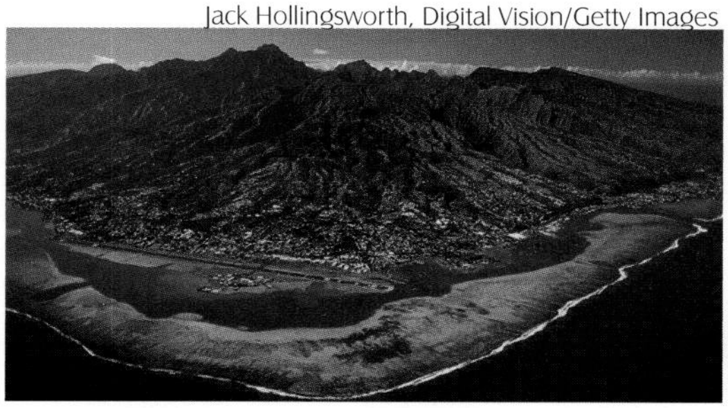

Figure 15-25

Fringing reefs.

Fringing reefs lie along an island or mainland coast and are composed of the fore reef, reef crest, and back reef. The fringing reef in this photograph surrounds Moorea in French Polynesia.

A barrier reef has a similar structure to a fringing reef, but it is further from shore. Whereas a fringing reef is part of the main coast, a barrier reef has a lagoon between it and the main coast. Barrier reefs are usually much larger and occur where there is rock or other large substrate for the reef to begin growing

STUDY QUESTIONS

Find the answers as you read.

1. What part of a coral polyp creates the structure of a coral reef?
2. What are the differences between *fringing reefs, barrier reefs,* and *atolls*?
3. What wave characteristic can allow plant communities to dominate the coast?
4. How do mangroves affect the coast?
5. What are the primary motivations for humans to modify the coastline?
6. What are the differences between *groins, jetties, breakwaters,* and *seawalls*?
7. What changes and problems occur due to human structures intended to protect the coastline?
8. What is *beach renourisment*?
9. What is the likely solution to the problems created by human coastal structures?

Earth Observatory, NASA

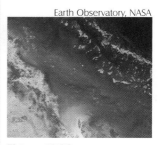

Figure 15-26

Barrier reef.

Barrier reefs are similar to fringing reefs but they are further from shore and are usually separated from it by a lagoon, as shown in this photograph of the Great Barrier Reef in Australia.

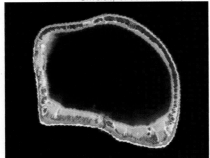

Serge Andrefouet,
Unversity of South Florida/NASA

Figure 15-27

Atoll.

An atoll is a ring-shaped coral reef that encircles a shallow lagoon. This true-color image of Tuanake Atoll in French Polynesia was taken by the Landsat 7 satellite.

on. It is called a barrier reef because it creates a barrier between the open ocean and the main coastline.

An atoll is a ring-shaped coral reef that encircles a shallow lagoon. Darwin was one of the first scientists to ponder how atolls (from the Maldives aboriginal word *atollon*) could form. They stand in deep water with no other landmasses nearby. With depths too deep for corals to grow, atolls could not simply grow up from the bottom.

Darwin theorized that atolls form on the remains of volcanic islands. A volcanic island in tropical water will naturally acquire a fringing reef. After the volcano becomes extinct, it sinks over hundreds of thousands of years. It sinks because it is carried by plate tectonics away from the mid-ocean ridge crest where it formed, into deep water. The coral animals keep building the reef as the top of the volcano slips below the ocean surface. Eventually only the circular atoll remains near the surface.

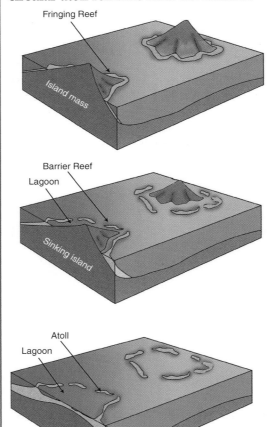

Figure 15-28

Atoll formation.

Darwin's atoll formation theory says that volcanic islands in tropical water naturally acquire fringing reefs. After the volcano goes extinct, it sinks (over hundreds of thousands of years) while the fringing reef continues to grow and becomes a barrier reef. When the volcano slips under the water's surface, an atoll is left.

Plant Communities

What wave characteristic can allow plant communities to dominate the coast?

How do mangroves affect the coast?

Coral reefs can grow in areas with relatively high wave energy. In areas where the waves have generally low energy, plant communities can dominate the coast. Seagrasses can live entirely under water in the ocean, but most marine plants live partly out of the water. In both cases, plants provide structure that helps hold sediment in place and absorb energy.

Among the most important of the plant-dominated shorelines are the mangrove swamps. As discussed in Chapter 5 and in Chapter 16, mangrove swamps provide a biologically important environment. Mangroves provide a habitat in which many juvenile organisms survive until they are large enough to compete on adjacent coral reefs.

Mangroves affect the coast directly by holding sediment in place and by absorbing wave energy. Mangroves and coral reefs commonly coexist. The coral reef absorbs much of the wave energy. This provides water calm enough for the mangroves to grow. The mangroves further absorb wave energy and hold sediment with their roots. This slows erosion. Many tropical islands would not exist if it were not for the combination of coral reefs and mangroves protecting them from erosion by waves and currents.

Human Activities

What are the primary motivations for humans to modify the coastline?

What are the differences between groins, jetties, breakwaters, *and* seawalls?

What changes and problems occur due to human structures intended to protect the coastline?

What is beach renourishment?

What is the likely solution to the problems created by human coastal structures?

Just as we shape other environments to our purposes, we also alter the coastline. There are two primary motivations for humans to modify the coastline. The first is to create new coastal structures. An example would be building a harbor. The second motivation is to protect buildings or other structures on existing coasts from natural coastal changes. An example of this would be putting up a

US Geological Survey

Figure 15-29a

Groins.

We shape other environments to our purposes, we also alter the coastline. An example would be building a harbor or be putting up a protective wall.

Bonnie M. Bendell

Figure 15-29b

Groins.

Groins are artificial protrusions that jut out into the water perpendicular from shore. They are often used to create an area protected from longshore current or for recreational purposes. Note the saw-toothed appearance of the beach created by sand accumulation on the upside drift and depletion on the downside drift.

INTERNET PORTAL

SCiLINKS. NSTA

Topic: Costal Changes
Go To: www.scilinks.org
Code: LOP2370

Figure 15-30

Jetties.

Jetties are similar to groins except they are built to protect or reinforce a harbor entrance.

protective wall so that high tide and seas cannot destroy a condominium community built just above the beach.

Human-built coastal structures include *groins, jetties, breakwaters,* and *seawalls.* A groin is an artificial protrusion jutting out perpendicular to the shore. These may be built to create an area relatively protected from longshore current, or for recreation, such as fishing. They are commonly built from piles of boulders and stone, though they can be made from sand bags, concrete, and other materials.

A jetty is essentially the same as a groin, except that it is built to reinforce a harbor entrance. A breakwater runs parallel to shore or starts on shore and curves into the sea. Its purpose is to create an artificial lagoon to use as a harbor or beach. A seawall stands either at the water along the shore or at the top of a beach. It acts as a barrier to block waves from coming ashore and eroding the land.

It is easy to understand why a hotel owner would want a seawall to protect a multimillion-dollar high-rise building, or a developer would want a harbor where tourists can anchor their boats. However, human coastal structures interfere with natural coastal processes. This particularly includes sand flow.

Human structures intended to protect the coastline create changes and problems. Jetties and groins block longshore drift. This tends to cause sand to accumulate on the upside drift and to become depleted on the downside drift. Spits may form at the upside drift ends of a jetty as shown in Figure 15-30.

Seawalls reflect wave energy, creating turbulence and more erosion when storm waves breach the wall. They also create problems at their ends. Unprotected land next to the seawall tends to suffer from increased erosion.

The result of these and other structures is that beaches may erode away from where they used to naturally exist. This unin-

Rick Crawford, National Estaurine Research Reserve Collection, NOAA

tended effect often leads to more human action. In this case, the response may be *beach renourishment*. Beach renourishment is transporting sand or sediment from a different location to replenish eroded sand.

Dana J. Seagars, NMFS, Fisheries Collection, NOAA

Beach renourishment has several problems, unfortunately. First, it is very expensive. Second, it is not really a solution, but instead, a temporary fix. If the structure that is causing the erosion remains in place, the beach will continue to erode. Eventually, the beach will need to be renourished again. Third, taking sand from somewhere else affects the source environment. Dredging sand from offshore may damage biological communities. Also, offshore sand has finer grain than onshore sand due to natural sorting. The same sorting action carries offshore sand away more quickly than the original sand eroded.

The likely solution to problems created by human structures is a change in coastal attitudes and management. Attempting to protect the beach with artificial structures and using renourishment provide only a short-term benefit. A policy change that emphasizes coastal development that accepts natural coastal processes instead of trying to change them appears a better answer. It will be inconvenient in the short term, especially in established coastal communities that depend on artificial structures. But, in the long term it is more effective and less costly to work with nature instead of against it. More than half of the world's population lives along coastal areas. The sea level appears to be rising and climate change models forecast increases in intense weather events. Both of these would mean loss of coastal areas and increasing damages from storm surge. A comprehensive approach to solving coastal management problems is urgently needed. An effective management program of the coastal zone must balance the demands for coastal resources, economic development, and conservation.

Figure 15-31

Breakwaters.

Breakwaters are constructions that run parallel to shore or start on shore and curve into the sea. They are built to create an artificial lagoon for a harbor or beach. This breakwater is in Eastport, Maine.

INTERNET PORTAL

SCiLINKS. NSTA

Topic: Beach Renourishment
Go To: www.scilinks.org
Code: LOP2375

Photo courtesy of PDPhoto.org

Figure 15-32

Seawall.

Seawalls are artificial barriers standing along a shore or at the top of a beach. They are used as a barrier to block waves from coming ashore and eroding the land.

1. The part of a coral polyp that creates the structure of a coral reef is

   A. its external skeleton.

   B. its fecal waste.

   C. coral sand.

   D. all of the above

2. A(n) _____ stands away from shore and has a lagoon between it and the main coast.

   A. fringing reef

   B. barrier reef

   C. atoll

   D. all of the above

3. Plants will dominate a coast if the waves that strike the coast

   A. originate at the equator.

   B. bend as they approach the shoreline.

   C. have low energy.

   D. none of the above

4. Mangroves affect the coast by (choose all that apply)

   A. absorbing wave energy.

   B. holding sediment in place.

   C. generating backwash.

   D. creating tombolos.

5. The primary motivations for humans to modify a coastline include (choose all that apply)

   A. to restore natural conditions.

   B. to create new coastal structures.

   C. to protect existing coastal structures.

   D. to build new fishing grounds.

6. A _____ protrudes perpendicular from shore to protect a harbor. A _____ creates an artificial calm water lagoon.

   A. jetty, seawall

   B. groin, breakwater

   C. groin, seawall

   D. jetty, breakwater

7. Building structures to protect coastlines can create changes and problems that include

   A. blocking longshore drift.

   B. causing unnatural sand depletion and accumulation.

   C. increasing erosion.

   D. all of the above

8. Beach renourishment is

   A. feeding beach organisms by adding nutrients to the sand.

   B. transporting sand away from where it is going to erode anyway.

   C. transporting in sand from a different location to replenish eroded sand.

   D. none of the above

9. The likely solution to problems created by human coastal structures appears to be

   A. increased funding for beach renourishment.

   B. totally abandoning coastal living.

   C. new technologies that counter natural processes.

   D. none of the above

New Terms You Learned

- **active coast** a coast where plates collide, resulting in volcanic activity and earthquakes (p. 15-4)
- **atolls** ring-shaped coral reefs that encircle shallow lagoons (p. 15-21)
- **back reef** the inner, land side of a coral reef with less biological activity (p. 15-21)
- **backshore** the region of a beach rarely touched by seawater, including dunes or grasses all the way to "non-beach" ground (p. 15-14)
- **barrier flat** a broad, relatively level area behind the dunes of a barrier island, with vegetation ranging from grasses to woodlands (p. 15-18)
- **barrier islands** form when material accumulates parallel to shore, forming a barrier between the ocean and the existing coast (p. 15-10)
- **barrier reefs** coral reefs that grow some distance from shore and create a barrier between the open ocean and the main coast (p. 15-21)
- **bay mouth barrier** a sand barrier created by a spit accumulating so much sediment that it blocks the mouth of the bay (p. 15-16)
- **beach** an accumulation of loose sediment near the edge of a large water body (p. 15-10)
- **beach renourishment** transporting in sand or sediment from a different location to replenish eroded sand (p. 15-25)
- **bioerosion** erosion caused by species eating coral polyps and excreting sand as digestive waste; the parrotfish is one species that performs this process (p. 15-14)
- **breakwaters** structures built parallel to shore or attached to the shore and curving into the sea; their purpose is to create artificial, calm water lagoons (p. 15-24)
- **coastal cell** a local region of material transport mechanisms that, when combined, form an area with no net sand gain or loss (p. 15-15)
- **combination coast** a coast formed by both non-marine forces and marine forces (both primary and secondary coastal development) (p. 15-5)

- **drowned river valley** a coast formed by a rising sea level flooding an area eroded by a river during a period of low sea level (p. 15-6)
- **estuaries** partially enclosed water bodies where fresh and salt water mix (p. 15-7)
- **fault coasts** coasts formed by tectonic activity caused by seafloor uplifting or the sea flooding areas of fault spreading (p. 15-9)
- **fjord coast** a coast formed by a rising sea level flooding an area eroded by glaciers during the last ice age (p. 15-6)
- **fore reef** the outer, ocean side of a coral reef with most of the biological activity (p. 15-21)
- **foreshore** the region of a beach from the high tide mark to the low tide mark (p. 15-14)
- **fringing reefs** coral reefs that grow along an island or the mainland (p. 15-21)
- **groins** artificial protrusions jutting out perpendicular to the shore (p. 15-24)
- **jetties** artificial protrusions jutting out perpendicular to the shore at a harbor entrance, with the purpose of protecting the entrance (p. 15-24)
- **lagoon** an area of shallow water separated from the ocean by a barrier island or other obstruction (p. 15-18)
- **longshore current** a current parallel to shore caused by waves approaching the beach at an angle (p. 15-12)
- **longshore drift** the movement of sediment and materials along the coast, caused by a longshore current (p. 15-12)
- **longshore trough** a slightly deeper area in the offshore section of a beach, running parallel to shore (p. 15-14)
- **low-tide terrace** the flat portion of the foreshore of a beach where the waves break (p. 15-14)
- **offshore** the beach area beyond the low-tide terrace; it includes a longshore trough and shallow sandbar that both parallel the shore (p. 15-14)

- **passive coast** a coast located far away from active plate boundaries; it has little or no volcanic activity or earthquakes (p. 15-4)

- **primary coast** a coast formed by non-marine forces such as volcanic activity, glaciers, and erosion (p. 15-5)

- **reef crest** the upper, shallowest portion of a coral reef that experiences most of the wave energy (p. 15-21)

- **river-dominated delta** a delta with a strong river and mild wave and tidal action (p. 15-19)

- **salt marsh** an intertidal grassland that is usually biologically diverse and productive (p. 15-18)

- **salt wedge estuary** an estuary in which seawater forms a layer under the fresh water, resulting in a saltwater layer and a freshwater layer (p. 15-7)

- **seawalls** structures built at the water's edge or at the top of a beach that block waves from traveling any farther ashore (p. 15-24)

- **secondary coast** a coast formed by marine forces such as waves and marine life (p. 15-5)

- **spit** a length of accumulated sand attached to land at one end, pointing in the direction of the longshore drift (p. 15-16)

- **stratified estuary** an estuary in which salt water and fresh water form distinct layers, but the upper freshwater layer becomes saltier near the mouth of the river, and the lower saltwater layer becomes less salty toward the head of the river (p. 15-8)

- **tide-dominated delta** a delta in an area with strong tides that redistribute accumulating sediments (p. 15-19)

- **tombolo** a spit that extends between two islands or between an island and the mainland (p. 15-16)

- **vertically mixed estuary** an estuary in which water flow and topography cause fresh water and seawater to mix, resulting in brackish water (p. 15-8)

- **wave-dominated delta** a delta in an area with high wave energy that redistributes accumulating sediments as dunes and spits (p. 15-19)

- **weakly stratified estuary** an estuary in which salt water and fresh water mix vertically, but there are still distinct freshwater and saltwater layers (p. 15-8)

Chapter 15 in Review

1. List and describe the differences between active and passive coasts, and primary and secondary coasts. Include examples of each.

2. Explain what forces scientists theorize cause primary coasts. For each of the forces, give examples of the types of coasts it would form.

3. Explain what forces scientists theorize cause secondary coasts. For each of the forces, give examples of the types of coasts it would form.

4. Draw a diagram that explains what causes a longshore current and longshore drift. Include a written description of the process.

5. Explain where sand comes from. Where would you expect the sand in Palau to come from? Why? (Find Palau on a map if you do not know where it is.)

6. Diagram a beach and identify its three sections. Identify key features in those sections. What factors affect the shape and appearance of the beach? Assume the beach you are drawing is steep and has high-energy waves. Identify the relative grain sizes you would expect to find on various sections.

7. Explain how a coastal cell maintains the same amount of sand.

8. Describe and diagram what causes spits and tombolos.

9. Explain why barrier islands are temporary coastal features. What processes make them change over time?

10. Sketch a "typical" barrier island, identifying the five features found on it.

11. Diagram and explain the differences between river-dominated, tide-dominated, and wave-dominated deltas.

12. What part of the polyp creates the structure of a reef? Explain how coral reefs build.

13. Sketch a fringing reef, a barrier reef, and an atoll. List their differences.

14. What wave characteristic is necessary for plant communities to dominate a coast? How do mangroves affect the coast?

15. What motivates humans to modify the coastline?

16. Define groin, jetty, breakwater, and seawall. If you were building a harbor along a featureless coast with no natural inlets, which of these would you build? Why?

17. Describe some of the changes and problems that result from human structures intended to protect a coastline.

18. What is beach renourishment? Why is it not a permanent solution? What other problems are there with beach renourishment?

19. What is the likely solution to the problems created by human coastal structures?

Connecting Chapter Concepts – Science Scenarios

1. Scientists classify coasts as primary coasts and secondary coasts, depending upon what they think caused them. Each of these has subclassifications, and a particular coast can result from both primary and secondary coast processes.
   A. What is the difference between a primary coast and a secondary coast?
   B. What is the difference between a fjord coast and a drowned river valley coast?
   C. Some secondary coasts are thought to result from marine organisms. What is perhaps the most significant example of such a secondary coast?
2. Erosion by waves and currents is constantly moving sand. This results in changes to both primary and secondary coastal features.
   A. What process tends to move material along the coastline? What type of current is necessary for this process to take place?
   B. Where does sand come from?
   C. What are spits and tombolos? Why do they form in some areas, but not in others?
   D. What is a delta? Why do they not occur at the mouth of every river? Where do they usually form?

Marine Science and the Real World

1. Diagram a "typical" barrier island on the east coast of the United States. Based on what you have learned about wave refraction, longshore drift, and sand redistribution, show where you would expect the island to erode and sand to accumulate. Indicate how the barrier island may gradually move based on these processes.

2. Imagine you are a coastal engineer responsible for protecting a shoreline that is frequently subjected to large waves and storm surge. What recommendations would you make if your goal is to avoid building new structures that will create problems with coastal dynamics?

3. Sketch a groin constructed on the west coast of the United States. Diagram where you would expect a spit to form.

4. Imagine you are a boat captain. How might what you have learned about tombolos affect your thinking as you steer the boat?

5. The US military conducted early nuclear weapons tests on a fleet of obsolete warships in 1946. As a test site, they chose Bikini Atoll, a large atoll in the South Pacific. Based on what you know about atolls, why would scientists choose one as the location for these tests? In answering this, remember that as they were studying the explosive power of atomic bombs, they knew little about radioactive fallout.

References

Cunningham, William P., Mary Ann Cunningham and Barbara Woodworth Saigo. 1999. *Environmental Science: A Global Concern.* Boston: McGraw-Hill.

Garrison, T. 2004. *Oceanography: An Invitation to Marine Science.* Pacific Grove, CA: Brooks/Cole, a division of Thomson Learning, Inc.

Garrison, T. 2004. *Essentials of Oceanography.* Pacific Grove, CA: Brooks/Cole, a division of Thomson Learning, Inc.

Klemm, Barbara, Francis M. Pottenger III, Thomas W. Speitel, S. Arthur Reed and Ann E. Coopersmith. 1991. *Hawaii Marine Science Studies: The Fluid Earth. Physical Science and Technology of the Marine Environment.* Honolulu, HI: Curriculum Research and Development Group.

Sverdrup, Keith A., Alyn C. Duxbury and Alison B. Duxbury. 2000. *An Introduction to the World's Oceans.* Boston: McGraw-Hill.

Tarbuck, Edward J. and Frederick K. Lutgens. 2000. *Earth Science.* Upper Saddle River: Prentice Hall.

Thurman, Harold V., and Elizabeth A. Burton. 2001. *Introductory Oceanography.* New Jersey: Prentice Hall.

U.S. Army Corps of Engineers. 2002. *Coastal Engineering Manual: Engineer Manual.* 1110-2-1100. Washington, D.C.

UNIT 6   The Present and Futu

the Marine Environment

Damage Assessment, Remediation and Restoration Program, NOAA

Photo by Marty Snyderman

CHAPTER 16

Marine Ecosystems

Bob Wohlers

Al Hornsby

Searching for the Missing Link in Marine Caves

Thomas M. Iliffe, PhD
Professor, Department of Marine Biology, Texas A&M University at Galveston

Some say humans know more about outer space than about our own planet, particularly because 71% of it is hidden beneath the ocean. Marine biologists such as Tom Iliffe are working hard to balance this disparity. Iliffe is a professor in marine biology who specializes in diving exploration and scientific studies of marine caves.

"My primary research involves biodiversity surveys of the animals inhabiting saltwater caves. I've led research expeditions to study the biology of marine and freshwater caves to the Bahamas, Belize, Mexico, Jamaica, the Canary Islands, Iceland, Spain's Balearic Islands, Romania, Czechoslovakia, the Galapagos, Hawaii, and numerous other locations in the Indo-Pacific; in addition to nine years of studies on Bermuda's marine caves. This research has resulted in the discovery of more than 300 new species of marine animals. Amazingly, many of these cave-limited species have close relatives inhabiting caves on opposite sides of the world."

Iliffe's interest in science is a lifelong affair that began when he was a child growing up on the shores of Lake Erie. Though his masters degree was in oceanography, after moving from Florida to Texas and finding the diving there not as diverse, Iliffe decided to pursue another interest: caves.

"I had always had an interest in caves, and after moving to Texas, I went on several trips to explore dry caves in Central Texas and Northern Mexico. And, after I finished my PhD, my first job was as a research scientist at the Bermuda Biological Station studying tar washing up on the beaches. I soon discovered Bermuda had numerous limestone caves with deep and clear interior saltwater pools. At that time, most of what we knew about aquatic cave biology dealt with freshwater systems. Few scientists had ever seriously looked at marine caves. I was able to interest Boris Sket, a cave biologist from Slovenia who had studied caves along the Adriatic Sea's coast, to come to Bermuda on his way to a conference in the US. Together, we found some amazing new animals in the deeper, more saline cave waters. I was hooked. Within a few years of getting my cave-diving certification, we discovered and explored many new underwater caves and found dozens of new species of marine life."

Through his work, Iliffe has traveled the world and experienced the thrill of discovery of numerous new caves and cave animals. To students considering careers in marine science, Iliffe has this to say: "If you are interested in marine science as a potential career, you need to take as many math and science courses as possible, including biology, chemistry, geology, and so on. Your undergraduate program should train you first as a biologist, with secondary emphasis on marine biology. You should also enjoy being outdoors and be willing to do hard work. Getting certified as a scuba diver is also a good idea."

Treasures of the NOAA Library Collection

Figure 16-1a

Endurance in ice pack.

1922 *Scientific American*
profiling Shackleton's
expedition to Antarctica.

At the Ends of the Earth Collection, NOAA

Figure 16-1b

Antarctic exploration.

Ernest Shackleton's
expedition to Antarctica
in 1914 never got to the
South Pole. However, it
became one of the most
incredible tales of survival
in the history of exploration.
His vessel, *Endurance*,
is pictured before it was
crushed by ice flows.

One of the most famous stories of survival is that of Ernest Shackleton, Antarctic explorer. Shackleton arrived in Antarctica with a crew of 28 on his ship the *Endurance* in late 1914. His plan was to cross the Antarctic continent from sea to sea via the pole. Antarctica, history would show, had other plans.

Through January 1915, *Endurance* picked its way through the Antarctic ice pack, trying to make landfall. Shackleton sought the shortest route across the continent. However, with winter approaching, the ice pack blocked *Endurance* repeatedly. The pack grew thicker and, despite repeated attempts to progress, on January 19, 1915, *Endurance* was frozen solidly in the ice pack. Shackleton knew he and his men would be there through the long winter. The ice pack would not melt again until spring.

At first, the crew lived in *Endurance*, consuming the supplies brought for the expedition. A shrewd leader, Shackleton kept his crew continuously busy with various projects. He realized that they were better off being too busy to worry or entertain doubts.

Thinking long-term, Shackleton realized that his provisions would not likely last the many months they faced. Having his men hunt for food would keep them preoccupied and bolster their food supplies. However, they were in barren Antarctica, a land without forests or plants. Could humans live off the land here?

Shackleton knew, as we know today, that as barren as Antarctica appears to the eye, it is a rich ecosystem. Far from being devoid of life, its seas are one of the richest areas on Earth. Marine mammals, birds, and fish would provide Shackleton and his men with the food they needed.

At first they caught seals and penguins, which provided food for them and the dogs. But as winter came on, the seals and penguins became scarce. From their precarious position, Shackleton's men witnessed the seasonal ebb and flow of polar ecosystems. Antarctica explodes with life in the spring and summer, yet becomes nearly devoid of it in the winter.

Shackleton's crew remained stranded through 1915. In October, the men began finding seals and penguins again, but the ice flows crushed *Endurance* on the 27th. Shackleton moved his men over the ice on foot and by boat, making it to barren Elephant Island on April 16, 1916. After several weeks of planning, Shackleton and five other men set sail in a small, open boat for South Georgia Island, the closest human settlement. It was more than 1,289 kilometers (795 miles) away across one of the roughest seas on Earth. They reached the South Georgia Island's whaling stations in mid May.

It took until August 30 for Shackleton to outfit ships and return to Elephant Island for the rest of his men. He found that every one had survived the 105 days since his departure. They had existed primarily on seal and penguin meat – bounty from one of the world's most productive ecosystems.

Ecology and Ecosystems

The Science of Ecology

What is ecology?

With the rise of environmental awareness, the term *ecology* has become a buzzword thrown about by the media and politicians. You may already have a general idea of what ecology is, but to discuss marine ecology clearly, it is important to be precise and specific.

Ecology (from the Greek *ecos* meaning *home*) is the science that studies how organisms relate to each other and their environment. Ecology embraces the broad range of disciplines, including biology, physics, geology, climatology, oceanography, paleontology, and even astronomy. Beyond *biotic* (living) factors, the study of ecology considers the *abiotic* (nonliving) aspects of the environment. These include temperature, wind, pH, currents, minerals, and sunlight. Ecology also examines the number and type of organisms in an environment. And, ecology studies the relationships and interactions of the abiotic and biotic aspects of the environment. The goal is to understand how, through relationships and interactions, changes in an environment will affect those organisms in the environment. In marine ecology, the four branches of oceanography, biological, chemical, geological, and physical come together.

Ecology Terminology

What is an ecosystem?

What is a community?

What is a population?

What is a habitat?

What is a microhabitat?

What is a niche?

Ecologists use specific terms shared by biologists and other scientists. You may be familiar with some of these. However, it is useful to keep some of the precise meanings of these terms in mind as you go through this chapter.

At some level you are probably familiar with the concept of an *ecosystem*. An ecosystem is an entity usually with clearly defined

STUDY QUESTIONS

Find the answers as you read.

1. What is *ecology*?

2. What is an *ecosystem*?

3. What is a *community*?

4. What is a *population*?

5. What is a *habitat*?

6. What is a *microhabitat*?

7. What is a *niche*?

8. How does the flow of energy through the food web affect an ecosystem?

9. Which nutrient cycle is the basis for most of the biomass in all ecosystems?

10. Which nutrient cycle is thought to be limited in marine ecosystems compared to terrestrial ecosystems?

11. Why are the most productive marine ecosystems found in cold, temperate regions?

INTERNET PORTAL

SCiLINKS. NSTA

**Topic: Biotic/Abiotic Factors
Go To: www.scilinks.org
Code: LOP2380**

physical boundaries, distinct abiotic conditions, at least one energy source, and a community of interacting organisms through which energy is transferred. No ecosystem exists entirely in isolation (except under artificial conditions). In the ocean, ecosystems are often overlapping and interacting.

A *community* is a collection of different populations of organisms living and interacting in an ecosystem. This includes all species and types of organisms. A *population* is a group of the same species that live and interact within a community. "Interact" is part of the definition of a population because sometimes two populations of the same species live in a single community, but they do not interact. An example of this type of community exists off Vancouver Island, Canada. In those waters, orca pods live relatively closely together, yet maintain separate populations that rarely interact. These pods do not interbreed as far as scientists can tell. Therefore, separate pods would be considered separate populations within the same community.

Mary Hollinger, NODC biologist, NOAA

Figure 16-2a

Puddle.

PADI

Figure 16-2b

Reef.

NASA

Figure 16-2c

Earth and its ocean.

Defining an ecosystem.
An ecosystem can be as limited as a temporary puddle of water or as broad as the entire ocean because both are areas with clearly defined boundaries.

A *habitat* includes the area and physical conditions in which you find an organism. Some species are adapted to or occur in very specific habitats, whereas others range over a variety of habitats. Chitons, for example, live in the rocky intertidal zone, whereas octopuses live in a wide depth range and in many different parts of a reef. The chiton has a narrowly defined habitat compared to the octopus.

Figure 16-3a & b

Defining a habitat.

A habitat is the area and conditions in which you find an organism. In other words, its habitat is its address. Some species, such as the chiton, are adapted to very specific habitats. Most chitons live in the intertidal zone. Other species, such as the octopus, have more broad habitats.

A *microhabitat* exists on a very small scale. For example, tiny crustaceans and worms live in the spaces between sand grains on the sea floor. (Organisms in this microhabitat are called *meiofauna*, from the Greek *meion* meaning *less*, and *Faunus*, a woodlands god in Roman mythology – fauna, meaning animal.)

An organism's role in its habitat is called its *niche*. On coral reefs, for example, cleaner-shrimp and cleaner-fish both survive by feeding on the parasites and dead or injured skin of reef fish. To avoid confusing habitat and niche, think of the habitat as an organism's address, and the niche as its job.

Figure 16-4

Defining a niche.

An organism's role in its habitat, or its job, is called its *niche*. On coral reefs, the cleaner-fish eats the parasites and dead or injured skin of reef fish. Fish that want a cleaning will display specific behaviors to show the cleaner fish that they will not eat the cleaner.

Energy Flow and Nutrient Cycles

How does the flow of energy through the food web affect an ecosystem?

Which nutrient cycle is the basis for most of the biomass in all ecosystems?

Which nutrient cycle is thought to be limited in marine ecosystems compared to terrestrial ecosystems?

Why are the most productive marine ecosystems found in cold, temperate regions?

Trophic relationships, discussed in Chapter 4, and nutrient cycles, discussed in Chapter 8, are both concepts fundamental to ecology. They describe how energy and matter form the basis for interaction among organisms and between organisms and the environment.

As discussed in Chapter 4, photosynthesizers and chemosynthesizers bring energy from the sun and chemicals into the food web. This energy transfers up through the food web, but most of the energy gets lost as heat in the process. Only about 10% of the available energy passes from one trophic level to the next.

The energy flow through the food web affects an ecosystem by determining how much energy is available for organisms at higher

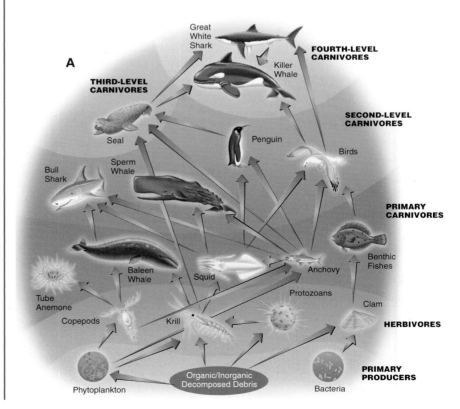

Figure 16-5a

Energy flow.

This illustration shows how energy flows through a functioning ecosystem.

trophic levels. In most ecosystems, there are fewer high-level predators than low-level prey. The amount of primary production shapes the ecosystem. High and diverse primary production creates the potential for more organisms at high trophic levels, and the potential for more trophic levels. Similarly, anything that affects energy flow will also affect the ecosystem. For example, if pollution causes a substantial decline in an ecosystem's primary consumers, it disrupts energy flow to higher trophic levels. Therefore, even with ample primary production, the ecosystem would lose many of the high-level organisms in its community.

Energy flows through an ecosystem, eventually being lost as heat into the water, atmosphere, and space. Nutrients, on the other hand, are not lost. As discussed in Chapter 8, carbon, nitrogen, phosphorus, and other crucial elements cycle through the Earth's ecosystems.

The carbon nutrient cycle is the basis for most of the biomass in all ecosystems. As discussed in Chapter 8, carbon is fundamental for all life. The ocean appears to play an important role in the global ecosystem by helping absorb the excess carbon released by the burning of fossil fuel.

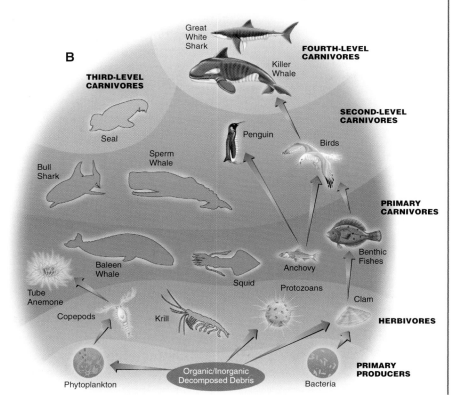

B

THIRD-LEVEL CARNIVORES

FOURTH-LEVEL CARNIVORES

Great White Shark

Killer Whale

SECOND-LEVEL CARNIVORES

Seal

Sperm Whale

Penguin

Birds

Bull Shark

PRIMARY CARNIVORES

Benthic Fishes

Baleen Whale

Anchovy

Squid

Protozoans

Clam

Tube Anemone

Copepods

Krill

HERBIVORES

Organic/Inorganic Decomposed Debris

Phytoplankton

Bacteria

PRIMARY PRODUCERS

Figure 16-5b

Interrupted energy flow.

A substantial decline in an ecosystem's primary consumers disrupts energy flow to higher trophic levels. Here we see a reduction of the amount and types of prey available to killer whales. The whale population will suffer in this ecosystem unless they move on to an area with more productivity, or more primary consumers to transfer energy to higher trophic levels.

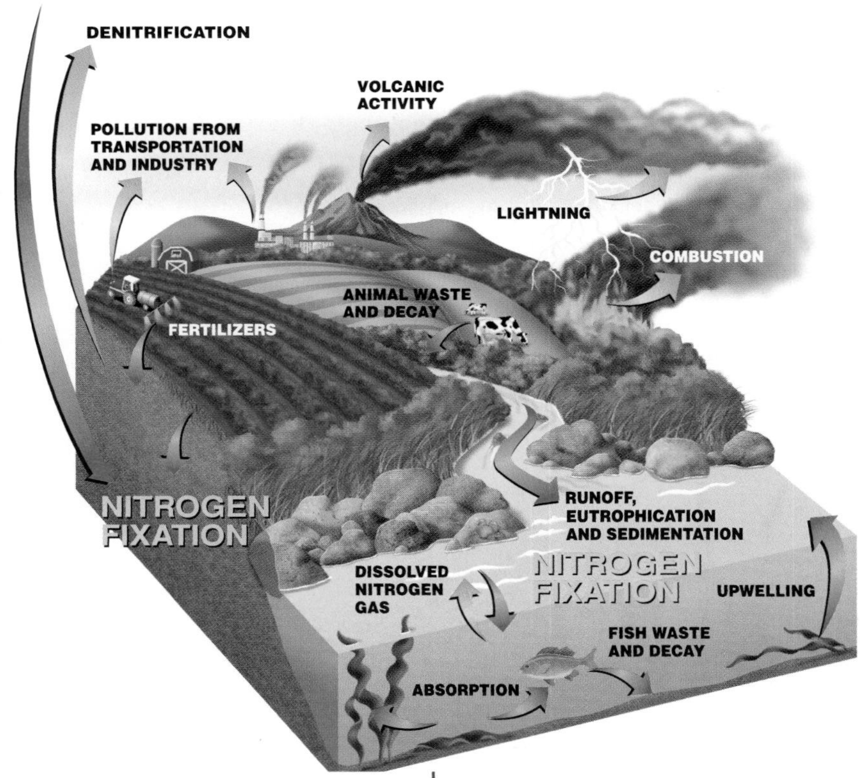

Figure 16-6

Nitrogen cycling.

Atmospheric nitrogen must be fixed into other compounds, such as nitrate or ammonia, before it can be used by organisms. The nitrogen-fixing bacteria that do this were once thought to live primarily in terrestrial ecosystems. However, recent evidence indicates that nitrogen-fixing bacteria are much more common in marine ecosystems than scientists first thought. Beyond natural sources, two of the biggest sources of organic nitrogen in coastal waters are fertilizer and industrial wastes from the land.

As discussed in Chapters 5 and 8, the nitrogen nutrient cycle is thought to be more limited in marine ecosystems than in terrestrial ecosystems. The reason is because inorganic nitrogen stored in the atmosphere must be fixed into organic compounds before it can be used by organisms. The nitrogen-fixing bacteria that do this live primarily in terrestrial ecosystems. (However, nitrogen-fixing bacteria are more common in marine ecosystems than previously thought.) Terrestrial sources of organic nitrogen are especially important in coastal water. Seabird droppings, erosion, and runoff carry organic nitrogen compounds (and phosphorus) from terrestrial environments into the marine environment. The source of a great amount of organic nitrogen in coastal waters is fertilizer and industrial waste. Runoff carries the nitrogen into rivers and on into coastal waters. Once there, the nitrogen fertilizes the water, creating algal blooms. This is an example of how ecosystems do not exist in isolation.

Nutrient cycles and energy flow are equally important to an ecosystem. However, nutrients are usually a limiting factor, whereas energy is usually not. You can see the importance of limiting factors by comparing warm, tropical marine ecosystems with cold, temperate marine ecosystems. Tropical ecosystems generally have more energy (sunlight) available, but fewer nutrients than temperate ecosystems. The reason for fewer nutrients is that in the tropics, the strong thermocline prevents vertical mixing that brings nutrients up from deeper water. One of the few highly productive marine ecosystems found in tropical waters is the coral reef. Temperate coastal waters, by comparison, have less overall sunlight, but receive far more nutrients. For this reason, the most highly productive marine ecosystems are found in colder water.

DENITRIFICATION

VOLCANIC ACTIVITY

POLLUTION FROM TRANSPORTATION AND INDUSTRY

LIGHTNING

COMBUSTION

ANIMAL WASTE AND DECAY

FERTILIZERS

NITROGEN FIXATION

RUNOFF, EUTROPHICATION AND SEDIMENTATION

DISSOLVED NITROGEN GAS

NITROGEN FIXATION

UPWELLING

FISH WASTE AND DECAY

ABSORPTION

1. **Ecology is**

   A. a term that means habitat.

   B. the study of how organisms relate to each other and their environment.

   C. a science that embraces only biology.

   D. all of the above

2. **A(n) _____ is a distinct area, usually with clearly defined boundaries, with distinct abiotic conditions, and a community of interacting organisms.**

   A. ecosystem

   B. community

   C. population

   D. habitat

3. **A collection of different organisms living in an ecosystem would be called a(n)**

   A. niche.

   B. population.

   C. community.

   D. ecosystem.

4. **A _____ is a group of the same species living and interacting within a community.**

   A. niche

   B. habitat

   C. population

   D. microhabitat

5. **The area and conditions in which you find an organism are called a(n)**

   A. ecosystem.

   B. habitat.

   C. community.

   D. niche.

6. **A _____ is a type of habitat that exists on a very small scale.**

   A. microhabitat

   B. community

   C. population

   D. niche

7. **An organism's role in its habitat is called its**

   A. community.

   B. microhabitat.

   C. population.

   D. niche.

8. **Energy flow through an ecosystem affects the ecosystem by**

   A. determining how much energy is available for high trophic levels.

   B. reducing the amount of primary production required.

   C. reversing and accumulating in secondary consumers.

   D. all of the above

9. **The _____ nutrient cycle is the basis for most of the biomass in all ecosystems.**

   A. carbon

   B. oxygen

   C. nitrogen

   D. phosphorus

10. **The _____ nutrient cycle is thought to be more limited in marine ecosystems compared to terrestrial ecosystems.**

    A. carbon

    B. oxygen

    C. nitrogen

    D. phosphorus

11. **Most highly productive marine ecosystems are found in cooler regions because**

    A. those regions have more abundant energy.

    B. those regions have more abundant nutrients.

    C. those regions lack high-level predators.

    D. those regions lack primary consumers.

STUDY QUESTIONS

Find the answers as you read.

1. In what way does the euphotic zone ecosystem interact with other ocean ecosystems?

2. How does the neuston ecosystem differ from deeper ecosystems in the euphotic zone ecosystem?

3. What factors may account for low primary productivity in the neuston ecosystem?

4. In what way can pollution in the euphotic zone ecosystem influence global warming?

5. What is the world's largest floating ecosystem?

6. Why is the neritic zone significant as a marine ecosystem?

7. Why is upwelling important to coastal ocean ecosystems?

Luis A. Solorzano/www.californiabiota.com

Figure 16-7

Neuston.

While most neuston are tiny or microscopic, some are larger. This small by-the-wind sailor, *Velella vellella*, floats on the surface and stings its prey.

Ecosystems in the Open Sea

Now that you are familiar with some of the basic terms and concepts related to marine ecosystems, let's look at specific ecosystems found in the open ocean.

Euphotic Zone Ecosystems

In what way does the euphotic zone ecosystem interact with other ocean ecosystems?

How does the neuston ecosystem differ from deeper ecosystems in the euphotic zone ecosystem?

What factors may account for low primary productivity in the neuston ecosystem?

In what way can pollution in the euphotic zone ecosystem influence global warming?

What is the world's largest floating ecosystem?

As discussed in Chapter 9, the euphotic zone comprises only about 1% of the ocean, yet the vast majority of marine life lives in this region. It is the zone that receives enough sunlight to support photosynthesis. In the open ocean, this ecosystem can extend to a depth of nearly 200 m (656 feet), but in coastal waters, where there is more turbidity due to particulate matter in the water, light may penetrate to about only 30 m (100 feet) or less. The euphotic zone is where photosynthetic organisms convert light energy into energy that transfers through food webs as chemical energy. It is also an ecosystem that pollutants affect profoundly.

Many smaller ecosystems exist within the euphotic zone ecosystem. As discussed in Chapter 3, neuston are the plankton that live in the uppermost layer of the ocean. The neuston ecosystem is very thin – only a few millimeters in many instances. It receives the maximum sunlight and it covers about 71% of the Earth's surface.

There have been surprisingly few studies to compare the neuston ecosystem to the other ecosystems in the euphotic zone. Those that have been made find that the first few millimeters to a few centimeters of water differ substantially from the water below. Generally, the neuston ecosystem holds significantly more nutrients, chlorophyll *a*, and carbon compounds. Surface tension supports eggs, larvae, and microscopic life on the top film of the water. The cyanophyte, diatom, and dinoflagellate populations in the neuston ecosystem may be 10,000 times more numerous than in the water just a few millimeters deeper. This makes the neuston zone an important ecosystem for primary productivity.

However, this is not true globally. In most places, photosynthesis and primary productivity are greater in deeper regions of the euphotic zone. One reason primary productivity is low in the neuston ecosystem is that this layer is very thin. It has a small volume compared with the mixed layers below it. Another reason may be photoinhibition, which is discussed in Chapter 4. Photoinhibition seems to be especially prevalent in tropical seas where there is little to protect neuston organisms from extended, direct exposure to ultraviolet light. Ozone depletion may make photoinhibition worse as even more UV light makes it to the Earth's surface.

An important factor that may reduce primary productivity throughout the euphotic zone ecosystem is pollution. A variety of pollutants from the atmosphere and runoff enter the euphotic zone. Scientists are concerned about how some of these pollutants will affect the ecosystem and global warming. The ocean plays an important role in moderating global climate. Carbon dioxide is removed from the air in two ways: during photosynthesis, and when carbon dioxide diffuses from the atmosphere into the water. Many oil-based pollutants float on water, creating a barrier that slows or stops carbon dioxide (and other gases) from entering the water column. Therefore, by affecting the euphotic zone ecosystem, these pollutants may also contribute to global warming.

Floating debris, whether natural or human-produced, act as potential shelter and attracts marine life. This creates distinct ecosystems that thrive around floating material in the water.

The world's largest floating ecosystem is the Sargasso Sea, which is discussed in Chapter 5. Strands of *Sargassum* sp. brown algae accumulate in the middle of the North Atlantic gyre, floating in massive mats that support a complex community. *Sargassum* mat organisms include tiny fish of many species, crustaceans, and other organisms. These

Ocean Explorer, NOAA

Art Howard/Ross et al, Ocean Explorer, NOAA/HBOI

Figure 16-8a   **Figure 16-8b**

The Sargasso Sea.

Perhaps the most famous neuston ecosystem in the ocean is the North Atlantic's Sargasso Sea. Named for a floating form of brown algae, *Sargassum* sp., this enormous ecosystem is kept in place by the constant motion of the North Atlantic Gyre. Massive mats of *Sargassum* support a complex and diverse community. Several species of fish and invertebrates live only in this ecosystem. Most of the organisms, like this *Sargassum* fish (*Histrio histrio*), are well camouflaged within the *Sargassum*.

include species you normally associate with ecosystems close to the shoreline. However, some species are found nowhere else in the world. The sargassumfish is a species of frogfish adapted specifically to this ecosystem. It blends in with the *Sargassum*, preying on small crustaceans and fish.

The Sargasso Sea, and other euphotic zone ecosystems found around floating debris, provide another example of how ecosystems interact. Predatory fish hide under *Sargassum* or debris, feeding on fish and neuston that live there. These predators in turn provide food for pelagic fish, sharks, dolphins, and other large predators.

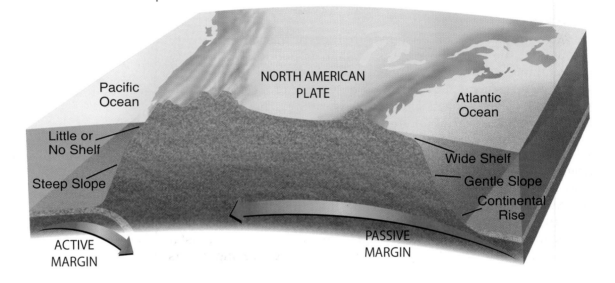

Figure 16-9

Neritic zone productivity.
The neritic zone is defined as the water column above the continental shelf. Off the east coast of North America, the continental shelf is wide. Off the west coast, the shelf is narrow. Since light can normally reach all the way to the bottom of the continental shelf, productivity near the coast is normally very high.

Continental Shelf Ecosystems

Why is the neritic zone significant as a marine ecosystem?

Why is upwelling important to coastal ocean ecosystems?

As discussed in Chapter 3, the neritic zone consists of the water between the low-tide mark and the edge of the continental shelf. This zone can range from only a few to several hundred kilometers or miles wide.

The neritic zone is a very important marine ecosystem because it is the most productive region in the ocean. Several factors combine to make it such a highly productive ecosystem. Continental shelf depth seldom exceeds 200 meters (656 feet). This tends to

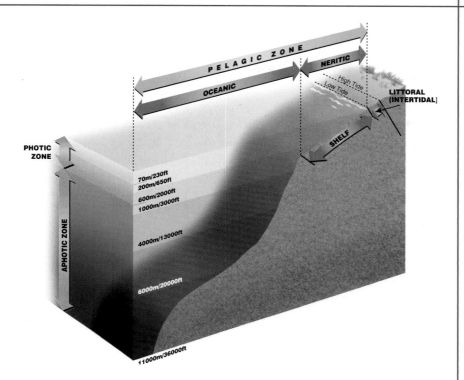

PELAGIC ZONE

NERITIC

OCEANIC

High Tide
Low Tide

LITTORAL
(INTERTIDAL)

SHELF

PHOTIC
ZONE

70m/230ft
200m/650ft
600m/2000ft
1000m/3000ft

4000m/13000ft

6000m/20000ft

11000m/36000ft

APHOTIC ZONE

Figure 16-10

Neritic versus oceanic productivity.

Because the neritic zone is in relatively shallow water, in most locations light reaches all the way to the bottom. This makes sunlight readily available to primary producers. Also, by being near the coasts, the neritic zone benefits from nutrients in runoff from the land and from deep water nutrients that upwell at the shelf edges. In contrast, productivity is much lower in the oceanic zone, where sunlight is available above about 200 meters (656 feet), but nutrients are less abundant.

keep nutrients in the shallow, photic zone and helps retain heat from the sun. Also, because of location, many neritic zone organisms benefit from nutrients in river runoff. Nutrients rising with currents from deep water at the shelf edges also make this zone biologically rich.

Upwelling plays a significant role in the balance of coastal ocean ecosystems. As discussed in Chapter 11, upwelling brings

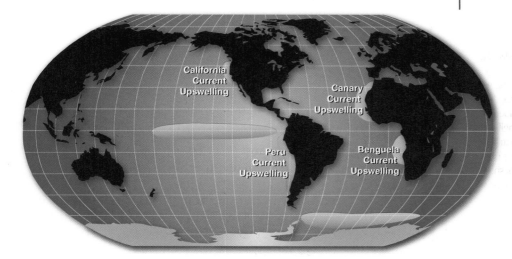

California
Current
Upswelling

Canary
Current
Upswelling

Peru
Current
Upswelling

Benguela
Current
Upswelling

Figure 16-11

Coastal upwelling.

Upwelling brings nutrients from the seafloor to shallow (lighted), productive depths. Therefore, areas with the highest upwelling activity also have the highest nutrient levels. These correspond with many of the ocean's most productive regions and major fisheries.

nutrients from deeper water to shallow, more productive depths. This is especially significant with respect to fecal pellets and other nutrients that sink to the relatively less productive bottom in the abyssal zone. Wind causes upwelling that returns nutrients to the upper ocean depths.

The role of upwelling is unmistakable. Areas with the highest upwelling activity also have the highest nutrient levels. These areas correspond with many of the ocean's highest productivity regions on continental shelves as well as regions far from the continental shelves. Examples include the waters offshore of Peru, the Bering Sea, the Grand Banks in the Atlantic, and the deep water surrounding Antarctica.

ARE YOU LEARNING?

1. The euphotic ecosystem interacts with other ecosystems by being the zone where photosynthetic organisms convert light into energy that transfers through the food web as chemical energy.

   A. true
   B. false

2. Differences between the neuston ecosystem and other ecosystems in the euphotic zone include _____ (choose all that apply).

   A. having significantly more nutrients.
   B. substantially higher populations of cyanophytes, diatoms and dinoflagellates.
   C. being the deepest euphotic zone.
   D. substantially higher populations of sharks and other apex predators.

3. _____ may account for low productivity in the neuston ecosystem (choose all that apply).

   A. Photoinhibition
   B. Predatory consumption
   C. Pollution
   D. *Sargassum*

4. Pollution in the euphotic zone ecosystem may influence global warming by decreasing the amount of carbon dioxide going into the water.

   A. true
   B. false

5. The world's largest floating ecosystem is the neritic zone.

   A. true
   B. false

6. The neritic zone is significant as a marine ecosystem because

   A. it is the largest ecosystem.
   B. it is home to the largest extremophile populations.
   C. it is the ocean's most productive region.
   D. all of the above

7. Upwellings are significant to coastal ocean ecosystems because

   A. they carry nutrients away from shore.
   B. they bring nutrients up from the seafloor.
   C. they carry *Sargassum* to warm water.
   D. none of the above

Coastal Ecosystems – Estuaries, Salt Marshes, Mangrove Swamps, Seagrasses

High Productivity Marine Environments

Why are coastal ecosystems generally highly productive?

Why do human activities have wide-ranging potential effects on coastal ecosystems?

What is eutrophication*?*

Generally, coastal ecosystems are highly productive ecosystems for several reasons. They benefit from nutrient-rich runoff from land. Tidal movement adds energy to the sun's energy. Because these systems are shallow and the bottom is in close contact with the water column, water movement resuspends nutrients, providing enhanced primary production. In these shallow areas, light can penetrate, stimulating benthic vascular plants to grow. These plant communities act as the foundation for several different types of ecosystems that cannot exist in the deep and open ocean.

The combination of certain nutrients, ample light, and shelter make coastal ecosystems diverse and rich. While you do not commonly find large organisms in coastal ecosystems (though there are some), these ecosystems provide a haven for juveniles of many open ocean species. As discussed in Chapter 5, mangrove swamps contribute to the health of coral reefs in this way.

Human activities have wide-ranging effects on coastal ecosystems. Historically, people have settled near coasts. With human proximity to coastal ecosystems, many human activities have adversely affected these ecosystems, though the effects have not always been obvious. Because people live adjacent to coasts, pollutants often reach coastal ecosystems in concentrated form. Agriculture, for example, alters these ecosystems when fertilizer washes seaward with runoff.

One particular concern with coastal ecosystems is *eutrophication*, which is an overabundance of nutrients that causes an ecological imbalance (from the Greek *eu* meaning *good*, and *trophos* meaning *feeding*). Eutrophication is an asset for some species and a detriment for others. Fertilizer in runoff adds excessive amounts of nutrients to the water. This stimulates excessive algae growth, called algae blooms. When the algae die, decomposition of the biomass consumes available oxygen. The depletion of oxygen kills fish and other sea life. Although there are other causes of harmful algal blooms (HABs), eutrophication is the most obvious.

STUDY QUESTIONS

Find the answers as you read.

1. Why are coastal ecosystems generally highly productive?

2. Why do human activities have wide-ranging potential effects on coastal ecosystems?

3. What is *eutrophication*?

4. What factors limit the productivity of estuary ecosystems?

5. What percentage of commercial fish species use estuary ecosystems as nurseries?

6. How do estuaries contribute to the productivity of surrounding marine ecosystems?

7. How do conditions differ in the upper and lower parts of a salt marsh?

8. What adaptations allow halophytes to survive in salt water?

9. What two characteristics of mangrove trees allow them to survive in the coastal environment?

10. How do seagrasses differ from other halophytes?

11. How do seagrass ecosystems differ from other halophyte-based ecosystems?

Estuaries

What factors limit the productivity of estuary ecosystems?

What percentage of commercial fish species do estuary ecosystems serve as nurseries?

How do estuaries contribute to the productivity of surrounding marine ecosystems?

Estuaries exist where the ocean meets rivers in a semi-enclosed area, allowing for the mixing of fresh and salt water. Tides help push seawater from the ocean into these semi-enclosed areas, while river currents flow from the landward side, bringing fresh water and nutrients. Estuaries may be large, with multiple inlets and lagoons, or they may be simple wide stretches of a river entering

National Estuarine Research Reserve Collection, NOAA

National Estuarine Research Reserve Collection, NOAA

Figure 16-12a

Where river meets sea.

Estuaries are the filter and absorber of nutrients (and pollutants). The continuous replenishment of nutrients causes them to have high primary productivity. Estuaries can be large with multiple inlets and lagoons with grasses or mangroves, **(16-12a)** or they can be simple wide stretches of a river entering the sea **(16-12b)**.

Figure 16-12b

the sea. Most of the major east coast North American rivers flowing into the Atlantic flow first into estuaries. This is why the North Atlantic does not have as much sediment flowing into it as other ocean basins with comparable rivers.

Because estuaries trap and accumulate nutrients and sediments from runoff, they tend to be rich with nutrients and biologically productive. The continuous replenishment of nutrients in estuaries results in ecosystems with high primary productivity. In an estuary, the primary producers are algae and *halophytes*—saltwater plants (from the Greek *hals* meaning *salt*, and *phyton* meaning *plant*). The algae and halophytes support a large community of primary and secondary consumers.

Some factors limit species diversity in estuaries. One limiting factor is an organism's tolerance to a wide salinity range. The osmotic stress caused by the mixing of fresh water and salt water proves fatal to many organisms. As discussed in Chapter 8, organisms that tolerate wide salinity ranges are called euryhaline organisms. Variations in salinity tend to reduce the diversity of species to only euryhaline organisms. Another limiting factor is eutrophication, which was explained earlier in this section. The tendency of decomposition to deplete oxygen in the bottom waters, coupled with stratification (separation of surface and bottom water), can lead to reduced habitats for estuarine organisms, especially benthic organisms. The rotten-eggs smell common to benthic areas comes from sulfides released by thriving anaerobic sulfur bacteria.

Estuaries contribute to the productivity of surrounding marine ecosystems in many ways. They filter and absorb nutrients (and pollutants). In fact, estuaries and their associated marshes are called the *kidneys* of the biosphere because of their ability to clean the water. Estuaries also provide a region of shallow, sheltered water and nutrients, making them excellent nurseries. By providing a rich haven, larvae and juveniles of open ocean species can elude predation and grow before venturing out to sea. Estimates show that estuary ecosystems serve as nurseries for more than 75% of commercial fish species. In this way, estuaries contribute to the productivity of adjacent marine ecosystems by increasing the number of individuals that survive the hazardous larval and juvenile stages. Surviving juveniles migrate from the estuaries to the open ocean as they grow and mature. Also, estuaries provide a pulse of nutrients to adjacent marine ecosystems, particularly during high runoff events. This release of nutrients contributes to the coastal ocean productivity.

Salt Marshes

How do conditions differ in the upper and lower parts of a salt marsh?

What adaptations allow halophytes to survive in saltwater?

Salt marshes are located in estuaries and along the coasts. They are found where flat, gently sloping shores are washed by the tides with nutrient-rich sediments. Rivers provide the salt marsh with a source of sediments and nutrients.

Conditions within a salt marsh vary, which affects the types of organisms that can inhabit different areas within the ecosystem. The upper marsh includes the areas only rarely flooded by the tides. Organisms there must tolerate extreme conditions due to the accumulation of salts left behind from evaporation. The lower marsh, however, includes areas flooded by salt water as a regular part of the tidal cycle. In many areas, that means twice daily.

As discussed in Chapter 5, most plants cannot live in seawater because osmosis dehydrates them. Halophytes, on the other hand,

INTERNET PORTAL

SCiLINKS. NSTA

Topic: Estuaries
Go To: www.scilinks.org
Code: LOP2390

have adaptations that allow them to survive in salt water. Thanks to these adaptations, halophytes occupy a niche with little competition from other plants, and become the dominant species.

Halophytes in the lower marsh deal with flooding from salt water. The hollow reed *Spartina* sp., called cordgrass, is a good example of halophyte adaptation to this part of the ecosystem.

Figure 16-13

Salt marsh plant community.

A cross-section of a typical temperate salt marsh community along the US east coast, showing common submerged and emergent aquatic vegetation.

Figure 16-14

Salt marsh food web.

This typical food web of a salt marsh outlines three ecosystems - Benthic, Aquatic and Terrestrial. Each depends on the other. Bacteria and fungi decompose dead vascular land plants (like pickleweed and cordgrass) to become the all important marine detritus. When these decomposers are consumed, energy flows throughout the web. In the food web, benthic, other aquatic, and terrestrial ecosystems overlap. Follow the lines to visualize the general energy flow. Green lines generally represent autotroph energy flow, red lines heterotroph energy.

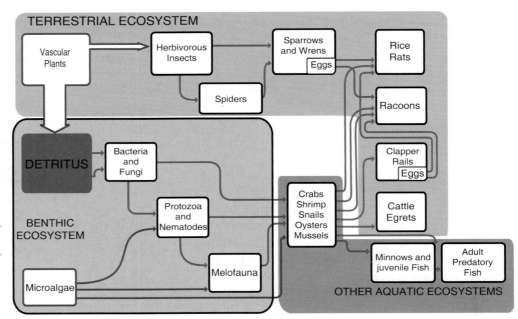

Spartina sp., excludes salt from its tissues and moves oxygen it produces by photosynthesis to its roots.

Plants in the upper marsh only rarely have to deal with seawater. When very high tides bring seawater into the upper marsh, it is easily diluted by the inflow of fresh water from the river. But as you learned earlier, they later have to deal with the accumulated salts left behind by evaporation. Organisms in this part of the ecosystem have different adaptations that help them survive. One example is *Salicornia* sp., or pickleweed. Pickleweed handles excess salt by storing it in sacrificial leaves. When the salt load accumulates to a certain point, the leaf drops away, taking the salt with it. *Salicornia* grows another leaf to take its place.

Halophytes dominate the salt marsh, yet they are not food for many organisms. Salt marsh plants are tough and salty, making them unsuitable for most herbivores. Their root systems hold sediment, which, along with the accumulation of dead halophytes, creates dense mats of *detritus*. In the salt marsh, *detrital mats* provide habitats for huge communities of invertebrates, water birds, juvenile fish, larva, eggs, and other organisms. As discussed in Chapter 4, bacteria and fungi decompose organic matter. In salt marshes, decomposition of detritus is an important part of the food web, as shown in Figure 16-14.

Mangrove Swamps

What two characteristics of mangrove trees allow them to survive in the coastal environment?

Chapter 5 discusses mangrove swamps (also called mangrove forests or just mangroves for short) and their important role in the marine environment, especially coral reefs. Mangrove trees are not a single species, but actually a group of more than 50 species from several families of halophytic trees and shrubs.

In many respects, mangroves occupy similar niches as the halophytes that characterize salt marshes, but they're bigger, tougher,

Mark Sramek, Restoration Center, SE Region, NOAA

Louise Kane, Restoration Center, NOAA

Figure 16-15

Estuarine plants.

Spartina sp., commonly known as cordgrass, is wide-ranging. A true halophyte, *Spartina* sp., excludes salt from its tissues and moves oxygen it produces by photosynthesis to its roots.

Figure 16-16

Estuarine plants.

Salicornia sp., commonly known as pickleweed, deals with excess salt by storing it in sacrificial leaves. These salt-laden leaves drop off, taking the salt with them. Another leaf then grows to take its place.

OAR, National Undersea Research Program, NOAA

Figure 16-17

Red mangroves.

Red mangroves (*Rhizopora mangale*) grow above the waterline on stilt-like roots. They obtain fresh water by a form of reverse osmosis, which allows fresh water from the sea to move into the roots while excluding the salts.

Figure 16-18

Black mangrove pneumatophores.

The roots of the black mangrove (*Avicennia germinans*) grow in the sediment below the waterline. Tubes called *pneumatophores* act as snorkels to provide air to the roots in the muck. The trees eliminate salt through special glands in their leaves.

Figure 16-19

White mangroves.

White mangroves (*Laguncularia racemosa*) lack specialized adaptations. They are very saltwater tolerant, but usually live above the high tide line where they do not need special root adaptations.

and found in tropical climates. Mangrove species have various adaptations that allow them to live in salt water and anaerobic mud.

Red mangroves, *Rhizopora* sp., grow in the intertidal zone on stilt-like roots. This allows oxygen to reach the roots. *Rhizopora* sp. obtains fresh water by filtering seawater through its adapted roots, which exclude the salt. This is an example of *reverse osmosis*, which is the process of transporting water through a semipermeable membrane against the natural osmotic pressure gradient. This is a form of active transport, which is the process of a cell moving materials from areas of low concentration to areas of high concentration.

Mangroves of the genus *Avicennia* sp. (black mangroves) have roots that grow in the sediment below the waterline. These mangroves aerate their roots with snorkel-like root structures called *pneumatophores*, which draw air from above the water's surface. Some *Avicennia* sp. eliminate salt through sacrificial leaves, like the pickleweed. Others have special glands in their leaves that excrete salt.

White mangroves, *Laguncularia* sp., lack such specialized adaptations. They are very saltwater tolerant, but usually grow above the high tide line where they do not need special root adaptations. These mangroves receive sufficient freshwater runoff to survive.

Regardless of the species or the adaptations, mangroves share two important characteristics that make them the basis of mangrove ecosystems. First, they have strong, tangled roots that provide habitats for juvenile fish and invertebrates. As in salt marshes, this tangled root habitat provides a nursery for nearby marine ecosystems, particularly coral reefs. Second, because of their intertangled root systems, mangroves hold the soil well, which protects the shoreline from erosion from tidal currents, waves, and storm surges. This is especially important in a tropical setting where violent storms are frequent. Without the strong mangrove root systems, tropical storms would quickly wash away many tropical islands and beaches.

As discussed in Chapter 5, mangroves trap nutrients, much as marshes do, helping to protect coral reefs and other nearby marine ecosystems from eutrophication. However, because they are swampy, sulfide-smelling mosquito havens, until relatively recently people viewed them as wastelands. Today we know they are ecosystems crucial to the global ecosystem, but mangroves continue to vanish because of social pressures covered in the next few chapters.

Randolph Femmer, National Biological Information Infrastruture

Figure 16-20

Coastal sentinels.

Mangroves are crucial ecosystems in the subtropics and tropics. In addition to their ecosystem function, they protect coastlines from erosion.

Seagrasses

How do seagrasses differ from other halophytes?

How do seagrass ecosystems differ from other halophyte-based ecosystems?

Seagrass ecosystems are similar to other halophyte-based ecosystems in that they stabilize sediments and provide shelter and habitats for other organisms. However, seagrasses differ from other halophytes in several important ways that make them and their ecosystems distinct.

Seagrasses are rooted, vascular, flowering plants that live entirely under water except during rare, very low tides. Seagrasses live in protected shallow coastal areas where light can penetrate to the bottom. Some species live as deep as 30 meters (100 feet), provided the water is clear enough to allow at least 20% of surface light to reach the bottom. You may find seagrasses growing adjacent to mangrove or salt marsh ecosystems. More commonly, though, seagrass grows in colonies spread across the bottom like underwater pastures. Their root systems intertwine, forming a mat below the sediment. Most species release pollen into the current to reproduce, much like terrestrial plants release pollen into the wind.

Unlike most halophytes, seagrasses are edible and provide food for some ecosystem inhabitants. They are heavily grazed by sea turtles, manatees and dugongs.

Heather Dine, Florida Keys National Marine Sanctuary, NOAA

Figure 16-21

Seagrasses.

Seagrasses grow in underwater pastures, sometimes spreading across vast areas of the sea bottom. Their root systems intertwine, forming a mat that helps to retain and stabilize the sediment. Most species release pollen into the current to reproduce, much like terrestrial plants release pollen into the wind.

1. **Coastal ecosystems are generally highly productive because (choose all that apply)**

   A. they benefit from nutrient-rich runoff from land.

   B. benthic organisms can live in the upper photic zone.

   C. plants provide shelter.

   D. large organisms typically dominate them.

2. **Human activities have wide-ranging potential effects on coastal ecosystems because (choose all that apply)**

   A. people have settled near coasts.

   B. agricultural fertilizer can cause eutrophication of coastal ecosystems.

   C. effects of the activities may not always be obvious.

   D. trophic pyramids are unstable in coastal ecosystems.

3. **Eutrophication is**

   A. the trophic pyramid common to European estuaries.

   B. pollution that results from dumping toxins into the ocean.

   C. pollution that results from excess nutrients in the ocean.

   D. none of the above

4. **Factors that limit the productivity of estuary ecosystems include (choose all that apply)**

   A. a lack of seawater.

   B. the need to survive osmotic stress.

   C. the depletion of the oxygen in the sediments.

   D. excessive growth of benthic organisms.

5. **Estuary ecosystems act as nurseries for more than_____% of commercial fish species.**

   A. 25

   B. 50

   C. 75

   D. 90

6. **Estuaries contribute to the productivity of surrounding marine ecosystems by (choose all that apply)**

   A. providing a nursery for juveniles of many species.

   B. providing a steady stream of nutrients.

   C. allowing all sediment from storm runoff to reach them.

   D. encouraging eutrophication.

7. **In the _____ marsh of a salt water marsh, organisms must deal with salt water as a regular part of the tidal cycle. The _____ marsh, by contrast, includes areas rarely flooded by tides.**

   A. upper, lower

   B. inner, upper

   C. lower, upper

   D. outer, lower

8. **Adaptations that allow halophytes to survive in salt water include (choose all that apply)**

   A. reverse osmosis.

   B. pneumatophores.

   C. sacrificial leaves.

   D. salt glands.

9. **Characteristics that allow all mangroves to survive in the coastal environment include (choose all that apply)**

   A. a strong, tangled root system.

   B. adaptations that draw air from above the water's surface.

   C. special leaves that do not require light for photosynthesis.

   D. the ability to hold soil well.

10. **Seagrasses differ from other halophytes because they (choose all that apply)**

    A. live entirely under water.

    B. can live in deeper water.

    C. provide shelter and habitats for other organisms.

    D. release pollen under water.

11. **Seagrass ecosystems differ from other halophyte-based ecosystems because (choose all that apply)**

    A. they do not require a freshwater source.

    B. they can exist in deeper water.

    C. the seagrasses provide food for ecosystem inhabitants.

    D. they do not require sunlight.

Coastal Ecosystems – Intertidal Zones, Beaches, Kelp and Seaweed, Coral Reefs

Intertidal Zones

What are the greatest challenges to life in supralittoral ecosystems?

What conditions challenge organisms in littoral ecosystems?

When we think of coastal ecosystems, we tend to think of mangroves, estuaries, and similar ecosystems. The numerous complex organisms make their productivity conspicuous. However, in *every* place the ocean touches land, you will find a coastal ecosystem with rich communities.

Ecosystems in the world's intertidal zones exist in areas that are above the waterline at times, and below at other times. Where tidal ranges are high, intertidal zones can reach depths of about 10 meters (33 feet).

The supralittoral zone, as discussed in Chapter 3, is the area only submerged during the highest tides. The greatest challenges facing organisms that live in supralittoral ecosystems are drying and thermal stress. A constant spray of seawater that evaporates also results in high salt levels.

Organisms with habitats in the supralittoral zone have adaptations that help them retain moisture. Unlike many marine organisms, they can either obtain oxygen from the air or store sufficient oxygen in their tissues to endure many hours out of the water.

Nancy Sefton, Earthwise Media

Capt. Albert E. Theberge, NOAA Corps

Figure 16-22a

Figure 16-22b

The supralittoral zone.

Organisms in the supralittoral zone have adaptations that help them retain moisture.
They can either obtain oxygen from the air or store sufficient oxygen in their tissues to endure
many hours out of the water. They are also hardy enough to withstand drying and thermal stress.

Topic: Intertidal Zone
Go To: www.scilinks.org
Code: LOP2400

Additionally, they need to be hardy enough to withstand periodic water motion and pounding by waves. Barnacles, periwinkles, and limpets are examples of organisms particularly well adapted to life in rocky supralitttoral zones.

The rest of the *littoral zone* (the area between high and low tide) faces similar challenges. However, life here is not left above the surface for extended periods like the supralittoral zone. Organisms in littoral ecosystems also face the challenges of drying out, thermal stress, increased salinity, decreased dissolved oxygen, and water motion. Progressing seaward, the environment becomes less stressful with respect to drying out and thermal stress, though waves and surge remain challenges. Many supralittoral organisms also thrive here, along with seaweeds, anemones, and mussels.

The lowest part of the littoral zone is rarely exposed to air—only at extremely low tides. With ample water, nutrients, and sunlight, this is a highly productive region in most coastal ecosystems. One challenge to life here, therefore, is intense competition.

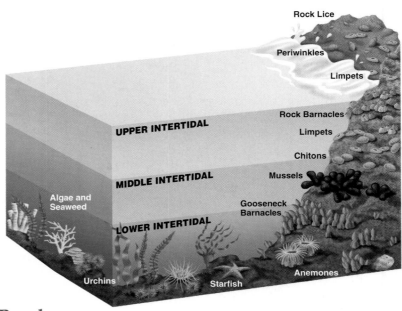

Figure 16-23

Rocky shore community.

Beaches

How do beaches affect other marine ecosystems?

To the untrained eye, the typical sandy beach appears nearly devoid of life. It looks almost like a desert, with only an occasional shell or sea star. The reality is that beaches are rich and productive ecosystems. They also have important characteristics that affect other marine ecosystems.

As discussed in Chapter 15, much of the sand results from weathering and erosion of the continents and from the tests of marine creatures. Scientists think that the sands on the world's beaches may have migrated for thousands of years before being deposited on a beach.

Sand protects the coastline. As a wave comes ashore, it picks up sand. Each sand grain dissipates a miniscule portion of wave energy. That portion times billions and billions of sand grains reduces the forces that wear away the coastline. This is one way that beaches affect ecosystems.

Beach ecosystems are rich in organisms living on the organic material in the sand mix. Complex organisms, including worms, mollusks, and fish live in the submerged beach sand. As you learned earlier in this chapter, meiofauna are the benthic organisms that live in the spaces between sand grains. They are so diverse that the community of a single beach ecosystem could take years to catalog. About a third of all known animal phyla have representatives in the meiofauna. Additionally, algae and other non-animal organisms live among the sand grains.

The interaction among water motion, meiofauna, and large scavengers on the beach provides a second way that beaches affect other marine ecosystems. They clean the water. Many organic and inorganic substances that wash onto a beach are broken down by the physical and organic processes in the beach ecosystem.

Ken Kurtis/www.reefseekers.com

Figure 16-24

Beach dwellers.

One of the largest infauna found on sandy beaches are the mole crabs (*Emerita sp.*), also known as sand crabs (crabs about as big as your thumb). They can be found quickly borrowing back into the sand as waves wash back to sea.

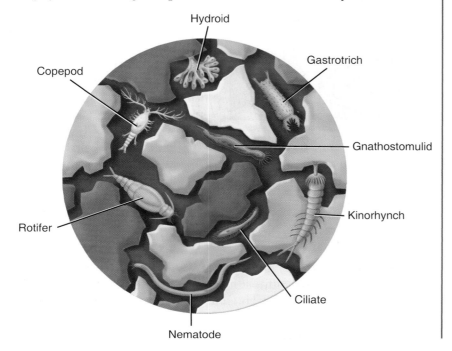

Figure 16-25

Life at the beach.

Beach ecosystems include worms, mollusks, and fish that live in the submerged beach sand. The organisms living among the sand grains, while tiny, are so diverse that about a third of all known animal phyla have representatives in the meiofauna.

Kelp and Seaweed Ecosystems

How has human hunting of sea otters disrupted the ecological balance of kelp forest ecosystems?

As discussed in Chapter 5, seaweed refers to a diverse group of red, green, and brown algae. All of these provide the bases for ecosystems among their stipes, holdfasts, and blades. Among these, kelp ecosystems are probably the most diverse.

You find kelp forests globally in cool water. They live there because they require the nutrients found in the cool ocean. The richest and most productive kelp ecosystems exist in coastal waters with upwellings. In clear water with ample sunlight and nutrients, giant kelp (*Macrocystis pyrifera*) can reach 60 meters (196.8 feet) long, providing habitats for a substantial ecosystem. Kelp forests and other seaweed-based ecosystems are among the most biologically productive ecosystems. Their primary production exceeds the primary productivity of terrestrial forests and is almost equal to the productivity of coral reefs.

Because of its dependence on sunlight, cool water, and nutrients, kelp responds noticeably to environmental changes. For example, during El Niño Southern Oscillation (ENSO) events (discussed in Chapter 11), there are massive die-offs of kelp along the California coast. The normal upwelling of cold, nutrient-rich water does not take place during ENSO. Instead, the water temperature is much higher than normal and the water has fewer nutrients available to the kelp. This disrupts the local ecosystems for a year or more.

Kelp provides a clear example of why it is important to study ecology, not simply individual organisms. Until protected, in some areas the sea otter was hunted nearly to extinction. Amazingly, in these areas, the kelp began to die off rapidly.

The explanation is that while few organisms eat kelp, one that does eat it is the sea urchin. These echinoderms graze on the rubbery holdfasts that anchor the kelp. Sea urchins are also one of the sea otter's primary foods. The energy required by a mammal living in cool seawater is considerable, so the average sea otter eats a substantial number of sea urchins.

Bob Wohlers

Figure 16-26

Underwater forests.

The fastest growing algae known, giant kelp (*Macrocystis pyrifera*) can reach 60 meters (196.8 feet) in length. It provides a lush habitat and supports or is an integral part of one of the most biologically productive ecosystems.

Killing the sea otters disrupted the kelp forest's ecological balance by removing the sea urchin's chief predator. This allowed the sea urchin population to rise relatively unchecked. More sea urchins meant more grazing on kelp holdfasts. Once the holdfasts were eaten away, the kelp floated off and died. In the end, the sea urchins ate the kelp faster than it could grow. This is an excellent example of the interdependence that exists within an ecosystem. It shows that each organism contributes to a balance that allows life to thrive there.

Coral Reefs

What marine ecosystem is thought by many scientists to be the most taxonomically diverse?

Why do coral ecosystems require water that is in moderate motion and free of nutrients?

Why is eutrophication one of the biggest threats to coral ecosystems?

What other threats do coral ecosystems face?

Of all the Earth's ecosystems, few compare to the coral reef. Many scientists believe they are the most taxonomically diverse ecosystems in the ocean. The Indo-West Pacific area between Papua New Guinea and the Sulu and Celebes Seas has the world's largest marine species diversity. More than 2,000 species of fish are known, with new species discovered every year. The further you go from this area, the less

Figure 16-27

Upsetting the balance.
Killing sea otters disrupted kelp forest ecology by removing the sea urchin's chief predator. Without predators, sea urchins can eat kelp faster than it can grow, denuding vast areas of once lush coastal habitat.

INTERNET PORTAL
SCiLINKS. NSTA
Topic: Coral Reefs
Go To: www.scilinks.org
Code: LOP2405

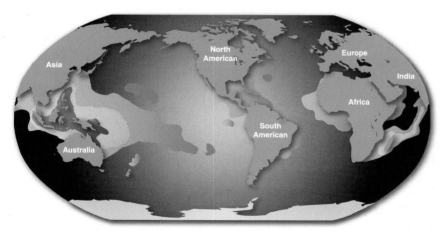

Species Diversity

| 0 | 10 | 50 | 100 | 150 | 200 | 250 | 300 | 350 | 400 | 450 |

Figure 16-28

Coral diversity.
The Indo-West Pacific area between Papua New Guinea and the Sulu and Celebes Seas has the world's largest marine species diversity. More than 500 species of coral are known. Diversity declines the further you go from this area.

diversity you find, which is why many scientists think that present-day species of corals and coral reefs originated in the Indo-West Pacific.

While supporting immense diversity, coral reef ecosystems are also fragile. For a couple of decades now, scientists, divers, and others familiar with coral have been worried about the health of these ecosystems. The conditions coral animals require for life are narrow and specific. These animals live in clear water so that dinoflagellates (zooxanthellae) coexisting in the polyps have light for photosynthesis. These animals also need water that is in moderate motion to prevent sediments from accumulating on the polyps. Particulate matter can clog and smother the polyps. The sediments also reduce the amount of light reaching the algae inside them.

Coral ecosystems also require water that is relatively free of nutrients. This may seem odd considering the high productivity of this ecosystem. However, coral ecosystems efficiently cycle nutrients and other materials within the ecosystem. The lack of nutrients in the water actually protects coral from competitive organisms.

This is why eutrophication is one of the biggest threats to coral ecosystems. A rise in water nutrient levels allows competitive algae to overgrow and smother coral colonies. It also allows plankton to grow, reducing water clarity and the amount of sunlight reaching the polyps. To some extent, these are natural processes, but over the last several decades, eutrophication levels have been rising. Correspondingly, many reefs once dominated by corals now have algae overgrowing them.

Besides eutrophication, thermal stress threatens coral reef ecosystems. A concern is that global climate may raise temperatures above coral's survival threshold. As discussed in Chapter 5, many reef die-offs are attributed to coral bleaching, which occurs when coral polyps reject the zooxanthellae dinoflagellates living in their tissue. Coral bleaching seems to be associated with high temperatures, but agricultural runoff may trigger the bleaching.

Another threat comes from sedimentation resulting from coastal dredging and construction. This causes sediment to accumulate on the polyps more quickly than water motion can remove it. Coral diseases also seem to be more common. These "attacks" by fungi, cyanophytes, bacteria, and algae damage and displace corals. Scientists are still trying to determine the likely sources and causes for many of these diseases.

Dr. James P. McVey, Sea Grant Program, NOAA

Figure 16-29

Coral versus algae.

A rise in nutrient levels allows algae to grow, displacing coral colonies. Today, many reefs once dominated by corals are now covered with mats of algae.

Chapter 18 discusses more about threats to the world's coral reefs. Regardless of the specific threat, it is important to apply the principles of ecology to the overall picture. The concern is not just for the coral alone, but the entire coral ecosystem. Just as the loss of sea otters threatens kelp, the loss of the corals threatens other organisms in the ecosystem.

Parrotfish, for example, feed on coral. If the coral dies, the parrotfish population will decrease as they lose their primary food source. Predators that feed on the parrotfish may similarly suffer. Other organisms will not survive because the competitive algae do not provide the same habitat as a coral reef. The decline of coral is likely to have a domino effect throughout the entire marine ecosystem. Ultimately, that means the loss of coral will affect the global ecosystem in ways that ecologists are still trying to predict.

ARE YOU LEARNING?

1. **The greatest challenges to life in supralittoral ecosystems are**

   A. drying out and thermal stress.

   B. predators and pollution.

   C. drowning and flooding.

   D. none of the above

2. **Conditions that challenge organisms in littoral ecosystems include (choose all that apply)**

   A. drying out.

   B. thermal stress.

   C. water motion.

   D. drowning.

3. **Beaches affect other marine ecosystems by (choose all that apply)**

   A. accelerating coastal erosion.

   B. reducing sedimentation caused by coastal erosion.

   C. breaking down organic and inorganic materials.

   D. acting as a filter that processes compounds entering the sea.

4. **Hunting sea otters disrupted the kelp forest ecological balance because**

   A. sea otters eat kelp, therefore the kelp overpopulated.

   B. sea otters eat sea urchins, which eat kelp.

   C. stray bullets hit and killed kelp.

   D. none of the above

5. **The marine ecosystem that many scientists think is the most taxonomically diverse marine is the _____ ecosystem.**

   A. coral reef

   B. kelp forest

   C. neuston

   D. none of the above

6. **Coral ecosystems require water that is in moderate motion and free of nutrients because**

   A. water motion keeps sediments from accumulating on the coral.

   B. still water with nutrients creates thermal stress.

   C. the presence of nutrients allows competitive algae to grow.

   D. all of the above

7. **Eutrophication is one of the biggest threats to coral ecosystems because it provides nutrients that allow plankton growth, depriving coral of sunlight.**

   A. true

   B. false

8. **Threats facing coral ecosystems include (choose all that apply)**

   A. global climate change.

   B. sedimentation.

   C. coral disease.

   D. competitive algae.

STUDY QUESTIONS

Find the answers as you read.

1. What conditions challenge marine ecosystems in the Arctic?

2. Where and when do you find the most productivity in the Arctic?

3. What makes the Antarctic seas some of the most productive marine ecosystems?

4. What is the northern limit of the Antarctic's productive seas?

INTERNET PORTAL

SCI**LINKS** NSTA

Topic: Polar Marine Ecosystems
Go To: www.scilinks.org
Code: LOP2410

Polar Ecosystems

Because of their nutrient-rich water, the ocean at both poles are among the Earth's most productive seas. The extreme cold and darkness of winter reduce bioproductivity. However, productivity during the warm, long days of summer more than offsets the winter lull. Every species of great whale and many other marine mammals feed in the polar regions. These are the only seas capable of supporting large populations of these energy-hungry giants. While coral reefs are characterized by high diversity of relatively small populations, the polar seas are the opposite. The have low diversity but high populations.

The Arctic

What conditions challenge marine ecosystems in the Arctic?

Where and when do you find the most productivity in the Arctic?

The Arctic Ocean is bordered by the shallow continental shelves of North America, Greenland, Eurasia, and Russia. This northernmost part of the ocean connects to the rest of the ocean at the Bering Straight and the upper North Atlantic. The Arctic is a deep basin, and much of it is a permanently frozen ice cap.

Marine ecosystems in the Arctic face the challenges of reduced sunlight under the ice and water that is barely above freezing. For these reasons, the diversity of organisms is limited under the permanent ice cap. Species that do live in these conditions have special adaptations. For example, Arctic fish have proteins in their blood that act like antifreeze and keep their blood from freezing. Many Arctic organisms have very slow metabolisms. As a result, some fish have no blood hemoglobin. Their blood carries sufficient oxygen without it.

At the edge of the ice cap, however, life intensifies, especially between March and September. As the sun melts ice in the spring, water flows off

Figure 16-30

The Arctic Ocean.

The Arctic is bordered by the shallow continental shelves of North America, Greenland, Eurasia, and Russia. This northern most part of the ocean connects to other parts of the ocean at the Bering Straight and the upper North Atlantic. Much of the Arctic is a permanently frozen ice cap.

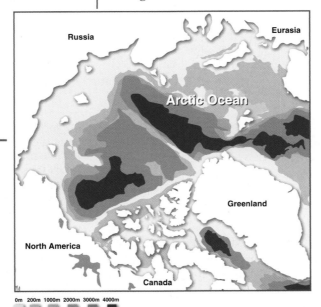

Russia

Eurasia

Arctic Ocean

Greenland

North America

Canada

0m 200m 1000m 2000m 3000m 4000m

the ice, sinking into deep water. Warmer currents from the south interact with the cold water at the continental shelf edges. This process churns up nutrients from the shelf bottom.

Extremely high productivity occurs along an arc in the North Pacific and across the North Atlantic from April to August. These waters support massive fisheries, marine mammals, and other organisms. This ecosystem flourishes from the nutrients churned up from the bottom.

The Antarctic

What makes the Antarctic seas some of the most productive marine ecosystems?

What is the northern limit of the Antarctic's productive seas?

Antarctica has a more extreme climate than the Arctic. Also, the Antarctic differs topographically from the Arctic. Antarctica, is a continent, not a frozen sea. It is also not enclosed by the continental shelves of other continents. Instead, it has its own continental shelf. The deepest and broadest ocean ring surrounds the Antarctic. For these reasons, the Antarctic ecosystem has differences and similarities compared to the Arctic.

During the winter, water at the edges of Antarctica freezes, forming ice sheets and adding an area about the size of North America to the edges of the continent. When summer comes, the melting of these ice sheets sets off an explosion of bioproductivity.

As the temperature of the seawater drops, water molecules join together to form sea ice. When the ice forms, the salts become concentrated in the remaining seawater. This very cold, very salty, very dense water flows down the continental margins of Antarctica and becomes Antarctic Bottom Water, the most dense water in the ocean, as discussed in Chapter 11. Winds blowing along the coast of Antarctica result in Ekman Transport which moves surface water away from the continent, causing upwelling in the area.

Figure 16-31

The Southern Ocean.

Home to the strongest current (the West Wind Drift) and the highest seas on Earth, the Southern Ocean is also highly productive. However, limited by the lack of sunlight through most of the year, this productivity occurs for only a short period during the austral (southern) summer (December through March). This productivity is especially pronounced in the region adjoining the Atlantic, where nutrient-rich water upwells to the surface after its long journey from the northern polar region.

Glenn Grant, National Science Foundation

Figure 16-32

Emperor Penguin.

The Emperor Penguin is the largest of all penguin species. Endemic (only found in) Antarctica, they feed primarily on krill and squid.

This nutrient-rich deep water reaches the surface at the *Antarctic Divergence*, an area located at approximately 65° to 70° south latitude (see Figure 16-31 for location). This is the largest nutrient-rich area on Earth. The Antarctic Divergence supports massive phytoplankton blooms from November through the southern summer. The copepod and krill populations are larger than any other species population found in any other ecosystem. Single krill swarms have been estimated as exceeding 100 million tons, which is more than the world's annual commercial fish catch.

The productive water zone extends northward until it meets the warm Atlantic, Indian, and Pacific waters. At this point, the cold Antarctic water sinks under the warm water. This area is called the Antarctic Convergence. It is located at approximately 50° to 60° south latitude.

As in the Arctic, organisms living in the coldest Antarctic ecosystems have special adaptations. Because the Antarctic is a relatively isolated ecosystem, most species are specialized and found only in the Antarctic.

ARE YOU LEARNING?

1. **Conditions that challenge marine ecosystems in the Arctic include (choose all that apply)**

   A. geothermal heating.

   B. reduced sunlight.

   C. krill swarms.

   D. near-freezing water.

2. **You find the most productivity in the Arctic**

   A. north of Canada from September to November.

   B. surrounding Alaska from April to August.

   C. along the North Pacific and North Atlantic from April to August.

   D. along the North Pacific and North Atlantic from September to November.

3. **The Antarctic seas are some of the most productive marine ecosystems because**

   A. there is no hunting permitted there.

   B. the ocean is warmer than you would expect for the latitude.

   C. rich, deep water surfaces to create the largest nutrient-rich area on Earth.

   D. all of the above

4. **The northern limit of the Antarctic seas is called the _____. It is found at approximately _____.**

   A. Antarctic Convergence, 50° to 60° south latitude

   B. Antarctic Divergence, 50° to 60° south latitude

   C. Antarctic Convergence, 65° to 70° south latitude

   D. Antarctic Divergence, 65° to 70° south latitude

Deep-Sea Ecosystems

The Abyssal Zone

Why is there no primary productivity in most of the deep ocean?

What provides nutrients for most of the deep ocean?

What types of organism are found most commonly in the abyssal zone?

In the deep ocean beyond the continental shelves, the sun's light and warmth never reach the bottom and the average temperature is 2°C (35.6°F). Without sunlight, there is no photosynthesis.

Much of the deep ocean gets its nutrients from *marine snow*. Marine snow is sediment consisting of dead organisms, fecal pellets and other nutrients that constantly falls into the deep ocean from the productive shallow waters above. Most of the deep ocean is the abyssal zone, which covers about 30% of the Earth's surface. This is one of the smoothest and flattest areas on Earth, found at depths between about 3,000 and 4,000 meters (9,843 and 13,123 feet). The abyssal zone lacks dense concentrations of life. However, there is a vast diversity of species.

Marine snow makes the deep ocean rich in nutrients. But, without photosynthesis, there is insufficient energy accumulated to support a great abundance of multicellular organisms. Those that do survive are primarily echinoderms, such as sea cucumbers, sea lilies, and brittle stars. Concentrations of large organisms are rare.

STUDY QUESTIONS

Find the answers as you read.

1. Why is there no primary productivity in most of the deep ocean?

2. What provides nutrients for most of the deep ocean?

3. What types of organism are found most commonly in the abyssal zone?

4. What is a *whale fall*?

5. What stages do whale fall ecosystems go through?

6. What two deep-sea ecosystems have primary productivity associated with chemicals emerging from the Earth?

7. Why do scientists know very little about ecosystems existing in the hadal zone?

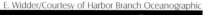
E. Widder/Courtesy of Harbor Branch Oceanographic

Figure 16-33a

Anglerfish.

Looking like something from a Hollywood horror film, this fish only grows to about 20 centimeters (8 inches) and lives in the abyssal zone around 1,000 meters (3,280 feet). Note the glowing "fishing rod" growing from the fish's snout. This organ is used to attract prey.

E. Widder/Courtesy of Harbor Branch Oceanographic

Figure 16-33b

Viperfish.

Although these abyssal zone "monsters" look like they should be huge animals, most are quite small. For example, this viperfish only grows to be about to 30 centimeters (12 inches). In the dark, other fish cannot see the viperfish's fanglike teeth so its mouth becomes an unseen trap.

However, submersibles have seen rattails, deep-sea dogfishes, cat-sharks, crustaceans, mollusks, and many species of deep ocean fish.

The greatest diversity of organisms in the abyssal zone has been found in the meiofauna. As in beach sand, there are representatives from almost all of the animal phyla living in the deep ocean sediments. The concentrations and populations are lower than in shallower seas, but the diversity is not. Scientists have explored only a small portion of the abyssal zone. It is not unusual for new species to be found whenever remotely operated vehicles explore these deep waters, and it is unclear exactly how many animals live there. ROVs are noisy and have bright lights, which may frighten animals away. The abyssal zone is one of the last frontiers on our planet to be explored. There is much left to be discovered about this ecosystem.

Whale Falls

What is a whale fall?

What stages do whale fall ecosystems go through?

Although the abyssal plains are typical of most of the deep ocean ecosystems, there are some important exceptions, including *whale falls*. A whale fall is exactly what the name says – a place where a dead whale comes to rest on the deep ocean floor.

Whale carcasses provide a massive concentration of nutrients in areas that normally only receive diffuse marine snow. Scientists think that the result is the development of a distinct local ecosystem that goes through three distinct stages.

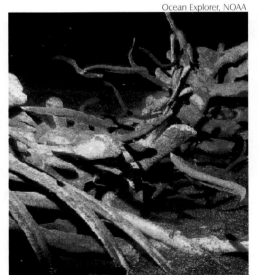

Ocean Explorer, NOAA

The first stage is when the scavengers arrive. They consume the whale's soft tissues in a few months. Hagfish, grenadiers, deep-sea spider crabs, and sleeper sharks are some of the scavengers associated with this stage.

The second stage lasts about a year. Worms, small crustaceans, and other small organisms feed on the remaining soft tissue and the tissue is dispersed

Figure 16-34

Whale fall in Monterey Canyon.

Crabs and an octopus were living on this skull of a dead whale when it was located in October 2002.

around the whale as detritus. Marine biologists are still trying to determine exactly how these organisms find their way to the whale. The current thinking is that larval stages of these animals are widely dispersed in the ocean. When food is available, they settle on to it and complete their development.

The final stage involves the decay of the whale skeleton. This can last several years or even decades. The bones provide a steady supply of sulfide as they are broken down. Chemosynthetic bacteria live on this sulfide, creating a food source for tubeworms, crustaceans, gastropods, and bivalves. These bacteria appear to be the

Ocean Explorer, NOAA

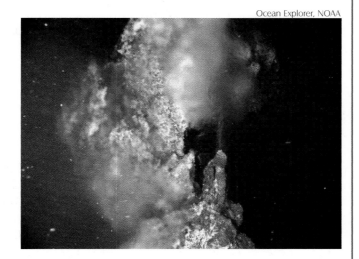

Figure 16-35

Life in the dark.
Hydrothermal vent communities are based on chemosynthesis rather than photosynthesis. Specialized bacteria act as the base of a trophic pyramid, forming a diverse community that includes giant tube worms.

same as those associated with hydrothermal vents. It may be that whale falls enable the colonization of these deep-sea ecosystems. If this is the case, the effects of whaling on these deep ecosystems may be substantial.

Other large organisms sinking to the deep ocean bottom have a similar effect. Wood, kelp, *Sargassum*, and large fish provide a nutrient concentration that supports a local ecosystem for several months to a year.

Hydrothermal Vents and Cold Seeps

What two deep-sea ecosystems have primary productivity associated with chemicals emerging from the Earth?

You have already learned that hydrothermal vents are sources of primary productivity. Around these vents, chemosynthesizing bacteria consume sulfides dissolved in the heated water emerging

INTERNET PORTAL

SCiLINKS. NSTA
Topic:
Chemosynthetic Ecosystems
Go To: www.scilinks.org
Code: LOP2415

from these vents. These bacteria act as the base of a trophic pyramid for a diverse community living in these deep ocean ecosystems.

Similar to hydrothermal vents, cold seeps are places where hydrocarbons and sulfide-rich fluids seep from the underlying rock in the ocean floor. Unlike hydrothermal vents, the water emitted from a cold seep is not hot. Cold seeps were first discovered in 1984 by Dr. Charles Paull in the Gulf of Mexico. Since that time, they have been discovered off the coasts of California, Japan, Costa Rica, Africa, and Alaska, and under an ice shelf in the Antarctica.

Like the hydrothermal vents, cold seeps support chemosynthetic-based ecosystems. In some cold seeps, the chemosythesizers include the same sulfide-consuming bacteria, but in others, the microbes consume methane or other hydrocarbons.

The Hadal Depths – Ocean Trenches

Why do scientists know very little about ecosystems existing in the hadal zone?

Figure 16-36

Another small step for man.
While humans have landed on the moon six times, we have visited the bottom of the deepest ocean only once. On January 23, 1960, Lt. Don Walsh and Dr. Jacques Piccard descended to 11,022 meters—that's 6.85 miles—into an area of the Marianas Trench known as the Challenger Deep. It was done in the bathyscaphe *Trieste* pictured here.

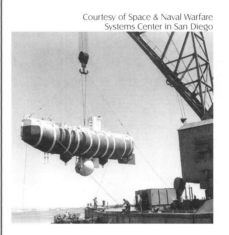

Courtesy of Space & Naval Warfare Systems Center in San Diego

The hadal zone makes up the deepest ocean depths, found in the deep ocean trenches where the oceanic plates collide with continental plates. Depths in this zone range from about 5,000 to 6,000 meters (16,400 to 19,700 feet), although some spots are deeper than 11,000 meters (36,000 feet).

· Scientists know very little about the hadal zone ecosystems primarily because of the limits of technology. The extreme pressure makes it expensive and difficult to make submersibles or instruments capable of observing these depths. Only a few submersibles have been built that can descend safely into the hadal zone, and only a single manned trip has been made to the deepest known spot in the ocean.

Therefore, what scientists know about life in the hadal zone is limited to fleeting glimpses. Most of these are from ROVs (Remote Operated Vehicles) and brief visits by submersibles. These brief observations have found organisms even in the Mariana Trench (the deepest known place on Earth), but the character and extent of the hadal ecosystems remain largely unknown.

1. **There is no primary productivity in most of the deep ocean because**

    A. there are no nutrients.

    B. there is no life there.

    C. there is no sunlight.

    D. it is too cold.

2. **Much of the deep ocean gets its nutrients from**

    A. marine snow.

    B. whale falls.

    C. hydrothermal vents.

    D. cold seeps.

3. **Organisms currently known to exist in the abyssal zone are (choose all that apply)**

    A. echinoderms.

    B. meiofauna.

    C. mammals.

    D. kelp and seagrass.

4. **A whale fall is a**

    A. trap used by whalers to catch whales in deep ocean.

    B. pre-winter period with many whale observations.

    C. place where a dead whale rests on the deep ocean floor.

    D. none of the above

5. **Whale fall ecosystems go through three stages. During the second of these**

    A. scavengers arrive and consume the soft tissues.

    B. small organisms feed on remaining soft tissue.

    C. chemosynthetic bacteria feed on sulfide from the bones.

    D. all of the above

6. **Deep-sea ecosystems that have primary productivity associated with chemicals emerging from the Earth include (choose all that apply)**

    A. the abyssal zone.

    B. whale falls.

    C. hydrothermal vents.

    D. cold seeps.

7. **Scientists know little about ecosystems existing in the hadal zone primarily because there is little interest in studying them.**

    A. true

    B. false

New Terms You Learned

- **abiotic** nonliving (p. 16-3)
- **Antarctic Divergence** an area located at approximately 65° to 70° south latitude where nutrient rich deep water reaches the surface (p. 16-32)
- **biotic** living (p. 16-3)
- **community** a collection of different populations of organisms living and interacting in an ecosystem (p. 16-4)
- **detrital mats** layers of partially decomposed organic matter that provide habitats for communities of invertebrates, water birds, juvenile fish, and other organisms (p. 16-19)
- **detritus** partially decomposed organic matter that makes up a portion of sediments in an aquatic environment; loose material from the break up of organic and inorganic material (p. 16-19)
- **ecology** the science that studies how organisms relate to each other and their environment (p. 16-3)
- **ecosystem** a distinct entity usually with clearly defined physical boundaries, distinct abiotic conditions, at least one energy source, and a community of interacting organism through which energy is transferred (p. 16-3)
- **eutrophication** an overabundance of nutrients that causes an ecological imbalance (p. 16-15)
- **habitat** the area and conditions in which you find an organism (p. 16-4)

- **halophytes** saltwater plants (p. 16-16)
- **littoral zone** area between the high tide mark and the low tide mark (p. 16-24)
- **marine snow** sediment consisting of dead organisms, fecal pellets and other nutrients that constantly fall into the deep ocean from the productive shallow water above (p. 16-33)
- **meiofauna** tiny organisms that live in the spaces between sand grains on the sea floor (p. 16-5)
- **microhabitat** a type of habitat that exists on a very small scale (p. 16-5)
- **niche** an organism's role in its habitat; its job (p. 16-5)
- **pneumatophores** snorkel-like root structures on some mangrove species that draw air from above the water's surface (p. 16-20)
- **population** a group of the same species living and interacting within a community (p. 16-4)
- **reverse osmosis** the process of transporting material through a semipermeable membrane against the natural flow of diffusion (p. 16-20)
- **whale falls** places where dead whales come to rest on the deep ocean floor, resulting in a high nutrient concentration and a local ecosystem (p. 16-34)

Chapter 16 in Review

1. Explain what ecology is, and how it differs from ecosystem.

2. Define the terms ecosystem, community, population, habitat, microhabitat and niche, with an example of each.

3. Explain how the flow of energy through the food web affects an ecosystem.

4. Which nutrient cycle is the basis for all biomass in all the ecosystems on Earth? Why? Which nutrient cycle is thought to be limited in marine ecosystems compared to terrestrial ecosystems. Why?

5. Explain why you generally find the most productive marine ecosystems in cold, temperate regions. Which marine ecosystem is the most productive on Earth? Does it conform to this principle? Why or why not?

6. How does the neuston ecosystem differ from deeper ecosystems in the euphotic zone ecosystem?

7. What organisms may be 10,000 times more numerous in the top few millimeters of water than in water just a few centimeters deeper? Why? List and explain the two factors that can account for low primary productivity in the neuston ecosystem. What is the world's largest floating ecosystem?

8. Explain the significance of the neritic zone as a marine ecosystem.

9. Explain why upwelling is significant to open ocean ecosystems. Explain how this relates to the Antarctic seas being some of the most productive marine ecosystems. How does upwelling relate to the northern limit of Antarctic's productive seas?

10. Explain why coastal ecosystems are generally highly productive. Why do human activities have wide-ranging potential effects on these ecosystems?

11. Explain eutrophication; what causes it, and why it is a big threat to coral reefs?

12. What factors limit the productivity of estuary ecosystems?

13. Explain how estuaries contribute to the productivity of surrounding marine ecosystems. About what percentage of commercial fish species use estuary ecosystems as nurseries?

14. Compare and contrast the differences in conditions between the upper and lower regions of a salt marsh.

15. List the adaptations halophytes use to survive in salt water. What is the advantage of being a halophyte?

16. What two characteristics of mangrove trees allow them to survive in the coastal environment?

17. Compare and contrast seagrasses with other halophytes. Compare and contrast seagrass ecosystems with other halophyte-based ecosystems.

18. Compare and contrast the challenges organisms in supralittoral and littoral ecosystems face.

19. Explain how beaches affect other marine ecosystems.

20. Explain why killing sea otters threatened kelp. What ecological principle does this illustrate?

21. Explain why coral reefs require water that is in moderate motion. What dangers other than eutrophication threaten coral reefs? Which one of these threats relates to this need for water motion?

22. Identify the conditions that challenge marine ecosystems in the Arctic. What adaptations do some organisms have to meet these challenges?

23. Where and when do you find the most productivity in the Arctic? Why?

24. Where does most of the deep ocean get its nutrients? Why is there no primary productivity in most of the deep ocean?

25. Describe the types of organisms found most commonly in the abyssal zone. Why do you find few large multicellular organisms there?

26. Describe the stages of a whale fall, and explain its significance to abyssal environments.

27. Compare and contrast the primary production of hydrothermal vent ecosystems with cold-seep ecosystems.

28. Explain why scientists know little about the ecosystems in the hadal zone.

Connecting Chapter Concepts – Science Scenarios

1. Every part of the ocean is an ecosystem, from where land meets sea to the bottom of the deepest trenches. The open ocean has ecosystems that have little or no contact with land or the bottom.
    A. What marine ecosystem covers more of the Earth than any other? Why is it important, and why is it under a lot of scrutiny by scientists?
    B. What zone is the most productive region in the ocean? Why?
    C. What and where is the Sargasso Sea? What keeps it in its place?
    D. Why are upwellings important to open ocean ecosystems?
2. Coral reefs are thought by many scientists to be the most taxonomically diverse ecosystems in the ocean. They are highly productive ecosystems that require conditions that are very narrow and specific.
    A. Coral reefs require water that is very low in nutrients, which may seem surprising considering their high productivity. Why is this? What allows such high productivity despite nutrient-free water?
    B. What are the two major threats to coral reefs? How do they threaten the reefs?
    C. Why are mangrove swamps important to coral reefs and other adjacent ecosystems?

Marine Science and the Real World

1. Earth is an ecosystem made up of millions and millions of smaller ecosystems. Is outer space part of Earth's ecosystem? Why or why not? Is Earth part of a solar system ecosystem? Why or why not?
2. The example of hunting sea otters is just one in which human activity has disrupted one part of an ecosystem with unanticipated consequences elsewhere in the system. Give some other examples, real or imagined.
3. If whale falls allow chemosynthesizing bacteria to spread from one area to another, then the whaling industry may be affecting the deep-sea ecological balance. Explain this.
4. Some people say that ecology is the most important natural science going into the 21st century. Do you agree or disagree? Defend your answer.

References

Atkinson, A., et al. 2001. *South Georgia, Antarctica: A Productive, Cold Water, Pelagic Ecosystem. Marine Ecology Progress Series.* 216.

Barnes, R.S.K. and R.N. Hughes. 1982. *An Introduction to Marine Ecology.* Blackwell Scientific Publications.

Constable, A.J. et al. 2003. Southern Ocean Productivity In Relation To Spatial And Temporal Variation In The Physical Environment. *Journal of Geophysical Research.* 108 (C4).

Jefferson, T.A., et al. 1993. *Marine Mammals of the World.* FAO Species Catalogues.

Korb, R.E, and M. Whitehouse. 2004. Contrasting Primary Production Regimes Around South Georgia, Southern Ocean: Large Blooms Versus High Nutrient, Low Chlorophyll Waters. *Deep-Sea Research and Oceanographic Abstracts.* I51.

Kurlansky, M. 1997. *Cod: A Biography Of The Fish That Changed The World.* New York: Walker and Company.

Mitsch, W. J. and J. G. Gosselink. 1993. *Wetlands*, 2nd edition. Van Nostrand Reinhold, New York.

Moore, J.K. and M.R. Abbott. 2000. Phytoplankton Chlorophyll Distributions And Primary Production In The Southern Ocean. *Journal of Geophysical Research.* 105 (C12).

Pauly, D., et al. 1998. Fishing Down Marine Food Webs. *Science.*

Peck, L. 2002. Ecophysiology Of Antarctic Marine Ectotherms: Limits To Life. *Polar Biology.* 25.

Priddle, J., et al. 1998. Reexamining The Antarctic Paradox : Speculation On The Southern Ocean As A Nutrient Limited System. *Annals Of Glaciology.* 27.

Smith, C. 2004. Whale Falls, Wood Or Kelp: A Bonanza For Life In The Deep Sea. http://www.oceanexplorer.noaa.gov/edu/oceanage/04baco_taylor/media/smithwhalefalls.pdf

UCMP. 2004. Berkeley Guides To Taxa. www.ucmp.berkeley.edu/help/taxaform.html

USGS. 1999. Exploring The Deep Ocean Floor: Hot Springs And Strange Creatures. http://pubs.usgs.gov/publications/text/exploring.html

Dover, Van, et al. 2002. Evolution And Biogeography Of Deep Sea Vent And Seep Invertebrates. *Science.* 295.

Wayne County Regional Educational Service Agency. 2004. Hydrothermal Environments of the Ocean Floor. www.resa.net/nasa/ocean_hydrothermal.htm

Whitehead, P.J.P., et al. 1985. *Clupeoid Fishes of the World.* FAO Species Catalogues.

CHAPTER 17

Marine Resources

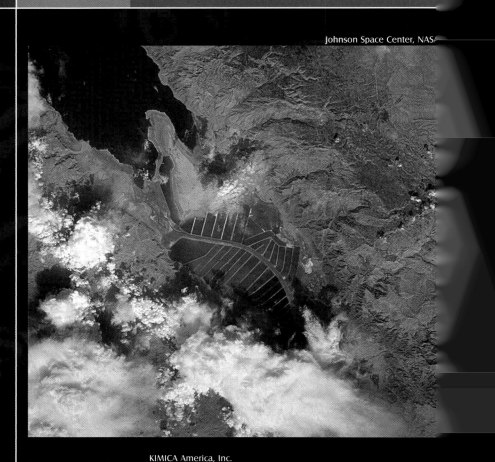

Johnson Space Center, NASA

KIMICA America, Inc.

Not Just for Dinner Anymore

From the common horseshoe crab (whose blood can detect harmful bacteria) to Fiji's exotic cone snail (whose toxin holds promise as a painkiller), aquatic organisms are becoming the laboratory animals of choice for medical research. In fact, research scientists including Amy Wright believe marine creatures may be the key to curing medical conditions such as cancer, heart disease, or even AIDS.

With her doctoral degree in organic chemistry, Wright searches for new medicines that can be derived from the tissues of marine invertebrates, algae, and microorganisms. In particular, she looks for small organic molecules that can be used to treat human disease and suffering. These types of medicines are known in her field as natural products.

"Most people are familiar with looking at terrestrial organisms for new medicines. An example of a plant-derived natural product is morphine, while erythromycin is an important antibiotic made by bacteria. We are looking for similar types of compounds, but from organisms that live in the sea, in the hopes of finding new treatments for cancer, drug-resistant bacterial infections, or neurodegenerative diseases such as Alzheimer's disease."

Among her proudest moments, Wright counts contributing to the delivery of new cancer drugs, such as ecteinascidin–743 and discodermolide, to clinical trials. These two drugs are at various stages of the approval process.

Science was a natural choice for Wright. She grew up, as she puts it, "surrounded by science." Her father was an aerospace engineer and her mother, armed with a mathematics degree, made sure Wright and her siblings learned the fundamentals of reading, writing, and arithmetic. Coupled with her love of boats and the ocean, a career in marine science seemed ideal.

"I grew up near the Pacific Ocean and I love being on, in, or around the water, either boating, swimming, diving, body-surfing, or even just looking at the ocean. From the time I was very small, my parents – who have always been a major inspiration – took us to tide pools and beaches all over the west coast of the US."

To students considering careers in marine science, Wright says: "Focus on the basics and get a sound background in chemistry, biology, math, physics, and computer science and then choose a specialty based upon what you like the best. You should also participate in as many research activities as possible: Volunteer at a museum or lab (company, university, etc.) if you can. Look for places that encourage young people to work with scientists conducting real research and apply for internships. There's so much to choose from when it comes to science. Take the time to get the experience you need so that you may choose well."

Amy E. Wright, PhD
Director, Center for Marine Biomedical and Biotechnology Research, Harbor Branch Oceanographic Institution at Florida Atlantic University

Seafood has shaped history. The history of North America and the growth of the early settlements in New England and Newfoundland can be told through the history of cod fishing. For centuries the Basques kept the secret of their source of cod, making the journey from the Bay of Biscay to Newfoundland and salting cod to preserve it for the markets of Europe. The story of human effects on biological resources such as fish stocks is a tale still being played out as fishing communities like Gloucester and New Bedford, Massachusetts that have flourished for 400 years. The industrial revolution changed fishing forever, evolving practices from hook and line to steam trawlers and beyond so that by the 1930s, the effect on fish stocks was already evident.

The history of cod includes the European push for exploration and modern disputes between countries. Chapter 7 discusses the dispute between the United Kingdom and Iceland over this fishery in the 1970s Cod Wars, though its significance goes back almost a thousand years.

Chapter 2 covers the warming of the global climate that opened normally frozen North Atlantic passages, allowing the Vikings to reach North America in approximately 985 A.D. According to some accounts, the Vikings survived on dried cod, which they also used for trade.

Throughout the European Middle Ages, cod and other fisheries were crucial. Under the feudal system, the common people couldn't hunt because the nobles owned the land and its wildlife. They farmed, but nobility owned or protected the farmland, so that a good portion of each crop went to the noble family. An important protein source that closed the gap between the limited crops and starvation was, again, cod. By the year 1000 the Basques had established an international trade in cod caught in distant waters and salted prior to transport. From the remains of fish bones around England, British archeologists have discovered that by 1050 A.D., a major shift in people's diet from eating freshwater fish to eating marine fish had taken place. Cod became so important that by the mid 1500s, it made up more than half the fish eaten in Europe, and the British had already been involved in the first of many disputes over cod fisheries.

Marine resources range from food to potential medicines to minerals on the seabed to potential energy. Chapter 2 also covers the search for resources that motivated much of the ocean's exploration. Sometimes the sea is a resource simply as a "highway" for carrying goods or military power across the globe.

All resources have environmental and political significance because they all have economic value. From the European voyages of discovery discussed in Chapter 2 to today's study of minerals and the ecosystems supporting the major fisheries, nearly all ocean investigation and exploration have been motivated directly or indirectly by economics. In this chapter, we'll look at the many resources that humans get from the sea and some of the international laws that have originated over these resources. You'll also see we're perilously close to losing some of them.

Resource Classification

What is the difference between a renewable resource *and a* nonrenewable resource?

What is the difference between a physical resource *and a* biological resource?

Why are some potentially renewable resources currently nonrenewable resources?

Because there is a broad range of marine resources, let's begin by classifying them into different areas. Two common categories are *renewable* and *nonrenewable resources* and *physical* and *biological resources.*

Renewable resources are those that growing organisms, sunlight, or other processes naturally replace. Nonrenewable resources are those that natural processes don't replace, or that do so at such a slow rate that they're not replenished in a human lifespan.

Biological resources are those that involve bioproductivity, such as fish stocks and kelp harvesting. Physical resources don't involve biological processes. These include minerals, energy production, and recreation.

Find the answers as you read.

1. What is the difference between a *renewable resource* and a *nonrenewable resource?*

2. What is the difference between a *physical resource* and a *biological resource?*

3. Why are some potentially renewable resources currently nonrenewable resources?

Figure 17-1

Taking too much.

This is a commercial fishing vessel with a full net. The ocean has its limits. Overfishing can turn marine organisms into a nonrenewable resource.

As you'll see in more detail, many physical resources, such as oil and natural gas, are nonrenewable. Some, such as wave energy, are renewable because the sun replenishes the energy source daily. People tend to think of biological resources as renewable, and in many cases they are. However, while most marine biological resources are *potentially* renewable, most are *effectively* nonrenewable. This happens when a fishery takes a species from the ocean faster than it can reproduce to maintain its population. Whaling and commercial fishing, which you'll read more about in this chapter, are two of many examples of unsustainable exploitation.

ARE YOU LEARNING?

1. Cod would be considered a _____ resource, whereas oil would be considered a _____ resource.

   A. biological, physical

   B. physical, biological

2. Oysters are currently a _____ resource, but whales are probably a _____ resource.

   A. renewable, nonrenewable

   B. nonrenewable, renewable

3. Some potentially renewable resources are currently nonrenewable because

   A. people don't live long enough.

   B. species are taken faster than they can reproduce and maintain their population.

Nonrenewable Resources

Energy

How are oil and natural gas formed?

Why are the physical characteristics of the surrounding rock important in the search for oil and natural gas?

How do oil companies extract oil and natural gas from the seabed?

What are methane hydrates?

Why aren't methane hydrates currently used as an energy source?

Among the nonrenewable marine resources, at present energy makes the most important economic contribution. Specifically, this refers to petroleum and natural gas.

Petroleum and Natural Gas. About one third of the world's crude oil and about a quarter of the natural gas presently come from offshore sources. Additionally, about a third of their reserves occur along the continental margins. In the US, these lie primarily along the continental shelf off of the central Gulf of Mexico, southern California, and Alaska.

Crude oil or petroleum (from the Greek *petro* meaning *rock* and the Latin *oleum* meaning *oil*) is a complex mix of thousands of different compounds. The most important are *hydrocarbons,* which consist of carbon and hydrogen chains. Hydrocarbons are the source of chemical energy from which refineries distill gasoline, diesel, kerosene, and other fuels. Natural gas, also called *methane* (CH_4), is a gaseous hydrocarbon.

Chapter 14 examines how geologists find petroleum and natural gas in marine and terrestrial sediments. Scientists think petroleum and natural gas originate from the remains of primarily marine organisms, such as plankton and soft-bodied benthic organisms. After these organisms die, they amass in depressions with little water motion, low oxygen, and few scavenging organisms. Anaerobic bacteria (species that don't use oxygen) break down the organic matter into simpler organic compounds, most of which doesn't dissolve in water.

As time passes, sediments accumulate on top of these compounds until they're under high pressure and high temperature. The compounds continue to undergo conversion into hydrocarbons in a process estimated to take millions of years. This completes the transition of these organisms into crude oil.

STUDY QUESTIONS

Find the answers as you read.

1. How are oil and natural gas formed?

2. Why are the physical characteristics of the surrounding rock important in the search for oil and natural gas?

3. How do oil companies extract oil and natural gas from the seabed?

4. What are *methane hydrates?*

5. Why aren't methane hydrates currently used as an energy source?

6. Other then iron and manganese, what other minerals exist in ferromanganese nodules ?

7. Despite their potential value, why aren't ferromanganese nodules exploited as a mineral resource?

8. From what marine resource does about half the worldwide production of magnesium come?

9. What products do manufacturers make using seawater evaporites?

10. What are phosphorite deposits?

11. Why will land-based phosphorite deposits likely remain the primary sources of phosphorus?

12. What potential resources exist at hydrothermal vents in marine muds?

13. What two physical marine resources are second only to gas and oil in terms of their economic value?

INTERNET PORTAL

SCiLINKS. NSTA

Topic: Oil Exploration
Go To: www.scilinks.org
Code: LOP2420

Scientists have concluded that this same process results in methane (natural gas – CH$_4$) along with petroleum. In the case of methane, however, the insoluble compounds progress from petroleum to methane when the process continues for longer periods, or at a higher temperature. This explains why geologists have found few oil deposits below 3,000 meters (9,800 feet), and only natural gas deeper than 7,000 meters (23,000 feet). The pressure and temperature are so high that only methane forms.

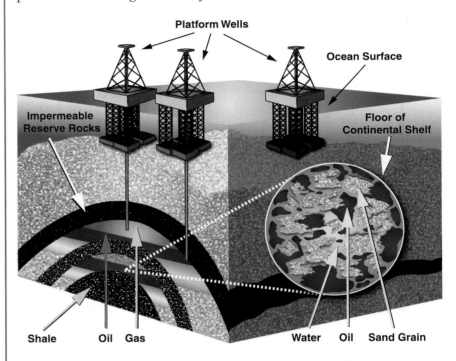

Figure 17-2

Drilling for oil.

Crude oil does not occur in large voids or caverns within the Earth but within the spaces of porous rock, such as sandstone. The oil is confined by impermeable rock, such as shale. Significant amounts of water and natural gas are also present within an oil field.

Chapter 14 explains how oceanographers study sediments with seismic instruments. By studying how sound waves travel and echo within sediment, they can determine variations in density and composition. This method applies well to the search for oil because it is less dense than surrounding sediments. The physical characteristics of the rock surrounding oil and natural gas are important because they determine where the oil or gas collects.

Hydrocarbons form surrounded by sediment called *source rock.* They don't necessarily stay there, however, and may travel through porous sediments lying over it. When hydrocarbons reach rock that they can't penetrate, called *reserve rock,* they collect in the spaces underneath it, allowing the oil or gas to pool. This is called an oil or gas reserve. Sound waves detect the reserves as low-density pockets in the reserve rock.

Oil companies extract petroleum and natural gas by drilling through sediment and rock into the reserve. However, drilling for oil and gas at sea costs substantially more than doing so on land. The most significant differences are that drilling at sea requires a platform from which to drill (oil rig) and special drilling equipment to minimize the risk of an oil spill or gas leak. To support this, offshore drilling frequently involves commercial diving and ROV (Remotely Operated Vehicle) operations to observe and maintain the underwater equipment sections. Offshore drilling platforms have significant safety and transportation costs that range from housing and feeding a crew to emergency medical care.

Despite the cost and complexity, however, offshore drilling continues to grow to meet the demand for oil and gas. Most oil rigs operate in water 100 meters (328 feet) deep or less, but underwater drilling technologies continue to advance to keep up with the world's thirst for oil.

Oil platforms range from relatively simple coastal structures to massive engineering projects with facilities comparable to a major ship or even a small town. They're also reaching into deeper and deeper water. Currently, the largest platform is Statfjord B, con-

Bob Wohlers

Figure 17-3

Oil giants.

The modern generation of oil platforms consists of some of the largest structures ever constructed by humans.

structed in 1981 in the Shetland Islands off the coast of Scotland. The tallest platform is named Ursa, operated by Shell Oil Company, off the Louisiana coast. Ursa is a tension-leg platform that drills in more than 1,220 meters (4,000 feet) of water. Tension-leg platforms float rather than stand on the bottom. Enormous cables anchored into the seabed hold these platforms in place.

Figure 17-4a

Platform Mars.

Figure 17-4b

Redefining big.
Like an iceberg, the size of an oil rig is hidden by the water beneath it. Compare the height of the Mars platform with the skyline of Houston, Texas.

One of the newest deep water platforms is Platform Mars. In 1996, Shell Oil Company found a large oil field in the Gulf of Mexico in about 815 meters (2,674 feet) of water. With an estimated 700 million barrels of oil, the Mars reserve is the largest found in the United States in more than 30 years, yet only represents about 10% of the oil the US consumes annually.

Today, oil companies are taking more risks and drilling ever deeper wells as their shallower wells run dry. In 2005, Chevron and its partners drilled the deepest oil well ever drilled in the Gulf of Mexico, 274 kilometers (170 miles) from New Orleans. The drilling ship hovered over 1,067 meters (3,500 feet) of water and drilled a well to a depth of 10,420 meters (34,189 feet).

Methane Hydrates. There's another form of nonrenewable marine energy source that you may not be familiar with. These are the *methane hydrates*, which are ice crystals containing methane found on the continental slope. The unusual hydrocarbon deposits consist of

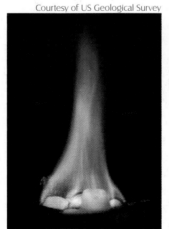

Figure 17-5

Hot rocks.

Although it looks like burning rock, this is methane hydrate. It's a piece of ice containing methane gas. When the ice melts, the methane is released and can burn.

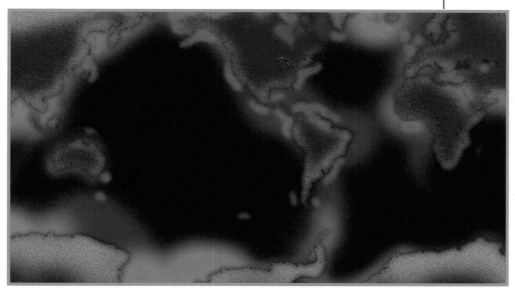

 **Methane Hydrate Deposits**

Figure 17-6

Worldwide locations of methane hydrate deposits.

Methane hydrate deposits have been found throughout the world, especially on the sea bottom. It's estimated that methane hydrate deposits exceed twice the amount of all crude oil and natural gas reserves on Earth.

frozen water molecules that create a "cage" within sediment. Each of these "cages" holds a single methane gas molecule. When you bring methane hydrates to the surface, the ice melts, releasing the methane. You can light a match and ignite the methane emerging from the sediments.

Exactly how methane hydrates form is still unknown, although they're thought to come from a multiple step process that includes both aerobic and anaerobic bacteria. They are normally found in polar sediments and on the continental slope at depths of about 300 to 500 meters (985 to 1,640 feet).

According to the US Geological Survey and US Department of Energy, methane hydrate deposits in US waters may hold from 3,169,000 *trillion* liters (112,000 *trillion* cubic feet) to 19,130,000 *trillion* liters (676,000 *trillion* cubic feet) of methane. Worldwide, more than 11,320 *million trillion* liters (400 *million trillion* cubic feet) of methane are thought to exist in methane hydrates.

Despite this tremendous energy resource potential, currently no one uses methane hydrates as fuel. This is because it's very expensive to recover them and they're relatively dangerous to handle. Technologies for handling methane hydrates are being developed, but there are significant challenges. Because methane is a greenhouse gas and there are vast quantities captured within the ice crystals, methane hydrates could be a problem if changing sea temperatures or the effects of mining caused a sudden release.

INTERNET PORTAL

SCiLINKS. NSTA

Topic: Methane Hydrates
Go To: www.scilinks.org
Code: LOP2425

Salts and Minerals

Other than iron and manganese, what other minerals exist in ferromanganese nodules?

Despite their potential value, why aren't ferromanganese nodules exploited as a mineral resource?

From what marine resource does about half the worldwide production of magnesium come?

What products do manufacturers make using seawater evaporites?

What are phosphorite deposits?

Why will land-based phosphorite deposits likely remain the primary sources of phosphorus?

What potential resources exist at hydrothermal vents in marine muds?

To date, most mineral resources come from terrestrial sources. Nonetheless, the ocean contributes, or has the potential to contribute, to the economic demand for minerals, metals, and salts.

Ferromanganese Nodules. The chapter on sediments discusses that ferromanganese nodules commonly form around shark teeth and volcanic fragments. In addition to iron and manganese, the nodules are rich in copper, nickel, and cobalt, making them tremendously valuable potential resources. Cobalt metal, in particular, has high value for use in many military and industrial applications, such as jet engines. The US armed forces consider cobalt resources in our national defense strategy because there are no adequate cobalt reserves within US borders.

Nodules form in all oceans. Current estimates suggest that the richest nodule deposits, in the Pacific Ocean, account for 16 billion metric tons of cobalt. That's more than all the known terrestrial reserves, and, based on current demand, a supply large enough to meet the world's needs for centuries. This fact alone continues to spark interest in these nodules as a resource.

So far, however, the cost of recovery exceeds the worth of the minerals. This will probably change with technology innovations and rising mineral demand. Japan and Korea presently lead in developing equipment for feasible deep-sea nodule recovery. Another challenge in mining the deep seafloor is international law. You'll read about these concerns near the end of this chapter.

Magnesium Compounds. Magnesium is a strong, lightweight metal essential for aerospace construction and other structural applications. It burns intensely, so it is used in flares and other processes requiring rapid, hot combustion. Magnesium compounds are important in various chemical processes

USAF

Figure 17-7

From sea to air.
Magnesium is an essential component of the metal alloy used in jet aircraft, including the new F-22 Raptor.

involving food, medicine, soil conditions, and other applications.

About half the worldwide magnesium production comes from seawater. Magnesium is the third most abundant element dissolved in seawater, occurring primarily as magnesium chloride ($MgCl_2$) and magnesium sulfate ($MgSO_4$). Electrical and chemical processes extract these compounds from seawater for further refinement and use.

Salts. *Evaporites,* as discussed in Chapter 14, are the salts left behind when seawater evaporates. These salts consist mostly of sodium chloride (NaCl – table salt), but also calcium carbonate, gypsum, and other magnesium-rich and potassium-rich compounds.

Extracting salts by evaporating seawater occurs in many of the world's arid regions. Normally accomplished in large, shallow ponds, the process involves extracting the salts as the brine concentrates through various stages of evaporation. Manufacturers use seawater evaporites in the production of fertilizers, medicines, wallboard and other building materials, and table salt. Table salt is used, in turn, for snow and ice removal, water softeners, agriculture, and food processing.

Phosphorite. Phosphorite (also known as phosphate rock) deposits are thought to be the remains of marine organisms that live in areas with extensive upwelling. The phosphorus in these organisms remains in phosphorite form when these creatures die. Extensive deposits exist off the coasts of the South American Pacific coast, California, Florida, and the African Atlantic coast. Major accumulations of phosphorite are found primarily in a depth range of about 30 to 300 meters (100 to 1,000 feet).

Because phosphorus is important for all life, phosphorite is important in fertilizers used for agriculture. However, much as ferromanganese nodules remain too costly to recover, offshore phosphorite deposits are similarly uneconomical to exploit. For this reason, the approximately 150 million tons of phosphate rock

Johnson Space Center, NASA

Figure 17-8

Salt's not just a seasoning.
Large evaporation ponds called salinas are used to collect salt deposits. Chemicals collected in this way are termed evaporites.

mined annually come from terrestrial sources, which will probably continue for the foreseeable future. Nonetheless, there's no substitute for phosphorus in living systems, and terrestrial reserves may be depleted by the mid 21st century. To avert a crisis in agriculture and industry, the offshore deposits may become important.

Marine Muds and Metals. As discussing in other chapters, hydrothermal vents play important roles in supporting chemosynthetic ecosystems and maintaining seawater chemistry. The superheated seawater ejected from the vents carries large quantities of dissolved metals and minerals. These muds include lead, zinc, copper, iron, silver, cadmium, and sulfur. When the heated water cools in the cold deep-sea water, these precipitate into mounds and chimneys around the vents. This creates a potential source for these minerals and metals.

Mineral sources also exist in places where geothermal heat reaches the seabed. In the Red Sea, for example, this process causes metals and other dissolved compounds to precipitate into basins on the bottom. These hot brines produce muds rich in metal sulfides, silicate, and other oxides in a high enough concentration to make recovering them economically feasible.

Seamounts also have important potential resources. In particular, cobalt deposits have been found throughout the Pacific, including within the US Economic Zone. Seamounts also have a high percentage of endemic fish (in this case meaning fish found only on a particular seamount or chain of seamounts) and unique deep-sea corals and sponges. This makes them particularly vulnerable to damage by ongoing commercial trawl fishing. In 2004, 1,136 representatives from 69 countries signed a proclamation urging the UN and fish-

P. Rona, OAR, National Undersea Research Program, NOAA

Figure 17-9

Hydrothermal vents and minerals.

Hydrothermal vents play important roles in supporting chemosynthetic ecosystems and maintaining seawater chemistry. The superheated seawater ejected from the vents carries large quantities of dissolved metals and minerals. These muds include lead, zinc, copper, iron, silver, cadmium, and sulfur.

ing management bodies to ban trawling in deep-sea ecosystems. In May of 2007, 20 nations including the United States signed an agreement to exclude bottom trawling from the southern Pacific – an area totaling one quarter of the world's ocean. The agreement covers the high seas from Australia to South America and from the Equator to the Antarctic, which is an area that includes many seamounts.

Gravel and Sand

What two physical marine resources are second only to gas and oil in terms of their economic value?

As examined in Chapter 14, sand and gravel are important marine resources. At present, they are the marine resources second only to gas and oil in their annual economic value. Without sand and gravel to make concrete, modern construction would be impossible. Other industries use sand rich in calcium carbonate to make glass, as an animal feed additive, and to reduce soil acidity.

To meet this need, each year industry mines more than 1 billion metric tons of sand and gravel from offshore deposits. Most of these deposits are considered nonrenewable relict deposits.

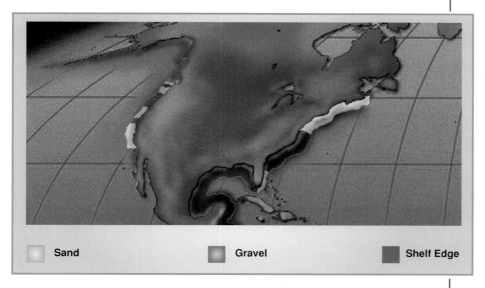

| Sand | Gravel | Shelf Edge |

Figure 17-10

Mining sand and gravel.

In terms of the quantity of minerals extracted from the sea, sand and gravel are second only to crude oil. The map shows the primary regions of the US continental shelf where these resources are mined.

The importance of offshore sand and gravel varies by region. Although about 99% of the world's sand and gravel comes from terrestrial sources, offshore sources account for significantly more in some nations that have better access to marine sources than terrestrial sources.

ARE YOU LEARNING?

1. **Scientists think oil and natural gas form (choose all that apply)**

   A. when coal liquifies.

   B. from methane hydrates.

   C. under high pressure and temperature over long periods.

   D. from the remains of marine organisms.

2. **The physical characteristics of surrounding rock are important in the search for oil and gas because**

   A. there's no way to drill through some types of rock.

   B. nonporous rock traps oil and gas allowing a reserve to form.

   C. seismic instruments can only "see" through sand.

   D. all of the above

3. **Oil companies extract oil and natural gas from the seabed by (choose all that apply)**

   A. drilling from oil rigs.

   B. using special equipment to reduce the risk of oil spills or gas leaks.

   C. using special submarines to dig into the ocean bottom.

   D. none of the above

4. **Methane hydrates are**

   A. a combination of methane and hydrogen.

   B. very scarce.

   C. ice crystals containing methane found on the continental slope.

   D. all of the above

5. **Methane hydrates are not currently used as an energy source because**

   A. they're too scarce to be a realistic resource.

   B. they're difficult to get and dangerous to handle with current technology.

   C. doing so is prohibited by international treaty.

   D. none of the above—methane hydrates are widely used

6. **Besides iron and manganese, ferromanganese nodules consist of (choose all that apply)**

   A. copper.

   B. petroleum.

   C. cobalt.

   D. carbohydrates.

7. **Despite their potential value, ferromanganese nodules aren't exploited as mineral resources currently primarily because**

   A. there are not enough of them to make it worthwhile.

   B. they would make some minerals so cheap that it would destabilize the world economy.

   C. they are an important food source for several whale species.

   D. none of the above

8. **About half of the world's magnesium production comes from**

   A. seawater.

   B. seabed sediments.

   C. methane hydrates.

   D. extraction from natural gas.

9. **Products made from seawater evaporites include (choose all that apply)**

   A. construction materials.

   B. water softeners.

   C. fertilizer.

   D. medicine.

10. **Phosphorite deposits are the remains of marine organisms that live in areas of extensive upwelling.**

    A. true   B. false

11. **Land-based phosphorite deposits will likely remain the primary sources of phosphorus because**

    A. offshore phosphorite deposits are too costly to recover.

    B. the need for phosphate rock is declining.

    C. phosphorite deposits sit directly over important oil reserves.

    D. none of the above

12. **Hydrothermal vents and marine muds are potential sources of minerals and metals including (choose all that apply)**

    A. cobalt.   B. copper.

    C. sulfur.   D. zinc.

13. **Among physical marine resources, _____ is/are second only to gas and oil in terms of their annual economic value.**

    A. methane hydrates

    B. magnesium

    C. sand and gravel

    D. evaporites

Renewable Resources

Energy

In what ways can the ocean supply renewable energy for human use?

Which of the renewable energy sources appears to be the most practical?

Although we customarily think of oil and natural gas when we think of energy from marine resources, the sea offers renewable energy options. Because it rises and falls with waves and tides and captures heat from the sun, the sea provides several types of renewable energy for human use.

There are many ways to capture wave energy, with at least two methods in use. One involves building a caisson (a watertight chamber filled with compressed air), as illustrated in Figure 17-11. The opening under water permits rising waves to compress the air in the chamber, forcing it through a turbine that spins to generate electricity. When the wave passes, the water level in the chamber drops, drawing air back in.

Another method involves a series of buoys attached by vertical rods to the sides of a wheel. As the buoys rise and fall in the waves, they crank the wheel. An axle attached to the wheel turns a generator to produce electricity.

STUDY QUESTIONS

Find the answers as you read.

1. In what ways can the ocean supply renewable energy for human use?

2. Which of the renewable energy sources appears to be the most practical?

3. Why are there growing concerns about fresh water as we move through this century?

4. How do we get fresh water from the sea?

5. What are *nonextractive resources*?

6. What revolutionized sea transport shipping after World War II?

7. What is *ecotourism*?

8. How has ecotourism affected environments both negatively and positively?

INTERNET PORTAL

SC*L*INKS. NSTA

Topic: Wave and Tidal Energy
Go To: www.scilinks.org
Code: LOP2430

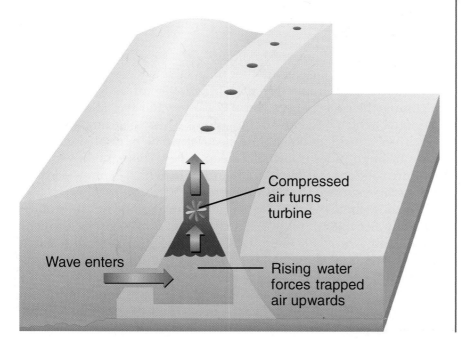

Figure 17-11

Harnessing wave energy.

In this caisson, water forced into the void of the breakwater by waves compresses the trapped air. This forces the compressed air through the hole in the top of the caisson, which turns the turbine blades and generates electricity.

Compressed air turns turbine

Wave enters

Rising water forces trapped air upwards

Tide can be used for energy where the tidal change is 3 meters (10 feet) or more. To generate power, engineers build barriers that act like two-way dams across bays or tidal rivers. When the tide rises, the water spins turbine generators as it flows into the bay. After the tide changes, the water generates power again it flows to the sea. The La Rance Tidal Power Station in France uses this principle to generate more than 500 kilowatts annually.

Figure 17-12

Ocean Thermal Energy Conversion.

Ocean Thermal Energy Conversion (OTEC) uses warm surface water to vaporize liquid ammonia, which has a low boiling point. Pressure from the expanding ammonia gas drives a turbine, which generates electricity. As the ammonia reaches deeper water, it cools and turns back into liquid. The liquid ammonia is then pumped back to the warm shallow water to repeat the process.

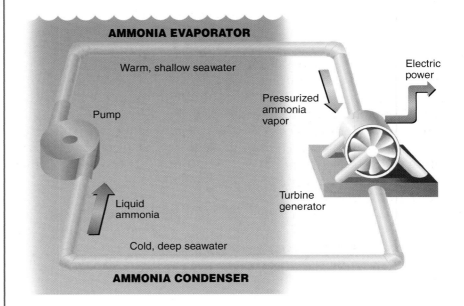

Thermal gradient technology, or *Ocean Thermal Energy Conversion* (OTEC), is yet another renewable energy source. It harnesses the energy trapped in the upper layers of seawater. In simple terms, the process uses warm surface water to vaporize liquid ammonia, which has a low boiling point. The expanding ammonia gas drives a turbine to generate electricity. The ammonia gas then flows through pipes into cooler deep water. There the lower temperature condenses it into liquid ammonia, which is pumped back to the warm surface to repeat the process.

Of these three renewable energy resources, none has been commercially feasible, though that's changing as the cost of conventional energy rises. Of these, tidal power seems the most feasible so far. Using tidal energy has widespread environmental concerns that include ecological damage caused by the massive dams and changes in the flow of nutrients to and from bays and tidal rivers. Thermal gradient technology has been tried experimentally but has largely been abandoned because it has low efficiency.

Fresh Water

Why are there growing concerns about fresh water as we move through this century?

How do we get fresh water from the sea?

It may seem odd to think of fresh water as a marine resource, but it certainly is. The introduction to Chapter 8 outlines the fact that although water covers the majority of the Earth's surface, only a fraction is potable (drinkable) fresh water, and it's not always in ample supply.

The single most important factor that determines how many people can live in a given area is the availability of fresh water. In some places, it costs more per volume than gasoline. The human population is rising, and the demand for fresh water with it. People not only need fresh water to drink and bathe, but for growing food (including livestock) and industry.

Unfortunately, the supply of fresh water isn't keeping pace and there is global concern about the privatization of water, making this resource a growing concern as we move through this century. Some scientists and environmentalists fear that freshwater shortages may become a mounting source of conflict among nations and cultures.

Richard Mass, Veolia Water Photo Library

Extracting fresh water from seawater involves *desalinization* – the removal of dissolved salts. At present, there are more than 7,500 desalinization plants worldwide, 60% of which are in the Middle East. The Western Hemisphere accounts for only about 12% of the fresh water produced by desalinization, with most of that in Florida and the Caribbean. These plants use primarily either *distillation* or *reverse osmosis* to desalinate seawater.

Distillation is the process of evaporating seawater and capturing the water vapor to leave the salts behind. Most plants simply boil seawater, capturing and condensing the water vapor. This is effective, but uses a lot of energy.

About a quarter of all desalinization uses *reverse osmosis*. Reverse osmosis pumps seawater through a semipermeable membrane under pressure. The membrane lets the water molecules through,

Figure 17-13

Turning salt water to fresh.
Because more than 97% of all water on Earth is seawater, desalinization plants offer great hope in supplying a growing world demand for fresh water - especially in arid regions.

but holds back the salt. This requires far less energy than boiling or freezing water, but the membranes are fragile and expensive.

There are inventors working on low-cost desalinization technologies. One example is covering large shallow pools of seawater with plastic and recovering the condensation that forms underneath the covers. There's even a bottled water company that melts icebergs on special barges to get fresh water.

Nonextractive Resources

What are nonextractive resources?

What revolutionized sea transport shipping after World War II?

What is ecotourism?

How has ecotourism affected environments both negatively and positively?

There's a class of resources that we describe in terms of use that you may not think of as resources, but they most certainly are. *Nonextractive resources* are those uses we make of the sea without removing anything from the sea. Therefore, they are renewable because there's nothing that needs renewing.

The three most conspicuous uses of the sea are for transport shipping, projection of state power and recreation. All of these uses are physical resources in that they involve the physical aspects of the sea. The original argument made in the 17th century by Hugo Grotius for the "freedom of the seas" was about the use of the sea as a corridor for shipping and movement of military vessels to secure trade routes.

Capt. Albert E. Theberge, NOAA Corps

Figure 17-14

Cargo-container revolution.
The introduction of containers revolutionized the shipping industry. Once cargo ships need to remain in port for weeks to unload and load. Today, modern container ships can load and unload in a matter of days or even hours.

Sea Transport Shipping. You need only look at history to realize what an important resource the ocean is for its use as a corridor for shipping. Blockades – closing access to the sea for shipping – have frequently been important strategies during war. During the American Civil War, the north blockaded the south to prevent it from obtaining war materials and food from Europe in exchange for cotton. During

World War II, Nazi Germany tried unsuccessfully to blockade the United Kingdom. During both wars with Iraq, the United States' blockades cut off Iraq's ability to receive materials in exchange for oil.

Sea transport has been vital for hundreds of years and remains so. Today, nearly half of the world's crude oil travels in tanker ships. About 25% of the world's shipping involves carrying iron, coal, and grain. Finished commodities, from automobiles and electronics to athletic wear and toys, travel between countries in day-to-day commerce.

At one time, cargo ships needed weeks to load and unload. This supported a trade called *longshoring* that still exists. Longshoremen load and unload cargo ships. Until World War II, this was a laborious, time-consuming task.

After World War II, the invention of the cargo container revolutionized sea transport shipping. The use of standardized cargo containers makes it possible to quickly load and unload prepacked containers with a special crane. These containers can also travel by truck or rail, significantly reducing handling requirements. Modern container ships can hold more than 4,000 containers that can be loaded or unloaded in only a day or two.

Projection of State Power. Another nonextractive use of the ocean with a long history is as a corridor for the projection of state military power far from home. Such military power is used for exploration, conquest, scientific research, to protect trade or to keep peace. Chapter 2 covers the voyages of exploration, conquest and research that were part of the search for resources and the desire to expand influence.

Another important function of navies is to keep shipping lanes open and ensure safe passage for trade across the ocean. There are narrow straits around the world that are vital shipping passageways. It is critical that these remain open to all vessels because the global economy depends on trade between countries. For example, the Straits of Malacca is one of the busiest passageways in the world. It connects the Indian and Pacific Ocean and is the fastest route between the East and West. It is 880 kilometers (550 miles) long and only 2.7 kilometers (1.7 miles) across at its narrowest point. Fifteen million barrels of oil per day travel by ship through this Strait from the Persian Gulf and West Africa to China, Japan, and all of the Asian Pacific countries.

Sea power and free movement of commerce on the ocean often play a role in international negotiations between governments when it comes to resource and environmental management deci-

Figure 17-15a

Marine Recreation –
Surfing.

Figure 17-15b

Marine Recreation –
Scuba Diving

Figure 17-15c

Marine Recreation –
Canoeing

sions. In fact, it was the key challenge when it came to the international negotiations for the United Nations Convention on the Law of the Sea (UNCLOS) – balancing the freedom of passage rights required by the world's navies with the need to manage the environment and resources effectively.

Recreation. People have enjoyed the ocean for recreation almost as far back as history records. However, in the 20th century rising standards of living and technologies have opened the door to more recreational pursuits. Activities include angling (sport fishing), snorkeling, scuba diving, sailing and boating, water skiing, parasailing, surfing, and more.

Marine recreation has become an important contributor to the fastest growing industry on Earth, tourism. In growing numbers, tourists travel to coastal and island destinations to enjoy their recreations. In many destinations, ocean-based tourism has replaced traditional ways of making a living off of the sea.

Nature-based tourism, or *ecotourism,* is now a major component of the international tourism industry. Ecotourism focuses on visiting and experiencing wildlife and natural environments. Much of it is on or near the sea.

Ecotourism has affected environments both positively and negatively. On the positive side, in a growing number of destinations, local people are realizing that to provide a popular ecotourism destination, they need to preserve the local environments. Consequently, for example, they no longer take as many fish for food because the fish produce more income as part of a living reef for snorkelers and scuba divers. This has been a particularly visible trend on many Caribbean islands.

Because ecotourism is growing quickly, many destinations have development problems. These areas have trouble keeping pace with the rising number of tourists. Rapid construction may progress with little long-term concern for the environment. As an example, there are rising problems with sewage seeping into underground freshwater supplies in some places. The Yucatan Peninsula in Mexico seems to be facing this problem.

Other negative consequences can arise from seemingly harmless activities. Feeding fish, for instance, might seem a positive activity for snorkelers and scuba divers. The reality proves quite different. Where people do this, fish and other wildlife behave unnaturally because they now view humans as a food source (but not as food, fortunately). Local populations may grow larger than would normally exist due to the excess abundance of food. This can cause localized ecological imbalances that disrupt normal natural processes.

ARE YOU LEARNING?

1. **The ocean can provide renewable energy by (choose all that apply)**

   A. using the energy in waves.

   B. using the energy in tides.

   C. using the energy in hurricanes and typhoons.

   D. using the energy in the upper layers of seawater.

2. **Of the possible renewable energy sources, the one that appears most feasible is**

   A. using the energy in waves.

   B. using the energy in tides.

   C. using the energy in hurricanes and typhoons.

   D. using the energy in the upper layers of seawater.

3. **There are growing concerns about fresh water as we move through this century because**

   A. melting ice caps may make fresh water too abundant and dilute the ocean.

   B. the supply of fresh water isn't keeping pace with the rising demand.

4. **We get fresh water from the sea through desalinization, which can involve**

   A. boiling seawater and condensing the vapor.

   B. forcing seawater through reverse osmosis filters.

   C. isolating salts by spinning seawater in a centrifuge.

   D. A and B but not C

5. **Nonextractive resources**

   A. are picked up off the seabed without extracting them from the sediments.

   B. precipitate from seawater without any extraction necessary.

   C. do not require taking anything from the sea.

   D. none of the above

6. **The invention of _____ after World War II revolutionized sea transport shipping.**

   A. steam

   B. nuclear power

   C. sonar

   D. the cargo container

7. **Ecotourism**

   A. focuses on visiting and experiencing wildlife and natural environments.

   B. is any type of tourism that involves the ocean.

   C. is a type of fishing.

   D. is none of the above

8. **Ecotourism has helped the environment in some cases by encouraging its preservation, but has hurt it in others by encouraging rapid construction and development.**

   A. true

   B. false

Submerged Cultural Resources

A Definition – Submerged Cultural Resources

What is a submerged cultural resource?

Chapter 2 provides and overview of the discipline of underwater archaeology. Much of what we know about ancient maritime cultures and naval history comes from what archaeologists find underwater. Once archaeological sites are found in aquatic environments, they are evaluated and set aside for protection and comprehensive research. At that point they are referred to as *submerged cultural resources* because they are part of a nation's material heritage that happens to be underwater.

Submerged cultural resources are typically shipwrecks, but they can also include submerged settlements, burial and disposal sites, and underwater areas with artifacts left by prehistoric and

Photo by Submerged Resources Center, National Park Service

historic cultures. In addition to the ocean, underwater sinkholes and caves are often rich in archaeology. Shipwrecks give archaeologists information about how people lived, died and constructed their ships. The remains of a particular wreck often provide clues about how it end up underwater, how many individuals may have perished in the accident, and who they were. Airplanes have also become increasingly important as part of the submerged cultural resources base. Some of the best-preserved planes, ships and prehistoric human remains have been discovered in underwater environments.

STUDY QUESTIONS

Find the answers as you read.

1. What is a *submerged cultural resource?*

2. Why protect submerged cultural resources?

Figure 17-16

What are Submerged Cultural Resources?

Submerged cultural resources are typically shipwrecks, but they can also include submerged settlements, burial and disposal sites, and underwater areas with artifacts left by prehistoric and historic cultures.

Protecting Submerged Cultural Resources

Why protect submerged cultural resources?

Photo by Submerged Resources Center, National Park Service

Preserving the scientific and historical integrity of submerged cultural resources is important to protect what scientists learn from them. Removing or even just disturbing the contents of terrestrial or submerged sites diminishes the information archaeologists can learn from them. Beyond this, submerged cultural resources are often protected for visiting by recreational scuba divers, much as terrestrial historic sites are protected to be enjoyed by visitors. Most underwater archaeologists approve of divers visiting sites in a respectful way. It increases their understanding and enjoyment of submerged heritage and gives them a sense of social ownership.

Often, national and international laws protect submerged cultural sites to keep them from being looted or defaced. Countries do this in a variety of ways. For example, in the United States, the US Department of the Interior, National Park Service has a Submerged Resources Center staffed by underwater archaeologists to provide the expertise required for managing these sites as or within national parks. The Submerged Resources Center's core mission is to inventory and evaluate submerged resources in the national park system and to assist other groups with underwater heritage resource issues.

Figure 17-17

Underwater archaeologists.
Pictured are underwater archaeologists measuring an historical shipwreck's anchor. Left undisturbed, sites like this can provide valuable clues for trained scientists to determine the history, fate and the sailors who worked on the ship.

ARE YOU LEARNING?

1. A submerged cultural resource can be (choose all that apply)

    A. an underwater city.

    B. a shipwreck.

    C. an underwater area that is littered with ancient artifacts discarded by a civilization.

    D. an underwater burial site.

2. Submerged cultural resources are protected to maintain the integrity of the site for scientists to study and to keep collectors and treasure hunters from looting the site.

    A. true

    B. false

Biological Resources – Marine Mammals

STUDY QUESTIONS

Find the answers as you read.

1. Were whale populations hunted sustainably before 1868?

2. What has happened to whale populations since 1900?

3. What has happened to whale populations since the International Whaling Commission (IWC) moratorium on whaling in 1986?

4. How does whaling continue despite the IWC moratorium?

5. What cetaceans are not protected by the IWC moratorium and are thought to be endangered?

6. What fur-bearing marine mammals are used as biological resources?

You probably think of biological, not physical resources, when you think of renewable resources. Biological resources can be renewable, if properly managed.

However, many of the primary biological resources exploited by humans have been taken with so much vigor that they have not been able to sustain themselves. Many biological resources are commercially extinct. The classic example and perhaps most immediately recognized example is whaling. For this reason, the use of whales and other marine mammals as biological resources is a suitable place to begin this discussion.

Whales

Were whale populations hunted sustainably before 1868?

What has happened to whale populations since 1900?

What has happened to whale populations since the International Whaling Commission (IWC) moratorium on whaling in 1986?

How does whaling continue despite the IWC moratorium?

Whaling dates back at least 2,000 years. The early peoples of Japan were among the first whalers. Scandinavians were whaling by 800 A.D., with the Basques of northern Spain and southern France engaged in whaling about the same time. By the 16th century whaling was common among European nations.

While the Japanese killed whales for the meat, the Europeans were primarily interested in *blubber.* Blubber is a protective fat layer

Figure 17-18

The Demise of Whales.

For centuries, technology powered by wind and muscle protected some, but not all whales from being overexploited. But, with the advent of steam, coal, and eventually diesel engines, along with the invention of the explosive-powered harpoon, whale populations plunged in a matter of decades.

Roy C. Andrews, Fisheries Collection, NOAA

that insulates whales, allowing them to thrive even in polar waters. Blubber was rendered into whale oil, which was important as a lubricant and fuel. Before the discovery of petroleum reserves, whale oil lit the world at night.

Until 1868, primitive technology made whaling dangerous

and difficult. Harpoons were little more than heavy spears hurled from small longshore boats. The wounded whale would drag the boat (or boats) at high speed in what came to be called a "Nantucket sleigh ride," named for the whaling port of Nantucket, Massachusetts. Often the whale towed the longshore boat for hours before it became exhausted enough to be killed. This limited the number of whales that whalers could take. Yet despite this, because whales reproduce in small numbers, much whaling was already being carried on at an unsustainable rate. By 1868 the Atlantic Grey Whale was hunted to extinction and the Right Whale had been completely removed from most of its range.

Everything changed in 1868 with the invention of the modern harpoon gun. Instead of a hand-thrown spear, the modern whale harpoon launches from a gun and explodes on impact inside the whale. Besides being a more damaging weapon, the modern harpoon can be launched from a ship. With no need for the longshore boats, whalers began pursing whales with fast steamships. This allowed them to harvest blue, fin, Sei, and Minke whales, which in the past had managed to survive being hunted. Attacking and killing a whale went from taking hours to taking minutes.

As whaling grew, the development of large factory ships allowed whalers to process the whales at sea. Although petroleum had become a primary fuel source by the end of the 1800s, whale oil still had a market in cosmetics, food products, fertilizer, and as an industrial lubricant. Baleen was even used for corset stays and buggy whips.

As with commercial fishing, whalers continued to use new technologies. International whaling was so successful that whale populations plunged during the 20th century. Populations declined prior to World War II, but managed to recover to some degree during the wartime halt to whaling. Even so, as early as the 1950s some countries began to convert whaling vessels into fishing vessels because there weren't enough whales to hunt. The use of the stern ramp, which was designed to drag a whale up to the deck, made it possible to use larger fishing nets than were possible on conventional fishing vessels which pulled nets up over the side.

The whalers who remained continued to improve their hunting with technology. By the late 1960s, whaling fleets had spotter airplanes looking for pods from the air. They used sonar to track whales trying to escape in the depths. From an estimated population of 4.4 million whales in 1900, today the estimated population is around 1 million. Eight of the 11 great whales species became commercially extinct. However, whalers often still took them if they happened across them.

HOW RIGHT WHALES GOT THEIR NAME

Especially before 1868, whalers favored right whales as targets. They made good targets for early whalers because they swam slowly, struggled little, and didn't sink after dying. Hence, they were the "right" whales to kill.

INTERNET PORTAL

SCiLINKS. NSTA

Topic: Whaling and Fishing
Go To: www.scilinks.org
Code: LOP2435

With whale populations already dwindling by World War II, in 1946 the International Whaling Commission (IWC) formed to set quotas in an effort to stay within maximum sustainable yields. However, the quotas were too high and whale populations continued to fall. As one species became commercially extinct, whalers went on to the next largest species.

As international attention focused on the plight of the whales, many non-whaling nations joined the IWC. As a result, in 1982 the IWC adopted a resolution that called for an indefinite moratorium on commercial whaling. It became effective in 1986.

The results of the moratorium provide a lesson in species recovery. It is something to consider in light of what you just read about overfishing. Since the moratorium, some species seem to be recovering. Gray, blue, and humpback whales seem to be on the rise in the Pacific. On the other hand, right and southern blue whales in the North Atlantic appear to still be declining. It's estimated that there are only about 300 northern right whales. Watchers saw only two females with calves on the calving grounds off the coast of Georgia in 1999. This compares to 17 calves in 1997 and six in 1998. The lesson appears to be that, given a chance, a species can recover. However, if ending commercial pressure takes too long, a species may not make it and continue into extinction.

Despite the moratorium and the continued low population levels, whaling still continues. It does so for several reasons. For one, the IWC is a voluntary organization and even members don't have to abide by its rulings. For example, in 1993 Norway resumed hunting Minke whales, which had shown a recovery in numbers.

Another way whaling continues is through the IWC's allowance for aboriginal hunting. This allows indigenous people in North America, Greenland, Russia, and other nations to preserve their cultural traditions related to whale hunting. This would not be a major threat to whales if it required the use of the traditional whaling methods. Unfortunately, often the "traditions" are carried out with modern equipment.

A third exemption is for scientific whaling. When studying whales, researchers must at times take specimens for study. Under this premise, Japan continues to hunt whales. Under the auspices of the Institute for Cetacean Research and despite international pressure, the Japanese government authorizes taking more than 400 whales annually. These "specimens" are sold to wholesalers and used as food in school lunches, among other purposes.

Courtesy of Australian Customs

Figure 17-19

"Scientific" Whaling?

When studying whales, researchers must at times take specimens for study. Under this premise, Japan continues to hunt whales. Under the auspices of the Institute for Cetacean Research and despite international pressure, the Japanese government authorizes taking more than 400 whales annually. These "specimens" are sold to wholesalers and used as food in school lunches, among other purposes. Interesting data has, however, been obtained from the taking of these whales.

Other Cetaceans

What cetaceans are not protected by the IWC moratorium and are thought to be endangered?

While large whales tend to be the focus in whaling, far more small cetaceans get taken than do large whales. The IWC doesn't protect dolphins, some which have become the most endangered of the cetaceans. Several species face immediate danger of extinction because many countries hunt dolphin for food. This includes the "vaquita" (Spanish for *little cow*) in the Gulf of California. In some countries, dolphin costs less than chicken or beef. When you see "dolphin" on a menu in the US, it is a fish also called mahi-mahi. In other countries, such as Peru, "dolphin," or rather "delfin" is the mammal dolphin.

Chapter 7 covered another threat to dolphins and small whales: they are caught in nets set by commercial fishers. The danger to dolphins comes from the fact that tuna are usually swimming below schools of dolphins and are caught in the process of tuna fishing. This has killed an estimated 6 million dolphins since 1971. The rate dropped significantly beginning in 1972 with the passage of the US Marine Mammals Protection Act. In one of the most successful environmental campaigns, consumers began boycotting tuna in response to the campaign to stop the dolphin deaths. In 1988 Congress imposed a ban on all tuna imports that weren't taken in accordance with US law. Consumers also boycotted tuna that didn't comply. Today US tuna fishers and foreign importers must comply with "dolphin safe" fishing techniques that reduce dolphin kills.

It is worth noting that today neither whales nor small cetaceans provide any material that's not available from some other source. US manufacturers demonstrate that there's no need for whale oil. The import and use of whale products or materials is illegal in the US, but this has not hindered any industry except whaling itself.

Seals and Sea Lions

What fur-bearing marine mammals are used as biological resources?

Historically, seals and sea lions have been biological resources exploited for their fur and for food. At the turn of the 19th century, fur seal populations were so decimated that Russia, Japan, Great Britain and the US entered into the Fur Seal Treaty of 1911, which remained in effect for 30 years. It was the first international treaty involving several countries that dealt with wildlife conservation and was a role model for future treaties. Within five years, the population rebounded and protection was extended in 1966.

US Department of Commerce/NOAA

Figure 17-20

Dolphin safe.

Perhaps the first and most successful consumer-based marine conservation campaign involved saving dolphins from tuna nets. The buying power of informed, like-minded people was shown to be a major force protecting the species.

Tom Breakfield, Photodisc/Getty Images

Figure 17-21

Hunting on the ice.

Seal hunting remains one of the most emotional and controversial issues in species conservation.

Not all seals are protected. The most famous fur hunt is the harp seal hunt, which takes place on the Canadian coast on the Labrador Sea. Hunters take the newborn harp pups for their dense, white fur. Older seals lose this white fur and are therefore not as valuable.

Worldwide opposition continues to pressure Canada to ban this practice, with efforts going so far as to also pressure the US White House to take the matter up with Canada. Supporters contend that the harp seal isn't endangered. They also say that hunters take seals in numbers far below the maximum sustainable yield. However, public opposition will probably continue, if for no other reason than that many consider it offensive to exploit these harmless and appealing pups.

ARE YOU LEARNING?

1. **Whale populations were sustainable until 1868 because**

   A. there was no whaling taking place.

   B. there was no demand for whale oil, so few were taken.

   C. the modern whale harpoon didn't exist.

   D. people protected whales to enjoy Nantucket sleigh rides.

2. **Since 1900, whale populations**

   A. fell from 4.4 million to about 1 million.

   B. stabilized in 1946 at about 2 million.

   C. have not been determined.

   D. have risen sharply.

3. **After the IWC moratorium on whaling in 1986, whale populations**

   A. have gone up significantly.

   B. have remained stable.

   C. have continued to decline.

   D. have improved for some species, but declined for others.

4. **Whaling continues despite the IWC moratorium because (choose all that apply)**

   A. the moratorium expired.

   B. IWC members don't have to abide by its rulings.

   C. there is an IWC exemption for research.

   D. there is an IWC exemption for aboriginal cultures.

5. **Dolphins are not protected by the IWC moratorium and are thought to be endangered.**

   A. true   B. false

6. **_____ and _____ are marine mammals taken for their fur.**

   A. Dolphins, whales

   B. Sea lions, seals

   C. Sea lions, dolphins

   D. Seals, whales

Biological Resources – Algae, Aquaculture and Medicine

Algae

How do we use algae as a food resource?

As discussed in Chapter 5, animals aren't the only biological resources people take from the sea. Marine algae is another resource used as food. Seaweeds and algae make up 10% of the Japanese diet; much of this is red algae nori. Nori is the most-consumed algae in the world and is often served with sushi.

You may be surprised to learn how much algae you consume. The commercial product *algin*, which comes from the mucus in kelp and other marine algae, has a complex molecular structure useful in food processing and other applications. Manufacturers use it as a thickening agent in salad dressing and ice cream, and to clarify beer and wine. You also find algin in paint and abrasives. With widespread applications in food and chemical processes, industry uses nearly $250 million worth of algin annually.

Farming the Sea

What is the growth trend in aquaculture?

About what percentage of the seafood consumed in the world is produced by aquaculture?

Commercial fishing is comparable to traditional terrestrial hunting and gathering. It entails living off what happens to grow in the wild. There is a long history of sustainable subsistence aquaculture as practiced by the Chinese and the early Hawaiians. *Aquaculture* is comparable to terrestrial farming and ranching. It uses farming techniques to grow and harvest aquatic organisms. *Mariculture* is aquaculture specific to the marine environment.

The growth trend in aquaculture is steeply upward. According to the Food and Agriculture Organization, the total contribution of aquaculture to global supplies of fish, crustaceans, mollusks and other aquatic animals grew from 4% in 1970 to 27% in 2000 and 32% in 2004.

In 2004, aquaculture produced more than 60 million tons of fish, seafood, and other biological resources. The estimated value was about $70 million. China alone accounts for about 70% of the total quantity of aquaculture production.

KIMICA America, Inc.

Figure 17-22

Mmmm, algae!

Kelp harvesting vessel in action. Most people are surprised to learn that algin, a byproduct of algae, is used as a thickener in hundreds of common food items.

INTERNET PORTAL

SCiLINKS. NSTA

Topic: Kelps Beds
Go To: www.scilinks.org
Code: LOP2440

Today more than 30% of the world's seafood comes from aquaculture. Most of this is freshwater fish, but aquaculture of marine species continues to grow. Mariculture, a branch of aquaculture that involves the farming of marine species for food and other uses in the ocean, is also growing.

Aquaculture may sound like the solution to overfishing, but it's not without its problems. For one, farmed species of carnivorous

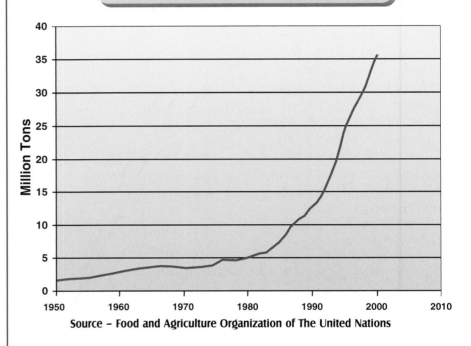

Figure 17-23

World Aquaculture Production 1950-2000.

As indicated by the graph, aquaculture has grown tremendously over the past 30 years and isn't expected to slow anytime soon.

fish such as salmon and shrimp, live on fish meal made from wild-caught fish. Chapter 4 covers trophic relationships and demonstrates that only about 10% of the biomass from one level makes it to the next. Therefore, 1 kilogram of salmon requires 10 kilograms of anchovies or other fish. In this sense, aquaculture is part of the problem instead of the solution. This is because wild fisheries continue to be depleted to make the food used in the aquaculture of some species. However, species like tilapia, which are omnivores, can live on food derived from plants. This creates a more sustainable alternative. Much research is being done to find an alternative feed for carnivorous species like shrimp and salmon.

But, this is not the only problem related to the sustainability of modern intensive aquaculture. Some problems are similar to those caused by raising livestock on land. Keeping many animals in close quarters tends to allow disease to spread rapidly. To prevent this, aquaculturists give antibiotics to farmed fish, but this means that eventually antibiotics pass through them into the environment.

Another problem is the concentrated animal waste. Many aquaculture pens release concentrated nitrates (including uneaten food), leading to plankton blooms. Like terrestrial farms, an aquatic farm consumes resources that wild organisms would use. Species raised by aquaculture may be from limited genetic stock. The health of wild stocks can be threatened by the accidental release of farm-raised stocks, which can compromise the gene pool of wild species if they breed together.

Despite these problems, aquaculture will probably continue to grow. There are already solutions proposed to the more serious drawbacks. Approached reasonably and responsibly, aquaculture can provide a renewable resource that is an alternative to commercial fishing.

US Geological Survey

Figure 17-24a

Salmon aquaculture.

U.S. Department of Agriculture

Figure 17-24b

Sea farming.
Many aquaculture pens release concentrated waste in the form of nitrates, sometimes leading to plankton blooms. Despite these problems, if approached responsibly, aquaculture can provide a renewable resource that is an alternative to commercial fishing.

New Medicines from the Ocean

What is bioprospecting *and how does it relate to the development of new drugs?*

About half of the drugs available to modern medicine come from nature. They're either natural substances or synthesized from natural substances, including those found in the sea. Marine scientists estimate that we've barely scratched the surface when it comes to identifying organisms with potential pharmacological importance.

The search for organisms with pharmacological or other chemical benefits is called *bioprospecting*. Bioprospecting is important in

INTERNET PORTAL

SCiLINKS NSTA

Topic: Drugs from the Sea
Go To: www.scilinks.org
Code: LOP2450

the development of new drugs because it is in nature that chemists often find new ways to fight disease. The potential exists for a wide range of drugs that combat viruses, inflammation, cancer, heart disease, AIDS/HIV, and others. Even insecticides and a new class of steroids have been found in sea organisms.

So as not to bioprospect from natural reefs, marine scientists are examining the possibility of harvesting marine organisms for possible drugs from artificial reefs. Shipwrecks and decommissioned oil platforms in particular are being examined as possible harvest sites for pharmacological products.

Biosprospecting can only continue with a healthy sea. It's frightening to think that we could accidentally cause the extinction of the organism that holds the cure to the disease that you or someone you love has. This is but one reason everyone has to preserve a healthy ocean.

ARE YOU LEARNING?

1. **One of the most common uses of algae is as**
   A. algin.
   B. a paper product.
   C. an aerospace structural material.
   D. all of the above

2. **The growth trend in aquaculture is**
   A. flat.
   B. downward.
   C. steeply upward.
   D. undetermined.

3. **About _____% of the world's seafood comes from aquaculture.**
   A. less than 30
   B. more than 30
   C. 10
   D. 100

4. **Bioprospecting is**
   A. looking for gold in the ocean.
   B. looking for gold in organisms.
   C. looking for pharmacological or other chemical benefits in organisms.
   D. none of the above

Biological Resources – Fish

Fisheries for Food and Industry

What proportion of the protein in the human diet comes from the ocean?

Where are commercially important fish found and why?

What fish group accounts for the largest commercial harvest?

What is a reduction fishery?

How much of the commercial worldwide fish catch is used for reduction?

Compared to terrestrial foods, seafood in its many forms may seem like a minor contribution to the human diet as it accounts for only about 4% of what people eat or an average of 14.2 kilograms per year. On the other hand, it accounts for about 18% of the protein we eat – 15% consumed directly as seafood and about 3% indirectly through fish meal and other seafood byproducts fed to livestock.

This varies by nation and culture. For example, in Japan the average consumption is 72.1 kilograms (159 pounds) of fish per year, while Americans average 29.7 kilograms (47 pounds) annually. About 89% of the world's wild-caught fish comes from the ocean, with the rest coming from freshwater sources. For some small island developing states, seafood provides more than 50% of people's annual protein intake.

STUDY QUESTIONS

Find the answers as you read.

1. What proportion of the protein in the human diet comes from the ocean?

2. Where are commercially important fish found and why?

3. What fish group accounts for the largest commercial harvest?

4. What is a *reduction fishery*?

5. How much of the commercial worldwide fish catch is used for reduction?

6. According to the United Nations Food and Agriculture Organization (FAO), what has the trend been in worldwide commercial fishing since World War II?

7. Why do many scientists have doubts about the accuracy of the FAO reports?

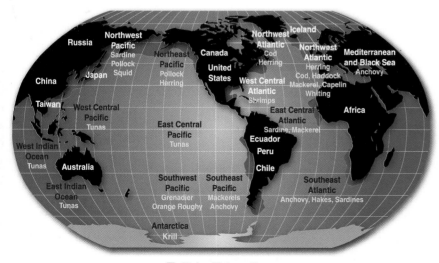

■ Major Fishery Zones

Figure 17-25

Global fisheries.

This illustration shows the major fishing regions of the world as defined by the United Nations Food and Agricultural Organization (FAO). The Northwest Pacific is now the region with the highest catches, both because of its high productivity, and because other regions have been fished so heavily. Recent evidence has also shown that China has greatly exaggerated its reported catch.

Northeast Fisheries Science Center, NOAA

Figure 17-26

Fishing on an industrial scale.

Huge factory ships follow many of the world's fleets, taking and processing the catch so it's filleted and frozen before reaching shore.

Commercial fishing targets both pelagic and groundfish. Pelagic fish live in the open water column. Groundfish live on or near the sea bottom. Yet of all the species in the sea, only about 500 make up the vast majority of the catch.

Commercially important fish are found primarily in two places: the waters of the continental shelves and a few offshore regions with abundant upwelling. The reason is that most of the ocean has relatively low bioproductivity. The continental shelves and the upwelling regions have high productivity because of the ample supply of nutrients and sunlight.

In 2005, the total world fisheries catch and aquaculture combined production was an estimated 142 million metric tons. This was made up of inland (freshwater) capture and aquaculture production as well as marine capture and aquaculture. The total amount of wild fish captured from the oceans in 2005 was 84 million metric tons. Of the total fisheries production, 108 million metric tons was used for direct human production and 34 million metric tons was used for non-food purposes.

Chapter 7 explains that fish in the order Clupeiformes are important commercial species. These include herring, sardines, and anchovies and account for the largest single group that is taken commercially. Although humans eat some of these fresh, much is processed into fish meal and fed to poultry and livestock, or used to make fish feed for aquaculture. Manufacturers also extract the oil and use it in products ranging from food products to cosmetics and paint.

A fishery catching fish for purposes other than direct human consumption is called a *reduction fishery*. In 1950, reduction fisheries accounted for only about 10% of commercial fishing. Today, about one-quarter of the world commercial fish catch is used for reduction.

WORLD COMMERCIAL CATCHES IN MILLIONS OF METRIC TONS

Catch	1975	1980	1985	1990	1995	1999
Fish						
Herrings, sardines, etc.	13.43	16.14	21.10	22.32	22.01	22.71
Miscellaneous marine fishes	7.42	7.97	8.41	9.82	9.80	10.72
Cods, haddocks, hakes	11.85	10.75	12.46	11.58	10.73	9.40
Jacks, mullets, sauries	6.08	7.30	8.31	9.78	10.79	7.71
Rockfishes, basses, congers	5.19	5.30	5.21	5.80	6.85	6.83
Tunas, bonitos, billfishes	2.06	2.55	3.18	4.43	4.93	5.97
Mackerels	4.15	4.03	3.83	3.54	4.69	5.11
Flounders and other flatfishes	1.16	1.08	1.35	1.23	0.92	0.96
Salmon, smelts	0.55	0.80	1.17	1.51	1.15	0.91
Sharks, rays	0.59	0.60	0.62	0.69	0.76	0.82
Total marine fishes	**51.93**	**55.73**	**64.40**	**69.36**	**71.66**	**70.26**
Molluscs						
Squids, octopuses	1.18	1.53	1.79	2.36	2.87	3.37
Clams, cockles	0.94	1.20	1.51	1.53	0.96	0.81
Scallops	0.29	0.37	0.60	0.87	0.51	0.57
Mussels	0.53	0.62	0.97	1.34	0.24	0.24
Oysters	0.85	0.97	1.09	1.00	0.19	0.16
Total marine molluscs	**4.03**	**4.91**	**6.18**	**7.73**	**6.27**	**6.79**
Crustacea						
Shrimps	1.33	1.70	2.12	2.63	2.34	2.89
Crabs	0.75	0.82	.89	.89	1.09	1.19
Lobsters	0.10	0.10	.20	0.21	0.22	0.23
Krill0.04	0.04	0.48	0.19	0.37	0.12	0.10
Total marine crustaceans	**2.35**	**3.20**	**3.42**	**4.50**	**4.80**	**5.76**
World total (all groups)	**66.13**	**72.38**	**86.26**	**97.97**	**91.37**	**92.87**

Note: Catches tabulated in groups defined by the Food and Agriculture Organization of the United Nations. Figures for catches are rounded to the nearest ten-thousandth and, when added, may not equal totals. Source: Food and Agriculture Organization of the United Nations, FAO Yearbook, Fisheries Statistics.

Trends in the Worldwide Commercial Fish Catch

According to the United Nations Food and Agriculture Organization (FAO), what has the trend been in worldwide commercial fishing since World War II?

Why do many scientists have doubts about the accuracy of the FAO reports?

About a billion people rely on fish as their primary protein source. According to estimates, worldwide commercial fishing and aquaculture related activities employ more than 40 million people directly. This number does not include people who catch fish in small quantities for their own consumption. Commercial fishing is a physically demanding occupation. In the United States, the annual fatality rate is 155 per 100,000 workers.

In addition to those directly involved in commercial fishing, another 200 million people have jobs related to commercial fish

Figure 17-27

World commercial catches in millions of metric tons.

This chart shows how the worldwide annual catch of many major marine food species has been increasing over the years. The predicted trend is that soon the worldwide fisheries will be unable to meet the rising demand for fish.

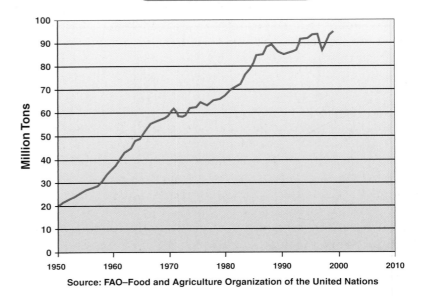

World Fish Catch, 1950-2000

Source: FAO–Food and Agriculture Organization of the United Nations

Figure 17-28

World fish catch from 1950 to 2004.

While the tonnage of fish seems to remain steady since around 1985, this graph does not reflect the significant increase in fishing effort needed to maintain this level of catch or the changes in size or target species of fish due to overfishing.

processing or distribution. By the end of 2004, the world's fishing fleet was made up of 4 million vessels. Of these, two-thirds were traditional fishing boats, and 1.3 million were mechanized with various types of engines.

The most modern fleets catch fish using scout planes, satellite-based sensors, current profilers, sonar, and other technologies. Huge factory ships follow many of these fleets, taking and processing the catch so it's filleted and frozen before reaching shore.

According to the United Nations Food and Agricultural Organization (FAO), the worldwide annual catch increased from 21 million metric tons after World War II to 40 million by 1960 and 70 million by 1970. Optimism about the potential output of the ocean was high and estimates of the potential of future catches were high.

In 1967 a Commission on Marine Science Engineering and Resources was appointed to investigate current and future US coastal and ocean resources. Known as the Stratton Commission for its Chairman, Julius A. Stratton of the Ford Foundation, the group released its report in 1969 entitled "Our Nations and the Sea: A Plan for National Action." The report said it would be realistic – even conservative – to expect to be able to harvest between 400 and 500 million metric tons of fish annually. This suggests that at the time, we still considered the ocean's resources almost limitless.

By 1989, the annual catch had reached 86 million metric tons and has held about level at between 70 to 85 million metric tons ever since. In 2005, the FAO estimated that about half the commercially targeted fish stocks were fully exploited, and about a quarter were overexploited, depleted or recovering from depletion. Its 2006 report confirmed earlier observations that the maximum capacity of wild capture fisheries from the ocean has been reached. So instead of reaching the 500 million metric ton catch level estimated in 1967, commercial fishing from the ocean was already nearing the probable maximum output.

A number of researchers and scientists in the past had concerns about the accuracies of reported catch numbers. The FAO is the only institution that maintains statistics for global fisheries. It relies on volunteer reporting by member countries to obtain its information, which may not be accurate. An independent analysis in 2001 showed a discrepancy. According to the figures, the worldwide catch statistics were distorted by major fluctuations of certain fish populations and inaccurate reporting. For example, in 1991 the official reported Chinese catch was 10.1 million metric tons. Independent analysis, however, calculated the catch at half that. Many fisheries scientists actually think that the worldwide catch has *declined* since 1988, but the statistics collected are too imprecise to answer this with certainty as present.

As fish stocks decline, overfishing causes shifts in the fish that are caught. For example, the average size of the fish caught declines. Eventually this leads to the collapse of the target fish populations. As the more favored species became depleted, commercial fishers then begin to target fish previously considered unappealing for human consumption. This is an important aspect of what is called fishing down the food web.

Additionally, bycatch – the catching of non-target species of fish, birds and turtles – has resulted in millions of tons of fish being dumped or discarded at sea. Bycatch is not included in the fishing statistics.

Another contributing factor to overfishing around the world is that there are too many boats. After World War II as commercial fishing was on the rise, many changes in technology dramatically increased how many fish factory trawlers could catch. Starting in the 1950's the use of stern ramps, bigger, stronger nylon nets, stronger engines, automated processing and freezer technology, improved navigational and fish finding equipment led to a dramatic increase in the amount of fish a fishing vessel could catch. Despite the fact that most of the major fishing nations have pledged to reduce the number of ships, the numbers of vessels continue to increase. As fuel prices increase, however, it has had the effect of making many of these vessels unprofitable.

1. **About _____% of the protein in the human diet comes from the ocean.**

   A. 4

   B. 10

   C. 18

   D. 34

2. **Commercial fish are found in the waters of _____ because _____.**

   A. the open ocean, there's little pollution

   B. the deep-sea, hydrothermal vents provide heat

   C. the continental shelf and offshore regions with upwelling, these are high bioproductivity regions

   D. none of the above

3. **The fish group that accounts for the largest commercial harvest is**

   A. the clupeiforms.

   B. the crustaceans.

   C. cod.

   D. mahi-mahi.

4. **Reduction fishing is**

   A. catching fish for anything other than for your own consumption.

   B. catching fish using technology such as satellites and sonar.

   C. catching fish in harbors and other waterways.

   D. catching fish for purposes other than direct human consumption.

5. **Reduction fishing accounts for _____ of the world commercial fish catch.**

   A. 90%

   B. half

   C. about a quarter

   D. very little

6. **According to the United Nations Food and Agriculture Organization (FAO), the trend in the world fish catch since World War II has been**

   A. a nearly steady increase.

   B. a stable, renewable catch rate.

   C. a steady increase until 1989, and has been about level since.

   D. widely fluctuating for no explainable reason.

7. **Many scientists doubt the accuracy of FAO reports because**

   A. the FAO is well known for being overly optimistic.

   B. fish catch yields appear substantially larger than the FAO says.

   C. worldwide catch statistics were distorted by major fluctuations of certain fish populations and inaccurate reporting.

   D. the FAO has not complied with scientific review requirements.

The State of the World's Fisheries – A Bleak Picture

Maximum Sustainable Yield, Overfishing and Ecosystem-Based Management

What is maximum sustainable yield? *How does this concept relate to the concept of overfishing?*

According to fisheries scientists, the FAO, the National Marine Fisheries Service, and other sources, what is the condition of the world's fisheries?

Until the 20th century, people believed that the sea was an infinite resource. In a sense, they were correct. Until the 20th century, there wasn't a huge demand on marine resources. Consequently, the sea renewed biological resources fast enough to replace what we took.

Today, however, we know that a limitless sea is a myth. Technology and rising demand have made it possible to exhaust biological resources. We can catch fish and other organisms more quickly than they can reproduce and maintain their populations. Given this problem and rising demand, the role of fisheries management is to prevent the day coming when there will be nothing to catch. Many fisheries scientists think that, unfortunately, we're not off to a very good start.

The concept of *maximum sustainable yield* lies at the heart of the challenge to manage fisheries sustainably. Maximum sustainable yield is the greatest yield (catch) of a target species that fisheries can take without jeopardizing future catches. *Overfishing* occurs when the quantity of fish taken exceeds the amount of fish that can be resupplied by the growth and reproduction of the remaining population.

Maximum sustainable yield isn't an easy number to establish. Scientific methods can never establish an exact number. so that scientists usually give a range that can be established. For example, the estimate may result in telling decision makers that fishers can be allowed to take between 10 to 15 thousand metric tons of a certain fish species or population. When establishing the total allowable catch that can be taken, decision makers have to consider not only the health of the population, but also the economic effect on the fishers and their families and communities. The pressure to choose the higher number in the range, or go above the range, results in continual overfishing.

Figure 17-29

An empty ocean?

The dilemma of the modern fishing industry is that technology has made it too efficient at catching fish. Fish stocks were once thought inexhaustible, but overfishing now has the potential of virtually emptying the sea of any desirable species.

Figure 17-30

Destructive methods.

Even when a fishery isn't overfished, the methods used can cause serious unintended harm to species such as sea turtles, marine mammals, and cetaceans.

Other factors also complicate the process and lead to overfishing. The use of maximum sustainable yield in the past has led to evaluating each target species without accounting for other factors such as environmental changes, the loss of habitat, the lack of prey fish for food, etc. All these factors can affect the future of a particular fish population. To make matters worse, illegal fishing (known as pirate fishing) occurs in many fisheries, and there is no way to account for how much illegal fishers take from a particular stock.

As a result of these and other factors, overfishing is occurring in virtually all the world's fisheries. Fleets catch less than in previous years, and so they have to range farther. As discussed earlier, FAO estimates that 50% of the marine fish populations are fully exploited and 25% are overfished or depleted. The National Marine Fisheries Service estimates that half of the fish stock in US waters is overfished. This estimate is based on species with known status. Because we lack data lacking on most fish stocks, the picture could be much worse.

Fisheries management is moving to ecosystem-based management. This means that the maximum sustainable yield of individual species cannot be calculated without considering the other species in the ecosystem. It also accounts for other factors, such as changes to habitats and food webs (whether there are enough prey for the fish to eat, or enough for higher level predators to feed on).

The Problems with Overfishing

What responses to declining fisheries appear to contribute to overfishing?

What potential problems result from commercial fishing for species low on the food web?

What indirect effects does overfishing have on the environment?

Clearly, the evidence shows that the world's fisheries can't sustain the present catch levels. Responding to declining species in the face of continued or rising demand, however, the fishing industry has become more efficient. By refining their technology, the fishing fleets are taking ever larger proportions of declining stocks. This response worsens the problem. Already several fisheries show the long-term consequences of this response.

One example is the Newfoundland cod fishery. Once one of the world's most productive fish stocks, cod populations became so low that the Canadian government closed the fishery in 1992. This put more than 35,000 people out of work. In 1993, the National

Marine Fisheries Service similarly closed large parts of the New England cod fishery.

Another example is the North Atlantic swordfish. Between 1982 and 1990, the US catch declined by 70%. The average fish weight fell from 52 kilograms (115 pounds) to 27 kilograms (60 pounds). The Atlantic bluefin tuna declined by 80% in just three years from 1990 to 1993. Today, this is the most valuable fish on Earth, selling for more than $100 per kilogram in Japan. Many fisheries scientists fear this fish is doomed to extinction.

Karen Ducey, National Marine Fisheries Service, NOAA

Figure 17-31

Gill netting.

Gill netting is used by fishermen to entangle either pelagic or groundfish. They haul the nets aboard, removing the desired catch and discarding the bycatch.

Besides becoming more efficient, fisheries also respond by turning to new, unexploited resources. These are fish that are usually lower in the trophic pyramid, leading to a problem called "fishing down the food chain." This creates problems with overfishing species such as the herrings, sardines and anchovies. The first problem is that these species are prey fish – food for higher species. Depleting them can deplete the population of predators that rely on them for food. A second problem is that fishing down the food chain allows the proliferation of other organisms low on the food web. For example, overfishing in the Black Sea removed fish species that feed on plankton. This allowed rapid plankton growth. The abundant plankton, in turn, resulted in a population explosion of jellyfish that feed on plankton. To make matters worse, the jellyfish aren't even native species to the Black Sea. They were introduced there in bilge water from ships from the Atlantic Ocean.

Another problem results when commercial fishing disregards how fast species reproduce. For example, the orange roughy in New Zealand's waters became a targeted fishery. Unfortunately, there was no consideration of the late reproduction of this species. Orange roughy live more than 100 years and don't reproduce until they're 25 to 30 years old. Because they reproduce so slowly, this resource was commercially extinct within only 13 years. A similar situation now exists with the Patagonian toothfish, which appears on restaurant menus as "Chilean seabass." Like the roughy, the toothfish is a long-lived, late-reproducing fish. It is already overfished and targeted by pirate fishers. If the demand continues, it, too, will be commercially extinct soon.

Bycatch, you recall, is the unintentional capture of organisms. Estimates suggest that 25% of the worldwide fish catch is bycatch.

This amounts to about 29 million tons of fish that are caught and discarded, yet not counted in the estimates of the total remaining population. For example, shrimp fisheries catch and kill more than 1.8 million tons of marine life annually according to Seafood Watch of the Monterey Bay Aquarium. This includes about 45,000 sea turtles each year. The US shrimp fleet is better than most because they use required exclusion devices to protect sea turtles. However, these aren't perfect devices and an estimated 12,000 turtles are killed each year despite them. Bycatch involves mammals, other fish species including commercial fish, sharks and reptiles. Hundreds of albatross and other birds die in nets and commercial fishing lines annually.

Recommendations for Sustaining the World's Fisheries

What four recommendations did the Pew Oceans Commission make for the restoration and preservation of US biological resources?

Given the state of the world's fisheries, it is not surprising that many environmental groups are disappointed with government fishery management. Among these is the Pew Oceans Commission, a respected group of US scientists, wildlife advocates, natural resource managers, and politicians. In June 2003, the Pew Oceans Commission released a report that criticized US fisheries policies and offered recommendations to restore US fisheries. In 2004, the US president's appointed US Oceans Commission also made fairly similar recommendations. In 2005, the two commissions formed the Joint Ocean Commission Initiative. Here are some of the key recommendations resulting from this process:

1. Enact legislation to create incentives for ecosystem-based management.
2. Rely more strongly on science to guide management actions to ensure the long term sustainability of US fisheries.
3. Accede to the United Nations Convention on the Law of the Sea, allowing the US to take advantage of economic opportunities, protect sovereign interests and freedom of navigation.
4. Establish a network of marine reserves or protected areas.

What international and US policies will follow these recommendations remains to be seen. If nothing is done, an entire industry and food source will probably collapse. This important topic is revisited in Chapter 19, which looks at the future of our ocean planet.

INTERNET PORTAL

SCiLINKS. NSTA

Topic: Marine Reserves
Go To: www.scilinks.org
Code: LOP2510

MARINE PROTECTED AREAS: THE CASE FOR MARINE RESERVES

Marine reserves are ocean areas fully protected from extractive activities such as removal of plants, animals or other resources. Despite strong evidence that marine reserves benefit the ocean, only 0.01% of the ocean worldwide is protected as marine reserves. Marine reserves work on four basic levels.

First, by excluding extractive activities, they protect the structure of the local ecosystem, which is the basis for biodiversity. In areas where no species are removed (except for scientific monitoring) and the ecosystem remains intact, all species continue to thrive. This helps assure a stock of the widest variety of species.

Second, marine reserves can improve local fisheries. Several examples demonstrate that the existence of reserve areas provides an area where breeding and growth can take place uninhibited. The result is that fishing yields improve in adjacent areas. This is not theory – it has been demonstrated in practice many times in several types of environments.

Third, marine reserves provide living laboratories for study. To understand how human activities affect the ocean, it's necessary to have something to compare with affected areas. Reserves provide an area that represents the local ocean in its least altered state.

Fourth, marine reserves often contribute to economic growth by enabling the use of the sea as a non-extractive resource. They provide a place for snorkelers, scuba divers, and other water enthusiasts to enjoy nature. So, while they're reserves, they still contribute to the local economy. Many island nations have found that the economic benefit of reserves with water sports greatly exceeds the economic benefits of conventional fisheries.

When properly managed, reserves have been shown to work quite well. One of these examples is the Merritt Island National Reserve in Florida. Established in 1962, this area wasn't initially set aside as a reserve. It just worked out that way because the area is next to the Cape Canaveral rocket launch site. For safety and security, the area was closed to all human access. Records show that the record sizes for black drum, red drum, and spotted sea trout, all popular sport fishing species, have all been set within 100 kilometers (62 miles) of the Merritt Island reserve. The rest of Florida has had no new world records since 1985, but catches near the reserve continue to produce fish.

This highlights the fact that big fish are in some ways more important than small fish. Large females produce substantially more eggs. Depending on the species, doubling the size of a fish can increase egg numbers by 20 to 200 times. Marine reserves provide a habitat in which fish can grow to their maximum potential size. This is one reason for the fish yield increase near reserves – fish in the reserve produce more offspring.

A similar result is occurring in the island nation of St. Lucia in the Caribbean. Following a long battle, St. Lucia closed 35% of the fishing grounds off the island's southern coast. The idea was specifically to rehabilitate local stocks. Within five years, catches in the open areas nearly doubled, and today fishermen catch more fish than before. The overall health of the local coral reefs has improved as well. Also, St. Lucia tourism benefits as a popular site for scuba diving thanks in part to its well preserved reefs.

While the evidence is conclusive that reserves help fish populations and other organisms recover substantially, unfortunately reserves don't reduce all global or regional threats. Pollution, global warming and overfishing effects outside of reserve boundaries don't avoid marine reserves.

1. _____ is taking no more fish than would affect future populations. Exceeding it is the precise definition of _____.

   A. Reduction fishing, maximum sustainable yield

   B. Subsidy fishing, overfishing

   C. Overfishing, reduction fishing

   D. Maximum sustainable yield, overfishing

2. According to fisheries scientists, the FAO, the National Marine Fisheries Services, and other sources, _____ of the world's fisheries are overfished or depleted.

   A. 25%

   B. 33%

   C. 75%

   D. 100%

3. Responses to declining fisheries that appear to contribute to the problem include (choose all that apply)

   A. farming fish stock.

   B. using new technologies and methods to catch fish more efficiently.

   C. turning to new, unexploited fisheries.

   D. establishing marine reserves.

4. Problems from commercial fishing for species low in the food web include that (choose all that apply)

   A. it can deplete species higher on the food web that consume them.

   B. it can allow other organisms to proliferate.

   C. there is no market for such species.

   D. none of the above

5. Indirect effects of commercial overfishing on the environment include (choose all that apply)

   A. declines in species that feed on the fish.

   B. bycatch.

   C. damage to oil reserves.

   D. none of the above

6. The Pew Oceans Commission 2003 recommendations for the restoration and preservation of the US biological marine resources specifically included establishing marine reserves and protected areas.

   A. true

   B. false

STUDY QUESTIONS

Find the answers as you read.

1. What are the five primary methods of commercial fishing?

2. How is it that the fishing industry thrives as a business despite estimates that the annual fish catch sells for less than it costs to catch?

Commercial Fishing

Commercial Fishing Methods

What are the five primary methods of commercial fishing?

Commercial fisheries primarily use five methods for taking their catch. One is to use gill nets, which fishermen deploy to entangle either pelagic or groundfish. They haul the nets aboard, removing the desired catch and discarding the bycatch.

The drift net is particularly destructive. Made of very fine, almost invisible mesh, these nets are suspended from the surface to about 10 meters (33 feet). These nets can be as long as 80 kilometers (50 miles), capturing almost every organism in their path. Drift nets lost in storms become "ghost" nets – essentially untended traps that haphazardly kill for years. At the peak of usage in the 1980s, an estimated 40,000 kilometers (25,000 miles) of drift nets stretched through the ocean – enough to circle the Earth. The use of drift nets has been outlawed internationally, although some "pirate fishers" still use them illegally.

Longline fishing uses hooked lines up to 20 or 30 kilometers (12 to 19 miles) long to capture target species such as swordfish. While they're more selective than nets, longlines still produce bycatch. Fisheries scientists suspect that longlines have played a part in the decline of sharks, marlin, and other pelagic species.

Commercial fishermen use purse seine nets to capture pelagic fish, including some species of tuna. The fishing vessel deploys the net around the school, closes the bottom and hauls up the net. This method has less bycatch than others, but bycatch is still a problem. This is the method responsible for dolphin bycatch. However, exclusion devices have reduced (but not eliminated) the problem.

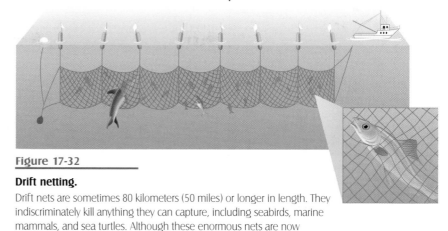

Figure 17-32

Drift netting.

Drift nets are sometimes 80 kilometers (50 miles) or longer in length. They indiscriminately kill anything they can capture, including seabirds, marine mammals, and sea turtles. Although these enormous nets are now banned by international law, they're still used illegally by some fishers.

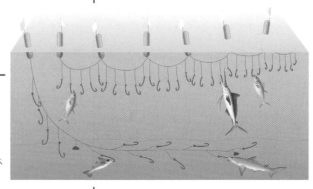

Figure 17-33

Longlining.

Longlining is also indiscriminate in that it captures any fish that will take the bait. This gear has been responsible for the decline of shark and billfish populations.

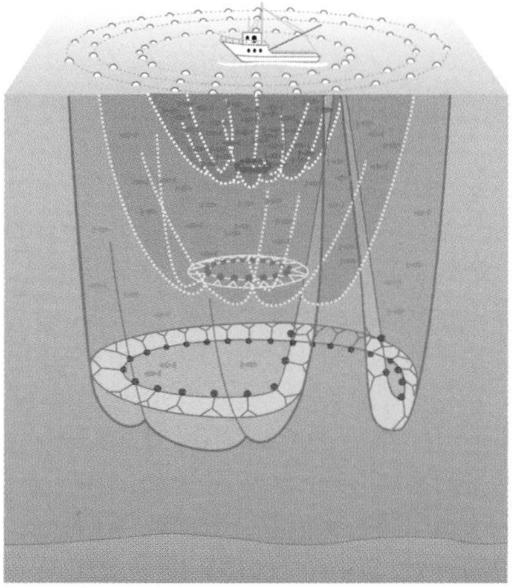

Figure 17-34

Purse seining.

As the name "purse" implies, a line draws the net into a smaller and smaller volume. This is the primary method of catching tuna. Although it can be a very selective form of fishing, tens of thousands of dolphins are killed each year when they are trapped in the nets along with the tuna.

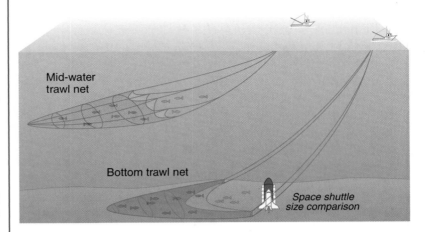

Figure 17-35

Trawling.
Mid-water trawls are capable of sweeping vast regions of the ocean clean of any sizable fish. Bottom trawls can be highly destructive to the benthos, which is the animal communities that live on the sea floor.

Trawling is a very old fishing technique used mid-water and on the bottom. It's estimated that the total ocean bottom area trawled each year equals the size of the continental United States. One concern is that the bottom consists of sensitive and easily disrupted benthic organisms and ecosystems that are crucial to the environment. In highly fished areas, the same bottom can be trawled six or more times in a year.

The Economics of Commercial Fishing

How is it that the fishing industry thrives as a business despite estimates that the annual fish catch sells for less than it costs to catch?

Compared to the industries involved with other marine resources, the worldwide fishing industry is unique in that, according to economic estimates, the worldwide fish catch sells for less than it costs to catch. According to estimates, the world's fishing fleets spend about $54 billion to catch $70 billion in fish. That's about $0.77 spent for every dollar earned.

Normally, this would be the recipe for business failure. No business can spend more than it earns and survive long – unless someone subsidizes it. It appears that the fishing industry survives because of global government subsidies. These subsidies take the form of grants, low- or no-interest loans, free or low-cost fuel, tax incentives, and price controls. In effect, taxpayers cover the overhead so that the fishing industry makes a profit.

Despite the apparent illogic, it's not hard to understand why governments do this. Fishing employs millions of people. A sudden loss of their jobs would destabilize many regional economies. It's not a simple matter to train millions of people for new careers or force them to do something different.

Fishing also represents food security for fishing nations. Governments, therefore, have a further incentive to support an industry vital to their own subsistence or environmental security.

Although commercial fishing in its present state appears unsustainable and very damaging to the environment, it would be wrong to characterize everyone in that trade as uncaring or unethical. Despite the problems, many people involved with it care deeply about the environment and the sustainability of their livelihood. It's worth considering that the problem lies as much with those of us who buy fish as with those who catch them.

Fishing is a long-standing trade with many hard-working individuals and families who struggle to earn a living. Fishing is enmeshed in many local cultures. It defines many people's existence, sometimes going back generations. Some choose this work because, despite the physical demands and risks, they love the sea and working on it. You can't simply tell people that their way of life is wrong and over and that they have to start learning computer programming next week.

For a number of years governments have attempted to negotiate a reduction in subsidies without much progress. Despite many government programs around the world aimed at reducing the number of fishing boats, the number of boats did not significantly change by 2004. Where the number of boats was reduced, it those eliminated were commonly replaced by boats with higher fishing capacity.

Ultimately, though, government, society, and the industry must face the facts. With fish stocks declining, eventually many people in the fishing industry will have to find other work. It can happen either because there are no more fish or by a planned transition. In the latter case, governments would withdraw fishing subsidies

COMMERCIAL FISHING AND THE LAWS OF ECONOMICS

The laws of economics provide a clear case that commercial fishing subsidies contribute to overfishing. While many economic principles remain debated, a few are rarely disputed. One of these, as paraphrased from Nobel-prize winning economist Milton Friedman, is that if you create a demand, you create a supply. This means that if you subsidize something so that it is cheaper than it would normally be, you create an artificial demand and a market surplus.

Because governments subsidize the profession of fishing, there's a surplus of those in that profession. Based on the economic estimates, the world has almost twice the fishing fleet that would exist without subsidies. This is surely a factor in the overfishing situation.

Based on current figures, fish prices should be as much as 77% higher than they are now. But, because fishing is subsidized, fish sells for less than it normally would. Also following the laws of economics, an artificially low price creates a higher demand than would normally exist. If subsidizing stopped, the price would rise and reduce the demand. This would reduce both fishing and fish consumption, perhaps creating economic incentives to develop alternative food sources.

in steps. This would allow economies and people to adjust over a period of years. Instead of subsidies, the money would go toward developing new industries and skill training for workers. It would also give fish stocks a chance to recover for a healthy environment and a sustainable resource.

ARE YOU LEARNING?

1. **The primary methods used in commercial fishing include (choose all that apply)**

   A. longline fishing.

   B. purse seine nets.

   C. gill nets.

   D. fly rods.

2. **The fishing industry thrives as a business despite estimates that the annual fish catch sells for less than it costs to catch because**

   A. the estimates are wrong.

   B. government subsidies make up the difference.

   C. the good catch years counterbalance the poor catch years.

   D. the fishing fleet owners bought shares of Microsoft in 1982.

STUDY QUESTIONS

Find the answers as you read.

1. What was the significance of *Mare Liberum*?

2. What was the original seaward boundary recognized by international law as marking territorial waters of a country?

3. How did the Truman Proclamation of 1945 change the concept of territorial waters?

4. What is *UNCLOS*?

5. What is an *Exclusive Economic Zone (EEZ)*?

6. What are the territorial seas and what are high seas?

7. What guarantee of freedom of navigation did UNCLOS include concerning straits?

8. What EEZ does the United States claim?

Who Owns the Sea?

The Origin of Territorial Waters

What was the significance of Mare Liberum*?*

What was the original seaward boundary recognized by international law as marking territorial waters of a country?

In discussing marine resources, a logical question is, "Who owns them?" If you find something in the sea, what country has a claim to it? Who, for that matter, owns the sea? How far from the coast does a country's territory extend?

These questions and the control of coastal waters have been issues between nations for almost as long as there have been ships. The foundations of western legal views of the ocean can be traced back to the 1490s. A Papal Bull issued by Pope Alexander VI in 1493, followed by the Treaty of Tordesillas in 1493, divided the ocean between Spain and Portugal, the two major sea powers of the day. This gave them a monopoly for exploration and exclusive trading privileges with the East and West Indies.

About 100 years later the British had defeated of the Spanish Armada and Holland successfully defended its trading rights in a dispute with Portugal. To establish the legality of Holland's right to trade, in 1604 Dutch jurist Hugo Grotius wrote *De Jure Praedae* (Latin for *On the Law of Prize and Booty*). The most important part of the paper defended the concept of a what has become known as "freedom of the seas"– freedom of navigation and access to the high seas by every nation. Five years later, Grotius' principle of free access was reprinted as *Mare Liberum* (Latin for *A Free Ocean*). One of his main arguments was that passage rights (freedom of navigation) were inexhaustible because navigation by others across the ocean did not result in loss to anyone. This was the basis of his argument that every nation should be allowed the freedom to sail to any part of the ocean – for trade as well as for their military. He also wrote that it was impossible to exhaust the supply of fish in the ocean.

Not everyone agreed. An English jurist, John Seldan published *Mare Clausum* (*Of the Dominion or Ownership of the Sea*) to establish England's right to protect resources. He acknowledged that it was possible that fishing and other activities could make the sea worse. In this way Grotius and Seldan laid down the critical concepts that 300 years later were to dominate the UNCLOS negotiations – the freedom of navigation versus the right to protect resources.

By the early 18th century, Mare Liberum was internationally recognized. Nations generally agreed to the principle of freedom of the seas for navigation. However, a concept of territorial waters had emerged. Territorial waters are the areas of ocean over which coastal nations have control. At the time, the limit of territorial waters was five kilometers (about three miles) from shore because this was the approximate effective range for cannon fire during this period.

Beyond five kilometers the ocean belonged to no one and was considered international waters – later defined as the "high seas." The concepts of territorial sea and high seas became legal conventions accepted for more than 200 years. They are still the basis for modern international laws of the sea, though today the accepted territorial limit is 19.2 kilometers (12 miles).

The Truman Proclamation

How did the Truman Proclamation of 1945 change the concept of territorial waters?

With the end of World War II came the first major change in the traditional definition of territorial waters. The change came as an extended claim to ocean resources without declaring territorial claims. New technologies had made oil and natural gas available

Figure 17-36

Father of the Law of the Sea.
Seventeenth-century Dutch jurist Hugo Grotius, who wrote De Jure Praedae (Latin for On the Law of Prize and Booty). In it he defended free access to the sea by all nations, a legal tenet that remains with us today.

on the continental shelf. To protect US interests, President Harry Truman issued the Truman Proclamation of 1945. The proclamation declared that "the United States regards the natural resources of the subsoil and sea bed of the continental shelf beneath the high seas but contiguous to the coasts of the United States as appertaining to the United States, subject to its jurisdiction and control." This gave the United States an important legal framework "with respect to the natural resources of the subsoil and sea bed of the continental shelf."

Exclusive Economic Zones

What is UNCLOS?

What is an Exclusive Economic Zone (EEZ)?

What are the territorial seas and what are high seas?

What guarantee of freedom of navigation did UNCLOS *include concerning straits?*

What EEZ does the United States claim?

The Truman Proclamation started a change in how the world sees protecting the ocean's resources. Concerned about the resources of the continental shelf including oil, the US had asserted exclusive jurisdiction over the natural resources of the continental shelf, but it did not claim this additional area as territorial sea. Rather, it laid claim only to the resources.

A number of developing nations also wanted to control their own important resources including fish stocks. This led the Latin American states to declare fishing zones – in some cases actually claiming 200 mile territorial seas. In 1952, Chile Ecuador and Peru signed the Declaration of Maritime Zone. The declaration asserted their jurisdiction over the sea, seabed, and subsoil for 350 kilometers (about 217 miles) from the coastline. In the early 1960s, Iceland extended its exclusive fishing zone by 50 miles, then more, to protect its cod fisheries – which led to the Cod War conflicts with Britain. These claims raised serious security concerns for nations like the United States and Russia, thanks in part to the Cold War. The Cold War gave both nations a pressing need to maintain freedom of navigation for their navies.

In 1958, the United Nations (UN) began a conference in Geneva to settle the issues. The negotiations for the UN Convention on the Law of the Sea (UNCLOS) strove to find a balance between maintaining freedom of the seas and control over natural resources. It took 24 years, but in April 1982, the UN adopted the United Nations

Topic: Law of the Sea
Go To: www.scilinks.org
Code: LOP2460

Convention of the Law of the Sea, also referred to as UNCLOS. UNCLOS was ratified within the UN by a vote of 130 for, 4 against. Due mainly to concerns about mining rights for the seabed, the United States was one of the four countries voting against it.

UNCLOS confirmed the 12 mile territorial sea that had been legally defined previously and established the concept of the *Exclusive Economic Zone* (EEZ). A nation's EEZ extends 370 kilometers (200 nautical miles or 230 statute miles) from the shoreline. Within the EEZ, a nation has complete control of all living resources, economic activity, and environmental protection, but not over the water itself. A nation may not interfere with the passage of vessels, unless the vessels threaten the natural resources or the environment. This differs from the territorial sea that is considered an extension of land territory. It is within the territorial sea that the nation can exercise all control, including its laws on land.

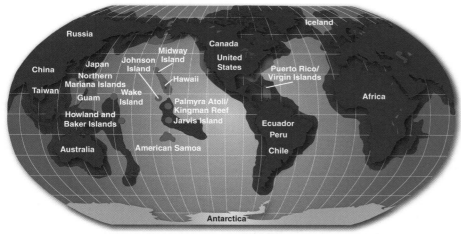

■ World Exclusive Economic Zones   ■ United States Exclusive Economic Zones

Figure 17-37

Exclusive Economic Zones (EEZs).

Shown here is a comparison between the EEZs of the United States and other nations. In 1983, the United States proclaimed its own EEZ within 200 nautical miles of its coasts. This effectively doubled the size of the United States.

Areas beyond the EEZs are the *high seas* or *international waters.* High seas belong to no nation. In particular, UNCLOS ensured the freedom of navigation rights through all of the Straits around the world. In a number of cases. like the Malacca Straits, the passageway is so narrow that these waters are well within the 19.2 kilometers (12 mile) territorial sea of adjacent nations. By including special rules about straits, freedom of navigation was guaranteed for all countries.

One of the more controversial aspects of UNCLOS, and the heart of the US objection, was the establishment of the International Seabed Authority plan. This plan said that mineral wealth that might one day be recovered from the deep seabed would be the common heritage of mankind and should be shared internationally. As a response, however, in 1983 Ronald Reagan issued Presidential Proclamation 5030, establishing for the United States an Exclusive Economic Zone within 200 nautical miles of its coasts. This effectively doubled the size of the United States. In 1994, an additional agreement was made that addressed the US concerns about the seabed portion of the agreement.

UNCLOS also established the basic framework for fisheries management within EEZs . It laid the groundwork for cooperation in management of fish stocks that "straddle" (overlap) adjacent EEZs, or are migratory and travel great distances, like tuna. In 1995, the US and many other key fishing nations signed the Straddling and Migratory Fish Stocks Agreement.

The establishment of EEZs is a milestone in international law. As is covered in Chapter 19, it is far more than a way that nations divide up the sea. It may well be a major step toward effectively maintaining the ocean and its resources for generations to come.

ARE YOU LEARNING?

1. **Mare Liberum established the concept of**

   A. free access to the sea by all nations.

   B. cannons that can fire 5 kilometers.

   C. the sea being split between Spain and Portugal.

   D. EEZs.

2. **The original seaward boundary recognized by international law as territorial waters of a country was**

   A. 3 kilometers (2 miles).

   B. 5 kilometers (3 miles).

   C. 320 kilometers (200 miles).

   D. 350 kilometers (217 miles).

3. **The Truman Proclamation of 1945 changed the concept of territorial waters by**

   A. extending claims to resources without claiming territory.

   B. extending territorial claims.

   C. both of the above

   D. none of the above

4. **UNCLOS is**

   A. the United Nations Convention of the Law of the Sea.

   B. the result of a 24-year effort to establish an international law of the sea.

   C. a UN document that establishes economic and international zones in the sea.

   D. all of the above

5. **According to UNCLOS, an Exclusive Economic Zone is within 200 nautical miles of a nation's shoreline in which it has control of all resources, economic activity, and environmental protection.**

   A. true

   B. false

6. **According to UNCLOS, high seas are waters beyond the EEZs that belong to whichever nations claim them and can enforce that claim.**

   A. true

   B. false

7. **The US claims an EEZ of**

   A. all ocean territory within 200 nautical miles of its coasts.

   B. only the UNCLOS EEZ definition in all respects.

   C. all ocean territory within 350 nautical miles of the continental US coast.

Biodiversity and the Future

The Ultimate Resource

What is biodiversity *and how does it relate to biological resources?*

The introduction to Chapter 5 raises the question of the importance of a single species. This is worth revisiting in light of biological resources and the future.

It's often hard to point to the importance of a single organism. However, it's not hard to point to the importance of having *all* of them. Harvard biologist E. O. Wilson coined the term *biodiversity*. It is the concept that the preservation of the Earth and its ecosystems relies on the broad genetic diversity of all the organisms on Earth.

Biologist Paul Eherlich proposed this analogy. Think of the biosphere with all its organisms as an airplane in flight. Imagine that each organism is a rivet holding the airplane together. Now think of a species going extinct as removing a rivet. As you might imagine, an airplane can lose a rivet or two without falling apart. It will continue to fly along. But, if it loses too many rivets, the structure fails and the plane crashes. Also, some rivets are more important than others. Losing just one– if it's an important one – can crash the plane just as easily as losing several.

The problem is, we don't know as much about organisms as we do about airplanes. An aerospace engineer can determine how many rivets the plane can lose without crashing, and which ones it can never lose. Biologists can't say that about the ecosystem. We don't know when losing one more species is losing too many or when losing this species will bring down our "plane." Ecologist Aldo Leopold once said, "A wise tinkerer saves all the parts."

The importance of biodiversity is that *every* organism is a biological resource. Even if there is no direct use of an organism, it is important because it is part of what keeps life going. It's a resource because it is one of the rivets that holds everything together.

In the end, the ultimate resource we get from the sea is life itself. Without a functional ocean with a thriving biosphere, only a few organisms would survive on Earth. We would not be among them.

STUDY QUESTIONS

Find the answers as you read.

1. What is *biodiversity* and how does it relate to biological resources?

INTERNET PORTAL

SCLINKS. NSTA

Topic: Biodiversity
Go To: www.scilinks.org
Code: LOP2455

ARE YOU LEARNING?

1. **According to the concept of biodiversity, every organism is a biological resource because**

   A. in some form or another, every organism is edible.

   B. all organisms contain oil.

   C. aerospace engineers use organisms as rivets.

   D. every organism is part of maintaining a healthy ecosystem.

New Terms You Learned

- **algin** complex molecule substance derived from algae used in food processing and other applications as a thickening agent (p. 17-29)
- **aquaculture** using farm techniques to grow and harvest aquatic organisms (p. 17-29)
- **biodiversity** the concept that the health of the Earth and its ecosystems relies on the broad genetic diversity found within many organisms (p. 17-53)
- **biological resources** resources that involve bioproductivity, such as fisheries and kelp harvesting (p. 17-3)
- **bioprospecting** the search for organisms with pharmacological or other chemical benefits (p. 17-31)
- **blubber** the protective fat layer that provides natural insulation for whales (p. 17-24)
- **desalinization** the removal of dissolved salts from seawater (p. 17-17)
- **distillation** the process of evaporating seawater and capturing the water vapor to leave salts behind (p. 17-17)
- **ecotourism** tourism that focuses on visiting and experiencing wildlife and natural environments (p. 17-20)
- **Exclusive Economic Zone (EEZ)** zone within 370 kilometers (200 nautical miles or 230 statute miles) from a nation's shoreline in which it has complete control of all resources, economic activity and environmental protection (p. 17-51)
- **hydrocarbon** compound of carbon and hydrogen chain commonly found in petroleum and natural gas (p. 17-5)
- **international waters** the regions beyond the EEZs that belong to no nation (p. 17-51)
- **longshoring** the trade of loading and unloading cargo ships (p. 17-19)
- **Mare Liberum** A free ocean, the principle that all nations have a right to free access to the seas (p. 17-49)
- **mariculture** aquaculture specific to the marine environment (p. 17-29)

- **maximum sustainable yield** the number of a target species fisheries can take without jeopardizing future populations (p. 17-39)
- **methane** natural gas, a gaseous hydrocarbon (p. 17-5)
- **methane hydrates** ice crystals containing methane found on the continental slope (p. 17-8)
- **nonextractive resources** resources obtained from the sea without removing anything from it, such as sea transport shipping and recreation (p. 17-18)
- **nonrenewable resources** resources that natural processes don't replace, or that do so at such a slow rate that they're not replenished in a human lifespan (p. 17-3)
- **Ocean Thermal Energy Conversion (OTEC)** a process that harnesses the energy trapped in the upper layers of seawater to generate electricity; a renewable resource (p. 17-16)
- **overfishing** taking more of a species than the maximum sustainable yield (p. 17-39)
- **physical resources** resources that don't involve biological processes (p. 17-3)
- **reduction fishery** a fishery catching fish for purposes other than direct human consumption (p. 17-34)
- **renewable resources** are those that growing organisms, sunlight, or other processes naturally replace (p. 17-3)
- **reserve rock** nonporous rock that traps migrating oil or gas, forming an oil or gas reserve (p. 17-6)
- **reverse osmosis** the process of transporting material through a semipermeable membrane against the natural flow of diffusion; commonly used as a method for desalinating seawater to create fresh water (p. 17-17)
- **source rock** the rock in which hydrocarbons (oil and natural gas) form (p. 17-6)
- **submerged cultural resource** underwater archaeological sites set aside for protection and comprehensive research (p. 17-22)

- **United Nations Convention of the Law of the Sea (UNCLOS)** convention that established Exclusive Economic Zones, now recognized as international law (p. 17-51)

Chapter 17 in Review

1. Identify the differences between physical and biological resources and renewable and nonrenewable resources. Give examples of each. Based on what you've learned in this chapter, explain why potentially renewable biological resources are currently nonrenewable.

2. Describe how scientists think oil and natural gas form, including the role of surrounding rock. Explain why the surrounding rock is important in searching for oil and natural gas.

3. How do oil companies extract oil and natural gas from the seabed? What are some of the challenges compared to doing so on land? How do oil companies meet those challenges?

4. Explain why methane hydrates aren't currently used as an energy source.

5. List the minerals found in ferromanganese nodules and explain why they're not currently exploited as a mineral resource. Explain how UNCLOS may affect a country's decision to mine the nodules.

6. What resources do we get from seawater? What products are they used for?

7. What is phosphorite and what is it used for? Why will terrestrial sources be the primary sources for phosphorite?

8. What potential resources exist at hydrothermal vents and in marine muds? Explain which of these resources is a strategic metal and why.

9. What physical marine resources are second only to gas and oil in terms of their annual economic value?

10. Describe three ways the ocean can supply renewable energy. Which of these has proved most practical? Why?

11. Describe why fresh water is a growing concern for the future and how we get it from the sea.

12. Define the uses of the sea as nonextractive resources and give two examples.

13. Why is sea transport shipping important? What revolutionized it after World War II?

14. What is ecotourism? How has it affected environments both positively and negatively?

15. What happened in 1868 that changed whaling? How has this affected whale populations since 1900? What has happened to whale populations since the IWC moratorium in 1986?

16. How does whaling continue despite the IWC moratorium? What other cetaceans are thought to be endangered? Why?

17. What types of fur-bearing marine mammals are used as biological resources?

18. Describe how algae is used as a resource and the products in which you might find it.

19. Describe the present state of aquaculture, including its growth and contribution to the world's seafood supply.

20. Explain what bioprospecting is and how it relates to the development of new drugs.

21. Where are commercially important fish found? Why? What proportion of protein in the human diet comes from fish?

22. Explain what reduction fisheries are. What is the purpose of reduction fishing and what proportion of the worldwide catch does it account for? What fish group accounts for the largest catch and how does this group relate to reduction fisheries? What are the environmental concerns related to reduction fisheries?

23. Describe the trend in commercial fishing since World War II according to the United Nations FAO. Why do many scientists doubt the FAO's figures? What is the predicted trend for the worldwide fisheries with respect to demand?

24. What are *maximum sustainable yield* and *overfishing?* What is the condition of the world's fisheries? What responses to declining fisheries appear to contribute to overfishing?

25. Explain why commercial fishing for species low in the food web has potential problems and what those problems are. What indirect effects does overfishing have on the environment?

26. Describe the five primary methods of commercial fishing.

27. Explain how the fishing industry survives despite estimates that it costs more to catch fish than they sell for. Why does this situation exist? What rec-

ommendations have been made to restore and preserve US biological marine resources?

28. What was the significance of Mare Liberum? What seaward boundary recognized by international law grew out of Mare Liberum?

29. How did the Truman Proclamation of 1945 change the concept of protecting resources of the continental shelf? How did it lead to UNCLOS?

30. What is an Exclusive Economic Zone and high seas according to UNCLOS? How does UNCLOS protect freedom of navigation through straits?

31. What EEZ does the United States claim? How does UNCLOS protect freedom of navigation?

32. Explain why, according to the concept of biodiversity, all organisms are biological resources.

Connecting Chapter Concepts – Science Scenarios

1. Renewable resources are resources that growing organisms, sunlight or other processes naturally replace.
   A. While many marine resources are potentially renewable resources, they're presently not renewable. Explain.
   B. The ocean can provide renewable energy in at least three ways. Which of these appears to be the most feasible at present? What concerns exist about using it?
   C. What are nonextractive resources? Give two examples. Are they renewable?
   D. About how much of the world's seafood comes from aquaculture? Are there any drawbacks to aquaculture? If so, what are they?

2. The world's fisheries provide about 18% of the world's protein and provide income for hundreds of millions of people. However, scientists are concerned that the world fish catch is on the brink of collapse due to overfishing.
   A. What is meant by *maximum sustainable yield?* Why is this a critical concept for fisheries management?
   B. How does overfishing a species low on the food web affect other species?
   C. Estimates suggest that commercial fishing costs more than it earns globally. If this is the case, why does it survive as an industry?
   D. About what percent of the world's fish is bycatch? What happens to bycatch?

Marine Science and the Real World

1. Suppose that, through new technology, methane hydrates become practical energy sources. What benefits would come from this? What problems would result?

2. Suppose you're in charge of a project to mine minerals that surround hydrothermal vents. What challenges do you need to be prepared to handle?

3. You are scuba diving off an island and you spot in the sand what looks like an old ship's cannon recently exposed by a fierce storm. As you begin to explore the site, you find other artifacts. The site seems unexplored by historians and archaeologists. Would you begin taking items off the site? Moving items around? Or, should you determine the location of the site and report it to scientists? Explain your reasoning.

4. Why do you think nonrenewable energy resources aren't used extensively? What would change this?

5. Make a case for sustainable commercial fishing and sustainable aquaculture. What factors have to be considered when using ecosystem-based management for fisheries? What makes some forms of commercial aquaculture sustainable while others are unsustainable?

6. The subsidization of commercial fishing highlights the complexities involved with culture, traditions, education, politics, and economies. Imagine you're a resource manager and politician and your job is to ensure that fishing in local waters does not exceed maximum sustainable yield. The problem is that at this level, half the fishing industry employees will lose their jobs. Assuming you have reasonable funding available, describe your plan for restoring fisheries, finding alternatives to commercial fishing, and accommodating the local economy.

7. Regarding your answer to Question 5, list six reasons why your plan won't work.

8. Regarding your answer to Question 6: Propose a solution to each of the six problems.

9. Do you agree that aboriginal cultures should be able to preserve their whaling traditions? Why or why not? Would you change anything about this provision in the IWC exemption for aboriginal cultures?

10. Commercial fishing with trawl nets can be destructive to seafloor organisms. Using today's methods of drilling for oil offshore, is there any data to show that this industry destroys the benthic environment like bottom trawlers? Research your answer.

References

Borgese, E. M. 1983. The Law of the Sea. Scientific American. March. 42. California Coastal Commission. www.coastal.ca.gov/desalpt/dchap1.thml

Canada Department of Fisheries and Oceans. 2008. A Recent Account of Canada's Atlantic Cod Fishery Access. www.dfo-mpo.gc.ca/kids-enfants/map-carte/map_e.htm

Costanza, R., et al. 1998. Principles for Sustainable Governance of the Oceans. *Science.* 281 (no. 5374).

Cramer, D. 1995. Troubled Waters. *The Atlantic Monthly.* June.

FAO. 2007. The State of World Fisheries and Aquaculture 2006, Rome: FAO Fisheries and Aquaculture Department. www.fao.org/docrep/009/A0699e/A0699e00.htm

Garmendia, Jenny Miller. 2005. The Global Fisheries Crisis. *The Undersea Journal.* 3rd Quarter.

Heilprin, John. 2007. 20 Nations Agree on New Fishing Limits. Associated Press. May 4.

Helvarg, D. 2001. Blue Frontier: Saving Americas Living Seas. New York: W.H. Freeman & Co.

Holmes, B. 1994. Biologists Sort the Lessons of Fisheries Collapse. *Science.* 264. 27 May.

Hunt, J. M. 1981. The Origin of Petroleum. *Oceanus.* 24 (no. 2.

Iudicello, S. 1999. *Fish, Markets, and Fishermen: The Economics of Overfishing.* Covelo, CA: Island Press.

Kurlansky, Mark. 1997. Cod: *A Biography of a Fish that Changed the World.* New York: Penguin Books.

Malakoff, D. 1997. Extinction on the High Seas. *Science.* 277 (no. 5325). July.

Maritime Conservation Biology Institute and Oceana. 2004. Scientists' Statement on Protecting the World's Deep-Sea Coral and Sponge Ecosystems. AAAS Annual Meeting. http://www.mcbi.org/what/dsc-statement.htm

McCloskey, W. 2000. *Their Father's Work: Casting Nets With the World's Fishermen.* New York: International Marine.

Milazzo, Matteo. 1998. Subsidies in World Fisheries, A Reexamination. World Bank Technical Paper No. 406 Fisheries Series. Washington DC: The World Bank.

Milne, D. 1995. *Marine Life and the Sea.* Belmont, CA: Wadsworth.

Nash, M. 1997. The Fish Crisis. *Time.* 11 August. 150 (no. 6).

NOAA. 2007. Fur Seal Treaty of 1911. NOAA Celebrating 200 Years. http://celebrating200years.noaa.gov/events/fursealtreaty/welcome.html#treaty

Parfit, M. 1995. Diminishing Returns. *National Geographic Magazine.* November.

Partnership for Interdisciplinary Studies of Coastal Ocean. 2007. The Science of Marine Reserves (2nd Edition, International Version). www.piscoweb.org

Pauly, D. & J.L. Maclean. 2003. *In a Perfect Ocean: The State of Fisheries and Ecosystems in the North Atlantic Ocean.* Washington, DC: Island Press.

Penney, T. R., and D. Bharathan. 1987. Power From the Sea. *Scientific American.* January.

Raloff, Janet. 1996. Fishing for Answers. *Science News.* 26 October. 150.

Roberts, C. 2007. *The Unnatural History of the Sea.* Washington D.C.: Island Press.

Robinson, A. 1999. Trawling for Cancer Cures. *Business Week.* 20 September.

Safina, C. 1999. *Song for the Blue Ocean.* New York: Henry Holt and Company.

Safina, C. (1995). The World's Imperiled Fish. *Scientific American.* 273 (no. 5), November, 46-52.

Seaweed Biotechnology Laboratory. Northeastern University, Marine Science Center. www.marinescience.neu.edu/facultystaff/cheney.html

Seitz, J. L. 1995. *Global Issues: An Introduction.* Cambridge, MA: Blackwell.

Steinberg, P. 2001. The Social Construction of the Ocean. Edited by Steven Smith. Vol. 78, Cambridge Studies in International Relations. Cambridge, MA: Cambridge University Press.

Stocks, K. 2004. Seamount Invertebrates: Composition and Vulnerability to Fishing. Morato, R. and D. Pauly, eds. Seamounts: Biodiversity and Fisheries. Fisheries Centre Research Reports, Vol. 12, No. 5. The University of British Colombia, Vancouver, B.C. Canada.

Stratton Commission. 1960. Our Nation and the Sea: A Plan for National Action. *Report of the Commission on Marine Science, Engineering and Resources.* 305. Washington D.C.: The Stratton Commission.

Suess, E. 1999. Flammable Ice. *Scientific American.* 281 (no. 5). November.

Sumaila, U.R., J. Alder and H. Keith. 2005. Global Scope and Economics of Illegal Fishing. Fisheries Centre Working Paper #2005-02. The University of British Columbia, Vancouver, B.C., Canada.http://www.fisheries.ubc.ca/publications/working/

Truman Proclamation on Conservation. 1945. Policy of the United States with Respect to Coastal Fisheries in Certain Areas of the High Seas. Paper presented at the Presidential Proclamation No. 2668. 28th September.

United Nations Conference on Straddling Fish Stocks and Highly Migratory Fish Stocks. Sixth Session. 1995. Agreement for the Implementation of the Provisions of the United Nations Convention on the Law of the Sea of 10 December 1982. Relating to the Conservation and Management of Straddling Fish Stocks and Highly Migratory Fish Stocks. September 8. A/CONF.164/37.

United Nations Convention on the Law of the Sea. 1982. U.N. Dec. 10. A/CONF.62/122. Reprinted in the Law of the Sea: Official Text of the United Nations Convention on the Law of the Sea with Annexes and Index, UN Sales No. E.83.V.5, 1983.

United Nations Food and Agriculture Organization. www.fao.org/fi/highligh/2010.asp

US Department of Energy. http://fossil.energy.gov/programs/oilgas/hydrates/

US Geological Survey Marine and Coastal Geology Program. http://marine.usgs.gov/fact-sheets/gas-hydrates/title.html

CHAPTER 18

Pollution and the Health of the Ocean

Budd Riker

Damage Assessment, Remediation and Restoration Program, NOAA

Tracing Metals

S ome chemical oceanographers study the behavior of trace metals, such as mercury, lead, barium, and cadmium in rivers and the ocean. To scientists such as John Trefry, trace metals are both friend and foe: friend because of their natural and economic value and foe because of their potential adverse effects on human health when they are released in pollutant discharges into the environment.

Trefry's interest in science evolved gradually and he credits his teachers for encouraging his interest in math and science, but he did not apply his talents to ocean-related studies until after he graduated from college.

"After college, I taught high-school chemistry and coached ice hockey. During that time, I was introduced to a friend of a friend who taught marine biology. He challenged me to think about applying my love of chemistry and nature to the ocean – it sounded really good! He said that too few chemists were studying the ocean, so I went on to graduate study in chemical oceanography within a year or so after that chance encounter."

Trefry's research focuses on the concentrations and cycling of trace metals in the ocean, estuaries, and rivers. These studies have taken place in a wide variety of places, including the Pacific and Atlantic Oceans, the Arctic, the Gulf of Mexico, the Mississippi River, and the Indian River Lagoon in Florida.

"I have had many exciting opportunities to dive 2,100 to 3,000 meters (7,000 to 10,000 feet) beneath the sea in the deep submergence vehicle Alvin and sample hydrothermal vent fluids at temperatures between 250° and 400° C (480°and 750° F). In an entirely different environment, I enjoyed the excitement of driving a snowmobile 16 kilometers (10 miles) out onto a frozen Arctic Ocean, drilling holes through the 2-meter (6-foot) thick ice and sampling the underlying water. As exciting as my work is and has been, it is also very important. We must understand and appreciate trace metals for their economic value, but we also must be wary of possible health problems from their release into the environment."

An educator himself, Trefry passes on his passion for the ocean and chemistry to new generations of scientists and offers this advice for anyone wanting to follow in his particular footsteps:

"Ask yourself the following questions: Do I like math, chemistry, physics, biology, and geology? Do I yearn to be out in nature? Am I challenged to seek answers to things that I don't know? Will enjoying my career in science be more important than material wealth? If the answers are 'yes,' chemical oceanography is worth a serious look."

John H. Trefry, PhD
Professor, Oceanography and Environmental Science, Florida Institute of Technology

Figure 18-1a

B-52 bomber.

Tom Reynolds, USAF

Figure 18-1b

KC-135 tanker.

The search and recovery operations for the H-bomb lost off the coast of Spain in 1966 cost more than $90 million. It proved a dramatic example of the financial, environmental, and geopolitical effects that pollution can have even when it is accidental.

Sometimes people put things in the sea intentionally, like tossing garbage overboard at sea. At other times, it happens by accident, like when a storm sinks a ship in water too deep for divers to reach or when things fall overboard. For a long time, intentional or accidental litter at sea was not a concern beyond the cost of the loss, if any. Once below the waves, it was out of sight and out of mind.

More recently, this perspective has changed. Much, but not all, of the change comes from how litter and pollution affect the ocean's global health. On January 17, 1966, the US Air Force experienced a Broken Arrow — the code for a missing nuclear weapon. They had lost a hydrogen bomb in the Mediterranean Sea off the coast of Spain.

The incident occurred when a B-52 bomber carrying four H-bombs collided with a fuel-laden KC-135 tanker, destroying both aircraft and breaking them into fragments that scattered over a wide area of coast and sea. Recovery teams found three of the bombs, each equal to a million tons of TNT, on land. The fourth was nowhere to be found on land. It had to be in the sea.

The immediate concern was that the weapon might be found by the Soviet Union or one of its satellite nations and US technology and other secrets would be revealed. A long-term concern was that the bomb contained plutonium, uranium, and tritium, all potentially toxic to the local environment if leaked into the water.

Within days, recovery experts and search teams were at work, along with the famous deep diving submersible Alvin. At a cost of nearly $1 million per day, it took almost three months to locate the missing weapon and recover it. As the teams searched, the Soviet Union mounted pressure for an "international search team," implying that the US could not be trusted. Diplomats scurried about to keep multinational pressure at bay and reassure Spain that the US Navy would recover the weapon. In the end, the search and recovery operations cost more than $90 million. It proved a dramatic example of the financial, environmental, and geopolitical effects that pollution can have — even accidental pollution.

This chapter covers the wide-ranging effects humans have on the health of the Earth as it relates to the sea. These effects range from global changes that affect the entire planet to damage to specific marine habitats. You will see how the relentless flow of contaminants into the sea, while less dramatic than losing an H-bomb, costs far more money and has the potential for far more long-term damage. You will see that pollution includes toxins, nutrients, heat, and sound. You will learn why pollution affects how much you will pay in taxes and for food in the future, and how pollution may create risks to your health.

Beyond the problems, this chapter looks at some of the possible remedies. You will also see how international relations play an important role in solving marine pollution problems. You will read about some of the steps already being taken to protect the sea, what we can do to preserve the sea, and what more we need to do.

Global Habitat Destruction

When most people hear about pollution and the ocean, they probably think that it is chiefly a sea-related problem. As explained in previous chapters, the ocean, the land, and the atmosphere link together. Through runoff, convection, evaporation, winds, and currents, they are all extensions of each other and the primary influences on our global ecosystem. Changes to the atmosphere or land affect the entire Earth, including the ocean. Moving a species from one body of water to another alters ecosystems. Overfishing affects local ecosystems and the world's food supply. The reality is that environmental damage anywhere on Earth usually affects the entire global habitat.

Global Warming

Which gases are greenhouse gases?

What data support the suggestion that the Earth's average surface temperature is on the rise?

What percent of the carbon dioxide released when fossil fuels are burned is absorbed by the ocean?

What are some of the possible effects of global warming?

What change in carbon dioxide emissions did the Kyoto Climate Change Conference agree to establish by 2012?

What is probably the only real solution to the global warming problem?

Previous chapters discussed global warming and greenhouse gases. As discussed in Chapter 10, the tendency for greenhouse gases to trap and hold solar heat is not a bad thing. These gases are essential to keep the Earth's climate stable and Earth habitable.

Scientists know that the Earth's surface temperature fluctuates naturally and they estimate that the Earth has been generally warming since the last ice age 18,000 years ago. This warming does not concern scientists as much as the increase in its rate since the beginning of the Industrial Revolution.

STUDY QUESTIONS

Find the answers as you read.

1. Which gases are greenhouse gases?

2. What data support the suggestion that the Earth's average surface temperature is on the rise?

3. What percent of the carbon dioxide released when fossil fuels are burned is absorbed by the ocean?

4. What are some of the possible effects of global warming?

5. What change in carbon dioxide emissions did the Kyoto Climate Change Conference agree to establish by 2012?

6. What is probably the only real solution to the global warming problem?

7. Why is the ozone layer vital to life on Earth?

8. How does ultraviolet radiation harm organisms?

9. What is the significance of the June 1990 international ban on ozone-depleting chemicals?

10. How do modern ships carry non-native species to new environments?

11. What kinds of damage do non-native species cause?

12. Why do some ecologists speculate that the Earth will become a more homogeneous ecosystem?

13. How does overfishing affect local ecosystems?

Several gases in the atmosphere produce the greenhouse effect. These include water vapor, carbon dioxide, methane, and CFCs. All of these, except CFCs, enter the atmosphere through natural processes, but under natural conditions do not cause the Earth to overheat. This is because photosynthesis and the ocean remove them (particularly the carbon dioxide), maintaining the balance.

With the beginning of the Industrial Revolution, humans began to upset the balance. When fossil fuels are burned, carbon in the form of carbon dioxide is released. Prior to the Industrial Revolution, the carbon in fossil fuels was relatively isolated from the carbon cycle. But, when fossil fuels are burned, "new" carbon is added to the atmosphere. This additional carbon in the form of carbon dioxide is more than photosynthesis can cycle. Thus, more carbon dioxide stays in the air. Additional carbon dioxide in the atmosphere increases the atmosphere's ability to retain heat.

Figure 18-2

Atmospheric carbon dioxide 1750-2000.

Note the sharp increase since 1750. Blue indicates data taken from samples of air trapped in ice from Antarctica. Green indicates data taken directly from the atmosphere in Mauna Kea, Hawaii.

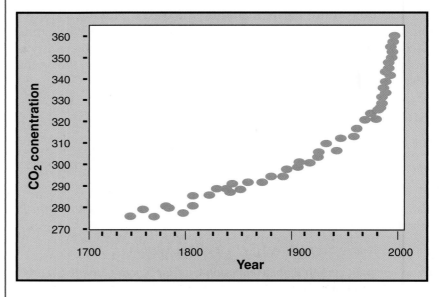

 Data from samples of atmosphere in Mauna Kea, Hawaii

 Data from samples of air trapped in ice in Antarctica

Data indicate that carbon dioxide is indeed rising. Scientists estimate that carbon dioxide in the atmosphere was about 290 parts-per-million (ppm) in 1850 compared to 386 ppm in 2008. This is a 33% increase. The ppm figure would be much higher without the ocean absorbing a lot of the released carbon dioxide. Climatologists calculate that the ocean currently absorbs from 30% to 50% of carbon dioxide from the atmosphere.

Scientists are concerned that the Earth's average surface temperature is rising. One indication of this increase in temperature comes from the overall rise in sea level. This rise can be attributed to melting of polar ice and to expansion of seawater due to warming. Records kept since the 1880s show a rise in sea level.

Historic temperatures can be calculated by examining glacial samples and tree rings. Based on these data, scientists can estimate the average temperature of individual years going back as far as 1,000 years. This data set indicates a marked rise in temperature beginning at the end of the 1800s. The warmest years in recorded history are within the last decade.

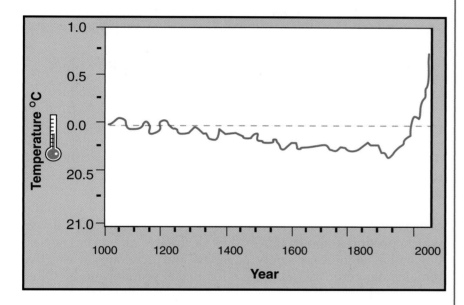

Figure 18-3

One thousand years of global temperature records. This chart shows the Earth's temperature record over the past 1,000 years. Note the steep upward trend since the beginning of the 20th century. Is this a natural variation or the result of human alteration of the atmosphere? A scientific consensus is building that it is the latter, however some believe that this rise may be a natural event. Currently, there is not complete consensus on the matter.

Some estimates suggest that the Earth's average temperature will rise about 2°C over the next 50 to 100 years. That does not sound like much, but the possible effects are significant. These include coral reef death and coral bleaching, changes in global weather patterns, habitat destruction from climate changes, and an increase in violent storms. Computer projections suggest that temperature increases of this nature may cause sea level to rise 0.3 to 1.5 meters (1 to 5 feet). That may not sound like much, but it is sufficient to flood low coastal areas in Florida, the Netherlands, and some small island nations. It would cause coastal wetlands to move inland and it would probably destroy many coral reefs. Coral may not be able to grow quickly enough to keep pace with the changing depth.

As discussed in Chapter 11, some scientists hypothesize that as global warming continues, melting glaciers and ice caps will dilute the seawater near the poles, preventing the high-density, salty water from forming. Without this water, there will be no down-welling to create the North Atlantic deep water currents. Without these currents, tropical regions will continue to warm and polar regions will eventually freeze all the way to the sea bottom. These events would result in wide-ranging damage to ecosystems.

In 1997, industrialized nations met to address the global warming problem in Kyoto, Japan. The Kyoto Climate Change Conference, as it was called, agreed that by 2012, industrial nations would need to reduce carbon dioxide emissions 6% to 8% below 1990 levels. This would require a substantial cutback in fossil fuel use by industry and consumers. However, several nations, including the US, viewed this as impractical and questionable in benefit and withdrew from the agreement. So far, no nation has been able to reach this goal.

Given the world's dependence on energy, changing the global warming trend poses a substantial international challenge. In the last century, the production of fossil fuels increased by a factor of 50. The demand for energy is expected to increase 350% from the present level in the next 25 years. Simply cutting off the supply of energy is not the answer. To do so would cause global economic depression. This would be accompanied by mass starvation and disease due to the inability to produce and transport food and medical care.

The only likely solution is to find and develop cost-effective alternatives to fossil fuels. One existing source is nuclear power, which produces about 17% of US electricity. However, nuclear power has significant safety concerns and generates waste that remains dangerously radioactive for 10,000 years or more. Other alternatives to fossil fuels are solar power, wind power, tidal and wave power, biofuels, and hydrogen fuel cells.

Damage to the Ozone Layer

Why is the ozone layer vital to life on Earth?

How does ultraviolet radiation harm organisms?

What is the significance of the June 1990 international ban on ozone-depleting chemicals?

Chapter 10 explains that the stratosphere has an ozone layer that is vital to life on Earth because it protects us from ultraviolet radiation. Without this protection, life in its current form could not exist.

Some chemicals (primarily CFCs) destroy ozone. They have caused the hole in the ozone layer above Antarctica. In September

INTERNET PORTAL

SC*i*LINKS. NSTA

Topic: Ozone Depletion
Go To: www.scilinks.org
Code: LOP2505

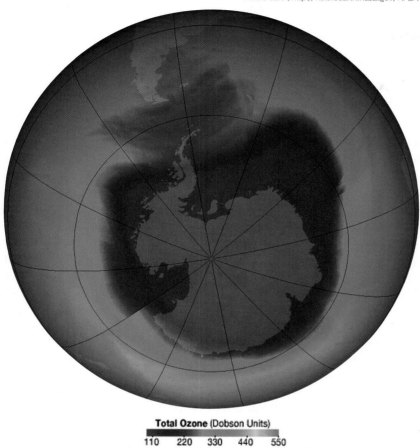

Total Ozone (Dobson Units)

110   220   330   440   550

Figure 18-4

A hole at the bottom of the world.

The release of CFCs destroys ozone, which has resulted in a hole in the ultraviolet-protective ozone layer above Antarctica. In September 2006, scientists recorded the largest hole there yet. It was larger than the size of North America. The picture shown here was made September 17, 2008.

2000, scientists recorded the largest hole there yet. It was about three times the size of the continental US.

Ozone is important because ultraviolet radiation (UV) damages DNA and protein. This is associated with mutations, cancer, and reduction in reproduction. Decreased protection from UV would therefore depress crop yields, reduce plankton growth, and probably cause similar productivity declines throughout all the world's ecosystems. Estimates suggest that a 1% decrease in ozone protection results in a 5% to 7% increase in human skin cancer. Strong ultraviolet radiation can cause cataracts and suppress the immune system.

In June 1990, 53 nations agreed on an international ban of ozone-depleting chemicals. The ban took effect in 2000, so it will be some time before we know how it affects the ozone layer. However, the significance of the ban was that it demonstrated that the international community can cooperate to solve global issues threatening us all.

Non-Native Species

How do modern ships carry non-native species to new environments?

What kinds of damage do non-native species cause?

Why do some ecologists speculate that the Earth will become a more homogeneous ecosystem?

Maritime trade has been an important part of the world economy for hundreds of years. Almost since the earliest days, humans have carried unintentional *passenger* organisms to new parts of the world. Many plants and animals that grow wild on land and in the ocean around the US were transplanted from abroad. Oranges and the kudzu vine are two examples of organisms transplanted from Asia.

Although non-native species sometimes enter a new environment by being carried there intentionally, today the most common mechanism is unintentional transportation. Modern ships may do this when they take on and release ballast water to maintain stability. They may take on water in one place – along with local organisms in the water – and travel thousands of kilometers to pick up cargo. Once they are loaded with cargo, they no longer need the ballast, so they pump the water out – along with the organisms that came on board. This does not always successfully transplant an organism. Changes in temperature, salinity, and the generally foul conditions in a ship bilge kill many organisms. Also, the new environment may not be well suited for the new organism, so it may fall prey to a predator or dies of starvation.

Sometimes, though, conditions are ideal for the passenger organism. The new species may have characteristics that allow it to out compete local organisms. They become biological invaders that can shift the ecological balance, sometimes even destroying an existing ecosystem. One of the best examples is the zebra mussel invasion of the Great Lakes. Their larvae probably entered the lakes in 1988 in ballast water from a vessel from Europe. Scientists think the mussels probably came from the Black Sea or near the Ukranian seaports of Kherson and Nikolayev, where they are native.

Although a marine species, the zebra mussel adapted to freshwater life in the Great Lakes, where they had neither competitors nor predators. In these conditions, they multiplied so quickly that in one year they existed in densities of 30,000 per square meter in some areas. The zebra mussel clogged water intake pipes, attached themselves to ships, and grew thick on docks and other structures. This filter feeder has been so prolific that it has

Simon van Mechelen, Great Lakes Environmental Research Laboratory, NOAA.

Figure 18-5

Foreign invaders.

An alien species introduced into US waters from ballast water, the zebra mussel clogs water intake pipes and grows in dense concentrations on docks and other structures. They are voracious secondary consumers, but without natural predators, they cut off the food supply to higher trophic levels.

Figure 18-6

Current range of zebra mussels.

One of the best and most serious examples of invasive species in the US is the zebra mussel. This map shows where they are now found in abundance.

actually improved the water clarity of the lakes by filtering out suspended matter.

Unfortunately, much of the suspended matter is algae, which is the base of the food chain for the lakes. The zebra mussels are proving to be voracious secondary consumers. Without natural predators, the food web stops with them. They are cutting off the supply of energy to higher trophic levels.

Similar to the zebra mussel, the green mussel is a non-native species being found in coastal regions of the Gulf of Mexico. It remains to be seen what the consequences of this organism will be. On the west coast of the US, the European green crab has been found in Pacific waters from San Francisco to Vancouver Island. This crab is a voracious competitor.

Animals are not the only problem. Water plants, algae, and even diseases are spread by accidental introduction. One example is hydrilla, a non-native plant that clogs Florida waterways. It was accidentally introduced into the environment by the aquarium trade in the 1960s. Once hydrilla populations explode, the plants smother and replace virtually every native bottom plant.

The green seaweed *Caulerpa taxifolia* is becoming a major problem in the Mediterranean. Accidentally transplanted from the Caribbean in 1984 to the Mediterranean, *Caulerpa taxifolia* now covers large areas of seafloor along Spain, France, Italy, and Croatia. San Francisco Bay is virtually an international zoo, with more than 300 introduced species that have altered the ecology.

The pace of species introduction is so rapid and countermeasures have been so ineffective that many ecologists think the world could have much more homogeneous ecosystems in the future. This means that for a given type of environment, the same species will be found worldwide. The concern is that introduced species extinguish existing competitive species, resulting in a significant reduction in biodiversity throughout the world.

Overfishing

How does overfishing affect local ecosystems?

Chapter 17 discussed the causes and problems with extensive overfishing. However, the topic deserves revisiting here because the effects of overfishing harm not only specific fisheries but also the overall global environment. One example you read about was the clupeids, which provide food for fish higher in the food web. Overfishing clupeids cuts off food from the upper-level predators

Topic: Overfishing
Go To: www.scilinks.org
Code: LOP2500

1900

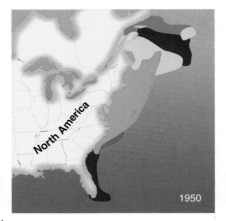

1950

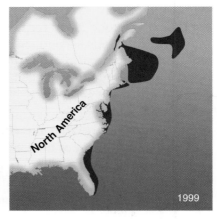

1999

Tons of fish per square km	10+	4-5
	8-9	3-4
	6-7	0-2

Figure 18-7

The results of one hundred years of fishing.

Although this illustration tells the tale of the fishery decline on the east coast of North America, this experience has been sadly repeated all over the world.

and also allows lower-level organisms that they feed on to overpopulate. This, in turn, has its own ecological effects.

The point is that overfishing affects local ecosystems by creating an imbalance. You cannot eliminate species from an environment without disrupting the ecological balance. As discussed in Chapter 17, estimates suggest that 70% of the worldwide fish stocks are overfished. This makes overfishing a global concern as well as a regional concern.

1. **Greenhouse gases include (choose all that apply)**

   A. carbon dioxide.

   B. oxygen.

   C. methane.

   D. water vapor.

2. **Evidence that supports the theory that the Earth's average surface temperature is on the rise include (choose all that apply)**

   A. polar ice sheets are melting.

   B. sea level is rising.

   C. bird populations are decreasing.

   D. tree rings show evidence that temperature is rising.

3. **Climatologists estimate that the ocean absorbs about _____% of the carbon dioxide released from burning fossil fuels.**

   A. 10 to 30

   B. 30 to 50

   C. 50 to 80

   D. 80 to 100

4. **Possible effects of global warming include (choose all that apply)**

   A. flooding coastal areas and island nations.

   B. restoration of coral reefs.

   C. loss of remaining coast wetlands.

   D. a decrease in the production of North Atlantic deep water currents.

5. **The Kyoto Climate Change Conference agreed to reduce carbon dioxide emissions to zero by 2012.**

   A. true

   B. false

6. **Most likely, the only real solution to the global warming problem is**

   A. artificially cool the atmosphere.

   B. to stop using energy.

   C. to develop cost-effective alternatives to fossil fuel.

   D. to find another planet to live on.

7. **The ozone layer is vital to life on Earth because**

   A. it supplies us with oxygen.

   B. it protects us from heavy rain.

   C. absorbs carbon dioxide.

   D. it protects us from ultraviolet radiation.

8. **Ultraviolet radiation is harmful because it**

   A. causes unchecked photosynthesis.

   B. damages DNA and protein.

   C. penetrates the aphotic zone.

   D. none of the above

9. **The significance of the June 1990 international ban on ozone-depleting chemicals is that it showed that the international community**

   A. can save the ozone layer.

   B. cannot agree to limit the use of CFCs.

   C. can cooperate to solve global issues that threaten everyone.

   D. none of the above

10. **The most common way that modern ships transplant non-native species to new environments is by**

    A. allowing ship mascots to escape.

    B. loading and discharging ballast water.

    C. deliberately sabotaging the local environment.

    D. none of the above

11. **Non-native species do damage by (choose all that apply)**

    A. disrupting the local ecosystem.

    B. outcompeting and replacing native species.

    C. reducing biodiversity.

    D. photosynthesizing.

12. **Some ecologists speculate that Earth could become a homogeneous ecosystem because**

    A. the spread of non-native species is so rapid.

    B. countermeasures have been relatively ineffective in stopping accidental introductions of species to new environments.

    C. some species are being found worldwide.

    D. upper-level predation is not taking place.

13. **Overfishing affects local ecosystems by creating the imbalance that must result if you eliminate a species from an environment.**

    A. true

    B. false

Sensitive Marine Habitat Destruction

STUDY QUESTIONS

Find the answers as you read.

1. What is the primary cause of coastal wetland destruction?

2. Why are estuaries particularly at risk of destruction?

3. Approximately what percent of the world's mangroves has been destroyed?

4. How do ENSO events relate to coral reef destruction?

5. What practices associated with capturing fish are destructive to coral?

6. Approximately what percent of the world's coral reefs do scientists estimate has been destroyed?

Coastal Wetland Destruction

What is the primary cause of coastal wetland destruction?

Why are estuaries particularly at risk of destruction?

Approximately what percent of the world's mangroves has been destroyed?

As discussed in Chapters 5 and 16, mangroves and other coastal wetlands are among the most biologically productive habitats on Earth. Unfortunately, they are rapidly being destroyed.

The primary cause of coastal wetland destruction is the tendency for people to live near the coast. About two-thirds of the world's population is concentrated along the coast. In the US, 70% of the population lives within a day's drive of the ocean. Most of the world's largest metropolitan areas are located directly in the coastal zone.

Considering the proximity of human population to coasts, it is no surprise that sewage and toxic materials pollute coastal waters. However, there are additional reasons human activities are destroying wetlands.

One of the most significant problems is that coastal areas are prime real estate. There is tremendous economic pressure to fill wetlands and use the area for housing, commercial zones, and even airports. Beyond the direct destruction that results when wetlands are filled, poor land use, poorly managed dredging, dams, and the removal of sand dunes can all affect and destroy wetlands.

Estuaries are particularly at risk of destruction for several reasons. The first is that they are not only potential real estate when filled in, but they are also potential harbors when dredged. This effectively doubles the incentive to destroy them. Second, estuaries are very sensitive environments. It takes only one part per 10 million of oil in water to seriously disrupt the growth and reproduction of some species that live in this type of wetland. Migrating birds stop over in estuaries. This means a single polluted estuary can affect the ecology of environments thousands of kilometers away.

Because of their proximity to urban centers, US estuaries are often badly damaged. The waters associated with US Gulf Coast estuaries account for about 40% of the most productive fisheries in the US. Due to pollution of these estuaries, about 60% of the gulf shellfish harvest areas are closed or restricted.

In tropical regions such as Florida, mangroves are a particular concern. These wetlands act as nurseries for the larvae and young of tropical species. The protection they find in a mangrove estuary gives them a chance to survive to maturity.

At one time, 60% to 75% of the Earth's tropical and semi-tropical coastline was mangrove forest. This is no longer true. It is estimated that today more than 50% of mangroves has been destroyed. To make matters worse, they are continuing to vanish. In South America and Southeast Asia, large areas of mangroves are destroyed to make shrimp ponds or are burned as firewood. In Ecuador, shrimp mariculture has displaced about a third of all mangrove forests. Scientists expect the Philippines to lose all of their mangroves to mariculture and other uses within the next decade. Many scientists estimate that, worldwide, mangroves are disappearing more quickly than tropical rainforests.

Coral Reef Destruction

How do ENSO events relate to coral reef destruction?

What practices associated with capturing fish are destructive to coral?

Approximately what percent of the world's coral reefs do scientists estimate has been destroyed?

Human activities are destroying one of the world's most productive ecosystems, the coral reefs. Some of the destruction comes from coral bleaching, which occurs when coral polyps reject the zooxanthellae dinoflagellates that live in their tissue. Bleaching seems to correlate with high surface temperatures, which in turn appear associated with ENSO events. (Chapter 11 discusses the global temperature shifts that take place during ENSO events.) Scientists noted the first widespread bleaching in the 1980s. Since then, they have recorded several bleaching incidents, with the worst so far in 1997-98. Some research also suggests that agricultural runoff triggers coral bleaching.

Besides coral bleaching, a host of other ailments that may be related to pollution attack coral. Disease nearly wiped out the Caribbean black spiny sea urchin during 1983-84. This caused a coral decline because the urchins feed on algae that, in turn, compete with and displace coral. The loss of the urchins allowed these algae to overrun coral in many places.

©Arne Johannessen/
www.arne-met-nelda.com

Figure 18-8

Cheap shrimp.

Much of the mangrove destruction around the world today is due to shrimp farming. It has already eradicated about a third of all mangrove forests in Ecuador; the Philippines is expected to lose all their mangroves to mariculture and other uses within the next decade.

Florida Fish and Wildlife Conservation Commission's Fish and Wildlife Research Institute

Figure 18-9

Troubled corals.

Bleaching occurs when coral polyps reject their symbiotic algae (zooxanthellae). It has been correlated with high surface temperatures, which appear to be associated with ENSO events. The worst incident so far recorded occurred in 1997-98.

Other human activities indirectly affect coral. In some areas, global warming is raising temperatures above coral's survival range. Construction and agriculture add sediments and fertilizers to runoff that reaches some reefs. The sediments clog and smother the polyps. The nutrient runoff allows competitive algae to displace coral on the reef. As explained in Chapter 16, the loss of mangrove forests removes the environment in which many coral reef juveniles evade predation until maturing.

Some human activities destroy the coral reef environment directly. Dredging harbors and collecting coral for sale to tourists are obvious examples. Two practices associated with capturing fish are especially destructive. Some people gathering tropical marine fish for the aquarium trade or as live food fish displayed in restaurants stun the fish with toxic substances, including cyanide. The toxic substances kill the nearby coral, plus hundreds of other fish and invertebrates in the area. Fish captured this way also commonly die, but very slowly. They die in transit or live just long enough to die in a home or restaurant aquarium. In some areas, people use

COOKED TO DEATH

The Queensland Center for Marine Studies in Australia released a report in 2004 with a bleak outlook for the survival of the Australian Great Barrier Reef. According to the report, the Great Barrier Reef, which is the largest coral reef in the world, will be 95% without coral by 2050. The Great Barrier Reef is more than 1,900 kilometers (1,200 miles) long.

According to the Center's report, the chief factor in destroying the coral will be global warming. Predictions suggest that the average local water temperature will rise by as much as 6° C, yet coral bleaching requires only an increase as small as 1° C.

Even before the report, the Australian government took steps to minimize damage to the reef. However, how this wider concern will affect the reef largely depends on how the international community deals with global warming.

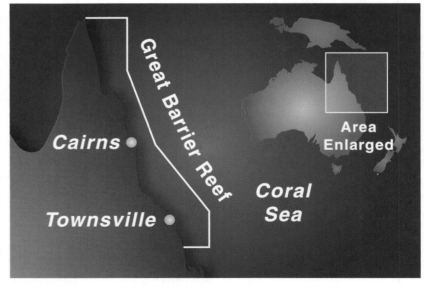

Figure 18-10

The Great Barrier Reef.

dynamite to stun and kill fish for food. This causes widespread death and damage in the coral community.

Scientists estimate that the indirect and direct effects of human activities have destroyed about 25% of the Earth's corals. These effects harm or threaten nearly 60% of the remaining coral reefs, causing some to fear whether there will be any at all in 50 years.

ARE YOU LEARNING?

1. **The primary cause of coastal wetland destruction is the tendency for**

   A. people to overfish.

   B. people to relocate coastal species inland.

   C. people to live near the coast.

   D. the coast to degrade naturally.

2. **Estuaries are particularly at risk of destruction because they (choose all that apply)**

   A. can be used for either real estate or harbors.

   B. are sensitive environments.

   C. do not naturally last very long anyway.

   D. tend to accumulate toxins from the open sea.

3. **According to estimates, more than _____% of mangroves has been destroyed.**

   A. 10

   B. 25

   C. 40

   D. 50

4. **ENSO events seem to correlate with**

   A. dynamite fishing.

   B. coral bleaching.

   C. mangrove destruction.

   D. all of the above

5. **Practices destructive to coral associated with capturing fish and fishing include (choose all that apply)**

   A. using dynamite to stun fish.

   B. using fishing poles.

   C. using toxic substances to stun fish.

   D. releasing bait fish.

6. **Scientists estimate that about _____% of the world's coral reefs has been destroyed.**

   A. 10

   B. 25

   C. 40

   D. 50

Pollutants and Their Effects

Definition of Pollution

With respect to the marine environment, how do we define "pollution"?

The ocean is not only a major food source and a wondrous ecosystem, but also a huge waste receptacle. As ironic as this sounds, it began with the belief in the late 1800s and early 1900s that "the solution to pollution is dilution." This meant that by diluting wastes, natural processes would break them down and eliminate them.

STUDY QUESTIONS

Find the answers as you read.

1. With respect to the marine environment, how do we define "pollution"?

2. What are the different sources for pollution in the ocean?

3. What is the percent of pollution contributed by each source?

Bob Wohlers

Figure 18-11

Definition of pollution.

With respect to the marine environment, it is useful to define pollution as "products of human activities that have harmful or objectionable effects to the water quality or affect the physical, chemical, or biological environment." Near every home are storm drains. Regardless of where you live, these drains dump into rivers or near coastal zones directly into the ocean. If you dump oil, pesticides, or other chemicals down the storm drains, they will eventually end up in the ocean.

From that perspective, the ocean is an obvious, unlimited answer to what to do with waste – that is, it has long been viewed as a sewer.

Each year we dump more than 22 billion tons of pollutants into the seas, but the seas have begun to show the effects. Dilution no longer works, and the ocean cannot provide life and food while also being a sewer. "Out of sight, out of mind" no longer applies to the marine environment.

With respect to the marine environment, *pollution* is defined as "products of human activities that have harmful or objectionable effects to the water quality or affect the physical, chemical, or biological environment." This definition includes organic or natural compounds like bacteria, as well as unnatural, manufactured substances like sound and hot water discharge.

Sources of Pollution

What are the different sources for pollution in the ocean?

What is the percent of pollution contributed by each source?

Today scientists find traces of synthetic compounds in virtually all ocean water. It's difficult to imagine what totally unpolluted conditions would be. In fact, scientists use samples recovered from polar ice packs and glaciers to try to create a model of a pristine ocean.

Researchers have growing data about the types and quantities of pollutants entering the ocean. According to the United Nations Environmental Programme, this is the estimated breakdown of marine chemical pollution:

- 44% - land run-off/discharge, agricultural and industrial runoff (nutrients).
- 33% - airborne emissions from land; propellants, hydrocarbons, and *biocides* (chemicals that kill, such as pesticides) that enter the ocean from the atmosphere as snow and rain.
- 12% - shipping spills and accidental spills; maritime accidents, ships dumping bilge water, ballast water and garbage.
- 10% - ocean dumping; industrial, municipal, and agricultural waste and dredging spills. A common pollutant in estuaries is bacteria, mostly from sewage dumped into bays and rivers.
- 1% - offshore mining, oil and gas drilling. Each year, we dump about 100 million tons of plastics, 17 million tons of sewage and sludge, 5 million tons of oil, and 5 trillion gallons of toxic waste into the marine environment.

Pollutants that enter the ocean in one place don't necessarily stay there. Through natural processes, they can return to the atmosphere, enter the food web or be transported by the *global conveyor belt* that circulates all the world's water. Consequently, no matter where they enter the sea, eventually pollutants go everywhere. Furthermore, since the conveyor belt circulation is slow, pollutants entering the ocean today may spread for more than 1,000 years before we know all their effects – or even that they exist.

Another problem is that pollutants affect sea life in various ways. Some are instantly lethal, whereas many only weaken organisms. These weakened organisms become easy prey, which can create a change in the environmental balance. Even if the pollutant doesn't significantly harm the organism that ingests it, the animal that eats it also consumes the pollutant.

INTERNET PORTAL

SCiLINKS. NSTA

Topic: Ocean Pollution
Go To: www.scilinks.org
Code: LOP2465

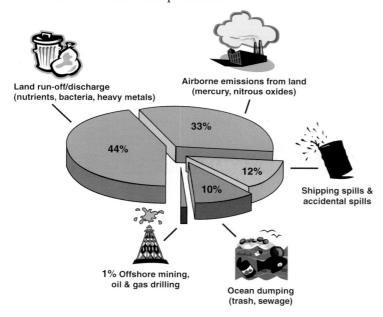

Land run-off/discharge
(nutrients, bacteria, heavy metals)

Airborne emissions from land
(mercury, nitrous oxides)

44%

33%

12%

10%

Shipping spills &
accidental spills

1% Offshore mining,
oil & gas drilling

Ocean dumping
(trash, sewage)

Figure 18-12

Sources of marine pollution.

A common misconception is that marine pollution comes primarily from oil spills and other easily identified industrial sources. In reality, most of the pollution is *non-point-source* (coming from multiple origins). This is a cocktail of hundreds of substances contributed from common everyday activities, like driving cars, landfill trash, and run-off from farms and parking lots. One third of the pollutants entering the sea come from the atmosphere, deposited by rainfall.

Pollutants vary in how long they persist in the environment. *Biodegradable* pollutants are those that microbes can render into harmless compounds relatively easily. Crude oil is an example of a biodegradable pollutant. Some synthetic compounds, including plastics, may remain in the environment for hundreds of years because there are no microbes that decompose them.

Some pollutants are not toxic, but instead, they are organic materials that provide nutrients for organisms. With added nutrients, there can be explosive population growth of some species, which creates an imbalance in the ecosystem. In coastal water, organic matter and agricultural fertilizers account for the greatest volume of waste. Bacteria eventually break down or consume these compounds, but the intense bacterial activity can deplete the local oxygen supply, causing massive kills of fish and other organisms. Nitrates and phosphates can cause phytoplankton blooms discussed in Chapter 4. The many dinoflagellates associated with plankton blooms have a neurotoxin that accumulates in oysters and clams. If people eat these bivalves after a plankton bloom, the accumulated toxins can cause illness and sometimes death.

Polluting the ocean contaminates our seafood. Besides toxins from plankton blooms and other pollutants you will read about, seafood can carry the organisms that cause typhoid, salmonella, viral hepatitis, and botulism. By eating some types of seafood, people are exposed to heavy metal poisoning. The cumulative effects of pollution are not well understood, so opinions vary greatly about their long-term effect on both the marine environment and human health.

ARE YOU LEARNING?

1. **With respect to the marine environment, we can define pollution as**

   A. substances created by all organisms that change water quality.

   B. products of human activities that have harmful or objectionable effects to the water quality or affect the physical, chemical, or biological environment.

   C. primarily crude oil or refined oil caused by tanker spills.

2. **Sources of pollution include (choose all that apply)**

   A. propellants, hydrocarbons, and biocides in the atmosphere.

   B. agricultural and industrial runoff.

   C. maritime accidents or ships dumping bilge water, ballast, and garbage.

   D. glacial melting releasing paleopetroleum wastes.

3. **About 44% of marine pollution comes from**

   A. propellants, hydrocarbons, and biocides in the atmosphere.

   B. agricultural and industrial runoff.

   C. maritime accidents or ships dumping bilge water, ballast, and garbage.

   D. glacial melting releasing paleopetroleum wastes.

Toxic Pollutants

Toxic pollutants damage the environment by being poisonous to organisms. As you will see, some pollutants are immediately lethal to any organism that comes in contact with them, while other pollutants must accumulate in the tissues of an organism before they become lethal.

Heavy Metals

What are heavy metals?

How do heavy metals affect organisms?

What risks do heavy metals present for humans?

Excluding oil, each year more than 19 trillion liters (5 trillion gallons) of potentially toxic waste, including *heavy metals*, hydrocarbons, industrial chemicals, and radioactive materials enter the ocean. Even small quantities of the heavy metals may be a major threat to organisms. The heavy metals that most concern scientists are lead, mercury, cadmium, arsenic, and copper.

Heavy metals damage organisms by interfering with cellular metabolism. They are not easily eliminated, so they tend to accumulate in organisms over time. *Bioaccumulation* is the concentration of heavy metals, synthetic organic chemicals, and natural organic chemicals that gradually accumulates in an organism's body throughout its lifetime. The amount of toxin that accumulates may or may not be great enough to kill the organism. If a higher trophic level animal consumes the organism, the toxins are passed on.

High trophic level animals can have high concentrations of toxic substances in their flesh due to bioaccumulation in their prey. Since high level animals eat many lower level organisms that have accumulated toxins, the toxins become more concentrated in higher level animals. The toxic substance concentrates yet further at the next trophic level and so on. This is called *biomagnification*.

Because of bioaccumulation and biomagnification, predators high on the food web, such as tuna, tend to have high concentrations of heavy metals. This presents a risk of heavy metal poisoning to humans who consume tuna and other high-level organisms.

Sources of heavy metals include coal combustion (used by electrical utilities and steel and iron manufacturers), fuel oil refining, fuel additive manufacturing, and urban waste incineration. Because they are so common and have widespread uses, mercury and lead

STUDY QUESTIONS

Find the answers as you read.

1. What are *heavy metals*?

2. How do heavy metals affect organisms?

3. What risks do heavy metals present for humans?

4. Why can many synthetic organic chemicals persist in the marine environment?

5. How do these synthetic chemicals concentrate into dangerous levels when they enter the sea in very low concentrations?

6. What are the major sources of oil pollution in the ocean?

7. How does oil pollution affect the marine environment?

8. Why is refined oil more hazardous to the environment than crude oil?

9. Why is it sometimes better to leave an oil spill alone rather than to clean it up?

10. How do radioactive materials presently affect marine organisms?

11. How do radioactive materials get into the ocean?

12. Why are radioactive materials a concern even though dumping them in the sea was banned by international law in 1975 and 1983?

13. What concerns exist regarding the dumping of munitions in the ocean?

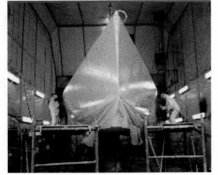

Figure 18-13

Avoiding foul substances.

For years, anti-fouling paints used on the bottoms of ships and boats contained some very toxic chemicals. One substance in these paints, TBT, is so toxic that paints containing it are banned from use in the US. Today, ships are being painted with antifouling paints free from TBT.

are particularly problematic. Both enter the environment naturally, but human processes release about five times as much mercury and 17 times as much lead as do natural sources.

Heavy metals present significant risks for humans. Research has shown that high levels of mercury are associated with birth defects, brain damage and behavior disorders. The US government advises limited consumption of some types of fish that accumulate the highest levels of heavy metals (tuna, swordfish, mackerel, and shark), but there are additional sources. Lead enters the environment from industrial waste, gasoline fumes and residue, landfills, and runoffs. At one time, house paint and leaded gasoline were a lead risk, but today, they are no longer allowed in the US.

Copper enters the environment by accident, but also intentionally. Copper oxides are used in special anti-fouling paints for boats and ships that keep organisms from growing on them. Another heavy metal anti-fouling compound called *tributyl tin* (TBT) is so toxic that the US banned it in the late 1980s. Unfortunately, other countries still use it. TBT is an *immunosuppressor*, which means that it compromises an organism's immune system. Findings suggest that high TBT levels in dolphins and small whales may account for the increased number of strandings of these species. Many scientists consider heavy metals a more serious public health threat than all other organic chemicals, or even radioactive waste.

SWEAT IT OUT

There is little doubt that regular exercise (three to five times weekly) is essential for good health. Mounting evidence shows that the human body lasts longer and works best with regular physical activity. Regular exercise is associated with lower obesity, reduced cancer risk, and less heart disease. It has even been demonstrated that people who exercise regularly improve their brain function – their ability to think. It is also becoming clear that the younger you begin an exercise habit, the better your health.

While there is almost no question about the benefits, scientists are still discovering all the reasons why exercise helps the body so much. Recent findings indicate that one reason is that exercise helps your body eliminate heavy metals. This is significant because the kidneys and liver do not readily eliminate heavy metals through normal excretion processes.

Analysis of athletes with a statistically low cancer incidence led researchers to analyze their perspiration. Scientists found that the athletes' sweat contained toxins and metals including cadmium, lead, zinc, nickel, and even cholesterol. It has also been noted that a conditioned athlete loses less of the desirable body salts in sweat compared to an unconditioned person. If regular exercise increases sweat production and helps eliminate heavy metals and other toxins, it sounds like a good idea for organisms high in the food web – like you – to be exercising regularly!

Synthetic Organic Chemicals

Why can many synthetic organic chemicals persist in the marine environment?

How do these synthetic chemicals concentrate into dangerous levels when they enter the sea in very low concentrations?

In addition to heavy metals, synthetic chemicals capable of interacting with organic processes enter the ocean. Known as *synthetic organic chemicals* because they are human-made but based on organic molecule structures, these substances are particularly dangerous because they can be toxic in even very small quantities. Many persist in the environment because bacteria and other processes do not break them down.

Synthetic organic chemicals normally exist in very low concentrations in seawater. However, just as they do with heavy metals and some natural chemicals, organisms bioaccumulate synthetic organic chemicals. A good example of this is dichlorodiphenyltrichloroethane, more commonly known as the pesticide DDT. Although DDT is barely detectable in seawater, it magnifies 200,000 times in just five trophic levels.

Substances that biomagnify are called *conservative materials*. They are called this because they are conserved rather than digested as they move through the food web. Conservative materials can cause harm at any trophic level, but they are the greatest risk to top-level predators, including humans.

TOXIC SOUP: OCEAN-BORNE SYNTHETIC ORGANIC CHEMICALS

Name	Major Health Effects
Aldicarb (Temik)	High toxicity to the nervous system
Benzene	Chromosomal damage, anemia, blood disorders, and leukemia
Carbon tetrachloride	Cancer; liver, kidney, lung: central nervous system damage
Chloroform	Liver and kidney damage; suspected cancer
Dioxin	Skin disorders, cancer, genetic mutations
Ethylene dibromide (EDB)	Cancer and male sterility
Polychlorinated biphenyls (PCBs)	Liver, kidney, and lung damage
Trichloroethylene (TCE)	In high concentrations, liver and kidney damage, central nervous system depression, skin problems, and suspected cancer and mutations
Vinyl chloride	Liver, kidney, and lung damage; lung, cardiovascular, and gastrointestinal problems; cancer and suspected mutations

DDT DEBATE RAGES ON

The US banned DDT due to its purported damage to the environment, but it remains in use as a pesticide in developing countries. Despite the concerns that led to the US ban, many health officials argue that the benefits of using DDT to eliminate mosquitoes and combat malaria far outweigh the potential risks.

This raises the question of whether low-income, developing countries can afford not to use DDT, despite concerns for the environment. Compared to alternative pesticides, DDT is significantly less expensive. Adding fuel to the controversy, some scientists point out that many of the supposed downsides of DDT have never been proven.

Other scientists state that since alternatives exist, a better strategy is to phase out DDT altogether. They propose that the risks are real, and that safer alternatives can be made economically feasible through support by developed countries.

Figure 18-14

Major synthetic organic chemicals found in the sea.

Synthetic organic chemicals are manufactured by humans, but based on organic molecule structures. These are particularly dangerous substances because they can be toxic in small quantities.

In sublethal levels, conservative materials have a wide range of effects on marine animals, from fin erosion, pre-cancerous growths, and skeletal deformities to abnormal larvae. One of the most dramatic examples is the effect of polychlorinated biphenyls (PCBs) on beluga whales in the St. Lawrence River. These belugas accumulate so much PCB through biomagnfication that, *by law*, their carcasses are classified as hazardous waste! A few, but not many, organisms have systems that detoxify conservative materials, but their ability to do so is limited.

DDT and PCBs belong to a group of problematic synthetic organic chemicals called *chlorinated hydrocarbons*. Chapter 17 explains that a hydrocarbon is an organic compound consisting of hydrogen and carbon. If chlorine replaces one or more hydrogen atoms, the resulting molecule is a chlorinated hydrocarbon. Chlorinated hydrocarbons do not break down with chemical oxidation or from bacterial action, so they persist in the environment for a long time.

Many industrial solvents, including those used for dry cleaning, are chlorinated hydrocarbons. DDT, PCBs, and a host of other pesticides and chemicals are used in agriculture. These enter the aquatic environment and eventually the ocean as runoff from aerial spraying, dust, and sewage. The problem with chlorinated hydrocarbons is that they are not soluble in water, but very soluble in fats. Water tends to cycle through organisms, carrying water-soluble wastes with it, but waste in lipids (fat) tends to be stored. Because they dissolve into body lipids, organisms can bioaccumulate chlorinated hydrocarbons by ingesting small amounts over long periods. Scientists blame chlorinated hydrocarbons for the decline of some seal and sea lion populations, among other effects to organisms.

INTERNET PORTAL

SCiLINKS. NSTA

Topic: Bioaccumulation
Go To: www.scilinks.org
Code: LOP2475

Figure 18-15

Biomagnification.

Organisms low on the food chain accumulate toxins, which concentrate when they are consumed by the next trophic level. The toxin concentrates more at the next level, and the process continues on up the food chain, Here, almost imperceptible quantities of the pesticide DDT in seawater eventually reach a concentration 202,368 times greater in just five levels of the food chain.

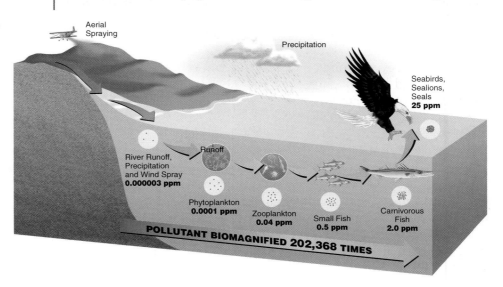

Aerial Spraying

Precipitation

Seabirds, Sealions, Seals **25 ppm**

River Runoff, Precipitation and Wind Spray **0.000003 ppm**

Runoff

Phytoplankton **0.0001 ppm**

Zooplankton **0.04 ppm**

Small Fish **0.5 ppm**

Carnivorous Fish **2.0 ppm**

POLLUTANT BIOMAGNIFIED 202,368 TIMES

There is at least one document-ed incident of PCB contami-nation affecting humans with skin darkening, dermatitis, and respiratory difficulties that per-sisted for years.

Karthik Lakshminarayanan

Figure 18-16

Mammalian biohazard.
Beluga whales accumulate so much PCB through bio-magnfication that in some countries their carcasses are legally classified as hazard-ous waste!

If fluorine is added to a chlorinated hydrocarbon, the result is a gas called a chloro-fluorocarbon (CFC). You may recall CFCs from the discussion on the hole in the ozone layer. CFCs play a role in the production of coolants, aerosol propellants, and foamed plastics. CFCs are not a significant threat to the marine environment directly. This is because they have a low molecular weight and do not appear to accumulate in organisms. They can, however, contaminate groundwater supplies when dumped into landfills or lagoons.

Oil

What are the major sources of oil pollution in the ocean?

How does oil pollution affect the marine environment?

Why is refined oil more hazardous to the environment than crude oil?

Why is it sometimes better to leave an oil spill alone rather than try to clean it up?

The primary origin of oil in the ocean is not from human pollu-tion, but instead from natural seeps. Undersea petroleum pockets naturally seep into the ocean, adding about as much as all the other sources combined (47%).

But, to many people, the word "oil" is synonymous with "oil slick" and "marine pollution." Unquestionably, oil pollution is a problem. However, while oil can be toxic (and have other effects), the causes and consequences surprise most people. Depending on location and other factors, an oil spill may actually be *less* of an envi-ronmental concern than most other forms of pollution.

Annually about 6 million tons of petroleum hydrocarbons enter the ocean and aquatic environments. The most widely publicized and dramatic causes are oil tanker accidents. In reality, tanker acci-dents only account for about 5% of oil pollution. People also point to oil platforms as a problem. While oil platforms have experienced accidental, uncontrolled releases, they rank behind oil shipping as a pollution source. Oil is spilled when filling or unloading tankers, but petroleum industry activities account for only a little more than 16% of the oil spilled.

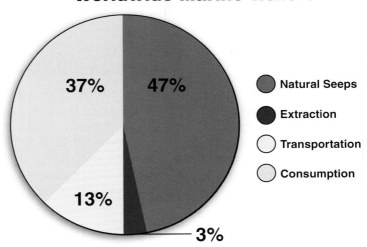

Worldwide Marine Waters

37%   47%

13%

3%

- Natural Seeps
- Extraction
- Transportation
- Consumption

Figure 18-17

Petroleum in ocean water.
Natural seeps contribute more oil to the ocean than any other source. Sources of pollution are far greater from consumption of oil than from extraction and transportation of oil.

The most common source of oil pollution (37%) is the consumers, not the producers. Oil enters aquatic environments through runoff from parking lots and streets and as waste from sewage treatment plants. Incomplete combustion in cars and other motorized vehicles releases waste petroleum hydrocarbons into the air. Eventually, these hydrocarbons wash out of the atmosphere with rain and snow, falling into the sea. Oil dripping from automobile engines drips onto highways and eventually washes out to sea. It is estimated that US treatment plants alone add about 900 million liters (237.8 million gallons) of oil to the sea annually. That is 22 times the famous 1989 *Exxon Valdez* spill in Alaska.

It does not take a lot of oil pollution to do damage in coastal water. Some species react to very low concentrations with behavioral changes ranging from lethargy to aggression. Lobsters and mussels react to oil at levels so much lower than the toxic level for other species that scientists want to study them as early pollution indicators.

Oil pollution can affect fisheries, with aquaculture particularly at risk because penned fish cannot flee from an oil spill. Among natural fisheries, even though the adults may avoid the oil, fish eggs and larvae often cannot. Fortunately, it seems that most fish produce so many eggs that oil is not a major threat to the fisheries stock. However, oil can contaminate seafood when fishing nets become fouled.

The seafood most affected by oil is shellfish. Clams and oysters absorb oil and take it into their tissues, making them inedible. Even

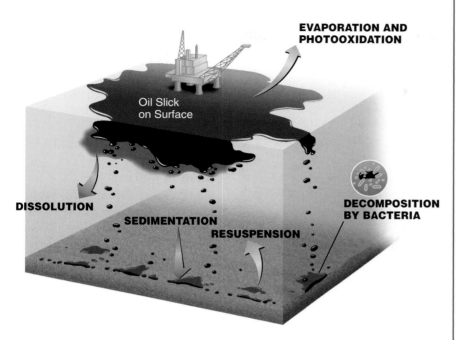

EVAPORATION AND PHOTOOXIDATION

Oil Slick on Surface

DISSOLUTION

SEDIMENTATION

RESUSPENSION

DECOMPOSITION BY BACTERIA

Figure 18-18

Fate of an oil spill.

In an oil spill, the volatile compounds evaporate, leaving behind the heavier oil components. Wave action helps accumulate the oil into tar balls, and emulsified oil sinks to the seafloor. On the bottom, benthic organisms consume the oil, or it becomes incorporated into sediments where bacteria eventually decompose it. Over time, the oil becomes part of the carbon cycle. However, residues can have long-lasting consequences, especially when refined petroleum is spilled.

small quantities of oil can ruin an entire shellfish catch. Damage to these fisheries can last a few years. Although some petroleum hydrocarbons are toxic to humans, it is rarely an issue because oil contaminated seafood has a foul taste that makes it inedible.

It is hard to generalize the effects of oil pollution because there are so many variables. What is the source and how close is it to shore? What is the composition of the oil, and what is the quantity? How will weather affect the spill? What kinds of biological communities are at risk, and how does oil affect them?

With so many variables, it is necessary to have different ways of dealing with oil once it enters the environment. Chemical agents speed up *emulsification*, which is the process of breaking up the oil slick into droplets, but this can kill many organisms. Sometimes the oil slick is burned, which can create an air pollution concern. Clean-up can involve absorbents that soak up the oil. Some chemicals sink the oil to the seabed to biodegrade naturally. Natural processes quickly degrade spilled oil within one to three years.

Ideally, oil pollution should be treated before it reaches shore. Oil is much less of a concern in the open ocean because the most sensitive environments are the intertidal shallows, estuaries, and other shore communities. Once oil reaches shore, removing it becomes difficult, expensive, and time consuming. It may be necessary to remove large quantities of sand and soil, which in turn becomes a disposal problem and removal harms the environment.

Damage Assessment, Remediation and Restoration Program, NOAA

Figure 18-19

Tanker Accidents.

While the incidents are highly dramatic and receive much press coverage, tanker accidents account for less than 5% of the oil spilled into the sea.

The degradation of the oil relies on bacteria and fungi, which may be a slow process.

Although it is helpful to use some of the previously described spill clean-up measures, some chemicals and methods cause more damage than the oil itself. One example of this was the 1989 *Exxon Valdez* oil spill. About 41 million liters (10.8 million gallons) spilled, of which skimmer ships, booms, scrapers, and absorbing sheets recovered about 17%. About 35% evaporated, 8% burned, 5% dissipated within five months, and chemicals dispersed about 5%. The remaining 30% fouled about 4,500 kilometers (2,800 miles) of coastline.

Surprisingly, recent analysis of the *Exxon Valdez* oil spill suggests that the cleaned areas fared worse than those left alone. In many areas, cleaners used water heated to 65°C (149°F) and high-pressure jets to remove oil from rocks. The high temperatures killed plankton and other organisms at the base of the food web. The jets smothered others with mud and sand. The effort cost more than $3.5 billion, yet some scientists now conclude that often the best thing to do (though admittedly the hardest politically) is to leave an oil spill alone.

In the public eye, the most dramatic oil spill damage results near shore. The loss of seabirds is very conspicuous and attracts public concern. Oil mats their feathers and destroys the ability of their plumage to repel water and maintain body heat. Birds and other animals swallow oil when trying to clean themselves, causing internal disorders and organ failure. Even minor exposure can depress egg laying and reduce hatches. Oil can transfer from a mother's feathers through an eggshell, killing the embryo. Oil can affect many marine mammals, including polar bears, though so far there is no evidence that whales are at significant risk.

Another consideration is that an oil spill can involve either crude oil or refined oil. Crude oil spills have so far been the more frequent and larger spills. Some components of crude oil evaporate or dissolve quickly and easily in water, but can harm organisms even in modest amounts. Insoluble components form a sticky surface layer that affects the local biosphere because it prevents gas diffusion and decreases sunlight penetration.

INTERNET PORTAL

SCiLINKS. NSTA

Topic: Oil Spills
Go To: www.scilinks.org
Code: LOP2470

Despite these problems, crude oil is biodegradable. Although crude oil spills look horrible and get lots of press coverage, most marine life in an affected area recovers in about five years. For example, Iraq dumped nearly 100 million liters (26.4 million gallons) of crude oil into the Persian Gulf during the 1991 Gulf War. This is the largest oil spill in history, yet it dissipated over a short period with little long-term biological damage.

Refined oil, however, poses a different problem. It disrupts the environment more extensively and for longer periods than crude oil. This is because refinement breaks up the heavy crude oil components and concentrates the lighter, biologically active ones. Refined oils also have added chemicals that make them more toxic. The primary concern is that the last 20 years have seen a marked increase in the amount of refined oil transported by sea.

Today scientists have a good grasp of what happens to an oil spill. Initially, the volatile compounds evaporate, leaving behind the heavier oil components. Wave action tends to cause this to accumulate into tar balls and emulsions that sink to the seafloor. There, benthic organisms consume these hydrocarbons, or the hydrocarbons become incorporated into sediments where they may eventually be decomposed by bacteria. Either way, eventually the oil becomes part of the carbon cycle. However, residues can have long-lasting consequences, especially if they are from a refined oil spill.

Figure 18-20

Air/sea pollution.
Several sources of ocean pollution come from your own car. Many atmospheric pollutants in car exhaust eventually end up in the ocean when they are cleared from the air by rainfall. Oil drips from cars onto roadways and runoff eventually carries it to the sea.

Figure 18-21

Oil spill legacy.

Unlike the effects of a refined oil spill, which can be devastating and last for decades, crude oil is often less of a problem. In fact, most marine life in an affected area recovers in about five years. Shown here, South Korean soldiers are attempting to remove crude oil from a beach near Seoul.

Photo courtesy of Exxon Valdez Oil Spill Trustee Council

Radioactive Waste

How do radioactive materials get into the ocean?

Why are radioactive materials a concern even though dumping them in the sea was banned by international law in 1975 and 1983?

How do radioactive materials presently affect marine organisms?

Despite the obvious danger radiation poses to living organisms, so far no widespread effects have been noted. It appears that marine organisms have a high tolerance to radioactivity. Regardless, scientists fear that it is just a matter of time before measurable effects to ecosystems or organisms become evident. A likely radioactive effect is genetic damage.

You may not realize it, but seawater is naturally radioactive. This is due primarily to the radioactive decay of potassium-40, uranium, and thorium. This natural radiation exists at a very low level, with the potential for dangerous radiation coming only from human activities. Radioactive material enters the ocean primarily from people dumping it there.

Human-produced radioactive materials began entering the ocean in the 1940s with the dawn of nuclear testing. Today radioactive substances entering the sea come primarily from nuclear-reactor cooling water and nuclear-power vessel discharges. But, the radiation has not yet caused any widespread effects.

Dumping high-level radioactive waste has been banned by international law since 1975, with low-level waste dumping banned in 1983. However, radioactive waste remains a concern for several reasons. For one, dumping began in 1946. The US alone dumped more than 110,000 barrels of plutonium and cesium into the sea, some near densely populated centers. This includes sites near Massachusetts Bay, the California Farallon Islands, and one dumpsite within 4.8 kilometers (3 miles) of Newark, New Jersey. In a study of the Farallon Islands, the US National Oceanic and Atmospheric Administration (NOAA) reported that 47,000 barrels of nuclear waste had ruptured in that area, posing a threat to local marine resources.

Nuclear waste exists in the Arctic, North Atlantic, and Barents Sea, as well as in many rivers in northern Russia.

Figure 18-22

Irradiated depths.

Before the ban in 1983, the US dumped more than 110,000 barrels of plutonium and cesium into the sea, some near densely populated centers. With the fall of the Soviet Union, concerns have been renewed about nuclear waste disposal at sea.

Courtesy of Bellona

Ironically, one of the ways scientists trace deep ocean circulation in the North Atlantic is by measuring the flow of tritium, the radioactive form of hydrogen.

Much has come to light since the fall of the Soviet Union. Russia admits that the former Soviet Union dumped thousands of tons of nuclear waste into their northern seas, including 17 nuclear reactors. Lake Karacy in central Russia was used as a nuclear dump and now holds 24 times more radioactive fallout than was released by the Chernobyl nuclear power station disaster. Because Russia lacks the funds to deal with their aging reactors, concerns include slowly deteriorating Russian nuclear-powered vessels. Another issue is what would happen in an accident that involved the considerable amount of radioactive material transported by ship.

Munitions

What concerns exist regarding the dumping of munitions in the ocean?

The remnants of war litter the ocean bottom. Today live shells and bombs exist in untold numbers in the ocean. Some went down with ships that were casualties of war, some were "duds" that did not explode, and some were dumped because they were obsolete or surplus. Besides explosives, chemical weapons have also been dumped or lost. At least one cache of dumped mustard gas from World War II has been located in North Atlantic coastal waters shallow enough for divers to reach.

The concerns for the environment regarding lost munitions range from minor to significant. Explosions may seem like a major concern, but environmentally speaking, they are not. Detonation of unexploded bombs is a safety concern for ships and divers, but not a long-term, wide-ranging environmental hazard. The leakage of chemical weapons, on the other hand, could pose a major threat by contaminating and killing local wildlife.

Today it is illegal to dispose of chemical weapons in coastal waters, except in an emergency. However, some people suspect that some countries do not enforce this and that coastal dumping continues.

Figure 18-23

Deadly depths.
Live shells and bombs exist in untold numbers in the ocean. As this photo from Truk Lagoon in the western Pacific shows, some sank with ships that were casualties of war.

Joe Liburdi

1. **Heavy metals include (choose all that apply)**

   A. lead.

   B. mercury.

   C. cadmium.

   D. copper.

2. **Heavy metals affect organisms by (choose all that apply)**

   A. interfering with cellular metabolism.

   B. giving them a foul taste.

   C. accumulating in the tissues.

   D. increasing reproductive behavior.

3. **Heavy metal risks to humans include (choose all that apply)**

   A. brain damage.

   B. behavioral disorders.

   C. birth defects.

   D. hearing loss.

4. **Synthetic organic chemicals can persist in the marine environment because**

   A. they naturally form there.

   B. they bind irreversibly with water.

   C. bacteria convert them into stable forms.

   D. bacteria and other processes don't break them down.

5. **Synthetic organic chemicals concentrate into dangerous levels from very low concentrations**

   A. due to evaporation in tide pools.

   B. through biomagnification at each trophic level.

   C. by attracting each other as charged ions.

   D. all of the above

6. **The major source of oil pollution in the sea is**

   A. oil rig spills.

   B. runoff from land.

   C. oil tanker accidents.

   D. the olive industry surrounding the Mediterranean Sea.

7. **Oil affects the environment by**

   A. changing organism behaviors.

   B. contaminating food fish.

   C. sinking to the bottom.

   D. all of the above

8. **Refined oil is more of a hazard than crude oil because refinement adds toxic chemicals and concentrates biologically active compounds.**

   A. true

   B. false

9. **It is sometimes better to leave an oil slick alone because it's too expensive to clean it up.**

   A. true

   B. false

10. **Radioactive materials get into the ocean primarily from**

    A. nuclear accidents.

    B. intentional dumping.

    C. uranium meteors.

    D. none of the above

11. **Despite the 1975 and 1983 bans on dumping radioactive materials at sea, they remain a concern because (choose all that apply)**

    A. so much was dumped prior to the bans.

    B. evidence suggests that radioactive waste barrels are leaking.

    C. after the bans, some nuclear powered vessels continued to dump nuclear waste.

    D. uranium meteors continue to raise radiation levels.

12. **So far, radioactive material has**

    A. had no noted widespread effects on marine life.

    B. caused extensive genetic damage to fish populations.

    C. caused one giant lizard named Godzilla.

    D. killed numerous whales.

13. **The main environmental concern regarding lost munitions is the**

    A. leakage of chemical weapons.

    B. detonation of unexploded bombs.

    C. creation of artificial reefs.

Nutrient Pollutants

When nutrients are introduced into an environment where they do not normally exist in high concentration, the nutrients are pollutants. Nutrient pollution causes some organisms to overpopulate an ecosystem, and that disrupts the ecological balance. As discussed in Chapter 16, coral polyps die when nutrients allow algae to reproduce in great numbers and cover the polyps.

Eutrophication

What causes eutrophication?

How does eutrophication hurt marine ecosystems?

One of the main effects of excess nutrients flowing into the sea, you may remember, is called eutrophication. Eutrophication may be a primary cause of harmful algal blooms (HABs – see Chapter 5 for more information on HABs). Nutrients and fertilizers enter the ocean and estuaries, providing an unnatural food source for diatoms and dinoflagellates. This food causes a population explosion during which these phytoplankton emit toxins that kill fish and other organisms.

Eutrophication occurs when bodies of water receive excess nutrients, which cause excessive plant growth. Excess nutrients come from wastewater plants (the plants make the water disease-free, but leave nutrients intact), home lawn fertilizers, septic systems, factory effluent, soil erosion, and agricultural runoff. River runoff transports enormous amounts of fertilizers and other nutrients to the ocean where they stimulate the growth of algae. This enhanced plant growth is called an algal bloom. When the massive amounts of algae die, they sink to the bottom of the ocean where they decompose. The aerobic bacteria that cause the decomposition remove much of the oxygen from the water creating *hypoxic* (low oxygen) and *anoxic* (no oxygen) zones. Today, many of the world's rivers cause eutrophication to some degree through this process.

The Mississippi River, which drains more than one-third of the US, is a prime example. The Mississippi dumps large amounts of nitrogen fertilizer runoff into the Gulf of Mexico. The resulting eutrophication has created hypoxic and anoxic zones on the bottom of the Louisiana coast continental shelf. The size of these zones varies from year to year, depending on rainfall and other conditions, but some years the combined area of the zones is about the same size as New Jersey. The low-oxygen zones either

STUDY QUESTIONS

Find the answers as you read.

1. What causes eutrophication?

2. How does eutrophication hurt marine ecosystems?

3. What are the process levels used to treat sewage before dumping?

4. What environmental concerns result from dumping sludge?

5. What concerns does livestock sewage present?

Topic: Eutrophication
Go To: www.scilinks.org
Code: LOP2485

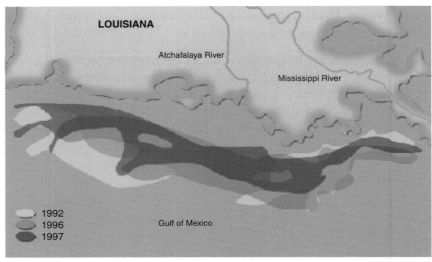

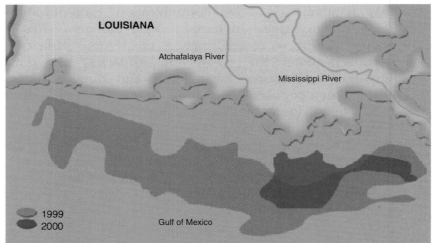

Figure 18-24

Louisiana's dead zone.
Louisiana has one of the largest coastal dead zones in the world. Since 1985, the dead zone has ranged in size from about 260 square kilometers (100 square miles) in 1988 to more than 22,100 square kilometers (8,500 square miles) in 2002. In 2007 it was 20,500 square kilometers (7,900 square miles), which is about the size of New Jersey. The small areas seen in 2000 do not represent an improvement in the situation. It was a drought year, so much less fresh water entered the Gulf of Mexico.

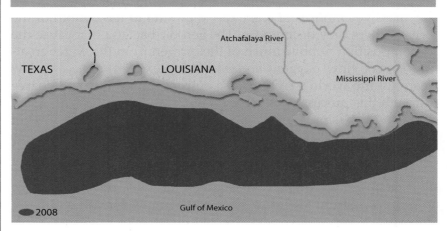

kill fish, shrimp, and other organisms, or cause those species that can to flee. Understandably, this is devastating to local fisheries and the environment.

Since the discovery of the hypoxic area off Louisiana during the 1990s, marine researchers have located several similar zones along both US coasts. All of these affect local fisheries, suggesting that handling this problem will have to be part of fishery management.

It is worth noting that even nontoxic algae blooms can cause lethal conditions in surface waters. The overabundance of algae from eutrophication clogs the gills of some species and consumes all the free oxygen. These anoxic conditions can cause massive fish kills. Today, in near-shore waters, anoxic and hypoxic events cause more massive fish kills than do oil spills.

Sewage

What are the process levels used to treat sewage before dumping?

What environmental concerns result from dumping sludge?

What concerns does livestock sewage present?

When discussing water pollution, sewage is the first thing that occurs to many people. Originally, sewage systems were little more than drains that carried raw sewage to the nearest body of water. Over time, urban governments combined these systems with modern wastewater treatment, but some of their old characteristics remain a problem.

Until 1972, a city in the US could discharge sewage into any body of water, provided it was not polluted sewage. The problem was that every state defined "polluted" differently. In 1972, the Federal Clean Water Act made the definition uniform with the goal of making US waters fishable and swimmable. Dumping of raw sewage is still allowed in many other parts of the world.

Today there are three basic processes used to treat sewage before dumping it. Level I processes remove solids. Level II is the removal of solids and *pathogens* (disease-causing microbes). Level III removes solids, pathogens, and nutrients. The Clean Water Act required that all sewage be treated with Level II processes or higher by 1977. However, sometimes sewage bypasses treatment when storm waters overwhelm the system capacity. When this happens, raw sewage can enter local water systems.

About 98% of sewage is actually water. After treatment, the isolated solids make up a material called *sewage sludge*. It is a mixture of organic material as well as bacteria, viruses, metals, and synthetic chemicals. After isolation, the processors may ship the sludge for use in landfills, and for burning to generate electricity, or dump it at sea.

US Environmental Protection Agency

Figure 18-25

Sludge dumping.
About 10 million tons of sludge are dumped each year at a site off the continental shelf from New York. While this is well offshore, scientists worry that it could contaminate the Gulf Stream, spreading eutrophication around the Atlantic basin.

Topic: Marine Ecosystems
Go To: www.scilinks.org
Code: LOP2490

The sludge can be as much of a problem as raw sewage. One example is the dump site in the Atlantic, just off the coast of New York. In use for decades, the bottom is covered with sludge, resulting in a hypoxic environment in which few organisms can survive. Storms dislodge the sludge, washing it onto local beaches, contaminating shellfish beds, and causing disease outbreaks. Public outcry resulted in a new dump site at the edge of the continental shelf. Today, about 10 million tons of sludge are transported to this new site each year. Scientists worry that it could contaminate the Gulf Stream, spreading eutrophication around the Atlantic basin.

In addition to human waste, animal waste creates sewage concerns, though sometimes on a larger scale. Livestock produces more waste than a comparable human population and it is not generally processed like human sewage. Much livestock sewage concentrates in ponds near large farms and ranches, the idea being to allow natural decomposition. Unfortunately, livestock sewage seeps into groundwater, and storms can wash out storage ponds. In one incident in 1995, a tropical storm washed 98.4 million liters (26 million gallons) of hog waste into the New River in North Carolina. This resulted in massive HABs and fish kills. Similarly, many scientists think a spill involving poultry sewage caused an HAB in Chesapeake Bay.

ARE YOU LEARNING?

1. _____ cause(s) eutrophication.

   A. HABs

   B. Thermal pollution

   C. Radiation

   D. Nutrients and fertilizers

2. **Eutrophication harms marine ecosystems by (choose all that apply)**

   A. causing HABs.

   B. draining rivers of their nutrients.

   C. raising oxygen levels too high.

   D. causing fish to grow too big.

3. **In sewage processing, Level II treatment**

   A. removes solids.

   B. removes solids and pathogens.

   C. removes solids, pathogens, and nutrients.

   D. removes solids, pathogens, nutrients, and toxins.

4. **Dumping sludge causes environmental concerns including**

   A. eutrophication.

   B. countercurrent backflow.

   C. pathogen resurgence.

   D. none of the above

5. **Livestock sewage concerns are the same as human sewage concerns, although sometimes on a larger scale.**

   A. true

   B. false

Energy Pollutants

STUDY QUESTIONS

Find the answers as you read.

1. How can heated water be a pollutant?

2. What sources of heated water can affect the marine environment?

Energy pollution is any energy introduced to the marine environment that affects biological or physical processes. Any form of energy is potentially a pollutant, though heat is the primary concern at present. Sound is also an issue; the effects of this pollution need a lot of research.

Heat Pollution

How can heated water be a pollutant?

What sources of heated water can affect the marine environment?

Heat can act as a pollutant in marine environments by raising the temperature in a local area. Most thermal (heat) pollution comes from electrical power plants, which draw water from the sea for cooling. By using heat exchangers, the discharged hot water remains free of radiation and contaminants. Usually the heat is the only pollutant. However, some industrial discharges pollute with both heat and substances.

In some cases, the heated water has benefits, such as in aquaculture. In Florida, warm water discharge from power plants has created an unintended but useful winter refuge for the endangered manatee.

But in most cases, thermal pollution has a tendency to harm the environment. During summer months, the natural temperature is often already close to the heat tolerance limit for many species. Added hot water can raise temperatures above the tolerance level and cause a decrease in the solubility of dissolved oxygen. This may cause a die-off or decline in the productivity within the immediate areas affected by the warm water.

Although it has not been an issue so far, there's a potential for these artificial heat sources to create an environment for non-native, warm-water species. As you learned, introducing new species to an area tends to throw the local ecology significantly out of balance.

Sound Pollution

A rising concern among some scientists is sound pollution. Some scientists have found that human-produced sounds ranging from ship engines to sonar may be detrimental to marine species. The US military uses low-frequency active sonar to detect submarines. Some of the suspected effects that this type of noise may have on marine mammals like whales include temporary or permanent hearing loss, disorientation/loss of direction, stranding, inability to communicate with one another, aggressive behavior, panic/stress, organ damage, and the inability to locate predators and prey. Sound pollution is likely to be an important study area in the near future as scientists research these and other possible effects of sound pollution in the sea.

ARE YOU LEARNING?

1. **Heated water can be a pollutant**
   A. by raising the temperature above the tolerance of organisms.
   B. by causing the ocean to evaporate and become a desert.
   C. by attracting manatees.
   D. all of the above

2. **The sources of heated water that can affect the marine environment include (choose all that apply)**
   A. agricultural runoff.
   B. power plant cooling.
   C. industrial discharges.
   D. HABs.

STUDY QUESTIONS

Find the answers as you read.

1. How do plastics enter the marine environment?

2. Why are plastics a hazard to the marine environment?

3. How do spoil and industrial solid waste damage marine communities?

Refuse Pollutants

Refuse pollutants cause problems that differ from problems created by toxic, nutrient, and energy pollution. Among the refuse pollutants, plastic is the most obvious, though other seemingly harmless materials such as fish nets also fit into this category.

Plastic

How do plastics enter the marine environment?

Why are plastics a hazard to the marine environment?

Plastics are not toxic and they do not bioaccumulate or biomagnify. People use a lot of plastics because they are lightweight, strong, and cannot be easily destroyed by natural processes. It is these same qualities that make plastics a big problem in the environment. The estimated lifespan for a plastic is more than 400 years. This is a real concern.

Depending on where samples are taken, oceanographers are finding plastics make up between 60% and 95% of marine debris. This plastic debris in the sea today will be around for the next four centuries unless someone removes it.

Plastics enter the marine environment primarily by being lost or dumped there. The most common plastics include fishing gear, plastic bags, packing materials, balloons, bottles, and syringes. In the 1990s, debris in the water near Britain doubled and in the Antarctic, the increase was hundredfold. The result of a 1999 study by Charles Moore, founder of Algalita Marine Research Foundation in Long Beach, California, showed that in the North Pacific Ocean there was six times more plastic debris than zooplankton. Considering the staggering amount of plastic being produced, without preventative measures, the amount going into the ocean will continue to increase.

Today you can go almost anywhere on the ocean and find plastic trash. Winds and currents carry it to the poles and to the most remote Pacific atolls. But, as ugly and unpleasant as it is, why is it a concern to the health of the ocean?

Plastics are a hazard in the marine environment because they look like food to some predators. Sea turtles and sea birds commonly die when they swallow plastic bags and similar items that resemble jellyfish, their natural prey. Filter feeders, including whales and whale sharks, swallow small pieces as they strain plankton from the water. Once swallowed, the plastic can cause internal blockage and a swift death, or it can accumulate in the gut, reducing hunger and inhibiting feeding. This keeps the animal from eating sufficiently, resulting in slow starvation. Another concern is that while plastics resist biodegrading, when swallowed some do release chemicals associated with eggshell thinning (in birds), abnormal behavior, and tissue damage.

Plastics entangle and entrap marine animals. Chapter 17 discusses "ghost" drift nets, which are lost nets that catch marine life as they float through the ocean. Lost fishing nets and traps can become "killing machines" that last for decades. As many as 30,000 seals die annually in lost or discarded nets and traps. Even household litter creates risks. People commonly find six-pack rings encircling the necks of marine mammals and birds, cutting their flesh, causing infection, and inhibiting feeding.

Figure 18-26

Ghost net tragedy.
Lost fishing nets can become "killing machines" that last for decades. Sea turtles and seals are especially vulnerable since they must surface for oxygen, or they drown.

Mike Tork, Office of Protected Resources, NOAA

Figure 18-27

Beach strewn with plastic debris.

Kamilo Beach, Big Island, Hawaii was strewn with plastics and dead animals when this 2006 photograph was taken. Death from ingestion of plastics is not swift. An animal normally dies a slow, agonizing death from gastrointestinal blockage, or starvation.

Agalita Marine Research Foundation/www.agalita.org

Fisheries Collection, NOAA

Figure 18-28

Six-pack death trap.

People commonly find six-pack rings encircling the necks of marine mammals, cutting their flesh, causing infection, and inhibiting feeding. Eventually, the entrapped animal dies of starvation, infection, or drowning.

In 1960, US plastics production was about 3 million tons, and by 2000 it had risen to more than 50 million tons. It has become such an important material that it is not likely that production will decline.

Solutions to the plastics issue will likely come from several approaches. One approach is to make plastic that degrades. This is done by making it sensitive to sunlight. Unfortunately, this is not an effective solution when plastic sinks into the underwater environment. However, it may be possible to create a plastic that will biodegrade effectively in the marine environment. Recycling is probably the most important step because the best solution to the plastics problem is to keep it out of the ocean altogether.

Dredge Spoil and Industrial Solids

How do spoil and industrial solid waste damage marine communities?

Few people realize that a major pollution source is *spoil*. Spoil is the name of the soft bottom material removed during the dredging of harbors and ports. Sometimes dredgers remove spoil from the ocean to use as landfill, but more often they dump it at sea.

Because of boats, coastal development, and the shipping industry, bottom sediments in harbors and ports tend to contain toxic chemicals. These chemicals damage the benthic communities when dumped with the spoil at sea. However, dumping spoil harms environments even when it contains no toxic substances.

The damage comes when spoil buries benthic organisms, killing them. Suspended particles carried from the spoil cloud the water and clog the feeding and respiratory organs of some organisms. This spreads the damage to other marine communties.

Solid industrial waste disposal at sea produces similar damage to spoil dumping. Scientists have found negative effects on natural communities where municipalities dump solid waste, including fly ash (from power stations that use coal) and mining wastes.

ARE YOU LEARNING?

1. **Plastics enter the marine environment primarily**

   A. by getting washed out of landfills.

   B. through debris carried in runoff.

   C. by being dumped or lost there.

   D. none of the above

2. **Plastic is a hazard in the environment because (choose all that apply)**

   A. it is ugly.

   B. animals mistake it for food.

   C. it traps and entangles animals.

   D. it is biodegradable.

3. **Spoil and industrial solid waste damage marine communities by**

   A. burying them.

   B. carrying toxins.

   C. clogging feeding and respiratory organs.

   D. all of the above

Efforts and Solutions

The world community recognizes the threats to the ocean's health and the potential consequences to the world and humanity. As demonstrated with the agreement to ban CFCs to protect the ozone layer, the international community does have the ability to work together to solve recognized problems.

Pollution is expensive and a threat to our health, and perhaps our existence. Fortunately, legislation and international conventions have already provided the first steps. But, there is more need for urgent action and agreement.

The Cost of Pollution

About how much per person does pollution cost the average US citizen?

Pollution is ugly, offensive, and destructive. If that were not enough, it is expensive. The US spends about $250 billion annually to control atmospheric, terrestrial, and marine pollution. That is about 2% of the gross national product, or $1,000 per US citizen on average. Estimates suggest that the US loses about 4% of its gross national product to environmental damage. This is not likely to end any time soon.

Besides direct costs, there are indirect costs that are likely to escalate. By threatening food supplies and creating health risks, food prices and medical costs will probably rise also.

STUDY QUESTIONS

Find the answers as you read.

1. About how much per person does pollution cost the average US citizen?

2. What does the Coastal Zone Management Act do to preserve coastal resources?

3. What powers did the Marine Protection Research and Sanctuaries Act grant the US federal government?

4. What agreement resulted from the 1972 Ocean Dumping Convention?

5. What two conventions in 1973 addressed pollution released by ships?

6. What is the 1980 World Conservation Strategy?

7. What agreement resulted from the 1991 Madrid Protocol on Environmental Protection of the Antarctic Treaty?

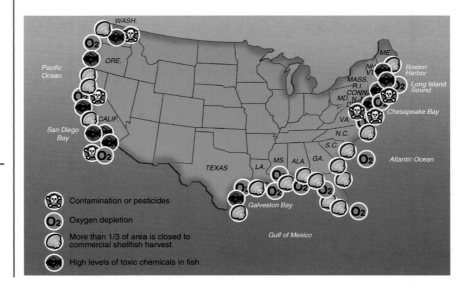

Figure 18-29

Coastal pollution in the US.

No coastal state of the US is immune to the effects of marine pollution. Above are the locations and types of some of the worst cases.

Contamination or pesticides

O2 Oxygen depletion

More than 1/3 of area is closed to commercial shellfish harvest

High levels of toxic chemicals in fish

Managing the Coastal Zone

What does the Coastal Zone Management Act do to preserve coastal resources?

What powers did the Marine Protection Research and Sanctuaries Act grant the US federal government?

Fortunately, scientists and regulators are becoming more aware of what is needed to solve some of the pollution problems. It is becoming clear that land and water cannot be managed separately. Coastal wetlands are one example of how closely land, sea, and even air interact. Solutions to environmental issues need to consider the far-reaching aspects of the problem.

Many countries, including the US, recognize that it is important to manage the entire coastline. This includes the waters flowing into the ocean, the lands that interact with the sea, and the ocean out to the edge of the continental shelf. Not all countries act to preserve these areas, unfortunately, and those that do need to do more. Interestingly,

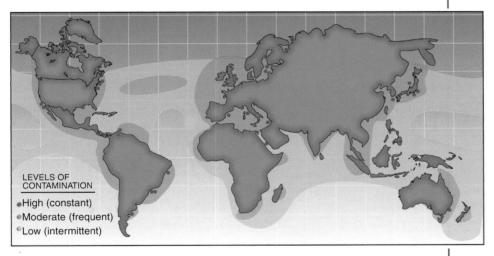

LEVELS OF
CONTAMINATION

● High (constant)
● Moderate (frequent)
● Low (intermittent)

the idea of coastal management is not new. People indigenous to Hawaii and some South Pacific islands have a long history of preserving coastal zones, allowing people to only take what they need at a sustainable rate.

The approach to managing coastal resources taken by the US is similar to one used by many countries. The Coastal Zone Management Act (CZMA) of 1972 provides economic incentives for states to take a strong role in preserving their coastal zone. It does not force them to do so, but helps to counterbalance the economic pressures that lead to coastal zone destruction. It also helps make coastal resource management more consistent from state to state.

Figure 18-30

Marine pollution is a worldwide problem.

Not surprisingly, pollution is concentrated around coastal regions and major population centers. But, even the open ocean is not immune. Why do you think there is so little pollution in the central north Pacific and north Atlantic?

Another significant piece of US legislation is the Marine Protection Research and Sanctuaries Act of 1972. This act gives the federal government the power to designate specific coastal zone areas for research, protection, or recreation. The act recognizes multiple interests and shareholders with respect to coastal resources and provides a voice for all.

Perhaps the most significant result of these acts has been the establishment of multiple marine sanctuaries on both coasts. These sanctuaries provide a natural refuge where marine organisms can thrive with reduced pressures from fishing and other human activities. They also provide a place where scientists can study marine environments in a more natural or protected state.

International Conservation Efforts

What agreement resulted from the 1972 Ocean Dumping Convention?

What two conventions in 1973 addressed pollution released by ships?

What is the 1980 World Conservation Strategy?

What agreement resulted from the 1991 Madrid Protocol on Environmental Protection of the Antarctic Treaty?

Topic: Marine Conservation
Go To: www.scilinks.org
Code: LOP2480

International cooperation to protect the ocean is nothing new. One example is a United Nations convention that assembled representatives from 110 nations to discuss international policies about marine pollution. This was the London Convention on the Prevention of Water Pollution by Dumping of Wastes and Other Matter, more commonly known as the 1972 Ocean Dumping Convention. This resulted in an international agreement that prohibited marine dumping of persistent (nonbiodegradable) plastic.

The same convention also resulted in the 1973 Marine Pollution Convention. Known formally as the London International Convention for the Prevention of Pollution from Ships, this established regulations that limit and control oil pollution, packaged substances, sewage, and garbage dumped from ships. Also in 1973, the International Convention for the Prevention of Pollution (also called *MARPOL*, which is an abbreviation for MARine POLlution) took place. It similarly regulates discharge from ships and has been adopted by more than 80 countries.

In 1980, the United Nations Environment Program, the International Union for the Conservation of Nature and Natural Resources, and the World Wildlife Fund released their World Conservation Strategy. This document provides a strategy and procedures by which nations can develop their economic potential without destroying their resources. It represents the consensus of more than 450 government agencies and the efforts of more than 700 scientists.

Among its results, the World Conservation Strategy recommends that countries with common seas work together to find common solutions to shared marine problems. This led to the Regional Seas Programmes, which have established zones for international cooperation around the world. In 1991, the Madrid Protocol on Environmental Protection of the Antarctic Treaty banned mining and oil exploration in Antarctica for at least 50 years. It further designated the entire continent as a natural reserve devoted to peace and science. This makes it the world's largest terrestrial and marine reserve.

ARE YOU LEARNING?

1. **Pollution costs the average US citizen about _____ annually.**

   A. $100

   B. $500

   C. $1,000

   D. $10,000

2. **The Coastal Zone Management Act preserves coastal resources by**

   A. forcing states to limit coastal development.

   B. taxing the destruction of coast development.

   C. requiring the US Navy to patrol the coast.

   D. providing economic incentives for states to preserve coastal resources.

3. **The Marine Protection Research and Sanctuaries Act granted the US federal government the power to**

   A. designate coastal zones for research, protection, and recreation.

   B. conduct research on whether sanctuaries would do anything.

   C. nothing, because the act didn't pass.

   D. none of the above

4. **The 1972 Ocean Dumping Convention resulted in agreements on**

   A. restrictions on dumping nonbiodegradable plastics at sea.

   B. establishing marine reserves.

   C. how much nuclear waste could be dumped.

   D. all of the above

5. **Two conventions in 1973 that addressed pollution released by ships were**

   A. the Ocean Dumping Convention and the Marine Sanctuaries Act.

   B. the Marine Pollution Convention and the Coastal Zone Management Act.

   C. the Marine Pollution Convention and the International Convention for the Prevention of Pollution.

   D. none of the above

6. **The 1980 World Conservation Strategy is a document that provides a strategy and procedures by which nations can develop their economic potential without destroying marine resources.**

   A. true

   B. false

7. **The 1991 Madrid Protocol on Environmental Protection of the Antarctic Treaty resulted in the agreement that**

   A. Antarctica may be used for coal mining.

   B. Antarctica is a natural reserve.

   C. treaties need shorter names.

   D. marine reserves are ineffective.

New Terms You Learned

- **anoxic** having no oxygen (p. 18-31)
- **bioaccumulation** the concentration of heavy metals, synthetic chemicals, and natural organic chemicals that gradually accumulates in an organism's body throughout its lifetime (p. 18-19)
- **biocides** chemicals that kill, such as pesticides (p. 18-16)
- **biodegradable** capable of being broken down into harmless substances by microbes (p. 18-17)
- **biomagnification** the process by which contamination becomes greater with each trophic level (p. 18-19)
- **chlorinated hydrocarbon** a compound consisting of hydrogen and carbon, in which chlorine replaces one or more of the hydrogen atoms; examples are DDT and PCBs (p. 18-22)
- **conservative materials** chemicals and heavy metals that biomagnify, so named because they are conserved rather than consumed as they move through the food web (p. 18-21)
- **coral bleaching** the white appearance of coral that has rejected its zooxanthellae dinoflagellates (symbiotic algae - Symbiodinum) due to stress (p. 18-13)
- **emulsification** with respect to oil spills, the breaking up of the slick into small droplets (p. 18-25)
- **hypoxic** having low oxygen (p. 18-31)
- **immunosuppressor** an agent that compromises or suppresses an organism's immune system, reducing its ability to fight disease (p. 18-20)
- **MARPOL** International Convention for the Prevention of Pollution (abbreviation for MARine POLlution); regulates discharge from ships (p. 18-42)
- **pathogens** microbes that cause disease (p. 18-33)
- **pollution** products of human activities that have harmful or objectionable effects to the water quality or affect the physical, chemical, or biological environment (p. 18-16)

- **sewage sludge** a mixture of organic material as well as bacteria, viruses, metals and synthetic chemicals from the isolated solids of sewage (p. 18-33)
- **spoil** the soft bottom material removed during the dredging of harbors and ports (p. 18-38)
- **synthetic organic chemicals** human-made chemicals that are based on organic molecule structures (p. 18-21)
- **tributyl tin (TBT)** an antifouling heavy metal compound banned by the US in the late 1980s (p. 18-20)

Chapter 18 in Review

1. List the basic greenhouse gases. Explain the evidence that supports the theory that the Earth's average surface temperature is rising. How has the ocean helped reduce this rise? What are the possible effects of global warming?

2. What change in carbon dioxide emissions did the Kyoto Climate Change Conference agree to establish by 2012? What is likely to be the only real solution to the global warming problem? Give examples of possibilities.

3. Explain what makes the ozone layer vital to life, and what would happen without it.

4. Besides reducing damage to the ozone layer, what was the significance of the June 1990 international ban on ozone-depleting chemicals?

5. Explain how ships carry non-native species to new environments.

6. Why are non-native species an environmental threat? What damage do they do? Why do some ecologists speculate that Earth will become a more homogeneous ecosystem?

7. How does overfishing affect local ecosystems?

8. What is the primary cause of coastal wetland destruction and why are estuaries particularly at risk? What has happened to mangrove forests? Approximately what percent of the world's mangroves has been destroyed?

9. How do ENSO and particular fish-capturing practices relate to coral reef destruction? Approximately what percent of the world's coral reefs has been destroyed?

10. Define pollution and list the different sources of pollution in the ocean. What is the percent of pollution contributed by each source?

11. Explain where oil pollution originates and how it affects the environment.

12. Explain what heavy metals are, what they do to organisms, and the risks they present to humans.

13. Explain why synthetic organic chemicals persist in the environment. Describe the processes of bioaccumulation and biomagnification.

14. Why is refined oil more hazardous to the environment than crude oil? Based on the *Exxon Valdez* oil spill, what conclusion have many scientists reached regarding cleaning up such spills? Why?

15. Explain how radioactive materials get into the ocean, even after the bans in 1975 and 1983. How has radioactive material affected marine organisms so far?

16. What are the concerns with respect to dumping munitions in the ocean? What type of munition presents the most potential for problems?

17. What causes eutrophication? How does it hurt marine ecosystems? What is an example?

18. What are the differences between the three process levels used to treat sewage?

19. What is sewage sludge? What environmental concerns result from dumping it at sea?

20. Explain why livestock sewage can be a greater hazard to the marine environment than human sewage.

21. Explain where thermal pollution originates and how it can affect the marine environment.

22. Explain how plastics enter the marine environment and why they are a hazard. Describe the steps being taken to control plastics pollution.

23. Explain how spoil and industrial solid waste damage marine communities.

24. How much per person does pollution cost the average US citizen each year? Why?

25. List and summarize the US laws and international agreements discussed in this chapter.

Connecting Chapter Concepts – Science Scenarios

1. Global warming has become a major concern due to its potential to affect all the Earth's environments, including the seas. Scientists think that the use of fossil fuels has increased the amount of carbon dioxide in the atmosphere, which increases the amount of heat it retains.

   A. Scientists think the ocean has reduced the effects of global warming to a large extent. How?
   B. What are the scientific estimates for temperature change and sea level change over the next 50 to 100 years based on current trends?
   C. What is the only likely solution to global warming?

2. Annually, about 6 million tons of petroleum hydrocarbons enter the ocean and aquatic environments, providing a major source of pollution and contamination to marine and aquatic ecosystems.

   A. What is the primary cause of oil in the ocean? About what percent do petroleum industry activities contribute?
   B. What food sources are most affected by oil pollution?
   C. From an environmental perspective, which appears to be the least damaging: a crude oil spill or a refined oil spill? Why?
   D. Based on findings from the site of the 1989 Exxon Valdez oil spill, what do some scientists think is the best way to deal with an oil spill? What supports this position?

Marine Science and the Real World

1. Someone once said that "out of sight, out of mind" means the same thing as "invisible and insane." How does this play on words relate to pollution?

2. Virtually everyone knows that pollution is expensive and is destroying the environment. Why does it still happen?

3. Sometimes it's better to leave an oil slick alone than to try to clean it up, but sometimes that's not easy to do. Why?

4. Why would people in the commercial fishing industry argue against making nets out of biodegradable plastic?

5. One solution to eutrophication would be to ban the materials that cause it. Why isn't this done?

6. Is there any way to lower the costs of pollution? Why or why not?

7. Why do you think that alternative energy sources have been so slow in becoming available? Does your family have an electric or hybrid car? Have you considered it? Why or why not?

8. Why do you think it was easier for the international community to agree to ban ozone-depleting chemicals than it has been to reach other environmental agreements?

9. Marine reserves clearly benefit fish populations and other organisms, yet some interest groups oppose them. What reasons might they have?

References

Anderson, D. M. 1994. Red Tides. Scientific American. August.

Brown, L. 2002. State of the World. New York: Norton.

Carson, R. 1962. Silent Spring. Boston: Houghton Mifflin.

Cherfas, J. 1990. The Fringe of the Ocean Under Siege from Land. Science. 248 (no. 4952).

Costanza, R., et al. 1998. Principles for Sustainable Governance of the Oceans. Science. 281 (no. 5374). 10 July.

Crowley, T. J. 2000. Causes of Climate Change Over the Past 1000 Years. Science. 289 (no. 5477). 14 July.

Duedall, I. 1990. A History of Ocean Disposal. Oceanus. 33 (no. 2, Summer).

Earle, S.A. 1995. Sea Change: A Message of the Oceans. New York: Fawcett Columbine Books.

Falkowski, P., et al. 2000. The Global Carbon Cycle: A Test of Our Knowledge of Earth as a System. Science. 290 (no. 5490). October.

Hardin, G. 1968. The Tragedy of the Commons. Science. 162. 13 December.

Houghton, R. A. and G. M. Woodwell. 1989. Global Climatic Change. Scientific American. April.

Kerr, R. A. 1991. A Lesson Learned, Again, at Valdez. Science. 252 (no. 5004).

Kerr, R. A. 2000. Can the Kyoto Climate Treaty Be Saved from Itself? Science. 290 (no. 5493). 3 November.

Kerr, R. A. 1995. Is the World Warming or Not? Science. 267 (no. 5198).

Lewis, Flora. 1967. One of Our H-Bombs is Missing. Toronto : McGraw Hill Book Company. Bantam Edition. 1987.

Mann, M. E. 2000. Lessons for a New Millennium. Science. 289 (no. 5477). 14 July.

McKibben, Bill. 1989. The End of Nature. New York: Random House.

Ocean Mammals Institution. What is UNP? www.oceanmammalinst.org

Ocean Link. Causes Of Oceanic Noise Pollution And Recommendations For Reduction. www.oceanlink.island.net

Toufexis, A. 1988. The Dirty Seas. Time. 1 August.

Weisskopf, M. 1988. Plastic Reaps a Grim Harvest in the Oceans of the World. Smithsonian. March.

Woodward, C. 2000. Ocean's End. New York: Basic Books.

Zwiers, F.W. and A.J. Weaver. 2000. The Causes of 20th Century Warming. Science. 290 (no. 5499). 15 December.

CHAPTER 19

Management, Research, and the Future of an Ocean Planet

The Tragedy of the Commons

Managing Ocean Resources

Research and Opportunities

You and the Future of an Ocean Planet

A Sea Turtle's Best Friend

Humans have taken a toll on sea turtle populations with hundreds of years of harvesting. Modern threats, including accidental entanglement, pollution, and the loss of nesting habitat due to coastal development have also hurt sea turtle populations. Some species, such as the Caribbean green turtle, have declined nearly 99% since the late 1400s.

Dr. Llewellyn Ehrhart, Distinguished Senior Research Fellow at the Hubbs-Sea World Research Institute in Orlando, Florida, is working to conserve marine turtle populations and to measure the success of existing efforts.

"I didn't become interested in science until I was a college sophomore. And, it wasn't until the early 1970s when I was working on Kennedy Space Center lands and discovered them nesting on the space center's beaches that I became interested in sea turtles. Upon discovering the turtle nests, I got in touch with Dr. Archie Carr, who was the best-known sea turtle biologist in the world at the time. He sent me some tags and encouraged me to study the sea turtles, and the rest, as they say, is history."

Ehrhart's primary area of research is sea turtle conservation biology, which includes population dynamics and reproductive trends. His research helps define the overall status of sea turtle stocks and discover long-term trends. This allows legislators and conservation managers to track and assess existing conservation and management efforts.

One of Ehrhart's most rewarding moments was the establishment of the Archie Carr National Wildlife Refuge on Florida's east coast. The refuge, located along a 32 kilometer (20 mile) section of coastline, is the most important loggerhead turtle nesting area in the western hemisphere and the second most important nesting beach in the world. About 25% of all loggerhead sea turtle and 35% of all green sea turtle nests in the United States are in this refuge.

"The Archie Carr National Wildlife Refuge is a direct result of the work my students and I did in the 1980s. We submitted a report to Congress that showed how important this beach was and a new national wildlife refuge was created because of what we did. It's an incredible achievement that also sends an important message to future scientists and environmentalists that their work can make a difference."

To those future scientists and environmentalists, Ehrhart gives the following recommendations: "Get a good, well-rounded bachelors degree and don't specialize too soon. Study biology, math, and chemistry along with other sciences and don't neglect the humanities and fine arts, then hone your interests as they develop. Once you're certain this is what you want to do, find a good masters program that lets you work in the field as you're moving towards your degree. This is an exciting field to be in, but it does take dedication and commitment. New generations will need to work harder than ever to ensure we leave something behind for our children. It's a huge responsibility but I can't imagine doing anything else."

Llewellyn M. Ehrhart, PhD
**Distinguished Senior Research Fellow,
Hubbs-Sea World Research Institute**

On March 9, 1862, during the US Civil War, the Union warship *Monitor* clashed with the Confederate warship *Virginia* in the waters of Hampton Roads, *Virginia*. The two ships pounded each other for hours, with neither inflicting any significant damage to the other.

Monitor Collection, NOAA

Figure 19-1

Battle of Hampton Roads.

The Civil War battle of the *Monitor* and the *Virginia* near Hampton Roads.

Although a struggle between only two warships and with no clear winner, it was a battle that brought about significant change. For one, it was the first time that ironclad, armored ships fought each other. This ushered out the era of wooden warships and in the era of armored ships. This was also the first use of a cannon turret on a warship, allowing the *Monitor*'s two guns to match the *Virginia*'s 12 guns.

A second reason we remember the *Monitor* is that it helped bring about a major change in social thinking. Although there was no winner to the battle, the *Monitor* kept the North's blockade of the South intact. This was important because many European nations had hinted that they might disregard the blockade and trade with the South if the North couldn't enforce it. Therefore, counterbalancing the *Virginia*'s threat to the blockade made a major contribution to winning the war and toppling the institution of slavery.

We also remember the *Monitor* as a milestone in yet another change in US social thinking. Impervious to Confederate naval tactics, it took a storm to send the innovative little warship to her grave in December 1862. Her exact resting place remained unknown for more than 100 years – and a lot changed about how we think of the ocean in that time.

When the *Monitor* sank, people viewed the seas as inexhaustible and limitless. You could take as much from the sea as you wanted without compromising its bounty. The world saw the seas as "self-cleaning" – able to absorb anything dumped into them. But, by the mid 20th century, scientists and environmentalists had started to realize that the ocean is neither inexhaustible nor indestructible. By the 1950s, overfishing and whaling had demonstrated that humans could overexploit the sea. A rise in detectable toxins demonstrated that we actually can over pollute the sea. By the 1960s, a major shift in social thinking was underway. With an increase in the environmental awareness, we were beginning to realize that the sea is not limitless and that we have to change the ways we think about and use the ocean.

In the United States, the passing of Marine Protection, Research and Sanctuaries Act in 1972 was an early step in this new direction. This law recognized the fragility of the sea and for the first time empowered the federal government to create protected areas in US waters. However, no one expected that the *Monitor*, a submerged cultural resource and an icon of social change from the previous century, would enter the picture.

In 1975, 113 years after her launching and two years after it was located, the *Monitor* and the waters around her were designated as the first National Marine Sanctuary. This made the *Monitor* central to another national and global change. Hopefully, it is only the start of changes that will replace indiscriminate ocean exploitation with exploration and governance for current and future generations.

This chapter looks at the challenges and opportunities that face the world and the ocean. It gives a perspective on ocean resources, why they're important, and how they may best be managed. We'll look at some of the current ocean research efforts, and some ideas about finding your place in the future of an ocean planet.

Figure 19-2a

Divers exploring the Monitor.

Figure 19-2b

Divers exploring the Monitor.
Underwater archaeologists exploring and mapping the Monitor. The Monitor is one of America's most famous submerged cultural resources.

The Tragedy of the Commons

STUDY QUESTIONS

Find the answers as you read.

1. What does the Tragedy of the Commons suggest causes overfishing and the other pending biological resource crises?

2. What does the Tragedy of the Commons suggest about the international management of marine biological resources?

3. What changes must take place to avoid the Tragedy of the Commons?

A Metaphor for Our Times

What does the Tragedy of the Commons suggest causes overfishing and the other pending biological resource crises?

What does the Tragedy of the Commons suggest about the international management of marine biological resources?

The challenges and trends that exist with overfishing and our use of other biological resources are discussed in Chapter 17. Broadly speaking, as the world fish catch has fallen, our response has been to find new ways to catch fish and to switch to new fisheries. Despite clear evidence that we're taking more from the sea than it can provide, our answer to fewer fish is to catch more. What could explain such a strange behavior?

In 1968, a biologist named Garrett Hardin published an article called "The Tragedy of the Commons." His article used a metaphor to explain how individuals acting in their best self interest can unwillingly destroy the natural resources upon which they depend, leading to a collapse of their community and the destruction of their own way of life in the process.

Hardin described a hypothetical community of farmers that used a "common" pasture, which was something often available to English farmers in the Middle Ages. All farmers had cattle that freely grazed in the pasture, and they all added as many cattle to the pasture as they could afford.

At first, everything went well. The community grew and prospered, so new farmers and their children joined in, adding their cattle to pasture. The existing farmers reinvested their earnings by buying more cattle. Soon, the pasture had more cattle than it could sustain. There were so many cattle that they ate the grass faster than it could grow. With not enough grass to feed the growing numbers of cattle, it became harder and harder for cattle to live in the pasture. In the end, the pasture could not be used anymore and the entire community failed.

What had happened, and why didn't the community stop it? Since the field was open to all, there wasn't much incentive for each individual to manage it. But, investing individually in more cattle would provide a return, at least as long as the field held out.

You can see how this metaphor applies to the ocean. The Tragedy of the Commons suggests that free access to a finite resource by many people combined with their normal pursuit of self-interest misplaces incentives and responsibilities. This ultimately destroys the resource.

In the case of faulty fishery management, there's little incentive for one individual, group, or a country to stop fishing so that fish stocks can rebound. The reason for this lack of incentive is because somebody else is likely to continue fishing and deplete the fishery anyway. There's no incentive to fish less or close certain areas of the ocean because those who invest will recapture only a fraction of their investment. Others benefit just as much without carrying any burden of cost associated with fishing less or the expense enforcing reserve areas.

Therefore, under such scenarios, the only action that makes sense economically is to get as many of the remaining fish as possible before they're all gone. To be fair, it's not likely that many, if any, fishers consciously think that way. Like most people, many of those who overfish are simply working hard to maintain their lifestyle and pay the bills. But, because the ocean is a common resource, the very costs and limits that would preserve the fisheries run contrary to making a living and supporting a business. They add costs and work, with little return on the investment.

There's little dispute that our ocean is overfished, polluted, and damaged by human activities. Finding solutions is an economic, political and social challenge. If you accept the Tragedy of the Commons metaphor as a suitable picture of what is happening in our ocean, it suggests that to continue to benefit from all the ocean has to offer, the way we manage it must change. Fortunately, it is.

Avoiding the Tragedy

What changes must take place to avoid the Tragedy of the Commons?

National and international legal initiatives, such as the 1945 Truman Proclamation and the 1982 UNCLOS discussed in Chapter 17, have shifted the Tragedy of the Commons scenario from an international to national arenas. Today, while many countries recognize that the responsibility and need to protect their coastal waters rests with them, the national and international challenges remain. Some countries are trying to renew their fisheries, others continue to take fish indiscriminately.

Pollution prevention is costly and the consequences of pollution are often most deeply felt by those who contribute the least to its creation. Since fish, waste and pollution don't recognize political boundaries, we need management solutions that work across political boundaries, economies and ecosystems. In addition, when

INTERNET PORTAL

SCiLINKS. NSTA

Topic: Ocean Governance
Go To: www.scilinks.org
Code: LOP2520

it comes to areas beyond national jurisdiction, we need innovative, international management approaches to avoid the Tragedy of the Commons scenario.

Broadly speaking the substantial changes in policy and management strategies center around the need to:

1. Move from management focused on single resource (tuna, whales, etc) or activity (navigation, recreational fishing, etc) to a comprehensive place or area-based management (the Gulf of Mexico, the Bering Sea, etc). This allows managers to account for the broad political, economic and social dimensions.

2. Address the global and cross-boundary effects of pollution in the ocean.

3. Shift subsidies and create incentives to emphasize and reward renewable resource management strategies.

4. Increase investment in ocean research with respect to its role in providing biological resources and in survival of life on Earth. Similar investments in terrestrial agriculture have paid off handsomely.

5. Address management of ocean resources in high seas. Pelagic, open ocean, and highly migratory species, such as tuna, and deep-sea ecosystems, such as cold water corals, remain vulnerable as long as these areas remain unmanaged.

ARE YOU LEARNING?

1. The Tragedy of the Commons suggests that _____ cause overfishing and other pending biological crises.

   A. free access to a finite resource and properly structured incentives and responsibilities

   B. closed access to an infinite resource and misplaced incentives and responsibilities

   C. free access to a finite resource and misplaced incentives and responsibilities

   D. free access to an infinite resource and properly structured incentives and responsibilities

2. The Tragedy of the Commons metaphor suggests that international management of marine biological resources_____.

   A. is effective

   B. must change

3. Changes needed to avoid the Tragedy of the Commons include (choose all that apply)

   A. focusing management on one species or issue.

   B. addressing global and cross-boundary effects of pollution.

   C. shifting subsidies and incentives to favor sustainable management strategies.

   D. addressing biological resources in international waters.

Managing Ocean Resources

The Precautionary Principle

What is the Precautionary Principle?

Considering the declining health of the ocean and the extent of detrimental human effects on our environment, a growing number of scientists advocate use of the Precautionary Principle when it comes to our decisions regarding the environment.

The principle can be expressed:

When an activity threatens human health or the environment, we need to take precautions even if we don't understand all the cause-and-effect relationships scientifically. In this context, those who want to conduct the activity, not the public, should be the ones to prove that the activity they plan to conduct will not harm the environment. Applying this precautionary principle must be an open, informed, and impartial process that includes all those who may experience the effects of such action. The process must also consider all reasonable alternatives, including the option of not allowing any activity.

In a nutshell, the Precautionary Principle says that even without enough information, we should not hesitate to take action to *avoid* potentially serious or irreversible harm to the environment. Many scientists believe that it's time to take this stance when it comes to the ocean in particular and the environment in general.

Managing Resources Sustainably

What are the two approaches to using renewable ocean resources?

What examples demonstrate ineffective and effective renewable resource management?

Why are scientific research and political, social and economic understanding crucial to sustainable management of ocean resources?

When it comes to renewable ocean resources, there are only two ways to use them: 1) take them until they're gone or 2) manage them so that they're sustainable. The second approach may mean taking nothing at all, like in the case of some marine reserves. The advantage of the first approach is that you get more in the short run and you don't have to manage anything. The drawback, as elaborated in Chapter 17, is that soon you don't have the resource at all.

STUDY QUESTIONS

Find the answers as you read.

1. What is the Precautionary Principle?

2. What are the two approaches to using renewable ocean resources?

3. What examples demonstrate ineffective and effective renewable resource management?

4. Why are scientific research and political, social and eco-nomic understanding crucial to sustainable management of ocean resources?

5. What is *ecosystem-based management (EBM)*?

6. What are the characteristics of EBM?

Topic: Precautionary Principle
Go To: www.scilinks.org
Code: LOP2670

Animals Collection, NOAA's Ark

Figure 19-3

California gray whale.

Thanks to effective management, the California gray whale population has increased enough to be removed from the endangered species list.

The advantage of the second approach is that, with effective management, in exchange for taking less or nothing for some time and/or in some areas, you get more in the long run.

Imagine you have $2 million in the bank. This principal earns interest income. If you take money from the bank faster than it earns interest, you reduce the principal and you earn even less interest. Eventually, you have nothing. If, on the other hand, you make sure you never touch the principal and only spend the interest, you have income indefinitely. Better yet, if you choose to spend *less* than the earned interest and add some of it to the principal your interest earnings would continually *increase*.

The state of the world fisheries and the decline of many whale species provide examples of ineffective management – taking money from the bank faster than the principal earns interest. These examples show that we can wipe out biological resources at a rate not though to have existed before in Earth's history. The rebounds of the California gray whale and other success stories show that effective management makes a difference. Biological resources stocks can recover if we change our ways and "reinvest the interest."

Here's why the world's oceans have a problem. In the bank account example, you sustain your income by never spending the principal – only the interest. With respect to the ocean, we continue to spend the "principal" so the "interest rate" for most of the resources we extract everyday is getting smaller and smaller. This means the longer we spend "principal," the longer we'll have to take little or nothing to allow the resources to restore. More importantly, social, political and economic pressures, often conflict, further complicating successful resource management because at least in the short term, they demand we take more instead of less.

In managing ocean resources, an understanding of social, economic and political dimensions of resource management must complement marine science research. Management informed by multidisciplinary science is the only way to manage the ocean for now and for the future. No management plan will work unless we address the social, economic and political effects that come with enacting the plan.

INTERNET PORTAL

SCiLINKS. NSTA

Topic: Marine Protected Areas
Go To: www.scilinks.org
Code: LOP2565

MARINE PROTECTED AREAS: A TOOL FOR OCEAN MANAGEMENT

Terrestrial parks and reserves that encompass almost 13% of Earth's landmass have been around for more than 100 years. In contrast, only 0.7% of the world's ocean is presently designated as protected areas.

According to the International Union for Conservation of Nature, (IUCN) a protected area is "a clearly defined geographical space, recognized, dedicated and managed, through legal or other effective means, to achieve the long-term conservation of nature with associated ecosystem services and cultural values." Depending on their management objective, the over 5,000 Marine Protected Areas (MPAs) created around the world to date do a great deal to preserve ocean resources. Basically, if managed effectively, MPAs can do four things:

First, they can protect the structure of the local ecosystem, by properly managing extractive uses.

Second, they can lead to improved local fisheries. MPAs that protect spawning areas or nursery grounds can help species thrive in adjacent areas.

Third, they are living laboratories for study. To understand how human activities affect the ocean, it's necessary to have something to compare with affected areas. Many of the MPAs represent some aspect of the local ocean in its least altered state.

Fourth, they can provide economic growth opportunities and alternative livelihoods when extractive uses are prohibited in the given area. In that case, MPAs can provide a place for snorkelers, scuba divers, other watersports enthusiasts, and other tourists, to enjoy nature.

However, the effectiveness of marine protected areas varies greatly around the world. One study found that only 6% of MPAs in the Caribbean have an effective management. One problem is the existence of "paper parks", MPAs with little or no financial resources, limited or non existent enforcement or poor management.

Marine Protected Areas aren't a panacea but they are a necessary tool in our ocean management toolbox. Since global environmental problems such as pollution and climate change don't avoid marine protected areas we need an array of tools to better manage our ocean.

A New Era in Ocean Management

What is ecosystem-based management (EBM)*?*

What are the characteristics of EBM*?*

Today, there is no place in the ocean that remains unaffected by our activities. Human activities on land and in the ocean are changing coastal and marine ecosystems at an unprecedented rate. These changes threaten the ocean's ability to provide us with important benefits, *or ecosystem services*, such as healthy and abundant food sources, clean beaches, and protection from storms and flooding.

In 2005, more than 220 scientists and policy experts issued a Scientific Consensus Statement on Marine *Ecosystem-Based Management* highlighting current scientific understanding of marine ecosystems. In the statement, the scientists explained that we need a new management approach. The statement defines and describes ecosystem-based management (EBM) as the foundation of this new approach. Both the Pew Oceans Commission and the U.S. Commission on Ocean Policy, discussed in Chapter 17, called on the US to adopt EBM as the cornerstone of a new era of ocean policy.

EBM is a type of place-based management that looks at whole ecosystems. Most importantly, humans and our interactions with the environment are key components of the ecosystem-based management. For example, instead of managing one issue (such as fishing) or resource (such as grouper population) in isolation, the EBM considers the whole ecosystem (such as the Great Barrier Reef). It integrates a particular ecosystem and the diverse stakeholders, which are groups or individuals who affect or can be affected by the ecosystem changes. The idea is to create a holistic management scheme. In particular, the EBM

- recognizes that human and ecological systems depend on one another.
- is concerned with the ecological integrity and sustainability of these interdependent systems.
- integrates ecological, social, and economic goals.
- engages multiple stakeholders in a collaborative process to define problems and seek solutions.
- addresses the complexity of natural processes and social systems.
- uses ecosystem processes, interdependencies and boundaries to guide and inform management decisions.

ARE YOU LEARNING?

1. **The Precautionary Principle states that**

   A. we should not hesitate to take action to avoid potentially serious or irreversible harm to the environment, even when we don't have all the information.

   B. we should never take action without enough information.

   C. free access to a finite resource and misplaced incentives and responsibilities.

   D. free access to an infinite resource and properly structured incentives and responsibilities.

2. **There are only two approaches to using renewable resources. With either, eventually the resource is gone.**

   A. true

   B. false

3. **Examples of ineffective biological resource management include _____, and examples of effective management include _____.**

   A. the decline of fisheries, the recovery of the gray whale

   B. the overpopulation of the gray whale, the recovery of the cod fishery

   C. shifting subsidies and incentives to favor sustainable management strategies

   D. addressing biological resources in international waters

4. **Scientific research and political, social and economic understanding are crucial to sustainable ocean resource management because no management plan will work unless we address the political, social and economic effects of the plan.**

   A. true

   B. false

5. **Ecosystem-based management is**

   A. a place-based system that looks at whole ecosystems.

   B. a system that looks at a single species within an ecosystem.

   C. disregarding anything that is not part of the natural environment.

   D. all of the above

6. **Ecosystem-based management (choose all that apply)**

   A. addresses the complexity of natural and social processes and systems.

   B. engages few stakeholders in a collaborative process.

   C. integrates ecological, social, and economic goals.

   D. recognizes that human and ecological systems are interdependent.

Research and Opportunities

The Door Opens

Why is there a greater need and more potential for marine research now than at any other time in history?

Why do we refer to the ocean as the Earth's "last frontier"?

As discussed in Chapter 2, humans have been exploring the ocean since the dawn of civilization. With thousands of years behind us, you might think that we know the ocean like the backs of our hands. Surprisingly, this isn't true. With 95% of the ocean largely unexplored, we've barely scratched the surface when it comes to studying the ocean. The reality is that there's a greater need and more potential for marine research now than at any time in history. This need exists for two primary reasons: 1) what we know is almost nothing compared to what we need and want to know 2) we have the technology available to study all ocean realms.

There's never been a greater need for marine science research. Critical research needs exist in understanding the effects of global climate change, the long-term effects of various types of pollution on the ocean, and the interdependencies between humans and ocean ecosystems. There's an immediate demand for applied science in energy development. This includes the search for and sustainable extraction of oil and natural gas, as well as engineering to develop renewable energy from the sea. There's a growing need for applied biology in aquaculture and fisheries management.

Beyond resource development, there's a need to explore the virtually unknown biosphere of the deep seas. Current estimates suggest that 80% of the life being found on the ocean floor is unknown and there may be *millions* of undiscovered species.

It has only been in the last half of the 20th century that we've had widespread access to practical and cost-effective tools for underwater exploration. Through electronic instrument packages in the sea and in orbit, we can study the sea locally and globally like never before. Modern submersibles, remotely operated vehicles, and new diving technologies provide cost-effective access to the underwater world. For example, in a span of a lifetime scuba diving has gone from a dangerous, difficult activity to something almost anyone in average health can enjoy.

The ocean is the Earth's last frontier. The terrestrial environment has little opportunity left for true exploration. There are very few places on land where no one has ever been before. The opposite

STUDY QUESTIONS

Find the answers as you read.

1. Why is there a greater need and more potential for marine research now than at any other time in history?

2. Why do we refer to the ocean as the Earth's "last frontier"?

3. Why is it important that scientists understand the ocean acidification – global warming connection?

4. Beyond their potential as an energy resource, why do methane hydrates interest scientists?

5. Why is *paleoclimatology* important in studying changes in the atmosphere?

6. Why are scientists trying to learn more about the biodiversity of the ocean?

7. Why is there so much potential for discovering new drugs among benthic organisms?

8. How does undersea research apply to space research?

Topic: Marine Research
Go To: www.scilinks.org
Code: LOP2525

Figure 19-4a

Astronauts and _Trieste_ submarine.

We know more about our moon than our ocean. Only two people have ever visited the bottom of the Marianas trench; whereas 12 people have walked on the moon.

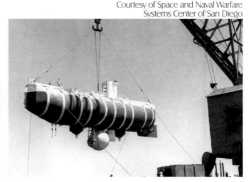

Figure 19-4b

Figure 19-4c

INTERNET PORTAL

SC*L*INKS. NSTA

Topic: Climate Change
Go To: www.scilinks.org
Code: LOP2530

is true for the underwater environment. In the ocean, explorers routinely go where no one has gone before. Even now, more than 30 years after the Apollo program, more people have been to the moon than to the deepest place in the ocean. Twelve people have walked on the surface of the moon, but only two have been to the bottom of the Marianas Trench.

With new research demand and new exploration technologies available, the door is open to the sea. It's time to step through and see what's there to explore.

Ocean and Climate Interplay

Why is it important that scientists understand the ocean acidification - global warming connection?

Chapter 18 discusses global warming and the ocean. Ocean acidification – the increase in the acidity of the ocean – is a phenomenon discussed in Chapter 8. Marine scientists are currently trying to understand the feedback mechanisms at play between the ocean and the climate.

Ocean acidification is one of the most interesting and challenging ocean and climate change research questions to be tackled now and in the future. Scientists studying coral reefs want to know how the increasing acidity of the ocean may affect coral reefs. In laboratory experiments, scientists have demonstrated that corals grown in acidified environments can sustain basic life functions and resume skeleton building after they've been reintroduced to normal marine conditions. However, under current scenarios, global warming and ocean acidification will slow calcification rates and corals may become increasingly rare on reefs in the 21st century.

In another example, scientists studying Pacific continental shelf area in North America found large quantities of acidic water upwelling close to the shelf. These acidic waters upwelling so close to continental shelf may pose a direct threat to marine organisms because most of them live or are spawned on continental shelves where ocean acidity is much lower.

Methane Hydrates and Global Climate Changes

Beyond their potential as an energy resource, why do methane hydrates interest scientists?

Chapter 17 explains that methane hydrates interest scientists because they are a potential energy resource. That's certainly an incentive for studying them but methane hydrates may help answer many other important questions, and you could build an entire career on studying them.

In addition to being a potential energy resource, methane hydrates interest scientists for their role in the biosphere and global climate changes. Some scientists estimate that a full one-third of all the Earth's biomass consists of microbes living under the ocean floor without oxygen. Recent evidence suggests that these microbes transform a significant amount of organic carbon into methane, which raises vital questions.

US Geological Survey

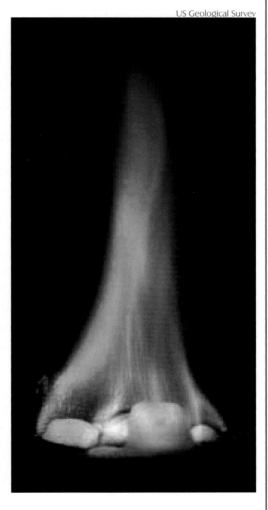

Figure 19-5

Burning methane hydrate.
Besides being a potential energy source, methane hydrates interest scientists because of their role in the biosphere and global climate change. Some scientists estimate that a full one-third of all the Earth's biomass consists of microbes living under the ocean floor, and that these microbes may convert organic carbon to methane.

How much do these life processes protect us from global climate changes? There's little dispute that the Earth is getting warmer due to the greenhouse effect. Scientists also think that the ocean is taking up a lot of the carbon released by burning fossil fuels. It may be that microbes are converting some of this carbon as methane hydrates, and thereby protecting us somewhat from climate change.

However, there's another side to this question. Methane is a greenhouse gas that contributes 20 times more to global warming than does the same amount of carbon dioxide. Can methane hydrates release their methane? Some scientists fear that an earthquake or other geologic event could cause a massive methane release. As discussed in Chapter 18, methane is one of the key contributors to global climate change. Therefore, such release could significantly accelerate global temperature increases. Many marine geochemists think such massive methane release has happened in the past and will probably happen again. Research may be able to tell us how likely this event is to occur, when it could happen, and what to prepare for if it does. We may even be able to prevent it.

The Atmosphere Yesterday, Today, and Tomorrow

Why is paleoclimatology *important in studying changes in the atmosphere?*

Related to the study of methane hydrates and global climate changes is the study of our atmosphere. When you think about it, air is a particularly important resource. If you don't think so, see how long you can go without it!

To help explain present and future trends, scientists study climates of the past, before instrumental weather measurements were taking place. This is called *paleoclimatology.* This study of ancient atmospheres is important because it provides a baseline of conditions to compare with the present atmosphere. This information allows scientists to predict changes to the atmosphere and likely changes to the climate.

Researchers study many aspects of the ocean world to get clues about ancient climates. By examining the chemical or biological composition of coral skeletons, biogenous layers on the ocean floor or air trapped in ice, scientists can infer climate conditions of the past. Scientists examine the layers of coral skeletons making up coral reefs to determine climate trends over the years, much as you can from the rings of a tree. The layers of ocean sediment accumulated over the millennia also provide vital information about the past climates. A key element of biogenous sediments, discussed in Chapter 14, is foraminiferan tests (their skeleton shells). Because species of foraminiferans require specific temperatures or depths to survive, particular species present in the sediment indicate the water conditions when the sediment was deposited. Additionally, by sampling gases trapped within ice, scientists can estimate the amount of atmospheric gases such as carbon dioxide or oxygen that were ambient in the atmosphere when that particular ice layer was formed.

Based on these and other data, climatologists use computers to model how the Earth has changed from millions of years ago to today. Understanding how the Earth's climate has changed in the past is a critical component in understanding the present and the future of climate change.

Understanding Ocean Biodiversity

Why are scientists trying to learn more about the biodiversity of the ocean?

Since the vast majority of the ocean remains largely unexplored, scientists want to learn more about the past, present and the future of marine biodiversity. Although we already know of millions of species, scientists think millions more remain to be discovered.

Chapter 17 discusses why biodiversity is the ultimate resource in safeguarding our future. Scientists are trying to grasp the scope of this ultimate resource. They are trying to discover and catalog new species so they can understand biodiversity trends and encourage conservation. (For more on the topic of species cataloging, see the discussion in Chapter 5 regarding cybertaxonomy.)

There are several ongoing efforts that address ocean biodiversity. FishBase – a global information system on everything about fish – is a database with practically all known fish species. It is indispensible to professionals such as research scientists, fisheries managers, zoologists and students interested in learning about the interrelations of fish species.

A ten year research effort called the Census of Marine Life (CoML) began in 2000 under the leadership of an international scientific committee of experts from all fields of marine science. CoML hopes to answer three basic, yet very large questions: What lived in the ocean in the past? What lives in the ocean now? What will live in the ocean in the future? Answering this will help scientists understand the diversity, distribution, and abundance of species in the ocean. It will also help us improve the tools and methodologies we use for the study of life in the ocean, to better management of marine resources, and to educate the public in general.

The Encyclopedia of Life (EOL), is another collaborative scientific effort to catalog the biodiversity of life, including the ocean. EOL's goal is to have an online database for all 1.8 million species now known to live on Earth. The plan is to have 230,000 marine species pages by 2013, with support by the CoML effort. When completed, EOL will provide scientists, policymakers, students, and citizens with information needed to study, manage and protect our ocean planet.

Census of Marine Life/www.coml.org

Figure 19-6a

Encyclopedia of Life/www.eol.org

Figure 19-6b

The Census of Marine Life (www.coml.org) and the Encyclopedia of Life (www.eol.org) are trying to catalog new species so scientists can understand biodiversity trends and encourage conservation. For more information on the use of these web sites by scientists, go to Chapter 5 and read the sidebar "Cybertaxonomy."

INTERNET PORTAL
SCiLINKS. NSTA
Topic: Biodiversity
Go To: www.scilinks.org
Code: LOP2455

Cures from the Ocean

Why is there so much potential for discovering new drugs among benthic organisms?

As discussed in Chapter 17, the wealth of biodiversity found and yet to be discovered in the ocean holds a tremendous potential for drug discovery and research. Researchers have found literally thousands of biochemical compounds with medical potential. For example, scientists are studying the anti-tumor properties of a compound named discodermolide found in a marine sponge, *Discodermia dissolute.*

Considering the vast diversity of benthic organisms, the potential for cures from the sea is vast. Because so many of these organisms don't move, they often use chemicals for self-defense against everything from larger, multicellular predators to bacteria. They have powerful immune systems loaded with literally millions of potential drugs.

RISING SCUBA TECHNOLOGIES

The scuba diving that most marine scientist use and that you've seen on television (or perhaps even tried) is primarily open circuit scuba diving. Open circuit scuba (from the acronym SCUBA, meaning Self Contained Underwater Breathing Apparatus) was refined by undersea explorer Jacques Cousteau in the 1940s. It works by delivering compressed air from a cylinder when you inhale. When you exhale, your breath goes into the water, producing bubbles.

Open circuit scuba opened the ocean realm to exploration by providing a simple, reliable, and relatively inexpensive way to spend time under water. Because of its simplicity and reliability, it will probably remain the most popular underwater breathing system for the immediate future. However, it does have some disadvantages.

PADI

Figure 19-5a

Open circuit scuba.

The primary disadvantage is that the deeper you go, the faster you use up your air. This is because the scuba regulator supplies air at the surrounding water pressure. Since the deeper you go, the higher the pressure, each breath takes more air molecules from your cylinder. This isn't much of a problem for most recreational diving because you don't stay under water much longer than an hour, and you don't dive deeper then 40 meters/130 feet. But, it is a limitation for the scientist who needs to stay under water for longer times or wants to venture deeper.

The alternative is closed circuit scuba. Closed circuit scuba doesn't waste your exhalation as bubbles. Instead, it re-circulates each breath, which is why these units are often referred to as rebreathers. Special chemicals remove waste carbon dioxide and a small cylinder replenishes the small amount of oxygen your body actually uses from each breath. These devices can also change the ratio of oxygen and nitrogen to reduce the risk of decompression sickness.

Although closed circuit scuba has been around for some time, it is only recently that modern electronics have made it practical. These devices require special training and aren't quite as simple to master as open circuit scuba. However, closed circuit scuba provides a new tool to explore deeper water for longer periods. As the technology advances and prices drop, closed circuit scuba may become more common in recreational diving as well. For an example of a scientist using this technology, see the biography of Dr. Richard Pyle in Chapter 5.

Kenny Schneider, Courtesy of Steam Machines, Inc.

Figure 19-7b

Closed circuit scuba.

It is generally far more economical for manufacturers to synthesize drugs than to harvest them from the sea. This makes the ocean the place to discover new pharmaceuticals to manufacture. With a rising population, lengthening life spans, and fears of epidemics, the demand for underwater drug research is likely to be high.

Courtesy of PharmaMar

Ocean Explorer, NOAA

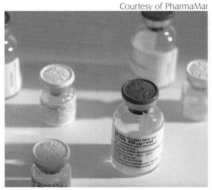

Figure 19-8a

Drugs from the sea.
Discodermolide was discovered from the composition of a species of deep water sponge shown in **Figure 19-8b**.

Figure 19-8b

Miracle Sponge.
Discodermolide (the drug) was isolated from the sponge *Discodermia dissoluta.*

Feet in the Water and an Eye on the Sky

How does undersea research apply to space research?

In addition to exploring the sea, humans are increasingly interested in exploring space. As it happens, undersea research applies to space research by providing analogous environments for study. These range from the search for life in the solar system to the dynamics of human space flight.

Hydrothermal vents are one such example. By showing that life exists in a chemosynthetic ecosystem that doesn't rely on the sun, biologists hope that similar life exists in nearby space. Jupiter's moon, Europa, is thought to have a saltwater ocean covered with miles of ice. The tidal effect from Jupiter may be strong enough to provide sufficient energy for a chemosynthetic ecosystem. It may do this by creating tides that are so powerful that they create friction heat sufficient to keep water in liquid state. Methane-hydrate-producing organisms provide a similar example for life that may exist in conditions significantly different from those we're used to.

When humans eventually get to explore other planets in our universe, another challenge will be exploring them without contaminating them. Again, the sea provides a place to study this challenge. In the 1980s, scientists discovered a lake under the Antarctic ice cap that's thought to have been isolated from the surface for tens of millions of years. Lake Vostock, as it's called, has become a focal point for research about the past, but also for studying how to research an isolated, uncontaminated environment.

OAR, NURP, NOAA

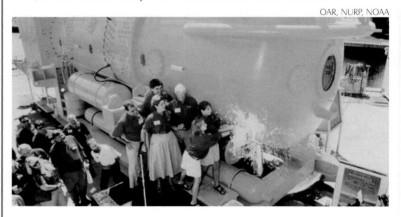

Figure 19-9

After complete overhaul, *Aquarius* is christened and readied for sea.

With the rise in interest in sending humans to explore Mars and return to the moon, the sea again offers a place to learn. Living in an undersea environment has many of the same psychological, environmental, and logistical problems as living in space. Like being in space, working from an underwater habitat requires learn to research while in an isolated environment. Based on these analogous challenges, the NASA Extreme Environment Mission Operations (NEEMO) team studies human spaceflight issues in the *Aquarius* underwater habitat in Key Largo, Florida. Located in 18

University of North Carolina Wilmington,
Undersea Research Center/NURP, NOAA

Figure 19-10

NEEMO 3 team with NURC instructor Mark Hulsbeck on *Aquarius*' deck.

National Undersea Research Center, NOAA/NASA

Figure 19-11

NEEMO I team in the *Aquarius* bunk room.

meters (60 feet) of water, *Aquarius* is currently the only operating underwater research habitat in the world.

NEEMO missions put astronauts and scientists under water in the habitat for durations from five to 14 days. During these missions, the scientists research performance psychology, biomedical questions, interaction with ground-based support and other space-related problems. What the NEEMO teams learn here, in a better controlled and less costly environment for the explorers, reduces the lessons that need to be learned on the moon or Mars.

ARE YOU LEARNING?

1. **There is a greater need for marine research now than at any time in history because (choose all that apply)**

   A. people have finally discovered there's an ocean.

   B. we know almost nothing compared to what we need and want to know.

   C. we have the technology to study all ocean realms.

   D. the seas are common property.

2. **The ocean is the Earth's "last frontier" because**

   A. after we go there, no one will be allowed to go anywhere else.

   B. explorers in the sea routinely go where no one has gone before.

   C. it is the final thing humans have left to do before the end of time.

   D. none of the above

3. **It is important that scientists understand the ocean acidification - global warming connection because (choose all that apply)**

   A. acidified environments may affect coral reefs.

   B. acidic water upwellings may pose a threat to marine organisms on the continental shelf.

   C. acidic water may be able to eat through the holes of ships.

4. **Beyond their potential as an energy resource, methane hydrates interest scientists because**

   A. the organisms that produce them have a role in global climate changes.

   B. it is likely that the U.N. will ban methane hydrates.

   C. the organisms that produce them are the likely cause of overfishing.

5. **Paleoclimatology is important in studying changes in the atmosphere because**

   A. it proves that the atmosphere has never changed.

   B. it provides evidence that the dinosaurs changed the atmosphere.

   C. it provides a baseline of conditions in the past for comparison.

   D. none of the above

6. **Scientists are trying to learn about ocean biodiversity because (choose all that apply)**

   A. they are trying to grasp the scope of biodiversity.

   B. they want to understand biodiversity trends.

   C. it helps them encourage conservation.

7. **Benthic organisms provide tremendous potential for new drugs because**

   A. they often rely on chemical defenses and have strong immune systems.

   B. they get sick and make good subjects for studying drug effectiveness.

   C. they're easier to catch than pelagic organisms that swim.

   D. all of the above

8. **Undersea research applies to space research by (choose all that apply)**

   A. providing analogous environments to study.

   B. examining types of chemosynthetic life.

   C. studying how to research an isolated environment.

   D. providing analogous challenges when living in an underwater habitat.

You and the Future of an Ocean Planet

The Ocean Is Our Future

Why should the future of the ocean interest you?

Based on what you've learned in this course, you should now realize that life on Earth is tied directly to the ocean. Even if you decide to live on the top of a mountain, as far away from the sea as you can get, the ocean affects you and you affect the ocean. The ocean provides oxygen, absorbs carbon, provides a livable climate, redistributes heat, is the water from which rain forms and helps feed the world. Your everyday actions, from the type of seafood you eat to how you get to school, what you dump into neighboring water sheds or where you wash your car affect the ocean. The future of the ocean must interest you because your future relies on the health of the ocean.

With overfishing, pollution, global climate changes, overdevelopment, and other challenges facing us, it may seem overwhelming. Is it too late to save the seas? No, it's not.

If we act now, we can have a healthy ocean with rich stocks of biological resources. We can benefit from all the services that the ocean provides without undermining the environment. There are many challenges, but more opportunities and resources exist now to do things right than ever before. No single person can solve all the problems, but many people working together can. And, we must do so for the sake of ourselves, the ocean, and the future of the ocean planet.

Ocean Conservation and You

What can you do to help preserve and protect the ocean?

Because your everyday choices and long term choices affect the ocean, the first step you can take to preserve the ocean is to choose wisely. This doesn't usually require major research or major inconveniences. But, it does mean making the best choices regarding things like the seafood you catch or buy, the type of laundry detergent you use, and the companies you do business with. To help protect the ocean, you need to understand the problems, recognize the solutions and, most importantly, act accordingly.

There are three basic steps to take to help preserve and protect the ocean.

INTERNET PORTAL

SCiLINKS. NSTA

Topic: Marine Conservation
Go To: www.scilinks.org
Code: LOP2480

Stay informed about the ocean:

- Read scientific and popular publications on ocean issues. Go beyond what you learn about the ocean in this course and keep learning. You and every person on this planet must be ocean literate.
- Subscribe to marine conservation organizations' news-letters and podcasts.
- Listen to the current political and economic news and events.
- Share your knowledge in ways that will inspire action among your classmates, friends, family and community.

Be an ocean advocate:

- Support research and responsible environmental causes through contribution and membership in marine conservation organizations.
- Communicate your care and concern for the ocean to your local, regional, and national political representatives.
- When you're old enough to vote, be sure candidates know that ocean issues are important to you and that they affect how you cast your vote.

Act to protect:

- Be a discriminating consumer by choosing products and services that do not deplete ocean resources. Many conservation organizations have created guides to help you make the choices that are good for you and the ocean planet.
- Volunteer for local environmental activities and marine research institutions.
- Become a scuba diver, snorkeler, or surfer and share your passion for the ocean. People who spend time on the water love the ocean, and people protect what they love.

A Career in Marine Science

How do you discover whether a career in marine science is right for you?

What should you do now to prepare for a career in marine science?

If you have a passion for the ocean, you probably already know it. You may be thinking about investing your future in the sea. There are several steps you can take to discover whether a career in marine science is right for you.

Brenda Konar, University of Alaska Fairbanks

Figure 19-12

Students on a marine science field trip.

Courtesy of Richard Pyle

Figure 19-13

Scientific Diver.

Figure 19-14a

Coral researcher taking photos of a study site.

Figure 19-14b

Scientific divers.

Submersible pilot transporting researcher to a study site below which he can dive.

Figure 19-14c

Marine Archaeologists.

First, get involved with marine sciences. Seaquariums, zoos, not-for-profit foundations, and many other marine institutions rely on volunteers to get things done. There's no better way to decide whether a career is for you than by being part of it.

Second, follow your heart. Marine science is a huge discipline – too big for anyone to be an expert in all of it. You may find you're most interested in fish, or perhaps in undersea technology or submerged cultural resources. In the first case, your study would emphasize biology, in the second engineering and the third archaeology or maritime history. As you get involved, let your passion guide your choices. That's how most people make their biggest contributions and find the most satisfaction.

Third, read everything you can find in the areas of marine science that interest you. Watch television programs and check out the internet. If a career in marine sciences is right for you, seeking ocean related information will come naturally.

Assuming you've decided that you do want to pursue a marine science career, what do you do next? You probably realize that you'll choose a college or university with a marine science program in your interest area. However, there's a lot you can do before college.

First, keep your grades up. The better you do in high school, the more options you have in choosing a college. Math is a very important part of science, so develop your abilities with it. Even if you aren't good in math, work at it harder. Persistence will pay off. You don't need to love it (many scientists don't), but you have to be able to use it. Scientists use math daily.

Second, go beyond your required coursework. Colleges favor those students who do extracurricular work. Ask your teachers about opportunities to enter science fairs with marine science projects. If there's a marine science club, join it and be an active participant. You may even be able to start a club if your school doesn't have one yet.

Third, volunteer in marine science programs as mentioned above. Colleges know that students who are involved in their passion in high school are serious about their career choice. They make some of the best college students and move on to some of the most rewarding careers.

Fourth, learn to snorkel or, better yet, to scuba dive. Diving isn't required in some marine sciences, but it may help you apply many of the concepts you have learned in this text. It's also one of the best ways to experience the undersea world firsthand. Scuba diving is a tool for aquatic research.

Fifth, remember to have fun. If being a marine scientist is the right thing for you, you'll enjoy the challenging work and will be able to keep your life balanced. You'll rarely have a boring day at work as a marine researcher.

Finally, no matter which career path you choose, how many times it changes and how long you're in it, remember that you need to keep learning. Stay engaged in the constantly evolving world of marine science. You need to do this to keep your research current, to improve your communication skills and to make your work relevant to world's needs. The more you grow your understanding of how the ocean-human system works, the more you can contribute.

An Ocean Related Career

How can your career involve the ocean apart from being a marine scientist?

You may already know that being a marine scientist isn't for you. However, even if you choose not to be a marine scientist, you can have a great career tied to the ocean. There are many jobs in various fields that are specifically related to the ocean, and many broadly applied professions have specialized application related to the ocean. These opportunities exist in the private, government, and non-profit sectors of the world economy. You could work for a private firm, the federal government or a marine conservation organization. You could be a commercial diver, but you could also be a lawyer who specializes in the environmental law. Vocational, research and service opportunities abound as long as you remain curious and passionate about the ocean. Here are just a few of the possibilities:

Commander John Bortniak, NOAA Corps

Figure 19-14d

Scientists departing in skiff on marine mammal study.

- Marine educator
- Ecotourism guide
- Beach superintendent
- Maritime or environmental lawyer
- Coastal or ocean policy analyst
- Economist
- Marine archaeologist
- Marine historian
- Fundraiser for marine conservation organization
- Aquaculture specialist

- Marine management consultant
- Marina manager
- Marine artist
- Museum curator
- Environmental planner
- Manager of a land conservation organization
- Botanist
- Computer specialist with a marine or environmental organization
- Ecologist

- Hatchery specialist
- Landscape or maritime architect
- Merchant ship crew or officer
- US Navy or Coast Guard crew or officer
- Cruise operator
- Scuba, snorkeling, sail boarding, wake boarding, or surfing instructor
- Aquaculturist
- Fishing or dive charter boat operator
- Resort operator
- Park ranger
- Marine engineer or architect
- Marine insurance
- Customs inspector

- Marine surveyor
- Vessel design, construction, and maintenance
- Oil platform worker
- Commercial diver
- ROV operator
- Submersible pilot
- Underwater photographer or cinematographer
- Nature journalist or outdoor sports writer
- Travel writer
- Travel agent
- Science writer
- Watersports or scuba manufacturer or sales representative

ARE YOU LEARNING?

1. **The future of the ocean should interest you because**

   A. your future depends on the health of the ocean.

   B. there's a lot of money to be made as a marine scientist.

   C. we said so.

2. **Ways to preserve and protect the ocean include (choose all that apply)**

   A. staying informed.

   B. being an ocean advocate.

   C. acting to protect the ocean.

3. **To discover whether a career in marine science is right for you (choose all that apply)**

   A. get involved as a volunteer in marine sciences.

   B. follow your heart to discover your particular interest.

   C. read everything you can in your area of interest.

   D. join the army.

4. **To begin preparing now for a career in marine science (choose all that apply)**

   A. keep your grades up.

   B. go beyond your required coursework.

   C. volunteer for marine science programs.

   D. learn to snorkel or scuba dive.

5. **Careers involving the ocean apart from marine science include (choose all that apply)**

   A. merchant ship crew or officer.

   B. scuba, snorkeling, sail boarding, or surfing instructor.

   C. ship builder, marine engineer, or architect.

   D. ROV operator or research submarine pilot.

New Terms You Learned

- **ecosystem-based management** A type of management that considers whole ecosystem in a given place including humans and their interactions with the environment (p. 19-9)
- **ecosystem services** resources and processes needed by humans, such as food or protection from storms, that are provided by natural systems (p. 19-9)
- **paleoclimatology** the study of past climate, for times prior to instrumental weather measurements (p. 19-14)
- **Precautionary Principle** Where there are threats of serious or irreversible damage, lack of full scientific certainty shall not be used as a reason for postponing cost-effective measures to prevent environmental degradation (Rio Declaration 1992) (p. 19-7)
- **stakeholder** A person, group, organization, who effects or can be affected by any particular system (p. 19-9)

Chapter 19 in Review

1. In your own words, describe the Tragedy of the Commons. What part of the metaphor corresponds to managing fisheries?
2. Explain what the Tragedy of the Commons metaphor suggests about the management of marine biological resources.
3. What changes need to take place to avoid the destructive results of Tragedy of the Commons? Why are these changes essential?
4. What is the Precautionary Principle? What does it tell us about when to take action to protect the ocean?
5. Describe the only two approaches to using biological ocean resources and give examples that demonstrate ineffective and effective management of them. Why is scientific research and political, social and economic understanding crucial to keeping biological ocean resources sustainable?
6. Define ecosystem-based management. Explain how differs from some of the current management strategies?
7. Why is the ocean the Earth's "final frontier"? How does this relate to the potential for marine research now than at any time in history?
8. Why is it important that scientists understand the global warming - ocean acidification connection?
9. Explain the biological interest in methane hydrates specific to global climate changes.
10. Explain why paleoclimatology is important in studying changes to the atmosphere.
11. Describe the two scientific efforts to understand ocean's biodiversity. Explain how are they important.
12. Explain why there's so much potential for discovering new drugs among benthic organisms. Why is there not likely as much potential for mass producing new drugs from benthic organisms?
13. How does undersea research apply to space research? Give some specific examples.
14. Why is the future of the ocean important to you?
15. Explain the steps you can take to help preserve and protect the ocean. For each step, give an example of something you can do today.

16. What can you do to determine whether a career in marine sciences is right for you? What can you do now to prepare for such a career?

17. List and briefly describe five possible careers related to the ocean, other than being a marine scientist, that are not listed in this chapter.

Connecting Chapter Concepts – Science Scenarios

1. "Tragedy of the Commons," a 1968 article by biologist Garrett Hardin, is often cited as a metaphor for the problems associated with managing ocean resources. In his metaphor, Hardin describes The Commons as a pasture in which a group of farmers can have as many cattle as they want and profit from their individual cattle, with no responsibility for managing the pasture as a whole.

   A. Why do the farmers in the metaphor have no incentive to care for the pasture? How does this relate to fisheries?

   B. What is the only action that makes sense economically for the farmers of The Common? How does this relate to fisheries?

   C. What does the Tragedy of the Commons suggest is the problem that causes overfishing? What is the solution?

   D. What shifted the Tragedy of the Commons scenario from the international to the national arenas?

2. Today there are more opportunities for marine research than at any time in history. These opportunities range from understanding the ocean's biodiversity through resource development and space exploration.

   A. Why it is important to understand ocean biodiversity?

   B. What are methane hydrates? Why do they interest scientists?

   C. In what ways does the sea help us study space exploration?

3. How do you discover whether a career as a marine scientist is right for you? What should you do now to prepare for such a career?

Marine Science and the Real World

1. Explain how the wreck of the USS *Monitor* serves as an important symbol for marine resource management in the United States.

2. Imagine you're a United Nations delegate trying to eliminate the Tragedy of the Commons scenario for international waters. What changes to international law would you suggest? What arguments against these suggestions would you expect?

3. List five tasks that you perform every day (such as washing dishes) that affect the ocean and describe how you can change what you do to minimize the negative effects of those tasks on the ocean environment.

4. Choose five different careers listed in this chapter and explain why you think they would be right for you?

5. What do you dream of doing as an adult? Describe your career and list the skills you need to succeed. How can you start developing those skills now? No matter what it is, explain how your role in it relates to the ocean.

References

Duxbury, A. and A. Duxbury. 1994. An Introduction to the World's Oceans. Dubuque, IA: William C. Brown Publishers.

Garrison, T. 2004. *Oceanography: An Invitation to Marine Science.* Pacific Grove, CA: Brooks/Cole, a division of Thomson Learning, Inc.

Garrett Hardin. 1968. The Tragedy of the Commons. *Science.* 162 (No. 3859). December 13.

McLeod, K.L., J. Lubchenco, S.R. Palumbi, and A.A. Rosenberg. 2005. Scientific Consensus Statement on Marine Ecosystem-Based Management. Signed by 221 academic scientists and policy experts with relevant expertise and published by the Communication Partnership for Science and the Sea at http://compassonline. org/?q=EBM

Segar, D.A. 1998. *Introduction to Ocean Sciences.* Belmont, CA: Wadsworth Publishing Company.

Thurman, Harold V. and Elizabeth A. Burton. 2001. *Introductory Oceanography.* New Jersey: Prentice Hall.

Partnership for Interdisciplinary Studies of Coastal Oceans. 2007. The Science of Marine Reserves (2nd Edition, United States Version). www. piscoweb.org

Halpern, S., Shaun Walbridge, Kimberly A. Selkoe, Carrie V. Kappel, Fiorenza Micheli, Caterina D'Agrosa, John F. Bruno, Kenneth S. Casey, Colin Ebert, Helen E. Fox, Rod Fujita, Dennis Heinemann, Hunter S. Lenihan, Elizabeth M. P. Madin, Matthew T. Perry, Elizabeth R. Selig, Mark Spalding, Robert Steneck and Reg Watson. 2008. A Global Map of Human Impact on Marine Ecosystems Benjamin. *Science.* 15 February. 319 (5865).

Feely, Richard; Christopher L. Sabine, J. Martin Hernandez-Ayon, Debby Ianson and Burke Hales. 2008. Evidence for Upwelling of Corrosive "Acidified" Seawater onto the Continental Shelf. *Science.* 10.

Hoegh-Guldberg, O., P.J. Mumby, A.J. Hooten, R.S. Steneck, P. Greenfield, E. Gomez, C.D. Harvell, P.F. Sale, A.J. Edwards, K. Caldeira, N. Knowlton, C.M. Eakin, R. Iglesias-Prieto, N. Muthiga, R.H. Bradbury, A. Dubi, and M.E. Hatziolos. 2007. Coral Reefs Under Rapid Climate Change and Ocean Acidification. *Science.* 318 (5857).

Fine, Maoz and Dan Tchernov. 2007. Scleractinian Coral Species Survive and Recover from Decalcification. *Science.* 315 (5820).

CHAPTER 1–Introduction to Marine Science

Life on an Ocean Planet   Page 1-7

1. someone who uses the processes of science to find answers.
2. weather; climate.
3. food; oxygen; natural resources including oil.
4. No, humans have seen very, very little of it.
5. depleted fisheries; pollution; the loss of crucial marine environment
6. it allows you to make responsible decisions related to the ocean.

Defining Your Study   Page 1-17

1. the process of discovering the facts, processes, and unifying principles that explain the nature of the ocean and its associated life forms.
2. recording and describing the ocean's processes and contents.
3. biological oceanography; physical oceanography.
4. technology
5. physical science; life science; Earth and space science.
6. true
7. science as inquiry; science and technology; science in personal and social perspectives; the historical nature of science.
8. none of the above
9. atmospheric science; ecology; astronomy.
10. mathematics; history; technology; social sciences.

Science, Technology, Society, and You   Page 1-34

1. both A and C – a body of knowledge; an organized method.
2. true
3. by improving many aspects of life; by threatening and degrading life in many ways.
4. prioritize the consequences to the environment in applying technologies.
5. identifying the problem; constructing models; comparing observations; predicting outcomes.
6. Identify the problem (or question); Make a hypothesis; Test the hypothesis; Interpret and analyze results; Report results, procedures, and conclusions.
7. an educated scientific guess that you can test.
8. inductive, deductive
9. a scientific explanation with observable supporting evidence.
10. both A and B – it allows scientists to verify your work; it allows scientists to build on what you've learned.
11. true
12. the changes affect all walks of life; doing so can help you advance your career; failing to do so can put you behind in your career; you can help society adjust to the effects.

How to Learn Marine Science Most Efficiently   Page 1-43

1. six
2. theories on the foundation of life in the ocean; the present and the future of the marine environment.
3. showing you different marine sciences and what their careers involve.
4. learning objectives.
5. none of the above; Examining Life on an Ocean Planet before reading it makes learning more efficient and effective. It does this by establishing your mental framework about marine science. Research on how people learn shows that this is important because your brain builds on this framework as you study.

6. recite
7. explore the provided references; explore connections that relate to other subjects or everyday life; apply what you learn in the labs and activities; follow your curiosity.

CHAPTER 2–History of Ocean Exploration and Marine Sciences

The History of Oceanography – Why Study It?   Page 2-3

1. it is part of understanding how the ocean has affected society; it explains how and why marine sciences are conducted today, it's interesting
2. ancient uses and explorations; European voyages of discovery

Ancient Uses and Explorations (5000 B.C.-800 A.D.)   Page 2-15

1. true
2. Egyptians, 3200 B.C
3. establishing the first trade routes through the Mediterranean.
4. it is the earliest known regular open-ocean seafaring beyond sight of land.
5. true
6. using the North Star to determine how far north or south you are.
7. the first latitude/longitude system and calculating the Earth's circumference
8. false; Herodotus' map was one of the earliest published maps of the world. Strabo's map demonstrated the Greek's expanding knowledge, and its accuracy, about the world.
9. identify specific locations on the Earth's surface.
10. a latitude line, the equator
11. a longitude line, Greenwich England

The Middle Ages (800 A.D.-1400)   Page 2-19

1. suppressing advancements.
2. false; Global warming freed the North Atlantic of sea ice and allowed the Vikings to explore westward.
3. the compass.
4. the central rudder and watertight compartments.

European Voyages of Discovery (1400-1700)   Page 2-22

1. economics, politics, and religion.
2. Prince Henry, Dias, and da Gama.
3. to find a route to Asia and East India.
4. Vespucci.
5. crossing the Isthmus of Panama and finding the Pacific Ocean.
6. Magellan, 1519-1522
7. Drake, 1577-1580

The Birth of Marine Science (1700-1900)   Page 2-32

1. they had science and exploration as their only goals.
2. chronometer
3. many south Pacific islands; Hawaii
4. none of the above; The United States Exploring Expedition proved the existence of Antarctica.
5. true
6. the seafloor subsides
7. the theory of natural selection; the theory of evolution of species.

8. the Challenger expedition.

9. the first soundings deeper than 4,000 meters; discovering marine organisms in the deep ocean; sampling and illustrating plankton; and documenting physical, chemical, geological, and biological information in 362 stations in 36 million square kilometers (14 million square miles) of ocean.

Twentieth-Century Marine Science   Page 2-48

1. the Industrial Revolution.

2. mapping the Atlantic seafloor.

3. the first ship constructed specifically for marine science.

4. both A and B

5. to pick specific samples; take living samples without killing them; directly observe organism behaviors; directly observe phenomena in their natural setting.

6. bathyspheres, bathyscaphes, and deep-diving submersibles.

7. depth, logistics

8. ROV/AUV

9. false; Drifters collect data adrift and transmit it to satellites.

10. sea-surface height; color; temperature; shape.

11. making navigation significantly more accurate.

CHAPTER 3–Theories of the Origins of Life

The Universe, Solar System, and Earth   Page 3-9

1. the theorized beginning of the universe from a single point.

2. the theorized beginning of a star caused by gases accumulating and condensing into a dense core.

3. when protostars became so dense that nuclear fusion began in their cores.

4. when light atoms within stars fused, becoming heavier atoms.

5. the star consumes all the hydrogen fueling it.

6. resulted when a supernova shock wave caused a nebula to condense and spin.

7. when some condensing gas revolving around the sun collapsed into masses too small to become stars.

8. the solar system formed from a nebula.

9. accretion.

10. density stratification.

11. that a planet-sized object struck young Earth, sending material into orbit that eventually became the moon.

12. only after Earth cooled enough to have a crust.

13. only after Earth cooled enough for water to accumulate on the surface.

14. created the atmospheric changes required for terrestrial life to form.

Origins of Life   Page 3-16

1. based on how scientists interpret the fossil record.

2. are readily formed under certain conditions by natural processes.

3. a large, stable molecule formed by chance and became capable of reproducing itself.

4. the origin of life from nonliving matter.

5. heterotroph, autotroph

6. true

7. mutation, natural selection

Ocean Zones and Lifestyles   Page 3-22

1. true

2. pelagic, benthic

3. neritic zone.

4. midnight, bathypelagic and abyssalpelagic zones

5. lighted, nonlighted

6. supralittoral

7. nekton.

8. float, plankton

9. Epifauna and epiflora, Infauna

CHAPTER 4–The Energy of Life

The Nature of Life   Page 4-6

1. organizes matter, uses energy to perform useful work, uses energy to create temporary order within itself. Note: Choice "D" isn't true because even non-life obeys the second law of thermodynamics.

2. to accomplish useful work—the processes of life.

3. true

4. true

How Matter and Energy Enter Living Systems   Page 4-12

1. true

2. the conversion of carbohydrate to usable energy.

3. organisms that create energy-rich compounds. Note: Choice "B" is incorrect because all organisms respire, not just primary producers.

4. false; Photosynthesis is the process of using light energy to produce carbohydrates.

5. true

6. false; Chemosynthesis is similar to photosynthesis because it produces carbohydrates from inorganic compounds. It differs because it does not use sunlight for energy.

The Ocean's Primary Productivity   Page 4-22

1. carbohydrates, grams of carbon per square meter of surface area per year

2. mass of living tissue; mass of living tissue at a given time

3. true

4. a wide variety of organisms that share a habitat and lifestyle.

5. phytoplankton.

6. a rigid cell wall made of silica.

7. one or two flagella.

8. a calcium carbonate shell.

9. true

10. picoplankton; the most common type of bacteria in the ocean; important in producing oxygen and taking up carbon dioxide.

11. physiological or biological necessities that affect survival.

12. coastal temperate regions and subpolar regions.

13. less

14. the oxygen produced by autotrophs equals the oxygen they need for cellular respiration.

continued on page A-4

Energy Flow Through the Biosphere — Page 4-27

1. a representation of how energy transfers from one level of organisms to another.
2. an organism that consumes primary producers.
3. an organism that consumes primary consumers.
4. 10%
5. organisms often eat across the theoretical levels of the trophic pyramid.
6. organic compounds are recycled into the inorganic compounds that primary producers use.

CHAPTER 5—A Survey of Life in the Sea – Introduction, Prokaryotes, Eukaryotes, Chromalveolates, Marine Plants, Rhizaria

The Linnaeus Classification System – Putting Life in Its Place — Page 5-15

1. it helps identify relationships between organisms.; it requires them to clearly identify key characteristics of each organism.; it avoids confusion.
2. genus and species.
3. kingdom, species, family, class, phylum
4. anatomical features; genetics.
5. false; A common problem is that some organisms don't fit cleanly into the different classifications. Taxonomists solve the problem by creating intermediate super and sub classifications.
6. Archaea, Bacteria, Eukarya
7. are the smallest forms of what could be considered marine life, are very abundant in the world's oceans, and have more biomass than that of marine mammals.

Prokaryotes – Small Yet Vital — Page 5-20

1. simpler
2. have similar cell structures
3. fix inorganic nitrogen into organic nitrogen
4. photosynthesis evolved in cyanobacteria.; cyanobacteria created most of the oxygen in the atmosphere.

Eukaryotes – Diversity of Body Forms — Page 5-22

1. animals, algae
2. false: plants have cell walls and chloroplasts and animal cells do not.

Chromalveolates – Dinoflagellates, Coccolithophores, Diatoms and Brown Algae — Page 5-30

1. being unicellular; using a flagella to move; being planktonic.
2. true
3. as plankton.
4. true
5. diatoms; brown algae.
6. 25%
7. kelp; it is the foundation of temperate coastal ecosystems
8. is multicellular, are unicellular; are mostly anchored to the bottom, are planktonic
9. thickening agents in the textile, dental, cosmetic, and food industries

Marine Plants – Red Algae, Green Algae, Seagrasses and Mangroves — Page 5-38

1. that assists chlorophyll a to capture light.
2. false; Red algae can live deeper because they have phycoerythrins, which are red pigments that allow them to photosynthesize much deeper than they otherwise would
3. they help to cement the reef together.
4. land plants may have evolved from green algae.
5. water salinity.
6. emergent, submergent
7. habitats
8. they're nurseries for adjacent marine ecosystems; they filter runoff water; they hold sediments in place.

Rhizaria – Foraminiferans and Radiolarians — Page 5-41

1. having planktonic species; being microscopic; having amoeboid form; building intricate mineral shells or skeletons.

CHAPTER 6—A Survey of Life in the Sea – Introduction to Marine Animals - Invertebrates

Sponges – Filters of the Sea — Page 6-6

1. collar cells and amoebocytes.
2. false; Sponges feed by drawing water in through it's pores and filtering out nutrient particles as the flow continues out through the oscula.
3. by breaking off buds – asexually; sexually by producing sperm that is released into the water.
4. they're free-swimming organisms.

Corals, Anemones, Sea Fans, and Jellyfish – Aquatic Stinging Nettles — Page 6-14

1. jellyfish; anemone; hard corals; sea fans
2. true
3. Anthozoa, corals and anemones
4. Scyphozoa, Cubozoa
5. false; Box jellyfish are stronger swimmers and more active hunters than jellyfish.
6. Hydrozoa

Comb Jellies – Gelatinous Carnivores — Page 6-16

1. using cilia for movement.
2. having oval or pear-shaped, nearly colorless bodies; being generally small – only a few millimeters to several centimeters long.
3. planktonic animals.

Simple Marine Worms – Flat, Ribbon-Like and Round — Page 6-19

1. a flattened shape with a single opening that is both mouth and anus.
2. a flattened shape with a one-way digestive system.
3. a round, structurally simple body, and a one-way digestive system.
4. Lineus longissimus.

Mollusks – A Bag, a Scraper and a Foot — Page 6-26

1. seal slugs, snails, squid
2. mantle, foot, radula

3. single-shelled mollusks, snails, and whelks.

4. false; During torsion, a gastropod's body twists into a permanent loop that brings the organs together.

5. all of the above

6. none of the above; Mollusks in the class Cephalopoda include squid, octopuses, cuttlefish and nautilus.

7. true

8. octopus

Complex Worms – Segments and a Simple Heart   Page 6-28

1. nephridia, a heart, and, in some cases, jaws; metamerism.

2. Polychaeta.

Crustaceans – Underwater Arthropods   Page 6-34

1. chitinous exoskeleton; jointed legs; segmented bodies

2. two pairs of antennae; teardrop-shaped larvae; molting their exoskeletons as they grow; a pair of appendages on each body segment.

3. their unique lifestyle of living "upside down" attached to something

4. they form a link between the smaller plankton and the larger animals.

5. none of the above

6. False; The crustaceans in order Decapoda are important to the fishing industry because they include the lobsters, shrimp, and crabs currently harvested for food.

7. they are important primary and secondary consumers that link plankton to large animals high on the food web.

Echinoderms – Stars of the Sea   Page 6-40

1. radially symmetrical bodies; bilaterally symmetrical larvae; five-segment bodies; tube feet.

2. their larvae are bilaterally symmetrical.

3. Crinoidea, upward-facing mouth, long feather-like arms

4. Asteroidea, five arms with equal share of organs, downward-facing mouth.

5. Ophiuroidea, long thin legs, single organ set in central disk

6. Echinoidea, no arms, ball or disk shape

7. Holothuroidea, elongated body, tentacles around the mouth

Invertebrate Chordates   Page 6-42

1. notochord, dorsal nerve cord

2. tunicates, salps

3. lancelets, vertebrates

CHAPTER 7–A Survey of Life in the Sea – Introduction to Marine Animals - Vertebrates

Subphylum Vertebrata   Page 7-4

1. false; Organisms in subphylum Vertebrata are those with dorsal nerve cords that develop into a spinal cord protected by vertebrae.

2. scientists think they may resemble the early ancestor of ray-finned fish and sharks.

3. jaws

Sharks and Rays – Teeth and Wings   Page 7-10

1. sharks, rays

2. cartilaginous skeletons; no swim bladder.

3. a light cartilage skeleton; backward-pointing denticles; ampullae of Lorenzini; lateral lines.

4. internally.

5. none of the above; The largest shark is the whale shark, which eats plankton.

6. all of the above

7. the same basic anatomy with adaptation to life on sandy bottoms.

Ray-Finned Fish – Half the World's Vertebrates   Page 7-16

1. bony skeletons, scales, swim bladders

2. externally

3. true

4. Clupeiformes, Gadiformes, herring and cod

Marine Reptiles – Cold Blood and Warm Water   Page 7-19

1. all of the above

2. true

3. sea snakes; saltwater crocodiles; seven species of marine turtle.

Seabirds – At Flight Over and In the Ocean   Page 7-22

1. feathers; forelimbs that are wings; laying internally fertilized eggs.

2. being predators; being prey; providing nitrogen compounds to the ocean.

3. webbed feet; the ability to "fly" under water; bill adaptations, such as the pelican's pouch; the ability to fly over wide expanses of water.

4. near the equator, only in the Southern Hemisphere

Marine Mammals – Warm Blood in Cold Water   Page 7-30

1. hair; nourishing their young with milk provided by mammary glands; being homeothermic; that almost all give birth to live young.

2. all of the above: the mammalian diving reflex; myglobin for storing oxygen; breathing air to meet oxygen demands.

3. Pinnipedia, lack ear flaps, have ear flaps

4. Cetacea

5. manatees; dugongs.

6. whaling; overfishing; tuna fishing; fur hunting.

CHAPTER 8–The Nature of Water

The Water Planet   Page 8-8

1. a molecule with a configuration that causes it to have a positively charged end and a negatively charged end

2. being a liquid at room temperature, surface tension, and that ice floats.

3. true

The Inorganic Chemistry of Water   Page 8-23

1. a mixture with a uniform appearance in which atom- or molecule-sized particles of one substance are evenly distributed throughout another

2. all the inorganic dissolved solids in seawater.

3. the characteristics caused by the dissolved solids in seawater.

4. It is the principle that, regardless of the salinity of seawater, the proportion of inorganic dissolved solids remains the same relative to each other.

5. chloride.

6. true

continued on page A-6

7. that the oceans are becoming no more or less salty .
8. higher
9. the amount of carbon dioxide tends to vary with depth.

The Organic Chemistry of Water   Page 8-30

1. false
2. the process of elements and compounds moving continuously to and from organisms and the Earth.
3. Carbon
4. it provides a versatile foundation for diverse chemicals.
5. for the formation of organic compounds such as proteins, chlorophyll, and nucleic acids.
6. it is an important component of DNA and other nucleic acids.
7. because it is used for shells and skeletons in some organisms.
8. constructing specialized proteins, such as hemoglobin and enzymes.

Chemical Factors That Affect Marine Life   Page 8-34

1. true
2. Passive, Active
3. Osmoregulators, osmoconformers

CHAPTER 9–
Water: A Physically Unique Molecule

The Physics of Water   Page 9-15

1. the total energy in the random motion of molecules and atoms, a measurement of average molecular motion speed
2. Celsius
3. a. the amount of heat required to raise the temperature of a substance by a given amount.
4. allows the oceans to heat areas that would otherwise be cooler, and cool areas that would otherwise be hotter.
5. less dense, different from 6. latent heat of fusion.
7. latent heat of vaporization.
8. thermal inertia, thermal equilibrium 9. more
10. denser, less dense
11. 2
12. temperatures

How Water Physics Affect Marine Life   Page 9-33

1. absorb and scatter, absorbs
2. aphotic
3. true
4. ectotherm
5. it allows the organism to live in habitats with wider temperature ranges.
6. about five times faster than
7. insignificant, equal to
8. decreases
9. it affects the efficiency of nutrients, gas, and wastes passing through the cell membrane.
10. minimizing the effect of their weight.
11. streamlining.
12. carry organisms to new habitats.

CHAPTER 10–Air-Sea interaction

The Solar Connection   Page 10-14

1. 78
2. troposphere, thermosphere
3. decreases.
4. Rain or snow
5. 50
6. the Earth would grow hotter and hotter.
7. the Earth is a sphere; the Earth is tilted on its axis; the Earth is in an elliptical orbit.
8. warm air rising and cool air flowing in to replace it.

The Coriolis Effect   Page 10-19

1. true
2. the rotation of the Earth.

The Winds   Page 10-25

1. circular flow pattern.
2. false; An atmospheric circulation cell is a distinct air mass with an individual airflow pattern.
3. 0° and 30° latitude, toward the equator
4. 30° and 60° latitude, toward the poles
5. geographic, ITCZ/meteorological
6. at about 30º latitude; where the vertical airflow is downward; where the Hadley and Ferrel cells meet.
7. higher
8. a local seasonal weather pattern that causes winters to be very dry.
9. none of the above; The sentence cannot be answered with any term(s).
10. wind is drawn into a low-pressure area at the Earth's surface, forming a spiral pattern.
11. true

CHAPTER 11–Highways in the Sea

Surface Currents   Page 11-25

1. wind.
2. true
3. five, each major ocean basin
4. of the elevated surface level in the center and the Coriolis effect.
5. geostrophic, clockwise in the Northern Hemisphere and counterclockwise in the Southern Hemisphere.
6. true
7. false; The overall effect is to move the water 90° to the right or left, depending on the hemisphere.
8. current that runs in the opposite direction of an adjacent current, current that runs in the opposite direction and beneath a surface current
9. beneath, unclear
10. true
11. more extreme.
12. accumulates in the Eastern Pacific, dramatic weather changes

Deep Currents   Page 11-32

1. the mixing of water masses of different water densities.
2. central water, intermediate water, and deep water.

3. high latitudes, where freezing and cooling cause an increase in salinity and density.
4. true
5. it redistributes heat and moderates the Earth's climate.

Studying Ocean Currents
Page 11-37

1. Lagrangian, Eulerian
2. drogues; Argo float; flow meters; Doppler Acoustic Current Meters; satellites; radioactive chemicals; rubber ducks.

CHAPTER 12–Waves and Tides

The Nature of Waves
Page 12-11

1. false; A wave is energy transmission through matter. The matter moves as the wave passes, but returns to its place of origin.
2. Orbital, Longitudinal
3. Wavelength
4. wavelength divided by period
5. wind; gravity; seismic activity
6. gravity, Coriolis effect
7. greater than half the wavelength, less than one-twentieth of the wavelength
8. wind speed, wind duration, fetch
9. constructive or destructive interference
10. true.

When Waves Hit the Shore
Page 12-19

1. all of the above
2. The H:L ratio exceeds 1:7; the water depth is 1.3 times the height; the top of the wave is traveling more quickly than the bottom; contact with the bottom decreases the wavelength and increases the height.
3. refraction, reflection
4. a vertical wave that doesn't travel, but has a trough and crest that alternate
5. heavy winds; cyclonic storms
6. earthquakes; heavy winds
7. earthquakes; landslides,
8. they have such long wavelengths that no water is deep enough for them to be deep waves,
9. tsunami periods are so long that ships rise and fall very slowly when a tsunami passes under them.

Tides
Page 12-27

1. primarily the moon's gravity, with some effect from the sun.
2. false; Newton's theory assumed that Earth was perfectly spherical and primarily the moon's gravity influenced the tides. Laplace's dynamic theory accounts for other influences and better explains tidal variations.
3. the season, the Coriolis effect; ocean basin shape; that the Earth is not perfectly spherical.
4. points with no net water motion around which tides occur.
5. diurnal, mixed
6. false; Tidal currents are incoming and outgoing currents created by the tides. A tidal bore is a wave created by an incoming tide moving through a narrow area.
7. spring, neap

CHAPTER 13–A Revolution in Science: The Theory of Plate Tectonics

The Earth Inside and Out
Page 13-9

1. the inner core, the outer core, the mantle, and the crust.
2. the uppermost solid portion of the mantle and the crust.
3. sedimentary.
4. true
5. false; Isostatic equilibrium is the balance between the weight of the crust and the buoyancy provided by the mantle.
6. rising or falling along a fault.

The Theory of Continental Drift
Page 13-13

1. all of the continents were once one continent that broke up and drifted apart over hundreds of millions of years.
2. single continent hundreds of millions of years ago, single sea that surrounded it
3. that the shapes of the continents fit together, the discovery of coal in Antarctica, the distribution of fossils.
4. what forces could move continents

The Theory of Seafloor Spreading
Page 13-20

1. giving scientists a way to map the bottom terrain.
2. mid-ocean ridge, rift valley
3. emerges from the rift valley, magma pushing up from the asthenosphere
4. the pattern of sediment layers; radiometric dating of seafloor and mid-continent rocks; the magnetic patterns found on the seafloor.

The Unifying Theory: Plate Tectonics
Page 13-29

1. false; It unites the theory of seafloor spreading and the theory of continental drift.
2. several rigid plates that float on the asthenosphere.
3. mark the boundaries between tectonic plates.
4. plates spread apart from each other.
5. plates collide with each other.
6. plates slide past each other.
7. is a local rising column of magma that does not move with the plate above it.
8. convection.
9. a new ocean will form in the East Africa rift valley.

CHAPTER 14–Sediments in the Sea

The Study of Sediments
Page 14-8

1. clamshell sampler; piston corer; drilling ships.
2. true

Types of Sediment
Page 14-15

1. biogenous
2. Lithogenous sediments, are the most abundant by volume
3. the diameter of an individual particle.
4. true

continued on page A-8

ARE YOU LEARNING? ANSWER KEY

Continental-Shelf Sediments   Page 14-19

1. tides, waves, and currents.
2. relict sediments.
3. faster than

Deep-Ocean Sediments   Page 14-25

1. more
2. at or below the carbonate compensation depth, calcareous material dissolves as quickly as it accumulates.
3. the dense fecal pellets of larger planktonic organisms carry material to the bottom relatively quickly.
4. true

Sediments as Economic Resources   Page 14-29

1. the cost of mining the sediment is less than the economic value of the sediment
2. to make mild abrasives.
3. such as calcium carbonate, calcium sulfate, gypsum, and sodium chloride (table salt) forms when the process of water evaporation of occurs in landlocked and isolated seas.

CHAPTER 15–The Dynamic Coast

Coastal Classification   Page 15-11

1. active, passive
2. primary, secondary
3. land-based erosion. volcanic activity. tectonic activity.
4. fjord coasts. drowned river valleys.
5. deltas.
6. volcanic islands.
7. fault coasts.
8. marine life.
9. as wave energy focuses on areas that protrude.
10. as a result of the accumulation of ocean sediments in one place.
11. none of the above; Scientists think that marine organisms build coasts by providing a structure that reduces the effects of waves and current.

Coastal Dynamics   Page 15-20

1. because of the effect of a longshore current; primarily with the prevailing winds.
2. the digestive wastes of organisms, such as parrotfish; wave erosion of the shoreline; sources that are inland and carried to the ocean by streams and rivers.
3. foreshore
4. sediment grain size; wave energy; beach slope.
5. a local region with no net sand gain or loss.
6. true
7. false; A tombolo forms when longshore current slows around two islands or an island and the mainland. This allows sand to settle into two spits that grow together.
8. the sea erodes the coast of a barrier island; rising sea level gradually moves a barrier island shoreward; storms move a barrier island shoreward.
9. an ocean beach; a barrier flat; a lagoon.
10. river-dominated

Biological Processes and Human Activity   Page 15-26

1. its external skeleton.
2. barrier reef
3. have low energy.
4. absorbing wave energy; holding sediment in place.
5. to create new coastal structures. to protect existing coastal structures.
6. jetty, breakwater
7. all of the above
8. transporting in sand from a different location to replenish eroded sand.
9. none of the above; The likely solution to problems created by human structures is a change in coastal attitudes and management.

CHAPTER 16–Marine Ecosystems

Ecology and Ecosystems   Page 16-9

1. the study of how organisms relate to each other and their environment.
2. ecosystem
3. community.
4. population
5. habitat.
6. microhabitat
7. niche.
8. determining how much energy is available for high trophic levels.
9. carbon
10. nitrogen
11. those regions have more abundant nutrients.

Ecosystems in the Open Sea   Page 16-14

1. true
2. having significantly more nutrients; substantially higher populations of cyanophytes, diatoms and dinoflagellates.
3. Photoinhibition, Pollution
4. true
5. false The world's largest floating ecosystem is the Sargasso Sea.
6. it is the ocean's most productive region.
7. they bring nutrients up from the seafloor.

Coastal Ecosystems – Estuaries, Salt Marshes, Mangrove Swamps, Seagrasses   Page 16-22

1. they benefit from nutrient-rich runoff from land., benthic organisms can live in the upper photic zone., plants provide shelter.
2. people have settled near coasts., agricultural fertilizer can cause eutrophication of coastal ecosystems., effects of the activities may not always be obvious.
3. pollution that results from excess nutrients in the ocean.
4. the need to survive osmotic stress., the depletion of the oxygen in the sediments.
5. 75
6. providing a nursery for juveniles of many species., providing a steady stream of nutrients.
7. lower, upper
8. reverse osmosis., pneumatophores., sacrificial leaves., salt glands.
9. a strong, tangled root system; the ability to hold soil well.

A–7   Are You Learning Answer Key   Life on an Ocean Planet

10. live entirely under water; can live in deeper water; release pollen under water.

11. they do not require a freshwater source; they can exist in deeper water; the seagrasses provide food for ecosystem inhabitants.

Coastal Ecosystems – Intertidal Zones, Beaches, Kelp and Seaweed, Coral Reefs   Page 16-29

1. drying out and thermal stress.

2. drying out., thermal stress., water motion.

3. reducing sedimentation caused by coastal erosion., breaking down organic and inorganic materials., acting as a filter that processes compounds entering the sea.

4. sea otters eat sea urchins, which eat kelp.

5. coral reef

6. water motion keeps sediments from accumulating on the coral., the presence of nutrients allows competitive algae to grow.

7. true

8. global climate change, sedimentation, coral disease, competitive algae.

Polar Ecosystems   Page 16-32

1. reduced sunlight., near-freezing water.

2. along the North Pacific and North Atlantic from April to August.

3. rich, deep water surfaces to create the largest nutrient-rich area on Earth.

4. Antarctic Convergence, 50° to 60° south latitude

Deep-Sea Ecosystems   Page 16-37

1. there is no sunlight.

2. marine snow.

3. echinoderms., meiofauna.

4. place where a dead whale rests on the deep ocean floor.

5. small organisms feed on remaining soft tissue.

6. hydrothermal vents., cold seeps.

7. false; They know little about hadal zone ecosystems primarily because of the difficulties and expense of making submersibles or instruments that can go that deep.

CHAPTER 17–Marine Resources

Resource Classification   Page 17-4

1. biological, physical

2. renewable, nonrenewable

3. species are taken faster than they can reproduce and maintain their population.

Nonrenewable Resources   Page 17-14

1. under high pressure and temperature over long periods; from the remains of marine organisms.

2. nonporous rock traps oil and gas allowing a reserve to form.

3. drilling from oil rigs; using special equipment to reduce the risk of oil spills or gas leaks.

4. ice crystals containing methane found on the continental slope.

5. they're difficult to get and dangerous to handle with current technology.

6. copper; cobalt.

7. none of the above; Despite their potential value, ferromanganese nodules aren't exploited as mineral resources currently primarily because the cost of recovery exceeds the worth of the minerals.

8. seawater.

9. construction materials; water softeners; fertilizer; medicine.

10. true

11. offshore phosphorite deposits are too costly to recover.

12. cobalt; copper; sulfur; zinc.

13. sand and gravel

Renewable Resources   Page 17-21

1. using the energy in waves; using the energy in tides; using the energy in the upper layers of seawater.

2. using the energy in tides.

3. the supply of fresh water isn't keeping pace with the rising demand.

4. A and B but not C

5. do not require taking anything from the sea.

6. the cargo container

7. focuses on visiting and experiencing wildlife and natural environments.

8. true

Submerged Cultural Resources   Page 17-23

1. an underwater city; a shipwreck; an underwater area that is littered with ancient artifacts discarded by a civilization; an underwater burial site.

2. true

Biological Resources – Marine Mammals   Page 17-28

1. the modern whale harpoon didn't exist.

2. fell from 4.4 million to about 1 million.

3. have improved for some species, but declined for others.

4. IWC members don't have to abide by its rulings; there is an IWC exemption for research; there is an IWC exemption for aboriginal cultures.

5. true

6. Sea lions, seals

Biological Resources – Algae, Aquaculture, and Medicine   Page 17-32

1. algin.

2. steeply upward.

3. more than 30

4. the feeding of some organisms contributes to overfishing; farmed animals can promote the spread of disease; farmed animals release concentrated nitrates and other waste.

5. looking for pharmacological or other chemical benefits in organisms.

6. false; Bioprospecting relates to the development of the potential for finding new drugs within marine organisms.

Biological Resources – Fish   Page 17-38

1. 18

2. in continental shelf and offshore regions with upwelling, these are high bioproductivity regions

3. the clupeiforms.

4. catching fish for purposes other than direct human consumption.

5. about a quarter

6. a steady increase until 1989, and has been about level since.

7. worldwide catch statistics were distorted by major fluctuations of certain fish populations and inaccurate reporting.

continued on page A-10

The State of the World's Fisheries – A Bleak Picture
Page 17-44

1. Maximum sustainable yield, overfishing
2. 25%
3. using new technologies and methods to catch fish more efficiently; turning to new, unexploited fisheries.
4. it can deplete species higher on the food web than consume them; it can allow other organisms to proliferate.
5. declines in species that feed on the fish; bycatch
6. true

Commercial Fishing
Page 17-48

1. longline fishing.; purse seine nets.; gill nets.
2. government subsidies make up the difference.

Who Owns the Sea?
Page 17-52

1. free access to the sea by all nations.
2. 5 kilometers (3 miles).
3. extending claims to resources without claiming territory.
4. all of the above
5. true
6. False. According to UNCLOS, international waters are waters beyond the EEZs that belong to no one.
7. all ocean territory within 200 nautical miles of its coasts.

Biodiversity and the Future
Page 17-53

1. every organisms is part of maintaining a healthy ecosystem.

CHAPTER 18–Pollution and the Health of the Ocean

Global Habitat Destruction
Page 18-11

1. carbon dioxide; methane; water vapor.
2. polar ice sheets are melting; sea level is rising; tree rings show evidence that temperature is rising.
3. 30 to 50
4. the flooding of coastal areas and island nations; the loss of remaining coastal wetlands; a decrease in the production of North Atlantic deep-water currents.
5. false; The goal was to reduce carbon dioxide emissions to 6% to 8% below 1990 levels by 2012.
6. develop cost-effective alternatives to fossil fuel.
7. protects us from ultraviolet radiation.
8. damages DNA and protein.
9. can cooperate to solve global issues that threaten everyone.
10. loading and discharging ballast water.
11. disrupting the local ecosystem; out competing and replacing native species, reducing biodiversity.
12. the spread of non-native species is so rapid; countermeasures have been relatively ineffective in stopping accidental introductions of species to new environments; some species are being found worldwide.
13. true

Sensitive Marine Habitat Destruction
Page 18-15

1. people to live near the coast.
2. can be used for either real estate or harbor; they are sensitive environments.

3. 50
4. coral bleaching.
5. using dynamite to stun fish; using toxic substances to stun fish.
6. 25

Pollutants and Their Effects
Page 18-18

1. products of human activities that have harmful or objectionable effects to the water quality or affect the physical, chemical, or biological environment.
2. propellants, hydrocarbons, and biocides in the atmosphere; agricultural and industrial runoff; maritime accidents or ships dumping bilge water, ballast, and garbage.
3. agricultural and industrial runoff.

Toxic Pollutants
Page 18-30

1. lead; mercury; cadmium; copper.
2. interfering with cellular metabolism; accumulating in the tissues.
3. brain damage; behavioral disorders; birth defects.
4. bacteria and other processes don't break them down.
5. through biomagnification at each trophic level.
6. runoff from land.
7. all of the above
8. true
9. false. It is sometimes better to leave an oil slick alone because clean-up processes can be more damaging than the oil.
10. intentional dumping.
11. so much was dumped prior to the bans; evidence suggests that radioactive waste barrels are leaking; after the bans, some nuclear powered vessels continued to dump nuclear waste.
12. has had no noted widespread effects on marine life.
13. leakage of chemical weapons.

Nutrient Pollutants
Page 18-34

1. Nutrients and fertilizers
2. causing HABs.
3. removes solids and pathogens.
4. eutrophication.
5. true

Energy Pollutants
Page 18-36

1. by raising the temperature above the tolerance of organisms.
2. power plant cooling; industrial discharges.

Refuse Pollutants
Page 18-39

1. by being dumped or lost there.
2. animals mistake it for food; it traps and entangles animals.
3. all of the above

Efforts and Solutions
Page 18-43

1. $1,000
2. providing economic incentives for states to preserve coastal resources.
3. designate coastal zones for research, protection, and recreation.
4. restrictions on dumping nonbiodegradable plastics at sea.
5. the Marine Pollution Convention and the International Convention for the Prevention of Pollution.
6. true
7. Antarctica is a natural reserve.

CHAPTER 19—Management, Research, and the Future of an Ocean Planet

The Tragedy of the Commons   Page 19-6

1. free access to a finite resource and misplaced incentives and responsibilities

2. must change.

3. addressing global and cross-boundary effects of pollution; shifting subsidies and incentives to favor sustainable management strategies; addressing biological resources in international waters.

Managing Ocean Resources   Page 19-10

1. we should not hesitate to take action to avoid potentially serious or irreversible harm to the environment, even when we don't have all the information.

2. false; One approach is to manage ocean resources so they are renewable.

3. the decline of fisheries; the recovery of the gray whale.

4. true

5. a place-based system that looks at whole ecosystems.

6. addresses the complexity of natural and social processes and systems; integrates ecological, social, and economic goals; recognizes that human and ecological systems are interdependent.

Research and Opportunities   Page 19-19

1. we know almost nothing compare to what we need and want to know; we have the technology to study all ocean realms.

2. explorers in the sea routinely go where no one has gone before.

3. acidified environments may affect coral reefs; acidic water upwellings may pose a threat to marine organisms on the continental shelf.

4. the organisms that produce them have a role in global climate changes.

5. it provides a baseline of conditions in the past for comparison.

6. they are trying to grasp the scope of bidiversity; they want to understand biodiversity trends; it helps them encourage conservation.

7. they often rely on chemical defenses and have strong immune systems.

8. providing analogous environments to study; examining types of chemosynthetic life; studying how to research an isolated environment; providing analogous challenges when living in an underwater habitat.

You and the Future of an Ocean Planet   Page 19-24

1. your future depends on the health of the oceans.

2. staying informed; being an ocean advocate; acting to protect the ocean.

3. get involved as a volunteer in marine sciences; follow your heart to discover your particular interest; read everything you can in your area of interest.

4. keep your grades up; go beyond your required coursework; volunteer for marine science programs; learn to snorkel or scuba dive.

5. merchant ship crew or officer; scuba, snorkeling, sail boarding, or surfing instructor; ship builder, marine engineer, or architect; ROV operator or research submarine pilot.

Glossary

A

abiogenesis the formation of life from nonliving matter, also called spontaneous generation

abiotic nonliving

absolute pressure the total pressure, so that the zero point is a vacuum

abyssal zone a division of the benthic zone, the ocean bottom in deep water

abyssalpelagic zone a division of the oceanic zone consisting of the deepest water found in oceanic trenches; between 4,000 and 6,000 meters (13,123 and 19,685 feet)

accretion the process in which small particles clump together due to gravity to form a solid body, such as a planet

Actinopterygii the class of all ray-finned fish; jawed fish with skeletons made of bone; most have a swim bladder and scales

active coast a coast where plates collide, resulting in volcanic activity and earthquakes

active transport the process of a cell moving materials from low concentration to high concentration

adhesion the tendency of water molecules to stick to other substances due to water's polar nature

aerobic respiration respiration that uses oxygen in the release of energy

aerosols suspensions of fine liquid and/or solid droplets in the air

agnathan a group of Vertebrata, characterized by marine animals similar to fish, but lacking both jaws and paired fins; includes two classes Petromyzontida, the lampreys, and Myxini, the hagfish.

albedo a measure of reflectivity; the higher the albedo, the higher the reflectivity

algae a loose, non-scientific term for aquatic organisms that can produce carbohydrates by photosynthesis; taxonomists usually define eukaryote algae as those organisms that belong in one of several specific groups, notably Dinoflagellata, Heterokontophyta (diatoms, brown algae), Rhodophyta, and Chlorophyta

algin complex molecule substance derived from algae used in food processing and other applications as a thickening agent

amino acids the component molecules used by living systems to build proteins

amoebocytes mobile cells in sponges that pick up and distribute nutrients from water drawn into a sponge

amphidromic points location with no net water motion, about which the tides move away in a pinwheel type pattern

ampullae of Lorenzini organ in sharks and rays that detects weak electrical currents; see electroreception

anadromous describes fish such as salmon and shad that return from the sea to the rivers where they were born in order to breed

anaerobic respiration respiration that does not use oxygen in the release of energy

angiosperm flowering plants; one of the major groups of seed plants including marine seagrasses

anoxic having no oxygen

Antarctic Convergence Zone an area located at approximately 50° to 60° south latitude where the nutrient rich Antarctic water sinks under the warmer water of the more northern ocean

Antarctic Divergence an area located at approximately 65° to 70° south latitude where nutrient rich deep water reaches the surface

anthropomorphism subconsciously or consciously assigning human traits to inanimate objects or animals

antinodes in a standing wave, the points where there is maximum vertical change in the water level

aphotic zone the ocean zone of perpetual darkness below the photic zone beginning at approximately 1,000 meters/3,280 feet

aphotic zone the ocean zone of perpetual darkness below the photic zone beginning at approximately 1,000 meters/3,280 feet

aquaculture using farm techniques to grow and harvest aquatic organisms

aqualung brand name for the first practical scuba introduced by Jacques Cousteau

Archaea domain of prokaryotes consisting of primitive organisms noted for being extremophiles

archaebacteria one of the three domains of living organisms, recognized as the oldest living organisms on earth; are prokaryotes and unicellular

Argo float a global array of 3,000 free-drifting profiling floats that measures the temperature and salinity of the upper 2000 m of the ocean.

asexual reproduction in which there is no fusion of male and female sex cells (gametes); as in sponge budding

asthenosphere theorized upper layer of the mantle characterized by hot solid material that flows slowly over time, much like old glass

astrology the study of the supposed influence of the stars and planets on human affairs

astronomy the scientific study of the universe, especially of the motions, positions, sizes, composition, and behavior of celestial objects

atmospheric circulation cells six distinct air masses (three in each hemisphere) with individual air flow patterns

atmospheric pressure measurement equal to the air pressure at sea level, roughly equal to one bar

atolls ring-shaped coral reefs that encircle shallow lagoons

autotrophs organisms that can create organic chemical energy compounds from inorganic compounds and an external energy source

autotrophy the process of self-feeding by producing energy-rich organic compounds (carbohydrates)

Aves a class in the phylum Chordata, animals characterized by having feathers, forelimbs that are wings, a four-chambered heart and laying internally fertilized eggs

axial inclination the angle of tilt measured with 0° at perpendicular between a planet's rotation axis and the plane of its orbit around the sun

B

back reef the inner, land side of a coral reef with less biological activity

backshore the region of a beach rarely touched by seawater, including dunes or grasses all the way to "non-beach" ground

bacteria unicellular microorganisms found in the Domain Bacteria

bar pressure measurement equal to the air pressure at sea level, roughly equal to one atmosphere

barrier flat a broad, relatively level area behind the dunes of a barrier island, with vegetation ranging from grasses to woodlands

barrier islands form when material accumulates parallel to shore, forming a barrier between the ocean and the existing coast

barrier reefs coral reefs that grow some distance from shore and create a barrier between the open ocean and the main coast

bathyal zone a division of the benthic zone, the ocean bottom along the continental slope to the open ocean bottom

bathypelagic zone a division of the oceanic zone consisting of deep water in open ocean; between 1,000 and 4,000 meters (3,280 and 13,123 feet)

bathyscaphe extremely deep diving vessels that operate much like a blimp airship, descending and rising without connection to the surface and with limited ability for horizontal movement; Trieste is an example

bathysphere extremely deep diving underwater vessel, connected to a support ship by a cable, only capable of vertical movement

bay mouth barrier a sand barrier created by a spit accumulating so much sediment that it blocks the mouth of the bay

beach an accumulation of loose sediment near the edge of a large water body

beach renourishment transporting in sand or sediment from a different location to replenish eroded sand

benthic zone the bottom portion of the ocean; pertaining to areas of water (and organisms) at the bottom of a water body, like the bottom of the ocean

benthos marine organisms that live on or in the sea bottom

Big Bang the theorized moment in which the universe began to expand from a single concentrated point

bilateral symmetry symmetry along a vertical axis, as seen in mammals, fish, reptiles and most of the more complex organisms

binomial Latin name from Latin *bis* meaning twice and *nomen* meaning name; a species' scientific name consisting of genus and species, e.g., Carcharhinus leucas (common name: bull shark)

bioaccumulation the concentration of heavy metals, synthetic chemicals, and natural organic chemicals that gradually accumulates in an organism's body throughout its lifetime

biocides chemicals that kill, such as pesticides

biodegradable capable of being broken down into harmless substances by microbes

biodiversity the concept that the health of the Earth and its ecosystems relies on the broad genetic diversity found within many organisms

bioerosion erosion caused by species eating coral polyps and excreting sand as digestive waste; the parrotfish is one species that performs this process

biogenous sediment sediment that originates from life, consisting of primarily shells and hard skeleton

biogeochemical cycle the process of elements and compounds moving continuously to and from organisms and the earth

biological oceanography (marine biology) the study of the life in the ocean and the ocean's role as a habitat for that life

biological resources resources that involve bioproductivity, such as fisheries and kelp harvesting

bioluminescence the ability of an organism to emit light

biomagnification the process by which contamination becomes greater with each trophic level

biomass the mass of living tissue; tissue and other organic material created by living systems

bioprospecting the search for organisms with pharmacological or other chemical benefits

biosphere the outer part of the Earth—land, water and atmosphere—where all organisms live; the habitable space on Earth

biosynthesis a synonym for abiogenesis; also means the use of biological processes in the manufacture of products

Glossary

biotic living

blades in brown algae, structures equivalent to leaves on plants

blubber thick fat layer found in members of order Cetacea that provides insulation and reserve energy

boulder the largest grain size on the Wentworth Scale

brackish water water with a salinity of 0.6 to 30‰

breakwaters structures built parallel to shore or attached to the shore and curving into the sea; their purpose is to create artificial, calm water lagoons

brine water saturated or nearly saturated with dissolved salts

brown algae members of the phylum Heterokontophyta, multicellular algae characterized by having holdfasts, blades, stipes and pneumatocysts

buffer a substance that lessens the tendency for a solution to become too acid or too alkaline

buoyancy the upward force on an object immersed in a gas or liquid that is equal to weight of the displace gas or liquid

bycatch marine life caught in a net or trap that is not the organism intended for capture

C

caisson disease name for decompression sickness, name originated when the condition developed in workers emerging from pressurized caissons used for building bridge foundations

calcareous calcium carbonate containing

calcareous ooze ooze composed primarily of planktonic organisms that have calcium carbonate skeletons or shells

calorie the amount of heat needed to raise one gram of water one degree Celsius

capillary waves waves with wavelengths of 1.73 centimeters (.68 inches) or smaller, with surface tension being the primary restoring force that acts on them

carapace a shell or hard surface on all or part of an animal used for protection

carbohydrate an organic compound derived from carbon, hydrogen, and oxygen that is an important source of food and energy for organisms; the primary units of usable energy in living systems and a source of carbon used in an organism's tissues

Carbonate Compensation Depth (CCD) the depth at which calcium carbonate dissolves as fast as it accumulates, generally considered to be about 4,500 meters (14,760 feet)

cartographer person who practices cartography map making

cell the smallest whole structure that can be defined as a living system

cellular respiration the process of releasing energy from carbohydrates to perform the functions of life

cellulose a complex carbohydrate that gives plants their hardness and structure

cerata organ on nudibranch back that functions as a gill and as a defensive weapon with nematocysts from consumed prey

chemical equilibrium the state in which processes add and remove solutes from a solution at the same rate

chemical oceanography the study of seawater chemistry

chemosynthesis the process of using chemicals to create energy-rich organic compounds, such as carbohydrates

chitin the hard carbohydrate material that makes up arthropod exoskeleton

chlorinated hydrocarbon a compound consisting of hydrogen and carbon, in which chlorine replaces one or more of the hydrogen atoms; examples are DDT and PCBs

chlorofluorocarbon (CFC) a hydrocarbon gas that includes fluorine and chlorine in the hydrocarbon molecule; used in the manufacture of aerosol sprays, packing materials, solvents and refrigerants; known to destroy ozone in the atmosphere

chlorophyll compound that allows an organism to use sunlight energy to convert inorganic material into energy-rich organic compounds (carbohydrates)

chlorophyll a and b chlorophyll a is a pigment directly involved with photosynthesis; chlorophyll b assists chlorophyll a in capturing light for use in photosynthesis; each absorb different colors of light, meaning that organisms with both chlorophyll a and b use light more efficiently than organisms with either pigment alone.

chloroplasts organelles (structures) within cells used in photosynthesis

Chondrichthyes a class in the subphylum Vertebrata, fish characterized by lacking true bone and having a skeleton made of cartilage and having five to seven gill slits on each side of the body; includes sharks, skates and rays

chromatophores pigment sacs found in some organisms that allow them to change their skin color and pattern

chronometer sea going clock or watch used to determine longitude – time piece introduced in 1735 that would run accurately even in rough seas

cilia short, hair-like structures similar to flagella that protrude from a cell for propulsion or to move liquid past the cell

circumnavigation the act of going completely around something

cirri short, hook-like legs on some echinoderm and arthropod species

clamshell sampler ocean sediment sampler with a set of jaws, designed to scoop up bottom sediment for research purposes; also called a grab sampler

claspers male copulatory organs found on sharks and rays

class a major category in the taxonomic classification of related organisms, comprising a group of orders

clay the smallest grain size on the Wentworth Scale

cnidocytes in Cnidarians, specialized stinging cells made up of nematocysts

coastal cell a local region of material transport mechanisms that, when combined, form an area with no net sand gain or loss

coccolithophores single-celled autotrophs characterized by shells of calcium carbonate

coccoliths calcium carbonate scales that surround coccolithophores for protection

coevolution when two organisms evolve together because they have a relationship

cohesion the tendency of water molecules to stick together due to hydrogen bonding

cold-core eddies circular loops of water that break away from currents, flow counterclockwise in the Northern Hemisphere, and have cool water centers

collar cells cells with flagella that direct water though a sponge's epithelium

colligative properties the properties of a liquid that may be altered by the presence of a solute

colloid a homogeneous mixture such as fog or smoke consisting of very small particles that are larger than atoms and molecules

combination coast a coast formed by both non-marine forces and marine forces (both primary and secondary coastal development)

commercial extinction the reduction of a species to a population too low to exploit commercially

community a collection of different populations of organisms living and interacting in an ecosystem

compensation depth the depth at which the production of carbohydrates by photosynthesizing autotrophs equals the carbohydrates the autotrophs need for cellular respiration; at this depth, no energy is available to pass to higher trophic levels

concept map a representation of a topic made by arranging key ideas or concepts to show their relationships

conservative constituents dissolved inorganic salts in seawater that do not change proportion over time

conservative materials chemicals and heavy metals that biomagnify, so named because they are conserved rather than consumed as they move through the food web

continental crust the crust under the continents

continental drift, theory of the theory that the continents were once a single land mass that drifted apart and are still moving

continental shelf the extended, underwater perimeter of a continent; an area that can stretch for many kilometers out to sea in some areas

contour currents bottom currents that flow around obstacles and that are influenced by bottom topography

convection a vertical circulation pattern in a gas or liquid caused by hot material rising and cold material sinking

convergent boundary in the theory of plate tectonics, the boundary between two tectonic plates that are coming together; also called a colliding boundary

convergent evolution the process where two unrelated structures in unrelated organisms evolve to perform similar functions

coral bleaching the white appearance of coral that has rejected its zooxanthellae dinoflagellates (symbiotic algae - Symbiodinium) due to stress

Coriolis effect the tendency for the path of an object moving in the North Hemisphere to deflect to the right, or to deflect left when moving in the Southern Hemisphere

cosmogenous sediments sediment that originates from outer space

countercurrent current that runs in the opposite direction of an adjacent current

countershading natural coloration of organism that conceals them against the bottom when viewed from above and against the surface when viewed from below

covalent bond a bond formed by atoms sharing electrons

crest the highest wave point above the average water level

CTD conductivity, temperature, and depth sensor; a device often attached to a watersampling device

cyanobacteria a picoplankton bacteria belonging to a large group that have a photosynthetic pigment to carry out photosynthesis

cybertaxonomy a mixture of the science of taxonomy, internet technology, computer engineering an global partnership on the identification and cataloging of new and existing species

cyclone large rotating storm system of low pressure air with converging winds at the center

 D

decomposers primarily bacteria and fungi that break down organic material into inorganic form

decompression the release of pressure; in diving, the term refers to the process of the body releasing gas absorbed during the dive when surfacing

decompression sickness the conditions caused by inert nitrogen or other gas coming out of solution and forming bubbles with in the body

decompression stops stops that divers make to release nitrogen or other gas accumulated at depth so they may safely surface

Glossary

deductive reasoning concluding what facts will be observed as the result of a known process

deep circulation movement of water created by the mixing of water masses of different densities

deep sea floor collective term that refers to the bathyal, abyssal and the hadal zones

deepwater waves waves in water that is deeper than half their wavelength

denitrification the release of free nitrogen into the atmosphere from the breakdown of nitrogen compounds

density stratification in the nebular theory, the process by which matter became layered according to density during the Earth's formation, with heavier matter near the core and lighter material closer to the crust

denticles shark and ray scales, named for their characteristics that are much like shark teeth

deposit feeders organisms that feed off detritus drifting down from above

dermal branchiae in some echinoderms, structures on the exoskeleton that absorb oxygen much like gills

desalinization the removal of dissolved salts from seawater

detrital mats layers of partially decomposed organic matter that provide habitats for communities of invertebrates, water birds, juvenile fish, and other organisms

detritus partially decomposed organic matter that makes up a portion of sediments in an aquatic environment; loose material from the break up of organic and inorganic material

diatom microscopic, one-celled photosynthetic plankton characterized by a rigid cell wall made of silica

diatomaceous earth soil composed of diatom remains; thought to have been created by the uplifting of siliceous sediments

diffraction, wave the tendency of energy to shift within a wave upon reaching an obstacle, allowing a new wave pattern to form

dinoflagellates phytoplankton characterized by flagella that allow them to orient themselves or swim

dissociation the separation of a molecule into atoms and/or smaller molecules while in solution

dissolved salts the sodium chloride and other dissolved inorganic solids in seawater

disturbing forces energy sources that cause waves to form

diurnal tide the tidal pattern of a single high and low tide daily

divergent boundary in the theory of plate tectonics, the boundary between two tectonic plates that are spreading apart; also called a spreading boundary

divergent evolution when two or more related species develop adaptations that make them increasingly different due to differences in their environments

division in botany and microbiology, may be used in place of phylum; a major category in the taxonomic classification of plants, comprising a group of classes

DNA deoxyribonucleic acid contains the genetic instructions used in the development and functioning of all known living organisms and some viruses

doldrums a region near the equator where the Trade Winds cease for extended periods

Doppler shift the change in a wave frequency caused by a change in speed or direction

dorsal nerve chord a tube of nervous tissue just above the notochord

downwelling a downward vertical current that pushes surface water toward the bottom

drag resistance to movement caused by friction from contact with a fluid (or any gas or fluid)

drowned river valley a coast formed by a rising sea level flooding an area eroded by a river during a period of low sea level

dynamic theory (of tides) tide theory that accounts for various influences in explaining why there are multiple tidal bulges

dysphotic zone the dimly lit, deeper and less biologically productive portion of the photic zone

E

Earth and space science the study of the physical earth, the solar system, the universe and their interrelationships

echolocation natural click transmissions from some marine mammals who listen to the echoes to determine an object's distance, size, density, and shape

ecology the science that studies how organisms relate to each other and their environment

ecosystem a distinct entity usually with clearly defined physical boundaries, distinct abiotic conditions, at least one energy source, and a community of interacting organism through which energy is transferred

ecosystem services resources and processes needed by humans, such as food or protection from storms, that are provided by natural systems

ecosystem-based management A type of management that considers whole ecosystem in a given place including humans and their interactions with the environment.

ecotourism tourism that focuses on visiting and experiencing wildlife and natural environments

ectotherm an organism with an internal temperature that is close to and varies with the external temperature

eddies large circular loops that break away from currents; caused by friction from the flow of a current

Ekman spiral the spiral of water layers flowing to the right of the layer above in the Northern Hemisphere and to the left of the layer above in the Southern Hemisphere due to Ekman transport

Ekman transport the net motion of the water column down to friction depth, which is 90° to the right in the Northern Hemisphere or 90° to the left in the Southern Hemisphere

electrolyte a solution that can conduct an electrical current

electroreception the ability to sense the tiny, minute electricity created by muscles and nerves of other organisms

emergent marine plant a marine plant that lives partially submerged with its roots underwater and leaves and branches above water

empirical that which is based on something observed or experienced

emulsification with respect to oil spills, the breaking up of the slick into small droplets

endosymbiosis symbiosis in which one organism lives inside another and both organisms benefit

endotherm an organism with an internal temperature that varies with, but is constantly higher than, the surrounding temperature

energy the capacity to do work

ENSO abbreviation for El Niño-South Oscillation and commonly referred to as El Niño; during ENSO, characterized by the build up of high pressure in the Western Pacific and low pressure to the east; trade winds weaken, and upwelling along the South American coast stops

entomologist scientist specializing in the study of insects

entropy a measure of the disorder that exists in a system; the measure of how much unavailable energy exists in a system due to even distribution; high entropy means low organization and low energy potential

epifauna benthic animals that live on the sea floor; includes some species of crabs, sea stars, sea urchins

epiflora benthic plants that live on the sea floor; includes seagrasses, some species of algae

epipelagic zone the upper portion of the oceanic zone that sunlight reaches; between 0 and 70 meters (230 feet)

epithelium a thin layer of tightly packed cells lining internal cavities, ducts and organs of animals and covering exposed bodily surfaces

equalizing the technique divers use to add air to a body air space to balance it with the increased pressure outside the air space

equator 0° parallel latitude running around the earth at its widest point

equilibrium theory (of tides) simplistic tide theory that assumes earth is perfectly uniform and that solar and lunar gravity are the only tidal influences

erosion the process of water, wind, glaciers, and gravity carrying away rock, soil and organic particles

estuaries partially enclosed water bodies where fresh and salt water mix

eukaryote domain taxon of those organisms with complex cell structures

eulerian method the study of currents through the use of fixed instruments that measure water characteristics as it flows by

euphotic zone the upper, most biologically productive portion of the photic zone

eutrophication an overabundance of nutrients that causes an ecological imbalance

evaporites the salts/compounds left behind when seawater evaporates

Exclusive Economic Zone (EEZ) zone within 370 kilometers (200 nautical miles or 230 statute miles) from a nation's shoreline in which it has complete control of all resources, economic activity and environmental protection

exoskeleton a hard protective covering the provides support and protection for some invertebrates

extratropical cyclone large rotating storm system of low pressure air that forms where the Ferrel and Polar cells meet

extremophiles organisms that live in environments that have conditions fatal to most forms of life

F

family a category in the taxonomic classification of related organisms comprising of one or more genera

fault a weak area in the crust where landmasses will sink, rise, or slide by one another

fault coasts coasts formed by tectonic activity caused by seafloor uplifting or the sea flooding areas of fault spreading

fauna animal life

Ferrel cells atmospheric circulation cells between approximately 30° and 60° latitude

ferromanganese nodules irregular lumps of iron and manganese with small amounts of cobalt, nickel, chromium, copper, molybdenum, and zinc found on some deep ocean bottoms

fetch the area over which the wind blows

fissures seafloor cracks that act as passageways for seawater and molten rock to rise from Earth's mantle

fixation the process of converting, or fixing, an inorganic compound into a usable organic compound

fjord coast a coast formed by a rising sea level flooding an area eroded by glaciers during the last ice age

flagella whip-like protrusion from a cell used for swimming, orientation or other motion

flood current the incoming tidal flow

flora plant life

Glossary

flotsam method the studying of currents by tracking the highly identifiable items accidentally or naturally adrift in the water

food web an illustration that shows that organisms often have different choices of prey; represents the flow of energy through consumption in nature

fore reef the outer, ocean side of a coral reef with most of the biological activity

foreshore the region of a beach from the high tide mark to the low tide mark

frequency the number of waves that pass a fixed point in one second

friction depth the depth in an Ekman Spiral at which there is insufficient wind energy to overcome friction and move the water below

fringing reefs coral reefs that grow along an island or the mainland

frustule silica cell wall of diatom

fucoxanthin pigment that gives brown algae their characteristic olive-green/brown coloration

fully developed sea an area where the waves have reached the maximum possible size for the wind speed, duration and fetch

fusiform shape open ocean fish shape characterized by spindle shape, slightly larger head and V-shaped tail; as in tuna

G

gametes male and female reproductive cells that fuse to initiate the development of offspring

gas gland organ in ray-finned fish that, along with another organ called the rete mirabile, takes oxygen from the bloodstream to inflate the swim bladder

gastrovascular cavity internal cavity of Cnidaria where digestion and reproduction takes place

gauge pressure useable pressure, as when using gas from a cylinder, so that the zero point is one atmosphere

genera biological classification consisting of structurally similar or related species. This classification lies between family and species

genus a category in the taxonomic classification of related organisms, comprising one or more species

geodesist a person who engages in geodesy

geodesy a branch of earth science that deals with measurement of Earth's gravitational field, crustal motion, tides, and polar motion

geographic information systems (GIS) software oceanographers use to map the seafloor

geographic equator an imaginary line around the Earth that separates the Northern and Southern hemispheres and is at 0° latitude

geological oceanography the study of the geology (see geology) of the ocean

geology the study of the structure of the Earth or another planet, in particular its rocks, soil, and minerals, and its history and origins

geostrophic related to the Earth's rotation (Coriolis effect)

geostrophic currents currents created by the rotation of the Earth (Coriolis effect)

Global Positioning System (GPS) satellite-based navigation system made up of a network of 24 satellites placed into orbit by the US Department of Defense

grab sampler ocean sediment sampler with a set of jaws, designed to scoop up bottom sediment for research purposes; also called a clamshell sampler

grain size the diameter of an individual sediment particle

gravity waves waves with wavelengths longer than 1.73 centimeters (.68 inches); gravity is their primary restoring force

green algae members of the phylum Chlorophyta, multicellular algae characterized by sharing the same green color as land plants; typically found in shallow water

greenhouse effect the ability of the Earth's atmosphere to hold and reuse energy close to the Earth's surface

groins artificial protrusions jutting out perpendicular to the shore

gross primary productivity the measure of all the organic material produced in an area by autotrophs

gyre the circular flow of currents in an ocean basin due to the Coriolis effect

H

H:L symbol for the ratio of the wave height to wavelength

habitat the area and conditions in which you find an organism

hadal zone The deepest zone, areas below 6,000 meters (19,685 feet)

hadalpelagic zone a division of the oceanic zone, the deeper water in the ocean trenches, below 6,000 meters (19,685 feet)

Hadley cells atmospheric circulation cells between the equator and approximately 30° latitude

half-life the rate of radioactive decay of an unstable element expressed as the time required for half the element present to decay into a stable element

halite table or rock salt, which is sodium chloride (NaCl)

halocline an abrupt change in salinity that marks two different water layers

halophytes saltwater plants

hard-hat diving diving that supplies air from the surface through a hose to a helmet the diver wears

Harmful Algal Blooms (HABs) inappropriately called red tides; a rapid growth of certain marine algae due to the addition of nutrients in a local offshore area

heat the kinetic energy in the random movement or vibration of individual atoms and molecules in a substance

heat capacity how much heat energy it takes to raise one gram of a substance 1° Celsius

height, wave the vertical measurement from the trough to the crest of a wave

heliox a mix of helium and oxygen as a breathing gas for very deep diving

herbivore an animal that eats plants

heterogeneous mixture a mixture that is not uniform, consisting of visibly different substances

heterotrophs organisms that rely on external energy sources by digesting plant or animal matter

heterotrophy the process of obtaining energy-rich organic compounds by consuming other plants or animals

Hjulström's diagram a graph that illustrates the relationship of transportation, erosion, and deposition of particles of different sizes

holdfast an algae appendage that anchors the organism to rocks

homeotherm an organism with a stable internal temperature ("warm-blooded" organisms)

homeothermic designation for organisms that maintain a constant internal temperature; also called warm-blooded

homogeneous mixture a mixture that has a uniform appearance throughout, such as a solution

horse latitudes region at 30° latitude in both hemispheres where dry air sinks along the boundary of the Hadley and Ferrel cells; winds can cease for extended periods; name came from carcasses of horses thrown overboard by stranded ships

hot spot theory the theory that small melting spots in the mantle send magma up through the crust; these spots do not move in relation to the tectonic plate above it

hydrocarbon compound of carbon and hydrogen chain commonly found in petroleum and natural gas

hydrogen bond bond between water molecules caused by attraction of positive hydrogen end of one molecule to the negative oxygen of another

hydrogenous sediment sediment that originates from chemical reactions in seawater

hydrophone an underwater microphone

hydrostatic pressure pressure exerted by water

hydrothermal vent a fissure in the Earth's surface from which geothermically heated water is forced out – found near volcanically active places, areas where tectonic plates are moving

hypertonic the condition of having a higher concentration of water or other substance that exerts osmotic pressure; a solution that contains a higher concentration of electrolytes than that found in living cells

hypothesis a scientific guess based on observation, but with little data to support it; an untested scientific explanation for an observed phenomenon

hypotonic the condition of having a lower concentration of water or other substance that exerts osmotic pressure; a solution in which the concentration of an electrolyte is below that in cells

hypoxic having low oxygen

I

ice rafting the process by which polar ice floats to sea carrying sediments that sink when the ice melts

igneous rock rock created by cooling magma or lava

immunosuppressor an agent that compromises or suppresses an organism's immune system, reducing its ability to fight disease

in situ on location or at the actual site of something rather than in the laboratory or an artificial condition

inductive reasoning concluding what process caused an observed fact or facts

infauna benthic organisms that live buried or partially buried in the sea floor; includes some types of clams, tube worms, sea pens

internal ocean waves energy that occurs within different density layers

international waters the regions beyond the EEZs that belong to no nation

intertropical convergence zone (ITCZ) an area where weather and climate are affected by the meeting of the Northern and Southern Hadley cells

intertropical convergence zone equator (ITCZ equator) an imaginary line marking temperature equilibrium between the hemispheres that shifts slightly north and south of the geographic equator with seasonal changes; roughly the same as the meteorological equator

invertebrate animal lacking a backbone or spinal column; includes crabs, jellyfish, sea urchins, sea stars

ion a charged particle (atom or molecule)

ionic bond an electrical attraction between two oppositely charged atoms or groups of atoms; as in sodium chloride

island arc a chain of volcanic islands created at a subduction zone

isotonic the condition of having an equal concentration of water or other substance that exerts osmotic pressure

isostatic equilibrium the balance between the weight of the crust and the force of buoyancy provided by the mantle

Glossary

isostatic rebound   a deflection in the Earth's crust thought to be a cause of earthquakes that results from a change in weight distribution between the oceanic crust and continental crust

J

jetties   artificial protrusions jutting out perpendicular to the shore at a harbor entrance, with the purpose of protecting the entrance

joule   a unit of energy measure; 4.2 joules = 1 calorie

K

kelp   a typically used common name for many larger species of brown algae in the phylum Phaeophyta; characterized by having holdfasts, stipes, blades and pneumatocysts

kingdom   in taxonomy, a group of similar phyla or divisions

L

lagoon   an area of shallow water separated from the ocean by a barrier island or other obstruction

Lagrangian method   also known as the float method; a study of currents performed by tracking a drifting object

latent   present, not noticeable, but capable of being active

latent heat of fusion   the non-sensible heat lost when water goes from liquid to ice

latent heat of vaporization   the heat required to vaporize a substance

lateral line   lines of sensory pores along the length of the body of fish that detect differences in water pressure; allows fish to detect vibrations of an approaching predator or struggling prey

lava   molten rock that emerges through the crust via a volcano or other opening

life science   the study of living things and their interactions with their environments; a principal branch of science concerned with plants, animals, and other living organisms and including biology, botany, and zoology.

limiting factor   a physical or biological necessity that will limit an organism's normal function if present in inappropriate amounts

lithification   the formation of rock

lithogenous sediments   (also known as terrigenous sediments) sediment that originates on land, primarily through erosion carrying particles into the sea

lithosphere   the uppermost, rigid part of the upper mantle and the crust; cool solid rock portion of the outer Earth

littoral zone   ocean bottom zone between the high tide and low tide marks

longitudinal wave   wave in which the energy moves in the same direction that the energy travels through the compression and decompression of particles.

longshore current   a current parallel to shore caused by waves approaching the beach at an angle

longshore drift   the movement of sediment and materials along the coast, caused by a longshore current

longshore trough   a slightly deeper area in the offshore section of a beach, running parallel to shore

longshoring   the trade of loading and unloading cargo ships

Loran-C   electronic navigation system that was based on radio signal transmitters along the coast

low-tide terrace   the flat portion of the foreshore of a beach where the waves break

luciferase   enzyme found in a photophore; used in the production of bioluminescent light by mixing with luciferin

luciferin   compound found in a photophore that produces light when mixed the enzyme luciferase

M

machine   a combination of matter capable of using energy to perform useful work; a device with moving parts, often powered to perform a task

macro algae   multicellular species of algae

magma   molten rock inside the Earth

magnetometer   instrument that measures the polar orientation and intensity of magnetism of minerals

Mammalia   class in the phylum Vertebrata, animals characterized by hair on the body, nourishing young with milk provided by mammary glands, being warm-blooded and with the majority giving live birth; includes whales, dolphin, sea lions, seals, walrus

mammalian diving reflex   especially pronounced in marine mammals, an adaptation to immersion in water that slows the pulse and diverts blood flow to extend breath-hold time

mantle   in mollusks, a muscular bag that surrounds the gills and most organs, and is used to circulate water through the organism or as in squid and octopus, propulsion

Mare Liberum   A free ocean, the principle that all nations have a right to free access to the seas

mariculture   aquaculture specific to the marine environment

marine science   the process of discovering the facts, processes and unifying principles that explain the nature of the ocean and its associated life forms

marine snow   sediment consisting of dead organisms, fecal pellets and other nutrients that constantly fall into the deep ocean from the productive shallow water above

MARPOL   International Convention for the Prevention of Pollution (abbreviation for MARine POLlution); regulates discharge from ships

mathematics   the universal "language" of science; the study of the relationships among numbers, shapes and quantities

maximum sustainable yield   the number of a target species fisheries can take without jeopardizing future populations

medusa   in Cnidarians, free-swimming, bell-shaped life cycle stage; such as a jellyfish

meiofauna tiny organisms that live in the spaces between sand grains on the sea floor

meridians longitude lines

mesoglea in Cnidaria, the jellylike material located between the two body tissues

mesopelagic zone the division of the oceanic zone that sunlight reaches, but not strongly enough to support much life; between 200 and 1,000 meters (656 and 3,280 feet)

mesosphere layer of atmosphere from 50,000 to 90,000 meters (31 to 56 miles) above sea level

metabolism the energy-releasing chemical processes within an organism

metamerism the division of the body into repeating segments, as found in phylum Annelida (worms)

metamorphic rock rock that forms when pressure and heat become great enough to change the rock chemically

meteor material entering the Earth's atmosphere from space

meteorite a meteor that strikes the ground

meteorological equator an imaginary line marking temperature equilibrium between the hemispheres that shifts slightly north and south of the geographic equator with seasonal changes; roughly the same as the ITCZ equator

methane natural gas, a gaseous hydrocarbon

methane hydrates ice crystals containing methane found on the continental slope

microhabitat a type of habitat that exists on a very small scale

micronutrients essential substances that organisms use in very small amounts

microplankton plankton that is between 20 and 200 microns in size

microtektites glass particles that form when a large meteorite impacts the Earth

midnight zone that zone of the deep ocean that is entirely dark—there is no light; also loosely associated with the aphotic, abyssalpelagic and hadalpelagic zones.

mid-ocean ridge a mountain range on the bottom of the ocean, created where plates diverge; each mid-ocean ridge has a rift valley running through its center

mitochondria organelles (structures) within cells that process oxygen to produce energy

mixed tides the tidal pattern of two unequal high and low tides daily

mixture the combination of two or more substances that are not chemically bonded, and not in fixed proportions to each other

monsoon local seasonal wind pattern caused by heat from the continents that results in summers with significant rainfall and winters with very little rainfall

mud a mixture of clay and silt

mutation an abnormal characteristic in an individual organism caused by an error in the organism's DNA

myoglobin protein similar to hemoglobin that binds reversibly with oxygen, allowing marine mammals to extend their breath-hold time underwater.

Myxini class that include lampreys

N

natural selection the process by which organisms with favorable characteristics tend to live longer and reproduce more

neap tides the weaker monthly tidal extremes of high and low tide, created when the arrangement in space of the moon, sun, and Earth form a right angle; they result when the gravitational force of the sun pulls in a perpendicular direction to the gravitational force of the moon

nebula a large, hazy bright or dark cloud of hydrogen, helium, and interstellar dust in space

nebular theory the theory that the solar system developed from a nebula

nekton swimming organisms that are able to move independently of water currents; most fish, mammals, turtles, sea snakes

nematocysts stinging cells of Cnidarian organisms

nephridia simple kidney organs found in less complex organisms

neritic zone the water area between the low tide mark and the edge of the continental shelf

net primary productivity the quantity of energy remaining after autotrophs have satisfied their respiratory needs

neuston plankton that lives on the water's surface; includes Portuguese man-of-war

niche an organism's role in its habitat; its job

nitrification when microorganisms convert ammonia into nitrates and nitrites

node in a standing wave, the point where there is no vertical change in the water level

nodules irregular lumps of rock about the size of potatoes that are found in deep water; classified as hydrogenous sediments and thought to be produced by some of the slowest chemical reactions in nature; types of nodules include ferromanganese and phosphorite

nonconservative constituents dissolved substances in seawater that change over time and vary in proportion due to biological and geological activity

nonextractive resources resources obtained from the sea without removing anything from it, such as sea transport shipping and recreation

non-ionic a solution in which solute particles remain intact and do not separate into ions

Glossary

nonrenewable resources resources that natural processes don't replace, or that do so at such a slow rate that they're not replenished in a human lifespan

non-sensible heat heat change at a substance's state change that does not cause a temperature change and cannot be measured with a thermometer

notochord a firm tissue mass along the organism's dorsal

nuclear fusion atomic reaction in which lighter atoms unite to form heavier atoms, releasing tremendous energy in the process

nutrients elements and compounds required for life, other than oxygen or carbon dioxide used for respiration or photosynthesis

Occam's razor the guideline that when you have two competing explanations for something and no evidence to support either, the simpler explanation is more likely to be correct

ocean from the Greek word *okeanos* and the Latin *oceanus*; a large expanse of salt water; includes any of the Earth's five largest oceans – Atlantic, Pacific, Indian, Arctic and Antarctic; covering about 71% of the Earth's surface

ocean conveyor belt the interconnected surface and deep-water currents that redistribute heat throughout the world

ocean crust the crust under the ocean basins

ocean literacy understanding the basic concepts related to how the ocean functions as an ecosystem, its importance to the Earth's ecosystem, and how and why it is vital to human existence

Ocean Thermal Energy Conversion (OTEC) a process that harnesses the energy trapped in the upper layers of seawater to generate electricity; a renewable resource

oceanic zone the open water area beyond the continental shelf

oceanography the science of recording and describing the ocean's contents and processes; four main branches – biological, chemical, geological, and physical

offshore the beach area beyond the low-tide terrace; it includes a longshore trough and shallow sandbar that both parallel the shore

ooliths (ooids) round, white grains that form when calcium carbonate is deposited around shell fragments or other particles.

ooze deep ocean sediments that contain 30% or more biogenous sediments; includes calcareous and siliceous oozes

orbital wave a wave that only transmits through fluids; a wave that occurs when energy moves the fluid in a circular motion as it passes

order a taxonomic classification made up of related families or organisms

organelle microscopic structures ("organs") within an individual cell

Orpheus theory the theory that a planetary object struck the Earth and hurled material into orbit, forming the moon

oscula (singular osculum) openings in a sponge through which filtered water exits

osmoconformers marine organisms that cannot regulate the water concentration inside their cells

osmoregulators marine organisms that can regulate the water concentration inside their cells

osmosis diffusion through a semipermeable membrane, such as a cell wall

osmotic pressure the pressure differential caused when a substance exists in differing concentrations on two sides of a semipermeable membrane

Osteichthyes a superclass in the phylum Vertebrata, animals characterized by having jaws and true bone; ray-finned fish, includes bass, eels, snappers, sea horses, tuna, flounder

outer sublittoral zone a division of the littoral zone, the ocean bottom away from shore out to the edge of the continental shelf

outrigger an elongated float such as a shaped log extended from the side of the boat to prevent capsizing

overfishing taking more of a species than the maximum sustainable yield

oviparous reproduction in which the mother lays eggs that mature and hatch outside the mother's body

ovoviviparous reproduction in which eggs hatch and develop inside the mother with the young born live; as in some sharks and rays

ozone highly reactive oxygen gas molecule made up of three oxygen atoms

paleoceanography the study of prehistoric oceans

paleoclimatology the study of past climate, for times prior to instrumental weather measurements.

Pangaea the theorized single continent in the distant past before the continents broke apart and drifted away from each other

Panthalassa the theorized single large ocean that existed when the Earth's landmasses consisted of the single continent Pangaea

parallels latitude lines

passive coast a coast located far away from active plate boundaries; it has little or no volcanic activity or earthquakes

passive transport the process of moving substances into or out of a cell by normal diffusion

pathogens microbes that cause disease

pedicellaria in echinoderms, pincher-like pairs of organs on the exoskeleton used to pluck foreign objects off the exterior of the organism

pelagic zone the water portion of the ocean; pertaining to areas of water that are not near the surface or bottom of the water body (compare with benthic zone)

period the time it takes for the same spot on two waves to pass a single point

Petromyzontida class that includes sea lampreys

pH a scale that represents the balance between the positive hydrogen ions (H+) and the negative hydroxide ions (OH-) in a liquid, thereby measuring the acidity or alkalinity, with 7 being neutral, lower numbers acidic and higher numbers alkaline

photic zone upper sunlit zone of the ocean

photoinhibition the condition in which excess light overwhelms an autotroph's ability to photosynthesize

photophore specialized structure on an organism used to emit bioluminescent light

photosynthesis the organic synthesis of carbohydrates from light energy and inorganic compounds

phycoerythrins red pigments found in red algae and in some Cyanobacteria that allow the organism to photosynthesize much deeper than they otherwise would

phylogeny the evolutionary history of a particular group of organisms or their genes

phylum a major taxonomic group into which animals are divided, made up of several classes

physical oceanography the study of physics within the marine environment

physical resources resources that don't involve biological processes

physical science the study of matter and energy; any of the sciences such as physics and chemistry that study non-living things

phytoplankton planktonic organisms that photosynthesize; autotrophic plankton

picoplankton a community of extremely tiny plankton

piloting navigating by using references on shore

piston corer research device used to study bottom sediment; an open tube on a cable that is dropped from a ship, retrieves layers of bottom sediment

plankton organisms that exist adrift in the ocean, unable to swim against currents and waves, most, but not all, are very small or microscopic; includes dinoflagellates, diatoms, jellyfish, fish larva

plankton bloom periods of explosive reproduction and growth of particular plankton species

plate tectonics, theory of theory states that the continents float on the Earth's molten interior, gradually moving over millions of years

plunging breakers surf waves characterized by a curl that forms as the top of the wave pitches through the air and then splashes into the bottom of the wave

pneumatocysts natural, gas-filled float structures that provide certain species of marine algae with buoyancy, lifting it off the bottom

pneumatophores snorkel-like root structures on some mangrove species that draw air from above the water's surface

poikilotherm endotherms (warm-blooded animals) such as large fish and reptiles that lack a layer of insulation and whose body temperature varies with the temperature of its surroundings

Polar cells atmospheric circulation cell between approximately 50° to 60° latitude and the North or South pole

polar molecule a molecule with positively and negatively charged ends

polarity the characteristic of having positive and negative poles

pollution products of human activities that have harmful or objectionable effects to the water quality or affect the physical, chemical, or biological environment

polyp in Cnidarians, a sessile, vase-shaped life cycle stage

polysaccharide a complex carbohydrate (starch)

poorly sorted sediment sediment of mixed grain sizes created when water movement changes frequently

population a group of the same species living and interacting within a community

Precautionary Principle where there are threats of serious or irreversible damage, lack of full scientific certainty shall not be used as a reason for postponing cost-effective measures to prevent environmental degradation. (Rio Declaration 1992)

pressure gradient force the force of water flowing away from a mound water where a current interrupts its flow

primary coast a coast formed by non-marine forces such as volcanic activity, glaciers, and erosion

primary consumers the first level of heterotrophs that eats the primary producers and photosynthesizing bacteria

primary producers autotrophic organisms capable of synthesizing energy-rich organic compounds from inorganic material, effectively introducing new organic material into the environment that the primary consumers can feed upon and so forth

principle of constant proportions principle that the proportions of dissolved elements in sea water are constant

principle of uniformitarianism the principle that processes acting on the Earth's surface today were the same in the past

Glossary

progressive wave a wave that allows you to observe its energy moving from one point to another; progressive waves are classified as longitudinal, transverse, and orbital

prokaryote structurally simple single celled organisms; thought to be the oldest forms of life

protostar theorized accumulation of gases that, due to gravitational attraction, forms a dense core that may, given enough mass, begin nuclear reactions and become a star

pseudopod long, slender branching treads of a cell body used to catch food and provide locomotion in unicellular, amoeboidtype organisms

pycnocline a thermocline and halocline together creating a boundary between layers of differing water density

R

radial symmetry symmetry around a point, like pie slices or a clock face

radiolarians tiny amoeba-like marine animals whose complex skeletons are made of silica and contribute to siliceous ooze

radiometric dating method of estimating a rock's age based on the decay rate of radioactive elements in the rock

radula specialized "tongue" in mollusks that is adapted for the particular species' feeding needs

recent sediments sediments that have accumulated since sea level stabilized (about 5,000 years ago) where it is today

red algae members of the phylum Rhodophyta, multicellular algae characterized by having the red pigment phycoerythrin, allowing this group to use blue light available in deeper water for photosynthesis; within this group is coralline algae – reef building species

red tide extreme plankton bloom that makes it difficult for organisms to survive due to oxygen consumption and toxin release

reduction fishery a fishery catching fish for purposes other than direct human consumption

reef crest the upper, shallowest portion of a coral reef that experiences most of the wave energy

reflection, wave wave energy bouncing off a nearly perpendicular object in the water; may cause a standing wave

refraction, wave bending of waves

refractometer optimal instrument that determines salinity based on light refraction through a seawater sample

relict sediments sediments that accumulated and were left stranded when the sea level was lower than present day (about 5,000 years ago); much of the continental shelf is blanketed with sand deposits that are mainly relict sands

Remotely Operated Vehicle (ROV) an unmanned submersible that is remotely controlled

renewable resources are those that growing organisms, sunlight, or other processes naturally replace.

Reptilia class in the phylum Vertebrata, animals characterized by air breathing, coldblooded species that reproduce by laying internally fertilized eggs; includes alligators, crocodiles, turtles, lizards, snakes

reserve rock nonporous rock that traps migrating oil or gas, forming an oil or gas reserve

restoring forces energy sources that resists wave formation

rete mirabile organ in ray-finned fish that, along with another organ called the gas gland, takes gas from the bloodstream to inflate the swim bladder

reverse osmosis the process of transporting material through a semipermeable membrane against the natural flow of diffusion; commonly used as a method for desalinating seawater to create fresh water

rheology the study of how matter flows

Rhodophyta a phyla characterized by multicellular red algae having only chlorophyll "a" and red pigments called phycoerythrins

rift valley valley running through the center of mid-ocean ridges thought to be the origin of new seafloor in the process of seafloor spreading

Ring of Fire an area bordering the Pacific Ocean where many earthquakes and volcanoes occur

river-dominated delta a delta with a strong river and mild wave and tidal action

RNA ribonucleic acid made from a long chain of nucleotide units; similar to DNA, but usually exists in cells as a single strand; is central to the translation of some RNAs into proteins

rock cycle the processes that account for the changes in the types of rock

rogue wave wave that exceeds the maximum theoretical size in a fully developed sea

S

saccharide a simple carbohydrate (includes sugars, such as glucose)

salinity the total quantity or concentration of all dissolved inorganic solids

salinometer electronic instrument that determines salinity based on the conductivity of seawater

salt marsh an intertidal grassland that is usually biologically diverse and productive

salt wedge estuary an estuary in which seawater forms a layer under the fresh water, resulting in a saltwater layer and a freshwater layer

saturated air air in which the rate of evaporation balances the rate of condensation

science a body of knowledge and an organized method used to gain knowledge about the observable universe

scientific method the formal, organized steps that scientists follow in proposing explanations for their observations and then testing their explanations

scientific process skills skills used in conducting the scientific method, such as comparing, relating, inferring, applying, measuring, modeling, recording, etc.

scientist someone who uses the processes of science to find answers about how things work and why in the observable universe

sea beans seeds that redistribute themselves by drifting in current

seafloor spreading the theory that the seafloor forms in and spreads from rift valleys in mid-ocean ridges, eventually pushing underground in trenches

sea level the average level of the sea's surface at its mean level between high and low tide

seawalls structures built at the water's edge or at the top of a beach that block waves from traveling any farther ashore

secondary coast a coast formed by marine forces such as waves and marine life

secondary consumers organisms that eat primary consumers

sediment organic and inorganic particles accumulated together in a loose, unconsolidated form

sedimentary rock rock formed by the compression and cementing together of sediments

seiche a form of standing wave that can be destructive; formed in large bays, harbors, and lakes as a wave that rocks back and forth as a result of a strong wind or local earthquake

seismic refraction a technique used to study marine sediments; equipment includes an air gun aboard a vessel to produce the reflected sound and a towed hydrophone to detect the reflected sound waves

seismic waves waves that travel through the Earth that result from movement of the plates; also known as earthquake waves

semidiurnal tides the tidal pattern of two roughly equal high and low tides daily

semipermeable membrane a membrane that will allow some substances to pass through, but not others

sensible heat heat that is measurable as a change in temperature and readable with a thermometer

sepia the natural, black ink-like substance found in cuttlefish, squid and octopuses

sessile term for an organism that is permanently attached in place on the sea bottom; includes corals, barnacles, sea fans, mussels

sewage sludge a mixture of organic material as well as bacteria, viruses, metals and synthetic chemicals from the isolated solids of sewage

shallow-water waves waves in water that is shallower than one-twentieth their wavelength

silica common name for silicon dioxide

siliceous silicon containing

siliceous ooze ooze composed primarily of planktonic organisms that have silica skeletons

siphon in cephalopods (squids, octopus, nautilus), structure derived from the ancestral molluscan foot; used to manipulate the movement/direction of the animal

situatedness the explanation of when, where, and why a concept came about

slack current an outgoing tidal flow

slack tide the relative lack of water motion between tides

solute the part of a solution that is less abundant

solution the state in which the molecules of a solute are evenly dispersed amid the molecules of a solvent

solvent the part of a solution that is more abundant, usually a liquid

source rock the rock in which hydrocarbons (oil and natural gas) form

southern oscillation part of the ENSO event ; a "seesaw" in air pressure. When air pressure is high in the eastern Pacific, it is low in the Western Pacific and vice-versa

species a group of organisms that can reproduce together to produce fertile offspring

speed, wave wavelength divided by period

spicules in sponges, tiny structures providing support; made of glass or calcium material

spilling breakers surf waves characterized by the top of the wave tumbling and sliding down the front of the wave as it decelerates slowly on gentle slope beaches

spit a length of accumulated sand attached to land at one end, pointing in the direction of the longshore drift

spoil the soft bottom material removed during the dredging of harbors and ports

spontaneous generation the formation of life from non living matter, also called abiogenesis

spring tides the highest and lowest monthly tides, caused by the alignment of the sun and moon with respect to Earth

SQ3R A well researched study method than can help anyone learn from a textbook; stands for Survey, Question, Read, Recite and Review.

stakeholder A person, group, organization, who effects or can be affected by any particular system

standing crop the biomass, total weight, or energy content of organisms at a given time

standing wave a vertical oscillation in which water rises and falls with alternating trough and crests in a single position

state an expression of a substance's form as solid, liquid, or gas

Glossary

statistical significance a calculation that determines how likely a result is by mere chance (p 1-29)

stipes stem-like structure that supports algae but lacks the vascular system found in plants

storm surge bulge or wave caused by low pressure at the center of a cyclonic storm

stratified estuary an estuary in which salt water and fresh water form distinct layers, but the upper freshwater layer becomes saltier near the mouth of the river, and the lower saltwater layer becomes less salty toward the head of the river

stratigraphy the study of sediment layers

stratosphere layer of atmosphere from 15,000 to 50,000 meters (9 to 31 miles) above sea level

streamlining having the characteristic of a shape that reduces drag

subducted sinks beneath

subduction in the theory of plate tectonics, where one plate sinks beneath another during plate collision

sublittoral zone a division of the littoral zone, the ocean bottom close to shore

submerged cultural resource underwater archaeological sites set aside for protection and comprehensive research

submergent plant · a marine plant that lives entirely underwater

submersible typically two and three-person, independently self-propelled vessels that dive in moderate to deep depths

sunlit zone the top layer of the ocean, nearest the surface; also called the euphotic or epipelagic zone

supernova a catastrophic explosion of a large star in the latter stages of stellar evolution, with a resulting short-lived luminosity from 10 to 100 million times that of the Sun

supralittoral zone shore bottom that is splashed, but not submerged by water

surface tension water's resistance to being penetrated by something trying to break through the surface

surging breaker surf waves that rise onto an abrupt, near vertical beach rising out of deep water; so named because they surge ashore before breaking

suspension a hetergeneous mixture with solid particles that tend to settle

suspension feeders organisms that filter particles (mostly plankton) suspended in the water for food

sverdrup unit of measurement for current flow that equals one million cubic meters per second

swell a long line of waves that have the same frequency and wavelength

synthetic organic chemicals human-made chemicals that are based on organic molecule structures

T

taxa plural of taxon

taxon any of the groups to which organisms are assigned according to the principles of taxonomy, including species, genus, family, order, class, and phylum; the divisions and subdivisions used to classify organisms

taxonomists scientists who study the relationships between organisms and classify them

technology the study, development, and application of devices, machines, and techniques for manufacturing and productive processes

temperature the measurement of how fast molecules/ atoms in a substance move (vibrate)

terrigenous sediment (also known as lithogenous sediments) sediment that originates on land, primarily through erosion carrying particles into the sea

test a shell or other hard covering on an invertebrate; in sea urchins, the globular external skeleton/shell on which the spines are attached

theory a scientific explanation with observable evidence to support it

thermal equilibrium the state in which heating and cooling balance so that temperature neither increases nor decreases substantially

thermal inertia the tendency for water to resist temperature changes

thermal plumes localized areas of high heat release in the outer core thought to be associated with volcanic activity

thermistor a semiconductor that has current flow resistance that varies predictably with temperature

thermocline transition between a colder, deeper water layer and a warmer, upper layer of water)

thermodynamics (second law of) in a closed system (one that lets no new energy in or out), order decreases as time passes

thermosphere outermost layer of atmosphere; from 90,000 meters (56 miles) above sea level into space

tidal bore a wave created where an incoming tide flows into a narrow area

tide-dominated delta a delta in an area with strong tides that redistribute accumulating sediments

tombolo a spit that extends between two islands or between an island and the mainland

torsion in gastropods, the developmental process that forms the body into a permanent loop so that the organism fits into a spiral shell

transform boundary in the theory of plate tectonics, the boundary between two tectonic plates that are sliding past each other

transpiration the passage of water vapor from living organisms

transverse wave wave in which the energy motion is perpendicular to the travel direction

trench deep ravine in the ocean floor thought to mark where two tectonic plates meet, one being pushed under the other

tributyl tin (TBT) an antifouling heavy metal compound banned by the US in the late 1980s

trochophore initial larval stage of mollusks

trophic pyramid a representation of how energy transfers from one level of organisms to the next as they consume each other

tropical cyclone inward circulation of air around a low-pressure system; it forms within a single atmospheric cell, usually in low latitudes

troposphere layer of atmosphere in contact with the surface Earth up to 15,000 meters (9 miles) above sea level

trough the lowest wave point above the average water level

tsunami a destructive wave caused by a sudden water displacement that results from an underwater landslide, volcanic eruption, earthquake or an iceberg falling into the sea from a glacier

turbidites sediment deposits created by turbidity currents; they consist of layers of lithogenous sand embedded with fine deep-sea sediments

turbidity currents underwater avalanches of thick, muddy sediments accumulated on the continental shelf that speed down the continental slope into deep water

turbulence chaotic water movement caused by an object passing through the water

turnover the time required for the photosynthesis/respiration cycle in an ecosystem

twilight zone the zone where only a small amount of light can penetrate the water; also loosely known as the dysphotic, mesopelagic and bathypelagic zones.

U

undercurrent current that runs in the opposite direction and beneath a surface current

unikont a Supergroup above the Kingdom Animalia. Unikonts are defined as eukaryotes, whose flagella, if present, are singular. The major groups of unikonts include amoebozoans, fungi and all animals groups.

United Nations Convention of the Law of the Sea (UNCLOS) convention that established Exclusive Economic Zones, now recognized as international law

upwelling upward vertical current that brings deep water to the surface

V

veliger planktonic larval stage of mollusks

vertebrate animal with a backbone or spinal column; includes fish, whales, sea lions

vertically mixed estuary an estuary in which water flow and topography cause fresh water and seawater to mix, resulting in brackish water

viscosity the tendency for a fluid to resist flow

viviparous reproduction in which the young develop inside the mother and are born live; mammalian live birth

W

warm-core eddies circular loops of water that break away from currents, flow clockwise in the Northern Hemisphere, and have warm water centers

wave the transmission of energy through matter

wave diffraction the tendency of energy to shift within a wave upon reaching an obstacle, allowing a new wave pattern to form

wave height the vertical measurement from the trough to the crest of a wave

wave reflection wave energy bouncing off a nearly perpendicular object in the water; may cause a standing wave

wave refraction bending of waves

wave speed wavelength divided by period

wave trains a series of swells traveling together with the leading wave dissipating and the following waves forming

wave-dominated delta a delta in an area with high wave energy that redistributes accumulating sediments as dunes and spits

wavelength the horizontal distance between the identical point on two waves

weakly stratified estuary an estuary in which salt water and fresh water mix vertically, but there are still distinct freshwater and saltwater layers

weathering involves mechanical and chemical processes that break rocks into smaller particles

well sorted sediment sediment of primarily one-grain size, resulting when water movement in a region does not fluctuate very much

Wentworth Scale the classification of sediments by size; a boulder is the largest grain size and clay is the smallest grain size in this classification system

western intensification the flow of major ocean currents against western ocean basin boundaries caused by the Coriolis effect

whale falls places where dead whales come to rest on the deep ocean floor, resulting in a high nutrient concentration and a local ecosystem

Z

zooplankton planktonic animals that eat phytoplankton or other heterotrophic plankton

zooxanthellae golden-brown, autotrophic dinoflagellates that live intracellular (in the tissues) of various marine animals – especially corals and anemones.

Index

A

Abbe, Ernst Karl, 8:16
Abiogenesis, 3:10–12
Aboriginal hunting, 17:23
Abraham, Edward, 1:22
Absolute pressure, 9:26
Absorption of light, 9:17
Abyssal zone, 3:18–20; 14:21; 16:33–34
Abyssalpelagic zone, 3:18
Acceptance of theories, 3:15
Accretion, 3:6
Acetone, 9:5
Acidification of ocean, 19:12
Acidity, 8:10–22
Actinopterygii, 7:3
Active coasts, 15:4
Active sonar, 9:23
Active transport, 8:32–33
Actniopterygii, 7:11
Adaptation(s)
  of brown algae species, 5:28
  of deep-ocean life, 9:26
  of echinoderms, 6:36
  in littoral zone, 16:24
  to maintain internal temperature, 9:22
  of mangroves, 16:19, 20
  of marine mammals, 7:23–25
  of plants to marine environment, 5:34
  related to tides, 12:26
  in salt marshes, 16:18
  of seabirds, 7:20–21
  in supralittoral zone, 16:23–24
Adhesion, 8:6–7
ADP/ATP cycle, 8:28
Advocacy, 19:21
ADW (Atlantic Deep Water), 16:31
Aerobic respiration, 4:9
Aerosols, 10:6, 7
Africa, 2:19–20; 13:11, 12, 27, 29; 14:13
African flamingos, 5:20
Agnatha, 7:4
Agnathans, 7:2–3
Agriculture, 16:15; 18:22
Agulhas Current, 11:10
Air
  composition of, 10:3–4, 6
  and sun, 10:3–8
Air cylinders, 2:54–55
Air pollution, 8:7–8; 10:7; 18:25, 27
Air pressure, 10:23–24
Air quality, 10:2
Air reservoirs, 2:52
Airborne emissions, 18:16
Airplanes
  for whaling, 17:25
  wrecks of, 17:22
Air-sea interaction, 10:1–24
  and Coriolis effect, 10:15–19
  and sun, 10:3–14
  and wind, 10:19–24
Akhet, 15:3
Alabama, freshwater in, 8:3
Alaska, 15:6; 17:5; 18:24
Alaskan pollock, 7:15
Albedo, 10:9
Aldicarb, 18:21
Aleutian Islands, 13:24; 15:9
Alexander the Great, 1:18; 2:49
Alexandria, 2:11
Algae, 5:31; 18:9. *See also* Marine algae
  brown, 5:21, 28–30
  definition of, 5:31
  green, 5:33–34
  macro, 5:32

red, 5:32–33; 17:29
Algalita Marine Research Foundation, 18:37
Algin, 17:29
Alkalinity, 8:10–22
Alligators, 7:16, 17
Aluminum, 9:5
Alvarez, Luis and Walter, 14:9
Alvin submersible, 1:2; 2:59–61; 13:21
  Broken Arrow recovery using, 18:2
  and hydrothermal vent research, 4:11; 8:1
  research using, 2:39
  and seafloor spreading, 13:17
  and *Titanic* wreck exploration, 2:43
Amazon River, 2:21; 12:23
Amblyrhynchus cristatus, 7:19
American lobsters, 6:33
Amhioxus, 6:42
Amino acids, 3:10, 11
Ammonia, 3:11; 8:26–27; 9:5; 17:16
Ammonium chloride, 9:30
Amoebocytes (sponges), 6:4, 5
Amphidromic points, 12:21
Ampulae of Lorenzini, 7:6–7
Anadromous, 5:3
Anaerobic bacteria, 17:5
Analysis step (scientific method), 1:27–29
Anchored buoys, 2:45
Anchovies, 7:14; 17:34
Ancient Egypt, 2:4–5; 14:12; 15:2, 3
Ancient Greece, 1:23; 2:49; 3:10; 3:2
Ancient historical oceanography, 2:4–14
  Greek, 2:8–10
  Phoenician, 2:5–6
  Polynesian, 2:7–8
  prehistory and rise of seafaring, 2:4–5
Ancient Rome, 1:2; 2:49
Ancient Syria, 2:5
Andes Mountains, 13:25
Andrea Doria, 1:2
Anemonefish, 6:10
Anemones, 6:10. *See also* Sea anemones
Anerobic respiration, 4:9–10
Angelfish, 5:3, 21; 7:13
Angle of incidence, 10:10–12
Angle of sun, 4:21
Anglerfish, 16:33
Animal waste, 17:31; 18:34
Animalia, 5:13
Animals, 7:2
  marine. *See* Marine animals.
  in phylogenetic tree of life, 5:14
Annelida, 6:28
Annelids, 6:3, 27–28
Anoxic zones, 18:31
Antarctic, 10:10; 13:27
  debris in water near, 18:37
  as ecosystem, 16:31–32
  mining/oil ban in, 18:43
  waves in, 12:9
Antarctic birds, 7:21
Antarctic Bottom Water, 11:28–30, 32; 16:31
Antarctic Circle, 2:25, 26
Antarctic Circumpolar Current, 1:14; 11:5, 9, 14, 15, 30
Antarctic Convergence Zone, 4:20; 16:32
Antarctic Divergence, 16:32
Antarctic ice cap, lake under, 19:18
Antarctic krill, 5:9; 6:33
Antarctica
  coal in, 13:13
  and continental drift, 13:11, 28, 29

ozone "hole" over, 10:5; 18:6–7
primary production in, 4:19, 20
sediment deposition around, 14:20
Ernest Shackleton's expedition to, 16:2
siliceous oozes in, 14:23
upwelling around, 16:14
Wilkes Exploration of, 2:27
Anthropomorphism, 7:2
Anti-fouling compounds, 18:20
Antifreezing compounds, 16:30, 32
Antinodes, 12:14
Aphotic zone, 3:20; 9:19
Aplysina fistularis, 6:5
Apollo 8, 5:4
Appalachian Mountains, 13:12; 15:13
Apparent deflection, 10:17
Applied research, 2:34; 19:11
Aquaculture, 17:29–31, 34; 18:13
Aqualungs, 2:40, 55–57
Aquanauts, 2:59
Aquarium fish, 18:14
Aquarius habitat, 2:61, 62; 19:18, 19
Aquifers, 10:7–8
Arabian Peninsula, 2:4
Archaea, 4:26–27; 5:13, 18
  age of, 5:16
  Bacteria vs., 5:18–20
  as domain of prokaryotes, 5:16
  in phylogenetic tree of life, 5:14
Archaeological oceanography, 1:1–2; 2:6
Archaeology, 1:1–2
  definition of, 2:6
  maritime, 2:1
  underwater, 2:6, 58
Archeabacteria, 5:13
Arches, 15:9, 10
Archie Carr National Wildlife Refuge, 19:1
Archimedes' Principle, 9:29; 13:8
Archimedes submersible, 1:2
Arctic
  as ecosystem, 16:30–31
  and Ekman transport, 11:6–7
  and heat, 10:10, 12
  nuclear waste in, 18:28
  productivity in, 4:20
Arctic Circle, 9:12
Arctic Ocean, 18:1
Argentina, 14:24
Argo, 1:1, 2; 8:16; 11:34
Argo profiling float project, 2:63
Aristotle, 1:23; 2:49; 3:2
Arizona State University, 5:12
ARKive, 5:12
Arsenic, 18:19
Arthropoda, 6:3, 29
Artifacts, underwater, 17:22
Artificial reefs, 7:1
Asherah submersible, 2:36
Asia, 13:28
Assimilation, 8:26–27
Assisted escapes, 2:56
Asteroidea, 6:37
Asteroids, 14:9
Asthenosphere, 13:5, 6, 8, 16, 22
Astrobiology, 3:1
Astrology, 3:2
Astronauts, 2:61; 19:12
Astronomers, 2:24
Astronomy, 1:12; 3:2
Astrophysics, 1:12
Aswan Dam, 15:3
Ata. *See* Atmosphere of pressure
Atlantic bluefin tuna, 17:41

Atlantic Countercurrent, 11:16
Atlantic Deep Water (ADW), 16:31
Atlantic Ocean
  calcareous oozes in, 14:25
  carbonate compensation depth in, 14:23
  and continental drift, 13:27–29
  deep-water in, 11:28, 29
  depth measurement of, 2:35
  exploration of, 2:27
  mapping floor of, 2:35
  Meteor research of, 2:34–35
  sediment thickness in, 14:21
Atlantis, 2:35
Atmosphere, 3:8. *See also* Air-sea interaction
  heating of, 10:22
  oxygen in, 8:26
  study of, 19:14–15
Atmosphere of pressure (ata), 9:25, 26
Atmospheric circulation cells, 10:19–21
Atolls, 15:22
Augerville, Lemaire D', 2:51
Australia, 2:24, 27; 13:11, 12, 27–29; 18:14
Automobiles, 18:24, 27
Autonomous Underwater Vehicle (AUV), 2:43–44
Autotrophs, 3:12; 4:7, 9, 16, 20–21, 23; 5:24
Autotrophy, 4:7
Autumn, 10:12
AUV (Autonomous Underwater Vehicle), 2:43–44
Aves, 7:20
Axis of rotation, 10:10

B

B-52 bombers, 18:2
Back reefs, 15:21
Backshore, 15:14
Bacon, Sir Francis, 13:10
Bacteria, 1:22; 4:26–27; 5:13, 19–20; 16:35
  Archaea vs., 5:18–20
  as domain of prokaryotes, 5:16
  in phylogenetic tree of life, 5:14
Bahamas Banks, 14:28
Baja Peninsula, 10:13; 13:28
Baking soda, 8:21
Balboa, Vasco Nuñez de, 2:21
Baleen, 17:25
Baleen whales, 4:24; 7:26
Ballard, Robert, 1:1–2, 37; 2:39, 43, 61, 62
Ballast, 2:51; 18:8, 16
Baltic Sea, 8:18
Bar of pressure, 9:25, 27
Barents Sea, 18:28
Barnacles, 6:30–31; 16:24
Barometers, 13:2
Barracuda, 5:25; 7:13
Barrier flats, 15:17, 18
Barrier islands, 15:9, 10, 17–18
Barrier reefs, 15:21–22
Barriers, tidal-power, 17:16
Barton, Otis, 2:36, 37, 55
Basaltic rock, 13:7, 8
Basic solutions, 8:21
Basket stars, 6:35, 38
Basking sharks, 7:8
Basques, 17:2, 24
Bass, George, 2:5, 6, 58, 60
Bass, George, 2:5, 6, 58, 60
Bathyal zone, 3:20
Bathypelagic zone, 3:18
Bathyscaphes, 2:37–38, 57; 16:36
Bathyspheres, 2:36, 37, 55
Batidoidimorpha, 5:10; 7:9
Bats, 9:23

Index

Index

Index

sciences, 2:1–63
  and ancient uses/explorations, 2:4–14
  birth of marine science, 2:23–31
  European voyages of discovery, 2:19–22
  Middle Ages, 2:16–18
  reasons for study of, 2:2–3
  relevance of, 2:2
  in twentieth-century, 2:33–47
  underwater exploration timeline, 2:48–63
Hjulström's diagram, 14:14, 15
H:L ratio, 12:4–5, 12, 13
HMRG (Hawaii Mapping Research Group) Deep, 8:3
H.M.S. *Beagle*, 2:29
H.M.S. *Challenger*, 2:30–32; 14:24
H.M.S. *Challenger II*, 2:35
Holden, John, 13:28
Holdfasts, 5:28, 29, 34
"Holey sock," 11:34
Holistic management of oceans, 19:10
Holocephali, 5:10
Holothuroidea, 6:39
Homeothermic organisms, 7:22
Homeotherms, 9:21, 22
Homer, 1:16
Homogeneous mixtures, 8:9–10
Horned shark, 7:7
Horse latitudes, 10:22
Horseshoe crabs, 17:1
Hot spot theory, 13:26
Hot water vents, 1:22
Hotels, underwater, 2:61
Household litter, 18:37
Houston, Texas, 12:15
Hughes Corporation, 14:6
Human activities
  and coastal ecosystems, 16:15–16
  and coasts, 15:23–25
  and coral reef destruction, 18:14, 15
  oceans affected by, 19:9
  and pollution, 18:16
Human cloning, 1:32, 33
Human performance, underwater, 2:62
Humbolt squid, 6:24
Humpback whales (Megaptera novaeangliae), 6:33; 9:23; 17:23
Humus, 16:19
Hunley submarine, 2:53, 62
Hunnu, 2:4
Hunting Underwater with Harpoon and Camera (Hans Hass), 2:56
Hurricane Andrew, 10:23
Hurricane Eloise, 12:15
Hurricane Ike, 12:15
Hurricane Isabel, 15:18
Hurricane Katrina, 14:26–27
Hurricane Rita, 14:26–27
Hurricanes, 10:23; 12:1, 2, 15–16; 15:18
Hutton, James, 13:3
Hydrilla, 18:9
Hydrocarbons, 17:5–8; 18:16, 22–25
Hydrocarbon-vent tubeworms, 13:21
Hydrocharitaceae, 5:35
Hydrodynamics, 7:24
Hydrogen, 3:3–4, 10, 11; 4:3, 4; 8:5–6
Hydrogen bombs, 18:2
Hydrogen bonding, 8:5–8, 10
Hydrogen sulfide, 13:21
Hydrogenous sediments, 14:11, 24, 28
Hydroids, 6:7
Hydrolab, 2:59
Hydrological cycle, 9:10; 10:7–8
Hydrostatic pressure, 9:25–27

Hydrothermal vents, 2:60; 3:12; 4:11, 12; 8:1, 4, 16, 18; 13:1; 16:35–36; 18:1
  animals living near, 13:21
  chemosynthesis in, 16:35
  as ecosystems, 16:35–36
  exploration of, 13:21
  metal sulfides found at, 14:28
  as mineral resources, 17:12
  space applications of research on, 19:17–18
Hydroxide ions, 8:20
Hydrozoa, 6:12–14
Hyperbaric conditions, 2:53
Hyperthermophiles, 5:17, 18
Hypertonic state, 8:31
Hypotheses, 1:3, 25, 29
Hypothesis step (scientific method), 1:25
Hypotonic state, 8:31, 32
Hypoxic zones, 18:31, 33, 34

I

Ice, 9:7–8; 18:5
Ice core drilling, 11:1
Ice floats, 8:8
Iceland, 2:17; 13:22, 24; 17:50
Identification step (scientific method), 1:25
Igneous rocks, 13:6–7
Iliffe, Thomas M., 16:1
Illustrations, 1:36
Immunosuppressors, 18:20
In phase (waves), 12:9
In situ, 8:17
Incas, 8:26
India, 2:20; 10:23; 12:18; 13:11, 28, 29; 14:9
Indian Ocean, 11:10; 13:28, 29
  calcareous oozes in, 14:25
  depth measurement of, 2:35
  eastern boundary currents in, 11:12
  mutualistic anemone relationships in, 6:10
  tsunamis in, 12:2
  2004 earthquake, 12:18
Indian Ocean Gyre, 11:9
Indo-Australian Plate, 13:25
Indonesia, 12:18
Indo-West Pacific area, 6:10; 16:27
Inductive reasoning, 1:25
Industrial fishing, 17:34
Industrial Revolution, 2:33–34; 8:26, 27; 13:3; 17:2; 18:3, 4
Industrial solids, 18:38–39
Industrial solvents, 18:22
Inertia, thermal, 9:11–12
Infauna, 3:21, 22
Infrared light, 10:9
Infrared radiation, 10:9
Inner core, 13:4, 5
Inorganic chemistry of water, 8:9–22
  acidity/alkalinity, 8:10–22
  colligative properties of seawater, 8:12–13
  dissolved solids in seawater, 8:1
  measurement of salinity/temperature/depth, 8:14–17
  principle of constant proportions, 8:1
  salinity/temperature/density relationships, 8:18–19
  salts/salinity, 8:11–12
  solutions/mixtures, 8:9–10
  sources of salt, 8:16, 18
An Inquiry into the Nature and Causes of the Wealth of Nations (Adam Smith), 13:3
Insects, 5:3, 11

Institute for Archeological Oceanography, 1:1
Institute for Cetacean Research, 17:23
Institute of Nautical Archaeology, Texas A & M University, 2:60
Institute of Research and Exploitation of the Sea, 2:39
Instrumentation, 9:1
Integrated Ocean Drilling Program, 14:5
Intermediate water, 11:29
Internal combustion fuels, 18:6
Internal temperature
  of animals, 9:21–22
  of marine mammals, 7:23
Internal waves, 12:10
International Commission on Zoological Nomenclature, 5:12
International conservation efforts, 18:42–43; 19:5
International Convention for the Prevention of Pollution (MARPOL), 18:4
International Hydrodynamics, 2:39
International Institute for Species Exploration, Arizona State University, 5:12
International Seabed Authority, 17:51–52
International Space Station, 2:61
International Tsunami Warning System, 12:2
International Union for the Conservation of Nature, World Commission on Protected Areas, 19:9
International Union for the Conservation of Nature and Natural Resources, 18:42
International waters, 17:49
International Whaling Commission (IWC), 17:26
Intertidal zones, 16:23–24
Intertropical convergence zones (ITCZs), 10:21–22
Invertebrate nekton, 3:20
Invertebrates, 3:21; 6:1–42
  chordates, 6:41–42
  classification of, 6:3
  complex worms, 6:27–28
  crustaceans, 6:29–34
  defensive compounds produced by, 6:1
  echinoderms, 6:35–40
  mollusks, 6:20–26
  in phylum Cnidaria, 6:7–14
  in phylum Ctenophora, 6:15–16
  simple marine worms, 6:17–19
  sponges, 6:4–6
Ionic bonding, 8:10
Ions, 8:10
Iraq, 17:19; 18:27
Ireland, 7:15
Iridium, 14:9
Irish moss, 5:33
Iron, 4:3; 8:24, 29; 14:13, 24; 16:11; 17:10, 12, 19
Iron ships, 2:33, 34
Ironclad ships, 2:1
Island arcs, 13:24
Isostatic equilibrium, 13:7–9
Isostatic rebound, 13:8
Isotonic state, 8:31, 32
Isotopes, 14:1
ITCZ equator, 10:21
ITCZs (intertropical convergence zones), 10:21–22
Italy, 2:19
IWC (International Whaling Commission), 17:26

J

J. Craig Venter Institute, 2:63
Jamaica, 6:1
James, William, 2:51
Japan, 14:24; 17:10, 24–26, 29, 41
Japanese Navy, 2:54; 13:24
Japanese spider crabs, 6:33
Jason Project, 1:2
Jason ROV, 1:2
Jawbones, 9:23
Jawless fish, 7:2–3
Jayne, Steven, 11:1
Jeffries, Harold, 13:13
Jellyfish, 4:1; 6:7, 8, 10–12, 13; 9:20; 16:10
Jetties, 15:24
JIM one-atmosphere dive suit, 2:59
Johnson *SeaLink* (JSL) submersibles, 1:10, 18; 2:39; 8:17
JOIDES *Resolution*, 14:5
Joules, 9:5
Journal des Scavans, 2:50
Journal of the Franklin Institute, 2:52
Journals, 1:30–31
Journey to the Center of the Earth (Jules Verne), 13:4
JSL. *See* Johnson *SeaLink* submersibles
Juan de Fuca Plate, 13:25
Juan de Fuca Ridge, 13:20
Jules Undersea Lodge, 2:61
Jupiter, 19:17
Jurassic Park (Michael Crichton), 3:18

K

Kalnejais, Linda, 15: 1
Kamchatka Peninsula, 11:29
Kangaroos, 13:12
Karcy, Lake, 18:29
KC-135 tankers, 18:2
KCl (potassium chloride), 8:11
Keller, Hannes, 2:58
Kelp, 5:28–29; 16:26–27
Kelp forests, 4:14; 6:39; 16:26
Kennedy Space Center, 19:1
Key Largo, 2:61, 62
Kherson, Ukraine, 18:8
Kingdoms, 5:8, 9
  controversy over division into, 5:13
  defined, 5:6
  number of, 5:8–9
  supergroups as, 5:11
Klamath Lake, 8:2
Klingert, Karl Heinrich, 2:50
Kodia, Alaska, 12:17, 18
Kola Peninsula, 13:4
Korea, 17:10
Krill, 4:24; 6:33–34; 10:12; 16:32
K-T extinction hypothesis, 14:9
Kudzu vine, 18:8
Kuroshio Current, 11:10, 16
Kyoto Climate Change Conference, 18:6

L

La Chalupa habitat, 2:61
La Niña, 2:60; 11:24
La Rance Tidal Power Station, 17:16
La Spirotechnique, 2:57
Labrador Sea, 17:28
Lady with a Spear (Eugenie Clark), 2:57
Lagoons, 15:22
Lagrange, Joseph-Louis, 11:33
Lagrangian method, 11:33, 34
L'Aire Liquide et Cie., 2:56
Lambert, Alexander, 2:53
Lamnidae, 7:8
Lampreys, 7:3

Index

Index